ARCHBO

2012

THIRD SUPPLEMENT TO THE 2012 EDITION

EDITOR

P. J. RICHARDSON, Q.C., LL.M. (Lond.), Dip.Crim. (CANTAB.)
of Gray's Inn and the Inner Temple, Barrister

SUPPLEMENT EDITORS

WILLIAM CARTER, B.A. (OXON.)
of Gray's Inn, Barrister

STEPHEN SHAY, B.A. (OXON.)
of the Middle Temple, Barrister

SWEET & MAXWELL

THOMSON REUTERS

*Published in 2012 by Sweet & Maxwell, 100 Avenue Road, London NW3
3PF*
Part of Thomson Reuters (Professional) UK Limited
(Registered in England & Wales, Company No 1679046.
Registered Office and address for service:
Aldgate House, 33 Aldgate High Street, London EC3N 1DL)
Printed and bound in Great Britain by Ashford Colour Press Ltd
Typeset by Sweet & Maxwell Ltd, 100 Avenue Road, London, NW3 3PF
Tables typeset by YHT Ltd, London
For further information on our products and services, visit:
http://www.sweetandmaxwell.co.uk

No natural forests were destroyed to make this product; only farmed
timber was used and replanted.

**A CIP catalogue record for this book is available from the British
Library**

ISBN MAIN WORK 978–0–414–04822–5
ISBN THIRD SUPPLEMENT 978–0–414–04825–6

SERVICE INFORMATION

The Archbold service

Archbold: Criminal Pleading, Evidence and Practice consists of one main text volume (including the tables and index). This volume is re-issued annually, and is updated by cumulative supplements and *Archbold Review*.

The supplement

Three cumulative supplements, containing updating material for the main volume, are published in each year as part of the service.

This is the third supplement of 2012.

New material is incorporated into this supplement using the same paragraph numbers as appear in the main work. All material new to this supplement is marked in the text by ★ a **bold** star in the margin.

After consulting the main work on any given subject, reference should always be made to the same paragraph number in the current supplement to check that there have been no new developments since the main text volume was published. The supplement will also track material which has been removed or relocated as part of the re-issue process.

The back cover contains a list of all important developments included in this supplement for the first time and where they can be found.

All references in the text to cases, statutes and statutory instruments are contained in the tables printed at the beginning of this supplement.

Please email *smg.archbold@thomson.com* with comments/suggestions for any of the Archbold services, particularly any notes on the index to the mainwork.

Archbold e-update activation code

As a subscriber to Archbold 2012 you have free and unlimited access to the accompanying weekly e-update service and online archive. If you are a new user accessing the service for the first time then please visit **www.sweetandmaxwell.co.uk/archbold** where you will be asked to complete a simple short registration process, and to enter the following activation code to start receiving updates:

> AB2012

If you are an existing user of the e-update then your access will automatically be updated for the new edition and there is no need to re-register.

TABLE OF CONTENTS

ABBREVIATIONS OF LEGISLATION

The following abbreviations have been adopted throughout.

AFA	Armed Forces Act
CAA	Criminal Appeal Act
CDA	Crime and Disorder Act
CDDA	Company Directors Disqualification Act
CEMA	Customs and Excise Management Act
CJA	Criminal Justice Act
CJCSA	Criminal Justice and Court Services Act
CJIA	Criminal Justice and Immigration Act
CJPA	Criminal Justice and Police Act
CJPOA	Criminal Justice and Public Order Act
CLA	Criminal Law Act
CLW	Criminal Law Week
CPIA	Criminal Procedure and Investigations Act
C(S)A	Crime (Sentences) Act
CYPA	Children and Young Persons Act
DTA	Drug Trafficking Act
DTOA	Drug Trafficking Offences Act
ECHR	European Convention on Human Rights
FSMA	Financial Services and Markets Act
MCA	Magistrates' Courts Act
MHA	Mental Health Act
PACE	Police and Criminal Evidence
PCA	Proceeds of Crime Act
PCCA	Powers of Criminal Courts Act
PCC(S)A	Powers of Criminal Courts (Sentencing) Act
PJA	Police and Justice Act
RIPA	Regulation of Investigatory Powers Act
RSA	Road Safety Act
RSC	Rules of the Supreme Court (Revision)
RTA	Road Traffic Act
RTOA	Road Traffic Offenders Act
SCA	Serious Crime Act
SOA	Sexual Offences Act
SOCPA	Serious Organised Crime and Police Act
VCRA	Violent Crime Reduction Act
YJCEA	Youth Justice and Criminal Evidence Act

TABLE OF STATUTES

References in bold indicate where legislation is reproduced in full

TABLE OF NON–UK LEGISLATION

TABLE OF EUROPEAN AND INTERNATIONAL TREATIES AND CONVENTIONS

References in bold indicate where legislation is reproduced in full

TABLE OF EUROPEAN DIRECTIVES AND REGULATIONS

TABLE OF STATUTORY INSTRUMENTS

References in bold indicate where legislation is reproduced in full

TABLE OF CASES

TABLE OF EUROPEAN HUMAN RIGHTS CASES

TABLE OF PRACTICE DIRECTIONS

References in bold indicate where legislation is reproduced in full

CHAPTER 1

THE INDICTMENT

III. SENDINGS, TRANSFERS AND COMMITTALS FOR TRIAL OF INDICTABLE OFFENCES

B. SENDINGS FOR TRIAL

(1) Introduction

With effect from April 2, 2012, the *Criminal Procedure Rules* 2011 (S.I. 2011 No. 1709) are **1-22** amended by the *Criminal Procedure (Amendment) Rules* 2011 (S.I. 2011 No. 3075), r.6, so as to insert a new Part 9 (set out in the schedule to the amending rules) which applies to the allocation and sending of cases for trial under sections 17A to 26 of the *MCA* 1980 (§§ 1–88 *et seq.* in the main work) and sections 50A to 52 of the *CDA* 1998 (§§ 1–23 *et seq.* in the main work). For the full text of Part 9, see *post*, §§ 1–45a *et seq.* As to the application of Part 9, see new rule 2.1(4) (inserted by r.3(a) of the amending rules).

(2) Sending of cases to the Crown Court

Crime and Disorder Act 1998, ss.50A, 51–51E

[Order of consideration for either-way offences
With effect from June 18, 2012 (*Criminal Justice Act 2003 (Commencement No. 28 and Sav-* ★**1-23** *ing Provisions) Order* 2012 (S.I. 2012 No. 1320)), section 41 of, and paragraphs 15 and 17 of Schedule 3 to, the 2003 Act are brought into force in certain areas (as to which, see *post*, § 1–88). There are associated saving provisions, as to which, see article 5 of the order (*post*, § 1–88).

No committal proceedings for indictable-only offences
With effect from June 18, 2012 (*Criminal Justice Act 2003 (Commencement No. 28 and Sav-* ★**1-24** *ing Provisions) Order* 2012 (S.I. 2012 No. 1320)), section 41 of, and paragraphs 15 and 18 of Schedule 3 to, the 2003 Act are brought into force in certain areas (as to which, see *post*, § 1–88), to the extent that they are not already in force. There are associated saving provisions, as to which, see article 5 of the order (*post*, § 1–88).

[Sending cases to the Crown Court: children and young persons
As from a day to be appointed, section 51A(3)(d) of the 1998 Act is amended by the *Legal* ★**1-26** *Aid, Sentencing and Punishment of Offenders Act* 2012, s.126, and Sched. 21, para. 6, so as to substitute "226B" for "226(3) or 228(2)".

[Notices in serious or complex fraud cases
As from a day to be appointed, section 51B(6)(b) of the 1998 Act is amended by the *Legal* ★**1-27** *Aid, Sentencing and Punishment of Offenders Act* 2012, s.39(1), and Sched. 5, paras 46 and 48, so as to substitute the words "regulations under section 19 of the *Legal Aid, Sentencing and Punishment of Offenders Act* 2012" for the words "paragraph 2 of Schedule 3 to the *Access to Justice Act* 1999".

(3) Supplementary provision

Crime and Disorder Act 1998, s.52

Provisions supplementing section 51 [and 51A]

★**1–32**   With effect from June 18, 2012 (*Criminal Justice Act 2003 (Commencement No. 28 and Saving Provisions) Order* 2012 (S.I. 2012 No. 1320)), section 41 of, and paragraphs 68 and 69 of Schedule 3 to, the 2003 Act are brought into force in certain areas (as to which, see *post*, § 1–88), to the extent that they are not already in force. There are associated saving provisions, as to which, see article 5 of the order (*post*, § 1–88).

(4) Reporting restrictions

Crime and Disorder Act 1998, ss.52A, 52B

[Restrictions on reporting

★**1–33**   As from a day to be appointed, section 52A(7) of the 1998 Act is amended by the *Legal Aid, Sentencing and Punishment of Offenders Act* 2012, s.39(1), and Sched. 5, paras 46 and 49, so as to substitute a new paragraph (h), as follows—

> "(h) whether, for the purposes of the proceedings, representation was provided to the accused or any of the accused under Part 1 of the *Legal Aid, Sentencing and Punishment of Offenders Act* 2012".

[Offences in connection with reporting

★**1–34**   With effect from June 18, 2012 (*Criminal Justice Act 2003 (Commencement No. 28 and Saving Provisions) Order* 2012 (S.I. 2012 No. 1320)), section 41 of, and paragraph 19(1) of Schedule 3 to, the 2003 Act are brought into force, except in so far as paragraph 19(1) would insert section 52B(4) of the 1998 Act.

(5) Procedure

Crime and Disorder Act 1998, Sched. 3

Reporting restrictions

★**1–37**   As from a day to be appointed, paragraph 3(8) of Schedule 3 to the 1998 Act is amended by the *Legal Aid, Sentencing and Punishment of Offenders Act* 2012, s.39(1), and Sched. 5, paras 46 and 50, so as to substitute a new paragraph (g), as follows—

> "(g) whether, for the purposes of the proceedings, representation was provided to the accused or any of the accused under Part 1 of the *Legal Aid, Sentencing and Punishment of Offenders Act* 2012".

★**1–44**   With effect from May 18, 2012 (*Criminal Justice Act 2003 (Commencement No. 28 and Saving Provisions) Order* 2012 (S.I. 2012 No. 1320), art. 2), section 41 of, and paragraph 20(1) and (2) of Schedule 3 to, the 2003 Act (see the main work) are brought into force. With effect from June 18, 2012 (*ibid.*, art 4), sections 41 and 332 of, the remainder of paragraph 20, and paragraphs 68, 71(a) to (c) and 72 of Schedule 3, and Part 4 of Schedule 37 to, the 2003 Act are brought into force by the same order in certain areas (as to which, see *post*, § 1–88). There are associated saving provisions: for those relating to the provisions brought into force in certain areas only, see article 5 of the order (*post*, § 1–88). As to the amendments coming into force on May 18, 2012, article 6(1) of the order provides that they do not affect the power to make regulations under paragraph 1 of Schedule 3 in relation to a person sent for trial under section 51 of the 1998 Act before the substitution of that section by the 2003 Act is fully in force in relation to the whole of England and Wales.

**Criminal Procedure Rules 2011 (S.I. 2011 No. 1709), Pt 9 (as inserted by the Criminal
Procedure (Amendment) Rules 2011 (S.I. 2011 No. 3075), r.6)**

Section 1:

General Rules

When this Part applies

9.1—(1) This Part applies to the allocation and sending of cases for trial under—   **1–45a**
 (a) sections 17A to 26 of the *Magistrates' Courts Act* 1980; and
 (b) sections 50A to 52 of the *Crime and Disorder Act* 1998.

(2) Section 2 of this Part applies in a magistrates' court where the court must, or can, send a defendant to the Crown Court for trial, without allocating the case for trial there.

(3) Section 3 of this Part applies in a magistrates' court where the court must allocate the case to a magistrates' court or to the Crown Court for trial.

(4) Section 4 of this Part applies in the Crown Court, where a defendant is sent for trial there.

Exercise of magistrates' court's powers

9.2—(1) This rule applies to the exercise of the powers to which Sections 2 and 3 apply.   **1–45b**

(2) The general rule is that the court must exercise its powers at a hearing in public, but it may exercise any power it has to—
 (a) withhold information from the public; or
 (b) order a hearing in private.

(3) The general rule is that the court must exercise its powers in the defendant's presence, but it may exercise the powers to which the following rules apply in the defendant's absence on the conditions specified—
 (a) where rule 9.8 (adult defendant: request for plea), rule 9.9 (adult defendant: guilty plea) or rule 9.13 (young defendant) applies, if—
  (i) the defendant is represented, and
  (ii) the defendant's disorderly conduct makes his or her presence in the courtroom impracticable;
 (b) where rule 9.10 (adult defendant: not guilty plea) or rule 9.11 (adult defendant: allocation for magistrates' court trial) applies, if—
  (i) the defendant is represented and waives the right to be present, or
  (ii) the defendant's disorderly conduct makes his or her presence in the courtroom impracticable.

(4) The court may exercise its power to adjourn—
 (a) if either party asks; or
 (b) on its own initiative.

(5) Where the court on the same occasion deals with more than one offence alleged against the same defendant, it must deal with them in the following sequence—
 (a) any to which rule 9.6 applies (prosecutor's notice requiring Crown Court trial);
 (b) any to which rule 9.7 applies (sending for Crown Court trial, without allocation there), in this sequence—
  (i) any the court must send for trial, then
  (ii) any the court can send for trial; and
 (c) any to which rule 9.14 applies (allocation for Crown Court trial).

Matters to be specified on sending for trial

9.3—(1) Where the court sends a defendant to the Crown Court for trial, it must specify—   **1–45c**
 (a) each offence to be tried;
 (b) in respect of each, the power exercised to send it; and
 (c) the Crown Court centre at which the trial will take place.

(2) In a case in which the prosecutor serves a notice to which rule 9.6(1)(a) applies (notice requiring Crown Court trial in a case of serious or complex fraud), the court must specify the Crown Court centre identified by that notice.

(3) In any other case, in deciding the Crown Court centre at which the trial will take place, the court must take into account—

(a) the convenience of the parties and witnesses;

(b) how soon a suitable courtroom will be available; and

(c) the directions on the allocation of Crown Court business contained in the Practice Direction.

Duty of justices' legal adviser

1–45d   **9.4**—(1) This rule applies—

    (a) only in a magistrates' court; and

    (b) unless the court—

        (i) includes a District Judge (Magistrates' Courts), and

        (ii) otherwise directs.

(2) On the court's behalf, a justices' legal adviser may—

    (a) read the allegation of the offence to the defendant;

    (b) give any explanation and ask any question required by the rules in this Part;

    (c) make any announcement required by the rules in this Part, other than an announcement of—

        (i) the court's decisions about allocation and sending,

        (ii) any indication by the court of likely sentence, or

        (iii) sentence.

(3) A justices' legal adviser must—

    (a) assist an unrepresented defendant;

    (b) give the court such advice as is required to enable it to exercise its powers;

    (c) if required, attend the members of the court outside the courtroom to give such advice, but inform the parties of any advice so given.

Duty of magistrates' court officer

1–45e   **9.5**—(1) The magistrates' court officer must—

    (a) serve notice of a sending for Crown Court trial on—

        (i) the Crown Court officer, and

        (ii) the parties;

    (b) in that notice record—

        (i) the matters specified by the court under rule 9.3 (matters to be specified on sending for trial),

        (ii) any indication of intended guilty plea given by the defendant under rule 9.7 (sending for Crown Court trial),

        (iii) any decision by the defendant to decline magistrates' court trial under rule 9.11 (adult defendant: allocation to magistrates' court for trial), and

        (iv) the date on which any custody time limit will expire;

    (c) record any indication of likely sentence to which rule 9.11 applies; and

    (d) give the court such other assistance as it requires.

(2) The magistrates' court officer must include with the notice served on the Crown Court officer—

    (a) the initial details of the prosecution case served by the prosecutor under rule 21.2;

    (b) a record of any—

        (i) listing or case management direction affecting the Crown Court,

        (ii) direction about reporting restrictions,

        (iii) decision about bail, for the purposes of section 5 of the *Bail Act* 1976,

        (iv) recognizance given by a surety, or

        (v) representation order; and

    (c) if relevant, any available details of any—

        (i) interpreter,

        (ii) intermediary, or

        (iii) other supporting adult, where the defendant is assisted by such a person.

SECTION 2:

SENDING WITHOUT ALLOCATION FOR CROWN COURT TRIAL

Prosecutor's notice requiring Crown Court trial

1–45f   **9.6**—(1) This rule applies where a prosecutor with power to do so requires a magistrates' court to send for trial in the Crown Court—

4

(a) a case of serious or complex fraud; or

(b) a case which will involve a child witness.

(2) The prosecutor must serve written notice of that requirement—

(a) on the magistrates' court officer and on the defendant; and

(b) before trial in a magistrates' court begins under Part 37 (trial and sentence in a magistrates' court).

(3) The notice must identify—

(a) the power on which the prosecutor relies; and

(b) the Crown Court centre at which the prosecutor wants the trial to take place.

(4) The prosecutor—

(a) must, when choosing a Crown Court centre, take into account the matters listed in rule 9.3(3) (court deciding to which Crown Court centre to send a case); and

(b) may change the centre identified before the case is sent for trial.

As to the application of this rule, see rule 2.1(4), *post*, § 2–206.

Sending for Crown Court trial

9.7—(1) This rule applies where a magistrates' court must, or can, send a defendant to the   **1–45g** Crown Court for trial without allocating the case for trial there.

(2) The court must read the allegation of the offence to the defendant.

(3) The court must explain, in terms the defendant can understand (with help, if necessary)—

(a) the allegation, unless it is self-explanatory;

(b) that the offence is one for which the court, as appropriate—

(i) must send the defendant to the Crown Court for trial, or

(ii) can send the defendant to the Crown Court for trial because the offence is related to one already sent for trial there;

(c) that the court is about to ask whether the defendant intends to plead guilty;

(d) that if the answer is "yes", then the Crown Court will arrange a hearing to take the defendant's plea; and

(e) that reporting restrictions apply, which the defendant may ask the court to vary or remove.

(4) In the following sequence, the court must then—

(a) ask whether the defendant intends to plead guilty;

(b) invite the prosecutor to—

(i) identify the court's power to send the defendant to the Crown Court for trial for the offence, and

(ii) make representations about any ancillary matters, including bail and directions for the management of the case in the Crown Court;

(c) invite the defendant to make representations about—

(i) the court's power to send the defendant to the Crown Court, and

(ii) any ancillary matters; and

(d) exercise its powers to—

(i) send the defendant to the Crown Court for trial, and

(ii) give any ancillary directions.

It is submitted that this rule is *ultra vires* to the extent that it may be construed as imposing an obligation on a defendant who must be sent to the Crown Court for trial to indicate his intended plea. Whilst there are provisions in the primary legislation that require a defendant, in specified circumstances, to indicate his intended plea (*e.g.* the *MCA* 1980, s.24A (§ 1–111 in the main work)), where a defendant must be sent for trial, it is the duty of the magistrates' court so to send him "forthwith" (see s.51(1) of the *CDA* 1998 (§ 1–25 in the main work)). Requiring a defendant to indicate his intended plea risks violating his privilege against self-incrimination; at the least, he should be advised that he is under no obligation to respond, and he should also be advised as to the course to be taken if he chooses to indicate a "Not Guilty" plea.

It is not entirely clear what situation is envisaged by "or can", but presumably one where the magistrates' court has a power, but not a duty, to send the defendant for trial in the Crown Court. An example would be where he appears for an either-way offence that is related to an offence for which he has been sent for trial on an earlier occasion: see s.51(4) of the 1998 Act. To the extent that this rule suggests that the decision as to whether or not to send such a defendant for trial may be dictated by his intended plea, it is misleading. Such a defendant should plainly be advised what the options are; and it is entirely illogical to tell the defendant that if he indicates an intention to plead guilty, a hearing will be arranged in the Crown Court, and then — after he has been asked what he intends to do — to invite representations from his legal representative about the court's power to send the case to the Crown Court for trial (see the sequence set out in para. (4)).

Section 3:

Allocation for Magistrates' or Crown Court Trial

Adult defendant: request for plea

1–45h   9.8—(1) This rule applies where—
   (a) the defendant is 18 or over; and
   (b) the court must decide whether a case is more suitable for trial in a magistrates' court or in the Crown Court.
(2) The court must read the allegation of the offence to the defendant.
(3) The court must explain, in terms the defendant can understand (with help, if necessary)—
   (a) the allegation, unless it is self-explanatory;
   (b) that the offence is one which can be tried in a magistrates' court or in the Crown Court;
   (c) that the court is about to ask whether the defendant intends to plead guilty;
   (d) that if the answer is "yes", then the court must treat that as a guilty plea and must sentence the defendant, or commit the defendant to the Crown Court for sentence;
   (e) that if the defendant does not answer, or the answer is "no", then—
      (i) the court must decide whether to allocate the case to a magistrates' court or to the Crown Court for trial,
      (ii) the value involved may require the court to order trial in a magistrates' court (where the offence is one to which section 22 of the *Magistrates' Courts Act* 1980 applies), and
      (iii) if the court allocates the case to a magistrates' court for trial, the defendant can nonetheless require trial in the Crown Court (unless the offence is one to which section 22 of the *Magistrates' Courts Act* 1980 applies and the value involved requires magistrates' court trial); and
   (f) that reporting restrictions apply, which the defendant may ask the court to vary or remove.
(4) The court must then ask whether the defendant intends to plead guilty.

As to the application of the rules in this section, see rule 2.1(4), *post*, § 2–206.

Adult defendant: guilty plea

1–45i   9.9—(1) This rule applies where—
   (a) rule 9.8 applies; and
   (b) the defendant indicates an intention to plead guilty.
(2) The court must exercise its power to deal with the case—
   (a) as if the defendant had just pleaded guilty to an offence that can be tried only in a magistrates' court; and
   (b) in accordance with rule 37.10 (procedure if the court convicts).

Adult defendant: not guilty plea

1–45j   9.10—(1) This rule applies where—
   (a) rule 9.8 applies; and
   (b) the defendant—
      (i) indicates an intention to plead not guilty, or
      (ii) gives no indication of intended plea.
(2) In the following sequence, the court must then—
   (a) where the offence is one to which section 22 of the *Magistrates' Courts Act* 1980 applies, explain in terms the defendant can understand (with help, if necessary) that—
      (i) if the court decides that the value involved clearly is less than £5,000, the court must order trial in a magistrates' court,

      (ii) if the court decides that it is not clear whether that value is more or less than £5,000, then the court will ask whether the defendant agrees to be tried in a magistrates' court, and

      (iii) if the answer to that question is "yes", then the court must order such a trial and if the defendant is convicted then the maximum sentence is limited;

  (b) invite the prosecutor to—

      (i) identify any previous convictions of which it can take account, and

      (ii) make representations about how the court should allocate the case for trial, including representations about the value involved, if relevant;

  (c) invite the defendant to make such representations;

  (d) where the offence is one to which section 22 of the *Magistrates' Courts Act* 1980 applies—

      (i) if it is not clear whether the value involved is more or less than £5,000, ask whether the defendant agrees to be tried in a magistrates' court,

      (ii) if the defendant's answer to that question is "yes", or if that value clearly is less than £5,000, order a trial in a magistrates' court,

      (iii) if the defendant does not answer that question, or the answer is "no", or if that value clearly is more than £5,000, apply paragraph (2)(e);

  (e) exercise its power to allocate the case for trial, taking into account—

      (i) the adequacy of a magistrates' court's sentencing powers,

      (ii) any representations by the parties, and

      (iii) any allocation guidelines issued by the Sentencing Council.

Adult defendant: allocation for magistrates' court trial

9.11—(1) This rule applies where—   **1–45k**

  (a) rule 9.10 applies; and

  (b) the court allocates the case to a magistrates' court for trial.

(2) The court must explain, in terms the defendant can understand (with help, if necessary) that—

  (a) the court considers the case more suitable for trial in a magistrates' court than in the Crown Court;

  (b) if the defendant is convicted at a magistrates' court trial, then in some circumstances the court may commit the defendant to the Crown Court for sentence;

  (c) if the defendant does not agree to a magistrates' court trial, then the court must send the defendant to the Crown Court for trial; and

  (d) before deciding whether to accept magistrates' court trial, the defendant may ask the court for an indication of whether a custodial or non-custodial sentence is more likely in the event of a guilty plea at such a trial, but the court need not give such an indication.

(3) If the defendant asks for such an indication of sentence and the court gives such an indication—

  (a) the court must then ask again whether the defendant intends to plead guilty;

  (b) if, in answer to that question, the defendant indicates an intention to plead guilty, then the court must exercise its power to deal with the case—

      (i) as if the defendant had just pleaded guilty to an offence that can be tried only in a magistrates' court, and

      (ii) in accordance with rule 37.10 (procedure if the court convicts);

  (c) if, in answer to that question, the defendant indicates an intention to plead not guilty, or gives no indication of intended plea, in the following sequence the court must then—

      (i) ask whether the defendant agrees to trial in a magistrates' court,

      (ii) if the defendant's answer to that question is "yes", order such a trial,

      (iii) if the defendant does not answer that question, or the answer is "no", apply rule 9.14.

(4) If the defendant asks for an indication of sentence but the court gives none, or if the defendant does not ask for such an indication, in the following sequence the court must then—

  (a) ask whether the defendant agrees to trial in a magistrates' court;

  (b) if the defendant's answer to that question is "yes", order such a trial;

  (c) if the defendant does not answer that question, or the answer is "no", apply rule 9.14.

Adult defendant: prosecutor's application for Crown Court trial

9.12—(1) This rule applies where—   **1–45j**

  (a) rule 9.11 applies;

(b) the defendant agrees to trial in a magistrates' court; but

(c) the prosecutor wants the court to exercise its power to send the defendant to the Crown Court for trial instead.

(2) The prosecutor must—

(a) apply before trial in a magistrates' court begins under Part 37 (trial and sentence in a magistrates' court); and

(b) notify—

(i) the defendant, and

(ii) the magistrates' court officer.

(3) The court must determine an application to which this rule applies before it deals with any other pre-trial application.

Young defendant

1–45m   **9.13**—(1) This rule applies where—

(a) the defendant is under 18; and

(b) the court must decide whether to send the defendant for Crown Court trial instead of ordering trial in a youth court.

(2) The court must read the allegation of the offence to the defendant.

(3) The court must explain, in terms the defendant can understand (with help, if necessary)—

(a) the allegation, unless it is self-explanatory;

(b) that the offence is one which can be tried in the Crown Court instead of in a youth court;

(c) that the court is about to ask whether the defendant intends to plead guilty;

(d) that if the answer is "yes", then the court must treat that as a guilty plea and must sentence the defendant, or commit the defendant to the Crown Court for sentence;

(e) that if the defendant does not answer, or the answer is "no", then the court must decide whether to send the defendant for Crown Court trial instead of ordering trial in a youth court; and

(f) that reporting restrictions apply, which the defendant may ask the court to vary or remove.

(4) The court must then ask whether the defendant intends to plead guilty.

(5) If the defendant's answer to that question is "yes", the court must exercise its power to deal with the case—

(a) as if the defendant had just pleaded guilty to an offence that can be tried only in a magistrates' court; and

(b) in accordance with rule 37.10 (procedure if the court convicts).

(6) If the defendant does not answer that question, or the answer is "no", in the following sequence the court must then—

(a) invite the prosecutor to make representations about whether Crown Court or youth court trial is more appropriate;

(b) invite the defendant to make such representations;

(c) exercise its power to allocate the case for trial, taking into account—

(i) the offence and the circumstances of the offence,

(ii) the suitability of a youth court's sentencing powers,

(iii) where the defendant is jointly charged with an adult, whether it is necessary in the interests of justice for them to be tried together in the Crown Court, and

(iv) any representations by the parties.

Allocation and sending for Crown Court trial

1–45n   **9.14**—(1) This rule applies where—

(a) under rule 9.10 or rule 9.13, the court allocates the case to the Crown Court for trial;

(b) under rule 9.11, the defendant does not agree to trial in a magistrates' court; or

(c) under rule 9.12, the court grants the prosecutor's application for Crown Court trial.

(2) In the following sequence, the court must—

(a) invite the prosecutor to make representations about any ancillary matters, including bail and directions for the management of the case in the Crown Court;

(b) invite the defendant to make any such representations; and

(c) exercise its powers to—

(i) send the defendant to the Crown Court for trial, and

(ii) give any ancillary directions.

CROWN COURT INITIAL PROCEDURE AFTER SENDING FOR TRIAL

Service of prosecution evidence

9.15—(1) This rule applies where— **1–45o**

(a) a magistrates' court sends the defendant to the Crown Court for trial; and

(b) the prosecutor serves on the defendant copies of the documents containing the evidence on which the prosecution case relies.

(2) The prosecutor must at the same time serve copies of those documents on the Crown Court officer.

(6) First appearance in Crown Court

Criminal Procedure Rules 2011 (S.I. 2011 No. 1709), r.12.2

Time for first appearance of accused sent for trial

With effect from April 2, 2012, Part 12 of the *Criminal Procedure Rules* 2011 (S.I. 2011 **1–46** No. 1709) is revoked by the *Criminal Procedure (Amendment) Rules* 2011 (S.I. 2011 No. 3075), r.7.

(7) Service of prosecution evidence

As to the amendment of the *Crime and Disorder Act 1998 (Service of Prosecution Evidence)* **★1–47** *Regulations* 2005 (S.I. 2005 No. 902), see *post*, § 1–48.

S.I. 2005 No. 902, regs 2–6

With effect from June 18, 2012, the *Crime and Disorder Act 1998 (Service of Prosecution Ev-* **★1–48** *idence) Regulations* 2005 (S.I. 2005 No. 902) are amended by the *Crime and Disorder Act 1998 (Service of Prosecution Evidence) (Amendment) Regulations* 2012 (S.I. 2012 No. 1345), so as (i) to omit the words "under section 51 of the 1998 Act" from regulation 2, (ii) to insert "1998" after the words "section 52(1)(a) of the" in regulation 2, (iii) to substitute the words "at which that person is to be tried" for the words from "specified" to the end of regulation 2, and (iv) to substitute the words "at which the person sent for trial is to be tried" for the words from "specified" to "Act" in regulation 3.

(8) Dismissal applications

Written notice of oral application for dismissal

With effect from April 2, 2012, rule 13.2(2) of the *Criminal Procedure Rules* 2011 (S.I. **1–51** 2011 No. 1709) is amended by the *Criminal Procedure (Amendment) Rules* 2011 (S.I. 2011 No. 3075), r.8, so as to substitute "28" for "14" in sub-paragraphs (b) and (c).

Written application for dismissal

With effect from April 2, 2012, rule 13.3(4) of the *Criminal Procedure Rules* 2011 (S.I. **1–52** 2011 No. 1709) is amended by the *Criminal Procedure (Amendment) Rules* 2011 (S.I. 2011 No. 3075), r.8, so as to substitute "28" for "14" in sub-paragraphs (b) and (c).

C. TRANSFERS FOR TRIAL

(1) Serious fraud cases

(a) *Notices of transfer*

Criminal Justice Act 1987, ss.4, 5

Notices of transfer and designated authorities

★**1–57**   As from a day to be appointed, section 4(1) of the 1987 Act is amended by the *Legal Aid, Sentencing and Punishment of Offenders Act* 2012, s.39(1), and Sched. 5, paras 34 and 35, so as to substitute the words "*regulations under section 19 of the* Legal Aid, Sentencing and Punishment of Offenders Act *2012*" for the words "*paragraph 2 of Schedule 3 to the* Access to Justice Act *1999*".

★   With effect from June 18, 2012 (*Criminal Justice Act 2003 (Commencement No. 28 and Saving Provisions) Order* 2012 (S.I. 2012 No. 1320)), section 41 of, and paragraph 58 of Schedule 3 to, the 2003 Act (see the main work) are brought into force in certain areas (as to which, see *post*, § 1–88). There are associated saving provisions, as to which, see article 5 of the order (*post*, § 1–88).

Notices of transfer-procedure

★**1–58**   As to the commencement of sections 41 and 332 of, and paragraph 58 of Schedule 3, and Part 4 of Schedule 37 to, the 2003 Act (see the main work), see *ante*, § 1–57.

(b) *Dismissal applications*

Criminal Justice Act 1987, s.6

Applications for dismissal

★**1–70**   As to the commencement of sections 41 and 332 of, and paragraph 58 of Schedule 3, and Part 4 of Schedule 37 to, the 2003 Act (see the main work), see *ante*, § 1–57.

(2) Cases involving children

(a) *Notices of transfer*

Criminal Justice Act 1991, s.53 and Sched. 6

Notices of transfer in certain cases involving children

★**1–73**   As from a day to be appointed, section 53(3) of the 1991 Act (see the main work) is amended by the *Legal Aid, Sentencing and Punishment of Offenders Act* 2012, s.39, and Sched. 5, para. 40, so as to substitute the words "*regulations under section 19 of the* Legal Aid, Sentencing and Punishment of Offenders Act *2012*" for the words "*paragraph 2 of Schedule 3 to the* Access to Justice Act *1999*".

With effect from June 18, 2012 (*Criminal Justice Act 2003 (Commencement No. 28 and Saving Provisions) Order* 2012 (S.I. 2012 No. 1320)), sections 41 and 332 of, and paragraph 62 of Schedule 3, and Part 4 of Schedule 37 to, the 2003 Act are brought into force in certain areas (as to which, see *post*, § 1–88). There are associated saving provisions, as to which, see article 5 of the order (*post*, § 1–88).

Notices of transfer: procedure in lieu of committal

★**1–79**   As to the commencement of sections 41 and 332 of, and paragraph 62 of Schedule 3, and Part 4 of Schedule 37 to, the 2003 Act (see the main work), see *ante*, § 1–73.

D. Committals for Trial

(1) Introduction

With effect from April 2, 2012, the *Criminal Procedure Rules* 2011 (S.I. 2011 No. 1709) are **1-86**
amended by the *Criminal Procedure (Amendment) Rules* 2011 (S.I. 2011 No. 3075), r.6, so as
to insert a new Part 9 (set out in the schedule to the amending rules) which applies to the
allocation and sending of cases for trial under sections 17A to 26 of the *MCA* 1980 (§§ 1–88
et seq. in the main work) and sections 50A to 52 of the *CDA* 1998 (see §§ 1–23 *et seq.* in the
main work). For the full text of Part 9, see *ante*, §§ 1–45a *et seq.* As to the application of Part
9, see new rule 2.1(4) (inserted by r.3(a) of the amending rules (*post*, § 2–206)).

(2) Determination of mode of trial

(a) *Statutory provisions*

Procedure for indication of intention as to plea

Magistrates' Courts Act 1980, ss.17A–17E

Initial procedure: accused to indicate intention as to plea
With effect from June 18, 2012 (*Criminal Justice Act 2003 (Commencement No. 28 and Sav-* ★**1-88**
ing Provisions) Order 2012 (S.I. 2012 No. 1320)), section 41 of, and paragraphs 1 and 2 of
Schedule 3 to, the 2003 Act are brought into force in the local justice areas of Bath and
Wansdyke, Berkshire, Bristol, Liverpool and Knowsley, North Avon, North Hampshire,
North Somerset, Ormskirk, Sefton, St Helens, Wigan and Leigh, and Wirral, and in relation
to the Crown Court where it deals with a person sent for trial or committed for sentence by
a magistrates' court in those local justice areas.
The amendments brought into force in these areas have no effect in relation to an offence
if either (a) a person first appeared in respect of the offence before June 18, 2012, or (b) a
person first appeared in respect of the offence on or after that date, but the offence is related to an indictable-only offence and the person who is charged with the latter offence first
appeared in respect of it before that date: S.I. 2012 No. 1320, art.5(1)–(3). For these
purposes, a person first appears in respect of an offence where he appears or is brought
before a magistrates' court for the first time in the proceedings in respect of which he is
charged with the offence, and an offence is related to an indictable-only offence if, were a
magistrates' court to apply section 51 of the *CDA* 1998, as it was in force immediately
before June 18, 2012 (as to which, see § 1–24 in the main work), that court would be
required to send the person charged with the first offence to the Crown Court for trial
for that offence, or could have done so: art. 5(4).

[Functions under sections 17A to 17D capable of exercise by single justice
With effect from June 18, 2012 (*Criminal Justice Act 2003 (Commencement No. 28 and Sav-* ★**1-92**
ing Provisions) Order 2012 (S.I. 2012 No. 1320)), section 41 of, and paragraphs 1 and 3 of
Schedule 3 to, the 2003 Act are brought into force in certain areas (as to which, see *ante*,
§ 1–88). There are associated saving provisions, as to which, see article 5 of the order (*ante*,
§ 1–88).

Procedure for determining mode of trial of offences triable either way

Magistrates' Courts Act 1980, s.18

Initial procedure on information for offence triable either way
With effect from June 18, 2012 (*Criminal Justice Act 2003 (Commencement No. 28 and Sav-* ★**1-94**
ing Provisions) Order 2012 (S.I. 2012 No. 1320)), section 41 of, and paragraphs 1 and 4 of

Schedule 3 to, the 2003 Act (see the main work) are brought into force in certain areas (as to which, see *ante*, § 1–88). There are associated saving provisions, as to which, see article 5 of the order (*ante*, § 1–88).

Magistrates' Courts Act 1980, s.19

Court to begin by considering which mode of trial appears more suitable

★**1–96**   With effect from June 18, 2012 (*Criminal Justice Act 2003 (Commencement No. 28 and Saving Provisions) Order* 2012 (S.I. 2012 No. 1320)), section 41 of, and paragraphs 1 and 5 of Schedule 3 to, the 2003 Act are brought into force in certain areas (as to which, see *ante*, § 1–88). There are associated saving provisions, as to which, see article 5 of the order (*ante*, § 1–88).

★**1–97**   As from June 11, 2012, a seventh update to the sentencing guidelines for magistrates' courts comes into force in relation to all offenders aged 18 or over who are sentenced on or after that date, regardless of the date of their offence. One of the principal effects is to import a new definitive allocation guideline, which includes, in particular, guidance on when either-way offences should be tried summarily. The guideline emphasises that, in general, either-way offences should be tried summarily unless it is likely that the court's sentencing powers will be insufficient, taking into account all aspects of the case, including the facts alleged by the prosecution case and those advanced by the defence.

Magistrates' Courts Act 1980, ss.20, 20A

[Procedure where summary trial appears more suitable: supplementary

★**1–99**   With effect from June 18, 2012 (*Criminal Justice Act 2003 (Commencement No. 28 and Saving Provisions) Order* 2012 (S.I. 2012 No. 1320)), section 41 of, and paragraphs 1 and 6 of Schedule 3 to, the 2003 Act are brought into force in certain areas (as to which, see *ante*, § 1–88). There are associated saving provisions, as to which, see article 5 of the order (*ante*, § 1–88).

Magistrates' Courts Act 1980, s.21

Procedure where trial on indictment appears more suitable

★**1–105**   With effect from June 18, 2012 (*Criminal Justice Act 2003 (Commencement No. 28 and Saving Provisions) Order* 2012 (S.I. 2012 No. 1320)), section 41 of, and paragraphs 1 and 7 of Schedule 3 to, the 2003 Act are brought into force in certain areas (as to which, see *ante*, § 1–88). There are associated saving provisions, as to which, see article 5 of the order (*ante*, § 1–88).

Proceedings in the absence of the accused

★**1–109**   The amendments to section 23 of the *MCA* 1980 effected by the *CJA* 2003, s.41, and Sched. 3, para. 8, are brought into force in certain areas (as to which, see *ante*, § 1–88) on June 18, 2012 (*Criminal Justice Act 2003 (Commencement No. 28 and Saving Provisions) Order* 2012 (S.I. 2012 No. 1320)). There are associated saving provisions, as to which see article 5 of the order (*ante*, § 1–88).

Magistrates' Courts Act 1980, ss.24–24D

Summary trial of information against child or young person for indictable offence

★**1–110**   With effect from June 18, 2012 (*Criminal Justice Act 2003 (Commencement No. 28 and Saving Provisions) Order* 2012 (S.I. 2012 No. 1320)), sections 41 and 332 of, and paragraphs 1 and 9 of Schedule 3 to, and Part 4 of Schedule 37 to, the 2003 Act are brought into force in certain areas (as to which, see *ante*, § 1–88). There are associated saving provisions, as to which, see article 5 of the order (*ante*, § 1–88).

[Functions under sections 24A to 24C capable of exercise by single justice

★**1–114**   With effect from June 18, 2012 (*Criminal Justice Act 2003 (Commencement No. 28 and Sav-*

ing Provisions) Order 2012 (S.I. 2012 No. 1320)), section 41 of, and paragraphs 1 and 10 of Schedule 3 to, the 2003 Act are brought into force in certain areas (as to which, see *ante*, § 1–88). There are associated saving provisions, as to which, see article 5 of the order (*ante*, § 1–88).

As from June 11, 2012, a seventh update to the sentencing guidelines for magistrates'   ★**1–115** courts comes into force. One of the principal effects is to import a new definitive allocation guideline, which includes, in particular, guidance on decisions as to mode of trial of young offenders jointly charged with an adult. As well as restating the current state of the law, it gives examples of factors to be taken into account when deciding whether to separate a youth from an adult with whom he is jointly charged, *viz.* whether separate trials can take place without causing undue inconvenience to witnesses or injustice to the case as a whole, the age of the youth particularly where the difference in age is substantial, the maturity level of the youth, the alleged role of the youth, and the record of the youth.

Juvenile charged with adult

The statement of the law in the penultimate paragraph in the main work was approved   **1–117** in *R. (W. (a minor)) v. Leeds Crown Court* [2012] 1 Cr.App.R. 13, DC.

(3) Changing from summary trial to committal proceedings, and vice versa

Magistrates' Courts Act 1980, s.25

Power to change from summary trial to committal proceedings, and vice versa

With effect from June 18, 2012 (*Criminal Justice Act 2003 (Commencement No. 28 and Sav-*   ★**1–120** *ing Provisions) Order* 2012 (S.I. 2012 No. 1320)), sections 41 and 332 of, and paragraphs 1 and 11 of Schedule 3 to, and Part 4 of Schedule 37 to, the 2003 Act are brought into force in certain areas (as to which, see *ante*, § 1–88). There are associated saving provisions, as to which, see article 5 of the order (*ante*, § 1–88).

(4) Power to issue summons to accused

Magistrates' Courts Act 1980, s.26

Power to issue summons to accused in certain circumstances

With effect from June 18, 2012 (*Criminal Justice Act 2003 (Commencement No. 28 and Sav-*   ★**1–122** *ing Provisions) Order* 2012 (S.I. 2012 No. 1320)), section 41 of, and paragraphs 1 and 12 of Schedule 3 to, the 2003 Act are brought into force in certain areas (as to which, see *ante*, § 1–88). There are associated saving provisions, as to which, see article 5 of the order (*ante*, § 1–88).

(5) Remittal to youth court

Magistrates' Courts Act 1980, s.29

Power to remit person under 18 for trial to youth court

With effect from June 18, 2012 (*Criminal Justice Act 2003 (Commencement No. 28 and Sav-*   ★**1–123** *ing Provisions) Order* 2012 (S.I. 2012 No. 1320)), section 41 of, and paragraph 51 of Schedule 3 to, the 2003 Act are brought into force (so far as not already in force) in certain areas (as to which, see *ante*, § 1–88). There are associated saving provisions, as to which, see article 5 of the order (*ante*, § 1–88).

As to section 29 having no application in the Crown Court, see *R. (W. (a minor)) v. Leeds Crown Court* [2012] 1 Cr.App.R. 13, DC (as to which, see also *ante*, § 1–117).

(6) Penalties on summary conviction

Magistrates' Courts Act 1980, s.32

Penalties on summary conviction for offences triable either way

★1–125   As from a day to be appointed, the upper limit on a fine by way of penalty on summary conviction of an offence triable either way is removed by the *Legal Aid, Sentencing and Punishment of Offenders Act* 2012, s.85(1), which provides that where "on the commencement day, a relevant offence would, apart from this subsection, be punishable on summary conviction by a fine or maximum fine of £5,000 or more (however expressed), the offence is punishable on summary conviction on or after that day by a fine of any amount." Subsection (3) provides that, for the purposes of the section "an offence is relevant if, immediately before the commencement day, it is a common law offence or it is contained in an Act or an instrument made under an Act (whether or not the offence is in force at the time)". Subsection (4) stipulates that nothing in subsection (1) affects (i) fines for offences committed before the commencement day, (ii) the operation of restrictions on fines that may be imposed on a person aged under 18, or (iii) fines that may be imposed on a person convicted by a magistrates' court who is to be sentenced as if convicted on indictment. The "commencement day" is the day on which subsection (1) is brought into force: s.85(17).

(8) Joinder of certain summary offences in an indictment

Criminal Justice Act 1988, s.40

Power to join in indictment count for common assault etc.

★1–133   With effect from June 18, 2012 (*Criminal Justice Act 2003 (Commencement No. 28 and Saving Provisions) Order* 2012 (S.I. 2012 No. 1320)), sections 41 and 332 of, and paragraph 60 of Schedule 3, and Part 4 of Schedule 37 to, the 2003 Act are brought into force (so far as not already in force) in certain areas (as to which, see *ante*, § 1–88). There are associated saving provisions, as to which, see article 5 of the order (*ante*, § 1–88).

(9) Committal for trial of summary offence connected with either way offence

Criminal Justice Act 1988, s.41

Power of Crown Court to deal with summary offence where person committed for either way offence

★1–137   As to the commencement of sections 41 and 332 of, and paragraph 60 of Schedule 3 to, and Part 4 of Schedule 37 to, the 2003 Act, see *ante*, § 1–133.

IV. AGAINST WHOM AN INDICTMENT LIES

B. Exemptions

(2) Diplomatic and international immunities

Diplomatic missions

1–147   In *Bat v. Germany* [2011] A.C.D. 111, DC, it was held: (i) under rules of customary international law, a civil servant will be entitled to inviolability of the person and immunity from suit if he is sent on a "special mission" by his government to the United Kingdom with the prior consent of the United Kingdom (Art. 1(a) of the Special Missions Convention of 1960 providing that "(a) a 'special mission' is a temporary mission, representing the State, which is sent by one State to another State with the consent of the latter for the purpose of dealing with it on specific questions or of performing in relation to it a specific task; …"); it is, however, for the United Kingdom government, and not the courts, to decide whether to recognise a mission as a special mission; (ii) whilst, under customary international law, certain holders of high-ranking office are entitled to immunity *ratione personae* during their term of office, the claimant (equivalent, in the Foreign and Commonwealth Office, to some-one of director level, at a mid-rank), was far removed from the narrow circle of those who hold the high-ranking office to be equated with the state they personify (*e.g.* Head of State, Head of Government or Minister for Foreign Affairs); however, the fact that he was not engaged on foreign affairs was not itself grounds for rejection of his claim; had he held a sufficiently high rank, the fact that he was intending to discuss matters of mutual security concern would not have entitled the United Kingdom to deprive him of immunity; and (iii) there is no customary international law that affords a person immunity from criminal pros-ecution or extradition *ratione materiae* as opposed to *ratione personae* (*i.e.* by virtue of his ac-tions on behalf of that state as opposed to his status).

C. Indicting Extradited and Repatriated Persons

(1) Introduction

Repatriated prisoners

As from a day to be appointed, the *Legal Aid, Sentencing and Punishment of Offenders Act* 2012, s.130, inserts a new section 3A in the *Repatriation of Prisoners Act* 1984 to provide statutory protection from prosecution of prisoners transferred to Great Britain under international prisoner transfer arrangements in certain circumstances.

★**1–173a**

Repatriation of Prisoners Act 1984, s.3A

[Prosecution of other offences

3A.—(1) This section applies where—

    (a) a person has been transferred into Great Britain under a warrant under section 1, and

    (b) the international arrangements in accordance with which the person has been transferred contain a speciality provision.

(2) The person must not, unless a condition in subsection (3) is met—

    (a) be prosecuted for any offence committed before the departure of that person from the country or territory from which that person has been transferred, or

    (b) be detained or otherwise subjected to any restriction of liberty for any offence committed before the departure of that person from the country or territory from which that person has been transferred, other than the offence in respect of which the person has been transferred.

(3) For the purposes of subsection (2), the conditions are as follows—

    (a) the person has consented to the transfer;

    (b) the offence is an offence which is not punishable with imprisonment or another form of detention;

    (c) the offence is an offence in respect of which the person will not be detained in connection with the person's trial, sentence or appeal;

    (d) the person is given an opportunity to leave Great Britain and—

        (i) the person does not do so before the end of the permitted period, or

        (ii) if the person does so before the end of the permitted period, the person subsequently returns to Great Britain;

    (e) after the transfer has taken place, the person has made a renunciation of the application of subsection (2) to the offence;

    (f) the appropriate authority of the country or territory from which the person has been transferred consents to the prosecution of the offence.

(4) For the purpose of subsection (3)(d) the "permitted period" is 45 days starting with the day on which the person's sentence ends.

(5) For the purpose of subsection (3)(e) a renunciation must be made before a court before which the person may be prosecuted for that offence.

15

(6) In this section a "speciality provision" means a provision preventing or limiting the prosecution, detention or other restriction of liberty of the person ("P") for any offence committed before the departure of P from the country or territory from which P has been transferred, other than for the offence in respect of which P has been transferred.]

V. THE FORM OF AN INDICTMENT

B. DRAWING THE INDICTMENT

(2) Number of counts

1–181   *R. v. Hartley* is now reported at [2012] 1 Cr.App.R. 7, *sub nom. R. v. Hartley (Practice Note)*.

D. SPECIFIC AVERMENTS

(5) Date and place

Specimen charges; identifying the incident charged

1–208   *R. v. Hartley* is now reported at [2012] 1 Cr.App.R. 7, *sub nom. R. v. Hartley (Practice Note)*.

E. DUPLICITY

(4) Rule 14.2(2) of the Criminal Procedure Rules 2011 (S.I. 2011 No. 1709)

Application of the rule and potential problems arising from it

1–225   *R. v. Hartley* is now reported at [2012] 1 Cr.App.R. 7, *sub nom. R. v. Hartley (Practice Note)*.

F. AMENDMENT

When an amendment may be made

1–230   In *R. v. Thompson (Richard)* [2012] 1 Cr.App.R. 12, CA, the court considered *R. v. Osieh* (see the main work), and concluded that what was said there as to the power to amend an indictment to include a count that is disclosed only in a notice of additional evidence was not *obiter* (as asserted in the main work), and was correct. The point must now be taken to be settled, subject only to the possibility of an appeal to the Supreme Court, but for criticism of this conclusion (along the lines of that in the main work), see CLW/11/38/1.

G. JOINDER

(5) Separate trials of counts lawfully joined and of defendants jointly charged

The approach to severance in cases alleging scandalous conduct

★**1–253**   To the extent that *R. v. D.* (see the main work) suggested that there was a rule of law that where two or more complainants give evidence in relation to similar (sexual) offending, and where it is not suggested that their evidence is cross-admissible, the judge must give a specific direction to the jury that they should not treat the evidence of one complainant as supportive of the evidence of another, it went too far; whilst the precise direction that is appropriate will depend on the facts of the particular case, here it had been sufficient for the judge to have given the jury a strong direction as to the need to consider each count and the evidence on each count separately, and to point out to the jury that the evidence on each count was different and that therefore their verdicts need not be the same: *R. v. H.* [2012] 1 Cr.App.R. 30, CA. As to this case, see also *post*, § 11–40.

H. Consequences of a Defect Being Left Uncorrected

The decision of the House of Lords in *Seal v. Chief Constable of South Wales Police* (see the **1–266** main work) was considered by the European Court of Human Rights in *Seal v. U.K.* (2012) 54 E.H.R.R. 6. That court accepted that restrictions on the right of access to a court (whether by way of imposition of a time limit on the institution of proceedings, or by way of a requirement that leave to institute proceedings be obtained from an independent judge) were permissible in principle. It also held that the manner in which they had operated in the particular circumstances had been proportionate; but the very fact that the court considered proportionality allows of the possibility that domestic law will deem proceedings to have been a nullity in circumstances where the Strasbourg court would hold the restriction to be a disproportionate interference with the right of access to a court.

VI. TIME FOR COMMENCEMENT OF PROSECUTION

B. Statutory Limitations on the Prosecution of Offences

(1) General time limits

Magistrates' Courts Act 1980, s.127

As to the further commencement of section 30 of the *CJA* 2003, see *post*, § 1–276. ★**1–272**

(2) Particular provisions as to time

A statute (*Social Security Administration Act* 1992, s.116(2)) that allowed for a prosecution ★**1–275** to be instituted at any time within the period of three months from when the Secretary of State knew of evidence to justify a prosecution, or within 12 months from the offence itself, "whichever period last expires", was unequivocal; thus, if a benefit offence only came to light 12 months after it was committed, the Secretary of State had another three months in which to launch proceedings: *Bennett v. Secretary of State for Work and Pensions*, 176 J.P. 181, DC.

C. Commencement of Prosecution

With effect from March 19, 2012, sections 29(1) to (3) and (5) and 30 of the *CJA* 2003 ★**1–276** come into force, but only for the purposes of criminal proceedings instituted by the Director of the Serious Fraud Office or the DPP, or a person authorised by either of them: *Criminal Justice Act 2003 (Commencement No. 27) Order* 2012 (S.I. 2012 No. 825).

VII. PREFERRING THE BILL OF INDICTMENT

A. When a Bill of Indictment may be Preferred

Administration of Justice (Miscellaneous Provisions) Act 1933, s.2(1), (2)

With effect from June 18, 2012 (*Criminal Justice Act 2003 (Commencement No. 28 and Sav-* ★**1–277**

ing Provisions) Order 2012 (S.I. 2012 No. 1320)), sections 41 and 332 of, and paragraph 34 of Schedule 3 to, and Part 4 of Schedule 37 to, the 2003 Act are brought into force (so far as they are not already in force) in certain areas (as to which, see *ante*, § 1–88). There are associated saving provisions, as to which, see article 5 of the order (*ante*, § 1–88).

Indictment based on committal

Committal defective

1-284   *R. v. Hall* (see the main work) was considered in *R. v. Ayhan, post,* § 5–38, where the issue related to the validity of a committal for sentence.

Administration of Justice (Miscellaneous Provisions) Act 1933, s.2(3)–(8) and Sched. 2

★**1-296**   With effect from June 18, 2012 (*Criminal Justice Act 2003 (Commencement No. 28 and Saving Provisions) Order* 2012 (S.I. 2012 No. 1320)), section 41 of, and paragraph 34 of Schedule 3 to, the 2003 Act are brought into force (so far as they are not already in force) in certain areas (as to which, see *ante*, § 1–88). There are associated saving provisions, as to which, see article 5 of the order (*ante*, § 1–88).

IX. PROCEEDINGS AGAINST CORPORATIONS

Procedure on charge of offence against corporation

Magistrates' Courts Act 1980, s.46, and Sched. 3

★**1-315**   With effect from June 18, 2012 (*Criminal Justice Act 2003 (Commencement No. 28 and Saving Provisions) Order* 2012 (S.I. 2012 No. 1320)), sections 41 and 332 of, and paragraph 51(1) and (13) of Schedule 3 to, and Part 4 of Schedule 37 to, the 2003 Act are brought into force in certain areas (as to which, see *ante*, § 1–88). There are associated saving provisions, as to which, see article 5 of the order (*ante*, § 1–88).

XI. POWERS AND DUTIES OF PARTICULAR PROSECUTION AGENCIES

A. CROWN PROSECUTION SERVICE

(2) Functions of Director of Public Prosecutions

Prosecution of Offences Act 1985, s.3

1-326   The amendment of section 3 of the 1985 Act by the *Police Reform and Social Responsibility Act* 2011, s.99, and Sched. 16, para. 171 (see the main work), came into force on January 16, 2012: *Police Reform and Social Responsibility Act 2011 (Commencement No. 3 and Transitional Provisions) Order* 2011 (S.I. 2011 No. 3019).

(8) Guidelines for crown prosecutors

Prosecution of Offences Act 1985, s.10

1-338   *R. (E.) v. DPP*; *R. (S. and R.) v. DPP* is now reported at [2012] 1 Cr.App.R. 6.

(11) Power of Secretary of State to set time limits in relation to preliminary stages of criminal proceedings

Prosecution of Offences Act 1985, s.22

★**1-342**   With effect from June 18, 2012 (*Criminal Justice Act 2003 (Commencement No. 28 and Sav-*

ing Provisions) Order 2012 (S.I. 2012 No. 1320)), section 41 of, and paragraph 57(1) and (5) of Schedule 3 to, the 2003 Act are brought into force (so far as they are not already in force) in certain areas (as to which, see *ante,* § 1–88). There are associated saving provisions, as to which, see article 5 of the order (*ante,* § 1–88).

As from a day to be appointed, section 22(11) of the 1985 Act is amended by the *Legal* ★ *Aid, Sentencing and Punishment of Offenders Act* 2012, s.105, and Sched. 12, para. 22, so as to substitute, in the definition of "custody", the words "or youth detention accommodation to which a person is remanded under section 91 of the *Legal Aid, Sentencing and Punishment of Offenders Act* 2012" for the words from "to which" to "Act of 1969".

Requirements of the European Convention on Human Rights

O'Dowd v. U.K. is now reported at (2012) 54 E.H.R.R. 8.   **1-345**

Criteria to be satisfied before extension granted

Whereas defendants in custody are to be tried within the custody time limits set out in ★**1-357** regulations made under section 22 of the 1985 Act (§ 1–342 in the main work), and whereas a Crown Court judge may extend the time limit if there is "good and sufficient cause" (s.22(3)(iii)), the approach the Crown Court should take is as follows: (i) if in a routine case, where there should ordinarily be no difficulty about the availability of a judge or a physical court room, an issue as to the availability of money by way of "sitting day allocation" (*viz.* the budget allocated by Her Majesty's Courts and Tribunals Service to each court) arises, then the case must be referred to the resident judge well in advance of any issue arising as to the custody time limit; listing is a judicial responsibility for the resident judge, under the guidance of the presiding judges; the listing officer carries out the day-to-day listing operation under the direction of the resident judge; (ii) as the extension of custody time limits involves the liberty of a defendant, the resident judge must be provided with sufficient information on a regular basis such that there can be proper monitoring of cases nearing their limit; provided the listing officer at each court centre gives the resident judge such regular information and there is close co-operation between centres, routine cases should be managed in such a way that money is always available to enable a case to be heard within its time limit; if more funds or judges are needed at a court centre, then that information must be passed to those responsible for the provision of money; (iii) if, despite such careful management, an application has to be made to extend a time limit in a routine case because the funds by way of allocated sitting days are insufficient to enable the case to be heard within the time limit, then the application must be heard in open court on the basis of detailed evidence; it is clear from *ex p. McDonald* (see the main work), that it is for the prosecution to satisfy the court of the need to extend the time limit; it must follow that evidence from the senior management of the courts and tribunals service must be provided well in advance of the hearing to the defendant and adduced by the prosecution to the court; the judge must then subject the application and the evidence to that rigorous level of scrutiny that is required where a trial is to be delayed and a person confined to prison because of the lack of money to try the case; although other considerations may apply to cases that are not routine, lack of money provided by Parliament will rarely, if ever, justify an extension of a time limit; (iv) the judge hearing the application must give a full and detailed judgment; on judicial review, the Divisional Court, whilst recognising that the decision is for the judge, will scrutinise the matter rigorously; without a full and detailed judgment, such review cannot be done speedily and economically: *R. (McAuley) v. Crown Court at Coventry* [2012] 4 *Archbold Review* 2, DC (also considering *R. (Gibson) v. Winchester Crown Court* (see the main work).

(12) Discontinuance of proceedings in magistrates' court

Prosecution of Offences Act 1985, s.23

With effect from June 18, 2012 (*Criminal Justice Act 2003 (Commencement No. 28 and Sav-* ★**1-360** *ing Provisions) Order* 2012 (S.I. 2012 No. 1320)), section 41 of, and paragraph 57(1) and (6) of Schedule 3 to, the 2003 Act are brought into force (so far as they are not already in force) in certain areas (as to which, see *ante*, § 1–88). There are associated saving provisions, as to which, see article 5 of the order (*ante*, § 1–88).

(13) Discontinuance of proceedings in Crown Court

Prosecution of Offences Act 1985, s.23A

Discontinuance of proceedings after accused has been sent for trial

★**1–363**   With effect from June 18, 2012 (*Criminal Justice Act 2003 (Commencement No. 28 and Saving Provisions) Order* 2012 (S.I. 2012 No. 1320)), sections 41 and 332 of, and paragraph 57(1) and (7) (not "(2)" as erroneously stated in the main work) of Schedule 3, and Part 4 of Schedule 37 to, the 2003 Act are brought into force (so far as they are not already in force) in certain areas (as to which, see *ante*, § 1–88). There are associated saving provisions, as to which, see article 5 of the order (*ante*, § 1–88).

CHAPTER 2

THE CRIMINAL JURISDICTION OF THE CROWN COURT

I. THE CROWN COURT

C. CONSTITUTION

(1) Judges of the Crown Court

Senior Courts Act 1981, s.8

★**2–3**   As from April 2, 2012 (*Armed Forces Act 2011 (Commencement No. 1, Transitional and Transitory Provisions) Order* 2012 (S.I. 2012 No. 669)), the *Armed Forces Act* 2011, s.26, and Sched. 2, para. 1(1) to (3), amend section 8(1) of the 1981 Act so as: (i) to substitute for the words ", Recorder or District Judge (Magistrates' Courts)" in paragraph (b), the words ", Recorder, qualifying judge advocate or District Judge (Magistrates' Courts)", and (ii) to substitute for the words "or Recorder" in paragraph (c), the words ", Recorder or qualifying judge advocate".

★   As from April 2, 2012 (*Armed Forces Act 2011 (Commencement No. 1, Transitional and Transitory Provisions) Order* 2012 (S.I. 2012 No. 669)), the *Armed Forces Act* 2011, s.26*Armed Forces Act* 2011, s.26, and Sched. 2, para. 1(1) and (4), and Sched. 2, para. 1(1) and (4), amend section 8 of the 1981 Act so as to insert a new subsection (1A), as follows—

"(1A) The jurisdiction of the Crown Court exercisable by a qualifying judge advocate by virtue of subsection (1) is the jurisdiction of the Court in relation to any criminal cause or matter other than an appeal from a youth court.".

★   As from April 2, 2012 (*Armed Forces Act 2011 (Commencement No. 1, Transitional and Transitory Provisions) Order* 2012 (S.I. 2012 No. 669)), the *Armed Forces Act* 2011, s.26, and Sched. 2, para. 1(1) and (5), amend section 8(3) of the 1981 Act so as substitute for the words ", Circuit judge, Recorder or District Judge (Magistrates' Courts)" the words ", Circuit judge, Recorder, qualifying judge advocate or District Judge (Magistrates' Courts)".

★   As from April 2, 2012 (*Armed Forces Act 2011 (Commencement No. 1, Transitional and Transitory Provisions) Order* 2012 (S.I. 2012 No. 669)), the *Armed Forces Act* 2011, s.26, and Sched. 2, para. 1(1) and (6), amend section 8 of the 1981 Act so as to insert a new subsection (4), as follows—

"(4) Subsection (1A) does not affect the jurisdiction of the Crown Court exercisable by a person who holds an office mentioned in subsection (1)(a) or (b) where that person is also a qualifying judge advocate.".

Senior Courts Act 1981, ss.73, 74

General provisions

As from April 2, 2012 (*Armed Forces Act 2011 (Commencement No. 1, Transitional and Transitory Provisions) Order* 2012 (S.I. 2012 No. 669)), the *Armed Forces Act* 2011, s.26, and Sched. 2, para. 2, amend section 73(2) and (3) of the 1981 Act so as to substitute the words ", Recorder or qualifying judge advocate" for the words "or Recorder" (wherever they occur). ★**2–4**

Appeals and committals for sentence

As from April 2, 2012 (*Armed Forces Act 2011 (Commencement No. 1, Transitional and Transitory Provisions) Order* 2012 (S.I. 2012 No. 669)), the *Armed Forces Act* 2011, s.26, and Sched. 2, para. 3, amend section 74 of the 1981 Act so as: (i) to insert the words "or a qualifying judge advocate" after the word "Recorder" in subsection (1), and (ii) to substitute the words ", Recorder or qualifying judge advocate," for the words "or Recorder," in subsection (3). ★**2–5**

Criminal Procedure Rules 2011 (S.I. 2011 No. 1709), r.63.10

Constitution of the Crown Court

As from April 2, 2012, rule 63.10(a)(i) of the 2011 rules is amended by the substitution of ", a Recorder or a qualifying judge advocate" for the words "or a Recorder": *Criminal Procedure (Amendment) Rules* 2011 (S.I. 2011 No. 3075), r.16(a). **2–6**

(2) Additional powers

Courts Act 2003, s.66

Judges having powers of District Judges (Magistrates' Courts)

As from April 2, 2012 (*Armed Forces Act 2011 (Commencement No. 1, Transitional and Transitory Provisions) Order* 2012 (S.I. 2012 No. 669)), the *Armed Forces Act* 2011, s.26, and Sched. 2, para. 6(a), amend section 66 of the 2003 Act so as to insert a new subsection (2A), as follows— ★**2–8**

"(2A) A qualifying judge advocate has the powers of a justice of the peace who is a District Judge (Magistrates' Courts) in relation to criminal causes and matters.".

As from April 2, 2012 (*Armed Forces Act 2011 (Commencement No. 1, Transitional and Transitory Provisions) Order* 2012 (S.I. 2012 No. 669)), the *Armed Forces Act* 2011, s.26, and Sched. 2, para. 6(b), amend section 66 of the 2003 Act so as to insert new subsections (5) and (6), as follows— ★

"(5) In this section 'qualifying judge advocate' means—
　the Judge Advocate General; or
　a person appointed under section 30(1)(a) or (b) of the *Courts-Martial (Appeals) Act* 1951 (assistants to the Judge Advocate General).
(6) Subsection (2A) is without prejudice to the powers conferred by this section on a person within subsection (2) where that person is also a qualifying judge advocate.".

In *R. (W. (a minor)) v. Leeds Crown Court* [2012] 1 Cr.App.R. 13, DC, a magistrates' court had committed a juvenile to the Crown Court alongside an adult co-accused, under section 24(1)(b) of the *MCA* 1980 (see § 1–110 in the main work). At the Crown Court the co-accused pleaded guilty. It was submitted that the judge could and should have remitted the case to the youth court for trial, either by deciding to sit as a district judge of the magistrates' court under section 66 of the 2003 Act and, in that capacity, revisiting the issue of mode of trial under section 24, or by interpreting section 29 of the 1980 Act (see

§ 1–123 in the main work) so as to give him power to do so. It was held that once a juvenile had been validly committed for trial with an adult, he had to be tried in the Crown Court even if the adult pleaded guilty. Given the detailed and complex provisions setting out the powers of the Crown Court and of magistrates' courts to determine mode of trial and to revisit previous decisions, it could not be contended that the absence of the power to remit was due to legislative inadvertence. The section 66 argument did not work because the matter was no longer in the magistrates' court to be revisited. The Crown Court was seized of the matter and the powers of magistrates' courts were no longer relevant. The Crown Court judge had to sit as a judge of the Crown Court.

It is submitted that this decision brings into question the decision in *R. v. Ashton*; *R. v. Draz*; *R. v. O'Reilly* [2006] 2 Cr.App.R. 15, CA. See the commentary in the main work.

D. ALLOCATION OF BUSINESS AND LOCATION OF CROWN COURT SITTINGS

(1) Statutory provisions

Magistrates' Courts Act 1980, s.7

Place of trial on indictment

★**2–11**   With effect from June 18, 2012 (*Criminal Justice Act 2003 (Commencement No. 28 and Saving Provisions) Order* 2012 (S.I. 2012 No. 1320)), sections 41 and 332 of, and paragraph 51(1) and (3) of Schedule 3 to, and Part 4 of Schedule 37 to, the 2003 Act are brought into force in certain areas (as to which, see *ante*, § 1–88). There are associated saving provisions, as to which, see article 5 of the order (*ante*, § 1–88).

Senior Courts Act 1981, ss.75, 76

Allocation of cases according to composition of court, etc.

★**2–12**   As from April 2, 2012 (*Armed Forces Act 2011 (Commencement No. 1, Transitional and Transitory Provisions) Order* 2012 (S.I. 2012 No. 669)), the *Armed Forces Act* 2011, s.26, and Sched. 2, para. 4, amend section 75(1) of the 1981 Act so as to substitute the words ", Circuit judge, Recorder, qualifying judge advocate or District Judge (Magistrates' Courts)" for the words ", Circuit judge, Recorder or District Judge (Magistrates' Courts)".

Committal [Sending] for trial: alteration of place of trial

★**2–13**   With effect from June 18, 2012 (*Criminal Justice Act 2003 (Commencement No. 28 and Saving Provisions) Order* 2012 (S.I. 2012 No. 1320)), sections 41 and 332 of, and paragraph 54(1) and (2) of Schedule 3 to, and Part 4 of Schedule 37 to, the 2003 Act are brought into force in certain areas (as to which, see *ante*, § 1–88). There are associated saving provisions, as to which, see article 5 of the order (*ante*, § 1–88).

E. RIGHTS OF AUDIENCE AND COURT DRESS

Court dress of advocates

2–28   As from November 21, 2011, advocates appearing before the Supreme Court or the Judicial Committee of the Privy Council may, by agreement, dispense with any or all of the elements of traditional court dress. Provided that all the advocates in any particular case agree, they may communicate to the registrar their wish to dispense with part or all of court dress, and the court will normally agree: *Revised guidance on court dress at the United Kingdom Supreme Court*, unreported, November 21, 2011, SC.

V. APPELLATE JURISDICTION OF CROWN COURT IN CRIMINAL CASES

F. Procedure

(4) Appeal is by way of rehearing

Senior Courts Act 1981, s.79(3)

Where a judge hears an appeal to the Crown Court against conviction with lay magis-   **2–184**
trates, any pre-sentence report should not be read until the trial stage has been concluded;
such reports are prepared on the assumption that the defendant is guilty and can contain
opinion and hearsay, which is either inadmissible or only admissible under certain conditions; and they may refer to the defendant's antecedents; since an appeal against conviction
to the Crown Court is by way of rehearing, it is important for the tribunal of fact not to see
such inadmissible evidence: *Barnard v. DPP* [2011] A.C.D. 108, DC ([2011] EWHC 1648
(Admin.)). As to this case, see also *post*, § 13–110a.

VI. CRIMINAL PROCEDURE RULES

Criminal Procedure Rules 2011 (S.I. 2011 No. 1709), Pt 2

When the rules apply

As from April 2, 2012, the *Criminal Procedure (Amendment) Rules* 2011 (S.I. 2011 No.   **2–206**
3075), r.3(a), amends rule 2(1) of the 2011 rules so as to insert a new paragraph (4), as follows—

"(4) Rule 9.6, and the rules in Section 3 of Part 9 (allocation and sending for trial), apply only
where there have come into force the amendments made by Schedule 3 to the *Criminal Justice Act*
2003 (allocation of cases triable either way, and sending cases to the Crown Court, etc.) which confer
the powers to which those rules apply.".

As from April 2, 2012, the *Criminal Procedure (Amendment) Rules* 2011 (S.I. 2011 No.
3075), r.3(b), amends rule 2(3) of the 2011 rules so as to substitute "2011" for "1997" in
both places.

Criminal Procedure Rules 2011 (S.I. 2011 No. 1709), Pt 5

Forms

Consolidated Criminal Practice Direction (Amendment No. 26) (Criminal Proceedings: Forms) is   **★2–219**
now reported at [2012] 1 Cr.App.R. 28, *sub nom. Amendment No. 26 to the Consolidated Criminal Practice Direction (Criminal Proceedings: Forms)*.

As from February 20, 2012, expanded versions of the plea and case management hearing   **★**
form for use in connection with Part 3 of the *Criminal Procedure Rules* 2011 (S.I. 2011 No.
1709) (see §§ 4–115 *et seq.* in the main work), for cases involving two to 10 defendants, are
available on the Ministry of Justice's website (http://www.justice.gov.uk/courts/procedure-
rules/criminal/formspage).

The Lord Chief Justice has authorised the withdrawal of four forms used in connection   **★**
with Part 3 of the 2011 rules by magistrates' courts and youth courts when committing or
sending a case for trial in the Crown Court, and one form used in connection with rule
41.11 or 41.12 (retrial following acquittal for serious offence), and the amendment of six
other forms for use in connection with rules 41.2, 41.3, 41.4, 41.8, 41.15 and 41.16.

Supply to the public, including reporters, of information about a case

In *R. (Guardian News and Media Ltd) v. City of Westminster Magistrates' Court* [2012] 4   **★2–219g**
Archbold Review 1, CA (Civ. Div.) (*post*, § 4–4), both Lord Neuberger M.R. and Hooper L.J.
expressed the view that the reference to "a document ... about the case" in rule 5.8(7) of the
2011 rules was wide enough to embrace witness statements and exhibits. Hooper L.J. fur-

ther expressed the view that this rule could be relied on to reach the same result in relation to the power to order the disclosure of documents to non-parties as the court had reached by application of the common law (as to which, see *post*, § 4–4). However, the Master of the Rolls declined to express any view on this, the court having heard no argument on the point, and Toulson L.J. did not touch on the issue.

CHAPTER 3

BAIL, APPEARANCE OF ACCUSED FOR TRIAL, PRESENCE DURING TRIAL

I. BAIL

A. GENERAL

(2) The Bail Act 1976

(c) *Text of the Act*

Bail Act 1976, ss.1, 2

Other definitions

★3–7   As from a day to be appointed, section 2(2) of the 1976 Act is amended by the *Legal Aid, Sentencing and Punishment of Offenders Act* 2012, s.90, and Sched. 11, paras 1 and 2, so as (i) to substitute "eighteen" for "seventeen" in the definition of "young person"; and (ii) to insert the following definitions at the appropriate places—

> "'bail in non-extradition proceedings' means bail in criminal proceedings of the kind mentioned in section 1(1)(a),";
>
> "'custodial sentence' means a sentence or order mentioned in section 76(1) of the *Powers of Criminal Courts (Sentencing) Act* 2000 or any corresponding sentence or order imposed or made under any earlier enactment,";
>
> "'imprisonable offence' means an offence punishable in the case of an adult with imprisonment,";
>
> "'sexual offence' means an offence specified in Part 2 of Schedule 15 to the *Criminal Justice Act* 2003,";
>
> "'violent offence' means murder or an offence specified in Part 1 of Schedule 15 to the *Criminal Justice Act* 2003,".

Bail Act 1976, s.3

General provisions

★3–9   As from a day to be appointed, section 3 of the 1976 Act is amended by the *Legal Aid, Sentencing and Punishment of Offenders Act* 2012, s.90, and Sched. 11, paras 1 and 3, so as (i) to substitute, in subsection (6ZAA), the words "person granted bail in criminal proceedings of the kind mentioned in section 1(1)(a) or (b)), section 3AAA (in the case of a child or young person granted bail in connection with extradition proceedings)," for the word "person)"; (ii) to substitute, in subsection (7), the words "a person under the age of seventeen" for the words "a child or young person"; (iii) to substitute, in the same subsection, the words "the person" for the words "the child or young person" in both places where they occur, and (iv) in subsection (7)(a), to omit the words "of a young person" and the word "young" in the second place it appears.

★3–11   With effect from June 18, 2012 (*Criminal Justice Act 2003 (Commencement No. 28 and Sav-*

ing Provisions) Order 2012 (S.I. 2012 No. 1320)), section 41 of, and paragraph 48 of Schedule 3 to, the 2003 Act are brought into force (so far as they are not already in force) in certain areas (as to which, see *ante*, § 1–88). There are associated saving provisions, as to which, see article 5 of the order (*ante*, § 1–88).

Conditions of bail

Mangouras v. Spain is now reported at (2012) 54 E.H.R.R. 25.   ★3–11a

Bail Act 1976, s.3AA

Conditions for the imposition of electronic monitoring requirements: children and young persons

As from a day to be appointed, section 3AA of the 1976 Act is amended by the *Legal Aid,*   ★3–12
Sentencing and Punishment of Offenders Act 2012, s.90, and Sched. 11, paras 1 and 4, so as (i) to add at the end of the heading "*released on bail other than in extradition proceedings*", and (ii) to insert the words "released on bail in criminal proceedings of the kind mentioned in section 1(1)(a) or (b)" after the words "young person" in subsection (1).

As from a day to be appointed, section 3AA of the 1976 Act is amended by the *Legal Aid,*   ★
Sentencing and Punishment of Offenders Act 2012, s.105, and Sched. 12, paras 14 and 15, so as (i) to substitute the words "subject to a custodial remand" for the words "to local authority accommodation" in subsection (3)(b), and (ii) to insert new subsections (11) and (12), as follows—

"(11) The references in subsection (3)(b) to an imprisonable offence include a reference to an offence—
    (a) of which the child or young person has been convicted outside England and Wales, and
    (b) which is equivalent to an offence that is punishable with imprisonment in England and Wales.

(12) The reference in subsection (3)(b) to a child or young person being subject to a custodial remand is to the child or young person being—
    (a) remanded to local authority accommodation or youth detention accommodation under section 91 of the *Legal Aid, Sentencing and Punishment of Offenders Act* 2012,
    (b) remanded to local authority accommodation under section 23 of the *Children and Young Persons Act* 1969 or to prison under that section as modified by section 98 of the *Crime and Disorder Act* 1998 or undersection 27 of the *Criminal Justice Act* 1948, or
    (c) subject to a form of custodial detention in a country or territory outside England and Wales while awaiting trial or sentence in that country or territory or during a trial in that country or territory.".

As from a day to be appointed, a new section 3AAA (conditions for the imposition of electronic monitoring requirements: children and young persons released on bail in extradition proceedings) is inserted in the 1976 Act after section 3AA by the *Legal Aid, Sentencing and Punishment of Offenders Act* 2012, s.90, and Sched. 11, paras 1 and 5.

Bail Act 1976, ss.3AB, 3AC

Conditions for the imposition of electronic monitoring requirements: other persons

As from a day to be appointed, section 3AB of the 1976 Act is amended by the *Legal Aid,*   ★3–12a
Sentencing and Punishment of Offenders Act 2012, s.90, and Sched. 11, paras 1 and 6, so as (i) to substitute "eighteen" for "seventeen" in subsection (1), and (ii) to omit subsection (4).

Electronic monitoring: general provisions

As from a day to be appointed, section 3AC of the 1976 Act is amended by the *Legal Aid,*   ★3–12b
Sentencing and Punishment of Offenders Act 2012, s.90, and Sched. 11, paras 1 and 7, so as to insert ", 3AAA" after "3AA" in each of subsections (7) and (8).

Bail Act 1976, s.5

Supplementary provisions about decisions on bail

As to the commencement of section 41 of, and paragraph 48 of Schedule 3 to, the 2003   ★3–24
Act (see the main work), see *ante*, § 3–11.

Bail Act 1976, ss.5B, 6

Offence of absconding by person released on bail

★**3–29**   As to the commencement of section 41 of, and paragraph 48 of Schedule 3 to, the 2003 Act (see the main work), see *ante*, § 3–11.

"Surrender to custody"

3–30   In the absence of special arrangements particular either to the court or to the individual case, surrender to the Crown Court for the purposes of section 6(1) of the 1976 Act (§ 3–27 in the main work) is accomplished when the defendant presents himself to the custody officer by entering the dock or where a hearing before the judge commences at which he is formally identified as being present; if there has been no previous surrender, as ordinarily there will have been, it is also accomplished by arraignment (*R. v. Central Criminal Court, ex p. Guney* (see the main work)); the position in a magistrates' court may be the same, but may easily differ (as to which, see *DPP v. Richards* (see the main work)); reporting to the court usher (either by the defendant or the defendant's advocate), however, does not amount to surrender: *R. v. Evans* [2012] 1 W.L.R. 1192, CA.

Bail Act 1976, s.7

Liability to arrest for absconding or breaking conditions of bail

★**3–37**   As from a day to be appointed, section 7 of the 1976 Act is amended by the *Legal Aid, Sentencing and Punishment of Offenders Act* 2012, s.90, and Sched. 11, paras 1 and 8, so as (i) to substitute the words "subsections (5A) and (6)" for "subsection (6)" in subsection (5); (ii) to substitute the words "a person brought before a justice under subsection (4) or (4B)" for the words "the person so brought before the justice" in subsection (6); and (iii) to insert a new subsection (5A), as follows—

> "(5A) A justice of the peace may not remand a person in, or commit a person to, custody under subsection (5) if—
>> (a) the person has attained the age of eighteen,
>> (b) the person was released on bail in non-extradition proceedings,
>> (c) the person has not been convicted of an offence in those proceedings, and
>> (d) it appears to the justice of the peace that there is no real prospect that the person will be sentenced to a custodial sentence in the proceedings.".

★   As from a day to be appointed, section 7 of the 1976 Act is amended by the *Legal Aid, Sentencing and Punishment of Offenders Act* 2012, s.105, and Sched. 12, paras 14 and 16, so as to substitute, in subsection (6), the words "section 91 of the *Legal Aid, Sentencing and Punishment of Offenders Act* 2012 (remands of children otherwise than on bail)" for the words from "section 23" to the end of the subsection.

3–39   For the Grand Chamber decision in *Al-Khawaja v. U.K.*, see *post*, § 11–3a. If the *Havering Magistrates' Court* decision was not overtaken by the chamber decision (see the main work), it certainly will not have been overtaken by that of the Grand Chamber.

Bail Act 1976, s.9

Offence of agreeing to indemnify sureties in criminal proceedings

★**3–46**   As to the commencement of section 41 of, and paragraph 48 of Schedule 3 to, the 2003 Act (see the main work), see *ante*, § 3–11.

Bail Act 1976, s.9A

Bail decisions relating to persons aged under 18 who are accused of offences mentioned in Schedule 2 to the Magistrates' Courts Act 1980

★**3–47a**   As from a day to be appointed, section 9A of the 1976 Act is amended by the *Legal Aid, Sentencing and Punishment of Offenders Act* 2012, s.90, and Sched. 11, paras 1 and 9, so as (i) to substitute "children or young persons" for "persons under 18" in the heading; (ii) to substitute the words "child or young person" for the words "person under 18" in subsection (1)(a); and (iii) to insert the words "child or young" after the word "accused" in subsections (2) and (3)(b).

Bail Act 1976, Sched. 1

Defendants to whom Part I applies

As from a day to be appointed,paragraph 1 of Part I of Schedule 1 to the 1976 Act, and the heading preceding it, are amended by the *Legal Aid, Sentencing and Punishment of Offenders Act* 2012, s.90, and Sched. 11, paras 1, and 10 to 12, so as (i) to change the heading to "Application of Part I"; and (ii) to insert the words "and paragraph 1A" after "sub-paragraph (2)".   ★3–48

As from a day to be appointed, a new paragraph 1A is inserted in Part I of Schedule 1 to   ★
the 1976 Act by the *Legal Aid, Sentencing and Punishment of Offenders Act* 2012, s.90, and Sched. 11, paras 1, 10 and 13, as follows—

"1A.—(1) The paragraphs of this Part of this Schedule mentioned in sub-paragraph (2) do not apply in relation to bail in non-extradition proceedings where—
(a) the defendant has attained the age of 18,
(b) the defendant has not been convicted of an offence in those proceedings, and
(c) it appears to the court that there is no real prospect that the defendant will be sentenced to a custodial sentence in the proceedings.
(2) The paragraphs are—
(a) paragraph 2 (refusal of bail where defendant may fail to surrender to custody, commit offences on bail or interfere with witnesses),
(b) paragraph 2A (refusal of bail where defendant appears to have committed indictable or either way offence while on bail), and
(c) paragraph 6 (refusal of bail where defendant has been arrested under section 7).".

Exceptions to right to bail

As from a day to be appointed,paragraph 2 of Part I of Schedule 1 to the 1976 Act is   ★
amended by the *Legal Aid, Sentencing and Punishment of Offenders Act* 2012, s.90, and Sched. 11, paras 1, 10 and 14, so as to substitute a new sub-paragraph (2), as follows—
"(2) Where the defendant falls within paragraph 6B, this paragraph does not apply unless—
(a) the court is of the opinion mentioned in paragraph 6A, or
(b) paragraph 6A does not apply by virtue of paragraph 6C.".

As from a day to be appointed, a new paragraph 2ZA is inserted (after para. 2) in Part I   ★
of Schedule 1 to the 1976 Act by the *Legal Aid, Sentencing and Punishment of Offenders Act* 2012, s.90, and Sched. 11, paras 1, 10 and 15, as follows—
"2ZA.—(1) The defendant need not be granted bail if the court is satisfied that there are substantial grounds for believing that the defendant, if released on bail (whether subject to conditions or not), would commit an offence while on bail by engaging in conduct that would, or would be likely to, cause—
(a) physical or mental injury to an associated person; or
(b) an associated person to fear physical or mental injury.
(2) In sub-paragraph (1) 'associated person' means a person who is associated with the defendant within the meaning of section 62 of the *Family Law Act* 1996.".

As from a day to be appointed, a new paragraph 2A of Part I of Schedule 1 to the 1976   ★
Act is substituted by the *Legal Aid, Sentencing and Punishment of Offenders Act* 2012, s.90, and Sched. 11, paras 1, 10 and 16. The draftsman has not specified whether this is intended to be by way of substitution of the original paragraph 2A or of the paragraph 2A that was substituted for that paragraph by the *CJA* 2003, but which is in force for certain purposes only (as to which, see the main work). Since the new paragraph is in identical terms to the original paragraph 2A (in italics in the main work), save only for the use of "the defendant" instead of the word "he" in sub-paragraph (b), it might be thought that the intention was merely to abandon the version that was inserted by the 2003 Act and to revert to the original. If that were the case, however, the expectation would have been

that the relevant provision of the 2003 Act that inserted the replacement paragraph 2A would have been repealed, but it has not; and it also has to be asked why the draftsman would have troubled to replace a provision with an effectively identical provision. Neither explanation makes much (if any) sense.

★   As from a day to be appointed, a new paragraph 6 of Part I of Schedule 1 to the 1976 Act is substituted by the *Legal Aid, Sentencing and Punishment of Offenders Act* 2012, s.90, and Sched. 11, paras 1, 10 and 17, as follows—

> "6. The defendant need not be granted bail if, having previously been released on bail in, or in connection with, the proceedings, the defendant has been arrested in pursuance of section 7.".

As with the new paragraph 2A, it is anything but clear as to whether the draftsman had in mind the original paragraph 6 or the replacement paragraph 6 (as to which, see the main work). If it was the original paragraph 6 that was to be replaced, then the draftsman has replaced one provision with an almost identical provision (the sense is in fact identical), which seems pointless. If it was the replacement paragraph 6 that he had in mind, then there will be two versions of paragraph 6 with identical meanings and almost identical wording, which seems even more pointless. The courts will have to do what they can to make sense of it.

Exception applicable to drug users in certain areas

★3–48a   As from a day to be appointed, paragraph 6A of Part I of Schedule 1 to the 1976 Act is amended by the *Legal Aid, Sentencing and Punishment of Offenders Act* 2012, s.90, and Sched. 11, paras 1, 10 and 18, so as to substitute the words "of the opinion" for the word "satisfied".

Decisions under paragraph 2

★3–50   As from a day to be appointed, paragraph 9 of Part I of Schedule 1 to the 1976 Act is amended by the *Legal Aid, Sentencing and Punishment of Offenders Act* 2012, s.90, and Sched. 11, paras 1, 10 and 19, so as (i) to substitute "2ZA(1)" for ""2A(1), 6(1) or 6A", and (ii) to insert "or 6A" after "paragraph 6ZA". As with the amendments to paragraph 2A and 6 (*ante*, § 3–48), the draftsman seems to have overlooked the fact that the 2003 Act amendments are not fully in force (hence the text in double square brackets as well as the text in single square brackets in the main work); and, as to this, see also the amendments to paragraph 2 of Part III of Schedule 1 (*post*, § 3–52), which are suggestive of the same oversight.

★   As from a day to be appointed, paragraph 9AA of Part I of Schedule 1 to the 1976 Act is amended by the *Legal Aid, Sentencing and Punishment of Offenders Act* 2012, s.90, and Sched. 11, paras 1, 10 and 20, so as to substitute the words "a child or young person" for the words "under the age of eighteen".

★   As from a day to be appointed, paragraph 9AB(1)(a) of Part I of Schedule 1 to the 1976 Act is amended by the *Legal Aid, Sentencing and Punishment of Offenders Act* 2012, s.90, and Sched. 11, paras 1, 10 and 21, so as to substitute the words "a child or young person" for the words "under the age of eighteen".

Defendants to whom Part IA applies

★3–50a   As from a day to be appointed, paragraph 1 of Part IA of Schedule 1 to the 1976 Act, and the heading preceding it, are amended by the *Legal Aid, Sentencing and Punishment of Offenders Act* 2012, s.90, and Sched. 11, paras 1, and 22 to 24, so as (i) to change the heading to "Application of Part IA"; and (ii) to substitute the words "Subject to paragraph 1A, the" for the word "The".

★   As from a day to be appointed, a new paragraph 1A is inserted in Part IA of Schedule 1 to the 1976 Act by the *Legal Aid, Sentencing and Punishment of Offenders Act* 2012, s.90, and Sched. 11, paras 1, and 22 to 25, as follows—

> "1A.—(1) The paragraphs of this Part of this Schedule mentioned in sub-paragraph (2) do not apply in relation to bail in, or in connection with, proceedings where—
>> (a) the defendant has attained the age of 18,
>> (b) the defendant has not been convicted of an offence in those proceedings, and
>> (c) it appears to the court that there is no real prospect that the defendant will be sentenced to a custodial sentence in the proceedings.

(2) The paragraphs are—
(a) paragraph 2 (refusal of bail for failure to surrender to custody),
(b) paragraph 3 (refusal of bail where defendant would commit further offences on bail), and
(c) paragraph 7 (refusal of bail in certain circumstances when arrested under section 7).".

As from a day to be appointed, paragraph 4 of Part IA of Schedule 1 to the 1976 Act is ★
amended by the *Legal Aid, Sentencing and Punishment of Offenders Act* 2012, s.90, andSched.
11, paras 1, 22 and 26, so as (i) to make the existing text sub-paragraph (1); (ii) to substitute
the words "an associated person" for the words "any person other than the defendant" in
paragraphs (a) and (b); and (iii) to insert a new paragraph (2), as follows—

"(2) In sub-paragraph (1) 'associated person' means a person who is associated with the defendant
within the meaning of section 62 of the *Family Law Act* 1996.".

Exceptions to right to bail

As from a day to be appointed, paragraph 2 of Part II of Schedule 1 to the 1976 Act is ★**3–51**
amended by the *Legal Aid, Sentencing and Punishment of Offenders Act* 2012, s.90, and Sched.
11, paras 1, 27 and 28, so as to insert a new sub-paragraph (za) before sub-paragraph (a), as
follows—

"(za) the defendant—
(i) is a child or young person, or
(ii) has been convicted in the proceedings of an offence;".

As from a day to be appointed, paragraph 5 of Part II of Schedule 1 to the 1976 Act is ★
subjected to an identical amendment as that for paragraph 2 (*ante*) by the *Legal Aid, Sentencing and Punishment of Offenders Act* 2012, s.90, and Sched. 11, paras 1, 27 and 29.

As from a day to be appointed, a new paragraph 6 is inserted in Part II of Schedule 1 to ★
the 1976 Act by the *Legal Aid, Sentencing and Punishment of Offenders Act* 2012, s.90, and
Sched. 11, paras 1, 27 and 30, as follows—

"6.—(1) The defendant need not be granted bail if—
(a) having been released on bail in, or in connection with, the proceedings for the offence, the
defendant has been arrested in pursuance of section 7, and
(b) the court is satisfied that there are substantial grounds for believing that the defendant, if
released on bail (whether subject to conditions or not), would commit an offence while on
bail by engaging in conduct that would, or would be likely to, cause—
(i) physical or mental injury to an associated person, or
(ii) an associated person to fear physical or mental injury.
(2) In sub-paragraph (1) 'associated person' means a person who is associated with the defendant
within the meaning of section 62 of the *Family Law Act* 1996.".

Interpretation

As from a day to be appointed, paragraph 2 of Part III of Schedule 1 to the 1976 Act is ★**3–52**
amended by the *Legal Aid, Sentencing and Punishment of Offenders Act* 2012, s.90, and Sched.
11, paras 1 and 31, so as (i) to substitute the words "paragraph 16 of Schedule 11 to the
Legal Aid, Sentencing and Punishment of Offenders Act 2012" for the words "section 14(1) of
the *Criminal Justice Act* 2003" in paragraph (b); (ii) to substitute the words "paragraph 17 of
Schedule 11 to the *Legal Aid, Sentencing and Punishment of Offenders Act* 2012" for the words
"section 15(1) of the *Criminal Justice Act* 2003" in paragraph (c); and (iii) to insert at the end
a new sub-paragraph (g), as follows—

"(g) as respects the reference in paragraph 6 of Part 2 of this Schedule, bail granted before the
coming into force of that paragraph".

As to the amendments in (i) and (ii), see also the amendments relating to paragraphs 2A
and 6 of Part I of Schedule 1 (*ante*, §§ 3–48, 3–50).

As from a day to be appointed, paragraph 3 of Part III of Schedule 1 to the 1976 Act is ★
amended by the *Legal Aid, Sentencing and Punishment of Offenders Act* 2012, s.105, and
Sched. 12, paras 14 and 17, to substitute the words "accommodation pursuant to a remand
under section 91(3) or (4) of the *Legal Aid, Sentencing and Punishment of Offenders Act* 2012
(remands to local authority accommodation or youth detention accommodation)" for the
words from "the care of" to the end of the paragraph.

(3) Limitation on right to bail

Criminal Justice and Public Order Act 1994, s.25

No bail for defendants charged with or convicted of homicide or rape after previous conviction of such offences

★**3–55**   As from a day to be appointed, section 25(1) of the 1994 Act is amended by the *Legal Aid, Sentencing and Punishment of Offenders Act* 2012, s.90, and Sched. 11, para. 33, so as to substitute the words "of the opinion" for the word "satisfied".

O'Dowd v. U.K. is now reported at (2012) 54 E.H.R.R. 8.

Coroners and Justice Act 2009, s.115

Bail decisions in murder cases to be made by Crown Court judge

3–55a   *R. (A.) v. Lewisham Youth Court, DPP (Interested party)* (see the main work) is now reported at [2012] 1 W.L.R. 34, *sub nom. R. (A.) v. Lewisham Youth Court.*

(4) Custody time limits

S.I. 1987 No. 299, regs 2, 4–8

Custody time limits in the Crown Court

★**3–59**   With effect from June 18, 2012, regulation 5 of the *Prosecution of Offences (Custody Time Limits) Regulations* 1987 (S.I. 1987 No. 299) is amended by the *Prosecution of Offences (Custody Time Limits) (Amendment) Regulations* 2012 (S.I. 2012 No. 1344), so as to omit (i) the words "under section 51 of the *Crime and Disorder Act* 1998 ('the 1998 Act')" in paragraph (6B), (ii) the words "under section 51 of the 1998 Act" in paragraph (6C), and (iii) the words "under section 51 of the 1998 Act" in paragraph (6D).

(6) Place of remand

(b) *Persons under 21 years*

Persons aged 17 to 20

Criminal Justice Act 1948, s.27

★**3–68**   With effect from June 18, 2012 (*Criminal Justice Act 2003 (Commencement No. 28 and Saving Provisions) Order* 2012 (S.I. 2012 No. 1320)), section 41 of, and paragraphs 35 and 36 of Schedule 3 to, the 2003 Act are brought into force (so far as they are not already in force) in certain areas (as to which, see *ante*, § 1–88). There are associated saving provisions, as to which, see article 5 of the order (*ante*, § 1–88).

★   As from a day to be appointed, section 27 of the 1948 Act is amended by the *Legal Aid, Sentencing and Punishment of Offenders Act* 2012, s.105, and Sched. 12, paras 1 to 3, so as (i) to substitute "18" for "17" in the heading; and (ii) to substitute "eighteen" for "seventeen" in subsection (1).

Persons under 17

Children and Young Persons Act 1969, s.23

Remands and committals to local authority accommodation

★**3–69**   As from a day to be appointed, section 23 of the 1969 Act is repealed by the *Legal Aid, Sentencing and Punishment of Offenders Act* 2012, s.105, and Sched. 12, paras 5 and 6. For the replacement provisions, see the following provisions in particular of Chapter 3 (ss.91–107) of the *Legal Aid, Sentencing and Punishment of Offenders Act* 2012: ss.91 (remands of children otherwise than on bail), 92 (remands to local authority accommodation), 93 (conditions, etc., on remands to local authority accommodation), 94 (requirements for electronic monitoring), 96 (further provisions about electronic monitoring), 97 (liability to arrest for breaking conditions of remand), 98 (first set of conditions for a remand to youth detention accommodation), 99 (second set of conditions for a remand to youth detention accommodation), 102 (remands to youth detention accommodation) and 107 (interpretation). For the text of the new provisions, see *post*, §§ 3–80b *et seq.*

As from a day to be appointed, section 23(5A) of the 1969 Act is amended (subject to the   ★**3–70**
repeal of the entire section (as to which, see *ante*, § 3–69) not having already taken effect) by the *Legal Aid, Sentencing and Punishment of Offenders Act* 2012, s.39(1), and Sched. 5, para. 4, so as to substitute (i) the words "representation was provided to the child or young person under Part 1 of the *Legal Aid, Sentencing and Punishment of Offenders Act* 2012 for the purposes of the proceedings but" for the words from the beginning of paragraph (a) to the words "but the right", (ii) the words "for such representation" for the words "to be granted such a right" in the same paragraph, and (iii) the words "for such representation" for the words "to be granted a right to it" in paragraph (aa).

As from a day to be appointed, section 23(4A) of the 1969 Act (as it has effect by virtue of   ★**3–71**
the modifications in the *CDA* 1998 (as to which, see § 3–75 in the main work)) is amended (subject to the repeal of the entire section (as to which, see *ante*, § 3–69) not having already taken effect) by the *Legal Aid, Sentencing and Punishment of Offenders Act* 2012, s.39(1), and Sched. 5, para. 5, so as to substitute (i) the words "representation was provided to the person under Part 1 of the *Legal Aid, Sentencing and Punishment of Offenders Act* 2012 for the purposes of the proceedings but" for the words from the beginning of paragraph (a) to the words "but the right", (ii) the words "for such representation" for the words "to be granted such a right" in the same paragraph, and (iii) the words "for such representation" for the words "to be granted a right to it" in paragraph (aa).

R. (A.) v. Lewisham Youth Court, DPP (Interested party) (see the main work) is now reported   **3–74**
at [2012] 1 W.L.R. 34, *sub nom. R. (A.) v. Lewisham Youth Court.*

Modifications

As from a day to be appointed, section 98 of the *CDA* 1998 is repealed by the *Legal Aid,*   ★**3–75**
Sentencing and Punishment of Offenders Act 2012, s.105, and Sched. 12, paras 36 and 40; and section 130 of the *CJPA* 2001 is repealed by *ibid.*, para. 47.

Children and Young Persons Act 1969, s.23AA

Electronic monitoring of conditions of remand
As from a day to be appointed, section 23AA of the 1969 Act is repealed by the *Legal Aid,*   ★**3–76a**
Sentencing and Punishment of Offenders Act 2012, s.105, and Sched. 12, paras 5 and 7.

Provision of accommodation for children in police protection or detention or on remand, etc.

As to the prospective amendment and repeal of section 23 of the *CYPA* 1969 Act, see   ★**3–77**
ante, §§ 3–69 *et seq.*

As from a day to be appointed, section 21(2)(c) of the *Children Act* 1989 is amended by the *Legal Aid, Sentencing and Punishment of Offenders Act* 2012, s.105, and Sched. 12, paras 23 and 24, so as to omit sub-paragraph (i) (children on remand under the *CYPA* 1969, s.23).

As from a day to be appointed, section 61 of the *CJA* 1991 is repealed by the *Legal Aid,*   ★**3–78**
Sentencing and Punishment of Offenders Act 2012, s.105, and Sched. 12, paras 26 and 29.

As from a day to be appointed, section 60(3) of the *CJA* 1991 is amended by the *Legal*   ★**3–79**
Aid, Sentencing and Punishment of Offenders Act 2012, s.105, and Sched. 12, paras 26 and 28, so as (i) to omit the words "or committed", and (ii) to insert the words "under section 91(3)

of the *Legal Aid, Sentencing and Punishment of Offenders Act* 2012" after the words "local authority accommodation". As to section 91 of the 2012 Act, see *post*, § 3–80c.

Children and Young Persons Act 1969, ss.23A, 23B

Liability to arrest for breaking conditions of bail

★**3–80**   As from a day to be appointed, section 23A of the 1969 Act is repealed by the *Legal Aid, Sentencing and Punishment of Offenders Act* 2012, s.105, and Sched. 12, paras 5 and 8.

Report by local authority in certain cases where person remanded on bail

★**3–80a**   As from a day to be appointed, section 23B of the 1969 Act is amended by the *Legal Aid, Sentencing and Punishment of Offenders Act* 2012, s.105, and Sched. 12, paras 1 and 9, so as (i) to insert, at the end of subsection (2), the words "under section 91(3) of the *Legal Aid, Sentencing and Punishment of Offenders Act* 2012", (ii) to substitute, in subsection (3), the words "section 92(2) of the *Legal Aid, Sentencing and Punishment of Offenders Act* 2012" for the words "section 23(2) of this Act", (iii) to substitute, in subsection (6)(a), "18" for "17", (iv) to substitute, in subsection (6)(b), for the words from "requirement" to "fulfilled", the words "requirements in section 94(3) and (4) or 95(3) and (4) of the *Legal Aid, Sentencing and Punishment of Offenders Act* 2012 would have been fulfilled if the person had not been remanded on bail", (v) to insert the words "(subject to subsection (8))" after the word "means" in the definition of "serious offence" in subsection (7), and (vi) to insert a new subsection (8), as follows—

> "(8) For the purposes of the application of this section to a person remanded on bail in connection with proceedings under the *Extradition Act* 2003—
>> (a) an offence is a 'serious offence' if the conduct constituting the offence would, if committed in England and Wales, constitute an offence punishable in the case of an adult with imprisonment for a term of two years or more, and
>> (b) the reference in subsection (1)(a) to a person being charged with a serious offence includes a reference to the person having been accused of such an offence.".

Remands of children otherwise than on bail (replacement provisions)

★**3–80b**   As to the replacement, as from a day to be appointed, of section 23 of the *CYPA* 1969, and its associated legislation (§§ 3–69 *et seq.* in the main work) by Chapter 3 (ss.91–107) of Part 3 of the *Legal Aid, Sentencing and Punishment of Offenders Act* 2012, see *ante*, § 3–69.

Legal Aid, Sentencing and Punishment of Offenders Act 2012, ss.91–94, 96-99, 102, 107

[Remands of children otherwise than on bail

★**3–80c**   **91.**—(1) This section applies where—
> (a) a court deals with a child charged with or convicted of one or more offences by remanding the child, and
> (b) the child is not released on bail.

(2) This section also applies where—
> (a) a court remands a child in connection with extradition proceedings, and
> (b) the child is not released on bail.

(3) Subject to subsection (4), the court must remand the child to local authority accommodation in accordance with section 92.

(4) The court may instead remand the child to youth detention accommodation in accordance with section 102 where—
> (a) in the case of a child remanded under subsection (1), the first or second set of conditions for such a remand (see sections 98 and 99) is met in relation to the child, or
> (b) in the case of a child remanded under subsection (2), the first or second set of conditions for such a remand in an extradition case (see sections 100 and 101) is met in relation to the child.

(5) This section is subject to section 128(7) of the *Magistrates' Courts Act* 1980 (remands to police detention for periods of not more than 3 days); but that provision has effect in relation to a child as if for the reference to 3 clear days there were substituted a reference to 24 hours.

(6) In this Chapter, "child" means a person under the age of 18.

(7) References in this Chapter (other than in relation to extradition proceedings) to the remand of a child include a reference to—

    (a) the sending of a child for trial, and

    (b) the committal of a child for sentence,

and related expressions are to be construed accordingly.

(8) Before the insertion of section 51A of the *Crime and Disorder Act* 1998 (sending cases to the Crown Court: children and young persons) by Schedule 3 to the *Criminal Justice Act* 2003 is fully in force, subsection (7) has effect as if it also referred to the committal of a child for trial.

(9) Subsection (7) also applies to any provision of an Act other than this Act that refers (directly or indirectly) to the remand of a child under this section.]

Remands to local authority accommodation

[Remands to local authority accommodation

    92.—(1) A remand to local authority accommodation is a remand to accommodation provided   ★**3–80d** by or on behalf of a local authority.

(2) A court that remands a child to local authority accommodation must designate the local authority that is to receive the child.

(3) That authority must be—

    (a) in the case of a child who is being looked after by a local authority, that authority, and

    (b) in any other case, the local authority in whose area it appears to the court that the child habitually resides or the offence or one of the offences was committed.

(4) The designated authority must—

    (a) receive the child, and

    (b) provide or arrange for the provision of accommodation for the child whilst the child is remanded to local authority accommodation.

(5) Where a child is remanded to local authority accommodation, it is lawful for any person acting on behalf of the designated authority to detain the child.]

[Conditions etc on remands to local authority accommodation

    93.—(1) A court remanding a child to local authority accommodation may require the child to   ★**3–80e** comply with any conditions that could be imposed under section 3(6) of the *Bail Act* 1976 if the child were then being granted bail.

(2) The court may also require the child to comply with any conditions imposed for the purpose of securing the electronic monitoring of the child's compliance with the conditions imposed under subsection (1) if—

    (a) in the case of a child remanded under section 91(1) (proceedings other than extradition proceedings), the requirements in section 94 are met, or

    (b) in the case of a child remanded under section 91(2) (extradition proceedings), the requirements in section 95 are met.

(3) A court remanding a child to local authority accommodation may impose on the designated authority—

    (a) requirements for securing compliance with any conditions imposed on the child under subsection (1) or (2), or

    (b) requirements stipulating that the child must not be placed with a named person.

(4) A court may only impose a condition under subsection (1) or (2), or a requirement under subsection (3), after consultation with the designated authority.

(5) Where a child has been remanded to local authority accommodation, a relevant court—

    (a) may, on the application of the designated authority, impose on that child any conditions that could be imposed under subsection (1) or (2) if the court were then remanding the child to local authority accommodation, and

    (b) where it does so, may impose on the authority requirements for securing compliance with the conditions imposed under paragraph (a).

(6) Where a child has been remanded to local authority accommodation, a relevant court may, on the application of the designated authority or that child, vary or revoke any conditions or requirements imposed under this section (including as previously varied under this subsection).

(7) A court that imposes conditions on a child under this section or varies conditions so imposed—

    (a) must explain to the child in open court and in ordinary language why it is imposing or varying those conditions, and

(b) if the court is a magistrates' court, must cause a reason given under paragraph (a) to be specified in the warrant of commitment and entered in the register.

(8) In this section "relevant court"—

(a) in relation to a child remanded to local authority accommodation by virtue of section 91(1) (proceedings other than extradition proceedings), means—

(i) the court by which the child was so remanded, or

(ii) any magistrates' court that has jurisdiction in the place where the child is for the time being;

(b) in relation to a child remanded to local authority accommodation by virtue of section 91(2) (extradition proceedings), means the court by which the child was so remanded.

(9) References in this section to consultation are to such consultation (if any) as is reasonably practicable in all the circumstances of the case.]

[Requirements for electronic monitoring

★**3–80f**   **94.**—(1) The requirements referred to in section 93(2)(a) (requirements for imposing electronic monitoring condition: non-extradition cases) are those set out in subsections (2) to (6).

(2) The first requirement is that the child has reached the age of twelve.

(3) The second requirement is that the offence mentioned in section 91(1), or one or more of those offences, is an imprisonable offence.

(4) The third requirement is that—

(a) the offence mentioned in section 91(1), or one or more of those offences, is a violent or sexual offence or an offence punishable in the case of an adult with imprisonment for a term of 14 years or more, or

(b) the offence or offences mentioned in section 91(1), together with any other imprisonable offences of which the child has been convicted in any proceedings, amount or would, if the child were convicted of that offence or those offences, amount to a recent history of committing imprisonable offences while on bail or subject to a custodial remand.

(5) The fourth requirement is that the court is satisfied that the necessary provision for electronic monitoring can be made under arrangements currently available in each local justice area which is a relevant area.

(6) The fifth requirement is that a youth offending team has informed the court that, in its opinion, the imposition of an electronic monitoring condition will be suitable in the child's case.

(7) For the purposes of this section, a local justice area is a relevant area in relation to a proposed electronic monitoring condition if the court considers that it will not be practicable to secure the electronic monitoring in question unless electronic monitoring arrangements are available in that area.

(8) In this Chapter—

"electronic monitoring condition" means a condition imposed on a child remanded to local authority accommodation for the purpose of securing the electronic monitoring of the child's compliance with conditions imposed under section 93(1) or (5);

"imprisonable offence" means—

(a) an offence punishable in the case of an adult with imprisonment, or

(b) in relation to an offence of which a child has been accused or convicted outside England and Wales, an offence equivalent to an offence that, in England and Wales, is punishable in the case of an adult with imprisonment;

"sexual offence" means an offence specified in Part 2 of Schedule 15 to the *Criminal Justice Act 2003*;

"violent offence" means murder or an offence specified in Part 1 of Schedule 15 to the *Criminal Justice Act 2003*;

"youth offending team" means a team established under section 39 of the *Crime and Disorder Act 1998*.

(9) References in this Chapter to a child being subject to a custodial remand are to the child being—

(a) remanded to local authority accommodation or youth detention accommodation, or

(b) subject to a form of custodial detention in a country or territory outside England and Wales while awaiting trial or sentence in that country or territory or during a trial in that country or territory.

(10) The reference in subsection (9) to a child being remanded to local authority accommodation or youth detention accommodation includes—

(a) a child being remanded to local authority accommodation under section 23 of the *Children and Young Persons Act* 1969, and

(b) a child being remanded to prison under that section as modified by section 98 of the *Crime and Disorder Act* 1998 or under section 27 of the *Criminal Justice Act* 1948.]

[Further provisions about electronic monitoring

96.—(1) Where a court imposes an electronic monitoring condition, the condition must include provision making a person responsible for the monitoring. ★**3–80g**

(2) A person who is made responsible by virtue of subsection (1) must be of a description specified in an order made by the Secretary of State.

(3)–(6) [*Making of rules by Secretary of State for regulation of electronic monitoring.*]]

[Liability to arrest for breaking conditions of remand

97.—(1) A child may be arrested without warrant by a constable if— ★**3–80h**

(a) the child has been remanded to local authority accommodation,

(b) conditions under section 93 have been imposed in respect of the child, and

(c) the constable has reasonable grounds for suspecting that the child has broken any of those conditions.

(2) Subject to subsection (3), a child arrested under subsection (1) must be brought before a justice of the peace—

(a) as soon as practicable, and

(b) in any event within the period of 24 hours beginning with the child's arrest.

(3) If the child was arrested during the period of 24 hours ending with the time appointed for the child to appear before the court in pursuance of the remand, the child must be brought before the court before which the child was to have appeared.

(4) In reckoning a period of 24 hours for the purposes of subsection (2) or (3), no account is to be taken of Christmas Day, Good Friday or any Sunday.

(5) If a justice of the peace before whom a child is brought under subsection (2) is of the opinion that the child has broken any condition imposed in respect of the child under section 93, the justice of the peace must remand the child.

(6) Section 91 applies to a child in relation to whom subsection (5) applies as if—

(a) except in a case within paragraph (b), the child was then charged with or convicted of the offence for which the child had been remanded, or

(b) in the case of a child remanded in connection with extradition proceedings, the child was then appearing before the justice of the peace in connection with those proceedings.

(7) If a justice of the peace before whom a child is brought under subsection (2) is not of the opinion mentioned in subsection (5), the justice of the peace must remand the child to the place to which the child had been remanded at the time of the child's arrest subject to the same conditions as those which had been imposed on the child at that time.]

Remands to youth detention accommodation

[First set of conditions for a remand to youth detention accommodation

98.—(1) For the purposes of section 91(4)(a), the first set of conditions for a remand to youth detention accommodation is met in relation to a child if each of the following is met in relation to the child— ★**3–80i**

(a) the age condition (see subsection (2)),

(b) the offence condition (see subsection (3)),

(c) the necessity condition (see subsection (4)), and

(d) the first or second legal representation condition (see subsections (5) and (6)).

(2) The age condition is that the child has reached the age of twelve.

(3) The offence condition is that the offence mentioned in section 91(1), or one or more of those offences—

(a) is a violent or sexual offence, or

(b) is an offence punishable in the case of an adult with imprisonment for a term of 14 years or more.

(4) The necessity condition is that the court is of the opinion, after considering all the options for the remand of the child, that only remanding the child to youth detention accommodation would be adequate—

(a) to protect the public from death or serious personal injury (whether physical or psychological) occasioned by further offences committed by the child, or

35

(b) to prevent the commission by the child of imprisonable offences.

(5) The first legal representation condition is that the child is legally represented before the court.

(6) The second legal representation condition is that the child is not legally represented before the court and—

    (a) representation was provided to the child under Part 1 of this Act for the purposes of the proceedings, but was withdrawn—

        (i) because of the child's conduct, or

        (ii) because it appeared that the child's financial resources were such that the child was not eligible for such representation,

    (b) the child applied for such representation and the application was refused because it appeared that the child's financial resources were such that the child was not eligible for such representation, or

    (c) having been informed of the right to apply for such representation and having had the opportunity to do so, the child refused or failed to apply.]

[Second set of conditions for a remand to youth detention accommodation

★3–80j   **99.**—(1) For the purposes of section 91(4)(a), the second set of conditions for a remand to youth detention accommodation is met in relation to a child if each of the following is met in relation to the child—

    (a) the age condition (see subsection (2)),

    (b) the sentencing condition (see subsection (3)),

    (c) the offence condition (see subsection (4)),

    (d) the first or second history condition or both (see subsections (5) and (6)),

    (e) the necessity condition (see subsection (7)), and

    (f) the first or second legal representation condition (see subsections (8) and (9)).

(2) The age condition is that the child has reached the age of twelve.

(3) The sentencing condition is that it appears to the court that there is a real prospect that the child will be sentenced to a custodial sentence for the offence mentioned in section 91(1) or one or more of those offences.

(4) The offence condition is that the offence mentioned in section 91(1), or one or more of those offences, is an imprisonable offence.

(5) The first history condition is that—

    (a) the child has a recent history of absconding while subject to a custodial remand, and

    (b) the offence mentioned in section 91(1), or one or more of those offences, is alleged to be or has been found to have been committed while the child was remanded to local authority accommodation or youth detention accommodation.

(6) The second history condition is that the offence or offences mentioned in section 91(1), together with any other imprisonable offences of which the child has been convicted in any proceedings, amount or would, if the child were convicted of that offence or those offences, amount to a recent history of committing imprisonable offences while on bail or subject to a custodial remand.

(7)–(9) *[Identical to s.98(4)-(6), ante, § 3–80i.]*

(10) In this Chapter "custodial sentence" means a sentence or order mentioned in section 76(1) of the *Powers of Criminal Courts (Sentencing) Act* 2000.

(11) The reference in subsection (5)(b) to a child being remanded to local authority accommodation or youth detention accommodation includes—

(a), (b) *[identical to s.94(10)(a), (b), ante, § 3–80f].]*

[Remands to youth detention accommodation

★3–80k   **102.**—(1) A remand to youth detention accommodation is a remand to such accommodation of a kind listed in subsection (2) as the Secretary of State directs in the child's case.

(2) Those kinds of accommodation are—

    (a) a secure children's home,

    (b) a secure training centre,

    (c) a young offender institution, and

    (d) accommodation, or accommodation of a description, for the time being specified by order under section 107(1)(e) of the *Powers of Criminal Courts (Sentencing) Act* 2000 (youth detention accommodation for purposes of detention and training order provisions).

(3) A child's detention in one of those kinds of accommodation pursuant to a remand to youth detention accommodation is lawful.

(4) Where a court remands a child to youth detention accommodation, the court must—

    (a) state in open court that it is of the opinion mentioned in section 98(4), 99(7), 100(4) or 101(7) (as the case may be), and

    (b) explain to the child in open court and in ordinary language why it is of that opinion.

(5) A magistrates' court must ensure a reason that it gives under subsection (4)(b)—

    (a) is specified in the warrant of commitment, and

    (b) is entered in the register.

(6) Where a court remands a child to youth detention accommodation, the court must designate a local authority as the designated authority for the child for the purposes of—

    (a) subsection (8),

    (b) regulations under section 103 (arrangements for remands), and

    (c) section 104 (looked after child status).

(7) That authority must be—

    (a) in the case of a child who is being looked after by a local authority, that authority, and

    (b) in any other case, the local authority in whose area it appears to the court that the child habitually resides or the offence or one of the offences was committed.

(8) Before giving a direction under subsection (1), the Secretary of State must consult the designated authority.

(9) A function of the Secretary of State under this section (other than the function of making regulations) is exercisable by the Youth Justice Board for England and Wales concurrently with the Secretary of State.

(10) The Secretary of State may by regulations provide that subsection (9) is not to apply, either generally or in relation to a particular description of case.

(11) In this Chapter "secure children's home" means accommodation which is provided in a children's home, within the meaning of the *Care Standards Act* 2000—

    (a) which provides accommodation for the purposes of restricting liberty, and

    (b) in respect of which a person is registered under Part 2 of that Act.

(12) Before the coming into force in relation to England of section 107(2) of the *Health and Social Care (Community Health and Standards) Act* 2003, subsection (11) has effect as if it defined "secure children's home" in relation to England as accommodation which—

    (a) is provided in a children's home, within the meaning of the *Care Standards Act* 2000, in respect of which a person is registered under Part 2 of that Act, and

    (b) is approved by the Secretary of State for the purpose of restricting the liberty of children.]

Supplementary

[*Interpretation of Chapter*

  107.—(1) In this Chapter— ★**3–801**

    "child" has the meaning given by section 91(6);

    "court" and "magistrates' court" include a justice of the peace;

    "custodial sentence" has the meaning given by section 99(10);

    "the designated authority—

        (a) in relation to a child remanded to local authority accommodation, means the local authority that is designated by the court under section 92(2) to receive the child;

        (b) in relation to a child remanded to youth detention accommodation, means the local authority that is designated by the court under section 102(6) as the designated authority for the child;

    "electronic monitoring condition" has the meaning given by section 94(8);

    "extradition proceedings" means proceedings under the *Extradition Act* 2003;

    "imprisonable offence" has the meaning given by section 94(8);

    "local authority" mean—

        (a) a county council;

        (b) a county borough council;

        (c) a district council for an area for which there is no county council;

        (d) a London borough council;

        (e) the Common Council of the City of London;

        (f) the Council of the Isles of Scilly;

    "secure children's home" has the meaning given by section 102(11);

"sexual offence" has the meaning given by section 94(8);

"violent offence" has the meaning given by section 94(8);

"youth offending team" has the meaning given by section 94(8).

(2) In this Chapter, references to the remand of a child, and related expressions, are to be construed in accordance with section 91(7) and (8).

(3) In this Chapter, references to a remand to local authority accommodation, and related expressions, are to be construed in accordance with section 92(1).

(4) In this Chapter, references to a child being subject to a custodial remand are to be construed in accordance with section 94(9).

(5) In this Chapter, references to a remand to youth detention accommodation, and related expressions, are to be construed in accordance with section 102(1).

(6) In this Chapter, references to a child who is looked after by a local authority are to be construed in accordance with section 22 of the *Children Act* 1989.

(7) Subsections (3) and (5) are subject to sections 94(10) and 99(11) (references to remand to local authority accommodation or youth detention accommodation to include such a remand under section 23 of the *Children and Young Persons Act* 1969 or a remand to prison).]

(7) Transfer to hospital of persons in custody otherwise than under sentence

Mental Health Act 1983, s.52

Further provisions as to persons remanded by magistrates' courts

★**3–85** With effect from June 18, 2012 (*Criminal Justice Act 2003 (Commencement No. 28 and Saving Provisions) Order* 2012 (S.I. 2012 No. 1320)), section 41 of, and paragraph 55(1) and (3) of Schedule 3 to, the 2003 Act are brought into force (so far as not already in force) in certain areas (as to which, see *ante*, § 1–88). There are associated saving provisions, as to which, see article 5 of the order (*ante*, § 1–88).

(8) Appeal against grant of bail

Bail (Amendment) Act 1993, s.1

Prosecution right of appeal

★**3–86** As from a day to be appointed, section 1 of the 1993 Act is amended by the *Legal Aid, Sentencing and Punishment of Offenders Act* 2012, s.90, and Sched. 11, para. 32, so as (i) to substitute, in subsection (2), the words "Subsections (1) and (1B) above apply" for the words "Subsection (1) above applies", (ii) to substitute, in subsections (3), (4) and (8), ", (1A) or (1B)" for "or (1A)", (iii) to substitute, in subsection (10)(a), the words "references in subsections (1) and (1B)" for the words "reference in subsection (1)" and the words "are to be read as references" for the words "is to be read as a reference", and (iv) to insert new subsections (1B) and (1C), as follows—

> "(1B) Where a judge of the Crown Court grants bail to a person who is charged with, or convicted of, an offence punishable by imprisonment, the prosecution may appeal to the High Court against the granting of bail.
>
> (1C) An appeal under subsection (1B) may not be made where a judge of the Crown Court has granted bail on an appeal under subsection (1).".

★ As from a day to be appointed, section 1(10) of the 1993 Act is further amended by the *Legal Aid, Sentencing and Punishment of Offenders Act* 2012, s.105, and Sched. 12, para. 32, so as (i) to substitute the words "person under the age of 18" for the words from "child" to "*Act* 1969", and (ii) to substitute, in paragraph (b), the words "Chapter 3 of Part 3 of the *Legal Aid, Sentencing and Punishment of Offenders Act* 2012 (remands of children otherwise than on bail)" for the words from "section 23" to "accommodation)".

B. Specific Provisions

(1) The police

(a) *The Police and Criminal Evidence Act 1984*

Police and Criminal Evidence Act 1984, s.34

Limitations on police detention

As from a day to be appointed, section 34(5)(b) of the 1984 Act is amended by the *Legal*   ★3-93
Aid, Sentencing and Punishment of Offenders Act 2012, s.135(3), and Sched. 24, paras 4 and 5,
so as to substitute the words "given a youth caution under section 66ZA" for the words from
"reprimanded" to "65".

Police and Criminal Evidence Act 1984, s.36

Custody officers at police station

The amendment of section 36(9) of the 1984 Act by the *Police Reform and Social*   3-96
Responsibility Act 2011, s.99, and Sched. 16, paras 160 and 162 (substituting "local policing
body" for "police authority" (see the main work)), came into force on January 16, 2012: *Police Reform and Social Responsibility Act 2011 (Commencement No. 3 and Transitional Provisions) Order* 2011 (S.I. 2011 No. 3019).

Police and Criminal Evidence Act 1984, ss.37A–37D

Consultation with the Director of Public Prosecutions

As from a day to be appointed, section 37B(9)(b) of the 1984 Act is amended by the *Legal*   ★3-101b
Aid, Sentencing and Punishment of Offenders Act 2012, s.135(3), and Sched. 24, paras 4 and 6,
so as to substitute the words "youth caution under section 66ZA" for the words "warning or
reprimand under section 65".

Police and Criminal Evidence Act 1984, s.38

Duties of custody officer after charge

As from a day to be appointed, section 38(2A) of the 1984 Act is amended by the *Legal*   ★3-102
Aid, Sentencing and Punishment of Offenders Act 2012, s.90, and Sched. 11, para. 34, to
substitute "paragraphs 1A and 2(2)" for "paragraph 2(2)".

Police and Criminal Evidence Act 1984, s.40

Review of police detention

The reference in section 40(13) of the 1984 Act to the detainee's solicitor shall be taken as   3-110
including a reference to a licensed body acting for the detainee, *i.e.* a body that holds a
licence issued by the Law Society under Part 5 of the *Legal Services Act* 2007: *Legal Services
Act 2007 (Designation as a Licensing Authority) (No. 2) Order* 2011 (S.I. 2011 No. 2866), arts
1(3) and 8(1) and (2)(b), and Sched. 2.

Police and Criminal Evidence Act 1984, s.42

Authorisation of continued detention

The reference in section 42(7) of the 1984 Act to the detainee's solicitor shall be taken as   3-115
including a reference to a licensed body acting for the detainee, *i.e.* a body that holds a
licence issued by the Law Society under Part 5 of the *Legal Services Act* 2007: *Legal Services
Act 2007 (Designation as a Licensing Authority) (No. 2) Order* 2011 (S.I. 2011 No. 2866), arts
1(3) and 8(1) and (2)(b), and Sched. 2.

(2) Magistrates' courts

(a) *The Magistrates' Courts Act 1980*

Jurisdiction

Magistrates' Courts Act 1980, s.6(3), (4)

Discharge or committal for trial

★**3–134**   With effect from June 18, 2012 (*Criminal Justice Act 2003 (Commencement No. 28 and Saving Provisions) Order* 2012 (S.I. 2012 No. 1320)), section 332 of, and Part 4 of Schedule 37 to, the 2003 Act are brought into force in certain areas (as to which, see *ante*, § 1–88). There are associated saving provisions, as to which, see article 5 of the order (*ante*, § 1–88).

Restriction on justices sitting after dealing with bail

★**3–136**   With effect from June 18, 2012 (*Criminal Justice Act 2003 (Commencement No. 28 and Saving Provisions) Order* 2012 (S.I. 2012 No. 1320)), section 332 of, and Part 4 of Schedule 37 to, the 2003 Act are brought into force.

Magistrates' Courts Act 1980, s.120

★**3–144a**   As to the repeal of sections 1 to 26 of, and Schedules 1 to 3A and 14, Pt II, to, the *Access to Justice Act* 1999, see *post*, § 6–130.

Remand

Magistrates' Courts Act 1980, s.128

Remand in custody or on bail

★**3–152**   With effect from June 18, 2012 (*Criminal Justice Act 2003 (Commencement No. 28 and Saving Provisions) Order* 2012 (S.I. 2012 No. 1320)), section 41 of, and paragraph 51(1) and (7) of Schedule 3 to, the 2003 Act are brought into force in certain areas (as to which, see *ante*, § 1–88). There are associated saving provisions, as to which, see article 5 of the order (*ante*, § 1–88).

Further remand

★**3–155**   The amendment of section 129(4) by the *CJA* 2003 comes into force on June 18, 2012 (*Criminal Justice Act 2003 (Commencement No. 28 and Saving Provisions) Order* 2012 (S.I. 2012 No. 1320)) in certain areas (as to which, see *ante*, § 1–88). There are associated saving provisions, as to which, see article 5 of the order (*ante*, § 1–88).

Magistrates' Courts Act 1980, s.130

Transfer of remand hearings

★**3–156**   As from a day to be appointed, section 130(3) of the 1980 Act is amended by the *Legal Aid, Sentencing and Punishment of Offenders Act* 2012, s.39(1), and Sched. 5, paras 12 and 17, so as to substitute, for the words from "all the powers" to the end, new text as follows—

> "all of the following powers which that court would have had but for the order—
> (a) powers in relation to further remand (whether in custody or on bail), and
> (b) powers under Part 1 of the *Legal Aid, Sentencing and Punishment of Offenders Act* 2012".

★**3–157**   With effect from June 18, 2012 (*Criminal Justice Act 2003 (Commencement No. 28 and Saving Provisions) Order* 2012 (S.I. 2012 No. 1320)), section 41 of, and paragraph 51(1) and (9) of Schedule 3 to, the 2003 Act are brought into force in certain areas (as to which, see *ante*, § 1–88). There are associated saving provisions, as to which, see article 5 of the order (*ante*, § 1–88).

Magistrates' Courts Act 1980, s.131

Remand of accused already in custody

As from a day to be appointed, section 131(2A) of the 1980 Act is repealed by the *Legal Aid, Sentencing and Punishment of Offenders Act* 2012, s.89(2), and Sched. 10, para. 4.   ★3–158

(3) The Crown Court

(a) *Preliminaries*

Right to representation

As to the repeal of section 26 of the *Access to Justice Act* 1999, see *post*, § 6–130.   ★3–167

(b) *Jurisdiction in respect of cases before magistrates*

Senior Courts Act 1981, s.80

Process to compel appearance

With effect from June 18, 2012 (*Criminal Justice Act 2003 (Commencement No. 28 and Saving Provisions) Order* 2012 (S.I. 2012 No. 1320)), section 41 of, and paragraph 54(1) and (4) of Schedule 3 to, the 2003 Act are brought into force in certain areas (as to which, see *ante*, § 1–88), to the extent that they are not already in force. There are associated saving provisions, as to which, see article 5 of the order (*ante*, § 1–88).   ★3–174

(c) *Jurisdiction in respect of cases of which the Crown Court is then seised*

Senior Courts Act 1981, s.81

Bail

With effect from June 18, 2012 (*Criminal Justice Act 2003 (Commencement No. 28 and Saving Provisions) Order* 2012 (S.I. 2012 No. 1320)), paragraph 4 of Schedule 36 to the *CJA* 2003 is brought into force (together with s.331 so far as relating thereto).   ★3–177

With effect from June 18, 2012 (S.I. 2012 No. 1320 (*ante*)), section 41 of, and paragraph 54(1) and (5) of Schedule 3 to, the 2003 Act are brought into force in certain areas (as to which, see *ante*, § 1–88), to the extent that they are not already in force. There are associated saving provisions, as to which, see article 5 of the order (*ante*, § 1–88).   ★

III. *PRESENCE OF THE ACCUSED IN COURT DURING THE TRIAL*

B. LIMITATIONS

(1) Preliminary and sentencing hearings

Crime and Disorder Act 1998, ss.57A–57E

Introductory

As from a day to be appointed, section 57A(3) of the 1998 Act is amended by the *Legal Aid, Sentencing and Punishment of Offenders Act* 2012, s.105, and Sched. 12, paras 36 and 39, so as to substitute in paragraph (a) of the definition of "custody", the words "or youth detention accommodation to which a person is remanded under section 91 of the *Legal Aid, Sentencing and Punishment of Offenders Act* 2012" for the words from "to which" to "1969".   ★3–200

CHAPTER 4

TRIAL

I. PRELIMINARIES

A. COMMENCEMENT DATE

Senior Courts Act 1981, s.77

Committal [Sending] for trial: date of trial

★**4–1**   With effect from June 18, 2012 (*Criminal Justice Act 2003 (Commencement No. 28 and Saving Provisions) Order* 2012 (S.I. 2012 No. 1320)), section 41 of, and paragraph 54(1) and (3) of Schedule 3 to, the 2003 Act are brought into force in certain areas (as to which, see *ante*, § 1–88), to the extent that they are not already in force. There are associated saving provisions, as to which, see article 5 of the order (*ante*, § 1–88).

B. HEARING IN OPEN COURT

(1) European Convention on Human Rights

Practical application

★**4–4**   In a case where documents have been placed before a judge and referred to in the course of the proceedings, the default position should henceforth be that access by non-parties should be permitted on the common law principle of open justice; and where access is sought for a proper journalistic purpose, the case for allowing it will be particularly strong; however, there may be countervailing reasons; it is not sensible or practical to look for a standard formula for determining how strong the grounds of opposition need to be in order to outweigh the merits of the application; the court has to carry out a proportionality exercise, which will be fact-specific; and central to the court's evaluation will be the purpose of the open justice principle, the potential value of the material in advancing that purpose and, conversely, any risk of harm which access to the documents may cause to the legitimate interests of others: *R. (Guardian News and Media Ltd) v. City of Westminster Magistrates' Court* [2012] 4 *Archbold Review* 1, CA (Civ. Div.) (reversing the decision of the Divisional Court (as to which, see the main work)).

C. PUBLICITY

(1) General right to publish reports

4–15   Lord Judge C.J. has issued the following guidance which replaces the interim guidance referred to in the main work: (i) a representative of the media or a legal commentator who wishes to use live, text-based communications from court may do so without making an application to the court (it being presumed that this will not interfere with the proper administration of justice); (ii) however, where a member of the public, who is in court, wishes to use live text-based communications during court proceedings, an application for permission to activate and use, in silent mode, a mobile phone, small laptop or similar piece of equipment, solely in order to make such communications of the proceedings, will need to be made, formally or informally; (iii) when considering, either generally of its own motion, or following a formal application or informal request by a member of the public, whether to permit such communications, and if so by whom, the paramount question for the judge will be whether they may interfere with the proper administration of justice, in which respect, the factors identified in paragraph I.2.2 of the consolidated criminal practice direction (*Practice Direction (Criminal Proceedings: Consolidation)* [2002] 1 W.L.R. 2870, CA (§ 28–93 in the main work)) are likely to be relevant; (iv) without being exhaustive, the danger to the administration of justice is likely to be at its most acute in the context of criminal trials; (v) it may be necessary for the judge to limit live, text-based communications to representatives of the media for journalistic purposes, because of the potential for electronic interference with the court's own sound recording equipment, or because the widespread use of such devices in court may cause a distraction; (vi) subject to these considerations, the use of an unobtrusive, hand-held, silent piece of modern equipment for the purposes of simultaneous reporting of proceedings to the outside world as they unfold in court is generally unlikely to interfere with the proper administration of justice; (vii) any permission given may be withdrawn by the court at any time: *Practice Guidance: the Use of Live Text-based Forms of Communication (including Twitter) from Court for the Purposes of Fair and Accurate Reporting* [2012] 1 Cr.App.R. 21.

(2) Restrictions

(aa) *Pre-proceedings*

Apart from investigation anonymity orders (as to which, see § 8–150 in the main work), it **4–16a** should be noted that, as from a day to be appointed, section 13 of the *Education Act* 2011 inserts new sections 141F to 141H, relating to restrictions on reporting allegations of offences committed by teachers, into Part 8 of the *Education Act* 2002. Section 141F applies where a person employed or engaged as a teacher at a school is the subject of an allegation that he is, or may be, guilty of a "relevant criminal offence" (*viz.* an offence against the law of England and Wales where the victim of the offence is a registered pupil at the school where the person is employed or engaged as a teacher: s.141F(14)), and the allegation is made by or on behalf of a registered pupil at the school (s.141F(1) and (2)). Section 141F(3) prohibits the inclusion of any matter relating to the person in any publication (as to which, see s.141F(14)) if it is likely to lead members of the public to identify the person as the teacher who is the subject of the allegation. The restrictions cease to apply in various circumstances, including once proceedings for the offence have been instituted (s.141F(10), as to which, see also s.141F(15)).

(a) *Hearings before trial*

Magistrates' Courts Act 1980, s.8

Restrictions on reports of committal proceedings

As from a day to be appointed, section 8(4) of the 1980 Act is amended by the *Legal Aid,* ★**4–19** *Sentencing and Punishment of Offenders Act* 2012, s.39(1), and Sched. 5, paras 12 and 13, so as to substitute a new paragraph (i), as follows—

> "(i) *whether, for the purposes of the proceedings, representation was provided to the accused or any of the accused under Part 1 of the* Legal Aid, Sentencing and Punishment of Offenders Act *2012*".

With effect from June 18, 2012 (*Criminal Justice Act 2003 (Commencement No. 28 and Sav-* ★**4–20** *ing Provisions) Order* 2012 (S.I. 2012 No. 1320)), section 332 of, and Part 4 of Schedule 37 to, the 2003 Act are brought into force in certain areas (as to which, see *ante*, § 1–88). There are associated saving provisions, as to which, see article 5 of the order (*ante*, § 1–88).

D. IDENTITY AND IMPARTIALITY OF JUDGE

Impartiality

Where the defendant unsuccessfully applied for leave to change his plea on the basis that **4–53** the advice of his original counsel was unduly pessimistic, the fair-minded and informed observer would not have suspected the judge who refused the application of bias, given that the relationship between judge and the original counsel was essentially professional (counsel having appeared in front of the judge on seven occasions, none of which were a trial), supplemented by occasional meetings of no consequence when the judge had been at the bar; any competent judge would be well able to put his relationship with counsel out of his mind and evaluate the evidence of counsel, the defendant, and the other witnesses fairly; the fair-minded and informed observer would be aware that judges have years of relevant training and experience, and would be aware of the terms of the judicial oath: *R. v. Oldfield* [2012] 1 Cr.App.R. 17, CA (considering *Porter v. Magill; Weeks v. Magill* (see the main work)). As to this case, see also *post*, § 4–252.

F. Interpreters

(4) For the accused at trial

4–61   Considering the right to a fair trial and to the assistance of an interpreter under the *New Zealand Bill of Rights Act* 1990 (in similar terms to Art. 6 of the ECHR (§ 16–57 in the main work)), the Supreme Court of New Zealand in *R. v. Abdula*, unreported, November 1, 2011 ([2011] NZSC 130), said that the nature of the interpreter's task is such that even the highest quality of trial interpretation cannot achieve perfection in conveying information and ideas spoken in a foreign language into the language of the court and vice versa; but the standard that must be attained reflects the accused's entitlement to full contemporaneous knowledge of what is happening at his trial; and interpretation will not be compliant if, as a result of its poor quality, an accused is unable to understand sufficiently the trial process or any part of the trial that affects his interests, to the extent that there is a real risk of an impediment to the conduct of the defence. The court said that trial judges should at all times be alert to the quality of interpretation; where the quality is challenged, the cumulative effect of any deficiencies in the interpretation must be evaluated in the overall context of the trial to determine whether its standard was, nevertheless, such that there was compliance with the accused's rights; but the consequence of a breach of the right to the assistance of an interpreter will be a breach of the right to a fair trial. It was the court's view that consecutive interpretation at all times is highly desirable; it enables an accused to react in response to what is said in court immediately and without being distracted by the voices of counsel and witnesses speaking at the same time as the interpreter; it also avoids the very real risk that the interpreter will fall behind and miss passages of evidence; the interpreter should, at all times, speak in a voice loud enough for all in the courtroom to hear; this meets the needs of all present in court who are likely to require interpretative assistance, and will help the judge to ensure that interpretation does not become the subject of simultaneous overspeaking; finally, the court said that an audio recording should be made of all trials in which there is an interpreter providing assistance for an accused person; the recording would be the appropriate and best means of resolving issues about the accuracy and general competence of interpretation.

K. Limited Discretionary Power to Prevent Prosecution Proceeding

(2) Abuse of process

(a) *Jurisdiction*

General

4–75   *R. v. Maxwell* is now reported at [2011] 2 Cr.App.R. 31.
    Warren v. Att.-Gen. for Jersey is now reported at [2012] 1 A.C. 22.

(b) *Where it will be impossible to give the defendant a fair trial*

Evidential matters

In *R. v. M.O.* [2012] 1 *Archbold Review* 1, CA ([2011] EWCA Crim. 2854), it was said that,   **4–78**
while an appellate court must be cautious before interfering with a terminating ruling staying a trial on the ground that failures of disclosure by the prosecution have led to an abuse
of process, such a ruling will require an exceptional case, particularly where the charges are
serious; deficiencies in disclosure may be censured, but it does not follow that the trial
should not proceed. Given that there was no allegation of bad faith on the part of the prosecution, it was held that the judge should not have made such a ruling unless it was
established that the defendants would not have had a fair trial; the failure was late, rather
than non-disclosure, and there was nothing to indicate that this could not have been accommodated during the trial (*e.g.* by adjournment).

Delay and the right to trial "within a reasonable time"

Common law principles
    R. v. F. (S.) is now reported at [2011] 2 Cr.App.R. 28.   **4–79**

Application of principles
    See *R. v. Killick, post,* § 4–93.   **4–81**

Delay by victim in reporting offence
    R. v. F. (S.) is now reported at [2011] 2 Cr.App.R. 28.   **4–83**

(c) *Where a stay is necessary to protect the integrity of the criminal justice system*

General

    R. v. Maxwell is now reported at [2011] 2 Cr.App.R. 31.   **4–87**
    Warren v. Att.-Gen. for Jersey is now reported at [2012] 1 A.C. 22.

Situations akin to autrefois

In *R. v. Dwyer* [2012] 2 *Archbold Review* 1, CA, it was held: (i) that the plea of *autrefois*   ★**4–88**
convict was not available to a defendant, charged with conspiracy to supply a Class A drug in
respect of a period of about six months, who had already been convicted of possession of
the same Class A drug with intent to supply and sentenced (in accordance with current
sentencing practice) on the basis of his admissions to the court that he had engaged in
small-scale supply to feed his own habit and had been doing so for the same six-month period; as stated in *R. v. Beedie* (see the main work), *autrefois convict* only applies when the
second indictment charges the same offence as the first; however (ii), in deciding whether
the second set of proceedings should have been stayed as an abuse on the basis that they
arose out of the same or substantially the same facts as the first (*Connelly v. DPP* (see the
main work), and *R. v. Beedie*), the terms of the defendant's admissions were capable of
constituting, and did constitute, the facts upon which the first set of proceedings was
concluded (in that they formed the factual basis upon which sentence was passed); given
that the second set of proceedings was founded on almost precisely the same conduct as had
been the foundation of the sentencing decision in the first prosecution, and given that there
were no special circumstances to justify their pursuit, they were oppressive and should have
been stayed as an abuse.

Other unfairness in the decision to institute or continue proceedings

    R. (E.) v. DPP; R. (S. and R.) v. DPP is now reported at [2012] 1 Cr.App.R. 6.   **4–90**

Jones (Craig Nicholas) v. DPP is now reported at [2012] R.T.R. 3, *sub nom. Jones v. DPP.*

★   *R. v. M. (L.), B. (M.) and G. (D.); R. v. Tabot; R. v. Tijani* (see the main work) was further considered in *R. v. N. (A.); R. v. Le* (as to which, see *post*, Appendix E–12d).

★   A prosecution that did not constitute an abuse of process at the date of conviction could not then become an abuse on the basis of new or amended prosecutorial guidance or policy issued subsequently: *R. v. A. (R.J.)* [2012] 2 Cr.App.R. 8, CA.

Prosecution going back on promise, etc.

4–93   In *R. v. Killick* [2012] 1 Cr.App.R. 10, CA, it was held to be plain on the authorities (as set out in *R. v. Abu Hamza* (see the main work)) that if a clear and unequivocal representation has been made to a defendant that he will not be prosecuted, upon which he relies to his detriment, it will be open to a court to find that to proceed against him would be an abuse of process, although there will be circumstances where, even in that situation, it will not be an abuse to proceed; however, an email sent by the police to a defendant's solicitors to the effect that, following a review by the CPS of an initial decision not to proceed against him, it had been decided that the matter would be discontinued, did not amount to an unequivocal representation that there would be no prosecution; the email went to the solicitors, not the defendant, and it could be inferred that the solicitors would have been aware of the right of the complainants in the case to seek a further review of the decision, and that they would have so informed the defendant when they passed on the information in the email; and where the complainants had in fact sought a further review, the CPS had had a duty to review the decision, impartially, not only because of the service's own guidance but because they were responding to the rights of the complainants in the prosecution process; on the facts, the review itself, and the decision after all to prosecute, could not be criticised. It was further held that the "lamentable" delay of almost four years between first arrest and the defendant finally being informed that he would be prosecuted (which was also over two years after the email), for which no excuse had or could have been put forward, did not in the circumstances itself amount to an abuse or cause prejudice or detriment to the defendant (although there was evidence to show that it had caused the defendant clear strain); and nor was the overall delay such that it had been an affront to justice to allow the case to proceed.

In *R. v. Nixon* [2011] 2 S.C.R. 566, the Supreme Court of Canada held that a prosecution decision to resile from a plea agreement in relation to a lesser charge and to continue the prosecution constitutes an act of prosecutorial discretion that will only be reviewable for abuse of process, either because it results in trial unfairness or meets the narrow residual category of abuse that undermines the integrity of the judicial process. The court ruled that prosecutorial discretion is not spent with the decision to initiate proceedings, nor does it terminate with a plea agreement; but, given that acts of prosecutorial discretion are generally beyond the reach of the court, there is good reason to impose a threshold evidentiary burden on an applicant who alleges abuse of process; evidence that a plea agreement has been entered into and subsequently reneged on by the prosecution will, however, meet the requisite threshold; further, to the extent that the prosecution are the only party who are privy to the information, the evidentiary burden then shifts to them to enlighten the court on the circumstances and reasons behind their decision to resile from the agreement; but the ultimate burden of proving abuse, nevertheless, remains with the defendant. The court added that it is the circumstances surrounding the repudiation of an agreement that should be reviewed to determine whether that decision amounts to an abuse, not the reasonableness of the decision to enter into the agreement; reviewing for reasonableness a decision made in the exercise of prosecutorial discretion runs contrary to the constitutionally separate role of the prosecutor; what has to be decided is whether the Crown's conduct in repudiating the agreement was, in all the circumstances, so unfair or oppressive, or so tainted by bad faith or improper motive, that to allow the Crown to proceed would tarnish the integrity of the criminal justice system.

Abuse of executive power

4–99   *R. v. Maxwell* is now reported at [2011] 2 Cr.App.R. 31.

Warren v. Att.-Gen. for Jersey is now reported at [2012] 1 A.C. 22.

Making the application

R. v. F. (S.) is now reported at [2011] 2 Cr.App.R. 28.   **4-101**

N. Pre-Trial Hearings

(1) The court's case management powers and duties

For a new practice direction setting out the correct method of citation of authorities for   **★4-112**
written and oral submissions in the Senior Courts of England and Wales, county courts and
magistrates' courts, see *Practice Direction (Citation of Authorities), post,* § 7–200.

Criminal Procedure Rules 2011 (S.I. 2011 No. 1709), Pt 3

The court's case management powers
With effect from April 2, 2012, rule 3.5 of the *Criminal Procedure Rules* 2011 (S.I. 2011   **4-116**
No. 1709) is amended by the *Criminal Procedure (Amendment) Rules* 2011 (S.I. 2011 No.
3075), r.4(a), so as to substitute a new paragraph (2)(h), as follows—

"(h) require that issues in the case should be—
  (i) identified in writing,
  (ii) determined separately, and decide in what order they will be determined;".

(2) Plea and case management hearings

Practice Direction (Criminal Proceedings: Consolidation), paras IV.41.1-IV.41.11 (as substituted by Practice Direction (Criminal Proceedings: Further Directions) [2007] 1 W.L.R. 1790)

PCMH form
Expanded versions of the plea and case management hearing form, for use in connection   **★4-123**
with Part 3 of the *Criminal Procedure Rules* 2011 (S.I. 2011 No. 1709) (§§ 4–115 *et seq.* in the
main work), and for cases involving two to five defendants, and cases involving six to 10
defendants, are now available on the Ministry of Justice website: http://www.justice.gov.uk/
courts/procedure-rules/criminal/formspage.
  R. (Firth) v. Epping Magistrates' Court (see the main work) was considered in *R. v. Newell,*   **★4-124**
176 J.P. 273, CA. The court said that a statement written by defence counsel on a plea and
case management hearing form is, in principle, admissible against a defendant under the
common law rules relating to admissions by agents, which are preserved by section 118(1)
of the *CJA* 2003 (§ 11–70 in the main work), but that , provided a case is conducted in accordance with the letter and spirit of the *Criminal Procedure Rules* 2011 (S.I. 2011 No.
1709), then, in the exercise of the court's discretion under section 78 of the *PACE Act* 1984
(§ 15–401 in the main work), such statement should not be admitted in evidence against
the defendant. The court added that, given the statutory regime in the Crown Court,
embedded primarily in the *CPIA* 1996 and the 2011 rules, and the obligation to put
"cards on the table" through the attendance of the trial advocate at the plea and case
management hearing, the requirements of the plea and case management hearing form
should be seen primarily as a means for the provision of information to enable a judge
actively to manage the case up to and throughout the trial, and for the parties to know
the issues that have to be addressed and the witnesses who are to attend; the nature of
the defence should appear from the defence statement, and a breach of the requirements
relating to such a statement will have statutory consequences (see the 1996 Act, ss.5 and
11 (§§ 12–56, 12–62 in the main work)); and the trial advocate at the plea and case
management hearing should see it as part of his duty to help the court with the management of the case by setting out information on the form, without the risk of the informa-

tion provided being used in evidence against his client. The court noted that there may be fact-specific cases where it would be right not to exercise the discretion in section 78, and to admit such statements (*e.g.*, where no defence statement is provided, despite the judge asking for one, and there is an attempted ambush inconsistent with what was stated on the form), but such cases should be "very, very rare". As to magistrates' courts, the court said that statements made on the trial preparation form (other than in the section relating to admissions) should not be used at trial as statements of the defendant admissible in evidence against him, provided the advocate follows the letter and spirit of the 2011 rules.

(3) Preparatory hearings

(a) *Serious or complex fraud cases*

Criminal Justice Act 1987, ss.7–10

The preparatory hearing

★**4-127**   With effect from May 1, 2012, section 9(11) of the 1987 Act is repealed in part by the *Protection of Freedoms Act* 2012, s.115(2), and Sched. 10, Pt 10. See *post*, § 7–309.

(b) *Long, complex or serious cases*

Criminal Procedure and Investigations Act 1996, s.28

★**4-130**   With effect from June 18, 2012 (*Criminal Justice Act 2003 (Commencement No. 28 and Saving Provisions) Order* 2012 (S.I. 2012 No. 1320)), sections 41 and 332 of, and paragraph 66(1) and (6) of Schedule 3 to, and Part 4 of Schedule 37 to, the 2003 Act are brought into force (so far as not already in force) in certain areas (as to which, see *ante*, § 1–88). There are associated saving provisions, as to which, see article 5 of the order (*ante*, § 1–88).

Criminal Procedure and Investigations Act 1996, ss.35, 36

Appeals to Court of Appeal

★**4-137**   With effect from May 1, 2012, the insertion of "43 or" in section 35(1) of the 1996 Act is repealed (along with such part of the *CJA* 2003, s.45(9), as inserted that text) by the *Protection of Freedoms Act* 2012, s.115(2), and Sched. 10, Pt 10.

(e) *Reporting restrictions*

Criminal Justice Act 1987, s.11

Restrictions on reporting

★**4-149**   With effect from June 18, 2012 (*Criminal Justice Act 2003 (Commencement No. 28 and Saving Provisions) Order* 2012 (S.I. 2012 No. 1320)), section 41 of, and paragraph 58 of Schedule 3 to, the 2003 Act are brought into force in certain areas (as to which, see *ante*, § 1–88). There are associated saving provisions, as to which, see article 5 of the order (*ante*, § 1–88).

As from a day to be appointed, section 11(12) of the 1987 Act is amended by the *Legal Aid, Sentencing and Punishment of Offenders Act* 2012, s.39(1), and Sched. 5, paras 34 and 36, so as to substitute a new paragraph (h), as follows—

> "(h) whether, for the purposes of the proceedings, representation was provided to the accused or any of the accused under Part 1 of the *Legal Aid, Sentencing and Punishment of Offenders Act* 2012".

★**4-150**   As from a day to be appointed, section 37(9) of the *CPIA* 1996 is amended by the *Legal Aid, Sentencing and Punishment of Offenders Act* 2012, s.39(1), and Sched. 5, para. 42. The amendment is identical to that made to section 11(12) of the *CJA* 1987 (as to which, see *ante*, § 4–149).

(4) Statutory pre-trial hearings

Criminal Procedure and Investigations Act 1996, ss.39–42

Meaning of pre-trial hearing

With effect from June 18, 2012 (*Criminal Justice Act 2003 (Commencement No. 28 and Saving Provisions) Order* 2012 (S.I. 2012 No. 1320)), section 41 of, and paragraph 66(1) and (7) of Schedule 3 to, the 2003 Act are brought into force (so far as not already in force) in certain areas (as to which, see *ante*, § 1–88). There are associated saving provisions, as to which, see article 5 of the order (*ante*, § 1–88). ★4–152

R. Vulnerable Defendants: Special Arrangements

In *R. v. Cox (Practice Note)* [2012] 2 Cr.App.R. 6, CA, it was said that the overall responsibility of the trial judge for the fairness of the trial has not been altered because of the increased availability of intermediaries (under the *YJCEA* 1999, s.29 (§ 8–94 in the main work)) or indeed the wide band of possible measures provided for by that Act. In the context of a defendant with communication problems, the court said that, when every sensible step taken to identify an available intermediary has been unsuccessful, the next stage is not for the proceedings to be stayed, but for the judge to make an informed assessment of whether the absence of an intermediary would make the proposed trial unfair or whether fairness can be safeguarded by procedural modifications to the ordinary trial process (*e.g.* frequent breaks, simply phrased questions and answers, playing tape-recordings of the defendant's police interview to accustom the jury to his patterns of speech, judge maintaining close control over questioning, intervening where any possible unfairness might arise, and playing "part of the role which an intermediary, if available, would otherwise have played"). The court added that it would be most unusual for a defendant who is fit to plead to be found to be so disadvantaged by his condition that a properly brought prosecution would have to be stayed. ★4–165

II. ARRAIGNMENT AND PLEA

B. Plea

(9) Autrefois acquit and convict

(a) *Scope*

As to whether the plea of *autrefois convict* was available where a defendant, charged with conspiracy to supply a Class A drug over a period of about six months, had already been convicted of possession of the same drug with intent to supply and had been sentenced on the basis of his admissions to the court that he had engaged in small-scale supply to feed his own habit and had been doing so for the same six-month period, see *R. v. Dwyer, ante*, § 4–88. ★4–183

(13) Defendant unfit to plead or take his trial

(a) *Procedure, evidence and burden of proof*

Criminal Procedure (Insanity) Act 1964, ss.4, 4A

Finding that the accused did the act or made the omission charged against him

As from a day to be appointed, section 8 of the *Criminal Procedure (Insanity) Act* 1964 is amended by the *Health and Social Care Act* 2012, s.38(5)(a), so as to insert the words ", or by ★4–232 another person by virtue of section 12ZA or 12ZB of that Act," after the words "Secretary of State" in the definition of "duly approved".

"did the act or made the omission charged"

★**4–237**   As to what constitutes the relevant "act ... charged against him as the offence" under section 4A(2) of the 1964 Act (§ 4–232 in the main work) for the purposes of an offence of voyeurism, contrary to the *SOA* 2003, s.67(1) (§ 20–212 in the main work), see *R. v. M.B.*, *post*, § 20–217 (in which the court considered *R. v. Antoine* (see the main work)).

C. CHANGE OF PLEA

4–252   If an application to change a plea of guilty is likely to involve a conflict of evidence between the defendant and his former counsel, the practice of bringing in, to deal with the matter, a judge from another court centre, who has no personal knowledge of the counsel involved, is to be commended: *R. v. Oldfield* [2012] 1 Cr.App.R. 17, CA. As to this case, see also *ante*, § 4–53.

VI. THE JURY

B. QUALIFICATION

Juries Act 1974, Sched. 1

Persons disqualified

★**4–269**   As from a day to be appointed, paragraph 6(d) of Schedule 1 to the 1974 Act is amended by the *Legal Aid, Sentencing and Punishment of Offenders Act* 2012, ss.126 and 127, Sched. 21, para. 1 (insertion of "226A, 226B" before "227"), and Sched. 22, para. 11 (insertion of "(including such a sentence imposed as a result of section 219A, 220, 221A or 222 of the *Armed Forces Act* 2006)" after "2003").

D. ATTENDANCE, SERVICE, EXCUSALS, DEFERRAL

Juries Act 1974, s.9B

Discharge of summonses to disabled persons only if incapable of acting effectively as a juror

★**4–290**   As from April 2, 2012 (*Armed Forces Act 2011 (Commencement No. 1, Transitional and Transitory Provisions) Order* 2012 (S.I. 2012 No. 669), section 9B of the *Juries Act* 1974 (as prospectively amended by the *Courts Act* 2003) is amended by the *AFA* 2011, s.26, and Sched. 2, para. 9, so as to omit the word "or" at the end of subsection (3)(c) (this has been inadvertently omitted from the main work), and to insert at the end of subsection (3)(d), the following—

> ", or
> (e) subject to subsection (4), a qualifying judge advocate (within the meaning of the *Senior Courts Act* 1981).
>
> (4) Subsection (3)(e) applies only where the case relates to a summons to attend for jury service in the Crown Court".

If the amendment effected by the 2003 Act has not come into force at the time of the coming into force of paragraph 1 of Schedule 2 to the 2011 Act, then paragraph 10 of Schedule 2 provides that, pending the commencement of that amendment, section 9B(3) of the 1974 Act shall be amended as follows: (i) the words from "any judge" to the end become paragraph (a), and (ii) at the end of paragraph (a), there is inserted the following—

", or
    (b) subject to subsection (4), any qualifying judge advocate (within the meaning of the *Senior Courts Act* 1981).
   (4) Subsection (3)(b) applies only where the case relates to a summons to attend for jury service in the Crown Court".

F. The Judge's Discretion to Stand Jurors Down

Impartiality

Where, during the summing up, it was discovered that a juror's fiancé had been sitting in **4–293** court on several days of the trial, including during proceedings that took place in the jury's absence, where the juror had been in communication with her fiancé, with whom she lived, during the course of the trial, and where the juror admitted she had received texts from her fiancé when in the jury room and had passed on information received from him to at least one juror on a few occasions, the judge, in dismissing an application to discharge the jury, had correctly identified the test (whether a fair-minded, independent and informed observer would conclude that there was a real danger that the jury might be biased, *i.e.* that their decision might be affected by information that they ought not to have received: *Porter v. Magill; Weeks v. Magill* (see § 4–53 in the main work)), but had failed to apply it properly because he substituted his own view of the facts for that of the independent observer; the independent observer must reach his decision on the likelihood of bias by considering the facts in their context; in this case, the judge made some findings about what had, or rather had not, been communicated to the other jurors, but, being no more than findings based on his own assessment of the evidence, they were not facts of which knowledge could be attributed to the independent observer; such an observer must make his own assessment of the risk of bias based on all the available raw material; and here, such an observer, knowing that jurors must be, and must be seen to be, unbiased, would have concluded that there was a real risk that during the course of the trial the jury had received information and views emanating from an extraneous source that they could not put out of their mind; the convictions were thus unsafe: *R. v. Mears and Mears* [2011] 10 *Archbold Review* 3, CA.

Leaving aside the question whether the presence of a police officer on a jury could ever be compatible with the right to a fair trial by an independent and impartial tribunal, as guaranteed by Article 6 of the ECHR (§ 16–57 in the main work), where there is an important conflict regarding police evidence in the case and the police officer witness giving the relevant evidence is personally acquainted with a police officer who is a member of the jury, jury directions and judicial warnings will be insufficient to guard against the risk that the juror may, albeit subconsciously, favour the evidence of the police: *Hanif and Khan v. U.K.* [2012] Crim.L.R. 295, ECtHR (finding — in proceedings arising out of *R. v. Khan* (see the main work) — that Article 6 had been violated where the police officer juror had known the police officer witness for 10 years and, although not from the same police station, had on three occasions worked with him on an investigation).

J. Discharge of Juror or Jury

(2) Investigation

Practice Direction (Crown Court: Guidance to Jurors) **[2004] 1 W.L.R. 665** (amending *Practice Direction (Criminal Proceedings: Consolidation)* **[2002] 1 W.L.R. 2870**)

As to whether it was appropriate for the court to inquire into the deliberations of a jury, **4–310** where it had emerged that there had been a conversation between a co-defendant (who had been convicted and who was on bail pending sentence) and two jurors in a public house, in which the co-defendant gave them material information about the appellant (whose case the jury were still considering), and that the jurors did not report the conversation to the judge but, the following day, disseminated the information to at least three other jurors, and as to the conclusion that would be reached by the informed observer regarding such conduct, see

4–310 *Archbold's Criminal Pleading—2012 ed.*

R. v. Hewgill (Michael), post, § 7–102 (considering *R. v. Thompson*; *R. v. Crawford*; *R. v. Gomulu*; *R. v. Allen*; *R. v. Blake*; *R. v. Kasunga* (§§ 4–315, 4–325 and 7–102 in the main work), *Re Medicaments and Related Classes of Goods (No. 2)* and *Porter v. Magill*; *Weeks v. Magill* (as to both of which, see §§ 4–53, 7–89 and 16–74 in the main work).

(4) Misconduct or bias

4–315   For consideration as to when a court should or should not conduct investigations with the jury where jurors fail to observe the judge's directions as to how to approach their role, see *R. v. Hewgill (Michael), post,* § 7–102.

L. MISCELLANEOUS

(2) Direction to jury as to how to approach their role

4–325   *R. v. Thompson*; *R. v. Crawford*; *R. v. Gomulu*; *R. v. Allen*; *R. v. Blake*; *R. v. Kasunga* (see the main work) was considered in *R. v. Hewgill (Michael), post,* § 7–102.

VIII. TRIAL ON INDICTMENT WITHOUT A JURY

A. FRAUD CASES AND JURY TAMPERING

Criminal Justice Act 2003, ss.43–49

[Applications by prosecution for certain fraud cases to be conducted without a jury
★4–329   With effect from May 1, 2012, section 43 of the 2003 Act is repealed by the *Protection of Freedoms Act* 2012, s.115(2), and Sched. 10, Pt 10.

Procedure for applications under sections 43 and 44
★4–332   With effect from May 1, 2012, section 45 of the 2003 Act is amended by the *Protection of Freedoms Act* 2012, s.115(1) and (2), Sched. 9, para. 148(1) and (2), and Sched. 10, Pt 10, so as (i) to change "sections 43 and 44" in the heading to "section 44", (ii) to omit subsection (1)(a), and (iii) to repeal in part the amendments made by subsections (5) and (9).

Discharge of jury because of jury tampering
★4–333   With effect from May 1, 2012, section 46(7) of the 2003 Act is amended by the *Protection of Freedoms Act* 2012, s.115(1) and (2), Sched. 9, para. 148(1) and (3), and Sched. 10, Pt 10, so as to omit "43 or".

Further provision about trials without a jury
★4–336   With effect from May 1, 2012, section 48(1) of the 2003 Act is amended by the *Protection of Freedoms Act* 2012, s.115(1) and (2), Sched. 9, para. 148(1) and (4), and Sched. 10, Pt 10, so as to omit "43,".

XII. SUBMISSION OF INSUFFICIENT EVIDENCE

C. R. V. GALBRAITH

4–365   *R. v. F. (S.)* is now reported at [2011] 2 Cr.App.R. 28.

XIV. *EXTENT TO WHICH EVIDENCE OTHER THAN DEFENCE EVIDENCE MAY BE ADDUCED AFTER THE PROSECUTION HAVE CLOSED THEIR CASE*

B. Evidence in Rebuttal

(4) Evidence available to the prosecution ab initio, the relevance of which though not arising ex improviso was marginal, is admissible subject to trial judge's discretion

In *R. v. Grocott* [2012] Crim.L.R. 210, CA, it was held that the fundamental principles ★4–407 underlying *R. v. Scott* (see the main work), and *R. v. Pilcher*, 60 Cr.App.R. 1, CA, that a defendant ought not to be ambushed and that the prosecution should present their entire case in one piece from the outset, are valid principles, but they have to be applied in the context of the additional procedures and protections that the courts now have and use to ensure a fair trial in which proper disclosure takes place in advance so as to avoid either side being caught unfairly by surprise; whether or not something should be allowed to be put in cross-examination when the evidence of a defendant brings out some matter more clearly than the prosecution might earlier have appreciated, can be something of a grey area and the judge is best placed, having the whole feel of the case, to determine what course accords with the overriding objective (that criminal cases be dealt with justly); on appeal, therefore, the court will be cautious before deciding that the judge was positively wrong to permit such questioning.

XIV. CLOSING SPEECHES

A. Prosecution

(1) Entitlement and timing

In *R. v. Williams (James)* [2012] R.T.R. 18, CA, the fact that the prosecution had made a ★4–424 closing speech in case where the defendant had been unrepresented and had called no witnesses when they had no entitlement to do so was one factor leading to the court's conclusion (considering *R. v. Mondon* and *R. v. Stovell* (see the main work)) that the conviction was unsafe. As to this case, see also *post*, §§ 7–64, 7–87.

XVII. SUMMING UP

C. Miscellaneous

(6) Scope of judge's task

As to *R. v. D.* (see the main work), see *R. v. H.*, *ante*, § 1–253. As to this case, see also *post*, ★4–441 § 11–40.

I. Corroboration

(3) Practice

(d) *Supporting evidence*

R. v. Islam (see the main work) was considered in *R. v. A. (Ashraf)*, *post*, § 11–40; and both ★4–481 *R. v. Islam* and *R. v. A. (Ashraf)* were considered in *R. v. H.*, *post*, § 11–40.

K. Defendant's Character

(1) Good character

★4–484   In *R. v. D. (P.)* [2012] 1 Cr.App.R. 33, CA, it was said that when directing a jury as to the relevance of a defendant's good character, the principles to be applied are those set out in *R. v. Vye*; *R. v. Wise*; *R. v. Stephenson* (see the main work), *R. v. Aziz* (§ 4–485 in the main work), *R. v. Gray* (§ 4–485 in the main work), and *R. v. Doncaster* (§§ 4–485, 13–68 in the main work); even where a defendant has been shown to be guilty of criminal conduct and thus cannot pray in aid absolutely good character, the prima facie rule of practice is to qualify the *Vye* direction, rather than withhold it. Accordingly, it was held that where a defendant on various charges of physical and sexual violence against his wife (including anal rape) had had no previous convictions for sexual offences, the judge's failure to give a modified direction (going to propensity) had been a serious misdirection rendering the defendant's conviction on those charges unsafe, even though he would not have been entitled to directions relating to credibility (because of limited admissions he had made about using violence against his wife and because of evidence that he had misused charitable money) and even though there was other powerful evidence that his wife had been telling the truth (including an internet article in which the defendant described anal rape as "the ultimate punishment"); the fact that a good character direction might be undermined by the facts of a particular case is no warrant for declining to give any such direction; it is for the jury to decide what weight to give the absence of previous convictions; and while it is possible to envisage a case where a verdict might be safe despite a failure to give a *Vye* direction (*e.g.* where the character of the defendant casts no light upon his guilt or innocence), this was not such a case.

★4–487   As to the effect on the safety of a conviction of a failure to give a good character direction, see *Brown (Nigel) v. State of Trinidad and Tobago* and *R. v. Williams (James)*, *post*, § 7–64. As to the latter case, see also *ante*, § 4–424; and *post*, § 7–87.

XIX. VERDICT

I. Special Verdict

Special verdict of insanity

Trial of Lunatics Act 1883, s.2

★4–535   For a case considering *R. v. Antoine* (see the main work), see *R. v. M.B.*, *post*, § 20–217.

Criminal Procedure (Insanity and Unfitness to Plead) Act 1991, s.1

Acquittals on grounds of insanity

★4–536   As from a day to be appointed, section 6(1) of the *Criminal Procedure (Insanity and Unfitness to Plead) Act* 1991 is amended by the *Health and Social Care Act* 2012, s.38(5)(c). The amendment is identical to the amendment made to section 8 of the *Criminal Procedure (Insanity) Act* 1964 (as to which, see *ante*, § 4–232).

CHAPTER 5

SENTENCES AND ORDERS ON CONVICTION

I. GENERAL INTERPRETATION

(1) Introduction

(a) Legislative framework

As from a day to be appointed, the headings to Chapters 3 and 6 of Part 12 of the *CJA*   ★**5–1**
2003 are substituted by the *Legal Aid, Sentencing and Punishment of Offenders Act* 2012,
ss.68(6) and 111(2), Sched. 9, para. 3, and Sched. 14, paras 5 and 16, to become "Suspended
sentence orders" and "Release, licences and recall" respectively.

(2) Legislation

Powers of Criminal Courts (Sentencing) Act 2000, ss.161, 163, 164

General definitions

As from a day to be appointed, section 163(1) of the *PCC(S)A* 2000 is amended by the   ★**5–4**
Legal Aid, Sentencing and Punishment of Offenders Act 2012, s.68(6), and Sched. 9, para. 1, so
as to omit the definition of "operational period". Section 68(7) of the 2012 Act provides that
the amendments and modifications made by section 68 and Schedule 9 apply in relation to
offences committed before or after the coming into force of any provision of that section or
that schedule.

Further interpretative provisions

As from a day to be appointed, section 164 of the 2000 Act is amended by the *Legal Aid,*   ★**5–6**
Sentencing and Punishment of Offenders Act 2012, s.122(3), and Sched. 19, paras 3 and 7, so as
to insert "224A," after "section" in subsection (3)(c).

As from a day to be appointed, section 164(3) of the 2000 Act is further amended by the   ★
2012 Act, s.142(3), and Sched. 26, paras 9 and 14(1) and (2), so as to insert a new paragraph
(aa) after paragraph (a), as follows—

     "(aa) under section 1A(5) of the *Prevention of Crime Act* 1953,".

As from a day to be appointed, section 164(3) of the 2000 Act is further amended by the   ★
2012 Act, s.142(3), and Sched. 26, paras 9 and 14(1) and (3), so as to insert a new paragraph
(ba) after paragraph (b), as follows—

     "(ba) under section 139AA(7) of the *Criminal Justice Act* 1988,".

Criminal Justice Act 2003, ss.176, 305

Interpretation of Part 12

As from a day to be appointed, section 305(1) of the 2003 Act is amended by the *Legal*   ★**5–8**
Aid, Sentencing and Punishment of Offenders Act 2012, s.72(6), so as to insert, at the appropriate place, a new definition, as follows—

     "'foreign travel prohibition requirement', in relation to a community order or suspended
       sentence order, has the meaning given by section 206A;".

As from a day to be appointed, section 305(1) of the 2003 Act is further amended by the   ★
2012 Act, s.76(8), so as to insert, at the appropriate place, a new definition, as follows—

"'alcohol abstinence and monitoring requirement', in relation to a community order or suspended sentence order, has the meaning given by section 212A;".

★ Section 77 of the 2012 Act (which itself came into force on May 1, 2012) provides for section 76 to be piloted in a specified area or areas before it can be brought into force generally.

★ As from a day to be appointed, section 305(1) of the 2003 Act is further amended by the 2012 Act, s.89(2), and Sched. 10, paras 12 and 37, so as to omit (i) the definition of "custody plus order", (ii) the definition of "intermittent custody order", (iii) the words "custody plus order" and "intermittent custody order" (wherever they appear), and (iv) in the definition of "responsible officer", the words "a custody plus order, an intermittent custody plus order".

★ As from a day to be appointed, section 305(1A) of the 2003 Act is amended by the 2012 Act, s.110(11), so as to substitute for the words "In the definition of 'sentence of imprisonment' in subsection (1) the" the words "In this Part any".

★ As from a day to be appointed, section 305(4) of the 2003 Act is amended by the 2012 Act, s.122(3), and Sched. 19, paras 8 and 22, so as to insert a new paragraph (bb), as follows—

"(bb) a sentence falls to be imposed under section 224A if the court is obliged by that section to pass a sentence of imprisonment for life,".

★ Paragraph 24(1) and (3) of Schedule 19 to the 2012 Act provide that, in relation to any time before the coming into force of section 61 of the *CJCSA* 2000, section 305(4) is to have effect as if the words "or, if the person is aged at least 18 but under 21, custody for life" were inserted after the words "imprisonment for life" in paragraph (bb).

★ As from a day to be appointed, section 305(4) of the 2003 Act is further amended by the 2012 Act, s.142(3), and Sched. 26, paras 15 and 22(1) and (2), so as to insert before paragraph (a), a new paragraph (za), as follows—

"(za) a sentence falls to be imposed under subsection (5) of section 1A of the *Prevention of Crime Act* 1953 if it is required by that subsection and the court is not of the opinion there mentioned,".

★ As from a day to be appointed, section 305(4) of the 2003 Act is further amended by the 2012 Act, s.142(3), and Sched. 26, paras 15 and 22(1) and (3), so as to insert after paragraph (a), a new paragraph (aa), as follows—

"(aa) a sentence falls to be imposed under subsection (7) of section 139AA of the *Criminal Justice Act* 1988 if it is required by that subsection and the court is not of the opinion there mentioned,".

II. PRELIMINARIES

(1) Legal representation

Powers of Criminal Courts (Sentencing) Act 2000, s.83

Restrictions on imposing custodial sentences on persons not legally represented

★5–12 As from a day to be appointed, section 83(3) of the 2000 Act is amended by the *Legal Aid, Sentencing and Punishment of Offenders Act* 2012, s.39(1), and Sched. 5, paras 52 and 53, so as (i) to substitute for the words from the beginning of paragraph (a) to "but the right", the words "representation was made available to him for the purposes of the proceedings under Part 1 of the *Legal Aid, Sentencing and Punishment of Offenders Act* 2012 but", (ii) to substitute the words "for such representation" for the words "to be granted such a right" in paragraph (a), and (iii) to substitute the words "for such representation" for the words "to be granted a right to it" in paragraph (aa).

(4) Pre-sentence reports

Criminal Justice Act 2003, ss.156–158

Procedural requirements for imposing community sentences and discretionary custodial sentences

★5–19 As from a day to be appointed, section 156 of the 2003 Act is amended by the *Legal Aid,*

Sentencing and Punishment of Offenders Act 2012, s.122(3), and Sched. 19, paras 8 and 13, so as to insert a new subsection (9), as follows—

"(9) References in subsections (1) and (3) to a court forming the opinions mentioned in sections 152(2) and 153(2) include a court forming those opinions for the purposes of section 224A(3).".

As from a day to be appointed, section 156 of the 2003 Act is further amended by the ★ 2012 Act, s.126, and Sched. 21, paras 20 and 22, so as (i) to substitute the words "section 226A(1)(b) or section 226B(1)(b)" for the words "section 227(1)(b) or section 228(1)(b)(i)" in subsection (3)(a), and (ii) to insert a new subsection (10), as follows—

"(10) The reference in subsection (1) to a court forming the opinion mentioned in section 153(2) includes a court forming that opinion for the purposes of section 226A(6) or 226B(4).".

Additional requirements in case of mentally disordered offender

As from a day to be appointed, section 157(6) of the *CJA* 2003 is amended by the *Health* ★5–20 *and Social Care Act* 2012, s.38(5)(d), so as to insert the words ", or by another person by virtue of section 12ZA or 12ZB of that Act," after the words "Secretary of State".

(6) Committal for sentence

Powers of Criminal Courts (Sentencing) Act 2000, ss.3–7

Committal for sentence on summary trial of offence triable either way

With effect from June 18, 2012 (*Criminal Justice Act 2003 (Commencement No. 28 and Sav-* ★5–25 *ing Provisions) Order* 2012 (S.I. 2012 No. 1320)), section 41 of, and paragraph 22A of Schedule 3 to, the 2003 Act are brought into force in certain areas (as to which, see *ante*, § 1–88). There are associated saving provisions, as to which, see article 5 of the order (*ante*, § 1–88).

Committal for sentence of dangerous adult offenders

As from a day to be appointed, section 3A(2) of the 2000 Act is amended by the *Legal Aid,* ★5–26 *Sentencing and Punishment of Offenders Act* 2012, s.126, and Sched. 21, paras 7 and 8, so as to substitute "226A" for "225(3) or 227(2)".

Committal for sentence of dangerous young offenders

With effect from June 18, 2012 (*Criminal Justice Act 2003 (Commencement No. 28 and Sav-* ★5–28 *ing Provisions) Order* 2012 (S.I. 2012 No. 1320)), section 41 of, and paragraphs 21 and 23 of Schedule 3 to, the 2003 Act are brought into force in certain areas (as to which, see *ante*, § 1–88), and to the extent that they are not already in force. There are associated saving provisions, as to which, see article 5 of the order (*ante*, § 1–88).

As from a day to be appointed, section 3C(2) of the 2000 Act is amended by the *Legal Aid,* ★ *Sentencing and Punishment of Offenders Act* 2012, s.126, and Sched. 21, paras 7 and 9, so as to substitute "226B" for "226(3) or 228(2)".

Committal for sentence on indication of guilty plea to offence triable either way

With effect from June 18, 2012 (*Criminal Justice Act 2003 (Commencement No. 28 and Sav-* ★5–29 *ing Provisions) Order* 2012 (S.I. 2012 No. 1320)), section 41 of, and paragraphs 21 and 24 of Schedule 3 to, the 2003 Act are brought into force in certain areas (as to which, see *ante*, § 1–88). There are associated saving provisions, as to which, see article 5 of the order (*ante*, § 1–88).

[Committal for sentence on indication of guilty plea by child or young person with related offences

With effect from June 18, 2012 (*Criminal Justice Act 2003 (Commencement No. 28 and Sav-* ★5–30 *ing Provisions) Order* 2012 (S.I. 2012 No. 1320)), section 41 of, and paragraphs 21 and 25 of Schedule 3 to, the 2003 Act are brought into force in certain areas (as to which, see *ante*, § 1–88). There are associated saving provisions, as to which, see article 5 of the order (*ante*, § 1–88).

Power of Crown Court on committal for sentence under sections 3 and 4

★5–31   With effect from June 18, 2012 (*Criminal Justice Act 2003 (Commencement No. 28 and Saving Provisions) Order* 2012 (S.I. 2012 No. 1320)), section 41 of, and paragraphs 21 and 26 of Schedule 3 to, the 2003 Act are brought into force in certain areas (as to which, see *ante*, § 1–88). There are associated saving provisions, as to which, see article 5 of the order (*ante*, § 1–88).

Power of Crown Court on committal for sentence under sections 3B, 3C and 4A

★5–32   With effect from June 18, 2012 (*Criminal Justice Act 2003 (Commencement No. 28 and Saving Provisions) Order* 2012 (S.I. 2012 No. 1320)), section 41 of, and paragraphs 21 and 27 of Schedule 3 to, the 2003 Act are brought into force in certain areas (as to which, see *ante*, § 1–88). There are associated saving provisions, as to which, see article 5 of the order (*ante*, § 1–88).

Committal for sentence in certain cases where offender committed in respect of another offence

★5–33   With effect from June 18, 2012 (*Criminal Justice Act 2003 (Commencement No. 28 and Saving Provisions) Order* 2012 (S.I. 2012 No. 1320)), section 41 of, and paragraphs 21 and 28 of Schedule 3 to, the 2003 Act are brought into force in certain areas (as to which, see *ante*, § 1–88), and to the extent that they are not already in force. There are associated saving provisions, as to which, see article 5 of the order (*ante*, § 1–88).

Power of Crown Court on committal for sentence under section 6

★5–34   As to the removal (as from a day to be appointed) of £5,000 as the upper limit on a fine on summary conviction (see s.7(6)(a) of the 2000 Act), see the *Legal Aid, Sentencing and Punishment of Offenders Act* 2012, s.85(1) (*ante*, § 1–125).

Effect of unlawful committal

5–38   Where the memorandum of conviction recorded that the offender had been committed to the Crown Court for sentence under section 3 of the *PCC(S)A* 2000 (§ 5–25 in the main work), but where two of the four offences were summary offences, the essential question was not what the memorandum of conviction recorded as the power that the committing justices had used, but the power that they had actually used; the right approach was to examine the question whether the magistrates' court had been vested with the necessary jurisdiction; if it had been (as here, where it could have committed under s.6 of the 2000 Act (§ 5–33 in the main work)), then an omission from, or inaccuracy in, the memorandum of conviction about the statutory powers which had been available to be exercised, or which had been exercised, did not affect the validity of the committal; it followed that the only remaining question was whether the sentences imposed for the summary offences exceeded the powers of the magistrates' court; if they did, they would fall to be reduced accordingly: *R. v. Ayhan* [2012] 1 Cr.App.R. 27, CA (considering, *inter alia, R. v. Hall* (§ 1–284 in the main work)).

(7) Remission for sentence of young offenders

Powers of Criminal Courts (Sentencing) Act 2000, s.8

Power and duty to remit young offenders to youth courts for sentence

★5–42   With effect from June 18, 2012 (*Criminal Justice Act 2003 (Commencement No. 28 and Saving Provisions) Order* 2012 (S.I. 2012 No. 1320)), section 41 of, and paragraph 74 of Schedule 3 to, the 2003 Act are brought into force (so far as not already in force) in certain areas (as to which, see *ante*, § 1–88). There are associated saving provisions, as to which, see article 5 of the order (*ante*, § 1–88).

Section 8 provides only for remittal for sentence. It cannot be construed as conferring on the Crown Court a power to remit a juvenile to a youth court for trial where he was jointly charged with an adult and where both were committed for trial to the Crown Court under the *MCA* 1980, s.6, pursuant to a mode of trial decision under section 24(1)(b) of that Act (§ 1–110 in the main work), and where the adult subsequently pleaded guilty: *R. (W. (a minor)) v. Leeds Crown Court* [2012] 1 Cr.App.R. 13, DC.

(8) Deferment of sentence

Sentence following deferment

Any curfew requirement to be complied with in conjunction with deferment of sentence **5–53** under the *PCC(S)A* 2000, s.1 (§ 5–45 in the main work), does not represent part of the sentence that is imposed at the end of the period of deferment; therefore, considering section 1D(2) of the 2000 Act (*ibid.*, § 5–49) and section 204(3) of the *CJA* 2003 (*ibid.*, § 5–270), there is no legislative restriction on imposing another curfew requirement as part of a community sentence: *R. v. Saeed Ali*, 176 J.P. 1, CA.

III. GENERAL PRINCIPLES

A. PURPOSES OF SENTENCING

(1) Offenders generally

Criminal Justice Act 2003, s.142

Purposes of sentencing [: offenders aged 18 or over]
As from a day to be appointed, section 142(2)(c) of the 2003 Act is amended by the *Legal* **★5–61** *Aid, Sentencing and Punishment of Offenders Act* 2012, s.122(3), and Sched. 19, paras 8 and 9, so as (i) to insert after "weapon)", the words ", under section 224A of this Act (life sentence for second listed offence for certain dangerous offenders)", and (ii) to insert the words "imprisonment or detention for life for certain" before "dangerous offenders".

As from a day to be appointed, section 142(2)(c) of the 2003 Act is further amended by ★ the 2012 Act, s.142(3), and Sched. 26, paras 15 and 16, so as (i) to insert the words "under section 1A(5) of the *Prevention of Crime Act* 1953 (minimum sentence for offence of threatening with offensive weapon in public)" after the words "falls to be imposed", and (ii) to insert the words "under section 139AA(7) of the *Criminal Justice Act* 1988 (minimum sentence for offence of threatening with article with blade or point or offensive weapon)" after the words "firearms offences)".

(2) Children and young persons

Criminal Justice Act 2003, s.142A

[Purposes etc. of sentencing: offenders under 18
As from a day to be appointed, section 142A(4)(b) of the 2003 Act is amended by the **★5–66** *Legal Aid, Sentencing and Punishment of Offenders Act* 2012, s.142(3), and Sched. 26, paras 15 and 17(1) and (2), so as to insert a new sub-paragraph (zi) before sub-paragraph (i), as follows—

> "(zi) section 1A(5) of the *Prevention of Crime Act* 1953 (minimum sentence for offence of threatening with offensive weapon in public),".

As from a day to be appointed, section 142A(4)(b) of the 2003 Act is further amended by ★ the 2012 Act, s.142(3), and Sched. 26, paras 15 and 17(1) and (3), so as to insert a new sub-paragraph (ia) after sub-paragraph (i), as follows—

"(ia) section 139AA(7) of the *Criminal Justice Act* 1988 (minimum sentence for offence of threatening with article with blade or point or offensive weapon),".

B. Determining the Seriousness of the Offence

(1) Statute

Previous convictions

Relevance

5–70   Where a judge proposes to implement a suspended sentence in full, and consecutively to the sentence to be imposed for the fresh offence, it is not legitimate to treat the seriousness of the fresh offence as aggravated by the mere fact that it was committed during the operational period of the suspended sentence; whilst section 143(2) of the *CJA* 2003 (§ 5–67 in the main work) requires a court to treat a previous conviction as an aggravating factor if it can reasonably be so treated, a court must be careful to guard against treating the fact that the fresh offence was committed during the operational period of a suspended sentence as a further aggravating factor; that it was so committed is dealt with by the implementation of the suspended sentence; to increase the sentence for the new offence on this account would involve an element of double counting: *R. v. Levesconte* [2012] 2 Cr.App.R.(S.) 19, CA.

(2) Factual basis of sentence

(a) *On conviction following a plea of not guilty*

Sample counts and specimen charges

5–84   *R. v. Hartley* is now reported at [2012] 1 Cr.App.R. 7, *sub nom. R. v. Hartley (Practice Note)*.

Strict liability offences

★5–88   Where an offender is convicted of, or pleads guilty to, an offence under regulatory legislation that requires proof of neglect, but not of dishonesty, it is not open to the judge to pass sentence on the basis that he was acting dishonestly, however fortunate he may have been that the prosecution agreed to a count that did allege dishonesty being ordered to lie on the file: *R. v. Stone and Moore*, unreported, January 24, 2012, CA ([2012] EWCA Crim. 186).

(b) *Following plea of guilty*

Agreed basis of plea

★5–90   *Att.-Gen.'s Reference (No. 23 of 2011)* is now reported at [2012] 1 Cr.App.R.(S.) 45, *sub nom. Att.-Gen.'s Reference (No. 23 of 2011) (R. v. Sanchez Williams)*.

Evidence given in trial of co-defendant(s)

★5–102   *R. v. Smith (Patrick)* (see the main work) was considered in *R. v. Dudley* [2012] 2 Cr.App.R.(S.) 15, CA. It was said that although not rigidly confined by the terms of the basis of plea, a sentencing judge had erred where he had passed sentence on the appellant on a substantially different basis from that set out in the basis of plea without first proposing a *Newton* hearing (§ 5–99 in the main work); although he had heard much evidence at the trial of the appellant's co-conspirators, none of it had been called on his behalf and much of it came from people whose interests would be well served if blame were to be directed towards him.

C. Reduction in Sentence for Guilty Plea

Criminal Justice Act 2003, s.144

Reduction in sentences for guilty pleas

As from a day to be appointed, section 144(2) of the 2003 Act is amended by the *Legal Aid, Sentencing and Punishment of Offenders Act* 2012, s.142(3), and Sched. 26, paras 15 and 18(1) and (2), so as to (i) substitute the words "a provision mentioned in subsection (3)" for the words "subsection (2) of section 110 or 111 of the *Sentencing Act*", and (ii) to substitute the words "that provision" for the words "that subsection" in both places.   **★5–107**

As from a day to be appointed, section 144 of the 2003 Act is further amended by the 2012 Act, s.142(3), and Sched. 26, paras 15 and 18(1) and (3), so as to insert new subsections (3) to (5), as follows—

    "(3) The provisions referred to in subsection (2) are—
        section 1A(6)(a) of the *Prevention of Crime Act* 1953;
        section 110(2) of the *Sentencing Act*;
        section 111(2) of the *Sentencing Act*;
        section 139AA(8)(a) of the *Criminal Justice Act* 1988.

    (4) In the case of an offence the sentence for which falls to be imposed under a provision mentioned in subsection (5), nothing in that provision prevents the court from imposing any sentence that it considers appropriate after taking into account any matter referred to in subsection (1) of this section.

    (5) The provisions referred to in subsection (4) are—
        section 1A(6)(b) of the *Prevention of Crime Act* 1953;
        section 139AA(8)(b) of the *Criminal Justice Act* 1988.".

Advance indication of sentence

R. v. Omole is now reported at [2012] 1 Cr.App.R.(S.) 41.   **5–111**

General entitlement to discount

As to the substitution of section 174 of the *CJA* 2003, see *post*, § 5–165.   **★5–112**

Extent of discount

In *R. v. James* [2011] L.S. Gazette, October 6, 19, CA the court held that an indication of a willingness to plead guilty to a particular count that was conditional on the prosecution not proceeding with a more serious count was not, for the purposes of the Sentencing Guidelines Council's guideline (Appendix K–1), an indication of a willingness to plead guilty to the offence in question; where, therefore, the prosecution, at the time of the conditional offer, indicated their intention to proceed with the more serious count, as a consequence of which the defendant only entered his plea to the lesser offence on the day of trial, the judge had been entitled to give a discount of just one-sixth.   **5–113**

Withholding the discount

See *R. v. Wilson (Paul)*, *post*, Appendix K–351.   **★5–115**

D. Increase in Sentences for Racial or Religious Aggravation or Aggravation Related to Disability or Sexual Orientation

Criminal Justice Act 2003, ss.145, 146

Increase in sentences for aggravation related to disability or sexual orientation

As from a day to be appointed, section 146 of the *CJA* 2003 is amended by the *Legal Aid,*   **★5–121**

Sentencing and Punishment of Offenders Act 2012, s.65(1) to (4), so as (i) to substitute, in the heading, ", sexual orientation or transgender identity" for "or sexual orientation", (ii) in subsection (2)(a), to omit the word "or" at the end of sub-paragraph (i), and (iii) to insert a new sub-paragraph (iii), in subsection (2)(a), as follows—

> "(iii) the victim being (or being presumed to be) transgender, or".

★   As from a day to be appointed, section 146 of the *CJA* 2003 is further amended by the 2012 Act, s.65(1) and (5), so as (i) to omit the word "or" at the end of subsection (2)(b)(i), and (ii) to insert at the end of subsection (2)(b), the word "or," followed by a new sub-paragraph (iii), as follows—

> "(iii) by hostility towards persons who are transgender".

★   As from a day to be appointed, section 146 of the *CJA* 2003 is further amended by the 2012 Act, s.65(1) and (6), so as to insert a new subsection (6), as follows—

> "(6) In this section references to being transgender include references to being transsexual, or undergoing, proposing to undergo or having undergone a process or part of a process of gender reassignment.".

E. Mitigation

(3) Selected mitigating factors

Assistance to law enforcement agencies

Assistance given otherwise than in accordance with the 2005 Act

★**5-139**   For an example of a case where the Court of Appeal approved a total discount that was on a par with that recommended in *R. v. P.*; *R. v. Blackburn* (a case under the 2005 Act (see § 5–137 in the main work)) where the appellant had not entered into an agreement under that Act, but had given evidence against members of his family in a murder trial (having pleaded guilty himself to causing or allowing the death of a vulnerable adult, contrary to the *Domestic Violence, Crime and Victims Act* 2004, s.5 (§ 19–118a in the main work), and conspiracy to pervert the course of justice), see *R. v. Watt* [2012] 1 Cr.App.R.(S.) 31, CA.

F. Sentencing Guidelines

Court of Appeal guidelines

5-144   *R. v. Anigbugu (Att.-Gen.'s Reference (No. 73 of 2010))*; *R. v. Pyo (Att.-Gen.'s Reference (No. 75 of 2010))*; *R. v. McGee (Att.-Gen.'s Reference (No. 3 of 2011))* is now reported at [2011] 2 Cr.App.R.(S.) 100, *sub nom. Att.-Gen.'s References (Nos 73, 75 of 2010, and 03 of 2011) (R. v. Anigbugu)*.

Sentencing Guidelines Council

5-145   Where sentence is passed on or after January, 16, 2012, the Sentencing Guidelines Council's guideline on non-domestic burglary will be superseded by the guideline of the Sentencing Council for England and Wales (*post*).

Sentencing Council for England and Wales

5-147   On October 13, 2011, the Sentencing Council for England and Wales issued a definitive guideline on burglary, applying to all offenders aged 18 or over who are sentenced on or after January 16, 2012, regardless of the date of their offence. The guideline covers both aggravated burglary (*Theft Act* 1968, s.10 (§ 21–129 in the main work)), and burglary, whether of a dwelling or non-dwelling (1968 Act, s.9 (*ibid.*, § 21–108)). For the details, see *post*, Appendix K–259 *et seq.*

The Sentencing Council for England and Wales issued a definitive guideline on drug offences on January 24, 2012, applying to all offenders aged 18 or over, who are sentenced on or after February 27, 2012, regardless of the date of their offence and covering a number of offences. For the details, see *post*, Appendix K–271 *et seq.*

The Sentencing Council for England and Wales has issued two further guidelines: on the ★ related topics of taking offences into consideration and totality, which applies to all offenders who are sentenced on or after June 11, 2012 (as to which, see *post*, §§ 5–160 *et seq.*, and Appendix K–280 *et seq.*), and on dangerous dog offences, which applies to all offenders aged 18 or over who are sentenced on or after August 20, 2012, regardless of the date of the offence (as to which, see *post*, Appendix K–291 *et seq.*).

Coroners and Justice Act 2009, ss.121, 125, 126

Sentencing guidelines: duty of court

As from a day to be appointed, section 125(6) of the 2009 Act is amended by the *Legal* ★**5–149** *Aid, Sentencing and Punishment of Offenders Act* 2012, s.122(3), and Sched. 19, para. 23, so as to insert a new paragraph (da), as follows—

> "(da) section 224A of that Act (life sentence for second listed offence for certain dangerous offenders);".

As from a day to be appointed, section 125(6) of the 2009 Act is further amended by the ★ 2012 Act, s.142(3), and Sched. 26, para. 31, so as to insert new paragraphs (ea) and (fa) after paragraphs (e) and (f) respectively, as follows—

> "(ea) section 1A(5) of the *Prevention of Crime Act* 1953 (minimum sentence for offence of threatening with offensive weapon in public);";
> "(fa) section 139AA(7) of the *Criminal Justice Act* 1988 (minimum sentence for offence of threatening with article with blade or point or offensive weapon);".

Determination of tariffs, etc.

As from a day to be appointed, section 126(1) of the 2009 Act is amended by the *Legal* ★**5–150** *Aid, Sentencing and Punishment of Offenders Act* 2012, s.126, and Sched. 21, para. 34(1) and (2), so as (i) to omit paragraphs (a) and (b), (ii) to substitute the words "226A of the *Criminal Justice Act* 2003" for the words "227 of that Act" in paragraph (c), and (iii) to substitute "226B" for "228" in paragraph (d).

As from a day to be appointed, section 126(2) of the 2009 Act is amended by the 2012 ★ Act, s.126, and Sched. 21, para. 34(1) and (3), so as (i) to omit paragraph (b), (ii) to substitute the words "226A(6) of the *Criminal Justice Act* 2003" for the words "227(3) of that Act" in paragraph (c), and (iii) to substitute "226B(4)" for "228(3)" in paragraph (d).

As from a day to be appointed, section 126(4) of the 2009 Act is amended by the 2012 ★ Act, s.126, and Sched. 21, para. 34(1) and (4), so as to substitute the words "means a sentence mentioned in subsection (2) of section 34 of the *Crime (Sentences) Act* 1997 other than a sentence mentioned in paragraph (d) or (e) of that subsection" for the words from "has" to the end.

Effect of guidelines

As to the substitution of section 174 of the *CJA* 2003, see *post*, § 5–165.   ★**5–152**

In *R. v. Heathcote-Smith and Melton* [2012] Crim.L.R. 304, CA, where the appellants ★ pleaded guilty to conspiracy to distribute indecent images of children (*Protection of Children Act* 1978, s.1 (§ 31–107 in the main work)), it was held that the judge had erred in going above the Sentencing Guidelines Council's guideline (*post*, Appendix K–101) on the basis that, at the time the guideline was published (2007), the council had no real idea of the scale of this type of offending "many years later in 2011". This, the court said, was an error of principle because reconsideration of a guideline is a matter for the council, not a judge.

G. Parity of Sentence

Disparity of sentence as ground of appeal

R. v. Cshako is now reported at [2012] 1 Cr.App.R.(S.) 39.   **5–159**

H. Taking Offences into Consideration

Practice

★**5–160**   The Sentencing Council for England and Wales has issued a guideline on the topic of taking offences into consideration (TICs) (as well as on the related topic of totality), which applies to all offenders who are sentenced on or after June 11, 2012. Essentially the guideline reiterates current case law. In putting this into the context of statutory guidelines for particular offences, however, it emphasises that a court should not have regard to offences taken into consideration when determining the starting point for the conviction offence, but should generally treat them as an aggravating feature. Where there is a large number of such offences, it may be appropriate to move outside the category range, although this must be considered in the context of the case and subject to the principle of totality. Next, the court should consider whether the frank admission of a number of offences is an indication of a defendant's remorse or determination to address addiction or offending behaviour, before going on to apply, first, a reduction for any guilty plea to the overall sentence and, secondly, the totality principle. Where permissible, ancillary orders (*e.g.* compensation and restitution) can be considered in relation to any or all of the offences taken into consideration.

Matters which should not be taken into consideration

★**5–161**   In addition to the matters set out in the main work, the Sentencing Council's guideline (*ante*) says that it would generally be undesirable for an offence to be taken into consideration: (i) where it is likely to attract a greater sentence than the conviction offence, (ii) where it is a specified offence for the purposes of the *CJA* 2003, s.224 (§ 5–495 in the main work), but the conviction offence is non-specified, and (iii) where it is not founded on the same facts or evidence or is not part of a series of offences of the same or similar character (unless the court is satisfied that it is in the interests of justice to do so).

Procedure

★**5–162**   As to procedure, the guideline of the Sentencing Council (*ante*) reflects what is said in the main work, but adds that there is there is a requirement that the TIC schedule should set out the nature and date of each offence, relevant details about the offence and any other brief details that the court should be aware of.

I. Duty of Court to Give Reasons for, and Explain Effect of, Sentence

Criminal Justice Act 2003, s.174

★**5–165**   As from a day to be appointed, section 174 of the *CJA* 2003 is substituted in its entirety by the *Legal Aid, Sentencing and Punishment of Offenders Act* 2012, s.64(1) and (2).

Criminal Justice Act 2003, s.174

[Duty to give reasons for and to explain effect of sentence
    174.—(1) A court passing sentence on an offender has the duties in subsections (2) and (3).
    (2) The court must state in open court, in ordinary language and in general terms, the court's reasons for deciding on the sentence.
    (3) The court must explain to the offender in ordinary language—
        (a) the effect of the sentence,
        (b) the effects of non-compliance with any order that the offender is required to comply with and that forms part of the sentence,
        (c) any power of the court to vary or review any order that forms part of the sentence, and
        (d) the effects of failure to pay a fine, if the sentence consists of or includes a fine.

(4) *Criminal Procedure Rules* may—

    (a) prescribe cases in which either duty does not apply, and

    (b) make provision about how an explanation under subsection (3) is to be given.

(5) Subsections (6) to (8) are particular duties of the court in complying with the duty in subsection (2).

(6) The court must identify any definitive sentencing guidelines relevant to the offender's case and—

    (a) explain how the court discharged any duty imposed on it by section 125 of the *Coroners and Justice Act* 2009 (duty to follow guidelines unless satisfied it would be contrary to the interests of justice to do so);

    (b) where the court was satisfied it would be contrary to the interests of justice to follow the guidelines, state why.

(7) Where, as a result of taking into account any matter referred to in section 144(1) (guilty pleas), the court imposes a punishment on the offender which is less severe than the punishment it would otherwise have imposed, the court must state that fact.

(8) Where the offender is under 18 and the court imposes a sentence that may only be imposed in the offender's case if the court is of the opinion mentioned in—

    (a) section 1(4)(a) to (c) of the *Criminal Justice and Immigration Act* 2008 and section 148(1) of this Act (youth rehabilitation order with intensive supervision and surveillance or with fostering), or

    (b) section 152(2) of this Act (discretionary custodial sentence),

the court must state why it is of that opinion.

(9) In this section "definitive sentencing guidelines" means sentencing guidelines issued by the Sentencing Council for England and Wales under section 120 of the *Coroners and Justice Act* 2009 as definitive guidelines, as revised by any subsequent guidelines so issued.]

IV. DISCHARGE AND BINDING OVER

(1) **Discharge**

Powers of Criminal Courts (Sentencing) Act 2000, s.12

Absolute and conditional discharge

As from a day to be appointed, section 12(1) of the 2000 Act is amended by the *Legal Aid,* ★**5–169** *Sentencing and Punishment of Offenders Act* 2012, s.122(3), and Sched. 19, paras 3 and 4, so as to insert "224A," before "225(2)".

As from a day to be appointed, section 12(1) of the 2000 Act is further amended by the ★ 2012 Act, s.142(3), and Sched. 26, paras 9 and 10, so as to substitute the words "section 1A(5) of the *Prevention of Crime Act* 1953, section 51A(2) of the *Firearms Act* 1968, section 139AA(7) of the *Criminal Justice Act* 1988" for the words "section 51A(2) of the *Firearms Act* 1968".

As from a day to be appointed, section 12(2) of the 2000 Act is amended by the 2012 Act, ★ s.135(3), and Sched. 24, paras 18 and 19, so as (i) to substitute "66ZB(6)" for "66(4)", and (ii) to substitute "youth cautions" for "reprimands and warnings". Section 66ZB(6) of the *CDA* 1998 (inserted as from a day to be appointed by the 2012 Act, s.135(2)) provides that where a person who has received two or more youth cautions (under section 66ZA) is convicted of an offence committed within two years beginning with the date of the last of those cautions, or a person who has received a youth conditional caution followed by a youth caution is convicted of an offence committed within two years beginning with the date of the youth caution, he is not to be conditionally discharged unless the court is of the opinion that "there are exceptional circumstances relating to the offence or the person that justify" such a disposal, in which case the court is to state in open court that it is of that opinion and give its reasons. As to the treatment of a reprimand or warning under section 65 of the 1998 Act, or any caution treated as such by virtue of paragraph 5 of Schedule 9 to that Act, as a youth caution under section 66ZA, see section 135(5) of the 2012 Act.

V. COMMUNITY SENTENCES

AA. Community Rehabilitation, Community Punishment, Drug Treatment and Testing, and Drug Abstinence Orders

(1) General provisions

Powers of Criminal Courts (Sentencing) Act 2000, ss.33–36

Meaning of "community order" and "community sentence"

5-187   **33.**—(1) In this Act, "community order" means any of the following orders—

    (a) a curfew order;

    (aa) an exclusion order;

    (b) a community rehabilitation order;

    (c) a community punishment order;

    (d) a community punishment and rehabilitation order;

    (e) a drug treatment and testing order;

    (ee) a drug abstinence order;

    (f) an attendance centre order;

    (g) a supervision order;

    (h) an action plan order.

    (2) In this Act, "community sentence" means a sentence which consists of or includes one or more community orders.

[This section is printed as amended by the *CJCSA* 2000, s.74, and Sched. 7, paras 1 to 3 and 161. It was substituted by a new section by the *CJA* 2003, s.304, and Sched. 32, paras 90 and 95, but this substitution was of no effect in relation to offences committed before April 4, 2005: see § 5–2 in the main work. The new subsection (1) was in similar terms, only it was defining "youth community order" as any of the orders in paragraphs (a), (aa), (f), (g) and (h), which became (a), (b), (c), (d) and (e). Subsection (2) defined a community sentence as a community order under section 177 of the *CJA* 2003 or one or more youth community orders. The substituted section 33 is repealed by the *CJIA* 2008, s.149, and Sched. 28, Pt 1. Save to the extent that subsection (1) defines a "youth community order" as including an attendance centre order, this repeal came into effect on November 30, 2009 (*Criminal Justice and Immigration Act 2008 (Commencement No. 13 and Transitory Provision) Order* 2009 (S.I. 2009 No. 3074)), but this repeal has no effect in relation to any offence committed before that date or to any failure to comply with an order in respect of an offence committed before that date: 2008 Act, Sched. 27, para. 1.]

Community orders not available where sentence fixed by law etc.

5-188   **34.** None of the powers to make community orders which are conferred by this Part is exercisable in respect of an offence for which the sentence—

    (a) is fixed by law; or

    (b) falls to be imposed under section 109(2), 110(2) or 111(2) below (requirement to impose custodial sentences for certain repeated offences committed by offenders aged 18 or over).

[This section was repealed as from April 4, 2005 (*Criminal Justice Act 2003 (Commencement No. 8 and Transitional and Saving Provisions) Order* 2005 (S.I. 2005 No. 950)): *CJA* 2003, s.332, and Sched. 7, Pt 7. For the relevant saving provisions, see *ante*, § 5–2.]

As to (b), see section 164(3), § 5–6 in the main work.

Restrictions on imposing community sentences

5-189   **35.**—(1) A court shall not pass a community sentence on an offender unless it is of the opinion that the offence, or the combination of the offence and one or more offences associated with it, was serious enough to warrant such a sentence.

    (2) In consequence of the provision made by section 51 below with respect to community punish-

ment and rehabilitation orders, a community sentence shall not consist of or include both a community rehabilitation order and a community punishment order.

(3) Subject to subsection (2) above and to section 69(5) below (which limits the community orders that may be combined with an action plan order), where a court passes a community sentence—

(a) the particular order or orders comprising or forming part of the sentence shall be such as in the opinion of the court is, or taken together are, the most suitable for the offender; and

(b) the restrictions on liberty imposed by the order or orders shall be such as in the opinion of the court are commensurate with the seriousness of the offence, or the combination of the offence and one or more offences associated with it.

(4) Subsections (1) and (3)(b) above have effect subject to section 59 below (curfew orders and community punishment orders for persistent petty offenders).

[This section is printed as amended by the *CJCSA* 2000, s.74 and Sched. 7, paras 1 to 3. It is repealed as from April 4, 2005 (*Criminal Justice Act 2003 (Commencement No. 8 and Transitional and Saving Provisions) Order* 2005 (S.I. 2005 No. 950)): *CJA* 2003, s.332, and Sched. 7, Pt 7. For the relevant saving provisions, see § 5–2 in the main work.]

Procedural requirements for community sentences: pre-sentence reports etc.

36.—(1) In forming any such opinion as is mentioned in subsection (1) or (3)(b) of section 35 **5–190** above, a court shall take into account all such information as is available to it about the circumstances of the offence or (as the case may be) of the offence and the offence or offences associated with it, including any aggravating or mitigating factors.

(2) In forming any such opinion as is mentioned in subsection (3)(a) of that section, a court may take into account any information about the offender which is before it.

(3) The following provisions of this section apply in relation to—

(a) a community rehabilitation order which includes additional requirements authorised by Schedule 2 to this Act;

(b) a community punishment order;

(c) a community punishment and rehabilitation order;

(d) a drug treatment and testing order;

(e) a supervision order which includes requirements authorised by Schedule 6 to this Act.

(4) Subject to subsection (5) below, a court shall obtain and consider a pre-sentence report before forming an opinion as to the suitability for the offender of one or more of the orders mentioned in subsection (3) above.

(5) Subsection (4) above does not apply if, in the circumstances of the case, the court is of the opinion that it is unnecessary to obtain a pre-sentence report.

(6) In a case where the offender is aged under 18 and the offence is not triable only on indictment and there is no other offence associated with it that is triable only on indictment, the court shall not form such an opinion as is mentioned in subsection (5) above unless—

(a) there exists a previous pre-sentence report obtained in respect of the offender; and

(b) the court has had regard to the information contained in that report, or, if there is more than one such report, the most recent report.

(7) No community sentence which consists of or includes such an order as is mentioned in subsection (3) above shall be invalidated by the failure of a court to obtain and consider a pre-sentence report before forming an opinion as to the suitability of the order for the offender, but any court on an appeal against such a sentence—

(a) shall, subject to subsection (8) below, obtain a pre-sentence report if none was obtained by the court below; and

(b) shall consider any such report obtained by it or by that court.

(8) Subsection (7)(a) above does not apply if the court is of the opinion—

(a) that the court below was justified in forming an opinion that it was unnecessary to obtain a pre-sentence report; or

(b) that, although the court below was not justified in forming that opinion, in the circumstances of the case at the time it is before the court, it is unnecessary to obtain a pre-sentence report.

(9) In a case where the offender is aged under 18 and the offence is not triable only on indictment and there is no other offence associated with it that is triable only on indictment, the court shall not form such an opinion as is mentioned in subsection (8) above unless—

(a) there exists a previous pre-sentence report obtained in respect of the offender; and

(b) the court has had regard to the information contained in that report, or, if there is more than one such report, the most recent report.

(10) Section 156 below (disclosure of pre-sentence report to offender etc.) applies to any pre-sentence report obtained in pursuance of this section.

[This section is printed as amended by the *CJCSA* 2000, s.74, and Sched. 7, paras 1 to 3. It is repealed as from April 4, 2005 (*Criminal Justice Act 2003 (Commencement No. 8 and Transitional and Saving Provisions) Order* 2005 (S.I. 2005 No. 950)): *CJA* 2003, s.332, and Sched. 7, Pt 7. For the relevant saving provisions, see § 5–2 in the main work.]

5–191   Apart from the matters specifically referred to in section 36, a court, in forming an opinion as to the suitability of a community order, should have regard, in particular to sections 151 (effect of previous convictions and offending while on bail) (now section 143 of the *CJA* 2003 (§ 5–67 in the main work)) and 158 (savings for mitigation and mentally disordered offenders) of the *PCC(S)A* 2000 (now section 166 of the *CJA* 2003 (§ 5–126 in the main work)).

Powers of Criminal Courts (Sentencing) Act 2000, s.36A

Pre-sentence drug testing

5–192   **36A.**—(1) Where a person aged 18 or over is convicted of an offence and the court is considering passing a community sentence, it may make an order under subsection (2) below for the purpose of ascertaining whether the offender has any specified Class A drug in his body.

(2) The order shall require the offender to provide, in accordance with the order, samples of any description specified in the order.

(3) If it is proved to the satisfaction of the court that the offender has, without reasonable excuse, failed to comply with the order it may impose on him a fine of an amount not exceeding level 4.

In this subsection, "level 4" means the amount which, in relation to a fine for a summary offence, is level 4 on the standard scale.

(4) The court shall not make an order under subsection (2) above unless it has been notified by the Secretary of State that the power to make such orders is exercisable by the court and the notice has not been withdrawn.

[This section was inserted by the *CJCSA* 2000, s.48. It is repealed as from April 4, 2005 (*Criminal Justice Act 2003 (Commencement No. 8 and Transitional and Saving Provisions) Order* 2005 (S.I. 2005 No. 950)): *CJA* 2003, s.332, and Sched. 7, Pt 7. For the relevant saving provisions, see § 5–2 in the main work.]

The court may make a similar order under section 52(4) (*post*, § 5–216), if it is contemplating a drug treatment and testing order. Failure to express willingness to comply with an order under section 52(4) may empower the court to pass a custodial sentence: see the *PCC(S)A* 2000, s.79(3) (*post*, § 5–469).

(2) Particular orders

(a) *Community rehabilitation orders*

Powers of Criminal Courts (Sentencing) Act 2000, ss.41–44

Community rehabilitation orders

5–193   **41.**—(1) Where a person aged 16 or over is convicted of an offence and the court by or before which he is convicted is of the opinion that his supervision is desirable in the interests of—

(a) securing his rehabilitation, or

(b) protecting the public from harm from him or preventing the commission by him of further offences,

the court may (subject to sections 34 to 36 above) make an order requiring him to be under supervision for a period specified in the order of not less than six months nor more than three years.

(2) An order under subsection (1) above is in this Act referred to as a "community rehabilitation order".

(3) A community rehabilitation order shall specify the petty sessions area in which the offender resides or will reside.

(4) If the offender is aged 18 or over at the time when the community rehabilitation order is made, he shall, subject to paragraph 18 of Schedule 3 to this Act (offender's change of area), be required to be under the supervision of an officer of a local probation board appointed for or assigned to the petty sessions area specified in the order, or (as the case may be) an officer of a provider of probation services acting in the local justice area specified in the order.

(5) If the offender is aged under 18 at that time, he shall, subject to paragraph 18 of Schedule 3, be required to be under the supervision of—

(a) an officer of a local probation board appointed for or assigned to the petty sessions area specified in the order, or (as the case may be) an officer of a provider of probation services acting in the local justice area specified in the order; or

(b) a member of a youth offending team established by a local authority specified in the order;

and if an order specifies a local authority for the purposes of paragraph (b) above, the authority specified must be the local authority within whose area it appears to the court that the offender resides or will reside.

(6) In this Act, "responsible officer", in relation to an offender who is subject to a community rehabilitation order, means the officer of a local probation board, officer of a provider of probation services or member of a youth offending team responsible for his supervision.

(7) Before making a community rehabilitation order, the court shall explain to the offender in ordinary language—

(a) the effect of the order (including any additional requirements proposed to be included in the order in accordance with section 42 below);

(b) the consequences which may follow (under Part II of Schedule 3 to this Act) if he fails to comply with any of the requirements of the order; and

(c) that the court has power (under Parts III and IV of that Schedule) to review the order on the application *either* of the offender *or of the responsible officer* [, of the responsible officer or any affected person].

(8) On making a community rehabilitation order, the court may, if it thinks it expedient for the purpose of the offender's reformation, allow any person who consents to do so to give security for the good behaviour of the offender.

(9) The court by which a community rehabilitation order is made shall forthwith give copies of the order to—

(a) if the offender is aged 18 or over, an officer of a local probation board assigned to the court or an officer of a provider of probation services acting at the court (as the case may be), or

(b) if the offender is aged under 18—

(i) an officer of a local probation board assigned to the court or an officer of a provider of probation services acting at the court (as the case may be); or

(ii) a member of a youth offending team assigned to the court,

and he shall give a copy to the offender, to the responsible officer and to the person in charge of any institution in which the offender is required by the order to reside.

[(9A) The court by which such an order is made shall give to any affected person any information relating to the order which the court considers it appropriate for him to have.]

(10) The court by which such an order is made shall also, except where it itself acts for the petty sessions area specified in the order, send to the clerk to the justices for that area—

(a) a copy of the order; and

(b) such documents and information relating to the case as it considers likely to be of assistance to a court acting for that area in the exercise of its functions in relation to the order.

(11) An offender in respect of whom a community rehabilitation order is made shall keep in touch with the responsible officer in accordance with such instructions as he may from time to time be given by that officer, and shall notify him of any change of address.

[(12) For the purposes of this Act, a person is an affected person in relation to a community rehabilitation order if—

(a) a requirement under section 36B(1) above is included in the order by virtue of his consent; or

(b) a requirement is included in the order under paragraph 8(1) of Schedule 2 to this Act for the purpose (or partly for the purpose) of protecting him from being approached by the offender.]

[This section is printed as amended by the *CJCSA* 2000, ss.43 and 74, and Sched. 7, para. 1; and the *Offender Management Act 2007 (Consequential Amendments) Order* 2008 (S.I. 2008 No. 912), art. 3, and Sched. 1, para. 14(1) and (4); and as amended, as from a day to be appointed, by the *CJCSA* 2000, s.74, and Sched. 7, para. 165 (omission of italicised words, insertion of words in square brackets). It is repealed as from April 4, 2005 (*Criminal Justice Act 2003 (Commencement No. 8 and Transitional and Saving Provisions) Order* 2005 (S.I. 2005 No. 950)): *CJA* 2003, s.332, and Sched. 7, Pt 7. For the relevant saving provisions, see § 5–2 in the main work; and *post*, §§ 5–255 *et seq.*]

A community rehabilitation order is a "community order" (s.33(1)), and thus a court must not make such an order without complying with sections 35 and 36 (*ante*, §§ 5–189, 5–190).

Additional requirements which may be included in community rehabilitation orders

5–194   42.—(1) Subject to subsection (3) below, a community rehabilitation order may in addition require the offender to comply during the whole or any part of the community rehabilitation period with such requirements as the court, having regard to the circumstances of the case, considers desirable in the interests of—

    (a) securing the rehabilitation of the offender; or

    (b) protecting the public from harm from him or preventing the commission by him of further offences.

(2) Without prejudice to the generality of subsection (1) above,

    (a) the additional requirements which may be included in a community rehabilitation order shall include the requirements which are authorised by Schedule 2 to this Act.

    (b) subject to subsections (2D) and (2F) below, the order shall, if the first set of conditions is satisfied, include a drug abstinence requirement and may include such a requirement if the second set of conditions is satisfied.

(2A) For the purposes of this Part of this Act, a drug abstinence requirement is a requirement for the offender—

    (a) to abstain from misusing specified Class A drugs; and

    (b) to provide, when instructed to do so by the responsible officer, any sample mentioned in the instruction for the purpose of ascertaining whether he has any specified Class A drug in his body.

(2B) The first set of conditions is—

    (a) that the offender was aged 18 or over on the date of his conviction for the offence;

    (b) that, in the opinion of the court, the offender is dependent on or has a propensity to misuse specified Class A drugs; and

    (c) that the offence is a trigger offence.

(2C) The second set of conditions is—

    (a) that the offender was aged 18 or over on the date of his conviction for the offence; and

    (b) that, in the opinion of the court—

        (i) the offender is dependent on or has a propensity to misuse specified Class A drugs; and

        (ii) the misuse by the offender of any specified Class A drug caused or contributed to the offence.

(2D) The order may not include a drug abstinence requirement if—

    (a) the community rehabilitation order includes any requirement in respect of drugs under paragraph 6 of Schedule 2 to this Act; or

    (b) the community sentence includes a drug treatment and testing order or a drug abstinence order.

(2E) The function of giving instructions for the purposes of subsection (2A)(b) above shall be exercised in accordance with guidance given from time to time by the Secretary of State; and the Secretary of State may make rules for regulating the provision of samples in pursuance of such instructions.

(2F) The court shall not include a drug abstinence requirement in the order unless the court has been notified by the Secretary of State that arrangements for implementing such requirements are available in the area proposed to be specified under section 41(3) above and the notice has not been withdrawn.

(3) Without prejudice to the power of the court under section 130 below to make a compensation order, the payment of sums by way of damages for injury or compensation for loss shall not be included among the additional requirements of a community rehabilitation order.

[This section is printed as amended by the *CJCSA* 2000, ss.49 and 74, and Sched. 7, paras 1 and 166. It is repealed as from April 4, 2005 (*Criminal Justice Act 2003 (Commencement No. 8 and Transitional and Saving Provisions) Order* 2005 (S.I. 2005 No. 950)): *CJA* 2003, s.332, and Sched. 7, Pt 7. For the relevant saving provisions, see § 5–2 in the main work; and *post*, §§ 5–255 *et seq.*]

As to what is a "trigger offence", see the *CJCSA* 2000, Sched. 6 (§ 15–194 in the main work).

As to "specified Class A drugs", see § 15–195 in the main work.

Breach, revocation and amendment of community rehabilitation order
43. [*Gives effect to Sched. 3, post, §§ 5–228 et seq.*]   **5–195**

Offenders residing in Scotland or Northern Ireland
44. [*Gives effect to Sched. 4.*]   **5–196**

Powers of Criminal Courts (Sentencing) Act 2000, Sched. 2

SCHEDULE 2

ADDITIONAL REQUIREMENTS WHICH MAY BE INCLUDED IN COMMUNITY
REHABILITATION ORDERS

Requirements as to residence

1.—(1) Subject to sub-paragraphs (2) and (3) below, a community rehabilitation order may include   **5–197** requirements as to the residence of the offender.

(2) Before making a community rehabilitation order containing any such requirement, the court shall consider the home surroundings of the offender.

(3) Where a community rehabilitation order requires the offender to reside in an approved hostel or any other institution, the period for which he is required to reside there shall be specified in the order.

Requirements as to activities etc.

2.—(1) Subject to the provisions of this paragraph, a community rehabilitation order may require   **5–198** the offender—

    (a) to present himself to a person or persons specified in the order at a place or places so specified;

    (b) to participate or refrain from participating in activities specified in the order—

        (i) on a day or days so specified; or

        (ii) during the community rehabilitation period or such portion of it as may be so specified.

(2) A court shall not include in a community rehabilitation order a requirement such as is mentioned in sub-paragraph (1) above unless—

    (a) it has consulted—

        (i) in the case of an offender aged 18 or over, an officer of a local probation board; or

        (ii) in the case of an offender aged under 18, either an officer of a local probation board or a member of a youth offending team; and

    (b) it is satisfied that it is feasible to secure compliance with the requirement.

(3) A court shall not include a requirement such as is mentioned in sub-paragraph (1)(a) above or a requirement to participate in activities if it would involve the co-operation of a person other than the offender and the offender's responsible officer, unless that other person consents to its inclusion.

(4) A requirement such as is mentioned in sub-paragraph (1)(a) above shall operate to require the offender—

    (a) in accordance with instructions given by his responsible officer, to present himself at a place or places for not more than 60 days in the aggregate; and

    (b) while at any place, to comply with instructions given by, or under the authority of, the person in charge of that place.

(5) A place specified in an order shall have been approved by the local probation board for the area in which the premises are situated as providing facilities suitable for persons subject to community rehabilitation orders.

(6) A requirement to participate in activities shall operate to require the offender—

(a) in accordance with instructions given by his responsible officer, to participate in activities for not more than 60 days in the aggregate; and

(b) while participating, to comply with instructions given by, or under the authority of, the person in charge of the activities.

(7) Instructions given by the offender's responsible officer under sub-paragraph (4) or (6) above shall, as far as practicable, be such as to avoid—

(a) any conflict with the offender's religious beliefs or with the requirements of any other community order to which he may be subject; and

(b) any interference with the times, if any, at which he normally works or attends school or any other educational establishment.

Requirements as to attendance at community rehabilitation centre

5-199   3.—(1) Subject to the provisions of this paragraph, a community rehabilitation order may require the offender during the community rehabilitation period to attend at a community rehabilitation centre specified in the order.

(2) A court shall not include in a community rehabilitation order such a requirement as is mentioned in sub-paragraph (1) above unless it has consulted—

(a) in the case of an offender aged 18 or over, an officer of a local probation board; or

(b) in the case of an offender aged under 18, either an officer of a local probation board or a member of a youth offending team.

(3) A court shall not include such a requirement in a community rehabilitation order unless it is satisfied—

(a) that arrangements can be made for the offender's attendance at a centre; and

(b) that the person in charge of the centre consents to the inclusion of the requirement.

(4) A requirement under sub-paragraph (1) above shall operate to require the offender—

(a) in accordance with instructions given by his responsible officer, to attend on not more than 60 days at the centre specified in the order; and

(b) while attending there to comply with instructions given by, or under the authority of, the person in charge of the centre.

(5) Instructions given by the offender's responsible officer under sub-paragraph (4) above shall, as far as practicable, be such as to avoid—

(a) any conflict with the offender's religious beliefs or with the requirements of any other community order to which he may be subject; and

(b) any interference with the times, if any, at which he normally works or attends school or any other educational establishment.

(6) References in this paragraph to attendance at a community rehabilitation centre include references to attendance elsewhere than at the centre for the purpose of participating in activities in accordance with instructions given by, or under the authority of, the person in charge of the centre.

(7) The Secretary of State may make rules for regulating the provision and carrying on of community rehabilitation centres and the attendance at such centres of persons subject to community rehabilitation orders; and such rules may in particular include provision with respect to hours of attendance, the reckoning of days of attendance and the keeping of attendance records.

(8) In this paragraph "community rehabilitation centre" means premises—

(a) at which non-residential facilities are provided for use in connection with the rehabilitation of offenders; and

(b) which are for the time being approved by the Secretary of State as providing facilities suitable for persons subject to probation orders.

Extension of requirements for sexual offenders

5-200   4. If the court so directs in the case of an offender who has been convicted of a sexual offence—

(a) sub-paragraphs (4) and (6) of paragraph 2 above, and

(b) sub-paragraph (4) of paragraph 3 above,

shall each have effect as if for the reference to 60 days there were substituted a reference to such greater number of days as may be specified in the direction.

Requirements as to treatment for mental condition etc.

5.—(1) This paragraph applies where a court proposing to make a community rehabilitation or-   **5–201**
der is satisfied, on the evidence of a registered medical practitioner approved for the purposes of
section 12 of the *Mental Health Act* 1983, that the mental condition of the offender—

    (a) is such as requires and may be susceptible to treatment; but

    (b) is not such as to warrant the making of a hospital order or guardianship order within the
        meaning of that Act.

(2) Subject to sub-paragraph (4) below, the community rehabilitation order may include a requirement that the offender shall submit, during the whole of the community rehabilitation period or
during such part or parts of that period as may be specified in the order, to treatment by or under
the direction of a registered medical practitioner or a chartered psychologist (or both, for different
parts) with a view to the improvement of the offender's mental condition.

(3) The treatment required by any such order shall be such one of the following kinds of treatment as may be specified in the order, that is to say—

    (a) treatment as a resident patient in an independent hospital or care home within the mean-
        ing of the *Care Standards Act* 2000 or a hospital within the meaning of the *Mental Health
        Act* 1983, but not hospital premises at which high security psychiatric services within the
        meaning of that Act are provided;

    (b) treatment as a non-resident patient at such institution or place as may be specified in the
        order;

    (c) treatment by or under the direction of such registered medical practitioner or chartered
        psychologist (or both) as may be so specified;

but the nature of the treatment shall not be specified in the order except as mentioned in
paragraph (a), (b) or (c) above.

(4) A court shall not by virtue of this paragraph include in a community rehabilitation order a
requirement that the offender shall submit to treatment for his mental condition unless—

    (a) it is satisfied that arrangements have been or can be made for the treatment intended to
        be specified in the order (including arrangements for the reception of the offender where
        he is to be required to submit to treatment as a resident patient); and

    (b) the offender has expressed his willingness to comply with such a requirement.

(5) While the offender is under treatment as a resident patient in pursuance of a requirement of
the community rehabilitation order, his responsible officer shall carry out the supervision of the offender to such extent only as may be necessary for the purpose of the revocation or amendment of
the order.

(6) Where the medical practitioner or chartered psychologist by whom or under whose direction
an offender is being treated for his mental condition in pursuance of a community rehabilitation order is of the opinion that part of the treatment can be better or more conveniently given in or at an
institution or place which—

    (a) is not specified in the order, and

    (b) is one in or at which the treatment of the offender will be given by or under the direction
        of a registered medical practitioner or chartered psychologist,

he may, with the consent of the offender, make arrangements for him to be treated accordingly.

(7) Such arrangements as are mentioned in sub-paragraph (6) above may provide for the offender to receive part of his treatment as a resident patient in an institution or place notwithstanding
that the institution or place is not one which could have been specified for that purpose in the community rehabilitation order.

(8) Where any such arrangements as are mentioned in sub-paragraph (6) above are made for the
treatment of an offender—

    (a) the medical practitioner or chartered psychologist by whom the arrangements are made
        shall give notice in writing to the offender's responsible officer, specifying the institution
        or place in or at which the treatment is to be carried out; and

    (b) the treatment provided for by the arrangements shall be deemed to be treatment to which
        he is required to submit in pursuance of the community rehabilitation order.

(9) Subsections (2) and (3) of section 54 of the *Mental Health Act* 1983 shall have effect with respect to proof for the purposes of sub-paragraph (1) above of an offender's mental condition as they
have effect with respect to proof of an offender's mental condition for the purposes of section
37(2)(a) of that Act.

(10) In this paragraph, "chartered psychologist" means a person for the time being listed in the
British Psychological Society's Register of Chartered Psychologists.

Requirements as to treatment for drug or alcohol dependency

5–202

6.—(1) Subject to sub-paragraph (2) below, this paragraph applies where a court proposing to make a community rehabilitation order is satisfied—

(a) that the offender is dependent on drugs or alcohol;

(b) that his dependency caused or contributed to the offence in respect of which the order is proposed to be made; and

(c) that his dependency is such as requires and may be susceptible to treatment.

(2) If the court has been notified by the Secretary of State that arrangements for implementing drug treatment and testing orders are available in the area proposed to be specified in the probation order, and the notice has not been withdrawn, this paragraph shall have effect as if the words "drugs or", in each place where they occur, were omitted.

(3) Subject to sub-paragraph (5) below, the community rehabilitation order may include a requirement that the offender shall submit, during the whole of the community rehabilitation period or during such part of that period as may be specified in the order, to treatment by or under the direction of a person having the necessary qualifications or experience with a view to the reduction or elimination of the offender's dependency on drugs or alcohol.

(4) The treatment required by any such order shall be such one of the following kinds of treatment as may be specified in the order, that is to say—

(a) treatment as a resident in such institution or place as may be specified in the order;

(b) treatment as a non-resident in or at such institution or place as may be so specified;

(c) treatment by or under the direction of such person having the necessary qualifications or experience as may be so specified;

but the nature of the treatment shall not be specified in the order except as mentioned in paragraph (a), (b) or (c) above.

(5) A court shall not by virtue of this paragraph include in a community rehabilitation order a requirement that the offender shall submit to treatment for his dependency on drugs or alcohol unless—

(a) it is satisfied that arrangements have been or can be made for the treatment intended to be specified in the order (including arrangements for the reception of the offender where he is to be required to submit to treatment as a resident); and

(b) the offender has expressed his willingness to comply with such a requirement.

(6) While the offender is under treatment as a resident in pursuance of a requirement of the community rehabilitation order, his responsible officer shall carry out the offender's supervision to such extent only as may be necessary for the purpose of the revocation or amendment of the order.

(7) Where the person by whom or under whose direction an offender is being treated for dependency on drugs or alcohol in pursuance of a community rehabilitation order is of the opinion that part of the treatment can be better or more conveniently given in or at an institution or place which—

(a) is not specified in the order, and

(b) is one in or at which the treatment of the offender will be given by or under the direction of a person having the necessary qualifications or experience,

he may, with the consent of the offender, make arrangements for him to be treated accordingly.

(8) Where any such arrangements as are mentioned in sub-paragraph (7) above are made for the treatment of an offender—

(a) the person by whom the arrangements are made shall give notice in writing to the offender's responsible officer, specifying the institution or place in or at which the treatment is to be carried out; and

(b) the treatment provided for by the arrangements shall be deemed to be treatment to which he is required to submit in pursuance of the community rehabilitation order.

(9) In this paragraph, the reference to the offender being dependent on drugs or alcohol includes a reference to his having a propensity towards the misuse of drugs or alcohol; and references to his dependency on drugs or alcohol shall be construed accordingly.

Curfew requirements

5–203

7.—(1) Subject to the provisions of this paragraph, a community rehabilitation order may include a requirement that the offender remain, for periods specified in the requirement, at a place so specified.

(2) A requirement under sub-paragraph (1) above may specify different places or different periods for different days, but shall not specify—

(a) periods which fall outside the period of six months beginning with the day on which the order is made; or

(b) periods which amount to less than two hours or more than twelve hours in any one day.

(3) A requirement under sub-paragraph (1) above shall, as far as practicable, be such as to avoid—

(a) any conflict with the offender's religious beliefs or with the requirements of any other community order to which he may be subject; and

(b) any interference with the times, if any, at which he normally works or attends school or any other educational establishment.

(4) An order which includes a requirement under sub-paragraph (1) above shall include provision for making a person responsible for monitoring the offender's whereabouts during the curfew periods specified in the requirement; and a person who is made so responsible shall be of a description specified in an order made by the Secretary of State.

(5) A court shall not include in a community rehabilitation order such a requirement as is mentioned in sub-paragraph (1) above unless the court has been notified by the Secretary of State that arrangements for monitoring the offender's whereabouts are available in the area in which the place proposed to be specified in the requirement is situated and the notice has not been withdrawn.

(6) A court shall not include in a community rehabilitation order such a requirement as is mentioned in sub-paragraph (1) above if the community sentence includes a curfew order.

(7) Before including in a community rehabilitation order such a requirement as is mentioned in sub-paragraph (1) above, the court shall obtain and consider information about the place proposed to be specified in the requirement (including information as to the attitude of persons likely to be affected by the enforced presence there of the offender).

(8) The Secretary of State may make rules for regulating—

(a) the monitoring of the whereabouts of an offender who is subject to a requirement under sub-paragraph (1) above; and

(b) without prejudice to the generality of paragraph (a) above, the functions of any person responsible for monitoring the offender's whereabouts during the curfew periods specified in the requirement.

(9) The Secretary of State may by order direct that sub-paragraph (3) above shall have effect with such additional restrictions as may be specified in the order.

[Exclusion requirements

8.—(1) Subject to the provisions of this paragraph, a community rehabilitation order may include **5–204** a requirement prohibiting the offender from entering a place specified in the requirement for a period so specified of not more than two years.

(2) A requirement under sub-paragraph (1) above—

(a) may provide for the prohibition to operate only during the periods specified in the order;

(b) may specify different places for different periods or days.

(3) *[Identical to para. 7(3), ante.]*

(4) An order which includes a requirement under sub-paragraph (1) above shall include provision for making a person responsible for monitoring the offender's whereabouts during the periods when the prohibition operates; and a person who is made so responsible shall be of a description specified in an order made by the Secretary of State.

(5) A court shall not include in a community rehabilitation order such a requirement as is mentioned in sub-paragraph (1) above unless the court has been notified by the Secretary of State that arrangements for monitoring the offender's whereabouts are available in the area in which the place proposed to be specified in the order is situated and the notice has not been withdrawn.

(6) A court shall not include in a community rehabilitation order such a requirement as is mentioned in sub-paragraph (1) above if the community sentence includes an exclusion order.

(7) The Secretary of State may make rules for regulating—

(a) the monitoring of the whereabouts of an offender who is subject to a requirement under sub-paragraph (1) above; and

(b) without prejudice to the generality of paragraph (a) above, the functions of any person responsible for monitoring the offender's whereabouts during the periods when the prohibition operates.

(8) *[Identical to para. 7(8), ante.]*

(9) In this paragraph, "place" includes an area.]

[This schedule is printed as amended by the *CJCSA* 2000, s.49, 50 and 74, and Sched. 7, paras 1, 4 and 198; and the *Care Standards Act* 2000, s.116 and Sched. 4, para. 28(2); and as amended, as from a day to be appointed, by the *CJCSA* 2000, s.51 (insertion of para. 8). It is repealed as from April 4, 2005 (*Criminal Justice Act 2003 (Commencement No. 8 and Transitional and Saving Provisions) Order* 2005 (S.I. 2005 No. 950)): *CJA* 2003, s.332, and Sched. 7, Pt 7. For the relevant saving provisions, see § 5–2 in the main work; and *post*, §§ 5–255 *et seq.*]

Willingness to comply with requirements of order

5-205   The general requirement that an offender should express his willingness to comply with the requirements of a probation order was abolished by the *C(S)A* 1997, s.38(2), with reference to probation orders made for offences committed on or after October 1, 1997 (*Crime (Sentences) Act 1997 (Commencement No. 2 and Transitional Provisions) Order* 1997 (S.I. 1997 No. 2200)). Where a court proposes to make a community rehabilitation order for an offence committed before that date, the requirement remains: see Sched. 11, para. 4(1)(b) to the 2000 Act. An offender must still express his willingness to comply with requirements relating to psychiatric treatment, or treatment for drug or alcohol dependency (Sched. 2, paras 5(4) and 6(5)).

For cases on the meaning of "willingness", see *R. v. Marquis*, 59 Cr.App.R. 228, CA, and *R. v. Barnett*, 8 Cr.App.R.(S.) 200, CA.

Combined with custodial sentence

5-206   A community sentence may not be imposed on the same occasion as an offender is made the subject of a suspended sentence: s.118(6) of the 2000 Act. There is no such express bar on a community sentence being imposed at the same time as an immediate custodial sentence, but the spirit of section 118(6) would seem to apply *a fortiori*.

Where, however, the offender is already serving a custodial sentence, it has been held that there is no objection to the imposition of a community sentence provided that the sentence could have practical effect, as where the custodial sentence had only a short time to run: see *Fontenau v. DPP* [2001] 1 Cr.App.R.(S.) 15, DC. This is contrary to the approach of the Court of Appeal in *R. v. Carr Thompson* [2000] 2 Cr.App.R.(S.) 335, where a probation order which had been made on the same occasion as the Crown Court dismissed an appeal against a custodial sentence was quashed. The court relied on *R. v. Evans*, 43 Cr.App.R. 66, CCA. *Evans* was, however, decided at a time when the legislation expressly declared that probation was instead of punishment. The rationale of the decision, *viz.* that it was fundamentally inconsistent to impose an avowedly punitive sentence at the same time as making a probation order, disappeared with the legislative changes made by the *CJA* 1991. Probation then became a form of punishment, and the rationale underlying *Evans* disappeared. It is submitted that the more flexible approach in *Fontenau* is to be preferred to that in *Carr Thompson*.

Contempt of court

5-207   A community rehabilitation order may not be made against a person adjudged guilty of contempt of court: *R. v. Palmer*, 95 Cr.App.R. 170, CA.

Electronic monitoring

5-208   As to the electronic monitoring of a curfew requirement under paragraph 7, see section 36B (*post*, § 5–313). Rule 42.2 of the *Criminal Procedure Rules* 2011 (S.I. 2011 No. 1709) makes provision as to notification of the defendant, the person responsible for electronically monitoring compliance, and the responsible officer.

Enforcement

5-209   See Schedule 3 to the 2000 Act, see *post*, §§ 5–228 *et seq.*

(b) *Community punishment orders*

Powers of Criminal Courts (Sentencing) Act 2000, ss.46–49

Community punishment orders

46.—(1) Where a person aged 16 or over is convicted of an offence punishable with imprison-   **5-210**
ment, the court by or before which he is convicted may (subject to sections 34 to 36 above) make
an order requiring him to perform unpaid work in accordance with section 47 below.

(2) An order under subsection (1) above is in this Act referred to as a "community punishment
order".

(3) The number of hours which a person may be required to work under a community punishment order shall be specified in the order and shall be in the aggregate—

(a) not less than 40; and

(b) not more than 240.

(3A) Subject to subsection (3B) below, the community punishment order shall, if the set of conditions in section 42(2B) above is satisfied, include a drug abstinence requirement and may include
such a requirement if the set of conditions in section 42(2C) above is satisfied.

(3B) The order may not include a drug abstinence requirement if the community sentence
includes a drug treatment and testing order or a drug abstinence order.

(3C) Subsections (2E) and (2F) of section 42 above apply for the purposes of this section as they
apply for the purposes of that.

(4) A court shall not make a community punishment order in respect of an offender unless, after
hearing (if the court thinks it necessary) an appropriate officer, the court is satisfied that the offender
is a suitable person to perform work under such an order.

(5) In subsection (4) above "an appropriate officer" means—

(a) in the case of an offender aged 18 or over, an officer of a local probation board, an officer
of a provider of probation services or social worker of a local authority social services
department; and

(b) in the case of an offender aged under 18, an officer of a local probation board, an officer of
a provider of probation services, a social worker of a local authority social services department or a member of a youth offending team.

(6) A court shall not make a community punishment order in respect of an offender unless it is
satisfied that provision for him to perform work under such an order can be made under the arrangements for persons to perform work under such orders which exist in the petty sessions area in
which he resides or will reside.

(7) Subsection (6) above has effect subject to paragraphs 3 and 4 of Schedule 4 to this Act (transfer
of order to Scotland or Northern Ireland).

(8) Where a court makes community punishment orders in respect of two or more offences of
which the offender has been convicted by or before the court, the court may direct that the hours of
work specified in any of those orders shall be concurrent with or additional to those specified in any
other of those orders, but so that the total number of hours which are not concurrent shall not
exceed the maximum specified in subsection (3)(b) above.

(9) A community punishment order—

(a) shall specify the petty sessions area in which the offender resides or will reside; and

(b) where the offender is aged under 18 at the time the order is made, may also specify a local
authority for the purposes of section 47(5)(b) below (cases where functions are to be
discharged by member of a youth offending team);

and if the order specifies a local authority for those purposes; the authority specified must be the
local authority within whose area it appears to the court that the offender resides or will reside.

(10) Before making a community punishment order, the court shall explain to the offender in
ordinary language—

(a) the purpose and effect of the order (and in particular the requirements of the order as
specified in section 47(1) to (3) below);

(b) the consequences which may follow (under Part II of Schedule 3 to this Act) if he fails to
comply with any of those requirements; and

(c) that the court has power (under Parts III and IV of that Schedule) to review the order on
the application either of the offender or of the responsible officer.

(11) The court by which a community punishment order is made shall forthwith give copies of
the order to—

(a) if the offender is aged 18 or over, an officer of a local probation board assigned to the court or an officer of a provider of probation services acting at the court (as the case may be), or

(b) if the offender is under 18—

    (i) an officer of a local probation board assigned to the court or an officer of a provider of probation services acting at the court; or

    (ii) a member of a youth offending team assigned to the court,

and he shall give a copy to the offender and to the responsible officer.

(12) The court by which such an order is made shall also, except where it itself acts for the petty sessions area specified in the order, send to the clerk to the justices for that area—

(a) a copy of the order; and

(b) such documents and information relating to the case as it considers likely to be of assistance to a court acting for that area in the exercise of its functions in relation to the order.

(13) In this section and Schedule 3 to this Act "responsible officer", in relation to an offender subject to a community punishment order, means the person mentioned in subsection (4)(a) or (b) or (5)(b) of section 47 below who, as respects the order, is responsible for discharging the functions conferred by that section.

[This section is printed as amended by the *CJCSA* 2000, ss.45, 49(2) and 74, and Sched. 7, paras 2, 4 and 168; and the *Offender Management Act 2007 (Consequential Amendments) Order* 2008 (S.I. 2008 No. 912), art. 3, and Sched. 1, para. 14(1) and (5). It is repealed as from April 4, 2005 (*Criminal Justice Act 2003 (Commencement No. 8 and Transitional and Saving Provisions) Order* 2005 (S.I. 2005 No. 950)): *CJA* 2003, s.332, and Sched. 7, Pt 7. For the relevant saving provisions, see § 5–2 in the main work; and *post*, §§ 5–255 *et seq.*]

A community punishment order is a "community order" within Part IV of the Act (s.33(1), *ante*, § 5–187), and thus a court must not make such an order without complying with sections 35 and 36 (*ante*, §§ 5–189, 5–190), unless the case falls within section 59 (*post*, § 5–227).

Obligations of person subject to community punishment order

5-211

47.—(1) An offender in respect of whom a community punishment order is in force shall—

(a) keep in touch with the responsible officer in accordance with such instructions as he may from time to time be given by that officer and notify him of any change of address; and

(b) perform for the number of hours specified in the order such work at such times as he may be instructed by the responsible officer.

(2) The instructions given by the responsible officer under this section shall, as far as practicable, be such as to avoid—

(a) any conflict with the offender's religious beliefs or with the requirements of any other community order to which he may be subject; and

(b) any interference with the times, if any, at which he normally works or attends school or any other educational establishment.

(3) Subject to paragraph 22 of Schedule 3 to this Act (power to extend order), the work required to be performed under a community punishment order shall be performed during the period of twelve months beginning with the date of the order; but, unless revoked, the order shall remain in force until the offender has worked under it for the number of hours specified in it.

(4) If the offender is aged 18 or over at the time when the order is made, the functions conferred by this section on "the responsible officer" shall be discharged by an officer of a local probation board or (as the case may be) an officer of a provider of probation services acting in the local justice area specified in the order.

(5) If the offender is aged under 18 at that time, those functions shall be discharged by—

(a) a person mentioned in subsection (4) above; or

(b) a member of a youth offending team established by a local authority specified in the order.

(6) The reference in subsection (4) above to the petty sessions area specified in the order and the reference in subsection (5) above to a local authority so specified are references to the area or an authority for the time being so specified, whether under section 46(9) above or by virtue of Part IV of Schedule 3 to this Act (power to amend orders).

[This section is printed as amended by the *CJCSA* 2000, s.74 and Sched. 7, paras 2, 5 and 169; and the *Offender Management Act 2007 (Consequential Amendments) Order* 2008 (S.I. 2008 No. 912), art. 3, and Sched. 1, para. 14(1) and (6). It is repealed as from April 4, 2005 (*Criminal Justice Act 2003 (Commencement No. 8 and Transitional and Saving Provisions) Order*

2005 (S.I. 2005 No. 950)): *CJA* 2003, s.332, and Sched. 7, Pt 7. For the relevant saving provisions, see § 5–2 in the main work; and *post*, §§ 5–255 *et seq.*]

Breach, revocation and amendment of community punishment orders
    48. [*Gives effect to Sched. 3*, post, §§ 5–228 et seq.]

Offenders residing in Scotland or Northern Ireland
    49. [*Gives effect to Sched. 4.*]

Combined with other forms of sentence

Section 118(6) of the *PCC(S)A* 2000 provides that a court which imposes a suspended **5–212** sentence may not make any form of community order on the same occasion. A magistrates' court should not make a community punishment order in respect of an offence committed while the offender is subject to a suspended sentence imposed by the Crown Court: the offender should be committed to the Crown Court for both matters to be dealt with together (see *R. v. Stewart*, 6 Cr.App.R.(S.) 166, CA). Where a community punishment order is made by one court for one offence, the making of the order does not prevent another court, dealing with the offender for offences committed before the order was made, from imposing a custodial sentence (see *R. v. Bennett*, 2 Cr.App.R.(S.) 96, CA).

Consecutive orders

See section 46(2), *ante*. **5–213**

When a community punishment order is made against an offender who is subject to an existing community punishment order which has been partly performed, the total number of hours outstanding should not generally exceed 240 (see *R. v. Siha*, 13 Cr.App.R.(S.) 588, CA). The Court of Appeal held in *R. v. Meredith*, 15 Cr.App.R.(S.) 528, that where an offender was ordered to perform a number of hours of community service by a magistrates' court and then ordered to perform a further number of hours by the Crown Court in the form of a consecutive community service order, both orders became for all practical purposes one order and a breach of one became a breach of both. It is submitted that this case is wrongly decided, at least where one order is made by a magistrates' court and the other by the Crown Court, as an order made by a magistrates' court can be revoked (following a failure to comply with the order) only by a magistrates' court, and an order made by the Crown Court can be revoked only by the Crown Court: see Sched. 3, paras 4 and 5 (*post*, §§ 5–231, 5–232).

Enforcement

The enforcement of community punishment orders is governed by the provisions of **5–214** Schedule 3 (*post*, §§ 5–228 *et seq.*).

(c) *Community punishment and rehabilitation orders*

Powers of Criminal Courts (Sentencing) Act 2000, s.51

Community punishment and rehabilitation orders
    51.—(1) Where a person aged 16 or over is convicted of an offence punishable with imprison- **5–215** ment and the court by or before which he is convicted is of the opinion mentioned in subsection (3) below, the court may (subject to sections 34 to 36 above) make an order requiring him both—
        (a) to be under supervision for a period specified in the order, being not less than twelve months nor more than three years; and
        (b) to perform unpaid work for a number of hours so specified, being in the aggregate not less than 40 nor more than 100.
  (2) An order under subsection (1) above is in this Act referred to as a "community punishment and rehabilitation order".

(3) The opinion referred to in subsection (1) above is that the making of a community punishment and rehabilitation order is desirable in the interests of—

  (a) securing the rehabilitation of the offender; or

  (b) protecting the public from harm from him or preventing the commission by him of further offences.

(4) Subject to subsection (1) above, sections 41, 42, 46 and 47 above and Schedule 2 to this Act shall apply in relation to community punishment and rehabilitation orders—

  (a) in so far as those orders impose such a requirement as is mentioned in paragraph (a) of subsection (1) above, as if they were community rehabilitation orders; and

  (b) in so far as they impose such a requirement as is mentioned in paragraph (b) of that subsection, as if they were community punishment orders.

(5) [*Gives effect to Sched. 3 (enforcement), post, §§ 5–228 et seq.*]

(6) [*Gives effect to Sched. 4 (offenders residing in Scotland or Northern Ireland).*]

[This section is printed as amended by the *CJCSA* 2000, ss.45 and 75, and Sched. 7, para. 3. It is repealed as from April 4, 2005 (*Criminal Justice Act 2003 (Commencement No. 8 and Transitional and Saving Provisions) Order* 2005 (S.I. 2005 No. 950)): *CJA* 2003, s.332, and Sched. 7, Pt 7. For the relevant saving provisions, see § 5–2 in the main work; and *post*, §§ 5–255 *et seq.*]

A community punishment and rehabilitation order is a "community order" (s.33(1), *ante*, § 5–187) and thus a court must not make such an order without complying with sections 35 and 36 (*ante*, §§ 5–189, 5–190).

As to the enforcement of community punishment and rehabilitation orders, see Schedule 3, *post*, §§ 5–228 *et seq.*

(d) *Drug treatment and testing orders*

Powers of Criminal Courts (Sentencing) Act 2000, ss.52–57

Drug treatment and testing orders

5-216   52.—(1) Where a person aged 16 or over is convicted of an offence, the court by or before which he is convicted may (subject to sections 34 to 36 above) make an order which—

  (a) has effect for a period specified in the order of not less than six months nor more than three years ("the treatment and testing period"); and

  (b) includes the requirements and provisions mentioned in sections 53 and 54 below;

but this section does not apply in relation to an offence committed before 30th September 1998.

(2) An order under subsection (1) above is in this Act referred to as a "drug treatment and testing order".

(3) A court shall not make a drug treatment and testing order in respect of an offender unless it is satisfied—

  (a) that he is dependent on or has a propensity to misuse drugs; and

  (b) that his dependency or propensity is such as requires and may be susceptible to treatment.

(4) For the purpose of ascertaining for the purposes of subsection (3) above whether the offender has any drug in his body [(in a case where, at the time of conviction, he was aged under 18)], the court may by order require him to provide samples of such description as it may specify; but the court shall not make such an order unless the offender expresses his willingness to comply with its requirements.

(5) A court shall not make a drug treatment and testing order unless it has been notified by the Secretary of State that arrangements for implementing such orders are available in the area proposed to be specified in the order under section 54(1) below and the notice has not been withdrawn.

(6) Before making a drug treatment and testing order, the court shall explain to the offender in ordinary language—

  (a) the effect of the order and of the requirements proposed to be included in it;

  (b) the consequences which may follow (under Part II of Schedule 3 to this Act) if he fails to comply with any of those requirements;

  (c) that the order will be periodically reviewed at intervals as provided for in the order (by virtue of section 54(6) below); and

(d) that the order may be reviewed (under Parts III and IV of Schedule 3) on the application
either of the offender or of the responsible officer;
and "responsible officer" here has the meaning given by section 54(3) below.

(7) A court shall not make a drug treatment and testing order unless the offender expresses his
willingness to comply with its requirements.

[This section is printed as amended, as from a day to be appointed, by the *CJCSA* 2000,
s.74, and Sched. 7, para. 170 (insertion of words in square brackets). It is repealed as
from April 4, 2005 (*Criminal Justice Act 2003 (Commencement No. 8 and Transitional and Saving Provisions) Order* 2005 (S.I. 2005 No. 950)): *CJA* 2003, s.332, and Sched. 7, Pt 7. For
the relevant saving provisions, see § 5–2 in the main work; and *post*, §§ 5–255 *et seq.*]

A drug treatment and testing order is a "community order" (s.33(1), *ante*, § 5–187) and
thus a court must not make such an order without complying with sections 35 and 36 (*ante*,
§§ 5–189, 5–190).

The treatment and testing requirements

53.—(1) A drug treatment and testing order shall include a requirement ("the treatment   **5–217**
requirement") that the offender shall submit, during the whole of the treatment and testing period, to treatment by or under the direction of a specified person having the necessary qualifications or experience ("the treatment provider") with a view to the reduction or elimination of the
offender's dependency on or propensity to misuse drugs.

(2) The required treatment for any particular period shall be—
    (a) treatment as a resident in such institution or place as may be specified in the order; or
    (b) treatment as a non-resident in or at such institution or place, and at such intervals, as may
        be so specified;
but the nature of the treatment shall not be specified in the order except as mentioned in
paragraph (a) or (b) above.

(3) A court shall not make a drug treatment and testing order unless it is satisfied that arrangements have been or can be made for the treatment intended to be specified in the order (including
arrangements for the reception of the offender where he is to be required to submit to treatment as
a resident).

(4) A drug treatment and testing order shall include a requirement ("the testing requirement")
that, for the purpose of ascertaining whether he has any drug in his body during the treatment and
testing period, the offender shall during that period, at such times or in such circumstances as may
(subject to the provisions of the order) be determined by the treatment provider, provide samples of
such description as may be so determined.

(5) The testing requirement shall specify for each month the minimum number of occasions on
which samples are to be provided.

[This section was repealed as from April 4, 2005 (*Criminal Justice Act 2003 (Commencement
No. 8 and Transitional and Saving Provisions) Order* 2005 (S.I. 2005 No. 950)): *CJA* 2003,
s.332, and Sched. 7, Pt 7. For the relevant saving provisions, see § 5–2 in the main work;
and *post*, §§ 5–255 *et seq.*]

Provisions of order as to supervision and periodic review

54.—(1) A drug treatment and testing order shall include a provision specifying the petty ses-   **5–218**
sions area in which it appears to the court making the order that the offender resides or will
reside.

(2) A drug treatment and testing order shall provide that, for the treatment and testing period,
the offender shall be under the supervision of an officer of a local probation board appointed for or
assigned to the petty sessions area specified in the order or (as the case may be) an officer of a
provider of probation services acting in the local justice area specified in the order.

(3) In this Act "responsible officer", in relation to an offender who is subject to a drug treatment
and testing order, means the officer of a local probation board or officer of a provider of probation
services responsible for his supervision.

(4) A drug treatment and testing order shall—
    (a) require the offender to keep in touch with the responsible officer in accordance with such
        instructions as he may from time to time be given by that officer, and to notify him of any
        change of address; and

(b) provide that the results of the tests carried out on the samples provided by the offender in pursuance of the testing requirement shall be communicated to the responsible officer.

(5) Supervision by the responsible officer shall be carried out to such extent only as may be necessary for the purpose of enabling him—

    (a) to report on the offender's progress to the court responsible for the order;

    (b) to report to that court any failure by the offender to comply with the requirements of the order; and

    (c) to determine whether the circumstances are such that he should apply to that court for the revocation or amendment of the order.

(6) A drug treatment and testing order shall—

    (a) provide for the order to be reviewed periodically at intervals of not less than one month;

    (b) provide for each review of the order to be made, subject to section 55(6) below, at a hearing held for the purpose by the court responsible for the order (a "review hearing");

    (c) require the offender to attend each review hearing;

    (d) provide for the responsible officer to make to the court responsible for the order, before each review, a report in writing on the offender's progress under the order; and

    (e) provide for each such report to include the test results communicated to the responsible officer under subsection (4)(b) above and the views of the treatment provider as to the treatment and testing of the offender.

(7) In this section references to the court responsible for a drug treatment and testing order are references to—

    (a) where a court is specified in the order in accordance with subsection (8) below, that court;

    (b) in any other case, the court by which the order is made.

(8) Where the area specified in a drug treatment and testing order made by a magistrates' court is not the area for which the court acts, the court may, if it thinks fit, include in the order provision specifying for the purposes of subsection (7) above a magistrates' court which acts for the area specified in the order.

(9) Where a drug treatment and testing order has been made on an appeal brought from the Crown Court or from the criminal division of the Court of Appeal, for the purposes of subsection (7)(b) above it shall be deemed to have been made by the Crown Court.

[This section is printed as amended by the *CJCSA* 2000, s.74, and Sched. 7, para. 4; and the *Offender Management Act 2007 (Consequential Amendments) Order* 2008 (S.I. 2008 No. 912), art. 3, and Sched. 1, para. 14(1) and (7). It is repealed as from April 4, 2005 (*Criminal Justice Act 2003 (Commencement No. 8 and Transitional and Saving Provisions) Order* 2005 (S.I. 2005 No. 950)): *CJA* 2003, s.332, and Sched. 7, Pt 7. For the relevant saving provisions, see § 5–2 in the main work; and *post*, §§ 5–255 *et seq.*]

Periodic reviews

5-219   55.—(1) At a review hearing (within the meaning given by subsection (6) of section 54 above) the court may, after considering the responsible officer's report referred to in that subsection, amend any requirement or provision of the drug treatment and testing order.

(2) The court—

    (a) shall not amend the treatment or testing requirement unless the offender expresses his willingness to comply with the requirement as amended;

    (b) shall not amend any provision of the order so as to reduce the treatment and testing period below the minimum specified in section 52(1) above, or to increase it above the maximum so specified; and

    (c) except with the consent of the offender, shall not amend any requirement or provision of the order while an appeal against the order is pending.

(3) If the offender fails to express his willingness to comply with the treatment or testing requirement as proposed to be amended by the court, the court may—

    (a) revoke the order; and

    (b) deal with him, for the offence in respect of which the order was made, in any way in which it could deal with him if he had just been convicted by the court of the offence.

(4) In dealing with the offender under subsection (3)(b) above, the court—

    (a) shall take into account the extent to which the offender has complied with the requirements of the order; and

    (b) may impose a custodial sentence (where the order was made in respect of an offence punishable with such a sentence) notwithstanding anything in section 79(2) below.

(5) Where the order was made by a magistrates' court in the case of an offender under 18 years of age in respect of an offence triable only on indictment in the case of an adult, any powers exercisable under subsection (3)(b) above in respect of the offender after he attains the age of 18 shall be powers to do either or both of the following—

(a) to impose a fine not exceeding £5,000 for the offence in respect of which the order was made;

(b) to deal with the offender for that offence in any way in which the court could deal with him if it had just convicted him of an offence punishable with imprisonment for a term not exceeding six months.

(6) If at a review hearing the court, after considering the responsible officer's report, is of the opinion that the offender's progress under the order is satisfactory, the court may so amend the order as to provide for each subsequent review to be made by the court without a hearing.

(7) If at a review without a hearing the court, after considering the responsible officer's report, is of the opinion that the offender's progress under the order is no longer satisfactory, the court may require the offender to attend a hearing of the court at a specified time and place.

(8) At that hearing the court, after considering that report, may—

(a) exercise the powers conferred by this section as if the hearing were a review hearing; and

(b) so amend the order as to provide for each subsequent review to be made at a review hearing.

(9) In this section any reference to the court, in relation to a review without a hearing, shall be construed—

(a) in the case of the Crown Court, as a reference to a judge of the court;

(b) in the case of magistrates' court, as a reference to a justice of the peace acting for the commission area for which the court acts.

[This section was repealed as from April 4, 2005 (*Criminal Justice Act 2003 (Commencement No. 8 and Transitional and Saving Provisions) Order* 2005 (S.I. 2005 No. 950)): *CJA* 2003, s.332, and Sched. 7, Pt 7. For the relevant saving provisions, see § 5–2 in the main work; and *post*, §§ 5–255 *et seq*.]

Breach, revocation and amendment of drug treatment and testing orders
56. [*Gives effect to Sched. 3*, post, §§ 5–228 et seq.]   **5-220**

Copies of orders
57.—(1) Where a drug treatment and testing order is made, the court making the order shall   **5-221** (subject to subsection (3) below) forthwith give copies of the order to an officer of a local probation board assigned to the court, or (as the case may be) an officer of a provider of probation services acting at the court.

(2) Where such an order is amended under section 55(1) above, the court amending the order shall (subject to subsection (3A) below) forthwith give copies of the order as amended to an officer of a local probation board assigned to the court, or (as the case may be) an officer of a provider of probation services operating at the court.

(3) Where a drug treatment and testing order is made by a magistrates' court and another magistrates' court is responsible for the order (within the meaning given by section 54(7) above) by virtue of being specified in the order in accordance with section 54(8)—

(a) the court making the order shall not give copies of it as mentioned in subsection (1) above but shall forthwith send copies of it to the court responsible for the order; and

(b) the court shall, as soon as reasonably practicable after the order is made, give copies of it to a probation officer assigned to that court, or (as the case may be) an officer of a provider of probation services acting at that court.

(3A) Where—

(a) a magistrates' court amends a drug treatment and testing order under section 55(1) above; and

(b) the order as amended provides for a magistrates' court other than that mentioned in paragraph (a) above to be responsible for the order;

the court amending the order shall not give copies of the order as amended as mentioned in subsection (2) above but shall forthwith send copies of it to the court responsible for the order and that court shall, as soon as reasonably practicable after the order is amended, give copies to an officer of a local probabion board assigned to that court, or (as the case may be) an officer of a provider of probation services acting at that court.

(4) An officer of a local probation board or officer of a provider of probation services to whom copies of an order are given under this section shall give a copy to—

    (a) the offender;

    (b) the treatment provider; and

    (c) the responsible officer.

[This section is printed as amended by the *CJCSA* 2000, s.74, and Sched. 7, paras 4 and 71; and the *Offender Management Act 2007 (Consequential Amendments) Order* 2008 (S.I. 2008 No. 912), art. 3, and Sched. 1, para. 14(1) and (8). It is repealed as from April 4, 2005 (*Criminal Justice Act 2003 (Commencement No. 8 and Transitional and Saving Provisions) Order* 2005 (S.I. 2005 No. 950)): *CJA* 2003, s.332, and Sched. 7, Pt 7. For the relevant saving provisions, see § 5–2 in the main work; and *post*, §§ 5–255 *et seq*.]

5-222   A drug treatment and testing order may be made only by a court which has been notified that arrangements for implementing the order have been made in the relevant area, and if the general requirements of sections 35 and 36 (*ante*, §§ 5–189, 5–190), relating to community orders are satisfied.

In order to ascertain whether an offender has drugs in his body, the court may order him to provide samples of such description as may be specified (s.52(4)), provided that the offender expresses his willingness to comply with the requirements of the order. A similar order may be made in respect of an offender over 18 by virtue of section 36A (*ante*, § 5–192).

The order must be for a period of between six months and three years, and must contain the requirements specified in section 53. An order may not be made unless the offender expresses his willingness to comply with the requirements of the order (s.52(7)). An offender who fails to express his willingness to comply with a requirement proposed to be included in such an order may be sentenced to a custodial sentence for the offence (s.79(3), *post*, § 5–469). There is no power to include requirements in a drug treatment and testing order other than those specified in section 53, but there appears to be no restriction on making such an order in conjunction with any other form of sentence, including a community punishment order or community rehabilitation order. For an analysis of the statutory requirements which must be satisfied before a drug treatment and testing order may be made, see *R. (Inner London Probation Service) v. Tower Bridge Magistrates' Court* [2002] 1 Cr.App.R.(S.) 43, DC.

Regular reviews of drug treatment and testing orders will be carried out by the court which made the order. An order made by the Court of Appeal, on appeal from the Crown Court, or by the House of Lords on an appeal from the Court of Appeal, is treated as if it had been made by the Crown Court (s.54(9)). The frequency of review hearings must be specified in the order (intervals of not less than one month), and the offender must attend unless the court subsequently releases him from the obligation to do so. At a review hearing, the court may amend the requirements of the order, but may not reduce the period of the order to less than the minimum or extend it beyond the maximum permissible period.

Where a defendant is to be sentenced shortly after being made the subject of a drug treatment and testing order by another court, and whether in respect of an offence committed before or after the order was imposed, the normal course to adopt where the court wishes the drug treatment and testing order to continue in effect, would be to make a further such order in identical terms (assuming the statutory criteria are met); if the court felt that further requirements were necessary, a community rehabilitation order would be an appropriate alternative; if, however, a custodial sentence is to be imposed, three options are open to the Crown Court in relation to the drug treatment and testing order; the first, and normal, option would be to revoke it and pass a custodial sentence for the original offence (*PCC(S)A* 2000, Sched. 3, para. 11 (*post*, § 5–238)); the second possibility would be to leave the order in force, but, whilst there is no statutory bar to such course, it is unlikely ever to be appropriate and feasible; thirdly, it would be possible to revoke the order and to impose a drug abstinence order under section 58A of the 2000 Act (provided the statutory criteria were met); but, as with the second option, this is unlikely ever to be practical: *R. v. Robinson* [2002] 2 Cr.App.R.(S.) 95, CA.

In *R. v. Woods and Collins* [2006] 1 Cr.App.R.(S.) 83, CA, the authorities in relation to drug treatment and testing orders were reviewed. It was said: (i) that these orders were designed for, amongst others, repeat offenders whose offending is driven by drug dependence; such offenders will often be those who would otherwise have to be sent to prison, and, it may well be, not for a short period; that the defendant was a prolific offender did not necessarily militate against an order, but there would be cases in which the nature of the offence or the scale of the offending was such that only a custodial sentence was justified; such orders are expensive and it is in the interests neither of the public nor the offender for one to be made where there are no reasonable prospects of it succeeding; that said, 100 per cent success rate should not be expected (some lapse often being a feature of an order which turns out to be substantially successful); (ii) as to the decisions to be made by a sentencer, these are (a) whether the case warrants adjournment for a report on the availability of such an order and (b) where such a report has been obtained and is favourable, whether such an order is appropriate; (iii) as to whether to adjourn for a report, there is no obligation to do so in every case in which it is represented to the sentencer that the cause of the offending was drug dependence and that the offender would welcome an order (where there is no prospect of such an order being made, obtaining a report would be wasteful and would unjustifiably raise false expectations); experienced sentencers know to look, *inter alia*, for signs that such an order might be effective; generally they will have the assistance of the standard pre-sentence report and they will look for indications that the defendant is likely to engage with the order, and that he has sufficient stability in his home life for there to be a reasonable prospect of its succeeding; it is also right at this stage to consider the nature of the offending, since the gravity of the offences or the personal characteristics of the defendant (*e.g.* repeated breaches of community orders) might demonstrate that such an order would plainly be inappropriate; but the possibility of such an order should not be rejected simply on the ground that the defendant is a repeat offender for whom otherwise a custodial sentence would be inevitable (such an offender being precisely the person for whom an order may be suitable), (iv) as to whether to make an order following a favourable report, this is for the court and not the probation officer; the public interest as well as the interests of the defendant are to be weighed in the balance, together with the criminality of the defendant and the desirability and prospects of rehabilitation; (v) as to appeals, if at either stage, the sentencer has properly addressed the issue before him and exercised his judgment, the cases in which it would be right for the Court of Appeal to say that he erred in principle would be comparatively rare.

In *Att.-Gen.'s Reference (No. 82 of 2005) (R. v. Toulson)* [2006] 1 Cr.App.R.(S.) 118, CA, it was said that whilst the general principle in *Att.-Gen.'s Reference (No. 28 of 2001) (R. v. McCollins)* [2002] 1 Cr.App.R.(S.) 59, CA, and *Att.-Gen.'s Reference (No. 64 of 2003)* [2004] 2 Cr.App.R.(S.) 22, CA, was that a drug treatment and testing order would be inappropriate in cases of serious offending (particularly where significant violence or threats were involved), no straitjacket had been imposed on sentencers in cases where they considered that in the public interest some course other than a deterrent sentence should at least be tried.

Pre-sentence drug testing

The *PCC(S)A* 2000, s.36A (*ante*, § 5–192) empowers a court which is dealing with an offender over the age of 18 and considering whether to pass any community sentence, to make an order requiring the offender to provide samples of any description specified in the order for the purpose of ascertaining whether the offender has any specified Class A drugs (heroin or cocaine) in his body. Such an order may be made only if the court has been notified that the power is available. The power is limited to testing for heroin and cocaine, and not any other kind of drug. The power contained in section 52(4), *ante*, allows a court which is considering a drug treatment and testing order in respect of an offender over 16 to order a defendant to provide samples to ascertain whether he has any drug in his body. As the consequence of failing to comply with an order to provide a specimen differ according to the power which is exercised, it is important for the court to specify whether the order is made under section 36A or section 52(4). When (and if) the amendment to section 52(4) effected by the *CJCSA* 2000 takes effect, there will be no overlap in the powers as section 52(4) will be restricted to offenders aged under 18 at the time of conviction. **5–223**

(e) *Drug abstinence orders*

Powers of Criminal Courts (Sentencing) Act 2000, ss.58A, 58B

Drug abstinence orders

5–224　　**58A.**—(1) Where a person aged 18 or over is convicted of an offence, the court by or before which he is convicted may (subject to sections 34 to 36 above) make an order which requires the offender—

　　(a) to abstain from misusing specified Class A drugs; and

　　(b) to provide, when instructed to do so by the responsible officer, any sample mentioned in the instruction for the purpose of ascertaining whether he has any specified Class A drug in his body.

　　(2) An order under subsection (1) above is in this Act referred to as a "drug abstinence order".

　　(3) The court shall not make a drug abstinence order in respect of an offender unless—

　　(a) in the opinion of the court, the offender is dependent on, or has a propensity to misuse, specified Class A drugs; and

　　(b) the offence in question is a trigger offence or, in the opinion of the court, the misuse by the offender of any specified Class A drug caused or contributed to the offence in question.

　　(4) A drug abstinence order shall provide that, for the period for which the order has effect, the offender shall be under the supervision of a person, being a person of a description specified in an order made by the Secretary of State.

　　(5) In this Act, "responsible officer", in relation to an offender who is subject to a drug abstinence order, means the person who is responsible for his supervision.

　　(6) The function of giving instructions for the purposes of subsection (1)(b) above shall be exercised in accordance with guidance given from time to time by the Secretary of State.

　　(7) A drug abstinence order shall have effect for a period specified in the order of not less than six months nor more than three years.

　　(8) The Secretary of State may make rules for regulating the provision of samples in pursuance of such instructions.

　　(9) A court shall not make a drug abstinence order unless the court has been notified by the Secretary of State that arrangements for implementing such orders are available in the area proposed to be specified in the order under section 54(1) above (as applied by section 58B(2) below) and the notice has not been withdrawn.

[See the note to s.58B, *post.*]

Drug abstinence orders: supplementary

5–225　　**58B.**—(1) Before making a drug abstinence order, the court shall explain to the offender in ordinary language—

　　(a) the effect of the order and of the requirements proposed to be included in it;

　　(b) the consequences which may follow (under Part II of Schedule 3 to this Act) if he fails to comply with any of those requirements; and

　　(c) that the order may be reviewed (under Parts III and IV of that Schedule) on the application either of the offender or of the responsible officer.

　　(2) Section 54 above (except subsections (2), (3) and (6)) and section 57 above (except subsections (2), (3A) and (4)(b)) shall apply for the purposes of section 58A above and this section as if references to drug treatment and testing orders were references to drug abstinence orders.]

　　(3) [*Gives effect to Sched. 3 (enforcement), post, §§ 5–228 et seq.*]

[Sections 58A and 58B were inserted as from July 2, 2001, by the *CJCSA* 2000, s.47. They were repealed as from April 4, 2005 (*Criminal Justice Act 2003 (Commencement No. 8 and Transitional and Saving Provisions) Order* 2005 (S.I. 2005 No. 950)): *CJA* 2003, s.332, and Sched. 7, Pt 7. For the relevant saving provisions, see § 5–2 in the main work; and *post*, §§ 5–255 *et seq.*]

(3) Persistent petty offenders

5–226　　If the conditions specified in section 59 are satisfied, the court may make a community punishment order or curfew order even though the offences concerned are not serious enough to warrant a community order, as would otherwise be required by section 35.

Powers of Criminal Courts (Sentencing) Act 2000, s.59

Curfew orders and community punishment orders for persistent petty offenders

59.—(1) This section applies where—

(a) a person aged 16 or over is convicted of an offence;

(b) the court by or before which he is convicted is satisfied that each of the conditions mentioned in subsection (2) below is fulfilled; and

(c) if it were not so satisfied, the court would be minded to impose a fine in respect of the offence.

(2) The conditions are that—

(a) one or more fines imposed on the offender in respect of one or more previous offences have not been paid; and

(b) if a fine were imposed in an amount which was commensurate with the seriousness of the offence, the offender would not have sufficient means to pay it.

(3) The court may—

(a) subject to subsections (5) and (7) below, make a curfew order under section 37(1) above, or

(b) subject to subsections (6) and (7) below, make a community punishment order under section 46(1) above,

in respect of the offender instead of imposing a fine.

(4) Subsection (3) above applies notwithstanding anything in subsections (1) and (3)(b) of section 35 above (restrictions on imposing community sentences).

(5) Section 37(1) above (curfew orders) shall apply for the purposes of subsection (3)(a) above as if for the words from the beginning to "make" there were substituted "Where section 59 below applies, the court may make in respect of the offender"; and—

(a) section 37(3), (5) to (8) and (10) to (12), and

(b) so far as applicable, the other provisions of this Part relating to curfew orders,

have effect in relation to a curfew order made by virtue of this section as they have effect in relation to any other curfew order.

(6) Section 46(1) above (community punishment orders) shall apply for the purposes of subsection (3)(b) above as if for the words from the beginning to "make" there were substituted "Where section 59 below applies, the court may make in respect of the offender"; and—

(a) section 46(3) and (4), and

(b) so far as applicable, the following provisions of section 46 and the other provisions of this Part relating to community punishment orders,

have effect in relation to a community punishment order made by virtue of this section as they have effect in relation to any other community punishment order.

(7) A court shall not make an order by virtue of subsection (3)(a) or (b) above unless the court has been notified by the Secretary of State that arrangements for implementing orders so made are available in the relevant area and the notice has not been withdrawn.

(8) In subsection (7) above "the relevant area" means—

(a) in relation to a curfew order, the area in which the place proposed to be specified in the order is situated;

(b) in relation to a community punishment order, the area proposed to be specified in the order.

[This section is printed as amended by the *CJCSA* 2000, s.74, and Sched. 7, para. 2. It is repealed as from April 4, 2005 (*Criminal Justice Act 2003 (Commencement No. 8 and Transitional and Saving Provisions) Order* 2005 (S.I. 2005 No. 950)): *CJA* 2003, s.332, and Sched. 7, Pt 7. For the relevant saving provisions, see § 5–2 in the main work; and *post*, §§ 5–255 *et seq.*]

For section 37 of the Act, see *post*, § 5–291.

(4) Enforcement, etc.

Powers of Criminal Courts (Sentencing) Act 2000, Sched. 3, Pts I–III

SCHEDULE 3

BREACH, REVOCATION AND AMENDMENT OF CERTAIN COMMUNITY ORDERS

PART I

PRELIMINARY

Definitions

5-228   1.—(1) In this Schedule "relevant order" means any of the following orders—

(a) a curfew order;

(aa) an exclusion order;

(b) a community rehabilitation order;

(c) a community punishment order;

(d) a community punishment and rehabilitation order;

(e) a drug treatment and testing order;

(f) a drug abstinence order.

(2) In this Schedule "the local justice area concerned" means—

(a) in relation to a curfew order, the local justice area in which the place for the time being specified in the order is situated; and

(b) in relation to an exclusion, community rehabilitation, community punishment, community punishment and rehabilitation, drug treatment and testing or drug abstinence order, the local justice area for the time being specified in the order.

(3) In this Schedule, references to the court responsible for a drug treatment and testing order or drug abstinence order shall be construed in accordance with section 54(7) of this Act (or that subsection as applied by section 58B(2) of this Act).

(4) In this Schedule—

(a) references to the community rehabilitation element of a community punishment and rehabilitation order are references to the order in so far as it imposes such a requirement as is mentioned in section 51(1)(a) of this Act (and in so far as it imposes any additional requirements included in the order by virtue of section 42); and

(b) references to the community punishment element of such an order are references to the order in so far as it imposes such a requirement as is mentioned in section 51(1)(b).

Orders made on appeal

5-229   2.—(1) Where a curfew, exclusion, community rehabilitation, community punishment, community punishment and rehabilitation or drug abstinence order has been made on appeal, for the purposes of this Schedule it shall be deemed—

(a) if it was made on an appeal brought from a magistrates' court, to have been made by a magistrates' court;

(b) if it was made on an appeal brought from the Crown Court or from the criminal division of the Court of Appeal, to have been made by the Crown Court.

(2) Where a drug treatment and testing order has been made on an appeal brought from the Crown Court or from the criminal division of the Court of Appeal, for the purposes of this Schedule it shall be deemed to have been made by the Crown Court.

PART II

BREACH OF REQUIREMENT OF ORDER

Issue of summons or warrant

5-230   3.—(1) If at any time while a relevant order is in force in respect of an offender it appears on information to a justice of the peace that the offender has failed to comply with any of the requirements of the order, the justice may—

(a) issue a summons requiring the offender to appear at the place and time specified in it; or

(b) if the information is in writing and on oath, issue a warrant for his arrest.

(2) Any summons or warrant issued under this paragraph shall direct the offender to appear or be brought—

(a) in the case of a drug treatment and testing order or a drug abstinence order, before the court responsible for the order;

(b) in the case of any other relevant order which was made by the Crown Court and included a direction that any failure to comply with any of the requirements of the order be dealt with by the Crown Court, before the Crown Court; and

(c) in the case of a relevant order which is not an order to which paragraph (a) or (b) applies, before a magistrates' court acting for the local justice area in which the offender resides or, if it is not known where he resides, before a magistrates' court acting for the local justice area concerned.

(3) Where a summons issued under sub-paragraph (1)(a) above requires an offender to appear before the Crown Court and the offender does not appear in answer to the summons, the Crown Court may issue a further summons requiring the offender to appear at the place and time specified in it.

(4) Where a summons issued under sub-paragraph (1)(a) above or a further summons issued under sub-paragraph (3) above requires an offender to appear before the Crown Court and the offender does not appear in answer to the summons, the Crown Court may issue a warrant for the arrest of the offender.

Powers of magistrates' court

4.—(1) If it is proved to the satisfaction of a magistrates' court before which an offender appears **5–231** or is brought under paragraph 3 above that he has failed without reasonable excuse to comply with any of the requirements of the relevant order, the court may deal with him in respect of the failure in any one of the following ways—

(a) it may impose on him a fine not exceeding £1,000;

(b) where the offender is aged 16 or over it may, subject to paragraph 7 below, make a community service order in respect of him;

(c) where—

   (i) the relevant order is a curfew order and the offender is aged under 16, or

   (ii) the relevant order is a probation order or combination order and the offender is aged under 21,

   it may, subject to paragraph 8 below, make an attendance centre order in respect of him; or

(d) where the relevant order was made by a magistrates' court, it may deal with him, for the offence in respect of which the order was made, in any way in which it could deal with him if he had just been convicted by the court of the offence.

(2) In dealing with an offender under sub-paragraph (1)(d) above, a magistrates' court—

(a) shall take into account the extent to which the offender has complied with the requirements of the relevant order; and

(b) in the case of an offender who has wilfully and persistently failed to comply with those requirements, may impose a custodial sentence (where the relevant order was made in respect of an offence punishable with such a sentence) notwithstanding anything in section 79(2) of this Act.

(3) Where a magistrates' court deals with an offender under sub-paragraph (1)(d) above, it shall revoke the relevant order if it is still in force.

(3A) Where a magistrates' court dealing with an offender under sub-paragraph (1)(a), (b) or (c) above would not otherwise have the power to amend the relevant order under paragraph 18 below (amendment by reason of change of residence), that paragraph has effect as if the reference to a magistrates' court acting for the local justice area concerned were a reference to the court dealing with the offender.

(4) Where a relevant order was made by the Crown Court and a magistrates' court has power to deal with the offender under sub-paragraph (1)(a) (b) or (c) above, it may instead commit him to custody or release him on bail until he can be brought or appear before the Crown Court.

(5) A magistrates' court which deals with an offender's case under sub-paragraph (4) above shall send to the Crown Court—

(a) a certificate signed by a justice of the peace certifying that the offender has failed to comply with the requirements of the relevant order in the respect specified in the certificate; and

(b) such other particulars of the case as may be desirable;

and a certificate purporting to be so signed shall be admissible as evidence of the failure before the Crown Court.

(6) A person sentenced under sub-paragraph (1)(d) above for an offence may appeal to the Crown Court against the sentence.

Powers of Crown Court

5–232   5.—(1) Where under paragraph 3 or by virtue of paragraph 4(4) above an offender is brought or appears before the Crown Court and it is proved to the satisfaction of that court that he has failed without reasonable excuse to comply with any of the requirements of the relevant order, the Crown Court may deal with him in respect of the failure in any one of the following ways—

(a)–(c) [*identical to para. 4(1)(a)–(c), ante*];

(d) it may deal with him, for the offence in respect of which the order was made, in any way in which it could deal with him if he had just been convicted before the Crown Court of the offence.

(2) In dealing with an offender under sub-paragraph (1)(d) above, the Crown Court—

(a), (b) [*identical to para. 4(2)(a), (b), ante, save that for the reference to* "section 79(2) of this Act" *there is substituted a reference to* "section 152(3) of the *Criminal Justice Act* 2003"];

(3) Where the Crown Court deals with an offender under sub-paragraph (1)(d) above, it shall revoke the relevant order if it is still in force.

(4) In proceedings before the Crown Court under this paragraph any question whether the offender has failed to comply with the requirements of the relevant order shall be determined by the court and not by the verdict of a jury.

Exclusions from paragraphs 4 and 5

5–233   6.—(1) Without prejudice to paragraphs 10 and 11 below, an offender who is convicted of a further offence while a relevant order is in force in respect of him shall not on that account be liable to be dealt with under paragraph 4 or 5 above in respect of a failure to comply with any requirement of the order.

(2) An offender who—

(a) is required by a community rehabilitation order or community punishment and rehabilitation order to submit to treatment for his mental condition, or his dependency on or propensity to misuse drugs or alcohol, or

(b) is required by a drug treatment and testing order to submit to treatment for his dependency on or propensity to misuse drugs,

shall not be treated for the purposes of paragraph 4 or 5 above as having failed to comply with that requirement on the ground only that he has refused to undergo any surgical, electrical or other treatment if, in the opinion of the court, his refusal was reasonable having regard to all the circumstances.

Community punishment orders imposed for breach of relevant order

5–234   7.—(1) Section 46(1) of this Act (community punishment orders) shall apply for the purposes of paragraphs 4(1)(b) and 5(1)(b) above as if for the words from the beginning to "make" there were substituted "Where a court has power to deal with an offender aged 16 or over under Part II of Schedule 3 to this Act for failure to comply with any of the requirements of a relevant order, the court may make in respect of the offender".

(2) In this paragraph a "secondary order" means a community punishment order made by virtue of paragraph 4(1)(b) or 5(1)(b) above.

(3) The number of hours which an offender may be required to work under a secondary order shall be specified in the order and shall not exceed 60 in the aggregate; and—

(a) where the relevant order is a community punishment order, the number of hours which the offender may be required to work under the secondary order shall not be such that the total number of hours under both orders exceeds the maximum specified in section 46(3) of this Act; and

(b) where the relevant order is a community punishment and rehabilitation order, the number of hours which the offender may be required to work under the secondary order shall not be such that the total number of hours under—

(i) the secondary order, and

(ii) the community punishment element of the community punishment and rehabilitation order,

exceeds the maximum specified in section 51(1)(b) of this Act.

(4) Section 46(4) of this Act and, so far as applicable—

(a) section 46(5) to (7) and (9) to (13), and

(b) section 47 and the provisions of this Schedule so far as relating to community service orders,

have effect in relation to a secondary order as they have effect in relation to any other community service order, subject to sub-paragraph (6) below.

(5) Sections 148 and 156 of the *Criminal Justice Act* 2003 (restrictions and procedural requirements for community sentences) do not apply in relation to a secondary order.

(6) Where the provisions of this Schedule have effect as mentioned in sub-paragraph (4) above in relation to a secondary order—

(a) the power conferred on the court by each of paragraphs 4(1)(d) and 5(1)(d) above and paragraph 10(3)(b) below to deal with the offender for the offence in respect of which the order was made shall be construed as a power to deal with the offender, for his failure to comply with the original order, in any way in which the court could deal with him if that failure had just been proved to the satisfaction of the court;

(b) the references in paragraphs 10(1)(b) and 11(1)(a) below to the offence in respect of which the order was made shall be construed as references to the failure to comply in respect of which the order was made; and

(c) the power conferred on the Crown Court by paragraph 11(2)(b) below to deal with the offender for the offence in respect of which the order was made shall be construed as a power to deal with the offender, for his failure to comply with the original order, in any way in which a magistrates' court (if the original order was made by a magistrates' court) or the Crown Court (if the original order was made by the Crown Court) could deal with him if that failure had just been proved to its satisfaction;

and in this sub-paragraph "the original order" means the relevant order the failure to comply with which led to the making of the secondary order.

Attendance centre orders imposed for breach of relevant order

8.—(1) Section 60(1) of this Act (attendance centre orders) shall apply for the purposes of **5-235** paragraphs 4(1)(c) and 5(1)(c) above as if for the words from the beginning to "the court may," there were substituted

"Where a court—

(a) has power to deal with an offender aged under 16 under Part II of Schedule 3 to this Act for failure to comply with any of the requirements of a curfew order, or

(b) has power to deal with an offender aged under 21 under that Part of that Schedule for failure to comply with any of the requirements of a probation or combination order,

the court may,".

(2) The following provisions of this Act, namely—

(a) subsections (3) to (11) of section 60, and

(b) so far as applicable, section 36B and Schedule 5,

have effect in relation to an attendance centre order made by virtue of paragraph 4(1)(c) or 5(1)(c) above as they have effect in relation to any other attendance centre order, but as if there were omitted from each of paragraphs 2(1)(b), 3(1) and 4(3) of Schedule 5 the words ", for the offence in respect of which the order was made," and "for that offence".

(3) Sections 148 and 156 of the *Criminal Justice Act* 2003 (restrictions and procedural requirements for community sentences) do not apply in relation to an attendance centre order made by virtue of paragraph 4(1)(c) or 5(1)(c) above.

Supplementary

9.—(1) Any exercise by a court of its powers under paragraph 4(1)(a), (b) or (c) or 5(1)(a), (b) or **5-236** (c) above shall be without prejudice to the continuance of the relevant order.

(2) A fine imposed under paragraph 4(1)(a) or 5(1)(a) above shall be deemed, for the purposes of any enactment, to be a sum adjudged to be paid by a conviction.

(3) Where a relevant order was made by a magistrates' court in the case of an offender under 18 years of age in respect of an offence triable only on indictment in the case of an adult, any powers exercisable under paragraph 4(1)(d) above in respect of the offender after he attains the age of 18 shall be powers to do either or both of the following—

(a) to impose a fine not exceeding £5,000 for the offence in respect of which the order was made;

(b) to deal with the offender for that offence in any way in which a magistrates' court could deal with him if it had just convicted him of an offence punishable with imprisonment for a term not exceeding six months.

PART III

REVOCATION OF ORDER

Revocation of order with or without re-sentencing: powers of magistrates' court

5–237   10.—(1) This paragraph applies where a relevant order made by a magistrates' court is in force in respect of any offender and on the application of the offender or the responsible officer it appears to the appropriate magistrates' court that, having regard to circumstances which have arisen since the order was made, it would be in the interests of justice—

(a) for the order to be revoked; or

(b) for the offender to be dealt with in some other way for the offence in respect of which the order was made.

(2) In this paragraph "the appropriate magistrates court" means—

(a) in the case of a drug treatment and testing order or a drug abstinence order, the magistrates' court responsible for the order;

(b) in the case of any other relevant order, a magistrates' court acting in the local justice area concerned.

(3) The appropriate magistrates' court may—

(a) revoke the order; or

(b) both—

(i) revoke the order; and

(ii) deal with the offender, for the offence in respect of which the order was made, in any way in which it could deal with him if he had just been convicted by the court of the offence.

(4) The circumstances in which a community rehabilitation, community punishment and rehabilitation or drug treatment and testing order may be revoked under sub-paragraph (3)(a) above shall include the offender's making good progress or his responding satisfactorily to supervision or, as the case may be, treatment.

(5) In dealing with an offender under sub-paragraph (3)(b) above, a magistrates' court shall take into account the extent to which the offender has complied with the requirements of the relevant order.

(6) A person sentenced under sub-paragraph (3)(b) above for an offence may appeal to the Crown Court against the sentence.

(7) Where a magistrates' court proposes to exercise its powers under this paragraph otherwise than on the application of the offender, it shall summon him to appear before the court and, if he does not appear in answer to the summons, may issue a warrant for his arrest.

(8) No application may be made by the offender under sub-paragraph (1) above while an appeal against the relevant order is pending.

*Revocation of order with or without re-sentencing: powers of
Crown Court on conviction etc.*

5–238   11.—(1) This paragraph applies where—

(a) a relevant order made by the Crown Court is in force in respect of an offender and the offender or the responsible officer applies to the Crown Court for the order to be revoked or for the offender to be dealt with in some other way for the offence in respect of which the order was made; or

(b) an offender in respect of whom a relevant order is in force is convicted of an offence before the Crown Court or, having been committed by a magistrates' court to the Crown Court for sentence, is brought or appears before the Crown Court.

(2) If it appears to the Crown Court to be in the interests of justice to do so, having regard to circumstances which have arisen since the order was made, the Crown Court may—

(a) revoke the order; or

(b) both—

(i) revoke the order; and

  (ii) deal with the offender, for the offence in respect of which the order was made, in any way in which the court which made the order could deal with him if he had just been convicted of that offence by or before the court which made the order.

(3) The circumstances in which a community rehabilitation, community punishment and rehabilitation or drug treatment and testing order may be revoked under sub-paragraph (2)(a) above shall include the offender's making good progress or his responding satisfactorily to supervision or, as the case may be, treatment.

(4) In dealing with an offender under sub-paragraph (2)(b) above, the Crown Court shall take into account the extent to which the offender has complied with the requirements of the relevant order.

*Substitution of conditional discharge for community rehabilitation
or community punishment and rehabilitation order*

12.—(1) This paragraph applies where a community rehabilitation order or community punish- **5-239**
ment and rehabilitation order is in force in respect of any offender and on the application of the offender or the responsible officer to the appropriate court it appears to the court that, having regard to circumstances which have arisen since the order was made, it would be in the interests of justice—

  (a) for the order to be revoked; and

  (b) for an order to be made under section 12(1)(b) of this Act discharging the offender conditionally for the offence for which the community rehabilitation or community punishment and rehabilitation order was made.

(2) In this paragraph "the appropriate court" means—

  (a) where the community rehabilitation or community punishment and rehabilitation order was made by a magistrates' court, a magistrates' court acting for the petty sessions area concerned;

  (b) where the community rehabilitation or community punishment and rehabilitation order was made by the Crown Court, the Crown Court.

(3) No application may be made under paragraph 10 or 11 above for a community rehabilitation order or community punishment and rehabilitation order to be revoked and replaced with an order for conditional discharge under section 12(1)(b); but otherwise nothing in this paragraph shall affect the operation of paragraphs 10 and 11 above.

(4) Where this paragraph applies—

  (a) the appropriate court may revoke the community rehabilitation or community punishment and rehabilitation order and make an order under section 12(1)(b) of this Act discharging the offender in respect of the offence for which the community rehabilitation or community punishment and rehabilitation order was made, subject to the condition that he commits no offence during the period specified in the order under section 12(1)(b); and

  (b) the period specified in the order under section 12(1)(b) shall be the period beginning with the making of that order and ending with the date when the community rehabilitation period specified in the community rehabilitation or community punishment and rehabilitation order would have ended.

(5) For the purposes of sub-paragraph (4) above, subsection (1) of section 12 of this Act shall apply as if—

  (a) for the words from the beginning to "may make an order either" there were substituted the words "Where paragraph 12 of Schedule 3 to this Act applies, the appropriate court may (subject to the provisions of sub-paragraph (4) of that paragraph) make an order in respect of the offender"; and

  (b) paragraph (a) of that subsection were omitted.

(6) An application under this paragraph may be heard in the offender's absence if—

  (a) the application is made by the responsible officer; and

  (b) that officer produces to the court a statement by the offender that he understands the effect of an order for conditional discharge and consents to the making of the application;

and where the application is so heard section 12(4) of this Act shall not apply.

(7) No application may be made under this paragraph while an appeal against the community rehabilitation or community punishment and rehabilitation order is pending.

(8) Without prejudice to paragraph 15 below, on the making of an order under section 12(1)(b) of this Act by virtue of this paragraph the court shall forthwith give copies of the order to the responsible officer, and the responsible officer shall give a copy to the offender.

(9) Each of sections 1(11), 2(9) and 66(4) of the *Crime and Disorder Act* 1998 (which prevent a

court from making an order for conditional discharge in certain cases) shall have effect as if the reference to the court by or before which a person is convicted of an offence there mentioned included a reference to a court dealing with an application under this paragraph in respect of the offence.

Revocation following custodial sentence by magistrates' court unconnected with order

5–240   13.—(1) This paragraph applies where—

(a) an offender in respect of whom a relevant order is in force is convicted of an offence by a magistrates' court unconnected with the order;

(b) the court imposes a custodial sentence on the offender; and

(c) it appears to the court, on the application of the offender or the responsible officer, that it would be in the interests of justice to exercise its powers under this paragraph, having regard to circumstances which have arisen since the order was made.

(2) In sub-paragraph (1) above "a magistrates' court unconnected with the order" means—

(a) in the case of a drug treatment and testing order or a drug abstinence order, a magistrates' court which is not responsible for the order;

(b) in the case of any other relevant order, a magistrates' court not acting for the petty sessions area concerned.

(3) The court may—

(a) if the order was made by a magistrates' court, revoke it;

(b) if the order was made by the Crown Court, commit the offender in custody or release him on bail until he can be brought or appear before the Crown Court.

(4) Where the court deals with an offender's case under sub-paragraph (3)(b) above, it shall send to the Crown Court such particulars of the case as may be desirable.

14. Where by virtue of paragraph 13(3)(b) above an offender is brought or appears before the Crown Court and it appears to the Crown Court to be in the interests of justice to do so, having regard to circumstances which have arisen since the relevant order was made, the Crown Court may revoke the order.

Supplementary

5–241   15.—(1) On the making under this Part of this Schedule of an order revoking a relevant order, the proper officer of the court shall forthwith give copies of the revoking order to the responsible officer.

(2) In sub-paragraph (1) above "proper officer" means—

(a) in relation to a magistrates' court, the designated officer for the court; and

(b) in relation to the Crown Court, the appropriate officer.

(3) A responsible officer to whom in accordance with sub-paragraph (1) above copies of a revoking order are given shall give a copy to the offender and to the person in charge of any institution in which the offender was required by the order to reside.

16. Paragraph 9(3) above shall apply for the purposes of paragraphs 10 and 11 above as it applies for the purposes of paragraph 4 above, but as if for the words "paragraph 4(1)(d) above" there were substituted "paragraph 10(3)(b)(ii) or 11(2)(b)(ii) below".

17. Where under this Part of this Schedule a relevant order is revoked and replaced by an order for conditional discharge under section 12(1)(b) of this Act and—

(a) the order for conditional discharge is not made in the circumstances mentioned in section 13(9) of this Act (order made by magistrates' court in the case of an offender under 18 in respect of offence triable only on indictment in the case of an adult), but

(b) the relevant order was made in those circumstances,

section 13(9) shall have effect as if the order for conditional discharge had been made in those circumstances.

5–242   [Paras 1 to 17 are printed as amended by the *CJCSA* 2000, ss.54 and 74, and Sched. 7, paras 1 to 3, and 199(1)–(6), (11)(b)(i), and (13)–(18); the *Domestic Violence, Crime and Victims Act* 2004, s.29, and Sched. 5, para. 4; and the *Courts Act 2003 (Consequential Provisions) Order* 2005 (S.I. 2005 No. 886), Sched., paras 82 and 113.

It should be further noted in relation to this schedule: (i) that its substitution by a new Schedule 3 by the *CJA* 2003, s.304, and Sched. 32, para. 125, will never take effect, the substituting provision in the 2003 Act having itself been repealed (without ever coming into force) by the *CJIA* 2008, s.148, and Sched. 28, Pt 1, with effect from November 30,

2009 (*Criminal Justice and Immigration Act 2008 (Commencement No. 13 and Transitory Provision) Order* 2009 (S.I. 2009 No. 3074)); (ii) that article 11 of, and Schedule 2 to, the *Criminal Justice Act 2003 (Commencement No. 8 and Transitional and Saving Provisions) Order* 2005 (S.I. 2005 No. 950), as amended by the *Criminal Justice Act 2003 (Commencement No. 8 and Transitional and Saving Provisions) (Amendment No. 2) Order* 2009 (S.I. 2009 No. 3111), art. 2(e), provides (see *post*, § 5–259) that "(n)otwithstanding the coming into force of section 1 of the *Criminal Justice and Immigration Act* 2008 in relation to any offence committed before 30 November 2009 or any failure to comply with an order made in respect of an offence committed before 30 November 2009", the schedule "shall continue to have effect (subject to any necessary modifications) as if" the reference in paragraphs 5(2) and 21(6)(b) to "section 79(2) of this Act" were to "section 152(3)" of the 2003 Act, and as if the reference in paragraphs 7(5) and 8(3) to "sections 35 and 36 of this Act" were to "sections 148 and 156" of the 2003 Act; and (iii) the modifications referred to in (ii) have been incorporated into the text of the schedule (*ante*), but the first of these modifications raises the issue whether paragraph 4(2) should be read as being similarly so modified.]

The criminal standard of proof applies where an information is laid alleging a failure to **5–243** comply with a community rehabilitation order; upon proof of a breach, the defendant was at risk of being sentenced to imprisonment (a sharp potential increase in penalty), and that should not occur unless the factual basis of the breach had been proved beyond reasonable doubt: *West Yorkshire Probation Board v. Boulter* [2006] 1 W.L.R. 232, DC.

Where a court re-sentences under paragraph 4(1)(d), 5(1)(d), 10(3)(b) or 11(2)(b) it must observe the provisions of sections 79 and 80 of the *PCC(S)A* 2000 (*post*, §§ 5–469, 5–470) before imposing a custodial sentence; but paragraphs 4(2)(b) and 5(2)(b) permit a custodial sentence notwithstanding anything in section 79(2). The fact that the offence was originally dealt with by a community sentence does not exclude the possibility of a custodial sentence under section 79(2) ("so serious that only such a sentence can be justified"): see *R. v. Webster*, 12 Cr.App.R.(S.) 760, CA; *R. v. Oliver and Little*, 96 Cr.App.R. 426, CA.

Where an offender has spent time in custody on remand before being sentenced to a community rehabilitation or community punishment order, and is later sentenced to a custodial sentence for the offence for which the community order was made, time spent in custody on remand will not count as part of that sentence for the purposes of the *CJA* 1967, s.67 (*rep.*). The Court of Appeal has held that the custodial sentence imposed in such circumstances should be reduced by an appropriate amount to compensate the offender for this time. (For cases dealing with probation orders, see *R. v. McDonald*, 10 Cr.App.R.(S.) 458, CA; *R. v. Gyorgy*, 11 Cr.App.R.(S.) 1, CA; *R. v. Needham*, *ibid.* at 506, CA; for cases dealing with community service orders, see *R. v. McIntyre*, 7 Cr.App.R.(S.) 196, CA; *R. v. MacKenzie*, 10 Cr.App.R.(S.) 299, CA.) In normal circumstances, it will be appropriate to reduce the intended sentence by a period equivalent to twice the time spent in custody on remand in connection with the original proceedings.

In *R. v. Henderson* [1997] 2 Cr.App.R.(S.) 266, CA, it was held that the amount of time to be allowed is a matter for the sentencer's discretion. If a court takes into account time spent in custody before the making of a community order, it should state that fact when passing sentence, and indicate the extent to which the matter has been taken into account. See also *R. v. Armstrong* [2002] 2 Cr.App.R.(S.) 87, CA (court not bound to reduce sentence by fixed amount).

The requirement that a court which re-sentences for an offence for which a community order was originally imposed should have regard to the extent to which the offender has complied with the requirements of the order (see paras 4(2)(a), 5(2)(a), 10(5) and 11(4)) was considered in *R. v. Neville*, 14 Cr.App.R.(S.) 768, CA.

Where a court makes a community order in a case where there is power to disqualify the offender from driving, and that power is exercised at the time the community order is made, there is no power to impose a further period of disqualification if the offender is later sentenced for a breach of the order: see *R. v. Coy*, 13 Cr.App.R.(S.) 619, CA, decided on the *PCCA* 1973, s.16 (*rep.*).

Where an offender commits an offence during the period of a community order, but is not convicted of that offence until after the community order has expired, there is no power to revoke the community order and pass a further sentence for the original offence: see *R. v. Bennett*, 15 Cr.App.R.(S.) 213; and *R. v. Cousin, ibid.* at 516, CA.

Where an offender is subject to a "relevant order" (see Sched. 3, para. 1) at the time of conviction by, or of being brought or appearing before, the Crown Court, that court has power to revoke the community order or to revoke and re-sentence for the original offence even though the community order had not been made at the time of the commission of the new offence (para. 11); what order should be made in any given case should be decided according to the demands of justice and not according to any prescriptive principle: *R. v. Newton* [1999] 2 Cr.App.R.(S.) 172, CA.

Where an offender applies for a community order to be revoked on the ground that he is unable to perform the order because of injury or ill health, the court should not, on revoking the order, impose a custodial sentence for the original offence, or a suspended sentence: *R. v. Fielding*, 14 Cr.App.R.(S.) 494, CA; *R. v. Jackson* [2000] 1 Cr.App.R.(S.) 405, CA.

Where an offender consents to a community service order, knowing that he is subject to a medical condition which will make performance of the order impossible, or will limit the type of work which he can perform, and the offence would justify a custodial sentence, the court may, on application to vary the order, revoke the order and substitute a custodial sentence: see *R. v. Hammon* [1998] 2 Cr.App.R.(S.) 202, CA.

(5) Amendment

5–244   Part IV (paras 18–25) of Schedule 3 to the *PCC(S)A* 2000 provides for the amendment of community orders. Paragraph 18 relates to amendment on the ground of the offender's change of residence, but does not apply to a drug treatment and testing order. Paragraphs 19 and 20 make provision for the amendment of the requirements of a community rehabilitation order or curfew order, and amendment of particular requirements of a community rehabilitation order or community punishment and rehabilitation order. Paragraph 22 provides for the extension of a community punishment or community punishment and rehabilitation order. Orders under paragraphs 18 to 20 and 22 are to be made by the magistrates' court acting for the petty sessions area concerned. The amendment of drug treatment and testing orders is regulated by paragraph 21 (*post*). Paragraphs 23 to 25 contain supplemental provisions.

**Powers of Criminal Courts (Sentencing) Act 2000, Sched. 3, Pt IV,
paras 21, 23–25**

Amendment of drug treatment and testing order

5–245   21.—(1) Without prejudice to the provisions of section 55(1), (6) and (8) of this Act, the court responsible for a drug treatment and testing order may by order—

(a) vary or cancel any of the requirements or provisions of the order on an application by the responsible officer under sub-paragraph (2) or (3)(a) or (b) below; or

(b) amend the order on an application by that officer under sub-paragraph (3)(c) below.

(2) Where the treatment provider is of the opinion that the treatment or testing requirement of the order should be varied or cancelled—

(a) he shall make a report in writing to that effect to the responsible officer; and

(b) that officer shall apply to the court for the variation or cancellation of the requirement.

(3) Where the responsible officer is of the opinion—

(a) that the treatment or testing requirement of the order should be so varied as to specify a different treatment provider,

(b) that any other requirement of the order, or a provision of the order, should be varied or cancelled, or

(c) that the order should be so amended as to provide for each subsequent periodic review (required by section 54(6)(a) of this Act) to be made without a hearing instead of at a review hearing, or vice versa,

he shall apply to the court for the variation or cancellation of the requirement or provision or the amendment of the order.

(4) The court—

(a) shall not amend the treatment or testing requirement unless the offender expresses his willingness to comply with the requirement as amended; and

(b) shall not amend any provision of the order so as to reduce the treatment and testing period below the minimum specified in section 52(1) of this Act, or to increase it above the maximum so specified.

(5) If the offender fails to express his willingness to comply with the treatment or testing requirement as proposed to be amended by the court, the court may—

(a) revoke the order; and

(b) deal with him, for the offence in respect of which the order was made, in any way in which it could deal with him if he had just been convicted by or before the court of the offence.

(6) In dealing with the offender under sub-paragraph (5)(b) above, the court—

(a) shall take into account the extent to which the offender has complied with the requirements of the order; and

(b) may impose a custodial sentence (where the order was made in respect of an offence punishable with such a sentence) notwithstanding anything in section 152(3) of the *Criminal Justice Act* 2003.

(7) Paragraph 9(3) above shall apply for the purposes of this paragraph as it applies for the purposes of paragraph 4 above, but as if for the words "paragraph 4(1)(d) above" there were substituted "paragraph 21(5)(b) below".

Supplementary

23. No order may be made under paragraph 18 above, and no application may be made under **5–246** paragraph 19 or 22 above or, except with the consent of the offender, under paragraph 21 above, while an appeal against the relevant order is pending.

24.—(1) Subject to sub-paragraph (2) below, where a court proposes to exercise its powers under this Part of this Schedule, otherwise than on the application of the offender, the court—

(a) shall summon him to appear before the court; and

(b) if he does not appear in answer to the summons, may issue a warrant for his arrest.

(2) This paragraph shall not apply to an order cancelling a requirement of a relevant order or reducing the period of any requirement, or to an order under paragraph 18 above substituting a new petty sessions area or a new place for the one specified in a relevant order.

25. [*Copies of amending orders.*]

26. [*Copies of orders amending drug treatment and testing orders.*]

[Paras 21 and 24 are printed as amended, as from a day to be appointed, by the *CJCSA* 2000, s.74, and Sched. 7, para. 199(24). As to this schedule, see the annotations to paras 1 to 17, *ante*, § 5–242.]

B. General Restrictions

Criminal Justice Act 2003, ss.147–151

Community sentence not available where sentence fixed by law etc.

As from a day to be appointed, section 150 of the 2003 Act is amended by the *Legal Aid,* ★**5–250** *Sentencing and Punishment of Offenders Act* 2012, s.142(3), and Sched. 26, paras 15 and 19, so as to insert new paragraphs (aa) and (ba) after paragraphs (a) and (b) respectively, as follows—

"(aa) falls to be imposed under section 1A(5) of the *Prevention of Crime Act* 1953 (minimum sentence for offence of threatening with offensive weapon in public),";

"(ba) falls to be imposed under section 139AA(7) of the *Criminal Justice Act* 1988 (minimum sentence for offence of threatening with article with blade or point or offensive weapon),".

As from a day to be appointed, section 150 of the 2003 Act is further amended by the ★ 2012 Act, s.122(3), and Sched. 19, paras 8 and 10, so as to insert a new paragraph (cb) after paragraph (ca), as follows—

"(cb) falls to be imposed under section 224A of this Act (life sentence for second listed offence for certain dangerous offenders),".

C. Community Orders

(1) General

Criminal Justice Act 2003, s.177

Community orders

★5–253   As from a day to be appointed, section 177 of the *CJA* 2003 is amended by the *Legal Aid, Sentencing and Punishment of Offenders Act* 2012, s.66(1) and (2), so as to (i) to insert "('the end date')" after the word "date" where it first appears in subsection (5), (ii) to omit the words from "; and" to the end of that subsection; and (iii) to insert new subsections (5A) and (5B), as follows—

"(5A) If a community order imposes two or more different requirements falling within subsection (1), the order may also specify a date by which each of those requirements must have been complied with; and the last of those dates must be the same as the end date.

(5B) Subject to section 200(3) (duration of community order imposing unpaid work requirement), a community order ceases to be in force on the end date.".

★   As from a day to be appointed, section 177 of the *CJA* 2003 is further amended by the 2012 Act, s.70(1), so as to omit subsection (2)(c).

★   As from a day to be appointed, section 177 of the *CJA* 2003 is further amended by the 2012 Act, s.72(1), so as to insert a new paragraph (ga) in subsection (1), as follows—

"(ga) a foreign travel prohibition order requirement (as defined by section 206A),".

★   As from a day to be appointed, section 177 of the *CJA* 2003 is further amended by the 2012 Act, s.72(2), so as to insert the words "a foreign travel prohibition requirement," after the words "a residence requirement," in subsection (4).

★   As from a day to be appointed (as to which, see *post*), section 177 of the *CJA* 2003 is further amended by the 2012 Act, s.76(2), so as to insert a new paragraph (ja) in subsection (1), as follows—

"(ja) an alcohol abstinence and monitoring requirement (as defined by section 212A),".

★   As from a day to be appointed (as to which, see *post*), section 177 of the *CJA* 2003 is further amended by the 2012 Act, s.76(3), so as to (i) to omit "and" at the end of subsection (2)(f), and (ii) to insert the word "and" at the end of paragraph (g), followed by a new paragraph (h), as follows—

"(h) section 212A(8) to (12) (alcohol abstinence and monitoring requirement)".

★   Section 77 of the 2012 Act (which itself came into force on May 1, 2012) provides for section 76 to be piloted in a specified area or areas before it can be brought into force generally.

★   As from a day to be appointed, section 182(4) of the *AFA* 2006 is amended by the *Legal Aid, Sentencing and Punishment of Offenders Act* 2012, s.78(1) and (4), so as to refer to subsections (5A) and (5B) as well as to subsections (5) and (6) of section 177.

Criminal Justice Act 2003 (Commencement No. 8 and Transitional and Saving Provisions) Order 2005 (S.I. 2005 No. 950), Sched. 2, paras 7–13

Transitional provisions

5–255   7. Notwithstanding the coming into force of section 1 of the *Criminal Justice and Immigration Act* 2008, paragraphs 8 to 10 shall have effect in relation to—
     (a) any offence committed before 30 November 2009; or
     (b) any failure to comply with an order made in respect of an offence committed before 30 November 2009.

[This paragraph is printed as substituted by the *Criminal Justice Act 2003 (Commencement No. 8 and Transitional and Saving Provisions) (Amendment No. 2) Order* 2009 (S.I. 2009 No. 3111), art. 2(d).]

8. Sections 41 to 58 of and Schedules 2 and 4 to the *Sentencing Act* shall continue to have effect   **5–256**
(subject to any necessary modifications) where a person aged 16 or 17 is convicted of an offence as
if—

    (a) for "sections 34 to 36 above" in sections 41(1), 46(1), 51(1) and 52(1) there were substituted
        "sections 148, 150 and 156 of the *Criminal Justice Act* 2003";

    (b) sections 41(4), (7) and (9)(a); 42(2)(b) to (3); 46(5)(a), (10), 11(a); 47(3A) to (4); and 52(6)
        were omitted;

    (c) paragraphs 2(2)(a)(i) and 3(2)(a) of Schedule 2 were omitted; and

    (d) paragraphs 1(3)(a) and 2(3)(a) of Schedule 4, in so far as they relate to paragraph 2(2)(a)(i)
        of Schedule 2 to the *Sentencing Act*, were omitted.

9. Notwithstanding the substitution of section 33 (community orders) and the amendment to sec-   **5–257**
tion 165 (interpretation) of the *Sentencing Act* by Schedule 32 to the 2003 Act, orders made under
sections 41 to 58 of the *Sentencing Act* (community rehabilitation orders, community punishment
orders, community punishment and rehabilitation orders and drug treating and testing orders) shall
continue to be regarded as community orders and community sentences for the purposes of the
Sentencing Act.

10. Notwithstanding sections 147 (meaning of community sentence), 177 (community orders) and   **5–258**
305 (interpretation) of the 2003 Act, orders made under sections 41 to 58 of the *Sentencing Act* shall
also be regarded as community orders and community sentences for the purposes of the provisions
specified in paragraphs (a) and (b)—

    (a) sections 148 to 150, 152, 156, 166 and 174 of the 2003 Act; and

    (b) the amendments made by paragraphs 8, 12(4) and 5, 13(2) and (3), 18(3), 21(3), 31, 38,
        73, 89, 123(4), 131, 132 and 134(a) of Schedule 32 to the 2003 Act.

11. Notwithstanding the coming into force of section 1 of the *Criminal Justice and Immigration Act*   **5–259**
2008 in relation to any offence committed before 30 November 2009 or any failure to comply with
an order made in respect of an offence committed before 30 November 2009, Schedule 3 to the
Sentencing Act shall continue to have effect (subject to any necessary modifications) as if—

    (a) the reference in paragraphs 5(2) and 21(6)(b) to "section 79(2) of this Act" were to "section
        152(3) of the *Criminal Justice Act* 2003"; and

    (b) the reference in paragraphs 7(5) and 8(3) to "sections 35 and 36 of this Act" were to "sec-
        tions 148 and 156 of the *Criminal Justice Act* 2003".

[This paragraph is printed as amended by S.I. 2009 No. 3111 (*ante*, § 5–255), art. 2(e).]

Savings

12. Notwithstanding the coming into force of section 1 of the *Criminal Justice and Immigration Act*   **5–260**
2008, in relation to any offence committed before 30 November 2009 or any failure to comply with
an order made in respect of an offence committed before 30 November 2009, the provisions of the
2003 Act specified in paragraph 13 shall have no effect where a person aged 16 or 17 is convicted of
an offence or in relation to orders made under sections 41 to 58 of the *Sentencing Act* by virtue of
paragraph 8.

[This paragraph is printed as amended by S.I. 2009 No. 3111 (*ante*, § 5–255), art. 2(f).]

13. The provisions referred to paragraph 12 are—   **5–261**

    (a) section 303(d)(i) (repeal of Chapter 3 of Part 4 of the *Sentencing Act*);

    (b) in Schedule 32, the amendments made by paragraphs 5, 14, 32, 36, 64, 69 to 72, 78(3),
        96, 97(2)(a) and (3), 98, 100(2)(a) in so far as it substitutes "16" for "21", (2)(c) and (3),
        101, 102(2)(a) and (4), 104(3) and 106(2);

    (c) in Schedule 37, the entries relating to—

        (i) section 94(1) of the *Social Work (Scotland) Act* 1968;

        (ii) sections 35(2), 36B, 37(9) and 41 to 58 of and Schedules 2 and 4 to the *Sentencing
           Act*.

(2) Definitions

Criminal Justice Act 2003, s.196

As from a day to be appointed, section 196 of the 2003 Act is amended by the *Legal Aid,*   ★**5–262**

Sentencing and Punishment of Offenders Act 2012, s.68(6), and Sched. 9, para. 7, so as (i) to insert "etc." at the end of the heading, and (ii) to insert a new subsection (1A), as follows—

> "(1A) In this Chapter 'suspended sentence order" means a suspended sentence order that imposes one or more community requirements.".

As to the application of the amendment under Schedule 9, see *ante*, § 5–4.

★   As from a day to be appointed, section 196 of the 2003 Act is further amended by the 2012 Act, s.89(2), and Sched. 10, paras 12 and 14, so as (i) to insert the word "or" at the end of subsection (1)(a), (ii) to omit subsection (1)(b), (iii) to omit subsection (1)(d) and the word "or" preceding it, and (iv) to omit subsection (2).

★   As from a day to be appointed, sections 181 to 188 of the 2003 Act are repealed by the *Legal Aid, Sentencing and Punishment of Offenders Act* 2012, s.89(1)(a).

Meaning of "responsible officer"

★**5–263**   As from a day to be appointed, section 182 of the *CJA* 2003 is repealed by the *Legal Aid, Sentencing and Punishment of Offenders Act* 2012, s.89(1)(a); and section 197(1)(a)(i) is amended so as to repeal the words "182(1) or" by the 2012 Act, s.89(2), and Sched. 10, paras 12 and 15.

(3) Requirements available in the case of all offenders

Criminal Justice Act 2003, ss.199–213

Obligations of person subject to unpaid work requirement

★**5–266**   As from a day to be appointed, section 200(4) of the 2003 Act is amended by the *Legal Aid, Sentencing and Punishment of Offenders Act* 2012, s.68(6), and Sched. 9, para. 8, so as (i) to substitute "189(1A)" for "189(1)(a)" and (ii) to substitute "189(1)(a)" for "189(1)(b)(ii)". As to the application of these amendments, see *ante*, § 5–4.

Programme requirement

★**5–268**   As from a day to be appointed, section 202 of the 2003 Act is amended by the *Legal Aid, Sentencing and Punishment of Offenders Act* 2012, s.70(3) to (7), so as (i) to insert the words "in accordance with this subsection" after the word "participate" in subsection (1), (ii) to substitute the words "on the number of days specified in the order" for the words from "specified in the order" to the end of that subsection, (iii) to omit subsections (4) and (5), (iv) in the opening words of subsection (6), to substitute the words "programme requirement" for the words "requirement to attend an accredited programme", (v) in subsection (6)(a), to substitute the words "that is from time to time specified by the responsible officer at the place that is so specified" for the words "at the place specified in the order", and (vi) in subsection (7), to substitute the words "by a responsible officer" for the words "in an order".

★   As from a day to be appointed, section 202(4)(b) of the 2003 Act is amended by the 2012 Act, s.89(2), and Sched. 10, paras. 12 and 16, so as to omit the words "(or, where the relevant order is a custody plus order or an intermittent custody order, will be)". This amendment will naturally only take effect if it is brought into force prior to the repeal of the entire subsection (*ante*).

Curfew requirement

★**5–270**   As from a day to be appointed, section 204 of the 2003 Act is amended by the *Legal Aid, Sentencing and Punishment of Offenders Act* 2012, s.71, so as (i) to substitute "sixteen" for "twelve" in subsection (2), and (ii) to substitute "twelve" for "six" in subsection (3).

★   As from a day to be appointed, section 204 of the 2003 Act is further amended by the 2012 Act, s.89(2), and Sched. 10, paras 12 and 17, so as to omit subsections (4) and (5).

Foreign travel prohibition requirement

★**5–272a**   As from a day to be appointed, a new section 206A is inserted in the 2003 Act by the *Legal Aid, Sentencing and Punishment of Offenders Act* 2012, s.72(5).

Criminal Justice Act 2003, s.206A

[Foreign travel prohibition requirement

206A.—(1) In this Part "foreign travel prohibition requirement", in relation to a relevant order, means a requirement prohibiting the offender from travelling, on a day or days specified in the order, or for a period so specified—

(a) to any country or territory outside the British Islands specified or described in the order,

(b) to any country or territory outside the British Islands other than a country or territory specified or described in the order, or

(c) to any country or territory outside the British Islands.

(2) A day specified under subsection (1) may not fall outside the period of 12 months beginning with the day on which the relevant order is made.

(3) A period specified under that subsection may not exceed 12 months beginning with the day on which the relevant order is made.]

Mental health treatment requirement

As from a day to be appointed, section 207(3)(a) of the 2003 Act is amended (to omit the words from ", on the evidence" to "1983," and to substitute "*Mental Health Act* 1983" for "that Act"), and section 207(5) is repealed, by the *Legal Aid, Sentencing and Punishment of Offenders Act* 2012, s.73.   ★**5–273**

With effect from August 1, 2012 (*Health and Social Care Act 2012 (Commencement No. 1 and Transitory Provision) Order* 2012 (S.I. 2012 No. 1319)), section 207(6) of the *CJA* 2003 is amended by the *Health and Social Care Act* 2012, s.213(8)(b), so as to substitute the words "the *Health and Social Work Professions Order*" for the words the "the *Health Professions Order*".   ★

Drug rehabilitation requirement

As from a day to be appointed, section 209(3) of the 2003 Act is repealed by the *Legal Aid, Sentencing and Punishment of Offenders Act* 2012, s.74(1).   ★**5–275**

Periodic review of drug rehabilitation requirement

As from a day to be appointed, section 211(2) of the 2003 Act is amended by the *Legal Aid, Sentencing and Punishment of Offenders Act* 2012, s.74(2), so as (i) to insert the word "and" at the end of paragraph (a), and (ii) to omit paragraph (b).   ★**5–277**

Alcohol treatment requirement

As from a day to be appointed, section 212(4) of the 2003 Act is repealed by the *Legal Aid, Sentencing and Punishment of Offenders Act* 2012, s.75(1).   ★**5–278**

Alcohol abstinence and monitoring requirement

As from a day to be appointed, a new section 212A is inserted in the 2003 Act by the *Legal Aid, Sentencing and Punishment of Offenders Act* 2012, s.76(1).   ★**5–278a**

Criminal Justice Act 2003, s.212A

[Alcohol abstinence and monitoring requirement

212A.—(1) In this Part "alcohol abstinence and monitoring requirement", in relation to a relevant order, means a requirement—

(a) that, subject to such exceptions (if any) as are specified—

(i) the offender must abstain from consuming alcohol throughout a specified period, or

(ii) the offender must not consume alcohol so that at any time during a specified period there is more than a specified level of alcohol in the offender's body, and

(b) that the offender must, for the purpose of ascertaining whether the offender is complying with provision under paragraph (a), submit during the specified period to monitoring in accordance with specified arrangements.

(2) A period specified under subsection (1)(a) must not exceed 120 days.

(3) If the Secretary of State by order prescribes a minimum period for the purposes of subsection (1)(a), a period specified under that provision must be at least as long as the period prescribed.

(4) The level of alcohol specified under subsection (1)(a)(ii) must be that prescribed by the Secretary of State by order for the purposes of that provision (and a requirement under that provision may not be imposed unless such an order is in force).

(5) An order under subsection (4) may prescribe a level—

(a) by reference to the proportion of alcohol in any one or more of an offender's breath, blood, urine or sweat, or

(b) by some other means.

(6) The arrangements for monitoring specified under subsection (1)(b) must be consistent with those prescribed by the Secretary of State by order (and an alcohol abstinence and monitoring requirement may not be imposed unless such an order is in force).

(7) An order under subsection (6) may in particular prescribe—

(a) arrangements for monitoring by electronic means;

(b) arrangements for monitoring by other means of testing.

(8) A court may not include an alcohol abstinence and monitoring requirement in a relevant order unless the following conditions are met.

(9) The first condition is that—

(a) the consumption of alcohol by the offender is an element of the offence for which the order is to be imposed or an associated offence, or

(b) the court is satisfied that the consumption of alcohol by the offender was a factor that contributed to the commission of that offence or an associated offence.

(10) The second condition is that the court is satisfied that the offender is not dependent on alcohol.

(11) The third condition is that the court does not include an alcohol treatment requirement in the order.

(12) The fourth condition is that the court has been notified by the Secretary of State that arrangements for monitoring of the kind to be specified are available in the local justice area to be specified.

(13) In this section—

"alcohol" includes anything containing alcohol;

"specified", in relation to a relevant order, means specified in the order.]

Supervision requirement

★**5–279**   As from a day to be appointed, section 213(3) of the 2003 Act is amended by the *Legal Aid, Sentencing and Punishment of Offenders Act* 2012, s.68(6), and Sched. 9, paras 2 and 9, so as to substitute "189(1A)"for "189(1)(a)" in paragraph (d). As to the application of this amendment under Schedule 9, see *ante*, § 5–4.

★   As from a day to be appointed, section 213(3) of the 2003 Act is further amended by the 2012 Act, s.89(2), and Sched. 10, paras 12 and 18, so as to omit paragraphs (b) and (c).

(5) Electronic monitoring

Criminal Justice Act 2003, s.215

Electronic monitoring requirement

★**5–281**   As from a day to be appointed (as to which, see *post*), section 215 of the 2003 Act is amended by the *Legal Aid, Sentencing and Punishment of Offenders Act* 2012, s.76(6), so as to insert new subsections (5) and (6), as follows—

"(5) An electronic monitoring requirement may not be included in a relevant order for the purposes of securing the electronic monitoring of the offender's compliance with an alcohol abstinence and monitoring requirement.

(6) Subsection (5) does not prevent the inclusion of an electronic monitoring requirement in a relevant order which includes an alcohol abstinence and monitoring requirement where this is for the purpose of securing the electronic monitoring of an offender's compliance with a requirement other than the alcohol abstinence and monitoring requirement.".

Section 77 of the 2012 Act (which itself came into force on May 1, 2012) provides for sec- ★
tion 76 to be piloted in a specified area or areas before it can be brought into force generally.

(9) Authorities

R. v. Rakib is now reported at [2012] 1 Cr.App.R.(S.) 1. **5–289**
As to whether a curfew requirement may be imposed as part of a community sentence
where sentence was previously deferred under section 1 of the *PCC(S)A* 2000 (§ 5–45 in the
main work), subject to compliance with a curfew requirement, see *R. v. Saeed Ali, ante,*
§ 5–53.

D. YOUTH COMMUNITY ORDERS

(1) Curfew orders

Powers of Criminal Courts (Sentencing) Act 2000, s.37

Curfew orders
37.—(1) Where a person [aged under 16] is convicted of an offence, the court by or before **5–291**
which he is convicted may (subject to sections 148, 150 and 156 of the *Criminal Justice Act* 2003)
make an order requiring him to remain, for periods specified in the order, at a place so specified.

(2) An order under subsection (1) above is in this Act referred to as a "curfew order".

(3) A curfew order may specify different places or different periods for different days, but shall
not specify—
    (a) periods which fall outside the period of six months beginning with the day on which it is
        made; or
    (b) periods which amount to less than two hours or more than twelve hours in any one day.

(4) *In relation to an offender aged under 16 on conviction, subsection (3)(a) above shall have effect as if
the reference to six months were a reference to three months.*

(5) The requirements in a curfew order shall, as far as practicable, be such as to avoid—
    (a) any conflict with the offender's religious beliefs or with the requirements of any other
        [youth] community order to which he may be subject; and
    (b) any interference with the times, if any, at which he normally works or attends school or any
        other educational establishment.

(6) A curfew order shall include provision for making a person responsible for monitoring the offender's whereabouts during the curfew periods specified in the order; and a person who is made so
responsible shall be of a description specified in an order made by the Secretary of State.

(7) A court shall not make a curfew order unless the court has been notified by the Secretary of
State that arrangements for monitoring the offender's whereabouts are available in the area in which
the place proposed to be specified in the order is situated and the notice has not been withdrawn.

(8) Before making a curfew order, the court shall obtain and consider information about the
place proposed to be specified in the order (including information as to the attitude of persons likely
to be affected by the enforced presence there of the offender).

(9) Before making a curfew order in respect of an offender who on conviction is under 16, the
court shall obtain and consider information about his family circumstances and the likely effect of
such an order on those circumstances.

(11) The court by which a curfew order is made shall give a copy of the order to the offender and
to the responsible officer.

(12) In this Act, "responsible officer", in relation to an offender subject to a curfew order, means—
    (a) where the offender is also subject to a supervision order, the person who is the supervisor
        in relation to the supervision order;
    (b) in any other case, the person who is responsible for monitoring the offender's whereabouts
        during the curfew periods specified in the order.

[This section is printed as amended, and repealed in part, by the *CJCSA* 2000, s.74, and
Sched. 7, para. 162; the *Anti-Social Behaviour Act* 2003, s.88, and Sched. 2, para. 2(1) and
(3); and the *CJA* 2003, s.302, and Sched. 32, paras 90 and 97(1), (2)(b) and (4). As to the

words in square brackets in subss. (1) and (5)(a), these were inserted as from April 4, 2005 (S.I. 2005 No. 950, *ante*, § 5–242) by *ibid.*, paras 90 and 97(1), (2)(a) and (3), but these insertions are of no effect in the case of 16- and 17-year-olds convicted of an offence prior to April 4, 2010 (as to which, see §§ 5–185, 5–186, 5–254 in the main work): S.I. 2005 No. 950, Sched. 2, paras 12 and 13 (*ante*, §§ 5–260, 5–261). Subs. (4) is repealed by the *Anti-social Behaviour Act* 2003, s.88, and Sched. 2, para. 2(1) and (2). This repeal came into force on September 30, 2004, in the areas of 33 specified local authorities: *Anti-social Behaviour Act (Commencement No. 4) Order* 2004 (S.I. 2004 No. 2168). For the local authorities concerned, see art. 3(2) of that order. Otherwise, it comes into force on a day to be appointed. Subject to saving provisions (as to which, see §§ 5–1, 5–185, 5–186 in the main work), this section was repealed, with effect from November 30, 2009 (*Criminal Justice and Immigration Act 2008 (Commencement No. 13 and Transitory Provision) Order* 2009 (S.I. 2009 No. 3074)), by the *CJIA* 2008, ss.6(1) and 149, and Sched. 28, Pt 1.]

5–292   As to the requirements to be complied with before imposing a curfew order, see sections 35 and 36 of the *PCC(S)A* 2000 (*ante*, §§ 5–189, 5–190) (it being a "community order" within that Act), and section 148 of the *CJA* 2003 (§ 5–248 in the main work) (it being a "community sentence" within that Act).

As to the making of a curfew order with an electronic monitoring requirement, see section 36B, *post*, § 5–313. Rule 42.2 of the *Criminal Procedure Rules* 2011 (S.I. 2011 No. 1709) makes provision as to notification to the defendant, the responsible officer and, if different, the person responsible for monitoring compliance, of the details of the order.

As to breach, revocation and amendment, see the Schedule 3 to the 2000 Act (*ante*, §§ 5–228 *et seq.*).

(2) Exclusion orders

Powers of Criminal Courts (Sentencing) Act 2000, s.40A

Exclusion orders

5–293   **40A.**—(1) Where a person [aged under 16] is convicted of an offence, the court by or before which he is convicted may (subject to sections 148, 150 and 156 of the *Criminal Justice Act* 2003) make an order prohibiting him from entering a place specified in the order for a period so specified of not more than *two years* [three months].

(2) An order under subsection (1) above is in this Act referred to as an "exclusion order".

(3) An exclusion order—

(a) may provide for the prohibition to operate only during the periods specified in the order;

(b) may specify different places for different periods or days.

(5) The requirements in an exclusion order shall, as far as practicable, be such as to avoid—

(a) any conflict with the offender's religious beliefs or with the requirements of any other [youth] community order to which he may be subject; and

(b) any interference with the times, if any, at which he normally works or attends school or any other educational establishment.

(6) An exclusion order shall include provision for making a person responsible for monitoring the offender's whereabouts during the periods when the prohibition operates; and a person who is made so responsible shall be of a description specified in an order made by the Secretary of State.

(7) An exclusion order shall specify the petty sessions area in which the offender resides or will reside.

(8) A court shall not make an exclusion order unless the court has been notified by the Secretary of State that arrangements for monitoring the offender's whereabouts are available in the area in which the place proposed to be specified in the order is situated and the notice has not been withdrawn.

(9) Before making an exclusion order in respect of an offender, the court shall obtain and consider information about his family circumstances and the likely effect of such an order on those circumstances.

(11) The court by which an exclusion order is made shall—

(a) give a copy of the order to the offender and the responsible officer; and

    (b) give to any affected person any information relating to the order which the court considers it appropriate for him to have.

(12) In this section, "place" includes an area.

(13) For the purposes of this Act, a person is an affected person in relation to an exclusion order if—

    (a) a requirement under section 36B(1) above is included in the order by virtue of his consent; or

    (b) a prohibition is included in the order for the purpose (or partly for the purpose) of protecting him from being approached by the offender.

(14) In this Act, "responsible officer", in relation to an offender subject to an exclusion order, means the person who is responsible for monitoring the offender's whereabouts during the periods when the prohibition operates.

[This section is inserted by the *CJCSA* 2000, s.46. It is printed as amended, and repealed in part, by the *CJA* 2003, ss.304 and 332, and Sched. 32, paras 90 and 100(1), (2)(b) and (4), and Sched. 37, Pt 7. As to the words in square brackets in subss. (1) and (5)(a), these were inserted, and the italicised words were omitted, as from April 4, 2005 (S.I. 2005 No. 950, *ante*, § 5–242) by the 2003 Act, s.304, and Sched. 32, paras 90 and 100(1), (2)(a) and (c), and (3), but these insertions are of no effect in the case of 16- and 17-year-olds convicted of an offence prior to April 4, 2010 (as to which, see §§ 5–185, 5–186, 5–254 in the main work): S.I. 2005 No. 950, Sched. 2, paras 12 and 13 (*ante*, §§ 5–260, 5–261). Subject to saving provisions (as to which, see §§ 5–1, 5–185, 5–186 in the main work), this section was repealed, with effect from November 30, 2009 (*Criminal Justice and Immigration Act 2008 (Commencement No. 13 and Transitory Provision) Order* 2009 (S.I. 2009 No. 3074)), by the *CJIA* 2008, ss.6(1) and 149, and Sched. 28, Pt 1.]

For breach, revocation and amendment of certain community orders, see Schedule 3 to the 2000 Act, *ante*, §§ 5–228 *et seq.*

(3) Attendance centre orders

Powers of Criminal Courts (Sentencing) Act 2000, s.60

Attendance centre orders

  60.—(1) Where—   **5–294**

    (a) (subject to 148, 150 and 156 of the *Criminal Justice Act* 2003) a person aged under *21* [16] is convicted by or before a court of an offence punishable with imprisonment, or

    (b) a court [has power or] would have power, but for section 89 below (restrictions on imprisonment of young offenders and defaulters), to commit a person aged under *21* [16] to prison in default of payment of any sum of money or for failing to do or abstain from doing anything required to be done or left undone, *or*

    (c) *a court has power to commit a person aged at least 21 but under 25 to prison in default of payment of any sum of money,*

the court may, if it has been notified by the Secretary of State that an attendance centre is available for the reception of persons of his description, order him to attend at such a centre, to be specified in the order, for such number of hours as may be so specified.

(2) An order under subsection (1) above is in this Act referred to as an "attendance centre order".

(3) The aggregate number of hours for which an attendance centre order may require a person to attend at an attendance centre shall not be less than 12 except where—

    (a) he is aged under 14; and

    (b) the court is of the opinion that 12 hours would be excessive, having regard to his age or any other circumstances.

(4) The aggregate number of hours shall not exceed 12 except where the court is of the opinion, having regard to all the circumstances, that 12 hours would be inadequate, and in that case [shall not exceed 24]—

    (a) *shall not exceed 24 where the person is aged under 16; and*

    (b) *shall not exceed 36 where the person is aged 16 or over but under 21 or (where subsection (1)(c) above applies) under 25.*

(5) A court may make an attendance centre order in respect of a person before a previous atten-

dance centre order made in respect of him has ceased to have effect, and may determine the number of hours to be specified in the order without regard—

(a) to the number specified in the previous order; or

(b) to the fact that order is still in effect.

(6) An attendance centre order shall not be made unless the court is satisfied that the attendance centre to be specified in it is reasonably accessible to the person concerned, having regard to his age, the means of access available to him and any other circumstances.

(7) The times at which a person is required to attend at an attendance centre shall, as for as practicable, be such as to avoid—

(a) any conflict with his religious beliefs or with the requirements of any other [youth] community order to which he may be subject; and

(b) any interference with the times, if any, at which he normally works or attends school or any other educational establishment.

(8) The first time at which the person is required to attend at an attendance centre shall be a time at which the centre is available for his attendance in accordance with the notification of the Secretary of State, and shall be specified in the order.

(9) The subsequent times shall be fixed by the officer in charge of the centre, having regard to the person's circumstances.

(10) A person shall not be required under this section to attend at an attendance centre on more than one occasion on any day, or for more than three hours on any occasion.

(11) Where a court makes an attendance centre order, the clerk of the court shall—

(a) deliver or send a copy of the order to the officer in charge of the attendance centre specified in it; and

(b) deliver a copy of the order to the person in respect of whom it is made or send a copy by registered post or the recorded delivery service addressed to his last or usual place of abode.

(12) Where a person ("the defaulter") has been ordered to attend at an attendance centre in default of the payment of any sum of money—

(a) on payment of the whole sum to any person authorised to receive it, the attendance centre order shall cease to have effect;

(b) on payment of a part of the sum to any such person, the total number of hours for which the defaulter is required to attend at the centre shall be reduced proportionately, that is to say by such number of complete hours as bears to the total number the proportion most nearly approximating to, without exceeding, the proportion which the part bears to the whole sum.

[This section is printed as amended by the *CJA* 2003, s.304, and Sched. 32, para. 102(1), (2)(a) (substitution of references to sections 148, 150 and 156 of the 2003 Act for references to corresponding provisions of the 2000 Act, and substitution of "16" for "21" in subs. (1)(a)), and (4) (substitution of "youth community order" for "community order" in subs. (7)); and as amended, as from a day to be appointed, by the *CJCSA* 2000, s.74 and Sched. 7, para. 173 (insertion of words in first set of square brackets in subs. (1)(b)); and the *CJA* 2003, s.304, and Sched. 32, paras 90 and 102(1), and (2)(b) and (c), and (3) (substitution of "16" for "21" in subs. (1)(b), omission of subs. (1)(c) and the word "or" immediately preceding it, substitution of words in square brackets for italicised words in subs. (4)). The amendments to subss. (1)(a) and (7) came into force on April 4, 2005: S.I. 2005 No. 950 (*ante*, § 5–242), save that, in the case of persons aged 16 or 17 upon conviction, the substitution of "16" for "21" in subs. (1)(a) and the insertion of the word "youth" before "community order" in subs. (7) have no application in relation to offences committed before November 30, 2009, or in relation to any failure to comply with an order made in respect of an offence committed before that date: *ibid.*, Sched. 2, paras 12 and 13 (*ante*, §§ 5–260, 5–261). The whole of this section is repealed as from a day to be appointed (as to which, see §§ 5–1, 5–185, 5–186 in the main work) by the *CJIA* 2008, ss.6(1) and 149, and Sched. 28, Pt 1. To the extent that this repeal relates to subs. (1)(a), it was brought into force on November 30, 2009: *Criminal Justice and Immigration Act 2008 (Commencement No. 13 and Transitory Provision) Order* 2009 (S.I. 2009 No. 3074).]

5-295   As to the requirements to be complied with before imposing an attendance centre order, see (for offences committed before April 4, 2005) sections 35 and 36 of the *PCC(S)A* 2000 (*ante*, §§ 5–189, 5–190) (it being a "community order" within that Act), and (for offences committed after that date) section 148 of the *CJA* 2003 (§ 5–248 in the main work) (it being a "community sentence" within that Act).

It is not entirely clear whether a court may make attendance centre orders on the same occasion in respect of a number of offences with an aggregate in excess of the limits in subsection (4). It is submitted that the better view is that it cannot; section 60(1) appears to be concerned with defining an *occasion* when an attendance centre order may be made. On any such occasion *one* order may be made. Subsection (5) appears to confirm the correctness of this approach: if it were incorrect, subsection (5) would not be needed.

Section 61 gives effect to Schedule 5 (*post*, §§ 5–365 *et seq*.).

(4) Supervision orders

Powers of Criminal Courts (Sentencing) Act 2000, ss.63, 64

Supervision orders

63.—(1) Where a child or young person (that is to say, any person aged under 18) is convicted **5–296** of an offence, the court by or before which he is convicted may (subject to sections 148, 150 and 156 of the *Criminal Justice Act* 2003) make an order placing him under the supervision of—

    (a) a local authority designated by the order;

    (b) an officer of a local probation board or an officer of a provider of probation services (as the case may be); or

    (c) a member of a youth offending team.

(2) An order under subsection (1) above is in this Act referred to as a "supervision order".

(3) In this Act "supervisor", in relation to a supervision order, means the person under whose supervision the offender is placed or to be placed by the order.

(4) Schedule 6 to this Act (which specifies requirements that may be included in supervision orders) shall have effect.

(5) A court shall not make a supervision order unless it is satisfied that the offender resides or will reside in the area of a local authority; and a court shall be entitled to be satisfied that the offender will so reside if he is to be required so to reside by a provision to be included in the order in pursuance of paragraph 1 of Schedule 6 to this Act.

(6) A supervision order—

    (a) shall name the area of the local authority and the petty sessions area in which it appears to the court making the order (or to the court amending under Schedule 7 to this Act any provision included in the order in pursuance of this paragraph) that the offender resides or will reside; and

    (b) may contain such prescribed provisions as the court making the order (or amending it under that Schedule) considers appropriate for facilitating the performance by the supervisor of his functions under section 64(4) below, including any prescribed provisions for requiring visits to be made by the offender to the supervisor;

and in paragraph (b) above "prescribed" means prescribed by Criminal Procedure Rules.

(7) A supervision order shall, unless it has previously been revoked, cease to have effect at the end of the period of three years, or such shorter period as may be specified in the order, beginning with the date on which the order was originally made.

(8) A court which makes a supervision order shall forthwith send a copy of its order—

    (a) to the offender and, if the offender is aged under 14, to his parent or guardian;

    (b) to the supervisor;

    (c) to any local authority who are not entitled by virtue of paragraph (b) above to such a copy and whose area is named in the supervision order in pursuance of subsection (6) above;

    (d) where the offender is required by the order to reside with an individual or to undergo treatment by or under the direction of an individual or at any place, to the individual or the person in charge of that place; and

    (e) where a petty sessions area named in the order in pursuance of subsection (6) above is not that for which the court acts, to the justices' chief executive for the petty sessions area so named;

and, in a case falling within paragraph (e) above, shall also send to the justices' chief executive in question such documents and information relating to the case as the court considers likely to be of assistance to them.

(9) If a court makes a supervision order while another such order made by any court is in force in respect of the offender, the court making the new order may revoke the earlier order (and paragraph 10 of Schedule 7 to this Act (supplementary provision) shall apply to the revocation).

[This section is printed as amended by the *CJCSA* 2000, s.74, and Sched. 7, para. 4; the *CJA* 2003, s.304, and Sched. 32, paras 90 and 103; the *Courts Act 2003 (Consequential Amendments) Order* 2004 (S.I. 2004 No. 2035); and the *Offender Management Act 2007 (Consequential Amendments) Order* 2008 (S.I. 2008 No. 912), art. 3, and Sched. 1, para. 14(1) and (9). Subject to saving provisions (as to which, see §§ 5–1, 5–185, 5–186 in the main work), this section was repealed, with effect from November 30, 2009 (*Criminal Justice and Immigration Act 2008 (Commencement No. 13 and Transitory Provision) Order* 2009 (S.I. 2009 No. 3074)), by the *CJIA* 2008, ss.6(1) and 149, and Sched. 28, Pt 1.]

As to the requirements to be complied with before imposing a supervision order, see sections 35 and 36 of the *PCC(S)A* 2000 (*ante*, §§ 5–189, 5–190) (it being a "community order" within that Act), and section 148 of the *CJA* 2003 (§ 5–248 in the main work) (it being a "community sentence" within that Act).

For Schedule 6, see *post*, §§ 5–300 *et seq.*

Selection and duty of supervisor and certain expenditure of his

5–297   **64.**—(1) A court shall not designate a local authority as the supervisor by a provision of a supervision order unless—

   (a) the authority agree; or

   (b) it appears to the court that the offender resides or will reside in the area of the authority.

   (2) Where a provision of a supervision order places the offender under the supervision of an officer of a local probation board, the supervisor shall be an officer of a local probation board appointed for or assigned to the petty sessions area named in the order in pursuance of section 63(6) above.

   (2A) Where a provision of a supervision order places the offender under the supervision of an officer of a provider of probation services, the supervisor shall be an officer of a provider of probation services acting in the local justice area named in the order in pursuance of section 63(6) above.

   (3) Where a provision of a supervision order places the offender under the supervision of a member of a youth offending team, the supervisor shall be a member of a team established by the local authority within whose area it appears to the court that the offender resides or will reside.

   (4) While a supervision order is in force, the supervisor shall advise, assist and befriend the offender.

   (5) [*Defrayment of expenditure.*]

[This section is printed as amended and repealed in part by the *CJCSA* 2000, s.74, and Sched. 7, paras 4 and 174; and S.I. 2008 No. 912 (*ante*, § 5–296), art. 3, and Sched. 1, para. 14(1) and (10). Subject to saving provisions (as to which, see §§ 5–1, 5–185, 5–186 in the main work), this section was repealed, with effect from November 30, 2009 (*Criminal Justice and Immigration Act 2008 (Commencement No. 13 and Transitory Provision) Order* 2009 (S.I. 2009 No. 3074)), by the *CJIA* 2008, ss.6(1) and 149, and Sched. 28, Pt 1.]

5–298   Section 64A (inserted by the *Anti-social Behaviour Act* 2003, s.88, and Sched. 2, para. 3) provides that nothing in Chapter V of Part IV of the Act prevents a court which makes a supervision order in respect of an offender from also making a curfew order in respect of him. Section 65 gives effect to Schedule 7 (*post*, §§ 5–371 *et seq.*). This makes provision for dealing with failures to comply with supervision orders and for revoking and amending such orders. Section 66 makes provision for facilities for implementing supervision orders. All these provisions were repealed, subject to savings (as to which, see §§ 5–1, 5–185, 5–186 in the main work), with effect from November 30, 2009 (*Criminal Justice and Immigration Act 2008 (Commencement No. 13 and Transitory Provision) Order* 2009 (S.I. 2009 No. 3074)), by the *CJIA* 2008, ss.6(1) and 149, and Sched. 28, Pt 1.

Powers of Criminal Courts (Sentencing) Act 2000, s.67

Meaning of "local authority", "reside" and "parent"

5–299   **67.**—(1) Unless the contrary intention appears, in sections 63 to 66 above and Schedules 6 and 7 to this Act—

"local authority" means the council of a county or of a county borough, metropolitan district or London borough or the Common Council of the City of London;

"reside" means habitually reside, and cognate expressions shall be construed accordingly except in paragraph 6(2) and (3) of Schedule 6.

(2) In the case of a child or young person—

    (a) whose father and mother were not married to each other at the time of his birth, and

    (b) with respect to whom a residence order is in force in favour of the father,

any reference in sections 63 to 66 and Schedules 6 and 7 to the parent of the child or young person includes a reference to the father.

(3) In subsection (2) above "residence order" has the meaning given by section 8(1) of the Children Act 1989, and subsection (2) above is without prejudice to the operation of section 1(1) of the *Family Law Reform Act* 1987 (construction of references to relationships) in relation to the provisions of this Act other than those mentioned in subsection (2).

[This section was repealed, subject to saving provisions (as to which, see §§ 5–1, 5–185, 5–186 in the main work), with effect from November 30, 2009 (*Criminal Justice and Immigration Act 2008 (Commencement No. 13 and Transitory Provision) Order* 2009 (S.I. 2009 No. 3074)), by the *CJIA* 2008, ss.6(1) and 149, and Sched. 28, Pt 1.]

Section 63   SCHEDULE 6

REQUIREMENTS WHICH MAY BE INCLUDED IN SUPERVISION ORDERS

Requirement to reside with named individual

1. A supervision order may require the offender to reside with an individual named in the order   **5–300** who agrees to the requirement, but a requirement imposed by a supervision order in pursuance of this paragraph shall be subject to any such requirement of the order as is authorised by paragraph 2, 3, 6 [, 6A] or 7 below.

[Para. 1 is printed as amended, as from a day to be appointed, by the *CJA* 2003, s.279, and Sched. 24, para. 2(1) and (2) (insertion of reference to para. 6A). The whole of Schedule 6 was repealed, subject to saving provisions (as to which, see §§ 5–1, 5–185, 5–186 in the main work), with effect from November 30, 2009 (*Criminal Justice and Immigration Act 2008 (Commencement No. 13 and Transitory Provision) Order* 2009 (S.I. 2009 No. 3074)), by the *CJIA* 2008, ss.6(1) and 149, and Sched. 28, Pt 1.]

Requirement to comply with directions of supervisor

2.—(1) Subject to sub-paragraph (2) below, a supervision order may require the offender to   **5–301** comply with any directions given from time to time by the supervisor and requiring him to do all or any of the following things—

    (a) to live at a place or places specified in the directions for a period or periods so specified;

    (b) to present himself to a person or persons specified in the directions at a place or places and on a day or days so specified;

    (c) to participate in activities specified in the directions on a day or days so specified.

(2) A supervision order shall not require compliance with directions given by virtue of sub-paragraph (1) above unless the court making it is satisfied that a scheme under section 66 of this Act (local authority schemes) is in force for the area where the offender resides or will reside; and no such directions may involve the use of facilities which are not for the time being specified in a scheme in force under that section for that area.

(3) A requirement imposed by a supervision order in pursuance of sub-paragraph (1) above shall be subject to any such requirement of the order as is authorised by paragraph 6 below (treatment for offender's mental condition).

(4) It shall be for the supervisor to decide—

    (a) whether and to what extent he exercises any power to give directions conferred on him by virtue of sub-paragraph (1) above; and

    (b) the form of any directions.

(5) The total number of days in respect of which an offender may be required to comply with directions given by virtue of paragraph (a), (b) or (c) of sub-paragraph (1) above shall not exceed 180 or such lesser number, if any, as the order may specify for the purposes of this sub-paragraph.

(6) For the purpose of calculating the total number of days in respect of which such directions may be given, the supervisor shall be entitled to disregard any day in respect of which directions were previously given in pursuance of the order and on which the directions were not complied with.

(7) Directions given by the supervisor by virtue of sub-paragraph (1)(b) or (c) above shall, as far as practicable, be such as to avoid—

    (a) any conflict with the offender's religious beliefs or with the requirements of any other youth community order or any community order to which he may be subject; and

    (b) any interference with the times, if any, at which he normally works or attends school or any other educational establishment.

[Para. 2 is printed as amended by the *Anti-social Behaviour Act* 2003, s.88, and Sched. 2, para. 4(1) and (2); and the *CJA* 2003, s.304, and Sched. 32, para. 127(a). As to the repeal of the whole of Schedule 6, see *ante*, § 5–300.]

Requirements as to activities, reparation, night restrictions etc.

5–302   3.—(1) This paragraph applies to a supervision order unless the order requires the offender to comply with directions given by the supervisor under paragraph 2(1) above.

(2) Subject to the following provisions of this paragraph ..., a supervision order to which this paragraph applies may require the offender—

    (a) to live at a place or places specified in the order for a period or periods so specified;

    (b) to present himself to a person or persons specified in the order at a place or places and on a day or days so specified;

    (c) to participate in activities specified in the order on a day or days so specified;

    (d) to make reparation specified in the order to a person or persons so specified or to the community at large;

    (e) [*repealed by* Anti-social Behaviour Act *2003, s.88, and Sched. 2, para. 4(1) and (3)(a)*];

    (f) to refrain from participating in activities specified in the order—

        (i) on a specified day or days during the period for which the supervision order is in force; or

        (ii) during the whole of that period or a specified portion of it;

    and in this paragraph "make reparation" means make reparation for the offence otherwise than by the payment of compensation.

(3) The total number of days in respect of which an offender may be subject to requirements imposed by virtue of paragraph (a), (b), (c) or (d) of sub-paragraph (2) above shall not exceed 180.

(4) The court may not include requirements under sub-paragraph (2) above in a supervision order unless—

    (a) it has first consulted the supervisor as to—

        (i) the offender's circumstances, and

        (ii) the feasibility of securing compliance with the requirements,

    and is satisfied, having regard to the supervisor's report, that it is feasible to secure compliance with them;

    (b) having regard to the circumstances of the case, it considers the requirements necessary for securing the good conduct of the offender or for preventing a repetition by him of the same offence or the commission of other offences; and

    (c) if the offender is aged under 16, it has obtained and considered information about his family circumstances and the likely effect of the requirements on those circumstances.

(5) The court shall not by virtue of sub-paragraph (2) above include in a supervision order—

    (a) any requirement that would involve the co-operation of a person other than the supervisor and the offender, unless that other person consents to its inclusion;

    (b) any requirement to make reparation to any person unless that person—

        (i) is identified by the court as a victim of the offence or a person otherwise affected by it; and

        (ii) consents to the inclusion of the requirement;

    (c) any requirement requiring the offender to reside with a specified individual; or

    (d) any such requirement as is mentioned in paragraph 6(2) below (treatment for offender's mental condition).

(6) Requirements included in a supervision order by virtue of sub-paragraph (2)(b) or (c) above shall, as far as practicable, be such as to avoid—

(a) any conflict with the offender's religious beliefs or with the requirements of any other youth community order to which he may be subject; and

(b) any interference with the times, if any, at which he normally works or attends school or any other educational establishment;

and sub-paragraphs (7) and (8) below are without prejudice to this sub-paragraph.

(7) Subject to sub-paragraph (8) below, a supervision order may not by virtue of sub-paragraph (2) above include—

(a) any requirement that would involve the offender in absence from home—

    (i) for more than two consecutive nights, or

    (ii) for more than two nights in any one week, or

(b) if the offender is of compulsory school age, any requirement to participate in activities during normal school hours,

unless the court making the order is satisfied that the facilities whose use would be involved are for the time being specified in a scheme in force under section 66 of this Act for the area in which the offender resides or will reside.

(8) Sub-paragraph (7)(b) above does not apply to activities carried out in accordance with arrangements made or approved by the local authority in whose area the offender resides or will reside.

(9) Expressions used in sub-paragraphs (7) and (8) above and in the *Education Act* 1996 have the same meaning in those sub-paragraphs as in that Act.

[Para. 3 is printed as amended and repealed in part by the *Anti-social Behaviour Act* 2003, ss.88 and 92, and Scheds 2, para. 4(1) and (3), and 3; the *CJA* 2003, s.304, and Sched. 32, para. 127(b); and the *Local Education Authorities and Children's Services Authorities (Integration of Functions) Order* 2010 (S.I. 2010 No. 1158). As to the repeal of the whole of Schedule 6, see *ante*, § 5–300.]

4. [*Repealed by* Anti-social Behaviour Act *2003, s.92, and Sched. 3.*]

Requirement to live for specified period in local authority accommodation

5.—(1) Where the conditions mentioned in sub-paragraph (2) below are satisfied, a supervision order may impose a requirement ("a local authority residence requirement") that the offender shall live for a specified period in local authority accommodation (as defined by section 163 of this Act). **5-303**

(2) The conditions are that—

(a) a supervision order has previously been made in respect of the offender;

(b) that order imposed—

    (i) a requirement under paragraph 1, 2, 3 or 7 of this Schedule; or

    (ii) a local authority residence requirement;

(c) the offender fails to comply with that requirement, or is convicted of an offence committed while that order was in force; and

(d) the court is satisfied that—

    (i) the failure to comply with the requirement, or the behaviour which constituted the offence, was due to a significant extent to the circumstances in which the offender was living; and

    (ii) the imposition of a local authority residence requirement will assist in his rehabilitation;

    except that sub-paragraph (i) of paragraph (d) above does not apply where the condition in paragraph (b)(ii) above is satisfied.

(3) A local authority residence requirement shall designate the local authority who are to receive the offender, and that authority shall be the authority in whose area the offender resides.

(4) The court shall not impose a local authority residence requirement without first consulting the designated authority.

(5) A local authority residence requirement may stipulate that the offender shall not live with a named person.

(6) The maximum period which may be specified in a local authority residence requirement is six months.

(7) A court shall not impose a local authority residence requirement in respect of an offender who is not legally represented at the relevant time in that court unless—

(a) he was granted a right to representation funded by the Legal Services Commission as part of the Criminal Defence Service for the purposes of the proceedings but the right was withdrawn because of his conduct or because it appeared that his financial resources were such that he was not eligible to be granted such a right;

(aa) he applied for such representation and the application was refused because it appeared that his financial resources were such that he was not eligible to be granted a right to it; or

(b) he has been informed of his right to apply for such representation for the purposes of the proceedings and has had the opportunity to do so, but nevertheless refused or failed to apply.

(8) In sub-paragraph (7) above—

(a) "the relevant time" means the time when the court is considering whether or not to impose the requirement; and

(b) "the proceedings" means—

(i) the whole proceedings; or

(ii) the part of the proceedings relating to the imposition of the requirement.

(9) A supervision order imposing a local authority residence requirement may also impose any of the requirements mentioned in paragraphs 2, 3, 6 and 7 of this Schedule.

[Para. 5(7) is printed as amended by the *Criminal Defence Service Act* 2006, s.4(2) and (3). As to the repeal of the whole of Schedule 6, see *ante*, § 5–300.]

Requirement to live for specified period with local authority foster parent

5–304   5A.—(1) Where the conditions mentioned in sub-paragraph (2) below are satisfied, a supervision order may impose a requirement ("a foster parent residence requirement") that the offender shall live for a specified period with a local authority foster parent.

(2) The conditions are that—

(a) the offence is punishable with imprisonment in the case of an offender aged 18 or over;

(b) the offence, or the combination of the offence and one or more offences associated with it, was so serious that a custodial sentence would normally be appropriate (or, where the offender is aged 10 or 11, would normally be appropriate if the offender were aged 12 or over); and

(c) the court is satisfied that—

(i) the behaviour which constituted the offence was due to a significant extent to the circumstances in which the offender was living, and

(ii) the imposition of a foster parent residence requirement will assist in his rehabilitation.

(3) A foster parent residence requirement shall designate the local authority who are to place the offender with a local authority foster parent under section 22C of the *Children Act* 1989, and that authority shall be the authority in whose area the offender resides.

(4) A court shall not impose a foster parent residence requirement unless—

(a) the court has been notified by the Secretary of State that arrangements for implementing such a requirement are available in the area of the designated authority;

(b) the notice has not been withdrawn; and

(c) the court has consulted the designated authority.

(5) Subject to paragraph 5(2A) of Schedule 7 to this Act, the maximum period which may be specified in a foster parent residence requirement is twelve months.

(6) A court shall not impose a foster parent residence requirement [*otherwise identical to para. 5(7), ante*].

(7) In sub-paragraph (6) [*otherwise identical to para. 5(8), ante.*]

(8) A supervision order imposing a foster parent residence requirement may also impose any of the requirements mentioned in paragraphs 2, 3, 6 and 7 of this Schedule.

(9) If at any time while a supervision order imposing a foster parent residence requirement is in force, the supervisor notifies the offender—

(a) that no suitable local authority foster parent is available, and

(b) that the supervisor has applied or proposes to apply under paragraph 5 of Schedule 7 for the variation or revocation of the order,

the foster parent residence requirement shall, until the determination of the application, be taken to require the offender to live in local authority accommodation (as defined by section 163 of this Act).

(10) This paragraph does not affect the power of a local authority to place with a local authority

foster parent an offender to whom a local authority residence requirement under paragraph 5 above relates.

(11) In this paragraph "local authority foster parent" has the same meaning as in the *Children Act* 1989.

[Para. 5A was inserted by the *Anti-social Behaviour Act* 2003, s.88, and Sched. 2, para. 4(1) and (5). Sub-para. (3) is printed as amended by the *CYPA* 2008, s.8(2), and Sched. 1, para. 10 (effective April 1, 2011 (*Children and Young Persons Act 2008 (Commencement No. 3, Saving and Transitional Provisions) Order* 2010 (S.I. 2010 No. 2981)). The *Criminal Defence Service Act* 2006, s.4(2) and (3), effected an identical amendment to sub-para. (6), as that made to para. 5(7), *ante*. As to the repeal of the whole of Schedule 6, see *ante*, § 5–300.]

Requirements as to treatment for mental condition

6.—(1) This paragraph applies where a court which proposes to make a supervision order is satis-   **5–305**
fied, on the evidence of a registered medical practitioner approved for the purposes of section 12 of the *Mental Health Act* 1983, that the mental condition of the offender—

    (a) is such as requires and may be susceptible to treatment; but

    (b) is not such as to warrant the making of a hospital order or guardianship order within the meaning of that Act.

(2) Where this paragraph applies, the court may include in the supervision order a requirement that the offender shall, for a period specified in the order, submit to treatment of one of the following descriptions so specified, that is to say—

    (a) treatment as a resident patient in a care home within the meaning of the *Care Standards Act* 2000, an independent hospital or a hospital within the meaning of the *Mental Health Act* 1983, but not a hospital at which high security psychiatric services within the meaning of that Act are provided;

    (b) treatment as a non-resident patient at an institution or place specified in the order;

    (c) treatment by or under the direction of a registered medical practitioner specified in the order; or

    (d) treatment by or under the direction of a registered psychologist specified in the order.

(3) A requirement shall not be included in a supervision order by virtue of sub-paragraph (2) above—

    (a) in any case, unless the court is satisfied that arrangements have been or can be made for the treatment in question and, in the case of treatment as a resident patient, for the reception of the patient;

    (b) in the case of an order made or to be made in respect of a person aged 14 or over, unless he consents to its inclusion;

and a requirement so included shall not in any case continue in force after the offender attains the age of 18.

(4) Subsections (2) and (3) of section 54 of the *Mental Health Act* 1983 shall have effect with respect to proof for the purposes of sub-paragraph (1) above of an offender's mental condition as they have effect with respect to proof of an offender's mental condition for the purposes of section 37(2)(a) of that Act.

(5) In sub-paragraph (2)—

    (a) "independent hospital"—

        (i) in relation to England, means a hospital as defined by section 275 of the *National Health Service Act* 2006 that is not a health service hospital as defined by that section, and

        (ii) in relation to Wales, has the same meaning as in the *Care Standards Act* 2000; and

    (b) "registered psychologist" means a person registered in the part of the register maintained under the *Health Professions Order 2001* (S.I. 2002 No. 251) which relates to practitioner psychologists.

[Para. 6 is printed as amended by the *Care Standards Act* 2000, s.116, and Sched. 4, para. 28(3); the *Health Care and Associated Professions (Miscellaneous Amendments and Practitioner Psychologists) Order* 2009 (S.I. 2009 No. 1182), Sched. 5, para. 5; and the *Health and Social Care Act 2008 (Consequential Amendments No. 2) Order* 2010 (S.I. 2010 No. 813), art. 10. As to the repeal of the whole of Schedule 6, see *ante*, § 5–300.]

[Requirements as to drug treatment and testing

6A.—(1) This paragraph applies where a court proposing to make a supervision order is satis-   **5–306**
fied—

(a) that the offender is dependent on, or has a propensity to misuse, drugs, and

(b) that his dependency or propensity is such as requires and may be susceptible to treatment.

(2) Where this paragraph applies, the court may include in the supervision order a requirement that the offender shall, for a period specified in the order ("the treatment period"), submit to treatment by or under the direction of a specified person having the necessary qualifications and experience ("the treatment provider") with a view to the reduction or elimination of the offender's dependency on or propensity to misuse drugs.

(3) The required treatment shall be—

(a) treatment as a resident in such institution or place as may be specified in the order, or

(b) treatment as a non-resident at such institution or place, and at such intervals, as may be so specified;

but the nature of the treatment shall not be specified in the order except as mentioned in paragraph (a) or (b) above.

(4) A requirement shall not be included in a supervision order by virtue of sub-paragraph (2) above—

(a) in any case, unless—

(i) the court is satisfied that arrangements have been or can be made for the treatment intended to be specified in the order (including arrangements for the reception of the offender where he is to be required to submit to treatment as a resident), and

(ii) the requirement has been recommended to the court as suitable for the offender by an officer of a local probation board, by an officer of a provider of probation services or by a member of a youth offending team; and

(b) in the case of an order made or to be made in respect of a person aged 14 or over, unless he consents to its inclusion.

(5) Subject to sub-paragraph (6), a supervision order which includes a treatment requirement may also include a requirement ("a testing requirement") that, for the purpose of ascertaining whether he has any drug in his body during the treatment period, the offender shall during that period, at such times or in such circumstances as may (subject to the provisions of the order) be determined by the supervisor or the treatment provider, provide samples of such description as may be so determined.

(6) A testing requirement shall not be included in a supervision order by virtue of sub-paragraph (5) above unless—

(a) the offender is aged 14 or over and consents to its inclusion, and

(b) the court has been notified by the Secretary of State that arrangements for implementing such requirements are in force in the area proposed to be specified in the order.

(7) A testing requirement shall specify for each month the minimum number of occasions on which samples are to be provided.

(8) A supervision order including a testing requirement shall provide for the results of tests carried out on any samples provided by the offender in pursuance of the requirement to a person other than the supervisor to be communicated to the supervisor.]

[Para. 6A was inserted by the *CJA* 2003, s.279, and Sched. 24, para. 2(1) and (3). For the purpose of sentencing persons resident in Bradford, Calderdale, Keighley, Manchester, Newham and the part of the Teesside petty sessions area that is coterminous with the borough of Middlesborough, this insertion took effect on December 1, 2004, but not in relation to offences committed before that date (and where an offence is found to have been committed over a period of two or more days or at some time during that period, it shall be taken to have been committed on the last of those days): *Criminal Justice Act 2003 (Commencement No. 6 and Transitional Provisions) Order* 2004 (S.I. 2004 No. 3033). Otherwise, it was not in force as at October 19, 2009. It is printed as amended by S.I. 2008 No. 912 (*ante*, § 5–242), art. 3, and Sched. 1, para. 14(1) and (17). As to the repeal of the whole of Schedule 6, see *ante*, § 5–300.]

Requirements as to education

5–307   7.—(1) This paragraph applies to a supervision order unless the order requires the offender to comply with directions given by the supervisor under paragraph 2(1) above.

(2) Subject to the following provisions of this paragraph, a supervision order to which this paragraph applies may require the offender, if he is of compulsory school age, to comply, for as long as he is of that age and the order remains in force, with such arrangements for his education as may

from time to time be made by his parent, being arrangements for the time being approved by the local authority.

(3) The court shall not include such a requirement in a supervision order unless—

(a) it has consulted the local authority with regard to its proposal to include the requirement; and

(b) it is satisfied that in the view of the local authority arrangements exist for the offender to receive efficient full-time education suitable to his age, ability and aptitude and to any special educational need he may have.

(4) Expressions used in sub-paragraphs (2) and (3) above and in the *Education Act* 1996 have the same meaning in those sub-paragraphs as in that Act.

(5) The court may not include a requirement under sub-paragraph (2) above unless it has first consulted the supervisor as to the offender's circumstances and, having regard to the circumstances of the case, it considers the requirement necessary for securing the good conduct of the offender or for preventing a repetition by him of the same offence or the commission of other offences.

[Para. 7 is printed as amended by the *Local Education Authorities and Children's Services Authorities (Integration of Functions) Order* 2010 (S.I. 2010 No. 1158). As to the repeal of the whole of Schedule 6, see *ante*, § 5–300.]

Exercise of powers under paragraphs 3, 6 and 7

8.—(1) Any power to include a requirement in a supervision order which is exercisable in relation to a person by virtue of paragraph 3, 6 or 7 above may be exercised in relation to him whether or not any other such power is exercised.

(2) Sub-paragraph (1) above is without prejudice to the power to include in a supervision order any other combination of requirements under different paragraphs of this Schedule that is authorised by this Schedule.

5–308

[As to the repeal of the whole of Schedule 6, see *ante*, § 5–300.]

(5) Action plan orders

Powers of Criminal Courts (Sentencing) Act 2000, ss.69–72

Action plan orders

69.—(1) Where a child or young person (that is to say, any person aged under 18) is convicted of an offence and the court by or before which he is convicted is of the opinion mentioned in subsection (3) below, the court may (subject to sections 148, 150 and 156 of the *Criminal Justice Act* 2003) make an order which—

5–309

(a) requires the offender, for a period of three months beginning with the date of the order, to comply with an action plan, that is to say, a series of requirements with respect to his actions and whereabouts during that period;

(b) places the offender for that period under the supervision of the responsible officer; and

(c) requires the offender to comply with any directions given by the responsible officer with a view to the implementation of that plan;

and the requirements included in the order, and any directions given by the responsible officer, may include requirements authorised by section 70 below.

(2) An order under subsection (1) above is in this Act referred to as an "action plan order".

(3) The opinion referred to in subsection (1) above is that the making of an action plan order is desirable in the interests of—

(a) securing the rehabilitation of the offender; or

(b) preventing the commission by him of further offences.

(4) In this Act "responsible officer", in relation to an offender subject to an action plan order, means one of the following who is specified in the order, namely—

(a) an officer of a local probation board or an officer of a provider of probation services (as the case may be);

(b) a social worker of a local authority social services department;

(c) a member of a youth offending team.

(5) The court shall not make an action plan order in respect of the offender if—

(a) he is already the subject of such an order; or

(b) the court proposes to pass on him a custodial sentence or to make in respect of him a *community rehabilitation order, a community punishment order, a community punishment and rehabilitation order* [community order under section 177 of the *Criminal Justice Act* 2003], an attendance centre order, a supervision order or a referral order.

(6) Before making an action plan order, the court shall obtain and consider—

(a) a written report by an officer of a local probation board, an officer of a provider of probation services, a social worker of a local authority social services department or a member of a youth offending team indicating—

(i) the requirements proposed by that person to be included in the order;

(ii) the benefits to the offender that the proposed requirements are designed to achieve; and

(iii) the attitude of a parent or guardian of the offender to the proposed requirements; and

(b) where the offender is aged under 16, information about the offender's family circumstances and the likely effect of the order on those circumstances.

(7) The court shall not make an action plan order unless it has been notified by the Secretary of State that arrangements for implementing such orders are available in the area proposed to be named in the order under subsection (8) below and the notice has not been withdrawn.

(8) An action plan order shall name the petty sessions area in which it appears to the court making the order (or to the court amending under Schedule 8 to this Act any provision included in the order in pursuance of this subsection) that the offender resides or will reside.

(9) Where an action plan order specifies an officer of a local probation board under subsection (4) above, the officer specified must be an officer appointed for or assigned to the petty sessions area named in the order.

(9A) Where an action plan order specifies an officer of a provider of probation services under subsection (4) above, the officer specified must be an officer acting in the local justice area named in the order.

(10) Where an action plan order specifies under that subsection—

(a) a social worker of a local authority social services department, or

(b) a member of a youth offending team,

the social worker or member specified must be a social worker of, or a member of a youth offending team established by, the local authority within whose area it appears to the court that the offender resides or will reside.

[This section is printed as amended by the *CJCSA* 2000, s.74 and Sched. 7, paras 1–4; the *CJA* 2003, s.304, and Sched. 32, paras 90 and 104(1), (2) and (4); and S.I. 2008 No. 912 (*ante*, § 5–242), art. 3, and Sched. 1, para. 14(1) and (12). The words in square brackets in subs. (5)(b) were substituted for the italicised words as from April 4, 2005 (S.I. 2005 No. 950, *ante*, § 5–188): *CJA* 2003, s.304, and Sched. 32, paras 90 and 104(1) and (3); but, in the case of persons aged 16 or 17 upon conviction, this amendment only comes into force on April 4, 2010 (as to which, see §§ 5–185, 5–186, 5–254 in the main work): S.I. 2005 No. 950, Sched. 2, paras 12 and 13 (*ante*, §§ 5–260, 5–261). Subject to saving provisions (as to which, see §§ 5–1, 5–185, 5–186 in the main work), this section was repealed, with effect from November 30, 2009 (*Criminal Justice and Immigration Act* 2008 (*Commencement No. 13 and Transitory Provision) Order* 2009 (S.I. 2009 No. 3074)), by the *CJIA* 2008, ss.6(1) and 149, and Sched. 28, Pt 1.]

Requirements which may be included in action plan orders and directions

5–310   **70.**—(1) Requirements included in an action plan order, or directions given by a responsible officer, may require the offender to do all or any of the following things, namely—

(a) to participate in activities specified in the requirements or directions at a time or times so specified;

(b) to present himself to a person or persons specified in the requirements or directions at a place or places and at a time or times so specified;

(c) subject to subsection (2) below, to attend at an attendance centre specified in the requirements or directions for a number of hours so specified;

(d) to stay away from a place or places specified in the requirements or directions;

(e) to comply with any arrangements for his education specified in the requirements or directions;

(f) to make reparation specified in the requirements or directions to a person or persons so specified or to the community at large; and

(g) to attend any hearing fixed by the court under section 71 below.

(2) Subsection (1)(c) above applies only where the offence committed by the offender is an offence punishable with imprisonment.

(3) In subsection (1)(f) above "make reparation", in relation to an offender, means make reparation for the offence otherwise than by the payment of compensation.

(4) A person shall not be specified in requirements or directions under subsection (1)(f) above unless—

(a) he is identified by the court or (as the case may be) the responsible officer as a victim of the offence or a person otherwise affected by it; and

(b) he consents to the reparation being made.

[(4A) Subsection (4B) below applies where a court proposing to make an action plan order is satisfied—

(a) that the offender is dependent on, or has a propensity to misuse, drugs, and

(b) that his dependency or propensity is such as requires and may be susceptible to treatment.

(4B) Where this subsection applies, requirements included in an action plan order may require the offender for a period specified in the order ("the treatment period") to submit to treatment by or under the direction of a specified person having the necessary qualifications and experience ("the treatment provider") with a view to the reduction or elimination of the offender's dependency on or propensity to misuse drugs.

(4C) The required treatment shall be—

(a) treatment as a resident in such institution or place as may be specified in the order, or

(b) treatment as a non-resident at such institution or place, and at such intervals, as may be so specified;

but the nature of the treatment shall not be specified in the order except as mentioned in paragraph (a) or (b) above.

(4D) A requirement shall not be included in an action plan order by virtue of subsection (4B) above—

(a) in any case, unless—

(i) the court is satisfied that arrangements have been or can be made for the treatment intended to be specified in the order (including arrangements for the reception of the offender where he is to be required to submit to treatment as a resident), and

(ii) the requirement has been recommended to the court as suitable for the offender by an officer of a local probation board, by an officer of a provider of probation services or by a member of a youth offending team; and

(b) in the case of an order made or to be made in respect of a person aged 14 or over, unless he consents to its inclusion.

(4E) Subject to subsection (4F), an action plan order which includes a requirement by virtue of subsection (4B) above may, if the offender is aged 14 or over, also include a requirement ("a testing requirement") that, for the purpose of ascertaining whether he has any drug in his body during the treatment period, the offender shall during that period, at such times or in such circumstances as may (subject to the provisions of the order) be determined by the responsible officer or the treatment provider, provide samples of such description as may be so determined.

(4F) A testing requirement shall not be included in an action plan order by virtue of subsection (4E) above unless—

(a) the offender is aged 14 or over and consents to its inclusion, and

(b) the court has been notified by the Secretary of State that arrangements for implementing such requirements are in force in the area proposed to be specified in the order.

(4G) A testing requirement shall specify for each month the minimum number of occasions on which samples are to be provided.

(4H) An action plan order including a testing requirement shall provide for the results of tests carried out on any samples provided by the offender in pursuance of the requirement to a person other than the responsible officer to be communicated to the responsible officer.]

(5) Requirements included in an action plan order and directions given by a responsible officer shall, as far as practicable, be such as to avoid—

(a) any conflict with the offender's religious beliefs or with the requirements of any other youth community order or any community order to which he may be subject; and

(b) any interference with the times, if any, at which he normally works or attends school or any other educational establishment.

[This section is printed as amended by the *CJA* 2003, s.302, and Sched. 32, paras 90 and

105; and S.I. 2008 No. 912 (*ante*, § 5–242), art. 3, and Sched. 1, para. 14(1) and (13); and as amended, as from a day to be appointed, by *ibid.*, s.279 and Sched. 24, para. 1 (insertion of subss. (4A) to (4H)). As to the commencement of section 279 and Schedule 24 in certain areas on December 1, 2004, see *ante*, § 5–306. Subject to saving provisions (as to which, see §§ 5–1, 5–185, 5–186 in the main work), this section was repealed, with effect from November 30, 2009 (*Criminal Justice and Immigration Act 2008 (Commencement No. 13 and Transitory Provision) Order* 2009 (S.I. 2009 No. 3074)), by the *CJIA* 2008, ss.6(1) and 149, and Sched. 28, Pt 1.]

Action plan orders: power to fix further hearings

5–311   **71.**—(1) Immediately after making an action plan order, a court may—

(a) fix a further hearing for a date not more than 21 days after the making of the order; and

(b) direct the responsible officer to make, at that hearing, a report as to the effectiveness of the order and the extent to which it has been implemented.

(2) At a hearing fixed under subsection (1) above, the court—

(a) shall consider the responsible officer's report; and

(b) may, on the application of the responsible officer or the offender, amend the order—

(i) by cancelling any provision included in it; or

(ii) by inserting in it (either in addition to or in substitution for any of its provisions) any provision that the court could originally have included in it.

[Subject to saving provisions (as to which, see §§ 5–1, 5–185, 5–186 in the main work), this section was repealed, with effect from November 30, 2009 (*Criminal Justice and Immigration Act 2008 (Commencement No. 13 and Transitory Provision) Order* 2009 (S.I. 2009 No. 3074)), by the *CJIA* 2008, ss.6(1) and 149, and Sched. 28, Pt 1.]

Breach, revocation and amendment

5–312   As to breach, revocation, and amendment, see Schedule 8 to the 2000 Act (§§ 5–721 *et seq.* in the main work).

(6) Electronic monitoring

Powers of Criminal Courts (Sentencing) Act 2000, s.36B

Electronic monitoring of requirements in [youth] community orders

5–313   **36B.**—(1) Subject to subsections (2) *to* (4) [and (3)] below, a [youth] community order may include requirements for securing the electronic monitoring of the offender's compliance with any other requirements imposed by the order.

(2) A court shall not include in a [youth] community order a requirement under subsection (1) above unless the court—

(a) has been notified by the Secretary of State that electronic monitoring arrangements are available in the relevant areas specified in subsections (7) to (10) below; and

(b) is satisfied that the necessary provisions can be made under those arrangements.

(3) Where—

(a) it is proposed to include in an exclusion order a requirement for securing electronic monitoring in accordance with this section; but

(b) there is a person (other than the offender) without whose co-operation it will not be practicable to secure the monitoring,

the requirement shall not be included in the order without that person's consent.

(4) *Where—*

(a) *it is proposed to include in a community rehabilitation order or a community punishment and rehabilitation order a requirement for securing the electronic monitoring of the offender's compliance with a requirement such as is mentioned in paragraph 8(1) of Schedule 2 to this Act; but*

(b) *there is a person (other than the offender) without whose co-operation it will not be practicable to secure the monitoring,*

the requirement shall not be included in the order without that person's consent.

(5) An order which includes requirements under subsection (1) above shall include provision for

making a person responsible for the monitoring; and a person who is made so responsible shall be of a description specified in an order made by the Secretary of State.

(6) The Secretary of State may make rules for regulating—

(a) the electronic monitoring of compliance with requirements included in a [youth] community order; and

(b) without prejudice to the generality of paragraph (a) above, the functions of persons made responsible for securing the electronic monitoring of compliance with requirements included in the order.

(7) In the case of a curfew order or an exclusion order, the relevant area is the area in which the place proposed to be specified in the order is situated.

In this subsection, "place", in relation to an exclusion order, has the same meaning as in section 40A below.

(8) *In the case of a community rehabilitation order or a community punishment and rehabilitation order, the relevant areas are each of the following—*

(a) *where it is proposed to include in the order a requirement for securing compliance with a requirement such as is mentioned in sub-paragraph (1) of paragraph 7 of Schedule 2 to this Act, the area mentioned in sub-paragraph (5) of that paragraph;*

(b) *where it is proposed to include in the order a requirement for securing compliance with a requirement such as is mentioned in sub-paragraph (1) of paragraph 8 of that Schedule, the area mentioned in sub-paragraph (5) of that paragraph;*

(c) *where it is proposed to include in the order a requirement for securing compliance with any other requirement, the area prposed to be specified under section 41(3) below.*

(9) In the case of *a community punishment order, a drug treatment and testing order, a drug abstinence order,* a supervision order or an action plan order, the relevant area is the petty sessions area proposed to be specified in the order.

(10) In the case of an attendance centre order, the relevant area is the petty sessions area in which the attendance centre proposed to be specified in the order is situated.

[This section was inserted by the *CJCSA* 2000, s.52, as from July 2, 2001 (except to the extent that it relates to exclusion orders and exclusion requirements); and from September 2, 2004 (except to the extent that it relates to exclusion requirements): *Criminal Justice and Court Services Act 2000 (Commencemenet No. 13) Order* 2004 (S.I. 2004 No. 2171). It is printed as amended and repealed in part by the *CJA* 2003, ss.304 and 332, Sched. 32, paras 90 and 96, and Sched. 37, Pt 7 (omission of italicised words, insertion of words in square brackets). These amendments came into force on April 4, 2005 (S.I. 2005 No. 950, *ante*, § 5–242), but (i) they have no application in relation to any offence committed before that date (see para. 5 of Sched. 2 to S.I. 2005 No. 950 (§ 5–2 in the main work)), and (ii) they have no effect where a person aged 16 or 17 is convicted of an offence committed before November 30, 2009, or in relation to any failure to comply with an order made in respect of such an offence (see paras 12 and 13 of Sched. 2 to S.I. 2005 No. 950 (*ante*, §§ 5–260, 5–261)). The repeal of the whole section is provided for by the *CJIA* 2008, ss.6(1) and 149, and Sched. 28, Pt 1. As at February 10, 2010, this repeal had not been brought into force.]

E. YOUTH REHABILITATION ORDERS

Criminal Justice and Immigration Act 2008, Sched. 1

Curfew requirement

As from a day to be appointed, paragraph 14 of Schedule 1 to the 2008 Act is amended ★**5-323** by the *Legal Aid, Sentencing and Punishment of Offenders Act* 2012, s.81, so as to substitute "16" for "12" in sub-paragraph (2), and to substitute "12" for "6" in sub-paragraph (3).

Pre-conditions to imposing local authority residence requirement or fostering requirement

As from a day to be appointed, paragraph 19(2) of Schedule 1 to the 2008 Act is amended ★**5-327** by the *Legal Aid, Sentencing and Punishment of Offenders Act* 2012, s.39(1), and Sched. 5, para. 69, so as to substitute the words "representation was made available to the offender for the purposes of the proceedings under Part 1 of the *Legal Aid, Sentencing and Punishment of Offenders Act* 2012 but" for the words from "the offender" to "the right" in sub-paragraph (a).

★   As from a day to be appointed, paragraph 20 of Schedule 1 to the 2008 Act is amended by the *Legal Aid, Sentencing and Punishment of Offenders Act* 2012, s.82, so as (i) to omit the words from ", on the evidence" to "1983," in sub-paragraph (3)(a), (ii) to substitute "the *Mental Health Act* 1983" for "that Act" in sub-paragraph (3)(a)(ii), and (iii) to omit sub-paragraph (5).

Date for compliance with requirements to be specified in order

★5–337   As from a day to be appointed, paragraph 32 of Schedule 1 to the 2008 Act is amended by the *Legal Aid, Sentencing and Punishment of Offenders Act* 2012, s.83(1)(a), so as to insert, in sub-paragraph (1), the words "('the end date')" after the word "date" where it first appears.

★   As from a day to be appointed, paragraph 32 of Schedule 1 to the 2008 Act is further amended by the 2012 Act, s.83(1)(b), so as to substitute a new sub-paragraph (2), as follows—

"(2) If a youth rehabilitation order imposes two or more different requirements falling within Part 2 of this Schedule, the order may also specify a date by which each of those requirements must have been complied with; and the last of those dates must be the same as the end date.".

★   As from a day to be appointed, paragraph 32 of Schedule 1 to the 2008 Act is further amended by the 2012 Act, s.83(1)(c), so as to insert a new sub-paragraph (4), as follows—

"(4) Subject to paragraph 10(7) (duration of youth rehabilitation order imposing unpaid work requirement), a youth rehabilitation order ceases to be in force on the end date.".

F. Enforcement

(1) Of community orders

Criminal Justice Act 2003, Sched. 8

Powers of magistrates' court

★5–345   As from a day to be appointed, paragraph 9(1) of Schedule 8 to the *CJA* 2003 is amended by the *Legal Aid, Sentencing and Punishment of Offenders Act* 2012, s.67(1) and (2), so as (i) to substitute the word "may" for the word "must" in the opening words, and (ii) to insert a new paragraph (aa), as follows—

"(aa) by ordering the offender to pay a fine of an amount not exceeding £2,500;".

★   As from a day to be appointed, paragraph 9(3) of Schedule 8 to the *CJA* 2003 is amended by the 2012 Act, s.66(3)(a), so as to substitute for the words from "but may" to the end, the words "but may only amend the order to substitute a later date for that specified under section 177(5) in accordance with sub-paragraphs (3ZA) and (3ZB)".

★   As from a day to be appointed, paragraph 9 of Schedule 8 to the *CJA* 2003 is further amended by the 2012 Act, s.66(3)(b), so as to insert new sub-paragraphs (3ZA) to (3ZC) after paragraph (3), as follows—

"(3ZA) A date substituted under sub-paragraph (3)—
    (a) may not fall outside the period of six months beginning with the date previously specified under section 177(5);
    (b) subject to that, may fall more than three years after the date of the order.
(3ZB) The power under sub-paragraph (3) to substitute a date may not be exercised in relation to an order if that power or the power in paragraph 10(3) to substitute a date has previously been exercised in relation to that order.
(3ZC) A date substituted under sub-paragraph (3) is to be treated as having been specified in relation to the order under section 177(5).".

★   As from a day to be appointed, paragraph 9 of Schedule 8 to the *CJA* 2003 is further amended by the 2012 Act, s.67(1) and (3), so as to insert a new sub-paragraph (3B) after paragraph (3A), as follows—

"(3B) A fine imposed under sub-paragraph (1)(aa) is to be treated, for the purposes of any enactment, as being a sum adjudged to be paid by a conviction.".

As from a day to be appointed, paragraph 9(6) of Schedule 8 to the *CJA* 2003 is amended ★ by the 2012 Act, s.67(1) and (4), so as to substitute the words "have the power to deal with the offender under sub-paragraph (1)(a), (aa), (b) or (c)" for the words from "be required to" to "or (c)".

Powers of Crown Court

As from a day to be appointed, paragraph 10(1) of Schedule 8 to the *CJA* 2003 is **★5–346** amended by the *Legal Aid, Sentencing and Punishment of Offenders Act* 2012, s.67(1) and (5), so as to (i) substitute the word "may" for the word "must" in the opening words, and (ii) to insert a new paragraph (aa), as follows—

"(aa) by ordering the offender to pay a fine of an amount not exceeding £2,500;".

As from a day to be appointed, paragraph 10(3) of Schedule 8 to the *CJA* 2003 is ★ amended by the 2012 Act, s.66(4)(a), so as to substitute for the words from "but may" to the end, the words "but may only amend the order to substitute a later date for that specified under section 177(5) in accordance with sub-paragraphs (3ZA) and (3ZB)".

As from a day to be appointed, paragraph 10 of Schedule 8 to the *CJA* 2003 is further ★ amended by the 2012 Act, s.66(4)(b), so as to insert new sub-paragraphs (3ZA) to (3ZC) after paragraph (3), as follows—

"(3ZA) A date substituted under sub-paragraph (3)—
    (a) may not fall outside the period of six months beginning with the date previously specified under section 177(5);
    (b) subject to that, may fall more than three years after the date of the order.
(3ZB) The power under sub-paragraph (3) to substitute a date may not be exercised in relation to an order if that power or the power in paragraph 9(3) to substitute a date has previously been exercised in relation to that order.
(3ZC) A date substituted under sub-paragraph (3) is to be treated as having been specified in relation to the order under section 177(5).".

As from a day to be appointed, paragraph 10 of Schedule 8 to the *CJA* 2003 is further ★ amended by the 2012 Act, s.67(1) and (6), so as to insert a new sub-paragraph (3B) after paragraph (3A), as follows—

"(3B) A fine imposed under sub-paragraph (1)(aa) is to be treated, for the purposes of any enactment, as being a sum adjudged to be paid by a conviction.".

Power to amend amounts of fines

As from a day to be appointed, a new paragraph 11A is inserted in Schedule 8 to the *CJA* **★5–347a** 2003 by the *Legal Aid, Sentencing and Punishment of Offenders Act* 2012, s.67(1) and (7), as follows—

"Power to amend amounts of fines
11A.—(1) The Secretary of State may by order amend any sum for the time being specified in paragraph 9(1)(aa) or 10(1)(aa).
(2) The power conferred by sub-paragraph (1) may be exercised only if it appears to the Secretary of State that there has been a change in the value of money since the relevant date which justifies the change.
(3) In sub-paragraph (2), 'the relevant date' means—
    (a) if the sum specified in paragraph 9(1)(aa) or 10(1)(aa) (as the case may be) has been substituted by an order under sub-paragraph (1), the date on which the sum was last so substituted;
    (b) otherwise, the date on which section 67 of the *Legal Aid, Sentencing and Punishment of Offenders Act* 2012 (which inserted this paragraph) came into force.
(4) An order under sub-paragraph (1) (a 'fine amendment order') must not have effect in relation to any community order made in respect of an offence committed before the fine amendment order comes into force.".

Extension of order

As from a day to be appointed, a new paragraph 19A is inserted in Schedule 8 to the *CJA* **★5–353a** 2003 by the *Legal Aid, Sentencing and Punishment of Offenders Act* 2012, s.66(5), as follows—

"Extension of order

19A.—(1) The appropriate court may, on the application of the offender or the responsible officer, amend a community order by substituting a later date for that specified under section 177(5).

(2) A date substituted under sub-paragraph (1)—

(a) may not fall outside the period of six months beginning with the date previously specified under section 177(5);

(b) subject to that, may fall more than three years after the date of the order.

(3) The power under sub-paragraph (1) may not be exercised in relation to an order if it has previously been exercised in relation to that order.

(4) A date substituted under sub-paragraph (1) is to be treated as having been specified in relation to the order under section 177(5).

(5) In this paragraph 'the appropriate court' has the same meaning as in paragraph 16.".

★5–358   As from a day to be appointed, paragraph 1(2) of Part 1 of Schedule 5 to the *AFA* 2006 is amended by the *Legal Aid, Sentencing and Punishment of Offenders Act* 2012, s.78(6), so as to insert a reference to paragraph 19A(5) after the reference to paragraph 18(4).

(2) Of youth community orders

(a) *Curfew and exclusion orders*

5–364   As to breach, revocation and amendment of curfew and exclusion orders, see Schedule 3 to the *PCC(S)A* 2000 (*ante*, §§ 5–228 *et seq.*).

(b) *Attendance centre orders*

Powers of Criminal Courts (Sentencing) Act 2000, Sched. 5

Section 61   SCHEDULE 5

Breach, Revocation and Amendment of Attendance Centre Orders

Breach of order or attendance centre rules

5–365   1.—(1) Where an attendance centre order is in force and it appears on information to a justice that the offender—

(a) has failed to attend in accordance with the order, or

(b) while attending has committed a breach of rules made under section 222(1)(d) or (e) of the *Criminal Justice Act* 2003 which cannot be adequately dealt with under those rules,

the justice may issue a summons requiring the offender to appear at the place and time specified in the summons or, if the information is in writing and on oath, may issue a warrant for the offender's arrest.

(2) Any summons or warrant issued under this paragraph shall direct the offender to appear or be brought—

(a) before a magistrates' court acting for the petty sessions area in which the offender resides; or

(b) if it is not known where the offender resides, before a magistrates' court acting for the petty sessions area in which is situated the attendance centre which the offender is required to attend by the order or by virtue of an order under paragraph 5(1)(b) below.

2.—(1) If it is proved to the satisfaction of the magistrates' court before which an offender appears or is brought under paragraph 1 above that he has failed without reasonable excuse to attend as mentioned in sub-paragraph (1)(a) of that paragraph or has committed such a breach of rules as is mentioned in sub-paragraph (1)(b) of that paragraph, that court may deal with him in any one of the following ways—

(a) it may impose on him a fine not exceeding £1,000;

(b) where the attendance centre order was made by a magistrates' court, it may deal with him, for the offence in respect of which the order was made, in any way in which he could have been dealt with for that offence by the court which made the order if the order had not been made; or

(c) where the order was made by the Crown Court, it may commit him to custody or release him on bail until he can be brought or appear before the Crown Court.

(2) Any exercise by the court of its power under sub-paragraph (1)(a) above shall be without prejudice to the continuation of the order.

(3) A fine imposed under sub-paragraph (1)(a) above shall be deemed, for the purposes of any enactment, to be a sum adjudged to be paid by a conviction.

(4) Where a magistrates' court deals with an offender under sub-paragraph (1)(b) above, it shall revoke the attendance centre order if it is still in force.

(5) In dealing with an offender under sub-paragraph (1)(b) above, a magistrates' court—

    (a) shall take into account the extent to which the offender has complied with the requirements of the attendance centre order; and

    (b) in the case of an offender who has wilfully and persistently failed to comply with those requirements, may impose a custodial sentence notwithstanding anything in section 152(2) of the *Criminal Justice Act* 2003.

(5A) Where a magistrates' court dealing with an offender under sub-paragraph (1)(a) above would not otherwise have the power to amend the order under paragraph 5(1)(b) below (substitution of different attendance centre), that paragraph has effect as if references to an appropriate magistrates' court were references to the court dealing with an offender.

(6) A person sentenced under sub-paragraph (1)(b) above for an offence may appeal to the Crown Court against the sentence.

(7) A magistrates' court which deals with an offender's case under sub-paragraph (1)(c) above shall send to the Crown Court—

    (a) a certificate signed by a justice of the peace giving particulars of the offender's failure to attend or, as the case may be, the breach of the rules which he has committed; and

    (b) such other particulars of the case as may be desirable;

and a certificate purporting to be so signed shall be admissible as evidence of the failure or the breach before the Crown Court.

3.—(1) Where by virtue of paragraph 2(1)(c) above the offender is brought or appears before the Crown Court and it is proved to the satisfaction of the court—

    (a) that he has failed without reasonable excuse to attend as mentioned in paragraph 1(1)(a) above, or

    (b) that he has committed such a breach of rules as is mentioned in paragraph 1(1)(b) above,

that court may deal with him, for the offence in respect of which the order was made, in any way in which it could have dealt with him for that offence if it had not made the order.

(2) Where the Crown Court deals with an offender under sub-paragraph (1) above, it shall revoke the attendance centre order if it is still in force.

(3) In dealing with an offender under sub-paragraph (1) above, the Crown Court—

    (a) shall take into account the extent to which the offender has complied with the requirements of the attendance centre order; and

    (b) in the case of an offender who has willfully and persistently failed to comply with those requirements, may impose a custodial sentence notwithstanding anything in section 152(2) of the *Criminal Justice Act* 2003.

(4) In proceedings before the Crown Court under this paragraph any question whether there has been a failure to attend or a breach of the rules shall be determined by the court and not by the verdict of a jury.

Revocation of order with or without re-sentencing

4.—(1) Where an attendance centre order is in force in respect of an offender, an appropriate **5–366** court may, on an application made by the offender or by the officer in charge of the relevant attendance centre, revoke the order.

(2) In sub-paragraph (1) above "an appropriate court" means—

    (a) where the court which made the order was the Crown Court and there is included in the order a direction that the power to revoke the order is reserved to that court, the Crown Court;

    (b) in any other case, either of the following—

        (i) a magistrates' court acting for the petty sessions area in which the relevant attendance centre is situated;

        (ii) the court which made the order.

(3) Any power conferred by this paragraph—

    (a) on a magistrates' court to revoke an attendance centre order made by such a court, or

    (b) on the Crown Court to revoke an attendance centre order made by the Crown Court,

includes power to deal with the offender, for the offence in respect of which the order was made, in any way in which he could have been dealt with for that offence by the court which made the order if the order had not been made.

(4) A person sentenced by a magistrates' court under sub-paragraph (3) above for an offence may appeal to the Crown Court against the sentence.

(5) The proper officer of a court which makes an order under this paragraph revoking an attendance centre order shall—

    (a) deliver a copy of the revoking order to the offender or send a copy by registered post or the recorded delivery service addressed to the offender's last or usual place of abode; and

    (b) deliver or send a copy to the officer in charge of the relevant attendance centre.

(6) In this paragraph "the relevant attendance centre", in relation to an attendance centre order, means the attendance centre specified in the order or substituted for the attendance centre so specified by an order made by virtue of paragraph 5(1)(b) below.

(7) In this paragraph "proper officer" means—

    (a) in relation to a magistrates' court, the justices' chief executive for the court; and

    (b) in relation to the Crown Court, the appropriate officer.

Amendment of order

5–367
5.—(1) Where an attendance centre order is in force in respect of an offender, an appropriate magistrates' court may, on application made by the offender or by the officer in charge of the relevant attendance centre, by order—

    (a) vary the day or hour specified in the order for the offender's first attendance at the relevant attendance centre; or

    (b) substitute for the relevant attendance centre an attendance centre which the court is satisfied is reasonably accessible to the offender, having regard to his age, the means of access available to him and any other circumstances.

(2) In sub-paragraph (1) above "an appropriate magistrates' court" means—

    (a) a magistrates' court acting for the petty sessions area in which the relevant attendance centre is situated; or

    (b) (except where the attendance centre order was made by the Crown Court) the magistrates' court which made the order.

(3) The justices' chief executive for a court which makes an order under this paragraph shall—

    (a) deliver a copy to the offender or send a copy by registered post or the recorded delivery service addressed to the offender's last or usual place of abode; and

    (b) deliver or send a copy—

        (i) if the order is made by virtue of sub-paragraph (1)(a) above, to the officer in charge of the relevant attendance centre; and

        (ii) if it is made by virtue of sub-paragraph (1)(b) above, to the officer in charge of the attendance centre which the order as amended will require the offender to attend.

(4) In this paragraph "the relevant attendance centre" has the meaning given by paragraph 4(6) above.

Orders made on appeal

5–368
6.—(1) Where an attendance centre order has been made on appeal, for the purposes of this Schedule it shall be deemed—

    (a) if it was made on an appeal brought from a magistrates' court, to have been made by that magistrates' court;

    (b) if it was made on an appeal brought from the Crown Court or from the criminal division of the Court of Appeal, to have been made by the Crown Court.

(2) In relation to an attendance centre order made on appeal, paragraphs 2(1)(b) and 4(3) above shall each have effect as if the words "if the order had not been made" were omitted and paragraph 3(1) above shall have effect as if the words "if it had not made the order" were omitted.

Orders for defaulters

5–369
7.—(1) References in this Schedule to an "offender" include a person who has been ordered to attend at an attendance centre for such a default or failure as is mentioned in section 60(1)(b) or (c) of this Act.

(2) Where a person has been ordered to attend at an attendance centre for such a default or failure—

    (a) paragraphs 2(1)(b), 3(1) and 4(3) above shall each have effect in relation to the order as if the words ", for the offence in respect of which the order was made," and "for that offence" were omitted; and

    (b) paragraphs 2(5)(b) and 3(3)(b) above (which relate to custodial sentences for offences) do not apply.

[This schedule is printed as amended by the *CJA* 2003, s.304, and Sched. 32, paras 90 and 126; and the *Domestic Violence, Crime and Victims Act* 2004, s.29, and Sched. 5, para. 6. The whole schedule is repealed as from a day to be appointed (as to which, see §§ 5–1, 5–185, 5–186 in the main work) by the *CJIA* 2008, ss.6(1) and 149, and Sched. 28, Pt 1.]

When dealing with an offender under paragraph 3(1), the court must observe any limita-　**5–370** tions related to his age which applied at the time when he was sentenced: he must be sentenced on the basis of his age when he was originally convicted of the offence for which the attendance centre order was made.

In a case coming within paragraph 4, the failure to attend the attendance centre, or breach of the rules, must be proved to the satisfaction of the Crown Court: the certificate of the magistrates' court is merely evidence.

(c) *Supervision orders*

Powers of Criminal Courts (Sentencing) Act 2000, Sched. 7

Section 65　　　　　　　　　　　　SCHEDULE 7

BREACH, REVOCATION AND AMENDMENT OF SUPERVISION ORDERS

Meaning of "relevant court", etc.

1.—(1) In this Schedule, "relevant court", in relation to a supervision order, means—　**5–371**

    (a) where the offender is under the age of 18, a youth court acting for the petty sessions area for the time being named in the order in pursuance of section 63(6) of this Act;

    (b) where the offender has attained that age, a magistrates' court other than a youth court, being a magistrates' court acting for the petty sessions area for the time being so named.

(2) If an application to a youth court is made in pursuance of this Schedule and while it is pending the offender to whom it relates attains the age of 18, the youth court shall deal with the application as if he had not attained that age.

Breach of requirement of supervision order

2.—(1) This paragraph applies if while a supervision order is in force in respect of an offender it is　**5–372** proved to the satisfaction of a relevant court, on the application of the supervisor, that the offender has failed to comply with any requirement included in the supervision order in pursuance of paragraph 1, 2, 3, 5, 5A [, 6A] or 7 of Schedule 6 to this Act or section 63(6)(b) of this Act.

(2) Where this paragraph applies, the court—

    (a) whether or not it also makes an order under paragraph 5(1) below (revocation or amendment of supervision order)—

        (i) may order the offender to pay a fine of an amount not exceeding £1,000; or

        (ii) subject to sub-paragraph (2A) below and paragraph 3 below, may make a curfew order in respect of him; or

        (iii) subject to paragraph 4 below, may make an attendance centre order in respect of him; or

    (b) if the supervision order was made by a magistrates' court, may revoke the supervision order and deal with the offender, for the offence in respect of which the order was made, in any way in which he could have been dealt with for that offence by the court which made the order if the order had not been made; or

    (c) if the supervision order was made by the Crown Court, may commit him in custody or release him on bail until he can be brought or appear before the Crown Court.

(2A) The court may not make a curfew order under sub-paragraph (2)(a)(ii) above in respect of an offender who is already subject to a curfew order.

(3) Where a court deals with an offender under sub-paragraph (2)(c) above, it shall send to the Crown Court a certificate signed by a justice of the peace giving—

(a) particulars of the offender's failure to comply with the requirement in question; and

(b) such other particulars of the case as may be desirable;

and a certificate purporting to be so signed shall be admissible as evidence of the failure before the Crown Court.

(4) Where—

(a) by virtue of sub-paragraph (2)(c) above the offender is brought or appears before the Crown Court, and

(b) it is proved to the satisfaction of the court that he has failed to comply with the requirement in question,

that court may deal with him, for the offence in respect of which the supervision order was made, in any way in which it could have dealt with him for that offence if it had not made the order.

(5) Where the Crown Court deals with an offender under sub-paragraph (4) above, it shall revoke the supervision order if it is still in force.

(6) A fine imposed under this paragraph shall be deemed, for the purposes of any enactment, to be a sum adjudged to be paid by a conviction.

(7) In dealing with an offender under this paragraph, a court shall take into account the extent to which he has complied with the requirements of the supervision order.

(8) Where a supervision order has been made on appeal, for the purposes of this paragraph it shall be deemed—

(a) if it was made on an appeal brought from a magistrates' court, to have been made by that magistrates' court;

(b) if it was made on an appeal brought from the Crown Court or from the criminal division of the Court of Appeal, to have been made by the Crown Court;

and, in relation to a supervision order made on appeal, sub-paragraph (2)(b) above shall have effect as if the words "if the order had not been made" were omitted and sub-paragraph (4) above shall have effect as if the words "if it had not made the order" were omitted.

(9) This paragraph has effect subject to paragraph 7 below.

Curfew orders imposed for breach of supervision order

5-373   3.—(1) Section 37(1) of this Act (curfew orders) shall apply for the purposes of paragraph 2(2)(a)(ii) above as if for the words from the beginning to "make" there were substituted "Where a court considers it appropriate to make an order in respect of any person in pursuance of paragraph 2(2)(a)(ii) of Schedule 7 to this Act, it may make".

(2) The following provisions of this Act, namely—

(a) section 37(3) to (12), and

(b) so far as applicable, sections 36B and 40 and Schedule 3 so far as relating to curfew orders,

have effect in relation to a curfew order made by virtue of paragraph 2(2)(a)(ii) above as they have effect in relation to any other curfew order, subject to sub-paragraph (5) below.

(3) Sections 148 and 156 of the *Criminal Justice Act* 2003 (restrictions and procedural requirements for community sentences) do not apply in relation to a curfew order made by virtue of paragraph 2(2)(a)(ii) above.

(5) Schedule 3 to this Act (breach, revocation and amendment of orders) shall have effect in relation to such a curfew order as if—

(a) the power conferred on the court by each of paragraphs 4(2)(c) and 10(3)(b) to deal with the offender for the offence in respect of which the order was made were a power to deal with the offender, for his failure to comply with the supervision order, in any way in which a relevant court could deal with him for that failure if it had just been proved to the satisfaction of that court;

(b) the reference in paragraph 10(1)(b) to the offence in respect of which the order was made were a reference to the failure to comply in respect of which the curfew order was made; and

(c) the power conferred on the Crown Court by paragraph 11(2)(b) to deal with the offender for the offence in respect of which the order was made were a power to deal with the offender, for his failure to comply with the supervision order, in any way in which a relevant court (if the supervision order was made by a magistrates' court) or the Crown Court (if the supervision order was made by the Crown Court) could deal with him for that failure if it had just been proved to its satisfaction.

(6) For the purposes of the provisions mentioned in paragraphs (a) and (c) of sub-paragraph (5) above, as applied by that sub-paragraph, if the supervision order is no longer in force the relevant court's powers shall be determined on the assumption that it is still in force.

Attendance centre orders imposed for breach of supervision order

4.—(1) Section 60(1) of this Act (attendance centre orders) shall apply for the purposes of **5-374** paragraph 2(2)(a)(iii) above as if for the words from the beginning to "the court may," there were substituted "Where a court considers it appropriate to make an order in respect of any person in pursuance of paragraph 2(2)(a)(iii) of Schedule 7 to this Act, the court may,".

(2) The following provisions of this Act, namely—

(a) subsections (3) to (11) of section 60, and

(b) so far as applicable, Schedule 5,

have effect in relation to an attendance centre order made by virtue of paragraph 2(2)(a)(iii) above as they have effect in relation to any other attendance centre order, subject to sub-paragraph (4) below.

(3) Sections 148 and 156 of the *Criminal Justice Act* 2003 (restrictions and procedural requirements for community sentences) do not apply in relation to an attendance centre order made by virtue of paragraph 2(2)(a)(iii) above.

(4) Schedule 5 to this Act (breach, revocation and amendment of attendance centre orders) shall have effect in relation to such an attendance centre order as if there were omitted—

(a) from each of paragraphs 2(1)(b) and 4(3) the words ", for the offence in respect of which the order was made," and "for that offence"; and

(b) from paragraphs 2(6) and 4(4) the words "for an offence".

Revocation and amendment of supervision order

5.—(1) If while a supervision order is in force in respect of an offender it appears to a relevant **5-375** court, on the application of the supervisor or the offender, that it is appropriate to make an order under this sub-paragraph, the court may—

(a) make an order revoking the supervision order; or

(b) make an order amending it—

(i) by cancelling any requirement included in it in pursuance of Schedule 6 to, or section 63(6)(b) of, this Act; or

(ii) by inserting in it (either in addition to or in substitution for any of its provisions) any provision which could have been included in the order if the court had then had power to make it and were exercising the power.

(2) Sub-paragraph (1) above has effect subject to paragraphs 7 to 9 below.

(2A) In relation to a supervision order imposing a foster parent residence requirement under paragraph 5A of Schedule 6 to this Act, the power conferred by sub-paragraph (1)(b)(ii) above includes power to extend the period specified in the requirement to a period of not more than 18 months beginning with the day on which the requirement first had effect.

(3) The powers of amendment conferred by sub-paragraph (1) above do not include power—

(a) to insert in the supervision order, after the end of three months beginning with the date when the order was originally made, a requirement in pursuance of paragraph 6 of Schedule 6 to this Act (treatment for mental condition), unless it is in substitution for such a requirement already included in the order;

(b) [*repealed by* Anti-social Behaviour Act 2003, s.88, and Sched. 2, para. 6(3)(b)].

(4) Where an application under sub-paragraph (1) above for the revocation of a supervision order is dismissed, no further application for its revocation shall be made under that sub-paragraph by any person during the period of three months beginning with the date of the dismissal except with the consent of a court having jurisdiction to entertain such an application.

Amendment of order on report of medical practitioner

6.—(1) If a medical practitioner by whom or under whose direction an offender is being treated for his mental condition in pursuance of a requirement included in a supervision order by virtue of paragraph 6 of Schedule 6 to this Act—

    (a) is unwilling to continue to treat or direct the treatment of the offender, or

    (b) is of the opinion mentioned in sub-paragraph (2) below,

the practitioner shall make a report in writing to that effect to the supervisor.

    (2) The opinion referred to in sub-paragraph (1) above is—

      (a) that the treatment of the offender should be continued beyond the period specified in that behalf in the order;

      (b) that the offender needs different treatment;

      (c) that the offender is not susceptible to treatment; or

      (d) that the offender does not require further treatment.

    (3) On receiving a report under sub-paragraph (1) above the supervisor shall refer it to a relevant court; and on such a reference the court may make an order cancelling or varying the requirement.

    (4) Sub-paragraph (3) above has effect subject to paragraphs 7 to 9 below.

Presence of offender in court, remands etc.

5-376   7.—(1) Where the supervisor makes an application or reference under paragraph 2(1), 5(1) or 6(3) above to a court he may bring the offender before the court; and, subject to sub-paragraph (9) below, a court shall not make an order under paragraph 2, 5(1) or 6(3) above unless the offender is present before the court.

    (2) Without prejudice to any power to issue a summons or warrant apart from this sub-paragraph, a justice may issue a summons or warrant for the purpose of securing the attendance of an offender before the court to which any application or reference in respect of him is made under paragraph 2(1), 5(1) or 6(3) above.

    (3) Subsections (3) and (4) of section 55 of the *Magistrates' Courts Act* 1980 (which among other things restrict the circumstances in which a warrant may be issued) shall apply with the necessary modifications to a warrant under sub-paragraph (2) above as they apply to a warrant under that section, but as if in subsection (3) after the word "summons" there were inserted the words "cannot be served or".

    (4) Where the offender is arrested in pursuance of a warrant issued by virtue of sub-paragraph (2) above and cannot be brought immediately before the court referred to in that sub-paragraph, the person in whose custody he is—

      (a) may make arrangements for his detention in a place of safety for a period of not more than 72 hours from the time of the arrest (and it shall be lawful for him to be detained in pursuance of the arrangements); and

      (b) shall within that period, unless within it the offender is brought before the court referred to in sub-paragraph (2) above, bring him before a justice;

and in paragraph (a) above "place of safety" has the same meaning as in the *Children and Young Persons Act* 1933.

    (5) Where an offender is brought before a justice under sub-paragraph (4)(b) above, the justice may—

      (a) direct that he be released forthwith; or

      (b) subject to sub-paragraph (7) below, remand him to local authority accommodation.

    (6) Subject to sub-paragraph (7) below, where an application is made to a youth court under paragraph 5(1) above, the court may remand (or further remand) the offender to local authority accommodation if—

      (a) a warrant has been issued under sub-paragraph (2) above for the purpose of securing the attendance of the offender before the court; or

      (b) the court considers that remanding (or further remanding) him will enable information to be obtained which is likely to assist the court in deciding whether and, if so, how to exercise its powers under paragraph 5(1) above.

    (7) Where the offender is aged 18 or over at the time when he is brought before a justice under sub-paragraph (4)(b) above, or is aged 18 or over at a time when (apart from this sub-paragraph) a youth court could exercise its powers under sub-paragraph (6) above in respect of him, he shall not be remanded to local authority accommodation but may instead be remanded—

      (a) *to a remand centre, if the justice or youth court has been notified that such a centre is available for the reception of persons under this sub-paragraph; or*

      (b) *to a prison, if the justice or youth court has not been so notified.*

    (8) A justice or court remanding a person to local authority accommodation under this paragraph shall designate, as the authority who are to receive him, the authority named in the supervision order.

(9) A court may make an order under paragraph 5(1) or 6(3) above in the absence of the offender if the effect of the order is confined to one or more of the following, that is to say—

(a) revoking the supervision order;

(b) cancelling a provision included in the supervision order in pursuance of Schedule 6 to, or section 63(6)(b) of, this Act;

(c) reducing the duration of the supervision order or any provision included in it in pursuance of that Schedule;

(d) altering in the supervision order the name of any area;

(e) changing the supervisor.

Restrictions on court's powers to revoke or amend order

8.—(1) A youth court shall not—   **5-377**

(a) exercise its powers under paragraph 5(1) above to make an order—

(i) revoking a supervision order, or

(ii) inserting in it a requirement authorised by Schedule 6 to this Act, or

(iii) varying or cancelling such a requirement,

except in a case where the court is satisfied that the offender either is unlikely to receive the care or control he needs unless the court makes the order or is likely to receive it notwithstanding the order;

(b) exercise its powers to make an order under paragraph 6(3) above except in such a case as is mentioned in paragraph (a) above;

(c) exercise its powers under paragraph 5(1) above to make an order inserting a requirement authorised by paragraph 6 of Schedule 6 to this Act in a supervision order which does not already contain such a requirement, unless the court is satisfied as mentioned in paragraph 6(1) of that Schedule on such evidence as is there mentioned.

(2) For the purposes of this paragraph "care" includes protection and guidance and "control" includes discipline.

9. Where the offender has attained the age of 14, then except with his consent a court shall not make an order under paragraph 5(1) or 6(3) above containing provisions—

(a) which insert in the supervision order a requirement authorised by paragraph 6 of Schedule 6 to this Act; or

(b) which alter such a requirement already included in the supervision order otherwise than by removing it or reducing its duration.

10. [*Copies of revoking or amending orders.*]

Appeals

11. The offender may appeal to the Crown Court against—   **5-378**

(a) any order made under paragraph 2(2), 5(1) or 6(3) above by a relevant court, except—

(i) an order made or which could have been made in the absence of the offender (by virtue of paragraph 7(9) above); and

(ii) an order containing only provisions to which the offender consented in pursuance of paragraph 9 above;

(b) the dismissal of an application under paragraph 5(1) above to revoke a supervision order.

Power of parent or guardian to make application on behalf of young person

12.—(1) Without prejudice to any power apart from this sub-paragraph to bring proceedings on   **5-379** behalf of another person, any power to make an application which is exercisable by a child or young person by virtue of paragraph 5(1) above shall also be exercisable on his behalf by his parent or guardian.

(2) In this paragraph "guardian" includes any person who was a guardian of the child or young person in question at the time when any supervision order to which the application relates was originally made.

[This schedule is printed as amended by the *CJCSA* 2000, s.74, and Sched. 7, para. 201(1) and (2)(a); the *Anti-social Behaviour Act* 2003, s.88, and Sched. 2, para. 6; and the *CJA* 2003, s.302, and Sched. 32, para. 128. The italicised words in para. 7(7) are omitted as from a day to be appointed: *CJCSA* 2000, s.74, and Sched. 7, para. 201(1) and (3). The paragraph number in square brackets in para. 2(1) was inserted by the *CJA* 2003, s.279, and Sched. 24, para. 7. As to the commencement of section 279 and Schedule 24 in certain areas on December 1, 2004, see *ante*, § 5–306. Subject to saving provisions (as to which, see §§ 5–1, 5–185, 5–186 in the main work), this schedule was repealed, with effect from November 30, 2009 (*Criminal Justice and Immigration Act 2008 (Commencement No. 13 and Transitory Provision) Order* 2009 (S.I. 2009 No. 3074)), by the *CJIA* 2008, ss.6(1) and 149, and Sched. 28, Pt 1.]

(3) Of youth rehabilitation orders

Criminal Justice and Immigration Act 2008, Sched. 2

Powers of magistrates' court

★5–382   As from a day to be appointed, paragraph 6(2)(a) of Schedule 2 to the 2008 Act is amended by the *Legal Aid, Sentencing and Punishment of Offenders Act* 2012, s.84(1) and (2), so as to substitute for sub-paragraphs (i) and (ii), "£2,500".

★   As from a day to be appointed, paragraph 6 of Schedule 2 to the 2008 Act is further amended by the 2012 Act, s.83(2), so as to insert (i) at the beginning of sub-paragraph (6), the words "Subject to sub-paragraph (6A),", and (ii) new sub-paragraphs (6A) to (6D), as follows—

"(6A) When imposing a requirement under sub-paragraph (2)(b), the court may amend the order to substitute a later date for that specified under paragraph 32(1) of Schedule 1.

(6B) A date substituted under sub-paragraph (6A)—

(a) may not fall outside the period of six months beginning with the date previously specified under paragraph 32(1) of Schedule 1;

(b) subject to that, may fall more than three years after the date on which the order took effect.

(6C) The power under sub-paragraph (6A) may not be exercised in relation to an order if that power or the power in paragraph 8(6A) has previously been exercised in relation to that order.

(6D) A date substituted under sub-paragraph (6A) is to be treated as having been specified in relation to the order under paragraph 32(1) of Schedule 1.".

Powers of Crown Court

★5–384   As from a day to be appointed, paragraph 8(2) of Schedule 2 to the 2008 Act is amended by the *Legal Aid, Sentencing and Punishment of Offenders Act* 2012, s.84(1) and (3), so as to substitute for sub-paragraphs (i) and (ii), "£2,500".

Power to amend amounts of fines

★5–385   As from a day to be appointed, paragraph 10 of Schedule 2 to the 2008 Act is amended by the *Legal Aid, Sentencing and Punishment of Offenders Act* 2012, s.84(4), so as (i) to omit "(i) or (ii)" in both places in sub-paragraph (1); (ii) to omit "(i) or (ii)" in both places in sub-paragraph (3)(a); and (iii) to substitute the words "section 84 of the *Legal Aid, Sentencing and Punishment of Offenders Act* 2012 came into force" for the words "this Act was passed".

Exercise of powers under paragraph 13(4) or 14(4): further provisions

★5–389   As from a day to be appointed, paragraph 16(1) of Schedule 2 to the 2008 Act is amended by the *Legal Aid, Sentencing and Punishment of Offenders Act* 2012, s.83(4), so as to insert at the beginning, the words "Subject to paragraph 16A".

★   As from a day to be appointed, a new paragraph 16A is inserted in Schedule 2 to the 2008 Act by the *Legal Aid, Sentencing and Punishment of Offenders Act* 2012, s.83(5), as follows—

"*Extension of order*

16A.—(1) The appropriate court may, on the application of the offender or the responsible officer, amend a youth rehabilitation order by substituting a later date for that specified under paragraph 32(1) of Schedule 1.

(2) A date substituted under sub-paragraph (1)—

(a) may not fall outside the period of six months beginning with the date previously specified under paragraph 32(1) of Schedule 1;

(b) subject to that, may fall more than three years after the date on which the order took effect.

(3) The power under sub-paragraph (1) may not be exercised in relation to an order if it has previously been exercised in relation to that order.

(4) A date substituted under sub-paragraph (1) is to be treated as having been specified in relation to the order under paragraph 32(1) of Schedule 1.

(5) In this paragraph 'the appropriate court' means—

(a) if the order was made by a youth court or other magistrates' court, or was made by the Crown Court and contains a direction under paragraph 36 of Schedule 1, the court determined under sub-paragraph (6), and

(b) if the order was made by the Crown Court and does not contain a direction under paragraph 36 of Schedule 1, the Crown Court.

(6) The court referred to in sub-paragraph (5)(a) is—

(a) if the offender is aged under 18 when the application is made, a youth court acting in the local justice area specified in the youth rehabilitation order, and

(b) if the offender is aged 18 or over at that time, a magistrates' court (other than a youth court) acting in that local justice area.".

VI. CUSTODIAL SENTENCES

A. MANDATORY LIFE SENTENCE

(2) Legislation

Criminal Justice Act 2003, ss.269, 270, 276, 277

Determination of minimum term in relation to mandatory life sentence

As from a day to be appointed, section 269 of the 2003 Act is amended by the *Legal Aid,* ★5–403
Sentencing and Punishment of Offenders Act 2012, s.110(1) and (10), so as (i) to substitute the words "section 240ZA (crediting periods of remand in custody) or of any direction which it would have given under section 240A (crediting periods of remand on certain types of bail)" for the words from "any direction which it would have given" to "certain types of condition)" in subsection (3)(b), and (ii) to insert a new subsection (3A), as follows—

"(3A) The reference in subsection (3)(b) to section 240ZA includes section 246 of the *Armed Forces Act* 2006 (crediting periods in service custody).".

These amendments apply in relation (i) to any person who falls to be released under Chapter 6 of Part 12 of the 2003 Act on or after the date on which section 110 comes into force (so far as they relate to section 240ZA of the 2003 Act), and (ii) to any person who is sentenced on or after that date (so far as they relate to section 240A of the 2003 Act): 2012 Act, s.120, and Sched. 15, paras 2(1) and 3.

Fixing the minimum term

The whole life starting point

R. v. Bieber and Kafkaris v. Cyprus (as to both of which, see the main work) were further **5–406**
considered in *Vinter v. U.K., post,* § 16–40.

The 25-year starting point and taking a knife or other weapon to the scene

R. v. Kelly is now reported at [2012] 1 Cr.App.R.(S.) 56. **5–410**

Youthfulness/ the prescribed starting points/ disparity

R. v. Miah is now reported at [2012] 1 Cr.App.R.(S.) 11, *sub nom. R. v. Miah and Choudhury.* **5–412**

Starting points generally

R. v. Kelly is now reported at [2012] 1 Cr.App.R.(S.) 56. **5–414**

Mitigating factors

★**5–416** *Att.-Gen.'s Reference (No. 23 of 2011)* is now reported at [2012] 1 Cr.App.R.(S.) 45, *sub nom. Att.-Gen.'s Reference (No. 23 of 2011) (R. v. Sanchez Williams)*.

Duty to give reasons

★**5–420** As from a day to be appointed, section 270 of the 2003 Act is amended by the *Legal Aid, Sentencing and Punishment of Offenders Act* 2012, s.64(1) and (3)(a), so as to substitute a new subsection (1), as follows—

"(1) Subsection (2) applies where a court makes an order under or (4).".

★ As from a day to be appointed, section 270(2) of the 2003 Act is amended by the 2012, s.64(1) and (3)(b), so as to substitute the words "In complying with the duty under section 174(2) to state its reasons for deciding on the order made," for the words "In stating its reasons".

Crime (Sentences) Act 1997, s.34

★**5–424** As from a day to be appointed, section 34(2)(d) of the *C(S)A* 1997 is amended by the *Legal Aid, Sentencing and Punishment of Offenders Act* 2012, s.117(10)(b), so as to insert the words "or detention in a young offender institution" after the words "a sentence of imprisonment".

★ As from a day to be appointed, the modification of section 34(2)(d) of the 1997 Act effected by the *Criminal Justice Act 2003 (Sentencing) (Transitory Provisions) Order* 2005 (S.I. 2005 No. 643) is revoked by the *Legal Aid, Sentencing and Punishment of Offenders Act* 2012, s.117(11).

Criminal Justice Act 2003, Sched. 21

Determination of minimum term in relation to mandatory life sentence

★**5–425** As from a day to be appointed, Schedule 21 to the *CJA* 2003 is amended by the *Legal Aid, Sentencing and Punishment of Offenders Act* 2012, s.65(1), (7) and (8), so as to substitute a new paragraph (3), as follows—

"3. For the purposes of this Schedule—
   (a) an offence is aggravated by sexual orientation if it is committed in circumstances mentioned in section 146(2)(a)(i) or (b)(i);
   (b) an offence is aggravated by disability if it is committed in circumstances mentioned in section 146(2)(a)(ii) or (b)(ii);
   (c) an offence is aggravated by transgender identity if it is committed in circumstances mentioned in section 146(2)(a)(iii) or (b)(iii).".

★**5–426** As from a day to be appointed, Schedule 21(5) to the *CJA* 2003 is amended by the *Legal Aid, Sentencing and Punishment of Offenders Act* 2012, s.65(1), (7) and (9), so as to insert the words ", disability or transgender identity" after the words "aggravated by sexual orientation" in sub-paragraph (2)(g).

Criminal Justice Act 2003, Sched. 22, paras 1, 2, 9 and 10

Section 276   SCHEDULE 22

Mandatory Life Sentences: Transitional Cases

Interpretation

5–428 1. In this Schedule—
   "the commencement date" means the day on which section 269 comes into force;
   "the early release provisions" means the provisions of section 28(5) to (8) of the *Crime (Sentences) Act* 1997;
   "existing prisoner" means a person serving one or more mandatory life sentences passed before the commencement date (whether or not he is also serving any other sentence);

"life sentence" means a sentence of imprisonment for life or custody for life passed in England and Wales or by a court-martial outside England and Wales;

"mandatory life sentence" means a life sentence passed in circumstances where the sentence was fixed by law.

Existing prisoners notified by Secretary of State

2. Paragraph 3 applies in relation to any existing prisoner who, in respect of any mandatory life sentence, has before the commencement date been notified in writing by the Secretary of State (otherwise than in a notice that is expressed to be provisional) either— **5–429**

   (a) of a minimum period which in the view of the Secretary of State should be served before the prisoner's release on licence, or

   (b) that the Secretary of State does not intend that the prisoner should ever be released on licence.

Sentences passed on or after commencement date in respect of offences committed before that date

9. Paragraph 10 applies where— **5–430**

   (a) on or after the commencement date a court passes a life sentence in circumstances where the sentence is fixed by law, and

   (b) the offence to which the sentence relates was committed before the commencement date.

10. The court—

   (a) may not make an order under subsection (2) of section 269 specifying a part of the sentence which in the opinion of the court is greater than that which, under the practice followed by the Secretary of State before December 2002, the Secretary of State would have been likely to notify as mentioned in paragraph 2(a), and

   (b) may not make an order under subsection (4) of section 269 unless the court is of the opinion that, under the practice followed by the Secretary of State before December 2002, the Secretary of State would have been likely to give the prisoner a notification falling within paragraph 2(b).

(3) Practice

Practice Direction (Criminal Proceedings: Consolidation), para. IV.49.14–IV.49.37 (as substituted by Practice Direction (Crime: Mandatory Life Sentences) (No. 2) [2004] 1 W.L.R. 2551

Transitional arrangements for new sentences where the offence was committed before 18 December 2003

IV.49.14 Where the court is passing a sentence of mandatory life imprisonment for an offence committed before 18 December 2003, the court should take a fourth step in determining the minimum term in accordance with section 276 and Schedule 22 ... . **5–432**

IV.49.15 The purpose of those provisions is to ensure that the sentence does not breach the principle of non-retroactivity by ensuring that a lower minimum term would not have been imposed for the offence when it was committed. Before setting the minimum term the court must check whether the proposed term is greater than that which the term [*sic*] the Secretary of State would probably have notified under the practice followed by the Secretary of State before December 2002.

IV.49.16 The decision in *Sullivan* ... gives detailed guidance as to the correct approach to this practice and judges passing mandatory life sentences where the murder was committed prior to 18 December 2003 are well advised to read that judgment before proceeding.

IV.49.17 The practical result of that judgment is that in sentences where the murder was committed before 31 May 2002, the best guide to what would have been the practice of the Secretary of State is the letter sent to judges by Lord Bingham C.J. on 10th February 1997, the relevant parts of which are set out at paras IV.49.18 to IV.49.21 below.

IV.49.18 The practice of Lord Bingham, as set out in his letter ... was to take 14 years as the period actually to be served for the "average", "normal" or "unexceptional" murder. Examples of factors he outlined as capable, in appropriate cases, of mitigating the normal penalty were:

   Youth.

   Age (where relevant to physical capacity on release or the likelihood of the defendant dying in prison).

Subnormality or mental abnormality.

Provocation (in a non-technical sense), or an excessive response to a personal threat.

The absence of an intention to kill.

Spontaneity and lack of premeditation (beyond that necessary to constitute the offence: *e.g.* a sudden response to family pressure or to prolonged and eventually unsupportable stress).

Mercy killing.

A plea of guilty, or hard evidence of remorse or contrition.

IV.49.19 Lord Bingham then listed the following factors as likely to call for a sentence more severe than the norm:

Evidence of a planned, professional, revenge or contract killing.

The killing of a child or a very old or otherwise vulnerable victim.

Evidence of sadism, gratuitous violence, or sexual maltreatment, humiliation or degradation before the killing.

Killing for gain (in the course of burglary, robbery, blackmail, insurance fraud, etc.).

Multiple killings.

The killing of a witness or potential witness to defeat the ends of justice.

The killing of those doing their public duty (policemen, prison officers, postmasters, firemen, judges, etc).

Terrorist or politically motivated killings.

The use of firearms or other dangerous weapons, whether carried for defensive or offensive reasons.

A substantial record of serious violence.

Macabre attempts to dismember or conceal the body.

IV.49.20 Lord Bingham further stated that the fact that a defendant was under the influence of drink or drugs at the time of the killing is so common he would be inclined to treat it as neutral. But in the not unfamiliar case in which a married couple, or two derelicts, or two homosexuals, inflamed by drink, indulge in a violent quarrel in which one dies, often against a background of long-standing drunken violence, then he would tend to recommend a term somewhat below the norm.

IV.49.21 Lord Bingham went on to say that given the intent necessary for proof of murder, the consequences of taking life and the understandable reaction of relatives of the deceased, a substantial term will almost always be called for, save perhaps in a truly venial case of mercy killing. While a recommendation of a punitive term longer than, say, 30 years will be very rare indeed, there should not be any upper limit. Some crimes will certainly call for terms very well in excess of the norm.

5–433   **IV.49.22** For the purposes of sentences where the murder was committed after 31 May 2002 and before 18 December 2003, the judge should apply the practice statement handed down on 31 May 2002 reproduced at paras 49.23 to 49.33 below.

IV.49.23 This statement replaces the previous single normal tariff of 14 years by substituting: a higher and a normal starting point of respectively 16 (comparable to 32 years) and 12 years (comparable to 24 years). These starting points have then to be increased or reduced because of aggravating or mitigating factors such as those referred to below. It is emphasised that they are no more than starting points.

The normal starting point of 12 years

5–434   **IV.49.24** Cases falling within this starting point will normally involve the killing of an adult victim, arising from a quarrel or loss of temper between two people known to each other. It will not have the characteristics referred to in paragraph 49.26. Exceptionally, the starting point may be reduced because of the sort of circumstances described in the next paragraph.

IV.49.25 The normal starting point can be reduced because the murder is one where the offender's culpability is significantly reduced, for example, because: the case came close to the borderline between murder and manslaughter; or the offender suffered from mental disorder, or from a mental disability which lowered the degree of his criminal responsibility for the killing, although not affording a defence of diminished responsibility; or the offender was provoked (in a non-technical sense), such as by prolonged and eventually unsupportable stress; or the case involved an over reaction in self-defence; or the offence was a mercy killing. These factors could justify a reduction to 8/9 years (equivalent to 16/18 years).

The higher starting point of 15/16 years

5–435   **IV.49.26** The higher starting point will apply to cases where the offender's culpability was exceptionally high or the victim was in a particularly vulnerable position. Such cases will be characterised by a feature which makes the crime especially serious, such as: the killing was "professional" or a contract killing; the killing was politically motivated; the killing was done for gain (in the course of a burglary, robbery etc.); the killing was intended to defeat the ends of justice (as in the killing of a witness or potential witness); the victim was providing a public service; the victim was a child or was otherwise vulnerable; the killing was racially aggravated; the victim was deliberately targeted because of his or her sexual orientation; there was evidence of sadism, gratuitous violence or sexual maltreatment, humiliation or degradation of the victim before the killing; extensive and/or multiple injuries were inflicted on the victim before death; the offender committed multiple murders.

Variation of the starting point

IV.49.27 Whichever starting point is selected in a particular case, it may be appropriate for the trial judge to vary the starting point upwards or downwards, to take account of aggravating or mitigating factors, which relate to either the offence or the offender, in the particular case.   **5–436**

IV.49.28 Aggravating factors relating to the offence can include: the fact that the killing was planned; the use of a firearm; arming with a weapon in advance; concealment of the body, destruction of the crime scene and/or dismemberment of the body; particularly in domestic violence cases, the fact that the murder was the culmination of cruel and violent behaviour by the offender over a period of time.

IV.49.29 Aggravating factors relating to the offender will include the offender's previous record and failures to respond to previous sentences, to the extent that this is relevant to culpability rather than to risk.

IV.49.30 Mitigating factors relating to the offence will include: an intention to cause grievous bodily harm, rather than to kill; spontaneity and lack of pre-meditation.

IV.49.31 Mitigating factors relating to the offender may include: the offender's age; clear evidence of remorse or contrition; a timely plea of guilt.

Very serious cases

IV.49.32 A substantial upward adjustment may be appropriate in the most serious cases, for example, those involving a substantial number of murders, or if there are several factors identified as attracting the higher starting point present. In suitable cases, the result might even be a minimum term of 30 years (equivalent to 60 years) which would offer little or no hope of the offender's eventual release. In cases of exceptional gravity, the judge, rather than setting a whole life minimum term, can state that there is no minimum period which could properly be set in that particular case.   **5–437**

IV.49.33 Among the categories of case referred to in paragraph IV.49.26 some offences may be especially grave. These include cases where the victim was performing his duties as a prison officer at the time of the crime or the offence was a terrorist or sexual or sadistic murder or involved a young child. In such a case, a term of 20 years and upwards could be appropriate.

IV.49.34 In following this guidance, judges should bear in mind the conclusion of the court in *Sullivan* that the general effect of both these statements is the same. While Lord Bingham does not identify as many starting points, it is open to the judge to come to exactly the same decision irrespective of which was followed. Both pieces of guidance give the judge a considerable degree of discretion.

Procedure for announcing the minimum term in open court

IV.49.35 Having gone through the three or four steps outlined above, the court is then under a duty under section 270 of the Act, to state in open court, in ordinary language, its reasons for deciding on the minimum term or for passing a whole life order.   **5–438**

IV.49.36 In order to comply with this duty the court should state clearly the minimum term it has determined. In doing so, it should state which of the starting points it has chosen and its reasons for doing so. Where the court has departed from that starting point due to mitigating or aggravating features it must state the reasons for that departure and any aggravating or mitigating features which have led to that departure. At that point the court should also declare how much, if any, time is being deducted for time spent in custody. The court must then explain that the minimum term is the minimum amount of time the prisoner will spend in prison, from the date of sentence, before the Parole Board can order early release. If it remains necessary for the protection of the public, the prisoner will continue to be detained after that date. The court should also state that where the prisoner has served the minimum term and the Parole Board has decided to direct release the prisoner will remain on licence for the rest of his life and may be recalled to prison at any time.

IV.49.37 Where the offender was 21 or over when he committed the offence and the court considers that the seriousness of the offence is so exceptionally high that a "whole life order" is appropriate, the court should state clearly its reasons for reaching this conclusion. It should also explain that the early release provisions will not apply.

As to the authority referred to in IV.49.16, see *R. v. Sullivan*; *R. v. Gibbs*; *R. v. Elener (Barry) and Elener (Derek)* [2005] 1 Cr.App.R. 3, CA.

B. Automatic Life Sentences

Powers of Criminal Courts (Sentencing) Act 2000, s.109

Life sentence for second serious offence

5–440   **109.**—(1) This section applies where—

    (a) a person is convicted of a serious offence committed after 30th September 1997; and

    (b) at the time when that offence was committed, he was 18 or over and had been convicted in any part of the United Kingdom of another serious offence.

    (2) The court shall impose a life sentence, that is to say—

      (a) *where the offender is 21 or over when convicted of the offence mentioned in subsection (1)(a) above, a sentence of imprisonment for life,*

      (b) *where he is under 21 at that time, a sentence of custody for life under section 94 above,*

[a sentence of imprisonment for life] unless the court is of the opinion that there are exceptional circumstances relating to either of the offences or to the offender which justify its not doing so.

    (3) Where the court does not impose a life sentence, it shall state in open court that it is of that opinion and what the exceptional circumstances are.

    (4) An offence the sentence for which is imposed under *subsection (2)* above shall not be regarded as an offence the sentence for which is fixed by law.

    (5) An offence committed in England and Wales is a serious offence for the purposes of this section if it is any of the following, namely—

      (a) an attempt to commit murder, a conspiracy to commit murder or an incitement to murder;

      (b) an offence under section 4 of the *Offences Against the Person Act* 1861 (soliciting murder);

      (c) manslaughter;

      (d) an offence under section 18 of the *Offences Against the Person Act* 1861 (wounding, or causing grievous bodily harm, with intent);

      (e) rape or an attempt to commit rape;

      (f) an offence under section 5 of the *Sexual Offences Act* 1956 (intercourse with a girl under 13);

      (g) an offence under section 16 (possession of a firearm with intent to injure), section 17 (use of a firearm to resist arrest) or section 18 (carrying a firearm with criminal intent) of the *Firearms Act* 1968; and

      (h) robbery where, at some time during the commission of the offence, the offender had in his possession a firearm or imitation firearm within the meaning of that Act.

    (6) An offence committed in Scotland is a serious offence for the purposes of this section if the conviction for it was obtained on indictment in the High Court of Justiciary and it is any of the following, namely—

      (a) culpable homicide;

      (b) attempted murder, incitement to commit murder or conspiracy to commit murder;

      (c) rape or attempted rape;

      (d) clandestine injury to women or an attempt to cause such injury;

      (e) sodomy, or an attempt to commit sodomy, where the complainer, that is to say, the person against whom the offence was committed, did not consent;

      (f) assault where the assault—

        (i) is aggravated because it was carried out to the victim's severe injury or the danger of the victim's life; or

        (ii) was carried out with an intention to rape or to ravish the victim;

      (g) robbery where, at some time during the commission of the offence, the offender had in his possession a firearm or imitation firearm within the meaning of the *Firearms Act* 1968;

      (h) an offence under section 16 (possession of a firearm with intent to injure), section 17 (use of a firearm to resist arrest) or section 18 (carrying a firearm with criminal intent) of that Act;

      (i) lewd, libidinous or indecent behaviour or practices; and

      (j) an offence under section 5(1) of the *Criminal Law (Consolidation) (Scotland) Act* 1995 (unlawful intercourse with a girl under 13).

    (7) An offence committed in Northern Ireland is a serious offence for the purposes of this section if it is any of the following, namely—

      (a) an offence falling within any of paragraphs (a) to (e) of subsection (5) above;

      (b) an offence under section 4 of the *Criminal Law Amendment Act* 1885 (intercourse with a girl under 14);

(c) an offence under Article 17 (possession of a firearm with intent to injure), Article 18(1) (use of a firearm to resist arrest) or Article 19 (carrying a firearm with criminal intent) of the *Firearms (Northern Ireland) Order* 1981; and

(d) robbery where, at some time during the commission of the offence, the offender had in his possession a firearm or imitation firearm within the meaning of that Order.

[This section is printed as amended, as from a day to be appointed, by the *CJCSA* 2000, s.74, and Sched. 7, para. 189 (substitution of words in square brackets for paras (a) and (b) in subs. (2)). It is repealed, as from April 4, 2005 (*Criminal Justice Act 2003 (Commencement No. 8 and Transitional and Saving Provisions) Order* 2005 (S.I. 2005 No. 950), by the *CJA* 2003, s.332, and Sched. 37 Pt 7. For the saving provisions in relation to an offence committed before April 4, 2005, see § 5–2 in the main work.]

Serious offences

The only attempts which are serious offences are those specifically mentioned: *R. v. Buck-* **5–441**
land; *R. v. Newman* [2000] 1 Cr.App.R. 471, CA. Offences under the *Firearms Act* 1968, s.17(2) are serious offences: *ibid.*; as are offences under sections 16, 17 and 18 of that Act where the firearm was an imitation only: *ibid.*

An offence of robbery is a "serious offence" within section 109(2)(h) if the offence was committed as a joint enterprise where a firearm or imitation was used, even though the offender himself had never had possession of it, provided that there was joint possession of it; where, in relation to the alleged index offence, there is an issue as to whether this was established against the offender, the court must be satisfied that at the earlier hearing the offender admitted, or it was admitted on his behalf, that he was in joint possession of the firearm: *R. v. Flamson* [2002] 2 Cr.App.R.(S.) 48, CA. The court considered that *R. v. Eubank* [2002] 1 Cr.App.R.(S.) 4, CA (§ 24–49 in the main work) had no application to the facts of the case. In *R. v. Murphy* [2003] 1 Cr.App.R.(S.) 39, CA, however, it was held, without reference to *Flamson*, that where there was an issue as to whether the defendant had been in possession of a firearm, the proper way to resolve the issue was, in accordance with *Eubank*, for an appropriate count under the *Firearms Act* 1968 to be included in the indictment. Where this course had not been adopted, it was not open to the judge to conclude in relation to either the index offence or the fresh offence that it fell within section 109(1)(h); absent an unequivocal admission on the part of the defendant (see *R. v. Benfield*; *R. v. Sobers* [2004] 1 Cr.App.R.(S.) 52, CA).

R. v. Benfield; *R. v. Sobers* was followed in *R. v. Hylands* [2005] 2 Cr.App.R.(S.) 25, CA, where it was said that for an offence of robbery to fall within section 109(5)(h) of the 2000 Act, the qualifying condition relating to a firearm or imitation firearm had to be established either by means of an appropriate count under the *Firearms Act* 1968 being included in the indictment, or there had to be an unequivocal admission in relation thereto; and this applies where the only issue in relation to the robbery is identity (there being unchallenged evidence before the jury that the robber was in possession of a firearm at the time of the robbery); if there was any doubt about the matter, it was to be resolved in favour of the defendant.

As to whether a conviction at a court-martial in Germany for an offence of wounding with intent to cause grievous bodily harm committed whilst a serving member of the armed forces in Germany may qualify as a "serious offence" within the meaning of section 109(1)(a) of the *PCC(S)A* 2000, see *R. v. Sanders*, *post*, § 5–447.

"exceptional circumstances"

The meaning of "exceptional circumstances" (s.109(2)) was reconsidered in *R. v. Offen* **5–442**
[2001] 1 W.L.R. 253, CA. Lord Woolf C.J. said that quite apart from the impact of the *Human Rights Act* 1998, the rationale of the section should be highly relevant in deciding whether or not exceptional circumstances existed. The question whether circumstances were appropriately regarded as "exceptional" must be influenced by the context in which the question was being asked. The policy and intention of Parliament were to protect the public against a person who had committed two serious offences. It therefore could be as-

sumed that the section was not intended to apply to someone in relation to whom it was established that there would be no need for protection in the future. In other words, if the facts showed the statutory assumption was misplaced, then this, in the statutory context, was not the normal situation and in consequence, for the purposes of the section, the position was exceptional. The time that elapsed between the two offences could, but would not necessarily, reflect on whether, after the second serious offence was committed, there was any danger against which the public would need protection. The same was true of two differing offences, and the age of the offender. These were all circumstances which could give rise to the conclusion that what could be normal and not exceptional in a different context was exceptional in this context. If this approach was not adopted, then in the case of the serious offences listed in the section, the gravity of which could vary greatly, the approach to "exceptional circumstances" could be unduly restrictive. The aim of section 2 was not to increase the time offenders spent in prison as a punishment for the offence they had committed, but to provide for an assessment to be made to see whether the offender posed a real risk to the public, in which event his release was deferred. Section 109 established a norm. The norm was that those who commit two serious offences were a danger or risk to the public. If in fact, taking into account all the circumstances relating to a particular offender, he did not create an unacceptable risk to the public, he was an exception to this norm.

Construing section 109 in accordance with the duty imposed on the court by section 3 of the 1998 Act, and taking into account the rationale of the section, gave content to "exceptional circumstances". In the court's judgment, section 109 would not contravene Convention rights if courts applied the section so that it did not result in offenders being sentenced to life imprisonment when they did not constitute a significant risk to the public. Whether there was a significant risk would depend on the evidence which was before the court. If the offender was a significant risk, the court could impose a life sentence under section 109 without contravening the Convention. It would be part of the responsibility of judges to assess the risk to the public that offenders constituted. In many cases the degree of risk that an offender constituted would be established by his record, with or without the assistance of assessments made in reports which were available to the court. If courts needed further assistance, they could call for it when deciding whether a discretionary life sentence should be imposed. There should be no undue difficulty in making a similar assessment when considering whether the court was required to impose an automatic life sentence, although the task would not be straightforward, because of the lack of information as to the first serious offence which will sometimes exist because of the passage of time. This did not mean that the court was approaching the passing of an automatic life sentence as if it was no different from the imposition of a discretionary life sentence. Notwithstanding the interpretation resulting from the application of section 3(1) of the 1998 Act suggested, section 109 would give effect to the intention of Parliament. It would do so, however, in a more just, less arbitrary and more proportionate manner. Section 109 would still mean that a judge was obliged to pass a life sentence in accordance with its terms unless, in all the circumstances, the offender posed no significant risk to the public. There was no such obligation in cases where section 109 did not apply. In addition, if the judge decided not to impose a life sentence under section 109, he would have to give reasons as required by section 109(3). Furthermore, the issue of dangerousness would have to be addressed in every case and a decision made as to whether or not to impose a life sentence.

Offen has since been applied in *R. v. McDonald* [2001] 2 Cr.App.R.(S.) 127, CA (having regard, in particular, to the length of time since the appellant's conviction for his previous "serious" offences (14 years) and to the fact that it was not the appellant but a co-defendant who had produced an imitation firearm in the course of the robbery, although it belonged to the appellant, it would be wrong to conclude that the appellant presented a serious risk of harm to the public so as to justify the imposition of an automatic life sentence); and in *R. v. Kelly (No. 2)* [2002] 1 Cr.App.R.(S.) 85, CA, it was held that the statutory presumption that arises under section 109(2), and which flows from the existence of two qualifying offences remains in place, and has to be displaced by the defendant in any given case; and such displacement may be achieved in a number of ways, including scrutiny of the offending and behaviour pattern, or by positive psychiatric or similar evidence, such evidence being likely to be required if the court is to be persuaded that the presumption cannot apply since the criterion to be established is that there is "no need to protect the public in the future" or "no significant risk to the public".

In *R. v. Baff* [2003] 2 Cr.App.R.(S.) 37, CA, it was said that the use of imitation firearms for the purpose of robbery caused as much fear and alarm to vulnerable members of the public as robbery with a real firearm; and that, if the court were to rule that section 109 did not as a matter of principle apply where the offender limited his offending to robberies with an imitation firearm, it would be creating an exception to an express provision flatly contradicting an aspect of sentencing policy laid down by Parliament.

In *R. v. Richards* [2002] 2 Cr.App.R.(S.) 26, CA, it was held that in considering whether a defendant who qualifies for an automatic life sentence under section 109 presents a significant risk to the public, the judge may take account of a significant risk of the commission of serious offences other than those listed as "serious" in the section itself, for example, burglaries of dwellings or a conspiracy to import hard drugs. For a criticism of this decision, see the commentary in the *Criminal Law Review*. It is inconsistent with the view of the court in *R. v. Fletcher*; *R. v. Smith* [2002] 1 Cr.App.R.(S.) 82, CA, to the effect that the "danger in point is that of violent or sexual offending."

Richards was not cited in *R. v. Stark* [2002] 2 Cr.App.R.(S.) 104, CA, where there was a high risk of further offences being committed by the appellant, but no significant risk of danger to the public by way of either violent or sexual offences; accordingly, it was held that the case was to be regarded as an exception to the norm, which was that those who committed two serious offences were a danger or risk to the public.

The approach in *R. v. Stark* and *R. v. Fletcher*; *R. v. Smith* was followed, and that in *Richards* expressly disapproved in *R. v. Magalhaes* [2005] 2 Cr.App.R.(S.) 13, CA.

In *R. v. Frost* [2001] 2 Cr.App.R.(S.) 26, CA, the appellant had been found guilty by a youth court in 1991 of wounding with intent to resist arrest. He was later convicted of wounding with intent to cause grievous bodily harm. The court held that the finding of guilt by the youth court amounted to a "conviction" for the purposes of *PCC(S)A* 2000, s.109(1), by virtue of the *CYPA* 1933, s.59. If the appellant had been older and had been subject to a probation order, the "conviction" would have been deemed not to be a conviction by virtue of the *PCCA* 1973, s.13(1) (*rep.*), but this provision did not apply to a supervision order. The anomaly which resulted from this amounted to an "exceptional circumstance" for the purposes of section 109, and the sentence of life imprisonment was quashed, even though it could not be said that the offender presented no significant risk to the public.

The fact that the offender is mentally ill and eligible for a hospital order does not in itself amount to an "exceptional circumstance" for this purpose: see *R. v. Newman* [2000] 2 Cr.App.R.(S.) 227, CA; *R. v. Drew* [2003] 2 Cr.App.R. 24, HL (where a submission that an automatic life sentence on conviction of wounding with intent constituted inhuman or degrading treatment was rejected; having been transferred administratively to hospital within a few days of the passing of sentence, the appellant was receiving the same treatment as he would have received had he been made subject to a hospital order, and he could not complain of the stigma attaching to the sentence as he had been convicted by a jury, who must therefore have been satisfied as to his intent).

On appeal, the issue is whether the offender created an unacceptable risk to the public at the time when he was sentenced, not at the time when the Court of Appeal is considering the matter: see *R. v. Watkins* [2003] 1 Cr.App.R.(S.) 16, CA; *R. v. Noorkoiv* [2002] 2 Cr.App.R.(S.) 91, CA.

C. Minimum Fixed Term Sentences

(1) Legislation

Powers of Criminal Courts (Sentencing) Act 2000, ss.112–115

Offences under service law

5–447　　In *R. v. Sanders* [2007] 1 Cr.App.R.(S.) 74, CA, it was held that the effect of section 114 of the *PCC(S)A* 2000 was limited to deeming the conviction to have been in England and Wales; it did not deem the offence to have been committed in England and Wales; where, therefore, the appellant had previously been convicted of an offence under section 70 of the *Army Act* 1955 and the corresponding civil offence had been one of those listed in section 109(5), but the offence had been committed abroad, he was not to be regarded as having previously been convicted of a serious offence, since, under section 109(5), an offence would only be "serious" if committed in England and Wales; section 114 would bite only in relation to convictions under section 70 where the offence occurred in England and Wales. It should be noted that the repeal of the words "a serious offence" in section 114(1)(b) is of no effect where an offender is being dealt with for an offence committed prior to April 4, 2005.

(2) Practice

"unjust"

5–452　　*R. v. Sparkes* is now reported at [2011] 2 Cr.App.R.(S.) 107.

★　　While section 110 of the *PCC(S)A* 2000 can be harsh in its operation, that does not enable a court to treat perfectly normal circumstances as being "particular circumstances" in order to circumvent its operation; neither the fact that an offender had been nearly 16 at the time of his first relevant drug conviction and 18 at the time of the current Class A drug trafficking offence, nor that he had got sucked into gang culture and was forced to continue to deal in drugs to repay drug debts, could possibly entitle the court to disapply section 110: *R. v. Lucas* [2012] 2 Cr.App.R.(S.) 14, CA.

"exceptional circumstances" (1968 Act, s.51A(2))

5–453　　*R. v. Boateng* is now reported at [2011] 2 Cr.App.R.(S.) 104.

★　　For an example of a case in which the Court of Appeal found "exceptional circumstances", in accordance with section 51A(2) of the *Firearms Act* 1968 (§ 5–449 in the main work), for not imposing the minimum sentence on an offender convicted of being in possession of a prohibited weapon, together with ammunition for use in that weapon, see *R. v. Jones* [2012] 1 Cr.App.R.(S.) 25, CA (offender had been threatened and her will overborne at the time she took receipt of bag containing the weapon and ammunition, but she was not under duress 17 days later when the bag was found in her possession). For the suggestion that the offender was fortunate, and that the court's approach was out of line with that taken in *R. v. Edwards (Michelle Marie), Att.-Gen.'s Reference (No. 23 of 2009) (R. v. Merrion)* (as to both of which, see § 4–454 in the main work), and *R. v. Ocran* [2011] 1 Cr.App.R.(S.) 36, CA, see CLW/12/07/13.

★　　In *R. v. Brereton (Matthew)* [2012] Crim.L.R. 396, CA, where the offender fell to be dealt with for possession of a disguised stun gun, it was acknowledged by the court that there had been an inconsistent and potentially arbitrary policy as to whether to prosecute for the "greater" offence of possession of a disguised firearm (*Firearms Act* 1968, s.5(1A)(a) (§ 24–19 in the main work), subject to the five-year minimum sentence provisions in s.51A (*ibid.*, § 5–449)) or the "lesser" offence of possession of a weapon designed to discharge a noxious liquid, gas or other thing (s.5(1)(b)), or at the very least to accept a plea to the lesser offence by way of disposing of such a case. In the particular circumstances, the court said that the judge had been justified in reducing the minimum sentence by one year because of (i) "a lamentable series of switches of decision by the prosecution" from one position to the other, raising and then dashing the expectations of the offender on more than one occasion, and (ii) the inappropriate manner in which other offences had been dealt with. However, the court ruled that it would not be right, in the absence of a prosecution policy demonstrated to be arbitrary, to reduce the sentence to the level it would have been had the offender been convicted of the lesser offence. The court stressed that the case was confined to its own facts and should not be cited as a precedent on the application of the exceptionality test.

D. DISCRETIONARY CUSTODIAL SENTENCES

(1) General restrictions

(a) *Legislation*

Powers of Criminal Courts (Sentencing) Act 2000, s.76

Section 76(1) of the 2000 Act was amended (with effect from April 4, 2005: *Criminal*   ★**5–457**
Justice Act 2003 (Commencement No. 8 and Transitional and Saving Provisions) Order 2005
(S.I. 2005 No. 950)) by the *CJA* 2003, s.304, and Sched. 32, paras 90 and 108, so as to
insert new paragraphs (bb) and (bc) as follows—

> "(bb) a sentence of detention for public protection under section 226 of the *Criminal Justice Act*
>   2003;
>   (bc) a sentence of detention under section 228 of that Act;".

As from a day to be appointed, section 76(1)(bc) of the 2000 Act is amended by the *Legal*   ★
Aid, Sentencing and Punishment of Offenders Act 2012, s.126, and Sched. 21, paras 7 and 10,
so as to insert "226B or" after "section".

Criminal Justice Act 2003, ss.152, 153

General restrictions on imposing discretionary custodial sentences
As from a day to be appointed, section 152(1)(b) of the 2003 Act is amended by the *Legal*   ★**5–458**
Aid, Sentencing and Punishment of Offenders Act 2012, s.122(3), and Sched. 19, paras 8 and
11, so as to insert "224A," before "225(2)".

As from a day to be appointed, section 152(1)(b) of the 2003 Act is further amended by   ★
the 2012 Act, s.142(3), and Sched. 26, paras 15 and 20, so as to substitute the words "section
1A(5) of the *Prevention of Crime Act* 1953, under section 51A(2) of the *Firearms Act* 1968,
under section 139AA(7) of the *Criminal Justice Act* 1988," for the words "section 51A(2) of
the *Firearms Act* 1968,".

Length of discretionary custodial sentences: general provisions
As from a day to be appointed, section 153(1) of the 2003 Act is amended by the *Legal*   ★**5–459**
Aid, Sentencing and Punishment of Offenders Act 2012, s.122(3), and Sched. 19, paras 8 and
12, so as to insert "224A," before "225".

As from a day to be appointed, section 153(2) of the 2003 Act is amended by the 2012   ★
Act, s.126, and Sched. 21, paras 20 and 21, so as to substitute "226A(4) and 226B(2)" for
"227(2) and 228(2)".

As from a day to be appointed, section 153(2) of the 2003 Act is further amended by the   ★
2012 Act, s.142(3), and Sched. 26, paras 15 and 21, so as to substitute the words "section
1A(5) of the *Prevention of Crime Act* 1953, section 51A(2) of the *Firearms Act* 1968, section
139AA(7) of the *Criminal Justice Act* 1988," for the words "section 51A(2) of the *Firearms Act*
1968,".

(c) *Legislation (offences committed before April 4, 2005)*

Powers of Criminal Courts (Sentencing) Act 2000, ss.79, 80

General restrictions on imposing discretionary custodial sentences

5–469   **79.**—(1) This section applies where a person is convicted of an offence punishable with a custodial sentence other than one—

(a) fixed by law; or

(b) falling to be imposed under section 109(2), 110(2) *or* 111(2) below.

(2) Subject to subsection (3) below, the court shall not pass a custodial sentence on the offender unless it is of the opinion—

(a) that the offence, or the combination of the offence and one or more offences associated with it, was so serious that only such a sentence can be justified for the offence; or

(b) where the offence is a violent or sexual offence, that only such a sentence would be adequate to protect the public from serious harm from him.

(3) Nothing in subsection (2) above shall prevent the court from passing a custodial sentence on the offender if he fails to express his willingness to comply with—

(a) a requirement which is proposed by the court to be included in a community rehabilitation order or supervision order and which requires an expression of such willingness; or

(b) a requirement which is proposed by the court to be included in a drug treatment and testing order or an order under section 52(4) above (order to provide samples). In relation to an offence committed before 1st October 1997:

(4) Where a court passes a custodial sentence, it shall—

(a) in a case not falling within subsection (3) above, state in open court that it is of the opinion that either or both of paragraphs (a) and (b) of subsection (2) above apply and why it is of that opinion; and

(b) in any case, explain to the offender in open court and in ordinary language why it is passing a custodial sentence on him.

(5) A magistrates' court shall cause a reason stated by it under subsection (4) above to be specified in the warrant of commitment and to be entered in the register.

[This section is printed as amended by the *CJCSA* 2000, s.74 and Sched. 7, para. 1. It is repealed, as from April 4, 2005 (*Criminal Justice Act 2003 (Commencement No. 8 and Transitional and Saving Provisions) Order* 2005 (S.I. 2005 No. 950)), by the *CJA* 2003, s.332, and Sched. 37, Pt 7. As to the saving provision in relation to offences committed before April 4, 2005, see § 5–2 in the main work.]

In relation to an offence committed before October 1, 1997, see the transitional provision in Sched. 11, para. 4(d).

Length of discretionary custodial sentences: general provision.

5–470   **80.**—(1) This section applies where a court passes a custodial sentence other than one fixed by law or falling to be imposed under section 109(2) below.

(2) Subject to sections 110(2) and 111(2) below, the custodial sentence shall be—

(a) for such term (not exceeding the permitted maximum) as in the opinion of the court is commensurate with the seriousness of the offence, or the combination of the offence and one or more offences associated with it; or

(b) where the offence is a violent or sexual offence, for such longer term (not exceeding that maximum) as in the opinion of the court is necessary to protect the public from serious harm from the offender.

(3) Where the court passes a custodial sentence for a term longer than is commensurate with the seriousness of the offence, or the combination of the offence and one or more offences associated with it, the court shall—

(a) state in open court that it is of the opinion that subsection (2)(b) above applies and why it is of that opinion; and

(b) explain to the offender in open court and in ordinary language why the sentence is for such a term.

(4) A custodial sentence for an indeterminate period shall be regarded for the purposes of subsections (2) and (3) above as a custodial sentence for a term longer than any actual term.

(5) Subsection (3) above shall not apply in any case where the court passes a custodial sentence falling to be imposed under subsection (2) of section 110 or 111 below which is for the minimum term specified in that subsection.

[This section is repealed, as from April 4, 2005 (*Criminal Justice Act 2003 (Commencement No. 8 and Transitional and Saving Provisions) Order* 2005 (S.I. 2005 No. 950)), by the *CJA* 2003, s.332, and Sched. 37, Pt 7. As to the saving provision in relation to offences committed before April 4, 2005, see § 5–2 in the main work.]

Powers of Criminal Courts (Sentencing) Act 2000, s.161

Meaning of "associated offence", "sexual offence", "violent offence" and "protecting the public from serious harm".

161.—(1) [*See § 5–2 in the main work.*]   **5-471**

(2) In this Act, "sexual offence" means any of the following—

(f) an offence under the *Protection of Children Act* 1978;

(fa) an offence under section 3 of the *Sexual Offences (Amendment) Act* 2000;

(fa) an offence under any provision of Part 1 of the *Sexual Offences Act* 2003; except section 52, 53 or 71

(g) an offence under section 1 of the *Criminal Law Act* 1977; of conspiracy to commit any of the offences in paragraphs (a) to (f) above;

(h) an offence under section 1 of the *Criminal Attempts Act* 1981; of attempting to commit any of those offences;

(i) an offence of inciting another to commit any of those offences.

(3) In this Act, "violent offence" means an offence which leads, or is intended or likely to lead, to a person's death or to physical injury to a person, and includes an offence which is required to be charged as arson (whether or not it would otherwise fall within this definition).

(4) In this Act any reference, in relation to an offender convicted of a violent or sexual offence, to protecting the public from serious harm from him shall be construed as a reference to protecting members of the public from death or serious personal injury, whether physical or psychological, occasioned by further such offences committed by him.

[Subss. (2) to (4) are printed as amended and repealed in part, by the *Sexual Offences (Amendment) Act* 2000, s.6(1); and the *SOA* 2003, ss.139 and 140, and Sched. 6, para. 4 (insertion of second para. (fa) in subs. (2)), and Sched. 7 (repeal of subs. (2)(a)–(e), the failure to repeal the first para. (fa) being accounted for by the draftsman having overlooked the amendment made by the 2000 Act). The amendments effected by the 2003 Act took effect on May 1, 2004 (*Sexual Offences Act 2003 (Commencement) Order* 2004 (S.I. 2004 No. 874)). For the former provisions, which will continue to apply in relation to offences committed before that date (*Interpretation Act* 1978, s.16 (Appendix B–16)), see the 2004 edition of this work. Subss. (2) to (4) are repealed, as from April 4, 2005 (*Criminal Justice Act 2003 (Commencement No. 8 and Transitional and Saving Provisions) Order* 2005 (S.I. 2005 No. 950)), by the *CJA* 2003, s.332, and Sched. 7. As to the saving provision in relation to offences committed before April 4, 2005, see § 5–2 in the main work.]

"Violent" and "sexual" offences

Whether any particular offence is a violent offence depends on the facts of the individual   **5-472** offence. An offence which leads to or is intended to lead only to psychological injury is not a "violent offence" but it is not necessary that serious harm should have been caused (see *R. v. Robinson* [1994] 1 W.L.R. 168, CA). Nor does it have to be established that physical injury was a probability: *R. v. Szczerba* [2002] 2 Cr.App.R.(S.) 86, CA.

In *R. v. Cochrane*, 15 Cr.App.R.(S.) 708, CA, it was held that a robbery in which the victim was threatened with a knife was a "violent offence" as the incident could have resulted in injury, either accidentally or if the victim had resisted. See also *R. v. Bibby*, 16 Cr.App.R.(S.) 127, CA. For cases of robbery by persons armed with a firearm, see *R. v. Touriq Khan*, 16 Cr.App.R.(S.) 180, CA, *R. v. Palin*, 16 Cr.App.R.(S.) 888, CA, and *R. v. Baker* [2001] 1 Cr.App.R.(S.) 55, CA. An offence of threatening to kill which does not involve the infliction of physical injury will not normally be a "violent offence": see *R. v. Richart*, 16 Cr.App.R.(S.) 977, CA, *R. v. Ragg* [1996] 1 Cr.App.R.(S.) 176, CA and *R. v. Birch* [2002] 1 Cr.App.R.(S.) 129, CA; but see *R. v. Wilson* [1998] 1 Cr.App.R.(S.) 341, CA.

Attempted arson is "an offence which is required to be charged as arson" and is accordingly a "violent offence" within section 161(3): *R. v. Guirke* [1997] 1 Cr.App.R.(S.) 170, CA.

"Serious harm" (s.161(4) of the Act of 2000)

5–473   See § 5–495 in the main work.

The criterion of seriousness

5–474   For discussion of the relevant authorities in relation to section 79(1), see § 5–465 in the main work.

Sentences commensurate with the seriousness of the offence

5–475   For relevant considerations where a court is deciding what term of custody is commensurate with an offence or group of offences, see § 5–466 in the main work.

Longer than normal sentences

5–476   For the definitions of "sexual offence" and "violent offence", see section 161(2) and (3) of the *PCC(S)A* 2000 (*ante*, § 5–471); and for the authorities in relation thereto, see *ante*, § 5–472. For the construction of references to "protecting the public from serious harm", see section 161(4) of the 2000 Act (*ante*, § 5–471); and the authorities referred to at §§ 5–495 *et seq.* in the main work.

An isolated offence, however serious, will rarely be sufficient to justify a longer than normal sentence under section 80(2)(b), whether the offence is violent or sexual, or both: *R. v. Walsh*, 16 Cr.App.R.(S.) 204, CA; *R. v. Mumtaz Ali*, 16 Cr.App.R.(S.) 692, CA. A longer than commensurate sentence may be passed on an offender with no previous convictions: *R. v. Thomas*, 16 Cr.App.R.(S.) 616, CA.

A court deciding whether to draw the inference that the offender is likely to commit further violent or sexual offences may need to examine the circumstances of the current offence in some detail, going beyond what would be necessary if only a commensurate sentence were in issue: *R. v. Oudkerk*, 16 Cr.App.R.(S.) 172, CA. Equally, if the inference is to be based on a previous conviction, the court may need to examine the circumstances of that offence in detail: *R. v. Samuels*, 16 Cr.App.R.(S.) 856, CA.

An offender may satisfy the requirements of section 80(2)(b) even though the members of the public who are at risk from him are a small group, or possibly an individual: *R. v. Hashi*, 16 Cr.App.R.(S.) 121, CA. Where the offender's behaviour is directed at a small group of people, who can be protected from him by other means, a longer than commensurate sentence may not be justified: *R. v. Nicholas*, 15 Cr.App.R.(S.) 381, CA; *R. v. Swain*, 15 Cr.App.R.(S.) 765, CA; *R. v. L.*, 15 Cr.App.R.(S.) 501, CA.

In many cases the inference of dangerousness will be based in part on psychiatric evidence: *R. v. Lyons*, 15 Cr.App.R.(S.) 460, CA; *R. v. Fawcett*, 16 Cr.App.R.(S.) 55, CA; *R. v. Etchells* [1996] 1 Cr.App.R.(S.) 163, CA.

The principles which should be applied in deciding the length of a longer than commensurate sentence were considered in *R. v. Mansell*, 15 Cr.App.R.(S.) 771, CA; and *R. v. Crow; R. v. Pennington*, 16 Cr.App.R.(S.) 409, CA. Lord Taylor C.J. said that some allowance should usually be made, even in the worst cases, for a plea of guilty. A sentence imposed under section 80(2)(b), whilst long enough to give necessary protection for the public, should still bear a reasonable relationship to the offence for which it was imposed.

This principle was not applied in *R. v. Chapman* [2000] 1 Cr.App.R. 77, CA, where it was said that there was no necessary ratio between the part of the sentence intended to punish and the part intended to protect. There was no objection in principle if the court regarded a sentence of two years as necessary to punish, but an additional term of six or eight years as necessary to protect, making a total term of eight or 10 years. *Chapman* was followed in *R. v. Wilson* [2000] 2 Cr.App.R.(S.) 323, CA, but not apparently in *R. v. De Silva* [2000] 2 Cr.App.R.(S.) 408, CA.

The question whether a longer than commensurate sentence may properly be imposed to run consecutively to a sentence of imprisonment was considered by the Court of Appeal in *R. v. Everleigh* [2002] 1 Cr.App.R.(S.) 32. The court considered *R. v. King*, 16 Cr.App.R.(S.) 987; *R. v. Walters* [1997] 2 Cr.App.R.(S.) 87; *R. v. Johnson* [1998] 1 Cr.App.R.(S.) 126; *R. v. Cuthbertson and Jenks* [2000] 1 Cr.App.R.(S.) 359; *R. v. Parsons* [2000] 1 Cr.App.R.(S.) 428; *R. v. Blades* [2000] 1 Cr.App.R.(S.) 463; *R. v. Sullivan* [2000] 2 Cr.App.R.(S.) 318; *R. v. Sowden* [2000] 2 Cr.App.R.(S.) 360; *R. v. Wilson* [2000] 2 Cr.App.R.(S.) 323; and *R. v. Ellis* [2001] 1 Cr.App.R.(S.) 43. Accepting that not all of these of authorities could be reconciled, the court held that they showed that it was inappropriate to pass a longer than the normal sentence to run consecutively to another sentence imposed on the same occasion, because a longer than normal sentence is intended in itself to protect the public from serious harm, without the need for any additional penalty in relation to other conduct punishable at the same time. Secondly, there was nothing inappropriate, but on the contrary it might be desirable, for a longer than normal sentence to be passed consecutively either to a sentence passed on an earlier occasion (*Wilson*) or to a period of return to custody ordered under the *PCC(S)A* 2000, s.116 (*post*, § 5–633), which was a consequence of a sentence passed on an earlier occasion (*Blades*). As was pointed out in *Blades*, it was important that both the public and the defendant should know that a sentence once passed would have to be served (subject to any reduction which might be appropriate in accordance with *R. v. Taylor* [1998] 1 Cr.App.R.(S.) 312). It was desirable that the sentencing judge, if imposing a consecutive sentence, should make it plain what were the factors which he had taken into consideration in so passing the sentence under section 80(2)(b).

In *R. v. Christie*, 16 Cr.App.R.(S.) 469, CA, it was said to be wrong to add an additional period to the sentence under section 80(2)(b) if the commensurate sentence already incorporated an element for the protection of the public. In *R. v. Campbell* [1997] 1 Cr.App.R.(S.) 119, CA, it was held that if the sentencing guidelines for a particular offence included an element for the protection of the public, the sentencer should decide what was the appropriate sentence, leaving out of account any element for the protection of the public, and should then add the greater element needed for the protection of the public from serious harm under section 80(2)(b). This would avoid the risk of imposing an element of the sentence twice over. In *R. v. Gabbidon and Bramble* [1997] 2 Cr.App.R.(S.) 19, CA, this approach was described as too difficult an exercise in forensic archaeology; it was better that the sentencer simply applied the principle of balance stated by Lord Taylor C.J. in *R. v. Mansell*, 15 Cr.App.R.(S.) 771.

In a case where a longer than normal sentence is passed on one offender and a commensurate sentence on the other, it does not necessarily follow that there is any disparity of sentence, provided that there is evidence of continuing dangerousness on the part of one offender and not in the case of the other: *R. v. Bestwick and Huddlestone*, 16 Cr.App.R.(S.) 168, CA.

A longer than commensurate sentence may be imposed on an offender under section 80(2)(b) even though he does not qualify for a sentence of life imprisonment under the criteria established for that form of sentence: *R. v. Helm*, 16 Cr.App.R.(S.) 834, CA. The enactment of section 80(2)(b) has not reduced the requirements for a life sentence: *R. v. Roche*, 16 Cr.App.R.(S.) 849, CA.

Where a sentencer has in mind the possibility of passing a longer than commensurate sentence, he should warn counsel for the defendant of his intentions and invite submissions on the question: *R. v. Baverstock*, 96 Cr.App.R. 435, CA. This point has been repeated in many cases; it is particularly important when any question arises as to whether the offence is a "violent offence" for the purposes of the Act. Where a court passes a longer than commensurate sentence it is required by the *PCC(S)A* 2000, s.80(3) to state in open court that it is of the opinion that subsection (2)(b) applies and why it is of that opinion, and explain to the offender in open court and in ordinary language why the sentence is for such a term. Failure to comply with this obligation does not invalidate the sentence:

Baverstock, ante; *R. v. Thomas*, 16 Cr.App.R.(S.) 616, CA. Even where the nature of the expected future harm is obvious, the sentencer should ensure that he has properly identified what the harm was before he proceeded to sentence, and should point out clearly and in straightforward terms what it was that he considered to be the serious harm in question: *R. v. Bacon*, 16 Cr.App.R.(S.) 1031, CA.

Where a court fails to pass a longer than commensurate sentence where such a sentence should be passed, the resulting sentence may be "unduly lenient" and may be the subject of a reference by the Attorney-General under the *CJA* 1988, s.36: *Att-Gen.'s Reference (No. 9 of 1994) (R. v. Groves)*, 16 Cr.App.R.(S.) 366, CA. Where a person sentenced to a longer than commensurate sentence persuades the Court of Appeal that the case is not one in which a longer than commensurate sentence should have been passed, the court is not bound to substitute a shorter sentence; its powers are at large, and it may approve the sentence passed as a commensurate sentence if it considers it appropriate to do so: *R. v. Palmer* [1996] 2 Cr.App.R.(S.) 68, CA; and see also *R. v. Henshaw* [1996] 2 Cr.App.R.(S.) 310, CA; and *R. v. Rai and Robinson* [2000] 2 Cr.App.R.(S.) 120, CA.

(2) Imprisonment

(a) *Age*

Power of Criminal Courts (Sentencing) Act 2000, s.89

Restriction on imposing imprisonment on persons under 21

★**5-478**   As to the commencement of section 41 of, and paragraph 74 of Schedule 3 to, the 2003 Act, see *ante*, § 5–42.

(c) *Life sentences, sentences for public protection and extended sentences for dangerous offenders*

Introduction

5-488   As to the transitional provisions in the *Criminal Justice and Immigration Act 2008 (Commencement No. 2 and Transitional and Saving Provisions) Order* 2008 (S.I. 2008 No. 1586) (see the main work), the amendments effected by the *CJIA* 2008 have no effect in relation to a person sentenced before the commencement date, and "sentenced" for this purpose refers to the date of sentence in the Crown Court, not to the date of any substituted sentence imposed by the Court of Appeal: *R. (Modhej) v. Secretary of State for Justice* [2012] A.C.D. 16, DC ([2011] EWHC 2267 (Admin.)).

Extended sentences (offences committed before April 4, 2005)

5-489   The *CJA* 2003 introduced a new scheme of custodial sentences for dangerous offenders. Offenders being sentenced after April 4, 2005, in respect of offences committed before that date will, however, continue to receive extended sentences under the former regime (*PCC(S)A* 2000, s.85 (*post*)) if appropriate. For the definitions of "sexual" and "violent" offence, see section 161 of the *PCC(S)A* 2000, *ante* § 5–471.

Powers of Criminal Courts (Sentencing) Act 2000, s.85

Sexual or violent offences: extension of certain custodial sentences for licence purposes

5-490   85.—(1) This section applies where a court—

(a) proposes to impose a custodial sentence for a sexual or violent offence committed on or after 30th September 1998; and

(b) considers that the period (if any) for which the offender would, apart from this section, be subject to a licence would not be adequate for the purpose of preventing the commission by him of further offences and securing his rehabilitation.

(2) Subject to subsections (3) to (5) below, the court may pass on the offender an extended sentence, that is to say, a custodial sentence the term of which is equal to the aggregate of—

    (a) the term of the custodial sentence that the court would have imposed if it had passed a custodial sentence otherwise than under this section ("the custodial term"); and

    (b) a further period ("the extension period") for which the offender is to be subject to a licence and which is of such length as the court considers necessary for the purpose mentioned in subsection (1) above.

(3) Where the offence is a violent offence, the court shall not pass an extended sentence the custodial term of which is less than four years.

(4) The extension period shall not exceed—

    (a) ten years in the case of a sexual offence; and

    (b) five years in the case of a violent offence.

(5) The term of an extended sentence passed in respect of an offence shall not exceed the maximum term permitted for that offence.

(6) Subsection (2) of section 80 above (length of discretionary custodial sentences) shall apply as if the term of an extended sentence did not include the extension period.

(7) The Secretary of State may by order amend paragraph (b) of subsection (4) above by substituting a different period, not exceeding ten years, for the period for the time being specified in that paragraph.

(8) In this section "licence" means a licence under Part II of the *Criminal Justice Act* 1991 (early release of prisoners).

[This section is repealed, as from April 4, 2005 (*Criminal Justice Act 2003 (Commencement No. 8 and Transitional and Saving Provisions) Order* 2005 (S.I. 2005 No. 950)), by the *CJA* 2003, s.332, and Sched. 37, Pt 7. As to the saving provision in relation to offences committed before April 4, 2005, see § 5–2 in the main work.]

General guidance on the use of the power to impose an extended sentence under section **5–491** 85 was given in *R. v. Nelson* [2002] 1 Cr.App.R.(S.) 134, CA. When dealing with a violent or sexual offence, the court should consider the matter in three stages. The first stage was to decide on the sentence which would be commensurate. The second stage was to consider whether a longer period in custody was needed to protect the public from serious harm from the offender. If so, a longer than commensurate custodial sentence would be called for. The third stage, in relation to a sexual offence, or a violent offence for which the appropriate custodial sentence was four years or longer, was to consider whether that sentence was adequate to prevent the commission by the offender of further offences and secure his rehabilitation. If not, an extended sentence was called for. It was not appropriate to reduce the custodial term because an extended licence period was being imposed.

The risk of further offences being committed by the offender did not justify a longer than commensurate sentence unless those further offences might cause death or some physical or psychological injury. There might be cases in which, because of the power to impose an extended licence period, a longer than commensurate sentence might not be necessary. One purpose of an extended sentence was to reduce the likelihood of re-offending, and it was therefore particularly suitable where a commensurate custodial term was too short for this to be done in prison and where the normal licence period, if any, would not be long enough to permit attendance at a treatment programme in the community. This would arise particularly in relation to less serious sexual offences, where the likelihood of re-offending appeared high, but where a longer than commensurate sentence could not be justified because the offender does not present a risk of serious harm to the public. The use of an extended sentence, with a relatively short custodial term, less than 12 months, had been endorsed in *R v. Ajaib* [2001] 1 Cr.App.R.(S.) 31, CA.

Extended sentences with longer than commensurate custodial terms would be appropriate, at the other end of the spectrum, where a violent or sexual offence is committed by a seriously dangerous offender, in relation to whom a life sentence, if available, might well have been passed. There might also be cases in which a discretionary life sentence was available for the offence but the criteria which have to be established before such a sentence can be passed may not all be present. Where a longer than commensurate sentence was called for, it should usually be accompanied by an extension period because a seriously dangerous offender, attracting a longer than commensurate sentence, might well commit further offences.

5–492   In determining the length of an extended sentence, the court must decide what period would be adequate to secure the offender's rehabilitation and to prevent re-offending. This would often be difficult. In some cases, involving less serious sexual offences where the custodial term was relatively short, the court might be able to take advice on the availability and length of treatment programmes and tailor the extension period accordingly. In all cases the court should consider whether a particular extension period could be justified on the evidence available. A long extension period should usually be based on a clear implication from the offender's criminal record or on what was said in a pre-sentence report or a psychiatric report. The objective, where possible, should be to fix the length of the extension period by reference to what could realistically be achieved within it. When the offender was clearly dangerous the custodial term would usually be longer than commensurate and a long period of extended licence would often be called for. It was clear from *R. v. Gould* [2000] 2 Cr.App.R.(S.) 173, CA, that a court imposing an extended sentence should bear in mind that the offender may ultimately serve the whole or part of the extension period in custody. But, as the legislature's intention in introducing extended sentences was clearly to place an offender at risk of recall for some considerable time, it would be illogical to require strict proportionality between the duration of the extension period and the seriousness of the offence. Proportionality with the seriousness of the offence was of central importance to a custodial term. It should not be a primary factor in determining the length of an extension period. It did, however, have some relevance and the implications of the overall sentence should be borne in mind.

There had been conflicting views as to whether the legislation permitted the imposition of consecutive extended sentences. The court was in no doubt that sensible practice required that extended sentences should not, generally, be imposed consecutively.

Where a sentencer was considering imposing an extended sentence, counsel should be warned of this, so that argument can be heard on the point. Judges should always take care to use the correct terminology when passing sentence. In particular, a longer than commensurate sentence should be so described: it was not an extended sentence. Judges should also seek to explain to a defendant the effect of the sentence passed.

Powers of Criminal Courts (Sentencing) Act 2000, s.86

Sexual offences committed before 30th September 1998

★**5–493**   As from a day to be appointed, section 86 of the 2000 Act is repealed by the *Legal Aid, Sentencing and Punishment of Offenders Act* 2012, s.121(4).

Criminal Justice Act 2003, ss.224–229

Meaning of "specified offence" etc.

★**5–495**   As from a day to be appointed, the 2003 Act is amended by the *Legal Aid, Sentencing and Punishment of Offenders Act* 2012, s.122(3), and Sched. 19, paras 8, 15 and 16, so as (i) to insert the cross-heading "*Interpretation*" before section 224, and (ii) to substitute "224A" for "225" in that section.

Life sentence for second listed offence

★**5–495a**   As from a day to be appointed, a new section 224A is inserted in the 2003 Act by the *Legal Aid, Sentencing and Punishment of Offenders Act* 2012, s.122(1); and, before that section, there is inserted, as from a day to be appointed, the heading "*Life sentences*" by *ibid.*, s.122(3), and Sched. 19, paras 8 and 17.

Criminal Justice Act 2003, s.224A

[Life sentence for second listed offence
    224A.—(1) This section applies where—

(a) a person aged 18 or over is convicted of an offence listed in Part 1 of Schedule 15B,

(b) the offence was committed after this section comes into force, and

(c) the sentence condition and the previous offence condition are met.

(2) The court must impose a sentence of imprisonment for life unless the court is of the opinion that there are particular circumstances which—

(a) relate to the offence, to the previous offence referred to in subsection (4) or to the offender, and

(b) would make it unjust to do so in all the circumstances.

(3) The sentence condition is that, but for this section, the court would, in compliance with sections 152(2) and 153(2), impose a sentence of imprisonment for 10 years or more, disregarding any extension period imposed under section 226A.

(4) The previous offence condition is that —

(a) at the time the offence was committed, the offender had been convicted of an offence listed in Schedule 15B ("the previous offence"), and

(b) a relevant life sentence or a relevant sentence of imprisonment or detention for a determinate period was imposed on the offender for the previous offence.

(5) A life sentence is relevant for the purposes of subsection (4)(b) if—

(a) the offender was not eligible for release during the first 5 years of the sentence, or

(b) the offender would not have been eligible for release during that period but for the reduction of the period of ineligibility to take account of a relevant pre-sentence period.

(6) An extended sentence imposed under this Act (including one imposed as a result of the *Armed Forces Act* 2006) is relevant for the purposes of subsection (4)(b) if the appropriate custodial term imposed was 10 years or more.

(7) Any other extended sentence is relevant for the purposes of subsection (4)(b) if the custodial term imposed was 10 years or more.

(8) Any other sentence of imprisonment or detention for a determinate period is relevant for the purposes of subsection (4)(b) if it was for a period of 10 years or more.

(9) An extended sentence or other sentence of imprisonment or detention is also relevant if it would have been relevant under subsection (7) or (8) but for the reduction of the sentence, or any part of the sentence, to take account of a relevant pre-sentence period.

(10) For the purposes of subsections (4) to (9)—

"extended sentence" means—

(a) a sentence imposed under section 85 of the *Sentencing Act* or under section 226A, 226B, 227 or 228 of this Act (including one imposed as a result of section 219A, 220, 221A or 222 of the *Armed Forces Act* 2006), or

(b) an equivalent sentence imposed under the law of Scotland, Northern Ireland or a member State (other than the United Kingdom);

"life sentence" means—

(a) a life sentence as defined in section 34 of the *Crime (Sentences) Act* 1997, or

(b) an equivalent sentence imposed under the law of Scotland, Northern Ireland or a member State (other than the United Kingdom);

"relevant pre-sentence period", in relation to the previous offence referred to in subsection (4), means any period which the offender spent in custody or on bail before the sentence for that offence was imposed;

"sentence of imprisonment or detention" includes any sentence of a period in custody (however expressed).

(11) An offence the sentence for which is imposed under this section is not to be regarded as an offence the sentence for which is fixed by law.]

In relation to any time before the coming into force of section 61 of the *CJCSA* 2000, sec- ★
tion 224A has effect with the insertion of the words "or, in the case of a person aged at least 18 but under 21, custody for life under section 94 of the *Sentencing Act*" after the words "imprisonment for life" in subsection (2), and with the insertion of the words "or, if the person is aged at least 18 but under 21, a sentence of detention in a young offender institution for such a period" after the word "more" in subsection (3): *Legal Aid, Sentencing and Punishment of Offenders Act* 2012, s.122(3), and Sched. 19, para. 24(1) and (2).

Life sentence or imprisonment for public protection for serious offences

As from a day to be appointed, section 225 of the *CJA 2003* is amended by the *Legal Aid,*　★**5–496**

Sentencing and Punishment of Offenders Act 2012, ss.123(a) (omission of subsections (3) to (4)) and 126, and Sched. 21, paras 20 and 23 (omission of "*or imprisonment for public protection*" from the heading).

Detention for life or detention for public protection for serious offences committed by those under 18

★**5–497**   As from a day to be appointed, section 226 of the *CJA* 2003 is amended by the *Legal Aid, Sentencing and Punishment of Offenders Act* 2012, ss.123(b) (omission of subsections (3) to (4)) and 126, and Sched. 21, paras 20 and 24 (omission of "*or detention for public protection*" from the heading).

New extended sentences

★**5–497a**   As from a day to be appointed, (i) new sections 226A and 226B are inserted in the *CJA* 2003 by the *Legal Aid, Sentencing and Punishment of Offenders Act* 2012, s.124; and (ii) above those new sections, there is inserted the heading "*Extended sentences*" by *ibid.*, s.122(3), and Sched. 19, paras 8 and 18.

Criminal Justice Act 2003, ss.226A, 226B

[Extended sentence for certain violent or sexual offences: persons 18 or over
   226A.—(1) This section applies where—
      (a) a person aged 18 or over is convicted of a specified offence (whether the offence was committed before or after this section comes into force),
      (b) the court considers that there is a significant risk to members of the public of serious harm occasioned by the commission by the offender of further specified offences,
      (c) the court is not required by section 224A or 225(2) to impose a sentence of imprisonment for life, and
      (d) condition A or B is met.
   (2) Condition A is that, at the time the offence was committed, the offender had been convicted of an offence listed in Schedule 15B.
   (3) Condition B is that, if the court were to impose an extended sentence of imprisonment, the term that it would specify as the appropriate custodial term would be at least 4 years.
   (4) The court may impose an extended sentence of imprisonment on the offender.
   (5) An extended sentence of imprisonment is a sentence of imprisonment the term of which is equal to the aggregate of—
      (a) the appropriate custodial term, and
      (b) a further period (the "extension period") for which the offender is to be subject to a licence.
   (6) The appropriate custodial term is the term of imprisonment that would (apart from this section) be imposed in compliance with section 153(2).
   (7) The extension period must be a period of such length as the court considers necessary for the purpose of protecting members of the public from serious harm occasioned by the commission by the offender of further specified offences, subject to subsections (8) and (9).
   (8) The extension period must not exceed—
      (a) 5 years in the case of a specified violent offence, and
      (b) 8 years in the case of a specified sexual offence.
   (9) The term of an extended sentence of imprisonment imposed under this section in respect of an offence must not exceed the term that, at the time the offence was committed, was the maximum term permitted for the offence.
   (10) In subsections (1)(a) and (8), references to a specified offence, a specified violent offence and a specified sexual offence include an offence that—
      (a) was abolished before 4 April 2005, and
      (b) would have constituted such an offence if committed on the day on which the offender was convicted of the offence.
   (11) Where the offence mentioned in subsection (1)(a) was committed before 4 April 2005—
      (a) subsection (1)(c) has effect as if the words "by section 224A or 225(2)" were omitted, and
      (b) subsection (6) has effect as if the words "in compliance with section 153(2)" were omitted.]

[Extended sentence for certain violent or sexual offences: persons under 18
★**5–497b**   **226B.**—(1) This section applies where—

(a) a person aged under 18 is convicted of a specified offence (whether the offence was committed before or after this section comes into force),

(b) the court considers that there is a significant risk to members of the public of serious harm occasioned by the commission by the offender of further specified offences,

(c) the court is not required by section 226(2) to impose a sentence of detention for life under section 91 of the *Sentencing Act*, and

(d) if the court were to impose an extended sentence of detention, the term that it would specify as the appropriate custodial term would be at least 4 years.

(2) The court may impose an extended sentence of detention on the offender.

(3) An extended sentence of detention is a sentence of detention the term of which is equal to the aggregate of—

(a) the appropriate custodial term, and

(b) a further period (the "extension period") for which the offender is to be subject to a licence.

(4) The appropriate custodial term is the term of detention that would (apart from this section) be imposed in compliance with section 153(2).

(5) The extension period must be a period of such length as the court considers necessary for the purpose of protecting members of the public from serious harm occasioned by the commission by the offender of further specified offences, subject to subsections (6) and (7).

(6) The extension period must not exceed—

(a) 5 years in the case of a specified violent offence, and

(b) 8 years in the case of a specified sexual offence.

(7) The term of an extended sentence of detention imposed under this section in respect of an offence may not exceed the term that, at the time the offence was committed, was the maximum term of imprisonment permitted for the offence in the case of a person aged 18 or over.

(8) In subsections (1)(a) and (6), references to a specified offence, a specified violent offence and a specified sexual offence include an offence that—

(a) was abolished before 4 April 2005, and

(b) would have constituted such an offence if committed on the day on which the offender was convicted of the offence.

(9) Where the offence mentioned in subsection (1)(a) was committed before 4 April 2005—

(a) subsection (1) has effect as if paragraph (c) were omitted, and

(b) subsection (4) has effect as if the words "in compliance with section 153(2)" were omitted.]

In relation to any time before the coming into force of section 61 of the *CJCSA* 2000, the ★ 2012 Act, s.126, and Sched. 21, para. 36(1) and (2), provide that section 226A is to have effect with the insertion of subsection (12), as follows—

"(12) In the case of a person aged at least 18 but under 21, this section has effect as if—

(a) the reference in subsection (1)(c) to imprisonment for life were to custody for life, and

(b) other references to imprisonment (including in the expression 'extended sentence of imprisonment') were to detention in a young offender institution.".

In relation to any time before the coming into force of section 61 of the *CJCSA* 2000, section 226B is also to have effect with the substitution of "21" for "18" in subsection (7): 2012 Act, s.126, and Sched. 21, para. 36(1) and (3). ★

Extended sentence for certain violent or sexual offences: persons 18 or over

As from a day to be appointed, section 227 of the *CJA* 2003 is repealed by the *Legal Aid,* ★5–498 *Sentencing and Punishment of Offenders Act* 2012, s.123(c).

Extended sentences for certain violent or sexual offences: persons under 18

As from a day to be appointed, section 228 of the *CJA* 2003 is repealed by the *Legal Aid,* ★5–499 *Sentencing and Punishment of Offenders Act* 2012, s.123(d).

Criminal Justice Act 2003, ss.231, 232

Appeals where previous convictions set aside

As from a day to be appointed, the 2003 Act is amended by the *Legal Aid, Sentencing and* ★5–501

Punishment of Offenders Act 2012, s.122(3), and Sched. 19, paras 8 and 19, so as to insert "*Supplementary*" as a new cross-heading before section 231.

★   As from a day to be appointed, section 231 of the 2003 Act is amended by the 2012 Act, s.122(3), and Sched. 19, paras 8 and 20(1) and (2), so as to insert a new subsection (A1) at the beginning, as follows—

"(A1) Subsection (2) applies where—
  (a) a sentence has been imposed on a person under section 224A,
  (b) a previous conviction of that person has been subsequently set aside on appeal, and
  (c) without that conviction, the previous offence condition in section 224A(4) would not have been met.".

★   As from a day to be appointed, section 231(1) of the 2003 Act is amended by the 2012 Act, s.122(3), Sched. 19, paras 8 and 20 (1) and (3), so as to substitute the words "Subsection (2) also" for the words "This section".

★   As from a day to be appointed, section 231(1) of the 2003 Act is further amended by the 2012 Act, s.126, and Sched. 21, paras 20 and 25, so as to insert (i) ", 226A" after "225(3) in paragraph (a), (ii) "226A(2) or" before "227(2A)" in paragraph (b), (iii) "226A(3) or" before "227(2B)" in paragraph (b), and (iv) "226A(2) or" after "may be)" in paragraph (c).

★   As from a day to be appointed, section 231 of the 2003 Act is further amended by the 2012 Act, s.122(3), and Sched. 19, paras 8 and 20(1) and (4), so as to insert new subsections (3) and (4), as follows—

"(3) Subsection (4) applies where—
  (a) a sentence has been imposed on a person under section 224A,
  (b) a previous sentence imposed on that person has been subsequently modified on appeal, and
  (c) taking account of that modification, the previous offence condition in section 224A(4) would not have been met.
(4) Notwithstanding anything in section 18 of the *Criminal Appeal Act* 1968, notice of appeal against the sentence mentioned in subsection (3)(a) may be given at any time within 28 days from the date on which the previous sentence was modified.".

Certificates of convictions for purposes of sections 225 and 227

★5–502   As from a day to be appointed, section 232 of the 2003 Act is repealed by the *Legal Aid, Sentencing and Punishment of Offenders Act* 2012, s.126, and Sched. 21, paras 20 and 26.

Certificates of conviction

★5–502a   As from a day to be appointed, a new section 232A is inserted in the 2003 Act by the *Legal Aid, Sentencing and Punishment of Offenders Act* 2012, s.122(3), and Sched. 19, paras 8 and 21.

Criminal Justice Act 2003, ss.232A

[Certificates of conviction
  232A. Where—
    (a) on any date after the commencement of Schedule 15B a person is convicted in England and Wales of an offence listed in that Schedule, and
    (b) the court by or before which the person is so convicted states in open court that the person has been convicted of such an offence on that date, and
    (c) that court subsequently certifies that fact,
  that certificate is evidence, for the purposes of section 224A, that the person was convicted of such an offence on that date.]

Specified violent and sexual offences

★5–503   As from July 2, 2012 (*Domestic Violence, Crime and Victims (Amendment) Act 2012 (Commencement) Order* 2012 (S.I. 2012 No. 1432)), Part 1 of Schedule 15 to the 2003 Act is amended by the *Domestic Violence, Crime and Victims (Amendment) Act* 2012, s.3, and Sched., para. 6, to take account of the extended ambit of the offence under section 5 of the *Domestic Violence, Crime and Victims Act* 2004 (not "2005" as incorrectly stated in the main work). As to the extension of section 5, see *post*, § 19–118a.

As from a day to be appointed, Part 1 of Schedule 15 to the 2003 Act is further amended by the *Protection of Freedoms Act* 2012, s.115(1), and Sched. 9, para. 147, so as to insert a reference to an offence under section 4A of the *Protection from Harassment Act* 1997.

As from a day to be appointed, Part 2 of Schedule 15 to the 2003 Act is amended by the 2012 Act, s.115(1), and Sched. 9, para. 139, so as to add a reference to an offence under section 59A of the *SOA* 2003.

Schedule 15A offences (ss.225(3A), 227(2A))

As from a day to be appointed, Schedule 15A to the *CJA* 2003 is repealed by the *Legal Aid, Sentencing and Punishment of Offenders Act* 2012, s.126, and Sched. 21, paras 20 and 31.   ★5–504

Offences listed for the purposes of sections 224A, 226A and 246A

As from a day to be appointed, a new Schedule 15B to the 2003 Act is inserted by the   ★5–505a
Legal Aid, Sentencing and Punishment of Offenders Act 2012, s.122(2), and Sched. 18. Part 1 lists (for the purposes of sections 224A(1) and (4), 226A and 246A) the following offences to the extent that they are offences under the law of England and Wales: manslaughter, an offence under section 4 or 18 of the *Offences against the Person Act* 1861, an offence under section 16, 17(1) or 18 of the *Firearms Act* 1968, an offence of robbery (*Theft Act* 1968, s.8) where, at some time during the commission of the offence, the offender had in his possession a firearm or imitation firearm within the meaning of the *Firearms Act* 1968, an offence under section 1 of the *Protection of Children Act* 1978, an offence under section 1, 56, 57 or 59 of the *Terrorism Act* 2000, an offence under section 47, 50 or 113 of the *Anti-terrorism, Crime and Security Act* 2001, an offence under section 1, 2, 4, 5 to 12, 14 or 15 of the *SOA* 2003, an offence under section 25 or 26 of that Act if the offender is aged 18 or over at the time of the offence, an offence under section 30, 31, 34 or 35 of that Act if the offender is liable to imprisonment for life on conviction on indictment, an offence under section 47 of that Act against a person aged under 16, an offence under section 48, 49 or 50 of that Act, an offence under 62 of that Act if the offender is liable to imprisonment for life on conviction on indictment, an offence under section 5 of the *Domestic Violence, Crime and Victims Act* 2004, an offence under section 5, 9, 10 or 11 of the *Terrorism Act* 2006, attempting to commit, conspiring to commit, or inciting the commission of any of these offences ("listed offences") or murder, an offence under Part 2 of the *SCA* 2007 in relation to which a listed offence or murder is the offence which the person intended or believed would be committed and aiding, abetting, counselling or procuring a listed offence.

Part 2 lists (for the purposes of sections 224A(4), 226A and 246A) the following offences to   ★
the extent that they are offences under the law of England and Wales: murder, any offence that was abolished before the coming into force of Schedule 15B and would have constituted an offence specified in Part 1 if committed on the relevant day (para. 46(1)). Paragraph 46(2) provides that "relevant day", in relation to an offence, "means—

> "(a) for the purposes of this paragraph as it applies for the purposes of section 246A(2), the day on which the offender was convicted of that offence, and
> (b) for the purposes of this paragraph as it applies for the purposes of sections 224A(4) and 226A(2), the day on which the offender was convicted of the offence referred to in section 224A(1)(a) or 226A(1)(a) (as appropriate)."

Part 3 lists the following offences under service law for the purposes of sections 224A(4),   ★
226A and 246A: an offence under section 70 of the *Army Act* 1955 or of the *Air Force Act* 1955, an offence under section 42 of the *Naval Discipline Act* 1957, as respects which the corresponding civil offence is an offence specified in Part 1 or 2 (para. 47), and an offence under section 42 of the *AFA* 2006 as respects which the corresponding offence under the law of England and Wales (within the meaning given by that section) is an offence specified in Part 1 or 2 (para. 48(1)). Paragraph 48(2) stipulates that section 48 of the 2006 Act (attempts, conspiracy, etc.) "applies for the purposes of this paragraph as if the reference in subsection (3)(b) of that section to any of the following provisions of that Act were a reference to this paragraph."

★   Part 4 lists offences under the law of Scotland, Northern Ireland or a member state other than the United Kingdom for the purposes of sections 224A(4) and 226A: an offence for which a person was convicted in any of those jurisdictions and which, if committed in England and Wales at the time of conviction, would have constituted an offence specified in Part 1 or 2.

★   Part 5 (para. 50) provides that in the schedule "imprisonment for life" includes "custody for life".

Life sentences, sentences for public protection, extended sentences

(iv) Assessment of significant risk

5–514   *R. v. Anigbugu (Att.-Gen.'s Reference (No. 73 of 2010)); R. v. Pyo (Att.-Gen.'s Reference (No. 75 of 2010)); R. v. McGee (Att.-Gen.'s Reference (No. 3 of 2011))* is now reported at [2011] 2 Cr.App.R.(S.) 100, *sub nom. Att.-Gen.'s References (Nos 73, 75 of 2010, and 03 of 2011) (R. v. Anigbugu).*

Att.-Gen.'s Reference (No. 5 of 2011) (R. v. Troninas) is now reported at [2012] 1 Cr.App.R.(S.) 20.

5–515   **Present or future risk?** In *R. v. M.J.* [2012] Crim.L.R. 390, CA ([2012] EWCA Crim. 132), the court considered *R. v. Smith (Nicholas)* (as to which, see the main work (and now reported at [2012] 1 Cr.App.R.(S.) 83)), and concluded that there was nothing said by the Supreme Court that was out of kilter with the previous practice of the Court of Appeal. In particular, it was held that nothing that was said in *Smith* excludes from consideration questions about the likely impact on a young offender of the process of maturation or the possible impact of alternative sentencing options which would sufficiently address the risk posed by the offender so as to make an indeterminate sentence unnecessary. It is submitted that, whilst this is convenient and it may reflect what Lord Phillips, who delivered the unanimous judgment of the Supreme Court, would have said, had the particular point been present to his mind, or it may be that this is indeed what he meant to say, it is not what he actually said. As to this, see the commentary in CLW/12/07/25.

5–516   *R. v. Beesley and Coyle; R. v. Rehman* is now reported at [2012] 1 Cr.App.R.(S.) 15.

5–517   **Availability of other sentences and orders.** As to *R. v. Smith (Nicholas)* (referred to in the main work), see now the decision of the Court of Appeal in *R. v. M.J., ante,* § 5–515.

Application of principles

★5–520   Where an offender falls to be sentenced for an offence of manslaughter by reason of provocation, it has to be assumed that the offender's loss of self-control was reasonable, even bearing in mind that people are expected to exercise reasonable control over their emotions; given this assumption, it is difficult to see how such a loss of self-control could, on its own, provide the basis for a conclusion (within s.225 of the 2003 Act) that the defendant represents a significant risk to members of the public of serious harm occasioned by the commission of further specified offences: *R. v. Brook (Neil)* [2012] Crim.L.R. 394, CA.

Consecutive/concurrent sentences

5–523   *R. v. Hills* (see the main work) was considered in *R. v. Taylor, post,* § 5–593.

Fixing the minimum term (life sentences not fixed by law)

Powers of Criminal Courts (Sentencing) Act 2000, s.82A

Determination of tariffs

★5–531   As from a day to be appointed, section 82A(3)(b) of the 2000 Act is amended by the *Legal Aid, Sentencing and Punishment of Offenders Act* 2012, s.110(13), and Sched. 13, paras 9 and 10, so as to substitute "240ZA" for "240".

★   As from a day to be appointed, section 82A of the 2000 Act is further amended by the

2012 Act, s.126, and Sched. 21, paras 7 and 11, so as (i) to omit subsection (4), and (ii) to substitute a new definition of "life sentence" in subsection (7) as follows—

"'life sentence' means a sentence mentioned in subsection (2) of section 34 of the *Crime (Sentences) Act* 1997 other than a sentence mentioned in paragraph (d) or (e) of that subsection".

(e) *Prison sentences of less than 12 months*

Introduction

Custody plus

As from a day to be appointed, sections 181 to 188 of the *CJA* 2003 are repealed by the *Legal Aid, Sentencing and Punishment of Offenders Act* 2012, s.89(1)(a).   ★5–536

Intermittent custody

As from a day to be appointed, sections 181 to 188 of the *CJA* 2003 are repealed by the *Legal Aid, Sentencing and Punishment of Offenders Act* 2012, s.89(1)(a).   ★5–537

Statutory provisions

As from a day to be appointed, sections 181 to 188 of, and Schedules 10 and 11 to, the *CJA* 2003 are repealed by the *Legal Aid, Sentencing and Punishment of Offenders Act* 2012, s.89(1)(a) and (b).   ★5–539

Criminal Justice Act 2003, ss.181, 182

CHAPTER 3

PRISON SENTENCES OF LESS THAN 12 MONTHS

Prison sentences of less than twelve months

[Prison sentences of less than 12 months

181.—(1) *Any power of a court to impose a sentence of imprisonment for a term of less than 12 months on an offender may be exercised only in accordance with the following provisions of this section unless the court makes an intermittent custody order (as defined by section 183).*   **5–540**

(2) *The term of the sentence—*

    (a) *must be expressed in weeks,*

    (b) *must be at least 28 weeks,*

    (c) *must not be more than 51 weeks in respect of any one offence, and*

    (d) *must not exceed the maximum term permitted for the offence.*

(3) *The court, when passing sentence, must—*

    (a) *specify a period (in this Chapter referred to as "the custodial period") at the end of which the offender is to be released on a licence, and*

    (b) *by order require the licence to be granted subject to conditions requiring the offender's compliance during the remainder of the term (in this Chapter referred to as "the licence period") or any part of it with one or more requirements falling within section 182(1) and specified in the order.*

(4) *In this Part "custody plus order" means an order under subsection (3)(b).*

(5) *The custodial period—*

    (a) *must be at least 2 weeks, and*

    (b) *in respect of any one offence, must not be more than 13 weeks.*

(6) *In determining the term of the sentence and the length of the custodial period, the court must ensure that the licence period is at least 26 weeks in length.*

(7) *Where a court imposes two or more terms of imprisonment in accordance with this section to be served consecutively—*

(a) *the aggregate length of the terms of imprisonment must not be more than 65 weeks, and*

(b) *the aggregate length of the custodial periods must not be more than 26 weeks.*

(7A) *For the purposes of subsection (7)(a) the aggregate length of the terms of imprisonment is not to be regarded as being more than 65 weeks if the aggregate of all the custodial periods and the longest of the licence periods in relation to those terms is not more than 65 weeks.*

(8) *A custody plus order which specifies two or more requirements may, in relation to any requirement, re-fer to compliance within such part of the licence period as is specified in the order.*

(9) *Subsection (3)(b) does not apply where the sentence is a suspended sentence.*]

This section comes into force on a day to be appointed. It is printed as amended by the *CJIA* 2008, s.20(1) and (2). The *AFA* 2006, s.196, provides that in sections 181 and 182, "court" includes a relevant service court. As from a further day to be appointed, sections 181 to 188 of, and Schedules 10 and 11 to, the *CJA* 2003 are repealed by the *Legal Aid, Sentencing and Punishment of Offenders Act* 2012, s.89(1)(a) and (b).

Licence conditions

5–541   **182.**—(1) *The requirements falling within this subsection are—*

(a) *an unpaid work requirement (as defined by section 199),*

(b) *an activity requirement (as defined by section 201),*

(c) *a programme requirement (as defined by section 202),*

(d) *a prohibited activity requirement (as defined by section 203),*

(e) *a curfew requirement (as defined by section 204),*

(f) *an exclusion requirement (as defined by section 205),*

(g) *a supervision requirement (as defined by section 213), and*

(h) *in a case where the offender is aged under 25, an attendance centre requirement (as defined by section 214).*

[(2) *The power under section 181(3)(b) to determine the conditions of the licence has effect subject to section 218 and to the following provisions of Chapter 4 relating to particular requirements—*

(a) *section 199(3) (unpaid work requirement),*

(b) *section 201(3) and (4) (activity requirement),*

(c) *section 202(4) and (5) (programme requirement), and*

(d) *section 203(2) (prohibited activity requirement).]*

(3) *Where the court makes a custody plus order requiring a licence to contain a curfew requirement or an exclusion requirement, the court must also require the licence to contain an electronic monitoring requirement (as defined by section 215) unless—*

(a) *the court is prevented from doing so by section 215(2) or 218(4), or*

(b) *in the particular circumstances of the case, it considers it inappropriate to do so.*

(4) *Where the court makes a custody plus order requiring a licence to contain an unpaid work require-ment, an activity requirement, a programme requirement, a prohibited activity requirement, a supervision requirement or an attendance centre requirement, the court may also require the licence to contain an electronic monitoring requirement unless the court is prevented from doing so by section 215(2) or 218(4).*

(5) *Before making a custody plus order requiring a licence to contain two or more different requirements falling within subsection (1), the court must consider whether, in the circumstances of the case, the require-ments are compatible with each other.*

Subsections (1) and (3) to (5) came into force on January 26, 2004, for the purposes of the passing of a sentence of imprisonment to which an intermittent custody order relates and the release on licence of a person serving such a sentence: *Criminal Justice Act 2003 (Commencement No. 1) Order* 2003 (S.I. 2003 No. 3282). See, however, §§ 5–537, 5–539 in the main work.

★   As to the prospective repeal of the whole section, see *ante*, § 5–540.

As to the word "court", see *ante*, § 5–540.

Criminal Justice Act 2003, ss.183–185

Intermittent custody

Intermittent custody

5–542   **183.**—(1) *A court may, when passing a sentence of imprisonment for a term complying with subsection (4)—*

   (a) *specify the number of days that the offender must serve in prison under the sentence before being released on licence for the remainder of the term, and*

   (b) *by order—*

      (i) *specify periods during which the offender is to be released temporarily on licence before he has served that number of days in prison, and*

      (ii) *require any licence to be granted subject to conditions requiring the offender's compliance during the licence periods with one or more requirements falling within section 182(1) and specified in the order.*

  (2) *In this Part "intermittent custody order" means an order under subsection (1)(b).*

  (3) *In this Chapter—*

  "licence period", in relation to a term of imprisonment to which an intermittent custody order relates, means any period during which the offender is released on licence by virtue of subsection (1)(a) or (b)(i);

  "the number of custodial days", in relation to a term of imprisonment to which an intermittent custody order relates, means the number of days specified under subsection (1)(a).

  (4) *The term of the sentence—*

   (a) *must be expressed in weeks,*

   (b) *must be at least 28 weeks,*

   (c) *must not be more than 51 weeks in respect of any one offence, and*

   (d) *must not exceed the maximum term permitted for the offence.*

  (5) *The number of custodial days—*

   (a) *must be at least 14, and*

   (b) *in respect of any one offence, must not be more than 90.*

  (6) *A court may not exercise its powers under subsection (1) unless the offender has expressed his willingness to serve the custodial part of the proposed sentence intermittently, during the parts of the sentence that are not to be licence periods.*

  (7) *Where a court exercises its powers under subsection (1) in respect of two or more terms of imprisonment that are to be served consecutively—*

   (a) *the aggregate length of the terms of imprisonment must not be more than 65 weeks, and*

   (b) *the aggregate of the numbers of custodial days must not be more than 180.*

  (8) *The Secretary of State may by order require a court, in specifying licence periods under subsection (1)(b)(i), to specify only—*

   (a) *periods of a prescribed duration,*

   (b) *periods beginning or ending at prescribed times, or*

   (c) *periods including, or not including, specified parts of the week.*

  (9) *An intermittent custody order which specifies two or more requirements may, in relation to any requirement, refer to compliance within such licence period or periods, or part of a licence period, as is specified in the order.*

Subsection (8) came into force on Royal Assent (November 20, 2003): s.336(1). The remainder of the section came into force on January 26, 2004, for the purposes of the passing of a sentence of imprisonment to which an intermittent custody order relates and the release on licence of a person serving such a sentence: S.I. 2003 No. 3282 (*ante*, § 5–541). See, however, §§ 5–537, 5–539 in the main work.

The *Intermittent Custody (Transitory Provisions) Order* 2003 (S.I. 2003 No. 3283) modifies section 183 (in relation to any time before the commencement of the repeal of section 78 of the *PCC(S)A* 2000 (§ 5–460 in the main work)) by substituting "14" for "28", "26" for "51", "45" for "90", "52" for "65" and "90" for "180" in subsections (4)(b), (4)(c), (5)(b), (7)(a) and (7)(b) respectively.

As to the prospective repeal of the whole section, see *ante*, § 5–540.   ★

Restrictions on power to make intermittent custody order

  184.—(1) *A court may not make an intermittent custody order unless it has been notified by the Secretary of State that arrangements for implementing such orders are available in the area proposed to be specified in the intermittent custody order and the notice has not been withdrawn.*   **5–543**

  (2) *The court may not make an intermittent custody order in respect of any offender unless—*

   (a) *it has consulted an officer of a local probation board or an officer of a provider of probation services,*

    (b) *it has received from the Secretary of State notification that suitable prison accommodation is available for the offender during the custodial periods, and*

    (c) *it appears to the court that the offender will have suitable accommodation available to him during the licence periods.*

    (3) *In this section "custodial period", in relation to a sentence to which an intermittent custody order relates, means any part of the sentence that is not a licence period.*

Intermittent custody: licence conditions

5-544   **185.**—(1) *Section 183(1)(b) has effect subject to section 218 and to the following provisions of Chapter 4 limiting the power to require the licence to contain particular requirements—*

    (a) *section 199(3) (unpaid work requirement),*

    (b) *section 201(3) and (4) (activity requirement),*

    (c) *section 202(4) and (5) (programme requirement), and*

    (d) *section 203(2) (prohibited activity requirement).*

    (2) *Subsections (3) to (5) of section 182 have effect in relation to an intermittent custody order as they have effect in relation to a custody plus order.*

Sections 184 and 185 came into force on January 26, 2004, for the purposes of the passing of a sentence of imprisonment to which an intermittent custody order relates and the release on licence of a person serving such a sentence: S.I. 2003 No. 3282 (*ante*, § 5–541). See, however, §§ 5–537, 5–539 in the main work. Section 184 is printed as amended by the *Offender Management Act 2007 (Consequential Amendments) Order* 2008 (S.I. 2008 No. 912), art. 3, and Sched. 1, para. 19(1) and (4).

★   As to the prospective repeal of the whole of both sections, see *ante*, § 5–540.

Revocation or amendment

★5-545   Section 187 gives effect to Schedule 10 (*post*, §§ 5–558 *et seq.*), which contains provisions relating to the revocation or amendment of custody plus orders and the amendment of intermittent custody orders. As to the prospective repeal of this section, see *ante*, § 5–540.

Transfer of orders

★5-546   Section 188 gives effect to Schedule 11 (not set out in this work), which makes provision for the transfer of custody plus orders and intermittent custody orders to Scotland or Northern Ireland. As to the prospective repeal of this section, see *ante*, § 5–540.

Criminal Justice Act 2003, ss.189–192

Suspended sentences of imprisonment

★5-547   As from a day to be appointed, section 189 of the *CJA* 2003 is amended by the *Legal Aid, Sentencing and Punishment of Offenders Act* 2012, s.68(1), so as to substitute for subsection (1), new subsections (1), (1A) and (1B), as follows—

"(1) If a court passes a sentence of imprisonment for a term of least 14 days but not more than 2 years, it may make an order providing that the sentence of imprisonment is not to take effect unless—

    (a) during a period specified in the order for the purposes of this paragraph ('the operational period') the offender commits another offence in the United Kingdom (whether or not punishable with imprisonment), and

    (b) a court having power to do so subsequently orders under paragraph 8 of Schedule 12 that the original sentence is to take effect.

(1A) An order under subsection (1) may also provide that the offender must comply during a period specified in the order for the purposes of this subsection ('the supervision period') with one or more requirements falling within section 190(1) and specified in the order.

(1B) Where an order under subsection (1) contains provision under subsection (1A), it must provide that the sentence of imprisonment will also take effect if—

    (a) during the supervision period the offender fails to comply with a requirement imposed under subsection (1A), and

(b) a court having power to do so subsequently orders under paragraph 8 of Schedule 12 that the original sentence is to take effect.".

As to the modification of these provisions pending the commencement of section 61 of the ★ *CJCSA* 2000, see *post*, § 5–548.

The amendments and modifications made by section 68 (and Schedule 9 (given effect by ★ s.68(6))) apply in relation to offences committed before the coming into force of any provision of the section or of that schedule: s.68(7).

As from a day to be appointed, section 189(2) of the 2003 Act is amended by the 2012 ★ Act, s.68(2), so as to substitute the words "does not exceed 2 years" for the words from "does not exceed" to the end of the subsection. As to the application of this amendment, see *ante*.

As from a day to be appointed, section 189(3) of the 2003 Act is amended by the 2012 ★ Act, s.68(3), so as to insert the words "(if any)" after the words "supervision period". As to the application of this amendment, see *ante*.

As from a day to be appointed, section 189(4) of the 2003 Act is amended by the 2012 ★ Act, s.68(4), so as to insert at the beginning, "Where an order under subsection (1) imposes one or more community requirements,". As to the application of this amendment, see *ante*.

As from a day to be appointed, section 189(7)(c) of the 2003 Act is amended by the 2012 ★ Act, s.68(5), so as to substitute "(1A)" for "(1)(a)". As to the application of this amendment, see *ante*.

As from a day to be appointed, the modifications of section 189 effected by the *Criminal* ★**5–548** *Justice Act 2003 (Sentencing) (Transitory Provisions) Order* 2005 (S.I. 2005 No. 643) (other than the modification of subs. (6)) are revoked by the *Legal Aid, Sentencing and Punishment of Offenders Act* 2012, s.68(6), and Sched. 9, para. 13. As to the application of this revocation, see section 68(7) of the 2012 Act (*ante*, § 5–547).

In relation to any time before the coming into force of section 61 of the *CJCSA* 2000, it is ★ now provided by section 68(6) of, and Schedule 9, para. 20, to, the *Legal Aid, Sentencing and Punishment of Offenders Act* 2012 that the new subsections (1) and (1B) (*ante*, § 5–547) of section 189 of the 2003 Act shall have effect with the insertion of (i) "or, in the case of a person aged at least 18 but under 21, a sentence of detention in a young offender institution" after the word "imprisonment" where it first appears in subsection (1), (ii) "or detention in a young offender institution" after the word "imprisonment" where it next appears in subsection (1), and (iii) "or detention in a young offender institution" after "imprisonment" in subsection (1B).

As from a day to be appointed, paragraph 2(2) of Schedule 2 to the *Armed Forces Act* ★ *2006 (Transitional Provisions etc.) Order* 2009 (S.I. 2009 No. 1059) is revoked by the *Legal Aid, Sentencing and Punishment of Offenders Act* 2012, s.68(6), and Sched. 9, para. 19.

R. v. Hewitt is now reported at [2011] 2 Cr.App.R.(S.) 111. **5–549**

R. v. Rakib is now reported at [2012] 1 Cr.App.R.(S.) 1.

Imposition of requirements by suspended sentence order

As from a day to be appointed, section 190(1) of the *CJA* 2003 is amended by the *Legal* ★**5–550** *Aid, Sentencing and Punishment of Offenders Act* 2012, s.72(3), so as to insert a new paragraph (ga), as follows—

"(ga) a foreign travel prohibition requirement (as defined by section 206A),".

As from a day to be appointed, section 190(1) of the *CJA* 2003 is further amended by the ★ 2012 Act, s.76(4), so as to insert a new paragraph (ja), as follows—

"(ja) an alcohol abstinence and monitoring requirement (as defined by section 212A),".

Section 77 of the Act (which itself came into force on May 1, 2012) provides for section 76 ★ to be piloted in a specified area or areas before it can be brought into force generally.

As from a day to be appointed, section 190(2) of the 2003 Act is amended by the 2012 ★ Act, s.68(6), and Sched. 9, para. 4, so as to substitute "189(1A)" for "189(1)(a)". As to the application of this amendment, see section 68(7) (*ante*, § 5–547).

As from a day to be appointed, section 190(2)(c) of the 2003 Act is repealed by the 2012 ★ Act, s.70(2).

★   As from a day to be appointed, section 190(2) of the 2003 Act is further amended by the
2012 Act, s.76(5), so as to (i) to omit "and" at the end of paragraph (f), (ii) to insert "and" at
the end of paragraph (g), and (iii) to insert a new paragraph (h), as follows—

"(h) section 212A(8) to (12) (alcohol abstinence and monitoring requirement)".

★   Section 77 of the Act (which itself came into force on May 1, 2012) provides for section 76
to be piloted in a specified area or areas before it can be brought into force generally.

★   As from a day to be appointed, section 190(4) of the 2003 Act is amended by the 2012
Act, s.72(4), so as to insert the words "a foreign travel prohibition requirement," after the
words "a residence requirement,".

Power to provide for review of suspended sentence order

★**5–551**   As from a day to be appointed, section 191(1) of the *CJA* 2003 is amended by the *Legal
Aid, Sentencing and Punishment of Offenders Act* 2012, s.68(6), and Sched. 9, para. 5, so as to
insert the words "that imposes one or more community requirements" after the words
"suspended sentence order". As to the application of this amendment, see section 68(7)
(*ante*, § 5–547).

Criminal Justice Act 2003, s.195

Interpretation of Chapter 3

★**5–556**   As from a day to be appointed, sections 181 to 188 of the 2003 Act are repealed by the
Legal Aid, Sentencing and Punishment of Offenders Act 2012, s.89(1)(a).

★   As from a day to be appointed, section 195 of the 2003 Act is amended by the *Legal Aid,
Sentencing and Punishment of Offenders Act* 2012, s.68(6), and Sched. 9, para. 6(1) and (2), so
as to substitute for the definition of "'operational period' and 'supervision period'" a new
definition, as follows—

"'the operational period', in relation to a suspended sentence, has the meaning given by section
189(1)(a);".

★   As from a day to be appointed, section 195 of the 2003 Act is further amended by the
2012 Act, s.68(6), and Sched. 9, para. 6(1) and (3), so as to insert a new definition at the
end, as follows—

"'the supervision period', in relation to a suspended sentence, has the meaning given by section
189(1A);".

★   As to the application of the amendments made by Schedule 9, see section 68(7) (*ante*, § 5–
547).

★   As from a day to be appointed, section 195 of the 2003 Act is further amended by the
2012 Act, s.89(2), and Sched. 10, paras 12 and 13, so as to omit the definitions of "custodial
period", "licence period" and "the number of custodial days".

Criminal Justice Act 2003, Sched. 10

Section 187   SCHEDULE 10

REVOCATION OR AMENDMENT OF CUSTODY PLUS ORDERS AND AMENDMENT OF INTERMITTENT
CUSTODY ORDERS

Interpretation

5–558   1.—(1) *In this Schedule—*
"*the appropriate court" means —*
(a) *where the custody plus order or intermittent custody order was made by the Crown Court, the
Crown Court, and*
(b) *in any other case, a magistrates' court acting in the local justice area concerned;*
"*the offender", in relation to a custody plus order or intermittent custody order, means the person in respect
of whom the order is made;*

"the local justice area concerned", in relation to a custody plus order or intermittent custody order, means the local justice area for the time being specified in the order;

"the responsible officer" has the meaning given by section 197.

(2) *In this Schedule any reference to a requirement being imposed by, or included in, a custody plus order or intermittent custody order is to be read as a reference to compliance with the requirement being required by the order to be a condition of a licence.*

Orders made on appeal

2. *Where a custody plus order or intermittent custody order has been made on appeal, it is to be taken for the purposes of this Schedule to have been made by the Crown Court.* **5–559**

Revocation of custody plus order or removal from intermittent custody order of requirements as to licence conditions

3.—(1) *Where at any time while a custody plus order or intermittent custody order is in force, it appears to the appropriate court on the application of the offender or the responsible officer that, having regard to circumstances which have arisen since the order was made, it would be in the interests of justice to do so, the court may—* **5–560**

(a) *in the case of a custody plus order, revoke the order, and*

(b) *in the case of an intermittent custody order, amend the order so that it contains only provision specifying periods for the purposes of section 183(1)(b)(i).*

(2) *The revocation under this paragraph of a custody plus order does not affect the sentence of imprisonment to which the order relates, except in relation to the conditions of the licence.*

Amendment by reason of change of residence

4.—(1) *This paragraph applies where, at any time during the term of imprisonment to which a custody plus order or intermittent custody order relates, the appropriate court is satisfied that the offender proposes to change, or has changed, his residence during the licence period from the local justice area concerned to another local justice area.* **5–561**

(2) *Subject to sub-paragraphs (3) and (4), the appropriate court may, and on the application of the Secretary of State or the responsible officer must, amend the custody plus order or intermittent custody order by substituting the other local justice area for the area specified in the order.*

(3) *The court may not amend under this paragraph a custody plus order or intermittent custody order which contains requirements which, in the opinion of the court, cannot be complied with unless the offender resides in the local justice area concerned unless, in accordance with paragraph 5, it either—*

(a) *cancels those requirements, or*

(b) *substitutes for those requirements other requirements which can be complied with if the offender does not reside in that area.*

(4) *The court may not amend under this paragraph any custody plus order or intermittent custody order imposing a programme requirement unless it appears to the court that the accredited programme specified in the requirement is available in the other local justice area.*

Amendment of requirements of custody plus order or intermittent custody order

5.—(1) *At any time during the term of imprisonment to which a custody plus order or intermittent custody order relates, the appropriate court may, on the application of the offender, the Secretary of State or the responsible officer, by order amend any requirement of the custody plus order or intermittent custody order—* **5–562**

(a) *by cancelling the requirement, or*

(b) *by replacing it with a requirement of the same kind imposing different obligations, which the court could include if it were then making the order.*

(2) *For the purposes of sub-paragraph (1)—*

(a) *a requirement falling within any paragraph of section 182(1) is of the same kind as any other requirement falling within that paragraph, and*

(b) *an electronic monitoring requirement is a requirement of the same kind as any requirement falling within section 182(1) to which it relates.*

(3) *Sub-paragraph (1)(b) has effect subject to the provisions mentioned in subsection (2) of section 182, and to subsections (3) and (5) of that section.*

Alteration of pattern of temporary release

6.—(1) *At any time during the term of imprisonment to which an intermittent custody order relates, the appropriate court may, on the application of the offender, the Secretary of State or the responsible officer, amend the order—* **5–563**

(a) *so as to specify different periods for the purposes of section 183(1)(b)(i), or*

(b) *so as to provide that he is to remain in prison until the number of days served by him in prison is equal to the number of custodial days.*

(2) *The appropriate court may not by virtue of sub-paragraph (1) amend an intermittent custody order unless it has received from the Secretary of State notification that suitable prison accommodation is available for the offender during the periods which, under the order as amended, will be custodial periods.*

(3) *In this paragraph "custodial period" has the same meaning as in section 184(3).*

Supplementary

5–564   7. *No application may be made under paragraph 3(1), 5(1) or 6(1) while an appeal against the sentence of which the custody plus or intermittent custody order forms part is pending.*

8.—(1) *Subject to sub-paragraph (2), where a court proposes to exercise its powers under paragraph 5 or 6, otherwise than on the application of the offender, the court—*

(a) *must summon him to appear before the court, and*

(b) *if he does not appear in answer to the summons, may issue a warrant for his arrest.*

(2) *This paragraph does not apply to an order cancelling any requirement of a custody plus or intermittent custody order.*

9.—(1) *On the making under this Schedule of an order revoking or amending a custody plus order or amending an intermittent custody order, the proper officer of the court must—*

(a) *provide copies of the revoking or amending order to the offender and the responsible officer,*

(b) *in the case of an amending order which substitutes a new local justice area, provide a copy of the amending order to—*

   (i) *the local probation board acting for that area, or (as the case may be) a provider of probation services operating in that area, and*

   (ii) *the magistrates' court acting in that area,*

(c) *in the case of an order which cancels or amends a requirement specified in the first column of Schedule 14, provide a copy of so much of the amending order as relates to that requirement to the person specified in relation to that requirement in the second column of that Schedule.*

(2) *Where under sub-paragraph (1)(b) the proper officer of the court provides a copy of an amending order to a magistrates' court acting in a different area, the officer must also provide to that court such documents and information relating to the case as it considers likely to be of assistance to a court acting in that area in the exercise of its functions in relation to the order.*

[Sched. 10 is printed as amended by the *Courts Act 2003 (Consequential Provisions) Order* 2005 (S.I. 2005 No. 886), art. 2, and Sched., para. 108; and the *Offender Management Act 2007 (Consequential Amendments) Order* 2008 (S.I. 2008 No. 912), art. 3, Sched. 1, para. 19(1) and (18).]

★   Schedule 10 (and section 187, which gives effect to it) came into force on January 26, 2004, for the purposes of the passing of a sentence of imprisonment to which an intermittent custody order relates and the release on licence of a person serving such a sentence: S.I. 2003 No. 3282 (*ante*, § 5–541). As to the prospective repeal of the whole of Schedule 10, see *ante*, § 5–540.

The *AFA* 2006, s.199(1) provides that in Schedule 10, as it applies to a custody plus order made by a relevant service court, "the appropriate court" means the Crown Court and the definition of the "appropriate court", in paragraph 1(1), and paragraph 2 are to be treated as omitted; and section 199(2) provides that paragraph 9(1)(b)(ii) and (2) do not apply in relation to a custody plus order made by a relevant service court.

Criminal Justice Act 2003, Sched. 12

Powers of court on breach of community requirement or conviction of further offence

★**5–570**   As from a day to be appointed, paragraph 8(2) of Schedule 12 to the 2003 Act is amended by the *Legal Aid, Sentencing and Punishment of Offenders Act* 2012, s.68(6), and Sched. 9, paras 2 and 10(1) to (3), so as (i) to insert at the beginning of sub-paragraph (c), the words "in the case of a suspended sentence order that imposes one or more community requirements," and (ii) to insert a new paragraph (d) as follows—

"(d) in the case of a suspended sentence order that does not impose any community requirements, the court may, subject to section 189(3), amend the order by extending the operational period".

As to the application of the amendments made by Schedule 9, see section 68(7) (*ante*, § 5– ★ 547).

As from a day to be appointed, paragraph 8(2) of Schedule 12 to the 2003 Act is further ★ amended by the 2012 Act, s.69(1) and (2)(a), so as to insert a new sub-paragraph (ba), as follows—

"(ba) the court may order the offender to pay a fine of an amount not exceeding £2,500,".

As from a day to be appointed, paragraph 8(2) of Schedule 12 to the 2003 Act is further ★ amended by the 2012 Act, s.89(2), and Sched. 10, paras 12 and 38(1) and (2), so as (i) to omit the words "and custodial period" from sub-paragraph (a), and (ii) to substitute, in sub-paragraph (b), the words "with the substitution for the original term of a lesser term" for the words from "with either or both" to the end of the sub-paragraph.

As from a day to be appointed, paragraph 8 of Schedule 12 to the 2003 Act is further ★ amended by the 2012 Act, s.68(6), and Sched. 9, paras 2 and 10(1) and (4), so as to substitute the words "any community requirements" for the words "the community requirements" in sub-paragraph (4)(a). As to the application of the amendments made by Schedule 9, see section 68(7) (*ante*, § 5–547).

As from a day to be appointed, paragraph 8 of Schedule 12 to the 2003 Act is further ★ amended by the 2012 Act, s.69(1) and (2)(b), so as to insert a new sub-paragraph (4ZA) after sub-paragraph (4), as follows—

"(4ZA) A fine imposed under sub-paragraph (2)(ba) is to be treated, for the purposes of any enactment, as being a sum adjudged to be paid by a conviction.".

As from a day to be appointed, paragraph 8(6) of Schedule 12 to the 2003 Act is amended ★ by the 2012 Act, s.69(1) and (2)(c), so as to insert ", (ba)" after "(b)".

As from a day to be appointed, paragraph 8 of Schedule 12 to the 2003 Act is further ★ amended by the 2012 Act, s.68(6), and Sched. 9, paras 2 and 10(1) and (5), so as to substitute the words "any community" for "the community" in sub-paragraph (8). As to the application of the amendments made by Schedule 9, see section 68(7) (*ante*, § 5–547).

Further provisions as to order that suspended sentence is to take effect

As from a day to be appointed, paragraph 9(1) of Schedule 12 to the 2003 Act is amended ★5–571 by the *Legal Aid, Sentencing and Punishment of Offenders Act* 2012, s.89(2), and Sched. 10, paras 12 and 38(1) and (3), so as to omit (i) the words "and custodial period", and (ii) sub-paragraph (a).

Power to amend amount of fine

As from a day to be appointed, a new paragraph 12A is inserted in Schedule 12 to the ★5–574a 2003 Act by the *Legal Aid, Sentencing and Punishment of Offenders Act* 2012, s.69(1) and (3). This gives the Secretary of State the power, by order, to amend the sum for the time being specified in paragraph 8(2)(ba) (as to which, see *ante*, § 5–570).

Application of Part

As from a day to be appointed, a new paragraph 12B is inserted at the beginning of Part ★5–574b 3 of Schedule 12 to the 2003 Act by the *Legal Aid, Sentencing and Punishment of Offenders Act* 2012, s.68(6), and Sched. 9, para. 11, as follows—

"*Application of Part*
12B. This Part of this Schedule applies only in relation to a suspended sentence order that imposes one or more community requirements.".

As to the application of the amendments made by Schedule 9, see section 68(7) (*ante*, § 5– 547).

Transitory provisions, etc.

As from a day to be appointed, the provisions of the *Criminal Justice Act 2003 (Sentencing)* ★5–582

(Transitory Provisions) Order 2005 (S.I. 2005 No. 643) that modify paragraphs 8 and 9 of Schedule 12 to the 2003 Act are repealed by the *Legal Aid, Sentencing and Punishment of Offenders Act* 2012, s.89(2), and Sched. 10, para. 44.

★   As from April 2, 2012 *(Armed Forces Act 2011 (Commencement No. 1, Transitional and Transitory Provisions) Order* 2012 (S.I. 2012 No. 669)), Schedule 7 to the *AFA* 2006 is amended by the *AFA* 2011, s.29, and Sched. 3, para. 24.

★   As from a day to be appointed, the *Armed Forces Act* 2006, Sched. 7, is further amended by the *Legal Aid, Sentencing and Punishment of Offenders Act* 2012, ss.68(6) and 89(2), Sched. 9, paras 14 and 18, and Sched. 10, para. 41(1) and (5).

Authorities

The decision as to implementation

5–584   As to whether it is legitimate, where a judge proposes to implement a suspended sentence in full and consecutively to the sentence to be imposed for a new offence, to treat the seriousness of the new offence as aggravated by the fact that it was committed during the operational period of the suspended sentence, see *R. v. Levesconte, ante,* § 5–70.

★   As to the amendment of paragraph 8 of Schedule 12 to the *CJA* 2003, see *ante,* § 5–570.

(f) Consecutive sentences

Totality of sentences

★5–592   The Sentencing Council for England and Wales has issued a guideline on the related topics of taking offences into consideration and totality, which applies to all offenders who are sentenced on or after June 11, 2012, and which includes consideration as to whether a case calls for concurrent or consecutive sentence. For further detail, see *post,* Appendix K–280 *et seq.*

Other forms of sentence

5–593   In *R. v. Taylor* [2012] 1 Cr.App.R.(S.) 75, CA, the question was whether it was permissible to order a determinate sentence to run from the date on which a minimum term for murder would expire. Following *R. v. Hills* (§ 5–523 in the main work) and considering *R. v. Jumah* (see the main work), it was held that there is no legal inhibition on the imposition of a determinate sentence to be served at a time commencing at the end of a minimum term specified under section 269 of, and Schedule 21 to, the 2003 Act (determination of minimum term in relation to mandatory life sentence *(ibid.,* §§ 5–403, 5–425 *et seq.*)); the power to order a consecutive sentence under section 154 of the *PCC(S)A* 2000 (commencement of Crown Court sentence *(ibid.,* § 5–59)) is restricted only by section 265 of the 2003 Act (restriction on consecutive sentences for released prisoners *(ibid.,* § 5–668)), which has no application to cases other than those where a person has been sentenced but has been released on licence from that sentence. *R. v. Foy* (see the main work) was distinguished on the ground that the statutory scheme that applied at that time was totally different, in that the only possibility of early release was in pursuit of an executive power conferred on the Home Secretary.

(4) Detention and training orders

Powers of Criminal Courts (Sentencing) Act 2000, s.100

Offenders under 18: detention and training orders

★5–597   As from a day to be appointed, section 100(1) of the 2000 Act is amended by the *Legal Aid, Sentencing and Punishment of Offenders Act* 2012, s.126, and Sched. 21, paras 7 and 13, so as to substitute "226B" for "228".

★   As from a day to be appointed, section 100 of the 2000 Act is further amended by the

2012 Act, s.142(3), and Sched. 26, paras 9 and 11, so as to insert a new subsection (1A), as follows—

"(1A) Subsection (1) applies with the omission of paragraph (b) in the case of an offence the sentence for which falls to be imposed under these provisions—
(a) section 1A(5) of the *Prevention of Crime Act* 1953 (minimum sentence for offence of threatening with offensive weapon in public);
(b) section 139AA(7) of the *Criminal Justice Act* 1988 (minimum sentence for offence of threatening with article with blade or point or offensive weapon).".

Powers of Criminal Courts (Sentencing) Act 2000, ss.101, 102

Term of order, consecutive terms and taking account of remands

As from a day to be appointed, section 101 of the 2000 Act is amended by the *Legal Aid, Sentencing and Punishment of Offenders Act* 2012, s.105, and Sched. 12, paras 42 and 43, so as (i) to omit the words from "and in that subsection" in subsection (12) to the end of the subsection, and (ii) to substitute a new paragraph (c) in subsection (11), as follows— ★5–598

"(c) remanded to youth detention accommodation under section 91(4) of the *Legal Aid, Sentencing and Punishment of Offenders Act* 2012; or".

As from a day to be appointed, section 101 of the 2000 Act is further amended by the 2012 Act, s.110(13), and Sched. 13, paras 9 and 11, so as to substitute, in subsection (12A), the words "(2A) of that section to section 240ZA" for the words "(2) of that section to section 240". ★

As from April 2, 2012 (*Armed Forces Act 2011 (Commencement No. 1, Transitional and Transitory Provisions) Order* 2012 (S.I. 2012 No. 669)), section 213 of the *AFA* 2006 is amended by the *AFA* 2011, s.29, and Sched. 3, para. 18, so as: (i) to insert a reference to section 106(4) to (6) of the 2000 Act in subsection (1); and (ii) to insert a reference to section 106(6) of the 2000 Act in subsection (2). ★

As from a day to be appointed, section 213(2) of the *AFA 2006* is further amended by the *Legal Aid, Sentencing and Punishment of Offenders Act* 2012, s.80(9)(a), so as to include a reference to section 104B(1). As to the application of the amendments made by section 80, see section 80(10) and (11) of the 2012 Act. ★

Powers of Criminal Courts (Sentencing) Act 2000, ss.103, 104

Breach of supervision requirements

As from a day to be appointed, section 104(3) of the 2000 Act is amended by the *Legal Aid, Sentencing and Punishment of Offenders Act* 2012, s.80(1) and (2), so as to substitute for paragraph (a), two new paragraphs, as follows— ★5–601

"(a) order the offender to be detained, in such youth detention accommodation as the Secretary of State may determine, for such period, not exceeding the maximum period found under subsection (3A) below, as the court may specify;
(aa) order the offender to be subject to such period of supervision, not exceeding the maximum period found under subsection (3A) below, as the court may specify; or".

Section 80(10) of the 2012 Act provides that the amendments made by section 80 apply in relation to a failure to comply with requirements under section 103(6)(b) of the 2000 Act that occurs after the section comes into force, and subsection (11) stipulates that where a failure is found to have occurred over two or more days, it is to be taken for the purposes of subsection (10) to have occurred on the first of those days. ★

As from a day to be appointed, section 104 of the 2000 Act is further amended by the 2012 Act, s.80(1) and (3), so as to insert new subsections (3A) to (3D), as follows— ★

"(3A) The maximum period referred to in subsection (3)(a) and (aa) above is the shorter of—
(a) three months, and
(b) the period beginning with the date of the offender's failure and ending with the last day of the term of the detention and training order.
(3B) For the purposes of subsection (3A) above a failure that is found to have occurred over two or more days is to be taken to have occurred on the first of those days.

(3C) A court may order a period of detention or supervision, or impose a fine, under subsection (3) above before or after the end of the term of the detention and training order.

(3D) A period of detention or supervision ordered under subsection (3) above—

(a) begins on the date the order is made, and

(b) may overlap to any extent with the period of supervision under the detention and training order.".

As to the application of the amendments made by section 80, see *ante.*

★ As from a day to be appointed, section 104 of the 2000 Act is further amended by the 2012 Act, s.80(1) and (4), so as to insert a new subsection (4A), as follows—

"(4A) Where an order under subsection (3)(a) above is made in the case of a person who has attained the age of 18, the order has effect to require the person to be detained in prison for the period specified by the court.".

As to the application of the amendments made by section 80, see *ante.* Section 80(8) of the 2012 Act provides that, pending the commencement of section 61 of the *CJCSA* 2000, this subsection is to have effect as if it referred to a person who has attained the age of 21.

★ As from a day to be appointed, section 104 of the 2000 Act is further amended by the 2012 Act, s.80(1) and (5), so as to insert a new subsection (5A), as follows—

"(5A) Sections 104A and 104B below make further provision about the operation of orders under subsection (3) above.".

As to the application of the amendments made by section 80, see *ante.*

★ As from a day to be appointed, section 104(6) of the 2000 Act is amended by the 2012 Act, s.80(1) and (6), so as to insert ", (aa)" after "(a)". As to the application of the amendments made by section 80, see *ante.*

Application of sections 103 to 105 in relation to orders under section 104(3)(aa)

★5–601a   As from a day to be appointed, a new section 104A is inserted in the 2000 Act by the *Legal Aid, Sentencing and Punishment of Offenders Act* 2012, s.80(1) and (7). As to the application of the amendments made by section 80, see *ante,* § 5–601.

Powers of Criminal Courts (Sentencing) Act 2000, s.104A

[Application of sections 103 to 105 in relation to orders under section 104(3)(aa)

104A.—(1) Subsections (3) to (7) of section 103 above apply in relation to a period of supervision to which an offender is subject by virtue of an order under section 104(3)(aa) above as they apply to the period of supervision under a detention and training order.

(2) In the application of section 103 above by virtue of subsection (1) above, subsection (7)(a) of that section is to be read as requiring a notice to be given to the offender as soon as is reasonably practicable after the order under section 104(3)(aa) above is made.

(3) Section 104 above and section 105 below apply where an offender is subject to a period of supervision under section 104(3)(aa) above as they apply where a detention and training order is in force in respect of an offender.

(4) In the application of section 104 above by virtue of subsection (3) above—

(a) the references in that section to section 103(6)(b) above are to be read as references to that provision as applied by subsection (1) above,

(b) the references in subsections (3A)(b) and (3C) of that section to the term of the detention and training order are to be read as references to the term of the period of supervision under section 104(3)(aa) above, and

(c) the reference in subsection (3D)(b) of that section to the period of supervision under the detention and training order is to be read as including a reference to the period of supervision under section 104(3)(aa) above.

(5) In the application of section 105 below by virtue of subsection (3) above—

(a) paragraph (a) of subsection (1) of that section is to be read as if the words 'after his release and' were omitted, and

(b) the reference in that paragraph to the date on which the term of the detention and training order ends is to be read as a reference to the date on which the period of supervision under section 104(3)(aa) ends.]

Interaction of orders under section 104(3)(a) with other sentences

★5–601b   As from a day to be appointed, a new section 104B is inserted in the 2000 Act by the

Legal Aid, Sentencing and Punishment of Offenders Act 2012, s.80(1) and (7). As to the application of the amendments made by section 80, see *ante*, § 5–601.

Powers of Criminal Courts (Sentencing) Act 2000, s.104B

[Interaction of orders under section 104(3)(a) with other sentences
   104B.—(1) Where a court makes a detention and training order in the case of an offender who is subject to a period of detention under section 104(3)(a) above, the detention and training order takes effect—
   (a) at the beginning of the day on which it is made, or
   (b) if the court so orders, at the time when the period of detention under section 104(3)(a) above ends.
   (2) Where a court orders an offender who is subject to a detention and training order to be subject to a period of detention under section 104(3)(a) above for a failure to comply with requirements under a different detention and training order, the period of detention takes effect as follows—
   (a) if the offender has been released by virtue of subsection (2), (3), (4) or (5) of section 102 above, at the beginning of the day on which the order for the period of detention is made, and
   (b) if not, either as mentioned in paragraph (a) above or, if the court so orders, at the time when the offender would otherwise be released by virtue of subsection (2), (3), (4) or (5) of section 102 above.
   (3) Subject to subsection (4) below, where at any time an offender is subject concurrently—
   (a) to a detention and training order, and
   (b) to a period of detention under section 104(3)(a) above,
the offender is to be treated for the purposes of sections 102 to 105 of this Act as if the offender were subject only to the detention and training order.
   (4) Nothing in subsection (3) above requires the offender to be released in respect of either the order or the period of detention unless and until the offender is required to be released in respect of each of them.
   (5)–(8) [*Power of Secretary of State to make regulations about the interaction between a period of detention under section 104(3)(a) above and a custodial sentence in a case where an offender who is subject to such a period of detention becomes subject to a custodial sentence, or an offender who is subject to a custodial sentence becomes subject to such a period of detention.*]

As from a day to be appointed, section 80(9)(b) of the *Legal Aid, Sentencing and Punish-* ★
ment of Offenders Act 2012 inserts new subsections (4) to (7) in the *AFA* 2006, s.213. Subsection (4) stipulates that subsection (5) applies where an order under section 104(3) is made against an offender for breach of supervision requirements during a period of supervision under an order under section 211 of that Act (or during a further period of supervision imposed for breach of supervision requirements where the original period of supervision was under section 211). Subsection (5) provides that in the application of sections 104A and 104B of the 2000 Act in relation to the offender, references to section 105 include references to section 214 of the 2006 Act. Subsection (6) makes provision for the interpretation of the expressions "further period of supervision" and "supervision requirements" and subsection (7) provides that in section 104B of the 2000 Act, references to a custodial sentence within the meaning of that Act include a custodial sentence within the meaning of the 2006 Act.

Powers of Criminal Courts (Sentencing) Act 2000, ss.105–107

Interaction with sentences of detention
   As from a day to be appointed, section 106A(1) of the 2000 Act is amended by the *Legal* ★**5-604**
Aid, Sentencing and Punishment of Offenders Act 2012, s.126, and Sched. 21, paras 7 and 14(1) and (2), so as to insert "226B or" after "section" in paragraph (b) of the definition of "sentence of detention".
   As from a day to be appointed, the definition of "sentence of detention" in section 106A(1) ★
of the 2000 Act is further amended by the 2012 Act, s.127, and Sched. 22, paras 14 and 16,

so as (i) to insert "226B or" before "228" in the second place it appears, and (ii) to insert "221A or" before "222".

★   As from a day to be appointed, section 106A(6) of the 2000 Act is amended by the 2012 Act, s.126, and Sched. 21, paras 7 and 14(1) and (3), so as (i) to insert "226B or" before "228", and (ii) to insert "subsection (5)(b) of section 264A or (as the case may be)" after "Board under".

(5) Detention of offenders under 18 convicted of certain serious offences

Powers of Criminal Courts (Sentencing) Act 2000, s.92

Use of the power in cases of dangerous young offenders

★5–612   As to the amendment of section 226 of the 2003 Act, and the repeal of section 228 of that Act, see *ante*, §§ 5–497, 5–499.

E. Release on Licence

Introduction

★5–616   As from a day to be appointed, section 121(1) of the *Legal Aid, Sentencing and Punishment of Offenders Act* 2012 provides that Chapter 6 of Part 12 of the *CJA* 2003 is to apply to any person serving a sentence for an offence committed before April 4, 2005, whenever that sentence was imposed; and, accordingly, section 121(3)(a) stipulates that the repeal of Part II of the *CJA* 1991 by section 303(a) of the 2003 Act has effect in relation to any such person. However, it should be noted that new section 267B of the 2003 Act (inserted, as from a day to be appointed, by the 2012 Act, s.121(6), and Sched. 17, paras 1 and 9) gives effect to new Schedule 20B (which modifies Chapter 6 so as to restate, with minor amendments, the effect of transitional provisions relating to the coming into force of that chapter). The new Schedule 20B is inserted into the 2003 Act by the 2012 Act, s.121(6), and Sched. 17, para. 10. It appears that the only post-commencement sentences to which it will have any application will be extended sentences imposed under section 85 of the *PCC(S)A* 2000 (*ante*, § 5–490).

Saving and transitional provisions

S.I. 2005 No. 950, Sched. 2, paras 14–31

Saving for prisoners serving sentences of imprisonment of less than 12 months

★5–618   As from a day to be appointed, paragraph 14 of Schedule 2 to S.I. 2005 No. 950 is revoked by the *Legal Aid, Sentencing and Punishment of Offenders Act* 2012, s.111(2), and Sched. 14, para. 17, which also provides that the repeal by the *CJA* 2003, s.303(a), of sections 33 to 51 of the *CJA* 1991 has effect in relation to any sentence of imprisonment which is in respect of an offence committed on or after April 4, 2005, and is of less than 12 months (whether or not it is imposed to run concurrently or consecutively with another such sentence).

Power of court to recommend licence conditions for certain prisoners

★5–619   As from a day to be appointed, paragraphs 15 to 18, 19(a), (c) and (d), 20, 22 to 28 and 30 to 34 of Schedule 2 to S.I. 2005 No. 950 are revoked by the *Legal Aid, Sentencing and Punishment of Offenders Act* 2012, s.121(3)(b).

Remand time

★5–620   As to the revocation of paragraphs 17 and 18 of Schedule 2 to S.I. 2005 No. 950, see *ante*, § 5–619.

Savings for prisoners convicted of offences committed before April 4, 2005

As to the revocation of paragraph 19(a), (c) and (d) of Schedule 2 to S.I. 2005 No. 950, see *ante*, § 5–619. ★**5–621**

As from a day to be appointed, sections 27 and 32 of the *CJIA* 2008 are repealed by the *Legal Aid, Sentencing and Punishment of Offenders Act* 2012, s.121(5), and Sched. 16, para. 20. ★

As to the revocation of paragraph 20 of Schedule 2 to S.I. 2005 No. 950, see *ante*, § 5–619. ★**5–622**

As to the revocation of paragraph 22 of Schedule 2 to S.I. 2005 No. 950, see *ante*, § 5–619. ★**5–624**

Transitional arrangements for recall after release

As to the revocation of paragraph 23 of Schedule 2 to S.I. 2005 No. 950, see *ante*, § 5–619. ★**5–625**

Fine defaulters and contemnors

As to the revocation of paragraph 24 of Schedule 2 to S.I. 2005 No. 950, see *ante*, § 5–619. ★**5–626**

Consecutive or concurrent terms

As to the revocation of paragraph 25 of Schedule 2 to S.I. 2005 No. 950, see *ante*, § 5–619. ★**5–627**

As to the revocation of paragraph 26 of Schedule 2 to S.I. 2005 No. 950, see *ante*, § 5–619. ★**5–628**

Crime (Sentences) Act 1997

As to the revocation of paragraph 28 of Schedule 2 to S.I. 2005 No. 950, see *ante*, § 5–619. ★**5–629**

The Criminal Justice and Court Services Act 2000

As to the revocation of paragraph 31 of Schedule 2 to S.I. 2005 No. 950, see *ante*, § 5–619. ★**5–631**

Order for return to prison (offences committed before April 4, 2005/short sentences)

The repeal of sections 116 and 117 of the *PCC(S)A* 2000 effected by the *CJA* 2003, "is of no effect in relation to a person in a case in which the sentence of imprisonment referred to in section 116(1)(a) ... is imposed in respect of an offence committed before April 4, 2005 or is for a term of less than twelve months" (*Criminal Justice Act 2003 (Commencement No. 8 and Transitional and Saving Provisions) Order* 2005 (S.I. 2005 No. 950), Sched. 2, para. 29 (§ 5–630 in the main work). **5–632**

The saving provision in paragraph 29 of Schedule 2 to S.I. 2005 No. 950 was considered in *R. v. Williams* [2010] 2 Cr.App.R.(S.) 6, CA. It was held that where an offender was released on licence in respect of an offence committed before April 4, 2005, and then committed fresh offences before the expiry of the whole term of his sentence, the judge had been entitled, pursuant to section 116 of the 2000 Act (*post*), to order him to return to custody to serve the relevant period in respect of the earlier offence, and to order that the sentences imposed in respect of the new offences be served consecutively to that period. It was clarified that the effect of S.I. 2005 No. 950, Sched. 2, para. 29, was that the repeal of section 116 was of no effect in relation to offences committed before the coming into effect of the repeal. Moreover, the court explained that the amendment of section 265 of the 2003 Act (§ 5–668 in the main work) by the *CJIA* 2008, s.20, so as to provide that subsection (1) applied to a person being sentenced to a term of imprisonment for an offence committed before April 4, 2005, had not had the effect of repealing the saving of section 116. The amendment of section 265, it was said, was necessitated by the amendment of section 116(1) (by the 2008 Act, Sched. 26, para. 45), which took prisoners who have been released under section 33(1A) of the 1991 Act (itself inserted by the 2008 Act, s.26) outside the reach of section 116 and who were then made subject to release and licence provisions which effectively match those of the *CJA* 2003 applying to sentences for offences committed on or after April 4, 2005.

As sections 116 and 117 will continue to apply for an indeterminate period, they are set out below.

Powers of Criminal Courts (Sentencing) Act 2000, s.116

Power to order return to prison etc. where offence committed during original sentence

5-633   **116.**—(1) This section applies to a person if—

    (a) he has been serving a determinate sentence of imprisonment which he began serving on or after 1st October 1992;

    (b) he is released under any provision of Part II of the *Criminal Justice Act* 1991 (early release of prisoners) other than section 33(1A);

    (c) before the date on which he would (but for his release) have served his sentence in full, he commits an offence punishable with imprisonment ("the new offence"); and

    (d) whether before or after that date, he is convicted of the new offence.

(2) Subject to subsection (3) below, the court by or before which a person to whom this section applies is convicted of the new offence may, whether or not it passes any other sentence on him, order him to be returned to prison for the whole or any part of the period which—

    (a) begins with the date of the order; and

    (b) is equal in length to the period between the date on which the new offence was committed and the date mentioned in subsection (1)(c) above.

(3) A magistrates' court—

    (a) shall not have power to order a person to whom this section applies to be returned to prison for a period of more than six months; but

    (b) subject to section 25 of the *Criminal Justice and Public Order Act* 1994 (restrictions on granting bail), may commit him in custody or on bail to the Crown Court to be dealt with under subsection (4) below.

(4) Where a person is committed to the Crown Court under subsection (3) above, the Crown Court may order him to be returned to prison for the whole or any part of the period which—

    (a) begins with the date of the order; and

    (b) is equal in length to the period between the date on which the new offence was committed and the date mentioned in subsection (1)(c) above.

(5) Subsection (3)(b) above shall not be taken to confer on the magistrates' court a power to commit the person to the Crown Court for sentence for the new offence, but this is without prejudice to any such power conferred on the magistrates' court by any other provision of this Act.

(6) The period for which a person to whom this section applies is ordered under subsection (2) or *(4)* above to be returned to prison—

    (a) shall be taken to be a sentence of imprisonment for the purposes of Part II of the *Criminal Justice Act* 1991 and this section;

    (b) shall, as the court may direct, either be served before and be followed by, or be served concurrently with, the sentence imposed for the new offence; and

    (c) in either case, shall be disregarded in determining the appropriate length of that sentence.

(7) As a consequence of subsection (6)(a) above, the court shall not be prevented by section 265 of the *Criminal Justice Act* 2003 (restriction on consecutive sentences for released prisoners) from making any direction authorised by subsection (6)(b) above.

(8) Where the new offence is found to have been committed over a period of two or more days, or at some time during a period of two or more days, it shall be taken for the purposes of this section to have been committed on the last of those days.

(9) For the purposes of sections 9 and 10 of the *Criminal Appeal Act* 1968 (rights of appeal), any order made in respect of a person by the Crown Court under subsection (2) or (4) above shall be treated as a sentence passed on him for the offence for which the sentence referred to in subsection (1) above was passed.

(10) This section and section 117 below apply to persons serving—

    (a) determinate sentences of detention under section 91 above, or

(b) sentences of detention in a young offender institution,
as they apply to persons serving equivalent sentences of imprisonment; and references in this
section and section 117 to imprisonment or prison shall be construed accordingly.

(11) In this section "sentence of imprisonment" does not include a committal for contempt of
court or any kindred offence.

[This section is printed as amended by the *CJIA* 2008, s.148(1), and Sched.26, paras 40
and 45. It is repealed, as from April 4, 2005, by the *CJA* 2003, s.332, and Sched. 37, Pt 7
(*Criminal Justice Act 2003 (Commencement No. 8 and Transitional and Saving Provisions) Order*
2005 (S.I. 2005 No. 950)). As to the saving and transitional provisions applicable to
Chapter 6 of Part 12, see §§ 5–618 *et seq.* in the main work.]

Powers of Criminal Courts (Sentencing) Act 2000, s.117

Treatment for purposes of section 116(1) of person serving two or more sentences or extended sentence

117.—(1) For the purposes of any reference in section 116(1) above (however expressed) to the **5–634**
term of imprisonment to which a person has been sentenced, consecutive terms and terms which
are wholly or partly concurrent shall be treated as a single term if—
  (a) the sentences were passed on the same occasion; or
  (b) where they were passed on different occasions, the person has not been released under
      Part II of the *Criminal Justice Act* 1991 at any time during the period beginning with the
      first and ending with the last of those occasions;
but this is subject to subsection (4) below.

(2) Where a suspended sentence of imprisonment is ordered to take effect, with or without any
variation of the original term, the occasion on which that order is made shall be treated for the
purposes of subsection (1) above as the occasion on which the sentence is passed.

(3) Where a person has been sentenced to two or more terms of imprisonment which are wholly
or partly concurrent and do not fall to be treated as a single term, the date mentioned in section
116(1)(c) above shall be taken to be that on which he would (but for his release) have served each of
the sentences in full.

(4) Subsections (1) to (3) above apply only where one or more of the sentences concerned were
passed on or after 30th September 1998; but where, by virtue of section 51(2) of the *Criminal Justice
Act* 1991 as enacted, the terms of two or more sentences passed before 30th September 1998 have
been treated as a single term for the purposes of Part II of that Act, they shall be treated as a single
term for the purposes of section 116(1) above.

(5) Section 116(1) and subsection (3) above shall each have effect as if the term of an extended
sentence (within the meaning of section 85 above) included the extension period (within the meaning of that section).

[This section is repealed, as from April 4, 2005, by the *CJA* 2003, s.332, and Sched. 37,
Pt 7 (*Criminal Justice Act 2003 (Commencement No. 8 and Transitional and Saving Provisions)
Order* 2005 (S.I. 2005 No. 950)). As to the saving and transitional provisions applicable to
Chapter 6 of Part 12, see §§ 5–618 *et seq.* in the main work.]

The power to order a return to custody applies only when the offender is convicted of an **5–635**
offence committed after his release from custody under Part II of the 1991 Act. It accordingly does not apply to an offence committed by an offender who is unlawfully at large following an escape from prison: *R. v. Matthews and Jacobs* [2002] 1 W.L.R. 2583, CA; nor to
an offence committed by an offender while still in custody serving the custodial part of the
sentence: *R. v. Qureshi* [2002] 2 Cr.App.R.(S.) 11, CA. But an offender may be made the
subject of more than one order under section 116 in respect of the same sentence, as where
he is released after being made the subject of a section 116 order and then commits a further offence before the date on which the sentence for the original offence would have
expired: *R. v. Pick and Dillon* [2006] 1 Cr.App.R.(S.) 61, CA.

In *R. v. Taylor* [1998] 1 Cr.App.R.(S.) 312, the Court of Appeal considered the principles
on which a court should act in deciding whether to order a return to custody under section
116. The sentencing tribunal should first decide what was the appropriate sentence for the
new offence, so that it received the sentence it merited. The possibility of an order under

section 116 should be disregarded at this stage, as section 116(6)(c) required. In considering whether an order under section 116 should be made, it would usually be appropriate to have regard to the nature and extent of any progress made by the defendant since his release and the nature and gravity of the new offence and whether it called for a custodial sentence. It would also be necessary to have regard to the totality, both in determining whether a return to prison should be ordered and whether such a period should be served before or concurrently with the sentence for the new offence, and in determining how long the return period should be. See also *R. v. Blades* [2000] 1 Cr.App.R.(S.) 463, CA; and *R. v. Martin* [2002] 2 Cr.App.R.(S.) 112, CA (order for return to prison for nearly three years in respect of previous sentence for robbery, consecutive to three-month sentence for theft, quashed and substituted by order for return for six months' consecutive).

Before making an order under section 116, the court should ascertain whether any time spent in custody on remand is to be deducted from the term of the original sentence under the *CJA* 1967, s.67 (§ 5–129 in the 2004 edition of this work), as this time will reduce the period which is relevant for the purposes of section 116. If there is any uncertainty about the relevant dates, the court should discount the period of return to allow for it: *R. v. Divers* [1999] 2 Cr.App.R.(S.) 421, CA.

A period which an offender is ordered to serve under section 116 must not be made to run consecutively to a new custodial sentence: *R. v. Jones* [1996] Crim.L.R. 524, CA; *R. v. Clerkenwell Magistrates' Court, ex p. Feely* [1996] 2 Cr.App.R.(S.) 309, DC. If orders are made under section 116 in respect of two different sentences, they must begin on the same day and run concurrently: *R. v. Divers, ante.*

In *R. v. Harrow JJ., ex p. Jordan* [1997] 1 W.L.R. 84, DC, it was held that where an offender was convicted summarily of an offence committed during the term of a sentence imposed by the Crown Court, the whole matter should be dealt with either in the magistrates' court or in the Crown Court. The magistrates' court should either deal with the sentence and the return, or commit both the question of sentence and the question of return to the Crown Court. The latter course should be adopted if there was a significant period of the whole term of the sentence unexpired and the new offence was of any gravity. *Ex p. Jordan* was followed in *R. v. Burton on Trent JJ. and Stafford Crown Court, ex p. Smith* [1998] 1 Cr.App.R.(S.) 223, DC.

5-636   Where an offender is committed to the Crown Court for sentence under the *PCC(S)A* 2000, s.3 (§ 5–25 in the main work), for an either way offence committed within the relevant period following his release from an earlier sentence, the Crown Court has power to make an order under section 116 by virtue of section 5, whether or not he is also committed to be dealt with under section 116(3): *R. v. Stephenson* [1999] 1 Cr.App.R.(S.) 177, CA. Where the offender is not committed for the later offence under section 3, but is committed to be dealt with under section 116, the Crown Court will have no power to sentence him for the later offence unless he is committed for that offence under section 6 (§ 5–33 in the main work).

The fact that an offender has been recalled to custody following the revocation of his licence does not prevent the court from making an order under section 116 in respect of the same sentence: *R. v. Sharkey* [2000] 1 Cr.App.R. 409, CA, disapproving *R. v. Governor of HMP Elmley, ex p. Moorton* [1999] 2 Cr.App.R.(S.) 165, DC.

The *PCC(S)A* 2000, s.84 (repealed and replaced by the *CJA* 2003, s.265 (to the same effect, and set out in the main work at § 5–668)) does not prevent the imposition of a sentence of imprisonment to run consecutively to a period of return to prison ordered under section 116: *R. v. Lowe; R. v. Leask* [1999] 2 Cr.App.R.(S.) 316, CA.

Where an offender who has been released on licence from a sentence of imprisonment commits an offence during the licence period, his licence may be revoked under the *CJA* 2003, s.254, before he comes before the court to be sentenced for the later offence. Any sentence imposed for the later offence must not be ordered to run consecutively to the original sentence which the offender is still serving following the revocation of his licence; but if the court makes an order under section 116 for his return to custody in respect of the original sentence, the sentence for the new offence may be ordered to run consecutively to the period of return so ordered: see *R. v. Laurent* [2001] 1 Cr.App.R.(S.)

65, CA; *R. v. Cawthorn* [2001] 1 Cr.App.R.(S.) 136, CA; and *R. v. Jesson* [2008] 1 Cr.App.R.(S.) 36, CA. It should be remembered that an offender ordered to return to custody under section 116 would normally serve half of the period ordered before release, unless it forms part of a long term sentence when added to the term of the new sentence, while an offender who has been recalled following the revocation of his licence is liable to be detained until the end of the licence period, unless he is released again on licence. See also *R. v. Stocker* [2003] 2 Cr.App.R.(S.) 54, CA; and *R. v. Teasdale* [2004] 1 Cr.App.R.(S.) 6, CA.

Criminal Justice Act 2003, s.237

Meaning of "fixed-term prisoner" etc.

As from a day to be appointed, section 237(1)(b) of the *CJA* 2003 is amended by the *Legal Aid, Sentencing and Punishment of Offenders Act* 2012, s.117(1) and (2), so as to insert (i) "or 96" after "91", and (ii) "227 or" before "228". ★**5–637**

As from a day to be appointed, section 237(1)(b) of the *CJA* 2003 is further amended by the 2012 Act, s.125(4), and Sched. 20, paras 1 and 2(1) and (2), to insert "226A, 226B" before "227". ★

As from a day to be appointed, section 237(1B) of the *CJA* 2003 is amended by the 2012 Act, s.127, and Sched. 22, para. 21, so as to insert new paragraphs (ba) and (bc), as follows—

> "(ba) references to a sentence under section 226A of this Act include a sentence under that section passed as a result of section 219A of the *Armed Forces Act* 2006;
> (bb) references to a sentence under section 226B of this Act include a sentence under that section passed as a result of section 221A of the *Armed Forces Act* 2006;".

As from a day to be appointed, section 237(1C) of the *CJA* 2003 is amended by the 2012 Act, s.110(1) and (2), so as (i) to substitute "240ZA" for "240", and (ii) to insert "or section 240A" after "*Armed Forces Act* 2006)". These amendments apply in relation (i) to any person who falls to be released under Chapter 6 of Part 12 of the 2003 Act on or after the date on which section 110 comes into force (so far as they relate to section 240ZA of the 2003 Act), and (ii) to any person who is sentenced on or after that date (so far as they relate to section 240A of the 2003 Act): 2012 Act, s.120, and Sched. 15, paras 2(1) and 3. ★

As from a day to be appointed, section 237 of the *CJA* 2003 is further amended by the 2012 Act, s.117(1) and (3), so as to insert a new subsection (3), as follows— ★

> "(3) In this Chapter, references to a sentence of detention under section 96 of the *Sentencing Act* or section 227 of this Act are references to a sentence of detention in a young offender institution.".

As from a day to be appointed, section 237(3) of the *CJA* 2003 (*ante*) is amended by the 2012, s.125(4), and Sched. 20, paras 1 and 2(1) and (3), so as to insert "226A or" before "227". ★

As from a day to be appointed, the modification of section 237 effected by the *Criminal Justice Act 2003 (Sentencing) (Transitory Provisions) Order* 2005 (S.I. 2005 No. 643) is revoked by the *Legal Aid, Sentencing and Punishment of Offenders Act* 2012, s.117(11). ★

Criminal Justice Act 2003, ss.238, 239

Power of court to recommend licence conditions for certain prisoners

As from a day to be appointed, section 238 of the 2003 Act is amended by the *Legal Aid, Sentencing and Punishment of Offenders Act* 2012, s.125(4), and Sched. 20, paras 1 and 3, so as to substitute "226B" for "228". ★**5–638**

Criminal Justice Act 2003, s.240

Crediting periods of remand in custody: terms of imprisonment and detention

As from a day to be appointed, section 240 of the *CJA* 2003 is repealed and replaced by a new section 240ZA (time remanded in custody to count as time served: terms of imprisonment and detention) by the *Legal Aid, Sentencing and Punishment of Offenders Act* 2012, s.108(1) and (2). The effect is that giving effect to days spent in custody on remand will be an entirely administrative matter. The sentencing court will have no role to play. ★**5–639**

Criminal Justice Act 2003, s.240ZA

[Time remanded in custody to count as time served: terms of imprisonment and detention

240ZA.—(1) This section applies where—

(a) an offender is serving a term of imprisonment in respect of an offence, and

(b) the offender has been remanded in custody (within the meaning given by section 242) in connection with the offence or a related offence.

(2) It is immaterial for that purpose whether, for all or part of the period during which the offender was remanded in custody, the offender was also remanded in custody in connection with other offences (but see subsection (5)).

(3) The number of days for which the offender was remanded in custody in connection with the offence or a related offence is to count as time served by the offender as part of the sentence.

But this is subject to subsections (4) to (6).

(4) If, on any day on which the offender was remanded in custody, the offender was also detained in connection with any other matter, that day is not to count as time served.

(5) A day counts as time served—

(a) in relation to only one sentence, and

(b) only once in relation to that sentence.

(6) A day is not to count as time served as part of any period of 28 days served by the offender before automatic release (see section 255B(1)).

(7) For the purposes of this section a suspended sentence—

(a) is to be treated as a sentence of imprisonment when it takes effect under paragraph 8(2)(a) or (b) of Schedule 12, and

(b) is to be treated as being imposed by the order under which it takes effect.

(8) In this section 'related offence' means an offence, other than the offence for which the sentence is imposed ('offence A'), with which the offender was charged and the charge for which was founded on the same facts or evidence as offence A.

(9) For the purposes of the references in subsections (3) and (5) to the term of imprisonment to which a person has been sentenced (that is to say, the reference to the offender's "sentence"), consecutive terms and terms which are wholly or partly concurrent are to be treated as a single term if—

(a) the sentences were passed on the same occasion, or

(b) where they were passed on different occasions, the person has not been released at any time during the period beginning with the first and ending with the last of those occasions.

(10) The reference in subsection (4) to detention in connection with any other matter does not include remand in custody in connection with another offence but includes—

(a) detention pursuant to any custodial sentence;

(b) committal in default of payment of any sum of money;

(c) committal for want of sufficient distress to satisfy any sum of money;

(d) committal for failure to do or abstain from doing anything required to be done or left undone.

(11) This section applies to a determinate sentence of detention under section 91 or 96 of the *Sentencing Act* or section 227 or 228 of this Act as it applies to an equivalent sentence of imprisonment.]

★   New section 240ZA is itself amended as from a day to be appointed by the 2012 Act, s.125(4), and Sched. 20, paras 1 and 4, so as to insert "226A, 226B" before "227" in subsection (11).

Re-sentencing following breach of suspended sentence or community order

5–641   *R. v. Hewitt* is now reported at [2011] 2 Cr.App.R.(S.) 111.

Criminal Justice Act 2003, s.240A

Crediting periods of remand on bail: terms of imprisonment and detention

★**5–645**   As from a day to be appointed, the heading for section 240A of the *CJA* 2003 is amended by the *Legal Aid, Sentencing and Punishment of Offenders Act* 2012, s.109(1) and (8), to substitute "*Time remanded on bail to count towards time served*" for "*Crediting periods of remand on bail*".

As from a day to be appointed, section 240A(1)(a) of the *CJA* 2003 is amended by the ★
2012 Act, s.121(5), and Sched. 16, paras 13 and 14, so as to omit the words "committed
on or after 4th April 2005".

As from a day to be appointed, section 240A(2) of the *CJA* 2003 is amended by the 2012 ★
Act, s.109(1) and (2), so as to substitute "subsections (3A) and (3B)" for "subsection (4)".
Section 109 applies in relation to any person sentenced on or after the date on which
that section comes into force: 2012 Act, s.120, and Sched. 15, para. 3.

As from a day to be appointed, section 240A of the *CJA* 2003 is further amended by the ★
2012 Act, s.109(1) and (3), so as to substitute, for subsections (3) to (7), new subsections
(3) to (3B), as follows—

> "(3) The credit period is calculated by taking the following steps.
> *Step 1*
> Add—
>> (a) the day on which the offender's bail was first subject to the relevant conditions (and for
>> this purpose a condition is not prevented from being a relevant condition by the fact that
>> it does not apply for the whole of the day in question), and
>> (b) the number of other days on which the offender's bail was subject to those conditions (but
>> exclude the last of those days if the offender spends the last part of it in custody).
> *Step 2*
> Deduct the number of days on which the offender, whilst on bail subject to the relevant condi-
> tions, was also—
>> (a) subject to any requirement imposed for the purpose of securing the electronic monitoring
>> of the offender's compliance with a curfew requirement, or
>> (b) on temporary release under rules made under section 47 of the *Prison Act* 1952.
> *Step 3*
> From the remainder, deduct the number of days during that remainder on which the offender
> has broken either or both of the relevant conditions.
> *Step 4*
> Divide the result by 2.
> *Step 5*
> If necessary, round up to the nearest whole number.
> (3A) A day of the credit period counts as time served—
>> (a) in relation to only one sentence, and
>> (b) only once in relation to that sentence.
> (3B) A day of the credit period is not to count as time served as part of any period of 28 days
> served by the offender before automatic release (see section 255B(1))."

As to the application of section 109 of the 2012 Act, see *ante*.

As from a day to be appointed, section 240A(8) of the *CJA* 2003 is amended by the 2012 ★
Act, s.109(1) and (4), so as (i) to omit "or (5)" and (ii) to substitute a new paragraph (b),
as follows—

> "(b) the number of days (if any) which it deducted under each of steps 2 and 3".

As to the application of section 109 of the 2012 Act, see *ante*.

As from a day to be appointed, section 240A(9) and (10) of the *CJA* 2003 are repealed by ★
the 2012 Act, s.109(1) and (5). As to the application of section 109 of the 2012 Act, see
ante.

As from a day to be appointed, section 240A(11) of the *CJA* 2003 is amended by the ★
2012 Act, s.109(1) and (6), so as (i) to substitute the words "Subsections (7) to (9) and (11)
of section 240ZA" for the words "Subsections (7) to (10) of section 240", and (ii) to
substitute for the words "(8) the reference to subsection (3) of sections 240 is", in
paragraph (b), the words "(9) the references to subsections (3) and (5) are". As to the application of section 109 of the 2012 Act, see *ante*.

As from a day to be appointed, section 240A(12) of the *CJA* 2003 is amended by the ★
2012 Act, s.109(1) and (7), so as (i) to omit the definition of "related offence" and the
"and" preceding it, and (ii) to insert a new definition before the definition of "electronic
monitoring requirement", as follows—

> "'curfew requirement' means a requirement (however described) to remain at one or more

specified places for a specified number of hours in any given day, provided that the requirement is imposed by a court or the Secretary of State and arises as a result of a conviction;".

As to the application of section 109 of the 2012 Act, see *ante*.

Offences committed before April 4, 2005

★**5-647**   As from a day to be appointed, section 23 of, and Schedule 6 to, the *CJIA* 2008 are repealed by the *Legal Aid, Sentencing and Punishment of Offenders Act* 2012, s.110(14)(c).

Criminal Justice Act 2003, ss.241–243

Effect of direction under section 240 or 240A on release on licence

★**5-650**   As from a day to be appointed, section 241 of the 2003 Act is amended by the *Legal Aid,
Sentencing and Punishment of Offenders Act* 2012, s.110(1) and (3) to (6), so as (i) to substitute,
in the heading, the words "*section 240ZA or direction under section 240A*" for the words
"*direction under section 240 or 240A*", (ii) to substitute, in subsection (1), the words "section
240ZA applies or a direction under section 240A relates" for the words "a direction under
section 240 or 240A relates", and the words "specified in section 240ZA or in the direction
under section 240A" for the words "specified in the direction", and (iii) to substitute, in
subsection (1A), the words "section 240ZA includes" for the words "a direction under section 240 or 240A includes a direction under". These amendments apply in relation (i) to
any person who falls to be released under Chapter 6 of Part 12 of the 2003 Act on or after
the date on which section 110 comes into force (so far as they relate to section 240ZA of the
2003 Act), and (ii) to any person who is sentenced on or after that date (so far as they relate
to section 240A of the 2003 Act): 2012 Act, s.120, and Sched. 15, paras 2(1) and 3.

★   As from a day to be appointed, section 241 of the 2003 Act is further amended by the
2012 Act, s.89(2), and Sched. 10, paras 12 and 20, so as to omit (i) the words "or Chapter 3
(prison sentences of less than 12 months)" in subsection (1), and (ii) subsection (2).

Interpretation of sections 240, 240A and 241

★**5-651**   As from a day to be appointed, section 242 of the *CJA* 2003 is amended by the *Legal Aid,
Sentencing and Punishment of Offenders Act* 2012, s.110(1) and (7), so as to substitute "240ZA"
for "240" in the heading and in subsections (1) and (2). These amendments apply in relation (i) to any person who falls to be released under Chapter 6 of Part 12 of the 2003 Act on
or after the date on which section 110 comes into force (so far as they relate to section
240ZA of the 2003 Act), and (ii) to any person who is sentenced on or after that date (so far
as they relate to section 240A of the 2003 Act): 2012 Act, s.120, and Sched. 15, paras 2(1)
and 3.

★   As from a day to be appointed, section 242 of the *CJA* 2003 is further amended by the
2012 Act, s.105, and Sched. 12, paras 50 and 51, so as (i) to substitute the words "to
youth detention accommodation under section 91(4) of the *Legal Aid, Sentencing and
Punishment of Offenders Act* 2012" for the words from "or committed" to "that section" in
subsection (2)(b), and (ii) to omit subsection (3).

Persons extradited to the United Kingdom

★**5-652**   As from a day to be appointed, section 243 of the *CJA* 2003 is amended by the *Legal Aid,
Sentencing and Punishment of Offenders Act* 2012, s.110(1) and (8), so as to substitute, for
subsection (2), new subsections (2) and (2A), as follows—

"(2) In the case of an extradited prisoner, the court must specify in open court the number of
days for which the prisoner was kept in custody while awaiting extradition.
(2A) Section 240ZA applies to days specified under subsection (2) as if they were days for which
the prisoner was remanded in custody in connection with the offence or a related offence.".

This amendment applies in relation to any person who is sentenced on or after the date
on which section 110 comes into force: 2012 Act, s.120, and Sched. 15, para. 3.

Duty to release prisoners serving less than 12 months

★**5-652a**   As from a day to be appointed, a new section 243A is inserted in the *CJA* 2003 by the
Legal Aid, Sentencing and Punishment of Offenders Act 2012, s.111(1).

Criminal Justice Act 2003, s.243A

[Duty to release prisoners serving less than 12 months

243A.—(1) This section applies to a fixed-term prisoner who is serving a sentence which is for a term of less than twelve months.

(2) As soon as a prisoner to whom this section applies has served the requisite custodial period for the purposes of this section, it is the duty of the Secretary of State to release that person unconditionally.

(3) For the purposes of this section "the requisite custodial period" is—

    (a) in relation to a person serving a sentence of imprisonment for a term of less than twelve months or a determinate sentence of detention under section 91 or 96 of the *Sentencing Act* for such a term, one-half of the sentence, and

    (b) in relation to a person serving two or more concurrent or consecutive sentences, the period determined under sections 263(2) and 264(2).

(4) This section is subject to—

    (a) section 256B (supervision of young offenders after release), and

    (b) paragraph 8 of Schedule 20B (transitional cases).]

Paragraph 8 of Schedule 20B (inserted, as from a day to be appointed, by the 2012 Act, ★
s.121(6), and Sched. 17, paras 1 and 10) provides for release on licence at the half-way point in the case of persons serving an extended sentence (under s.85 of the *PCC(S)A* 2000 (*ante*, § 5–490)) where the offence was committed after September 30, 1998, but before April 4, 2005, if the person has not previously been released on licence in respect of the sentence and he does not fall within paragraph 4 of Schedule 20B. As the premise is that the sentence is for less than 12 months, this provision will have extremely limited, if any, application.

Criminal Justice Act 2003, ss.244–253

Duty to release prisoners

As from a day to be appointed, section 244(1) of the 2003 Act is amended by the *Legal* ★**5–653**
Aid, Sentencing and Punishment of Offenders Act 2012, s.111(2), and Sched. 14, paras 5 and 6(1) and (2), so as to insert "243A or" after the word "section" where it first appears and the words "for the purposes of this section" after the words "the requisite custodial period".

As from a day to be appointed, section 244(1) of the 2003 Act is further amended by the ★
2012 Act, s.125(1) and (2), so as to insert ", 246A" after "243A".

As from a day to be appointed, section 244 of the 2003 Act is further amended by the ★
2012 Act, s.89(2), and Sched. 10, paras 12 and 21, so as (i) to omit subsection (2), and (ii) in subsection (3), to omit paragraphs (b) and (c) and the words "none of which falls within paragraph (c)" in paragraph (d).

As from a day to be appointed, section 244(3) of the 2003 Act is further amended by the ★
2012 Act, s.111(2), and Sched. 14, paras 5 and 6(1) and (3), so as (i) to substitute the words "For the purposes of this section" for the words "In this section", (ii) in paragraph (a), to substitute "a" for "any" and (iii) in the same paragraph, to insert the words "for such a term" after the words "the *Sentencing Act*".

As from a day to be appointed, section 244(3) of the 2003 Act is further amended by the ★
2012 Act, s.117(1) and (4), so as to insert "or 96" after "91" in paragraph (a).

As from a day to be appointed, section 244 of the 2003 Act is further amended by the ★
2012 Act, s.121(6) and Sched. 17, paras 1 and 2, so as to insert a new subsection (4), as follows—

    "(4) This section is subject to paragraphs 5, 6, 8, 25 and 28 of Schedule 20B (transitional cases).".

As to Schedule 20B, see *ante*, § 5–616.

As from a day to be appointed, the modification of section 244(3) effected by the *Criminal* ★
Justice Act 2003 (Sentencing) (Transitory Provisions) Order 2005 (S.I. 2005 No. 643) is revoked by the *Legal Aid, Sentencing and Punishment of Offenders Act* 2012, s.117(11).

Intermittent custody prisoners

As from a day to be appointed, section 245 of the 2003 Act is repealed by the *Legal Aid,* ★**5–654**
Sentencing and Punishment of Offenders Act 2012, s.89(2), and Sched. 10, paras 12 and 22.

Power to release prisoners on licence before required to do so

★**5–655**   As from a day to be appointed, section 246 of the 2003 Act is amended by the *Legal Aid, Sentencing and Punishment of Offenders Act* 2012, s.89(2), and Sched. 10, paras 12 and 23(1) and (2), so as to omit (i) the words ", other than an intermittent custody prisoner" in paragraph (a), and (ii) paragraph (b), and the word "and" that precedes it.

★   As from a day to be appointed, section 246(3) of the 2003 Act is repealed by the 2012 Act, s.89(2), and Sched. 10, paras 12 and 23(1) and (3).

★   As from a day to be appointed, section 246(4) of the 2003 Act is amended by the 2012 Act, s.125(4), and Sched. 20, paras 1 and 5(1) and (2), so as to insert "226A" after "section" in paragraph (a).

★   As from a day to be appointed, section 246(4) of the 2003 Act is amended by the 2012 Act, s.112(1) and (2), so as to insert a new paragraph (aa), as follows—

"(aa) the sentence is for a term of 4 years or more,".

★   As from a day to be appointed, section 246(4)(g) of the 2003 Act is amended by the 2012 Act, s.112(1) and (3), so as (i) to substitute the words "at any time" for the words "during the currency of the sentence", and (ii) to insert at the end, the words "(and the revocation has not been cancelled under section 255(3))".

★   As from a day to be appointed, section 246(4) of the 2003 Act is further amended by the 2012 Act, s.112(1) and (4), so as (i) to omit the word "or" at the end of paragraph (h), and (ii) to insert a new paragraph (ha), as follows—

"(ha) the prisoner has at any time been returned to prison under section 40 of the *Criminal Justice Act* 1991 or section 116 of the *Sentencing Act*, or".

★   As from a day to be appointed, section 246(4)(i) of the 2003 Act is amended by the 2012 Act, s.89(2), and Sched. 10, paras 12 and 23(1) and (4), so as to omit the words "or, where the sentence is one of intermittent custody" to the end of that paragraph.

★   As from a day to be appointed, section 246(4)(i) of the 2003 Act is further amended by the 2012 Act, s.110(1) and (9)(a), so as to substitute the words "to whom section 240ZA applies or a direction under section 240A relates" for the words "to whom a direction under section 240 or 240A relates". This amendment applies in relation (i) to any person who falls to be released under Chapter 6 of Part 12 of the 2003 Act on or after the date on which section 110 comes into force (so far as it relates to section 240ZA of the 2003 Act), and (ii) to any person who is sentenced on or after that date (so far as it relates to section 240A of the 2003 Act): 2012 Act, s.120, and Sched. 15, paras 2(1) and 3.

★   As from a day to be appointed, section 246 of the 2003 Act is further amended by the 2012 Act, s.112(1) and (5), so as to insert a new subsection (4ZA) after subsection (4), as follows—

"(4ZA) Where subsection (4)(aa) applies to a prisoner who is serving two or more terms of imprisonment, the reference to the term of the sentence is—
(a) if the terms are partly concurrent, a reference to the period which begins when the first term begins and ends when the last term ends;
(b) if the terms are to be served consecutively, a reference to the aggregate of the terms.".

★   As from a day to be appointed, section 246(4A)(b) of the 2003 Act is amended by the 2012 Act, s.110(1) and (9)(b), so as to substitute the words "section 240ZA includes" for the words "a direction under section 240 includes a direction under". This amendment applies in relation (i) to any person who falls to be released under Chapter 6 of Part 12 of the 2003 Act on or after the date on which section 110 comes into force (so far as it relates to section 240ZA of the 2003 Act), and (ii) to any person who is sentenced on or after that date (so far as it relates to section 240A of the 2003 Act): 2012 Act, s.120, and Sched. 15, paras 2(1) and 3.

★   As from a day to be appointed, section 246(5) of the 2003 Act is amended by the 2012 Act, s.89(2), and Sched. 10, paras 12 and 23(1) and (5), so as to omit (i) "or (b), (3)" in paragraph (a), and (ii) "or (3)(b)(ii)" in paragraph (c).

★   As from a day to be appointed, section 246(6) of the 2003 Act is amended by the 2012 Act, s.89(2), and Sched. 10, paras 12 and 23(1) and (6), so as to omit (i) the definition of "the required custodial days", (ii) the words "other than a sentence of intermittent custody" and ", (b)" in the definition of "the requisite custodial period" and (iii) the definition of "sentence of intermittent custody". The prospective repeal of the word "or" in the definition of "the required custodial days" in subsection (6) by the *Domestic Violence, Crime and Victims Act* 2004, Sched. 11, is itself repealed as from a day to be appointed by the 2012 Act, s.89(2), and Sched. 10, para. 40(1) and (3).

As from a day to be appointed, section 246(6) of the 2003 Act is further amended by the 2012 Act, s.111(2), and Sched. 14, paras 5 and 7, so as to insert the words "paragraph (a) or (b) of section 243A(3) or (as the case may be)" after the words "has the meaning given by" in the definition of "the requisite custodial period".

As from a day to be appointed, section 246(6) of the 2003 Act is further amended by the ★ 2012 Act, s.112(1) and (6), so as to insert a new definition at the end, as follows—

"'term of imprisonment' includes a determinate sentence of detention under section 91 or 96 of the *Sentencing Act* or under section 227 or 228 of this Act.".

As from a day to be appointed, section 246(6) of the 2003 Act is further amended by the ★ 2012 Act, s.125(4), and Sched. 20, paras 1 and 5(1) and (3), so as to insert "226A, 226B" before "227" in the definition of "term of imprisonment".

As to the modification of section 246 in its application to persons serving a sentence for an ★ offence committed before April 4, 2005, whenever the sentence was imposed, see paragraph 4 of Schedule 20A to the 2003 Act (inserted, as from a day to be appointed, by the *Legal Aid, Sentencing and Punishment of Offenders Act* 2012, s.121(5), and Sched. 16, paras 1 and 3).

Release on licence of prisoners serving extended sentence under section 226A or 226B

As from a day to be appointed, a new section 246A is inserted in the *CJA* 2003 by the ★5–655a *Legal Aid, Sentencing and Punishment of Offenders Act* 2012, s.125(1) and (3).

Criminal Justice Act 2003, s.246A

[Release on licence of prisoners serving extended sentence under section 226A or 226B

246A.—(1) This section applies to a prisoner ("P") who is serving an extended sentence imposed under section 226A or 226B.

(2) It is the duty of the Secretary of State to release P on licence under this section as soon as P has served the requisite custodial period for the purposes of this section unless either or both of the following conditions are met—

(a) the appropriate custodial term is 10 years or more;

(b) the sentence was imposed in respect of an offence listed in Parts 1 to 3 of Schedule 15B or in respect of offences that include one or more offences listed in those Parts of that Schedule.

(3) If either or both of those conditions are met, it is the duty of the Secretary of State to release P on licence in accordance with subsections (4) to (7).

(4) The Secretary of State must refer P's case to the Board—

(a) as soon as P has served the requisite custodial period, and

(b) where there has been a previous reference of P's case to the Board under this subsection and the Board did not direct P's release, not later than the second anniversary of the disposal of that reference.

(5) It is the duty of the Secretary of State to release P on licence under this section as soon as—

(a) P has served the requisite custodial period, and

(b) the Board has directed P's release under this section.

(6) The Board must not give a direction under subsection (5) unless—

(a) the Secretary of State has referred P's case to the Board, and

(b) the Board is satisfied that it is no longer necessary for the protection of the public that P should be confined.

(7) It is the duty of the Secretary of State to release P on licence under this section as soon as P has served the appropriate custodial term, unless P has previously been released on licence under this section and recalled under section 254 (provision for the release of such persons being made by section 255C).

(8) For the purposes of this section—

"appropriate custodial term" means the term determined as such by the court under section 226A or 226B (as appropriate);

"the requisite custodial period" means—
(a) in relation to a person serving one sentence, two-thirds of the appropriate custodial term, and
(b) in relation to a person serving two or more concurrent or consecutive sentences, the period determined under sections 263(2) and 264(2).]

Release on licence of prisoner serving extended sentence under section 227 or 228

★**5–657**   As from a day to be appointed, section 247 of the 2003 Act is amended by the *Legal Aid, Sentencing and Punishment of Offenders Act* 2012, s.121(6), and Sched. 17, paras 1 and 3, so as to insert a new subsection (8), as follows—

"(8) In its application to a person serving a sentence imposed before 14 July 2008, this section is subject to the modifications set out in paragraph 15 of Schedule 20B (transitional cases).".

★   As to Schedule 20B to the 2003 Act, see *ante*, § 5–616.

Duration of licence

★**5–659**   As from a day to be appointed, section 249 of the 2003 Act is amended by the *Legal Aid, Sentencing and Punishment of Offenders Act* 2012, s.89(2), and Sched. 10, paras 12 and 24, so as (i) to omit subsections (2) and (4) and the words, in subsection (3), from "and subsection (2)" to the end of the subsection, and (ii) to substitute "subsection (3)" for "subsections (2) and (3)" in subsection (1).

★   As from a day to be appointed, section 249 of the 2003 Act is further amended by the 2012 Act, s.111(2), and Sched. 14, paras 5 and 8(1) to (3), so as (i) to insert the words ", other than one to whom section 243A applies" after the words "a fixed-term prisoner" in subsection (1), and (ii) to insert a new subsection (1A) as follows—

"(1A) Where a prisoner to whom section 243A applies is released on licence, the licence shall, subject to any revocation under section 254 or 255, remain in force until the date on which, but for the release, the prisoner would have served one-half of the sentence.

This is subject to subsection (3).".

★   As from a day to be appointed, section 249 of the 2003 Act is further amended by the 2012 Act, s.111(2), and Sched. 14, paras 5 and 8(1) and (4), so as (i) to substitute "Subsections (1) and (1A) have" for "Subsection (1) has" in subsection (3), and (ii) to omit "and (4)" from the same subsection.

★   As from a day to be appointed, section 249 of the 2003 Act is further amended by the 2012 Act, s.121(6), and Sched. 17, paras 1 and 4, so as to insert a new subsection (5), as follows—

"(5) This section is subject to paragraphs 17, 19 and 26 of Schedule 20B (transitional cases).".

★   As to Schedule 20B to the 2003 Act, see *ante*, § 5–616.

Licence conditions

★**5–660**   As from a day to be appointed, section 250 of the 2003 Act is amended by the *Legal Aid, Sentencing and Punishment of Offenders Act* 2012, s.89(2), and Sched. 10, paras 12 and 25, so as (i) to omit subsections (2), (2A), (3) and (6), and (ii) to substitute the words "and section 264(3) (consecutive terms)" for the words from "section 264(3)" to the end of the subsection.

★   As from a day to be appointed, section 250(4) of the 2003 Act is amended by the 2012 Act, s.111(2), and Sched. 14, paras 5 and 9, so as to omit the words "for a term of twelve months or more" and the word "such" where it first appears.

★   As from a day to be appointed, section 250(4) of the 2003 Act is further amended by the 2012 Act, s.117(1) and (5), so as (i) to insert "or 96" after "91" and (ii) to insert "227 or" before "228".

★   As from a day to be appointed, section 250(4) of the 2003 Act is further amended by the 2012 Act, s.125(4), and Sched. 20, paras 1 and 6(1) and (2), so as (i) to insert before the first "227", "226A or", and (ii) to insert before the second "227", "226A, 226B,".

★   As from a day to be appointed, section 250 of the 2003 Act is further amended by the 2012 Act, s.125(4), and Sched. 20, paras 1 and 6(1) and (3), so as to insert a new subsection (5A), as follows—

"(5A) In respect of a prisoner serving an extended sentence imposed under section 226A or 226B whose release is directed by the Board under section 246A(5), a licence under—

(a) section 246A(5) (initial release), or

(b) section 255C (release after recall),

may not include conditions referred to in subsection (4)(b)(ii) unless the Board directs the Secretary of State to include them.".

As from a day to be appointed, the modification of section 250(4) effected by the *Criminal* ★ *Justice Act 2003 (Sentencing) (Transitory Provisions) Order* 2005 (S.I. 2005 No. 643) is revoked by the *Legal Aid, Sentencing and Punishment of Offenders Act* 2012, s.117(11).

Licence conditions on re-release of prisoner serving sentence of less than 12 months
As from a day to be appointed, section 251 of the 2003 Act is repealed by the *Legal Aid,* ★5–661 *Sentencing and Punishment of Offenders Act* 2012, s.89(2), and Sched. 10, paras 12 and 26.

Duty to comply with licence conditions
As from a day to be appointed, section 252(2) of the 2003 Act is amended by the *Legal* ★5–662 *Aid, Sentencing and Punishment of Offenders Act* 2012, s.89(2), and Sched. 10, paras 12 and 27.

Curfew condition to be included in licence under section 246
As from a day to be appointed, the heading to section 253 of the 2003 Act is amended by ★5–663 the *Legal Aid, Sentencing and Punishment of Offenders Act* 2012, s.114(3), so as to insert ", 255B or 255C" after "*section 246*".

As from a day to be appointed, section 253(3) of the 2003 Act is amended by the 2012 ★ Act, s.111(2), and Sched. 14, paras 5 and 10, so as to insert the words "unconditionally under section 243A or" after the words "fall to be released".

As from a day to be appointed, section 253(4) of the 2003 Act is repealed by the 2012 Act, ★ s.89(2), and Sched. 10, paras 12 and 28.

Recall after release
As from a day to be appointed, (i) sections 254 and 255 of the *CJA* 2003 are further ★5–664 amended by the *Legal Aid, Sentencing and Punishment of Offenders Act* 2012, s.113; (ii) new sections 255A to 255C of the 2003 Act are substituted for sections 255A to 255D by *ibid.*, s.114(1); and (iii) section 256 of the 2003 Act is amended by *ibid.*, s.114(4).

As from a day to be appointed, the substituted section 255A is amended by the 2012 Act, ★ s.125(4), and Sched. 20, paras 1 and 7.

Supervision of young offenders after release
As from a day to be appointed, the *Legal Aid, Sentencing and Punishment of Offenders Act* ★5–664a 2012, s.115, inserts new sections 256B (supervision of young offenders after release) and 256C (breach of supervision requirements) in the *CJA* 2003. Where a breach is proved to the satisfaction of a magistrates' court, that court may impose up to 30 days' detention or a fine not exceeding level 3. The offender has a right of appeal to the Crown Court (s.256C(7)).

Criminal Justice Act 2003, ss.263, 264, 264A

Concurrent terms
As from a day to be appointed, section 263(2) of the 2003 Act is amended by the *Legal* ★5–665 *Aid, Sentencing and Punishment of Offenders Act* 2012, s.111(2), and Sched. 14, paras 5 and 13, so as (i) to insert the words "to which that section applies" after the words "each of the others" in paragraph (b), (ii) to insert the words "(unless that release is unconditional)" after the words "release under this Chapter" in paragraph (c), and (iii) to insert a new paragraph (aa), as follows—

"(aa) the offender's release is to be unconditional if section 243A so requires in respect of each of the sentences (and in any other case is to be on licence),".

★   As from a day to be appointed, section 263(2) of the 2003 Act is further amended by the 2012 Act, s.116(1), (8) and (9), so as to (i) to substitute "246" for "244" in paragraph (b), and (ii) to substitute, in paragraph (c), for the words "licence for so long, and subject to such conditions, as is", new text, as follows—

"licence—
    (i)   until the last date on which the offender is required to be on licence in respect of any of the terms, and
    (ii) subject to such conditions as are".

★   As from a day to be appointed, section 263(3) of the 2003 Act is repealed by the 2012 Act, s.89(2), and Sched. 10, paras 12 and 31.

★   As from a day to be appointed, section 263(4) of the 2003 Act is amended by the 2012 Act, s.117(1) and (7), so as to insert "or 96" after "91" and "227 or" before "228".

★   As from a day to be appointed, section 263(4) of the 2003 Act is further amended by the 2012 Act, s.125(4), and Sched. 20, paras 1 and 11, so as to insert "226A, 226B," before "227".

★   As from a day to be appointed, section 263 of the 2003 Act is further amended by the 2012 Act, s.121(6), and Sched. 17, paras 1 and 7, so as to insert a new subsection (5), as follows—

"(5) This section is subject to paragraphs 21, 31 and 32 of Schedule 20B (transitional cases).".

As to Schedule 20B to the 2003 Act, see *ante*, § 5–616.

★   As from a day to be appointed, the modification of section 263(4) effected by the *Criminal Justice Act 2003 (Sentencing) (Transitory Provisions) Order* 2005 (S.I. 2005 No. 643) is revoked by the *Legal Aid, Sentencing and Punishment of Offenders Act* 2012, s.117(11).

Consecutive terms

★5–666   As from a day to be appointed, section 264(1) of the 2003 Act is amended by the *Legal Aid, Sentencing and Punishment of Offenders Act* 2012, s.89(2), and Sched. 10, paras 12 and 32(1) and (2), so as to omit paragraph (c), and the word "and" that precedes it. The prospective repeal of the word "and" at the end of subsection (1)(a) by the *Domestic Violence, Crime and Victims Act* 2004, Sched. 11, is itself repealed as from a day to be appointed by the 2012 Act, s.89(2), and Sched. 10, para. 40(1) and (3).

★   As from a day to be appointed, section 264(2) of the 2003 Act is amended by the 2012 Act, s.111(2), and Sched. 14, paras 5 and 14(a), so as to omit the words "on licence".

★   As from a day to be appointed, section 264(3) of the 2003 Act is amended by the 2012 Act, s.111(2), and Sched. 14, paras 5 and 14(b), so as to substitute the words "the aggregate length of the terms of imprisonment is 12 months or more" for the words "any of the terms of imprisonment is a term of twelve months or more".

★   As from a day to be appointed, section 264 of the 2003 Act is further amended by the 2012 Act, s.111(2), and Sched. 14, paras 5 and 14(c), so as to insert a new subsection (3A), as follows—

"(3A) Where the aggregate length of the terms of imprisonment is less than 12 months, the offender's release under this Chapter is to be unconditional.".

★   As from a day to be appointed, section 264(4) and (5) of the 2003 Act are repealed by the 2012 Act, s.111(2), and Sched. 14, paras 5 and 14(d).

★   As from a day to be appointed, section 264(6)(a)(ii) of the 2003 Act is amended by the 2012 Act, s.111(2), and Sched. 14, paras 5 and 14(e), so as to substitute the words "any other sentence" for the words "a term of twelve months or more", and the words "the sentence" for the words "the term".

★   As from a day to be appointed, section 264(6) of the 2003 Act is further amended by the 2012 Act, s.89(2), and Sched. 10, paras 12 and 32(1) and (3), so as to omit (i) paragraph (a)(iii) and the word "and" that precedes it, and (ii) paragraph (b).

★   As from a day to be appointed, section 264(6) of the 2003 Act is further amended by the 2012 Act, s.125(4), and Sched. 20, paras 1 and 12(1) and (2), so as to insert a new paragraph (zi) before sub-paragraph (a)(i), as follows—

"(zi) in relation to an extended sentence imposed under section 226A or 226B, means two-thirds of the appropriate custodial term determined by the court under that section,".

As from a day to be appointed, section 264(7) of the 2003 Act is amended by the 2012 ★ Act, s.111(2), and Sched. 14, paras 5 and 14(f), so as to omit the words "of 12 months or more".

As from a day to be appointed, section 264(7) of the 2003 Act is further amended by the ★ 2012 Act, s.117(1) and (8), so as to insert "or 96" after "91" and "227 or" before "228".

As from a day to be appointed, section 264(7) of the 2003 Act is further amended by the ★ 2012 Act, s.125(4), and Sched. 20, paras 1 and 12(1) and (3), so as to insert "226A, 226B," before "227".

As from a day to be appointed, section 264 of the 2003 Act is further amended by the ★ 2012 Act, s.121(6), and Sched. 17, paras 1 and 8, so as to insert a new subsection (8), as follows—

"(8) This section is subject to paragraphs 21, 22, 31, 32 and 33 of Schedule 20B (transitional cases).".

As to Schedule 20B to the 2003 Act, see *ante*, § 5–616.

As from a day to be appointed, the modification of section 264(7) effected by the *Criminal* ★ *Justice Act 2003 (Sentencing) (Transitory Provisions) Order* 2005 (S.I. 2005 No. 643) is revoked by the *Legal Aid, Sentencing and Punishment of Offenders Act* 2012, s.117(11).

As to the extended ambit of the definition of "custodial period" in section 264(6), see sec- ★ tion 267A of, and paragraph 10 of Schedule 20A to, the *CJA* 2003 (inserted, as from a day to be appointed, by the *Legal Aid, Sentencing and Punishment of Offenders Act* 2012, s.121(5), and Sched. 16, paras 1 to 3). Schedule 20A is expressed to modify certain provisions of Chapter 6 of Part 12 of the 2003 Act as they apply to persons serving a sentence for an offence committed before April 4, 2005. Paragraph 2 declares that paragraphs 3 to 9 apply in relation to any person serving a sentence for an offence committed before that date, whenever the sentence was imposed. The schedule is, therefore, silent as to the application of paragraph 10, which provides that section 264 applies as if the definition of "custodial period" in subsection (6) included, in relation to an extended sentence under the *PCC(S)A* 2000, s.85 (*ante*, § 5–490), one-half of the custodial term determined under that section.

Consecutive terms: intermittent custody

As from a day to be appointed, section 264A of the 2003 Act is repealed by the *Legal Aid,* ★**5–667** *Sentencing and Punishment of Offenders Act* 2012, s.89(2), and Sched. 10, paras 12 and 33.

Criminal Justice Act 2003, s.265

Restriction on consecutive sentences for released prisoners

As from a day to be appointed, section 265(1A) and (1B) of the 2003 Act are repealed by ★**5–668** the *Legal Aid, Sentencing and Punishment of Offenders Act* 2012, ss.89(2) and 121(5), Sched. 10, paras 12 and 34 (subs. 1B), and Sched. 16, paras 13 and 17 (subs. (1A)).

As from a day to be appointed, section 265(2) of the 2003 Act is amended by the 2012 ★ Act, s.117(1) and (9), so as to insert "or 96" after "91" and "227 or" before "228".

As from a day to be appointed, section 265(2) of the 2003 Act is further amended by the ★ 2012 Act, s.125(4), and Sched. 20, paras 1 and 13, so as to insert "226A, 226B," before "227".

As from a day to be appointed, the modification of section 265(2) effected by the *Criminal* ★ *Justice Act 2003 (Sentencing) (Transitory Provisions) Order* 2005 (S.I. 2005 No. 643) is revoked by the *Legal Aid, Sentencing and Punishment of Offenders Act* 2012, s.117(11).

Criminal Justice Act 2003, s.268

Interpretation of Chapter 6

As from a day to be appointed, section 268 of the 2003 Act is amended by the *Legal Aid,* ★**5–670** *Sentencing and Punishment of Offenders Act* 2012, s.89(2), and Sched. 10, paras 12 and 35, so as to omit the definitions of "intermittent custody prisoner", "release" and "relevant court order".

VII. FINES

Criminal Justice Act 2003, ss.163–165

General power of Crown Court to fine offender convicted on indictment

★**5–673**   As from a day to be appointed, section 163 of the 2003 Act is amended by the *Legal Aid, Sentencing and Punishment of Offenders Act* 2012, s.122(3), and Sched. 19, paras 8 and 14, so as to insert "224A," before "225(2)".

Power of Criminal Courts (Sentencing) Act 2000, ss.139, 140, 142

Enforcement of fines imposed and recognizances forfeited by Crown Court

★**5–677**   As to the commencement of section 41 of, and paragraph 74 of Schedule 3 to, the 2003 Act (see the main work), see *ante*, § 5–42.

Criminal Justice Act 1982, s.37

★**5–683**   As to the removal (as from a day to be appointed) of £5,000 as the upper limit on a fine on summary conviction of an offence, see the *Legal Aid, Sentencing and Punishment of Offenders Act* 2012, s.85 (*ante*, § 1–125).

★   As from a day to be appointed, section 37(3) of the 1982 Act is amended by the *Legal Aid, Sentencing and Punishment of Offenders Act* 2012, s.87(4), so as to insert at the end, the words "or section 87 of the *Legal Aid, Sentencing and Punishment of Offenders Act* 2012".

Terms of imprisonment in default

★**5–689**   The following principles emerge from the authorities for the guidance of courts fixing a period of imprisonment to be served in default of payment of a confiscation order, in accordance with the scale set out in the *PCC(S)A* 2000, s.139 (§ 5–676 in the main work): (i) it is of the first importance to have in mind that the purpose of a default term is to secure payment of the confiscation order; (ii) it is not the court's function to find an arithmetical match between the amount of the order and the length of the term, such that for any given band or bracket prescribed in the 2000 Act an order at the bottom of the band should attract a default term likewise at the bottom of the band, an order in the middle of the band should attract a term in the middle or an order at the top should attract a term at the top; (iii) the court is not to be influenced by the overall totality of the sentence passed for the crime plus the default term; but (iv), for any given band, the court should have regard to the maximum amount of a confiscation order within the band and the maximum default term within the band; (v) given principle (iv), and especially in a case falling within the top band (an amount exceeding £1 million) where there is no maximum confiscation order but only a maximum default term (10 years' imprisonment), regard must be had to the requirement of proportionality; however, it should be noted that the demands of proportionality are much weaker here, where the purpose of the default term is to secure satisfaction of the confiscation order, than where the court is punishing the offender: *R. v. Castillo (German)* [2012] Crim.L.R. 401, CA. It was held that, in the case before the court, where the amount of the order was £3 million and where the judge had imposed the maximum default term, some heed should have been paid to the fact that the maximum would be same for an order five times as great or more, and consideration should have been given to fixing a somewhat shorter period; in this context, proportionality did not define the right order; it merely adjusted what would otherwise be a wrong one. The default term was reduced to nine years.

VIII. COMPENSATION, RESTITUTION AND REPARATION

A. COMPENSATION ORDERS

Powers of Criminal Courts (Sentencing) Act 2000, ss.130–132

Compensation orders against convicted persons

As from a day to be appointed, section 130(2) of the *PCC(S)A* 2000 is amended by the　★**5–691**
Legal Aid, Sentencing and Punishment of Offenders Act 2012, s.122(3), and Sched. 19, paras 3
and 5, so as to insert "224A," before "225(2)".

As from a day to be appointed, section 130(2) of the 2000 Act is further amended by the　★
2012 Act, s.142(3), and Sched. 26, paras 9 and 12, so as to substitute the words "section
1A(5) of the *Prevention of Crime Act* 1953, section 51A(2) of the *Firearms Act* 1968, section
139AA(7) of the *Criminal Justice Act* 1988" for the words "section 51A(2) of the *Firearms Act*
1968".

As from a day to be appointed, section 130 of the 2000 Act is further amended by the　★
2012 Act, s.63(1), so as to insert a new subsection (2A), as follows—

"(2A) A court must consider making a compensation order in any case where this section empowers it to do so.".

The means of the offender (s.130(11))

For a further case considering the inquiries a court must make before imposing a　★**5–704**
compensation order, see *R. v. Ganyo (Molly) and Ganyo (Prize), post,* § 5–707.

Period of payment

Neither *R. v. Olliver and Olliver,* nor *R. v. Yehou* (see the main work), is authority for　★**5–707**
there being an outer limit for the period of repayment of a compensation order under the
PCC(S)A 2000, s.130 (§ 5–691 in the main work); under subsection (4), a court making
such an order must ask whether it is appropriate; and that requires an inquiry into
whether an order will be oppressive or an undue burden given the offender's means,
whether realistically he can be expected to repay in the terms proposed, and whether the
order accords with the nature of the offence and the nature of the offender: *R. v. Ganyo
(Molly) and Ganyo (Prize)* [2012] 1 Cr.App.R.(S.) 108, CA (upholding compensation orders
to repay N.H.S. bursaries of £10,000, at £100 per month (the defendant having obtained
professional qualifications as a result of her fraud), and of £3,298, at £50 per month).

B. RESTITUTION ORDERS

Powers of Criminal Courts (Sentencing) Act 2000, ss.148, 149

Restitution orders

With effect from June 18, 2012 (*Criminal Justice Act 2003 (Commencement No. 28 and Sav-*　★**5–711**
ing Provisions) Order 2012 (S.I. 2012 No. 1320)), sections 41 and 332 of, and paragraph 74
of Schedule 3 to, and Part 4 of Schedule 37 to, the 2003 Act are brought into force (so far as
not already in force) in certain areas (as to which, see *ante,* § 1–88). There are associated
saving provisions, as to which, see article 5 of the order (*ante,* § 1–88).

IX. DEPRIVATION AND CONFISCATION

A. DEPRIVATION

Powers of Criminal Courts (Sentencing) Act 2000, ss.143–145

Property subject to multiple ownership

5–734   *R. v. Kearney* is now reported at [2011] 2 Cr.App.R.(S.) 106.

Value of the property and the likely financial effects of the order on the offender (s.143(5))

5–735   Where a court, in making a deprivation order under the 2000 Act, s.143, fails to have regard to the value of the property and the likely financial and other effects on the offender of the making of the order, as required by section 143(5), such order is invalidly made and cannot stand: *Trans Berckx BVBA v. North Avon Magistrates' Court and Swindon Magistrates' Court and Other Interested Parties*, 176 J.P. 28, DC.

B. CONFISCATION UNDER THE DRUG TRAFFICKING ACT 1994

Assessment of benefit

5–737   When determining for the purposes of section 2 of the *DTA* 1994 (confiscation orders) whether an offender has benefited from an offence of drug trafficking in respect of which he has *not* been convicted at trial, the statutory assumptions provided for in section 4(3) are not the only way in which the Act permits the court to determine the fact (or extent) of such benefit; where those assumptions are not applicable, the court is entitled to rely on other evidence led at trial to show that one or more offences of drug trafficking (other than those charged) have been committed (and then to estimate the benefit that must have been obtained from those offences): *R. v. Briggs-Price* [2009] 1 A.C. 1026, HL. A majority of their Lordships held, however, that a judge should only rely on evidence of other offences not charged if he was satisfied to the criminal standard that they had been proved (the minority taking the view that the civil standard was the applicable standard).

Valuation of property

5–738   Where a judge assessed the value of the defendant's proceeds of drug trafficking at £3.2 million, he was correct in taking the view that he was required by the *DTA* 1994 to make a confiscation order in that amount, unless the defendant satisfied him (to the civil standard) that his realisable assets were less than that amount; and where the defendant had failed to do so, there was no obligation on the judge to assume that the defendant would have incurred some expenses to be set against that figure, and to make some discount in respect thereof; such approach was misconceived; his task under the statute was to assess the value of the proceeds in accord with the provisions of the statute (which was not the same as profit), and to make an order in that amount unless the value of the realisable assets was less than that amount, and the burden of proof in that regard was on the defendant: *R. v. Versluis* [2005] 2 Cr.App.R.(S.) 26, CA.

"drug trafficking offence"

5–739   Where the defendant was convicted of a conspiracy to convert the proceeds of drug trafficking "or" the proceeds of criminal conduct (the substantive offences being created by the *DTA* 1994, s.49, and the *CJA* 1988, s.93C, respectively), this was to be construed as a find-

ing that the agreement was not restricted to the laundering of the proceeds of drug trafficking or to the proceeds of criminal conduct other than drug trafficking, but was an
agreement to launder money, whatever its provenance; it was, in effect, an agreement to
launder both the proceeds of drug trafficking and the proceeds of other criminal conduct;
accordingly, the defendant was properly to be regarded as having been convicted of a
"drug trafficking offence" for the purposes of the confiscation provisions of the 1994 Act
as the definition of that expression extended to a conspiracy to commit an offence contrary to section 49; and the judge had, therefore, erred in declining to conduct confiscation proceedings under the 1994 Act: *R. v. Suchedina (Att.-Gen.'s Reference (No. 4 of 2003))*
[2005] 1 Cr.App.R. 2, CA.

Increase in realisable property

In *Re Peacock (Secretary of State for the Home Department intervening)* [2012] 1 W.L.R. 550, **★5–740**
SC, it was held that the High Court has power, under section 16(2) of the 1994 Act, to
certify that the amount that might be realised is greater than the amount taken into account
at the time a confiscation order under that Act was made, and to do so by reference to assets
honestly acquired since the date of the making of the order. As to the argument that
increasing a confiscation order by reference to after-acquired assets would militate against a
defendant's reform and rehabilitation, and be likely to discourage him from engaging in
lawful and openly profitable employment, the court pointed out that section 16(4) confers a
discretion on the Crown Court, rather than obliging it to order an increase in the amount
of the confiscation order in parallel with the assessment of the amount of increase in the
defendant's realisable property under section 16(2).

Certificate of inadequacy

It is unambiguously clear from the wording of sections 6 and 8(1) of the 1994 Act that the **5–741**
value of a gift made by a defendant will be included in the amount of a confiscation order
and will constitute "realisable property", even though it may not itself be realisable by the
defendant because it is no longer in his power or control; and it is implicit in the statutory
scheme that, where the value of a gift has been included in the amount of a confiscation order pursuant to section 6(1), it will not then be open to the defendant to seek a certificate of
inadequacy under section 17(1) on the basis that he cannot realise or recover that gift; section 17 cannot be used as a device for upsetting an original finding that an item is "realisable property" within section 6(2), and thus to be included in the "amount that might be realised" under section 6(1), and thus within the amount of the confiscation order: *Re L.*,
unreported, June 23, 2010, QBD (Hickinbottom J.) ([2010] EWHC 1531 (Admin.)).

Variation of realisable amount

Where, following the grant of a certificate of inadequacy by the High Court under section **5–742**
17 of the 1994 Act, the Crown Court had, pursuant to subsection (4) of that section,
substituted a nil amount as the amount to be recovered, it was possible, if the defendant
thereafter came into funds, for the amount to be varied upwards again if the High Court issued a certificate under section 16(2) that the amount that might be realised was now more
than the amount that had been substituted for the original amount; but the Crown Court
had a discretion as to whether to accede to an application for the amount to be increased
following such certification, and one factor to be taken into account by it in deciding how to
exercise its discretion would be whether the state had sat on its hands after significant and
clear evidence about the defendant's change in financial circumstances had come to its attention or had unreasonably delayed in re-opening the issue: *R. v. Griffin* [2009] 2
Cr.App.R.(S.) 89, CA.

Restraint orders; payment of legal expenses out of restrained assets

See *Revenue and Customs Prosecution Office v. Briggs-Price and O'Reilly, post*, § 5–761. **5–743**

C. Confiscation under the Criminal Justice Act 1988

Postponement of determinations

5–756   In *R. v. Haisman* [2004] 1 Cr.App.R.(S.) 63, CA, it was held that where prosecuting counsel had invited the judge to postpone confiscation proceedings and to proceed to sentence, and the judge responded by saying, "If everyone agrees to that, I will do that" and there was no dissent from any counsel to that course, the judge had "manifestly reached a decision"(*R. v. Ross* [2001] 2 Cr.App.R.(S.) 109, CA) to postpone the confiscation proceedings under section 72A of the *CJA* 1988, with the consequence that the confiscation orders made subsequent to the imposition of sentence were lawful.

In *R. v. Paivarinta-Taylor* [2010] 2 Cr.App.R.(S.) 64, CA, the court said that whereas section 72A(1) of the *CJA* 1988 enables a court to postpone making a determination as to a defendant's benefit for the purpose of a confiscation order, or as to the amount to be recovered from him under such an order, for such period as it may specify in certain circumstances, and whereas section 72A(9) provides that, in sentencing the defendant at any time during the specified postponement period, the court shall not impose any fine on him, the decision in *R. v. Soneji* [2006] 1 A.C. 340, HL (that where there is a breach of a procedural requirement in a statute, a court should ask itself what Parliament intended should be the consequences and whether it fairly could be taken to have intended total invalidity), remains binding authority, as do *R. v. Ruddick* [2004] 1 Cr.App.R.(S.) 7, CA, *R. v. Simpson* [2003] 2 Cr.App.R. 36, CA, and *R. v. Donohoe* [2007] 1 Cr.App.R.(S.) 88, CA, in so far as they add to the principles identified in *Soneji* as to the correct approach to the consequences of a breach of the procedural provisions relating to confiscation orders under the 1988 Act. Cases such as *R. v. Threapleton* [2002] 2 Cr.App.R.(S.) 46, CA, were decided without reference to *Soneji*, and the Court of Appeal said that they should in future be disregarded when considering the consequences of such a breach. It was held that Parliament could not be taken to have intended that a breach of section 72A(9) would lead to total invalidity, that the imposition of a fine before making a confiscation order would render the fine itself invalid, that, having imposed such a fine, the court could then no longer proceed to consider the making of a confiscation order, or that any confiscation order so made would itself be rendered invalid.

Assessment of benefit/making of assumptions

5–757   The assumption provided for in section 72AA(4)(a) of the 1988 Act (*viz.* that any property transferred to the defendant since the beginning of the relevant period was received by him "in connection with the commission of offences to which this Part of this Act applies") includes within its scope offences committed by persons other than the defendant; thus it is not sufficient to rebut the presumption to show that the property was obtained by the defendant as a result of somebody else's criminal conduct; but the defendant's knowledge or lack of knowledge would be highly material in deciding whether to apply the safety valve in subsection (5) (assumption not to be made if court is satisfied that there would be a serious risk of injustice): *R. v. Ilyas* [2009] 1 Cr.App.R.(S.) 59, CA. See the commentary by David Thomas Q.C. in the *Criminal Law Review* ([2008] Crim.L.R. 908) for the suggestion that this decision will not carry across to the *PCA* 2002 regime; and see the commentary in CLW/ 08/39/9 as to the limitations of the actual decision, and, in particular, for the suggestion that it is out of kilter with the decision of the House of Lords in *R. v. May* (§ 5–1044 in the main work).

★   Whereas section 72AA of the 1988 Act provided that in certain cases it was to be assumed against the defendant that he had committed offences other than those of which he had been convicted or which he had asked to be taken into consideration, and that this assumed criminal conduct should be included within his "relevant criminal conduct" (the assessed benefit from which would form the basis of any confiscation order, subject only to his realisable assets being insufficient), there was nothing objectionable in imposing on the defendant the burden of showing in the particular case that the assumptions should not be made; the assumptions were founded on his holding of property or expenditure of money, and there was nothing unfair in requiring him to show that the source of his property was legitimate: *R. v. Bagnall* [2012] L.S. Gazette, May 10, 21, CA ([2012] EWCA Crim. 677).

As to the assessment of benefit under the 1988 Act, see also *R. v. Ahmad, post,* § 5–1051. ★

Factual basis for making order

Where an agreement is reached as to the amount of a confiscation order, that agreement **5–758** will be binding on the defendant unless there are the sort of exceptional circumstances referred to in *R. v. Hirani,* unreported, June 11, 2008, CA ([2008] EWCA Crim. 1463) (save in most exceptional circumstances, a confiscation order based on an agreed amount will not be set aside where the essence of complaint is that, in seeking to secure the best deal available, erroneous advice was given to a party to the agreement; without exhaustively identifying such circumstances, there would need to be a well-founded submission that the whole process was unfair): *R. v. Ayankoya,* unreported, May 24, 2011, CA ([2011] EWCA Crim. 1488). The circumstances had, however, been wholly exceptional where: (i) the defendant had agreed to the amount after being incorrectly informed by his counsel that the judge had ruled that an adjournment to await bank statements supporting his claims would be impossible and that he therefore had a choice of either agreeing the amount or giving evidence without the statements with the inherent risk that a higher amount would result, and (ii) where the bank statements had in fact shown that there was force in the defendant's claims; in these circumstances, the erroneous advice had been of a potentially fundamental nature: *ibid.*

Amount that might be realised

In *R. v. Blee* [2004] 1 Cr.App.R.(S.) 33, CA, it was held that whereas section 74(3) of the **5–759** *CJA* 1988 provides that "the amount that might be realised at the time a confiscation order is made" includes "the total of the values at that time of all gifts caught by this Part of this Act" and whereas section 74(10) provides that a gift is caught by that part of the Act if "(a) it was made by the defendant at any time after the commission of the offence ...; and (b) the court considers it appropriate in all the circumstances to take the gift into account" it follows that the fact that the property held by the donee at the time of the confiscation order is less than the value of the gift does not *per se* preclude the court from taking the full value of the gift into account; the court is given a discretion by section 74(10) and the question for it to decide is whether it is "appropriate" to take the gift into account; if it considers it appropriate to take it into account (in whole or in part), then to the extent that it does so, the value of the gift is to be included in the computation of the amount that might be realised; in exercising the discretion, the court may have regard to the timing of the gift (here, made when the defendant, having been on the run, had decided to surrender), to the fact that it was made to a person from whom the defendant would be likely to be able to receive an equivalent benefit in return, if he wished, and to the fact that whilst the donee currently had assets worth considerably less than the value of the gift, he was in highly paid employment and would be likely again to hold substantial assets; and, where it is said that the gift has been dissipated prior to the confiscation order, this is a matter to be considered under section 74(10), rather than on a subsequent application for a certificate of inadequacy.

As to the approach to be taken where the prosecution allege that the defendant is the beneficial owner of property registered in the name of a third party, see *Revenue and Customs Prosecutions Office v. May* [2010] 3 All E.R. 1173, CA (Civ. Div.) (§ 5–1059 in the main work).

Valuation of property

In *R. v. Hedges* (2004) 148 S.J. 974, CA, it was held that in making a confiscation order **5–760** against a defendant whose only realisable asset was the house which he owned jointly with his wife, the correct approach to valuation of his interest in the property had been to determine the market value of the property, then deduct the outstanding mortgage and the reasonable costs of sale before making a confiscation order in respect of half the remaining amount; such an approach properly reflected the intention of section 74(4) of the *CJA* 1988 and was to be preferred to that of dividing the value of the house and then deducting the remaining mortgage and costs of sale from the defendant's half share, on the basis that he was responsible for payment of the mortgage; whilst it was true that the defendant was in theory liable to repay the whole mortgage, being jointly and severally liable, the reality was that the mortgage and the costs of sale would be discharged out of the proceeds of sale, the net effect of which would be to reduce his share in the value of the house by half the amount of the mortgage and costs of sale.

In *R. v. Ahmed* [2005] 1 All E.R. 128, CA, it was held that where a court concludes that an offender has benefited from relevant criminal conduct (*CJA* 1988, s.71(1A)), the court has no discretion, in valuing the realisable assets for the purposes of determining the amount of the confiscation order, to exclude from the computation, the value of the defendant's share in the matrimonial home, notwithstanding the probability that the home would have to be sold to meet the confiscation order; the words "the amount appearing to the court" in subsection (6)(b) ("... the sum which an order made by a court under this section requires an offender to pay shall be equal to (a) ...; or (b) the amount appearing to the court to be the amount that might be realised at the time the order is made, whichever is the less") did not give the court a discretion; it merely referred to the valuation process to be carried out under section 74, and section 3 of the *Human Rights Act* 1998 (§ 16–15 in the main work) did not require it to be read as construing such a discretion on the court on account of the possible interference with innocent third parties' rights under Article 8 of the ECHR (*ibid.*, § 16–101); the court is merely concerned with the arithmetic exercise of computing what is, in effect, a statutory debt; such process does not involve any assessment of the way in which the debt may ultimately be paid; different considerations would apply if the debt is not met and the prosecution determine to take enforcement action; if a court is asked to make an order for the sale of the matrimonial home then the third party's rights under Article 8 would clearly be engaged; and it would be at that stage that the court would have to consider whether or not it would be proportionate to make an order for the sale of the home. In connection with this case, see *Webber v. Webber (CPS intervening)*, § 5–1063 in the main work.

In the earlier case of *R. v. Goodenough* [2005] 1 Cr.App.R.(S.) 88, CA, it was held that where a defendant's only realisable asset was his equity in the matrimonial home, the making of a confiscation order in accordance with the requirements of the 1988 Act for the amount by which he had benefited from his offending (being an amount less than the value of his equity) did not infringe or interfere with his rights under Article 8 or under Article 1 of the First Protocol (right to peaceful enjoyment of possessions); the rights of the defendant's wife might be infringed if the house were to be sold in order to raise the money to pay the amount of the confiscation order, and it would be open to the wife to oppose any application to appoint a receiver to enforce the order.

Restraint orders; payment of legal expenses out of restrained assets

5–761   In *Revenue and Customs Prosecution Office v. Briggs-Price and O'Reilly* [2007] L.S. Gazette, June 28, 32, CA (Civ. Div.) ([2007] EWCA Civ. 568) it was held, in relation to the confiscation regimes under the *CJA* 1988 and the *DTA* 1994, that the principle in *Customs and Excise Commrs v. Norris* [1991] 2 Q.B. 293, CA (Civ. Div.) (defendant's legal expenses may be met from restrained assets), applies both to legal expenses incurred prior to conviction (and any appeal against conviction) and to legal expenses incurred in connection with the making of a confiscation order and an appeal against such order; there is a discretion in such cases, which will be exercised for a proper and legitimate purpose within the scope of the statutory regime where the released assets are to meet expenses for a prospective appeal which are neither excessive nor improperly incurred (such amount as is released being capable of control by assessment).

Restraint orders; appointment of receiver

5–762   See *Revenue and Customs Prosecutions Office v. Pigott (Lamb, interested party)* [2010] S.T.C. 1190, CA (Civ. Div.) (§ 5–874 in the main work).

Certificate of inadequacy

There is no rule of law that says that, on an application under section 83 of the 1988 Act   **5-763**
for a certificate of inadequacy, the High Court could not be persuaded that a defendant was
unable to pay the outstanding amount by reason of a worsening of his financial circumstances unless he gave full disclosure of what had happened in the meantime to all his assets, including previously unidentified assets (that the Crown Court had found to exist when
making the confiscation order); any such rule would trammel the width of section 83 by
imposing a restriction which was not in the statute; and it would also be capable of causing
not merely hardship, but hardship amounting to injustice; in the case of previously unidentified assets, it is possible that a defendant may genuinely have no idea or only a dim recollection of what originally happened to them; he should be allowed to try to persuade the
court, if this be the case, that his identified assets have shrunk in value and that as a result
he is not able to pay the amount outstanding: *Glaves v. CPS* [2011] Costs L.R. 556, CA (Civ.
Div.) (considering *Telli v. Revenue and Customs Prosecutions Office* (see § 5–1057 in the main
work)).

It was held in *Escobar v. DPP* [2009] 1 W.L.R. 64, DC, that when making an order under
section 83(4) of the *CJA* 1988 for the reduction of a sum payable under a confiscation order (following the issue of a certificate of inadequacy), the Crown Court has jurisdiction
to fix a time for payment (by way of extension of the original date). The court said that
although there is no express power to extend time in section 83, section 75(1) ("(1)
Where the Crown Court orders the defendant to pay an amount under this Part ..., sections 139(1) to (4) ... of the *Powers of Criminal Courts (Sentencing) Act* 2000 (powers of
Crown Court in relation to fines and enforcement of Crown Court fines) shall have effect as
if that amount were a fine imposed on him by the Crown Court.") operates so as to
incorporate section 139(1) of the 2000 Act (§ 5–676 in the main work), which in turn gives
the court power to extend the time for payment when it substitutes a lesser sum under section 83. When read as a whole, section 75 is generally concerned to make provision for
orders made under section 83 as well as those under other provisions in Part VI, and this is
consistent with the natural and grammatical meaning of the relevant provisions, in that the
Crown Court is making an order under section 83(4) and the effect of that order is that the
defendant has to pay an amount due under Part VI. For the suggestion that the court's
conclusion is out of kilter with the legislative structure, see CLW/09/02/5. For the relevant
provisions of the *PCA* 2002, see sections 23 and 39 (§§ 5–824, 5–840 in the main work),
neither of which contain any provision for an extension of the time allowed to pay.

Enforcement

See *Revenue and Customs Prosecutions Office v. May* [2010] 3 All E.R. 1173, CA (Civ. Div.)   **5-764**
(§ 5–1059 in the main work).

Presence of the accused

See *R. v. Spearing* (§ 3–199b in the main work).   **5-765**

D. Confiscation under the Proceeds of Crime Act 2002

(2) Legislation

(a) *Statute*

Proceeds of Crime Act 2002, ss.6–91

Making of order

With effect from June 18, 2012 (*Criminal Justice Act 2003 (Commencement No. 28 and Sav-*   **★5-805**
ing Provisions) Order 2012 (S.I. 2012 No. 1320)), section 41 of, and paragraph 75 of Schedule 3 to, the 2003 Act (see the main work) are brought into force in certain areas (as to
which, see *ante*, § 1–88). There are associated saving provisions, as to which, see article 5 of
the order (*ante*, § 1–88).

Postponement

R. v. Neish is reported at [2011] 1 Cr.App.R.(S.) 33, CA and not [2010] 1 Cr.App.R.(S.)   **5-815**
33, CA.

Defendant convicted or committed

★**5-828**   As to the commencement of section 41 of, and paragraph 75 of Schedule 3 to, the 2003 Act (see the main work), see *ante*, § 5–805.

Enforcement as fines

★**5-836**   For a case concerning a confiscation order under the *CJA* 1988 summarising the principles that have emerged from the authorities on fixing default terms, see *R. v. Castillo (German)*, *ante*, § 5–689.

Whereas section 35(2) of the 2002 Act deems a confiscation order to be a fine imposed by the court that made the order, whereas section 140(1)(b) of the *PCC(S)A* 2000 (§ 5–677 in the main work) deems a Crown Court fine as having been imposed on conviction by the magistrates' court that committed or sent the defendant to the Crown Court for trial, and whereas section 87(1) of the *MCA* 1980 deems a magistrates' court fine to be the equivalent of a High Court or county court judgment debt obtained by the designated officer of the relevant magistrates' court, these statutory provisions enabled the designated officer to use any of the civil enforcement measures available to a High Court or county court judgment creditor to enforce the confiscation order, including the obtaining and enforcement of a charging order over any beneficial interest in real property: *Designated Officer for Sunderland Magistrates' Court v. Krager* [2012] 1 W.L.R. 1291, Ch D (Briggs J.).

Sums received by justices' chief executive

5-881   The amendment of section 55(8) of the 2002 Act by the *Police Reform and Social Responsibility Act* 2011, s.99, and Sched. 16, paras 304 and 305 (see the main work), came into force on January 16, 2012: *Police Reform and Social Responsibility Act 2011 (Commencement No. 3 and Transitional Provisions) Order* 2011 (S.I. 2011 No. 3019).

Committal by magistrates' court

★**5-901**   As to the commencement of section 41 of, and paragraph 75 of Schedule 3 to, the 2003 Act (see the main work), see *ante*, § 5–805.

Criminal lifestyle

5-906   *R. v. Bajwa, Sahnan, Midgley, Sohi and Mallinson* is now reported at [2012] 1 Cr.App.R.(S.) 23, *sub nom. R. v. Bajwa*.

Proceeds of Crime Act 2002, Sched. 2

People trafficking

★**5-927**   As from a day to be appointed, paragraph 4 of Schedule 2 to the 2002 Act is amended by the *Protection of Freedoms Act* 2012, s.115(1), and Sched. 9, para. 138, so as to substitute a reference to "section 59A" for the references to "sections 57 to 59" of the *SOA* 2003.

(b) *Subordinate legislation*

Commencement

Proceeds of Crime Act 2002 (Commencement No. 5, Transitional Provisions, Savings and Amendment) Order 2003 (S.I. 2003 No. 333)

Citation and interpretation

5-937   **1.**—(1) [*Citation.*]

(2) In this Order, "the Act" means the *Proceeds of Crime Act* 2002.

(3) Where an offence is found to have been committed over a period of two or more days, or at some time during a period of two or more days, it shall be taken for the purposes of this Order to have been committed on the earliest of those days.

Commencement of provisions

2.—(1) The provisions of the Act listed in column 1 of the Schedule to this Order shall come   **5–938**
into force on 24th March 2003, subject to the transitional provisions and savings contained in
this Order.

(2) But where a particular purpose is specified in relation to any such provision in column 2 of
that Schedule, the provision concerned shall come into force only for that purpose.

Transitional provisions relating to confiscation orders—England and Wales

3.—(1) Section 6 of the Act (making of confiscation order) shall not have effect where the of-   **5–939**
fence, or any of the offences, mentioned in section 6(2) was committed before 24th March 2003.

(2) Section 27 of the Act (defendant convicted or committed absconds) shall not have effect where
the offence, or any of the offences, mentioned in section 27(2) was committed before 24th March
2003.

(3) Section 28 of the Act (defendant neither convicted nor acquitted absconds) shall not have effect where the offence, or any of the offences, in respect of which proceedings have been started but
not concluded was committed before 24th March 2003.

4. [*Transitional provisions relating to confiscation orders—Northern Ireland*]

It was held in *R. v. Moulden* [2009] 1 Cr.App.R. 27, CA, that where the respondent appeared before the Crown Court to be dealt with in respect of two indictments, one alleging
offences committed before March 24, 2003, and the other alleging offences committed after
that date, each indictment represented a separate set of "proceedings" for the purposes of
section 6(2)(a) of the 2002 Act (see § 5–805 in the main work) and accordingly, by virtue of
article 3(1), the 2002 Act had no application to the pre-March 24, 2003, indictment, but did
apply to the post-March 24, 2003, indictment. The judge had, therefore, been correct to apply the confiscation provisions of the *CJA* 1988 to the one indictment and the confiscation
provisions of the 2002 Act to the other indictment, and to reject the prosecution submission that the effect of these provisions was to disapply the 2002 Act in relation to both
indictments, thereby triggering the assumptions provided for by section 72AA of the
1988 Act.

Where the defendant pleaded guilty to a count of conspiracy to make false instruments,
the particulars of offence alleging that the offence took place "between the 1st day of January 2003 and the 16th day of May 2007", and where his written basis of plea was to the effect that his first admitted act in pursuance of the criminal agreement took place only on
October 29, 2003, his offence had begun before March 24, 2003, for the purposes of article
3(1) (having regard to article 1(3)), such that the applicable confiscation provisions were
those under Part VI of the *CJA* 1988, not Part 2 of the *PCA* 2002, see *R. v. Evwierhowa*
[2011] 2 Cr.App.R.(S.) 77, CA.

By virtue of articles 3(1) and 10(1)(e) (*post*, § 5–942), section 16 of the DTA 1994 (increase   ★
in realisable property) continues to have effect where an offence mentioned in section 6(2)
of the *PCA Act* 2002 (making of confiscation order (§ 5–805 in the main work)) was committed before March 24, 2003: *Re Peacock (Secretary of State for the Home Department
intervening)* [2012] 1 W.L.R. 550, SC. For the suggestion that the court misconstrued the order (albeit reaching the correct result), see CLW/12/08/5.

Transitional provisions relating to restraint orders and enforcement abroad—England and Wales

5. Sections 41 (restraint orders) and 74 (enforcement abroad) of the Act shall not have effect   **5–940**
where—
  (a) the powers in those sections would otherwise be exercisable by virtue of a condition in sec-
      tion 40(2) or (3) of the Act being satisfied; and
  (b) the offence mentioned in section 40(2)(a) or 40(3)(a), as the case may be, was committed
      before 24th March 2003.

6. [*Transitional provisions relating to restraint orders and enforcement abroad—Northern Ireland.*]

Transitional provisions relating to criminal lifestyle—England and Wales

7.—(1) This article applies where the court is determining under section 6(4)(a) of the Act   **5–941**
whether the defendant has a criminal lifestyle.

(2) Conduct shall not form part of a course of criminal activity under section 75(3)(a) of the Act
where any of the three or more offences mentioned in section 75(3)(a) was committed before 24th
March 2003.

(3) Where the court is applying the rule in section 75(5) of the Act on the calculation of relevant benefit for the purposes of determining whether or not the test in section 75(2)(b) of the Act is satisfied by virtue of conduct forming part of a course of criminal activity under section 75(3)(a) of the Act, the court must not take into account benefit from conduct constituting an offence mentioned in section 75(5)(c) of the Act which was committed before 24th March 2003.

(4) Conduct shall form part of a course of criminal activity under section 75(3)(b) of the Act, notwithstanding that any of the offences of which the defendant was convicted on at least two separate occasions in the period mentioned in section 75(3)(b) were committed before 24th March 2003.

(5) Where the court is applying the rule in section 75(5) of the Act on the calculation of relevant benefit for the purposes of determining whether or not the test in section 75(2)(b) of the Act is satisfied by virtue of conduct forming part of a course of criminal activity under section 75(3)(b) of the Act, the court may take into account benefit from conduct constituting an offence committed before 24th March 2003.

(6) Where the court is applying the rule in section 75(6) of the Act on the calculation of relevant benefit for the purposes of determining whether or not the test in section 75(2)(c) of the Act is satisfied, the court must not take into account benefit from conduct constituting an offence mentioned in section 75(6)(b) of the Act which was committed before 24th March 2003.

[This article is printed as substituted by the *Proceeds of Crime Act 2002 (Commencement No. 5) (Amendment of Transitional Provisions) Order* 2003 (S.I. 2003 No. 531).]

8. [*Transitional provisions relating to criminal lifestyle—Northern Ireland.*]

Transitional provisions relating to particular criminal conduct
9. Conduct which constitutes an offence which was committed before 24th March 2003 is not particular criminal conduct under section 76(3) or 224(3) of the Act.

Savings for England and Wales
5–942   **10.**—(1) Where, under article 3 or 5, a provision of the Act does not have effect, the following provisions shall continue to have effect—

   (a) sections 71 to 89 (including Schedule 4) and 102 of the *Criminal Justice Act* 1988;
   (b) paragraphs 83 and 84 of Schedule 17 to the *Housing Act* 1988;
   (c) sections 21(3)(e) to (g), 27, 28 and 34 of the *Criminal Justice Act* 1993;
   (d) paragraph 36 of Schedule 9 to the *Criminal Justice and Public Order Act* 1994;
   (e) sections 1 to 36 and 41 of the *Drug Trafficking Act* 1994;
   (f) sections 1 to 10, 15(1) and (3) (including Schedule 1), 16(2), (5) and (6) of the *Proceeds of Crime Act* 1995;
   (g) section 4(3) of the *Private International Law (Miscellaneous Provisions) Act* 1995;
   (h) sections 35 to 38 of the *Proceeds of Crime (Scotland) Act* 1995;
   (i) the *Proceeds of Crime (Enforcement of Confiscation Orders made in England and Wales or Scotland) Order (Northern Ireland) 1997* and the *Proceeds of Crime (Northern Ireland) Order* 1996, so far as necessary for the continued operation of the Proceeds of Crime (Enforcement of Confiscation Orders made in England and Wales or Scotland) Order (Northern Ireland) 1997;
   (j) paragraphs 23 and 36 of Schedule 5 to the *Justices of the Peace Act* 1997;
   (k) section 83 of, paragraph 114 of Schedule 8 to and paragraph 8 of Schedule 9 to the *Crime and Disorder Act* 1998;
   (l) paragraphs 139 and 172 of Schedule 13 to the *Access to Justice Act* 1999;
   (m) paragraphs 105 to 113 and 163 to 173 of Schedule 9 to the *Powers of Criminal Courts (Sentencing) Act* 2000;
   (n) paragraphs 6(1) to (3) and 10 of Schedule 15 to the *Terrorism Act* 2000.

(2) Where under article 3 or 5, a provision of the Act does not have effect, the following provisions shall continue to have effect as if they had not been amended by Schedule 11 to the Act—

   (a) section 13(6) of the *Criminal Justice (International Co-operation) Act* 1990;
   (b) paragraph 17(3) of Schedule 8 to the *Terrorism Act* 2000.

11. [*Savings for Northern Ireland.*]
12. [*Savings for enforcement of Scottish orders in England, Wales and Northern Ireland.*]
13. [*Savings in relation to external orders.*]
14. [*Amendment of arts 3 and 5 of S.I. 2003 No. 120, §§ 26–4, 26–5 in the main work.*]

Article 2   THE SCHEDULE

Column 1	*Column 2*
Part 2 (sections 6 to 91, including Schedule 2) (Confiscation: England and Wales).	So far as not already in force.
Part 4 (sections 156 to 239, including Schedule 5) (Confiscation: Northern Ireland).	
Part 9 (sections 417 to 434) (Insolvency etc.).	
Part 10 (sections 435 to 442) (Information).	So far as not already in force.
Section 444 (External requests and orders).	
Section 445 (External investigations).	
Section 447 (Interpretation).	
Section 456 (Amendments).	Commenced for the purposes of the provisions of Schedule 11 to the Act commenced by this Order.
Section 457 (Repeals).	Commenced for the purposes of the provisions of Schedule 12 to the Act commenced by this Order.
In Schedule 11, paragraphs 1, 4, 5, 7, 8, 9, 11, 14(2) and (3), 15, 16, 17(2), (4) and (6), 19(2) and (3), 20, 21, 25(2)(a) and (h) to (j), 26, 27, 28(1) and (2)(e) and (g), 31(2) and (3)(a) to (c), 32, 37 and 39.	Paragraphs 7, 11, 15, 16, 20, 21 and 39 are commenced except to the extent that they relate to Part 3 of the Act. Paragraph 17(2) is commenced so far as it repeals sections 71 to 89, 94 and 99 to 102 of the *Criminal Justice Act* 1988. Paragraph 25(2)(a) is commenced so far as it repeals sections 1 to 38 and 41 of the *Drug Trafficking Act* 1994. Paragraph 27 is commenced so far as not already in force. Paragraph 31(2) is commenced so far as it repeals articles 4 to 41 of the *Proceeds of Crime (Northern Ireland) Order* 1996.

Column 1

In Schedule 12, the following entries; the entry relating to the *Criminal Appeal (Northern Ireland) Act* 1980; the entry relating to the *Police and Criminal Evidence Act* 1984; the entry relating to the *Criminal Justice Act* 1988; the entry relating to the *Housing Act* 1988; the entry relating to the *Police and Criminal Evidence (Northern Ireland) Order* 1989; in the entry relating to the *Criminal Justice (International Co-operation) Act* 1990, the entry in the second column concerning section 13 of that Act; the entry relating to the *Criminal Justice (Confiscation) (Northern Ireland) Order 1990*; the entry relating to the *Criminal Justice Act* 1993; the entry relating to the *Drug Trafficking Act* 1994; the entry relating to the *Proceeds of Crime Act* 1995; in the entry relating to the *Criminal Procedure (Consequential Provisions) (Scotland) Act* 1995, the entry in the second column concerning Schedule 4 of that Act; the entry relating to the *Private International Law (Miscellaneous Provisions) Act* 1995; in the entry relating to the *Proceeds of Crime (Scotland) Act* 1995, the entry in the second column concerning sections 35 to 39 of that Act, the entry in the second column concerning section 40 of that Act and the entry in the second column concerning section 42 of that Act; the entry relating to the *Proceeds of Crime (Northern Ireland) Order* 1996; the entry relating to the *Justices of the Peace Act* 1997; in the entry relating to the *Crime and Disorder Act* 1998, the entry in the second column concerning section 83 of that Act, the entry in the second column concerning Schedule 8 of that Act and the entry in the second column concerning Schedule 9 of that Act; the entry relating to the *Access to Justice Act* 1999; the entry relating to the *Powers of Criminal Courts (Sentencing) Act* 2000; the entry relating to the *Terrorism Act* 2000; and the entry relating to the *Criminal Justice and Police Act* 2001.

Column 2

The entry relating to sections 71 to 102 of the *Criminal Justice Act* 1988 is commenced so far as it repeals sections 71 to 89, 94 and 99 to 102 of that Act. The entries relating to the *Criminal Justice Act* 1993, the *Proceeds of Crime Act* 1995 and the *Access to Justice Act* 1999 are commenced so far as not already in force. The entry relating to sections 1 to 54 of the *Drug Trafficking Act* 1994 is commenced so far as it repeals sections 1 to 38 and 41 of that Act. The entry relating to Parts II and III of the *Proceeds of Crime (Northern Ireland) Order* 1996 is commenced so far as it repeals articles 4 to 41 of that Order. The entry relating to the *Terrorism Act* 2000 is commenced so far as it repeals paragraphs 6 and 10 of Schedule 15 to that Act.

Rules of court relating to confiscation, restraint and receivership proceedings

Criminal Procedure Rules 2011 (S.I. 2011 No. 1709), Pt 57

Interpretation

5–944   With effect from April 2, 2012, rule 57.1 of the *Criminal Procedure Rules* 2011 (S.I. 2011 No. 1709) is amended by the *Criminal Procedure (Amendment) Rules* 2011 (S.I. 2011 No. 3075), r.13(b), so as to omit the definition of "business day".

Service of documents

5–954   With effect from April 2, 2012, rule 57.11 of the *Criminal Procedure Rules* 2011 (S.I. 2011 No. 1709) is amended by the *Criminal Procedure (Amendment) Rules* 2011 (S.I. 2011 No. 3075), r.13(c), so as: (i) to omit the words "Part 4 and" in paragraph (1); (ii) to omit paragraphs (2) and (3); and (iii) to substitute the words "Part 4 of these Rules" for the words "this rule" in paragraph (4).

Service by an alternative method

5–955   With effect from April 2, 2012, rule 57.12 of the *Criminal Procedure Rules* 2011 (S.I. 2011

No. 1709) is revoked by the *Criminal Procedure (Amendment) Rules* 2011 (S.I. 2011 No.
3075), r.13(d).

Certificates of service

With effect from April 2, 2012, rule 57.14(2)(c) of the *Criminal Procedure Rules* 2011 (S.I.   **5–957**
2011 No. 1709) is amended by the *Criminal Procedure (Amendment) Rules* 2011 (S.I. 2011
No. 3075), r.13(e), so as to substitute "4.9" for "57.12".

Criminal Procedure Rules 2011 (S.I. 2011 No. 1709), Pt 58

Payment of money in bank or building society account in satisfaction of confiscation order

With effect from April 2, 2012, rule 58.12(2) and (3) of the *Criminal Procedure Rules* 2011   **5–969**
(S.I. 2011 No. 1709) are revoked by the *Criminal Procedure (Amendment) Rules* 2011 (S.I.
2011 No. 3075), r.14.

Forms

Consolidated *Criminal Practice Direction (Amendment No. 26) (Criminal Proceedings: Forms)* is   **★5–1038**
now reported at [2012] 1 Cr.App.R. 28, *sub nom. Amendment No. 26 to the Consolidated Criminal Practice Direction (Criminal Proceedings: Forms)*.

(3) Authorities

Lack of discretion/abuse of process

Where the prosecution had declined to prosecute a defendant for additional offences, it   **★5–1042**
was not an abuse of process for them to adduce evidence of those additional offences in
confiscation proceedings in a criminal lifestyle case in order to rebut his assertion that the
assumptions in section 10 of the 2002 Act (§ 5–810 in the main work) should not apply: *R.
v. Bagnall* [2012] L.S. Gazette, May 10, 21, CA ([2012] EWCA Crim. 677).

Benefit

Property

It is not permissible for the Crown Court to apportion the benefit figure between two   **★5–1046**
defendants who entered into a joint venture, where to proceed on the basis of joint and several liability would mean that the total sum confiscated would be more than the total benefit
because the realisable assets of each exceed the benefit figure: *R. v. Lambert (Richard) and
Walding (Ian Alexander)* [2012] Crim.L.R. 476, CA (considering the statements of principle
in *R. v. May* (§§ 5–1044, 5–1046 in the main work) and *R. v. Green* (see the main work)).

In *R. v. James (Michael) and Blackburn (Raymond Francis)* [2012] Crim.L.R. 307, CA, it was   **5–1051**
held that items bought at the normal retail price from ordinary commercial suppliers by the
defendant for use in the course of an excise duty fraud relating to hand-rolled tobacco
(scales, cardboard boxes and building materials) were not obtained by the defendant as a
result of or in connection with his criminal conduct for the purposes of section 76(4) of the
2002 Act (§ 5–907 in the main work); and this applied also to a unit which was rented at
normal market rates and to the casual labouring services he obtained for the purposes of
the operation; *as to the equipment*, he did not obtain the items "as a result of" any criminal
conduct, but as a result of a lawful transaction with the supplier; nor did he obtain the items
"in connection with" any criminal conduct, as his criminal conduct in participating in the
conspiracy formed no part of the transactions by which he acquired them (distinguishing *R.
v. Waller* (see the main work)); the transactions were entered into for the purpose of criminal conduct, but that is not necessarily a state of affairs caught by section 76(4); *as to the unit*,
while the unit was rented for the purpose of enabling the criminal conduct to take place,
the arrangement to rent it was a contract that was not in itself in any way unlawful; the unit
could have been put to another purpose; because the payment of rent was a continuing

outlay, the connection with the criminal conduct was closer than in the case of the individual expenses, but, since the 2002 Act was a criminal statute and the confiscation process was not to be applied so as to operate as a fine (*Jennings v. CPS* (§ 5–1046 in the main work)), the words "in connection with" must be given a narrow construction; *as to the labouring services*, a person who pays for services at a market rate could not be said to have obtained a pecuniary advantage. As to this case, see also *post*, § 5–1052.

★   *R. v. Ahmad* [2012] 2 All E.R. 1204, CA, was a case under the *CJA* 1988. It was held that where the statutory assumptions relating to criminal lifestyle under section 72AA did not apply, the total amount of money received into bank accounts controlled by the defendants as a result of the sale or purported sale of goods by buffer companies in the furtherance of a missing-trader carousel fraud was not property obtained by them "as a result of or in connection with the commission of the offence", as defined by the 1988 Act, s.71(4), such as to constitute their (or part of their) "benefit" (disapproving *R. v. Waller, ante*); to commit the fraud it was necessary that an amount representing the value of the goods and the VAT thereon should pass through the accounts of the buffer companies, but the defendants' benefit constituted only the far lesser amount of VAT that they had fraudulently reclaimed (following *R. v. Olubitan* (§ 5–1049 in the main work), and *Jennings v. CPS, ante*); as *R. v. James (Michael) and Blackburn (Raymond Francis), ante*, shows, the words "in connection with" must be construed with the word "benefit" in mind; and to say that, in assessing the benefit, the court does not take into account the costs incurred by a criminal in committing the offence is very different from saying that the costs should be added on to the benefit; to make a confiscation order which includes within the benefit the costs of committing a crime would be contrary to the object of the legislation and it would operate as a fine (also considering *R. v. Smith (David)* (§ 5–1052 in the main work)).

Pecuniary advantage

5–1052   *R. v. Takkar* is now reported at [2011] 1 W.L.R. 3062.

R. v. Bajwa, Sahnan, Midgley, Sohi and Mallinson is now reported at [2012] 1 Cr.App.R.(S.) 23, *sub nom. R. v. Bajwa*.

Revenue and Customs Prosecutions Office v. Mitchell, and *R. v. White and other appeals* (as to both of which, see the main work) were considered in *R. v. Redmond* [2011] S.T.C. 1892, CA, in which the appellant had been convicted of being knowingly concerned in the fraudulent evasion of the duty payable on smuggled cigarettes (*CEMA* 1979, s.170(2) (§ 25–474 in the main work)), and where the issue, on appeal, was as to how to calculate the amount of VAT that had been evaded, it having been effectively agreed between the parties that the appellant himself had not incurred any liability in respect of the excise duty, but had been liable in respect of the VAT, and, to the extent that he was so liable, this represented a pecuniary advantage, the value of which constituted his benefit. In calculating the amount of VAT evaded, it was first necessary to determine the value of the cigarettes in accordance with section 21 of the *Value Added Tax Act* 1994. Subsection (1) required value to be determined in accordance with the Community Customs Code (Council Regulation No. 2913/92/EEC), articles 29 and 30 of which made reference to actual transaction value (the price actually paid) or, where this could not be determined, to the transaction value of identical or similar goods sold for export to the Community at or about the same time as the goods being valued. Where there was no evidence as to the actual price paid, the court said that it was not possible simply to take the retail price less excise duty; even in the hands of the eventual retailer, the price of a packet of cigarettes reflects many elements of which the value of the cigarettes is but one part; accordingly, the only safe course was to take the ex-factory price for those cigarettes that were not counterfeit, and to apply that price also to those of the cigarettes that were counterfeit. As to section 21(2) ("(2) ... the value of any goods imported from a place outside the member states shall be taken to include ... all taxes, duties and other charges levied either outside, or by reason of importation, within the United Kingdom (except VAT) ..."), it was held that this required that the excise duty that arose in respect of the cigarettes was to be included in the valuation exercise. As to the unsatisfactory nature of this case, see CLW/11/39/7.

In *R. v. James (Michael) and Blackburn (Raymond Francis), ante*, § 5–1051, it was held that only the person or persons who are personally liable to pay excise duty will have obtained a pecuniary advantage by evading its payment, and absent that liability, they will not have obtained a benefit in accordance with section 76 of the *PCA* 2002 (§ 5–907 in the main work) (*R. v. May* and *Jennings v. CPS* (§ 5–1046 in the main work)); however, it does not follow from the fact that a person evades a duty that he personally owes, that he necessarily obtained a benefit by evading it. Where, therefore, one defendant (who had been convicted of conspiracy to contravene the *CEMA* 1979, s.170 (*ibid.*, § 25–474), in respect of evasion of excise duty on hand-rolling tobacco, as a local "salaried" manager at the tobacco factory with no proprietary interest in the tobacco), had "held" the tobacco products at the time the excise duty became payable, or "caused" those products to reach the excise duty point whilst retaining a connection with the goods at that point of time thus making him personally liable for the duty, he did not obtain a pecuniary advantage, and therefore a "benefit" within the 2002 Act, because (following *R. v. Sivaraman* (*ibid.*, § 5–1045)), he was merely acting on behalf of his employer. It emerges from the judgment in this case that the Supreme Court may reconsider the correctness of the decision of the House of Lords in *R. v. Smith (David)* (see the main work), when it hears an appeal against the decision of the Court of Appeal in *R. v. Waya* (§ 5–1055 in the main work). For the suggestion, however, that the court's decision in this case is unsustainable if *R. v. Smith (David)* was correctly decided, see CLW/12/03/8.

As to the disapproval of *R. v. Waller* (see the main work), see *R. v. Ahmad, ante,* § 5–1051.   ★

Assumptions to be made in case of a criminal lifestyle

     R. v. Briggs-Price (see the main work) was distinguished in *R. v. Bagnall* [2012] L.S. Gazette, May 10, 21, CA ([2012] EWCA Crim. 677), in which it was held that where, in a criminal lifestyle case, the only question in the confiscation proceedings was the source of the assets held by the defendant, the mere fact that the prosecution had evidence that was suggestive of guilt of other offences to rebut the defendant's assertion that the assumptions should not apply did not mean that the prosecution shouldered the burden of proof. In reliance on *Phillips v. U.K.* (§§ 16–61, 16–77, 16–78 in the main work), the court also rejected objections to the legislation relating to the making of assumptions that were based on Article 6 of the ECHR (burden of proof in relation to a criminal charge and presumption of innocence (§ 16–57 in the main work)).   **★5-1054**

Valuation of benefit

As to the decision of the Court of Appeal in *R. v. Waya* being subject to an appeal to the Supreme Court, see *R. v. James (Michael)* and *Blackburn (Raymond Francis), ante,* § 5–1052.   **5-1055**

"Free property" (s.82), "realisable property" (s.83) and "property" (s.84)

R. v. McIntosh is now reported at [2012] 1 Cr.App.R.(S.) 60.   **5-1057**

In a hidden assets case, the court may conclude that a defendant's realisable assets are   ★ less than the full value of the benefit on the basis of the facts as a whole: *R. v. Ahmad* [2012] 2 All E.R. 1204, CA (preferring the approach in *R. v. McIntosh* to that in *Telli v. Revenue and Customs Prosecutions Office* (as to both of which, see the main work)).

X. DISQUALIFICATION, RESTRICTION, EXCLUSION, ETC., ORDERS

A. BANNING ORDERS UNDER THE FOOTBALL SPECTATORS ACT 1989

(2) Legislation

Football Spectators Act 1989, s.14

Definitions

     The *Football Spectators (2012 European Championship Control Period) Order* 2012 (S.I. 2012   **★5-1070**

No. 340) provides that, in relation to the UEFA 2012 European Championship tournament in Poland and Ukraine, section 14(6) of the 1989 Act (definition of "control period" in relation to an external tournament (§ 5–1069 in the main work)) shall have effect as if, for the reference to five days, there were substituted a reference to 10 days, and that the period beginning on May 29, 2012 (which is 10 days before the first match), and ending when the last match included in the tournament is finished or cancelled, is a control period for the purposes of Part II of the Act.

Football Spectators Act 1989, ss.14A–14H

Banning orders made on conviction of an offence

5–1072   *R. v. Boggild* is now reported at [2012] 1 Cr.App.R.(S.) 81.

★   In *R. v. Doyle, Wise (Ryan) and Wise (Darren)*, 176 J.P. 337, CA, it was said, in relation to the requirement in section 14A(2) of the 1989 Act, that the court should be satisfied that there are reasonable grounds to believe that making a banning order would help to prevent violence or disorder at, or in connection with, any regulated football matches, that no doubt the more the offence is linked to football grievances or the group "culture" of a set of fans linked by their support for a team, the more likely it will be that an order will help prevent violence or disorder; and the more there is a history of football-related offending, the greater will be the likelihood that the condition will be met; and although it is possible for this condition to be met by the commission of a single offence, there must be a risk of repetition of violence or disorder at a match; the test is not a high one, but it is clear that it is not automatically satisfied just because the instant offence was football-related. As to this case, see also *post*, § 5–1088.

Banning orders: general

★5–1076   As from a day to be appointed, section 14E(7) of the 1989 Act is repealed by the *Legal Aid, Sentencing and Punishment of Offenders Act* 2012, s.89(2), and Sched. 10, para. 6.

Information

★5–1082   As from a day to be appointed, section 18(5) of the 1989 Act is repealed by the *Legal Aid, Sentencing and Punishment of Offenders Act* 2012, s.89(2), and Sched. 10, para. 6.

Relevant offences

★5–1088   In *R. v. Doyle, Wise (Ryan) and Wise (Darren)*, 176 J.P. 337, CA, the court said that whether an offence was "related to football matches" within Schedule 1, paras (g) to (o), to the 1989 Act, called for a judgment of the court; such a judgment is not an assessment of the legal character of the offence, but a determination whether, on the particular facts of the offence as it was committed on the occasion in question, the offence was "related to football matches"; while the test is expressed in terms of "matches", it would appear that it would suffice if the behaviour was related to a single match; it would be wrong, however, to attempt to define when an offence is "related to football matches", as the facts that may occur will vary too much; in one or two reported cases (presumably *R. v. Elliott* and *R. v. Parkes* (as to which, see the main work)), the court had taken into account whether what was described as the "spark" of the offence of violence was a football factor, such as a dispute with opposing fans, but this is only an example of the kind of matter that may be relevant, and must not be taken as a substitute test; it is all too notorious that the "spark" for offences of violence may sometimes be illusory, or minimal, or simply irrelevant; it will not, of itself, be enough that the offence would not have occurred "but for" the fact that the defendant was en route to or from a match; however, if the offence is one committed by a group of football fans clearly acting as such, in a group whose identity was clearly football-oriented, their violence may well justify the expression "related to football matches", even if the particular *casus belli* is that exception is taken to another person for no particular reason. As to this case, see also *ante*, § 5–1072.

D. DISQUALIFICATION FROM DRIVING

(1) Legislation

Powers of Criminal Courts (Sentencing) Act 2000, ss.146, 147

Driving disqualification for any offence

As from a day to be appointed, section 146(2) of the 2000 Act is amended by the *Legal Aid, Sentencing and Punishment of Offenders Act* 2012, s.122(3), and Sched. 19, paras 3 and 6, so as to insert "224A," before 225(2)".   ★5–1106

As from a day to be appointed, section 146(2) of the 2000 Act is further amended by the 2012 Act, s.142(3), and Sched. 26, paras 9 and 13, so as to substitute "the words "section 1A(5) of the *Prevention of Crime Act* 1953, section 51A(2) of the *Firearms Act* 1968, section 139AA(7) of the *Criminal Justice Act* 1988" for the words "section 51A(2) of the *Firearms Act* 1968".   ★

Powers of Criminal Courts (Sentencing) Act 2000, ss.147A, 147B

[Extension of disqualification where custodial sentence also imposed

As from a day to be appointed, section 147A(4) of the 2000 Act is amended by the *Legal Aid, Sentencing and Punishment of Offenders Act* 2012, s.89(2), and Sched. 10, para. 10, so as to omit paragraphs (c) and (d).   ★5–1108

As from a day to be appointed, section 147A(4) of the 2000 Act is further amended by the 2012 Act, s.126, and Sched. 21, paras 7 and 15(1) to (3), so as (i) to substitute "226A" for "227", "two-thirds of" for "half" and "226A(5)(a)" for "227(2C)(a)" in paragraph (e), and (ii) to substitute "226B" for "228", "two-thirds of" for "half" and "226B(3)(a)" for "228(2B)(a)" in paragraph (f).   ★

As from a day to be appointed, section 147A(6) of the 2000 Act is amended by the 2012 Act, s.110(13), and Sched. 13, paras 9 and 12, so as (i) to omit the words "a direction under", (b) to substitute "section 240ZA" for "section 240" in paragraph (a), and (iii) to insert the words "a direction under" before "section 240A" in paragraph (b).   ★

As from a day to be appointed, section 147A(8) of the 2000 Act is amended by the 2012 Act, s.111(2), and Sched. 14, para. 3(a), so as to insert "243A(3)(a)," after "section".   ★

As from a day to be appointed, section 147A(8) of the 2000 Act is further amended by the 2012 Act, s.126, and Sched. 21, paras 7 and 15(1) and (4), so as to omit "or 247(2)".   ★

As from a day to be appointed, section 147A(9) of the 2000 Act is amended by the 2012 Act, s.111(2), and Sched. 14, para. 3(b), so as to insert "243A(3)(a)," after "in respect of section".   ★

As from a day to be appointed, section 147A(9) of the 2000 Act is further amended by the 2012 Act, s.126, and Sched. 21, paras 7 and 15(1) and (5), so as to omit paragraph (b).   ★

(3) Notes on disqualification from driving (s.147)

Relevance to offence

A judge was entitled to impose a period of disqualification under section 147 of the *PCC(S)A* 2000 (§ 5–1107 in the main work) upon an offender convicted of theft of diesel from a depot, where the offender, along with a group of professional criminals, went to the depot in one of two trucks, five times across two evenings, filled up plastic containers with diesel and drove the fuel away; the trucks were evidently being used for the purposes of the criminal activity; and it was no bar to disqualification that the offender was a passenger, rather than a driver: *R. v. Gilder* [2012] 1 Cr.App.R.(S.) 4, CA (considering *R. v. Sofekun* (§ 5–1110 in the main work)).   5–1111

F. Disqualification or Being Barred from Working with Children or Vulnerable Adults

(1) Background

S.I. 2009 No. 2611, art. 3 (as amended by the Policing and Crime Act 2009, s.81(5), and S.I. 2010 No. 1101 (post))

Repeal of provisions of the Criminal Justice and Court Services Act 2000

5–1122 R. v. C. is now reported at [2012] 1 Cr.App.R.(S.) 89.

Att.-Gen.'s Reference (No. 18 of 2011) is now reported at [2012] 1 Cr.App.R.(S.) 27.

(2) Bars on working with children or vulnerable adults

Summary

★5–1123 Section 88 of the *Protection of Freedoms Act* 2012 makes provision (with effect from May 1, 2012) for the dissolution of the Independent Safeguarding Authority and for the transfer of its functions to a new body corporate (established, as from a day to be appointed, under s.87) to be known as the Disclosure and Barring Service.

Schedule 3 to the *Safeguarding Vulnerable Groups Act* 2006 is extensively amended (as from a day to be appointed) by the *Protection of Freedoms Act* 2012. In particular, paragraphs 1 to 3, 5, 7 to 9 and 11 are amended by section 67. The general effect of the amendments is that (except in relation to automatic inclusion under para. 1 or 7) individuals are only considered for inclusion, and subsequently included in, the children's or adults' barred lists where there is reason to believe that the person is or has been, or might be in the future, engaged in regulated activity relating to children or vulnerable adults (as to which, see s.5 of, and Sched. 4 to, the 2006 Act). Paragraphs 2 and 8 (inclusion subject to consideration of representations) are further amended so that the person being considered for inclusion in a barred list is given the opportunity to make representations prior to his inclusion, rather than after.

★5–1124 As from a day to be appointed, paragraph 25(1) of Schedule 3 to the *Safeguarding Vulnerable Groups Act* 2006 is amended by the *Protection of Freedoms Act* 2012, s.115(1), and Sched. 9, para. 72(1) and (3), so as to insert, between the words "will" and "include", the words "or (as the case may be) may".

Compatibility with the ECHR

5–1127 *R. (Royal College of Nursing, O.O., C.W., A.A., and E.R.) v. Secretary of State for the Home Department and Independent Safeguarding Authority (Interested Party)* is now reported at [2011] 2 F.L.R. 1399, *sub nom. R. (Royal College of Nursing, O.O., C.E., A.A., and E.R.) v. Secretary of State for the Home Department and Independent Safeguarding Authority*.

(3) Disqualification orders

(a) Summary

5–1128 The *CJCSA* 2000, Part II introduced a new power to make a disqualification order by which a person convicted of an "offence against a child" would be disqualified indefinitely from working with children. "Offence against a child" was defined in section 26 and Schedule 4. A child for this purpose was a person under the age of 18. The conditions for making a disqualification order were set out in sections 28 and 29. The relevant provisions came into force on January 11, 2001. They were significantly amended by provisions of the *CJA* 2003.

As to the repeal of these provisions, subject to savings, from October 12, 2009, by the *Safeguarding Vulnerable Groups Act* 2006, see §§ 5–1119 *et seq.*, 5–1125 in the main work and *ante*.

In *R. v. Field*; *R. v. Young* [2003] 1 W.L.R. 882, CA, it was held that a disqualification order was not a "penalty" for the purposes of Article 7 of the ECHR (§ 16–97 in the main work). The effect of an order was entirely prospective, because it only affected future conduct. In such circumstances, the statute did not offend against the presumption against retrospective effect merely because it depended for its future application upon events that might have occurred before it came into force. The purpose of section 28 was plainly to protect children. That purpose would be severely undermined if a disqualification order could be imposed only in relation to offences committed after it came into force.

In *R. v. G.* [2006] 1 Cr.App.R.(S.) 30, CA, it was held that there was nothing in the Strasbourg jurisprudence to suggest that a disqualification order engaged Article 8 of the European Convention (right to respect for private and family life (§ 16–101 in the main work)), but, even if it did, such an inference was plainly in accordance with domestic law, pursued a legitimate purpose, and, in the circumstances, was proportionate (within Article 8(2)).

(b) *Legislation*

Criminal Justice and Court Services Act 2000, ss.26–31

Meaning of "offence against a child"

26.—(1) For the purposes of this Part, an individual commits an offence against a child if— **5-1129**
    (a) he commits any offence mentioned in paragraph 1 of Schedule 4,
    (b) he commits against a child any offence mentioned in paragraph 2 of that Schedule, or
    (c) he falls within paragraph 3 of that Schedule,
and references to being convicted of, or charged with, an offence against a child are to be read accordingly.

(2) The Secretary of State may by order amend Schedule 4 so as to add, modify or omit any entry.

[As to the repeal and saving for certain purposes of this section, see *ante*, § 5–1128.]

Equivalent armed forces offences

27.—(1) For the purposes of this Part, an individual is treated as being convicted of or (as the **5-1130** case may be) charged with an offence against a child if he is convicted of or charged with an equivalent armed forces offence.

(2) In subsection (1), "equivalent armed forces offence" means an offence under section 42 of the *Armed Forces Act* 2006 constituted by an act or omission which—
    (a) is an offence against a child, or
    (b) would, if committed in England or Wales, be an offence against a child.

(3) Section 48 of the *Armed Forces Act* 2006 (attempts, conspiracy, incitement and aiding and abetting outside England and Wales) applies for the purposes of subsection (2) of this section as if the reference in subsection (3)(b) of that section to any of the following provisions of that Act were a reference to subsection (2) of this section.

[This section is printed as amended by the *AFA* 2006, s.378(1), and Sched. 16, para. 179. As to its repeal and saving for certain purposes, see *ante*, § 5–1128.]

Disqualification from working with children: adults

28.—(1) This section applies where either of the conditions set out below is satisfied in the case **5-1131** of an individual.

(2) The first condition is that—
    (a) the individual is convicted of an offence against a child committed when he was aged 18 or over, and
    (b) a qualifying sentence is imposed by a superior court in respect of the conviction.

(3) The second condition is that—
    (a) the individual is charged with an offence against a child committed when he was aged 18 or over, and
    (b) a relevant order is made by a superior court in respect of the act or omission charged against him as the offence.

(4) Subject to subsection (5), the court must order the individual to be disqualified from working with children.

(5) An order shall not be made under this section if the court is satisfied, having regard to all the circumstances, that it is unlikely that the individual will commit any further offence against a child.

(6) If the court does not make an order under this section, it must state its reasons for not doing so and cause those reasons to be included in the record of the proceedings.

[This section is printed as amended by the *Constitutional Reform Act* 2005, s.59(5), and Sched. 11, para. 35. As to its repeal and saving for certain purposes, see *ante*, § 5-1128.]

Disqualification from working with children: juveniles

5-1132   **29.**—(1) This section applies where either of the conditions set out below is satisfied in the case of an individual.

(2) The first condition is that—

(a) the individual is convicted of an offence against a chld committed at a time when the individual was under the age of 18, and

(b) a qualifying sentence is imposed by a superior court in respect of the conviction.

(3) The second condition is that—

(a) the individual is charged with an offence against a child committed at a time when the individual was under the age of 18, and

(b) a relevant order is made by a superior court in respect of the act or omission charged against him as the offence.

(4) If the court is satisfied, having regard to all the circumstances, that it is likely that the individual will commit a further offence against a child it must order the individual to be disqualified from working with children.

(5) If the court makes an order under this section, it must state its reasons for doing so and cause those reasons to be included in the record of the proceedings.

[See the note to s.28, *ante*.]

Disqualification at discretion of court: adults and juveniles

5-1133   **29A.**—(1) This section applies where—

(a) an individual is convicted of an offence against a child (whether or not committed when he was aged 18 or over),

(b) the individual is sentenced by a senior [superior] court, and

(c) no qualifying sentence is imposed in respect of the conviction.

(2) If the court is satisfied, having regard to all the circumstances, that it is likely that the individual will commit a further offence against a child, it may order the individual to be disqualified from working with children.

(3) [*Identical to s.29(5), ante, § 5–863.*]

[This section was inserted by the *CJA* 2003, s.299, and Sched. 30, paras 1 and 2. As to its amendment by the *Constitutional Reform Act* 2005, see the note to s.28, *ante*. As to its repeal and saving for certain purposes, see *ante*, § 5-1128.]

Subsequent application for order under section 28 or 29

5-1134   **29B.**—(1) Where—

(a) section 28 applies but the court has neither made an order under that section nor complied with subsection (6) of that section, or

(b) section 29 applies but the court has not made an order under that section, and it appears to the prosecutor that the court has not considered the making of an order under that section,

the prosecutor may at any time apply to that court for an order under section 28 or 29.

(2) Subject to subsection (3), on an application under subsection (1)—

(a) in a case falling within subsection (1)(a), the court—

(i) must make an order under section 28 unless it is satisfied as mentioned in subsection (5) of that section, and

(ii) if it does not make an order under that section, must comply with subsection (6) of that section,

(b) in a case falling within subsection (1)(b), the court—

      (i) must make an order under section 29 if it is satisfied as mentioned in subsection (4) of that section, and

      (ii) if it does so, must comply with subsection (5) of that section.

   (3) Subsection (2) does not enable or require an order under section 28 or 29 to be made where the court is satisfied that it had considered the making of an order under that section at the time when it imposed the qualifying sentence or made the relevant order.

[This section was inserted by the *CJA* 2003, s.299, and Sched. 30, paras 1 and 2. As to its repeal and saving for certain purposes, see *ante*, § 5–1128.]

Sections 28 to 29B: supplemental

   30.—(1) In sections 28 to 29B and this section—   **5–1135**

    "guardianship order" means a guardianship order within the meaning of the *Mental Health Act* 1983,

    "qualifying sentence" means—

      (a) a sentence of imprisonment for a term of 12 months of more,

      (b) a sentence of detention in a young offender institution for a term of 12 months or more,

      (c) a sentence of detention during Her Majesty's pleasure,

      (d) a sentence of detention for a period of 12 months or more under section 91 of the *Powers of Criminal Courts (Sentencing) Act* 2000 or section 209 of the *Armed Forces Act* 2006 (offenders under 18 convicted of certain serious offences),

      (dd) a sentence of detention under section 226 or 228 of the *Criminal Justice Act* 2003,

      (e) a detention and training order for a term of 12 months or more under section 100 of the *Powers of Criminal Courts (Sentencing) Act* 2000 or section 211 of the *Armed Forces Act* 2006,

      (g) a hospital order within the meaning of the *Mental Health Act* 1983, or

      (h) a guardianship order,

    "relevant order" means—

      (a) an order made by the Crown Court, the Court of Appeal, the Court Martial or the Court Martial Appeal Court that the individual in question be admitted to hospital, or

      (b) a guardianship order,

    "superior court" means the Crown Court, the Court of Appeal, the Court Martial or the Court Martial Appeal Court.

   (3) In this Part, references to a sentence of imprisonment, include references to a suspended sentence.

   (4) If, for the purpose of making an order under section 28 or 29, the court determines, after considering any available evidence, that an individual was, or was not, under the age of 18 at the time when the offence in question was committed, his age at that time shall be taken, for the purposes of that sections [*sic*] (and in particular for the purpose of determining any question as to the validity of the order), to be that which the court determined it to be.

   (5) Below in this Part—

      (a) references to a disqualification order are to an order under section 28, 29 or 29A,

      (b) in relation to an individual on whom a sentence has been passed, or in relation to whom an order has been made, as mentioned in subsection (2) or (3) of section 28 or 29, references to his sentence are to that sentence or order,

      (c) in relation to an individual to whom section 29A applies and on whom a sentence has been passed, references to his sentence are to that sentence.

[This section is printed as amended by the *CJA* 2003, s.299, and Sched. 30, paras 1 and 3; the *Constitutional Reform Act* 2005, s.59(5), and Sched. 11, para. 35; and the *AFA* 2006, s.378(1), and Sched. 16, para. 180. As to its repeal and saving for certain purposes, see *ante*, § 5–1128.]

   In relation to any time before the repeal of section 30 has effect, it is to have effect (as   ★ from a day to be appointed) with the following modifications (i) the insertion of ", 226B" after "226" in paragraph (dd) of the definition of "qualifying offence" (*Legal Aid, Sentencing and Punishment of Offenders Act* 2012, s.126, and Sched. 21, para. 37), and (ii) the insertion in the same paragraph of "(including such a sentence imposed as a result of section 221, 221A or 222 of the *Armed Forces Act* 2006)" after "2003" (2012 Act, s.127, and Sched. 22, para. 39).

Appeals

5–1136   31.—(1) An individual may appeal against a disqualification order—

    (a) where the first condition mentioned in section 28 or 29 is satisfied in his case, as if the order were a sentence passed on him for the offence of which he has been convicted,

    (b) where the second condition mentioned in section 28 or 29 is satisfied in his case as if he had been convicted on indictment and the order were a sentence passed on him for that offence,

    (c) where an order is made under section 29A, as if the order were a sentence passed on him for the offence of which he has been convicted.

    (2) In relation to a disqualification order made by the Court Martial, subsection (1)(b) has effect as if the reference to conviction on indictment were a reference to a conviction by the Court Martial.

[This section is printed as amended by the *CJA* 2003, s.299, and Sched. 30, paras 1 and 4; and the *AFA* 2006, s.378(1), and Sched. 16, para. 181. As to its repeal and saving for certain purposes, see *ante*, § 5–1128.]

Criminal Justice and Court Services Act 2000, s.42

Interpretation of Part II

5–1137   42.—(1) In this Part—

"care home" has the same meaning as in the *Care Standards Act* 2000,

"charity trustee" has the same meaning as in the *Charities Act* 2011,

"child" means a person under the age of 18,

"children's home" has—

    (a) in relation to England and Wales, the same meaning as in the *Care Standards Act* 2000,

    (b) in relation to Northern Ireland, the meaning which would be given by Article 90(1) of the *Children (Northern Ireland) Order* 1995 if, in Article 91(2) of that *Order*, sub-paragraphs (a), (f) and (g) and the words after sub-paragraph (h) were omitted,

"Class A drug" has the same meaning as in the *Misuse of Drugs Act* 1971,

"day care premises" means—

    (a) in relation to England, premises in respect of which a person is registered, otherwise than as a childminder, under Part 3 of the *Childcare Act* 2006,

    (b) in relation to Wales, premises in respect of which a person is registered under Part 10A of the *Children Act* 1989 for providing day care,

"disqualification order" has the meaning given by section 30,

"educational institution" means an institution which is exclusively or mainly for the provision of full-time education to children,

"employment" means paid employment, whether under a contract of service or apprenticeship or under a contract for services,

"hospital" has—

    (a) in relation to England and Wales, the meaning given by section 128(1) of the *National Health Service Act* 2006 or the *National Health Service (Wales) Act* 2006,

    (b) in relation to Northern Ireland, the meaning given by Article 2(2) of the *Health and Personal Social Services (Northern Ireland) Order* 1972,

"local authority" has the same meaning as in the *Education Act* 1996,

"nursing home" has the meaning given by Article 16 of the *Registered Homes (Northern Ireland) Order* 1992,

"private hospital" has the meaning given by Article 90(2) of the *Mental Health (Northern Ireland) Order* 1986,

"residential care home" has the meaning given by Article 3 of the *Registered Homes (Northern Ireland) Order* 1992,

"the Tribunal" means the tribunal established by section 9 of the *Protection of Children Act* 1999,

"voluntary home" has the meaning given by Article 74(1) of the *Children (Northern Ireland) Order* 1995,

"work" includes—

    (a) work of any kind, whether paid or unpaid and whether under a contract of service or apprenticeship, under a contract for services, or otherwise than under a contract, and

(b) an office established by or by virtue of an enactment,and "working" is to be read accordingly.

[This section is printed as amended by the *CJA* 2003, s.304, and Sched. 32, paras 133 and 135; the *National Health Service (Consequential Provisions) Act* 2006, s.2, and Sched. 1, paras 212 and 213; the *Childcare Act* 2006, s.103(1), and Sched. 2, para. 40; the *AFA* 2006, s.378(1), and Sched. 16, para. 181; the *Charities (Pre-consolidation Amendments) Order* 2011 (S.I. 2011 No. 1396), art. 2, and Sched., para. 48(a); and the *Charities Act* 2011, s.354(1), and Sched. 7, para. 91. The definition of "disqualification order" is repealed by the *Safeguarding Vulnerable Groups Act* 2006, s.63(2), and Sched. 10, with effect from October 12, 2009. As to its saving for certain purposes, however, see *ante*, § 5–1128.]

Meaning of "offence against a child"

Schedule 4 to the *CJCSA* 2000 (as amended by the *Nationality, Immigration and Asylum Act* 2002, s.146(4), the *SOA* 2003, s.139, and Sched. 6, para. 44(1) and (5), and the *Domestic Violence, Crime and Victims Act* 2004, s.58(1), and Sched. 10, para. 56) lists the offences referred to in section 26. Schedule 4 is repealed (subject to savings: see *ante*, § 5–1128), as from October 12, 2009, by the *Safeguarding Vulnerable Groups Act* 2006, s.63(2), and Sched. 10. The offences mentioned in section 26(1)(a) are those under the *CYPA* 1933, s.1, the *Infanticide Act* 1938, s.1, the *SOA* 1956, ss.5, 6, 19, 20, 25, 26 and 28, the *Indecency with Children Act* 1960, s.1, the *CLA* 1977, s.54, the *Protection of Children Act* 1978, s.1, the *Child Abduction Act* 1984, s.1, the *CJA* 1988, s.160, and the *SOA* 2003, ss.5 to 26 and 47 to 50.

The offences mentioned in section 26(1)(b) are murder, manslaughter, kidnapping, false imprisonment, an offence under the *Offences against the Person Act* 1861, ss.18, 20 and 47, under the *SOA* 1956, ss.1 to 4, 14 to 17 and 24 and under the *SOA* 2003, ss.1 to 4, 30 to 41, 52, 53, 57 to 61, 66 and 67.

A person falls within paragraph 3 of Schedule 4 (see s.26(1)(c)) if he or she commits an offence, (a) under the *Offences Against the Person Act* 1861, s.16, by making a threat to kill a child; (b) under the *SOA* 1956, s.7, by having sexual intercourse with a child; (c) under the 1956 Act, s.9, by procuring a child to have sexual intercourse; (d) under the 1956 Act, s.10, by having sexual intercourse with a child; (e) being a woman, under the 1956 Act, s.11, by allowing a child to have sexual intercourse with her; (f) under the 1956 Act, s.12, by committing buggery with a child under 16; (g) under the 1956 Act, s.13, by committing an act of gross indecency with a child; (h) under the 1956 Act, s.21, by taking a child out of the possession of his parent or guardian; (i) under the 1956 Act, s.22, in relation to a child; (j) under the 1956 Act, s.23, by procuring a child to have sexual intercourse with a third person; (k) under the 1956 Act, s.27, by inducing or suffering a child to resort to or to be on premises for the purpose of having sexual intercourse; (l) under the 1956 Act, s.29, by causing or encouraging the prostitution of a child; (m) under the 1956 Act, s.30, in a case where the prostitute is a child; (n) under the 1956 Act, s.31, in a case where the prostitute is a child; (o) under the *MHA* 1983, s.128, by having sexual intercourse with a child; (p) under the *SOA* 1967, s.4, by procuring a child to commit an act of buggery with any person or procuring any person to commit an act of buggery with a child; (q) under the 1967 Act, s.5, by living on the earnings of a child prostitute; (r) under the *Theft Act* 1968, s.9(1)(a) by entering a building (or part thereof) with intent to rape a child; (s) under the *Misuse of Drugs Act* 1971, s.4(3), by supplying or offering to supply a Class A drug to a child, or being concerned in the supplying of such a drug to a child, or being concerned in making to a child of an offer to supply such drug; (sa) under the *SOA* 2003, ss.62 or 63, in a case where the intended offence was an offence against a child; (sb) under the *Domestic Violence, Crime and Victims Act* 2004, s.5 (as extended, as from July 2, 2012 (*Domestic Violence, Crime and Victims (Amendment) Act 2012 (Commencement) Order* 2012 (S.I. 2012 No. 1432)), by the *Domestic Violence, Crime and Victims (Amendment) Act* 2012: see para. 4 of the schedule to that Act for the relevant amendment of para. (sb)), in respect of a child; or (t) of aiding, abetting, counselling, procuring or inciting (to be construed as a reference to the offences under the *SCA* 2007, Pt 2: 2007 Act, s.63(1), and Sched. 6, para. 40) the commission of "an offence against a child" or of conspiring or attempting to commit such an offence. Whilst there is an obvious element of circularity about paragraph (t), it is submitted that the intended meaning is clear, *viz.* aiding and abetting, etc., the commission of any of the specific offences listed in any of the preceding paragraphs and subparagraphs of the schedule.

(c) *Notes on disqualification from working with children*

5-1139 In *R. v. M.G.* [2002] 2 Cr.App.R.(S.) 1, CA, it was held that the test to be applied by a court considering whether it was satisfied that it was unlikely that the individual would commit further offences against a child was not the criminal standard; where the judge found that the offender would probably not commit further offences against a child, but was not "satisfied" to this effect, a disqualification order was quashed.

 In considering whether an extended sentence imposed under the *PCC(S)A* 2000, s.85, is a "qualifying sentence" for the purposes of section 28, the relevant period is the whole length of the sentence, not the custodial term alone: *R. v. Wiles* [2004] 2 Cr.App.R.(S.) 88, CA.

H. Travel Restriction Orders

(3) Notes on travel restriction orders

★5-1147 The imposition of a travel restriction order under the *CJPA* 2001, s.33 (§ 5–1142 in the main work), on the basis that the court was required to do so unless it considered that it was inappropriate, had the effect of reversing the test in section 33; and the judge's reference to the offender possibly being tempted to re-offend was not an adequate basis for such an order; on the contrary, the imposition of a 10-year prison sentence would be a sufficient deterrent for a woman of the offender's age (58) and history: *R. v. Graham* [2012] 1 Cr.App.R.(S.) 57, CA (considering *R. v. Mee* (see the main work)).

I. Serious Crime Prevention Orders

(2) Legislation

Serious Crime Act 2007, ss.35–41

Compliance with orders: authorised monitors

5-1187 The amendments to section 39 of the 2007 Act effected by the *Police Reform and Social Responsibility Act* 2011, and noted in the main work, come into force on January 16, 2012: *Police Reform and Social Responsibility Act 2011 (Commencement No. 3 and Transitional Provisions) Order* 2011 (S.I. 2011 No. 3019). However, it should be noted that (i) the main work erroneously refers to paragraphs 304 and 305 of Schedule 16 to the 2011 Act, whereas it should refer to paragraph 370; and (ii) pending the commencement of section 1 of the 2011 Act, the amendment takes effect in modified form, as to which, see article 10(5) of, and Schedule 2, para. 79, to, the commencement order. The effect of the modification is that only the new paragraph (zb) comes into force, with this being temporarily denoted as paragraph "(za)".

Serious offences

★5-1192 As from a day to be appointed, Part 1 of Schedule 1 to the *SCA* 2007 is amended by the *Protection of Freedoms Act* 2012, s.115(1), and Sched. 9, para. 142, so as to substitute a reference to section 59A of the *SOA* 2003 for the reference to sections 57 to 59 of that Act.

J. Anti-Social Behaviour Orders

Authorities

Breach

Section 1(10) of the *CDA* 1998 (§ 5–1199 in the main work) does not require the prose-   ★5–1205
cution to prove a specific mental element on the part of the defendant at the time he did
that which he was prohibited from doing by the order; however, the defendant's state of
mind will usually be relevant if the issue of reasonable excuse is raised: *R. (J.B.) v. DPP*
[2012] 2 Cr.App.R. 2, DC (considering *R. v. Nicholson* (see the main work)).

K. Financial Reporting Orders

(2) Legislation

Serious Organised Crime and Police Act 2005, ss.76–81

Financial reporting orders: making

A court is entitled to look at a defendant's whole lifestyle when deciding whether to make   ★5–1213
a financial reporting order under section 76 of the 2005 Act (§ 5–1212 in the main work); it
is not confined to consideration of the offence or offences of which the offender has been
convicted: *R. v. Bagnall* [2012] L.S. Gazette, May 10, 21, CA ([2012] EWCA Crim. 677).

L. Procedure

Criminal Procedure Rules 2011 (S.I. 2011 No. 1709), Pt 50

Behaviour orders: general rules

With effect from April 2, 2012, rule 50.2(1) of the *Criminal Procedure Rules* 2011 (S.I.   **5–1221**
2011 No. 1709) is amended by the *Criminal Procedure (Amendment) Rules* 2011 (S.I. 2011
No. 3075), r.12(a), so as to substitute a new paragraph (a), as follows—

"(a) to consider—
(i) what order is proposed and why, and
(ii) the evidence in support;".

Evidence to assist the court: special rules

With effect from April 2, 2012, the *Criminal Procedure Rules* 2011 (S.I. 2011 No. 1709) are   **5–1223**
amended by the *Criminal Procedure (Amendment) Rules* 2011 (S.I. 2011 No. 3075), r.12(b), so
as to substitute a new rule 50.4, as follows—

"*Evidence to assist the court: special rules*
50.4—(1) This rule applies where the court can make on its own initiative—
(a) a football banning order;
(b) a restraining order;
(c) an anti-social behaviour order; or
(d) a drinking banning order.
(2) A party who wants the court to take account of evidence not already introduced must—
(a) serve notice in writing on—
(i) the court officer, and
(ii) every other party,
as soon as practicable (without waiting for the verdict);
(b) in the notice, identify that evidence; and
(c) attach any written statement containing such evidence.".

XI. ORDERS UNDER THE MENTAL HEALTH ACT 1983

(1) Hospital and guardianship orders

Mental Health Act 1983, s.37

Powers of courts to order hospital admission or guardianship

★5–1236 As from a day to be appointed, section 37(1A) of the 1983 Act is amended by the *Legal Aid, Sentencing and Punishment of Offenders Act* 2012, s.142(3), and Sched. 26, para. 2(1) and (2), so as to insert, before paragraph (a), a new paragraph (za), as follows—

"(za) under section 1A(5) of the *Prevention of Crime Act* 1953,".

★ As from a day to be appointed, section 37(1A) of the 1983 Act is further amended by the 2012 Act, s.142(3), and Sched. 26, para. 2(1) and (3), so as to insert, after paragraph (a), a new paragraph (aa), as follows—

"(aa) under section 139AA(7) of the *Criminal Justice Act* 1988,".

★ As from a day to be appointed, section 37(1A) of the 1983 Act is further amended by the 2012 Act, s.122(3), and Sched. 19, para. 1, so as to insert, after paragraph (b), a new paragraph (ba), as follows—

"(ba) under section 224A of the *Criminal Justice Act* 2003,".

Inter-relationship with discretionary life sentence

5–1238 In *Att.-Gen.'s Reference (No. 54 of 2011)* [2012] 1 Cr.App.R.(S.) 106, CA, the court emphasised that where a judge had been faced with a choice between a hospital order under section 37 of the 1983 Act, coupled with a restriction order under section 41 (§§ 5–1236, 5–1242 in the main work), and an indeterminate sentence of detention or imprisonment where it was anticipated that, if such a sentence were imposed, a transfer direction would be made under section 47 of the 1983 Act, the judge should take account of crucial differences in the release and recall regimes. First, under an indeterminate custodial sentence, release is dependent upon the responsible authority being satisfied that the defendant is no longer a danger to the public for any reason and principally not at risk of relapsing into dangerous crime, whereas under the hospital order regime release is dependent upon the responsible authority being satisfied that the defendant no longer presents any danger arising from his medical condition; similarly, and critically, release under the detention for public protection regime is on licence, and the licence can be revoked if the defendant shows that he remains a danger to the public from crime, whereas under the hospital order regime, recall is available, but only if the defendant's medical condition relapses; simple crime does not trigger a recall under the hospital order regime. Where, therefore, there was the plainest possible risk that the respondent might resume a criminal lifestyle once at large, it was essential that there was available to the authorities the power to recall him if that were to happen; accordingly, a sentence of detention for public protection would be substituted for the hospital order that had been imposed in the Crown Court.

(2) Restriction orders

Mental Health Act 1983, s.43

Power of magistrates' courts to commit for restriction order

★5–1243 With effect from June 18, 2012 (*Criminal Justice Act 2003 (Commencement No. 28 and Saving Provisions) Order* 2012 (S.I. 2012 No. 1320)), section 41 of, and paragraph 55(1) and (2) of Schedule 3 to, the 2003 Act are brought into force in certain areas (as to which, see *ante*, § 1–88). There are associated saving provisions, as to which, see article 5 of the order (*ante*, § 1–88).

XII. RECOMMENDATION FOR DEPORTATION

Immigration Act 1971, s.7

Exemption from deportation for certain existing residents

As from a day to be appointed, section 7(4) of the 1971 Act is amended by the *Legal Aid, Sentencing and Punishment of Offenders Act* 2012, s.110(13), and Sched. 13, para. 7, so as to insert ", 240ZA or 240A" after "section 240". ★5–1258

Immigration Act 1971, Sched. 3, paras 2–6

R. (Lumba) v. Secretary of State for the Home Department (JUSTICE intervening); *Same v. Same (No. 2) (Same intervening)*; *R. (Mighty) v. Same (Same intervening)* is now reported at [2012] 1 A.C. 245. ★5–1265

XV. MISCELLANEOUS MATTERS

B. ALTERATION OF SENTENCE

Powers of Criminal Courts (Sentencing) Act 2000, s.155

Alteration of Crown Court sentence

As from a day to be appointed, section 155(8) of the 2000 Act is amended by the *Legal Aid, Sentencing and Punishment of Offenders Act* 2012, s.39(1), and Sched. 5, paras 52 and 54, so as to substitute the words "relating to a requirement to make a payment under regulations under section 23 or 24 of the *Legal Aid, Sentencing and Punishment of Offenders Act* 2012" for the words "under section 17(2) of the *Access to Justice Act* 1999". ★5–1289

Variation after expiration of relevant time limit

R. v. Hudson is now reported at [2011] 2 Cr.App.R.(S.) 116. 5–1293

CHAPTER 6

COSTS AND CRIMINAL DEFENCE

I. COSTS

B. PROSECUTION OF OFFENCES ACT 1985

(1) Awards of costs out of central funds

(a) *Defence costs*

Prosecution of Offences Act 1985, s.16

As from a day to be appointed, section 16 of the 1985 Act is amended by the *Legal Aid, Sentencing and Punishment of Offenders Act* 2012, s.62(1), and Sched. 7, paras 1 and 2, so as to omit subsections (7) and (9), and to insert new subsections (6A) to (6D), as follows— ★6–3

> "(6A) Where the court considers that there are circumstances that make it inappropriate for the accused to recover the full amount mentioned in subsection (6), a defendant's costs order must be for the payment out of central funds of such lesser amount as the court considers just and reasonable.

(6B) Subsections (6) and (6A) have effect subject to—

(a) section 16A, and

(b) regulations under section 20(1A)(d).

(6C) When making a defendant's costs order, the court must fix the amount to be paid out of central funds in the order if it considers it appropriate to do so and—

(a) the accused agrees the amount, or

(b) subsection (6A) applies.

(6D) Where the court does not fix the amount to be paid out of central funds in the order—

(a) it must describe in the order any reduction required under subsection (6A), and

(b) the amount must be fixed by means of a determination made by or on behalf of the court in accordance with procedures specified in regulations made by the Lord Chancellor.".

★ Paragraphs 20 and 23 of Schedule 7 to the 2012 Act provide that the amendments made by paragraphs 2 to 5 do not have effect in relation to costs orders made by a court in proceedings which commenced before the day on which the amendment comes into force. Paragraph 24 provides that, for the purposes of paragraphs 20 and 22—

(a) proceedings commence in a magistrates' court when a warrant, requisition or summons relating to the proceedings is issued;

(b) proceedings commence on an appeal to the Crown Court when a notice of appeal is served;

(c) other proceedings commence in the Crown Court when they are committed, transferred or sent to that court;

(d) proceedings commence in the High Court when an application for leave to appeal by way of case stated is made or (in the absence of such an application) when notice of appeal is given;

(e) proceedings commence in the Court of Appeal when an application for leave to appeal is made or (in the absence of such an application) when notice of appeal is given;

(f) proceedings commence in the Supreme Court when an application for leave to appeal is made.

★**6–9** With effect from June 18, 2012 (*Criminal Justice Act 2003 (Commencement No. 28 and Saving Provisions) Order* 2012 (S.I. 2012 No. 1320)), section 41 of, and paragraph 57(1) and (3) of Schedule 3 to, the 2003 Act are brought into force (so far as they are not already in force) in certain areas (as to which, see *ante*, § 1–88). There are associated saving provisions, as to which, see article 5 of the order (*ante*, § 1–88).

Legal costs

★**6–9a** As from a day to be appointed, a new section 16A is inserted in the 1985 Act by the *Legal Aid, Sentencing and Punishment of Offenders Act* 2012, s.62(1), and Sched. 7, paras 1 and 3.

Prosecution of Offences Act 1985, s.16A

[Legal costs

16A.—(1) A defendant's costs order may not require the payment out of central funds of an amount that includes an amount in respect of the accused's legal costs, subject to the following provisions of this section.

(2) Subsection (1) does not apply where condition A, B or C is met.

(3) Condition A is that the accused is an individual and the order is made under—

(a) section 16(1),

(b) section 16(3), or

(c) section 16(4)(a)(ii) or (iii) or (d).

(4) Condition B is that the accused is an individual and the legal costs were incurred in proceedings in a court below which were—

(a) proceedings in a magistrates' court, or

(b) proceedings on an appeal to the Crown Court under section 108 of the *Magistrates' Courts Act* 1980 (right of appeal against conviction or sentence).

(5) Condition C is that the legal costs were incurred in proceedings in the Supreme Court.

(6) The Lord Chancellor may by regulations make provision about exceptions from the prohibition in subsection (1), including—

    (a) provision amending this section by adding, modifying or removing an exception, and

    (b) provision for an exception to arise where a determination has been made by a person specified in the regulations.

(7) Regulations under subsection (6) may not remove or limit the exception provided by condition C.

(8) Where a court makes a defendant's costs order requiring the payment out of central funds of an amount that includes an amount in respect of legal costs, the order must include a statement to that effect.

(9) Where, in a defendant's costs order, a court fixes an amount to be paid out of central funds that includes an amount in respect of legal costs incurred in proceedings in a court other than the Supreme Court, the latter amount must not exceed an amount specified by regulations made by the Lord Chancellor.

(10) In this section—

    "legal costs" means fees, charges, disbursements and other amounts payable in respect of advocacy services or litigation services including, in particular, expert witness costs;

    "advocacy services" means any services which it would be reasonable to expect a person who is exercising, or contemplating exercising, a right of audience in relation to any proceedings, or contemplated proceedings, to provide;

    "expert witness costs" means amounts payable in respect of the services of an expert witness, including amounts payable in connection with attendance by the witness at court or elsewhere;

    "litigation services" means any services which it would be reasonable to expect a person who is exercising, or contemplating exercising, a right to conduct litigation in relation to proceedings, or contemplated proceedings, to provide.]

As to the application of this amendment of the 1985 Act, see *ante*, § 16–3.

Principles governing exercise of discretion

Ashendon and Jones v. U.K. is now reported at (2012) 54 E.H.R.R. 13, *sub nom. Ashendon* **6–14**
v. U.K.; Jones v. U.K.

In *R. (Guney) v. Central Criminal Court* [2011] A.C.D. 90, DC, it was said that whereas the *Practice Direction (Criminal Proceedings: Costs)* [2004] 1 W.L.R. 2657, provided that a defendant's costs order (under the *Prosecution of Offences Act* 1985, s.16 (§ 6–3 in the main work)) should normally be made in respect of an acquitted defendant unless there were positive reasons for not doing so, *e.g.* where the defendant's conduct had brought suspicion on himself and had misled the prosecution into thinking that the case against him was stronger than it was, there is nothing in *R. (Spiteri) v. Basildon Crown Court* (see the main work), that requires there to be separate actions or conduct on the part of the acquitted defendant giving rise to suspicion being brought on himself on the one hand and to the prosecution being misled by his behaviour after arrest as to the strength of their case on the other. The practice direction of 2004 has since been replaced by *Practice Direction (Criminal Proceedings: Costs)* [2010] 1 W.L.R. 2351: see, in particular, paragraphs 2.1.1 and 2.2.1 (§ 6–105 in the main work).

Amount of award

As to the amendment of section 21(4A) of the 1985 Act, see *post*, § 6–50.   ★**6–18**

(b) *Prosecution costs*

Prosecution of Offences Act 1985, s.17

As from a day to be appointed, section 17 of the 1985 Act is amended by the *Legal Aid,*   ★**6–23**
Sentencing and Punishment of Offenders Act 2012, s.62(1), and Sched. 7, paras 1 and 4, so as (i) to substitute "subsections (2) and (2A)" for "subsection (2)" in subsection (1), (ii) to omit subsections (3) and (4), and (iii) to insert new subsections (2A) to (2C), as follows—

"(2A) Where the court considers that there are circumstances that make it inappropriate for the prosecution to recover the full amount mentioned in subsection (1), an order under this section must be for the payment out of central funds of such lesser amount as the court considers just and reasonable.

(2B) When making an order under this section, the court must fix the amount to be paid out of central funds in the order if it considers it appropriate to do so and—

> (a) the prosecutor agrees the amount, or
> (b) subsection (2A) applies.

(2C) Where the court does not fix the amount to be paid out of central funds in the order—

> (a) it must describe in the order any reduction required under subsection (2A), and
> (b) the amount must be fixed by means of a determination made by or on behalf of the court in accordance with procedures specified in regulations made by the Lord Chancellor.".

As to the application of these amendments, see *ante*, § 16–3.

★6–24   As to the amendment of section 21(4) of the 1985 Act, see *post*, § 6–50.

(2) Award of costs against accused

Relevance of means

6–29   *R. v. Rakib* is now reported at [2012] 1 Cr.App.R.(S.) 1.

R. v. Cotswold Geotechnical Holdings Ltd is now reported at [2012] 1 Cr.App.R.(S.) 26.

(3) Provision for orders as to costs in other circumstances

Prosecution of Offences Act 1985, s.19

★6–38   As from a day to be appointed, section 19(2) of the 1985 Act is amended by the *Legal Aid, Sentencing and Punishment of Offenders Act* 2012, s.39(1), and Sched 5, paras 22 and 23, so as to substitute the words "of whether, for the purposes of the proceedings, representation has been provided under Part 1 of the *Legal Aid, Sentencing and Punishment of Offenders Act* 2012" for the words "any grant of a right to representation funded by the Legal Services Commission as part of the Criminal Defence Service".

★6–39   As from a day to be appointed, section 19 of the 1985 Act is further amended by the *Legal Aid, Sentencing and Punishment of Offenders Act* 2012, s.62(1), and Sched 7, paras 1 and 5(1) and (2), so as to insert a new subsection (3ZA) after subsection (3), as follows—

"(3ZA) In relation to a sum that may be required by a court other than the Supreme Court to be paid out of central funds under regulations under subsection (3)—

> (a) the requirement under that subsection for the sum to be such sum as the court considers reasonably necessary to cover or compensate for expenses, fees, costs, trouble or losses is subject to regulations made under section 20(1A)(d), and
> (b) regulations under subsection (3) may make provision accordingly.".

★   As from a day to be appointed, section 19 of the 1985 Act is further amended by the 2012 Act, s.62(1), and Sched 7, paras 1 and 5(1) and (3), so as to insert a new subsection (3D) after subsection (3C), as follows—

"(3D) Regulations under subsection (3) may make provision generally or only in relation to particular descriptions of persons, expenses, fees, costs, trouble or losses.".

★   As from a day to be appointed, section 19 of the 1985 Act is further amended by the 2012 Act, s.62(1), and Sched 7, paras 1 and 5(1) and (4), so as to insert new subsections (4A) to (4C), as follows—

"(4A) Subsection (4) has effect subject to regulations under section 20(1A)(d).

(4B) An order under subsection (4) may not require the payment out of central funds of a sum that includes a sum in respect of legal costs (as defined in section 16A), except where regulations made by the Lord Chancellor provide otherwise.

(4C) Regulations under subsection (4B) may, in particular, include—

(a) provision for an exception to arise where a determination has been made by a person specified in the regulations,

(b) provision requiring the court, when it orders the payment of a sum that includes a sum in respect of legal costs, to include a statement to that effect in the order, and

(c) provision that the court may not order the payment of a sum in respect of legal costs exceeding an amount specified in the regulations.".

As to the application of these amendments, see *ante*, § 16–3.

(4) Costs against legal representatives, etc.

"improper", "unreasonable", "negligent"

In *R. v. Solicitors Reeves & Co.* [2011] Costs L.R. 616, CA, a wasted costs order against **6–43**
solicitors representing the defendant, made after the defence disclosed e-mails on the day of trial that led to the prosecution offering no evidence, was quashed. First, the solicitors had had no notice of the case against them; although defence counsel made representations, some of which were applicable to the solicitors, he was not in fact their representative; and this was a fundamental breach of the rules of natural justice, as well as a breach of the relevant procedural rules. Secondly, a judge must determine what costs have been wasted as a result of the relevant conduct and then decide whether all or part of those costs should be borne by the representative (*Re A Barrister (Wasted Costs Order) (No. 1 of 1991)* (§ 6–41 in the main work)), but here there had been no proper analysis of the loss caused at all; the judge's figure had apparently been picked out of nowhere. Thirdly, the judge was wrong to find that the solicitors' conduct was "negligent"; it was perfectly proper for the defence to decide that they would not volunteer the relevant documents (print-outs of certain emails), particularly since the prosecution knew of them and were not pressing for them, because they did not believe the prosecution would be able to prove their case; it was an entirely sensible decision, in the interests of their client, to put the prosecution to proof of their case and to keep the emails in reserve in order to advance a defence of lack of dishonesty, should that be necessary.

Where the prosecution serve a hearsay notice, if the defendant, having been advised by ★
his solicitors of his obligation (if he wishes to object to the evidence being admitted as hearsay) under Part 34 of the *Criminal Procedure Rules* 2011 (S.I. 2011 No. 1709) (§§ 11–52 *et seq.* in the main work) to give notice of his objection (detailing the facts in dispute and the basis of any objection), refuses to authorise the service of such a notice, the solicitors should withdraw; and their failure to do so in the instant case was not a mere error of judgment; by insisting on the attendance of the witness in question (who had moved to Australia) without serving a proper counter-notice, the defendant was manipulating the processes of the court, and the solicitors were complicit in that in a manner that amounted to "improper, unreasonable and negligent" conduct, so as to justify a wasted costs order being made against them, pursuant to section 19A of the 1985 Act (§ 6–40 in the main work) in respect of the cost of attendance of the witness: *R. v. S.V.S. Solicitors*, unreported, February 15, 2012, CA ([2012] EWCA Crim. 319). For criticism of this decision, see CLW/12/14/13.

(6) Supplemental provisions

Prosecution of Offences Act 1985, ss.20, 21

Regulations

As from a day to be appointed, section 20(1) of the 1985 Act is amended by the *Legal Aid,* ★**6–46**
Sentencing and Punishment of Offenders Act 2012, s.62(1), and Sched 7, paras 1 and 6(1) and (2), so as to omit the words from "and the regulations" to the end of the subsection.

As from a day to be appointed, section 20 of the 1985 Act is further amended by the 2012 ★
Act, s.62(1), and Sched 7, paras 1 and 6(1) and (3), so as to insert new subsections (1A) to (1C), as follows—

"(1A) The Lord Chancellor may by regulations—

> (a) make provision as to the amounts that may be ordered to be paid out of central funds in pursuance of a costs order, whether by specifying rates or scales or by making other provision as to the calculation of the amounts,
>
> (b) make provision as to the circumstances in which and conditions under which such amounts may be paid or ordered to be paid,
>
> (c) make provision requiring amounts required to be paid out of central funds by a costs order to be calculated having regard to regulations under paragraphs (a) and (b),
>
> (d) make provision requiring amounts required to be paid to a person out of central funds by a relevant costs order to be calculated in accordance with such regulations (whether or not that results in the fixing of an amount that the court considers reasonably sufficient or necessary to compensate the person), and
>
> (e) make provision as to the review of determinations of amounts required to be paid out of central funds by costs orders.
>
> (1B) In subsection (1A)(d) 'relevant costs order' means a costs order other than—
>
> (a) an order made by any court under section 17, and
>
> (b) so much of a costs order made by the Supreme Court as relates to expenses, fees, costs, trouble or losses incurred in proceedings in that court.
>
> (1C) Regulations under subsection (1A) may, in particular—
>
> (a) make different provision in relation to amounts to be paid in respect of different expenses, fees, costs, trouble and losses,
>
> (b) make different provision in relation to different costs orders and different areas, and
>
> (c) make different provision in relation to the fixing of an amount in a costs order and the fixing of an amount by means of a determination.".

★ As from a day to be appointed, section 20(2) of the 1985 Act is amended by the *Legal Aid, Sentencing and Punishment of Offenders Act* 2012, s.39(1), and Sched. 5, paras 22 and 24, so as to substitute the words "by the Lord Chancellor under arrangements made for the purposes of Part 1 of the *Legal Aid, Sentencing and Punishment of Offenders Act* 2012 or out of central funds in accordance with a costs order" for the words "by the Legal Services Commission or out of central funds".

★6–47 As from a day to be appointed, section 20(3) of the 1985 Act is amended by the *Legal Aid, Sentencing and Punishment of Offenders Act* 2012, s.62(1), and Sched 7, paras 1 and 6(1) and (4), so as (i) to substitute "subsection (1A)" for "subsection (1)", (ii) to substitute the words "provision as to the calculation of amounts" for "rates or scales of allowances", and (iii) to insert the words "(whether in the form of rates or scales or other provision)" after the word "order".

Interpretation

★6–49 As from a day to be appointed, the definition of "legally assisted person" in section 21(1) of the 1985 Act is amended by the *Legal Aid, Sentencing and Punishment of Offenders Act* 2012, s.39(1), and Sched. 5, paras 22 and 25(1) and (2), so as to substitute the words "for whom advice, assistance or representation is provided under arrangements made for the purposes of Part 1 of the *Legal Aid, Sentencing and Punishment of Offenders Act* 2012" for the words from "to whom" to the end of the definition.

★6–50 As from a day to be appointed, section 21(4) of the 1985 Act is amended by the *Legal Aid, Sentencing and Punishment of Offenders Act* 2012, s.62(1), and Sched 7, paras 1 and 7(1) and (2), so as to insert ", 16A" after "16".

★ As from a day to be appointed, section 21(4A) of the 1985 Act is amended by the 2012 Act, s.39(1), and Sched. 5, paras 22 and 25(1), (3) and (4), so as (i) to substitute the words "not to include the cost of advice, assistance or representation provided to the person under arrangements made for the purposes of Part 1 of the *Legal Aid, Sentencing and Punishment of Offenders Act* 2012" for the words from "not to" to "Service" in paragraph (a), and (ii) to substitute the words "the cost of such advice, assistance or representation" for the words from "the cost" in paragraph (b) to the end of that paragraph.

★ As from a day to be appointed, section 21(4A) of the 1985 Act is further amended by the 2012 Act, s.62(1), and Sched 7, paras 1 and 7(1) and (3), so as to insert ", 16A" after "16".

★6–51 With effect from June 18, 2012 (*Criminal Justice Act 2003 (Commencement No. 28 and Saving Provisions) Order* 2012 (S.I. 2012 No. 1320)), section 41 of, and paragraph 57(1) and (4) of Schedule 3 to, the 2003 Act are brought into force (so far as they are not already in force) in certain areas (as to which, see *ante*, § 1–88). There are associated saving provisions, as to which, see article 5 of the order (*ante*, § 1–88).

C. Costs in Criminal Cases (General) Regulations 1986 (S.I. 1986 No. 1335)

Part III—Costs out of central funds (regs 4–13)

Claims for costs

The reference in regulation 6 of the 1986 regulations to a solicitor shall be taken as including a reference to a licensed body, *i.e.* a body that holds a licence issued by the Law Society under Part 5 of the *Legal Services Act* 2007: *Legal Services Act 2007 (Designation as a Licensing Authority) (No. 2) Order* 2011 (S.I. 2011 No. 2866), arts 1(3) and 8(1) and (2)(a), and Sched. 2.   **6–58**

Part VI—Recovery of sums paid out of the legal aid fund or central funds (regs 26, 27)

Directions by the Lord Chancellor

As to the amendment of section 20(2) of the *Prosecution of Offences Act* 1985, see *ante*, § 6–46.   **★6–83**

E. Practice Direction

As to the grounds for refusing a defendant's costs order to an acquitted defendant, see *R. (Guney) v. Central Criminal Court*, *ante*, § 6–14.   **6–106**

II. CRIMINAL DEFENCE SERVICE

A. Introduction

Replacement of "legal aid"

As from a day to be appointed, sections 1 to 26 of, and Schedules 1 to 3A and 14, Pt II to, the *Access to Justice Act* 1999 are repealed by the *Legal Aid, Sentencing and Punishment of Offenders Act* 2012, s.39(1), and Sched. 5, para. 51.   **★6–130**

For the replacement provisions (effective from a day to be appointed), see Part I (ss.1–43) of the 2012 Act, and, in particular, sections 13 to 20 (criminal legal aid), 21 and 22 (financial resources), 23 (payment for services), 24 (enforcement), 31 (legal aid for legal persons) and 39 (consequential and transitional).

B. Primary Legislation

Access to Justice Act 1999

As to the repeal of the relevant provisions, see *ante*, § 6–130.   **★6–134**

Access to Justice Act 1999, ss.12–18

Criminal Defence Service

As to the repeal of section 12 of the 1999 Act, see *ante*, § 6–130.   **★6–135**

Advice and assistance

As to the repeal of section 13 of the 1999 Act, see *ante*, § 6–130.   **★6–137**

Representation

★**6–138**   As to the repeal of section 14 of the 1999 Act, see *ante*, § 6–130.

Selection of representative

★**6–139**   As to the repeal of section 15 of the 1999 Act, see *ante*, § 6–130.

Code of conduct

★**6–140**   As to the repeal of section 16 of the 1999 Act, see *ante*, § 6–130.

Terms of provision of funded services

★**6–141**   As to the repeal of section 17 of the 1999 Act, see *ante*, § 6–130.

Contribution orders

★**6–141a**   As to the repeal of section 17A of, and Schedule 3A to, the 1999 Act, see *ante*, § 6–130.

Funding

★**6–142**   As to the repeal of section 18 of the 1999 Act, see *ante*, § 6–130.

Pilot schemes

★**6–142a**   As to the repeal of section 18A of the 1999 Act, see *ante*, § 6–130. In consequence of this repeal, section 58 of the *CJIA* 2008 is similarly repealed as from a day to be appointed: *Legal Aid, Sentencing and Punishment of Offenders Act* 2012, s.39(1), and Sched. 5, Pt 2.

Access to Justice Act 1999, s.20

Restriction of disclosure of information

★**6–143**   As to the repeal of section 20 of the 1999 Act, see *ante*, § 6–130.

Misrepresentation

★**6–144**   As to the repeal of section 21 of the 1999 Act, see *ante*, § 6–130.

Access to Justice Act 1999, ss.22, 26

Position of service providers and other parties

★**6–145**   As to the repeal of section 22 of the 1999 Act, see *ante*, § 6–130.

Interpretation

★**6–146**   As to the repeal of section 26 of the 1999 Act, see *ante*, § 6–130.

Access to Justice Act 1999, Sched. 3

★**6–147**   As to the repeal of Schedule 3 to the 1999 Act, see *ante*, § 6–130.

Individuals to whom right may be granted

★**6–148**   As to the repeal of Schedule 3 to the 1999 Act, see *ante*, § 6–130.

Grant of right by court

★**6–149**   As to the repeal of Schedule 3 to the 1999 Act, see *ante*, § 6–130.

Financial eligibility

★**6–149a**   As to the repeal of Schedule 3 to the 1999 Act, see *ante*, § 6–130.

Information requests

As to the repeal of Schedule 3 to the 1999 Act, see *ante*, § 6–130.

Legal Aid, Sentencing and Punishment of Offenders Act 2012

Summary

Part 1 (ss.1–43) abolishes the Legal Services Commission (s.38) and places a duty on the Lord Chancellor to secure the availability of civil and criminal legal aid (s.1). An executive agency within the Ministry of Justice will administer the delivery of legal aid in England and Wales; however, the Lord Chancellor must designate a civil servant to be the Director of Legal Aid Casework with statutory responsibility for taking independent decisions on legal aid in individual cases (s.4). Sections 2 and 3 ensure that, together with the powers the Lord Chancellor has as a minister of the Crown, the Lord Chancellor has power to enter into appropriate arrangements with others for them to provide legal aid and the power to set quality standards for those providing legal aid services, including accreditation and monitoring. Sections 5 and 6 provide for the delegation of the Lord Chancellor's and the casework director's functions.

Sections 8 to 12 relate to civil legal aid. Section 9 provides that civil legal services (as ★ defined in s.8) are to be made available to an individual if they are described in Part 1 of Schedule 1, provided they do not fall within the excluded services in Part 2 or the excluded advocacy in Part 3. Included in Part 1 are legal services relating to the abuse of a child or vulnerable adult, working with vulnerable children or adults, domestic violence, anti-social behaviour, protection from harassment, gang-related violence, victims of sexual offences and of trafficking in human beings, proceeds of crime, and terrorism prevention and investigation measures.

Sections 13 to 20 relate to criminal legal aid. Section 13 stipulates that "initial advice" and ★ "initial assistance" (the meaning of which can be further prescribed by subordinate legislation) are to be made available to individuals who have been arrested and held in custody if the casework director has made a determination that the individual qualifies for such advice and assistance, having regard, in particular, to the interests of justice, and specifying the type of advice or assistance (or both) available. Regulations may make provision about the making and withdrawal of determinations. Section 15 gives the Lord Chancellor the power to prescribe in regulations the conditions for when advice and assistance must be made available to individuals in connection with criminal proceedings if the casework director has determined that the individual qualifies for such advice and assistance, having regard, in particular, to the interests of justice. This broadly reflects the provisions about advice and assistance in section 13(1)(b) of the *Access to Justice Act* 1999 (§ 6–137 in the main work). Regulations under section 15 may require the casework director to make a determination under this section in accordance with section 21 (financial resources) and other criteria, may make provision about the making and withdrawal of determinations, and may provide for the review of, or appeals against, the director's determinations. Section 14 broadly reflects the 1999 Act, s.12(2) (§ 6–135 in the main work), in defining "criminal proceedings" as including criminal trials, sentencing hearings, extradition hearings, binding over proceedings, appeals on behalf of a convicted person who has died, proceedings on a reference on a point of law following acquittal on indictment and proceedings for contempt in the face of a court, and allows for the prescription of further types of proceedings as criminal.

Section 16 provides that representation for the purposes of criminal proceedings (and re- ★ lated bail proceedings, and preliminary or incidental proceedings as specified by regulations) is to be made available to (i) individuals the subject of the proceedings defined in section 14, or (ii) individuals who are resisting an appeal to the Crown Court otherwise than in an official capacity, if a "relevant authority" has determined (provisionally or otherwise) that the individual qualifies for such representation (and has not withdrawn that determination). Section 17 provides that the relevant authority must determine whether an individual qualifies for representation (whether provisionally or otherwise) in accordance with section 21 and the interests of justice. The matters to be taken into account when deciding what the interests of justice require mirror paragraph 5 of Schedule 3 to the 1999 Act (§ 6–147 in the main work). By virtue of sections 18, 19 and 20, a "relevant authority" may be the casework director or, if regulations so allow, a court before which criminal proceedings take place or are to take place. Under section 18, a determination (except a provisional determination) may be made by the director except where the court is authorised to make the determination (but not a provisional determination) under regulations under section 19. A determination by the director must specify the criminal proceedings and regulations may make provision about the making and withdrawal of such determinations. Appeals against a negative determination will lie to such court, tribunal or other person as may be prescribed. Regulations under section 19 (determinations by a court) may likewise make provision as to the making and withdrawal of determinations. Section 20 provides for the making of regulations to enable the director or a court to make a provisional determination that an individual qualifies for representation where the individual is involved in any investigation that may result in criminal proceedings, the determination is made for the purposes of criminal proceedings that may result from the investigation, and any prescribed conditions are met. Section 21 provides for regulations to be made as to financial eligibility for services under Part 1 and section 22 provides for information requests to be made for the purposes of facilitating a determination about an individual's financial eligibility. Under section 23, regulations may be made requiring payment from individuals for whom services are made available under Part 1, largely reflecting sections 10, 17 and 17A (§§ 6–141, 6–141a in the main work) of the 1999 Act, and section 24 provides for regulations to make provision about the enforcement of payment obligations under section 23 (in particular to provide that overdue amounts are recoverable summarily as a civil debt or as if they were payable under an order of the High Court or a county court). Schedule 2 (s.24) enables regulations to be made to authorise a court to make clamping orders (that a motor vehicle be fitted with an immobilisation device) and vehicle sale orders as a form of enforcement action in relation to criminal legal aid. This is based on provisions in section 17(2A) to (2E) of, and Schedule 3A to, the 1999 Act.

★   Section 27 relates to the choice of provider of services under Part 1. The general rule is that the Lord Chancellor's duty under section 1(1) does not include a duty to secure that services are made available to an individual by the means selected by the individual or by the person selected by the individual; but subsection (4) provides that an individual who qualifies for representation for the purposes of criminal proceedings under section 16 may select any willing representative, although regulations may modify or extend this rule. Section 31 (and Sched. 3) deals with legal aid for legal persons. Section 32 relates to foreign law and provides, *inter alia*, that a determination under section 13, 15 or 16 does not impose a duty on the Lord Chancellor to secure that services are made available in respect of any law other than the law of England and Wales except where otherwise prescribed by the Lord Chancellor or where such law is relevant for determining any issue relating to the law of England and Wales. Section 33 makes it an either-way offence (maximum penalty on conviction on indictment, two years' imprisonment, or a fine, or both) to disclose information disclosed under section 22 in certain circumstances; and section 34 makes it a summary offence (level 4 fine, proceedings only to be brought with consent of the DPP) to disclose other information provided under Part 1, subject to certain exceptions (as to which, see also s.35). Section 36 makes it a summary offence (level 4) for a person intentionally to fail to comply with a requirement under Part 1 to provide documents or information, or to make a statement or representation in providing such documents or information that he knows or believes to be false. It also extends the time limit for prosecuting an offence under this section.

Legal Aid, Sentencing and Punishment of Offenders Act 2012, ss.13–20

[Advice and assistance for individuals in custody

★6–151d   **13.**—(1) Initial advice and initial assistance are to be available under this Part to an individual who is arrested and held in custody at a police station or other premises if the Director has determined that the individual qualifies for such advice and assistance in accordance with this Part (and has not withdrawn the determination).

(2) The Director must make a determination under this section having regard, in particular, to the interests of justice.

(3) A determination under this section must specify the type of advice or assistance (or both) to be available under this Part.

(4) Regulations may make provision about the making and withdrawal of determinations under this section.

(5) Regulations under subsection (4) may, in particular, include—

    (a) provision about the form and content of determinations and applications for determinations,

    (b) provision permitting or requiring applications and determinations to be made and withdrawn in writing, by telephone or by other prescribed means,

    (c) provision setting time limits for applications and determinations,

    (d) provision for a determination to be disregarded for the purposes of this Part if made in response to an application that is made otherwise than in accordance with the regulations,

    (e) provision about conditions which must be satisfied by an applicant before a determination is made,

    (f) provision about the circumstances in which a determination may or must be withdrawn,

    (g) provision requiring information and documents to be provided, and

    (h) provision requiring individuals who are the subject of a determination to be informed of the reasons for making or withdrawing the determination.

(6) The circumstances prescribed under subsection (5)(f) may, in particular, relate to whether the individual who is the subject of the determination has complied with requirements imposed by or under this Part.

(7) For the purposes of this section, in relation to an individual who is in custody—

    "initial advice" means advice as to how the law in relation to a matter relevant to the individual's arrest applies in particular circumstances and as to the steps that might be taken having regard to how it applies;

    "initial assistance" means assistance in taking any of those steps which the individual might reasonably take while in custody, including assistance in the form of advocacy.

(8) The Lord Chancellor may by regulations provide that prescribed advice or assistance is not initial advice or initial assistance for the purposes of this section.]

[Criminal proceedings

14. In this Part "criminal proceedings" means—   ★**6–151e**

    (a) proceedings before a court for dealing with an individual accused of an offence,

    (b) proceedings before a court for dealing with an individual convicted of an offence, including proceedings in respect of a sentence or order,

    (c) proceedings for dealing with an individual under the *Extradition Act* 2003,

    (d) proceedings for binding an individual over to keep the peace or to be of good behaviour under section 115 of the *Magistrates' Courts Act* 1980 and for dealing with an individual who fails to comply with an order under that section,

    (e) proceedings on an appeal brought by an individual under section 44A of the *Criminal Appeal Act* 1968 (appeal in case of death of appellant),

    (f) proceedings on a reference under section 36 of the *Criminal Justice Act* 1972 on a point of law following the acquittal of an individual on indictment,

    (g) proceedings for contempt committed, or alleged to have been committed, by an individual in the face of a court, and

    (h) such other proceedings, before any court, tribunal or other person, as may be prescribed.]

[Advice and assistance for criminal proceedings

15.—(1) Regulations may provide that prescribed advice and assistance is to be available under this Part to an individual described in subsection (2) if—   ★**6–151f**

    (a) prescribed conditions are met, and

    (b) the Director has determined that the individual qualifies for such advice and assistance in accordance with the regulations (and has not withdrawn the determination).

(2) Those individuals are—

    (a) individuals who are involved in investigations which may lead to criminal proceedings (other than individuals arrested and held in custody at a police station or other premises),

    (b) individuals who are before a court, tribunal or other person in criminal proceedings, and

(c) individuals who have been the subject of criminal proceedings.

(3) When making the regulations, the Lord Chancellor must have regard, in particular, to the interests of justice.

(4) The regulations must require the Director to make determinations under the regulations having regard, in particular, to the interests of justice.

(5) The regulations may require the Director to make such determinations in accordance with—

(a) section 21 (financial resources) and regulations under that section, and

(b) criteria set out in the regulations.

(6) The regulations may make provision about the making and withdrawal of determinations under the regulations.

(7) The regulations may, in particular, include—

(a)–(h) [*identical to s.13(5)(a)–(h)*, ante, § 6–151d].

(8) The circumstances prescribed under subsection (7)(f) may, in particular, relate to whether the individual who is the subject of the determination has complied with requirements imposed by or under this Part.

(9) The regulations may provide for the review of, or appeals to a court, tribunal or other person against, a decision by the Director—

(a) that the interests of justice do not require advice or assistance to be made available to an individual under the regulations, or

(b) that criteria prescribed under subsection (5)(b) are not met.

(10) In this section "assistance" includes, in particular, assistance in the form of advocacy.]

[Representation for criminal proceedings

★**6–151g**   **16.**—(1) Representation for the purposes of criminal proceedings is to be available under this Part to an individual if—

(a) the individual is a specified individual in relation to the proceedings, and

(b) the relevant authority has determined (provisionally or otherwise) that the individual qualifies for such representation in accordance with this Part (and has not withdrawn the determination).

(2) Representation for the purposes of criminal proceedings is to be available under this Part to an individual if—

(a) the proceedings involve the individual resisting an appeal to the Crown Court otherwise than in an official capacity, and

(b) the relevant authority has determined (provisionally or otherwise) that the individual qualifies for such representation in accordance with this Part (and has not withdrawn the determination).

(3) Where an individual qualifies under this Part for representation for the purposes of criminal proceedings ("the principal proceedings"), representation is also to be available to the individual for the purposes of—

(a) any related bail proceedings, and

(b) any preliminary or incidental proceedings.

(4) Regulations may—

(a) make provision specifying whether proceedings are or are not to be regarded as preliminary or incidental for the purposes of subsection (3), and

(b) make provision for exceptions from subsection (3).

(5) Regulations under subsection (4)(b) may, in particular, make exceptions for proceedings taking place more than a prescribed period of time before or after the principal proceedings.

(6) In this section—

"the relevant authority", in relation to a specified individual and criminal proceedings, means the person who is authorised by or under section 18, 19 or 20 to determine (provisionally or otherwise) whether the individual qualifies under this Part for representation for the purposes of the proceedings;

"specified individual" means—

(a) in relation to criminal proceedings mentioned in any of paragraphs (a) to (g) of section 14, an individual mentioned in that paragraph in relation to those proceedings, and

(b) in relation to criminal proceedings prescribed by regulations under section 14(h), a description of individual specified in the regulations in relation to those proceedings.]

[Qualifying for representation

★**6–151h**   **17.**—(1) The relevant authority must determine whether an individual qualifies under this Part for representation for the purposes of criminal proceedings (whether provisionally or otherwise) in accordance with—

(a) section 21 (financial resources) and regulations under that section, and

(b) the interests of justice.

(2) In deciding what the interests of justice consist of for the purposes of such a determination, the following factors must be taken into account—

(a) whether, if any matter arising in the proceedings is decided against the individual, the individual would be likely to lose his or her liberty or livelihood or to suffer serious damage to his or her reputation,

(b) whether the determination of any matter arising in the proceedings may involve consideration of a substantial question of law,

(c) whether the individual may be unable to understand the proceedings or to state his or her own case,

(d) whether the proceedings may involve the tracing, interviewing or expert cross-examination of witnesses on behalf of the individual, and

(e) whether it is in the interests of another person that the individual be represented.

(3) The Lord Chancellor may by order amend subsection (2) by adding or varying a factor.

(4) Regulations may prescribe circumstances in which making representation available to an individual for the purposes of criminal proceedings is to be taken to be in the interests of justice for the purposes of a determination under section 16.

(5) In this section "the relevant authority", in relation to an individual and criminal proceedings, means the person who is authorised by or under section 18, 19 or 20 to determine (provisionally or otherwise) whether the individual qualifies under this Part for representation for the purposes of the proceedings.]

[Determinations by Director

17.—(1) The Director is authorised to determine whether an individual qualifies under this Part for representation for the purposes of criminal proceedings, except in circumstances in which a court is authorised to make the determination under regulations under section 19. ★**6–151i**

(2) A determination by the Director under section 16 must specify the criminal proceedings.

(3) Regulations may make provision about the making and withdrawal of determinations by the Director under that section.

(4) Regulations under subsection (3) may, in particular, include—

(a)–(h) [*identical to s.13(5)(a)–(h), ante, § 6–151d*], and

(i) provision for the review of a decision by the Director that the interests of justice do not require representation to be made available, or to continue to be made available, to an individual under this Part for the purposes of criminal proceedings.

(5) The circumstances prescribed under subsection (4)(f) may, in particular, relate to whether the individual who is the subject of the determination has complied with requirements imposed by or under this Part.

(6) An appeal lies to such court, tribunal or other person as may be prescribed against a decision by the Director that the interests of justice do not require representation to be made available, or to continue to be made available, to an individual under this Part for the purposes of criminal proceedings, subject to subsection (7).

(7) Regulations may provide for exceptions from subsection (6).

(8) This section does not authorise the Director to make a provisional determination and accordingly—

(a) references in this section to a determination do not include a provisional determination, and

(b) references in this section to a decision do not include a decision made as part of such a determination.]

[Determinations by court

19.—(1) Regulations may— ★**6–151j**

(a) provide that a court before which criminal proceedings take place, or are to take place, is authorised to determine whether an individual qualifies under this Part for representation for the purposes of criminal proceedings of a prescribed description, and

(b) make provision about the making and withdrawal of such determinations by a court.

(2) The regulations may, in particular, include—

(a) provision about the form and content of determinations and applications for determinations,

(b) provision permitting or requiring applications and determinations to be made and withdrawn in writing, by telephone or by other prescribed means,

(c) provision setting time limits for applications and determinations,

(d) provision enabling a court to determine that an individual qualifies under this Part for representation for the purposes of criminal proceedings before another court,

(e) provision for the powers of a magistrates' court of any area under the regulations to be exercised by a single justice of the peace for the area, and

(f) provision about the circumstances in which a determination may or must be withdrawn.

(3) The circumstances prescribed under subsection (2)(f) may, in particular, relate to whether the individual who is the subject of the determination has complied with requirements imposed by or under this Part.

(4) The regulations must provide that, subject to prescribed exceptions, an appeal lies to such court, tribunal or other person as may be prescribed against a decision by a court that the interests of justice do not require representation to be made available, or to continue to be made available, to an individual under this Part for the purposes of criminal proceedings.

(5) The regulations may include consequential provision modifying an Act or instrument.

(6) Regulations under this section may not authorise a court to make a provisional determination and accordingly—

(a) references in this section to a determination do not include a provisional determination, and

(b) references in this section to a decision do not include a decision made as part of such a determination.]

[Provisional determinations

★**6–151k**   **20.**—(1) Regulations may provide that the Director or a court may make a provisional determination that an individual qualifies under this Part for representation for the purposes of criminal proceedings where—

(a) the individual is involved in an investigation which may result in criminal proceedings,

(b) the determination is made for the purposes of criminal proceedings that may result from the investigation, and

(c) any prescribed conditions are met.

(2) The regulations may, in particular, include—

(a) provision about the stage in an investigation at which a provisional determination may be made,

(b) provision about the making and withdrawal of provisional determinations, including provision equivalent to that described in section 18(4)(a) to (i) and (5),

(c) provision about the circumstances in which a provisional determination is to cease to be provisional, and

(d) provision about the circumstances in which a provisional determination is to be treated as if it were a determination made by the Director or a court in reliance on section 18 or 19.

(3) In this Part, as it applies in connection with a provisional determination made under regulations under this section as to whether an individual qualifies for representation for the purposes of criminal proceedings, references to proceedings include criminal proceedings that may result from the investigation concerned.]

Legal Aid, Sentencing and Punishment of Offenders Act 2012, ss.21–24, 27

Financial resources

[Financial resources

★**6–151l**   **21.**—(1) A person may not make a relevant determination that an individual qualifies under this Part for services unless the person has determined that the individual's financial resources are such that the individual is eligible for the services (and has not withdrawn the determination).

(2) Regulations may—

(a) make provision about when an individual's financial resources are such that the individual is eligible under this Part for services, and

(b) make provision for exceptions from subsection (1).

(3) Regulations may provide that an individual is to be treated, for the purposes of regulations under subsection (2), as having or not having financial resources of a prescribed description.

(4) Regulations under subsection (3) may, in particular, provide that the individual is to be treated as having prescribed financial resources of a person of a prescribed description.

(5) Regulations may make provision about the making and withdrawal of determinations under this section.

(6) Regulations under subsection (5) may, in particular, include—

    (a) provision about the form and content of determinations,

    (b) provision permitting or requiring determinations to be made and withdrawn in writing, by telephone or by other prescribed means,

    (c) provision setting time limits for determinations,

    (d) provision about conditions which must be satisfied before a determination is made,

    (e) provision about the circumstances in which a determination may or must be withdrawn,

    (f) provision requiring information and documents to be provided,

    (g) provision requiring individuals who are the subject of a determination to be informed of the reasons for making or withdrawing the determination, and

    (h) provision for the review of a determination in respect of an individual's financial resources.

(7) The circumstances prescribed under subsection (6)(e) may, in particular, relate to whether the individual who is the subject of the determination has complied with requirements imposed by or under this Part.

(8) In this section "relevant determination" means a determination that is required to be carried out in accordance with this section by—

    (a) section 11 or 17, or

    (b) regulations under section 15 or paragraph 4 of Schedule 3.]

[Information about financial resources

    22.—(1) The relevant authority may make an information request to—   **★6–151m**

    (a) the Secretary of State,

    (b) a relevant Northern Ireland Department, or

    (c) the Commissioners for Her Majesty's Revenue and Customs ("the Commissioners").

(2) An information request may be made only for the purposes of facilitating a determination about an individual's financial resources for the purposes of this Part.

(3) An information request made to the Secretary of State or a relevant Northern Ireland Department under this section may request the disclosure of some or all of the following information—

    (a) a relevant individual's full name and any previous names;

    (b) a relevant individual's address and any previous addresses;

    (c) a relevant individual's date of birth;

    (d) a relevant individual's national insurance number;

    (e) a relevant individual's benefit status at a time specified in the request;

    (f) information of a prescribed description.

(4) An information request made to the Commissioners under this section may request the disclosure of some or all of the following information—

    (a) whether or not a relevant individual is employed or was employed at a time specified in the request;

    (b) the name and address of the employer;

    (c) whether or not a relevant individual is carrying on a business, trade or profession or was doing so at a time specified in the request;

    (d) the name under which it is or was carried on;

    (e) the address of any premises used for the purposes of carrying it on;

    (f) a relevant individual's national insurance number;

    (g) a relevant individual's benefit status at a time specified in the request;

    (h) information of a prescribed description.

(5) The information that may be prescribed under subsections (3)(f) and (4)(h) includes, in particular, information relating to—

    (a) prescribed income of a relevant individual for a prescribed period, and

    (b) prescribed capital of a relevant individual.

(6) Information may not be prescribed under subsection (4)(h) without the Commissioners' consent.

(7) The Secretary of State, the relevant Northern Ireland Departments and the Commissioners may disclose to the relevant authority information specified in an information request made under this section.

(8) In this section—

"benefit status", in relation to an individual, means whether or not the individual is in receipt of
a prescribed benefit or benefits and, if so—

    (a) which benefit or benefits the individual is receiving,

    (b) whether the individual is entitled to the benefit or benefits alone or jointly,

    (c) in prescribed cases, the amount the individual is receiving by way of the benefit (or
each of the benefits) ("the benefit amount"), and

    (d) in prescribed cases, where the benefit consists of a number of elements, what those
elements are and the amount included in respect of each element in calculating the
benefit amount;

"the relevant authority" means—

    (a) a prescribed person, or

    (b) in relation to circumstances for which no person is prescribed, the Director;

"a relevant individual", in relation to an information request for the purposes of a determination about an individual's financial resources, means—

    (a) that individual, and

    (b) any other individual whose financial resources are or may be relevant for the
purposes of the determination;

"relevant Northern Ireland Department" means the Department for Social Development in
Northern Ireland or the Department of Finance and Personnel in Northern Ireland.]

Contributions and costs

[Payment for services

★6–151n   **23.**—(1) An individual to whom services are made available under this Part is not to be
required to make a payment in connection with the provision of the services, except where
regulations provide otherwise.

(2) The regulations may, in particular, provide that in prescribed circumstances an individual
must do one or more of the following—

    (a) pay the cost of the services;

    (b) pay a contribution in respect of the cost of the services of a prescribed amount;

    (c) pay a prescribed amount in respect of administration costs.

(3) The regulations may, in particular, provide that where—

    (a) civil legal services are provided to an individual under this Part in relation to a dispute,
and

    (b) prescribed conditions are met,

the individual must pay a prescribed amount which may exceed the cost of the civil legal services
provided.

(4) The regulations may, in particular, make provision about the determination of the cost of services for the purposes of the regulations.

(5) The regulations may, in particular—

    (a) provide for an individual's liability under the regulations to make a payment to change or
cease in prescribed circumstances,

    (b) provide for an individual's liability under the regulations to arise on a determination by a
prescribed person,

    (c) provide for such a determination to be varied or withdrawn by a prescribed person, and

    (d) provide for the review of such a determination in respect of an individual's liability to make
a payment.

(6) The regulations may, in particular, provide that an individual is to be treated, for the purposes
of the regulations, as having or not having financial resources of a prescribed description.

(7) Regulations under subsection (6) may, in particular, provide that the individual is to be
treated as having prescribed financial resources of a person of a prescribed description.

(8) The regulations may, in particular, include provision for an amount to be payable entirely or
partly—

    (a) by periodical payments;

    (b) by one or more lump sums;

    (c) out of income;

    (d) out of capital.

(9) The regulations may, in particular, include—

    (a) provision requiring information and documents to be provided,

    (b) provision about the time and manner in which payments must be made,

    (c) provision about the person to whom payments must be made, and

    (d) provision about what that person must do with the payments.

(10) The regulations may, in particular, make provision for the payment by an individual of interest, on such terms as may be prescribed, in respect of—

    (a) a loan made to the individual under this Part,

    (b) a payment in connection with the provision of services which is not required by the regulations to be made by the individual until after the time when the services are provided, and

    (c) so much of a payment as remains unpaid after the time when it is required by the regulations to be made by the individual.

(11) The regulations—

    (a) must make provision for the repayment to an individual of any amount in excess of the individual's liability under the regulations or under section 24, and

    (b) may make provision for the payment of interest on the excess.

(12) In this section—

    "administration costs" means costs in connection with the administration of legal aid, including the administration of charges arising under section 25;

    "prescribed amount" includes an amount calculated in a prescribed manner.]

[Enforcement

24.—(1) Regulations may make provision about the enforcement of an obligation to make a payment imposed under section 23.   ★**6–151o**

(2) The regulations may, in particular, make provision for costs incurred in connection with the enforcement of an individual's obligation to make a payment to be recovered from the individual.

(3) Regulations under this section may, in particular—

    (a) provide that overdue amounts are recoverable summarily as a civil debt;

    (b) provide that overdue amounts are recoverable as if they were payable under an order of the High Court or a county court, if the court in question so orders on the application of the person to whom the amounts are due.

(4) Regulations under this section may include provision requiring information and documents to be provided.

(5) Schedule 2 (criminal legal aid: motor vehicle orders) has effect.]

Providers of services, etc.

[Choice of provider of services etc

27.—(1) The Lord Chancellor's duty under section 1(1) does not include a duty to secure that, where services are made available to an individual under this Part, they are made available by the means selected by the individual.   ★**6–151p**

(2) The Lord Chancellor may discharge that duty, in particular, by arranging for the services to be provided by telephone or by other electronic means.

(3) The Lord Chancellor's duty under section 1(1) does not include a duty to secure that, where services are made available to an individual under this Part, they are made available by a person selected by the individual, subject to subsections (4) to (10).

(4) An individual who qualifies under this Part for representation for the purposes of criminal proceedings by virtue of a determination under section 16 may select any representative or representatives willing to act for the individual, subject to regulations under subsection (6).

(5) Where an individual exercises that right, representation by the selected representative or representatives is to be available under this Part for the purposes of the proceedings.

(6) Regulations may provide that in prescribed circumstances—

    (a) the right conferred by subsection (4) is not to apply in cases of prescribed descriptions,

    (b) an individual who has been provided with advice or assistance in accordance with section 13 or regulations under section 15 by a person selected by the individual is to be taken to have selected that person under subsection (4),

    (c) the right conferred by subsection (4) is not to include a right to select a representative of a prescribed description,

(d) that right is to select only a representative located in a prescribed area or of a prescribed description,

(e) that right is to select not more than a prescribed number of representatives to act at any one time, and

(f) that right is not to include a right to select a representative in place of a representative previously selected.

(7) Regulations under subsection (6)(b) may prescribe circumstances in which an individual is to be taken to have selected a person to provide advice or assistance.

(8) Regulations may provide that in prescribed circumstances the Lord Chancellor is not required to make available representation for an individual by a prescribed representative.

(9) Provision made under subsection (8) does not prejudice any right of the individual to select another representative.

(10) The circumstances which may be prescribed under this section include that a determination has been made by a prescribed person.]

Legal Aid, Sentencing and Punishment of Offenders Act 2012, ss.31, 39

[Legal aid for legal persons

★6–151q   **31.** Schedule 3 (legal aid for legal persons) has effect.]

[Consequential and transitional provision

★6–151r   **39.**—(1) Schedule 5 (legal aid: consequential amendments) has effect.

(2) Where the Lord Chancellor considers it appropriate as part of the arrangements for effecting the transition from the operation of Part 1 of the *Access to Justice Act* 1999 to the operation of this Part of this Act, the Lord Chancellor may by regulations make provision requiring or enabling prescribed 1999 Act services to be made available to individuals or other persons under this Part for a period specified or described in the regulations.

(3) In subsection (2) "1999 Act services" means services which, immediately before the day on which the first regulations under that subsection come into force, may be funded under Part 1 of the *Access to Justice Act* 1999.

(4) Where the Lord Chancellor considers it appropriate for the Legal Services Commission to cease to exist before this Part is brought fully into force, the Lord Chancellor may by regulations make provision for the purpose of requiring or enabling the Lord Chancellor and the Director, or persons authorised by the Lord Chancellor or the Director, to carry out LSC functions for a period specified or described in the regulations.

(5) In subsection (4) "LSC functions" means functions conferred or imposed on the Legal Services Commission by or under Part 1 of the *Access to Justice Act* 1999.

(6) Regulations under subsection (4) may not include provision requiring or enabling the Lord Chancellor—

(a) to take decisions about whether services should be funded in individual cases, or

(b) to give directions or guidance about the carrying out of functions under Part 1 of the *Access to Justice Act* 1999 in relation to individual cases.

(7) Regulations under this section—

(a) may amend, repeal, revoke or otherwise modify Part 1 of the *Access to Justice Act* 1999, this Part of this Act, any other Act and any instrument made under an Act;

(b) may describe a period, in particular, by reference to the coming into force of a provision of this Part of this Act or the repeal of a provision of Part 1 of the *Access to Justice Act* 1999.

(8) The requirement for regulations under this section to specify or describe a period does not prevent the making of further regulations under this section.

(9) The powers to make regulations under this section are without prejudice to the generality of the powers to make regulations under the other provisions of this Part and under section 149.

(10) In this section "Act" includes an Act or Measure of the National Assembly for Wales.]

Legal Aid, Sentencing and Punishment of Offenders Act 2012, Sched. 3

LEGAL AID FOR LEGAL PERSONS

[Legal persons

★6–151s   1. In this Schedule "legal person" means a person other than an individual.]

[Exceptional case determinations

★6–151t   2.—(1) For the purposes of this Schedule, in relation to a legal person and civil legal services, advice, assistance or representation for the purposes of criminal proceedings, an exceptional case determination is a determination that sub-paragraph (2) or (3) is satisfied.

(2) This sub-paragraph is satisfied if it is necessary to make the services available to the legal person under this Part because failure to do so would be a breach of—

    (a) the person's Convention rights (within the meaning of the *Human Rights Act* 1998), or

    (b) any rights of the person to the provision of legal services that are enforceable EU rights.

(3) This sub-paragraph is satisfied if it is appropriate to make the services available to the legal person under this Part, in the particular circumstances of the case, having regard to any risk that failure to do so would be such a breach.]

3. [*Civil legal aid.*]

[Advice and assistance for criminal proceedings

4.—(1) Regulations may provide that prescribed advice and assistance is to be available under this   ★**6–151u** Part to a legal person described in sub-paragraph (2) if—

    (a) prescribed conditions are met,

    (b) the Director has made an exceptional case determination in relation to the person and the advice and assistance (and has not withdrawn that determination), and

    (c) the Director has determined that the legal person qualifies for such advice and assistance in accordance with the regulations (and has not withdrawn that determination).

(2) Those legal persons are—

    (a) legal persons who are involved in investigations which may lead to criminal proceedings, and

    (b) legal persons who are before a court, tribunal or other person in criminal proceedings.

(3) Subsections (3) to (9) of section 15 apply in relation to regulations under this paragraph (and decisions made under such regulations) as they apply in relation to regulations under that section (and decisions made under such regulations).

(4) In those subsections as applied by this paragraph, references to an individual include a legal person.

(5) In this paragraph "assistance" includes, in particular, assistance in the form of advocacy.]

Representation for criminal proceedings

5.—(1) Representation for the purposes of criminal proceedings is to be available under this Part   ★**6–151v** to a legal person if—

    (a) the person is a specified legal person in relation to the proceedings, or

    (b) the proceedings involve the person resisting an appeal to the Crown Court otherwise than in an official capacity,

and the conditions in sub-paragraph (2) are met.

(2) Those conditions are that the Director—

    (a) has made an exceptional case determination in relation to the legal person and representation for the purposes of the proceedings, and

    (b) has determined (provisionally or otherwise) that the legal person qualifies for such representation in accordance with this Part,

(and has not withdrawn either determination).

(3) Where a legal person qualifies under this Part for representation for the purposes of criminal proceedings, representation is also to be available to the legal person for the purposes of any preliminary or incidental proceedings.

(4) Regulations under section 16(4) and (5) apply for the purposes of sub-paragraph (3) as they apply for the purposes of section 16(3), except to the extent that the regulations provide otherwise.

(5) Section 17(1)(b) applies in relation to an exceptional case determination under sub-paragraph (2)(a) as it applies in relation to a determination under section 16.

(6) Paragraphs (a) and (b) of section 17(1) apply in relation to a determination under sub-paragraph (2)(b) as they apply in relation to a determination under section 16.

(7) Subsections (2) to (7) of section 18 apply in relation to a determination under sub-paragraph (2) (and a decision in relation to the interests of justice for the purposes of such a determination) as they apply in relation to a determination under section 16 (and a decision for the purposes of such a determination).

(8) The Director may not make a provisional determination under sub-paragraph (2)(b) unless authorised to do so by regulations under sub-paragraph (9).

(9) Regulations may provide that the Director may make a provisional determination that a legal person qualifies under this Part for representation for the purposes of criminal proceedings where—

    (a) the legal person is involved in an investigation which may result in criminal proceedings,

    (b) the determination is made for the purposes of criminal proceedings that may result from the investigation, and

    (c) any prescribed conditions are met.

    (10) Subsections (2) and (3) of section 20 apply in relation to regulations under sub-paragraph (9) (and determinations and decisions made under such regulations) as they apply in relation to regulations under that section (and determinations and decisions made under such regulations).

    (11) In sections 17, 18 and 20 as applied by this paragraph—

    (a) references to an individual include a legal person,

    (b) references to the relevant authority have effect as if they were references to the Director, and

    (c) the reference in section 20(2)(d) to a determination made by the Director or a court in reliance on section 18 or 19 has effect as if it were a reference to a determination by the Director under sub-paragraph (2)(b) made otherwise than in reliance on regulations under sub-paragraph (9).

    (12) Regulations may prescribe circumstances in which making representation available to a legal person for the purposes of criminal proceedings is to be taken to be in the interests of justice for the purposes of a determination under this paragraph.

    (13) In this paragraph "specified legal person", in relation to criminal proceedings, means a description of legal person specified in regulations in relation to those proceedings.]

[Financial resources

★6–151w   6. Section 21 applies for the purposes of a determination under paragraph 3(1)(b) or 5(2)(b), or under regulations under paragraph 4 or 5(9), as if the references to an individual included a legal person.]

[Contributions and costs

★6–151x   7. In sections 23, 24, 25 and 26 and Schedule 2, references to an individual include a legal person to whom services are made available under this Part in accordance with this Schedule or regulations under this Schedule.

    8. In Schedule 2, references to criminal legal aid include advice, assistance and representation required to be made available under paragraph 4 or 5 of this Schedule.]

[Providers of services, etc.

★6–151y   9.—(1) Section 27 applies in relation to the provision of services to a legal person in accordance with this Schedule or regulations under this Schedule as it applies in relation to the provision of services to an individual under this Part.

    (2) In that section as applied by this paragraph—

    (a) references to an individual include a legal person,

    (b) the reference to a determination under section 16 includes a determination under paragraph 5(2)(b) of this Schedule, and

    (c) the reference to regulations under section 15 includes regulations under paragraph 4 of this Schedule.

    (3) In sections 28, 29 and 30, references to an individual include a legal person to whom services are made available under this Part in accordance with this Schedule or regulations under this Schedule.]

    10. [*Supplementary matters.*]]

C. Secondary Legislation

Criminal Defence Service (General) (No. 2) Regulations 2001 (S.I. 2001 No. 1437)

Change of representative

6–169   In *R. (Clive Rees Associates) v. Swansea Magistrates' Court and Rees Davies and Partners*, 176 J.P. 39, DC, it was said: (i) that paragraph (2)(a)(i) to (iii) of regulation 16 (grounds for change of litigator (see the main work)) address situations in which the application is initiated by the litigator, but an application made by an assisted party under paragraph (2)(a)(iv), on the grounds that a breakdown in the relationship meant that effective representation could no longer be provided, may amount to a "substantial compelling reason" even if the litigator does not share that view; (ii) that the power to transfer a representation order is conferred on the "court before which the proceedings are heard"; a magistrates' clerk lacks jurisdiction to make or confirm such an order; (iii) that it will normally be appropriate for a court to require a written application, although it may in exceptional circumstances consider an oral application; (iv) that, as noted in *R. v. Ulcay* [2008] 1 Cr.App.R. 27, CA (as to which, see § 4–67 in the main work), the party seeking a transfer must provide a full explanation of the reason which is said to justify it; simply to assert that there has been a breakdown in the relationship will not suffice; and an assisted party cannot obtain a transfer simply because he has received proper advice that he finds unpalatable; the duration of the relationship with, and the quantity of work undertaken by, the original representatives are likely to be relevant considerations; however, the mere fact that an application is made early in the proceedings, when only limited work has been done, is not of itself a reason for ordering a transfer; and (v) that where the defendant had received conflicting advice from two reputable firms, the justices were entitled to find, without further investigation, that there was such a conflict in advice and such a breakdown of trust with the original firm that he could no longer continue to be represented by them, and it was a relevant consideration that the second firm was already acting for him in other matters.

Recovery of defence costs orders

For an example of "exceptional circumstances" (within reg. 4(3)(a) of the *Criminal Defence*   **6–193** *Service (Recovery of Defence Costs Orders) Regulations* 2001 (S.I. 2001 No. 856) (§ 6–197 in the main work)) justifying the making of a recovery of defence costs order against a defendant who had been acquitted, see *R. (Guney) v. Central Criminal Court* [2011] A.C.D. 90, DC (the defence to a charge of soliciting to murder had been that the defendant knew that an undercover officer was a policeman and that he had been playing the role of a person who wanted someone murdered in order to expose police corruption).

As to regulation 4(3)(a) of the *Criminal Defence Service (Recovery of Defence Costs Orders)*   **6–197** *Regulations* 2001 (S.I. 2001 No. 856), see *R. (Guney) v. Central Criminal Court, ante,* § 6–193.

Contribution orders (Crown Court)

Criminal Defence Service (Contribution Orders) Regulations 2009 (S.I. 2009 No. 3328), regs 1–4, 6, 11, 21, 23

Application to judge

As to the need for advocates and litigators to submit a copy of an apportionment order   **6–230** under regulation 21 of the *Criminal Defence Service (Contribution Orders) Regulations* 2009 (S.I. 2009 No. 3328) (see the main work) with any claim for payment under the *Criminal Defence Service (Funding) Order* 2007 (S.I. 2007 No. 1174) (*post*, Appendix G–6 *et seq.*), see the website of the Legal Services Commission at http://www.legalservices.gov.uk/criminal/cds_news_13242.asp?page=1.

CHAPTER 7

CRIMINAL APPEAL

II. HIGH COURT JURISDICTION IN CROWN COURT PROCEEDINGS

A. JURISDICTION

(1) Appeal by way of case stated

Senior Courts Act 1981, s.28

Appeals from Crown Court and inferior courts

As from a day to be appointed, section 28(4) of the 1981 Act is amended by the *Legal Aid,*   **★7–2**

Sentencing and Punishment of Offenders Act 2012, s.39(1), and Sched. 5, paras 19 and 20, so as to substitute the words "a requirement to make a payment under regulations under section 23 or 24 of the *Legal Aid, Sentencing and Punishment of Offenders Act* 2012" for the words "an order under section 17 of the *Access to Justice Act* 1999".

(2) Judicial review

(a) *Statute*

Senior Courts Act 1981, ss.29, 31

Mandatory, prohibiting and quashing orders

★**7–4**   As from a day to be appointed, section 29(6) of the 1981 Act is amended by the *Legal Aid, Sentencing and Punishment of Offenders Act* 2012, s.39(1), and Sched. 5, paras 19 and 21, so as to substitute the words "requirements to make payments under regulations under section 23 or 24 of the *Legal Aid, Sentencing and Punishment of Offenders Act* 2012" for the words "orders under section 17 of the *Access to Justice Act* 1999".

B. Practice and Procedure

(1) Rules of court

Criminal Procedure Rules 2011 (S.I. 2011 No. 1709), r.64.6

★**7–19**   In *Tuthill v. DPP* [2012] A.C.D. 26, DC ([2011] EWHC 3760 (Admin.)), the court reiterated that rule 64.5 of the *Criminal Procedure Rules* 2011 (S.I. 2011 No. 1709) stipulates that, save in limited circumstances, a case stated must not contain a statement of evidence, that this rule could not be more clearly stated, and that, should there be a failure to comply in future, costs consequences (for justices' clerks) might follow.

C. Appeal from High Court

(2) Criminal cause or matter

7–22   In *R. (Guardian News and Media Ltd) v. City of Westminster Magistrates' Court*; *Guardian News and Media Ltd v. Government of the United States of America* [2011] 1 W.L.R. 3253, CA (Civ. Div.), it was said that the state of the law on the issue of what constitutes a "criminal cause or matter" for the purposes of section 18(1)(a) of the *Senior Courts Act* 1981 is less than satisfactory. The court took the view that where the applicant was attempting to appeal the dismissal by the Divisional Court of its appeal by way of case stated against a decision of a magistrates' court to refuse disclosure of documents referred to in the course of open extradition proceedings between two other parties, there was force in the two competing arguments; on the one hand, the refusal of the application was, as a matter of language, "in" a criminal matter, being made in the context of a criminal matter, namely extradition proceedings; and this approach had the benefit of being clear and of limiting the rights of appeal of a third party in criminal proceedings; on the other, the language of section 18(1)(a) was capable of being limited to a judgment that itself involves, or may lead to, a finding of criminality or one carrying criminal sanctions; and there was logic in the rules about civil appeals applying to an order or judgment that was purely civil in its nature and effect, as well as logic in a narrower construction being given to a rule restricting the right to appeal; in the absence of clear authority, justice would be best served by holding that the refusal to disclose was not "in any criminal cause or matter" and that the court therefore had jurisdiction to hear the appeal; the application for disclosure was wholly collateral to the extradition proceedings themselves, was made by a third party, and had not involved the High Court making an order that would have had any bearing on the extradition proceedings;

while this conclusion might be said to fall foul of the wide principle which had arguably been laid down in *Amand v. Home Secretary* (see the main work), it was consistent with *R. v. Southampton JJ., ex p. Green* (see § 7–24 in the main work), which, despite two opportunities (*Re Smalley* [1985] A.C. 622 and *Government of the United States of America v. Montgomery* [2001] 1 W.L.R. 196), the House of Lords had not overruled or disapproved; and, while the reasoning in *ex p. Green* was demonstrably flawed, this conclusion was consistent with *Carr v. Atkins* (see §§ 7–23, 7–24 in the main work), the most recent case on the issue in the Court of Appeal, in which Sir John Donaldson M.R. gave a suggested justification for the conclusion in *ex p. Green*, together with tentative guidance; any sort of final coherence in relation to the scope and effect of section 18(1)(a), however, could only be provided by the Supreme Court.

III. THE COURT OF APPEAL

D. STARE DECISIS IN THE CRIMINAL DIVISION OF THE COURT OF APPEAL

The Court of Appeal should not follow a Privy Council decision in preference to a decision of the Court of Appeal, unless there is domestic authority that shows that the Court of Appeal decision was *per incuriam* or at least of doubtful reliability; in *R. v. James*; *R. v. Karimi* (see the main work), where the Court of Appeal preferred a decision of the Privy Council to an earlier domestic decision that would normally be regarded as binding, this was justified as it was a foregone conclusion that, if the case had gone to the House of Lords, they would have followed the Privy Council decision: *Sinclair Investments (U.K.) Ltd v. Versailles Trade Finance Ltd (in administrative receivership)* [2011] 3 W.L.R. 1153, CA (Civ. Div.). **7–36**

IV. APPEAL TO COURT OF APPEAL BY THE DEFENDANT

A. APPEAL AGAINST CONVICTION ON INDICTMENT

(1) The right of appeal

Criminal Appeal Act 1968, s.1

Right of appeal against conviction on indictment

With effect from June 18, 2012 (*Criminal Justice Act 2003 (Commencement No. 28 and Saving Provisions) Order* 2012 (S.I. 2012 No. 1320)), section 41 of, and paragraph 44 of Schedule 3 to, the 2003 Act are brought into force (so far as they are not already in force) in certain areas (as to which, see *ante*, § 1–88). There are associated saving provisions, as to which, see article 5 of the order (*ante*, § 1–88). **★7–37**

(3) Determination of appeals

The safety test

R. v. F. (S.) is now reported at [2011] 2 Cr.App.R. 28. **7–49**

(4) Grounds of appeal

Misdirection

Non-direction

In *R. v. Williams (James)* [2012] R.T.R. 18, CA, it was held that the trial judge's failure to **★7–64** give a good character direction (or at least a modified one), combined with the fact that the prosecution had been allowed, inappropriately in a case where the defendant had not called any witnesses and was unrepresented, to give a closing speech (as to which, see *ante*, § 4–424), rendered the conviction unsafe; this was a case that turned to significant extent upon the defendant's credibility; and a good character direction was potentially of particular importance because it was one of the few supporting pieces of evidence in favour of the reliability and honesty of his account against an "army of prosecution witnesses who were contending for the contrary".

★ In *Brown (Nigel) v. State of Trinidad and Tobago* [2012] 1 W.L.R. 1577, PC, it was said to be well established that the omission of a good character direction is not necessarily fatal to the fairness of a trial or to the safety of a conviction; where there is a clash of credibility between the prosecution and the defendant, in the sense that the truthfulness and honesty of the witnesses on either side is directly in issue, the need for a good character direction is more acute; but where no such direct conflict is involved, it is appropriate to view the question of the need for such a direction on a broader plane and with a close eye on the significance of the evidence in the case. Whilst there will, of course, be cases where it is simply not possible to conclude with the necessary level of confidence that a good character direction would have made no difference, there will also be cases where the sheer force of the evidence against the defendant is overwhelming; in those cases it should not prove unduly difficult for an appellate court to conclude that a good character direction could not possibly have affected the verdict; whether a particular case comes within one category or the other will depend on a close examination of the nature of the issues and the strength of the evidence, as well as an assessment of the significance of a good character direction to those issues and evidence. In conclusion, the board referred approvingly to Lord Bingham's dictum in *Jagdeo Singh v. State of Trinidad and Tobago* (see the main work) that hard, inflexible rules are best avoided in this area.

Inconsistent verdicts

Of same court

7–70 A conviction will be quashed as unsafe on the ground of its inconsistency with the acquittal of the defendant on another count where the prosecution case was put on the basis that the jury must necessarily find the defendant guilty of both counts if they were to find him guilty of the count of which they actually found him guilty, and where the judge effectively directed them to that effect, even though, had the case been put differently, the differing verdicts could have stood together: *R. v. Mohammed* [2011] L.S. Gazette, October 6, 19, CA ([2011] EWCA Crim 2255); and *R. v. Dobson*, *The Times*, October 26, 2011, CA. In the latter case, the court said that whenever there is a possibility of inconsistent verdicts, the matter must be discussed between counsel and the judge before closing speeches; and the judge should thereafter sum the case up in the manner in which he has indicated during that discussion, whether or not that accords with the wishes of the parties.

Miscellaneous

(i) *Mistakes by, misconduct of, trial judge*

★**7–81** *R. v. Malcolm* is now reported at [2012] Crim.L.R. 238.

★ A judge's conduct during a trial, which included repeated interventions (in particular during examination of the defendant), and criticisms of defence counsel, did not threaten the safety of the defendant's convictions where the judge conceded in summing up that he had been "a little irritated during the evidence" but that his "irritations are not in any way related to the defence case" and that the jury should not "in any way … hold my grumpiness with his lawyers against the defendant"; the interventions were justifiable and, while there were occasions when the exchanges between bench and bar were "not warm", they formed no more than the rough and tumble of daily court life: *R. v. E.* [2012] Crim.L.R. 383, CA.

(ii) *Conduct of counsel*

7–83 *Campbell v. The Queen* is now reported at [2011] 2 A.C. 79.

(vi) Lack of legal representation

A defendant who had been given every opportunity before and at trial to obtain legal   ★7–87
representation and to challenge the written statements of prosecution witnesses, but who
had nevertheless elected to continue unrepresented and not to challenge their statements
directly, had not for this reason had an unfair trial, even though it had become apparent
during the trial (no defence statement having been produced and the trial having started
without any clear idea as to what exactly was in dispute between the parties) that his case
meant that he was, in effect, challenging the truthfulness of the prosecution witnesses; by
the time of the trial, the defendant fully understood the implications of his decisions, and it
was not for the court to compel him to take another course, notwithstanding that it might
have been in his best interests to do so: *R. v. Williams (James)* [2012] R.T.R. 18, CA. As to
this case, see also *ante*, §§ 4–424, 7–64.

(viii) Bias

See *R. v. Mears and Mears, ante*, § 4–293, and *Hanif and Khan v. U.K., ante*, § 4–293. In   **7–89**
the latter case, the European Court of Human Rights came to a different conclusion on the
facts to the Court of Appeal in the case referred to in the main work as *R. v. Khan*.

(xi) Prosecution improperly making second speech or commenting on failure to give evidence

See *R. v. Williams (James), ante*, § 4–424 (and, as to this case, see also *ante*, §§ 7–64, 7–87).   ★7–92

(xvi) Irregularity in relation to jury

See *R. v. Hewgill (Michael), post*, § 7–102.   **7–97**

Investigation of irregularities

The two exceptions to the ban on inquiring into a jury's deliberations (as to which, see   **7–102**
the main work) did not extend to a situation where, as a result of improper contact between
a co-defendant of the appellant and a juror (who had then discussed the communication
with other jurors), it was impossible to see how it could be said that an informed observer
could conclude that the jurors had returned their verdict without in any way taking into account, even subconsciously, what they had been told by the co-defendant (applying the test
in *In re Medicaments and Related Classes of Goods (No. 2)*, and *Porter v. Magill; Weeks v. Magill* (as to both of which, see § 4–53 in the main work)); the fact that the jury did not tell the
judge what had happened made it impossible to conclude objectively that they had reached
their verdict in an impartial manner, meaning that the verdict must be set aside: *R. v.
Hewgill (Michael)* [2012] Crim.L.R. 134, CA.

(9) Retrials

Criminal Appeal Act 1968, s.7

R. v. Maxwell is now reported at [2011] 2 Cr.App.R. 31.   **7–112**

As to whether it is open to the Court of Appeal to order a retrial after its order allowing   ★
an appeal against conviction has been finally recorded, see *R. v. Blackwood, post*, § 7–222.

Criminal Appeal Act 1968, Sched. 2

Sentence on conviction at retrial

As from a day to be appointed, paragraph 2(4) of Schedule 2 to the *CAA* 1968 is amended   ★7–117
by the *Legal Aid, Sentencing and Punishment of Offenders Act* 2012, s.110(13), and Sched. 13,
para. 6, so as to substitute "240ZA" for "240".

B. Appeal Against Sentence

(1) Who can appeal

Criminal Appeal Act 1968, s.9

Appeal against sentence following conviction on indictment

★**7–119**   With effect from June 18, 2012 (*Criminal Justice Act 2003 (Commencement No. 28 and Saving Provisions) Order* 2012 (S.I. 2012 No. 1320)), sections 41 and 332 of, paragraph 44 of Schedule 3 to, and Part 4 of Schedule 37 (erroneously referred to as "Schedule 7" in the main work) to, the 2003 Act are brought into force in certain areas (as to which, see *ante*, § 1–88). There are associated saving provisions, as to which, see article 5 of the order (*ante*, § 1–88).

Criminal Appeal Act 1968, s.50

Meaning of "sentence"

★**7–121**   As from a day to be appointed, section 50(3) of the *CAA* 1968 is amended by the *Legal Aid, Sentencing and Punishment of Offenders Act* 2012, s.39(1), and Sched. 5, para. 3, so as to substitute the words "relating to a requirement to make a payment under regulations under section 23 or 24 of the *Legal Aid, Sentencing and Punishment of Offenders Act* 2012" for the words "under section 17 of the *Access to Justice Act* 1999".

(2) Notes on appeal against sentence

Principles on which court acts

(v) *Sentence manifestly excessive or wrong in principle*

7–141   On October 13, 2011, the Sentencing Council for England and Wales issued a definitive guideline on burglary, applying to all offenders aged 18 or over who are sentenced on or after January 16, 2012, regardless of the date of their offence. The guideline covers both aggravated burglary (*Theft Act* 1968, s.10 (§ 21–129 in the main work)), and burglary, whether of a dwelling or non-dwelling (1968 Act, s.9 (*ibid.*, § 21–108)). For the details, see *post*, Appendix K–259 *et seq.*

★   The Sentencing Council for England and Wales has issued a definitive guideline, applying to all offenders aged 18 or over who are sentenced on or after February 27, 2012, regardless of the date of their offence. The offences covered are: (i) fraudulent evasion of a prohibition on the importation or exportation of a controlled drug (*CEMA* 1979, s.170(2) (§ 25–474 in the main work)), (ii) supplying or offering to supply such a drug (*Misuse of Drugs Act* 1971, s.4(3) (*ibid.*, § 27–28)) and possession of such a drug with intent to supply it to another (1971 Act, s.5(3) (*ibid.*, § 27–50)), (iii) production of such a drug (1971 Act, s.4(2)(a) or (b)) and cultivation of a cannabis plant (1971 Act, s.6(2) (*ibid.*, § 27–79)), (iv) permitting premises to be used for the production, supply, consumption, etc., of controlled drugs (1971 Act, s.8 (*ibid.*, § 27–84)), and (v) possession of a controlled drug (1971 Act, s.5(2)). For the detail, see *post*, Appendix K–271 *et seq.*

★   The Sentencing Council has issued a guideline on the related topics of taking offences into consideration and totality, applying to all offenders whose cases are dealt with on or after June 11, 2012. For the detail, see *ante*, §§ 5–160 *et seq.*, and *post*, Appendix K–280 *et seq.*

★   The Sentencing Council for England and Wales has issued a definitive guideline, applying to all offenders aged 18 or over who are sentenced on or after August 20, 2012, regardless of the date of the offence, and relating to offences under the *Dangerous Dogs Act* 1991. For the detail, see *post*, Appendix K–291 *et seq.*

G. Procedure from Notice of Appeal to Hearing

(2) **Right to representation**

As to the repeal of sections 1 to 26 of, and Schedules 1 to 3A and 14, Pt II, to, the *Access to Justice Act* 1999, see *ante*, § 6–130.

★7–165

Skeleton arguments and citation of authorities

Practice Direction (Criminal Proceedings: Consolidation), para. II.17 [2002] 1 W.L.R. 2870

Whether in written or oral submissions, the hierarchy for citing authorities should be first, the Law Reports, next, either the Weekly Law Reports or the All England Law Reports, and next, any of the authoritative specialist series of reports which contain a headnote and are made by individuals holding a Senior Courts qualification (for the purposes of the *Courts and Legal Services Act* 1990, s.115); where a judgment is not reported in any of these, other reports may be cited; where a judgment has not been reported, reference may be made to the official transcript if that is available (*e.g.* from BAILII), but not the handed-down text of a judgment; an unreported case should not usually be cited unless it contains a relevant statement of legal principle not found in reported authority; when one report is fuller than another, or when there are discrepancies between reports, the practice outlined above need not be followed, but the court should be given a brief explanation why this course is being taken, and the alternative references should be given; if a judgment under appeal has been reported before the hearing, but after skeleton arguments have been filed with the court, and counsel wish to argue from the published report, rather than from the official transcript, the court should be provided with photocopies of the report; judgments reported in any series of reports, including those of the Incorporated Council of Law Reporting, should be provided either by way of a photocopy of the published report or by way of a copy of a reproduction of the judgment in electronic form that has been authorised by the publisher of the relevant series; but in any event (i) the report must be presented to the court in an easily legible form (a 12-point font is preferred, but a 10- or 11-point font is acceptable) and (ii) the advocate presenting the report must be satisfied that it has not been reproduced in a garbled form from the data source; in any case of doubt, the court will rely on the printed text of the report (unless the editor of the report has certified that an electronic version is more accurate because it corrects an error contained in an earlier printed text): *Practice Direction (Citation of Authorities)* [2012] 1 W.L.R. 780, Senior Courts (applying to the Senior Courts of England and Wales, county courts and magistrates' courts). Paragraph II.19 of the consolidated criminal practice direction (*Practice Direction (Criminal Proceedings: Consolidation)* [2002] 1 W.L.R. 2870) is varied so as to refer to this practice direction (although it should be noted that as at June 5, 2012, no amendment had been made to the consolidated criminal practice direction as it appears on the website of the Ministry of Justice). For consideration as to how far this practice direction is intended to apply to criminal practice, see CLW/12/14/2.

★7–200

H. The Hearing

(7) **Leave to call additional evidence**

Criminal Appeal Act 1968, s.23

R. v. Malook is now reported at [2012] 1 W.L.R. 633, *sub nom. R. v. Malook (Sadakat)* (*Practice Note*).

★7–215

Practical application

Sentence appeals

R. v. Beesley and Coyle; *R. v. Rehman* is now reported at [2012] 1 Cr.App.R.(S.) 15.

7–215

★   *R. v. Malook* is now reported at [2012] 1 W.L.R. 633, *sub nom. R. v. Malook (Sadakat)* (*Practice Note*).

I. Notification of Result of Appeal and Matters Depending Thereon

(2) Alteration of decision, relisting of cases

★7-222   *R. v. Cross (Patrick)* (see the main work) determined that, once an order on an appeal has finally been recorded, the power to vary it is lost, and that an order on an appeal is finally recorded when it is recorded by the proper officer of the court of trial; where, therefore, the order recording the decision of the Court of Appeal to allow an appeal and quash a conviction must have been recorded by the Crown Court before the hearing of an application for a retrial, the order had become final by the time of the hearing; and it could not possibly be open to the court to order a retrial after the appellant's acquittal had been recorded in that way (s.2(3) of the *CAA* 1968 (§ 7–41 in the main work) providing that, save where a retrial is ordered, the quashing of a conviction shall operate as a direction to the court of trial to "enter ... a judgment and verdict of acquittal"): *R. v. Blackwood* [2012] 2 Cr.App.R. 1, CA.

V. APPEAL TO COURT OF APPEAL BY THE PROSECUTION

B. Terminating Rulings

General right of appeal in respect of rulings

★7-248   In order for the prosecution to appeal against a terminating ruling, section 58(4) and (8) of the *CJA* 2003 (§ 7–247 in the main work), and rule 67.2 of the *Criminal Procedure Rules* 2011 (S.I. 2011 No. 1709) (*ibid.*, § 7–266)), make it clear that either an adjournment must be sought immediately following the ruling, or the decision to appeal and the acquittal agreement (*viz.* the agreement that the defendant should be acquitted if leave to appeal is not obtained, or the appeal is abandoned) must be notified to the court immediately following the ruling; if an adjournment is sought and obtained, the acquittal agreement must be provided by, at latest, the time when an intention to appeal is notified; "immediately following the ruling" means there and then and, in any event, before anything important has happened; here, where the court had adjourned for the jury to be assembled to acquit the defendant (following a ruling that there was no case to answer) before anything at all was said on behalf of the Crown, and where the jury were discharged (without the defendant having been acquitted) before the prosecutor even attempted to notify the acquittal agreement to the court, the two conditions precedent in section 58(4) and (8) had not been fulfilled: *R. v. M.*, unreported, April 26, 2012, CA ([2012] EWCA Crim. 792) (considering *R. v. Arnold, C.P.S. v. C., M. and H.*, and *R. v. T. (N.)* (as to all of which, see the main work)).

D. Miscellaneous and Supplemental

Criminal Justice Act 2003, ss.71–74

Restrictions on reporting

★7-261   As from a day to be appointed, section 71(8) of the 2003 Act is amended by the *Legal Aid, Sentencing and Punishment of Offenders Act* 2012, s.39(1), and Sched. 5, para. 65, so as to substitute a new paragraph (g), as follows—

"(g) whether, for the purposes of the proceedings, representation was provided to the defendant or any of the defendants under Part 1 of the *Legal Aid, Sentencing and Punishment of Offenders Act* 2012".

VI. RETRIAL FOR SERIOUS OFFENCES

B. Application for Retrial

Criminal Justice Act 2003, ss.76–83

New and compelling evidence

Evidence that was available to be used in earlier proceedings, but which was not in fact ★**7–282**
used (in this instance crucial DNA evidence relied upon by the prosecution but excluded by the trial judge as inadmissible, a decision the House of Lords later ruled was wrong in *Att.-Gen.'s Reference (No. 3 of 1999)* (*post*, § 15–196b)), can constitute "new" evidence for the purposes of section 78(2) of the *CJA* 2003 (§ 7–281 in the main work): *R. v. B.* [2012] 2 Cr.App.R. 5, CA.

VII. INTERLOCUTORY, ETC., APPEALS

A. Serious or Complex Fraud Cases

Right of appeal

Criminal Justice Act 1987, s.9(1)

With effect from May 1, 2012, the words "43 or" in section 9(11) of the 1987 Act are re- ★**7–309**
pealed by the *Protection of Freedoms Act* 2012, s.115(2), and Sched. 10, Pt 10.

IX. APPEAL TO THE COURT OF APPEAL: PROCEDURE AND FORMS

A. Procedural Rules

Introduction

R. v. Boggild is now reported at [2012] 1 Cr.App.R.(S.) 81. **7–365**

Criminal Procedure Rules 2011 (S.I. 2011 No. 1709), Pt 68

When this part applies

R. v. Boggild is now reported at [2012] 1 Cr.App.R.(S.) 81. **7–380**

X. APPEAL TO THE SUPREME COURT FROM THE COURT OF APPEAL

D. Practice and Procedure in the Supreme Court

(3) Electronic communications from court

For further guidance regarding electronic communications in the lower courts, see *ante*, **7–423**
§ 4–15.

XI. GENERAL PROVISIONS RELATING TO APPEALS TO AND FROM THE COURT OF APPEAL

C. Interpretation

Criminal Appeal Act 1968, s.51

Interpretation

★**7–427**   As from a day to be appointed, the definition of "duly approved" in section 51(1) of the *CAA* 1968 is amended by the *Health and Social Care Act* 2012, s.38(5)(b), so as to insert the words ", or by another person by virtue of section 12ZA or 12ZB of that Act," after the words "Secretary of State".

XIII. REFERENCES TO THE COURT OF APPEAL BY THE ATTORNEY-GENERAL

A. Of Points of Law

Criminal Justice Act 1972, s.36

★**7–437**   As from a day to be appointed, section 36 of the *CJA* 1972 is amended by the *Legal Aid, Sentencing and Punishment of Offenders Act* 2012, s.62(1), and Sched. 7, para. 9, so as (i) to omit the words "to his costs, that is to say" from subsection (5), (ii) to substitute for subsection (5A), new subsections (5A) to (5C), as follows—

> "(5A) Subsection (5) has effect subject to—
>> (a) subsection (5B), and
>> (b) regulations under section 20(1A)(d) of the *Prosecution of Offences Act* 1985 (as applied by this section).
>
> (5B) A person is not entitled under subsection (5) to the payment of sums in respect of legal costs (as defined in section 16A of the *Prosecution of Offences Act* 1985) incurred in proceedings in the Court of Appeal.
>
> (5C) Subsections (1A) to (1C) and (3) of section 20 of the *Prosecution of Offences Act* 1985 (regulations as to amounts ordered to be paid out of central funds) apply in relation to amounts payable out of central funds under subsection (5) as they apply in relation to amounts payable out of central funds in pursuance of costs orders made under section 16 of that Act.".

★   Paragraphs 21 and 23 of Schedule 7 to the 2012 Act provide that the amendments made by paragraphs 9 to 11 do not have effect in relation to a person's entitlement to costs in connection with a reference made before the day on which the amendment comes into force.

B. Of Sentences

Criminal Justice Act 1988, s.36

Reviews of sentencing

★**7–442**   As from a day to be appointed, section 36(2)(b) of the 1988 Act is amended by the *Legal Aid, Sentencing and Punishment of Offenders Act* 2012, s.142(3), and Sched. 26, paras 4 and 5(1) and (2), so as to insert a new sub-paragraph (zi) before sub-paragraph (i), as follows—

> "(zi) section 1A(5) of the *Prevention of Crime Act* 1953;".

★   As from a day to be appointed, section 36(2)(b) of the 1988 Act is further amended by the 2012 Act, s.142(3), and Sched. 26, paras 4 and 5(1) and (3), so as to insert a new sub-paragraph (ia) after sub-paragraph (i), as follows—

> "(ia) section 139AA(7) of this Act;".

★   As from a day to be appointed, section 36(2)(b) of the 1988 Act is further amended by the 2012 Act, s.122(3), and Sched. 19, para. 2, so as to insert "224A," after the word "section" in sub-paragraph (iii).

Criminal Justice Act 1988, Sched. 3

As from a day to be appointed, paragraph 11 of Schedule 3 to the 1988 Act is amended ★**7–452**
by the *Legal Aid, Sentencing and Punishment of Offenders Act* 2012, s.62(1), and Sched. 7,
para. 11(1) and (2), so as (i) to number the existing provision as sub-paragraph (1), (ii) to
omit the words "to his costs, that is to say", and (iii) to insert new sub-paragraphs (2) to (4),
as follows—

"(2) Sub-paragraph (1) has effect subject to—
(a) sub-paragraph (3), and
(b) regulations under section 20(1A)(d) of the *Prosecution of Offences Act* 1985 (as applied by
this paragraph).
(3) A person is not entitled under sub-paragraph (1) to the payment of sums in respect of legal
costs (as defined in section 16A of the *Prosecution of Offences Act* 1985) incurred in proceedings in the
Court of Appeal.
(4) Subsections (1A) to (1C) and (3) of section 20 of the *Prosecution of Offences Act* 1985 (regulations as to amounts ordered to be paid out of central funds) apply in relation to funds payable out of
central funds under sub-paragraph (1) as they apply in relation to amounts payable out of central
funds in pursuance of costs orders made under section 16 of that Act.".

As to the application of this amendment, see *ante*, § 7–437. ★
As from a day to be appointed, paragraph 12 of Schedule 3 to the 1988 Act is amended ★
by the 2012 Act, s.62(1), and Sched. 7, para. 11(1) and (3).

CHAPTER 8

ORAL TESTIMONY OF WITNESSES

I. PRELIMINARIES

A. SECURING ATTENDANCE OF WITNESSES, PRODUCTION OF DOCUMENTS, ETC.

(2) Summons to witness to attend Crown Court

Criminal Procedure (Attendance of Witnesses) Act 1965, s.2

Issue of witness summons on application to Crown Court
With effect from June 18, 2012 (*Criminal Justice Act 2003 (Commencement No. 28 and Sav-* ★**8–2**
ing Provisions) Order 2012 (S.I. 2012 No. 1320)), sections 41 and 332 of, and paragraph 42
of Schedule 3 to, and Part 4 of Schedule 37 to, the 2003 Act (see the main work) are
brought into force (so far as they are not already in force) in certain areas (as to which, see
ante, § 1–88). There are associated saving provisions, as to which, see article 5 of the order
(*ante*, § 1–88).

(7) Evidence given in Children Act 1989, wardship or family proceedings

Necessity for leave

The effect of rule 12.73(1) of the *Family Procedure Rules* 2010 (S.I. 2010 No. 2955) (see ★**8–35**
the main work), is such that evidence given in care proceedings may be disclosed to solicitors acting for the parents in parallel criminal proceedings without leave of the court: *Re B.
(A Child: Disclosure of Evidence in Care Proceedings)* [2012] 1 F.L.R. 142, Fam D (Bodey J.).
As to this case, see also *post*, § 8–37.

Disclosure ordered to defence

For a further example of leave being given (if it was required, as to which, see *ante*, § 8– ★**8–37**

35) for disclosure of evidence given in care proceedings to solicitors acting for the parents in parallel criminal proceedings, see *Re B. (A Child: Disclosure of Evidence in Care Proceedings)* [2012] 1 F.L.R. 142, Fam D (Bodey J.) (considering *Re C. (A Minor) (Care Proceedings: Disclosure* (see § 8–38 in the main work)).

B. Issues Arising Prior to Entry into the Witness Box

(1) Presence in court

8–39   While it remains good practice for a factual witness who is intended to be called to remain out of court before giving evidence, and while section 78 of the *PACE Act* 1984 (§ 15–401 in the main work) might operate so to give the court a discretion to exclude the evidence of a prosecution witness if the witness's earlier presence in court could lead to the creation of an adverse effect on the fairness of the trial, that discretion would not apply to a defence witness (s.78 applying only to prosecution evidence): *R. v. Carty*, 175 J.P. 424, CA (considering *R. v. Briggs* (see the main work)).

III. COMPETENCE AND COMPELLABILITY

(2) Test of competence

Youth Justice and Criminal Evidence Act 1999, s.53

8–53   Under section 53(4) and (5) of the 1999 Act (see the main work), a defendant who has pleaded guilty and is not in the charge of the jury is competent to give evidence in criminal proceedings for the prosecution even though the basis of his plea may be the subject of dispute and even though he might, in evidence, suggest that he was not in fact a participant in the offence to which he had pleaded guilty; these were, however, matters which a judge could take account of on an application to exclude the evidence under section 78 of the *PACE Act* 1984 (§ 15–401 in the main work): *R. v. McEwan* [2012] Crim.L.R. 128, CA.

IV. RULES OF EVIDENCE AND PRACTICE RELATING TO THE QUESTIONING OF WITNESSES

A. General

(1) Special measures directions

Defendants

★8–72   As to the impact on proceedings where an intermediary is unavailable, see *R. v. Cox (Practice Note)*, *ante*, § 4–165.

Relevant offences

★8–76   As from a day to be appointed, new paragraphs 9A and 26A are inserted into Schedule 1A to the YJCEA 1999 by the *Legal Aid, Sentencing and Punishment of Offenders Act* 2012, s.142(3), and Sched. 26, para. 8. The two new paragraphs refer to offences under the *Prevention of Crime Act* 1953, s.1A, and the *CJA* 1988, s.139AA, respectively.

Youth Justice and Criminal Evidence Act 1999, ss.23–30

Video recorded evidence in chief

★8–89   With effect from June 18, 2012 (*Criminal Justice Act 2003 (Commencement No. 28 and Sav-*

ing Provisions) Order 2012 (S.I. 2012 No. 1320)), section 332 of, and Part 4 of Schedule 37 to, the 2003 Act are brought into force in certain areas (as to which, see *ante*, § 1–88). There are associated saving provisions, as to which, see article 5 of the order (*ante*, § 1–88).

Transcript for jury

The principles regulating the circumstances in which an "achieving best evidence" interview transcript should be shown to the jury, and the directions that a judge should give to the jury in the event that it is shown, were explained in *R. v. Popescu* (see the main work), which extrapolated six safeguards from well-established authority, all of which were founded on the central principle that a defendant is entitled to a fair trial without unfair procedural or evidential advantage being afforded to the prosecution; where, therefore, the judge had allowed the jury to retire with the transcript without good reason, this constituted a serious error, and the mere fact that the defence consented afforded no justification; the judge had compounded this error by failing to give the jury such directions as would be likely to guard against the risk of disproportionate weight being given to the transcript; even though, in this rape case, the issue was the simple one of consent, the danger that precludes a jury having the transcript is not merely that the jury might view the evidence-in-chief in the transcript in isolation from the other evidence, but that they will concentrate upon the written word rather their impression of the witness and their assessment of that witness as she gives her evidence, both in the form of the video recording and during cross-examination; the jury, under the English system of oral evidence, are required to assess the truth of a witness's evidence by reference to their assessment of him or her whilst giving that evidence; that is fundamental to the method by which a jury are expected to reach a conclusion as to guilt or innocence; accordingly, the defendant had been deprived of safeguards essential to the fairness of his trial, and his conviction was accordingly unsafe: *R. v. Sardar* [2012] 2 *Archbold Review* 2, CA. ★8-92

Examination of witness through intermediary
As to the use of an intermediary for a defendant, see *R. v. Cox (Practice Note)*, *ante*, § 4– 165. ★8-94

Youth Justice and Criminal Evidence Act 1999, ss.33A–33C

Examination of accused through intermediary
As to the use of an intermediary under the court's common law powers, see *R. v. Cox (Practice Note)*, *ante*, § 4–165. ★8-101

B. Examination-in-Chief

(3) Matters arising in examination-in-chief

(h) *Previous consistent statements*

Exceptions

Statement constituting recent complaint
R. v. Islam was considered in *R. v. A. (Ashraf)*, *post*, § 11–40; and both *R. v. Islam* and *R. v. A. (Ashraf)* were considered in *R. v. H.*, *post*, § 11–40. 8-210

C. Cross-Examination

(1) General principles

Form of questioning in cross-examination

In *R. v. Wills (Practice Note)* [2012] 1 Cr.App.R. 2, CA, it was said (having considered *R.* 8-217 *v. B.* (§§ 8–53, 8–55, 8–59 in the main work)) that: (i) where, in the case of vulnerable witnesses, it is necessary and appropriate to have limitations on the way in which an advocate conducts cross-examination, there is a duty on the judge to ensure that those limitations are complied with; where appropriate, the judge, in fairness to the defendant, should explain the limitations to the jury, and the reasons for them; this means that the limitations must be clearly defined; (ii) if counsel fails to comply with the limitations, it is important to give a relevant direction to the jury when that occurs; to leave it until the summing up will, in many cases, mean that it is much less effective; and (iii) for vulnerable witnesses, the traditional style of cross-examination, where comment is made on inconsistencies during cross-examination, must be replaced by a system where those inconsistencies can be drawn to the jury's attention at, or about, the time when evidence is being given and not, in longer or complex cases, for that comment to have to await the closing speeches at the end of the trial; one solution would be for important inconsistencies to be pointed out after the vulnerable witness has finished giving evidence, either by the advocate or by the judge after discussion with the advocates. As to (iii), see CLW/11/44/2; and as to the cross-examination of child witnesses generally, see David Caruso, *"I don't want to play follow the leader": Three Proposals for the Reform of the Cross-examination of Child Witnesses* [2011] J.C.C.L. 254.

(3) Restrictions

(b) *In proceedings for sexual offences*

Statutory restrictions

Youth Justice and Criminal Evidence Act 1999, ss.41–43

Interpretation and application of section 41

★8–239 With effect from June 18, 2012 (*Criminal Justice Act 2003 (Commencement No. 28 and Saving Provisions) Order* 2012 (S.I. 2012 No. 1320)), sections 41 and 332 of, and paragraph 73 of Schedule 3 to, and Part 4 of Schedule 37 to, the 2003 Act are brought into force (so far as not already in force) in certain areas (as to which, see *ante*, § 1–88). There are associated saving provisions, as to which, see article 5 of the order (*ante*, § 1–88).

Previous complaints and statements about sexual behaviour

8–248 *R. v. Ben-Rejab* is now reported at [2012] 1 Cr.App.R. 4, *sub nom. R. v. Ben-Rejab and Baccar.*

CHAPTER 9

DOCUMENTARY AND REAL EVIDENCE

II. PUBLIC DOCUMENTS

D. CATEGORIES OF PUBLIC DOCUMENTS

(1) Public registers

Births and Deaths Registration Act 1953, s.34

★9–49 With effect from May 21, 2012 (*Welfare Reform Act 2009 (Commencement No. 8) Order* 2012 (S.I. 2012 No. 1256)), section 56 of, and paragraph 14 of Schedule 6 to, the 2009 Act (see the main work) are brought into force.

III. PRIVATE DOCUMENTS

A. Proof of Contents

(1) Primary and secondary evidence

Police and Criminal Evidence Act 1984, ss.71, 72

Microfilm copies

With effect from June 18, 2012 (*Criminal Justice Act 2003 (Commencement No. 28 and Saving Provisions) Order* 2012 (S.I. 2012 No. 1320)), section 332 of, and Part 4 of Schedule 37 to, the 2003 Act are brought into force in certain areas (as to which, see *ante*, § 1–88). There are associated saving provisions, as to which, see article 5 of the order (*ante*, § 1–88). ★**9–102a**

CHAPTER 10

MISCELLANEOUS SOURCES OF EVIDENCE

II. ADMISSIONS

Criminal Justice Act 1967, s.10

The reference in section 10(2) of the 1967 Act to the defendant's solicitor shall be taken as including a reference to a licensed body acting for the defendant, *i.e.* a body that holds a licence issued by the Law Society under Part 5 of the *Legal Services Act* 2007: *Legal Services Act 2007 (Designation as a Licensing Authority) (No. 2) Order* 2011 (S.I. 2011 No. 2866), arts 1(3) and 8(1) and (2)(b), and Sched. 2. **10–7**

III. WRITTEN STATEMENTS AND DEPOSITIONS

A. Committal Proceedings

(1) General

Magistrates' Courts Act 1980, s.6(1), (2)

Discharge or committal for trial

With effect from June 18, 2012 (*Criminal Justice Act 2003 (Commencement No. 28 and Saving Provisions) Order* 2012 (S.I. 2012 No. 1320)), section 332 of, and Part 4 of Schedule 37 to, the 2003 Act are brought into force in certain areas (as to which, see *ante*, § 1–88). There are associated saving provisions, as to which, see article 5 of the order (*ante*, § 1–88). ★**10–9**

General requirement to sit in open court

As to the commencement of section 332 of, and Part 4 of Schedule 37 to, the 2003 Act (see the main work), see *ante*, § 10–9. ★**10–12**

Proceedings in absence of accused

Magistrates' Courts Act 1980, s.4(3), (4)

With effect from June 18, 2012 (*Criminal Justice Act 2003 (Commencement No. 28 and Saving Provisions) Order* 2012 (S.I. 2012 No. 1320)), sections 41 and 332 of, and paragraph 55 ★**10–13** of Schedule 3 to, and Part 4 of Schedule 37 to, the 2003 Act are brought into force in certain areas (as to which, see *ante*, § 1–88). There are associated saving provisions, as to which, see article 5 of the order (*ante*, § 1–88).

(3) Admissibility of evidence

Magistrates' Courts Act 1980, ss.5A–5F

Proof by production of copy

★**10–20**   As to the commencement of section 332 of, and Part 4 of Schedule 37 to, the 2003 Act (see the main work), see *ante*, § 10–9.

Magistrates' Courts Act 1980, s.97A

Summons or warrant to committal proceedings

★**10–21**   As to the commencement of section 332 of, and Part 4 of Schedule 37 to, the 2003 Act (see the main work), see *ante*, § 10–9.

Criminal Justice Act 1972, s.46

Admissibility of written statements made outside England and Wales

★**10–23**   As to the commencement of section 332 of, and Part 4 of Schedule 37 to, the 2003 Act (see the main work), see *ante*, § 10–9.

Magistrates' Courts Act 1980, s.103

Evidence of persons under 14 in committal proceedings for assault, sexual offences, etc.

10–24   As to the commencement of section 332 of, and Part 4 of Schedule 37 to, the 2003 Act (see the main work), see *ante*, § 10–9.

(4) Miscellaneous provisions relating to taking of depositions

Children and Young Persons Act 1933, s.42

Extension of power to take deposition of child or young person

★**10–26**   With effect from June 18, 2012 (*Criminal Justice Act 2003 (Commencement No. 28 and Saving Provisions) Order* 2012 (S.I. 2012 No. 1320)), section 41 of, and paragraph 33 of Schedule 3 to, the 2003 Act are brought into force in certain areas (as to which, see *ante*, § 1–88), and to the extent that they are not already in force. There are associated saving provisions, as to which, see article 5 of the order (*ante*, § 1–88).

(5) Relevant provisions of the Criminal Procedure Rules 2011 (S.I. 2011 No. 1709)

Criminal Procedure Rules 2011 (S.I. 2011 No. 1709), r.12.1

Documents to be sent to the Crown Court

10–35   With effect from April 2, 2012, rule 12.1 of the *Criminal Procedure Rules* 2011 (S.I. 2011 No. 1709) is revoked by the *Criminal Procedure (Amendment) Rules* 2011 (S.I. 2011 No. 3075), r.7.

B. Reading Depositions and Statements at Trial

(1) General permission in relation to committal evidence

Introduction

★**10–41**   As to the commencement of section 332 of, and Part 4 of Schedule 37 to, the 2003 Act (see the main work), see *ante*, § 10–9.

As to the commencement of section 332 of, and Part 4 of Schedule 37 to, the 2003 Act **★10–45** (see the main work), see *ante*, § 10–9.

(4) Statements served under the Criminal Justice Act 1967, s.9

Criminal Justice Act 1967, s.9

Proof by written statement

As to the commencement of section 332 of, and Part 4 of Schedule 37 (erroneously **★10–50** referred to as "Schedule 7" in the main work) to, the 2003 Act, see *ante*, § 10–9.

The references in section 9 of the 1967 Act to the defendant's solicitor shall be taken as including a reference to a licensed body acting for the defendant, *i.e.* a body that holds a licence issued by the Law Society under Part 5 of the *Legal Services Act* 2007: *Legal Services Act 2007 (Designation as a Licensing Authority) (No. 2) Order* 2011 (S.I. 2011 No. 2866), arts 1(3) and 8(1) and (2)(b), and Sched. 2.

As from April 2, 2012 (*Armed Forces Act 2011 (Commencement No. 1, Transitional and* **★** *Transitory Provisions) Order* 2012 (S.I. 2012 No. 669)), section 9 of the *CJA* 1967 is amended by the *AFA* 2011, s.26, and Sched. 2, para. 7, so as to insert a new paragraph (e) at the end of subsection (5) (as prospectively amended by the *Courts Act* 2003 (as to which, see the main work)), and a new subsection (5A), as follows—

> "(e) subject to subsection (5A), a qualifying judge advocate (within the meaning of the *Senior Courts Act* 1981).
> (5A) Subsection (5)(e) applies only where the application in question is to the Crown Court".

If the amendment made to section 9(5) of the 1967 Act by the 2003 Act has not come into force before the commencement of paragraph 1 of Schedule 2 to the 2011 Act, then paragraph 8 of that schedule provides that pending the commencement of that amendment: (i) paragraph 7 does not apply; and (ii) section 9(5) is amended so that the words from "by a puisne judge" to the end become paragraph (a), and there is inserted at the end of paragraph (a), the following—

> "; or
> (b) subject to subsection (5A), by a qualifying judge advocate (within the meaning of the *Senior Courts Act* 1981) sitting alone.
> (5A) Subsection (5)(b) applies only where the application in question is to the Crown Court".

IV. CERTIFICATES AND STATUTORY DECLARATIONS

A. Evidence by Certificate

As to the commencement of section 332 of, and Part 4 of Schedule 37 to, the 2003 Act **★10–53** (see the main work), see *ante*, § 10–9.

VI. LETTERS OF REQUEST

Designation of prosecuting authorities

The *Crime (International Co-operation) Act 2003 (Designation of Prosecuting Authorities)* **10–59** *(Amendment) Order* 2012 (S.I. 2012 No. 146) has further amended the *Crime (International Co-operation) Act 2003 (Designation of Prosecuting Authorities) Order* 2004 (S.I. 2004 No. 1034), so as to add to the list of designated prosecuting authorities for the purposes of section 7(5) of the 2003 Act, the Environment Agency and the Secretaries of State for Health, for Transport, and for Work and Pensions.

VII. EXPERT EVIDENCE

A. Legislation

Criminal Justice Act 1988, s.30

★**10–61** As to the commencement of section 332 of, and Part 4 of Schedule 37 (erroneously referred to as "Schedule 7" in the main work) to, the 2003 Act, see *ante*, § 10–9.

B. Opinion Evidence

Proper approach

10–67 Where two experts had agreed that DNA evidence provided some support for the proposition that the defendants had been present in a getaway car, but where they "respectfully disagreed" as to the strength of that evidence (with the expert for the defence stating that she believed that the weakness of the evidence meant that it was unsuitable for statistical interpretation), although they both agreed that the other's opinion was valid and tenable and reflected genuine and real differences in interpretational approach within the scientific community, it had been open to the judge to leave the jury to place what they considered to be the appropriate weight on the opinions of both experts; the case differed significantly from *R. v. Cannings* (see the main work), in which the Court of Appeal concluded that a prosecution following two or more sudden unexplained infant deaths in the same family should not be started or continued "exclusively or almost exclusively" on the basis of expert evidence where there was serious disagreement between reputable experts about the cause of death, and a body of such expert opinion had concluded that natural causes, whether explained or unexplained, could not be excluded as a reasonable (as opposed to a fanciful) possibility; in particular, the prosecution in the instant case did not depend "exclusively or almost exclusively" on the disputed DNA evidence, the disagreement was not as to whether there was any DNA evidence, but merely as to its strength, and, finally and significantly, the defendants had accepted that they might have been in the getaway car (although for innocent purposes): *R. v. Hookway and Noakes* [2012] Crim.L.R. 130, CA.

E. Immunity

10–70a *Jones v. Kaney* is now reported at [2011] 2 A.C. 398.

Chapter 11

HEARSAY EVIDENCE

II. STATUTE

A. Criminal Justice Act 1988

(2) The basic rules

Criminal Justice Act 2003, ss.114, 115, 133, 134

Hearsay and the right to fair trial

11–3a Having considered the decision of the Supreme Court in *R. v. Horncastle*; *R. v. Marquis*;

R. v. Carter (see the main work), the Grand Chamber of the European Court of Human Rights in *Al-Khawaja v. U.K.* (2012) 54 E.H.R.R. 23, reversed the chamber decision (as to which, see the main work) in part. It held that the guarantees in Article 6(3)(d) of the ECHR (§ 16–57 in the main work) are specific aspects of the right to a fair hearing that must be taken into account in any assessment of the fairness of proceedings; in making this assessment, the proceedings should be looked at as a whole, having regard to the rights of the defence, but also to the interest of the public and victims that crime is properly prosecuted and, where necessary, to the rights of witnesses; exceptions to the principle in Article 6(3)(d) are possible, but must not infringe the rights of the defence, which, as a rule, require that the accused should be given a proper opportunity to challenge and question a witness against him, either when the witness makes his statement or at a later stage. From this, the court held that it follows that: (a) there must be a good reason for the non-attendance of a witness; and (b) when a conviction is based solely or to a decisive degree on a statement made by a person whom the accused has had no opportunity to examine or to have examined, the rights of the defence may be restricted to an extent that is incompatible with Article 6. As to what constitutes good reason, while absence owing to the death of a witness will plainly be a good reason, whether the same will be the case for absence owing to fear will depend on whether the fear is attributable to the defendant or those acting on his behalf, or to a more general fear; if the former, it will be appropriate to allow the hearsay evidence of that witness to be introduced at trial, even if this is the sole or decisive evidence, because the defendant must be taken to have waived his right to question such a witness; if the latter, the court must conduct appropriate enquiries to determine, first, whether or not there are objective grounds for the fear, and, secondly, whether those grounds are supported by evidence; allowing the admission of a witness statement in lieu of live evidence at trial must be a measure of last resort; before a witness can be excused from testifying on grounds of fear, the court must be satisfied that all available alternatives, such as witness anonymity and other special measures, would be inappropriate or impracticable. As to the evidence being "sole or decisive", the court said that "decisive" should be narrowly understood as indicating evidence of such significance as is likely to be determinative of the outcome of the case; where the untested hearsay is corroborated by other evidence, the assessment of whether it is decisive will depend on the strength of the supporting evidence; where hearsay is the sole or decisive evidence against a defendant, its admission as evidence will not automatically result in a breach of Article 6, but because of the dangers of such evidence, its sole or decisive nature will constitute an important factor to balance in the scales, and one which would require sufficient counterbalancing factors, including the existence of strong procedural safeguards that permit a fair and proper assessment of the reliability of the evidence; in principle, the safeguards now contained in Chapter 2 of Part 11 of the *CJA* 2003, supported by those contained in the *PACE Act* 1984, s.78 (§ 15–401 in the main work), and the common law requirement to direct the jury on the burden of proof and as to the dangers of relying on a hearsay statement, are strong safeguards designed to ensure fairness.

Dealing with the two particular cases before it, the Grand Chamber held: (i) *Al-Khawaja* was a case that concerned the decisive statement of a witness who had died before trial, where there was strong corroborating evidence and where it would have been clear to the jury from the judge's direction that the statement should carry less weight; and there were sufficient counterbalancing factors to conclude that the admission of the statement did not result in a breach of Article 6; (ii) in *Tahery*, however, where the sole (if not decisive) statement of a witness to a stabbing who was in genuine fear of giving evidence had been admitted, and where there was only weak corroborating evidence, neither the fact that the defendant was in a position to challenge or rebut the statement by giving evidence himself or calling other witnesses who were present, nor the judicial warning to the jury to approach the statement with care, were, taken alone or in combination, sufficient counterbalance to the handicap under which the defence laboured, resulting in a violation of Article 6; a judicial warning, however clearly or forcibly expressed, cannot be a sufficient counterbalance where an untested statement of an eyewitness is the only direct evidence against the applicant; the jury were unable to conduct a fair and proper assessment of the absent witness.

★   In *R. v. Ibrahim* [2012] L.S. Gazette, May 24, 20, CA ([2012] EWCA Crim. 837), it was said that while there may be differences in approach to the admissibility of untested hearsay as between the Supreme Court and the Grand Chamber, these differences may be more of form than of substance; and that the combined effect of the decisions is that, first, there must be proper justification for admitting the evidence, which, under English law, depends on whether the conditions in the *CJA* 2003, s.116 (cases where a witness is unavailable (§ 11–15 in the main work)), are satisfied; secondly, there must be an inquiry as to whether that evidence can be shown to be reliable; it is therefore a pre-condition that untested hearsay is shown to be potentially safely reliable before it can be admitted; that is a matter for the judge to rule on, either at the admission stage or after the close of the prosecution case, pursuant to section 125 (stopping the case where evidence is unconvincing (§ 11–45 in the main work)); thirdly, there must be "counterbalancing measures", including all the statutory safeguards in the 2003 Act and any common law safeguards (*e.g.* proper directions in the summing-up). Ultimately, the court said, this all amounts to a single test, *viz.* whether or not the defendant has had a fair trial; when applying this test, it is important to assess the importance of the untested hearsay; the more central this is, the greater the need to ensure that there is proper justification for its admission, and the greater the need to ensure that it is reliable, and to ensure that there are adequate "counterbalancing measures" that have been properly applied; furthermore, if an untested hearsay statement is not shown to be reliable, and if it is a statement that is part of the "central corpus of evidence without which the case could not proceed" (*per* Professor J.R. Spencer Q.C. at [2012] 1 *Archbold Review* 5), the statement is almost bound to be "unconvincing" for the purposes of section 125(1)(b).

Section 114(1)(d)—admissibility as being "in the interests of justice"

11–3e   *R. v. Burton* is now reported at 175 J.P. 385.

R. v. Z. (see the main work) was applied in *R. v. Tindle*, 175 J.P. 462, CA. Where the complainant (the defendant's former partner) withdrew her allegation of assault because she was concerned about the effect of a possible custodial sentence on the defendant's children, where the prosecution applied to adduce her 999 call and witness statements as hearsay, and where the judge found that the condition under section 116(2)(d) of the *CJA* 2003 (absent witnesses (§ 11–15 in the main work)) was not met because the prosecution's attempts to locate the complainant had fallen well short of what was reasonable, it was held that the admission of the evidence under section 114(1)(d) (*ibid.*, § 11–3) circumvented the conditions laid down by Parliament in section 116; consideration of the important factor set out in section 114(2)(g) (court must have regard to whether oral evidence of the matter stated can be given and, if not, why not) should have led to the response that the oral evidence of the complainant could have been given, and, if it was unavailable, that was through the failure of the prosecution to take reasonable steps to secure her attendance; considering section 114(2)(c) (importance of the evidence in the context of the case as a whole), as the judge should have done, the evidence was virtually the entirety of the prosecution case; and only in rare circumstances, if any, could it be right to allow evidence of this importance to be adduced when there has been a failure to take reasonable steps to secure the attendance of the witness.

(3) Principal categories of admissibility

(a) *Absent witnesses*

Criminal Justice Act 2003, s.116

Cases where a witness is unavailable

★**11–15**   As to the combined effect of the decisions of the Supreme Court in *R. v. Horncastle; R. v.*

Marquis; *R. v. Carter* (§ 11–3a in the main work) and of the Grand Chamber of the European Court of Human Rights in *Al-Khawaja v. U.K.* (*ante*, § 11–3a), see *R. v. Ibrahim*, *ante*, § 11–3a.

Witness cannot be found (s.116(2)(d))

See *R. v. Tindle*, *ante*, § 11–3e.   11–21

Witness in fear (s.116(2)(e))

See *Al-Khawaja v. U.K.*, *ante*, § 11–3a.   11–22

The "interests of justice" (s.116(4))

For the Grand Chamber decision in *Al-Khawaja v. U.K.*, see *ante*, § 11–3a.   11–25

(d) *Previous statements of witnesses*

Criminal Justice Act 2003, ss.119, 120

Other prior statements (s.120)

Cross-examination on memory-refreshing documents (s.120(3))

In *R. v. Chinn* [2012] 2 Cr.App.R. 4, CA, it was said: (i) the word "which" in paragraphs ★**11–37**
(a) to (c) of section 120(3) of the 2003 Act refers to the document as a whole; but the words that follow paragraph (c) ("is admissible as evidence of any matter stated of which oral evidence by him would be admissible") refer only to the statement that has been made by the witness in the document; the document as a whole will not therefore be admissible as evidence of any matter stated in it under section 120(3); (ii) where a previous written statement is provided to a witness with a view to refreshing the witness's memory, but it fails to do so, section 120(3) cannot apply to make admissible as truth of the matters stated any or all of the statements made in the document; such a situation may, however, come within section 120(4); (iii) those parts of the statement that identify or describe a person, object or place will be admissible under section 120(5); and so will those parts that put the description or identification in the relevant context for the purpose of the proceedings; (iv) section 120(6) is not necessarily limited to "routine" matters; (v) where subsection (6) might apply, once the witness has said that the statement has failed to refresh his memory, counsel for the defence should be asked whether he objects to the witness statement (or identified parts of it) being adduced as evidence of the relevant matter stated in it; if objection is taken, then, in the absence of the jury, the witness should be examined on both the alleged failure of memory and the professed reasons for it; at this stage, any further arguments about excluding the evidence on grounds based on section 78 of the *PACE Act* 1984 (§ 15–401 in the main work) should also be addressed; the judge should then, in the absence of the jury, rule on those matters; if he accepts the submission that the witness statement (or a relevant part of it) should be adduced, it should be adduced in the presence of the jury as evidence of the matters stated, as if those matters had been adduced directly in oral evidence; when the judge sums up, he should explain shortly why the jury can consider the written material; no reference to hearsay or the 2003 Act will be necessary; the judge should, of course, also direct the jury to consider the reliability of the witness's earlier recollection of the subject matter of the statement that has been admitted and emphasise that it is for the jury to decide on the weight that they attribute to the evidence in the statement. For critical consideration of this decision, see CLW/12/13/2.

Statements identifying/ describing person, object or place (s.120(4), (5))
See *R. v. Chinn*, *ante*, § 11–37.   ★**11–38**

Witness who cannot reasonably be expected to remember events (s.120(4), (6))

★**11–39**   See *R. v. Chinn, ante,* § 11–37.

Recent complaint (s.120(4), (7) and (8))

11–40   Where recent complaint evidence is admitted under section 120(4) and (7) of the 2003 Act (§ 11–34 in the main work), the jury should be directed that such a previous consistent statement is, if they accept it was given or made and the conditions specified in section 120 are fulfilled, evidence of the truth of what was stated, but that, in deciding what weight it should bear, they should have in mind the fact that it is not evidence from a source independent of the complainant: *R. v. A. (Ashraf),* 175 J.P. 437, CA (considering *R. v. Islam* §§ 4–481, 8–210 in the main work).

★   *R. v. Islam* and *R. v. A. (Ashraf), ante,* were considered in *R. v. H.* [2012] 1 Cr.App.R. 30, CA. It was held that the lack of a direction as to the non-independence of the evidence of the mother of the complainants about the complaint that they had made to her did not render the appellant's convictions unsafe where it was clear from the judge's summing up that what mattered for the purpose of proving the case was the complainants' oral evidence, and where it was obvious that the mother's evidence of the complaint was not independent of the complainants.

(4) Supplementary

(e) *Stopping the case where evidence unconvincing*

Criminal Justice Act 2003, s.125

Stopping the case where evidence is unconvincing

★**11–45**   As to the need for an inquiry into the reliability of untested hearsay evidence either at the admission stage or after the close of the prosecution case, pursuant to section 125 of the 2003 Act (see the main work), see *R. v. Ibrahim, ante,* § 11–3a.

(5) Rules of court

Rules of court

★**11–51**   As to whether the failure of defence solicitors either to serve a notice objecting to hearsay evidence being admitted under Part 34 of the *Criminal Procedure Rules* 2011 (S.I. 2011 No. 1709) (§§ 11–52 *et seq.* in the main work) or to withdraw from the case (if the defendant refused to authorise them to serve one) amounted to "improper, unreasonable or negligent" conduct, so as to justify a wasted costs order being made against them, see *R. v. S.V.S. Solicitors, ante,* § 6–43.

C. BANKERS' BOOKS EVIDENCE ACT 1879

(3) Proof that book is a banker's book; verification of copy

Bankers' Books Evidence Act 1879, ss.4, 5

★**11–62**   As to the commencement of section 332 of, and Part 4 of Schedule 37 to, the 2003 Act (see the main work), see *ante,* § 10–9.

III. COMMON LAW

(7) Admissions by agents

★**11–85**   *R. (Firth) v. Epping Magistrates' Court* (see the main work) was considered in *R. v. Newell, ante,* § 4–124.

CHAPTER 12

PRIVILEGE, PUBLIC INTEREST IMMUNITY AND DISCLOSURE

I. PRIVILEGE

B. ANSWERS WHICH MAY INCRIMINATE A WITNESS

Taking and assessing the objection

The decision of the High Court in *Phillips v. Newsgroup Newspapers Ltd* has been upheld **12–5** by the Court of Appeal: see *Coogan v. News Group Newspapers Ltd; Phillips v. Same* [2012] 2 W.L.R. 848, CA (Civ. Div.). The point for which the decision of the High Court is cited in the main work was not in issue on the appeal.

C. LEGAL PROFESSIONAL PRIVILEGE

(1) The nature of legal professional privilege

If a communication or document qualifies for legal professional privilege, the privilege is **12–7** absolute and cannot be overridden by some supposedly greater public interest. It can be waived by the person entitled to it and can be overridden by statute but it is otherwise absolute. There is no balancing exercise that has to be carried out. Given the strength of that principle, it was hard, if not impossible, to envisage any circumstances where legal professional privilege could properly be directly overridden by an order of a court made in the exercise of its case management powers. However, since privilege has to be claimed, and since the onus is on the person claiming it to make good the claim, the possibility exists that, without waiving privilege, a person may nevertheless indirectly forfeit the right to claim it (if, for example, having been given every opportunity to do so within a reasonable period, he fails to do so). Similarly, a potentially valid claim may fail because it is not made with sufficient particularity, or because the evidence to support it is not available. Nevertheless, a court should be wary of allowing a potentially valid claim to privilege, however late it is made, to be indirectly overridden by exercise of a case management power. Otherwise, there is a danger of a litigant's substantive right to legal privilege being forced to yield, indirectly, to just the kind of balancing exercise that the highest authority (*viz. Three Rivers D.C. v. Governor and Company of the Bank of England (No. 6)* (see the main work)) says is impermissible: *J.S.C. B.T.A. Bank v. Shalabayev* [2011] L.S. Gazette, December 1, 19, Ch D (Henderson J.) ([2011] EWHC 2915 (Ch.)).

Legal advice privilege

Akzo Nobel Chemicals Ltd v. European Commission is now reported at [2011] 2 A.C. 338, *sub* **12–12** *nom. Akzo Nobel Chemicals Ltd (supported by Council of the Bars and Law Societies of the European Union, interveners) v. Commission of the European Communities.*

For legal advice privilege to be established the person claiming privilege must have the relationship of client to the lawyer concerned. Where a person was claiming joint privilege with another, it was necessary to distinguish between advice being given to an individual as a client and advice which is being given to another, but in which the first individual is interested because it impacts on his personal position. Only the former would support a claim for joint privilege. For joint privilege to arise it was necessary for the facts to demonstrate that all those sharing the privilege and the lawyers concerned knew, or ought to have known, that they enjoyed legal professional privilege with the others. Where there was no joint retainer, the individual claiming joint privilege would need to show that he communicated with the lawyer for the purpose of seeking advice in an individual capacity; that he made clear to the lawyer that he was seeking legal advice in that capacity, rather than as a representative of a corporate body; that those with whom the joint privilege was claimed knew or ought to have appreciated the legal position; that the lawyer knew or ought to have appreciated that he was communicating with the individual in that individual capacity; and, that the communication with the lawyer was confidential: *R. (Ford) v. Financial Services Authority (Johnson, interested parties)* [2012] 1 All E.R. 1238, QBD (Burnett J.).

★   Legal professional privilege did not extend to advice received from a person who was in fact a barrister or solicitor but who was not employed as such by the firm of claims consultants for whom he worked and where that firm did not hold itself out as a firm of solicitors or group of barristers, albeit that it employed some lawyers. The firm had not been retained as barristers or solicitors but as an organisation to provide claims and project handling advice. The protection of privilege was not intended to extend to the relationship between a person and another who is not in fact a qualified and practising lawyer, save in exceptional circumstances, and the fact that the person receiving the advice honestly understood that he was dealing with a qualified and practising barrister or solicitor was immaterial because the employer of the person giving the advice had not been retained to provide the services of barristers or solicitors: *Walter Lilly & Co. Ltd v. Mackay* [2012] L.S. Gazette, May 17, 25, QBD (Akenhead J.) ([2012] EWHC 649 (TCC)).

(3) Duration and waiver of privilege

Waiver

12–17   Where, in care proceedings, a mother had initially stated that injuries to a child had been occasioned accidentally by the father, and where she had subsequently given a different account stating that the injuries had been deliberately caused by him, and had sought to explain the change in account through a change of mind that had evolved through a number of conferences with her legal representatives, she was held to have waived privilege. The waiver was made through the words of her witness statement, and the effect of those words, objectively construed, prevailed notwithstanding the fact that they were drafted by a solicitor and that neither she nor her advisers appreciated the consequences. It would be unfair to allow her not to reveal all that passed between her and her lawyers between the times of the two statements, for to do so would be to risk the court and the other party having a partial and potentially misleading understanding of the material: *Re D. (a child)* [2011] 4 All E.R. 434, CA (Civ. Div.).

II. PUBLIC INTEREST IMMUNITY

B. Categories of Public Interest Immunity

Categories listed in the code of practice

★**12–34**   Where assurances are given to registered informants, to others or to the public in general (as in the case of a hotline) that their identity will be protected, those assurances should not be reneged on by the state without a judicial decision where the interests of the informant, the Crown, the defendant and the public interest can be carefully and impartially considered; the ordinary principle applicable to decisions by prosecutors is not applicable where the CPS seek to disclose the identity of a police informant who objects to that course; the disclosure of the identity of an informant without his consent is one of those cases where the prosecution have to apply to the court and the court has to consider carefully the issue and reach its own decision: *R. (W.V.) v. CPS* [2012] Crim.L.R. 456, DC. As to this case, see also *post*, § 12–54a.

III. DISCLOSURE

A. PRELIMINARY

Material produced by the police in the course of an investigation

R. v. Malook is now reported at [2012] 1 W.L.R. 633, *sub nom. R. v. Malook (Sadakat)* (*Practice Note*).   ★**12–50a**

B. LEGISLATION

(1) Criminal Procedure and Investigations Act 1996

Criminal Procedure and Investigations Act 1996, ss.1, 2

Application of this Part

With effect from June 18, 2012 (*Criminal Justice Act 2003 (Commencement No. 28 and Saving Provisions) Order* 2012 (S.I. 2012 No. 1320)), section 41 of, and paragraph 66(1) and (2) of Schedule 3 to, the 2003 Act are brought into force in certain areas (as to which, see *ante*, § 1–88), to the extent that they are not already in force. There are associated saving provisions, as to which, see article 5 of the order (*ante*, § 1–88).   ★**12–52**

Criminal Procedure and Investigations Act 1996, ss.3, 4

Initial duty of prosecutor to disclose

There is a potential conflict between the obligation of a prosecutor seeking to discharge his duty under section 3 of the 1996 Act, and not to risk a conviction being set aside for non-disclosure, and the need to uphold an agreement that an informant's identity should be kept confidential, the public interest in the flow of information from informers, and the rights of the informer under Article 2 of the ECHR (see § 16–36 in the main work); the duty to disclose under section 3(1) is expressly subject to section 3(6), and the disclosure of the identity of an informant without his consent is one of those cases where the prosecution must apply to the court and the court must consider carefully the issues and reach its own decision, taking account of the relevant interests by reference to the facts and issues in the case before the court and balancing the interests and risks: *R. (W.V.) v. CPS* [2012] Crim.L.R. 456, DC. As to this case, see also *ante*, § 12–34.   ★**12–54a**

Criminal Procedure and Investigations Act 1996, ss.5, 6

Compulsory disclosure by accused

With effect from June 18, 2012 (*Criminal Justice Act 2003 (Commencement No. 28 and Saving Provisions) Order* 2012 (S.I. 2012 No. 1320)), section 41 of, and paragraph 66(1) and (3) of Schedule 3 to, the 2003 Act are brought into force in certain areas (as to which, see *ante*, § 1–88), to the extent that they are not already in force. There are associated saving provisions, as to which, see article 5 of the order (*ante*, § 1–88).   ★**12–56**

Criminal Procedure and Investigations Act 1996, ss.10, 11

Prosecutor's failure to observe time limits

See *R. v. M.O.*, *ante*, § 4–78.   **12–61**

Criminal Procedure and Investigations Act 1996, ss.12, 13

Time limits: transitional

With effect from June 18, 2012 (*Criminal Justice Act 2003 (Commencement No. 28 and Sav-*   ★**12–64**

ing Provisions) Order 2012 (S.I. 2012 No. 1320)), the amendment (by the *CJA* 2003, s.41, and Sched. 3, para. 66) of the modified section 3(8) of the 1996 Act (as set out in section 13 of the 1996 Act) comes into force in certain areas (as to which, see *ante*, § 1–88), but not to the extent that it omits paragraph (a). There are associated saving provisions, as to which, see article 5 of the order (*ante*, § 1–88).

Criminal Procedure and Investigations Act 1996, ss.17, 18

Confidentiality: contravention

★**12–69**   As to the removal (as from a day to be appointed) of £5,000 as the upper limit on a fine on summary conviction (see s.18(3)(a) of the 1996 Act), see the *Legal Aid, Sentencing and Punishment of Offenders Act* 2012, s.85(1) (*ante*, § 1–125).

Criminal Procedure and Investigations Act 1996, ss.19-21

Common law rules as to disclosure

★**12–71**   With effect from June 18, 2012 (*Criminal Justice Act 2003 (Commencement No. 28 and Saving Provisions) Order* 2012 (S.I. 2012 No. 1320)), the amendment (by the *CJA* 2003, s.41, and Sched. 3, para. 66) of section 21 of the 1996 Act comes into force in certain areas (as to which, see *ante*, § 1–88). There are associated saving provisions, as to which, see article 5 of the order (*ante*, § 1–88).

(2) Rules and regulations

Criminal Procedure Rules 2011 (S.I. 2011 No. 1709), rr.22.1, 22.2, 22.3

12–85   *McKeown v. U.K.* is now reported at (2012) 54 E.H.R.R. 7.

(4) Sexual offences

Sexual Offences (Protected Material) Act 1997

Introductory

[Meaning of "protected material"

12–102   **1.**—(1) In this Act "protected material", in relation to proceedings for a sexual offence, means a copy (in whatever form) of any of the following material, namely—
(a) a statement relating to that or any other sexual offence made by any victim of the offence (whether the statement is recorded in writing or in any other form),
(b) a photograph or pseudo-photograph of any such victim, or
(c) a report of a medical examination of the physical condition of any such victim,
which is a copy given by the prosecutor to any person under this Act.
(2) For the purposes of subsection (1) a person is, in relation to any proceedings for a sexual offence, a victim of that offence if—
(a) the charge, summons or indictment by which the proceedings are instituted names that person as a person in relation to whom that offence was committed; or
(b) that offence can, in the prosecutor's opinion, be reasonably regarded as having been committed in relation to that person;
and a person is, in relation to any such proceedings, a victim of any other sexual offence if that offence can, in the prosecutor's opinion, be reasonably regarded as having been committed in relation to that person.
(3) In this Act, where the context so permits (and subject to subsection (4))—
(a) references to any protected material include references to any part of any such material; and
(b) references to a copy of any such material include references to any part of any such copy.

(4) Nothing in this Act—
   (a) so far as it refers to a defendant making any copy of—
      (i) any protected material, or
      (ii) a copy of any such material,
   applies to a manuscript copy which is not a verbatim copy of the whole of that material or copy; or
   (b) so far as it refers to a defendant having in his possession any copy of any protected material, applies to a manuscript copy made by him which is not a verbatim copy of the whole of that material.]

[Meaning of other expressions

12–103

2.—(1) In this Act—
   "contracted out prison" means a contracted out prison within the meaning of Part IV of the *Criminal Justice Act* 1991;
   "defendant", in relation to any proceedings for a sexual offence, means any person charged with that offence (whether or not he has been convicted);
   "governor", in relation to a contracted out prison, means the director of the prison;
   "inform" means inform in writing;
   "legal representative", in relation to a defendant, means a person who, for the purposes of the *Legal Services Act* 2007, is an authorised person in relation to an activity which constitutes the exercise of a right of audience or the conduct of litigation (within the meaning of that Act) and who is acting for the defendant in connection with any proceedings for the sexual offence in question;
   "photograph" and "pseudo-photograph" shall be construed in accordance with section 7(4) and (7) of the *Protection of Children Act* 1978;
   "prison" means any prison, young offender institution or remand centre which is under the general superintendence of, or is provided by, the Secretary of State under the *Prison Act* 1952, including a contracted out prison;
   "proceedings" means (subject to subsection (2)) criminal proceedings;
   "the prosecutor", in relation to any proceedings for a sexual offence, means any person acting as prosecutor (whether an individual or a body);
   "relevant proceedings", in relation to any material which has been disclosed by the prosecutor under this Act, means any proceedings for the purposes of which it has been so disclosed or any further proceedings for the sexual offence in question;
   "sexual offence" means one of the offences listed in the Schedule to this Act.
  (2) For the purposes of this Act references to proceedings for a sexual offence include references to—
   (a) any appeal or application for leave to appeal brought or made by or in relation to a defendant in such proceedings;
   (b) any application made to the Criminal Cases Review Commission for the reference under section 9 or 11 of the *Criminal Appeal Act* 1995 of any conviction, verdict, finding or sentence recorded or imposed in relation to any such defendant; and
   (c) any petition to the Secretary of State requesting him to recommend the exercise of Her Majesty's prerogative of mercy in relation to any such defendant.
  (3) In this Act, in the context of the prosecutor giving a copy of any material to any person—
   (a) references to the prosecutor include references to a person acting on behalf of the prosecutor; and
   (b) where any such copy falls to be given to the defendant's legal representative, references to the defendant's legal representative include references to a person acting on behalf of the defendant's legal representative.]

[The definition of "legal representative" is printed as amended by the *Legal Services Act* 2007, s.208(1), and Sched 21, para. 123.]

Regulation of disclosures to defendant

[Regulation of disclosures by prosecutor

3.—(1) Where, in connection with any proceedings for a sexual offence, any statement or other **12–104** material falling within any of paragraphs (a) to (c) of section 1(1) would (apart from this section) fall to be disclosed by the prosecutor to the defendant—

    (a) the prosecutor shall not disclose that material to the defendant; and

    (b) it shall instead be disclosed under this Act in accordance with whichever of subsections (2) and (3) below is applicable.

  (2) If—

    (a) the defendant has a legal representative, and

    (b) the defendant's legal representative gives the prosecutor the undertaking required by section 4 (disclosure to defendant's legal representative),

the prosecutor shall disclose the material in question by giving a copy of it to the defendant's legal representative.

  (3) If subsection (2) is not applicable, the prosecutor shall disclose the material in question by giving a copy of it to the appropriate person for the purposes of section 5 (disclosure to unrepresented defendant) in order for that person to show that copy to the defendant under that section.

  (4) Where under this Act a copy of any material falls to be given to any person by the prosecutor, any such copy—

    (a) may be in such form as the prosecutor thinks fit, and

    (b) where the material consists of information which has been recorded in any form, need not be in the same form as that in which the information has already been recorded.

  (5) Once a copy of any material is given to any person under this Act by the prosecutor, the copy shall (in accordance with section 1(1)) be protected material for the purposes of this Act.]

[Disclosure to defendant's legal representative

12–105   **4.**—(1) For the purposes of this Act the undertaking which a defendant's legal representative is required to give in relation to any protected material given to him under this Act is an undertaking by him to discharge the obligations set out in subsections (2) to (7).

  (2) He must take reasonable steps to ensure—

    (a) that the protected material, or any copy of it, is only shown to the defendant in circumstances where it is possible to exercise adequate supervision to prevent the defendant retaining possession of the material or copy or making a copy of it, and

    (b) that the protected material is not shown and no copy of it is given, and its contents are not otherwise revealed, to any person other than the defendant, except so far as it appears to him necessary to show the material or give a copy of it to any such person—

      (i) in connection with any relevant proceedings, or

      (ii) for the purposes of any assessment or treatment of the defendant (whether before or after conviction).

  (3) He must inform the defendant—

    (a) that the protected material is such material for the purposes of this Act,

    (b) that the defendant can only inspect that material, or any copy of it, in circumstances such as are described in subsection (2)(a), and

    (c) that it would be an offence for the defendant—

      (i) to have that material, or any copy of it, in his possession otherwise than while inspecting it or the copy in such circumstances, or

      (ii) to give that material or any copy of it, or otherwise reveal its contents, to any other person.

  (4) He must, where the protected material or a copy of it has been shown or given in accordance with subsection (2)(b)(i) or (ii) to a person other than the defendant, inform that person—

    (a) that that person must not give any copy of that material, or otherwise reveal its contents—

      (i) to any other person other than the defendant, or

      (ii) to the defendant otherwise than in circumstances such as are described in subsection (2)(a); and

    (b) that it would be an offence for that person to do so.

  (5) He must, where he ceases to act as the defendant's legal representative at a time when any relevant proceedings are current or in contemplation—

    (a) inform the prosecutor of that fact, and

    (b) if he is informed by the prosecutor that the defendant has a new legal representative who has given the prosecutor the undertaking required by this section, give the protected material, and any copies of it in his possession, to the defendant's new legal representative.

  (6) He must, at the time of giving the protected material to the new legal representative under subsection (5), inform that person—

    (a) that that material is protected material for the purposes of this Act, and

    (b) of the extent to which—
        (i) that material has been shown by him, and
        (ii) any copies of it have been given by him,
      to any other person (including the defendant).

    (7) He must keep a record of every occasion on which the protected material was shown, or a copy of it was given, as mentioned in subsection (6)(b).]

[Disclosure to unrepresented defendant

    5.—(1) This section applies where, in accordance with section 3(3), a copy of any material falls   **12–106** to be given by the prosecutor to the appropriate person for the purposes of this section in order for that person to show that copy to the defendant under this section.

    (2) Subject to subsection (3), the appropriate person in such a case is—
      (a) if the defendant is detained in a prison, the governor of the prison or any person nominated by the governor for the purposes of this section; and
      (b) otherwise the officer in charge of such police station as appears to the prosecutor to be suitable for enabling the defendant to have access to the material in accordance with this section or any person nominated by that officer for the purposes of this section.

    (3) The Secretary of State may by regulations provide that, in such circumstances as are specified in the regulations, the appropriate person for the purposes of this section shall be a person of any description so specified.

    (4) The appropriate person shall take reasonable steps to ensure—
      (a) that the protected material, or any copy of it, is only shown to the defendant in circumstances where it is possible to exercise adequate supervision to prevent the defendant retaining possession of the material or copy or making a copy of it,
      (b) that, subject to paragraph (a), the defendant is given such access to that material, or a copy of it, as he reasonably requires in connection with any relevant proceedings, and
      (c) that that material is not shown and no copy of it is given, and its contents are not otherwise revealed, to any person other than the defendant.

    (5) The prosecutor shall, at the time of giving the protected material to the appropriate person, inform him—
      (a) that that material is protected material for the purposes of this Act, and
      (b) that he is required to discharge the obligations set out in subsection (4) in relation to that material.

    (6) The prosecutor shall at that time also inform the defendant—
      (a) that that material is protected material for the purposes of this Act,
      (b) that the defendant can only inspect that material, or any copy of it, in circumstances such as are described in subsection (4)(a), and
      (c) that it would be an offence for the defendant—
        (i) to have that material, or any copy of it, in his possession otherwise than while inspecting it or the copy in such circumstances, or
        (ii) to give that material or any copy of it, or otherwise reveal its contents, to any other person,
as well as informing him of the effect of subsection (7).

    (7) If—
      (a) the defendant requests the prosecutor in writing to give a further copy of the material mentioned in subsection (1) to some other person, and
      (b) it appears to the prosecutor to be necessary to do so—
        (i) in connection with any relevant proceedings, or
        (ii) for the purposes of any assessment or treatment of the defendant (whether before or after conviction),
the prosecutor shall give such a copy to that other person.

    (8) The prosecutor may give such a copy to some other person where no request has been made under subsection (7) but it appears to him that in the interests of the defendant it is necessary to do so as mentioned in paragraph (b) of that subsection.

    (9) The prosecutor shall, at the time of giving such a copy to a person under subsection (7) or (8), inform that person—
      (a) that the copy is protected material for the purposes of this Act,
      (b) that he must not give any copy of the protected material or otherwise reveal its contents—
        (i) to any person other than the defendant, or

(ii) to the defendant otherwise than in circumstances such as are described in subsection (4)(a); and

(c) that it would be an offence for him to do so.

(10) If the prosecutor—

(a) receives a request from the defendant under subsection (7) to give a further copy of the material in question to another person, but

(b) does not consider it to be necessary to do so as mentioned in paragraph (b) of that subsection and accordingly refuses the request,

he shall inform the defendant of his refusal.

(11) [*Making of regulations under subs. (3).*]]

[Further disclosures by prosecutor

12–107   **6.**—(1) Where—

(a) any material has been disclosed in accordance with section 3(2) to the defendant's legal representative, and

(b) at a time when any relevant proceedings are current or in contemplation the legal representative either—

(i) ceases to act as the defendant's legal representative in circumstances where section 4(5)(b) does not apply, or

(ii) dies or becomes incapacitated,

that material shall be further disclosed under this Act in accordance with whichever of section 3(2) or (3) is for the time being applicable.

(2) Where—

(a) any material has been disclosed in accordance with section 3(3), and

(b) at a time when any relevant proceedings are current or in contemplation the defendant acquires a legal representative who gives the prosecutor the undertaking required by section 4,

that material shall be further disclosed under this Act, in accordance with section 3(2), to the defendant's legal representative.]

12–108   [**7.** [*Regulation of disclosures by Criminal Cases Review Commission.*]]

Supplementary

[Offences

12–109   **8.**—(1) Where any material has been disclosed under this Act in connection with any proceedings for a sexual offence, it is an offence for the defendant—

(a) to have the protected material, or any copy of it, in his possession otherwise than while inspecting it or the copy in circumstances such as are described in section 4(2)(a) or 5(4)(a), or

(b) to give that material or any copy of it, or otherwise reveal its contents, to any other person.

(2) Where any protected material, or any copy of any such material, has been shown or given to any person in accordance with section 4(2)(b)(i) or (ii) or section 5(7) or (8), it is an offence for that person to give any copy of that material or otherwise reveal its contents—

(a) to any person other than the defendant, or

(b) to the defendant otherwise than in circumstances such as are described in section 4(2)(a) or 5(4)(a).

(3) Subsections (1) and (2) apply whether or not any relevant proceedings are current or in contemplation (and references to the defendant shall be construed accordingly).

(4) A person guilty of an offence under this section is liable—

(a) on summary conviction, to imprisonment for a term not exceeding *six* [12] months or a fine not exceeding the statutory maximum or both;

(b) on conviction on indictment, to imprisonment for a term not exceeding two years or a fine or both.

(5) Where a person is charged with an offence under this section relating to any protected material or copy of any such material, it is a defence to prove that, at the time of the alleged offence, he was not aware, and neither suspected nor had reason to suspect, that the material or copy in question was protected material or (as the case may be) a copy of any such material.

(6) The court before which a person is tried for an offence under this section may (whether or not he is convicted of that offence) make an order requiring him to return any protected material, or any copy of any such material, in his possession to the prosecutor.

(7) Nothing in subsection (1) or (2) shall be taken to apply to—

(a) any disclosure made in the course of any proceedings before a court or in any report of any such proceedings, or

(b) any disclosure made or copy given by a person when returning any protected material, or a copy of any such material, to the prosecutor or the defendant's legal representative;

and accordingly nothing in section 4, or 5 shall be read as precluding the making of any disclosure or the giving of any copy in circumstances falling within paragraph (a) or (as the case may be) paragraph (b) above.]

[In subs. (4)(a), "12" is substituted for "six", as from a day to be appointed, by the *CJA* 2003, s.282(2) and (3). The increase has no application to offences committed before the substitution takes effect: s.282(4).]

[Modification and amendment of other enactments **12–110**

9.—(1) [*Modifies ss.5B to 5D of the* Magistrates' Courts Act *1980, §§ 10–16* et seq. *in the main work; and repealed, as from a day to be appointed, by the* CJA *2003, s.332, and Sched. 37, Pt 4.*]

(2) Despite section 20(1) of the *Criminal Procedure and Investigations Act* 1996 (disclosure provisions of the Act not affected by other statutory duties), section 3(3) to (5) of that Act (manner of disclosure) shall not apply in relation to any disclosure required by section 3, 7 or 9 of that Act if section 3(1) above applies in relation to that disclosure.

(3) [*See ss.17 and 18 of the* Criminal Procedure and Investigations Act *1996, §§ 12–68* et seq. *in the main work*]

(4) [*Inserts subs. 1(6) into the* Criminal Procedure and Investigations Act *1996, § 12–52 in the main work.*]]

[The repeal of subs. (1) came into force on June 18, 2012 (*Criminal Justice Act 2003 (Commencement No. 28 and Saving Provisions) Order* 2012 (S.I. 2012 No. 1320)), in certain areas (as to which, see *ante*, § 1–88).]

[10. [*Financial provision.*]] **12–111**

[Short title, commencement and extent **12–112**

11.—(1) [*Short title.*]

(2) This Act shall come into force on such day as the Secretary of State may appoint by order made by statutory instrument.

(3) Nothing in this Act applies to any proceedings for a sexual offence where the defendant was charged with the offence before the commencement of this Act.

(4) This Act extends to England and Wales only.]

[Section 2   SCHEDULE

SEXUAL OFFENCES FOR PURPOSES OF THIS ACT

5. Any offence under section 1 of the *Protection of Children Act* 1978 or section 160 of the *Criminal* **12–113** *Justice Act* 1988 (indecent photographs of children).

5A. Any offence under any provision of Part 1 of the *Sexual Offences Act* 2003 except section 64, 65, 69 or 71.

6. Any offence under section 1 of the *Criminal Law Act* 1977 of conspiracy to commit any of the offences mentioned in paragraphs 5 and 5A.

7. Any offence under section 1 of the *Criminal Attempts Act* 1981 of attempting to commit any of those offences.

8. Any offence of inciting another to commit any of those offences.]

[This schedule is printed as amended, and repealed in part, by the *SOA* 2003, ss.139 and 140, and Scheds 6, para. 36, and 7. The reference in para. 8 to inciting another to commit an offence has effect as a reference to the offences under Part 2 of the *SCA* 2007: 2007 Act, s.63(1), and Sched. 6, para. 34.]

CHAPTER 13

EVIDENCE OF BAD CHARACTER

I. INTRODUCTION

C. INTERPRETATION

Criminal Justice Act 2003, s.112

Interpretation of Chapter 1

★**13–8**   As to the definition of "important matter" in section 112(1) of the 2003 Act, see *R. v. Phillips (Paul Andrew), post,* § 13–70.

III. DEFENDANTS

A. ADMISSIBILITY

Criminal Justice Act 2003, ss.101, 108

Defendant's bad character

★**13–25**   As to "substantial probative value" in subsection (1)(e) of section 103 of the 2003 Act, see *R. v. Phillips (Paul Andrew), post,* § 13–70.

B. THE SEVEN GATEWAYS

(3) Important explanatory evidence (ss.101(1)(c), 102)

13–30   For an example of the admission of evidence of bad character to establish motive where, without the context thus provided, the suggestion that the defendant had murdered the deceased, as alleged, might have sounded implausible, see *Hudson v. R.* [2011] 3 N.Z.L.R. 289, Supreme Court of New Zealand ([2011] NZSC 51).

13–36   *R. v. D. (N.); R. v. P. (A.); R. v. U. (S.)* is now reported at [2012] 1 Cr.App.R. 8, *sub nom. R. v. D.; R. v. P.; R. v. U.*

★   *R. v. D.; R. v. P.; R. v. U.* was considered in *R. v. Lee (Peter Bruce),* 176 J.P. 231, CA. It was said that section 101(1)(c) of the *CJA* 2003 (§ 13–25 in the main work) must be read with section 102 (*ibid.,* § 13–29); to say that evidence fills out the picture is not the same as saying that the rest of the picture is either impossible or difficult to see without it; and the fact that the jury might wonder about a delay or time lag in reporting an incident is not a sufficient basis for the admission of bad character evidence via this gateway (as where a complainant says that an incident (not charged) many years after the alleged offences was what prompted her to go to the police). The court said that counsel and the judge must focus on the exact basis upon which bad character evidence is being admitted; a case which is truly one of propensity cannot and must not be dressed up as a case of important explanatory evidence; moreover, whatever the basis upon which evidence has been admitted, it is essential that the analysis of the evidence and use which can properly be made of it is considered before summing up; it sometimes happens that evidence that is admitted through one gateway becomes admissible on another basis, and the jury must have directions that focus on the use which they may properly make of such evidence.

262

(4) Important matter in issue between defendant and prosecution (ss.101(1)(d), 103)

(b) *Evidence that would have been admissible at common law*

Practical application

Accident, mistake, etc.

The common law has long accepted that evidence may be admitted at the behest of the ★**13–53** Crown to rebut a defence of mistake, accident or innocent association (considering *Makin v. Att.-Gen. for New South Wales*, and *DPP v. Boardman* (as to both of which, see § 13–40 in the main work)); and it is clear moreover that bad character evidence may be admitted under section 101(1)(d) of the *CJA* 2003 for a similar purpose: *R. v. Cambridge (Connor)* [2012] Crim.L.R. 373, CA. Where, therefore, the defendant's fingerprints were found on and in a plastic bag containing a firearm, where an incomplete DNA profile found on a swab taken from the gun matched the defendant's DNA, and where the defendant, claiming to know nothing about the gun, sought to explain this by saying that he was a frequent shopper at the shop from which the bag came, and he may have touched it whilst browsing there (with the DNA on the gun being a case of secondary transference), evidence of (i) his having been in possession of a pellet gun at the time of a fight between a large number of youths 30 months previously, and (ii) of his having been shot once in each leg at the top of the thigh six months previously, was correctly admitted; as a matter of logic and common sense, such evidence tended to rebut the defence of innocent association; the first incident showed a preparedness to at least carry a gun, and the second disclosed a possible motive for carrying one.

Allegation that prosecution witnesses mistaken or lying

R. v. D. (N.); R. v. P. (A.); R. v. U. (S.) is now reported at [2012] 1 Cr.App.R. 8, *sub nom.* **13–57** *R. v. D.; R. v. P.; R. v. U.*

Particular topics

Directing the jury

In any case where the evidence of complainants is treated as cross-admissible, the jury will **13–63a** need to exclude collusion or innocent contamination as an explanation for the similarity of the complaints before they can assess the force of the argument that they are unlikely to be the product of coincidence; save in an obvious case, in which the evidence has plainly excluded the risk of collusion and innocent contamination and no point is taken on behalf of the defendant, a direction to the jury will be required; if, however, the jury have been instructed that the evidence of each complainant must be judged separately, the occasion for a warning as to the risk of contamination will not, on that account, have arisen because the prosecution are not seeking to derive support for one allegation from the similarity of a separate complaint and the independence of the two complaints; but this is not to say that evidence of the circumstances may not reveal the real possibility of contamination; contamination (deliberate or innocent), if it has or may have occurred, may render unreliable the evidence of one or more complainants, whether or not the jury are invited to consider whether their evidence is mutually supportive; where such a real possibility is revealed by the development of the evidence at trial, there will be an obligation upon the trial judge to draw the jury's attention to the risk: *R. v. N. (H.)* [2012] Crim.L.R. 158, CA.

(c) *Propensity evidence*

Directing the jury

For further consideration of *R. v. Doncaster* (see the main work), and of the directions to ★**13–68** be given to the jury in the case of a defendant with no convictions or no relevant convictions, where non-conviction evidence of his bad character is adduced, see *R. v. D. (P.), ante*, § 4–484.

(5) Important matter in issue between defendant and co-defendant (ss.101(1)(e), 104))

★**13–70**   In *R. v. Phillips (Paul Andrew)* [2012] 1 Cr.App.R. 25, CA, it was held: (i) whereas section 101(1)(e) of the *CJA* 2003 provides "(1) In criminal proceedings evidence of the defendant's bad character is admissible if, but only if ... (e) it has substantial probative value in relation to an important matter in issue between the defendant and a co-defendant, ..." (§ 13–25 in the main work), and whereas section 112(1) defines "important matter" as "a matter of substantial importance in the context of the case as a whole ..." (*ibid.*, § 13–8), these provisions require separate consideration; as to the first, the term "substantial probative value" means that the evidence has an enhanced capability of proving or disproving a matter in issue; it is important that the threshold for admissibility is not understated, as the purpose of the requirement is to ensure so far as possible that the probative strength of the evidence removes the risk of unfair prejudice; and the issue upon which the bad character evidence must be substantially probative is an issue between the defendants; it is not the issue of whether the evidence itself is true, because that must be assumed (subject to clear cases) under section 109 (*ibid.*, § 13–104); nor will it be the question whether the co-accused has a propensity to commit similar offences, save to the extent that his having such a propensity may be probative of a matter in issue between them; the matter in issue will be a fact in issue between the defendants in the trial (such as, in this case, whether the appellant was an innocent dupe of the co-defendant); where the defendant is seeking to prove a relevant propensity, he must first establish that the evidence is substantially probative of the propensity (which it may not be if there is other evidence to the same effect) and, next, that the propensity is substantially probative of the fact in issue; as to the second, the judge is required to make an assessment of the importance of the issue between the defendants in the context of the case as a whole; an issue may be important as between the defendants and yet be of little importance in the context of the case as a whole; and (ii) once the statutory criteria for admission of bad character evidence against a co-accused are met, there is no discretion to exclude it on case management grounds or on account of unfair prejudice (but discretionary exclusion will be permissible if there has been a wilful refusal to comply with the notice requirements of the *Criminal Procedure Rules* 2011 (S.I. 2011 No. 1709) (*ibid.*, §§ 13–110 *et seq.*), and Article 6 of the ECHR (right to fair trial (*ibid.*, § 16–57)) requires it (considering *R. v. Musone* (*ibid.*, § 13–110a)); however, a judge is entitled to take steps to minimise the "satellite litigation" risk; first, by controlling the scope of the evidence, and the manner in which it is introduced; secondly, by imposing a timetable on its deployment; and, thirdly, by explaining to the jury the issues to which it is relevant and the need for a sequential approach ((a) is it true? (b) does it establish the propensity claimed? (c) does it assist in resolving the issue between the defendants? (d) does resolution of that issue assist with the ultimate issue?).

(6) Correcting a false impression (ss.101(1)(f), 105)

Criminal Justice Act 2003, s.105

Misleading impression about the defendant

13–74   *R. v. D. (N.); R. v. P. (A.); R. v. U. (S.)* is now reported at [2012] 1 Cr.App.R. 8, *sub nom. R. v. D.; R. v. P.; R. v. U.*

(7) Attack on another person's character (ss.101(1)(g), 106)

Directing the jury

13–101   In *R. v. Williams* [2011] L.S. Gazette, October 6, 19, CA it was held that where bad character evidence relating to the accused is admitted under section 101(1)(g) of the *CJA* 2003 (§ 13–25 in the main work), the judge must direct the jury that the issue to which such evidence goes is that of the defendant's credibility; and where there is a risk that the jury may use the evidence as propensity evidence, strong and clear directions are required as to the limited purpose for which the evidence has been put before them. Where, therefore, there had been a failure to direct the jury appropriately and a real possibility that the jury may have been inappropriately influenced by the evidence such that it could not be said that the error would have had no bearing on the outcome of the case, the conviction would be quashed as unsafe.

(8) Relationship between the seven gateways

R. v. D. (N.); R. v. P. (A.); R. v. U. (S.) is now reported at [2012] 1 Cr.App.R. 8, *sub nom.* **13–102** *R. v. D.; R. v. P.; R. v. U.*

As to the direction that must be given to the jury where evidence that is admitted through ★ one gateway becomes admissible on another basis, see *R. v. Lee (Peter Bruce), ante,* § 13–36.

IV. PROCEDURE

(5) Rules of court

Criminal Justice Act 2003, s.111

A judge should not question a witness as to the potential bad character of the defendant **13–110a** where there has been no application by the parties: *Barnard v. DPP* [2011] A.C.D. 108, DC ([2011] EWHC 1648 (Admin.)). As to this case, see also *ante,* § 2–184.

As to the discretion to exclude character evidence as between co-defendants where there ★ has been a wilful refusal to comply with the notice requirements of the *Criminal Procedure Rules* 2011 (S.I. 2011 No. 1709) (§§ 13–111 *et seq.* in the main work), and for consideration of *R. v. Musone* (see the main work), see *R. v. Phillips (Paul Andrew), ante,* § 13–70.

V. REHABILITATION OF OFFENDERS

(1) Introduction

As from November 30, 2011 the *Rehabilitation of Offenders Act 1974 (Exceptions) Order* **13–120** 1975 (S.I. 1975 No. 1023) (see the main work) was further amended so as to create a new exception to the general provisions in section 4(2) of, and Schedule 2, para. 3(3) to, the 1974 Act: *Rehabilitation of Offenders Act 1974 (Exceptions) (Amendment) (England and Wales) (No. 2) Order* 2011 (S.I. 2011 No. 2865).

(3) Statute

Rehabilitation of Offenders Act 1974, s.1

Rehabilitated persons and spent convictions

As from a day to be appointed, section 1 of the 1974 Act is amended by the *Legal Aid,* ★**13–123** *Sentencing and Punishment of Offenders Act* 2012, s.141(10), and Sched. 25, paras 1 and 2, so as to substitute "England and Wales" for "Great Britain" in subsection (4)(a). As to the application of this amendment, see section 141 of the 2012 Act (*post,* § 13–131a).

As from a day to be appointed, section 1 of the 1974 Act is further amended by the *Protection of Freedoms Act* 2012, s.115(1), and Sched. 9, para. 134, so as (i) to substitute "subsections (2), (5) and (6)" for "subsection (2)" in subsection (1), and (ii) to insert new subsections (5) and (6), as follows—

"(5) This Act does not apply to any disregarded conviction or caution within the meaning of Chapter 4 of Part 5 of the *Protection of Freedoms Act* 2012.

(6) Accordingly, references in this Act to a conviction or caution do not include references to any such disregarded conviction or caution.".

Rehabilitation of Offenders Act 1974, s.2

Rehabilitation of persons dealt with in service disciplinary proceedings

★**13–124**   As from a day to be appointed, section 2(5) of the 1974 Act is amended by the *Legal Aid, Sentencing and Punishment of Offenders Act* 2012, s.141(10), and Sched. 25, paras 1 and 3, so as to substitute "England and Wales" for "Great Britain". As to the application of this amendment, see section 141 of the 2012 Act (*post*, § 13–131a).

As from a day to be appointed, section 3 of the 1974 Act is repealed by the *Legal Aid, Sentencing and Punishment of Offenders Act* 2012, s.141(10), and Sched. 25, paras 1 and 4.

Rehabilitation of Offenders Act 1974, s.4

Effect of rehabilitation

★**13–125**   As from a day to be appointed, section 4(1)(a) of the 1974 Act is amended by the *Legal Aid, Sentencing and Punishment of Offenders Act* 2012, s.141(10), and Sched. 25, paras 1 and 5, so as to substitute "England and Wales" for "Great Britain". As to the application of this amendment, see section 141 of the 2012 Act (*post*, § 13–131a).

As to the disapplication of section 4(1) to (3) of the 1974 Act in relation to proceedings relating to certain decisions under the immigration and nationality legislation, see section 56A of the *UK Borders Act* 2007 (as inserted, as from a day to be appointed, by the 2012 Act, s.140).

Rehabilitation of Offenders Act 1974, s.5

Rehabilitation periods for particular sentences

★**13–127**   As from a day to be appointed, section 5(1)(f) of the 1974 Act is amended by the *Legal Aid, Sentencing and Punishment of Offenders Act* 2012, s.126, and Sched. 21, para. 2, so as to insert "226A, 226B," before "227".

As from a day to be appointed, section 5 of the 1974 Act is further amended by the 2012 Act, s.139(1) to (4), so as (i) to substitute "forty-eight" for "thirty" in subsection (1)(b) and (d), (ii) to substitute the words "In this section" for the words "In subsection (1)(d)" at the beginning of subsection (1A), and (iii) to substitute new subsections (2) to (8) for subsections (2) to (11), as follows—

"(2) For the purposes of this Act and subject to subsections (3) and (4), the rehabilitation period for a sentence is the period—

(a) beginning with the date of the conviction in respect of which the sentence is imposed, and

(b) ending at the time listed in the following Table in relation to that sentence:

Sentence	End of rehabilitation period for adult offenders	End of rehabilitation period for offenders under 18 at date of conviction
A custodial sentence of more than 30 months and up to, or consisting of, 48 months	The end of the period of 7 years beginning with the day on which the sentence (including any licence period) is completed	The end of the period of 42 months beginning with the day on which the sentence (including any licence period) is completed
A custodial sentence of more than 6 months and up to, or consisting of, 30 months	The end of the period of 48 months beginning with the day on which the sentence (including any licence period) is completed	The end of the period of 24 months beginning with the day on which the sentence (including any licence period) is completed
A custodial sentence of 6 months or less	The end of the period of 24 months beginning with the day on which the sentence (including any licence period) is completed	The end of the period of 18 months beginning with the day on which the sentence (including any licence period) is completed
Removal from Her Majesty's service	The end of the period of 12 months beginning with the date of the conviction in respect of which the sentence is imposed	The end of the period of 6 months beginning with the date of the conviction in respect of which the sentence is imposed
A sentence of service detention	The end of the period of 12 months beginning with the day on which the sentence is completed	The end of the period of 6 months beginning with the day on which the sentence is completed
A fine	The end of the period of 12 months beginning with the date of the conviction in respect of which the sentence is imposed	The end of the period of 6 months beginning with the date of the conviction in respect of which the sentence is imposed
A compensation order	The date on which the payment is made in full	The date on which the payment is made in full
A community or youth rehabilitation order	The end of the period of 12 months beginning with the day provided for by or under the order as the last day on which the order is to have effect	The end of the period of 6 months beginning with the day provided for by or under the order as the last day on which the order is to have effect
A relevant order	The day provided for by or under the order as the last day on which the order is to have effect	The day provided for by or under the order as the last day on which the order is to have effect

(3) Where no provision is made by or under a community or youth rehabilitation order or a relevant order for the last day on which the order is to have effect, the rehabilitation period for the order is to be the period of 24 months beginning with the date of conviction.

(4) There is no rehabilitation period for—

(a) an order discharging a person absolutely for an offence, or

(b) any other sentence in respect of a conviction where the sentence is not dealt with in the Table or under subsection (3),

and, in such cases, references in this Act to any rehabilitation period are to be read as if the period of time were nil.

(5) See also—

(a) section 8AA (protection afforded to spent alternatives to prosecution), and

(b) Schedule 2 (protection for spent cautions).

(6) The Secretary of State may by order amend column 2 or 3 of the Table or the number of months for the time being specified in subsection (3).

(7) For the purposes of this section—

(a) consecutive terms of imprisonment or other custodial sentences are to be treated as a single term,

(b) terms of imprisonment or other custodial sentences which are wholly or partly concurrent (that is terms of imprisonment or other custodial sentences imposed in respect of offences of which a person was convicted in the same proceedings) are to be treated as a single term,

    (c) no account is to be taken of any subsequent variation, made by a court dealing with a person in respect of a suspended sentence of imprisonment, of the term originally imposed,

    (d) no account is to be taken of any subsequent variation of the day originally provided for by or under an order as the last day on which the order is to have effect,

    (e) no account is to be taken of any detention or supervision ordered by a court under section 104(3) of the *Powers of Criminal Courts (Sentencing) Act* 2000,

    (f) a sentence imposed by a court outside England and Wales is to be treated as the sentence mentioned in this section to which it most closely corresponds.

(8) In this section—

'community or youth rehabilitation order' means—

    (a) a community order under section 177 of the *Criminal Justice Act* 2003,

    (b) a service community order or overseas community order under the *Armed Forces Act* 2006,

    (c) a youth rehabilitation order under Part 1 of the *Criminal Justice and Immigration Act* 2008, or

    (d) any order of a kind superseded (whether directly or indirectly) by an order mentioned in paragraph (a), (b) or (c),

'custodial sentence' means—

    (a) a sentence of imprisonment,

    (b) a sentence of detention in a young offender institution,

    (c) a sentence of Borstal training,

    (d) a sentence of youth custody,

    (e) a sentence of corrective training,

    (f) a sentence of detention under section 91 of the *Powers of Criminal Courts (Sentencing) Act* 2000 or section 209 of the *Armed Forces Act* 2006,

    (g) a detention and training order under section 100 of the *Powers of Criminal Courts (Sentencing) Act* 2000 or an order under section 211 of the *Armed Forces Act* 2006,

    (h) any sentence of a kind superseded (whether directly or indirectly) by a sentence mentioned in paragraph (f) or (g),

'earlier statutory order' means—

    (a) an order under section 54 of the *Children and Young Persons Act* 1933 committing the person convicted to custody in a remand home,

    (b) an approved school order under section 57 of that Act, or

    (c) any order of a kind superseded (whether directly or indirectly) by an order mentioned in any of paragraphs (c) to (e) of the definition of 'relevant order' or in paragraph (a) or (b) above,

'relevant order' means—

    (a) an order discharging a person conditionally for an offence,

    (b) an order binding a person over to keep the peace or be of good behaviour,

    (c) an order under section 1(2A) of the *Street Offences Act* 1959,

    (d) a hospital order under Part 3 of the *Mental Health Act* 1983 (with or without a restriction order),

    (e) a referral order under section 16 of the *Powers of Criminal Courts (Sentencing) Act* 2000,

    (f) an earlier statutory order, or

    (g) any order which imposes a disqualification, disability, prohibition or other penalty and is not otherwise dealt with in the Table or under subsection (3),

but does not include a reparation order under section 73 of the *Powers of Criminal Courts (Sentencing) Act* 2000,

'removal from Her Majesty's service' means a sentence of dismissal with disgrace from Her Majesty's service, a sentence of dismissal from Her Majesty's service or a sentence of cashiering or discharge with ignominy,

'sentence of imprisonment' includes a sentence of penal servitude (and 'term of imprisonment' is to be read accordingly),

'sentence of service detention' means—

    (a) a sentence of service detention (within the meaning given by section 374 of the *Armed Forces Act* 2006), or a sentence of detention corresponding to such a sentence, in respect of a conviction in service disciplinary proceedings, or

    (b) any sentence of a kind superseded (whether directly or indirectly) by a sentence mentioned in paragraph (a).".

As to the application of the amendments made by section 139, see section 141(1) to (6) ★ of the 2012 Act (*post*, § 13–131a).

Transitional

Section 141 of the *Legal Aid, Sentencing and Punishment of Offenders Act* 2012 (in force as ★**13–131a** from a day to be appointed) makes provision consequential on the enactment of section 139 (*ante*) and contains transitional provisions.

Legal Aid, Sentencing and Punishment of Offenders Act 2012, s.141

[Transitional and consequential provision
141.—(1) Section 139 applies in relation to convictions or (as the case may be) cautions before the commencement date (as well as in relation to convictions or cautions on or after that date).

(2) The *Rehabilitation of Offenders Act* 1974 ("the 1974 Act") applies in relation to convictions or cautions before the commencement date as if the amendments and repeals made by section 139 had always had effect.

(3) Where by virtue of subsection (2)—
(a) a person would, before the commencement date, have been treated for the purposes of the 1974 Act as a rehabilitated person in respect of a conviction, or
(b) a conviction would, before that date, have been treated for the purposes of that Act as spent,
the person or conviction concerned is (subject to any order made by virtue of section 4(4) or 7(4) of that Act) to be so treated on and after that date.

(4) Where by virtue of subsection (2)—
(a) a person would, before the commencement date, have been treated as mentioned in paragraph 3(1) of Schedule 2 to the 1974 Act in respect of a caution, or
(b) a caution would, before that date, have been treated for the purposes of that Act as spent,
the person or caution concerned is (subject to any order made by virtue of paragraph 4 or 6(1) and (4) of that Schedule to that Act) to be so treated on and after that date.

(5) But—
(a) no person who, immediately before the commencement date—
(i) is treated as a rehabilitated person for the purposes of the 1974 Act in respect of a conviction, or
(ii) is treated as mentioned in paragraph 3(1) of Schedule 2 to that Act in respect of a caution, and
(b) no conviction or caution which, immediately before the commencement date, is treated for the purposes of that Act as spent,
is to cease to be so treated merely because of section 139.

(6) Section 139 does not apply in relation to alternatives to prosecution given before the commencement date.

(7)–(9) [*Application of s.140 (as to which, see* ante, § 13–125.]

(10) Schedule 25 (consequential provision) has effect.

(11) Any reference in this section to section 139 is to be read as including a reference to Schedule 25.

(12) In this section "the commencement date" means such day as may be specified by order of the Secretary of State made by statutory instrument; and different days may be specified for different purposes.]

Rehabilitation of Offenders Act 1974, s.6

The rehabilitation period applicable to a conviction
As from a day to be appointed, section 6 of the 1974 Act is amended by the *Legal Aid,* ★**13–132** *Sentencing and Punishment of Offenders Act* 2012, s.139(1) and (5), so as (i) to substitute the words "by virtue of paragraph (g) of the definition of 'relevant order' in section 5(8) above" for the words "in accordance with section 5(8) above" in subsection (5), and (ii) to omit subsection (6). As to the application of the amendments made by section 139, see section 141 of the 2012 Act (*ante*, § 13–131a).

As from a day to be appointed, Schedule 1 to the 1974 Act is repealed by the *Legal Aid, Sentencing and Punishment of Offenders Act* 2012, s.141(10), and Sched. 25, paras 1 and 11. As to the application of this amendment, see section 141 of the 2012 Act (*ante*, § 13–131a).

Rehabilitation of Offenders Act 1974, s.7(1), (2), (4), (5)

Limitations on rehabilitation under this Act, etc.

★**13–133**   As from a day to be appointed, section 7 of the 1974 Act is amended by the *Legal Aid, Sentencing and Punishment of Offenders Act* 2012, s.141(10), and Sched. 25, paras 1 and 6, so as to substitute "England and Wales" for "Great Britain" in subsections (2)(a) and (3). As to the application of these amendments, see section 141 of the 2012 Act (*ante*, § 13–131a).

Summary offences relating to spent convictions

★**13–134**   As from a day to be appointed, section 9(3) and (8) of the 1974 Act are amended by the *Legal Aid, Sentencing and Punishment of Offenders Act* 2012, s.141(10), and Sched. 25, paras 1 and 9.

Cautions, etc.

★**13–135**   As from a day to be appointed, section 8A of the 1974 Act is amended by the *Legal Aid, Sentencing and Punishment of Offenders Act* 2012, ss.135(3) and 141(10), Sched. 24, paras 1 and 2, and Sched. 25, paras 1 and 8; and Schedule 2 to the 1974 Act is amended by *ibid.*, ss.135(3) and 139(1) and (7), and Sched. 24, paras 1 and 3. As to the application of the amendments made by section 139, see section 141(1) of the 2012 Act (*ante*, § 13–131a). The general effect of the amendments is to remove references to reprimands and warnings, to extend the ambit of section 8A and Schedule 2 to youth conditional cautions and to provide that a conditional caution becomes spent after three months or when it ceases to have effect, if earlier

★   As from a day to be appointed, a new section 8AA (protection afforded to spent alternatives to prosecution) is inserted in the 1974 Act by the *Legal Aid, Sentencing and Punishment of Offenders Act* 2012, s.139(1) and (6). An "alternative to prosecution" is to be interpreted in accordance with section 8B, as that section has effect in the law of Scotland: s.8AA(4). As to the application of the amendments made by section 139, see section 141(1) of the 2012 Act (*ante*, § 13–131a).

Disregarded convictions

★**13–136**   As to the enactment of provisions (as from a day to be appointed) allowing a person who has been convicted of, or cautioned for, an offence under section 12 (buggery) or 13 (gross indecency between men) of the *SOA* 1956, or corresponding earlier offences (and see s.101(3) and (4) for related military offences), to apply to the Secretary of State for the conviction or caution to become disregarded; and as to the effect of a conviction becoming disregarded, see the *Protection of Freedoms Act* 2012, ss.92 to 101.

CHAPTER 14

EVIDENCE OF IDENTIFICATION

I. VISUAL IDENTIFICATION

B. THE TURNBULL GUIDELINES

(4) When a Turnbull warning is appropriate

Issue as to veracity

The entirety of this paragraph in the main work was approved in *Grieves v. The Queen*   **14–15**
[2012] Crim.L.R. 212, PC ([2011] UKPC 39).

II. IDENTIFICATION BY OTHER PERSONAL CHARACTERISTICS

C. BLOOD, BODY SAMPLES, SECRETIONS SCENT AND ODONTOLOGY

DNA

See *R. v. Hookway and Noakes, ante*, § 10–67.   **14–58**

CHAPTER 15

INVESTIGATORY POWERS; CONFESSIONS; DISCRETION TO EXCLUDE EVIDENCE, ETC.

I. INVESTIGATORY POWERS

A. POLICE AND CRIMINAL EVIDENCE ACT 1984

(2) Codes of practice

(a) *Statute*

Police and Criminal Evidence Act 1984, ss.66, 67

As from July 10, 2012 (*Protection of Freedoms Act 2012 (Commencement No. 1) Order* 2012   **★15–2**
(S.I. 2012 No. 1205)), section 66 of the 1984 Act is amended by the *Protection of Freedoms Act* 2012, s.115(1), and Sched. 9, para. 21. The effect of the amendment is to replace section 66(3) as printed in the main work with a new subsection (3), as follows—

> "(3) Nothing in this section requires the Secretary of State to issue a code of practice in relation to any matter falling within the code of practice issued under section 47AB(2) of the *Terrorism Act* 2000 (as that code is altered or replaced from time to time) (code of practice in relation to terrorism powers to search persons and vehicles and to stop and search in specified locations).".

Codes of practice — supplementary

The amendments of section 67(4) and (9A) of the 1984 Act effected by the *Police Reform*   **15–3** *and Social Responsibility Act* 2011, s.99, and Sched. 16, paras 160 and 163 (see the main work), came into force on January 16, 2012: *Police Reform and Social Responsibility Act 2011 (Commencement No. 3 and Transitional Provisions) Order* 2011 (S.I. 2011 No. 3019); but this is subject to a temporary modification of the amendment to subsection (4) (as to which, see art. 10(5) of, and Sched. 2, para. 47, to, the commencement order) until section 1 of the 2011 Act comes into force.

(b) *Commencement*

★**15–6**   Revised Codes C, G and H were laid before Parliament on May 10, 2012. The new codes C and H will come into force on the day that the order giving them effect comes into force. As at June 20, this was expected to be in July, 2012. Under the terms of the draft order, new Code G will into force on November 12, 2012. For the text of Codes C and H, as laid before Parliament, see *post*, Appendix A. New Code G will be included in the first supplement to the 2013 edition. For the previous edition of Codes C and H, see the second supplement.

(3) "Reasonable grounds for suspicion"

★**15–14**   As to reasonable grounds for suspicion in the context of the police's powers to stop and search a group, see *Howarth v. Commr of Police of the Metropolis, post,* § 15–39.

(7) Application of Act to Armed Forces

Police and Criminal Evidence Act 1984, s.113

★**15–23**   As to the repeal of the original section 64 of the 1984 Act, see *post,* § 15–196a.

(8) Application of Act to Revenue and Customs

Provisions of the Act applied to Revenue and Customs

★**15–32**   As to the repeal of the original section 64 of the 1984 Act, see *post,* § 15–196a.

B. Stop and Search

(1) Police and Criminal Evidence Act 1984, Pt I (ss.1–7)

Police and Criminal Evidence Act 1984, s.1

Power of constable to stop, search persons, vehicles, etc.

★**15–39**   As from a day to be appointed, section 1(8A) of the 1984 Act is amended by the *Legal Aid, Sentencing and Punishment of Offenders Act* 2012, s.142(3), and Sched. 26, para. 3, so as to insert "or 139AA" after "139".

★   The test of lawfulness of a search by a police officer under section 1 of the 1984 Act is the same in all material respects as that for the lawfulness of an arrest set out in *Castorina v. Chief Constable of Surrey, The Times,* June 15, 1988, CA (Civ. Div.), *viz.* (i) the officer must suspect that he will find stolen, prohibited articles, etc.; (ii) he must have reasonable grounds for so suspecting; and (iii) he has a discretion which must be exercised reasonably in accordance with the principles laid down in *Associated Picture Houses Ltd v. Wednesbury Corporation* [1948] 1 K.B. 223, CA: *Howarth v. Commr of Police of the Metropolis* [2012] A.C.D. 41, DC. In the context of searches of a group of protesters on a train, it was not essential for the searching officer reasonably to suspect each and every individual member of the group to be carrying the offending items for a search of all members of the group to be lawful; where intelligence and past experience gave rise to a reasonable suspicion that if a search were carried out on the group, prohibited items would be found on one or more of the group members (and that such items would be used to cause significant damage), the feature of "group searching" went to the third *Castorina* question, namely whether the officer's decision to search individuals, given his suspicion of the group, reasonably held, went beyond the range of decisions open to him in the circumstances of the case; where steps were taken to ensure that those searched were protesters, where the searches were not excessive in character having regard to the nature of the suspicion held and where the organisers of the protest had not consulted with the police to assist in the orderly conduct of the event, the search did not go beyond the bounds of decision open to the officer: *ibid.* (followed in *Tuthill v. DPP* [2012] A.C.D. 26, DC).

C. Entry, Search and Seizure

(1) Introduction

As to the enactment of provisions (as from July 1, 2012 (*Protection of Freedoms Act 2012* *(Commencement No. 1) Order* 2012 (S.I. 2012 No. 1205)) allowing appropriate national authorities to repeal, add safeguards or rewrite powers of entry that are considered to be unnecessary or inappropriate, see the *Protection of Freedoms Act* 2012, ss.39 to 46; and as to a code of practice that must be prepared by the Secretary of State containing guidance about the exercise of powers of entry and associated powers (as from July 1 (*ibid.*)), see sections 47 to 52, and (as from a day to be appointed) 53 (relating to Wales) of the 2012 Act.   ★**15–52**

(2) Statute

Police and Criminal Evidence Act 1984, s.8

Power of justice of the peace to authorise entry and search of premises
In *R. (Glenn and Co. (Essex) Ltd) v. H.M. Commrs for Revenue and Customs* [2012] 1   **15–55**
Cr.App.R. 22, DC (considering the *Redknapp* and *Wood* cases cited in the main work), the court held that the ultimate question in deciding upon the validity of a warrant issued under section 8 of the 1984 Act is whether the statutory test has been applied, and on what basis; and if, despite the lack of full reasons, the court is able to discern a sufficient basis for the decision to issue a warrant, any challenge will fail. As to this case, see also *post*, §§ 15–85, 15–87.

Police and Criminal Evidence Act 1984, Sched. 1

Interpretation
As from April 2, 2012 (*Armed Forces Act 2011 (Commencement No. 1, Transitional and* *Transitory Provisions) Order* 2012 (S.I. 2012 No. 669)), the *PACE Act* 1984, Sched. 1, para. 17 (as prospectively amended by the *SOCPA* 2005), is amended by the *AFA* 2011, s.26, and Sched. 2, para. 11, so as to insert after "a Recorder" the words ", a qualifying judge advocate (within the meaning of the *Senior Courts Act* 1981)".   ★**15–61**

Police and Criminal Evidence Act 1984, ss.15, 16

Search warrants — safeguards
In determining whether a warrant has been drafted in sufficiently clear and precise terms   **15–85**
for the purposes of section 15 of the 1984 Act, the question of where the balance lies in an individual case will not be answered by reference to authority, since each case is likely to turn on particular facts; it will be answered by considering whether the warrant has identified the articles sought so far as practicable in the circumstances; the broad scope of an investigation may require a correspondingly broad power of search: *R. (Glenn and Co. (Es-*

sex) Ltd) v. H.M. Commrs for Revenue and Customs [2012] 1 Cr.App.R. 22, DC. As to this case, see also *ante*, § 15–55; and *post*, § 15–87.

Execution of warrants

15–87   Notwithstanding the apparently mandatory language of section 15(1) of the 1984 Act ("... an entry on or search of premises under a warrant is unlawful unless it complies with this section and section 16 below" (§ 15–84 in the main work)), in *R. (Glenn and Co. (Essex) Ltd) v. H.M. Commrs for Revenue and Customs* [2012] 1 Cr.App.R. 22, DC, where there had been a breach of section 16(5) (occupier not shown warrant or supplied with copy at point of entry on premises; merely allowed to inspect copy of warrant some minutes later, after arrest), the court (distinguishing *R. (Bhatti) v. Croydon Magistrates' Court* (see the main work) and *R. v. Chief Constable of Lancashire, ex p. Parker* (§ 15–85 in the main work)) would only grant a declaration of breach, and not a declaration that the execution of the warrant was unlawful or an order requiring the return of the material obtained; it would, said the court, still be open to the occupier to make an application to the Crown Court for return of property unlawfully seized (*CJPA* 2001, s.59 (§ 15–112 in the main work)) or for the exclusion of evidence (under the 1984 Act, s.78 (§ 15–401 in the main work)) in the event of a prosecution. As to this case, see also *ante*, §§ 15–55, 15–85.

Police and Criminal Evidence Act 1984, s.17

Entry for purposes of arrest, etc.

★**15–88**   As from a day to be appointed, section 17(1)(ca) of the 1984 Act is amended by the *Legal Aid, Sentencing and Punishment of Offenders Act* 2012, s.105, and Sched. 12, para. 21, so as to substitute the words "to local authority accommodation or youth detention accommodation under section 91 of the *Legal Aid, Sentencing and Punishment of Offenders Act* 2012" for the words from "or committed" to "that Act".

★   As from a day to be appointed, section 17 of the 1984 Act is further amended by the 2012 Act, s.144(8), so as (i) to substitute ", (iv) or (vi)" for "or (iv)" in subsection (3), and (ii) to insert a new sub-paragraph (vi) in subsection (1)(c), as follows—

> "(vi) section 144 of the *Legal Aid, Sentencing and Punishment of Offenders Act* 2012 (squatting in a residential building);".

Criminal Justice and Police Act 2001, ss.59–62

Application to the appropriate judicial authority

15–112   *R. (El-Kurd) v. Crown Court at Winchester and Serious Organised Crime Agency* is now reported at [2012] Crim.L.R. 138, *sub nom. R. (El-Kurd) v. Winchester Crown Court.*

Powers of seizure (Schedule 1, Parts 1, 2 and 3)

Powers to which section 50 applies (list 1)

15–121   With effect from March 14, 2012, the *Charities Act* 2011, s.354(1), and Sched 7, para. 92, amend Schedule 1 to the *CJPA* 2001 so as to substitute a new paragraph 56A (referring to s.48(3) of the 2011 Act).

★   As from a day to be appointed, the *Protection of Freedoms Act* 2012, s.115(1), and Sched. 9, para. 145, amend Schedule 1 to the *CJPA* 2001 so as to insert a new paragraph 63A (referring to section 2B(2) of the *Protection from Harrassment Act* 1997 (seizure of material relevant to stalking)).

★   As from July 10, 2012 (*Protection of Freedoms Act 2012 (Commencement No. 1) Order* 2012 (S.I. 2012 No. 1205)), the *Protection of Freedoms Act* 2012, s.115(1), and Sched. 9, para. 28, amend Schedule 1 to the *CJPA* 2001 so as to insert new paragraphs 69A and 69B (referring respectively to sections 43(4B)(b) and 43A(3) of the *Terrorism Act* 2000).

Powers to which section 51 applies (list 2)

★**15–123**   As from July 10, 2012 (*Protection of Freedoms Act 2012 (Commencement No. 1) Order* 2012

(S.I. 2012 No. 1205)), the *Protection of Freedoms Act* 2012, s.115(1), and Sched. 9, para. 29, amend Part 2 of Schedule 1 to the *CJPA* 2001 so as to insert a new paragraph 82A (referring to section 43A(3) of the *Terrorism Act* 2000).

D. Arrest

(2) The Police and Criminal Evidence Act 1984

Police and Criminal Evidence Act 1984, s.24

Hayes v. Chief Constable of Merseyside Police is now reported at [2011] 2 Cr.App.R. 30. It **15–131** was considered and applied in *Fitzpatrick, Wilkey and Thomas Boyd & White (a Firm) v. Commr of Police of the Metropolis* (2012) 156(3) S.J. 39, QBD. (arrest of solicitors on suspicion of commission of money laundering offences).

"Recordable offences"

As from July 1, 2012 (*Protection of Freedoms Act 2012 (Commencement No. 1) Order* 2012 ★**15–135** (S.I. 2012 No. 1205)), section 27 of the 1984 Act is amended by the *Protection of Freedoms Act* 2012, s.85, so as to insert a new subsection (4A), which provides that, in subsection (4), "conviction" includes a caution within the meaning of Part V of the *Police Act* 1997 and a reprimand or warning given under section 65 of the *CDA* 1998.

Police and Criminal Evidence Act 1984, ss.29, 30

Arrest elsewhere than at police station
The amendment of section 30(4) of the 1984 Act by the *Police Reform and Social* **15–142** *Responsibility Act* 2011, s.99, and Sched. 16, paras 160 and 161 (see the main work), came into force on January 16, 2012: *Police Reform and Social Responsibility Act 2011 (Commencement No. 3 and Transitional Provisions) Order* 2011 (S.I. 2011 No. 3019).

E. Questioning and Treatment of Persons

(1) Introduction

As to the repeal of the original section 64 of the 1984 Act and the non-implementation of ★**15–154** the replacement provisions, see *post*, §§ 15–196a, 15–197.

(5) Access to legal advice

Police and Criminal Evidence Act 1984, s.58

Consequences of breach of section 58

As to the admissibility of answers obtained through police questioning of an accused who **15–170** has not had access to a lawyer, in the context of the right to a fair trial and to legal representation under Article 6(1) and (3) of the ECHR (§ 16–57 in the main work), see *H.M. Advocate v. P* [2011] 1 W.L.R. 2497, SC (the fruits of such questioning), *Ambrose v. Harris (Procurator Fiscal, Oban); H.M. Advocate v. M.; H.M. Advocate v. G.* [2011] 1 W.L.R. 2435, SC (questioning other than at the police station), *McGowan (Procurator Fiscal, Edinburgh) v. B.* [2011] 1 W.L.R. 3121, SC, and *Jude v. H.M. Advocate; Hodgson v. H.M. Advocate; Birnie v. H.M. Advocate* [2011] L.S. Gazette, December 8, 21, SC ([2011] UKSC 55) (waiver of the right of access to a lawyer without the benefit of legal advice and without giving reasons), *post*, § 16–87.

Compatibility with the European Convention on Human Rights

15–172   As to whether it is compatible with the right to a fair trial and to legal representation under Article 6(1) and (3) of the ECHR (§ 16–57 in the main work), to give in evidence against the accused (a) answers to police questioning that takes place in the absence of a lawyer other than at a police station, (b) information or material that has been obtained as a result of police station questioning in the absence of a lawyer, or (c) statements made by a suspect who has waived his right of access to a lawyer without the benefit of legal advice and without giving reasons, see *Ambrose v. Harris (Procurator Fiscal, Oban)*; *H.M. Advocate v. M.*; *H.M. Advocate v. G.* [2011] 1 W.L.R. 2435, SC (as to (a)), *H.M. Advocate v. P.* [2011] 1 W.L.R. 2497, SC (as to (b)), and *Jude v. H.M. Advocate*; *Hodgson v. H.M. Advocate*; *Birnie v. H.M. Advocate* [2011] L.S. Gazette, December 8, 21, SC ([2011] UKSC 55); and *McGowan v. B.* [2011] 1 W.L.R. 3121, SC (as to (c) — and also as to the requirements of a valid waiver of the right to legal advice), *post*, § 16–87.

(8) Fingerprints, photographs, intimate and other samples

Police and Criminal Evidence Act 1984, s.61

Fingerprinting

15–178   Sections 10 and 13 of the *Counter-Terrorism Act* 2008 (see the main work) were repealed with effect from December 15, 2011, by the *Terrorism Prevention and Investigation Measures Act* 2011, s.29(3), and Sched. 7, para. 5(1) and (3).

★   As from a day to be appointed, section 61 of the 1984 Act is amended by the *Legal Aid, Sentencing and Punishment of Offenders Act* 2012, s.135(3), and Sched. 24, paras 4 and 7, so as (i) to insert "or" at the end of subsection (6)(a), (ii) to substitute "and" for "or" at the end of subsection (6)(b), (iii) to omit subsection (6)(c), and the word "and" at the end of that paragraph, and (iv) in subsection (6ZA)(a), to substitute the words "or cautioned" for the words ", cautioned or warned or reprimanded". It should be noted that subsection (6) is incorrectly formatted in the main work. It should be laid out as follows (text to be omitted is italicised, new text is in square brackets)—

> "(6) Subject to this section, the fingerprints of a person may be taken without the appropriate consent if (before or after the coming into force of this subsection)—
>> (a) he has been convicted of a recordable offence, [or]
>> (b) he has been given a caution in respect of a recordable offence which, at the time of the caution, he has admitted, *or* [and]
>> (c) *he has been warned or reprimanded under section 65 of the* Crime and Disorder Act *1998 for a recordable offence, and*
>
> either of the conditions mentioned in subsection (6ZA) below is met.]".

★15–179   As to the repeal of the original section 64 of the 1984 Act and the non-implementation of the replacement provisions, see *post*, §§ 15–196a, 15–197.

Police and Criminal Evidence Act 1984, s.62

Intimate samples

★15–181   With effect from June 18, 2012 (*Criminal Justice Act 2003 (Commencement No. 28 and Saving Provisions) Order* 2012 (S.I. 2012 No. 1320)), sections 41 and 332 of, and paragraph 56 of Schedule 3 to, and Part 4 of Schedule 37 to, the 2003 Act (see the main work) are brought into force (so far as they are not already in force) in certain areas (as to which, see *ante*, § 1–88). There are associated saving provisions, as to which, see article 5 of the order (*ante*, § 1–88).

★15–182   As to the repeal of the original section 64 of the 1984 Act and the non-implementation of the replacement provisions, see *post*, §§ 15–196a, 15–197.

Police and Criminal Evidence Act 1984, s.63

Other samples

15–183   Section 10 of the *Counter-Terrorism Act* 2008 (see the main work) was repealed with effect from December 15, 2011, by the *Terrorism Prevention and Investigation Measures Act* 2011, s.29(3), and Sched. 7, para. 5(1) and (3).

As from a day to be appointed, section 63(3A)(c)(i) of the 1984 Act is amended by the ★
Protection of Freedoms Act 2012, s.115(1), and Sched. 9, para. 3(1) and (2), to substitute "63R" for "64(ZA)".

As from a day to be appointed, section 63(3B) and (3BA) of the 1984 Act are amended by ★
the *Legal Aid, Sentencing and Punishment of Offenders Act* 2012, s.135(3), and Sched. 24, paras 4 and 8, so as (i) to add "or" at the end of subsection (3B)(a), (ii) to substitute "and" for "or" at the end of subsection (3B)(b), (iii) to omit subsection (3B)(c) and the word "and" at the end of that paragraph, and (iv) in subsection (3BA)(a) to substitute the words "or cautioned" for the words ", cautioned or warned or reprimanded".

Police and Criminal Evidence Act 1984, s.63A

Fingerprints and samples: supplementary provisions

Section 10(3)(a) of the *Counter-Terrorism Act* 2008 (inserting "or he is or has been subject **15–185** to a control order" into s.63A(1) of the 1984 Act (see the main work)) was repealed with effect from December 15, 2011, by the *Terrorism Prevention and Investigation Measures Act* 2011, s.29(3), and Sched. 7, para. 5(1) and (3).

Police and Criminal Evidence Act 1984, Sched. 2A

Fingerprinting: persons convicted etc. of an offence in England and Wales

As from a day to be appointed, paragraph 3 of Schedule 2A to the 1984 Act is amended ★**15–186** by the *Legal Aid, Sentencing and Punishment of Offenders Act* 2012, s.135(3), and Sched. 24, paras 4 and 11(1) and (2), so as (i) in sub-paragraph (2)(a), to substitute the words "or cautioned" for the words ", cautioned or warned or reprimanded", and (ii) in sub-paragraph (5), to substitute the words "or caution" for the words ", caution or warning or reprimand".

Fingerprinting: persons subject to a control order

Paragraph 4 of Schedule 2A to the 1984 Act was repealed with effect from December 15, 2011, by the *Terrorism Prevention and Investigation Measures Act* 2011, s.29(3), and Sched. 7, paras 2 and 6.

Non-intimate samples: persons convicted etc. of an offence in England and Wales

As from a day to be appointed, paragraph 11 of Schedule 2A to the 1984 Act is amended ★**15–188** by the *Legal Aid, Sentencing and Punishment of Offenders Act* 2012, s.135(3), and Sched. 24, paras 4 and 11(1) and (3), so as (i) in sub-paragraph (2)(a), to substitute the words "or cautioned" for the words ", cautioned or warned or reprimanded", and (ii) in sub-paragraph (5), to substitute the words "or caution" for the words ", caution or warning or reprimand".

Non-intimate samples: persons subject to a control order

Paragraph 12 of Schedule 2A to the 1984 Act was repealed with effect from December 15, 2011, by the *Terrorism Prevention and Investigation Measures Act* 2011, s.29(3), and Sched. 7, paras 2.

As to the repeal of paragraphs 4 and 12 of Schedule 2A to the 1984 Act, see *ante*, §§ 15– **15–189** 186, 15–188.

Police and Criminal Evidence Act 1984, ss.63AA, 63AB

National DNA database

As from a day to be appointed, new sections 63AA (inclusion of DNA profiles on National ★**15–189a** DNA Database) and 63AB (National DNA Database Strategy Board) are inserted in the 1984 Act after section 63A by the *Protection of Freedoms Act* 2012, ss.23 and 24. In connection with the coming into force of these sections, see section 25 of the 2012 Act (Secretary of State's duty to make statutory instrument relating to the destruction of material that would have been material to which section 63D or 63R of the 1984 Act applied if they had been in force at the time the material was taken, or, in the case of a DNA profile derived from such material, at the time it was so derived).

Police and Criminal Evidence Act 1984, s.63AA

[Inclusion of DNA profiles on National DNA Database
    63AA.—(1) This section applies to a DNA profile which is derived from a DNA sample and which is retained under any power conferred by any of sections 63E to 63L (including those sections as applied by section 63P).
    (2) A DNA profile to which this section applies must be recorded on the National DNA Database.]

Police and Criminal Evidence Act 1984, s.63AB

[National DNA Database Strategy Board
★**15–189b**   **63AB.**—(1) The Secretary of State must make arrangements for a National DNA Database Strategy Board to oversee the operation of the National DNA Database.
    (2) The National DNA Database Strategy Board must issue guidance about the destruction of DNA profiles which are, or may be, retained under this Part of this Act.
    (3) A chief officer of a police force in England and Wales must act in accordance with guidance issued under subsection (2).
    (4) The National DNA Database Strategy Board may issue guidance about the circumstances in which applications may be made to the Commissioner for the Retention and Use of Biometric Material under section 63G.
    (5) Before issuing any such guidance, the National DNA Database Strategy Board must consult the Commissioner for the Retention and Use of Biometric Material.
    (6) The Secretary of State must publish the governance rules of the National DNA Database Strategy Board and lay a copy of the rules before Parliament.
    (7) The National DNA Database Strategy Board must make an annual report to the Secretary of State about the exercise of its functions.
    (8) The Secretary of State must publish the report and lay a copy of the published report before Parliament.
    (9) The Secretary of State may exclude from publication any part of the report if, in the opinion of the Secretary of State, the publication of that part would be contrary to the public interest or prejudicial to national security.]

Police and Criminal Evidence Act 1984, ss.63B, 63C

Testing for presence of Class A drugs
15–191   With effect from January 16, 2012, minor drafting amendments are made to the *Police and Criminal Evidence Act 1984 (Drug Testing of Persons in Police Detention) (Prescribed Persons) Regulations* 2001 (S.I. 2001 No. 2645) (see the main work) by the *Local Policing Bodies (Consequential Amendments) Regulations* 2012 (S.I. 2012 No. 61).

Police and Criminal Evidence Act 1984, s.64

Retention of samples and fingerprints, etc generally
★**15–196**   As from a day to be appointed, section 14 of the *Crime and Security Act* 2010 (and hence the version of section 64 that that section would have substituted for the original section 64) is repealed by the *Protection of Freedoms Act* 2012, s.115(1) and (2), Sched. 9, para. 4, and Sched. 10, Pt 1.

Police and Criminal Evidence Act 1984, s.64

Destruction of fingerprints and samples
15–196a   **64.**—(1A) Where—

    (a) fingerprints, impressions of footwear or samples are taken from a person in connection with the investigation of an offence, and

    (b) subsection (3) below does not require them to be destroyed,

the fingerprints, impressions of footwear or samples may be retained after they have fulfilled the purposes for which they were taken but shall not be used by any person *except for purposes related to the prevention or detection of crime, the investigation of an offence, the conduct of a prosecution or the identification of a deceased person or of the person from whom a body part came* [except as described in subsection (1AB)].

    [(1AB) The fingerprints, impressions of footwear or samples may be used—

    (a) in the interests of national security,

    (b) for purposes related to the prevention or detection of crime, the investigation of an offence or the conduct of a prosecution, or

    (c) for purposes related to the identification of a deceased person or of the person from whom the material came.]

    (1B) In subsection (1A) [or (1AB)] above—

    (a) the reference to using a fingerprint or an impression of footwear includes a reference to allowing any check to be made against it under section 63A(1) or (1C) above and to disclosing it to any person;

    (b) the reference to using a sample includes a reference to allowing any check to be made under section 63A(1) or (1C) above against it or against information derived from it and to disclosing it or any such information to any person;

    (c) the reference to crime includes a reference to any conduct which—

        (i) constitutes one or more criminal offences (whether under the law of a part of the United Kingdom or of a country or territory outside the United Kingdom); or

        (ii) is, or corresponds to, any conduct which, if it all took place in any one part of the United Kingdom, would constitute one or more criminal offences; and

    (d) the references to an investigation and to a prosecution include references, respectively, to any investigation outside the United Kingdom of any crime or suspected crime and to a prosecution brought in respect of any crime in a country or territory outside the United Kingdom.

    (1BA) Fingerprints taken from a person by virtue of section 61(6A) above must be destroyed as soon as they have fulfilled the purpose for which they were taken.

    (3) If—

    (a) fingerprints, impressions of footwear or samples are taken from a person in connection with the investigation of an offence; and

    (b) that person is not suspected of having committed the offence,

they must, except as provided in the following provisions of this section, be destroyed as soon as they have fulfilled the purpose for which they were taken.

    (3AA) Samples, fingerprints and impressions of footwear are not required to be destroyed under subsection (3) above if—

    (a) they were taken for the purposes of the investigation of an offence of which a person has been convicted; and

    (b) a sample, fingerprint, (or as the case may be) an impression of footwear was also taken from the convicted person for the purposes of that investigation.

    (3AB) Subject to subsection (3AC) below, where a person is entitled under subsection (1BA) or (3) above to the destruction of any fingerprint, impression of footwear or sample taken from him (or would be but for subsection (3AA) above), neither the fingerprint, nor the impression of footwear, nor the sample, nor any information derived from the sample, shall be used—

    (a) in evidence against the person who is or would be entitled to the destruction of that fingerprint, impression of footwear or sample; or

    (b) for the purposes of the investigation of any offence;

and subsection (1B) above applies for the purposes of this subsection as it applies for the purposes of subsection (1A) above.

    (3AC) Where a person from whom a fingerprint, impression of footwear or sample has been taken consents in writing to its retention—

    (a) that fingerprint, impression of footwear or sample need not be destroyed under subsection (3) above;

    (b) subsection (3AB) above shall not restrict the use that may be made of the fingerprint, impression of footwear or sample or, in the case of a sample, of any information derived from it; and

(c) that consent shall be treated as comprising a consent for the purposes of section 63A(1C) above;

and a consent given for the purpose of this subsection shall not be capable of being withdrawn.

This subsection does not apply to fingerprints taken from a person by virtue of section 61(6A) above.

(3AD) For the purposes of subsection (3AC) above it shall be immaterial whether the consent is given at, before or after the time when the entitlement to the destruction of the fingerprint, impression of footwear or sample arises.

(4) [*Repealed by* Criminal Justice and Police Act *2001, s.137, and Sched. 7, Pt 2.*]

(5) If fingerprints or impressions of footwear are destroyed—

    (a) any copies of the fingerprints or impressions of footwear shall also be destroyed; and

    (b) any chief officer of police controlling access to computer data relating to the fingerprints or impressions of footwear shall make access to the data impossible, as soon as it is practicable to do so.

(6) A person who asks to be allowed to witness the destruction of his fingerprints or impressions of footwear or copies of them shall have a right to witness it.

(6A) If—

    (a) subsection (5)(b) above falls to be complied with; and

    (b) the person to whose fingerprints or impressions of footwear the data relate asks for a certificate that it has been complied with,

such a certificate shall be issued to him, not later than the end of the period of three months beginning with the day on which he asks for it, by the responsible chief officer of police or a person authorised by him or on his behalf for the purposes of this section.

(6B) In this section—

    ...

"the responsible chief officer of police" means the chief officer of police in whose police area the computer data were put onto the computer.

(7) Nothing in this section—

    (a) affects any power conferred by paragraph 18(2) of Schedule 2 to the *Immigration Act* 1971 or section 20 of the *Immigration and Asylum Act* 1999 (disclosure of police information to the Secretary of State for use for immigration purposes); or

    (b) applies to a person arrested or detained under the terrorism provisions.

★   [This version of section 64 (which had been due to be replaced by provisions to be inserted by the *Crime and Security Act* 2010, s.14 (as to which, see §§ 15–196, 15–196a in the main work)) remains in force until it is repealed, as from a day to be appointed, by the *Protection of Freedoms Act* 2012, s.115(1) and (2), Sched. 9, para. 3(1) and (3), and Sched. 10, Pt 1. It is printed as amended by the *CJA* 1988, s.148; the *CJPOA* 1994, s.57; the *Police Act* 1996, s.103, and Sched. 7, para. 37; the *CJPA* 2001, s.82; and the *SOCPA* 2005, ss.117(6)– (10) and 118(1) and (4); and as amended, as from a day to be appointed, by the *Counter-Terrorism Act* 2008, s.14(1) and (4) to (6) (insertion of words in square brackets in subs. (1A), omission of words from "except for purposes" to "body part came", insertion of subs. (1AB) and of "or (1AB)" in subs. (1B)).]

15-196b   The fingerprints, samples and information the retention and use of which, in accordance with section 64 is authorised by section 82 of the *CJPA* 2001, include (a) fingerprints and samples the destruction of which should have taken place before the commencement of section 82 (May 11, 2001), but did not, and (b) information deriving from any such samples or from samples the destruction of which did take place, in accordance with section 64, before the commencement of section 82: s.82(6).

For definitions of "fingerprints", "intimate sample", "non-intimate sample" and "the terrorism provisions", see section 65 (§ 15–201 in the main work).

The restriction in subsection (1A) on the use that may be made of retained fingerprints or samples, and information derived from them, applies to both fingerprints and samples taken from a suspect and also to fingerprints and samples taken from volunteers and victims: *Lambeth London Borough v. S., C., V. and J. (by his guardian)* [2007] 1 F.L.R. 152, Fam D (Ryder J.). Where a print or sample, or information relating to such print or sample, is improperly retained in breach of the requirements of this section, evidence derived therefrom will not be automatically excluded, but the breach will be a factor to be taken into account by the judge in exercising his discretion to exclude it: see *Att.-Gen.'s Reference (No. 3 of 1999)* [2001] 2 A.C. 91, HL (decided in relation to this section, as it read prior to its amendment by the 2001 Act).

Section 64 applies to DNA profiles: *R. v. Nathaniel* [1995] 2 Cr.App.R. 565, CA. The use of DNA profiles from destroyed samples to form a database for use for statistical purposes does not breach section 64: *R. v. Willoughby* [1997] 1 *Archbold News* 2, CA.

In *S. v. U.K.* (2009) 48 E.H.R.R. 50, ECtHR, it was held, contrary to the domestic courts' view (see *R. (S.) v. Chief Constable of South Yorkshire Police*; *R. (Marper) v. Same* [2004] 1 W.L.R. 2196, HL), that the indefinite retention of fingerprints and samples under section 64(1A), pursuant to guidelines issued by the Association of Chief Police Officers (ACPO), was incompatible with Article 8(1) of the ECHR, in that the blanket and indiscriminate nature of the power failed to strike a fair balance between the competing public and private interests and overstepped any acceptable margin of appreciation in that regard; of particular concern was that unconvicted persons, entitled to the presumption of innocence, were to be treated in the same way as convicted persons; and the retention of an unconvicted person's data was especially harmful in the case of minors, given their special situation and the importance of their development and integration into society. However, in *R. (G.C.) v. Commr of Police of the Metropolis (Liberty intervening)*; *R. (C.) v. Same (Same intervening)* [2011] 2 Cr.App.R. 18, SC, it was held by a majority that section 64(1A) does not require the police to hold the relevant data indefinitely; the discretion afforded by section 64(1A) is not necessarily incompatible with Article 8; but the existing ACPO guidelines (despite modification, after *S. v. U.K.*, to remove all samples relating to children under the age of 10) are unlawful, because they are in breach of Article 8 (in that they only allow for non-retention and destruction in exceptional circumstances). The court noted that the government was proposing to amend the legislative regime so that data in relation to unconvicted persons may only be retained for a limited time and only in relation to particular crimes. The new regime is provided for in the *Protection of Freedoms Act* 2012 and comes into force on a day to be appointed: see *post*, § 15–197a.

Destruction, etc., of samples

As from a day to be appointed, minor amendments are made to sections 64ZC(6)(a) and ★**15–197**
64ZI(3) of the 1984 by the *Legal Aid, Sentencing and Punishment of Offenders Act* 2012, s.135(3), and Sched. 24, paras 4, 9 and 10.

Note, however, that section 14(2) of the *Crime and Security Act* 2010 (inserting sections 64ZA to 64ZN as from a day to be appointed) is itself repealed, as from a day to be appointed, by the *Protection of Freedoms Act* 2012, s.115(1), and Sched. 9, para. 4(1) and (2).

The existing provisions relating to the destruction, retention, and use of fingerprints, etc. (as well as the provisions that would have been introduced by the 2010 Act (as to which, see the main work)) are replaced as from a day to be appointed by new sections 63D to 63U, which are inserted into the 1984 Act by the *Protection of Freedoms Act* 2012, ss.1 to 17. In connection with the coming into force of these provisions, see section 25 of that Act (*ante*, § 15–189a).

Section 63D applies to (i) fingerprints taken from a person under any power conferred by ★**15–197a**
Part V of the 1984 Act, or taken by the police, with the consent of the person from whom they were taken, in connection with the investigation of an offence by the police, and (ii) a DNA profile derived from a DNA sample taken as in (i). Such fingerprints and profiles must be destroyed if it appears to the responsible chief officer of police that either the taking of the fingerprint or sample was unlawful, or the fingerprint or sample was taken from a person in connection with that person's arrest, and the arrest was unlawful or based on mistaken identity (s.63D(2)). In any other case, such fingerprints and profiles must be destroyed unless they are retained under any power conferred by sections 63E to 63O (including those sections as applied by s.63P) (s.63D(3)). These sections concern the retention of material pending the conclusion of an investigation or proceedings (s.63E), of material taken from persons arrested for or charged with, but not convicted of, a qualifying of-

fence (ss.63F and 63G), of material taken from persons arrested for or charged with, but not convicted of, a minor offence (s.63H), of material taken from persons convicted of a recordable offence (s.63I), of material taken from persons convicted of an offence outside England and Wales (s.63J), of material taken from persons under 18 convicted of a first minor offence (s.63K), of material taken from persons given a penalty notice (s.63L), of material for purposes of national security (s.63M), of material given voluntarily (s.63N), and of material where consent has been given (s.63O). Under section 63P, where section 63D material taken from a person in connection with the investigation of an offence leads to that person being arrested for, charged with, or convicted of, an offence other than the offence under investigation, sections 63E to 63O and 63Q and 63T (*post*) have effect in relation to the material as if it had been taken in connection with the investigation of the offence in respect of which the person is arrested or charged.

Sections 63Q to 63S relate to the destruction of copies of fingerprints, samples, and impressions of footwear. Section 63Q provides that if fingerprints are required by section 63D to be destroyed, any copies of the fingerprints held by the police must also be destroyed, and that if a DNA profile is required by that section to be destroyed, no copy may be retained by the police except in a form which does not include information identifying the person to whom the profile relates. Section 63R applies to samples taken from a person under any power conferred by Part V of the 1984 Act, or taken by the police, with the consent of the person from whom they were taken, in connection with the investigation of an offence by the police. Section 63R(2) corresponds to section 63D(2) (*ante*). Otherwise, a sample must be destroyed before the end of the period of six months beginning with the date on which it was taken, or, in the case of a DNA sample, if sooner, as soon as a DNA profile has been derived from the sample (s.63R(3), (4) and (5)). However, the responsible chief officer of police may apply to a District Judge (Magistrates' Courts) for an order to retain a sample beyond the date on which it would otherwise be required to be destroyed by virtue of section 63R(4) or (5), if the sample is likely to be needed in any proceedings for an offence, for the purposes of disclosure to, or use by, a defendant, or for the purposes of responding to any challenge by a defendant in respect of the admissibility of material that is evidence on which the prosecution propose to rely (s.63R(6)–(8)). On such an application, the judge, if satisfied that the sample is likely to be so needed, may make an order that allows the sample to be retained for a period of 12 months beginning with the date on which the sample would otherwise be required to be destroyed (s.63R(9)(a)). This order may be renewed (on one or more occasions) for a further period of not more than 12 months from the end of the period when the order would otherwise cease to have effect (s.63(9)(b)). Impressions of footwear taken from a person under any power conferred by Part V of the 1984 Act, or taken by the police, with the consent of the person from whom they were taken, in connection with the investigation of an offence by the police, may be retained for as long as is necessary for purposes related to the prevention or detection of crime, the investigation of an offence, or the conduct of a prosecution; otherwise, they must be destroyed (s.63S).

Section 63T specifies the uses to which material retained under sections 63D, 63R and 63S may be put; material that is required by those sections to be destroyed must not, at any time after it is required to be destroyed, be used in evidence against the person to whom the material relates, or for the purposes of the investigation of any offence. Section 63U excludes the application of some or all of the above provisions in respect of material to which other specified regimes apply.

Material not subject to existing statutory restrictions

★**15-198**   As from a day to be appointed, a new section 18 of the *Counter-Terrorism Act* 2008 is substituted, and new sections 18A to 18E are inserted into that Act, by the *Protection of Freedoms Act* 2012, s.19, and Sched. 1, paras 3 and 4. Section 18 applies to fingerprints, DNA samples and DNA profiles that (a) are held for the purposes of national security by a law enforcement authority under the law of England and Wales or Northern Ireland and (b) are not held subject to "existing statutory restrictions" (as to which, see s.18(8)). Such material must be destroyed if it appears to the responsible officer (as to which, see s.18E(1))

that the material has not either been (i) obtained by the law enforcement authority pursuant
to an authorisation under the *Police Act* 1997, Pt III, (ii) obtained by the law enforcement
authority in the course of surveillance, or use of a covert human intelligence source,
authorised under the *RIPA* 2000, Pt II, (iii) supplied to the law enforcement authority by
another law enforcement authority, or (iv) otherwise lawfully obtained or acquired by the
law enforcement authority for any of the purposes mentioned in section 18D(1) (s.18(2),
(3)). In any other case, the material must be destroyed unless it is retained by the authority under any power conferred by section 18A or 18B (s.18(4)), but a DNA sample to
which section 18 applies must be destroyed as soon as a profile has been derived from it
or, if sooner, before the end of six months beginning with the date on which it was taken
(s.18(5)). Sections 18A and 18B relate to the retention of material generally and for
purposes of national security. Section 18C provides for the destruction of copies and section 18D makes provision as to the use that may be made of retained section 18 material,
with subsection (1) stipulating that it must not be used other than (a) in the interests of
national security, (b) for the purposes of a terrorist investigation, (c) for purposes related
to the prevention or detection of crime, the investigation of an offence or the conduct of
a prosecution, or (d) for purposes related to the identification of a deceased person or of
the person to whom the material relates, and subsection (3) prohibiting the use of material which is required by section 18 to be destroyed, at any time after it should have been
so destroyed, in evidence against the person to whom it relates or for the purposes of the
investigation of any offence. Section 18E contain supplementary provisions, including as
to the interpretation of sections 18 to 18D.

As from a day to be appointed, section 21 of the *Crime and Security Act* 2010 is repealed ★
by the *Protection of Freedoms Act* 2012, s.115(1) and (2), Sched. 9, para. 4, and Sched. 10, Pt
1.

Police and Criminal Evidence Act 1984, s.64A

Photographing of suspects etc.
As from a day to be appointed, section 64A(1B)(d) of the 1984 Act is amended by the   ★**15–199**
Legal Aid, Sentencing and Punishment of Offenders Act 2012, s.132, and Sched. 23, para. 13, so
as to omit the words "in uniform" where they first appear.

(9) Definitions

Police and Criminal Evidence Act 1984, s.65

Part V: supplementary
Section 10 of the *Counter-Terrorism Act* 2008 (see the main work) was repealed with effect   **15–201**
from December 15, 2011, by the *Terrorism Prevention and Investigation Measures Act* 2011,
s.29(3), and Sched. 7, para. 5(1) and (3).

As from a day to be appointed, section 65(1) of the 1984 Act is amended by the *Protection* ★
of Freedoms Act 2012, s.18(1) and (2), so as to insert definitions of "DNA profile", "DNA
sample" and "terrorist investigation" in identical terms to the definitions of those terms
inserted prospectively by the *Crime and Security Act* 2010 (save that the third of those definitions concludes "section 31 of that Act" rather than "section 32 of the *Terrorism Act* 2000"),
and to insert two new definitions after the definition of "registered health care professional",
as follows—

> "'the responsible chief officer of police', in relation to material to which section 63D or 63R ap-
>   plies, means the chief officer of police for the police area—
>   (a) in which the material concerned was taken, or
>   (b) in the case of a DNA profile, in which the sample from which the DNA profile was
>   derived was taken;
> "'section 63D material' means fingerprints or DNA profiles to which section 63D applies;".

As from a day to be appointed, section 65 of the 1984 Act is further amended by the ★
Protection of Freedoms Act 2012, s.18(1) and (3), so as to insert new subsections (2A) and (2B),
as follows—

"(2A) In subsection (2), the reference to the destruction of a sample does not include a reference to the destruction of a sample under section 63R (requirement to destroy samples).

(2B) Any reference in sections 63F, 63H, 63P or 63U to a person being charged with an offence includes a reference to a person being informed that the person will be reported for an offence.".

★ As from a day to be appointed, section 14 of the *Crime and Security Act* 2010 is repealed by the *Protection of Freedoms Act* 2012, s.115(1) and (2), Sched. 9, para. 4, and Sched. 10, Pt 1.

Police and Criminal Evidence Act 1984, s.65A

"Qualifying offence"

★**15–203**   As from a day to be appointed, section 65A(2) of the 1984 Act is amended by the *Protection of Freedoms Act* 2012, ss.18(1) and (4) and 115(1), and Sched. 9, para. 137, so as to substitute (i) in paragraph (j), "8, 9" for "9", and (ii) in paragraph (p), "59A" for "59".

"Persons convicted of an offence"

★**15–203a**   As from a day to be appointed, a new section 65B is inserted in the 1984 Act by the *Protection of Freedoms Act* 2012, s.18(1) and (5). In connection with the coming into force of this section, see section 25 of the 2012 Act (*ante*, § 15–189a).

Police and Criminal Evidence Act 1984, s.65B

["Persons convicted of an offence"

65B.—(1) For the purposes of this Part, any reference to a person who is convicted of an offence includes a reference to—

(a) a person who has been given a caution in respect of the offence which, at the time of the caution, the person has admitted,

(b) a person who has been warned or reprimanded under section 65 of the *Crime and Disorder Act* 1998 for the offence,

(c) a person who has been found not guilty of the offence by reason of insanity, or

(d) a person who has been found to be under a disability and to have done the act charged in respect of the offence.

(2) This Part, so far as it relates to persons convicted of an offence, has effect despite anything in the *Rehabilitation of Offenders Act* 1974.

(3) But a person is not to be treated as having been convicted of an offence if that conviction is a disregarded conviction or caution by virtue of section 92 of the *Protection of Freedoms Act* 2012.

(4) If a person is convicted of more than one offence arising out of a single course of action, those convictions are to be treated as a single conviction for the purposes of calculating under sections 63F, 63H and 63N whether the person has been convicted of only one offence.

(5) See also section 65(3) (which deals with findings equivalent to those mentioned in subsection (1)(c) or (d) by courts which exercise jurisdiction under the laws of countries or territories outside England and Wales).]

F. Police Act 1997 and Regulation of Investigatory Powers 2000

★**15–205**   New sections 32A and 32B of the 2000 Act (inserted, as from a day to be appointed, by the *Protection of Freedoms Act* 2012, s.38) make provision for judicial approval of authorisations granted under section 28 (authorisation of directed surveillance) or 29 (authorisation of covert human intelligence sources). New section 32A provides that an authorisation of directed surveillance or of covert human intelligence sources is not to take effect until a relevant judicial authority (in England and Wales, a justice of the peace: s.32A(7)) has made an order approving the grant of the authorisation. New section 32B sets out the procedure for obtaining judicial approval.

H. Proceeds of Crime Act 2002

(2) Statute

Proceeds of Crime Act 2002, ss.346–369

Search and seizure warrants

In the context of a confiscation order made under section 71 of the *CJA* 1988, while ★**15–239**
search warrants under section 352 (see the main work), and disclosure orders under section 357 (*ibid.*, § 15–244), of the 2002 Act can only be made for the purposes of a "confiscation investigation" (as defined in the 2002 Act, s.341 (*ibid.*, § 15–228)), and while a confiscation investigation is limited to the identification of the existence, quantification and location of benefit (*i.e.* any property or pecuniary advantage obtained as a result of or in connection with criminal conduct: 2002 Act, s.413(4) (*ibid.*, § 15–268)), there is nothing in either Act to prevent the use of such measures to investigate the extent or whereabouts of benefit at any time, and even long after a confiscation order has been made, provided the true and dominant purpose is indeed an investigation into the extent or whereabouts of the defendant's benefit, and not merely to locate realisable property for the purposes of satisfying the confiscation order: *R. (Horne) v. Central Criminal Court (CPS and H.M. Revenue and Customs (interested parties))*, unreported, May 22, 2012, DC ([2012] EWHC 1350 (Admin.)).

Disclosure orders

As to the use of disclosure orders under section 357 of the 2002 Act to investigate the ★**15–244**
extent or whereabouts of a defendant's benefit from criminal conduct at any time, see *R. (Horne) v. Central Criminal Court (CPS and H.M. Revenue and Customs (interested parties))*, *ante*, § 15–239.

J. Protection of Freedoms Act 2012

CCTV and surveillance cameras

Sections 29 to 36 of the *Protection of Freedoms Act* 2012 (in force as from a day to be ap- ★**15–309a**
pointed) make provision for a code of practice for surveillance camera systems. The Secretary of State must prepare such a code (s.29(1)). Relevant authorities that must have regard to the code, when exercising any functions to which the code relates, include a police and crime commissioner, the Mayor's Office for Policing and Crime, the Common Council of the City of London in its capacity as a police authority, and any chief officer of a police force in England and Wales (s.33(1) and (5)). While any failure on the part of any person to act in accordance with the code does not, of itself, make that person liable to criminal or civil proceedings (s.33(2)), the code is admissible in evidence in any such proceedings (s.33(3)), and a court or tribunal may take into account a failure by a relevant authority to have regard to the code in determining a question in any such proceedings (s.33(4)).

II. CONFESSIONS AND RELATED TOPICS

A. Confessions

(1) Police and Criminal Evidence Act 1984

(a) *Admissibility*

Police and Criminal Evidence Act 1984, ss.76, 76A

Confessions

With effect from June 18, 2012 (*Criminal Justice Act 2003 (Commencement No. 28 and Sav-* ★**15–311**

ing Provisions) Order 2012 (S.I. 2012 No. 1320)), sections 41 and 332 of, and paragraph 56(1) and (4) of Schedule 3 to, and Part 4 of Schedule 37 to, the 2003 Act are brought into force in certain areas (as to which, see *ante*, § 1–88). There are associated saving provisions, as to which, see article 5 of the order (*ante*, § 1–88).

(b) *Words and phrases*

"likely ... to render unreliable any confession which might be made by him in consequence thereof"

15–322   Where there had been a plain inducement to confess (here, a shop manager told his employee that, if the employee were to confess to stealing an item from the shop, the police would not be involved), any confession was likely to be rendered unreliable (*PACE Act* 1984, s.76(2) (§ 15–311 in the main work)); and the employee's subsequent silence while waiting for the police (the employer, contrary to his word, having summoned them) could not alter that: *R. v. Roberts (Neil)*, 176 J.P. 33, CA.

B. Accusations Made in the Presence of the Defendant

(3) Criminal Justice and Public Order Act 1994

Adverse inferences from a failure to mention facts

Criminal Justice and Public Order Act 1994, s.34

Effect of accused's failure to mention facts when questioned or charged

★15–361   With effect from June 18, 2012 (*Criminal Justice Act 2003 (Commencement No. 28 and Saving Provisions) Order* 2012 (S.I. 2012 No. 1320)), sections 41 and 332 of, and paragraph 64 of Schedule 3 to, and Part 4 of Schedule 37 to, the 2003 Act are brought into force (so far as they are not already in force) in certain areas (as to which, see *ante*, § 1–88). There are associated saving provisions, as to which, see article 5 of the order (*ante*, § 1–88).

Silence when questioned or charged

15–362   An error or other discrepancy by an interviewing officer as to the date of an offence will not necessarily preclude the application of section 34 of the 1994 Act, because the date is not normally an essential part of the charge: *R. v. M. (I.)* [2012] 1 Cr.App.R. 3, CA, where it was held that the first four conditions set out in *Argent* (see the main work) had been met, but not the fifth or sixth; and that in any event the judge had erred in failing to consider whether any section 34 direction should have been given at all. As to this case, see § 15–363 in the main work.

Fact relied on and unreasonable silence

15–365   For another example of a case where a section 34 direction was wrongly given in relation to facts which were not in issue, see *R. v. M. (I.)* [2012] 1 Cr.App.R. 3, CA. As to this case, see also *ante*, § 15–362, and *post*, §§ 15–366, 15–374.

"in the circumstances existing at the time"

15–366   In *R. v. M. (I.)* [2012] 1 Cr.App.R. 3, CA, it was held that it was difficult to see what more in the circumstances the defendant could have been expected to say, other than deny (in his prepared statement) what was being put in interview, namely that he had raped a particular person on a particular day, when in fact it was common ground at trial that the complainant was not alleging that she had been raped on that day (in fact she alleged that the defendant had raped her on a day about six weeks earlier and that on the day put to the defendant, he had attempted to assault her by penetration). As to this case, see also *ante*, §§ 15–362, 15–365, and *post*, § 15–374.

Directing the jury

It is wrong to direct the jury that a defendant relies on a number of facts, *including* those identified by the judge, because such a direction invites the jury to go beyond the facts which the judge identifies: *R. v. M. (I.)* [2012] 1 Cr.App.R. 3, CA. As to this case, see also *ante*, §§ 15–362, 15–365, 15–366. **15–374**

Criminal Justice and Public Order Act 1994, s.36

Effect of accused's failure or refusal to account for objects, substances or marks
With effect from June 18, 2012 (*Criminal Justice Act 2003 (Commencement No. 28 and Saving Provisions) Order* 2012 (S.I. 2012 No. 1320)), sections 41 and 332 of, and paragraph 64 of Schedule 3 to, and Part 4 of Schedule 37 to, the 2003 Act are brought into force (so far as they are not already in force) in certain areas (as to which, see *ante*, § 1–88). There are associated saving provisions, as to which, see article 5 of the order (*ante*, § 1–88). **★15–382**

Criminal Justice and Public Order Act 1994, s.37

Effect of accused's failure or refusal to account for presence at a particular place
With effect from June 18, 2012 (*Criminal Justice Act 2003 (Commencement No. 28 and Saving Provisions) Order* 2012 (S.I. 2012 No. 1320)), sections 41 and 332 of, and paragraph 64 of Schedule 3 to, and Part 4 of Schedule 37 to, the 2003 Act are brought into force (so far as they are not already in force) in certain areas (as to which, see *ante*, § 1–88). There are associated saving provisions, as to which, see article 5 of the order (*ante*, § 1–88). **★15–384**

C. Judicial Confessions

(2) Admission in proceedings for the same offence

(c) *Proceedings before justices*

Preliminary proceedings

R. (Firth) v. Epping Magistrates' Court was considered in *R. v. Newell*, *ante*, § 4–124. **★15–393**

III. DISCRETION TO EXCLUDE EVIDENCE

A. Under Statute

(1) General

Police and Criminal Evidence Act 1984, s.78

Exclusion of unfair evidence
With effect from June 18, 2012 (*Criminal Justice Act 2003 (Commencement No. 28 and Saving Provisions) Order* 2012 (S.I. 2012 No. 1320)), sections 41 and 332 of, and paragraph 56(1) and (5) of Schedule 3 to, and Part 4 of Schedule 37 to, the 2003 Act are brought into force in certain areas (as to which, see *ante*, § 1–88). There are associated saving provisions, as to which, see article 5 of the order (*ante*, § 1–88). **★15–401**

(7) Codes C and H and section 78

(a) *Introduction*

★**15–424**   As to new Codes C and H, see *ante*, § 15–2, and *post*, Appendix A.

(d) *Particular topics: authorities*

Failure to caution

★**15–429**   *R. v. Nelson and Rose* and *R. v. Hawkins* (both cited in the main work) were followed in *R. v. Williams (Michael)*, unreported, February 24, 2012, CA ([2012] EWCA Crim. 264), where it was confirmed that an objective test must be applied when considering whether there are "grounds to suspect" a person of an offence, so as to require a caution to be given under Code C:10.1 (Appendix A–69 in the second supplement: Appendix A, *post*, sets out the new Code C anticipated to come into force in July 2012).

CHAPTER 16

HUMAN RIGHTS

II. THE HUMAN RIGHTS ACT 1998

C. APPLICATION TO LEGISLATION

Human Rights Act 1998, ss.4, 5

★**16–20a**   *R. v. O.* and *R. v. M. (L.), B. (M.) and G. (D.); R. v. Tabot; R. v. Tijani* (as to both of which, see the main work) were further considered in *R. v. N. (A.); R. v. Le* (as to which, see *post*, Appendix E–12d).

IV. THE RIGHTS GUARANTEED

A. THE RIGHT TO LIFE

Permissible exceptions

16–38   The chamber decision in *Giuliani and Gaggio v. Italy* (see the main work) has been reversed in part by the Grand Chamber: see *Giuliani and Gaggio v. Italy* (2012) 54 E.H.R.R. 10. The Grand Chamber gave detailed guidance on the duty of the state to plan and manage public order operations, and concluded, on the facts, that there had been no violation of the procedural aspect of Article 2. Where a demonstrator had been shot and killed by a police officer, it was held that the criminal investigation into the shooting had been sufficiently effective to enable it to be determined whether the use of lethal force had been justified and whether the organisation and planning of the policing operation had been compatible with the obligation to protect life.

B. PROHIBITION OF TORTURE

Scope

16–40   *R. v. Bieber* and *Kafkaris v. Cyprus* (as to both of which, see the main work) were further considered in *Vinter v. U.K., The Times*, February 8, 2012, ECtHR. It was held that if a whole life order (under the *CJA* 2003, s.269, and Sched. 21 (§§ 5–403, 5–425 *et seq.* in the main work) is imposed on a defendant convicted of murder after due consideration of all relevant mitigating and aggravating factors, an Article 3 issue cannot arise at the moment when it is imposed. Any defendant who is convicted of an offence of the utmost severity must expect to serve a number of years in prison before he can realistically have any hope of release. An Article 3 issue will only arise when it can be shown that continued imprisonment can no longer be justified on any legitimate penological grounds (punishment, deterrence, public protection or rehabilitation), and the sentence is irreducible *de facto* and *de jure*.

To the list of cases in the main work in which consideration has been given to the questions whether the conditions of a person's detention gave rise to a breach of Article 3 may be added *M.S. v. U.K., The Times*, May 14, 2012, ECtHR (severely mentally ill applicant quickly descended into an abject condition when he was kept in a police cell for four days following his arrest for attacking his aunt). ★

C. Prohibition of Slavery and Forced Labour

R. v. K. is now reported at [2011] 2 Cr.App.R. 34, *sub nom. R. v K. (S.).*   **16–42b**

D. Right to Liberty and Security

General

R. (Moos and McClure) v. Commr of Police for the Metropolis (see the main work) has been   **16–45** reversed on appeal: see *R. (McClure and Moos) v. Commr of Police for the Metropolis* [2012] 2 *Archbold Review* 3, CA (Civ. Div.) ([2012] EWCA Civ. 12). As to this, see also *post*, § 19–344.

The decision of the House of Lords in *Austin v. Commr of Police of the Metropolis* (see the   ★ main work) has been vindicated in large part by that of the Grand Chamber of the European Court of Human Rights in *Austin v. U.K., The Times*, March 26, 2012. It was held that Article 5 is not concerned with mere restrictions on liberty of movement, which are governed by Article 2 of the Fourth Protocol, which has not been ratified by the United Kingdom; and Article 5 should not be interpreted in such a way as to incorporate the requirements of the protocol in respect of states that have not ratified it. Furthermore, Article 5 cannot be interpreted in such a way as to make it impracticable for the police to fulfil their duties of maintaining order and protecting the public, provided that they comply with the underlying principle of Article 5, which is to protect the individual from arbitrariness. In the particular circumstances, it was held that the putting of a cordon round a large group of protesters, and the maintenance thereof for seven hours, had not, on the specific and exceptional facts, involved any deprivation of liberty. Nevertheless, the court underlined that measures of crowd control must not be used by national authorities directly or indirectly to stifle or discourage protest.

Bail

O'Dowd v. U.K. is now reported at (2012) 54 E.H.R.R. 8.   **16–52**

E. Right to a Fair Trial

Application

For the Grand Chamber decision in *Al-Khawaja v. U.K.; Tahery v. U.K.*, see *Al-Khawaja v.*   **16–59** *U.K., ante,* § 11–3a. The court again considered whether the guarantees set out in Article 6(3)(a) to (e) of the ECHR (§ 16–57 in the main work) are specific aspects of the right to a fair trial, or whether they are mere illustrations of the requirements of a fair trial.

Scope

16–60   The *Prevention of Terrorism Act* 2005 has been repealed by the *Terrorism Prevention and Investigation Measures Act* 2011, s.1, with effect from December 15, 2011.

Trial within a reasonable time

16–73   Whilst it was reasonable for an appeal to the Court of Appeal to be stayed pending the outcome of an appeal raising the same point of law to the House of Lords in an earlier case, where there was unreasonable delay in hearing that earlier appeal, that delay could not be relied upon as justification for the delay in hearing the later appeal: *Minshall v. U.K.* [2012] S.T.C. 731, ECtHR (a confiscation appeal that had been stayed pending the outcome of the domestic proceedings that were under consideration in *Bullen and Soneji v. U.K.* (as to which, see the main work)). It should be noted that the Strasbourg court's conclusion that there had been unreasonable delay differed from that of Pitchford J. in *R. (Minshall) v. Marylebone Magistrates' Court* (see the main work) on the same facts, although his Lordship did not have the benefit of the Strasbourg court's decision in *Bullen and Soneji*, which was delivered some six weeks later. His Lordship's decision as to the principle of Article 6 applying to enforcement proceedings in relation to a confiscation order is entirely consistent with the Strasbourg decision.

Impartiality

16–74   See *R. v. Oldfield,ante*, § 4–53; *R. v. Mears and Mears, ante*, § 4–293; and *Hanif and Khan v. U.K., ante*, § 4–293.

Reasoned judgment

★**16–75**   *Taxquet v. Belgium* (see the main work) is now reported at (2012) 54 E.H.R.R. 26.

The presumption of innocence

16–78   In *G. v. U.K.* [2012] Crim.L.R. 46, ECtHR, a challenge to the decision of the House of Lords in *R. v. G. (Secretary of State for the Home Department intervening)* (see the main work) was rejected. It was held that, in principle, contracting states remain free to apply the criminal law to any act that is not carried out in the normal exercise of one of the rights protected by the ECHR; it is not the role of the European Court of Human Rights under Article 6(1) or (2) to dictate the content of domestic law, including whether or not a blameworthy state of mind should be one of the elements of an offence, or whether there should be any particular defence available to the accused; accordingly, whereas section 5 of the *SOA* 2003 (§ 20–49 in the main work) creates an offence of strict liability, Parliament's decision not to enact a defence based on reasonable belief that the complainant was aged 13 or over gave rise to no issue under Article 6. As to this case, see also *post*, § 16–108.

★   As to whether the presumption of innocence was engaged where the prosecution sought to suggest to the jury that persons previously acquitted of a conspiracy were "probably" guilty at the retrial of a co-defendant (in respect of whom the first jury had been unable to agree), see *R. v. Cook (Sam), post*, § 33–66.

The right to legal representation and legal aid

16–87   In *Ambrose v. Harris (Procurator Fiscal, Oban)*; *H.M. Advocate v. M.*; *H.M. Advocate v. G.* [2011] 1 W.L.R. 2435, SC, it was held that: (i) *Cadder v. H.M. Advocate (H.M. Advocate General for Scotland intervening)* (see the main work) is authority for the (virtually) absolute rule, derived from *Salduz v. Turkey* (see the main work), that where the prosecution lead and rely upon evidence of anything said by an accused without the benefit of legal advice during questioning under detention at a police station, this will violate Article 6(3) of the ECHR (§ 16–57 in the main work); (ii) but this rule does not extend to questioning before the suspect has been taken into police custody, or his freedom of action has been significantly curtailed; (iii) where that threshold has not been crossed, a more flexible approach is required; it will be necessary to identify the moment at which the individual has been "charged" for the purposes of Article 6(1), which is when his situation has been substantially affected; and this test must be taken to have been satisfied where he is subjected to the initial stages of police interrogation; the mere fact that a common law caution has been administered will not carry the necessary implication; but, when the surrounding circumstances or the actions that follow immediately afterwards are taken into account, it may well do so; (iv) as to what amounts to "police interrogation", it is not necessary that the questioning should amount to an "interrogation" in the formal sense, or amount to a detailed and sustained course of questioning; questions that the police need to put simply in order to decide what action to take with respect to the person whom they are questioning are unlikely to fall into this category; but they are likely to do so when the police have reason to think that they may well elicit an incriminating response; however (v), even if an individual has been "charged" (*e.g.* in the instant cases, the accused had been "charged", respectively, at the roadside, at home, and at home while forcibly restrained during a police search), the question still remains whether, taking all the circumstances into account, it is fair to admit the whole or any part of the evidence; the fact that an individual has had no access to legal advice, and that it was practicable for access to legal advice to be offered, will be material considerations in deciding this issue, but they are no more than that.

In *H.M. Advocate v. P.* [2011] 1 W.L.R. 2497, SC, it was held that: (i) no absolute rule can be derived from the Strasbourg jurisprudence (including *Salduz v. Turkey* (see the main work)) to the effect that use of the fruits of questioning an accused who has not had access to a lawyer will always be a violation of his rights under Article 6(1) and (3)(c) of the ECHR (§ 16–57 in the main work); (ii) it is one thing if the impugned evidence was created by answers given in reply to such impermissible questioning; the leading of such evidence would be a breach of the accused's convention rights unless there were compelling reasons to restrict the right of access (*Cadder v. H.M. Advocate (H.M. Advocate General for Scotland)* (see the main work)); (iii) it is another thing if the evidence existed independently of those answers, such that the evidence speaks for itself without it being necessary to refer, for support or explanation, to anything the accused said in his police interview; and (iv) the question of whether evidence of that kind is admissible has to be tested by considering whether the accused's right to a fair trial would be violated by the leading of the evidence.

In *McGowan (Procurator Fiscal, Edinburgh) v. B.* [2011] 1 W.L.R. 3121, SC, it was held that the jurisprudence of the Strasbourg court does not support the proposition that, as a rule, Article 6(1), read with Article 6(3)(c), dictates that the right of access to legal advice during police questioning can only be waived if the accused has received advice from a lawyer as to whether or not he should do so; in accordance with Strasbourg authority, a waiver must be established in an unequivocal manner and be attended by the minimum safeguards commensurate with the importance of the right; normally, an express waiver will be held to be effective. The court said that the minimum guarantees are that the accused has been told of his right, that he understands what the right is, that it is being waived, and that the waiver is made freely and voluntarily; however, a court must be alive to the possibility that the right may not be fully understood by everyone. The Supreme Court referred to *Pishchalnikov v. Russia*, unreported, September 24, 2009, ECtHR, where the court ruled that a waiver must not only be voluntary, but must also constitute a "knowing and intelligent relinquishment of a right", in that the accused must have been reasonably able to foresee what the consequences of his conduct would be. The Supreme Court said that when determining, therefore, what minimum safeguards are necessary, account should be taken of the fact that, for a variety of reasons, a suspect may not appreciate the consequences of his agreeing to be questioned in the absence of a solicitor; to minimise this risk, the court suggested that the police should follow (as a matter of best practice where it is not obligatory) paragraph 6.5 of Code C (*post*, Appendix A–54) and should also inform the suspect, even one with previous experience of the criminal process, of the arrangements that might be made if he wishes to exercise his right but is unable to name a solicitor or is concerned about the cost of employing one.

To similar effect, see *Jude v. H.M. Advocate; Hodgson v. H.M. Advocate; Birnie v. H.M.*

Advocate [2011] L.S. Gazette, December 8, 21, SC ([2011] UKSC 55) (there is no absolute rule to be derived from the Strasbourg jurisprudence that an accused must have been given legal advice on the question of whether or not he should exercise his right of access to a lawyer and have given reasons for his waiver before he can be held to have waived it, and it will not necessarily be incompatible with Article 6(1), read with Article 6(3)(c), to lead and rely on evidence of statements made by a suspect who has waived his right to access to a lawyer without the benefit of legal advice and without giving reasons).

The prohibition on hearsay evidence

16–91   For the Grand Chamber decision in *Al-Khawaja v. U.K.*; *Tahery v. U.K.*, see *Al-Khawaja v. U.K.*, *ante*, § 11–3a.

G. Right to Respect for Private and Family Life

Justification

★**16–107**   As to the repeal of the original section 64 of the *PACE Act* 1984, see *ante*, § 15–196a.

Consensual sexual offences

16–108   In *G. v. U.K.* [2012] Crim.L.R. 46, ECtHR, a challenge to the decision of the House of Lords in *R. v. G. (Secretary of State for the Home Department intervening)* (see the main work) was rejected. It was held that where, at the time of the events in question, the applicant and the complainant were respectively 15- and 12-years-old, and where the applicant was convicted under section 5 of the *SOA* 2003 (§ 20–49 in the main work) of "rape" of a child under 13, but was sentenced on the basis that the complainant had consented to intercourse and that the applicant had reasonably believed the complainant to be the same age as himself, the conduct in issue fell within the meaning of "private life" under Article 8 of the ECHR (*ibid.*, § 16–101); therefore, the criminal proceedings against the applicant constituted an "interference by a public authority" with his right to respect for private life. In determining whether such interference was "necessary in a democratic society", the court would, however, take into account that contracting states enjoy a wide margin of appreciation as regards the means of ensuring adequate protection against rape; and, given that, in this case, the public interest at stake was the need to protect the complainant and other children in her position against premature sexual activity, exploitation and abuse, the state's margin of appreciation must be wide; as Baroness Hale observed in the House of Lords, the consequences of penetrative sex for a child under 13 may be very harmful. The authorities could not be said to have exceeded the margin of appreciation available to them by creating a criminal offence that is called "rape" and which does not allow for any defence based either on apparent consent or on a mistaken belief about the child's age; nor had they exceeded their margin of appreciation by deciding to prosecute the applicant for the offence, particularly since the legislation permitted for a broad range of sentence, and the mitigating circumstances in the applicant's case were fully taken into account by the Court of Appeal (which had substituted a conditional discharge for the detention and training order imposed in the Crown Court). As to this case, see also *ante*, § 16–78.

H. Freedom of Thought, Conscience and Religion

Limitations

★**16–115**   Where a member of the armed forces applies for discharge on the grounds of conscientious objection, Article 9 of the ECHR is not violated if he is required to take part in active service pending the final determination of his claim; and the current procedure for dealing with claims by members of the armed forces of conscientious objection satisfies the requirements of Article 9(2) of being prescribed by law, and being necessary in a democratic society in the interests of public safety, the protection of public order, and the protection of others: *R. v. Lyons* [2012] 1 Cr.App.R. 20, CMAC.

I. Freedom of Expression

Election offences

R. (Woolas) v. Parliamentary Election Court is now reported at [2012] Q.B. 1. ★16–130

Chapter 17

THE MENTAL ELEMENT IN CRIME

I. MENS REA

E. "Transferred Malice"

R. (Jones) v. First-tier Tribunal (Social Entitlement Chamber) is now reported at [2011] 3 **17–24** W.L.R. 971.

F. Vicarious Liability

As to whether it is possible to extend the principle of delegation (where a corporation is **17–28** liable for the acts of its employees on the basis that it has delegated to that employee the performance of certain legislative duties it is under) to offences requiring proof of *mens rea* or to offences other than the licensing offences to which it has previously been held to apply (see the main work), see *R. v. St Regis Paper Company Ltd*, *post*, § 17–30.

G. Offences by Corporation

The lesson to be learned from *Meridian Global Funds Management Asia Ltd v. Securities* **17–30** *Commission* (§ 17–31 in the main work) is the importance of focusing on the statute that creates the offence in order to determine the rules of attribution applicable to the offence in question; as had been said in *Att.-Gen.'s Reference (No. 2 of 1999)* (§ 1–142 in the main work), Lord Hoffmann in *Meridian* had proceeded on the basis that the primary "directing mind and will" rule in *Tesco Supermarkets Ltd v. Nattrass* (see the main work), still prevails; he had merely fashioned an additional special rule of attribution geared to the purpose of the particular statute: *R. v. St Regis Paper Company Ltd* [2012] 1 Cr.App.R. 14, CA. Applying this lesson, it was held that, as a matter of statutory construction, it was impossible to impose criminal liability for a breach of regulation 32(1)(g) of the *Pollution Prevention and Control (England and Wales) Regulations* 2000 (S.I. 2000 No. 1973) ("(1) It is an offence for a person — (g) intentionally to make a false entry in any record required to be kept under the condition of a permit;") on a company save in accordance with the test in *Tesco Supermarkets Ltd v. Nattrass* (*viz.* a company can only be liable for offences requiring proof of *mens rea* in cases where the controlling officers of the corporation performed the proscribed conduct with relevant guilty intention); given the contrast between offences of strict liability such as in regulation 32(1)(b) to (e), and offences that require proof of *mens rea* such as in regulation 32(1)(g) and (h), there was no basis for suggesting that the regulations, designed as they were to protect the environment and prevent pollution, could not function without imposing liability on the company in respect of one who is not the directing will and mind of the company. As for vicarious liability, it was held, considering the structure of regulation 32, that it was not possible to rely upon any principle of delegation (*viz.* that a corporation is liable for the acts of its employee on the basis that it has delegated to that employee the performance of certain duties cast by the legislation on the employer), even if the principle could be applied to offences that require *mens rea*, and even if the principle could be applied in circumstances other than in the licensing cases from which the principle derives (as to which, see §§ 17–28, 17–29 in the main work). For the corresponding offence in the current regulations, see regulation 38(4)(c) of the *Environmental Permitting (England and Wales) Regulations* 2010 (S.I. 2010 No. 675). For criticism of the decision, see CLW/11/44/4.

III. MENTAL ELEMENT IN ACCESSORIES

A. INTENTION

★**17–67**   In *R. (Equality and Human Rights Commission) v. Prime Minister*; *R. (Al Bazzouni) v. Same* [2012] 1 W.L.R. 1389, DC, it was said that *R. v. Bryce* (see the main work), is not authority for the proposition that a person's liability to be convicted of murder as an accessory, where he has done an act that assists the principal in the commission of the substantive offence, depends on whether he foresaw that there was a *real* (as opposed to a *serious*) risk that the principal would commit the offence. The court said that the issues in *Bryce* had been as to the intent of the principal (was it necessary that he had formed the *mens rea* for murder at the time of the act of assistance?) and the intent of the alleged secondary party (deliberately to assist the principal); the court in *Bryce* had not been directly concerned with the degree of foresight that had to be proved against the alleged accessory in relation to the carrying out of the substantive offence by the principal. The Divisional Court observed, however, that the expressions "real possibility", "real or substantial risk" and "real or serious risk" are all to be found in *Bryce*, and that the expressions are used interchangeably in that and other authorities.

VI. DURESS

A. AVAILABILITY

★**17–119**   *R. v. O.* and *R. v. M. (L.), B. (M.) and G. (D.)*; *R. v. Tabot*; *R. v. Tijani* (as to both of which, see the main work) were further considered in *R. v. N. (A.)*; *R. v. Le* (as to which, see *post*, Appendix E–12d).

VII. NECESSITY

Availability and scope

★**17–128**   The defence of necessity is not available in respect of an offence under section 1 of the *Child Abduction Act* 1984 (§ 19–311 in the main work): *R. v. S. (C.)* [2012] 1 Cr.App.R. 31, CA (considering *R. v. Quayle*; *R. v. Wales*; *R. v. Kenny*; *R. v. Taylor and Lee*; *Att.-Gen.'s Reference (No. 2 of 2004)* (§ 17–131 in the main work)).

Chapter 19

OFFENCES AGAINST THE PERSON

I. HOMICIDE

A. Murder

(2) **Liability of secondary parties**

Principle

As to *R. v. Mendez and Thompson* (see the main work), see *post*, § 19–27.   **19–24**

R. v. Day (M.) and *R. v. Yemoh* (as to both of which, see the main work) were followed in   **19–27** *R. v. Carpenter* [2012] 1 Cr.App.R. 11, CA, where it was argued that their authority had been undermined by *R. v. Mendez and Thompson* (§§ 19–24, 19–32a in the main work). Where the defendant's son had been convicted of murder by stabbing and where the defendant and other members of her family had been present at the fight between her son and the victim, which was held at a pre-arranged location and also attended by members of the victim's family, it was held that the judge had not erred in directing the jury that they could find her guilty of manslaughter if she was aware that her son had the knife, and foresaw that he would use it to cause some harm or injury falling short of serious injury; this was in line with established authority (*e.g. R. v. Day (M.)* and *R. v. Yemoh*); and to the extent that superficial support to the contrary could be gained from *R. v. Mendez and Thompson* (§§ 19–24, 19–32a in the main work) (*viz.* that the defendant should be guilty of murder or nothing, because a secondary party can only be liable for a death where he shares the intention of the principal or foresees that the principal might act with that intention), that case does not in reality represent a departure from that established authority; the context in *Mendez* was different, being a case where use of a knife was not foreseen; it either had no bearing on the instant case, or was *obiter*.

The decision of the Court of Appeal in *R. v. Gnango* (see the main work) has been re-   **19–30** versed by the Supreme Court (see *R. v. Gnango* [2012] 2 W.L.R. 17). It was held: (i) that where D1 and D2 voluntarily engage in fighting each other, each intending to kill or cause grievous bodily harm to the other and each foreseeing that the other has a reciprocal intention, and where D1 mistakenly kills a third party in the course of the fight, D2 is guilty of the offence of murdering the third party; because, in this case, D1 and D2 formed a mutual plan or agreement (either beforehand, or on the spur of the moment when they saw each other and fired at each other) to have a gun fight, in which each would shoot at each other and be shot at, and in which each would attempt to kill or seriously injure the other, each was party to the other's attempt to kill or seriously injure him; therefore, D2 aided, abetted, counselled and procured D1 to shoot at him with murderous intent, making him guilty of aiding and abetting the attempted murder of himself; had D2 been killed by D1, he would have been party to his own murder; as it was, D1 accidentally shot a third party, and under the doctrine of transferred malice, D1 was liable for her murder; under the same doctrine, D2, because he had aided, abetted, counselled and procured the attempt (on his own life), was party to the murder that resulted; there is a close analogy between a consensual gun fight and a duel or a prize fight; and there is no statutory bar, or common law rule, that precludes conviction of a defendant of being party to a crime of which he was the actual or intended victim (considering *R. v. Tyrrell* [1894] 1 Q.B. 710); neither is there any reason to extend the common law so as to protect from conviction any defendant who is, or is intended to be, harmed by the crime that he commits, or attempts to commit; alternatively, (ii) that it could be said that D2 was liable as a principal to a joint enterprise (an agreement) to engage

in unlawful violence specifically designed to cause death or serious injury, where death occurred as a result; but this was not a difference of substance, and, in this case, whether D2
was correctly described as a principal or accessory was irrelevant to his guilt.

(3) Lawful homicide

Use of force in prevention of crime

Criminal Justice and Immigration Act 2008, s.76

Reasonable force for purposes of self-defence etc.

★**19–39a**   As from a day to be appointed, section 76 of the 2008 Act is amended by the *Legal Aid,
Sentencing and Punishment of Offenders Act* 2012, s.148(1) and (2), so as (i) to omit the word
"and" at the end of subsection (2)(a), and (ii) to insert a new paragraph (aa), as follows—

> "(aa) the common law defence of defence of property; and".

★   As from a day to be appointed, section 76 of the 2008 Act is further amended by the 2012
Act, s.148(1) and (3), so as to insert a new subsection (6A), as follows—

> "(6A) In deciding the question mentioned in subsection (3), a possibility that D could have
> retreated is to be considered (so far as relevant) as a factor to be taken into account, rather than as
> giving rise to a duty to retreat.".

★   As from a day to be appointed, section 76 of the 2008 Act is further amended by the 2012
Act, s.148(1), (4) and (5), so as (i) to substitute "Subsections (6A) and (7)" for "Subsection
(7)" in subsection (8), (ii) to omit the word "or" at the end of subsection (10)(a)(i), and (iii) to
insert a new sub-paragraph (ia) after subsection (10)(a)(i), as follows—

> "(ia) the purpose of defence of property under the common law, or".

★   Section 148(6) of the 2012 Act stipulates that paragraph 27 of Schedule 27 to the *CJIA*
2008 (as to which, see the main work) applies to any amendment made by section 148 as
it applies to section 76, but as if references to the date on which section 76 comes into
force were references to the date on which the amendment comes into force.

Use of force at schools, etc.

★**19–40**   As from April 1, 2012 (*Education Act 2011 (Commencement No. 3 and Transitional and Savings Provisions) Order* 2012 (S.I. 2012 No. 924)), section 2 of the *Education Act* 2011 amends
sections 550ZA to 550ZD of the *Education Act* 1996. The power of members of staff to search
pupils for prohibited items under section 550ZA of the 1996 Act is extended to include, as a
prohibited item, an article that the member of staff reasonably suspects has been, or is likely
to be, used to commit an offence (which includes anything that would be an offence but for
the operation of any presumption that a person under a particular age is incapable of committing an offence: s.550ZA(4A)) or to cause personal injury or damage to property
(s.550ZA(3)(ea)), and any other item that the school rules identify as an item for which a
search may be made (s.550ZA(3)(g)). Sections 550ZB to 550ZD, which relate to the seizure,
retention, return or disposal, or the delivery to a police constable, of any items found during a search, are amended so as to provide that the power to use such force as is reasonable
in the circumstances when searching under section 550ZA or seizing under section 550ZC
does not extend to searches for, and seizure of, an item that is a prohibited item by virtue of
section 550ZA(3)(g). Corresponding amendments (except in relation to section 550ZA(3)(g))
are made by section 3 to sections 85AA to 85AD of the *Further and Higher Education Act*
1992 in respect of an institution within the further education sector. Sections 85AA to 85AC
of the 1992 Act are further amended, as from the same date, by the 2011 Act, s.54, and
Sched. 13, para. 8, so as to extend them to 16 to 19 academies.

★   The *Schools (Specification and Disposal of Articles) Regulations* 2012 (S.I. 2012 No. 951)
specify prohibited items for which members of staff in schools can search pupils without
their consent under section 550ZA of the 1996 Act.

(4) Defences

(a) *"Loss of control"/provocation*

Introduction

The Court of Appeal gave detailed consideration to the new defence of "loss of control" **19–50**
in *R. v. Clinton*; *R. v. Parker*; *R. v. Evans*, *post*, § 19–56.

Qualifying triggers

Sexual infidelity

Att.-Gen.'s Reference (No. 23 of 2011) (see the main work) is now reported at [2012] 1 **★19–56**
Cr.App.R.(S.) 45 , *sub nom. Att.-Gen.'s Reference (No. 23 of 2011) (R. v. Sanchez Williams)*.

In *R. v. Clinton*; *R. v. Parker*; *R. v. Evans* [2012] 1 Cr.App.R. 26, CA, it was held: (i) that
the new partial defence to murder in sections 54 and 55 of the *Coroners and Justice Act* 2009
(§§ 19–51, 19–52 in the main work) of "loss of control" is self-contained, and its common
law heritage is irrelevant; (ii) that, as to the first component of the defence, "D's acts and
omissions ... resulted from D's loss of self-control" (s.54(1)(a)), the loss of self-control need
not be sudden (s.54(2)), but the defendant must not have been acting "in a considered
desire for revenge" (s.54(4)); in reality, the greater the level of deliberation, the less likely it
will be that the killing followed a true loss of self-control; (iii) that, as to the second
component, "the loss of self-control had a qualifying trigger" (s.54(1)(b)), this is self-
contained in section 55, but the practical application of section 55 will create considerable
difficulties; considering section 55(4), the defendant himself must have had a sense of having been seriously wronged, but the questions whether the circumstances were extremely
grave, and whether the defendant's sense of grievance was justifiable, require objective
evaluation; the process of objective evaluation in each individual case is hugely complicated
by the prohibitions in section 55(6), which identifies a number of features that are expressly
excluded from consideration as qualifying triggers, the most critical problem being in
paragraph (c), "the fact that a thing done or said constituted sexual infidelity is to be
disregarded"; whatever the anomalies to which it may give rise, section 55(6)(c) is unequivocal, and means that loss of control triggered by sexual infidelity cannot, on its own, qualify
as a trigger for the purposes of the second statutory component; and an admission of sexual
infidelity (even if untrue) as well as reports (by others) of sexual infidelity will be things
"said" that constitute sexual infidelity; however, where sexual infidelity is integral to, and
forms an essential part of, the context in which to make a just evaluation whether a qualifying trigger properly falls within the ambit of section 55(3) and (4), the prohibition in section
55(6)(c) does not operate to exclude it; and (iv) that, as to the third component, "a person
of D's sex and age, with a normal degree of tolerance and self-restraint and in the circumstances of D, might have reacted in the same or in a similar way to D" (s.54(1)(c)), the
impact on the defendant of sexual infidelity is not excluded; and this means that there will
be occasions when the jury would be both disregarding and considering the same evidence,
which is counter-intuitive.

Sentence

See *R. v. Brook (Neil)*, *ante*, § 5–520, a decision on provocation. As to whether it carries **★19–60**
across to the defence of "loss of control" under section 54 of the *Coroners and Justice Act*
2009 is open to argument.

Provocation

At common law, provocation reduced murder to manslaughter; and was available as a **19–61**
potential defence both for a principal and an accessory: *R. v. Marks* [1998] Crim.L.R. 676,
CA. It was irrelevant on the issue of guilt in all other crimes.

The jury should be directed that before they have to consider the issue of provocation the

Crown must have proved beyond reasonable doubt that all the other elements of murder were present, including the necessary intent: see *Lee Chun-Chuen v. R.* [1963] A.C. 220, PC; and *R. v. Martindale*, 50 Cr.App.R. 273, Ct-MAC.

The law as to provocation immediately prior to October 4, 2010 (as to which, see § 19–50 in the main work) was governed by a blend of common law and statute, *viz.* the *Homicide Act* 1957, s.3 (*post*, § 19–62).

Homicide Act 1957, s.3

Provocation

19–62   **3.** Where on a charge of murder there is evidence on which the jury can find that the person charged was provoked (whether by things done or by things said or by both together) to lose his self-control, the question whether the provocation was enough to make a reasonable man do as he did shall be left to be determined by the jury; and in determining that question the jury shall take into account everything both done and said according to the effect which, in their opinion, it would have on a reasonable man.

This section altered as well as clarified the common law on this subject.

Duty of judge

19–63   Section 3 involves two questions: (a) is there any evidence of specific provoking conduct of the accused, and (b) is there any evidence that the provocation caused him to lose his self-control? If both questions are answered in the affirmative, the issue of provocation should be left to the jury notwithstanding the fact that in the opinion of the judge no reasonable jury could conclude on the evidence that a reasonable person would have been provoked to lose his self-control: *R. v. Gilbert*, 66 Cr.App.R. 237, CA; *Franco v. R., The Times*, October 11, 2001, PC; notwithstanding that there may be circumstances suggesting that the accused acted in revenge, rather than as a result of a sudden and temporary loss of self-control: *R. v. Baillie* [1995] 2 Cr.App.R. 31, CA; and notwithstanding that the issue has not been raised by the defence: *Bullard v. R.* [1957] A.C. 635, PC; *DPP v. Camplin* [1978] A.C. 705, HL; *R. v. Rossiter*, 95 Cr.App.R. 326, CA; and would prefer it not to be left to the jury: *R. v. Dhillon* [1997] 2 Cr.App.R. 104, CA.

Where, however, there is only a speculative possibility of the accused having acted as a result of provoking conduct, the issue should not be left to the jury: *R. v. Acott* [1997] 2 Cr.App.R. 94, HL (there must be some evidence of specific provoking conduct resulting in a loss of control by the accused; the source of such evidence is immaterial as is reliance thereon by the accused); and *R. v. Evans (John Derek)* [2010] Crim.L.R. 491, CA (§ 19–58 in the main work). Evidence of a loss of self-control is insufficient, for a loss of self-control might be brought on by fear, panic or sheer bad temper, as well as by provoking conduct: *ibid.* Questions put in cross-examination are not evidence: *ibid.* The observations in *Acott* are equally apt when considering whether there is sufficient evidence that a defendant was provoked, as they are when considering whether there was evidence of provoking conduct: *R. v. Miao, The Times*, November 26, 2003, CA. For the issue to be left to the jury, there has to be evidence from which a reasonable jury might conclude that the defendant was or may have been provoked: *R. v. Cambridge*, 99 Cr.App.R. 142, CA. See also *R. v. Jones (Robert James)* [2000] 3 *Archbold News* 2, CA (where the defence is self-defence, with no reliance by the defence on provocation, the judge should not leave provocation to the jury where the evidence of provoking conduct by the deceased, or the evidence that such conduct caused a loss of self-control by the defendant is minimal or fanciful).

Where a judge is obliged to leave provocation to the jury, he should indicate to them, unless it is obvious, what evidence might support the conclusion that the defendant had lost his self-control; this is particularly important where the defence have not raised the issue: *R. v. Stewart* [1996] 1 Cr.App.R. 229, CA. See also *R. v. Humphreys* [1995] 4 All E.R. 1008, CA (similar duty where there is a complex history with several distinct strands of potentially provocative conduct, building up over time until the final encounter).

Where provocation is not left to the jury when it should have been, a conviction for manslaughter will be substituted unless the court is sure that the jury would inevitably have convicted: *R. v. Dhillon, ante*, but an appellate court should be cautious in drawing inferences or making findings about how the jury would have resolved issues which were never before them; and that is particularly so in the context of section 3, since Parliament had gone out of its way, unusually, to stipulate that resolution of the objective issue should be exclusively reserved to the jury; to the extent that an appellate court took it upon itself to decide that issue, it was doing what Parliament had said that the jury should do, and section 3 could not be read as applying only to the trial court: *Franco v. R., ante*.

In *R. v. Van Dongen and Van Dongen* [2005] 2 Cr.App.R. 38, CA, it was held that: (i) section 3 is concerned with provocative conduct, as opposed to merely causative conduct; yet a judgment that particular conduct was no more than causative risks straying into an evaluation of the objective element of the defence, which statute has left to the jury; accordingly, the prudent course for judges to take, in borderline cases, especially if the defence ask for a provocation direction to be given, is to leave the issue to the jury; (ii) where, therefore, in a case in which the defence had been self-defence and/or lack of intent and/or accident, but not provocation, there was evidence of conduct that was capable of being provoking conduct and there was evidence of a loss of self-control, the matter should have been left to the jury, more particularly as defence counsel had sought such a direction; but (iii) the failure to leave it did not mean that the conviction could not be upheld, notwithstanding that the Act specifically provides for the jury to determine the objective issue; *Franco v. R., ante*, was not authority for the proposition that a conviction could not be upheld in such circumstances; whilst it was necessary to be cautious in drawing inferences or making findings about how the jury would have resolved issues which were never before them, the court must not overlook the matter of justice for those concerned with the victim, nor the requirements of a proportionate appellate system, which included that those who were surely and fairly shown to be guilty of murder, and were so found by a jury, should not escape the consequences on gossamer grounds; where, therefore, the unavoidable facts of the case and the necessary logic of the jury's verdict ruled out any possibility of a miscarriage of justice, the conviction should be upheld.

Duty of counsel

See *R. v. Cox (A.M.)* [1995] 2 Cr.App.R. 513, CA (§ 19–57 in the main work).   **19–63a**

Onus of proof

Once there is evidence from any source, sufficient to be left to the jury on the issue of   **19–63b**
provocation, the onus remains throughout upon the Crown to prove absence of provocation beyond reasonable doubt: *R. v. McPherson*, 41 Cr.App.R. 213, CCA. As to the necessity for a careful direction on onus of proof, see *R. v. Wheeler*, 52 Cr.App.R. 28, CA (§ 19–44 in the main work).

"Provoked ... to lose his self control"

(i) *Meaning of "provocation"*

In *R. v. Whitfield*, 63 Cr.App.R. 39 at 42, the Court of Appeal said that the meaning of   **19–64**
provocation was still that given to it by Devlin J. in *R. v. Duffy* [1949] 1 All E.R. 932, as cited by Lord Goddard C.J. when giving the judgment of the Court of Criminal Appeal:

> "Provocation is some act, or series of acts, done [or words spoken] [by the dead man to the accused] which would cause in any reasonable person, and actually causes in the accused, a sudden and temporary loss of self-control, rendering the accused so subject to passion as to make him or her for the moment not master of his mind" (at p.932).

The words in the first pair of square brackets were not actually said by Devlin J. but appear in the quotation of him by Lord Lane C.J. as if spoken by him (presumably to take account of the express reference to "things said" in section 3 of the 1957 Act, *ante*, § 19–62); the words in the second pair of square brackets must be ignored in view of the wording of section 3. See also *post*, § 19–65.

(ii) Loss of self-control must be associated with the act which causes death

19–64a   The point was considered in *R. v. Ibrams and Gregory*, 74 Cr.App.R. 154, CA. Provocation is available only in the case of a sudden and temporary loss of self-control of such a kind as to make the accused for the moment not master of his mind: see *R. v. Duffy* and *R. v. Whitfield, ante*. Circumstances which induce a desire for revenge are inconsistent with provocation, since the conscious formulation of a desire for revenge means that a person has had time to think, to reflect and that would negative a sudden temporary loss of self-control, which is the essence of provocation. But the mere existence of such circumstances does not mean that the judge should not leave the issue to the jury if there is evidence that the accused was in fact provoked; it is for the jury to decide: see *R. v. Baillie* [1995] 2 Cr.App.R. 31, CA.

(iii) Cumulative provocation

19–64b   Although it is established that a temporary and sudden loss of self-control arising from an act of provocation is essential, it is less clear to what extent previous acts of provocation are admissible. Each case must be considered against the background of its own particular facts: *R. v. Thornton*, 96 Cr.App.R. 112, CA. In *R. v. Brown* [1972] 2 Q.B. 229, 56 Cr.App.R. 564, CA, a direction that the jury had to find provocation in something done on the morning of the killing was approved. In *R. v. Davies (P.)* [1975] Q.B. 691, 60 Cr.App.R. 253, the Court of Appeal described as "too generous" a direction that the jury could review the whole of the deceased's conduct throughout the years preceding death: and see *R. v. Ibrams and Gregory, ante*. In *R. v. Pearson* [1992] Crim.L.R. 193, the Court of Appeal substituted manslaughter for a conviction for murder on the grounds, *inter alia*, that the jury may have been left with the impression that an eight-year history of violent conduct by the deceased towards his younger son was not to be taken into account when considering the case of the elder son, who had spent much of that time away from home.

A general approach can, however, be discerned from the authorities, namely that evidence of previous provocative acts or past conduct, particularly in cases of domestic violence, is admissible in order to place in its appropriate context the reaction of the accused to the alleged provocation on the occasion of the killing: see *R. v. Thornton, ante*, at p. 118. For the proper approach in relation to a history of provocation leading to a post-traumatic stress syndrome or "battered woman syndrome", see *R. v. Ahluwalia*, 96 Cr.App.R. 133, CA, and *R. v. Thornton (No. 2)* [1996] 2 Cr.App.R. 108, CA (a jury might more easily find that there was a sudden loss of self-control triggered even by a minor incident if the defendant had endured abuse over a period, on a last-straw basis).

"Things done or said"

19–65   The things done or said may be done or said by the deceased or anyone else: *R. v. Davies (P.), ante*; *R. v. Doughty (S.)*, 83 Cr.App.R. 319, CA.

"Reasonable man"

19–65a   The "reasonable man" means "an ordinary person of either sex, not exceptionally excitable or pugnacious, but possessed of such powers of self-control as everyone is entitled to expect that his fellow citizens will exercise in society as it is today": *per* Lord Diplock in *DPP v. Camplin* [1978] A.C. 705 at 771, HL; means "a man of ordinary self-control": *ibid., per* Lord Simon at p.726. Both formulations were approved by the majority in *Att.-Gen. for Jersey v. Holley* [2005] 2 A.C. 580, PC, in which an enlarged board of nine was assembled for the purpose of considering the conflict between *Camplin* and *Luc Thiet Thuan v. R.* [1997] A.C. 131, PC, on the one hand, and *R. v. Smith (Morgan)* [2001] 1 A.C. 146, HL, on the other, and to "clarify definitively the present state of English law". That it had done so was accepted by the Court of Appeal in *R. v. James; R. v. Karimi* [2006] 1 Cr.App.R. 29.

The majority opinion in *Holley* was that the jury, in deciding whether the defendant lost his self-control and, if he did, whether he did so as a result of provocation, should take the defendant exactly as they find him ("warts and all" (including that he had a violent temperament: see *R. v. Mohammed (Faqir)* [2005] 9 *Archbold News* 3, CA)); but, having assessed the gravity of the provocation to the defendant (for which purpose they must, for example, take account of the fact that he is a homosexual if taunted for his homosexuality, that he is disabled if taunted for being a "cripple", *etc.*), the standard of self-control by which his conduct is to be evaluated is the external standard of a person having and exercising the ordinary powers of self-control to be expected of a person of the defendant's age and sex. The majority ruling in *Smith* was held to be wrong in that section 3 of the 1957 Act adopted a uniform, objective standard; whether the provocative act or words and the defendant's response met the "ordinary person" standard prescribed by the statute is the question the jury must consider, not the altogether looser question (suggested by *Smith*) of whether, having regard to all the circumstances, the jury consider the loss of self-control was sufficiently excusable; the statute, it was said, does not leave each jury free to set whatever standard they consider appropriate. Accordingly, it was held to follow that if the defendant had been taunted by reference to his being an alcoholic or a drug addict, his alcoholism or addiction might be relevant to the jury's consideration of the gravity of the taunt to the defendant, but it would not be relevant to the question whether he exercised ordinary self-control.

Self-induced provocation

The mere fact that the defendant caused a reaction in others which in turn led him to lose his self-control does not preclude a successful defence of provocation: *R. v. Johnson (C.)*, 89 Cr.App.R. 148, CA. **19–65b**

In *Edwards v. R.* [1973] A.C. 648, PC, the appellant's case was that the man whom he was blackmailing attacked him with a knife and he thereupon lost his temper and killed him. The relevant ordinance in Hong Kong was in the same terms as section 3 of the *Homicide Act* 1957, *ante*. The Board said (at p. 658):

> "No authority has been cited with regard to what may be called 'self-induced provocation'. On principle it seems reasonable to say that: (1) a blackmailer cannot rely on the predictable results of his own blackmailing conduct as constituting provocation sufficient to reduce his killing of the victim from murder to manslaughter, and the predictable results may include a considerable degree of hostile reaction by the person sought to be blackmailed, for instance vituperous words and even some hostile action such as blows with a fist; (2) but, if the hostile reaction by the person sought to be blackmailed goes to extreme lengths, it might constitute sufficient provocation even for a blackmailer; (3) there would in many cases be a question of degree to be decided by the jury."

Provocation and lies

Lies and attempts to cover up a killing are not necessarily inconsistent with provocation. In directions about lies, when the issue was murder or manslaughter, the jury should be alerted to the fact that, before they could treat lies as proof of guilt of the offence charged, they had to be sure that there was not some possible explanation which destroyed their potentially probative effect. A failure to give such a direction, coupled with an indication that the jury might regard lies as probative of murder rather than manslaughter, amounted to a material misdirection: *R. v. Richens*, 98 Cr.App.R. 43, CA; *R. v. Taylor* [1998] 7 *Archbold News* 3, CA. **19–65c**

Provocation and good character

Where there is evidence of the defendant's good character, the judge should direct the jury as to the relevance of that both to credibility and propensity; and, in particular, should remind them that, as a man of good character, the defendant might have been unlikely to indulge in serious violence without first being provoked: *Paria v. R.* [2004] Crim.L.R. 228, PC. **19–65d**

Sentence

See the guideline issued by the Sentencing Guidelines Council (*post*, K–71 *et seq.*). Of the **19–65e** pre-guideline authorities, see, in particular, *Att.-Gen.'s References (Nos 74, 95 and 118 of 2002) (R. v. Suratan; R. v. Humes; R. v. Wilkinson)* [2003] 2 Cr.App.R.(S.) 42, CA, which is summarised at paragraph 2.1 of the guideline (Appendix K–74).

★   See also *R. v. Brook (Neil)*, *ante*, § 5–520.

(b) *Diminished responsibility*

Homicide Act 1957, s.2

Persons suffering from diminished responsibility

19–66   As to the effect of the amendments to section 2 of the 1957 Act effected by the *Coroners and Justice Act* 2009, see *post*, § 19–69a.

Abnormality of "mind"/"mental functioning" — substantial impairment

(iv) *"Substantially"*

19–69a   In *R. v. Brown (Robert)* [2012] Crim.L.R. 223, CA, it was held that the amendments to section 2 of the *Homicide Act* 1957 effected by the *Coroners and Justice Act* 2009 (as to which, see § 19–66 in the main work) have not affected the test of "substantial impairment".

(v) *Drink and mental abnormality*

★**19–70**   The reformulation of the statutory conditions for diminished responsibility (by the *Coroners and Justice Act* 2009, s.52) was not intended to reverse the well-established rule that voluntary acute intoxication (whether caused by ingesting alcohol or drugs), uncomplicated by alcoholism or dependence, is not capable of being relied upon to found diminished responsibility (considering, *inter alia*, *R. v. Dietschmann* (see the main work), *R. v. Wood* (§ 19–72 in the main work), and *R. v. Stewart* (*ibid.*)); whilst "acute intoxication" is listed as a condition in the International Statistical Classification of Diseases and Related Health Problems, the presence of a "recognised medical condition" is a necessary, but not always sufficient, condition to raise the issue of diminished responsibility: *R. v. Dowds* [2012] 1 Cr.App.R. 34, CA.

Sentence

19–81   The approach to sentence adopted in *R. v. Wood* (see the main work) was held to apply equally to diminished responsibility cases arising under the amended version of section 2 of the *Homicide Act* 1957 (as to which, see § 19–66 in the main work) in *R. v. Brown (Robert)* [2012] Crim.L.R. 223, CA. In holding that the judge had been entitled to find that the defendant's responsibility for the killing remained substantial, the court said that it was not necessary for a judge to set out an exact arithmetical computation of the sentence that would have been passed had there been a conviction for murder, but that such an exercise was helpful.

★   When one is considering cases where responsibility is diminished, the significance of there being two killings is much minimised: *R. v. Dighton* [2012] 1 Cr.App.R.(S.) 30, CA.

(6) Restriction on prosecution

★**19–88a**   As from July 2, 2012 (*Domestic Violence, Crime and Victims (Amendment) Act 2012 (Commencement) Order* 2012 (S.I. 2012 No. 1432)), section 2 of the *Law Reform (Year and a Day Rule) Act* 1996 is amended by the *Domestic Violence, Crime and Victims (Amendment) Act* 2012, s.3, and Sched., para. 3, so as to ensure that a non-fatal offence under section 5 of the *Domestic Violence, Crime and Victims Act* 2004 is excluded from its ambit.

C. Corporate Manslaughter

(1) The offence

Corporate Manslaughter and Corporate Homicide Act 2007, s.1

The offence

As from April 1, 2012, section 26(2) of, and Schedule 5 to, the *Budget Responsibility and National Audit Act* 2011 (as to which, see the main work) are brought into force: *Budget Responsibility and National Audit Act 2011 (Commencement No. 2) Order* 2011 (S.I. 2011 No. 2576).   **19–117**

(2) Relevant duty of care

Corporate Manslaughter and Corporate Homicide Act 2007, ss.2–7

Emergencies

As from a day to be appointed, the definition of "relevant NHS body" in section 6(7) of the 2007 Act is amended by the *Health and Social Care Act* 2012, s.55(2), and Sched. 5, para. 147, so as (i) to insert the words "a clinical commissioning group," at the beginning of paragraph (a), (ii) to omit the words "a Strategic Health Authority," and "Primary Care Trust," from the same paragraph, and (iii) to insert a new paragraph (za) before paragraph (a), as follows—   **★19–117e**

"(za) the National Health Service Commissioning Board;".

(5) Application to particular categories of organisation

Corporate Manslaughter and Corporate Homicide Act 2007, ss.11–14

Application to police forces

The amendment of section 13(3) of the 2007 Act by the *Police Reform and Social Responsibility Act* 2011, s.99, and Sched. 16, para. 365 (see the main work), came into force on January 16, 2012: *Police Reform and Social Responsibility Act 2011 (Commencement No. 3 and Transitional Provisions) Order* 2011 (S.I. 2011 No. 3019).   **19–117l**

D. Causing or Allowing the Death of a Child or Vulnerable Adult

(1) Statute

Domestic Violence, Crime and Victims Act 2004, s.5

The offence

As from July 2, 2012 (*Domestic Violence, Crime and Victims (Amendment) Act 2012 (Commencement) Order* 2012 (S.I. 2012 No. 1432)), section 5 of the 2004 Act is amended by the *Domestic Violence, Crime and Victims (Amendment) Act* 2012, s.1(1) to (7), so as (i) to change the heading to "*Causing or allowing a child or vulnerable adult to die or suffer serious physical harm* ", (ii) to insert the words "or suffers serious physical harm" after the word "dies" in subsection (1)(a), (iii) to substitute the words "the death or serious physical harm" for "V's death" in subsections (1)(d), (3)(a) and (4)(b), (iv) to insert the words "of causing or allowing a person's death" after the words "this section" in subsection (7), and (v) to insert a new subsection (8), as follows—   **★19–118a**

"(8) A person guilty of an offence under this section of causing or allowing a person to suffer serious physical harm is liable on conviction on indictment to imprisonment for a term not exceeding 10 years or to a fine, or to both.".

Section 1(8) of the 2012 Act provides that the amendments made by this section do not apply in relation to any harm resulting from an act that occurs, or so much of an act as occurs, before the commencement of this section.

(6) Evidence and procedure

Domestic Violence, Crime and Victims Act 2004, ss.6, 6A

Evidence and procedure in cases of death: England and Wales

★**19–118f**   As from July 2, 2012 (*Domestic Violence, Crime and Victims (Amendment) Act 2012 (Commencement) Order* 2012 (S.I. 2012 No. 1432)), section 6 of the 2004 Act is amended by the *Domestic Violence, Crime and Victims (Amendment) Act* 2012, s.3, and Sched., para. 8, so as (i) to change the heading to "*Evidence and procedure in cases of death: England and Wales*"; and (ii) to insert the words "of causing or allowing a person's death" after "section 5" in subsection (5).

Evidence and procedure in cases of serious physical harm: England and Wales

★**19–118fa**   As from July 2, 2012 (*Domestic Violence, Crime and Victims (Amendment) Act 2012 (Commencement) Order* 2012 (S.I. 2012 No. 1432)), a new section 6A is inserted into the 2004 Act by section 2 of the *Domestic Violence, Crime and Victims (Amendment) Act* 2012.

[Evidence and procedure in cases of serious physical harm: England and Wales

6A.—(1) Subsections (3) to (5) apply where a person ("the defendant") is charged in the same proceedings with a relevant offence and with an offence under section 5 in respect of the same harm ("the section 5 offence").

(2) In this section "relevant offence" means—

(a) an offence under section 18 or 20 of the *Offences against the Person Act* 1861 (grievous bodily harm etc);

(b) an offence under section 1 of the *Criminal Attempts Act* 1981 of attempting to commit murder.

(3) Where by virtue of section 35(3) of the *Criminal Justice and Public Order Act* 1994 a court or jury is permitted, in relation to the section 5 offence, to draw such inferences as appear proper from the defendant's failure to give evidence or refusal to answer a question, the court or jury may also draw such inferences in determining whether the defendant is guilty of a relevant offence, even if there would otherwise be no case for the defendant to answer in relation to that offence.

(4) The charge of the relevant offence is not to be dismissed under paragraph 2 of Schedule 3 to the *Crime and Disorder Act* 1998 (unless the section 5 offence is dismissed).

(5) At the defendant's trial the question whether there is a case for the defendant to answer on the charge of the relevant offence is not to be considered before the close of all the evidence (or, if at some earlier time the defendant ceases to be charged with the section 5 offence, before that earlier time).]

III. ABORTION

(7) Defences

Abortion Act 1967, s.1

Medical termination of pregnancy

★**19–162**   As from a day to be appointed, section 1(3) of the 1967 Act is amended by the *Health and Social Care Act* 2012, ss.55(2) and 179(6), Sched. 5, para. 9 (omission of the words "a Primary Care Trust or"), and Sched. 14, para. 43 (insertion of the words "established under section 18 of the *National Health Service (Wales) Act* 2006 or the *National Health Service (Scotland) Act* 1978" after the words "National Health Service trust").

★**19–163**   *British Pregnancy Advisory Service v. Secretary of State for Health (Society for the Protection for Unborn Children, intervener)* (see the main work) is now reported at [2012] 1 W.L.R. 580, *sub nom. British Pregnancy Advisory Service v. Secretary of State for Health.*

IV. COMMON ASSAULT AND BATTERY

C. Defences

Consent

H. v. CPS is now reported at [2012] 2 W.L.R. 296.

★19–180

VI. WOUNDING, CAUSING GRIEVOUS BODILY HARM

(2) Indictment

As to evidence and procedure where a person is charged in the same proceedings with an offence under section 18 or 20 of the *Offences against the Person Act* 1861 and a non-fatal offence under section 5 of the *Domestic Violence, Crime and Victims Act* 2004, see section 6A of the 2004 Act, as inserted by section 2 of the *Domestic Violence, Crime and Victims (Amendment) Act* 2012 (*ante*, § 19–118fa).

19–201

(6) Ingredients of the offences

(c) *"Unlawfully and maliciously"*

R. (Jones) v. First-tier Tribunal (Social Entitlement Chamber) is now reported at [2011] 3 W.L.R. 971.

19–211

X. HARASSMENT

A. Introduction

As from a day to be appointed, new sections 2A (offence of stalking), 2B (power of entry in relation to offence of stalking) and 4A (stalking involving fear of violence or serious alarm or distress) are inserted in the *Protection from Harassment Act* 1997 by the *Protection of Freedoms Act* 2012, ss.111 and 112.

★19–277a

B. Statute

Protection from Harassment Act 1997, ss.1, 2

Prohibition of harassment

As from a day to be appointed, section 1(2) of the 1997 Act is amended by the *Protection of Freedoms Act* 2012, s.115(1), and Sched. 9, para. 143(1) and (2), so as to insert the words "or section 2A(2)(c)" after the words "this section".

★19–277b

For a defendant to succeed in bringing his case within section 1(3)(a) of the 1997 Act, he must show that the sole purpose of the course of conduct was the prevention or detection of crime; and it was the purpose of the course of conduct itself that mattered; the avowed purpose of the defendant was not determinative, but was merely part of the evidence which the court would have to assess: *Hayes v. Willoughby* [2012] 1 W.L.R. 1510, CA (Civ. Div.) (observing that a defendant will find it difficult to show that the purpose of his course of conduct was preventing or detecting crime if there was no reasonable or rational link between the purpose he asserts and the nature and extent of the conduct he pursued).

★

A course of conduct in the form of journalistic speech will fall within the protective ambit of section 1(3)(c) of the 1997 Act (harassment provisions do not apply to the pursuit of a course of conduct that was reasonable), unless, in the particular circumstances, the

★

journalistic content is so unreasonable that it is necessary (in the sense of a pressing social need) and proportionate to prohibit or sanction it in pursuit of one of the aims listed in Article 10(2) of the ECHR (freedom of expression (§ 16–119 in the main work)), including, in particular, the protection of the rights of others under Article 8 (right to respect for private and family life (*ibid.*, § 16–101)): *Trimingham v. Associated Newspapers Ltd* [2012] L.S. Gazette, June 21, 21, QBD (Tugendhat J.) ([2012] EWHC 1296 (QB)) (considering *Thomas v. News Group Newspapers Ltd* (as to which, see § 19–277a in the main work)).

Offence of harassment

★**19–277c**   As from a day to be appointed, new sections 2A (offence of stalking) and 2B (power of entry in relation to offence of stalking) are inserted in the 1997 Act by the *Protection of Freedoms Act* 2012, ss.111(1) and 112 respectively.

Protection from Harassment Act 1997, ss.2A, 2B

[Offence of stalking

2A.—(1) A person is guilty of an offence if—

    (a) the person pursues a course of conduct in breach of section 1(1), and

    (b) the course of conduct amounts to stalking.

(2) For the purposes of subsection (1)(b) (and section 4A(1)(a)) a person's course of conduct amounts to stalking of another person if—

    (a) it amounts to harassment of that person,

    (b) the acts or omissions involved are ones associated with stalking, and

    (c) the person whose course of conduct it is knows or ought to know that the course of conduct amounts to harassment of the other person.

(3) The following are examples of acts or omissions which, in particular circumstances, are ones associated with stalking—

    (a) following a person,

    (b) contacting, or attempting to contact, a person by any means,

    (c) publishing any statement or other material—

        (i) relating or purporting to relate to a person, or

        (ii) purporting to originate from a person,

    (d) monitoring the use by a person of the internet, email or any other form of electronic communication,

    (e) loitering in any place (whether public or private),

    (f) interfering with any property in the possession of a person,

    (g) watching or spying on a person.

(4) A person guilty of an offence under this section is liable on summary conviction to imprisonment for a term not exceeding 51 weeks, or a fine not exceeding level 5 on the standard scale, or both.

(5) In relation to an offence committed before the commencement of section 281(5) of the *Criminal Justice Act* 2003, the reference in subsection (4) to 51 weeks is to be read as a reference to six months.

(6) This section is without prejudice to the generality of section 2.]

[Power of entry in relation to offence of stalking

2B.—(1) A justice of the peace may, on an application by a constable, issue a warrant authorising a constable to enter and search premises if the justice of the peace is satisfied that there are reasonable grounds for believing that—

    (a) an offence under section 2A has been, or is being, committed,

    (b) there is material on the premises which is likely to be of substantial value (whether by itself or together with other material) to the investigation of the offence,

    (c) the material—

        (i) is likely to be admissible in evidence at a trial for the offence, and

        (ii) does not consist of, or include, items subject to legal privilege, excluded material or special procedure material (within the meanings given by sections 10, 11 and 14 of the *Police and Criminal Evidence Act* 1984), and

(d) either—

    (i) entry to the premises will not be granted unless a warrant is produced, or

    (ii) the purpose of a search may be frustrated or seriously prejudiced unless a constable arriving at the premises can secure immediate entry to them.

(2) A constable may seize and retain anything for which a search has been authorised under subsection (1).

(3) A constable may use reasonable force, if necessary, in the exercise of any power conferred by virtue of this section.

(4) In this section "premises" has the same meaning as in section 23 of the *Police and Criminal Evidence Act* 1984.]

Protection from Harassment Act 1997, ss.3–5

Putting people in fear of violence

As from a day to be appointed, section 4 of the 1997 Act is amended by the *Protection of*   ★**19-277e**
Freedoms Act 2012, s.115(1), and Sched. 9, para. 143(1) and (3), so as to insert (i) "or 2A" after "section 2" in subsection (5), and (ii) "or 2A" after "section 2" in subsection (6).

R. v. Haque is now reported at [2012] 1 Cr.App.R. 5.

As from a day to be appointed, a new section 4A (stalking involving fear of violence or serious alarm or distress) is inserted in the 1997 Act by the *Protection of Freedoms Act* 2012, s.111(2).

Protection from Harassment Act 1997, s.4A

[Stalking involving fear of violence or serious alarm or distress

4A.—(1) A person ("A") whose course of conduct—

    (a) amounts to stalking, and

    (b) either—

        (i) causes another ("B") to fear, on at least two occasions, that violence will be used against B, or

        (ii) causes B serious alarm or distress which has a substantial adverse effect on B's usual day-to-day activities,

is guilty of an offence if A knows or ought to know that A's course of conduct will cause B so to fear on each of those occasions or (as the case may be) will cause such alarm or distress.

(2) For the purposes of this section A ought to know that A's course of conduct will cause B to fear that violence will be used against B on any occasion if a reasonable person in possession of the same information would think the course of conduct would cause B so to fear on that occasion.

(3) For the purposes of this section A ought to know that A's course of conduct will cause B serious alarm or distress which has a substantial adverse effect on B's usual day-to-day activities if a reasonable person in possession of the same information would think the course of conduct would cause B such alarm or distress.

(4) It is a defence for A to show that—

    (a) A's course of conduct was pursued for the purpose of preventing or detecting crime,

    (b) A's course of conduct was pursued under any enactment or rule of law or to comply with any condition or requirement imposed by any person under any enactment, or

    (c) the pursuit of A's course of conduct was reasonable for the protection of A or another or for the protection of A's or another's property.

(5) A person guilty of an offence under this section is liable—

    (a) on conviction on indictment, to imprisonment for a term not exceeding five years, or a fine, or both, or

    (b) on summary conviction, to imprisonment for a term not exceeding twelve months, or a fine not exceeding the statutory maximum, or both.

(6) In relation to an offence committed before the commencement of section 154(1) of the *Criminal Justice Act* 2003, the reference in subsection (5)(b) to twelve months is to be read as a reference to six months.

(7) If on the trial on indictment of a person charged with an offence under this section the jury

find the person not guilty of the offence charged, they may find the person guilty of an offence under section 2 or 2A.

(8) The Crown Court has the same powers and duties in relation to a person who is by virtue of subsection (7) convicted before it of an offence under section 2 or 2A as a magistrates' court would have on convicting the person of the offence.

(9) This section is without prejudice to the generality of section 4.]

Restraining orders on conviction

★**19–277f** A person's right of access to a court under Article 6 of the ECHR (§ 16–57 in the main work) is not absolute; it is permissible, therefore, for a restraining order (under the 1997 Act, s.5) to be drafted in terms that are wide enough to prohibit the bringing of civil proceedings against the person for whose benefit the restraining order was made where they are brought for the sole purpose of causing that person vexation, anxiety and annoyance; and neither Article 8 (right to privacy (*ibid.*, § 16–101)) nor Article 10 (freedom of information (*ibid.*, § 16–119)) of the convention confer an absolute right to obtain publicly-available information about oneself; where, therefore, a restraining order had a prohibition on "retrieving or storing any information in any media or form whatsoever" relating to the person to be protected, the fact that compliance with this term might have the consequence that the defendant would be prohibited from obtaining publicly available information about himself did not mean that a prosecution for breaching this term of the order was bound to fail; the restriction of the defendant's Article 8 and 10 rights was plainly justifiable under Article 8(2) and 10(2), as being proportionate and necessary for the protection of the claimant from harassment at the hands of the defendant: *R. (Waxman) v. CPS*, 176 J.P. 121, QBD (Moore-Bick J.).

Protection from Harassment Act 1997, s.5A

Restraining orders on acquittal

★**19–277g** *R. v. Kapotra* is now reported at [2012] 1 Cr.App.R.(S.) 88, *sub nom. R. v. K. (Davinder)*.

In *R. v. Trott*, 175 J.P. 458, CA, a restraining order under section 5A of the 1997 Act was quashed because the procedure the judge had followed had effectively denied the defendant the opportunity to make any submissions on the propriety of the order, let alone its terms (considering *R. v. Major* and *R. v. K. (Davinder)* (as to both of which, see the main work)).

★ Where the prosecution offer no evidence against a defendant and, following his acquittal, invite the court to make a restraining order under section 5A, if the matter is contested, the judge should hear evidence on either side; having done so, the judge should then express his findings and explain (if it be the case) how those findings led him to conclude that a restraining order is necessary; he should then consider carefully the requisite length of the order, ensuring that it is proportionate: *R. v. Brough (Stuart)* [2012] 2 Cr.App.R.(S.) 8, CA (further considering *R. v. Major* and *R. v. K. (Davinder)*, *ante*).

C. Racial or Religious Aggravation

Crime and Disorder Act 1998, s.32

Racially or religiously aggravated harassment etc.

★**19–277k** As from a day to be appointed, section 32 of the 1998 Act is amended by the *Protection of Freedoms Act* 2012, s.115(1), and Sched. 9, para. 144, so as (i) to insert "or 2A" after "section 2" in subsection (1)(a), (ii) to substitute the words "offences of harassment and stalking" for the words "offence of harassment" in subsection (1)(a), (iii) to insert "or 4A" after "section 4" in subsection (1)(b), (iv) to insert the words "and stalking involving fear of violence or serious alarm or distress" after the word "violence" in subsection (1)(b), and (v) to substitute the words "either basic offence" for the words "the basic offence" in subsection (5).

XIII. OFFENCES RELATING TO CHILDREN AND YOUNG PERSONS

B. ABDUCTION OF CHILDREN

Child Abduction Act 1984, s.1

Offence of abduction of child by parent, etc.

As from a day to be appointed, section 1(8) of the 1984 Act is amended by the *Legal Aid,* ★**19–312**
Sentencing and Punishment of Offenders Act 2012, s.105, and Sched. 12, paras 18 and 19, so as
to substitute the words "otherwise than on bail" for the words "to a local authority
accommodation".

As to whether the defence of necessity is available in respect of an offence under section 1 ★
of the 1984 Act, see *R. v. S. (C.), ante,* § 17–128.

Child Abduction Act 1984, ss.3, 4

Penalties and prosecutions

The abduction of children from a loving parent is an offence of unspeakable cruelty, **19–316**
whatever the child may later think of the parent from whom he or she has been estranged
as a result of the abduction; it is cruel even if the offender is the other parent; and there are
cases that merit a sentence greater than the current maximum; any reference in mitigation
to the right to family life, whether at common law, or in accordance with Article 8 of the
ECHR (§ 16–101 in the main work), is misconceived, because, in effect, such a submission
involves praying in aid and seeking to rely on the very principle that the offender has
deliberately violated, depriving the other parent of his or her children and depriving the
children of contact with a loving parent; generally, where the only person available to care
for children commits serious offences, even allowing fully for the interests of the children, it
does not follow that a custodial sentence, of appropriate length, is inappropriate; and there
is no reason why the offence of child abduction should be placed in a special category of its
own when the interests of the children of the offender fall to be considered: *R. v. Kayani; R.
v. Solliman* [2012] 1 Cr.App.R. 16, CA. As to this case, see also *post,* § 19–335.

Child Abduction Act 1984, Sched.

Children in places of safety

As from a day to be appointed, paragraph 2(1) of the schedule to the 1984 Act is amended ★**19–317**
by the *Legal Aid, Sentencing and Punishment of Offenders Act* 2012, s.105, and Sched. 12,
paras 18 and 20(a) and (b), so as (i) to omit the words "section 23 of the *Children and Young
Persons Act* 1969," in sub-paragraph (1)(b), (ii) to insert "; or" at the end of sub-paragraph
(1)(ba), and (ii) to insert, after sub-paragraph (1)(ba), a new sub-paragraph (1)(bb), as follows—

"(bb) remanded to local authority accommodation or youth detention accommodation under
section 91 of the *Legal Aid, Sentencing and Punishment of Offenders Act* 2012".

As from a day to be appointed, paragraph 2(2) of the schedule to the 1984 Act is amended ★
by the 2012 Act, s.105, and Sched. 12, paras 18 and 20(c), so as to insert the words ", local
authority accommodation or youth detention accommodation" after the words "place of
safety".

C. GENERAL STATUTORY PROVISIONS RELATING TO CHILDREN IN CRIMINAL PROCEEDINGS

Offences to which special provisions apply

Children and Young Persons Act 1933, Sched. 1

Offences to which special provisions apply

As from a day to be appointed, Schedule 1 to the 1933 Act is amended by the *Protection of* ★**19–322**

Freedoms Act 2012, s.115(1), and Sched. 9, para. 136, so as to substitute a reference to section 59A of the *SOA* 2003 for the reference to section 57 of that Act, and to insert at the end, a new entry as follows—

> "Any offence against a child or young person under section 4 of the *Asylum and Immigration (Treatment of Claimants, etc.) Act* 2004, or any attempt to commit such an offence.".

XIV. FALSE IMPRISONMENT AND KIDNAPPING

(1) Offences

Kidnapping

19–333   Whereas two of the elements of the offence of kidnapping are (a) the taking or carrying away of the victim, and (b) by force or fraud, force includes the threat of force, and the taking or carrying away element can be established by proof that the victim was threatened with force to take and carry away both himself and the accused, as in the case of hijacking a car together with its driver: *R. v. Archer* [2012] Crim.L.R. 292, CA.

Force or fraud

19–335   In *R. v. Kayani*; *R. v. Solliman* [2012] 1 Cr.App.R. 16, CA, it was said that the observation in *R. v. C.* (see § 19–336 in the main work), to the effect that a parent who seizes a child from the other parent should be charged with child abduction (*Child Abduction Act* 1984, s.1 (*ibid.*, § 19–311)) and not kidnapping at common law, has been overtaken by events. However, the court recognised, that were a charge of kidnapping to be brought, there would be considerable difficulties of proof, particularly in relation to the element of force or fraud. The court added that there is also the separate evidential problem that proof of this ingredient, and of the absence of consent, may require interviews with a child who has already been damaged, and ultimately the giving of evidence by the child against the kidnapping parent, with considerable potential for adding to the child's trauma.

(2) Indictment

19–336   As to the observation in *R. v. C.* (see the main work) about not charging kidnapping where a count of child abduction encompassed the allegation made by the prosecution, see *R. v. Kayani*; *R. v. Solliman*, *ante*, § 19–335.

(5) Defences

Arrest under criminal process

(ii) *Without warrant*

19–344   The decision of the Divisional Court in *R. (Moos and McLure) v. Commr of Police for the Metropolis* (see the main work) has been reversed on appeal: see *R. (McClure and Moos) v. Commr of Police for the Metropolis* [2012] 2 *Archbold Review* 3. This does not affect the point for which the lower court's decision is cited in the main work. Where the Court of Appeal differed from the Divisional Court was as to the function of the court. Where, in judicial review proceedings, it was sought to justify strategic policing decisions made in connection with crowd control at two demonstrations on the ground that they were necessary in order to prevent a breach of the peace, the role of the court was to decide whether, in the light of what the responsible police officer knew and perceived at the time, it was satisfied that it was reasonable to fear an imminent breach of the peace; the court's function was not (as had been held by the lower court) to form its own view as to imminence.

★   The decision of the House of Lords in *Austin v. Commr of Police of the Metropolis* (see the main work) has been vindicated in large part by that of the Grand Chamber of the European Court of Human Rights in *Austin v. U.K.* (*ante*, § 16–45).

Foulkes v. Chief Constable of the Merseyside Police (§ 19–343 in the main work) and *McCon-* ★
nell v. Chief Constable of Greater Manchester Police (see the main work) were considered in
Demetriou v. DPP (2012) 156(18) S.J. 31, DC. The court said that to the extent that those
cases had drawn a distinction between violence in the home and violence in the street, this
was unjustifiable in current times; what was a relevant consideration was that a person in
the street might be able to walk away, an option that might well not be open to a person in
the confines of a domestic situation.

CHAPTER 20

SEXUAL OFFENCES

I. INTRODUCTION

Sexual Offences Acts 1956 to 1992

As to the enactment of provisions (as from a day to be appointed) allowing a person who ★**20–1**
has been convicted of, or cautioned for, an offence under section 12 (buggery) or 13 (gross
indecency between men) of the 1956 Act, or corresponding earlier offences (and see s.101(3)
and (4) for related military offences), to apply to the Secretary of State for the conviction or
caution to become disregarded; and as to the effect of a conviction becoming disregarded,
see the *Protection of Freedoms Act* 2012, ss.92 to 101.

II. OFFENCES

A. GENERAL INTERPRETATION

(1) Consent

Sexual Offences Act 2003, s.74

"Consent"

As to whether a failure to use a condom, where the complainant had made it clear she **20–10**
would only consent to protected sexual intercourse, went to the question of consent under
section 74 of the 2003 Act, see *Assange v. Swedish Judicial Authority, post,* § 20–15, in which *R.
v. B.* (see the main work was distinguished).

Sexual Offences Act 2003, ss.75, 76

Evidential presumptions about consent

Section 75 of the 2003 Act (§ 20–14 in the main work) does not reverse the ordinary **20–15**
principles relating to the burden of proof; it provides for evidential presumptions about
consent (and lack of reasonable belief in consent) in circumstances where, as a matter of
reality and common sense, the strong likelihood is that the complainant was not, in fact,
consenting; if, however, there is "sufficient evidence" for the jury to consider, then the
burden of proving lack of consent and/or of disproving reasonable belief in consent remains
on the prosecution; before the question of a defendant's reasonable belief in the
complainant's consent could be left to the jury, some evidence beyond the fanciful or
speculative must be adduced to support the reasonableness of his belief that she consented
to what he did when she was fast asleep; a mere assertion by the defendant of his belief in
consent was not sufficient: *R. v. Ciccarelli* [2012] 1 Cr.App.R. 15, CA. Accordingly, the court
held that the trial judge's conclusion that no sufficient evidence had been adduced in accor-

311

dance with section 75(1) to raise the issue of reasonable belief in consent was justified in the following circumstances. The defendant and the complainant, "effectively" strangers, had been at the house of a mutual friend, the defendant alleged that at that house the complainant "made an advance" on him, the defendant and his girlfriend took the complainant, who was drunk, back to their flat, the complainant fell asleep in the couple's spare room, and the defendant went into the spare room, saw the complainant was asleep, then touched her sexually prior to her waking up.

   R. v. Jheeta (see the main work), made clear that in most cases the absence of consent and the appropriate *mens rea* would be proved without reference to the evidential presumptions set out in sections 75 and 76 of the 2003 Act; in particular, section 76 (conclusive presumptions) should be given a stringent construction; section 76(2)(a) will only be relevant to those "comparatively rare cases where the defendant deliberately deceives the complainant about the nature or purpose" of intercourse (*Jheeta*); if the conduct of the defendant is not within section 76, the issue of consent must be decided by reference to section 74 (§ 20–10 in the main work). Where, therefore, it was alleged that the fugitive had knowingly had unprotected sexual intercourse with the complainant in circumstances where she had made it clear that she would only consent to protected sexual intercourse and had not then been aware that the fugitive had not used a condom (whether having removed or broken it or never having put it on), the materiality of the use or damage of the condom did not go to the nature or quality of the relevant act (intercourse) for the purposes of section 76, but it did go to the question of consent under section 74 (distinguishing *R. v. B.* (see § 20–10 in the main work)); and it would have been open to a jury in England and Wales in these circumstances to conclude that there had been no consent: *Assange v. Swedish Judicial Authority* [2011] L.S. Gazette, November 17, 17, DC ([2011] EWHC 2849 (Admin.)).

E. Rape and Other Offences against Children Under 13

(5) Elements of the offences

20–56   As to the compatibility of the strict liability offence of rape of a child under 13, contrary to section 5 of the *SOA* 2003 (§ 20–49 in the main work), with Articles 6 (right to a fair trial and presumption of innocence (§ 16–57 in the main work)) and 8 (right to respect for private life (§ 16–101 in the main work)) of the ECHR, see *G. v. U.K.* [2012] Crim.L.R. 46, ECtHR (*ante*, §§ 16–78, 16–108) (in which the decision of the House of Lords in *R. v. G. (Secretary of State for the Home Department intervening)* (see the main work) was upheld).

K. Offences by Care Workers for Persons with a Mental Disorder

(1) Statute

Sexual Offences Act 2003, ss.38-44

Care workers: interpretation

★20–147   As from a day to be appointed, the definition of "National Health Service body" in section 42(5) of the *SOA* 2003 is amended by the *Health and Social Care Act* 2012, s.55(2), and Sched. 5, para. 117, so as (i) to omit paragraph (c), and (ii) to insert new paragraphs (ba) and (bb), as follows—

   "(ba) the Secretary of State in relation to the exercise of functions under section 2A or 2B of, or paragraph 7C, 8 or 12 of Schedule 1 to, the *National Health Service Act* 2006, (bb) a local authority in relation to the exercise of functions under section 2B or 111 of, or any of paragraphs 1 to 7B, or 13 of Schedule 1 to, the National Health Service Act 2006,".

N. Trafficking

(1) Statute

Sexual Offences Act 2003, ss.57–60C

Trafficking into the UK for sexual exploitation
As from a day to be appointed, section 109(1) and (2) of the *Protection of Freedoms Act* 2012 substitute, for sections 57 to 59 of the 2003 Act, a new section 59A (trafficking people for sexual exploitation). ★20–179

Trafficking within the UK for sexual exploitation
As from a day to be appointed, section 109(1) and (2) of the *Protection of Freedoms Act* 2012 substitute, for sections 57 to 59 of the 2003 Act, a new section 59A (trafficking people for sexual exploitation). ★20–180

Trafficking out of the UK for sexual exploitation
As from a day to be appointed, section 109(1) and (2) of the *Protection of Freedoms Act* 2012 substitute, for sections 57 to 59 of the 2003 Act, a new section 59A (trafficking people for sexual exploitation). ★20–181

Trafficking people for sexual exploitation
As from a day to be appointed, section 109(1) and (2) of the *Protection of Freedoms Act* 2012 substitute, for sections 57 to 59 of the 2003 Act (§§ 20–179 *et seq.* in the main work), a new section 59A. ★20–181a

Sexual Offences Act 2003, s.59A

[Trafficking people for sexual exploitation
59A.—(1) A person ("A") commits an offence if A intentionally arranges or facilitates—
  (a) the arrival in, or entry into, the United Kingdom or another country of another person ("B"),
  (b) the travel of B within the United Kingdom or another country, or
  (c) the departure of B from the United Kingdom or another country,
with a view to the sexual exploitation of B.
(2) For the purposes of subsection (1)(a) and (c) A's arranging or facilitating is with a view to the sexual exploitation of B if, and only if—
  (a) A intends to do anything to or in respect of B, after B's arrival, entry or (as the case may be) departure but in any part of the world, which if done will involve the commission of a relevant offence, or
  (b) A believes that another person is likely to do something to or in respect of B, after B's arrival, entry or (as the case may be) departure but in any part of the world, which if done will involve the commission of a relevant offence.
(3) For the purposes of subsection (1)(b) A's arranging or facilitating is with a view to the sexual exploitation of B if, and only if—
  (a) A intends to do anything to or in respect of B, during or after the journey and in any part of the world, which if done will involve the commission of a relevant offence, or
  (b) A believes that another person is likely to do something to or in respect of B, during or after the journey and in any part of the world, which if done will involve the commission of a relevant offence.
(4) A person who is a UK national commits an offence under this section regardless of—
  (a) where the arranging or facilitating takes place, or

(b) which country is the country of arrival, entry, travel or (as the case may be) departure.

(5) A person who is not a UK national commits an offence under this section if—

(a) any part of the arranging or facilitating takes place in the United Kingdom, or

(b) the United Kingdom is the country of arrival, entry, travel or (as the case may be) departure.

(6) A person guilty of an offence under this section is liable—

(a) on summary conviction, to imprisonment for a term not exceeding 12 months or a fine not exceeding the statutory maximum or both;

(b) on conviction on indictment, to imprisonment for a term not exceeding 14 years.

(7) In relation to an offence committed before the commencement of section 154(1) of the *Criminal Justice Act* 2003, the reference in subsection (6)(a) to 12 months is to be read as a reference to 6 months.]

Sections 57 to 59: interpretation and jurisdiction

★**20–182**   As from a day to be appointed, section 60 of the 2003 Act is amended by the *Protection of Freedoms Act* 2012, ss.109(1) and (3) to (5), and 115(2), and Sched. 10, Pt 9, so as (i) to change the heading to "*Section 59A: interpretation*", (ii) to omit subsection (2), and (iii) to substitute a new subsection (1), as follows—

"(1) In section 59A—

'country' includes any territory or other part of the world;

'relevant offence' means—

(a) any offence under the law of England and Wales which is an offence under this Part or under section 1(1)(a) of the *Protection of Children Act* 1978, or

(b) anything done outside England and Wales which is not an offence within paragraph (a) but would be if done in England and Wales;

'UK national' means—

(a) a British citizen,

(b) a person who is a British subject by virtue of Part 4 of the *British Nationality Act* 1981 and who has the right of abode in the United Kingdom, or

(c) a person who is a British overseas territories citizen by virtue of a connection with Gibraltar.".

★   As from a day to be appointed, section 31 of the *UK Borders Act* 2007 is repealed by the *Protection of Freedoms Act* 2012, s.115(2), and Sched. 10, Pt 9.

Forfeiture of land vehicle, shop or aircraft

★**20–182a**   As from a day to be appointed, section 60A of the 2003 Act is amended by the *Protection of Freedoms Act* 2012, s.115(1), and Sched. 9, para. 140(1) and (2), so as to substitute "section 59A" for "sections 57 to 59" in each of subsections (1) and (5).

Detention of land vehicle, ship or aircraft

★**20–182b**   As from a day to be appointed, section 60B of the 2003 Act is amended by the *Protection of Freedoms Act* 2012, s.115(1), and Sched. 9, para. 140(1) and (3), so as to substitute "section 59A" for "sections 57 to 59" in subsection (1).

Q. OTHER STATUTORY OFFENCES

(2) Voyeurism

(e) *Elements of the offence*

★**20–217**   In *R. v. M.B.*, 176 J.P. 313, CA, it was held: (i) on a charge of voyeurism, the prosecution have to prove that (a) "for the purpose of obtaining sexual gratification", (b) the defendant "observed" (c) another person doing a private act, (d) knowing that the other person did not consent to being observed for the defendant's sexual gratification; *as to (a)*, the purpose can only be the result of the defendant's own subjective thought process; *as to (b)*, "observes" connotes a deliberate decision on the part of the defendant, as opposed to an accidental, careless, or reckless perception; *as to (c)*, whereas section 68(1) (interpretation (§ 20–213 in the main work)) requires the relevant act or state of affairs to take place "in a place which, in the circumstances, would reasonably be expected to provide privacy", whether a particular place is such would appear to be an objective test; as to (d), this requires proof of a specific state of mind; (ii) it is the purpose of sexual gratification that turns the deliberate observation of another doing an intimate act (such as undressing) in private into an "injurious act" (the phrase used by Lord Hutton in *R. v. Antoine* [2001] 1 A.C. 340, HL (§ 4–237 in the main work)); therefore, where a defendant charged with voyeurism is found unfit to be tried (*Criminal Procedure (Insanity) Act* 1964, s.4(5) (*ibid.*, § 4–231)), the relevant "act ... charged against him as the offence" under section 4A(2) of the 1964 Act (*ibid.*, § 4–232) is the deliberate observation of another doing a private act for the specific purpose of the observer obtaining sexual gratification; although the activity has two components, they are indissoluble, and together form the relevant "act"; but the observer's knowledge that the person observed does not consent is not directly linked to the outward component of the act; it refers to the state of mind the person must have, but it is not the reason for the observation; accordingly, for the purposes of section 4A(2), this element of the offence is not part of the "act ... charged against him as the offence". For critical consideration of the second aspect of this decision, see CLW/12/18/7.

R. Common Law Offences

(2) Keeping a disorderly house

Definition

In *R. v. Court and Gu* [2012] 1 Cr.App.R. 36, CA, it was held that the ancient common law offence of keeping a disorderly house should not be expanded beyond well-established parameters by judicial decision; and *R. v. Tan* (see the main work) had proceeded on the basis that the provision of "straightforward sexual intercourse" would not be sufficient to constitute this offence. Where, therefore, the case against the defendants was that, at the two properties they rented, only one woman was ever offering sexual services at any one time, that only one customer at a time was ever present at either house, and that the sexual services on offer did not go further than normal sexual intercourse, these circumstances, taken at their highest, were not capable of falling within the scope of the offence.

★20–246

III. ANONYMITY OF VICTIMS

Sexual Offences (Amendment) Act 1992, s.6

Interpretation

The *CJA* 2003, s.41, and Sched. 3, para. 63, amends subsection (3)(c) of the 1992 Act (see the main work), so as to substitute the words "sends him to the Crown Court" for the words "commits him". This amendment comes into force on June 18, 2012 (*Criminal Justice Act 2003 (Commencement No. 28 and Saving Provisions) Order* 2012 (S.I. 2012 No. 1320)) in certain areas (as to which, see *ante*, § 1–88). There are associated saving provisions, as to which, see article 5 of the order (*ante*, § 1–88).

★20–261

IV. NOTIFICATION AND ORDERS

A. Notification Requirements

(4) Legislation

The notification period

In *R. (Minter) v. Chief Constable of Hampshire Constabulary* [2012] 1 W.L.R. 1157, DC, it

20–267

was held that the whole term of an extended sentence imposed under the *PCC(S)A* 2000, s.85 (*ante*, § 5–490) constitutes the term for which a person is "sentenced to imprisonment" for the purpose of determining the period for which that person is subject to notification requirements pursuant to section 82(1) of the *SOA 2003*. The court disapproved *R. v. S. (Graham)* and approved what was said about that case in *Wiles* (as to both of which, see the main work).

★   As to the repeal of sections 227 and 228 of the *CJA* 2003, see *ante*, §§ 5–498, 5–499.

D. SEXUAL OFFENCES PREVENTION ORDERS

(2) Legislation

Sexual Offences Act 2003, ss.104–113

Sexual offences prevention orders: effect

20-327   In *R. v. Smith* [2012] 1 Cr.App.R.(S.) 82, the Court of Appeal, having considered, *inter alia*, *R. v. Hemsley* and *R. v. Mortimer* (as to both of which, see the main work), issued detailed guidance on the imposition, and appropriate terms, of a sexual offences prevention order. (i) Such an order must be necessary and proportionate and its terms must be sufficiently clear on their face for the offender and those who have to deal with him to understand, without difficulty or the need for expert legal advice, exactly what is prohibited. (ii) No order is needed if it merely duplicates another regime to which an offender is subject, and nor must it interfere with such a regime; the sex offender notification regime (*SOA* 2003, ss.80–102 (§§ 20–265 *et seq.* in the main work)), the prohibitions on working with children (*CJCSA* 2000, s.28 (*ante*, § 5–862), and *Safeguarding Vulnerable Groups Act* 2006 (§§ 5–854 *et seq.* in the main work)), and the conditions of an offender's licence must all be considered. (iii) The usual rule is that, absent some unusual feature, an indeterminate sentence will require no order; by contrast, an order may plainly be necessary in the case of any other custodial sentence, as it can be extended beyond the term of any licence or suspension period. (iv) There is no objection to an order extending beyond the duration of the notification requirements, or *vice versa*, if the circumstances require it, but, absent some unusual feature, it would be wrong to include a term, which although couched as a prohibition, amounted in effect to an extension of the notification requirements. (v) An order containing a blanket prohibition on computer use or internet access is impermissible; restricting internet use to job search, study, work, lawful recreation and purchases is also disproportionate; prohibiting the possession of any computer or other internet-capable device without first notifying the local police is too onerous both for offenders and the police; the prohibition most likely to be effective is one that has the effect of requiring the preservation of a readable internet history coupled with submission to inspection on request; but there is no need for the order to invest the police with powers of forcible entry into private premises beyond the statutory ones that they already have; where the risk includes the use of social networking sites or chatrooms to groom young people for sexual purposes, it may well be appropriate to prohibit communication via the internet with any young person known or believed to be under the age of 16, or even to prohibit use of such sites altogether. (vi) If contact with children needs to be restricted, it should relate to those under 16, not 18, unless there is a genuine risk of the offender committing offences under sections 16 to 19 (*ibid.*, §§ 20–96 *et seq.*)) or 25 and 26 (*ibid.*, §§ 20–110, 20–111)) of the 2003 Act; if an offender has been convicted of viewing child pornography, it is not legitimate to impose multiple prohibitions on him just in case he commits a different kind of offence; prohibitions on contact with children may be necessary for some predatory paedophiles who seek out children for sexual purposes, but care must be taken with their terms, as the offender may have children of his own, or within his extended family; even if there is a history of abuse within the family, any order ought ordinarily to be subject to any order made in family proceedings; where contact with children is prohibited, it is essential to include a saving for incidental contact such as is inherent in everyday life. (vii) There must be a written draft order, properly considered in advance of the sentencing hearing; such should be served on the court and the offender not less than two clear days before, but, in any event not at, the hearing.

SOPOs: variations, renewals and discharges

As from a day to be appointed, section 108 of the *SOA* 2003 is amended by section 17(2)   **20–328**
of the *AFA* 2011, so as to insert a new subsection (9), as follows—

"(9) Subsection (1) does not apply where section 232C(3)(a) of the *Armed Forces Act* 2006 (case where sexual offences prevention order in respect of person subject to service law, or civilian subject to service discipline, may be varied etc. by Court Martial) applies.".

Other offences for purposes of Part 2

As from July 2, 2012 (*Domestic Violence, Crime and Victims (Amendment) Act 2012 (Com-*   **★20–336**
mencement) Order 2012 (S.I. 2012 No. 1432)), Schedule 5 to the *SOA* 2003 is amended by the *Domestic Violence, Crime and Victims (Amendment) Act* 2012, s.3, and Sched., para. 5, to take account of the extended ambit of the offence under section 5 of the *Domestic Violence, Crime and Victims Act* 2004.

As from a day to be appointed, Schedule 5 to the *SOA* 2003 is further amended by the   **★**
Protection of Freedoms Act 2012, s.115(1), and Sched. 9, paras 140(1) and (4) (substituting a reference to section 59A of the *SOA* 2003 for the references to sections 57 to 59 of that Act) and 146 (inserting references to sections 2A and 4A of the *Protection from Harassment Act* 1997).

G. Interpretation, etc. of Part 2

Sexual Offences Act 2003, ss.131–136

Young offenders: application

As from a day to be appointed, section 131 of the 2003 Act is amended by the *Legal Aid,*   **★20–339**
Sentencing and Punishment of Offenders Act 2012, ss.126 and 127, Sched. 21, para. 19 (insertion of "226B or" before "228" in paragraph (l)), and Sched. 22, para. 20 (insertion of "221A or" before "222" in the same paragraph).

Offences with thresholds

As to the amendment of section 177(5) of the *CJA* 2003, see *ante*, § 5–253.   **★20–340**

Part 2: general interpretation

As from a day to be appointed, section 133 of the 2003 Act is amended by the *Legal Aid,*   **★20–341**
Sentencing and Punishment of Offenders Act 2012, s.135(3), and Sched. 24, para. 25, so as to omit paragraph (b) in the definition of "cautioned" together with the word "or" that precedes it.

CHAPTER 21

OFFENCES UNDER THE THEFT AND FRAUD ACTS

II. THEFT

(5) Elements of the offence of theft

(f) *"With the intention of permanently depriving the other of it"*

Theft Act 1968, s.6

21–77 Considering the first part of section 6(1) of the 1968 Act (§ 21–76 in the main work) in the context of a case where the defendants (charged with robbery) had taken a bicycle off another youth whom they had then chased away, and where the bicycle was found abandoned in a bus shelter about 50 yards from where it had been taken, it was held in *R. v. Vinall and J.* [2012] 1 Cr.App.R. 29, CA: (i) that if the prosecution are unable to establish an intent permanently to deprive at the moment of the taking, they may nevertheless establish that the defendant exercised such a dominion over the property that it can be inferred that, at the time of the taking, he intended to treat the property as his own to dispose of regardless of the owner's rights; and (ii) that subsequent disposal of the property may be evidence either of an intention at the time of the taking or of an intention at the time of disposal; and that when the allegation is theft, a later appropriation will suffice, whereas when the allegation is robbery, it almost certainly will not. The court preferred the approach taken in *R. v. Fernandes* (see the main work), in preference to the more restrictive approach taken in some of the earlier authorities, such as *R. v. Warner*, 55 Cr.App.R. 93, CA, and *R. v. Lloyd*, 81 Cr.App.R. 182, CA). As to this case, see also *post*, § 21–97.

III. ROBBERY AND ASSAULT WITH INTENT TO ROB

A. ROBBERY

(4) Sentence

Guideline cases

Armed robbery
21–91 *R. v. Thomas* is now reported at [2012] 1 Cr.App.R.(S.) 43.

(6) Elements of the offence of robbery

(a) *"Immediately before or at the time of doing so and in order to do steal"*

21–99 As to the importance of proving that the force used or threatened was used or threatened immediately before, or at the time of, the appropriation of the property with the necessary intention for theft, see *R. v. Vinall and J.* [2012] 1 Cr.App.R. 29, CA. As to this case, see also *ante*, § 21–77.

IV. BURGLARY AND AGGRAVATED BURGLARY

A. BURGLARY

(5) Sentence

Guideline (non-dwellings)

Where sentence is passed on or after January 16, 2012, the guideline of the Sentencing Guidelines Council will be superseded by the guideline issued on October 13, 2011, by the Sentencing Council for England and Wales which applies to all burglary offences. For the details thereof, see *post*, Appendix K–259 *et seq.* **21–114a**

Guideline (dwellings and non-dwellings)

On October 13, 2011, the Sentencing Council for England and Wales issued a definitive guideline on burglary, applying to all offenders aged 18 or over who are sentenced on or after January 16, 2012, regardless of the date of their offence. For the details, see *post*, Appendix K–259 *et seq.* **21–114b**

B. AGGRAVATED BURGLARY

(5) Sentence

On October 13, 2011, the Sentencing Council for England and Wales issued a definitive guideline on burglary and aggravated burglary, applying to all offenders aged 18 or over who are sentenced on or after January 16, 2012, regardless of the date of their offence. For the details, see *post*, Appendix K–259 *et seq.* **21–133**

(6) Evidence

R. v. Klass (see the main work) was applied in *R. v. Wiggins*, 176 J.P. 305, CA. **★21–134**

IX. FALSE ACCOUNTING

(5) Elements of the offence

(a) *Any account or any record or document made or required for an accounting purpose*

R. v. O. is now reported at [2011] 2 Cr.App.R. 33, CA, *sub nom. R. v. O. and H.* **21–232**

XIII. HANDLING STOLEN PROPERTY

(4) Sentence

Guidelines

In *R. v. Blackshaw* [2012] 1Cr.App.R.(S.) 114, CA, it was said that the guideline case on handling offences of *R. v. Webbe* (see the main work) did not contemplate that the offences with which it was concerned would take place within the context of public disorder such as seen in the riots that occurred around the country between August 6 and August 11, 2011. It followed that sentences beyond the range in that guideline for conventional offending (*i.e.* offending which lacked the aggravating features of widespread public disorder) were not only appropriate, but inevitable. The court said that, when dealing with offences of handling **21–279a** looted property, a line needed to be drawn between those that arose from, and were directly connected with, the disorder, and those that were intrinsic to the disorder; there was a significant difference between someone who handled stolen goods by way of encouragement of the commission of burglary and theft as part of the disorder, and someone whose offence represented opportunistic involvement after burglaries had occurred.

XVI. THEFT ACT 1968: GENERAL PROVISIONS

B. Evidence by Statutory Declaration

Theft Act 1968, s.27

★21–332   With effect from June 18, 2012 (*Criminal Justice Act 2003 (Commencement No. 28 and Saving Provisions) Order* 2012 (S.I. 2012 No. 1320)), section 332 of, and Part 4 of Schedule 37 (erroneously referred to as "Schedule 7" in the main work) to, the 2003 Act (see the main work) are brought into force in certain areas (as to which, see *ante*, § 1–88). There are associated saving provisions, as to which, see article 5 of the order (*ante*, § 1–88).

Chapter 22

FORGERY, PERSONATION AND CHEATING

I. FORGERY

B. Miscellaneous Offences Akin to Forgery

(2) Identity documents

(f) *Defences*

22–45j   *R. v. Unah* is now reported at [2011] 2 Cr.App.R. 32.

III. CHEATING

B. By Statute

Gambling Act 2005, s.42

Cheating

★22–71   There was jurisdiction to try a cricket agent who had engaged in spot-fixing cricket matches in return for cash for the offence of conspiracy to do an act or acts that would enable another person to cheat at gambling (contrary to the *CLA* 1977, s.1(1) (§ 33–2 in the main work), and the 2005 Act, s.42(1) (*ibid.*, § 22–70)) where the actual betting had taken place outside the jurisdiction but the "fix" was organised in England, see *R. v. Majeed*; *R. v. Westfield* [2012] L.S. Gazette, June 14, 23, CA ([2012] EWCA Crim. 1186). As to this case, see also *post*, § 31–140.

Chapter 23

CRIMINAL DAMAGE AND KINDRED OFFENCES

II. MALICIOUS DAMAGE ACT 1861

Class of offence and mode of trial

As to the removal (as from a day to be appointed) of the upper limit on a fine on sum-   ★**23–59**
mary conviction of an offence, see the *Legal Aid, Sentencing and Punishment of Offenders Act*
2012, s.85, *ante*, § 1–125.

Chapter 24

FIREARMS AND OFFENSIVE WEAPONS

I. FIREARMS

A. Firearms Act 1968

(4) Prohibited weapons and ammunition

Sentence

In *R. v. Brereton* [2012] Crim.L.R. 396, CA (as to which, see also *ante*, § 5–453), it was said   ★**24–23**
that it would help promote consistency in sentencing if a coherent and principled policy as
to prosecuting those found in possession of disguised stun guns were to be devised and
published, there being a choice between prosecuting for the offence under section 5(1)(b)
(to which the minimum sentence provisions in s.51A (§ 5–449 in the main work) do not apply) or for an offence under section 5(1A)(a) (to which the minimum sentence provisions do
apply).

(6) Prevention of crime and preservation of public safety

(a) *Possession with intent to endanger life*

Firearms Act 1968, s.16

Sentence

An offence under section 16 of the 1968 Act may on occasion call for a sentence that is as   **24–38**
long as, or even longer than, the sentence for attempted murder: *R. v. Sheen and Sheen*
[2012] 2 Cr.App.R.(S.) 3, CA (see also *post*, § 24–82a).

In *Att.-Gen.'s Reference (No. 6 of 2012) (R. v. Rollings)* [2012] Crim.L.R. 399, CA, it was   ★
held that the sentencing range for grave firearms cases had increased significantly since *Att.-
Gen.'s Reference (Nos 58–66 of 2002)* (cited in the main work). It would seem, therefore, that
seven to eight years' imprisonment is no longer the starting point for a contested case of
simple possession, contrary to section 16 of the 1968 Act.

(c) *Use of firearms to resist arrest*

Supplementary provisions as to trial and punishment of offences

Firearms Act 1968, Sched. 6, Pt II, paras 3–6

★**24–44** With effect from June 18, 2012 (*Criminal Justice Act 2003 (Commencement No. 28 and Saving Provisions) Order* 2012 (S.I. 2012 No. 1320)), sections 41 and 332 of, and paragraph 45 of Schedule 3 to, and Part 4 of Schedule 37 to, the 2003 Act are brought into force in certain areas (as to which, see *ante*, § 1–88). There are associated saving provisions, as to which, see article 5 of the order (*ante*, § 1–88).

(g) *Possession of firearms by persons previously convicted of crime*

Firearms Act 1968, s.21

★**24–65** As from a day to be appointed, section 21 of the 1968 Act is amended by the *Legal Aid, Sentencing and Punishment of Offenders Act* 2012, s.89(2), and Sched. 10, para. 3, so as to omit subsections (2A)(d) and (2B) and, in subsection (6), ", (2B)".

(13) Law enforcement and punishment of offences

Firearms Act 1968, ss.49, 51, 51A, 52

24–82a In *R. v. Sheen and Sheen* [2012] 2 Cr.App.R.(S.) 3, CA, it was held that two additional questions should be asked, in addition to the four posed in *R. v. Avis* (see the main work):

> 5. Where was the firearm (or were the firearms) discharged, and who and how many were exposed to danger by its or their use?

> 6. Was any injury or damage caused by the discharge of the firearm or firearms, and if so how serious was it?

(15) Definitions

Firearms Act 1968, s.57

24–85 The amendment of the definition of "civilian officer" in section 57(1) of the 1968 Act effected by the *Police Reform and Social Responsibility Act* 2011, s.99, and Sched. 16, paras 89 and 91 (see the main work), came into force on January 16, 2012: *Police Reform and Social Responsibility Act 2011 (Commencement No. 3 and Transitional Provisions) Order* 2011 (S.I. 2011 No. 3019); but this is subject to a temporary modification of the amendment (as to which, see art. 10(5) of, and Sched. 2, para. 22, to, the commencement order) until section 1 of the 2011 Act comes into force. The effect of the modification is that sub-paragraph (a)(i) is to read as follows:

> "(i) a person employed by a police authority established under section 3 of the *Police Act* 1996 who is under the direction and control of a chief officer of police,".

B. Prevention of Crime Act 1953

(5) Ingredients of the offence

(d) *"without lawful authority or reasonable excuse"*

Reasonable excuse

Self-defence

Where a defendant claims to have carried a weapon for his own protection, the jury   ★**24–122**
should be directed simply to find the facts, including any facts as to the defendant's state of
mind and the reason for it, and decide whether in their view, in the light of those facts (the
proof of which is on the defendant), the defence has been made out: *R. v. Clancy* [2012] 2
Cr.App.R. 7, CA (decided in relation to the defence of "good reason" under the *CJA* 1988,
s.139(4) (§ 24–128 in the main work)).

(6) Offence of threatening with offensive weapon in public

Prevention of Crime Act 1953, s.1A

As from a day to be appointed, a new section 1A is inserted in the 1953 Act by the *Legal*   ★**24–124a**
Aid, Sentencing and Punishment of Offenders Act 2012, s.142(1).

[Offence of threatening with offensive weapon in public
   1A.—(1) A person is guilty of an offence if that person—
      (a) has an offensive weapon with him or her in a public place,
      (b) unlawfully and intentionally threatens another person with the weapon, and
      (c) does so in such a way that there is an immediate risk of serious physical harm to that other
        person.
   (2) For the purposes of this section physical harm is serious if it amounts to grievous bodily harm
for the purposes of the *Offences against the Person Act* 1861.
   (3) In this section "public place" and "offensive weapon" have the same meaning as in section 1.
   (4) A person guilty of an offence under this section is liable—
      (a) on summary conviction, to imprisonment for a term not exceeding 12 months or to a fine
        not exceeding the statutory maximum, or to both;
      (b) on conviction on indictment, to imprisonment for a term not exceeding 4 years or to a fine,
        or to both.
   (5) Where a person aged 16 or over is convicted of an offence under this section, the court must
impose an appropriate custodial sentence (with or without a fine) unless the court is of the opinion
that there are particular circumstances which—
      (a) relate to the offence or to the offender, and
      (b) would make it unjust to do so in all the circumstances.
   (6) In this section "appropriate custodial sentence" means—
      (a) in the case of a person who is aged 18 or over when convicted, a sentence of imprisonment
        for a term of at least 6 months;
      (b) in the case of a person who is aged at least 16 but under 18 when convicted, a detention
        and training order of at least 4 months.
   (7) In considering whether it is of the opinion mentioned in subsection (5) in the case of a person
aged under 18, the court must have regard to its duty under section 44 of the *Children and Young
Persons Act* 1933.
   (8) In relation to an offence committed before the commencement of section 154(1) of the *Criminal Justice Act* 2003, the reference in subsection (4)(a) to 12 months is to be read as a reference to 6
months.
   (9) In relation to times before the coming into force of paragraph 180 of Schedule 7 to the *Criminal Justice and Court Services Act* 2000, the reference in subsection (6)(a) to a sentence of imprison-

ment, in relation to an offender aged under 21 at the time of conviction, is to be read as a reference to a sentence of detention in a young offender institution.

(10) If on a person's trial for an offence under this section (whether on indictment or not) the person is found not guilty of that offence but it is proved that the person committed an offence under section 1, the person may be convicted of the offence under that section.]

C. Criminal Justice Act 1988

(1) Having article with blade or point in public place

Criminal Justice Act 1988, s.139

Ingredients

★**24–128**   As to self-defence as a good reason, see *R. v. Clancy, ante,* § 24–122.

(2A) Threatening with article with blade or point or offensive weapon

Criminal Justice Act 1988, s.139AA

★**24–131b**   As from a day to be appointed, a new section 139AA is inserted in the 1988 Act by the *Legal Aid, Sentencing and Punishment of Offenders Act* 2012, s.142(2).

[Offence of threatening with article with blade or point or offensive weapon
    139AA.—(1) A person is guilty of an offence if that person—
        (a) has an article to which this section applies with him or her in a public place or on school premises,
        (b) unlawfully and intentionally threatens another person with the article, and
        (c) does so in such a way that there is an immediate risk of serious physical harm to that other person.
    (2) In relation to a public place this section applies to an article to which section 139 applies.
    (3) In relation to school premises this section applies to each of these—
        (a) an article to which section 139 applies;
        (b) an offensive weapon within the meaning of section 1 of the *Prevention of Crime Act* 1953.
    (4) For the purposes of this section physical harm is serious if it amounts to grievous bodily harm for the purposes of the *Offences against the Person Act* 1861.
    (5) In this section—
        "public place" has the same meaning as in section 139;
        "school premises" has the same meaning as in section 139A.
    (6) A person guilty of an offence under this section is liable—
        (a) on summary conviction, to imprisonment for a term not exceeding 12 months or to a fine not exceeding the statutory maximum, or to both;
        (b) on conviction on indictment, to imprisonment for a term not exceeding 4 years or to a fine, or to both.
    (7) Where a person aged 16 or over is convicted of an offence under this section, the court must impose an appropriate custodial sentence (with or without a fine) unless the court is of the opinion that there are particular circumstances which—
        (a) relate to the offence or to the offender, and
        (b) would make it unjust to do so in all the circumstances.
    (8) In this section "appropriate custodial sentence" means—
        (a) in the case of a person who is aged 18 or over when convicted, a sentence of imprisonment for a term of at least 6 months;
        (b) in the case of a person who is aged at least 16 but under 18 when convicted, a detention and training order of at least 4 months.
    (9) In considering whether it is of the opinion mentioned in subsection (7) in the case of a person

aged under 18, the court must have regard to its duty under section 44 of the *Children and Young Persons Act* 1933.

(10) In relation to an offence committed before the commencement of section 154(1) of the *Criminal Justice Act* 2003, the reference in subsection (6)(a) to 12 months is to be read as a reference to 6 months.

(11) In relation to times before the coming into force of paragraph 180 of Schedule 7 to the *Criminal Justice and Court Services Act* 2000, the reference in subsection (8)(a) to a sentence of imprisonment, in relation to an offender aged under 21 at the time of conviction, is to be read as a reference to a sentence of detention in a young offender institution.

(12) If on a person's trial for an offence under this section (whether on indictment or not) the person is found not guilty of that offence but it is proved that the person committed an offence under section 139 or 139A, the person may be convicted of the offence under that section.]

(3) Entry and search provisions

Criminal Justice Act 1988, s.139B

As from a day to be appointed, section 139B(1) of the 1988 Act is amended by the *Legal Aid, Sentencing and Punishment of Offenders Act* 2012, s.142(3), and Sched. 26, paras 4 and 6(1) and (2), so as to insert "or 139AA" after "139". Section 139B(4) is amended by the 2012 Act, s.142(3), and Sched. 26, paras 4 and 6(1) and (3). ★24–132

CHAPTER 25

OFFENCES AGAINST THE CROWN AND GOVERNMENT

III. TERRORISM

A. TERRORISM ACT 2000

Terrorism Act 2000, ss.15–23B

Business in the regulated sector

Since its substitution by the *Terrorism Act 2000 (Business in the Regulated Sector and Supervisory Authorities) Order* 2007 (S.I. 2007 No. 3288) (as to which see the main work), Schedule 3A to the 2000 Act has been amended by a number of instruments, the latest of which are the *Terrorism Act 2000 and Proceeds of Crime Act 2002 (Business in the Regulated Sector) Order* 2011 (S.I. 2011 No. 2701), which took effect on December 12, 2011, and the *Localism Act* 2011, ss.183 and 237, and Scheds 18, para. 1, and 25, Pt 29, which took effect on January 15, 2012. **25–26**

Terrorism Act 2000, s.1

Terrorism: interpretation

In *R. v. Gul* [2012] 1 Cr.App.R. 37, CA, it was held (considering *R. v. F.* (see the main work)) that: (i) the definition of "terrorism" in section 1 of the 2000 Act is comprehensive in its scope, and, on its face, acts by insurgents against the armed forces of a state anywhere in the world, where such acts seek to influence a government and are made for political purposes, fall within that definition; there is no exemption for those engaged in an armed insurrection and an armed struggle against a government; (ii) although international law may well develop through state practice or *opinio juris* a rule restricting the scope of terrorism so that it excludes some types of insurgents attacking the armed forces of government from the definition of terrorism, the necessary widespread and general state practice or the ★25–51 necessary *opinio juris* to that effect has not yet been established; therefore, there is no rule of international law that requires the court to read down section 1; and (iii) while decisions in two domestic asylum cases (*K.J. (Sri Lanka) v. Secretary of State for the Home Department*, unreported, April 2, 2009, CA (Civ. Div.) ([2009] EWCA Civ. 292), and *Secretary of State for the Home Department v. D.D. (Afghanistan)*, unreported, December 10, 2010, CA (Civ. Div.) ([2010] EWCA Civ. 1407)) suggested that military action directed against armed forces of the government did not, as such, constitute an act of terrorism or an act contrary to the purposes and principles of the United Nations, these decisions were not made with the benefit of detailed argument, and in neither case was the court applying the terms of section 1.

Search of persons

★**25–54**   As from July 10, 2012 (*Protection of Freedoms Act 2012 (Commencement No. 1) Order* 2012 (S.I. 2012 No. 1205)), section 43 of the 2000 Act is amended by the *Protection of Freedoms Act* 2012, ss.60(1) and (2) and 115(2), and Sched. 10, Pt 4, so as (i) to omit subsection (3), and (ii) to insert new subsections (4A) to (4C), as follows—

"(4A) Subsection (4B) applies if a constable, in exercising the power under subsection (1) to stop a person whom the constable reasonably suspects to be a terrorist, stops a vehicle (see section 116(2)).
　(4B) The constable—
　　(a) may search the vehicle and anything in or on it to discover whether there is anything which may constitute evidence that the person concerned is a terrorist, and
　　(b) may seize and retain anything which the constable—
　　　(i) discovers in the course of such a search, and
　　　(ii) reasonably suspects may constitute evidence that the person is a terrorist.
　(4C) Nothing in subsection (4B) confers a power to search any person but the power to search in that subsection is in addition to the power in subsection (1) to search a person whom the constable reasonably suspects to be a terrorist.".

Search of vehicles

★**25–54a**   As from July 10, 2012 (*Protection of Freedoms Act 2012 (Commencement No. 1) Order* 2012 (S.I. 2012 No. 1205)), a new section 43A is inserted in the 2000 Act by the *Protection of Freedoms Act* 2012, s.60(3).

Terrorism Act 2000, s.43A

Search of vehicles
　43A.—(1) Subsection (2) applies if a constable reasonably suspects that a vehicle is being used for the purposes of terrorism.
　(2) The constable may stop and search—
　　(a) the vehicle;
　　(b) the driver of the vehicle;
　　(c) a passenger in the vehicle;
　　(d) anything in or on the vehicle or carried by the driver or a passenger;
to discover whether there is anything which may constitute evidence that the vehicle is being used for the purposes of terrorism.
　(3) A constable may seize and retain anything which the constable—
　　(a) discovers in the course of a search under this section, and
　　(b) reasonably suspects may constitute evidence that the vehicle is being used for the purposes of terrorism.
　(4) A person who has the powers of a constable in one Part of the United Kingdom may exercise a power under this section in any Part of the United Kingdom.
　(5) In this section "driver", in relation to an aircraft, hovercraft or vessel, means the captain, pilot or other person with control of the aircraft, hovercraft or vessel or any member of its crew and, in relation to a train, includes any member of its crew.

Terrorism Act 2000, ss.40–43

25–55   The whole of the *Prevention of Terrorism Act* 2005 (see the main work) was repealed, with effect from December 15, 2011, by section 1 of the *Terrorism Prevention and Investigation Measures Act* 2011. For provisions broadly corresponding to sections 7A and 7C to 7E of the 2005 Act (but relating to the enforcement of terrorism prevention and investigation measures), see Schedule 5, paras 3, 4, 7, 8, 10 and 11, to the 2011 Act. Consequential amendments were made to section 1 of the *Counter-Terrorism Act* 2008 (see the main work), with effect from the same day, by the 2011 Act, s.29(3), and Sched. 7, para. 5 (references to the relevant provisions of the 2011 Act being substituted for the references to the repealed provisions of the 2005 Act).

As from July 10, 2012 (*Protection of Freedoms Act 2012 (Commencement No. 1) Order* 2012 ★ (S.I. 2012 No. 1205)), section 1(1) of the *Counter-Terrorism Act* 2008 is further amended by the *Protection of Freedoms Act* 2012, s.115(1), and Sched. 9, para. 33, to include references to searches under section 43(4B) and 43A of the *Terrorism Act* 2000.

Terrorism Act 2000, ss.47A–47C

Searches in specified areas or places

As from July 10, 2012 (*Protection of Freedoms Act 2012 (Commencement No. 1) Order* 2012 ★**25–56** (S.I. 2012 No. 1205)), the *Terrorism Act 2000 (Remedial) Order* 2011 (S.I. 2011 No. 631) (§ 25–58 in the main work) is revoked by the *Protection of Freedoms Act* 2012, s.115(1) and (2), Sched. 9, para. 34, and Sched. 10, Pt 4, with the consequence that the sections numbered 47A, 47B and 47C that were inserted by that order into the 2000 Act will lapse. In their stead, the 2012 Act, ss.61(1) and 62 insert (as from the same date) new sections 47A (searches in specified areas or places), 47B (code of practice relating to sections 43, 43A and 47A), 47AB (issuing of code), 47AC (alteration or replacement of code), 47AD (publication of code) and 47AE (effect of code).

Terrorism Act 2000, ss.47A–47AE

Searches in specified areas or places

47A.—(1) A senior police officer may give an authorisation under subsection (2) or (3) in relation to a specified area or place if the officer—

    (a) reasonably suspects that an act of terrorism will take place; and

    (b) reasonably considers that—

        (i) the authorisation is necessary to prevent such an act;

        (ii) the specified area or place is no greater than is necessary to prevent such an act; and

        (iii) the duration of the authorisation is no longer than is necessary to prevent such an act.

(2) An authorisation under this subsection authorises any constable in uniform to stop a vehicle in the specified area or place and to search—

    (a) the vehicle;

    (b) the driver of the vehicle;

    (c) a passenger in the vehicle;

    (d) anything in or on the vehicle or carried by the driver or a passenger.

(3) An authorisation under this subsection authorises any constable in uniform to stop a pedestrian in the specified area or place and to search—

    (a) the pedestrian;

    (b) anything carried by the pedestrian.

(4) A constable in uniform may exercise the power conferred by an authorisation under subsection (2) or (3) only for the purpose of discovering whether there is anything which may constitute evidence that the vehicle concerned is being used for the purposes of terrorism or (as the case may be) that the person concerned is a person falling within section 40(1)(b).

(5) But the power conferred by such an authorisation may be exercised whether or not the constable reasonably suspects that there is such evidence.

(6) A constable may seize and retain anything which the constable—

    (a) discovers in the course of a search under such an authorisation; and

    (b) reasonably suspects may constitute evidence that the vehicle concerned is being used for the purposes of terrorism or (as the case may be) that the person concerned is a person falling within section 40(1)(b).

(7) Schedule 6B (which makes supplementary provision about authorisations under this section) has effect.

(8) In this section—

"driver" has the meaning given by section 43A(5);

"senior police officer" has the same meaning as in Schedule 6B (see paragraph 14(1) and (2) of that Schedule);

"specified" means specified in an authorisation.

Code of practice relating to sections 43, 43A and 47A

Code of practice relating to sections 43, 43A and 47A

★**25–56a**   **47AA.**—(1) The Secretary of State must prepare a code of practice containing guidance about—

(a) the exercise of the powers conferred by sections 43 and 43A,

(b) the exercise of the powers to give an authorisation under section 47A(2) or (3),

(c) the exercise of the powers conferred by such an authorisation and section 47A(6), and

(d) such other matters in connection with the exercise of any of the powers mentioned in paragraphs (a) to (c) as the Secretary of State considers appropriate.

(2) Such a code may make different provision for different purposes.

(3) In the course of preparing such a code, the Secretary of State must consult the Lord Advocate and such other persons as the Secretary of State considers appropriate.

47AB. [*Procedure for issuing code.*]

47AC. [*Alteration or replacement of code.*]

47AD. [*Publication of code.*]

Effect of code.

★**25–56b**   **47AE.**—(1) A constable must have regard to the search powers code when exercising any powers to which the code relates.

(2) A failure on the part of a constable to act in accordance with any provision of the search powers code does not of itself make that person liable to criminal or civil proceedings.

(3) The search powers code is admissible in evidence in any such proceedings.

(4) A court or tribunal may, in particular, take into account a failure by a constable to have regard to the search powers code in determining a question in any such proceedings.

(5) The references in this section to a constable include, in relation to any functions exercisable by a person by virtue of paragraph 15 of Schedule 4 to the *Police Reform Act* 2002 or paragraph 16 of Schedule 2A to the *Police (Northern Ireland) Act* 2003 (search powers in specified areas or places for community support officers), references to that person.

(6) In this section "the search powers code" means the code of practice issued under section 47AB(2) (as altered or replaced from time to time).

Code of practice relating to section 47A

★**25–57**   As to section 47B of the 2000 Act, see *ante*, § 25–56.

Effect of code

★**25–58**   As to section 47B of the 2000 Act and S.I. 2011 No. 631, see *ante*, § 25–56.

★   As from July 10, 2012 (*Protection of Freedoms Act 2012 (Commencement No. 1) Order* 2012 (S.I. 2012 No. 1205)), sections 44 to 47 of the 2000 Act are repealed by the *Protection of Freedoms Act* 2012, ss.59 and 115(2), and Sched. 10, Pt 4.

★   As from July 10, 2012 (*Protection of Freedoms Act 2012 (Commencement No. 1) Order* 2012 (S.I. 2012 No. 1205)), a new Schedule 6B (searches in specified areas or places: supplementary) is substituted in the 2000 Act (for the Schedule 6B inserted by S.I. 2011 No. 631) by the *Protection of Freedoms Act* 2012, s.61(2), and Sched. 5.

Terrorism Act 2000, Sched. 2

SCHEDULE 2

PROSCRIBED ORGANISATIONS

As from November 11, 2011, the name "Muslims Against Crusades" (a name not specified **25–91**
in Schedule 2 to the *Terrorism Act* 2000 (see the main work)) is to be treated as another
name for the organisations "Al-Ghurabaa" and "The Saved Sect" which are listed in Schedule 2: *Proscribed Organisations (Name Changes) Order* 2011 (S.I. 2011 No. 2688).

Terrorism Act 2000, Sched. 6B

Searches in specified areas or places: supplementary

As to the substitution of the Schedule 6B set out in the main work, see *ante*, § 25–58. The **★25–122a**
new Schedule 6B is in identical terms to the current Schedule 6B, save that the statutory
reference in the definition of "driver" in paragraph 14(1) is now to section 43A(5); and it
should be noted that the text of paragraph 7(1) is incorrectly set out in the main work, and
that it should read "(1) The senior police officer who gives an authorisation must inform the
Secretary of State of it as soon as reasonably practicable."

Terrorism Act 2000, Sched. 7

Power to stop, question and detain

In *C.C. v. Commr of Police of the Metropolis* [2012] 2 All E.R. 1004, QBD, Collins J. held, in **25–124**
relation to paragraph 2(1) of Schedule 7 to the 2000 Act: (i) the power to question could not
be used if the predominant purpose was other than that specified; (ii) the definition of "terrorist" in section 40(1)(b) (§ 25–51 in the main work) is wide enough to allow for examination not only of whether the individual appears to be a terrorist but also of the way in which
or the act by which he so appears; (iii) an officer must be able to ask all questions that he
reasonably believes to be needed to enable him or others to reach the necessary determination; further examination may show that the officer's view (one way or the other) at a particular point was wrong; and (iv) where, the examining officers suspected before the commencement of the examination that the individual (being returned from Somalia) was a
terrorist, and where it was apparent that the purpose of their examination was not to
discover whether he was a terrorist or how he was a terrorist, but to obtain information —
which could not be regarded as tainted by allegations of torture — for the benefit of the security services (having been provided with a series of questions to ask) and which might
confirm the propriety of the control order that had been made against him (in advance of
his arrival), this was not a proper use of the power.

Modifications applicable to Channel Tunnel

Article 7 of the *Channel Tunnel (International Arrangements) Order* 1993 (S.I. 1993 No. **25–133**
1813) (Appendix F–13a, *post*) provides that the enactments mentioned in Schedule 4 to that
order shall (a) in their application to France by virtue of article 4(1) or (1B), and (b) in their
application to the United Kingdom within the tunnel system and elsewhere for the
authorised purposes (as to which, see article 2(2)), have effect with the modifications set out
in Schedule 4. As a result of the amendment of that schedule by the *Channel Tunnel
(International Arrangements) (Amendment) Order* 2001 (S.I. 2001 No. 178), Schedule 7 to the
2000 Act, being one of the enactments mentioned therein, has effect with the following
modifications—

(i) in paragraph 1(2) omit the references to "the border area", "captain", "ship" and
"vehicle" and for the words "an airport or hoverport" are substituted the words—
"a railway station or other place where
(a) persons embark or disembark or
(b) goods are loaded or unloaded,
on or from a through train or shuttle train, as the case may be";

(ii) in paragraph 1(3) for the words "ship or aircraft" wherever occurring, there are
substituted the words "through train or shuttle train";

(iii) in paragraph 2(2), the words "or in the border area", "or in the area" and "or
Northern Ireland" are omitted;

(iv) in paragraph 2(3) for the words "ship or aircraft" there are substituted "through train or shuttle train" and there are omitted the words "or Northern Ireland";

(v) after paragraph 2(3) there is inserted—

"**3A.** An examination under sub-paragraph (1) may be commenced in a train during the period when it is a control area.";

(vi) paragraphs 3 and 4 are omitted;

(vii) in paragraph 5 the words "or 3" are omitted;

(viii) in paragraph 6, in sub-paragraph (1), for the word "vehicle" there are substituted the words "through train or shuttle train" and, in sub-paragraph (2), for the words "ship, aircraft or vehicle" there are substituted the words "through train or shuttle train";

(ix) in paragraph 7 for the words "ship or aircraft", wherever occurring, there are substituted the words "through train or shuttle train";

(x) in paragraph 8 for the words "ship or aircraft", wherever occurring, there are substituted the words "through train or shuttle train", and sub-paragraph (2) is omitted;

(xi) in paragraph 9, in sub-paragraph (2), the words "or in Northern Ireland" are omitted and for the words "ship, aircraft or vehicle" there are substituted the words "through train or shuttle train" and, in sub-paragraph (4), for the words "ship or aircraft or enter a vehicle" there are substituted the words "through train or shuttle train";

(xii) paragraph 12 is omitted;

(xiii) in paragraph 13 for the words "ships or aircraft" and the words "ship or aircraft", wherever occurring, there are substituted the words "a through train or shuttle train" and for the words "United Kingdom" there are substituted the words "Tunnel System";

(xiv) for paragraph 14 there is substituted—

"**14.**—(1) The Secretary of State may from time to time give written notice to persons operating international services designating all or any through trains as control areas while they are within any area in the UK specified in the notice or while they constitute a control zone.

(2) The Secretary of State may from time to time give written notice designating a control area—

(i) to the Concessionaires as respects any part of the tunnel system in the UK or of a control zone within the tunnel system in France or Belgium, or

(ii) to any occupier or person concerned with the management of a terminal control point in the UK.

(3) A notice under sub-paragraph (1) or (2) above may specify facilities to be provided and conditions and restrictions to be observed in a control area, and any persons to whom such a notice is given shall take all reasonable steps to secure that any such facilities, conditions or restrictions are provided or observed.";

(xv) paragraphs 15, 16 and 17 are omitted, and

(xvi) the Table of Designated Ports is omitted.

Terrorism Act 2000, Sched. 8

Treatment of persons detained under section 41 or Schedule 7

★**25–141**   As from a day to be appointed, paragraph 11(1)(a) of Schedule 8 to the 2000 Act is amended by the *Protection of Freedoms Act* 2012, s.19, and Sched. 1, paras 1(1) and (5), so as to substitute the words "a relevant search (within the meaning given by paragraph 20A(6)) or for the purposes of" for "paragraph 14(4)".

★   As from a day to be appointed, the *Crime and Security Act* 2010, s.17, is repealed by the *Protection of Freedoms Act* 2012, s.115(1) and (2), Sched. 9, para. 4, and Sched. 10, Pt 1.

Terrorism Act 2000, Sched. 8, para. 14

25–143   14.—(1) This paragraph applies to—

(a) fingerprints or samples taken under paragraph 10 or 12, and

(b) information derived from those samples.

(2) The fingerprints and samples may be retained but shall not be used by any person except for the purposes of a terrorist investigation *or for purposes related to the prevention or detection of crime, the investigation of an offence or the conduct of a prosecution* [or as mentioned in sub-paragraph (2A)].

[(2A) The fingerprints or samples may be used—
  (a) in the interests of national security,
  (b) for purposes related to the prevention or detection of crime, the investigation of an offence or the conduct of a prosecution, or
  (c) for purposes related to the identification of a deceased person or of the person from whom the material came.]
(3) *In particular, a check may not be made against them under*—
  (a) *section 63A(1) of the* Police and Criminal Evidence Act *1984 (checking of fingerprints and samples), or*
  (b) *Article 63A(1) of the* Police and Criminal Evidence (Northern Ireland) Order *1989 (checking of fingerprints and samples),*
except for the purpose of a terrorist investigation or for purposes related to the prevention or detection of crime, the investigation of an offence or the conduct of a prosecution.
  (4) The fingerprints, samples or information may be checked, subject to sub-paragraph (2), against—
  (a) other fingerprints of samples taken under paragraph 10 or 12 or information derived from those samples,
  (b) relevant physical data or samples taken by virtue of paragraph 20,
  [(ba) material to which section 18 of the *Counter-Terrorism Act* 2008 applies,]
  (c) any of the fingerprints, samples and information mentioned in section 63A(1)(a) and (b) of the *Police and Criminal Evidence Act* 1984 (checking of fingerprints and samples),
  (d) any of the fingerprints, samples and information mentioned in Article 63A(1)(a) and (b) of the *Police and Criminal Evidence (Northern Ireland) Order* 1989 (checking of fingerprints and samples), and
  (e) fingerprints or samples taken under section 15(9) of, or paragraph 7(5) of Schedule 5 to, the *Prevention of Terrorism (Temporary Provisions) Act* 1989 or information derived from those samples.
  (4A) In this paragraph—
  (a) a reference to crime includes a reference to any conduct which—
    (i) constitutes one or more criminal offences (whether under the law of a part of the United Kingdom or of a country or territory outside the United Kingdom); or
    (ii) is, or corresponds to, any conduct which, if it all took place in any one part of the United Kingdom, would constitute one or more criminal offences; and
  (b) the references to an investigation and to a prosecution include references, respectively, to any investigation outside the United Kingdom of any crime or suspected crime and to a prosecution brought in respect of any crime in a country or territory outside the United Kingdom.
  (5) This paragraph (other than sub-paragraph (4)) shall apply to fingerprints or samples taken under section 15(9) of, or paragraph 7(5) of Schedule 5 to, the *Prevention of Terrorism (Temporary Provisions) Act* 1989 and information derived from those samples as it applies to fingerprints or samples taken under paragraph 10 or 12 and the information derived from those samples.

[This paragraph is printed as amended by the *CJPA* 2001, s.84; and as amended, as from a day to be appointed, by the *Counter-Terrorism Act* 2008, s.16 (omission of italicised words, insertion of words in square brackets). It is replaced by new paras 14 to 14I (as set out in the main work) as from a day to be appointed: *Crime and Security Act* 2010, s.17(1) and (2). As from a further day to be appointed, paragraph 14 is repealed (along with section 84 of the 2001 Act, section 16 of the 2008 Act and section 17 of the 2010 Act) by the *Protection of Freedoms Act* 2012, ss.19 and 115(1) and (2), Sched. 1, para. 1(1) and (2), Sched. 9, para. 4, and Sched. 10, Pt 1.]　★

As from a day to be appointed, paragraphs 14 to 14I of Schedule 8 to the 2000 Act, as　★ prospectively inserted by section 17 of the *Crime and Security Act* 2010, are effectively repealed by virtue of the repeal of section 17 of the 2010 Act by the *Protection of Freedoms Act* 2012, s.115(2), and Sched. 10, Pt 1.

As from a day to be appointed, paragraph 14F(3) of Schedule 8 to the 2000 Act is　★**25–144** amended by the *Legal Aid, Sentencing and Punishment of Offenders Act* 2012, s.135(3), and Sched. 24, paras 21 and 22, so as to omit paragraph (b) and the word "or" that precedes it.

As to the repeal of section 17 of the *Crime and Security Act* 2010, see *ante*, § 25–143.　★

As from a day to be appointed, paragraph 15 of Schedule 8 to the 2000 Act is amended　★**25–145** by the *Protection of Freedoms Act* 2012, s.19, and Sched. 1, para. 1(1) and (6) to (8), so as (i) to substitute "13" for "14" in sub-paragraphs (1) and (2), and (ii) to insert a new sub-paragraph (1A), as follows—

"(1A) In the application of section 65(2A) of the *Police and Criminal Evidence Act* 1984 for the purposes of sub-paragraph (1) of this paragraph, the reference to the destruction of a sample under section 63R of that Act is a reference to the destruction of a sample under paragraph 20G of this Schedule.".

★ As to the repeal of section 17 of the *Crime and Security Act* 2010, see *ante*, § 25–143.

Destruction and retention of fingerprints and samples etc: United Kingdom

★**25–145a** As from a day to be appointed, new paragraphs 20A to 20J are inserted in Schedule 8 to the 2000 Act by the *Protection of Freedoms Act* 2012, s.19, and Sched. 1, para. 1(1) and (4), as follows—

"*Destruction and retention of fingerprints and samples etc: United Kingdom*

20A.—(1) This paragraph applies to—
    (a) fingerprints taken under paragraph 10,
    (b) a DNA profile derived from a DNA sample taken under paragraph 10 or 12,
    (c) relevant physical data taken or provided by virtue of paragraph 20, and
    (d) a DNA profile derived from a DNA sample taken by virtue of paragraph 20.

(2) Fingerprints, relevant physical data and DNA profiles to which this paragraph applies ('paragraph 20A material') must be destroyed if it appears to the responsible chief officer of police that—
    (a) the taking or providing of the material or, in the case of a DNA profile, the taking of the sample from which the DNA profile was derived, was unlawful, or
    (b) the material was taken or provided, or (in the case of a DNA profile) was derived from a sample taken, from a person in connection with that person's arrest under section 41 and the arrest was unlawful or based on mistaken identity.

(3) In any other case, paragraph 20A material must be destroyed unless it is retained under any power conferred by paragraphs 20B to 20E.

(4) Paragraph 20A material which ceases to be retained under a power mentioned in sub-paragraph (3) may continue to be retained under any other such power which applies to it.

(5) Nothing in this paragraph prevents a relevant search, in relation to paragraph 20A material, from being carried out within such time as may reasonably be required for the search if the responsible chief officer of police considers the search to be desirable.

(6) For the purposes of sub-paragraph (5), 'a relevant search' is a search carried out for the purpose of checking the material against—
    (a) other fingerprints or samples taken under paragraph 10 or 12 or a DNA profile derived from such a sample,
    (b) any of the relevant physical data, samples or information mentioned in section 19C(1) of the *Criminal Procedure (Scotland) Act* 1995,
    (c) any of the relevant physical data, samples or information held by virtue of section 56 of the *Criminal Justice (Scotland) Act* 2003,
    (d) material to which section 18 of the *Counter-Terrorism Act* 2008 applies,
    (e) any of the fingerprints, data or samples obtained under paragraph 1 or 4 of Schedule 6 to the *Terrorism Prevention and Investigation Measures Act* 2011, or information derived from such samples,
    (f) any of the fingerprints, samples and information mentioned in section 63A(1)(a) and (b) of the *Police and Criminal Evidence Act* 1984 (checking of fingerprints and samples), and
    (g) any of the fingerprints, samples and information mentioned in Article 63A(1)(a) and (b) of the *Police and Criminal Evidence (Northern Ireland) Order* 1989 (checking of fingerprints and samples).

★**25–145b** 20B.—(1) This paragraph applies to paragraph 20A material relating to a person who is detained under section 41.

(2) In the case of a person who has previously been convicted of a recordable offence (other than a single exempt conviction), or an offence in Scotland which is punishable by imprisonment, or is so convicted before the end of the period within which the material may be retained by virtue of this paragraph, the material may be retained indefinitely.

(3) In the case of a person who has no previous convictions, or only one exempt conviction, the material may be retained until the end of the retention period specified in sub-paragraph (4).

(4) The retention period is—
- (a) in the case of fingerprints or relevant physical data, the period of 3 years beginning with the date on which the fingerprints or relevant physical data were taken or provided, and
- (b) in the case of a DNA profile, the period of 3 years beginning with the date on which the DNA sample from which the profile was derived was taken (or, if the profile was derived from more than one DNA sample, the date on which the first of those samples was taken).

(5) The responsible chief officer of police or a specified chief officer of police may apply to a relevant court for an order extending the retention period.

(6) An application for an order under sub-paragraph (5) must be made within the period of 3 months ending on the last day of the retention period.

(7) An order under sub-paragraph (5) may extend the retention period by a period which—
- (a) begins with the date on which the material would otherwise be required to be destroyed under this paragraph, and
- (b) ends with the end of the period of 2 years beginning with that date.

(8) The following persons may appeal to the relevant appeal court against an order under sub-paragraph (5), or a refusal to make such an order—
- (a) the responsible chief officer of police;
- (b) a specified chief officer of police;
- (c) the person from whom the material was taken.

(9) [*Scotland.*]

(10) In this paragraph—
'relevant court' means—
- (a) in England and Wales, a District Judge (Magistrates' Courts),
- (b) [*Scotland*]; and
- (c) [*Northern Ireland*];

'the relevant appeal court' means—
- (a) in England and Wales, the Crown Court,
- (b) [*Scotland*]; and
- (c) [*Northern Ireland*];

'a specified chief officer of police' means—
- (a) in England and Wales and Northern Ireland—
  - (i) the chief officer of the police force of the area in which the person from whom the material was taken resides, or
  - (ii) a chief officer of police who believes that the person is in, or is intending to come to, the chief officer's police area, and
- (b) [*Scotland*].

20C.—(1) This paragraph applies to paragraph 20A material relating to a person who is detained under Schedule 7. ★**25–145c**

(2) In the case of a person who has previously been convicted of a recordable offence (other than a single exempt conviction), or an offence in Scotland which is punishable by imprisonment, or is so convicted before the end of the period within which the material may be retained by virtue of this paragraph, the material may be retained indefinitely.

(3) In the case of a person who has no previous convictions, or only one exempt conviction, the material may be retained until the end of the retention period specified in sub-paragraph (4).

(4) The retention period is—
- (a) in the case of fingerprints or relevant physical data, the period of 6 months beginning with the date on which the fingerprints or relevant physical data were taken or provided, and
- (b) in the case of a DNA profile, the period of 6 months beginning with the date on which the DNA sample from which the profile was derived was taken (or, if the profile was derived from more than one DNA sample, the date on which the first of those samples was taken).

20D.—(1) For the purposes of paragraphs 20B and 20C, a person is to be treated as having been convicted of an offence if— ★**25–145d**
- (a) in relation to a recordable offence in England and Wales or Northern Ireland—
  - (i) the person has been given a caution in respect of the offence which, at the time of the caution, the person has admitted,
  - (ii) the person has been found not guilty of the offence by reason of insanity,
  - (iii) the person has been found to be under a disability and to have done the act charged in respect of the offence, or

(iv) the person has been warned or reprimanded under section 65 of the *Crime and Disorder Act* 1998 for the offence,

(b)–(f) [*Scotland*].

(2) Paragraphs 20B and 20C and this paragraph, so far as they relate to persons convicted of an offence, have effect despite anything in the *Rehabilitation of Offenders Act* 1974.

(3) But a person is not to be treated as having been convicted of an offence if that conviction is a disregarded conviction or caution by virtue of section 92 of the *Protection of Freedoms Act* 2012.

(4) For the purposes of paragraphs 20B and 20C—

    (a) a person has no previous convictions if the person has not previously been convicted—

        (i) in England and Wales or Northern Ireland of a recordable offence, or

        (ii) in Scotland of an offence which is punishable by imprisonment, and

    (b) if the person has previously been convicted of a recordable offence in England and Wales or Northern Ireland, the conviction is exempt if it is in respect of a recordable offence, other than a qualifying offence, committed when the person was aged under 18.

(5) In sub-paragraph (4), 'qualifying offence' has—

    (a) in relation to a conviction in respect of a recordable offence committed in England and Wales, the meaning given by section 65A of the *Police and Criminal Evidence Act* 1984, and

    (b) in relation to a conviction in respect of a recordable offence committed in Northern Ireland, the meaning given by article 53A of the *Police and Criminal Evidence (Northern Ireland) Order* 1989 (S.I. 1989 No. 1341 (N.I. 12)).

(6) If a person is convicted of more than one offence arising out of a single course of action, those convictions are to be treated as a single conviction for the purposes of calculating under paragraph 20B or 20C whether the person has been convicted of only one offence.

(7) Nothing in paragraph 20B or 20C prevents the start of a new retention period in relation to paragraph 20A material if a person is detained again under section 41 or (as the case may be) Schedule 7 when an existing retention period (whether or not extended) is still in force in relation to that material.

★**25–145e**   20E.—(1) Paragraph 20A material may be retained for as long as a national security determination made by the responsible chief officer of police has effect in relation to it.

(2) A national security determination is made if the responsible chief officer of police determines that it is necessary for any paragraph 20A material to be retained for the purposes of national security.

(3) A national security determination—

    (a) must be made in writing,

    (b) has effect for a maximum of 2 years beginning with the date on which the determination is made, and

    (c) may be renewed.

★**25–145f**   20F.—(1) If fingerprints or relevant physical data are required by paragraph 20A to be destroyed, any copies of the fingerprints or relevant physical data held by a police force must also be destroyed.

(2) If a DNA profile is required by that paragraph to be destroyed, no copy may be retained by a police force except in a form which does not include information which identifies the person to whom the DNA profile relates.

★**25–145g**   20G.—(1) This paragraph applies to—

    (a) samples taken under paragraph 10 or 12, or

    (b) samples taken by virtue of paragraph 20.

(2) Samples to which this paragraph applies must be destroyed if it appears to the responsible chief officer of police that—

    (a) the taking of the sample was unlawful, or

    (b) the sample was taken from a person in connection with that person's arrest under section 41 and the arrest was unlawful or based on mistaken identity.

(3) Subject to this, the rule in sub-paragraph (4) or (as the case may be) (5) applies.

(4) A DNA sample to which this paragraph applies must be destroyed—

    (a) as soon as a DNA profile has been derived from the sample, or

    (b) if sooner, before the end of the period of 6 months beginning with the date on which the sample was taken.

(5) Any other sample to which this paragraph applies must be destroyed before the end of the period of 6 months beginning with the date on which it was taken.

(6) The responsible chief officer of police may apply to a relevant court for an order to retain a sample to which this paragraph applies beyond the date on which the sample would otherwise be required to be destroyed by virtue of sub-paragraph (4) or (5) if—

(a) the sample was taken from a person detained under section 41 in connection with the investigation of a qualifying offence, and

(b) the responsible chief officer of police considers that the condition in sub-paragraph (7) is met.

(7) The condition is that, having regard to the nature and complexity of other material that is evidence in relation to the offence, the sample is likely to be needed in any proceedings for the offence for the purposes of—

(a) disclosure to, or use by, a defendant, or

(b) responding to any challenge by a defendant in respect of the admissibility of material that is evidence on which the prosecution proposes to rely.

(8) An application under sub-paragraph (6) must be made before the date on which the sample would otherwise be required to be destroyed by virtue of sub-paragraph (4) or (5).

(9) If, on an application made by the responsible chief officer of police under sub-paragraph (6), the relevant court is satisfied that the condition in sub-paragraph (7) is met, it may make an order under this sub-paragraph which—

(a) allows the sample to be retained for a period of 12 months beginning with the date on which the sample would otherwise be required to be destroyed by virtue of sub-paragraph (4) or (5), and

(b) may be renewed (on one or more occasions) for a further period of not more than 12 months from the end of the period when the order would otherwise cease to have effect.

(10) An application for an order under sub-paragraph (9) (other than an application for renewal)—

(a) may be made without notice of the application having been given to the person from whom the sample was taken, and

(b) may be heard and determined in private in the absence of that person.

(11) [*Scotland*.]

(12) A sample retained by virtue of an order under sub-paragraph (9) must not be used other than for the purposes of any proceedings for the offence in connection with which the sample was taken.

(13) A sample that ceases to be retained by virtue of an order under sub-paragraph (9) must be destroyed.

(14) Nothing in this paragraph prevents a relevant search, in relation to samples to which this paragraph applies, from being carried out within such time as may reasonably be required for the search if the responsible chief officer of police considers the search to be desirable.

(15) In this paragraph—

'ancillary offence', in relation to an offence for the time being listed in section 41(1) of the *Counter-Terrorism Act* 2008, means—

(a) aiding, abetting, counselling or procuring the commission of the offence, or

(b) inciting, attempting or conspiring to commit the offence;

'qualifying offence'—

(a) in relation to the investigation of an offence committed in England and Wales, has the meaning given by section 65A of the *Police and Criminal Evidence Act* 1984,

(b) [*Scotland*], and

(c) [*Northern Ireland*].

'relevant court' means—

(a) in England and Wales, a District Judge (Magistrates' Courts),

(b) [*Scotland*]; and

(c) [*Northern Ireland*];

'relevant offence' has the same meaning as in section 19A of the *Criminal Procedure (Scotland) Act* 1995;

'a relevant search' has the meaning given by paragraph 20A(6).

20H.—(1) Any material to which paragraph 20A or 20G applies must not be used other than—　★**25–145h**

(a) in the interests of national security,

(b) for the purposes of a terrorist investigation,

(c) for purposes related to the prevention or detection of crime, the investigation of an offence or the conduct of a prosecution, or

(d) for purposes related to the identification of a deceased person or of the person to whom the material relates.

(2) Subject to sub-paragraph (1), a relevant search (within the meaning given by paragraph

20A(6)) may be carried out in relation to material to which paragraph 20A or 20G applies if the responsible chief officer of police considers the search to be desirable.

(3) Material which is required by paragraph 20A or 20G to be destroyed must not at any time after it is required to be destroyed be used—

    (a) in evidence against the person to whom the material relates, or

    (b) for the purposes of the investigation of any offence.

(4) In this paragraph—

    (a) the reference to using material includes a reference to allowing any check to be made against it and to disclosing it to any person,

    (b) the reference to crime includes a reference to any conduct which—

        (i) constitutes one or more criminal offences (whether under the law of a part of the United Kingdom or of a country or territory outside the United Kingdom), or

        (ii) is, or corresponds to, any conduct which, if it all took place in any one part of the United Kingdom, would constitute one or more criminal offences, and

    (c) the references to an investigation and to a prosecution include references, respectively, to any investigation outside the United Kingdom of any crime or suspected crime and to a prosecution brought in respect of any crime in a country or territory outside the United Kingdom.

(5) Sub-paragraphs (1), (2) and (4) do not form part of the law of Scotland.

★**25–145i**   20I. Paragraphs 20A to 20F and 20H do not apply to paragraph 20A material relating to a person detained under section 41 which is, or may become, disclosable under—

    (a) the *Criminal Procedure and Investigations Act* 1996, or

    (b) a code of practice prepared under section 23 of that Act and in operation by virtue of an order under section 25 of that Act.

★**25–145j**   20J. In paragraphs 20A to 20I—

'DNA profile' means any information derived from a DNA sample;

'DNA sample' means any material that has come from a human body and consists of or includes human cells;

'fingerprints' has the meaning given by section 65(1) of the *Police and Criminal Evidence Act* 1984 (Part 5 definitions);

'paragraph 20A material' has the meaning given by paragraph 20A(2);

'police force' means any of the following—

    (a) the metropolitan police force;

    (b) a police force maintained under section 2 of the *Police Act* 1996 (police forces in England and Wales outside London);

    (c) the City of London police force;

    (d) any police force maintained under or by virtue of section 1 of the *Police (Scotland) Act* 1967;

    (e) the Scottish Police Services Authority;

    (f) the Police Service of Northern Ireland;

    (g) the Police Service of Northern Ireland Reserve;

    (h) the Ministry of Defence Police;

    (i) the Royal Navy Police;

    (j) the Royal Military Police;

    (k) the Royal Air Force Police;

    (l) the British Transport Police;

'recordable offence' has—

    (a) in relation to a conviction in England and Wales, the meaning given by section 118(1) of the *Police and Criminal Evidence Act* 1984, and

    (b) in relation to a conviction in Northern Ireland, the meaning given by article 2(2) of the *Police and Criminal Evidence (Northern Ireland) Order* 1989;

'relevant physical data' has the meaning given by section 18(7A) of the *Criminal Procedure (Scotland) Act* 1995;

'responsible chief officer of police' means, in relation to fingerprints or samples taken in England or Wales, or a DNA profile derived from a sample so taken, the chief officer of police for the police area—

    (a) in which the material concerned was taken, or

    (b) in the case of a DNA profile, in which the sample from which the DNA profile was derived was taken;

'responsible chief officer of police' means, in relation to relevant physical data or samples taken or provided in Scotland, or a DNA profile derived from a sample so taken or provided, the chief constable of the police force for the area—

(a) in which the material concerned was taken or provided, or

(b) in the case of a DNA profile, in which the sample from which the DNA profile was derived was taken;

'responsible chief officer of police' means, in relation to fingerprints or samples taken in Northern Ireland, or a DNA profile derived from a sample so taken, the Chief Constable of the Police Service of Northern Ireland.".

Extensions of warrants

As from July 10, 2012 (*Protection of Freedoms Act 2012 (Commencement No. 1) Order* 2012 (S.I. 2012 No. 1205)), paragraph 36 of Schedule 8 to the 2000 Act is amended by the *Protection of Freedoms Act* 2012, ss.57(1) and 115(1) and (2), Sched. 9, paras 23 and 26(1) to (3), and Sched. 10, Pt 4 (to make permanent the modifications under s.25 of the *Terrorism Act* 2006 (as to which, see § 25–163 in the main work)). As to the possibility of modification of paragraph 36 in an emergency, see Part 4 of Schedule 8 to the 2000 Act (*post*, § 25–163). ★**25–161**

As from July 10, 2012 (*Protection of Freedoms Act 2012 (Commencement No. 1) Order* 2012 (S.I. 2012 No. 1205)), section 25 of the *Terrorism Act* 2006 is itself repealed by the *Protection of Freedoms Act* 2012, ss.57(2) and 115(2), and Sched. 10, Pt 4. ★

Detention-conditions

As from July 10, 2012 (*Protection of Freedoms Act 2012 (Commencement No. 1) Order* 2012 (S.I. 2012 No. 1205)), paragraph 37(2) of Schedule 8 to the 2000 Act is amended by the *Protection of Freedoms Act* 2012, s.115(1) and (2), Sched. 9, paras 23 and 26(1) and (4), and Sched. 10, Pt 4 (to make permanent the modification under s.25 of the *Terrorism Act* 2006 (as to which, see § 25–163 in the main work)). ★**25–162**

Expiry or renewal of extended detention maximum period

As from July 10, 2012 (*Protection of Freedoms Act 2012 (Commencement No. 1) Order* 2012 (S.I. 2012 No. 1205)), section 25 of the *Terrorism Act* 2006 is repealed by the *Protection of Freedoms Act* 2012, ss.57(2) and 115(2), and Sched. 10, Pt 4. ★**25–163**

As from July 10, 2012 (*Protection of Freedoms Act 2012 (Commencement No. 1) Order* 2012 (S.I. 2012 No. 1205)), Part 4 (para. 38) of Schedule 8 is inserted in the 2000 Act by the *Protection of Freedoms Act* 2012, s.58, as follows— ★**25–163a**

"PART 4

EMERGENCY POWER WHEN PARLIAMENT DISSOLVED ETC. FOR TEMPORARY EXTENSION OF MAXIMUM PERIOD FOR DETENTION UNDER SECTION 41

38.—(1) The Secretary of State may make a temporary extension order if—

(a) either—

(i) Parliament is dissolved, or

(ii) Parliament has met after a dissolution but the first Queen's Speech of the Parliament has not yet taken place, and

(b) the Secretary of State considers that it is necessary by reason of urgency to make such an order.

(2) A temporary extension order is an order which provides, in relation to the period of three months beginning with the coming into force of the order, for paragraphs 36 and 37 to be read as if—

(a) in paragraph 36(3)(b)(ii) for '14 days' there were substituted '28 days', and

(b) the other modifications in sub-paragraphs (3) and (4) were made.

(3) The other modifications of paragraph 36 are—

(a) the insertion at the beginning of sub-paragraph (1) of 'Subject to sub-paragraphs (1ZA) to (1ZI),',

(b) the insertion, after sub-paragraph (1), of—

'(1ZA) Sub-paragraph (1ZB) applies in relation to any proposed application under sub-paragraph (1) for the further extension of the period specified in a warrant of further detention where the grant (otherwise than in accordance with sub-paragraph (3AA)(b)) of the application would extend the specified period to a time that is more than 14 days after the relevant time.

(1ZB) No person may make such an application—

(a) in England and Wales, without the consent of the Director of Public Prosecutions,

(b) in Scotland, without the consent of the Lord Advocate, and

(c) in Northern Ireland, without the consent of the Director of Public Prosecutions for Northern Ireland,

unless the person making the application is the person whose consent is required.

(1ZC) The Director of Public Prosecutions must exercise personally any function under sub-paragraph (1ZB) of giving consent.

(1ZD) The only exception is if—

(a) the Director is unavailable, and

(b) there is another person who is designated in writing by the Director acting personally as the person who is authorised to exercise any such function when the Director is unavailable.

(1ZE) In that case—

(a) the other person may exercise the function but must do so personally, and

(b) the Director acting personally—

(i) must review the exercise of the function as soon as practicable, and

(ii) may revoke any consent given.

(1ZF) Where the consent is so revoked after an application has been made or extension granted, the application is to be dismissed or (as the case may be) the extension is to be revoked.

(1ZG) Sub-paragraphs (1ZC) to (1ZF) apply instead of any other provisions which would otherwise have enabled any function of the Director of Public Prosecutions under sub-paragraph (1ZB) of giving consent to be exercised by a person other than the Director.

(1ZH) [*Northern Ireland.*]

(1ZI) [*Northern Ireland.*]'

(c) the substitution, for 'a judicial authority' in sub-paragraph (1A), of '—

(a) in the case of an application falling within sub-paragraph (1B), a judicial authority; and

(b) in any other case, a senior judge',

(d) the insertion, after sub-paragraph (1A), of—

'(1B) An application for the extension or further extension of a period falls within this sub-paragraph if—

(a) the grant of the application otherwise than in accordance with sub-paragraph (3AA)(b) would extend that period to a time that is no more than 14 days after the relevant time; and

(b) no application has previously been made to a senior judge in respect of that period.',

(e) the insertion, after 'judicial authority' in both places in sub-paragraph (3AA) where it appears, of 'or senior judge',

(f) the insertion, after 'detention' in sub-paragraph (4), of 'but, in relation to an application made by virtue of sub-paragraph (1A)(b) to a senior judge, as if—

(a) references to a judicial authority were references to a senior judge; and

(b) references to the judicial authority in question were references to the senior judge in question',

(g) the insertion, after 'judicial authority' in sub-paragraph (5), of 'or senior judge', and

(h) the insertion, after sub-paragraph (6), of—

'(7) In this paragraph and paragraph 37 "senior judge" means a judge of the High Court or of the High Court of Justiciary.'

(4) The modification of paragraph 37 is the insertion, in sub-paragraph (2), after 'judicial authority', of 'or senior judge'.

(5) A temporary extension order applies, except so far as it provides otherwise, to any person who is being detained under section 41 when the order comes into force (as well as any person who is subsequently detained under that section).

(6) The Secretary of State may by order revoke a temporary extension order if the Secretary of

State considers it appropriate to do so (whether or not the conditions mentioned in paragraphs (a) and (b) of sub-paragraph (1) are met).

(7) Sub-paragraph (8) applies if—

(a) any of the following events occurs—

(i) the revocation without replacement of a temporary extension order,

(ii) the expiry of the period of three months mentioned in sub-paragraph (2) in relation to such an order,

(iii) the ceasing to have effect of such an order by virtue of section 123(6B) and (6C), and

(b) at that time—

(i) a person is being detained by virtue of a further extension under paragraph 36,

(ii) the person's further detention was authorised by virtue of the temporary extension order concerned (before its revocation, expiry or ceasing to have effect) for a period ending more than 14 days after the relevant time (within the meaning given by paragraph 36(3B)),

(iii) that 14 days has expired, and

(iv) the person's detention is not otherwise authorised by law.

(8) The person with custody of that individual must release the individual immediately.

(9) Subject to sub-paragraphs (7) and (8), the fact that—

(a) a temporary extension order is revoked,

(b) the period of three months mentioned in sub-paragraph (2) has expired in relation to such an order, or

(c) such an order ceases to have effect by virtue of section 123(6B) and (6C),

is without prejudice to anything previously done by virtue of the order or to the making of a new order.".

Terrorism Act 2000, Sched. 14

Article 7 of the *Channel Tunnel (International Arrangements) Order* 1993 (S.I. 1993 No.   **25–167** 1813) (Appendix F–13a, *post*) provides that the enactments mentioned in Schedule 4 to that order shall (a) in their application to France by virtue of article 4(1) or (1B), and (b) in their application to the United Kingdom within the tunnel system and elsewhere for the authorised purposes (as to which, see article 2(2)), have effect with the modifications set out in Schedule 4. As a result of the amendment of that schedule by the *Channel Tunnel (International Arrangements) (Amendment) Order* 2001 (S.I. 2001 No. 178), Schedule 14 to the 2000 Act, being one of the enactments mentioned therein, has effect with the following modifications: in paragraphs 5 and 6, after the words "this Act", in each place where they occur, there are inserted the words "or the *Channel Tunnel (International Arrangements) Order* 1993".

C. Terrorism Act 2006

(2) Preparation of terrorist acts and training

Terrorism Act 2006, ss.5–8

Training for terrorism

With effect from October 1, 2012, Schedule 5 to the *Anti-terrorism, Crime and Security Act*   ★**25–194** 2001 (see the main work) is amended by the *Anti-terrorism, Crime and Security Act 2001 (Modification) Order* 2012 (S.I. 2012 No. 1466).

I. Aviation Security Act 1982

(3) Miscellaneous and general

As to the removal (as from a day to be appointed) of the upper limit on a fine on sum-   ★**25–255** mary conviction of an offence, see the *Legal Aid, Sentencing and Punishment of Offenders Act* 2012, s.85 (*ante*, § 1–125).

IV. IMMIGRATION

Immigration Act 1971, ss.25–25C

Assisting unlawful immigration to member State

★**25–286**   For the purposes of section 25(2) of the 1971 Act, an immigration law is a law that determines whether a person is lawfully or unlawfully either entering, in transit within, or in, the United Kingdom; therefore, section 2(1) of the *Asylum and Immigration (Treatment of Claimants, etc.) Act* 2004 ("(1) A person commits an offence if at a leave or asylum interview he does not have with him an immigration document which — (a) is in force, and (b) satisfactorily establishes his identity and nationality or citizenship.") is not an immigration law for these purposes: *R. v. Kapoor* [2012] 2 All E.R. 1205, CA (considering *R. v. Javaheri-fard and Miller* (§ 25–291 in the main work)).

IX. DISCLOSURE, ETC., OF GOVERNMENT SECRETS

C. Official Secrets Act 1989

"Prescribed" bodies or persons

★**25–371**   With effect from April 1, 2012, amendments are made to Schedules 1 and 2 to the *Official Secrets Act 1989 (Prescription) Order* 1990 (S.I. 1990 No. 200) by the *Budget Responsibility and National Audit Act 2011 (Consequential Amendments) Order* 2012 (S.I. 2012 No. 725), so as (i) to insert a reference to the National Audit Office at the end of the first column in Schedule 1, with a corresponding entry in the second column referring to the members and employees of that office, and (ii) to substitute, in Schedule 2, "Member of staff of the National Audit Office that was established by section 3 of the *National Audit Act* 1983" for "Member of staff of the National Audit Office".

XI. OFFENCES RELATING TO POSTS AND TELECOMMUNICATIONS

C. Regulation of Investigatory Powers Act 2000

Introduction

★**25–384**   As from a day to be appointed, section 71 of the 2000 Act is amended by the *Protection of Freedoms Act* 2012, s.115(1), and Sched. 9, paras 6 and 14, so as to insert "or the relevant judicial authority (within the meaning of section 23A or 32A)" immediately after the reference to the Surveillance Commissioners.

Regulation of Investigatory Powers Act 2000, ss.1–5

★**25–389**   As from a day to be appointed, section 4(5) of the 2000 Act is amended by the *Health and Social Care Act* 2012, s.55(2), and Sched. 5, para. 98, so as to substitute "section 4(3A)(a)" for "section 8".

Regulation of Investigatory Powers Act 2000, ss.15–19

Exceptions to section 17

25–396   Section 18(1) of the 2000 Act was amended, with effect from December 15, 2011, by the *Terrorism Prevention and Investigation Measures Act* 2011, s.29(3), and Sched. 7, para. 4(1) and (2), so as (i) to omit paragraph (da), and (ii) to insert a new paragraph (dd), as follows—

"(dd) any TPIM proceedings (within the meaning of the *Terrorism Prevention and Investigation Measures Act* 2011) or any proceedings arising out of such proceedings;".

Section 18(2) of the 2000 Act was amended, with effect from December 15, 2011, by the *Terrorism Prevention and Investigation Measures Act* 2011, s.29(3), and Sched. 7, para. 4(1) and (3), so as (i) to substitute "(db) to (f)" for "(da) to (f)" in the opening words, (ii) to omit paragraph (za), and (iii) to insert a new paragraph (zc), as follows—

"(zc) in the case of proceedings falling within paragraph (dd), to—
(i) a person, other than the Secretary of State, who is or was a party to the proceedings, or
(ii) any person who for the purposes of the proceedings (but otherwise than by virtue of appointment as a special advocate under Schedule 4 to the *Terrorism Prevention and Investigation Measures Act* 2011) represents a person falling within sub-paragraph (i);".

Regulation of Investigatory Powers Act 2000, ss.21–25

Obtaining and disclosing communications data

As from a day to be appointed, section 22(6) of the 2000 Act is amended by the *Protection of Freedoms Act* 2012, s.115(1), and Sched. 9, paras 6 and 7, so as to insert the words ", subject to section 23A," after the word "shall".   ★**25–400**

Form and duration of authorisations and notices

As from a day to be appointed, section 23 of the 2000 Act is amended by the *Protection of Freedoms Act* 2012, s.115(1), and Sched. 9, paras 6 and 8, so as to insert a new subsection (2A), as follows—   ★**25–401**

"(2A) The words in paragraph (a) of subsections (1) and (2) from 'or' to the end of the paragraph do not apply in relation to—
(a) an authorisation under section 22(3), (3B) or (3F) to which section 23A applies, or
(b) a notice under section 22(4) to which section 23A applies.".

Judicial approval for obtaining or disclosing communications data

As from a day to be appointed, sections 23A (authorisations requiring judicial approval) and 23B (procedure for judicial approval) are inserted in the 2000 Act by the *Protection of Freedoms Act* 2012, s.37.   ★**25–401a**

[Authorisations requiring judicial approval

23A.—(1) This section applies where a relevant person has—
(a) granted or renewed an authorisation under section 22(3), (3B) or (3F), or
(b) given or renewed a notice under section 22(4).

(2) The authorisation or notice is not to take effect until such time (if any) as the relevant judicial authority has made an order approving the grant or renewal of the authorisation or (as the case may be) the giving or renewal of the notice.

(3) The relevant judicial authority may give approval under this section to the granting or renewal of an authorisation under section 22(3), (3B) or (3F) if, and only if, the relevant judicial authority is satisfied that—
(a) at the time of the grant or renewal—
(i) there were reasonable grounds for believing that the requirements of section 22(1) and (5) were satisfied in relation to the authorisation, and
(ii) the relevant conditions were satisfied in relation to the authorisation, and
(b) at the time when the relevant judicial authority is considering the matter, there remain reasonable grounds for believing that the requirements of section 22(1) and (5) are satisfied in relation to the authorisation.

(4) The relevant judicial authority may give approval under this section to the giving or renewal of a notice under section 22(4) if, and only if, the relevant judicial authority is satisfied that—
(a) at the time of the giving or renewal of the notice—
(i) there were reasonable grounds for believing that the requirements of section 22(1) and (5) were satisfied in relation to the notice, and
(ii) the relevant conditions were satisfied in relation to the notice, and
(b) at the time when the relevant judicial authority is considering the matter, there remain rea-

sonable grounds for believing that the requirements of section 22(1) and (5) are satisfied in relation to the notice.

(5) For the purposes of subsections (3) and (4) the relevant conditions are—

  (a) in relation to any grant, giving or renewal by an individual holding an office, rank or position in a local authority in England, Wales or Scotland, that—

    (i) the individual was a designated person for the purposes of this Chapter,

    (ii) the grant, giving or renewal was not in breach of any restrictions imposed by virtue of section 25(3), and

    (iii) any other conditions that may be provided for by an order made by the Secretary of State were satisfied,

  (b) [*Northern Ireland*], and

  (c) in relation to any other grant, giving or renewal by a relevant person, that any conditions that may be provided for by an order made by the Secretary of State were satisfied.

(6) In this section—

"local authority in England" means—

    (a) a district or county council in England,

    (b) a London borough council,

    (c) the Common Council of the City of London in its capacity as a local authority, or

    (d) the Council of the Isles of Scilly,

"local authority in Scotland" means a council constituted under section 2 of the *Local Government etc. (Scotland) Act* 1994,

"local authority in Wales" means any county council or county borough council in Wales,

"Northern Ireland excepted or reserved matter" means an excepted or reserved matter (within the meaning of section 4(1) of the *Northern Ireland Act* 1998),

"Northern Ireland transferred matter" means a transferred matter (within the meaning of section 4(1) of the Act of 1998),

"relevant judicial authority" means—

    (a) in relation to England and Wales, a justice of the peace,

    (b) in relation to Scotland, a sheriff, and

    (c) in relation to Northern Ireland, a district judge (magistrates' courts) in Northern Ireland,

"relevant person" means—

    (a) an individual holding—

      (i) an office, rank or position in a local authority in England or Wales, or

      (ii) an office, rank or position in a local authority in Scotland (other than an office, rank or position in a fire and rescue authority),

    (b) also, in relation to a grant, giving or renewal for any purpose relating to a Northern Ireland excepted or reserved matter, an individual holding an office, rank or position in a district council in Northern Ireland, and

    (c) also, in relation to any grant, giving or renewal of a description that may be prescribed for the purposes of this subsection by an order made by the Secretary of State or every grant, giving or renewal if so prescribed, a person of a description so prescribed.

(7) [*Procedure for making order under subs. (6); and limitation on order-making power in relation to Northern Ireland.*]]

[Procedure for judicial approval

★25-401b   **23B.**—(1) The public authority with which the relevant person holds an office, rank or position may apply to the relevant judicial authority for an order under section 23A approving the grant or renewal of an authorisation or (as the case may be) the giving or renewal of a notice.

(2) The applicant is not required to give notice of the application to—

  (a) any person to whom the authorisation or notice which is the subject of the application relates, or

  (b) such a person's legal representatives.

(3) Where, on an application under this section, the relevant judicial authority refuses to approve the grant or renewal of the authorisation concerned or (as the case may be) the giving or renewal of the notice concerned, the relevant judicial authority may make an order quashing the authorisation or notice.

(4) In this section "relevant judicial authority" and "relevant person" have the same meaning as in section 23A.]

XIII. *REVENUE AND CUSTOMS OFFENCES*

B. CUSTOMS AND EXCISE MANAGEMENT ACT 1979

(2) Definitions and applications

Customs and Excise Management Act 1979, s.5

Time of importation, exportation, etc.

As to the application of section 5 of the 1979 Act to foreign postal packets carried by a **25–428**
universal service provider acting in that capacity, see the *Postal Packets (Revenue and
Customs) Regulations* 2011 (S.I. 2011 No. 3036), regs 9 and 10.

(4) Illegal importation

Customs and Excise Management Act 1979, s.50

Penalty for improper importation of goods

With effect from April 5, 2012, the maximum penalty for an offence under section 50 **★25–431**
of the 1979 Act (§ 25–430 in the main work) that is committed in relation to a prohibition
or restriction contained in article 6(a) or 11(a)(1)(b) of Council Regulation (EU) No. 36/
2012 concerning restrictive measures in relation to Syria (prohibition on importation) is
increased to 10 years' imprisonment: *Export Control (Syria Sanctions) and (Miscellaneous
Amendments) Order* 2012 (S.I. 2012 No. 810), art. 14(5).

With effect from June 1, 2012, the maximum penalty for an offence under section 50 ★
of the 1979 Act that is committed in connection with a prohibition on importation in
article 4, 11(1)(a), 13(1)(a) or 15(1)(b) of Council Regulation (EU) No. 267/2012 concerning restrictive measures in relation to Iran is increased to 10 years' imprisonment: *Export
Control (Iran Sanctions) Order* 2012 (S.I. 2012 No. 1243), art. 18(5).

(5) Illegal exportation

Customs and Excise Management Act 1979, s.68

Offences in relation to exportation of prohibited or restricted goods

With effect from April 5, 2012, the maximum penalty for an offence under section 68 **★25–436**
of the 1979 Act (§ 25–435 in the main work) that is committed in relation to a prohibition
or restriction on exportation contained in article 2(1)(a), 4(1), 8(1), 11, 11a(1)(a) or
12(1)(a) of Council Regulation (EU) No. 36/2012 concerning restrictive measures in relation to Syria (and repealing Council Regulation (EU) No. 442/2011 (see the main work))
is increased to 10 years' imprisonment: *Export Control (Syria Sanctions) and (Miscellaneous
Amendments) Order* 2012 (S.I. 2012 No. 810), art. 14(4).

With effect from June 1, 2012, the maximum penalty for an offence under section 68 ★
of the 1979 Act that is committed in connection with a prohibition or restriction on
exportation in article 2(1), 3(1) or 8(1), 15(1)(a) or 16 of Council Regulation (EU) No.
267/2012 (and repealing Council Regulation (EU) No. 961/2010 (see the main work)) or
of article 1a(a) or 1b(1) of Council Regulation (EU) No. 264/2012 concerning restrictive
measures in relation to Iran is increased to 10 years' imprisonment: *Export Control (Iran
Sanctions) Order* 2012 (S.I. 2012 No. 1243), art. 18(4). The *Export Control (Iran) Order* 2011
(S.I. 2011 No. 1297) (as to which, see the main work) is revoked by the 2012 order.

(9) Powers to seize and detain goods, etc.

Customs and Excise Management Act 1979, s.139

★**25–444**   In *Eastenders Cash & Carry plc v. Revenue and Customs Commrs* [2012] S.T.C. 817, CA (Civ. Div.) the Court of Appeal reversed the decision of the High Court (as to which, see the main work), and held that the power of detention of goods contained in section 139(1) of the 1979 Act is limited to cases in which the relevant facts empowering the court to condemn the goods as liable to forfeiture actually exist (*e.g.* where the goods in question are goods on which duty has in fact not been paid: s.49(1)).

(10) General provisions as to legal proceedings

Customs and Excise Management Act 1979, ss.147–149

Proceedings for offences

★**25–449**   With effect from June 18, 2012 (*Criminal Justice Act 2003 (Commencement No. 28 and Saving Provisions) Order* 2012 (S.I. 2012 No. 1320)), sections 41 and 332 of, and paragraph 50 of Schedule 3 to, and Part 4 of Schedule 37 to, the 2003 Act are brought into force in certain areas (as to which, see *ante*, § 1–88). There are associated saving provisions, as to which, see article 5 of the order (*ante*, § 1–88).

(13) Fraudulent evasion offences

Customs and Excise Management Act 1979, s.170

Penalty for fraudulent evasion of duty

★**25–475**   With effect from April 5, 2012, the maximum penalty for an offence under section 170 of the 1979 Act (§ 25–474 in the main work) that is committed in relation to a prohibition or restriction contained in article 2(1)(a), 4(1), 6(a), 8(1), 11, 11a(1)(a) or (b) or 12(1)(a) of Council Regulation (EU) No. 36/2012 concerning restrictive measures in relation to Syria (and repealing Council Regulation (EU) No. 442/2011 (see the main work)) is increased to 10 years' imprisonment: *Export Control (Syria Sanctions) and (Miscellaneous Amendments) Order* 2012 (S.I. 2012 No. 810), art. 14(4) and (5).

★   With effect from June 1, 2012, the maximum penalty for an offence under section 170 of the 1979 Act that is committed in connection with a prohibition or restriction on exportation in article 2(1), 3(1) or 8(1), 15(1)(a) or 16 of Council Regulation (EU) No. 267/2012 (repealing Council Regulation (EU) No. 961/2010 (as to which, see the main work)) or article 1a(a) or 1b(1) of Council Regulation No. 264/2012, or in connection with a prohibition or restriction on importation in article 4, 11(1)(a), 13(1)(a) or 15(1)(b) of the former regulation, concerning restrictive measures in relation to Iran, is increased to 10 years' imprisonment: *Export Control (Iran Sanctions) Order* 2012 (S.I. 2012 No. 1243), art. 18(4) and (5).

(11) General powers of examination and search

Customs and Excise Management Act 1979, s.159

Power to examine and take account of goods

25–460   As to the application of section 159 of the 1979 Act to foreign postal packets, see the *Postal Packets (Revenue and Customs) Regulations* 2011 (S.I. 2011 No. 3036), regs 6 and 7.

(14) Penalties and sentencing

Authorities

25–507   The Sentencing Council for England and Wales has issued a definitive guideline on drug offences, applying to all offenders aged 18 or over, who are sentenced on or after February 27, 2012, regardless of the date of their offence, and covering the offence of fraudulent evasion of the prohibition on the importation or exportation of a controlled drug, contrary to section 170(2) of the *CEMA* 1979 (§ 25–474 in the main work)). For the details, see *post*, Appendix K–271 *et seq.*

Customs and Excise Management Act 1979, Sched. 1

The amendment of Schedule 1 to the 1979 Act effected by the *Police Reform and Social*   **25–508**
Responsibility Act 2011 came into force on November 15, 2011: *Police Reform and Social Responsibility Act 2011 (Commencement No. 1) Order* 2011 (S.I. 2011 No. 2515). It should be noted, however, that the reference in the main work should be to paragraph 21 of Schedule 17 to the 2011 Act, not to paragraph 21 of Schedule 16.

C. Criminal Justice (International Co-operation) Act 1990

(3) Offences at sea

(a) *Offences*

Criminal Justice (International Co-operation) Act 1990, s.19

Ships used for illicit traffic

The amendment of the 1990 Act effected by the *Police Reform and Social Responsibility Act*   **25–521**
2011 came into force on November 15, 2011: *Police Reform and Social Responsibility Act 2011 (Commencement No. 1) Order* 2011 (S.I. 2011 No. 2515). It should be noted, however, that the reference in the main work should be to paragraph 22 of Schedule 17 to the 2011 Act, not to paragraph 22 of Schedule 16.

D. Value Added Tax Offences

(2) Offences and penalties

Sentence

In the context of missing-trader carousel fraud, the total value of identifiable VAT   **★25–538**
reclaims made or intended to be made, and the total amount actually paid out by way of VAT reclaim, will in most cases provide the most reliable starting point for sentencing; it will also provide the most reliable basis for a comparison with other cases, although sentencing decisions are inevitably fact-specific and a "like for like" comparison between cases will often be particularly difficult in frauds of this nature; however, it should not be thought that the total value of the transactions is irrelevant; on the contrary, it will assist in gauging the overall size, complexity and sophistication of the conspiracy; nor should it be thought that the total value of reclaims and repayments will always be a reliable indication of the true gain to the fraudsters or the true loss to Her Majesty's Revenue; a sophisticated carousel fraud may involve successful VAT reclaims that the revenue are unable to identify as linked to the conspirators: *R. v. Randhawa* [2012] S.T.C. 901, CA (noting also that the judge was right to make no allowance for a delay of five years between the offenders' arrest and their eventual sentence where their fraud was deliberately made as complicated as possible in order to maximise the difficulties for the prosecuting authority in obtaining the evidence necessary to prove their guilt).

CHAPTER 26

MONEY LAUNDERING OFFENCES

I. PROCEEDS OF CRIME ACT 2002

B. OFFENCES

(4) Legislation

Proceeds of Crime Act 2002, s.330

The regulated sector and supervisory authorities

26–16   Since its substitution by the *Proceeds of Crime Act 2002 (Business in the Regulated Sector and Supervisory Authorities) Order* 2007 (S.I. 2007 No. 3287) (as to which, see the main work), Schedule 9 to the 2002 Act has been amended by a number of instruments, the latest of which are the *Terrorism Act 2000 and Proceeds of Crime Act 2002 (Business in the Regulated Sector) Order* 2011 (S.I. 2011 No. 2701), which took effect on December 12, 2011, and the *Localism Act* 2011, ss.183 and 237, and Scheds 18, para. 2, and 25, Pt 29, which took effect on January 15, 2012.

E. SENTENCE

Proceeds of Crime Act 2002, s.334

★**26–42**   As to the appropriate sentence for the owner and a senior employee of a safe deposit company who were making the facilities available to anyone wishing to use them for obviously suspicious and potentially criminal activities, see *R. v. Swan and Woolf* [2012] 1 Cr.App.R.(S.) 90, CA. In upholding custodial sentences in both cases on pleas of guilty, the court observed that if it is important that professional people such as solicitors comply scrupulously with the legislation (as demonstrated by *R. v. Duff* and *R. v. Griffiths and Pattison* (as to both of which, see the main work)), it must be just as important that those whose business is to operate facilities that by their very nature provide opportunities for money laundering should do the same.

II. MONEY LAUNDERING REGULATIONS 2007

26–45   The *Money Laundering Regulations* 2007 (S.I. 2007 No. 2157) (see the main work) are further amended by the *Al-Qaida (Asset-Freezing) Regulations* 2011 (S.I. 2011 No. 2742), with effect from November 16, 2011, by the *Recognised Auction Platforms Regulations* 2011 (S.I. 2011 No. 2699), with effect from December 12, 2011, and by the *Money Laundering (Amendment No. 2) Regulations* 2011 (S.I. 2011 No. 2833), with effect from March 31, 2012.

CHAPTER 27

HARMFUL OR DANGEROUS DRUGS

A. INTRODUCTION

(3) Definition of a "controlled drug"

Controlled drugs and their classification for purposes of this Act

The *Police Reform and Social Responsibility Act* 2011, s.151, and Sched. 17, paras 1 and 2   **27–5**
(see the main work) came into force on November 15, 2011: *Police Reform and Social
Responsibility Act 2011 (Commencement No. 1) Order* 2011 (S.I. 2011 No. 2515).

Temporary class drug orders

The *Police Reform and Social Responsibility Act* 2011, s.151, and Sched. 17, paras 1 and 3   **27–5a**
(see the main work) came into force on November 15, 2011: *Police Reform and Social
Responsibility Act 2011 (Commencement No. 1) Order* 2011 (S.I. 2011 No. 2515).

As from April 5, 2012, the *Misuse of Drugs Act 1971 (Temporary Class Drug) Order* 2012   ★
(S.I. 2012 No. 980), specifies the following substances as drugs subject to temporary
control—

    (a) 2-(ethylamino)-2-(3-methoxyphenyl)cyclohexanone;
    (b) any stereoisomeric form of 2-(ethylamino)-2-(3-methoxyphenyl)cyclohexanone;
    (c) any ester or ether of a substance specified in paragraph (a) or (b);
    (d) any salt of a substance specified in any of paragraphs (a) to (c); and
    (e) any preparation or other product containing a substance specified in any of paragraphs
        (a) to (d).

The order stipulates that the provisions of the *Misuse of Drugs (Safe Custody) Regulations*
1973 (S.I. 1973 No. 798) (see § 27–91 in the main work) apply to these substances, and that
the *Misuse of Drugs Regulations* 2001 (S.I. 2001 No. 3998) (see § 27–83 in the main work)
are to apply to them as if they were specified as controlled drugs to which Schedule 1 to
those regulations applied.

(4) Classification of controlled drugs

Misuse of Drugs Act 1971, Sched. 2

Class B Drugs

As from June 13, 2012, the *Misuse of Drugs Act 1971 (Amendment) Order* 2012 (S.I. 2012   **★27–9**
No. 1390) amends Part II of Schedule 2 to the 1971 Act so as (i) to substitute for the words
"paragraph 1(c)" in paragraph 2A, the words "paragraph 1(ac) or (c)", and (ii) to insert a
new paragraph 1(ac) as follows—

    "(ac) any compound (not being pipradol) structurally derived from piperidine, pyrrolidine, az-
        epane, morpholine or pyridine by substitution at a ring carbon atom with a diphenylm-
        ethyl group, whether or not the compound is further modified in any of the following
        ways, that is to say,
        (i) by substitution in any of the phenyl rings to any extent with alkyl, alkoxy, haloalkyl, or
           halide groups;
      (ii) by substitution at the methyl carbon atom with an alkyl, hydroxyalkyl or hydroxy
          group;
     (iii) by substitution at the ring nitrogen atom with an alkyl, alkenyl, haloalkyl or hydroxyal-
         kyl group;".

Class C Drugs

★**27–10**   As from June 13, 2012, the *Misuse of Drugs Act 1971 (Amendment) Order* 2012 (S.I. 2012 No. 1390) amends Part III of Schedule 2 to the 1971 Act so as (i) to omit "Pipradrol" from paragraph 1(a); (ii) to insert "7-bromo-5-(2-chlorophenyl)-1,3-dihydro-2*H*-1,4-benzodiazepin-2-one" (commonly known as Phenazepam) after "Bromazepam" in paragraph 1(a); and (iii) to insert "Pipradrol" after "Oxymetholone" in paragraph 1(b).

B. RESTRICTION OF IMPORTATION AND EXPORTATION OF DRUGS

Misuse of Drugs Act 1971, s.3

27–26   The *Police Reform and Social Responsibility Act* 2011, s.151, and Sched. 17, paras 1 and 4 (see the main work) came into force on November 15, 2011: *Police Reform and Social Responsibility Act 2011 (Commencement No. 1) Order* 2011 (S.I. 2011 No. 2515).

C. RESTRICTION OF PRODUCTION AND SUPPLY OF CONTROLLED DRUGS

(1) Statute

Misuse of Drugs Act 1971, s.4

27–28   The *Police Reform and Social Responsibility Act* 2011, s.151, and Sched. 17, paras 1 and 5 (see the main work) came into force on November 15, 2011: *Police Reform and Social Responsibility Act 2011 (Commencement No. 1) Order* 2011 (S.I. 2011 No. 2515).

(2) Production

(b) *Class of offence, mode of trial and sentence*

27–31   The Sentencing Council for England and Wales has issued a definitive guideline on drug offences, applying to all offenders aged 18 or over, who are sentenced on or after February 27, 2012, regardless of the date of their offence, and covering the offences of production, or being concerned in the production of a controlled drug, contrary to section 4(2) of the *Misuse of Drugs Act* 1971 (§ 27–28 in the main work). For the detail, see *post*, Appendix K–271 *et seq.*

(3) Supply

(b) *Class of offence, mode of trial and sentence*

27–40   The Sentencing Council for England and Wales has issued a definitive guideline on drug offences, applying to all offenders aged 18 or over, who are sentenced on or after February 27, 2012, regardless of the date of their offence, and covering the offences of supplying, offering to supply, or being concerned in the supply of a controlled drug, contrary to section 4(3) of the *Misuse of Drugs Act* 1971 (§ 27–28 in the main work). For the detail, see *post*, Appendix K–271 *et seq.*

D. RESTRICTION OF POSSESSION OF CONTROLLED DRUGS

(1) Statute

Misuse of Drugs Act 1971, s.5

Restriction of possession of controlled drugs

27–50   The *Police Reform and Social Responsibility Act* 2011, s.151, and Sched. 17, paras 1 and 6 (see the main work) came into force on November 15, 2011: *Police Reform and Social Responsibility Act 2011 (Commencement No. 1) Order* 2011 (S.I. 2011 No. 2515).

(3) Class of offence, mode of trial and sentence

The Sentencing Council for England and Wales has issued a definitive guideline on drug **27–53** offences, applying to all offenders aged 18 or over, who are sentenced on or after February 27, 2012, regardless of the date of their offence, and covering the offences of possession of a controlled drug and possession of a controlled drug with intent to supply, contrary to section 5(2) and (3) of the *Misuse of Drugs Act* 1971 (§ 27–50 in the main work). For the detail, see *post*, Appendix K–271 *et seq.*

E. RESTRICTION OF CULTIVATION OF CANNABIS PLANT

(3) Class of offence, mode of trial and sentence

The Sentencing Council for England and Wales has issued a definitive guideline on drug **27–80** offences, applying to all offenders aged 18 or over, who are sentenced on or after February 27, 2012, regardless of the date of their offence, and covering the offences of cultivation of a cannabis plant, contrary to section 6(2) of the *Misuse of Drugs Act* 1971 (§ 27–79 in the main work). For the detail, see *post*, Appendix K–271 *et seq.*

F. AUTHORISATION OF ACTIVITIES OTHERWISE UNLAWFUL UNDER SECTIONS 3 TO 6

Misuse of Drugs Act 1971, ss.7, 7A

The *Police Reform and Social Responsibility Act* 2011, s.151, and Sched. 17, paras 1 and 7 **27–82** (see the main work) came into force on November 15, 2011: *Police Reform and Social Responsibility Act 2011 (Commencement No. 1) Order* 2011 (S.I. 2011 No. 2515).

The *Misuse of Drugs Regulations* 2001 (S.I. 2001 No. 3998) (see the main work) are fur- **★27–83** ther amended by the *Public Services Reform (Scotland) Act 2010 (Consequential Modifications of Enactments) Order* 2011 (S.I. 2011 No. 2581), with effect from October 28, 2011, the *Misuse of Drugs (Amendment No. 2) (England, Wales and Scotland) Regulations* 2012 (S.I. 2012 No. 973), with effect from April 23, 2012, and by the *Misuse of Drugs (Amendment No. 3) (England, Wales and Scotland) Regulations* 2012 (S.I. 2012 No. 1311), with effect from June 13, 2012. As to their application to drugs subject to a temporary class drug order, see the *Misuse of Drugs Act 1971 (Temporary Class Drug) Order* 2012 (S.I. 2012 No. 980) (*ante*, § 27–5a).

The *Misuse of Drugs (Designation) Order* 2001 (S.I. 2001 No. 3997) is further amended by ★ the *Misuse of Drugs (Designation) (Amendment No. 2) (England, Wales and Scotland) Order* 2012 (S.I. 2012 No. 1310), with effect from June 13, 2012.

Temporary class drug orders: power to make further provision

The *Police Reform and Social Responsibility Act* 2011, s.151, and Sched. 17, paras 1 and 8 **27–83a** (see the main work) came into force on November 15, 2011: *Police Reform and Social Responsibility Act 2011 (Commencement No. 1) Order* 2011 (S.I. 2011 No. 2515).

G. OCCUPIERS OF PREMISES

Misuse of Drugs Act 1971, s.8

Class of offence, mode of trial and sentence

The Sentencing Council for England and Wales has issued a definitive guideline on drug **27–85** offences, applying to all offenders aged 18 or over, who are sentenced on or after February 27, 2012, regardless of the date of their offence, and covering the offence of permitting premises to be used in the production or supply of a controlled drug, or the preparation of opium, or the smoking of cannabis or prepared opium, contrary to section 8 of the *Misuse of Drugs Act* 1971 (§ 27–84 in the main work). For the detail, see *post*, Appendix K–271 *et seq.*

I. Supplying Articles for Administering or Preparing Controlled Drugs

27–90   The *Police Reform and Social Responsibility Act* 2011, s.151, and Sched. 17, paras 1 and 9 (see the main work) came into force on November 15, 2011: *Police Reform and Social Responsibility Act 2011 (Commencement No. 1) Order* 2011 (S.I. 2011 No. 2515).

J. Powers of Secretary of State for Preventing Misuse of Controlled Drugs

Misuse of Drugs Act 1971, s.10

27–91   The *Police Reform and Social Responsibility Act* 2011, s.151, and Sched. 17, paras 1 and 10 (see the main work) came into force on November 15, 2011: *Police Reform and Social Responsibility Act 2011 (Commencement No. 1) Order* 2011 (S.I. 2011 No. 2515).

★   As from a day to be appointed, the *Scotland Act* 2012, s.19(1) and (2), amends section 10 of the 1971 Act so as: (i) to substitute for the words "Secretary of State" in subsection (2)(i), the words "appropriate authority", and (ii) to insert new subsections (2A) and (2B), as follows—

"(2A) Regulations made in pursuance of subsection (2)(i) must secure that under any licence a doctor may—
(a) administer, supply or prescribe a controlled drug, or
(b) authorise the administration or supply of a controlled drug,
only while at an address specified in the licence.
(2B) The appropriate authority for the purposes of subsection (2)(i) is—
(a) where the specified address for the purposes of subsection (2A) is in Scotland, the Scottish Ministers;
(b) otherwise, the Secretary of State.".

For the most recent amendments of the *Misuse of Drugs Regulations* 2001 (S.I. 2001 No. 3998), see *ante*, § 27–83.

★   The *Misuse of Drugs (Safe Custody) Regulations* 1973 (S.I. 1973 No. 798) are further amended by the *Postal Services Act 2011 (Consequential Modifications and Amendments) Order* 2011 (S.I. 2011 No. 2085), with effect from October 1, 2011; and by the *Public Services Reform (Scotland) Act 2010 (Consequential Modifications of Enactments) Order* 2011 (S.I. 2011 No. 2581), with effect from October 28, 2011. As to the application of the 1973 regulations to substances subject to a temporary class drug order, see *ante*, § 27–5a.

K. Power to Direct Special Precautions at Certain Premises

Misuse of Drugs Act 1971, s.11

27–92   The *Police Reform and Social Responsibility Act* 2011, s.151, and Sched. 17, paras 1 and 11 (see the main work) came into force on November 15, 2011: *Police Reform and Social Responsibility Act 2011 (Commencement No. 1) Order* 2011 (S.I. 2011 No. 2515).

L. Directions Relating to Prescribing by Practitioners

27–93   The *Police Reform and Social Responsibility Act* 2011, s.151, and Sched. 17, paras 1 and 12 (see the main work) came into force on November 15, 2011: *Police Reform and Social Responsibility Act 2011 (Commencement No. 1) Order* 2011 (S.I. 2011 No. 2515).

M. MISCELLANEOUS OFFENCES

Misuse of Drugs Act 1971, s.18

The *Police Reform and Social Responsibility Act* 2011, s.151, and Sched. 17, paras 1 and 13 **27–94** (see the main work) came into force on November 15, 2011: *Police Reform and Social Responsibility Act 2011 (Commencement No. 1) Order* 2011 (S.I. 2011 No. 2515).

Q. POWER OF SECRETARY OF STATE TO MAKE REGULATIONS

Misuse of Drugs Act 1971, s.22

The *Police Reform and Social Responsibility Act* 2011, s.151, and Sched. 17, paras 1 and 14 **27–101** (see the main work) came into force on November 15, 2011: *Police Reform and Social Responsibility Act 2011 (Commencement No. 1) Order* 2011 (S.I. 2011 No. 2515).

R. LAW ENFORCEMENT AND PUNISHMENT OF OFFENCES

(1) Search and seizure

Misuse of Drugs Act 1971, s.23

Powers to search and obtain evidence
The *Police Reform and Social Responsibility Act* 2011, s.151, and Sched. 17, paras 1 and 15 **27–103** (see the main work) came into force on November 15, 2011: *Police Reform and Social Responsibility Act 2011 (Commencement No. 1) Order* 2011 (S.I. 2011 No. 2515).

Misuse of Drugs Act 1971, s.23A

Temporary class drugs: further power to search, seize and detain
The *Police Reform and Social Responsibility Act* 2011, s.151, and Sched. 17, paras 1 and 16 **27–105a** (see the main work) came into force on November 15, 2011: *Police Reform and Social Responsibility Act 2011 (Commencement No. 1) Order* 2011 (S.I. 2011 No. 2515).

(2) Procedure and penalties

Misuse of Drugs Act 1971, s.25

Prosecution and punishment of offences
The *Police Reform and Social Responsibility Act* 2011, s.151, and Sched. 17, paras 1 and 17 **27–106** (see the main work) came into force on November 15, 2011: *Police Reform and Social Responsibility Act 2011 (Commencement No. 1) Order* 2011 (S.I. 2011 No. 2515).

Sentencing guidelines

The Sentencing Council for England and Wales has issued a definitive guideline on drug **27–107** offences, applying to all offenders aged 18 or over, who are sentenced on or after February 27, 2012, regardless of the date of their offence, and covering the following offences: fraudulent evasion of a prohibition on the importation or exportation of a controlled drug (*CEMA* 1979, s.170(2) (§ 25–474 in the main work)); supplying or offering to supply a controlled drug, or being concerned in such supply or offer (*Misuse of Drugs Act* 1971, s.4(3) (§ 27–28 in the main work)); possession of a controlled drug with intent to supply (1971 Act, s.5(3) (§ 27–50 in the main work)); production of a controlled drug, or being concerned in such production (1971 Act, s.4(2)(a) or (b) (§ 27–28 in the main work)); cultivation of a cannabis plant (1971 Act, s.6(2) (§ 27–79 in the main work)); permitting premises to be used (1971 Act, s.8 (§ 27–84 in the main work)); and possession of a controlled drug (1971 Act, s.5(2) (§ 27–50 in the main work)). For the detail, see *post*, Appendix K–271 *et seq.*

T. MISCELLANEOUS INTERPRETATION PROVISIONS

Misuse of Drugs Act 1971, ss.30, 36, 37

Interpretation

27–128   The *Police Reform and Social Responsibility Act* 2011, s.151, and Sched. 17, paras 1, 18 and 19 (see the main work) came into force on November 15, 2011: *Police Reform and Social Responsibility Act 2011 (Commencement No. 1) Order* 2011 (S.I. 2011 No. 2515).

CHAPTER 28

OFFENCES AGAINST PUBLIC JUSTICE

I. PERVERTING THE COURSE OF JUSTICE

A. CONDUCT CAPABLE OF AMOUNTING TO THE OFFENCE

(9) Interfering with witnesses, evidence and jurors

Informers

28–14a   The part of the decision summarised in the main work in *R. v. Barros* has been reversed: see *R. v. Barros*, unreported, October 26, 2011, Supreme Court of Canada ([2011] SCC 51). Although the identity of police informers is protected by a near absolute privilege, this should not trump the accused's right fully to answer the case against him; an accused and his representatives should not be prevented from identifying an informer for a lawful purpose and by lawful means; but, where the informer is in danger, any defence investigation must proceed responsibly, and any attempts to elicit privileged information from police officers will not be tolerated: *ibid.*

G. SENTENCE

28–28   Where an accused plants incriminating material on another person, with a view to that person being prosecuted and falsely convicted of a serious offence, the appropriate sentencing bracket after a trial is 10 to 12 years' imprisonment: *R. v. Weiner* [2012] 1 Cr.App.R.(S.) 6, CA (accused placed 177 indecent images on victim's computer, tipped off the police anonymously, and told the local press so that the victim would receive unwelcome publicity), following *Att.-Gen.'s References (Nos 6, 7 and 8 of 2000) (R. v. Rees, Warnes and James)* [2002] 2 Cr.App.R.(S.) 76, CA (estranged husband and others plotting to plant Class A drugs on wife to secure custody of child).

★   A sentence of 54 months' imprisonment on a guilty plea was upheld where the offender made false allegations of rape against nine males (all of whom were arrested and two of whom had had no dealings or contact with the offender of any sort): *R. v. Vine* [2012] 1 Cr.App.R.(S.) 78, CA (considering *R. v. Beeton* and *R. v. McKenning* (see the main work)).

III. CONTEMPT OF COURT

A. INTRODUCTION

In the context of an alleged contempt by or affecting a juror or jury, unless it is appropri-   **28–31** ate for the Crown Court to deal immediately with the contempt of its own motion (which in the light of many judicial warnings about the dangers inherent in a rushed process would be exceptional), such allegations should continue to be brought by the Attorney-General under *RSC*, Ord. 52 (§§ 28–129 *et seq.* in the main work)); trials for contempt of court on indictment are obsolete, and of historical interest only; neither the Attorney-General, nor the alleged contemnor, has any right to seek trial on indictment: *Att.-Gen. v. Dallas* [2012] 1 Cr.App.R. 32, DC, following *R. v. D.* and *Re Lonrho plc* (as to both of which, see the main work). As to this case, see also *post*, § 28–127.

C. CONTEMPT OF COURT ACT 1981

(2) The strict liability rule

Risk to be assessed by reference to time of publication

Att.-Gen. v. M.G.N. Ltd and News Group Newspapers Ltd is now reported at [2012] 1   **28–74** Cr.App.R. 1, *sub nom. Att.-Gen. v. M.G.N. Ltd and News Group International Ltd.*

Defences and power to order postponement of reporting

Contempt of Court Act 1981, ss.3, 4

Contemporary report of proceedings
With effect from June 18, 2012 (*Criminal Justice Act 2003 (Commencement No. 28 and Sav-*   **★28–78** *ing Provisions) Order* 2012 (S.I. 2012 No. 1320)), section 41 of, and paragraph 53 of Schedule 3 to, the 2003 Act are brought into force. This is subject to a saving provision in article 6 of the order, which provides that the substitution of section 4(3)(b) of the 1981 Act is to have no effect in the case of a report of committal proceedings.

D. SUMMARY POWERS TO DEAL WITH CONTEMPT

(5) Legal representation

As to the repeal of sections 1 to 26 of, and Schedules 1 to 3A and 14, Pt II, to, the *Access*   **★28–124** *to Justice Act* 1999, see *ante*, § 6–130.

(7) Sentence

For confirmation that an immediate custodial sentence is virtually inevitable for misuse of   **28–127** the internet by a juror, see *Att.-Gen. v. Dallas* [2012] 1 Cr.App.R 32, DC. As to this case, see also *ante*, § 28–31.

E. PROCEDURAL RULES

(1) Applications to magistrates' courts, the Crown Court and the Court of Appeal

Criminal Procedure Rules 2011 (S.I. 2011 No. 1709), Pt 62

Initial procedure on failure to comply with court order, etc.
With effect from April 2, 2012, rule 62.9(1)(a)(i) of the *Criminal Procedure Rules* 2011 (S.I.   **28–127i**

2011 No. 1709) is amended by the *Criminal Procedure (Amendment) Rules* 2011 (S.I. 2011 No. 3075), r.15, so as to substitute the words "restraint order or ancillary order" for the words "restraint order".

F. Appeals

Administration of Justice Act 1960, s.13

★**28–140**   Section 13(2) of the 1960 Act (§ 28–138 in the main work) should be construed on common law principles of rectification (following *Inco Europe Ltd v. First Choice Distribution (a firm)* [2000] 1 W.L.R. 586, HL), as permitting an appeal from the criminal division of the Court of Appeal to the Supreme Court in cases of contempt of court (such right of appeal having been removed in error by the draftsman of the *AFA* 2006, s.178, and Sched. 16, para. 45): *R. v. O.B.* [2012] L.S. Gazette, May 24, 17, CA ([2012] EWCA Crim. 901).

VI. OFFENCES AKIN TO PERJURY

D. False Written Statements Tendered in Evidence

Criminal Justice Act 1967, s.89

★**28–189**   With effect from June 18, 2012 (*Criminal Justice Act 2003 (Commencement No. 28 and Saving Provisions) Order* 2012 (S.I. 2012 No. 1320)), section 41 of, and paragraph 51(1) and (6) of Schedule 3 to, the 2003 Act are brought into force in certain areas (as to which, see *ante*, § 1–88). There are associated saving provisions, as to which, see article 5 of the order (*ante*, § 1–88).

VII. PRISON SECURITY

E. Smuggling and Unauthorised Photography, etc.

Prison Act 1952, ss.40A–40E

Other offences relating to prison security

★**28–222d**   With effect from March 26, 2012, section 45 of the *Crime and Security Act* 2010, which amends section 40D of the *Prison Act* 1952 (offences relating to electronic communication devices in prisons) (see § 28–222e in the main work), is brought into force: *Crime and Security Act 2010 (Commencement No. 5) Order* 2012 (S.I. 2012 No. 584).

Section 40D: meaning of "authorisation" and other interpretation

★**28–222e**   With effect from March 26, 2012, section 45 of the *Crime and Security Act* 2010, which amends section 40D of the *Prison Act* 1952 (offences relating to electronic communication devices in prisons) (see § 28–222d in the main work), is brought into force: *Crime and Security Act 2010 (Commencement No. 5) Order* 2012 (S.I. 2012 No. 584).

CHAPTER 29

PUBLIC ORDER OFFENCES

I. PUBLIC ORDER OFFENCES

B. NEW OFFENCES (PT I (SS.1–10))

(1) Riot

Public Order Act 1986, s.1

Sentence

In *R. v. Blackshaw* [2012] 1 Cr.App.R.(S.) 114, CA, in dealing with appeals against   **29–9**
sentence imposed for involvement in rioting that took place around the country in August 2011, the court identified the applicable principles. There was an overwhelming obligation on the courts to do what they could to ensure the protection of the public, whether in their homes or businesses or in the street. Those who deliberately participated in disturbances of this magnitude, causing injury and damage and fear to even the most stout-hearted of citizens, and who individually committed further crimes during the course of the riots, were committing aggravated crimes. The imposition of severe sentences, intended to provide both punishment and deterrence, must follow. Any participation whatever, irrespective of its precise form, in an unlawful or riotous assembly derived its gravity from becoming one of those who by weight of numbers pursued a common and unlawful purpose. The acts of any individual participator could not be approached in isolation. It was elementary that courts could not ignore the context in which a crime was committed. The fact that the involvement of some followed early criminal activity by others provided no mitigation at all. The reality was that the offenders were deriving support, comfort and encouragement from being together with other offenders. The sheer numbers involved may have led some to believe that they were untouchable and would escape detection. Nor should such public disorder be treated as "mindless" activity. It was stupid, irresponsible and dangerous, but the offenders were not mindless. Their actions were deliberate and each offender had known what he was doing.

As to sentencing guidelines, the Court of Appeal said that a sentencer should approach the sentencing decision by reference to any relevant guidelines. However, the aphorism that sentencing guidelines were guidelines not tramlines, continued to be fully reflected in the present legislative framework. None of the guidelines of relevance to the appeals in question, in relation to offences of theft or burglary or offences of violence, nor the guideline case on handling stolen goods, contemplated that the offences with which they were concerned would take place within the context of nationwide public disorder. Sentences beyond the range in the guidelines for conventional offending were not only appropriate but inevitable.

(2) Violent disorder

Public Order Act 1986, s.2

As to the removal (as from a day to be appointed) of £5,000 as the upper limit on a fine   **★29–10**
on summary conviction, see the *Legal Aid, Sentencing and Punishment of Offenders Act* 2012, s.85(1) (*ante*, § 1–125).

Sentence

29–14a   See *R. v. Blackshaw*, *ante*, § 29–9.

(4) Fear or provocation of violence

Public Order Act 1986, s.4

Ingredients of the offence

"with intent"

★**29–28a**   Where the defendant, in an unprovoked attack, approached the victim from behind and struck him a violent blow, knocking him unconscious, with the intention of doing so before he knew what was happening, there was no evidence from which the justices could have concluded that the defendant was guilty of an offence contrary to section 4 of the 1986 Act. There was no evidence that the defendant intended his victim to believe anything, let alone that he would suffer unlawful violence: *Hughes v. DPP*, 176 J.P. 237, DC.

(5) Harassment, alarm or distress

29–34a   It was not open to a court to infer that a person was likely to have been caused harassment, alarm or distress, where witnesses had given oral evidence as to an incident forming the basis of a charge under section 5 of the *Public Order Act* 1986, but had themselves said nothing about experiencing harassment, alarm or distress: *Harvey v. DPP*, 176 J.P. 265, QBD (Bean J.) (where the witnesses were police officers and the language complained of consisted of commonplace swear words which would be heard by police officers all too frequently as part of their job).

III. MAKING OF THREATS

D. PROTECTION OF ANIMAL RESEARCH ORGANISATIONS

Serious Organised Crime and Police Act 2005, ss.145–148

29–73   As from March 14, 2012, section 146(3)(b) of the 2005 Act is amended by the *Charities Act* 2011, s.354(1), and Sched. 7, para. 103, so as to substitute "charity trustee (within the meaning of the *Charities Act* 2011)" for "charity trustee (within the meaning of the *Charities Act* 1993)".

CHAPTER 30

COMMERCE, FINANCIAL MARKETS AND INSOLVENCY

II. OFFENCES IN RELATION TO COMMERCE, FINANCIAL MARKETS AND INSOLVENCY

E. FINANCIAL SERVICES AND MARKETS ACT 2000

(3) Carrying on unauthorised investment business

Financial Services and Markets Act 2000, ss.19, 21–25

30–212   The *Financial Services and Markets Act 2000 (Regulated Activities) Order* 2001 (S.I. 2001

No. 544) (see the main work) is further amended by the *Public Services Reform (Scotland) Act 2010 (Consequential Modifications of Enactments) Order* 2011 (S.I. 2011 No. 2581), with effect from October 28, 2011; and by the *Legislative Reform (Industrial and Provident Societies and Credit Unions) Order* 2011 (S.I. 2011 No. 2687), with effect from January 8, 2012.

The *Financial Services and Markets Act 2000 (Exemption) Order* 2001 (S.I. 2001 No. 1201) ★ (see the main work) is further amended by the *Financial Services and Markets Act 2000 (Exemption) (Amendment No. 2) Order* 2011 (S.I. 2011 No. 2716) with effect from March 31, 2012; and by the *Financial Services and Markets Act 2000 (Exemption) (Amendment) Order* 2012 (S.I. 2012 No. 763), with effect from the day on which articles 1(3) and 2 to 9 of the *Postal Services Act 2011 (Transfer of Assets) Order* 2012 (S.I. 2012 No. 688) come into force.

G. Insider Dealing

Class of offence, mode of trial and sentence

R. v. Rollins is now reported at [2012] 1 Cr.App.R.(S) 64.   **30–251**

Chapter 31

OFFENCES AGAINST PUBLIC MORALS AND POLICY

II. PUBLIC NUISANCE

A. Statute

(2) Dangerous Dogs Act 1991

Dangerous Dogs Act 1991, s.3(1)–(4)

Sentence

The Sentencing Council for England and Wales has issued a definitive guideline, apply-   ★**31–37b** ing to all offenders aged 18 or over, who are sentenced on or after August 20, 2012, regardless of the date of their offence, that covers, *inter alia*, the offences under section 3 of the 1991 Act (§ 31–35 in the main work). For the detail, see *post*, Appendix K–291 *et seq.*

Dangerous Dogs Act 1991, s.4(1)–(7)

Destruction and disqualification orders

The Sentencing Council for England and Wales has issued a definitive guideline, apply-   ★**31–38** ing to all offenders aged 18 or over, who are sentenced on or after August 20, 2012, regardless of the date of their offence. The guideline relates to offences under the 1991 Act and includes consideration as to when a court should make destruction and disqualification orders under section 4. For the detail, see *post*, Appendix K–291 *et seq.*

Dangerous Dogs Act 1991, s.4A

Contingent destruction orders

The Sentencing Council for England and Wales has issued a definitive guideline, apply-   ★**31–38b** ing to all offenders aged 18 or over, who are sentenced on or after August 20, 2012, regardless of the date of their offence. The guideline relates to offences under the 1991 Act and includes consideration as to when a court should make a contingent destruction order under section 4A. For the detail, see *post*, Appendix K–291 *et seq.*

III. OBSCENE OR INDECENT PUBLICATIONS AND DISPLAYS, ETC.

B. Statute

(1) Obscene Publications Acts 1959 and 1964

(b) *Definitions*

"publishes"

Obscene Publications Act 1959, s.1(3)–(6)

★**31–73**   "Publication" for the purposes of the *Obscene Publications Act* 1959 may be to a single person; so much is clear from section 1(3) of the Act (§ 31–72 in the main work), which provides, *inter alia*, that the transmission of electronically stored data amounts to publication: *R. v. G.S.*, *The Times*, February 16, 2012, CA.

(6) Criminal Justice and Immigration Act 2008

Criminal Justice and Immigration Act 2008, ss.63–68

Possession of extreme pornographic images

★**31–120**   The *Schools (Specification and Disposal of Articles) Regulations* 2012 (S.I. 2012 No. 951) specify items, including pornographic images as prohibited items for which members of staff in schools can search pupils without their consent under section 550ZA of the *Education Act* 1996 (as to which, see § 19–40 in the main work and *ante* in this supplement) and which they can seize under section 550ZC; and prescribe what must be done with any items so seized. In particular, an image that a member of staff has reasonable grounds for suspecting to be an image to which section 62(2) of the *Coroners and Justice Act* 2009 (§ 31–130 in the main work), or 63 of the 2008 Act applies, must be delivered to a police constable as soon as is reasonably practicable.

(7) Coroners and Justice Act 2009

Coroners and Justice Act 2009, ss.62–68

Possession of prohibited images of children

★**31–130**   See the *Schools (Specification and Disposal of Articles) Regulations* 2012 (S.I. 2012 No. 951) (*ante*, § 31–130) as to the duty of school staff to deliver to the police any item that they find and which they have reasonable grounds to suspect to be an image to which section 62(2) of the 2009 Act applies.

IV. BRIBERY AND CORRUPTION

B. Statute

(2) Public Bodies Corrupt Practices Act 1889 and Prevention of Corruption Acts 1906 and 1916

★**31–140**   In *R. v. Majeed*; *R. v. Westfield* [2012] L.S. Gazette, June 14, 23, CA ([2012] EWCA Crim.

1186), it was held that a cricketer and an agent (for several cricketers) who had engaged in spot-fixing of cricket matches in return for cash were correctly convicted of an offence of conspiracy to give corrupt payments (contrary to the *CLA* 1977, s.1(1) (§§ 33–1 *et seq.* in the main work), and section 1(1) of the 1906 Act, ("(1) If any agent corruptly accepts or obtains, or agrees to accept or attempts to obtain, from any person, for himself or for any other person, any gift or consideration as an inducement or reward for doing or forbearing to do ... any act in relation to his principal's affairs or business, ... he shall be guilty of a misdemeanour ...")) even though the bribes had not been intended to, and did not, influence the "principals" who employed the various cricketers (the Pakistan Cricket Board and the Essex County Cricket Club); the board and the club were victims of the corrupt activities and the conduct of the players on the field was integral to their affairs and business. As to this case, see also *ante*, § 22–71.

CHAPTER 32

MOTOR VEHICLE OFFENCES

II. DRIVING OFFENCES

A. CAUSING DEATH BY DANGEROUS DRIVING

(6) Ingredients of the offence

"dangerously"

Road Traffic Act 1988, s.2A

Meaning of dangerous driving
    As from a day to be appointed,section 2A of the *RTA* 1988 is amended by the *Legal Aid,*   ★**32–17**
Sentencing and Punishment of Offenders Act 2012, s.143(1) and (3), so as to insert ", 1A" after "sections 1".

"road or other public place"

    A car driven so that it encroaches on a road, even though its tyres remain on private   **32–18**
land, is capable of being on a "road" for the purpose of the offence under section 5(1)(a) of the 1988 Act (excess alcohol (§ 32–175 in the main work)), so long as the encroachment is material: *Avery v. DPP* [2012] R.T.R. 8, DC.

AA. CAUSING SERIOUS INJURY BY DANGEROUS DRIVING

(1) Statute

Road Traffic Act 1988, s.1A

Causing serious injury by dangerous driving
    As from a day to be appointed, a new section 1A is inserted in the *RTA* 1988 by the *Legal*   ★**32–26a**
Aid, Sentencing and Punishment of Offenders Act 2012, s.143(1) and (2). It has effect only in relation to driving after the section comes into force: s.143(4).

    [Causing serious injury by dangerous driving
        1A.—(1) A person who causes serious injury to another person by driving a mechanically propelled vehicle dangerously on a road or other public place is guilty of an offence.

(2) In this section "serious injury" means—

    (a) in England and Wales, physical harm which amounts to grievous bodily harm for the purposes of the *Offences against the Person Act* 1861, and

    (b) in Scotland, severe physical injury.]

E. Causing Death by Careless Driving when Under the Influence

(6) Ingredients of the offence

32–61   *Coates v. CPS* is now reported at 175 J.P. 401.

F. Causing Death by Driving: Unlicensed, Disqualified or Uninsured Persons

(6) Ingredients of the offence

32–63f   *R. v. M.H.* is now reported at [2011] 4 All E.R. 761, *sub nom. Prosecution Appeal; R. v. H.*

J. Failing to Provide Evidential Specimen

Warning of consequences of non-compliance

32–98   In *Bielecki v. DPP*, 175 J.P. 369, QBD (Foskett J.), it was held that a court may draw the inference, where the evidence supports it, that the warning as to the consequences of non-compliance with the requirement to provide a specimen for analysis under section 7 of the *RTA* 1988 (§ 32–93 in the main work) had been properly given and understood, in the case of a non-English speaker who had been assisted by an interpreter, without the need for any evidence from the interpreter.

M. Driving Without a License

(4) Interpretation

Road Traffic Act 1988, s.108

★32–111   With effect from January 19, 2013, section 108 of the *RTA* 1988 is amended by the *Motor Vehicles (Driving Licences) (Amendment) Regulations* 2012 (S.I. 2012 No. 977), reg. 2, and Sched. 1, paras 1 and 5: in subsection (1), (i) the definitions of "EEA Agreement" and "EEA State" are replaced by the words "'EEA agreement' and 'EEA state' have the meaning given by Schedule 1 to the *Interpretation Act* 1978;", (ii) a definition of "light quadricycle" is inserted (omitted from this supplement), and (iii) the definitions of "moped" and "motor bicycle" (neither of which is set out in the main work) are amended; and a new subsection (1A) is inserted, as follows—

    "(1A) In this Part of this Act, unless the context otherwise requires, a reference to the expiry of a licence is a reference to the time when it ceases to be in force (and 'expired' is to be interpreted accordingly).".

(5) Grant and form of licences

Road Traffic Act 1988, s.97

★32–112   With effect from January 19, 2013, section 97 of the *RTA* 1988 is amended by the *Motor Vehicles (Driving Licences) (Amendment) Regulations* 2012 (S.I. 2012 No. 977), reg. 2, and Sched. 1, paras 1 and 2, so as (i) to omit subsections (3)(d), (5) and (6), and (ii) to re-draft subsection (1)(d) as follows—

"(d) is not,

    (i) in accordance with section 88(1B) of this Act, subject to a current disqualification which is relevant to the licence he applies for, or

    (ii) subject to a current disqualification under the law of an EEA State (other than the United Kingdom) which relates to vehicles of the class, or of a class corresponding to the class, to which the application relates and was imposed while the person was the holder of a licence granted under the law of that State; and

(e) is not prevented from obtaining the licence by the provisions of section 89 of this Act or section 4 of or paragraphs 6 or 9 of Schedule 1 to the *Road Traffic (New Drivers) Act* 1995.".

The *Motor Vehicles (Driving Licences) Regulations* 1999 (S.I. 1999 No. 2864) (see the main work) are further amended by the *Motor Vehicles (Driving Licences) (Amendment) Regulations* 2011 (S.I. 2011 No. 2516) (from November 15, 2011); by the *Local Policing Bodies (Consequential Amendments) Regulations* 2011 (S.I. 2011 No. 3058) (from January 16, 2012); and by the *Motor Vehicles (Driving Licences) (Amendment) Regulations* 2012 (S.I. 2012 No. 977) (from January 19, 2013).

Road Traffic Act 1988, s.98

Form of licence

With effect from January 19, 2013, section 98 of the *RTA* 1988 is amended by the *Motor Vehicles (Driving Licences) (Amendment) Regulations* 2012 (S.I. 2012 No. 977), reg. 2, and Sched. 1, paras 1 and 4, so as to omit subsection (3)(b).   ★**32–113**

Q. FAILING TO GIVE INFORMATION AS TO IDENTITY OF DRIVER

(1) Statute

Road Traffic Act 1988, s.172

Duty to give information as to identity of driver in certain circumstances

R. (Purnell) v. Snaresbrook Crown Court, CPS (interested party) is now reported at [2011] **32–133** R.T.R. 35, *sub nom. R. (Purnell) v. Snaresbrook Crown Court.*

The offence under section 172(3) can be committed even though the keeper is unaware of ★ his obligation to comply with a requirement made under subsection (2); a requirement sent by post to the keeper's registered address, but not received by the keeper, is nonetheless validly served so as to give rise to the obligation under subsection (2)(a) (*Interpretation Act* 1978, s.7 (*post*, Appendix B–7)); and the defence under subsection (7)(b) will not succeed simply because the keeper did not know about the notice, but in an appropriate case a defendant may be able to show that it was not reasonably practicable for him to have become aware of the notice, in which case the defence will apply: *Whiteside v. DPP*, 176 J.P. 103, DC.

To make out the defence under section 172(4), the keeper of a vehicle must show that he ★ did not know the identity of the driver of his vehicle at the time the requirement for information was made by the police, and that reasonable diligence was exercised to ascertain the identity at that time; accordingly, the keeper of a vehicle is not to be condemned for failing first to make, and then to keep, a written record of the identity of each driver of the vehicle: *Atkinson v. DPP* [2012] R.T.R. 14, DC.

R. POLICE POWERS

(4) Power to seize, etc. vehicles driven without licence or insurance

Pryor v. Chief Constable of Manchester Police is now reported at [2011] R.T.R. 33.   **32–150a**

S. Procedure and Evidence

(5) Evidence

Road Traffic Offenders Act 1988, s.11

Evidence by certificate as to driver, user or owner

★**32–160**   With effect from June 18, 2012 (*Criminal Justice Act 2003 (Commencement No. 28 and Saving Provisions) Order* 2012 (S.I. 2012 No. 1320)), sections 41 and 332 of, and paragraph 61 of Schedule 3 to, and Part 4 of Schedule 37 to, the 2003 Act are brought into force in certain areas (as to which, see *ante*, § 1–88). There are associated saving provisions, as to which, see article 5 of the order (*ante*, § 1–88).

Road Traffic Offenders Act 1988, ss.13, 15, 16

Admissibility of records as evidence

★**32–161**   As to the commencement of sections 41 and 332 of, and paragraph 61 of Schedule 3 to, and Part 4 of Schedule 37 to, the 2003 Act (see the main work), see *ante*, § 32–160.

Documentary evidence as to specimens in such proceedings

★**32–163**   As to the commencement of sections 41 and 332 of, and paragraph 61 of Schedule 3 to, and Part 4 of Schedule 37 to, the 2003 Act (see the main work), see *ante*, § 32–160.

(7) Alternative verdicts

Road Traffic Offenders Act 1988, s.24

Alternative verdicts: general

★**32–165**   As from a day to be appointed, section 24 of the *RTOA* 1988 is amended by the *Legal Aid, Sentencing and Punishment of Offenders Act* 2012, s.143(7), and Sched. 27, paras 2 and 4, so as (i) to insert after section 24(A2)(a) a new paragraph (aa) referring to an offence under section 1A of the *RTA* 1988 (causing serious injury by dangerous driving), and (ii) to insert, in the table in section 24(1), an entry for section 1A, with corresponding alternative verdicts of section 2 (dangerous driving) and section 3 (careless, and inconsiderate, driving).

(8) Offences to which sections 1, 6, 11 and 12 apply

Road Traffic Offenders Act 1988, Sched. 1

★**32–166**   As from a day to be appointed, the table in Schedule 1 to the *RTOA* 1988 is amended by the *Legal Aid, Sentencing and Punishment of Offenders Act* 2012, s.143(7), and Sched. 27, paras 2 and 9, so as to insert an entry for section 1A of the *RTA* 1988 (causing serious injury by dangerous driving), with the applicable provisions of the *RTOA* 1988 stated to be sections 11 and 12(1).

T. Disqualification and Endorsement

(5) Statutory provisions-general

Road Traffic Offenders Act 1988, s.34

Disqualification for certain offences

★**32–181**   As from a day to be appointed, section 34(4) of the *RTOA* 1988 is amended by the *Legal*

Aid, Sentencing and Punishment of Offenders Act 2012, s.143(7), and Sched. 27, paras 2 and 5, so as to insert a new sub-paragraph after the word "or" at the end of section 34(4)(a)(ii), as follows—

> "(iia) an offence under section 1A of that Act (causing serious injury by dangerous driving), or".

(6) Special reasons

Emergency

Where "emergency" is relied on to support a plea of special reasons, the court should apply the test in *DPP v. Bristow* (§ 32–183 in the main work); while "life and limb" cases are not the only acceptable emergencies, they indicate the high hurdle that has to be crossed: *DPP v. Heathcote*, 175 J.P. 530, QBD (McCombe J.), quashing a finding of special reasons where the defendant (over twice the legal limit) had given chase when a vehicle belonging to his cousin was stolen late one evening. **32–188**

(8) Extension of disqualification where custodial sentence also imposed

As to the amendment of section 35A of the *RTOA* 1988, see *post*, § 32–196b. **★32–196a**

Road Traffic Offenders Act 1988, ss.35A, 35B

Extension of disqualification where custodial sentence also imposed

As from a day to be appointed, section 35A of the *RTOA* 1988 is amended by the *Legal Aid, Sentencing and Punishment of Offenders Act* 2012, s.89(2), and Sched. 10, para. 5, so as to omit subsection (4)(c) and (d). **★32–196b**

As from a day to be appointed, section 35A(6) of the 1988 Act is amended by the 2012 Act, s.110(13), and Sched. 13, para. 8, so as (i) to omit the words "a direction under", (ii) to substitute "section 240ZA" for "section 240" in paragraph (a), and (iii) to insert "a direction under" before "section 240A" in paragraph (b). **★**

As from a day to be appointed, section 35A of the 1988 is further amended by the 2012 Act, s.111(2), and Sched. 14, para. 1, so as (i) to insert "243A(3)(a)," after "section" in subsection (8), and (ii) to insert "243A(3)(a) or" after "in respect of section" in subsection (9)(a). **★**

As from a day to be appointed, section 35A of the 1988 Act is further amended by the 2012 Act, s.126, and Sched. 21, para. 4, so as (i) in subsection (4)(e), to substitute "226A" for "227", "two-thirds of" for "half", and "226A(5)(a)" for "227(2C)(a)", (ii) in subsection (4)(f), to substitute "226B" for "228", "two-thirds of" for "half", and "226B(3)(a)" for "228(2B)(a)", (iii) in subsection (8), to omit "or 247(2)", and (iv) to omit subsection (9)(b). **★**

(10) Disqualification until test is passed

Road Traffic Offenders Act 1988, s.36

Disqualification until test is passed

As from a day to be appointed, section 36(2)(b) of the *RTOA* 1988 is amended by the *Legal Aid, Sentencing and Punishment of Offenders Act* 2012, s.143(7), and Sched. 27, paras 2 and 6, so as to insert ", section 1A (causing serious injury by dangerous driving)" after "(causing death by dangerous driving)". **★32–198**

(16) Endorsement

Road Traffic Offenders Act 1988, s.45

Effects of endorsement of counterparts

As from a day to be appointed, section 45(6) of the *RTOA* 1988 is amended by the *Legal* **★32–211**

Aid, Sentencing and Punishment of Offenders Act 2012, s.143(7), and Sched. 27, paras 2and 7, so as to insert (i) ", 1A" after "section 1", and (ii) ", causing serious injury by dangerous driving" after "causing death by dangerous driving".

Road Traffic Offenders Act 1988, s.45A

Effect of endorsement of driving records

★**32–211a**   As from a day to be appointed, section 45A(4) of the *RTOA* 1988 (as prospectively substituted by the *RSA* 2006) is amended by the *Legal Aid, Sentencing and Punishment of Offenders Act* 2012, s.143(7), and Sched. 27, paras 2 and 8, so as to insert: (i) ", 1A" after "section 1", and (ii) ", causing serious injury by dangerous driving" after "causing death by dangerous driving".

U. Prosecution and Punishment Offences

Road Traffic Offenders Act 1988, Sched. 2

★**32–222**   As from a day to be appointed, Part I of Schedule 2 to the *RTOA* 1988 is amended by the *Legal Aid, Sentencing and Punishment of Offenders Act* 2012, s.143(5), to insert an entry relating to section 1A of the *RTA* 1988 (causing serious injury by dangerous driving). On summary conviction, the maximum penalty is 12 months' imprisonment or the statutory maximum or both; on indictment, five years' imprisonment or a fine or both. Disqualification and endorsement are obligatory and the offence carries 3 to 11 penalty points. By section 143(6) of the 2012 Act, the reference to "12 months" is to be read as "6 months (in England and Wales)" if the offence is committed before the commencement of section 154(1) of the *CJA* 2003.

III. DOCUMENT OFFENCES

B. Public Passenger Vehicles Act 1981

32–224   As from December 4, 2011, section 65 of the *Public Passenger Vehicles Act* 1981 is amended by the *Public Service Vehicles (Community Licences) Regulations* 2011 (S.I. 2011 No. 2634), reg. 17.

H. Goods Vehicles (Licensing of Operators) Act 1995

32–241   As from December 4, 2011, section 38 of the *Goods Vehicles (Licensing of Operators) Act* 1995 is amended by the *Road Transport Operator Regulations* 2011 (S.I. 2011 No. 2632), reg. 8, and Sched. 2, para. 12.

Chapter 33

CONSPIRACY, ENCOURAGEMENT AND ATTEMPT TO COMMIT CRIME

I. CONSPIRACY

D. Pleading, Evidence and Practice

(4) The trial of a single conspirator

★**33–64**   *R. v. Austin* is now reported at [2012] 1 Cr.App.R. 24, *sub nom. R. v. Austin and Tavakolinia.*

(5) Acts and declarations in furtherance of common design

R. v. Austin is now reported at [2012] 1 Cr.App.R. 24, *sub nom. R. v. Austin and Tavakolinia*. ★**33–66**

R. v. Austin and Tavakolinia, ante, was considered in *R. v. Cook (Sam)* [2012] 1 Cr.App.R. ★
23, CA, where an indictment alleged a conspiracy against five named persons, all of whom
were defendants. One pleaded guilty, three were acquitted and the jury disagreed in respect of the fifth. The prosecution conceded (on an interlocutory appeal) that, at the retrial
of the latter, the jury would have to be directed that he could only be convicted if they were
sure that he had conspired with the defendant who had pleaded guilty. The Court of Appeal held that it would be open to the prosecution, subject to considerations of fairness, to
put their case to the jury on the basis that the acquitted defendants were "probably" guilty.
For a submission to the effect that the prosecution's concession went further than necessary
in law, see the commentary at CLW/12/14/5.

II. SOLICITING OR INCITING A CRIME

(1) Common law

(a) Introduction

Definition

To solicit or incite another to commit a crime was indictable at common law. A person **33–78**
was guilty of incitement to commit an offence or offences if (a) he incited another to do or
cause to be done an act or acts which, if done, would involve the commission of an offence
or offences by the other; and (b) he intended or believed that the other, if he acted as
incited, should or would do so with the fault required for the offence or offences: *DPP v.
Armstrong (Andrew)* [2000] Crim.L.R. 379, DC; *R. v. Claydon* [2006] 1 Cr.App.R. 20, CA (approving, in both cases, the Law Commissions's definition (Criminal Law: A Criminal Code,
Law Com. No. 177, 1989)). In *Invicta Plastics Ltd v. Clare* [1976] R.T.R. 251, the Divisional
Court adopted *dicta* of Lord Denning M.R. in *Race Relations Board v. Applin* [1973] 1 Q.B.
815 at 825, CA (Civ. Div.), to the effect that "to incite" was not limited to urging or spurring
on by advice, encouragement or persuasion but included inciting another to do an act by
threats or by pressure. Incitement also included an offer of a bribe to a person to commit an
offence: *Wade v. Broughton* (1814) 3 V. & B. 172.

It was irrelevant whether the solicitation or incitement was effective: *Armstrong, ante*; or
whether the principal offence existed under the common law or was created by statute: see
1 Russ.Cr. 12th ed., 176. However, the offence had to be one which was capable of being
committed by the person incited: *R. v. Claydon, ante.*

Agents provocateurs

See §§ 15–452 *et seq.* in the main work, and see *R. v. Anderson* [1986] 1 A.C. 27 at 38, HL, **33–79**
and *R. v. Jones (James)* (§ 27–37a in the main work).

Mens rea

A person accused of incitement must be shown to have intended or believed that the **33–80**
person incited would, if he acted as incited to do, do so with the *mens rea* appropriate to the
offence (*ante*, § 33–78). As with conspiracy (§ 33–15 in the main work), it is submitted that
laudable ulterior motives are irrelevant. To the extent that *R. v. Shaw* [1994] Crim.L.R. 365,
CA (93 05976 W2) is authority to the contrary, it is submitted that it is wrong (see the commentary in the *Criminal Law Review*); and it was disapproved in *Claydon, ante,* § 33–78. The
explanation for the decision (that a person charged with inciting an offence of dishonesty
had to be proved to have been dishonest himself) may lie in the fact that the prosecution
had so put their case (transcript p.7F).

In *R. v. Curr*, 51 Cr.App.R. 113, CA, it was held that a person could only be convicted of incitement if the person incited knew that the conduct incited amounted to an offence. This was also disapproved of in *R. v. Claydon, ante*, where it was said that the actual knowledge or state of mind of the person incited was irrelevant. Albeit that this was *obiter*, it is submitted that this view is to be preferred, the offence being concerned with the state of mind of the incitor, not of the incitee.

(b) *Jurisdiction*

33–81   The common law jurisdiction in respect of incitement appears to be the same as that for conspiracy, as to which see §§ 33–21 *et seq.* in the main work. In *R. v. Tompkins* [2007] Crim.L.R. 235, CA, it was assumed that the courts of England and Wales have jurisdiction to try an allegation of incitement where the incitor was at all material times within the jurisdiction and the incitee was at all material times without the jurisdiction, provided that the *actus reus* of the offence was to occur, at least in part, within the jurisdiction.

As to the extended jurisdiction of the courts in relation to allegations of incitement to commit certain sexual acts outside the United Kingdom, see the *Sexual Offences (Conspiracy and Incitement) Act* 1996, s.2 (§ 2–36b in the main work); and as to their extended jurisdiction in relation to incitement to commit fraud and related offences, see Part I of the *CJA* 1993 (§§ 2–37 *et seq.* in the main work).

(c) *Indictment*

STATEMENT OF OFFENCE

33–82   *Incitement to steal.*

PARTICULARS OF OFFENCE

A B, on the —— day of ——, 20—, *unlawfully incited J N to steal property belonging to Y Z.*

Penalty—fine and/or imprisonment: *R. v. Higgins*, 2 East 5.

(d) *Particular offences*

To conspire or to incite

33–83   Section 5(7) of the *CLA* 1977 (§ 33–34 in the main work) abolished the offence of incitement to conspire.

In the course of giving the Court of Appeal's judgment in *R. v. Sirat*, 83 Cr.App.R. 41, Parker L.J. said:

> "There is no doubt that at comm on law incitement to commit a crime is an offence. This being so, it follows logically that if A incites B to incite C to commit a crime, *e.g.* to wound D, A is guilty of incitement to commit a crime, namely, incitement" (at p. 43).

Later in the judgment, however, his Lordship said, having read out the terms of section 5(7) of the 1977 Act:

> "If, therefore, A incites B to agree with C that C will wound D, A's incitement of B is by statute not an offence … . Where however the facts are that the accused's incitement of B is actually to enter into an agreement with C for the commission of a crime, it would in our judgment be impossible to hold that the accused can be guilty of incitement, on the ground that B must of necessity propose the crime to C on the way to making the agreement. Whether other forms of incitement to incite survive will fall for decision when the question arises. It may appear to be absurd that, where a person is inciting actual agreement to be made for the commission of a crime, he should be guilty of no offence, but that where he does not seek actual agreement but mere encouragement he should be guilty. This however is not necessarily absurd, for there may well be circumstances where there is no question of an agreement being sought but where the particular form of incitement is more effective than any attempt to secure agreement" (at pp. 44–45).

To attempt, and attempt to incite

On an indictment charging the defendants with inciting, counselling and procuring a **33–84** pregnant woman to administer to herself a noxious thing, namely an abortifacient, with intent to procure a miscarriage (see the *Offences against the Person Act* 1861, s.58 (§ 19–149 in the main work)), and with conspiracy to incite her to do the same, it was held (a) that if the woman, believing that she was taking a noxious thing within the meaning of the statute, did, with intent to procure her own abortion, take a thing in fact harmless, she was guilty of an attempt to commit an offence against section 58; but (b) that if the defendants in supplying the drug to the woman, though they well knew that she would take it in the belief that it was an abortifacient did not themselves believe that it was capable of procuring her own abortion, they could not be convicted of inciting her to commit the said offence, although if they had so believed it would have been otherwise: *R. v. Brown*, 63 J.P. 790.

In logic, it would seem that an incitement to attempt to commit an offence must necessarily be an incitement to commit that offence.

Where a letter was sent soliciting and inciting the addressee to commit a crime, but was not proved to have reached the intended recipient, the sender could properly be convicted of an attempt to incite the commission of the crime: *R. v. Banks* (1873) 12 Cox 393; *R. v. Ransford* (1874) 13 Cox 9; *R. v. Krause*, 66 J.P. 121; *R. v. Cope*, 16 Cr.App.R. 77, which may be distinguished from *R. v. Woods*, 22 Cr.App.R. 41, because in the former case the intended recipient of the letter would, if he had received it, have understood that he was being instigated to the commission of a crime, whereas in the latter case he would not; and *R. v. Goldman* [2001] Crim.L.R. 822, CA (defendant guilty of attempt to incite addressee to distribute indecent photographs of children, even where he was responding to an offer made by the addressee).

To do the impossible

A person cannot be convicted of incitement to commit a particular offence if the person **33–85** incited was incapable as a matter of law of committing the offence: *R. v. Claydon* [2006] 1 Cr.App.R. 20, CA. Nor can a person be convicted of incitement to commit a particular offence if its commission is factually impossible: see *R. v. Fitzmaurice* [1983] Q.B. 1083, 76 Cr.App.R. 17, CA (giving as an example incitement to murder a person who turned out to have been dead at the time of the incitement). Where it is contended that the offence incited was factually impossible, it is necessary to analyse the evidence with care to decide the precise offence which the defendant is alleged to have incited: *ibid.* At common law, the position was the same for conspiracy and attempts, but see now the *CLA* 1977, s.1(1)(b) (§ 33–2 in the main work), and the *Criminal Attempts Act* 1981, s.1(2) (§ 33–120 in the main work).

To commit a summary offence

Incitement to commit a summary offence was a summary offence, punishable as for the **33–86** offence incited: *MCA* 1980, s.45(1), (3).

To commit an offence triable either way

See the *MCA* 1980, s.17(1), and Sched. 1, paras 33 and 35. The effect is that incitement **33–87** to commit an offence triable either way is generally itself triable either way. Note that whilst paragraph 35 of Schedule 1 to the 1980 Act was repealed by the *SCA* 2007, ss.63(2) and 92, Sched. 6, para. 55(1) and (4), and Sched. 14, its effect has been preserved in relation to precommencement offences by the 2007 Act, s.91(1), and Sched. 13, para. 5(1)(b) (§ 33–118 in the main work).

(e) *Evidence*

33–88   Prove the soliciting or inciting as alleged in the indictment. Prove it in the same manner as the offence of being a counsellor and procurer would be proved, except that this offence is committed even though the offence solicited was not in fact committed. It is no defence to the above indictment that the person incited purposely submitted himself to the incitement with intent to betray the inciter: *R. v. Quail* (1866) 4 F. & F. 1076.

On a charge of inciting a person to receive stolen goods it is no defence that at the time of the incitement there did not exist stolen goods of the type mentioned: *R. v. McDonough*, 47 Cr.App.R. 37, CCA.

A charge of incitement to distribute indecent photographs of children could be founded on the defendant's entering the website of a commercial child pornography business and paying the required entrance fee with his credit card; it mattered not that the process was entirely automated by the computer; the computer merely facilitated the business, and it was irrelevant to say that only the computer was incited; someone lay behind the computer: *R. (O.) v. Coventry Magistrates' Court* [2004] Crim.L.R. 948, DC.

III. ENCOURAGING OR ASSISTING CRIME

(1) Introduction

Outline of Part 2

Inchoate offences

33–93   As to section 46 of the *SCA* 2007, see *R. v. Sadique and Hussain, post*, § 33–99.

(2) Legislation

(a) *Inchoate offences*

Serious Crime Act 2007, ss.44–49

Encouraging or assisting crime

33–99   In *Sadique and Hussain* [2012] 1 Cr.App.R. 19, CA, the court gave the following guidance in relation to section 46 of the *SCA* 2007 (encouraging or assisting offences believing one or more will be committed): (i) the offence should only be used when the prosecution allege that a defendant has done an act (which can be a course of conduct (s.67 (§ 33–116 in the main work)) or has failed to take reasonable steps to discharge certain duties (s.65(2)(b) (*ibid.*, § 33–114)) which act or failure was objectively capable of encouraging or assisting the commission of more than one offence (s.46(3)(a)) (which must be specified in the indictment) and where it may be that the defendant believed that one or more of those offences would be committed without having a belief as to which one or ones would be committed; although an act may have been capable of encouraging or assisting the commission of other offences, a defendant can only be convicted of the section 46 offence in relation to an offence specified in the indictment or (s.57 (*ibid.*, § 33–111)) which is a lesser included offence of an offence specified in the indictment; (ii) if a defendant pleads not guilty, there should be a separate count for each such offence, the first count worded as "Assisting in [offence X], contrary to section 46 of the *Serious Crime Act* 2007", and subsequent counts referring respectively to offence Y and offence Z, etc.; the particulars of each count should be the same and worded along the following lines "D ... did an act, namely ..., which was capable of assisting one or more offences of [X, Y, Z, etc.] believing that one or more of those offences would be committed but having no belief as to which and that his act would assist in the commission of one or more of those offences."; (iii) a defendant can be convicted under section 46 by reference to only one offence; to be convicted of a count relating to offence X (or a lesser included offence), he must (a) believe either that X will (and not might) be com-

mitted or that one or more of the offences specified in the indictment will be committed but
with no belief as to which, (b) believe that his act will encourage or assist the commission of
X, and (c) believe that X will be committed with the necessary fault for X; if (contrary to this
recommended practice) the indictment includes only one count for all specified offences, the
same principles will apply; (iv) the defendant will not need to know that the act or acts
which he believed would be done and which he believed he was assisting constitute an offence, nor will he need to know who was going to commit the offence or the identity of the
victim; however, full *mens rea* on his part in relation to the offence which he believed would
be committed will be required; that is, he must be proved to have believed that the act
constituting the offence would be done with the relevant fault, he was reckless as to whether
it would be done with the relevant fault or his state of mind was such that, if he were to do
it himself, he would do it with the relevant fault (see s.47(5) (*ibid.*, § 33–100)); (v) interpreting the provisions creating and defining section 46 in this way (including ss.47 and 48 (*ibid.*,
§ 33–101)), they are, albeit complex, neither vague nor uncertain, and are therefore not
incompatible with the certainty requirements of Article 7 of the ECHR (*ibid.*, § 16–97). For a
submission that the court may have misconstrued section 46(1)(b)(i), see CLW/12/01/6.

(d) *Jurisdiction and procedure*

Serious Crime Act 2007, ss.52–58

Penalties

For an example of sentencing under sections 44 and 46 of the 2007 Act, see *R. v. Black-*   **33–112**
shaw [2012] 1 Cr.App.R.(S.) 114, CA (four years' imprisonment upheld on guilty pleas for
encouraging crime via the social-networking website Facebook at the time of widespread
riots).

V. ATTEMPT TO COMMIT CRIME

B. STATUTORY OFFENCE OF ATTEMPT

Criminal Attempts Act 1981, ss.2, 3

Application of procedural and other provisions to offences under s.1

With effect from June 18, 2012 (*Criminal Justice Act 2003 (Commencement No. 28 and Sav-*   **★33–122**
ing Provisions) Order 2012 (S.I. 2012 No. 1320)), sections 41 and 332 of, and paragraph 52
of Schedule 3 to, and Part 4 of Schedule 37 to, the 2003 Act (see the main work) are
brought into force in certain areas (as to which, see *ante*, § 1–88). There are associated saving provisions, as to which, see article 5 of the order (*ante*, § 1–88).

D. PLEADING AND PRACTICE

Indictment

As to evidence and procedure where a person is charged in the same proceedings with an   **★33–135**
offence of attempted murder and a non-fatal offence under section 5 of the *Domestic Violence,
Crime and Victims Act* 2004 (§ 19–118a in the main work), see section 6A of the 2004 Act, as
inserted by section 2 of the *Domestic Violence, Crime and Victims (Amendment) Act* 2012, *ante*,
§ 19–118fa.

APPENDIX A

Codes of Practice and Attorney-General's Guidelines

I. CODES OF PRACTICE

A. Uɴᴅᴇʀ ᴛʜᴇ Pᴏʟɪᴄᴇ ᴀɴᴅ Cʀɪᴍɪɴᴀʟ Eᴠɪᴅᴇɴᴄᴇ Aᴄᴛ 1984

(1) Introduction

The *Police and Criminal Evidence Act* 1984 makes provision for the issuing by the Secre- **A–1**
tary of State of codes of practice in connection with the tape-recording of interviews (s.60,
§ 15–173 in the main work), the visual recording of interviews (s.60A, § 15–177 in the main
work), the exercise by police officers of statutory powers of "stop and search" (s.66(1)(a)(i)
and (ii), § 15–2 in the main work), the exercise by police officers of statutory powers to arrest a person (s.66(1)(a)(iii), § 15–2 in the main work) the detention, treatment, questioning
and identification of persons by police officers (s.66(1)(b), § 15–2 in the main work), and
searches of premises and seizure of property (s.66(1)(c) and (d), § 15–2 in the main work).

As at June 22, 2012, there were eight extant codes: Code A (stop and search); Code B
(search and seizure); Code C (detention, treatment and questioning of persons), Code D
(identification), Code E (tape-recording of interviews), Code F (visual recording of
interviews), Code G (arrest) and Code H (detention, treatment and questioning of persons
under section 41 of, and Schedule 8 to, the *Terrorism Act* 2000).

Code G (which was new) came into force on January 1, 2006: *Police and Criminal Evidence
Act 1984 (Codes of Practice) Order* 2005 (S.I. 2005 No. 3503). Code H (also new) came into
force on July 25, 2006: *Police and Criminal Evidence Act 1984 (Code of Practice C and Code of
Practice H) Order* 2006 (S.I. 2006 No. 1938). The current code C came into force on Febru-
ary 1, 2008: *Police and Criminal Evidence Act 1984 (Codes of Practice) Order* 2008 (S.I. 2008
No. 167). The current Codes E and F came into force on May 1, 2010: *Police and Criminal
Evidence Act 1984 (Codes of Practice) (Revisions to Codes E and F) Order* 2010 (S.I. 2010 No.
1108). The current codes A, B and D came into force on March 7, 2011: *Police and Criminal
Evidence Act 1984 (Codes of Practice) (Revision of Codes A, B and D) Order* 2011 (S.I. 2011 No.
412). For further details, see §§ 15–5, 15–6 in the main work.

It should be noted that the new Code A applies only in relation to a search commencing
after midnight on March 7, 2011; Code B applies only to applications for warrants made after midnight on March 7, 2011; and to searches and seizures made after midnight on
March 7, 2011; Code C applies only to people in police detention after midnight on January 31, 2008; Code D applies only to an identification procedure carried out after midnight
on March 7, 2011; Code E applies only to interviews carried out after midnight on May 1,
2010; and Code H applies only to people in police detention, following their arrest under
the *Terrorism Act* 2000, s.41, after midnight on July 24, 2006.

In relation to searches, *etc.*, taking place before the specified dates, the previous versions
of the codes will be the applicable provisions.

The *Terrorism Act 2000 (Remedial) Order* 2011 (S.I. 2011 No. 631), art. 5, and Sched. 2, para. 2, provided that as from March 18, 2011, Code A has effect as if paragraphs 2.18 to 2.26 were revoked. This is consequential on the effective repeal of sections 44 to 47 of the *Terrorism Act* 2000 by the 2011 order (as to which, see § 25–58 in the main work). There appears to be a drafting error in the statutory instrument, in that the intention must have been to provide that it is paragraphs 2.18A to 2.26 that are to be treated as revoked:

★ paragraph 2.18 has nothing to do with searches under the 2000 Act. As from a day to be appointed, the 2011 order is revoked by the *Protection of Freedoms Act* 2012, s.115(1) and (2), Sched. 9, para. 34, and Sched. 10, Pt 4.

★ A draft *Police and Criminal Evidence Act 1984 (Codes of Practice) (Revisions of Codes C, G and H) Order 2012* was laid before Parliament on May 10, 2012, along with the new codes. The order was approved by the House of Lords on June 18, 2012, and by the House of Commons on July 2, 2012. The order stipulates that it shall come into force on the day after the day on which it is made (anticipated to be July 10) and provides for the new Codes C and H to come into force on that day also, and for the new Code G to come into force on November 12. The explanatory note to the draft order states that the amendments to Code C "implement improvements and safeguards concerning the care and treatment of detainees and the right to legal advice", and that these are mirrored in the amendments to Code H, which also now includes provision relating to post-charge questioning under the *Counter-Terrorism Act* 2008 (as to which, see § 25–210 in the main work), and reflects changes to the terrorism detention legislation.

★ The text of the new Codes C and H, as laid before Parliament, is set out in this supplement (see *post*, A–38 *et seq.*, A–213 *et seq.*). Apart from the customary random punctuation and grammar (as to which, see *post*), the new codes as laid before Parliament are littered with drafting errors. The Home Office appear to regard it as acceptable to tidy up such errors after the codes have been laid before Parliament: thus, the text of the codes as they will eventually appear online on the Home Office website or in print, if published by the Stationery Office, will not necessarily coincide with the text of the codes laid before Parliament. The Home Office have also been singularly uncooperative in relation to the identification of any changes that they intend to make. Notwithstanding, the provision of a list of drafting errors to the Home Office, they continued to decline to confirm what changes were to be made until it was too late to publish this supplement with the definitive text of Codes C and H. It should be further pointed out that whilst the Home Office deny that the text of a code would ever be changed after publication, this is untrue. There has been at least one occasion when a substantive change was made (to correct an error in Code A) long after it had been published online.

★ In anticipation of the Home Office correcting the most obvious drafting errors prior to publication, minor changes have been made to the following paragraphs of Codes C and H as compared to the text as laid before Parliament: C:3B, C:5.7B, C:5F, C:6.11, C:6F, C:7.4, C:10F, Code C, Annex L, para. 4(c)(ii), H:1.2(c), H:1.3, H:1.4, H:1N, H:3.6, H:3G, H:3I, H:6.5, H:6.7(d)(iv), H:8.9, H:14.5, H:14I, H:15E, Code H, Annex B. In addition to these, (i) there are obvious errors in the drafting of C:8C and H:9.12, but it is not obvious what the correct wording should be; (ii) H:2.3A is out of order, but there is no way of knowing whether it will be re-numbered or re-positioned; (iii) there are references to the Legal Services Commission and the Criminal Defence Service notwithstanding that these are abolished by the *Legal Aid, Sentencing and Punishment of Offenders Act* 2012 (from a day to be appointed), (iv) there are references to reprimands and warnings notwithstanding these are abolished by the same Act (from a day to be appointed), (v) Code H refers to "the *Detention of Suspects (Temporary Extension) Bill* (notwithstanding that there is no such bill before Parliament (and fails to mention Part 4 of Schedule 8 to the *Terrorism Act* 2000 (inserted by the *Protection of Freedoms Act* 2012, s.58), which covers the same territory), and (vi) Code C:11.6 refers to out of date confiscation legislation (and there is no way of knowing whether the Home Office will deem it appropriate to amend this text, although this, along with all the other errors was pointed out to them in plenty of time for them to make their position plain).

For further details in relation to the codes generally, see the main work at §§ 15–2 *et seq.*

(primary legislation), § 15–5 (commencement), § 15–7 (status of codes), § 15–8 (who is
bound by the codes), § 15–10 (admissibility), and § 15–11 (breaches).

Apart from what has been said in relation to the text of the new Codes C and H, it should
be noted that the original text of the codes (as published by The Stationery Office and/or
available only on the Home Office website) is littered with errors of grammar and
punctuation. No change has been made to the words used, however obviously inappropriate, but limited changes have been made to the punctuation, use of case, use of italics and
paragraphing. This has been done with a view to injecting some consistency and
intelligibility.

(2) Stop and search

A. Code of Practice for the Exercise by:

**Police Officers of Statutory Powers of Stop and Search
Police Officers and Police Staff of Requirements to Record Public Encounters**

Commencement—Transitional arrangements

This code applies to any search by a police officer or any public encounter taking place after   **A–2**
midnight, twenty-one days after the day on which the *Police and Criminal Evidence Act 1984 (Codes of
Practice) (Revision of Codes A, B and D) Order* 2010 [*sic*] is made.

General

This code of practice must be readily available at all police stations for consultation by police officers, police staff, detained persons and members of the public.

The notes for guidance included are not provisions of this code, but are guidance to police officers
and others about its application and interpretation. Provisions in the annexes to the code are provisions of this code.

This code governs the exercise by police officers of statutory powers to search a person or a vehicle without first making an arrest. The main stop and search powers to which this code applies are
set out in Annex A, but that list should not be regarded as definitive. [See *Note 1*.] In addition, it covers requirements on police officers and police staff to record encounters not governed by statutory
powers.

This code does not apply to:

    (a) the powers of stop and search under;

        (i) *Aviation Security Act* 1982, s.27(2);

        (ii) *Police and Criminal Evidence Act* 1984, s.6(1) (which relates specifically to powers of
            constables employed by statutory undertakers on the premises of the statutory
            undertakers);

    (b) searches carried out for the purposes of examination under Schedule 7 to the *Terrorism
        Act* 2000 and to which the code of practice issued under paragraph 6 of Schedule 14 to
        the *Terrorism Act* 2000 applies.

A:1 Principles governing stop and search

A:1.1 Powers to stop and search must be used fairly, responsibly, with respect for people be-   **A–3**
ing searched and without unlawful discrimination. The *Equality Act* 2010 makes it unlawful for police officers to discriminate against, harass or victimise any person on the grounds of the "protected
characteristics" of age, disability, gender reassignment, race, religion or belief, sex and sexual
orientation, marriage and civil partnership, pregnancy and maternity when using their powers.
When police forces are carrying out their functions they also have a duty to have regard to the need
to eliminate unlawful discrimination, harassment and victimisation and to take steps to foster good
relations.

A:1.2 The intrusion on the liberty of the person stopped or searched must be brief and detention for the purposes of a search must take place at or near the location of the stop.

A:1.3 If these fundamental principles are not observed the use of powers to stop and search
may be drawn into question. Failure to use the powers in the proper manner reduces their
effectiveness. Stop and search can play an important role in the detection and prevention of
crime, and using the powers fairly makes them more effective.

A:1.4 The primary purpose of stop and search powers is to enable officers to allay or confirm suspicions about individuals without exercising their power of arrest. Officers may be required to justify the use or authorisation of such powers, in relation both to individual searches and the overall pattern of their activity in this regard, to their supervisory officers or in court. Any misuse of the powers is likely to be harmful to policing and lead to mistrust of the police. Officers must also be able to explain their actions to the member of the public searched. The misuse of these powers can lead to disciplinary action.

A:1.5 An officer must not search a person, even with his or her consent, where no power to search is applicable. Even where a person is prepared to submit to a search voluntarily, the person must not be searched unless the necessary legal power exists, and the search must be in accordance with the relevant power and the provisions of this code. The only exception, where an officer does not require a specific power, applies to searches of persons entering sports grounds or other premises carried out with their consent given as a condition of entry.

A:2 Explanation of powers to stop and search

A-4   A:2.1 This code applies to powers of stop and search as follows:

(a) powers which require reasonable grounds for suspicion, before they may be exercised; that articles unlawfully obtained or possessed are being carried, or under section 43 of the *Terrorism Act* 2000 that a person is a terrorist;

(b) authorised under section 60 of the *Criminal Justice and Public Order Act* 1994, based upon a reasonable belief that incidents involving serious violence may take place or that people are carrying dangerous instruments or offensive weapons within any locality in the police area or that it is expedient to use the powers to find such instruments or weapons that have been used in incidents of serious violence;

(c) authorised under section 44(1) and (2) of the *Terrorism Act* 2000 based upon a consideration that the exercise of the power is necessary for the prevention of acts of terrorism (see paragraph 2.18A), and;

(d) powers to search a person who has not been arrested in the exercise of a power to search premises (see Code B, paragraph 2.4).

Searches requiring reasonable grounds for suspicion

A-5   A:2.2 Reasonable grounds for suspicion depend on the circumstances in each case. There must be an objective basis for that suspicion based on facts, information, and/or intelligence which are relevant to the likelihood of finding an article of a certain kind or, in the case of searches under section 43 of the *Terrorism Act* 2000, to the likelihood that the person is a terrorist. Reasonable suspicion can never be supported on the basis of personal factors. It must rely on intelligence or information about, or some specific behaviour by the person concerned. For example, unless the police have a description of a suspect, a person's physical appearance (including any of the "protected characteristics" set out in the *Equality Act* 2010 (see paragraph 1.1)), or the fact that the person is known to have a previous conviction, cannot be used alone or in combination with each other, or in combination with any other factor, as the reason for searching that person. Reasonable suspicion cannot be based on generalisations or stereotypical images of certain groups or categories of people as more likely to be involved in criminal activity. A person's religion cannot be considered as reasonable grounds for suspicion and should never be considered as a reason to stop or stop and search an individual.

A:2.3 Reasonable suspicion can sometimes exist without specific information or intelligence and on the basis of the behaviour of a person. For example, if an officer encounters someone on the street at night who is obviously trying to hide something, the officer may (depending on the other surrounding circumstances) base such suspicion on the fact that this kind of behaviour is often linked to stolen or prohibited articles being carried. Similarly, for the purposes of section 43 of the *Terrorism Act* 2000, suspicion that a person is a terrorist may arise from the person's behaviour at or near a location which has been identified as a potential target for terrorists.

A:2.4 However, reasonable suspicion should normally be linked to accurate and current intelligence or information, such as information describing an article being carried, a suspected offender, or a person who has been seen carrying a type of article known to have been stolen recently from premises in the area. Searches based on accurate and current intelligence or information are more likely to be effective. Targeting searches in a particular area at specified crime problems increases their effectiveness and minimises inconvenience to law-abiding members of the public. It also helps in justifying the use of searches both to those who are searched and to the public. This does not however prevent stop and search powers being exercised in other locations where such powers may be exercised and reasonable suspicion exists.

A:2.5 Searches are more likely to be effective, legitimate, and secure public confidence when reasonable suspicion is based on a range of factors. The overall use of these powers is more likely to be effective when up to date and accurate intelligence or information is communicated to officers and they are well-informed about local crime patterns.

A:2.6 Where there is reliable information or intelligence that members of a group or gang habitually carry knives unlawfully or weapons or controlled drugs, and wear a distinctive item of clothing or other means of identification to indicate their membership of the group or gang, that distinctive item of clothing or other means of identification may provide reasonable grounds to stop and search a person. [See *Note 9*.]

A:2.7 A police officer may have reasonable grounds to suspect that a person is in innocent possession of a stolen or prohibited article or other item for which he or she is empowered to search. In that case the officer may stop and search the person even though there would be no power of arrest.

A:2.8 Under section 43(1) of the *Terrorism Act* 2000 a constable may stop and search a person whom the officer reasonably suspects to be a terrorist to discover whether the person is in possession of anything which may constitute evidence that the person is a terrorist. These searches may only be carried out by an officer of the same sex as the person searched (see Annex F). An authorisation under section 44(1) of the *Terrorism Act* 2000 allows vehicles to be stopped and searched by a constable in uniform who reasonably suspects that articles which could be used in connection with terrorism will be found in the vehicle or in anything in or on that vehicle. See paragraph 2.18A below.

A:2.9 An officer who has reasonable grounds for suspicion may detain the person concerned in order to carry out a search. Before carrying out a search the officer may ask questions about the person's behaviour or presence in circumstances which gave rise to the suspicion. As a result of questioning the detained person, the reasonable grounds for suspicion necessary to detain that person may be confirmed or, because of a satisfactory explanation, be eliminated. [See *Notes 2* and *3*.] Questioning may also reveal reasonable grounds to suspect the possession of a different kind of unlawful article from that originally suspected. Reasonable grounds for suspicion however cannot be provided retrospectively by such questioning during a person's detention or by refusal to answer any questions put.

A:2.10 If, as a result of questioning before a search, or other circumstances which come to the attention of the officer, there cease to be reasonable grounds for suspecting that an article is being carried of a kind for which there is a power to stop and search, no search may take place. [See *Note 3*.] In the absence of any other lawful power to detain, the person is free to leave at will and must be so informed.

A:2.11 There is no power to stop or detain a person in order to find grounds for a search. Police officers have many encounters with members of the public which do not involve detaining people against their will. If reasonable grounds for suspicion emerge during such an encounter, the officer may search the person, even though no grounds existed when the encounter began. If an officer is detaining someone for the purpose of a search, he or she should inform the person as soon as detention begins.

Searches authorised under section 60 of the Criminal Justice and Public Order Act 1994

A:2.12 Authority for a constable in uniform to stop and search under section 60 of the *Criminal Justice and Public Order Act* 1994 may be given if the authorising officer reasonably believes:

   (a) that incidents involving serious violence may take place in any locality in the officer's police area, and it is expedient to use these powers to prevent their occurrence;

   (b) that persons are carrying dangerous instruments or offensive weapons without good reason in any locality in the officer's police area; or

   (c) that an incident involving serious violence has taken place in the officer's police area, a dangerous incident or offensive weapon used in the incident is being carried by a person in any locality in that police area, and it is expedient to use these powers to find that instrument or weapon.

A:2.13 An authorisation under section 60 may only be given by an officer of the rank of inspector or above, in writing, or orally if paragraph 2.12(c) applies and it is not practicable to give the authorisation in writing. The authorisation (whether written or oral) must specify the grounds on which it was given, the locality in which the powers may be exercised and the period of time for which they are in force. The period authorised shall be no longer than appears reasonably necessary to prevent, or seek to prevent incidents of serious violence, or to deal with the problem of carrying dangerous instruments or offensive weapons. It may not exceed 24 hours. An oral authorisation given where paragraph 2.12(c) applies must be recorded in writing as soon as practicable. [See *Notes 10–13*.]

A:2.14 If an inspector gives an authorisation, he or she must, as soon as practicable, inform an officer of or above the rank of superintendent. This officer may direct that the authorisation shall be extended for a further 24 hours, if violence or the carrying of dangerous instruments or offensive weapons has occurred, or is suspected to have occurred, and the continued use of the powers is considered necessary to prevent or deal with further such activity. That direction must also be given in writing at the time or as soon as practicable afterwards. [See *Note 12*.]

A:2.14A The selection of persons and vehicles under section 60 to be stopped and, if appropriate, searched should reflect an objective assessment of the nature of the incident or weapon in question and the individuals and vehicles thought likely to be associated with that incident or those weapons [see *Notes 10 and 11*]. The powers must not be used to stop and search persons and vehicles for reasons unconnected with the purpose of the authorisation. When selecting persons and vehicles to be stopped in response to a specific threat or incident, officers must take care not to discriminate unlawfully against anyone on the grounds of any of the protected characteristics set out in the *Equality Act* 2010 (see paragraph 1.1).

A:2.14B The driver of a vehicle which is stopped under section 60 and any person who is searched under section 60 are entitled to a written statement to that effect if they apply within twelve months from the day the vehicle was stopped or the person was searched. This statement is a record which states that the vehicle was stopped or (as the case may be) that the person was searched under section 60 and it may form part of the search record or be supplied as a separate record.

Powers to require removal of face coverings

A–6   **A:2.15** Section 60AA of the *Criminal Justice and Public Order Act* 1994 also provides a power to demand the removal of disguises. The officer exercising the power must reasonably believe that someone is wearing an item wholly or mainly for the purpose of concealing identity. There is also a power to seize such items where the officer believes that a person intends to wear them for this purpose. There is no power to stop and search for disguises. An officer may seize any such item which is discovered when exercising a power of search for something else, or which is being carried, and which the officer reasonably believes is intended to be used for concealing anyone's identity. This power can only be used if an authorisation given under section 60, or under section 60AA, is in force. [See *Note 4*]

A:2.16 Authority under section 60AA for a constable in uniform to require the removal of disguises and to seize them may be given if the authorising officer reasonably believes that activities may take place in any locality in the officer's police area that are likely to involve the commission of offences and it is expedient to use these powers to prevent or control these activities.

A:2.17 An authorisation under section 60AA may only be given by an officer of the rank of inspector or above, in writing, specifying the grounds on which it was given, the locality in which the powers may be exercised and the period of time for which they are in force. The period authorised shall be no longer than appears reasonably necessary to prevent, or seek to prevent the commission of offences. It may not exceed 24 hours. [See *Notes 10–13*.]

A:2.18 An inspector who gives an authorisation must, as soon as practicable, inform an officer of or above the rank of superintendent. This officer may direct that the authorisation shall be extended for a further 24 hours, if crimes have been committed, or are suspected to have been committed, and the continued use of the powers is considered necessary to prevent or deal with further such activity. This direction must also be given in writing at the time or as soon as practicable afterwards. [See *Note 12*.]

As to this paragraph, see, *ante*, A–1 in relation to the effect of S.I. 2011 No. 631.

Searches authorised under section 44 of the Terrorism Act 2000

A–7   **A:2.18A–2.26** [*Note the effect of S.I. 2011 No. 631, ante, A–1.*]

Powers to search in the exercise of a power to search premises

A–8   **A:2.27** The following powers to search premises also authorise the search of a person, not under arrest, who is found on the premises during the course of the search:

    (a) section 139B of the *Criminal Justice Act* 1988 under which a constable may enter school premises and search the premises and any person on those premises for any bladed or pointed article or offensive weapon;

    (b) under a warrant issued under section 23(3) of the *Misuse of Drugs Act* 1971 to search premises for drugs or documents but only if the warrant specifically authorises the search of persons found on the premises; and

(c) under a search warrant or order issued under paragraph 1, 3 or 11 of Schedule 5 to the *Terrorism Act* 2000 to search premises and any person found there for material likely to be of substantial value to a terrorist investigation.

A:2.28 Before the power under section 139B of the *Criminal Justice Act* 1988 may be exercised, the constable must have reasonable grounds to believe that an offence under section 139A of the *Criminal Justice Act* 1988 (having a bladed or pointed article or offensive weapon on school premises) has been or is being committed. A warrant to search premises and persons found therein may be issued under section 23(3) of the *Misuse of Drugs Act* 1971 if there are reasonable grounds to suspect that controlled drugs or certain documents are in the possession of a person on the premises.

A:2.29 The powers in paragraph 2.27 do not require prior specific grounds to suspect that the person to be searched is in possession of an item for which there is an existing power to search. However, it is still necessary to ensure that the selection and treatment of those searched under these powers is based upon objective factors connected with the search of the premises, and not upon personal prejudice.

A:3 Conduct of searches

A:3.1 All stops and searches must be carried out with courtesy, consideration and respect for the person concerned. This has a significant impact on public confidence in the police. Every reasonable effort must be made to minimise the embarrassment that a person being searched may experience. [See *Note 4.*]　　**A–9**

A:3.2 The co-operation of the person to be searched must be sought in every case, even if the person initially objects to the search. A forcible search may be made only if it has been established that the person is unwilling to co-operate or resists. Reasonable force may be used as a last resort if necessary to conduct a search or to detain a person or vehicle for the purposes of a search.

A:3.3 The length of time for which a person or vehicle may be detained must be reasonable and kept to a minimum. Where the exercise of the power requires reasonable suspicion, the thoroughness and extent of a search must depend on what is suspected of being carried, and by whom. If the suspicion relates to a particular article which is seen to be slipped into a person's pocket, then, in the absence of other grounds for suspicion or an opportunity for the article to be moved elsewhere, the search must be confined to that pocket. In the case of a small article which can readily be concealed, such as a drug, and which might be concealed anywhere on the person, a more extensive search may be necessary. In the case of searches mentioned in paragraph 2.1(b), (c), and (d), which do not require reasonable grounds for suspicion, officers may make any reasonable search to look for items for which they are empowered to search. [See *Note 5.*]

A:3.4 The search must be carried out at or near the place where the person or vehicle was first detained. [See *Note 6.*]

A:3.5 There is no power to require a person to remove any clothing in public other than an outer coat, jacket or gloves, except under section 60AA of the *Criminal Justice and Public Order Act* 1994 (which empowers a constable to require a person to remove any item worn to conceal identity). [See *Notes 4* and *6.*] A search in public of a person's clothing which has not been removed must be restricted to superficial examination of outer garments. This does not, however, prevent an officer from placing his or her hand inside the pockets of the outer clothing, or feeling round the inside of collars, socks and shoes if this is reasonably necessary in the circumstances to look for the object of the search or to remove and examine any item reasonably suspected to be the object of the search. For the same reasons, subject to the restrictions on the removal of headgear, a person's hair may also be searched in public (see paragraphs 3.1 and 3.3).

A:3.6 Where on reasonable grounds it is considered necessary to conduct a more thorough search (*e.g.* by requiring a person to take off a T-shirt), this must be done out of public view, for example, in a police van unless paragraph 3.7 applies, or police station if there is one nearby. [See *Note 6.*] Any search involving the removal of more than an outer coat, jacket, gloves, headgear or footwear, or any other item concealing identity, may only be made by an officer of the same sex as the person searched and may not be made in the presence of anyone of the opposite sex unless the person being searched specifically requests it. [See *Notes 4, 7* and *8.*]

A:3.7 Searches involving exposure of intimate parts of the body must not be conducted as a routine extension of a less thorough search, simply because nothing is found in the course of the initial search. Searches involving exposure of intimate parts of the body may be carried out only at a nearby police station or other nearby location which is out of public view (but not a police vehicle). These searches must be conducted in accordance with paragraph 11 of Annex A to Code C except that an intimate search mentioned in paragraph 11(f) of Annex A to Code C may not be authorised or carried out under any stop and search powers. The other provisions of Code C do not apply to the conduct and recording of searches of persons detained at police stations in the exercise of stop and search powers. [See *Note 7.*]

Steps to be taken prior to a search

A–10
A:3.8 Before any search of a detained person or attended vehicle takes place the officer must take reasonable steps, if not in uniform (see paragraph 3.9), to show their warrant card to the person to be searched or in charge of the vehicle to be searched and whether or not in uniform, to give that person the following information:

(a) that they are being detained for the purposes of a search;

(b) the officer's name (except in the case of enquiries linked to the investigation of terrorism, or otherwise where the officer reasonably believes that giving his or her name might put him or her in danger, in which case a warrant or other identification number shall be given) and the name of the police station to which the officer is attached;

(c) the legal search power which is being exercised; and

(d) a clear explanation of:

(i) the object of the search in terms of the article or articles for which there is a power to search; and

(ii) in the case of:

- the power under section 60 of the *Criminal Justice and Public Order Act* 1994 (see paragraph 2.1(b)), the nature of the power, the authorisation and the fact that it has been given;

- the power under section 44 of the *Terrorism Act* 2000, the nature of the power, the authorisation and the fact that it has been given and the grounds for suspicion; (see paragraph 2.1(c) and 2.18A);

- all other powers requiring reasonable suspicion (see paragraph 2.1(a)), the grounds for that suspicion;

(e) that they are entitled to a copy of the record of the search if one is made (see section 4 below) if they ask within 3 months from the date of the search and:

(i) if they are not arrested and taken to a police station as a result of the search and it is practicable to make the record on the spot, that immediately after the search is completed they will be given, if they request, either:

- a copy of the record, or

- a receipt which explains how they can obtain a copy of the full record or access to an electronic copy of the record; or

(ii) if they are arrested and taken to a police station as a result of the search, that the record will be made at the station as part of their custody record and they will be given, if they request, a copy of their custody record which includes a record of the search as soon as practicable whilst they are at the station. [See *Note 16.*]

A:3.9 Stops and searches under the powers mentioned in paragraphs 2.1(b), and (c) may be undertaken only by a constable in uniform.

A:3.10 The person should also be given information about police powers to stop and search and the individual's rights in these circumstances.

A:3.11 If the person to be searched, or in charge of a vehicle to be searched, does not appear to understand what is being said, or there is any doubt about the person's ability to understand English, the officer must take reasonable steps to bring information regarding the person's rights and any relevant provisions of this code to his or her attention. If the person is deaf or cannot understand English and is accompanied by someone, then the officer must try to establish whether that person can interpret or otherwise help the officer to give the required information.

A:4 Recording requirements

(a) *Searches which do not result in an arrest*

A–11
A:4.1 When an officer carries out a search in the exercise of any power to which this code applies and the search does not result in the person searched or person in charge of the vehicle searched being arrested and taken to a police station, a record must be made of it, electronically or on paper, unless there are exceptional circumstances which make this wholly impracticable (*e.g.* in situations involving public disorder or when the recording officer's presence is urgently required elsewhere). If a record is to be made, the officer carrying out the search must make the record on the spot unless this is not practicable, in which case the officer must make the record as soon as practicable after the search is completed. [See *Note 16.*]

A:4.2 If the record is made at the time, the person who has been searched or who is in charge of the vehicle that has been searched must be asked if they want a copy and if they do, they must be given immediately, either:

- a copy of the record, or
- a receipt which explains how they can obtain a copy of the full record or access to an electronic copy of the record.

A:4.2A An officer is not required to provide a copy of the full record or a receipt at the time if they are called to an incident of higher priority. [See *Note 21*.]

(b) *Searches which result in an arrest*

A:4.2B If a search in the exercise of any power to which this code applies results in a person being arrested and taken to a police station, the officer carrying out the search is responsible for ensuring that a record of the search is made as part of their custody record. The custody officer must then ensure that the person is asked if they want a copy of the record and if they do, that they are given a copy as soon as practicable. [See *Note 16*.]

(c) *Record of search*

A:4.3 The record of a search must always include the following information:

- (a) a note of the self-defined ethnicity, and if different, the ethnicity as perceived by the officer making the search, of the person searched or of the person in charge of the vehicle searched (as the case may be) [see *Note 18*];
- (b) the date, time and place the person or vehicle was searched [see *Note 6*];
- (c) the object of the search in terms of the article or articles for which there is a power to search;
- (d) in the case of:
  - the power under section 60 of the *Criminal Justice and Public Order Act* 1994 (see paragraph 2.1(b)), the nature of the power, the authorisation and the fact that it has been given [see *Note 17*];
  - the power under section 44 of the *Terrorism Act* 2000, the nature of the power, the authorisation and the fact that it has been given and the grounds for suspicion [see paragraphs 2.1(c) and 2.18A and *Note 17*];
  - all other powers requiring reasonable suspicion (see paragraph 2.1(a)), the grounds for that suspicion;
- (e) subject to paragraph 3.8(b), the identity of the officer carrying out the search. [See *Note 15*.]

A:4.3A For the purposes of completing the search record, there is no requirement to record the name, address and date of birth of the person searched or the person in charge of a vehicle which is searched and the person is under no obligation to provide this information.

A:4.4 Nothing in paragraph 4.3 requires the names of police officers to be shown on the search record or any other record required to be made under this code in the case of enquiries linked to the investigation of terrorism or otherwise where an officer reasonably believes that recording names might endanger the officers. In such cases the record must show the officers' warrant or other identification number and duty station.

A:4.5 A record is required for each person and each vehicle searched. However, if a person is in a vehicle and both are searched, and the object and grounds of the search are the same, only one record need be completed. If more than one person in a vehicle is searched, separate records for each search of a person must be made. If only a vehicle is searched, the self-defined ethnic background of the person in charge of the vehicle must be recorded, unless the vehicle is unattended.

A:4.6 The record of the grounds for making a search must, briefly but informatively, explain the reason for suspecting the person concerned, by reference to the person's behaviour and/or other circumstances.

A:4.7 Where officers detain an individual with a view to performing a search, but the need to search is eliminated as a result of questioning the person detained, a search should not be carried out and a record is not required. [See paragraph 2.10, *Notes 3* and *22A*.]

A:4.8 After searching an unattended vehicle, or anything in or on it, an officer must leave a notice in it (or on it, if things on it have been searched without opening it) recording the fact that it has been searched.

A:4.9 The notice must include the name of the police station to which the officer concerned is attached and state where a copy of the record of the search may be obtained and how (if applicable) an electronic copy may be accessed and where any application for compensation should be directed.

A:4.10 The vehicle must if practicable be left secure.

Recording of encounters not governed by statutory powers

A:4.11 *Not used.*

A:4.12 There is no national requirement for an officer who requests a person in a public place to account for themselves, *i.e.* their actions, behaviour, presence in an area or possession of anything, to make any record of the encounter or to give the person a receipt. [See *Notes 22A* and *22B.*]

A:5 Monitoring and supervising the use of stop and search powers

A–12

A:5.1 Supervising officers must monitor the use of stop and search powers and should consider in particular whether there is any evidence that they are being exercised on the basis of stereotyped images or inappropriate generalisations. Supervising officers should satisfy themselves that the practice of officers under their supervision in stopping, searching and recording is fully in accordance with this code. Supervisors must also examine whether the records reveal any trends or patterns which give cause for concern, and if so take appropriate action to address this.

A:5.2 Senior officers with area or force-wide responsibilities must also monitor the broader use of stop and search powers and, where necessary, take action at the relevant level.

A:5.3 Supervision and monitoring must be supported by the compilation of comprehensive statistical records of stops and searches at force, area and local level. Any apparently disproportionate use of the powers by particular officers or groups of officers or in relation to specific sections of the community should be identified and investigated.

A:5.4 In order to promote public confidence in the use of the powers, forces in consultation with police authorities must make arrangements for the records to be scrutinised by representatives of the community, and to explain the use of the powers at a local level. [See *Note 19.*]

Notes for Guidance

Officers exercising stop and search powers

A–13

A:1 *This code does not affect the ability of an officer to speak to or question a person in the ordinary course of the officer's duties without detaining the person or exercising any element of compulsion. It is not the purpose of the code to prohibit such encounters between the police and the community with the co-operation of the person concerned and neither does it affect the principle that all citizens have a duty to help police officers to prevent crime and discover offenders. This is a civic rather than a legal duty; but when a police officer is trying to discover whether, or by whom, an offence has been committed he or she may question any person from whom useful information might be obtained, subject to the restrictions imposed by Code C. A person's unwillingness to reply does not alter this entitlement, but in the absence of a power to arrest, or to detain in order to search, the person is free to leave at will and cannot be compelled to remain with the officer.*

A:2 *In some circumstances preparatory questioning may be unnecessary, but in general a brief conversation or exchange will be desirable not only as a means of avoiding unsuccessful searches, but to explain the grounds for the stop/search, to gain cooperation and reduce any tension there might be surrounding the stop/search.*

A:3 *Where a person is lawfully detained for the purpose of a search, but no search in the event takes place, the detention will not thereby have been rendered unlawful.*

A:4 *Many people customarily cover their heads or faces for religious reasons—for example, Muslim women, Sikh men, Sikh or Hindu women, or Rastafarian men or women. A police officer cannot order the removal of a head or face covering except where there is reason to believe that the item is being worn by the individual wholly or mainly for the purpose of disguising identity, not simply because it disguises identity. Where there may be religious sensitivities about ordering the removal of such an item, the officer should permit the item to be removed out of public view. Where practicable, the item should be removed in the presence of an officer of the same sex as the person and out of sight of anyone of the opposite sex [see Annex F].*

A:5 *A search of a person in public should be completed as soon as possible.*

A:6 *A person may be detained under a stop and search power at a place other than where the person was first detained, only if that place, be it a police station or elsewhere, is nearby. Such a place should be located within a reasonable travelling distance using whatever mode of travel (on foot or by car) is appropriate. This applies to all searches under stop and search powers, whether or not they involve the removal of clothing or exposure of intimate parts of the body (see paragraphs 3.6 and 3.7) or take place in or out of public view. It means, for example, that a search under the stop and search power in section 23 of the* Misuse of Drugs Act *1971 which involves the compulsory removal of more than a person's outer coat, jacket or gloves cannot be* carried out unless a place which is both nearby the place they were first detained and out of public view, is available. If a search involves exposure of intimate parts of the body and a police station is not nearby, particular care must be taken to ensure that the location is suitable in that it enables the search to be conducted in accordance with the requirements of paragraph 11 of Annex A to Code C.

A:7 *A search in the street itself should be regarded as being in public for the purposes of paragraphs 3.6 and 3.7 above, even though it may be empty at the time a search begins. Although there is no power to require a person to do so, there is nothing to prevent an officer from asking a person voluntarily to remove more than an outer coat, jacket or gloves in public.*

A:8 Not used.

A:9 *Other means of identification might include jewellery, insignias, tattoos or other features which are known to identify members of the particular gang or group.*

Authorising officers

A:10 *The powers under section 60 are separate from and additional to the normal stop and search powers* **A–14** *which require reasonable grounds to suspect an individual of carrying an offensive weapon (or other article). Their overall purpose is to prevent serious violence and the widespread carrying of weapons which might lead to persons being seriously injured by disarming potential offenders or finding weapons that have been used in circumstances where other powers would not be sufficient. They should not therefore be used to replace or circumvent the normal powers for dealing with routine crime problems. A particular example might be an authorisation to prevent serious violence or the carrying of offensive weapons at a sports event by rival team supporters when the expected general appearance and age range of those likely to be responsible, alone, would not be sufficiently distinctive to support reasonable suspicion (see paragraph 2.6). The purpose of the powers under section 60AA is to prevent those involved in intimidatory or violent protests using face coverings to disguise identity.*

A:11 *Authorisations under section 60 require a reasonable belief on the part of the authorising officer. This must have an objective basis, for example: intelligence or relevant information such as a history of antagonism and violence between particular groups; previous incidents of violence at, or connected with, particular events or locations; a significant increase in knife-point robberies in a limited area; reports that individuals are regularly carrying weapons in a particular locality; information following an incident in which weapons were used about where the weapons might be found or in the case of section 60AA previous incidents of crimes being committed while wearing face coverings to conceal identity.*

A:12 *It is for the authorising officer to determine the period of time during which the powers mentioned in paragraph 2.1(b) and (c) may be exercised. The officer should set the minimum period he or she considers necessary to deal with the risk of violence, the carrying of knives or offensive weapons, or terrorism or to find dangerous instruments or weapons that have been used. A direction to extend the period authorised under the powers mentioned in paragraph 2.1(b) may be given only once. Thereafter further use of the powers requires a new authorisation. There is no provision to extend an authorisation of the powers mentioned in paragraph 2.1(c); further use of the powers requires a new authorisation.*

A:13 *It is for the authorising officer to determine the geographical area in which the use of the powers is to be authorised. In doing so the officer may wish to take into account factors such as the nature and venue of the anticipated incident or the incident which has taken place, the number of people who may be in the immediate area of that incident, their access to surrounding areas and the anticipated or actual level of violence. The officer should not set a geographical area which is wider than that he or she believes necessary for the purpose of preventing anticipated violence, the carrying of knives or offensive weapons, acts of terrorism, finding a dangerous instrument or weapon that has been used or, in the case of section 60AA, the prevention of commission of offences. It is particularly important to ensure that constables exercising such powers are fully aware of where they may be used. If the area specified is smaller than the whole force area, the officer giving the authorisation should specify either the streets which form the boundary of the area or a divisional boundary within the force area. If the power is to be used in response to a threat or incident that straddles police force areas, an officer from each of the forces concerned will need to give an authorisation.*

A:14 *An officer who has authorised the use of powers under section 44(1) of the* Terrorism Act 2000 *must take immediate steps to send a copy of the authorisation to the National Joint Unit, Metropolitan Police Special Branch, who will forward it to the Secretary of State. The Secretary of State should be informed of the reasons for the authorisation. The National Joint Unit will inform the force concerned, within 48 hours of the authorisation being made, whether the Secretary of State has confirmed or cancelled or altered the authorisation. See paragraph 2.18A.*

Recording

A:15 *Where a stop and search is conducted by more than one officer the identity of all the officers engaged* **A–15** *in the search must be recorded on the record. Nothing prevents an officer who is present but not directly involved in searching from completing the record during the course of the encounter.*

A:16 *When the search results in the person searched or in charge of a vehicle which is searched being arrested, the requirement to make the record of the search as part of the person's custody record does not apply if* the person is granted "street bail" after arrest (see section 30A of PACE) to attend a police station and is not taken in custody to the police station. An arrested person's entitlement to a copy of the search record which is made as part of their custody record does not affect their entitlement to a copy of their custody record or any other provisions of PACE *Code C section 2 (custody records).*

A:17 *It is important for monitoring purposes to specify whether the authority for exercising a stop and search power was given under section 60 of the* Criminal Justice and Public Order Act *1994, or under section 44(1) of the* Terrorism Act *2000.*

A:18 *Officers should record the self-defined ethnicity of every person stopped according to the categories used in the 2001 census question listed in Annex B. The person should be asked to select one of the five main categories representing broad ethnic groups and then a more specific cultural background from within this group. The ethnic classification should be coded for recording purposes using the coding system in Annex B. An additional "Not stated" box is available but should not be offered to respondents explicitly. Officers should be aware and explain to members of the public, especially where concerns are raised, that this information is required to obtain a true picture of stop and search activity and to help improve ethnic monitoring, tackle discriminatory practice, and promote effective use of the powers. If the person gives what appears to the officer to be an "incorrect" answer (e.g. a person who appears to be white states that they are black), the officer should record the response that has been given and then record their own perception of the person's ethnic background by using the PNC classification system. If the "Not stated" category is used the reason for this must be recorded on the form.*

A:19 *Arrangements for public scrutiny of records should take account of the right to confidentiality of those stopped and searched. Anonymised forms and/or statistics generated from records should be the focus of the examinations by members of the public.*

A:20 Not used.

A:21 *In situations where it is not practicable to provide a written copy of the record or immediate access to an electronic copy of the record or a receipt of the search at the time (see paragraph 4.2A above), the officer should consider giving the person details of the station which they may attend for a copy of the record. A receipt may take the form of a simple business card which includes sufficient information to locate the record should the person ask for copy [sic], for example, the date and place of the search, a reference number or the name of the officer who carried out the search (unless paragraph 4.4 applies).*

A:22 Not used.

A:22A *Where there are concerns which make it necessary to monitor any local disproportionality, forces have discretion to direct officers to record the self-defined ethnicity of persons they request to account for themselves in a public place or who they detain with a view to searching but do not search. Guidance should be provided locally and efforts made to minimise the bureaucracy involved. Records should be closely monitored and supervised in line with paragraphs 5.1 to 5.4 and forces can suspend or re-instate recording of these encounters as appropriate.*

A:22B *A person who is asked to account for themselves should, if they request, be given information about how they can report their dissatisfaction about how they have been treated.*

Definition of offensive weapon

A:23 *"Offensive weapon" is defined as any article made or adapted for use for causing injury to the person, or intended by the person having it with him for such use or by someone else. There are three categories of offensive weapons: those made for causing injury to the person; those adapted for such a purpose; and those not so made or adapted, but carried with the intention of causing injury to the person. A firearm, as defined by section 57 of the* Firearms Act *1968, would fall within the definition of offensive weapon if any of the criteria above apply.*

ANNEX A

Summary of main stop and search powers

This table relates to stop and search powers only. Individual statutes below may contain other police powers of entry, search and seizure.

POWER	Object of search	Extent of Search	Where Exercisable
Unlawful articles general			
1. *Public Stores Act* 1875, s.6	HM Stores stolen or unlawfully obtained	Persons, vehicles and vessels	Anywhere where the constabulary powers are exercisable
2. *Firearms Act* 1968, s.47	Firearms	Persons and vehicles	A public place, or anywhere in the case of reasonable suspicion of offences of carrying firearms with criminal intent or trespassing with firearms
3. *Misuse of Drugs Act* 1971, s.23	Controlled drugs	Persons and vehicles	Anywhere
4. *Customs and Excise Management Act* 1979, s.163	Goods: (a) on which duty has not been paid; (b) being unlawfully removed, imported or exported; (c) otherwise liable to forfeiture to HM Revenue and Customs	Vehicles and vessels only	Anywhere
5. *Aviation Security Act* 1982, s.27(1)	Stolen or unlawfully obtained goods	Airport employees and vehicles carrying airport employees or aircraft or any vehicle in a cargo area whether or not carrying an employee	Any designated airport
6. *Police and Criminal Evidence Act* 1984, s.1	Stolen goods; articles for use in certain *Theft Act* offences; offensive weapons, including bladed or sharply-pointed articles (except folding pocket knives with a bladed cutting edge not exceeding 3 inches); prohibited possession of a category 4 (display grade) firework, any person under 18 in possession of an adult firework in a public place.	Persons and vehicles	Where there is public access

			Where there is public access
7. *Sporting Events (Control of Alcohol etc.) Act* 1985, s.7	Intoxicating liquor	Persons, coaches and trains	Designated sports grounds or coaches and trains travelling to or from a designated sporting event.
8. *Crossbows Act* 1987, s.4	Crossbows or parts of crossbows (except crossbows with a draw weight of less than 1.4 kilograms)	Persons and vehicles	Anywhere except dwellings
9. *Criminal Justice Act* 1988 s.139B	Offensive weapons, bladed or sharply pointed article	Persons	School premises
Evidence of game and wildlife offences			
10. *Poaching Prevention Act* 1862, s.2	Game or poaching equipment	Persons and vehicles	A public place
11. *Deer Act* 1991, s.12	Evidence of offences under the Act	Persons and vehicles	Anywhere except dwellings
12. *Conservation of Seals Act* 1970, s.4	Seals or hunting equipment	Vehicles only	Anywhere
13. *Protection of Badgers Act* 1992, s.11	Evidence of offences under the Act	Persons and vehicles	Anywhere
14. *Wildlife and Countryside Act* 1981, s.19	Evidence of wildlife offences	Persons and vehicles	Anywhere except dwellings
Other			
15. *Terrorism Act* 2000, s.43(1)	Anything which may constitute evidence that the person is a terrorist	Persons	Anywhere
16. *Terrorism Act* 2000, s.44(1)	Articles of a kind which could be used in connection with terrorism	Vehicles and anything in or on vehicles (see paragraph 2.18A)	Anywhere within the area or locality authorised under subsection (1)
17. *[Not used.]*			
18. Paragraphs 7 and 8 of Schedule 7 to the *Terrorism Act* 2000	Anything relevant to determining if a person being examined falls within section 40(1)(b)	Persons, vehicles, vessels etc. (*Note: these searches are subject to the code of practice and issued under paragraph 6 of Schedule 14 to the Terrorism Act 2000*)	Ports and airports

| **19.** Section 60 *Criminal Justice and Public Order Act* 1994 | Offensive weapons or dangerous instruments to prevent incidents of serious violence or to deal with the carrying of such items or find such items which have been used in incidents of serious violence | Persons and vehicles | Anywhere within a locality authorised under subsection (1) |

ANNEX B

Self-Defined ethnic classification categories

A–17 White	**W**
A. *White—British*	W1
B. *White—Irish*	W2
C. *Any other White background*	W9
Mixed	**M**
D. *White and Black Caribbean*	M1
E. *White and Black African*	M2
F. *White and Asian*	M3
G. *Any other Mixed Background*	M9
Asian/ Asian—British	**A**
H. *Asian—Indian*	A1
I. *Asian—Pakistani*	A2
J. *Asian—Bangladeshi*	A3
K. *Any other Asian background*	A9
Black / Black—British	**B**
L. *Black—Caribbean*	B1
M. *Black African*	B2
N. *Any other Black background*	B9
Other	**O**
O. *Chinese*	O1
P. *Any other*	O9
Not stated	NS

ANNEX C

Summary of powers of community support officers to search and seize

A–17a   The following is a summary of the search and seizure powers that may be exercised by a community support officer (CSO) who has been designated with the relevant powers in accordance with Part 4 of the *Police Reform Act* 2002.

     When exercising any of these powers, a CSO must have regard to any relevant provisions of this code, including section 3 governing the conduct of searches and the steps to be taken prior to a search.

1. Power to stop and search not requiring consent

Designation	Power conferred	Object of Search	Extent of Search	Where Exercisable
Police Reform Act 2002, Schedule 4, paragraph 15	*Terrorism Act 2000*, s.44(1)(a) and (d) and 45(2) (see paragraph 2.18A)	Items intended to be used in connection with terrorism	(a) Vehicles or anything carried in or on the vehicle	Anywhere within area of locality authorised and in the company and under the supervision of a constable.

2. Powers to search requiring the consent of the person and seizure

A CSO may detain a person using reasonable force where necessary as set out in Part 1 of Schedule 4 to the *Police Reform Act* 2002. If the person has been lawfully detained, the CSO may search the person provided that person gives consent to such a search in relation to the following:

Designation	Powers conferred	Object of Search	Extent of Search	Where Exercisable
Police Reform Act 2002, Schedule 4, paragraph 7A	(a) *Criminal Justice and Police Act 2001*, s.12(2)	(a) Alcohol or a container for alcohol	(a) Persons	(a) Designated public place
	(b) *Confiscation of Alcohol (Young Persons) Act 1997*, s.1	(b) Alcohol	(b) Persons under 18 years old	(b) Public place
	(c) *Children and Young Persons Act 1933*, s.7(3)	(c) Tobacco or cigarette papers	(c) Persons under 16 years old found smoking	(c) Public place

3. Powers to search not requiring the consent of the person and seizure

A CSO may detain a person using reasonable force where necessary as set out in Part 1 of Schedule 4 to the *Police Reform Act* 2002. If the person has been lawfully detained, the CSO may search the person without the need for that person's consent in relation to the following:

Designation	Power conferred	Object of Search	Extent of Search	Where Exercisable
Police Reform Act 2002, Schedule 4, paragraph 2A	*Police and Criminal Evidence Act 1984*, s.32	(a) Objects that might be used to cause physical injury to the person or the CSO.	Persons made subject to a requirement to wait.	Any place where the requirement to wait has been made.
		(b) Items that might be used to assist escape.		

4. Powers to seize without consent

This power applies when drugs are found in the course of any search mentioned above.

Designation	Power conferred	Object of Seizure	Where Exercisable
Police Reform Act 2002, Schedule 4, paragraph 7B	*Police Reform Act 2002*, Schedule 4, paragraph 7B	Controlled drugs in a person's possession.	Any place where the person is in possession of the drug.

Annex D—Deleted

Annex E—Deleted

ANNEX F

Establishing gender of persons for the purpose of searching

A–17b   A:1. Certain provisions of this and other codes explicitly state that searches and other procedures may only be carried out by, or in the presence of, persons of the same sex as the person subject to the search or other procedure. (See paragraphs 2.8 and 3.6 and *Note 4* of this code, Code C, paragraph 4.1 and Annex A, paragraphs 5, 6, 11 and 12 (searches, strip and intimate searches of detainees under sections 54 and 55 of *PACE*), Code D, paragraph 5.5 and *Note 5F* (searches, examinations and photographing of detainees under section 54A of *PACE*) and 6.9 (taking samples) and Code H, paragraph 4.1 and Annex A, paragraphs 6, 7 and 12 (searches, strip and intimate searches under sections 54 and 55 of *PACE* and 43(2) of the *Terrorism Act* of persons arrested under section 41 of the *Terrorism Act* 2000.)

A:2. All searches should be carried out with courtesy, consideration and respect for the person concerned. Police officers should show particular sensitivity when dealing with transsexual or transvestite persons [see *Notes F1* and *F2*]. The following approach is designed to minimise embarrassment and secure the co-operation of the person subject to the search.

(a) *Consideration*

A–17c   A:3. At law, the gender of an individual is their gender as registered at birth unless they possess a gender recognition certificate as issued under section 9 of the *Gender Recognition Act* 2004, in which case the person's gender is the acquired gender.

   (a) If there is no doubt as to the sex of a person, or there is no reason to suspect that the person is not the sex that they appear to be, they should be dealt with as that sex.

   (b) A person who possesses a gender recognition certificate must be treated as their acquired gender.

   (c) If the police are not satisfied that the person possesses a gender recognition certificate and there is doubt as to a person's gender, the person should be asked what gender they consider themselves to be. If the person expresses a preference to be dealt with as a particular gender, they should be asked to sign the search record, the officer's notebook or, if applicable, their custody record, to indicate and confirm their preference. If appropriate, the person should be treated as being that gender.

   (d) If a person is unwilling to make such an election, efforts should be made to determine the predominant lifestyle of the person. For example, if they appear to live predominantly as a woman, they should be treated as such.

   (e) If there is still doubt, the person should be dealt with according to the sex that they were born.

A:5. [*sic*] Once a decision has been made about which gender an individual is to be treated as, where possible before an officer searches that person, the officer should be advised of the doubt as to the person's gender. This is important so as to maintain the dignity of the officer(s) concerned.

(b) *Documentation*

A–17d   A:6. Where the gender of the detainee is established under paragraphs 2(b) to (e) above the decision should be recorded either on the search record, in the officer's notebook or, if applicable, in the person's custody record.

A:7. Where the person elects which gender they consider themselves to be under paragraph 2(c) but is not treated as their elected gender, the reason must be recorded in the search record, in the officer's notebook or, if applicable, in the person's custody record.

Note for guidance

A–17e   A:F1 *Transsexual means a person who is proposing to undergo, is undergoing or has undergone a process (or part of a process) for the purpose of gender reassignment which is a protected characteristic under the Equality Act 2010 (see paragraph 1.1) by changing physiological or other attributes of their sex. It would apply to a woman making the transition to being a man and a man making the transition to being a woman* as well as to a person who has only just started out on the process of gender reassignment and to a person who has completed the process. Both would share the characteristic of gender reassignment with each having the characteristics of one sex, but with certain characteristics of the other sex.

A:F2 *Transvestite means a person of one gender who dresses in the clothes of a person of the opposite gender.*

A:F3 *Similar principles will apply to police officers and police staff whose duties involve carrying out, or being present at, any of the searches and other procedures mentioned in paragraph 1. Chief officers are responsible for providing corresponding operational guidance and instructions for the deployment of any transsexual officers and staff under their direction and control.*

(3) Search and seizure

The text that follows is of the version of the code that came into force on March 7, 2011: **A–18** see *ante*, Appendix A–1.

For authorities in relation to Code B, see, in particular, §§ 15–104 and 15–151 in the main work.

B. Code of Practice for Searches of Premises by Police Officers and the Seizure of Property Found by Police Officers on Persons or Premises

Commencement—transitional arrangements

This code applies to applications for warrants made after midnight, twenty-one days after the day **A–19** on which the *Police and Criminal Evidence Act 1984 (Codes of Practice) (Revision of Codes A, B and D) Order* 2010 [*sic*] is made, and to searches and seizures taking place after that time.

B:1 Introduction

B:1.1 This code of practice deals with police powers to: **A–20**
- search premises
- seize and retain property found on premises and persons.

B:1.1A These powers may be used to find:
- property and material relating to a crime
- wanted persons
- children who abscond from local authority accommodation where they have been remanded or committed by a court.

B:1.2 A justice of the peace may issue a search warrant granting powers of entry, search and seizure, *e.g.* warrants to search for stolen property, drugs, firearms and evidence of serious offences. Police also have powers without a search warrant. The main ones provided by the *Police and Criminal Evidence Act* 1984 (*PACE*) include powers to search premises:
- to make an arrest
- after an arrest.

B:1.3 The right to privacy and respect for personal property are key principles of the *Human Rights Act* 1998. Powers of entry, search and seizure should be fully and clearly justified before use because they may significantly interfere with the occupier's privacy. Officers should consider if the necessary objectives can be met by less intrusive means.

B:1.3A Powers to search and seize must be used fairly, responsibly, with respect for people who occupy premises being searched or are in charge of property being seized and without unlawful discrimination. The *Equality Act* 2010 makes it unlawful for police officers to discriminate against, harass or victimise any person on the grounds of the "protected characteristics" of age, disability, gender reassignment, race, religion or belief, sex and sexual orientation, marriage and civil partnership, pregnancy and maternity when using their powers. When police forces are carrying out their functions they also have a duty to have regard to the need to eliminate unlawful discrimination, harassment and victimisation and to take steps to foster good relations.

B:1.4 In all cases, police should therefore:
- exercise their powers courteously and with respect for persons and property
- only use reasonable force when this is considered necessary and proportionate to the circumstances.

B:1.5 If the provisions of *PACE* and this code are not observed, evidence obtained from a search may be open to question.

B:2 General

B:2.1 This code must be readily available at all police stations for consultation by:

- police officers
- police staff
- detained persons
- members of the public.

B:2.2 The *Notes for Guidance* included are not provisions of this code.

B:2.3 This code applies to searches of premises:

(a) by police for the purposes of an investigation into an alleged offence, with the occupier's consent, other than:

- routine scene of crime searches;
- calls to a fire or burglary made by or on behalf of an occupier or searches following the activation of fire or burglar alarms or discovery of insecure premises;
- searches when paragraph 5.4 applies;
- bomb threat calls;

(b) under powers conferred on police officers by *PACE*, ss.17, 18 and 32;

(c) undertaken in pursuance of search warrants issued to and executed by constables in accordance with *PACE*, ss.15 and 16; [see *Note 2A*];

(d) subject to paragraph 2.6, under any other power given to police to enter premises with or without a search warrant for any purpose connected with the investigation into an alleged or suspected offence. [See *Note 2B*].

For the purposes of this code, "premises" as defined in *PACE*, s.23, includes any place, vehicle, vessel, aircraft, hovercraft, tent or movable structure and any offshore installation as defined in the *Mineral Workings (Offshore Installations) Act* 1971, s.1. See *Note 2D*.

B:2.4 A person who has not been arrested but is searched during a search of premises should be searched in accordance with Code A. See *Note 2C*.

B:2.5 This code does not apply to the exercise of a statutory power to enter premises or to inspect goods, equipment or procedures if the exercise of that power is not dependent on the existence of grounds for suspecting that an offence may have been committed and the person exercising the power has no reasonable grounds for such suspicion.

B:2.6 This code does not affect any directions or requirements of a search warrant, order or other power to search and seize lawfully exercised in England or Wales that any item or evidence seized under that warrant, order or power be handed over to a police force, court, tribunal, or other authority outside England or Wales. For example, warrants and orders issued in Scotland or Northern Ireland, see *Note 2B(f)* and search warrants and powers provided for in sections 14 to 17 of the *Crime (International Co-operation) Act* 2003.

B:2.7 When this code requires the prior authority or agreement of an officer of at least inspector or superintendent rank, that authority may be given by a sergeant or chief inspector authorised to perform the functions of the higher rank under *PACE*, s.107.

B:2.8 Written records required under this code not made in the search record shall, unless otherwise specified, be made:

- in the recording officer's pocket book ("pocket book" includes any official report book issued to police officers), or
- on forms provided for the purpose.

B:2.9 Nothing in this code requires the identity of officers, or anyone accompanying them during a search of premises, to be recorded or disclosed:

(a) in the case of enquiries linked to the investigation of terrorism; or

(b) if officers reasonably believe recording or disclosing their names might put them in danger.

In these cases officers should use warrant or other identification numbers and the name of their police station. Police staff should use any identification number provided to them by the police force. See *Note 2E*.

B:2.10 The "officer in charge of the search" means the officer assigned specific duties and responsibilities under this code. Whenever there is a search of premises to which this code applies one officer must act as the officer in charge of the search. See *Note 2F*.

B:2.11 In this code:

(a) "designated person" means a person other than a police officer, designated under the *Police Reform Act* 2002, Pt 4 who has specified powers and duties of police officers conferred or imposed on them; [see *Note 2G*];

(b) any reference to a police officer includes a designated person acting in the exercise or performance of the powers and duties conferred or imposed on them by their designation;

(c) a person authorised to accompany police officers or designated persons in the execution of a warrant has the same powers as a constable in the execution of the warrant and the search and seizure of anything related to the warrant. These powers must be exercised in the company and under the supervision of a police officer. See *Note 3C*.

B:2.12 If a power conferred on a designated person:

(a) allows reasonable force to be used when exercised by a police officer, a designated person exercising that power has the same entitlement to use force;

(b) includes power to use force to enter any premises, that power is not exercisable by that designated person except:

  (i) in the company and under the supervision of a police officer; or

  (ii) for the purpose of:

   • saving life or limb; or

   • preventing serious damage to property.

B:2.13 Designated persons must have regard to any relevant provisions of the codes of practice.

Notes for guidance

B:2A PACE *ss.15 and 16 apply to all search warrants issued to and executed by constables under any* **A–22**
enactment, e.g. search warrants issued by a:

(a) *justice of the peace under the:*

  Theft Act *1968, s.26—stolen property*;

  Misuse of Drugs Act *1971, s.23—controlled drugs*;

  PACE, *s.8—evidence of an indictable offence*;

  Terrorism Act *2000, Sched. 5, para. 1*;

  Prevention of Terrorism Act *2005, s.7C—monitoring compliance with control order (see paragraph 10.1)*;

(b) *circuit judge under:*

  PACE, *Sched. 1*;

  Terrorism Act *2000, Sched. 5, para. 11.*

B:2B *Examples of the other powers in paragraph 2.3(d) include:*

(a) Road Traffic Act *1988, s.6E(1) giving police power to enter premises under section 6E(1) to:*

  • *require a person to provide a specimen of breath; or*

  • *arrest a person following:*

   – *a positive breath test;*

   – *failure to provide a specimen of breath;*

(b) Transport and Works Act *1992, s.30(4) giving police powers to enter premises mirroring the powers in (a) in relation to specified persons working on transport systems to which the Act applies;*

(c) Criminal Justice Act *1988, s.139B giving police power to enter and search school premises for offensive weapons, bladed or pointed articles;*

(d) Terrorism Act *2000, Sched. 5, paras 3 and 15 empowering a superintendent in urgent cases to give written authority for police to enter and search premises for the purposes of a terrorist investigation;*

(e) Explosives Act *1875, s.73(b) empowering a superintendent to give written authority for police to enter premises, examine and search them for explosives;*

(f) *search warrants and production orders or the equivalent issued in Scotland or Northern Ireland endorsed under the* Summary Jurisdiction (Process) Act *1881 or the* Petty Sessions (Ireland) Act *1851 respectively for execution in England and Wales;*

(g) *sections 7A and 7B of the* Prevention of Terrorism Act 2005, *searches connected with the enforcement of control orders (see paragraph 10.1).*

B:2C *The* Criminal Justice Act *1988, s.139B provides that a constable who has reasonable grounds to* *believe an offence under the* Criminal Justice Act *1988, s.139A has or is being committed may enter school premises and search the premises and any persons on the premises for any bladed or pointed article or offensive weapon. Persons may be searched under a warrant issued under the* Misuse of Drugs Act *1971, s.23(3) to search premises for drugs or documents only if the warrant specifically authorises the search of persons on the premises. Powers to search premises under certain terrorism provisions also authorise the search of persons on the premises, for example, under paragraphs 1, 2, 11 and 15 of Schedule 5 to the* Terrorism Act *2000 and section 52 of the* Anti-terrorism, Crime and Security Act *2001.*

B:2D *The* Immigration Act *1971, Pt III and Sched. 2 gives immigration officers powers to enter and search premises, seize and retain property, with and without a search warrant. These are similar to the powers available to police under search warrants issued by a justice of the peace and without a warrant under* PACE, ss.17, 18, 19 and 32 *except they only apply to specified offences under the* Immigration Act *1971 and immigration control powers. For certain types of investigations and enquiries these powers avoid the need for the Immigration Service to rely on police officers becoming directly involved. When exercising these powers, immigration officers are required by the* Immigration and Asylum Act *1999, s.145 to have regard to this code's corresponding provisions. When immigration officers are dealing with persons or property at police stations, police officers should give appropriate assistance to help them discharge their specific duties and responsibilities.*

B:2E *The purpose of paragraph 2.9(b) is to protect those involved in serious organised crime investigations or arrests of particularly violent suspects when there is reliable information that those arrested or their associates may threaten or cause harm to the officers or anyone accompanying them during a search of premises. In cases of doubt, an officer of inspector rank or above should be consulted.*

B:2F *For the purposes of paragraph 2.10, the officer in charge of the search should normally be the most senior officer present. Some exceptions are:*

(a) *a supervising officer who attends or assists at the scene of a premises search may appoint an officer of lower rank as officer in charge of the search if that officer is:*

- *more conversant with the facts;*
- *a more appropriate officer to be in charge of the search;*

(b) *when all officers in a premises search are the same rank. The supervising officer if available must make sure one of them is appointed officer in charge of the search, otherwise the officers themselves must nominate one of their number as the officer in charge;*

(c) *a senior officer assisting in a specialist role. This officer need not be regarded as having a general supervisory role over the conduct of the search or be appointed or expected to act as the officer in charge of the search.*

Except in (c), nothing in this note diminishes the role and responsibilities of a supervisory officer who is present at the search or knows of a search taking place.

B:2G *An officer of the rank of inspector or above may direct a designated investigating officer not to wear a uniform for the purposes of a specific operation.*

B:3 Search warrants and production orders

(a) *Before making an application*

A–23

B:3.1 When information appears to justify an application, the officer must take reasonable steps to check the information is accurate, recent and not provided maliciously or irresponsibly. An application may not be made on the basis of information from an anonymous source if corroboration has not been sought. See *Note 3A*.

B:3.2 The officer shall ascertain as specifically as possible the nature of the articles concerned and their location.

B:3.3 The officer shall make reasonable enquiries to:

(i) establish if:

- anything is known about the likely occupier of the premises and the nature of the premises themselves;
- the premises have been searched previously and how recently;

(ii) obtain any other relevant information.

B:3.4 An application:

(a) to a justice of the peace for a search warrant or to a circuit judge for a search warrant or production order under *PACE*, Sched. 1 must be supported by a signed written authority from an officer of inspector rank or above; [Note: if the case is an urgent application to a justice of the peace and an inspector or above is not readily available, the next most senior officer on duty can give the written authority];

  (b) to a circuit judge under the *Terrorism Act* 2000, Sched. 5 for:

- a production order;
- search warrant; or
- an order requiring an explanation of material seized or produced under such a warrant or production order

must be supported by a signed written authority from an officer of superintendent rank or above.

B:3.5 Except in a case of urgency, if there is reason to believe a search might have an adverse effect on relations between the police and the community, the officer in charge shall consult the local police/community liaison officer:

- before the search; or
- in urgent cases, as soon as practicable after the search.

(b) *Making an application*

  B:3.6 A search warrant application must be supported in writing, specifying:

    (a) the enactment under which the application is made, see *Note 2A*;

    (b) (i) whether the warrant is to authorise entry and search of:

- one set of premises; or
- if the application is under *PACE*, s.8, or Sched. 1, para. 12, more than one set of specified premises or all premises occupied or controlled by a specified person, and

      (ii) the premises to be searched;

    (c) the object of the search, see *Note 3B*;

    (d) the grounds for the application, including, when the purpose of the proposed search is to find evidence of an alleged offence, an indication of how the evidence relates to the investigation;

    (da) where the application is under *PACE*, s.8, or Sched. 1, para. 12 for a single warrant to enter and search:

      (i) more than one set of specified premises, the officer must specify each set of premises which it is desired to enter and search;

      (ii) all premises occupied or controlled by a specified person, the officer must specify:

- as many sets of premises which it is desired to enter and search as it is reasonably practicable to specify;
- the person who is in occupation or control of those premises and any others which it is desired to search;
- why it is necessary to search more premises than those which can be specified;
- why it is not reasonably practicable to specify all the premises which it is desired to enter and search;

    (db) whether an application under *PACE*, s.8 is for a warrant authorising entry and search on more than one occasion, and if so, the officer must state the grounds for this and whether the desired number of entries authorised is unlimited or a specified maximum;

    (e) there are no reasonable grounds to believe the material to be sought, when making application to a:

      (i) justice of the peace or a circuit judge consists of or includes items subject to legal privilege;

      (ii) justice of the peace, consists of or includes excluded material or special procedure material;

    [Note: this does not affect the additional powers of seizure in the *Criminal Justice and Police Act* 2001, Pt 2 covered in paragraph 7.7, see *Note 3B*];

    (f) if applicable, a request for the warrant to authorise a person or persons to accompany the officer who executes the warrant, see *Note 3C*.

B:3.7 A search warrant application under *PACE*, Sched. 1, para. 12(a), shall if appropriate indicate why it is believed service of notice of an application for a production order may seriously prejudice the investigation. Applications for search warrants under the *Terrorism Act* 2000, Schedule 5, paragraph 11 must indicate why a production order would not be appropriate.

B:3.8 If a search warrant application is refused, a further application may not be made for those premises unless supported by additional grounds.

Notes for guidance

B:3A *The identity of an informant need not be disclosed when making an application, but the officer should be prepared to answer any questions the magistrate or judge may have about:*

- *the accuracy of previous information from that source*
- *any other related matters.*

B:3B *The information supporting a search warrant application should be as specific as possible, particularly in relation to the articles or persons being sought and where in the premises it is suspected they may be found. The meaning of "items subject to legal privilege", "excluded material" and "special procedure material" are defined by PACE, ss.10, 11 and 14 respectively.*

B:3C *Under PACE, s.16(2), a search warrant may authorise persons other than police officers to accompany the constable who executes the warrant. This includes, e.g. any suitably qualified or skilled person or an expert in a particular field whose presence is needed to help accurately identify the material sought or to advise where certain evidence is most likely to be found and how it should be dealt with. It does not give them any right to force entry, but it gives them the right to be on the premises during the search and to search for or seize property without the occupier's permission.*

B:4 Entry without warrant—particular powers

(a) *Making an arrest etc*

B:4.1 The conditions under which an officer may enter and search premises without a warrant are set out in *PACE*, s.17. It should be noted that this section does not create or confer any powers of arrest. See other powers in *Note 2B(a).*

(b) *Search of premises where arrest takes place or the arrested person was immediately before arrest*

B:4.2 When a person has been arrested for an indictable offence, a police officer has power under *PACE*, s.32 to search the premises where the person was arrested or where the person was immediately before being arrested.

(c) *Search of premises occupied or controlled by the arrested person*

B:4.3 The specific powers to search premises which <u>are</u> occupied or controlled by a person arrested for an indictable offence are set out in *PACE*, s.18. They may not be exercised, except if section 18 (5) applies, unless an officer of inspector rank or above has given written authority. That authority should only be given when the authorising officer is satisfied that the premises <u>are</u> occupied or controlled by the arrested person and that the necessary grounds exist. If possible the authorising officer should record the authority on the Notice of Powers and Rights and, subject to paragraph 2.9, sign the notice. The record of the grounds for the search and the nature of the evidence sought as required by section 18(7) of the Act should be made in:

- the custody record if there is one, otherwise
- the officer's pocket book, or
- the search record.

B:5 Search with consent

B:5.1 Subject to paragraph 5.4, if it is proposed to search premises with the consent of a person entitled to grant entry the consent must, if practicable, be given in writing on the Notice of Powers and Rights before the search. The officer must make any necessary enquiries to be satisfied the person is in a position to give such consent. See *Notes 5A and 5B.*

B:5.2 Before seeking consent the officer in charge of the search shall state the purpose of the proposed search and its extent. This information must be as specific as possible, particularly regarding the articles or persons being sought and the parts of the premises to be searched. The person concerned must be clearly informed they are not obliged to consent, that any consent given can be withdrawn at any time, including before the search starts or while it is under way and anything seized may be produced in evidence. If at the time the person is not suspected of an offence, the officer shall say this when stating the purpose of the search.

B:5.3 An officer cannot enter and search or continue to search premises under paragraph 5.1 if consent is given under duress or withdrawn before the search is completed.

B:5.4 It is unnecessary to seek consent under paragraphs 5.1 and 5.2 if this would cause disproportionate inconvenience to the person concerned. See *Note 5C.*

Notes for guidance

B:5A *In a lodging house, hostel or similar accommodation, every reasonable effort should be made to* **A–27** *obtain the consent of the tenant, lodger or occupier. A search should not be made solely on the basis of the landlord's consent.*

B:5B *If the intention is to search premises under the authority of a warrant or a power of entry and search without warrant, and the occupier of the premises co-operates in accordance with paragraph 6.4, there is no need to obtain written consent.*

B:5C *Paragraph 5.4 is intended to apply when it is reasonable to assume innocent occupiers would agree to, and expect, police to take the proposed action, e.g. if:*

- *a suspect has fled the scene of a crime or to evade arrest and it is necessary quickly to check surrounding gardens and readily accessible places to see if the suspect is hiding*
- *police have arrested someone in the night after a pursuit and it is necessary to make a brief check of gardens along the pursuit route to see if stolen or incriminating articles have been discarded.*

B:6 Searching premises—general considerations

(a) *Time of searches*

B:6.1 Searches made under warrant must be made within three calendar months of the date **A–28** of the warrant's issue.

B:6.2 Searches must be made at a reasonable hour unless this might frustrate the purpose of the search.

B:6.3 When the extent or complexity of a search mean it is likely to take a long time, the officer in charge of the search may consider using the seize and sift powers referred to in section 7.

B:6.3A A warrant under *PACE*, s.8 may authorise entry to and search of premises on more than one occasion if, on the application, the justice of the peace is satisfied that it is necessary to authorise multiple entries in order to achieve the purpose for which the warrant is issued. No premises may be entered or searched on any subsequent occasions without the prior written authority of an officer of the rank of inspector who is not involved in the investigation. All other warrants authorise entry on one occasion only.

B:6.3B Where a warrant under *PACE*, s.8, or Sched. 1, para. 12 authorises entry to and search of all premises occupied or controlled by a specified person, no premises which are not specified in the warrant may be entered and searched without the prior written authority of an officer of the rank of inspector who is not involved in the investigation.

(b) *Entry other than with consent*

B:6.4 The officer in charge of the search shall first try to communicate with the occupier, or any other person entitled to grant access to the premises, explain the authority under which entry is sought and ask the occupier to allow entry, unless:

   (i) the search premises are unoccupied;

   (ii) the occupier and any other person entitled to grant access are absent;

   (iii) there are reasonable grounds for believing that alerting the occupier or any other person entitled to grant access would frustrate the object of the search or endanger officers or other people.

B:6.5 Unless sub-paragraph 6.4(iii) applies, if the premises are occupied the officer, subject to paragraph 2.9, shall, before the search begins:

   (i) identify him or herself, show their warrant card (if not in uniform) and state the purpose of and grounds for the search;

   (ii) identify and introduce any person accompanying the officer on the search (such persons should carry identification for production on request) and briefly describe that person's role in the process.

B:6.6 Reasonable and proportionate force may be used if necessary to enter premises if the officer in charge of the search is satisfied the premises are those specified in any warrant, or in exercise of the powers described in paragraph 4.1 to 4.3, and if:

   (i) the occupier or any other person entitled to grant access has refused entry;

   (ii) it is impossible to communicate with the occupier or any other person entitled to grant access; or

   (iii) any of the provisions of paragraph 6.4 apply.

(c) *Notice of powers and rights*

A–29   **B:**6.7 If an officer conducts a search to which this code applies the officer shall, unless it is impracticable to do so, provide the occupier with a copy of a notice in a standard format:

  (i) specifying if the search is made under warrant, with consent, or in the exercise of the powers described in paragraphs 4.1 to 4.3; [Note: the notice format shall provide for authority or consent to be indicated, see paragraphs 4.3 and 5.1];

  (ii) summarising the extent of the powers of search and seizure conferred by *PACE* and other relevant legislation as appropriate;

  (iii) explaining the rights of the occupier, and the owner of the property seized;

  (iv) explaining compensation may be payable in appropriate cases for damages [*sic*] caused entering and searching premises, and giving the address to send a compensation application, see *Note 6A*;

  (v) stating this code is available at any police station.

  B:6.8 If the occupier is:

  ● present, copies of the notice and warrant shall, if practicable, be given to them before the search begins, unless the officer in charge of the search reasonably believes this would frustrate the object of the search or endanger officers or other people;

  ● not present, copies of the notice and warrant shall be left in a prominent place on the premises or appropriate part of the premises and endorsed, subject to paragraph 2.9 with the name of the officer in charge of the search, the date and time of the search.

The warrant shall be endorsed to show this has been done.

(d) *Conduct of searches*

  B:6.9 Premises may be searched only to the extent necessary to achieve the purpose of the search, having regard to the size and nature of whatever is sought.

  B:6.9A A search may not continue under:

  ● a warrant's authority once all the things specified in that warrant have been found;

  ● any other power once the object of that search has been achieved.

  B:6.9B No search may continue once the officer in charge of the search is satisfied whatever is being sought is not on the premises. See *Note 6B*. This does not prevent a further search of the same premises if additional grounds come to light supporting a further application for a search warrant or exercise or further exercise of another power. For example, when, as a result of new information, it is believed articles previously not found or additional articles are on the premises.

  B:6.10 Searches must be conducted with due consideration for the property and privacy of the occupier and with no more disturbance than necessary. Reasonable force may be used only when necessary and proportionate because the co-operation of the occupier cannot be obtained or is insufficient for the purpose. See *Note 6C*.

  B:6.11 A friend, neighbour or other person must be allowed to witness the search if the occupier wishes unless the officer in charge of the search has reasonable grounds for believing the presence of the person asked for would seriously hinder the investigation or endanger officers or other people. A search need not be unreasonably delayed for this purpose. A record of the action taken should be made on the premises search record including the grounds for refusing the occupier's request.

  B:6.12 A person is not required to be cautioned prior to being asked questions that are solely necessary for the purpose of furthering the proper and effective conduct of a search, see Code C, paragraph 10.1(c). For example, questions to discover the occupier of specified premises, to find a key to open a locked drawer or cupboard or to otherwise seek co-operation during the search or to determine if a particular item is liable to be seized.

  B:6.12A If questioning goes beyond what is necessary for the purpose of the exemption in Code C, the exchange is likely to constitute an interview as defined by Code C, paragraph 11.1A and would require the associated safeguards included in Code C, section 10.

(e) *Leaving premises*

A–30   **B:**6.13 If premises have been entered by force, before leaving the officer in charge of the search must make sure they are secure by:

  ● arranging for the occupier or their agent to be present;

  ● any other appropriate means.

(f) *Searches under PACE, Schedule 1 or the Terrorism Act 2000, Schedule 5*

  B:6.14 An officer shall be appointed as the officer in charge of the search, see paragraph 2.10, in respect of any search made under a warrant issued under *PACE Act* 1984, Sched. 1 or the *Terrorism Act* 2000, Sched. 5. They are responsible for making sure the search is conducted with discretion and in a manner that causes the least possible disruption to any business or other activities carried out on the premises.

B:6.15 Once the officer in charge of the search is satisfied material may not be taken from the premises without their knowledge, they shall ask for the documents or other records concerned. The officer in charge of the search may also ask to see the index to files held on the premises, and the officers conducting the search may inspect any files which, according to the index, appear to contain the material sought. A more extensive search of the premises may be made only if:

- the person responsible for them refuses to:
  - produce the material sought, or
  - allow access to the index;
- it appears the index is:
  - inaccurate, or
  - incomplete;
- for any other reason the officer in charge of the search has reasonable grounds for believing such a search is necessary in order to find the material sought.

Notes for guidance

B:6A *Whether compensation is appropriate depends on the circumstances in each case. Compensation for* **A–31** *damage caused when effecting entry is unlikely to be appropriate if the search was lawful, and the force used can be shown to be reasonable, proportionate and necessary to effect entry. If the wrong premises are searched by mistake everything possible should be done at the earliest opportunity to allay any sense of grievance and there should normally be a strong presumption in favour of paying compensation.*

B:6B *It is important that, when possible, all those involved in a search are fully briefed about any powers to be exercised and the extent and limits within which it should be conducted.*

B:6C *In all cases the number of officers and other persons involved in executing the warrant should be determined by what is reasonable and necessary according to the particular circumstances.*

B:7 Seizure and retention of property

(a) *Seizure*

B:7.1 Subject to paragraph 7.2, an officer who is searching any person or premises under any **A–32** statutory power or with the consent of the occupier may seize anything:

(a) covered by a warrant;

(b) the officer has reasonable grounds for believing is evidence of an offence or has been obtained in consequence of the commission of an offence but only if seizure is necessary to prevent the items being concealed, lost, disposed of, altered, damaged, destroyed or tampered with;

(c) covered by the powers in the *Criminal Justice and Police Act* 2001, Pt 2 allowing an officer to seize property from persons or premises and retain it for sifting or examination elsewhere.

See *Note 7B.*

B:7.2 No item may be seized which an officer has reasonable grounds for believing to be subject to legal privilege, as defined in *PACE*, s.10, other than under the *Criminal Justice and Police Act* 2001, Pt 2.

B:7.3 Officers must be aware of the provisions in the *Criminal Justice and Police Act* 2001, s.59, allowing for applications to a judicial authority for the return of property seized and the subsequent duty to secure in section 60, see paragraph 7.12(iii).

B:7.4 An officer may decide it is not appropriate to seize property because of an explanation from the person holding it but may nevertheless have reasonable grounds for believing it was obtained in consequence of an offence by some person. In these circumstances, the officer should identify the property to the holder, inform the holder of their suspicions and explain the holder may be liable to civil or criminal proceedings if they dispose of, alter or destroy the property.

B:7.5 An officer may arrange to photograph, image or copy, any document or other article they have the power to seize in accordance with paragraph 7.1. This is subject to specific restrictions on the examination, imaging or copying of certain property seized under the *Criminal*

Justice and Police Act 2001, Pt 2. An officer must have regard to their statutory obligation to retain an original document or other article only when a photograph or copy is not sufficient.

B:7.6 If an officer considers information stored in any electronic form and accessible from the premises could be used in evidence, they may require the information to be produced in a form:

- which can be taken away and in which it is visible and legible; or
- from which it can readily be produced in a visible and legible form.

(b) *Criminal Justice and Police Act 2001: specific procedures for seize and sift powers*

B:7.7 The *Criminal Justice and Police Act* 2001, Pt 2 gives officers limited powers to seize property from premises or persons so they can sift or examine it elsewhere. Officers must be careful they only exercise these powers when it is essential and they do not remove any more material than necessary. The removal of large volumes of material, much of which may not ultimately be retainable, may have serious implications for the owners, particularly when they are involved in business or activities such as journalism or the provision of medical services. Officers must carefully consider if removing copies or images of relevant material or data would be a satisfactory alternative to removing originals. When originals are taken, officers must be prepared to facilitate the provision of copies or images for the owners when reasonably practicable. See *Note 7C*.

B:7.8 Property seized under the *Criminal Justice and Police Act* 2001, s.50 or 51 must be kept securely and separately from any material seized under other powers. An examination under section 53 to determine which elements may be retained must be carried out at the earliest practicable time, having due regard to the desirability of allowing the person from whom the property was seized, or a person with an interest in the property, an opportunity of being present or represented at the examination.

B:7.8A All reasonable steps should be taken to accommodate an interested person's request to be present, provided the request is reasonable and subject to the need to prevent harm to, interference with, or unreasonable delay to the investigatory process. If an examination proceeds in the absence of an interested person who asked to attend or their representative, the officer who exercised the relevant seizure power must give that person a written notice of why the examination was carried out in those circumstances. If it is necessary for security reasons or to maintain confidentiality officers may exclude interested persons from decryption or other processes which facilitate the examination but do not form part of it. See *Note 7D*.

B:7.9 It is the responsibility of the officer in charge of the investigation to make sure property is returned in accordance with sections 53 to 55. Material which there is no power to retain must be:

- separated from the rest of the seized property;
- returned as soon as reasonably practicable after examination of all the seized property.

B:7.9A Delay is only warranted if very clear and compelling reasons exist, *e.g.* the:

- unavailability of the person to whom the material is to be returned;
- need to agree a convenient time to return a large volume of material.

B:7.9B Legally privileged, excluded or special procedure material which cannot be retained must be returned:

- as soon as reasonably practicable;
- without waiting for the whole examination.

B:7.9C As set out in section 58, material must be returned to the person from whom it was seized, except when it is clear some other person has a better right to it. See *Note 7E*.

B:7.10 When an officer involved in the investigation has reasonable grounds to believe a person with a relevant interest in property seized under section 50 or 51 intends to make an application under section 59 for the return of any legally privileged, special procedure or excluded material, the officer in charge of the investigation should be informed as soon as practicable and the material seized should be kept secure in accordance with section 61. See *Note 7C*.

B:7.11 The officer in charge of the investigation is responsible for making sure property is properly secured. Securing involves making sure the property is not examined, copied, imaged or put to any other use except at the request, or with the consent, of the applicant or in accordance with the directions of the appropriate judicial authority. Any request, consent or directions must be recorded in writing and signed by both the initiator and the officer in charge of the investigation.

See *Notes 7F* and *7G*.

B:7.12 When an officer exercises a power of seizure conferred by sections 50 or 51 they shall provide the occupier of the premises or the person from whom the property is being seized with a written notice:

   (i) specifying what has been seized under the powers conferred by that section;

   (ii) specifying the grounds for those powers;

   (iii) setting out the effect of sections 59 to 61 covering the grounds for a person with a relevant interest in seized property to apply to a judicial authority for its return and the duty of officers to secure property in certain circumstances when an application is made;

   (iv) specifying the name and address of the person to whom:

- notice of an application to the appropriate judicial authority in respect of any of the seized property must be given;
- an application may be made to allow attendance at the initial examination of the property.

B:7.13 If the occupier is not present but there is someone in charge of the premises, the notice shall be given to them. If no suitable person is available, so the notice will easily be found it should either be:

- left in a prominent place on the premises;
- attached to the exterior of the premises.

(c) *Retention*

B:7.14 Subject to paragraph 7.15, anything seized in accordance with the above provisions   **A–34**
may be retained only for as long as is necessary. It may be retained, among other purposes:

   (i) for use as evidence at a trial for an offence;

   (ii) to facilitate the use in any investigation or proceedings of anything to which it is inextricably linked, see *Note 7H*;

   (iii) for forensic examination or other investigation in connection with an offence;

   (iv) in order to establish its lawful owner when there are reasonable grounds for believing it has been stolen or obtained by the commission of an offence.

B:7.15 Property shall not be retained under paragraph 7.14(i), (ii) or (iii) if a copy or image would be sufficient.

(d) *Rights of owners etc*

B:7.16 If property is retained, the person who had custody or control of it immediately before seizure must, on request, be provided with a list or description of the property within a reasonable time.

B:7.17 That person or their representative must be allowed supervised access to the property to examine it or have it photographed or copied, or must be provided with a photograph or copy, in either case within a reasonable time of any request and at their own expense, unless the officer in charge of an investigation has reasonable grounds for believing this would:

   (i) prejudice the investigation of any offence or criminal proceedings; or

   (ii) lead to the commission of an offence by providing access to unlawful material such as pornography.

A record of the grounds shall be made when access is denied.

Notes for guidance

B:7A *Any person claiming property seized by the police may apply to a magistrates' court under the* Police   **A–35**
(Property) Act *1897 for its possession and should, if appropriate, be advised of this procedure.*

B:7B *The powers of seizure conferred by* PACE, ss.*18(2) and 19(3) extend to the seizure of the whole premises when it is physically possible to seize and retain the premises in their totality and practical considerations make seizure desirable. For example, police may remove premises such as tents, vehicles or caravans to a police station for the purpose of preserving evidence.*

B:7C *Officers should consider reaching agreement with owners and/or other interested parties on the procedures for examining a specific set of property, rather than awaiting the judicial authority's determination. Agreement can sometimes give a quicker and more satisfactory route for all concerned and minimise costs and legal complexities.*

B:7D *What constitutes a relevant interest in specific material may depend on the nature of that material and the circumstances in which it is seized. Anyone with a reasonable claim to ownership of the material and anyone entrusted with its safe keeping by the owner should be considered.*

B:7E *Requirements to secure and return property apply equally to all copies, images or other material created because of seizure of the original property.*

B:7F *The mechanics of securing property vary according to the circumstances; "bagging up", i.e. placing* *material in sealed bags or containers and strict subsequent control of access is the appropriate procedure in many cases.*

B:7G *When material is seized under the powers of seizure conferred by* PACE, *the duty to retain it under the code of practice issued under the* Criminal Procedure and Investigations Act *1996 is subject to the provisions on retention of seized material in* PACE, *s.22.*

B:7H *Paragraph 7.14(ii) applies if inextricably linked material is seized under the* Criminal Justice and Police Act *2001, s.50 or 51. Inextricably linked material is material it is not reasonably practicable to separate from other linked material without prejudicing the use of that other material in any investigation or proceedings. For example, it may not be possible to separate items of data held on computer disk without damaging their evidential integrity. Inextricably linked material must not be examined, imaged, copied or used for any purpose other than for proving the source and/or integrity of the linked material.*

B:8 Action after searches

A–36 **B:8.1** If premises are searched in circumstances where this code applies, unless the exceptions in paragraph 2.3(a) apply, on arrival at a police station the officer in charge of the search shall make or have made a record of the search, to include:

  (i) the address of the searched premises;
  (ii) the date, time and duration of the search;
  (iii) the authority used for the search:
   - if the search was made in exercise of a statutory power to search premises without warrant, the power which was used for the search:
   - if the search was made under a warrant or with written consent;
    – a copy of the warrant and the written authority to apply for it, see paragraph 3.4; or
    – the written consent;
    shall be appended to the record or the record shall show the location of the copy warrant or consent;
  (iv) subject to paragraph 2.9, the names of:
   - the officer(s) in charge of the search;
   - all other officers and any authorised persons who conducted the search;
  (v) the names of any people on the premises if they are known;
  (vi) any grounds for refusing the occupier's request to have someone present during the search, see paragraph 6.11;
  (vii) a list of any articles seized or the location of a list and, if not covered by a warrant, the grounds for their seizure;
  (viii) whether force was used, and the reason;
  (ix) details of any damage caused during the search, and the circumstances;
  (x) if applicable, the reason it was not practicable:
    (a) to give the occupier a copy of the notice of powers and rights, see paragraph 6.7;
    (b) before the search to give the occupier a copy of the notice, see paragraph 6.8;
  (xi) when the occupier was not present, the place where copies of the notice of powers and rights and search warrant were left on the premises, see paragraph 6.8.

B:8.2 On each occasion when premises are searched under warrant, the warrant authorising the search on that occasion shall be endorsed to show:

  (i) if any articles specified in the warrant were found and the address where found;
  (ii) if any other articles were seized;
  (iii) the date and time it was executed and if present, the name of the occupier or if the occupier is not present the name of the person in charge of the premises;
  (iv) subject to paragraph 2.9, the names of the officers who executed it and any authorised persons who accompanied them;
  (v) if a copy, together with a copy of the notice of powers and rights was:
   - handed to the occupier;
   - or endorsed as required by paragraph 6.8; and left on the premises and where.

B:8.3 Any warrant shall be returned within three calendar months of its issue or sooner on completion of the search(es) authorised by that warrant, if it was issued by a:

- justice of the peace, to the designated officer for the local justice area in which the justice was acting when issuing the warrant; or
- judge, to the appropriate officer of the court concerned.

B:9 Search registers

B:9.1 A search register will be maintained at each sub-divisional or equivalent police station. All search records required under paragraph 8.1 shall be made, copied, or referred to in the register. See *Note 9A*.

Note for guidance

B:9A *Paragraph 9.1 also applies to search records made by immigration officers. In these cases, a search register must also be maintained at an immigration office. See also Note 2D.*

B:10 Searches under sections 7A, 7B and 7C of the Prevention of Terrorism Act 2005 in connection with control orders

B:10.1 This code applies to the powers under sections 7A, 7B and 7C of the *Prevention of Terrorism Act* 2005 to enter and search premises subject to the modifications in the following paragraphs.

B:10.2 In paragraph 2.3(d), the reference to the investigation into an alleged or suspected offence include [*sic*] the enforcement of obligations imposed by or under a control order made under the *Prevention of Terrorism Act* 2005.

B:10.3 References to the purpose and object of the search, the nature of articles sought and what may be seized and retained include (as appropriate):

- in relation section [*sic*] 7A (absconding), determining whether the controlled person has absconded and if it appears so, any material or information that may assist in the pursuit and arrest of the controlled person;
- in relation to section 7B (failure to grant access to premises), determining whether any control order obligations have been contravened and if it appears so, any material or information that may assist in determining whether the controlled person is complying with the obligations imposed by the control order or in investigating any apparent contravention of those obligations;
- in relation to section 7C (monitoring compliance), determining whether the controlled person is complying with their control order obligations, and any material that may assist in that determination;
- evidence in relation to an offence under section 9 of the *Prevention of Terrorism Act* 2005 (offences relating to control orders).

(4) Detention, treatment and questioning of persons

The text that follows is of the version of the code that was laid before Parliament in May, 2012 (but see *ante*, A–1), and is anticipated to come into force in early July, 2012: see *ante*, Appendix A–1.

For authorities in relation to Code C, see, in particular, §§ 15–167 *et seq.* (right of access to solicitor), § 15–204 (general), § 15–311 (confessions), § 15–372 (sufficient evidence for prosecution to succeed), §§ 15–401 *et seq.* (discretionary exclusion of evidence) in the main work.

C. Code of Practice for the Detention, Treatment and Questioning of Persons by Police Officers

Commencement—Transitional arrangements

This code applies to people in police detention after midnight on the day the *Police and Criminal Evidence Act 1984 (Codes of Practice) (Revision of Codes C, G and H) Order 2012* comes into force, notwithstanding that their period of detention may have commenced before that time.

C:1 General

C:1.0 The powers and procedures in this code must be used fairly, responsibly, with respect for the people to whom they apply and without unlawful discrimination. The *Equality Act* 2010 makes it unlawful for police officers to discriminate against, harass or victimise any person on the grounds of the "protected characteristics" of age, disability, gender reassignment, race, religion or

A–37

A–37a

★A–38

★A–39

★A–40

belief, sex and sexual orientation, marriage and civil partnership, pregnancy and maternity when using their powers. When police forces are carrying out their functions, they also have a duty to have regard to the need to eliminate unlawful discrimination, harassment and victimisation and to take steps to foster good relations.

C:1.1 All persons in custody must be dealt with expeditiously, and released as soon as the need for detention no longer applies.

C:1.1A A custody officer must perform the functions in this code as soon as practicable. A custody officer will not be in breach of this code if delay is justifiable and reasonable steps are taken to prevent unnecessary delay. The custody record shall show when a delay has occurred and the reason. See *Note 1H*.

C:1.2 This code of practice must be readily available at all police stations for consultation by:

- police officers;
- police staff;
- detained persons;
- members of the public.

C:1.3 The provisions of this code:

- include the *Annexes*;
- do not include the *Notes for Guidance*.

C:1.4 If an officer has any suspicion, or is told in good faith, that a person of any age may be mentally disordered or otherwise mentally vulnerable, in the absence of clear evidence to dispel that suspicion, the person shall be treated as such for the purposes of this code. See *Note 1G*.

C:1.5 If anyone appears to be under 17, they shall be treated as a juvenile for the purposes of this code in the absence of clear evidence that they are older.

C:1.6 If a person appears to be blind, seriously visually impaired, deaf, unable to read or speak or has difficulty orally because of a speech impediment, they shall be treated as such for the purposes of this code in the absence of clear evidence to the contrary.

★A–41 **C:**1.7 The "appropriate adult" means, in the case of a:

    (a) juvenile:

        (i) the parent, guardian or, if the juvenile is in the care of a local authority or voluntary organisation, a person representing that authority or organisation;

        (ii) a social worker of a local authority;

        (iii) failing these, some other responsible adult aged 18 or over who is not a police officer or employed by the police;

    (b) person who is mentally disordered or mentally vulnerable (see *Note 1D*);

        (i) a relative, guardian or other person responsible for their care or custody;

        (ii) someone experienced in dealing with mentally disordered or mentally vulnerable people but who is not a police officer or employed by the police;

        (iii) failing these, some other responsible adult aged 18 or over who is not a police officer or employed by the police.

C:1.8 If this code requires a person be given certain information, they do not have to be given it if at the time they are incapable of understanding what is said, are violent or may become violent or in urgent need of medical attention, but they must be given it as soon as practicable.

C:1.9 References to a custody officer include any police officer who for the time being, is performing the functions of a custody officer.

C:1.9A When this code requires the prior authority or agreement of an officer of at least inspector or superintendent rank, that authority may be given by a sergeant or chief inspector authorised to perform the functions of the higher rank under the *Police and Criminal Evidence Act* 1984 (*PACE*), s.107.

C:1.10 Subject to paragraph 1.12, this code applies to people in custody at police stations in England and Wales, whether or not they have been arrested, and to those removed to a police station as a place of safety under the *Mental Health Act* 1983, ss.135 and 136, as a last resort (see paragraph 3.16). Section 15 applies solely to people in police detention, *e.g.* those brought to a police station under arrest or arrested at a police station for an offence after going there voluntarily.

C:1.11 No part of this code applies to a detained person:

    (a) to whom *PACE* Code H applies because:

        - they are detained following arrest under section 41 of the *Terrorism Act* 2000 (*TACT*) and not charged; or

- an authorisation has been given under section 22 of the *Counter-Terrorism Act* 2008 (*CTACT*) (post-charge questioning of terrorist suspects) to interview them;

(b) to whom the code of practice issued under paragraph 6 of Schedule 14 to *TACT* applies because they are detained for examination under Schedule 7 to *TACT*.

C:1.12 This code does not apply to people in custody:

(i) arrested on warrants issued in Scotland by officers under the *Criminal Justice and Public Order Act* 1994, s.136(2), or arrested or detained without warrant by officers from a police force in Scotland under section 137(2); in these cases, police powers and duties and the person's rights and entitlements whilst at a police station in England or Wales are the same as those in Scotland;

(ii) arrested under the *Immigration and Asylum Act* 1999, s.142(3), in order to have their fingerprints taken;

(iii) whose detention is authorised by an immigration officer under the *Immigration Act* 1971;

(iv) who are convicted or remanded prisoners held in police cells on behalf of the Prison Service under the *Imprisonment (Temporary Provisions) Act* 1980;

(v) [*not used*];

(vi) detained for searches under stop and search powers except as required by Code A.

The provisions on conditions of detention and treatment in sections 8 and 9 must be considered as the minimum standards of treatment for such detainees.

C:1.13 In this code:

(a) "designated person" means a person other than a police officer, designated under the *Police Reform Act* 2002, Pt 4, who has specified powers and duties of police officers conferred or imposed on them;

(b) reference to a police officer includes a designated person acting in the exercise or performance of the powers and duties conferred or imposed on them by their designation;

(c) where a search or other procedure to which this code applies may only be carried out or observed by a person of the same sex as the detainee, the gender of the detainee and other parties present should be established and recorded in line with Annex L of this code.

C:1.14 Designated persons are entitled to use reasonable force as follows:— ★**A–42**

(a) when exercising a power conferred on them which allows a police officer exercising that power to use reasonable force, a designated person has the same entitlement to use force; and

(b) at other times when carrying out duties conferred or imposed on them that also entitle them to use reasonable force, for example:

- when at a police station carrying out the duty to keep detainees for whom they are responsible under control and to assist any other police officer or designated person to keep any detainee under control and to prevent their escape;

- when securing, or assisting any other police officer or designated person in securing, the detention of a person at a police station;

- when escorting, or assisting any other police officer or designated person in escorting, a detainee within a police station;

- for the purpose of saving life or limb; or

- preventing serious damage to property.

C:1.15 Nothing in this code prevents the custody officer, or other officer given custody of the detainee, from allowing police staff who are not designated persons to carry out individual procedures or tasks at the police station if the law allows. However, the officer remains responsible for making sure the procedures and tasks are carried out correctly in accordance with the codes of practice (see *Note 3F*). Any such person must be:

(a) a person employed by a police force and under the direction and control of the chief officer of that force; or

(b) employed by a person with whom a police force has a contract for the provision of services relating to persons arrested or otherwise in custody.

C:1.16 Designated persons and other police staff must have regard to any relevant provisions of the codes of practice.

C:1.17 References to pocket books include any official report book issued to police officers or other police staff.

Notes for guidance

★**A–43**   **C:**1A *Although certain sections of this code apply specifically to people in custody at police stations, those there voluntarily to assist with an investigation should be treated with no less consideration, e.g. offered refreshments at appropriate times, and enjoy an absolute right to obtain legal advice or communicate with anyone outside the police station.*

    C:1B *A person, including a parent or guardian, should not be an appropriate adult if they:*

- *are*
    - ~ *suspected of involvement in the offence;*
    - ~ *the victim;*
    - ~ *a witness;*
    - ~ *involved in the investigation;*
- *received admissions prior to attending to act as the appropriate adult.*

Note: if a juvenile's parent is estranged from the juvenile, they should not be asked to act as the appropriate adult if the juvenile expressly and specifically objects to their presence.

    C:1C *If a juvenile admits an offence to, or in the presence of, a social worker or member of a youth offending team other than during the time that person is acting as the juvenile's appropriate adult, another appropriate adult should be appointed in the interest of fairness.*

    C:1D *In the case of people who are mentally disordered or otherwise mentally vulnerable, it may be more satisfactory if the appropriate adult is someone experienced or trained in their care rather than a relative lacking such qualifications. But if the detainee prefers a relative to a better qualified stranger or objects to a particular person their wishes should, if practicable, be respected.*

    C:1E *A detainee should always be given an opportunity, when an appropriate adult is called to the police station, to consult privately with a solicitor in the appropriate adult's absence if they want. An appropriate adult is not subject to legal privilege.*

    C:1F *A solicitor or independent custody visitor (formerly a lay visitor) present at the police station in that capacity may not be the appropriate adult.*

    C:1G *"Mentally vulnerable" applies to any detainee who, because of their mental state or capacity, may not understand the significance of what is said, of questions or of their replies. "Mental disorder" is defined in the* Mental Health Act *1983, s.1(2), as "any disorder or disability of mind". When the custody officer has any doubt about the mental state or capacity of a detainee, that detainee should be treated as mentally vulnerable and an appropriate adult called.*

    C:1H *Paragraph 1.1A is intended to cover delays which may occur in processing detainees, e.g. if:*

- *a large number of suspects are brought into the station simultaneously to be placed in custody;*
- *interview rooms are all being used;*
- *there are difficulties contacting an appropriate adult, solicitor or interpreter.*

    C:1I *The custody officer must remind the appropriate adult and detainee about the right to legal advice and record any reasons for waiving it in accordance with section 6.*

    C:1J *[Not used.]*

    C:1K *This code does not affect the principle that all citizens have a duty to help police officers to prevent crime and discover offenders. This is a civic rather than a legal duty; but when police officers are trying to discover whether, or by whom, offences have been committed they are entitled to question any person from whom they think useful information can be obtained, subject to the restrictions imposed by this code. A person's declaration that they are unwilling to reply does not alter this entitlement.*

C:2 Custody records

★**A–44**   **C:**2.1A When a person is brought to a police station:

- under arrest;
- is arrested at the police station having attended there voluntarily; or
- attends a police station to answer bail;

they must be brought before the custody officer as soon as practicable after their arrival at the station or if applicable, following their arrest after attending the police station voluntarily. This applies to designated and non-designated police stations. A person is deemed to be "at a police station" for these purposes if they are within the boundary of any building or enclosed yard which forms part of that police station.

    C:2.1 A separate custody record must be opened as soon as practicable for each person brought to a police station under arrest or arrested at the station having gone there voluntarily or attending a police station in answer to street bail. All information recorded under this code must be recorded as soon as practicable in the custody record unless otherwise specified. Any audio or video recording made in the custody area is not part of the custody record.

C:2.2 If any action requires the authority of an officer of a specified rank, subject to paragraph 2.6A, their name and rank must be noted in the custody record.

C:2.3 The custody officer is responsible for the custody record's accuracy and completeness and for making sure the record or copy of the record accompanies a detainee if they are transferred to another police station. The record shall show the:

- time and reason for transfer;
- time a person is released from detention.

C:2.3A If a person is arrested and taken to a police station as a result of a search in the exercise of any stop and search power to which *PACE* Code A (stop and search) or the "search powers code" issued under *TACT* applies, the officer carrying out the search is responsible for ensuring that the record of that stop and search, is made as part of the person's custody record. The custody officer must then ensure that the person is asked if they want a copy of the search record and if they do, that they are given a copy as soon as practicable. The person's entitlement to a copy of the search record which is made as part of their custody record is in addition to, and does not affect, their entitlement to a copy of their custody record or any other provisions of section 2 (custody records) of this code. (See Code A, paragraph 4.2B, and the *TACT* search powers code, paragraph 5.3.5).

C:2.4 A solicitor or appropriate adult must be permitted to inspect a detainee's custody record as soon as practicable after their arrival at the station and at any other time whilst the person is detained. Arrangements for this access must be agreed with the custody officer and may not unreasonably interfere with the custody officer's duties.

C:2.4A When a detainee leaves police detention or is taken before a court they, their legal representative or appropriate adult shall be given, on request, a copy of the custody record as soon as practicable. This entitlement lasts for 12 months after release.

C:2.5 The detainee, appropriate adult or legal representative shall be permitted to inspect the original custody record after the detainee has left police detention provided they give reasonable notice of their request. Any such inspection shall be noted in the custody record.

C:2.6 Subject to paragraph 2.6A, all entries in custody records must be timed and signed by the maker. Records entered on computer shall be timed and contain the operator's identification.

C:2.6A Nothing in this code requires the identity of officers or other police staff to be recorded or disclosed:

(a) [*not used*];

(b) if the officer or police staff reasonably believe recording or disclosing their name might put them in danger.

In these cases, they shall use their warrant or other identification numbers and the name of their police station. See *Note 2A*.

C:2.7 The fact and time of any detainee's refusal to sign a custody record, when asked in accordance with this code, must be recorded.

Note for guidance

C:2A *The purpose of paragraph 2.6A(b) is to protect those involved in serious organised crime investigations or arrests of particularly violent suspects when there is reliable information that those arrested or their associates may threaten or cause harm to those involved. In cases of doubt, an officer of inspector rank or above should be consulted.* ★**A–45**

C:3 Initial action

(a) *Detained persons—normal procedure*

C:3.1 When a person is brought to a police station under arrest or arrested at the station having gone there voluntarily, the custody officer must make sure the person is told clearly about the following continuing rights which may be exercised at any stage during the period in custody: ★**A–46**

(i) the right to have someone informed of their arrest as in section 5;

(ii) the right to consult privately with a solicitor and that free independent legal advice is available;

(iii) the right to consult these codes of practice. See *Note 3D*.

C:3.2 The detainee must also be given:

- a written notice setting out:
  ~ the above three rights;

~ the arrangements for obtaining legal advice;

~ the right to a copy of the custody record as in paragraph 2.4A;

~ the caution in the terms prescribed in section 10;

● an additional written notice briefly setting out their entitlements while in custody. See *Notes 3A* and *3B*.

Note: the detainee shall be asked to sign the custody record to acknowledge receipt of these notices. Any refusal must be recorded on the custody record.

C:3.3 A citizen of an independent Commonwealth country or a national of a foreign country, including the Republic of Ireland, must be informed as soon as practicable about their rights of communication with their high commission, embassy or consulate. See section 7.

C:3.4 The custody officer shall:

● record the offence(s) that the detainee has been arrested for and the reason(s) for the arrest on the custody record; see paragraph 10.3 and Code G, paragraphs 2.2 and 4.3;

● note on the custody record any comment the detainee makes in relation to the arresting officer's account but shall not invite comment; if the arresting officer is not physically present when the detainee is brought to a police station, the arresting officer's account must be made available to the custody officer remotely or by a third party on the arresting officer's behalf; if the custody officer authorises a person's detention, subject to paragraph 1.8, that officer must record the grounds for detention in the detainee's presence and at the same time, inform them of the grounds; the detainee must be informed of the grounds for their detention before they are questioned about any offence;

● note any comment the detainee makes in respect of the decision to detain them but shall not invite comment;

● not put specific questions to the detainee regarding their involvement in any offence, nor in respect of any comments they may make in response to the arresting officer's account or the decision to place them in detention; such an exchange is likely to constitute an interview as in paragraph 11.1A and require the associated safeguards in section 11.

See paragraph 11.13 in respect of unsolicited comments.

C:3.5 The custody officer or other custody staff as directed by the custody officer shall:

(a) ask the detainee, whether at this time, they:

(i) would like legal advice, see paragraph 6.5;

(ii) want someone informed of their detention, see section 5;

(b) ask the detainee to sign the custody record to confirm their decisions in respect of (a);

(c) determine whether the detainee:

(i) is, or might be, in need of medical treatment or attention, see section 9;

(ii) requires:

● an appropriate adult;

● help to check documentation;

● an interpreter;

(d) record the decision in respect of (c).

Where any duties under this paragraph have been carried out by custody staff at the direction of the custody officer, the outcomes shall, as soon as practicable, be reported to the custody officer who retains overall responsibility for the detainee's care and treatment and ensuring that it complies with this code. See *Note 3F*.

C:3.6 When these needs are determined, the custody officer is responsible for initiating an assessment to consider whether the detainee is likely to present specific risks to custody staff or themselves. Such assessments should always include a check on the Police National Computer, to be carried out as soon as practicable, to identify any risks highlighted in relation to the detainee. Although such assessments are primarily the custody officer's responsibility, it may be necessary for them to consult and involve others, *e.g.* the arresting officer or an appropriate healthcare professional, see paragraph 9.13. Reasons for delaying the initiation or completion of the assessment must be recorded.

C:3.7 Chief officers should ensure that arrangements for proper and effective risk assessments required by paragraph 3.6 are implemented in respect of all detainees at police stations in their area.

C:3.8 Risk assessments must follow a structured process which clearly defines the categories of risk to be considered and the results must be incorporated in the detainee's custody record. The custody officer is responsible for making sure those responsible for the detainee's custody are appropriately briefed about the risks. If no specific risks are identified by the assessment, that should be noted in the custody record. See *Note 3E* and paragraph 9.14.

C:3.8A The content of any risk assessment and any analysis of the level of risk relating to the person's detention is not required to be shown or provided to the detainee or any person acting on behalf of the detainee. But information should not be withheld from any person acting on the detainee's behalf, for example, an appropriate adult, solicitor or interpreter, if to do so might put that person at risk.

C:3.9 The custody officer is responsible for implementing the response to any specific risk assessment, *e.g.*:

- reducing opportunities for self harm;
- calling an appropriate healthcare professional;
- increasing levels of monitoring or observation;
- reducing the risk to those who come into contact with the detainee.

See *Note 3E*.

C:3.10 Risk assessment is an ongoing process and assessments must always be subject to review if circumstances change.

C:3.11 If video cameras are installed in the custody area, notices shall be prominently displayed showing cameras are in use. Any request to have video cameras switched off shall be refused.

(b) *Detained persons—special groups*

C:3.12 If the detainee appears deaf or there is doubt about their hearing or speaking ability ★**A–47** or ability to understand English, and the custody officer cannot establish effective communication, the custody officer must, as soon as practicable, call an interpreter for assistance in the action under paragraphs 3.1–3.5. See section 13.

C:3.13 If the detainee is a juvenile, the custody officer must, if it is practicable, ascertain the identity of a person responsible for their welfare. That person:

- may be:
  - ~ the parent or guardian;
  - ~ if the juvenile is in local authority or voluntary organisation care, or is otherwise being looked after under the *Children Act* 1989, a person appointed by that authority or organisation to have responsibility for the juvenile's welfare;
  - ~ any other person who has, for the time being, assumed responsibility for the juvenile's welfare;
- must be informed as soon as practicable that the juvenile has been arrested, why they have been arrested and where they are detained. This right is in addition to the juvenile's right in section 5 not to be held incommunicado. See *Note 3C*.

C:3.14 If a juvenile is known to be subject to a court order under which a person or organisation is given any degree of statutory responsibility to supervise or otherwise monitor them, reasonable steps must also be taken to notify that person or organisation (the "responsible officer"). The responsible officer will normally be a member of a youth offending team, except for a curfew order which involves electronic monitoring when the contractor providing the monitoring will normally be the responsible officer.

C:3.15 If the detainee is a juvenile, mentally disordered or otherwise mentally vulnerable, the custody officer must, as soon as practicable:

- inform the appropriate adult, who in the case of a juvenile may or may not be a person responsible for their welfare, as in paragraph 3.13, of:
  - ~ the grounds for their detention;
  - ~ their whereabouts;
- ask the adult to come to the police station to see the detainee.

C:3.16 It is imperative that a mentally disordered or otherwise mentally vulnerable person, detained under the *Mental Health Act* 1983, s.136, be assessed as soon as possible. A police station should only be used as a place of safety as a last resort but if that assessment is to take place at the police station, an approved mental health professional and a registered medical practitioner shall be called to the station as soon as possible to carry it out. See *Note 9D*. The appropriate adult has no role in the assessment process and their presence is not required. Once the detainee has been assessed and suitable arrangements made for their treatment or care, they can no longer be detained under section 136. A detainee must be immediately discharged from detention under section 136 if a registered medical practitioner, having examined them, concludes they are not mentally disordered within the meaning of the Act.

C:3.17 If the appropriate adult is:

- already at the police station, the provisions of paragraphs 3.1 to 3.5 must be complied with in the appropriate adult's presence;
- not at the station when these provisions are complied with, they must be complied with again in the presence of the appropriate adult when they arrive.

C:3.18 The detainee shall be advised that:

- the duties of the appropriate adult include giving advice and assistance;
- they can consult privately with the appropriate adult at any time.

C:3.19 If the detainee, or appropriate adult on the detainee's behalf, asks for a solicitor to be called to give legal advice, the provisions of section 6 apply.

C:3.20 If the detainee is blind, seriously visually impaired or unable to read, the custody officer shall make sure their solicitor, relative, appropriate adult or some other person likely to take an interest in them and not involved in the investigation is available to help check any documentation. When this code requires written consent or signing the person assisting may be asked to sign instead, if the detainee prefers. This paragraph does not require an appropriate adult to be called solely to assist in checking and signing documentation for a person who is not a juvenile, or mentally disordered or otherwise mentally vulnerable (see paragraph 3.15).

(c) *Persons attending a police station or elsewhere voluntarily*

★**A–48**

C:3.21 Anybody attending a police station or other location (see paragraph 3.22) voluntarily to assist police with the investigation of an offence may leave at will unless arrested. See *Note 1K*. The person may only be prevented from leaving at will if their arrest on suspicion of committing the offence is necessary in accordance with Code G. See Code G, *Note 2G*.

If during an interview it is decided that their arrest is necessary, they must:

- be informed at once that they are under arrest and of the grounds and reasons as required by Code G, and
- be brought before the custody officer at the police station where they are arrested or, as the case may be, at the police station to which they are taken after being arrested elsewhere. The custody officer is then responsible for making sure that a custody record is opened and that they are notified of their rights in the same way as other detainees as required by this code.

If they are not arrested but are cautioned as in section 10, the person who gives the caution must, at the same time, inform them they are not under arrest, they are not obliged to remain at the station or other location but if they agree to remain, they may obtain free and independent legal advice if they want. They shall also be given a copy of the notice explaining the arrangements for obtaining legal advice and told that the right to legal advice includes the right to speak with a solicitor on the telephone and be asked if they want advice. If advice is requested, the interviewer is responsible for securing its provision without delay by contacting the defence solicitor call centre and for ensuring that the provisions of this code and Codes E and F concerning the conduct and recording of interviews of suspects are followed insofar as they can be applied to suspects who are not under arrest. See paragraph 3.2 and *Note 6B*.

C:3.22 If the other location mentioned in paragraph 3.21 is any place or premises for which the interviewer requires the person's informed consent to remain, for example, the person's home, then the references that the person is "not obliged to remain" and that they "may leave at will" mean that the person may also withdraw their consent and require the officer to leave.

(d) *Documentation*

C:3.23 The grounds for a person's detention shall be recorded, in the person's presence if practicable. See paragraph 1.8.

C:3.24 Action taken under paragraphs 3.12 to 3.20 shall be recorded.

(e) *Persons answering street bail*

C:3.25 When a person is answering street bail, the custody officer should link any documentation held in relation to arrest with the custody record. Any further action shall be recorded on the custody record in accordance with paragraphs 3.23 and 3.24 above.

Notes for guidance

C:3A *The notice of entitlements should:* ★A–49

- *list the entitlements in this code, including:*
  - ~ *visits and contact with outside parties, including special provisions for Commonwealth citizens and foreign nationals;*
  - ~ *reasonable standards of physical comfort;*
  - ~ *adequate food and drink;*
  - ~ *access to toilets and washing facilities, clothing, medical attention, and exercise when practicable;*
- *mention the:*
  - ~ *provisions relating to the conduct of interviews;*
  - ~ *circumstances in which an appropriate adult should be available to assist the detainee and their statutory rights to make representation whenever the period of their detention is reviewed.*

C:3B *In addition to notices in English, translations should be available in Welsh, the main minority ethnic languages and the principal European languages, whenever they are likely to be helpful. Audio versions of the notice should also be made available. Access to "easy read" illustrated versions should also be provided if they are available.*

C:3C *If the juvenile is in local authority or voluntary organisation care but living with their parents or other adults responsible for their welfare, although there is no legal obligation to inform them, they should normally be contacted, as well as the authority or organisation unless suspected of involvement in the offence concerned. Even if the juvenile is not living with their parents, consideration should be given to informing them.*

C:3D *The right to consult the codes of practice does not entitle the person concerned to delay unreasonably any necessary investigative or administrative action whilst they do so. Examples of action which need not be delayed unreasonably include:*

- *procedures requiring the provision of breath, blood or urine specimens under the* Road Traffic Act *1988 or the* Transport and Works Act *1992;*
- *searching detainees at the police station;*
- *taking fingerprints, footwear impressions or non-intimate samples without consent for evidential purposes.*

C:3E *Home Office Circular 32/2000 and the Guidance on the Safer Detention and Handling of Persons in Police Custody Second Edition (2012) produced on behalf of the Association of Chief Police Officers provide more detailed guidance on risk assessments and identify key risk areas which should always be considered.*

C:3F *A custody officer or other officer who, in accordance with this code, allows or directs the carrying out of any task or action relating to a detainee's care, treatment, rights and entitlements to another officer or any police staff must be satisfied that the officer or police staff concerned are suitable, trained and competent to carry out the task or action in question.*

C:4 Detainee's property

(a) *Action*

C:4.1 The custody officer is responsible for: ★A–50

- (a) ascertaining what property a detainee:
  - (i) has with them when they come to the police station, whether on:
    - arrest or re-detention on answering to bail;
    - commitment to prison custody on the order or sentence of a court;
    - lodgement at the police station with a view to their production in court from prison custody;
    - transfer from detention at another station or hospital;
    - detention under the *Mental Health Act* 1983, s.135 or 136;
    - remand into police custody on the authority of a court;
  - (ii) might have acquired for an unlawful or harmful purpose while in custody;
- (b) the safekeeping of any property taken from a detainee which remains at the police station.

The custody officer may search the detainee or authorise their being searched to the extent they consider necessary, provided a search of intimate parts of the body or involving the removal of more than outer clothing is only made as in Annex A. A search may only be carried out by an officer of the same sex as the detainee. See *Note 4A* and Annex L.

C:4.2 Detainees may retain clothing and personal effects at their own risk unless the custody officer considers they may use them to cause harm to themselves or others, interfere with evidence, damage property, effect an escape or they are needed as evidence. In this event the custody officer may withhold such articles as they consider necessary and must tell the detainee why.

C:4.3 Personal effects are those items a detainee may lawfully need, use or refer to while in detention but do not include cash and other items of value.

(b) *Documentation*

C:4.4 It is a matter for the custody officer to determine whether a record should be made of the property a detained person has with him or had taken from him on arrest. Any record made is not required to be kept as part of the custody record but the custody record should be noted as to where such a record exists. Whenever a record is made the detainee shall be allowed to check and sign the record of property as correct. Any refusal to sign shall be recorded.

C:4.5 If a detainee is not allowed to keep any article of clothing or personal effects, the reason must be recorded.

Notes for guidance

★**A–51**   **C:4A** *PACE, s.54(1), and paragraph 4.1 require a detainee to be searched when it is clear the custody officer will have continuing duties in relation to that detainee or when that detainee's behaviour or offence makes an inventory appropriate. They do not require every detainee to be searched, e.g. if it is clear a person will only be detained for a short period and is not to be placed in a cell, the custody officer may decide not to search them. In such a case the custody record will be endorsed "not searched", paragraph 4.4 will not apply, and the detainee will be invited to sign the entry. If the detainee refuses, the custody officer will be obliged to ascertain what property they have in accordance with paragraph 4.1.*

C:4B *Paragraph 4.4 does not require the custody officer to record on the custody record property in the detainee's possession on arrest if, by virtue of its nature, quantity or size, it is not practicable to remove it to the police station.*

C:4C *Paragraph 4.4 does not require items of clothing worn by the person be recorded unless withheld by the custody officer as in paragraph 4.2.*

C:5 Right not to be held incommunicado

(a) *Action*

★**A–52**   **C:5.1** Subject to paragraph 5.7B, any person arrested and held in custody at a police station or other premises may, on request, have one person known to them or likely to take an interest in their welfare informed at public expense of their whereabouts as soon as practicable. If the person cannot be contacted the detainee may choose up to two alternatives. If they cannot be contacted, the person in charge of detention or the investigation has discretion to allow further attempts until the information has been conveyed. See *Notes 5C* and *5D*.

C:5.2 The exercise of the above right in respect of each person nominated may be delayed only in accordance with Annex B.

C:5.3 The above right may be exercised each time a detainee is taken to another police station.

C:5.4 If the detainee agrees, they may at the custody officer's discretion, receive visits from friends, family or others likely to take an interest in their welfare, or in whose welfare the detainee has an interest. See *Note 5B*.

C:5.5 If a friend, relative or person with an interest in the detainee's welfare enquires about their whereabouts, this information shall be given if the suspect agrees and Annex B does not apply. See *Note 5D*.

C:5.6 The detainee shall be given writing materials, on request, and allowed to telephone one person for a reasonable time, see *Notes 5A* and *5E*. Either or both these privileges may be denied or delayed if an officer of inspector rank or above considers sending a letter or making a telephone call may result in any of the consequences in:

     (a) Annex B, paragraphs 1 and 2 and the person is detained in connection with an indictable offence;

     (b) [*not used*].

Nothing in this paragraph permits the restriction or denial of the rights in paragraphs 5.1 and 6.1.

C:5.7 Before any letter or message is sent, or telephone call made, the detainee shall be informed that what they say in any letter, call or message (other than in a communication to a solicitor) may be read or listened to and may be given in evidence. A telephone call may be terminated if it is being abused. The costs can be at public expense at the custody officer's discretion.

C:5.7A Any delay or denial of the rights in this section should be proportionate and should last no longer than necessary.

C:5.7B In the case of a person in police custody for specific purposes and periods in accordance with a direction under the *Crime (Sentences) Act* 1997, Sched. 1 (productions from prison etc.), the exercise of the rights in this section shall be subject to any additional conditions specified in the direction for the purpose of regulating the detainee's contact and communication with others whilst in police custody. See *Note 5F.*

(b) *Documentation*

C:5.8 A record must be kept of any:
- (a) request made under this section and the action taken;
- (b) letters, messages or telephone calls made or received or visit received;
- (c) refusal by the detainee to have information about them given to an outside enquirer. The detainee must be asked to countersign the record accordingly and any refusal recorded.

Notes for guidance

C:5A *A person may request an interpreter to interpret a telephone call or translate a letter.* ★**A–53**

C:5B *At the custody officer's discretion and subject to the detainee's consent, visits should be allowed when possible, subject to having sufficient personnel to supervise a visit and any possible hindrance to the investigation.*

C:5C *If the detainee does not know anyone to contact for advice or support or cannot contact a friend or relative, the custody officer should bear in mind any local voluntary bodies or other organisations who might be able to help. Paragraph 6.1 applies if legal advice is required.*

C:5D *In some circumstances it may not be appropriate to use the telephone to disclose information under paragraphs 5.1 and 5.5.*

C:5E *The telephone call at paragraph 5.6 is in addition to any communication under paragraphs 5.1 and 6.1.*

C:5F *Prison Service Order 1801 (production of prisoners at the request of police) provides detailed guidance and instructions for police officers and governors and directors of prisons regarding applications for prisoners to be transferred to police custody and their safe custody and treatments while in police custody.*

C:6 Right to legal advice

(a) *Action*

C:6.1 Unless Annex B applies, all detainees must be informed that they may at any time ★**A–54** consult and communicate privately with a solicitor, whether in person, in writing or by telephone, and that free independent legal advice is available. See paragraph 3.1, *Notes 1I, 6B* and *6J.*

C:6.2 [*Not used.*]

C:6.3 A poster advertising the right to legal advice must be prominently displayed in the charging area of every police station. See *Note 6H.*

C:6.4 No police officer should, at any time, do or say anything with the intention of dissuading any person who is entitled to legal advice in accordance with this code, whether or not they have been arrested and are detained, from obtaining legal advice. See *Note 6ZA.*

C:6.5 The exercise of the right of access to legal advice may be delayed only as in Annex B. Whenever legal advice is requested, and unless Annex B applies, the custody officer must act without delay to secure the provision of such advice. If the detainee has the right to speak to a solicitor in person but declines to exercise the right the officer should point out that the right includes the right to speak with a solicitor on the telephone. If the detainee continues to waive this right, or a detainee whose right to free legal advice is limited to telephone advice from the Criminal Defence Service (CDS) Direct (see *Note 6B*) declines to exercise that right, the officer should ask them why and any reasons should be recorded on the custody record or the interview record as appropriate. Reminders of the right to legal advice must be given as in paragraphs 3.5, 11.2, 15.4, 16.4, 2B of Annex A, 3 of Annex K and 16.5 of this code and Code D, paragraphs 3.17(ii) and 6.3. Once it is clear a detainee does not want to speak to a solicitor in person or by telephone they should cease to be asked their reasons. See *Note 6K.*

C:6.5A In the case of a person who is a juvenile or is mentally disordered or otherwise mentally vulnerable, an appropriate adult should consider whether legal advice from a solicitor is required. If the person indicates that they do not want legal advice, the appropriate adult has the right to ask for a solicitor to attend if this would be in the best interests of the person. However, the person cannot be forced to see the solicitor if they are adamant that they do not wish to do so.

C:6.6 A detainee who wants legal advice may not be interviewed or continue to be interviewed until they have received such advice unless:

> (a) Annex B applies, when the restriction on drawing adverse inferences from silence in Annex C will apply because the detainee is not allowed an opportunity to consult a solicitor; or
>
> (b) an officer of superintendent rank or above has reasonable grounds for believing that:
>
>> (i) the consequent delay might:
>>
>>> • lead to interference with, or harm to, evidence connected with an offence;
>>> • lead to interference with, or physical harm to, other people;
>>> • lead to serious loss of, or damage to, property;
>>> • lead to alerting other people suspected of having committed an offence but not yet arrested for it;
>>> • hinder the recovery of property obtained in consequence of the commission of an offence; see *Note 6A*;
>>
>> (ii) when a solicitor, including a duty solicitor, has been contacted and has agreed to attend, awaiting their arrival would cause unreasonable delay to the process of investigation;
>>
>> note: in these cases the restriction on drawing adverse inferences from silence in Annex C will apply because the detainee is not allowed an opportunity to consult a solicitor;
>
> (c) the solicitor the detainee has nominated or selected from a list:
>
>> (i) cannot be contacted;
>> (ii) has previously indicated they do not wish to be contacted; or
>> (iii) having been contacted, has declined to attend; and
>>
>>> • the detainee has been advised of the duty solicitor scheme but has declined to ask for the duty solicitor;
>>> • in these circumstances the interview may be started or continued without further delay provided an officer of inspector rank or above has agreed to the interview proceeding;
>>
>> note: the restriction on drawing adverse inferences from silence in Annex C will not apply because the detainee is allowed an opportunity to consult the duty solicitor;
>
> (d) the detainee changes their mind about wanting legal advice or (as the case may be) about wanting a solicitor present at the interview and states that they no longer wish to speak to a solicitor; in these circumstances, the interview may be started or continued without delay provided that:
>
>> (i) an officer of inspector rank or above:
>>
>>> • speaks to the detainee to enquire about the reasons for their change of mind (see *Note 6K*), and
>>> • makes, or directs the making of, reasonable efforts to ascertain the solicitor's expected time of arrival and to inform the solicitor that the suspect has stated that they wish to change their mind and the reason (if given);
>>
>> (ii) the detainee's reason for their change of mind (if given) and the outcome of the action in (i) are recorded in the custody record;
>>
>> (iii) the detainee, after being informed of the outcome of the action in (i) above, confirms in writing that they want the interview to proceed without speaking or further speaking to a solicitor or (as the case may be) without a solicitor being present and do not wish to wait for a solicitor by signing an entry to this effect in the custody record;
>>
>> (iv) an officer of inspector rank or above is satisfied that it is proper for the interview to proceed in these circumstances and:
>>
>>> • gives authority in writing for the interview to proceed and if the authority is not recorded in the custody record, the officer must ensure that the custody record shows the date and time of authority and where it is recorded, and

- takes or directs the taking of, reasonable steps to inform the solicitor that the authority has been given and the time when the interview is expected to commence, and records or causes to be recorded, the outcome of this action in the custody record;

(v) when the interview starts and the interviewer reminds the suspect of their right to legal advice (see paragraph 11.2, Code E, paragraph 4.5, and Code F, paragraph 4.5), the interviewer shall then ensure that the following is recorded in the written interview record or the interview record made in accordance with Code E or F:

- confirmation that the detainee has changed their mind about wanting legal advice or (as the case may be) about wanting a solicitor present and the reasons for it if given;
- the fact that authority for the interview to proceed has been given and, subject to paragraph 2.6A, the name of the authorising officer;
- that if the solicitor arrives at the station before the interview is completed, the detainee will be so informed without delay and a break will be taken to allow them to speak to the solicitor if they wish, unless paragraph 6.6(a) applies; and
- that at any time during the interview, the detainee may again ask for legal advice and that if they do, a break will be taken to allow them to speak to the solicitor, unless paragraph 6.6(a), (b), or (c) applies;

note: in these circumstances, the restriction on drawing adverse inferences from silence in Annex C will not apply because the detainee is allowed an opportunity to consult a solicitor if they wish.

C:6.7 If paragraph 6.6(a) applies, where the reason for authorising the delay ceases to apply, ★**A–55**
there may be no further delay in permitting the exercise of the right in the absence of a further authorisation unless paragraph 6.6(b), (c) or (d) applies. If paragraph 6.6(b)(i) applies, once sufficient information has been obtained to avert the risk, questioning must cease until the detainee has received legal advice unless paragraph 6.6(a), (b)(ii), (c) or (d) applies.

C:6.8 A detainee who has been permitted to consult a solicitor shall be entitled on request to have the solicitor present when they are interviewed unless one of the exceptions in paragraph 6.6 applies.

C:6.9 The solicitor may only be required to leave the interview if their conduct is such that the interviewer is unable properly to put questions to the suspect. See *Notes 6D* and *6E.*

C:6.10 If the interviewer considers a solicitor is acting in such a way, they will stop the interview and consult an officer not below superintendent rank, if one is readily available, and otherwise an officer not below inspector rank not connected with the investigation. After speaking to the solicitor, the officer consulted will decide if the interview should continue in the presence of that solicitor. If they decide it should not, the suspect will be given the opportunity to consult another solicitor before the interview continues and that solicitor given an opportunity to be present at the interview. See *Note 6E.*

C:6.11 The removal of a solicitor from an interview is a serious step and, if it occurs, the officer of superintendent rank or above who took the decision will consider if the incident should be reported to the Solicitors Regulation Authority. If the decision to remove the solicitor has been taken by an officer below superintendent rank, the facts must be reported to an officer of superintendent rank or above who will similarly consider whether a report to the Solicitors Regulation Authority would be appropriate. When the solicitor concerned is a duty solicitor, the report should be both to the Solicitors Regulation Authority and to the Legal Services Commission.

C:6.12 "Solicitor" in this code means:

- a solicitor who holds a current practising certificate;
- an accredited or probationary representative included on the register of representatives maintained by the Legal Services Commission.

C:6.12A An accredited or probationary representative sent to provide advice by, and on behalf of, a solicitor shall be admitted to the police station for this purpose unless an officer of inspector rank or above considers such a visit will hinder the investigation and directs otherwise. Hindering the investigation does not include giving proper legal advice to a detainee as in *Note 6D.* Once admitted to the police station, paragraphs 6.6 to 6.10 apply.

C:6.13 In exercising their discretion under paragraph 6.12A, the officer should take into account in particular:

● whether:

~ the identity and status of an accredited or probationary representative have been satisfactorily established;

~ they are of suitable character to provide legal advice, *e.g.* a person with a criminal record is unlikely to be suitable unless the conviction was for a minor offence and not recent;

● any other matters in any written letter of authorisation provided by the solicitor on whose behalf the person is attending the police station. See *Note 6F.*

C:6.14 If the inspector refuses access to an accredited or probationary representative or a decision is taken that such a person should not be permitted to remain at an interview, the inspector must notify the solicitor on whose behalf the representative was acting and give them an opportunity to make alternative arrangements. The detainee must be informed and the custody record noted.

C:6.15 If a solicitor arrives at the station to see a particular person, that person must, unless Annex B applies, be so informed whether or not they are being interviewed and asked if they would like to see the solicitor. This applies even if the detainee has declined legal advice or, having requested it, subsequently agreed to be interviewed without receiving advice. The solicitor's attendance and the detainee's decision must be noted in the custody record.

(b) *Documentation*

C:6.16 Any request for legal advice and the action taken shall be recorded.

C:6.17 A record shall be made in the interview record if a detainee asks for legal advice and an interview is begun either in the absence of a solicitor or their representative, or they have been required to leave an interview.

Notes for guidance

★**A–56**   **C:**6ZA *No police officer or police staff shall indicate to any suspect, except to answer a direct question, that period for which they are liable to be detained, or if not detained, the time taken to complete the interview, might be reduced:*

● *if they do not ask for legal advice or do not want a solicitor present when they are interviewed; or*

● *if they have asked for legal advice or (as the case may be) asked for a solicitor to be present when they are interviewed but change their mind and agree to be interviewed without waiting for a solicitor.*

C:6A *In considering if paragraph 6.6(b) applies, the officer should, if practicable, ask the solicitor for an estimate of how long it will take to come to the station and relate this to the time detention is permitted, the time of day (i.e. whether the rest period under paragraph 12.2 is imminent) and the requirements of other investigations. If the solicitor is on their way or is to set off immediately, it will not normally be appropriate to begin an interview before they arrive. If it appears necessary to begin an interview before the solicitor's arrival, they should be given an indication of how long the police would be able to wait before 6.6(b) applies so there is an opportunity to make arrangements for someone else to provide legal advice.*

C:6B *A detainee has a right to free legal advice and to be represented by a solicitor. This note for guidance explains the arrangements which enable detainees to obtain legal advice. An outline of these arrangements is also included in the Notice of Rights and Entitlements given to detainees in accordance with paragraph 3.2. The arrangements also apply, with appropriate modifications, to persons attending a police station or other location voluntarily who are cautioned prior to being interviewed. See paragraph 3.21.*

When a detainee asks for free legal advice, the Defence Solicitor Call Centre (DSCC) must be informed of the request.

Free legal advice will be limited to telephone advice provided by CDS Direct if a detainee is:

● *detained for a non-imprisonable offence;*

● *arrested on a bench warrant for failing to appear and being held for production at court (except where the solicitor has clear documentary evidence available that would result in the client being released from custody);*

● *arrested for drink driving (driving/in charge with excess alcohol, failing to provide a specimen, driving/in charge whilst unfit through drink); or*

● *detained in relation to breach of police or court bail conditions;*

unless one or more exceptions apply, in which case the DSCC should arrange for advice to be given by a solicitor at the police station, for example:

● *the police want to interview the detainee or carry out an eye-witness identification procedure;*

● *the detainee needs an appropriate adult;*

● *the detainee is unable to communicate over the telephone;*

- *the detainee alleges serious misconduct by the police;*
- *the investigation includes another offence not included in the list;*
- *the solicitor to be assigned is already at the police station.*

When free advice is not limited to telephone advice, a detainee can ask for free advice from a solicitor they know or if they do not know a solicitor or the solicitor they know cannot be contacted, from the duty solicitor.

To arrange free legal advice, the police should telephone the DSCC. The call centre will decide whether legal advice should be limited to telephone advice from CDS Direct, or whether a solicitor known to the detainee or the duty solicitor should speak to the detainee.

When a detainee wants to pay for legal advice themselves:

- *the DSCC will contact a solicitor of their choice on their behalf;*
- *they may, when free advice is only available by telephone from CDS Direct, still speak to a solicitor of their choice on the telephone for advice, but the solicitor would not be paid by legal aid and may ask the person to pay for the advice;*
- *they should be given an opportunity to consult a specific solicitor or another solicitor from that solicitor's firm; if this solicitor is not available, they may choose up to two alternatives; if these alternatives are not available, the custody officer has discretion to allow further attempts until a solicitor has been contacted and agreed to provide advice;*
- *they are entitled to a private consultation with their chosen solicitor on the telephone or the solicitor may decide to come to the police station;*
- *if their chosen solicitor cannot be contacted, the DSCC may still be called to arrange free legal advice.*

Apart from carrying out duties necessary to implement these arrangements, an officer must not advise the suspect about any particular firm of solicitors.

C:6C *[Not used.]*

C:6D *The solicitor's only role in the police station is to protect and advance the legal rights of their client. On occasions this may require the solicitor to give advice which has the effect of the client avoiding giving evidence which strengthens a prosecution case. The solicitor may intervene in order to seek clarification, challenge an improper question to their client or the manner in which it is put, advise their client not to reply to particular questions, or if they wish to give their client further legal advice. Paragraph 6.9 only applies if the solicitor's approach or conduct prevents or unreasonably obstructs proper questions being put to the suspect or the suspect's response being recorded. Examples of unacceptable conduct include answering questions on a suspect's behalf or providing written replies for the suspect to quote.*

C:6E *An officer who takes the decision to exclude a solicitor must be in a position to satisfy the court the decision was properly made. In order to do this they may need to witness what is happening.*

C:6F *If an officer of at least inspector rank considers a particular solicitor or firm of solicitors is persistently sending probationary representatives who are unsuited to provide legal advice, they should inform an officer of at least superintendent rank, who may wish to take the matter up with the Solicitors Regulation Authority.*

C:6G *Subject to the constraints of Annex B, a solicitor may advise more than one client in an investigation if they wish. Any question of a conflict of interest is for the solicitor under their professional code of conduct. If, however, waiting for a solicitor to give advice to one client may lead to unreasonable delay to the interview with another, the provisions of paragraph 6.6(b) may apply.*

★A–57

C:6H *In addition to a poster in English, a poster or posters containing translations into Welsh, the main minority ethnic languages and the principal European languages should be displayed wherever they are likely to be helpful and it is practicable to do so.*

C:6I *[Not used.]*

C:6J *Whenever a detainee exercises their right to legal advice by consulting or communicating with a solicitor, they must be allowed to do so in private. This right to consult or communicate in private is fundamental. If the requirement for privacy is compromised because what is said or written by the detainee or solicitor for the purpose of giving and receiving legal advice is overheard, listened to, or read by others without the informed consent of the detainee, the right will effectively have been denied. When a detainee speaks to a solicitor on the telephone, they should be allowed to do so in private unless this is impractical because of the design and layout of the custody area or the location of telephones. However, the normal expectation should be that facilities will be available, unless they are being used, at all police stations to enable detainees to speak in private to a solicitor either face to face or over the telephone.*

C:6K *A detainee is not obliged to give reasons for declining legal advice and should not be pressed to do so.*

C:7 Citizens of independent Commonwealth countries or foreign nationals

(a) *Action*

★**A–58**   **C:**7.1 A detainee who is a citizen of an independent Commonwealth country or a national of a foreign country, including the Republic of Ireland, has the right, upon request, to communicate at any time with the appropriate high commission, embassy or consulate. That detainee must be informed as soon as practicable of this right and asked if they want to have their high commission, embassy or consulate told of their whereabouts and the grounds for their detention. Such a request should be acted upon as soon as practicable. See *Note 7A.*

C:7.2 A detainee who is is a citizen of a country with which a bilateral consular convention or agreement is in force requiring notification of arrest, must also be informed that subject to paragraph 7.4, notification of their arrest will be sent to the appropriate high commission, embassy or consulate as soon as practicable, whether or not they request it. Details of the countries to which this requirement currently applies are available from:

http://www.fco.gov.uk/en/publications-and-documents/treaties/treaty-texts/prisoner-transfer-agreements.

C:7.3 Consular officers may, if the detainee agrees, visit one of their nationals in police detention to talk to them and, if required, to arrange for legal advice. Such visits shall take place out of the hearing of a police officer.

C:7.4 Notwithstanding the provisions of consular conventions, if the detainee claims that they are a refugee or have applied or intend to apply for asylum, the custody officer must ensure that the UK Border Agency (UKBA) is informed as soon as practicable of the claim. UKBA will then determine whether compliance with relevant international obligations requires notification of the arrest to be sent and will inform the custody officer as to what action police need to take.

(b) *Documentation*

★**A–59**   **C:**7.5 A record shall be made:

- when a detainee is informed of their rights under this section and of any requirement in paragraph 7.2;
- of any communications with a high commission, embassy or consulate; and
- of any communications with UKBA about a detainee's claim to be a refugee or to be seeking asylum and the resulting action taken by police.

Note for guidance

★**A–60**   **C:**7A *The exercise of the rights in this section may not be interfered with even though Annex B applies.*

C:8 Conditions of detention

(a) *Action*

★**A–61**   **C:**8.1 So far as it is practicable, not more than one detainee should be detained in each cell. See *Note 8C.*

C:8.2 Cells in use must be adequately heated, cleaned and ventilated. They must be adequately lit, subject to such dimming as is compatible with safety and security to allow people detained overnight to sleep. No additional restraints shall be used within a locked cell unless absolutely necessary and then only restraint equipment, approved for use in that force by the chief officer, which is reasonable and necessary in the circumstances having regard to the detainee's demeanour and with a view to ensuring their safety and the safety of others. If a detainee is deaf, mentally disordered or otherwise mentally vulnerable, particular care must be taken when deciding whether to use any form of approved restraints.

C:8.3 Blankets, mattresses, pillows and other bedding supplied shall be of a reasonable standard and in a clean and sanitary condition. See *Note 8A.*

C:8.4 Access to toilet and washing facilities must be provided.

C:8.5 If it is necessary to remove a detainee's clothes for the purposes of investigation, for hygiene, health reasons or cleaning, replacement clothing of a reasonable standard of comfort and cleanliness shall be provided. A detainee may not be interviewed unless adequate clothing has been offered.

C:8.6 At least two light meals and one main meal should be offered in any 24 hour period. See *Note 8B.* Drinks should be provided at meal times and upon reasonable request between meals. Whenever necessary, advice shall be sought from the appropriate healthcare professional, see *Note 9A,* on medical and dietary matters. As far as practicable, meals provided shall offer a varied diet and meet any specific dietary needs or religious beliefs the detainee may have. The detainee may, at the custody officer's discretion, have meals supplied by their family or friends at their expense. See *Note 8A*.

C:8.7 Brief outdoor exercise shall be offered daily if practicable.

C:8.8 A juvenile shall not be placed in a police cell unless no other secure accommodation is available and the custody officer considers it is not practicable to supervise them if they are not placed in a cell or that a cell provides more comfortable accommodation than other secure accommodation in the station. A juvenile may not be placed in a cell with a detained adult.

(b) *Documentation*

C:8.9 A record must be kept of replacement clothing and meals offered. ★**A–62**

C:8.10 If a juvenile is placed in a cell, the reason must be recorded.

C:8.11 The use of any restraints on a detainee whilst in a cell, the reasons for it and, if appropriate, the arrangements for enhanced supervision of the detainee whilst so restrained, shall be recorded. See paragraph 3.9.

Notes for guidance

C:8A *The provisions in paragraph 8.3 and 8.6 respectively are of particular importance in the case of a* ★**A–63** *person likely to be detained for an extended period. In deciding whether to allow meals to be supplied by family or friends, the custody officer is entitled to take account of the risk of items being concealed in any food or package and the officer's duties and responsibilities under food handling legislation.*

C:8B *Meals should, so far as practicable, be offered at recognised meal times, or at other times that take account of when the detainee last had a meal.*

C:8C *Guidance on the Safer Detention and Handling of Persons in Police Custody Second Edition (2012) produced on behalf of the Association of Chief Police Officers by the [sic] provides more detailed guidance on matters concerning detainee healthcare and treatment and associated forensic issues which should be read in conjunction with sections 8 and 9 of this code.*

C:9 Care and treatment of detained persons

(a) *General*

C:9.1 Nothing in this section prevents the police from calling an appropriate healthcare ★**A–64** professional to examine a detainee for the purposes of obtaining evidence relating to any offence in which the detainee is suspected of being involved. See *Notes 9A* and *8C*.

C:9.2 If a complaint is made by, or on behalf of, a detainee about their treatment since their arrest, or it comes to notice that a detainee may have been treated improperly, a report must be made as soon as practicable to an officer of inspector rank or above not connected with the investigation. If the matter concerns a possible assault or the possibility of the unnecessary or unreasonable use of force, an appropriate healthcare professional must also be called as soon as practicable.

C:9.3 Detainees should be visited at least every hour. If no reasonably foreseeable risk was identified in a risk assessment, see paragraphs 3.6–3.10, there is no need to wake a sleeping detainee. Those suspected of being under the influence of drink or drugs or both or of having swallowed drugs, see *Note 9CA*, or whose level of consciousness causes concern must, subject to any clinical directions given by the appropriate healthcare professional, see paragraph 9.13:

- be visited and roused at least every half hour;
- have their condition assessed as in Annex H;
- and clinical treatment arranged if appropriate.

See *Notes 9B, 9C* and *9H*.

C:9.4 When arrangements are made to secure clinical attention for a detainee, the custody officer must make sure all relevant information which might assist in the treatment of the detainee's condition is made available to the responsible healthcare professional. This applies whether or not the healthcare professional asks for such information. Any officer or police staff with relevant information must inform the custody officer as soon as practicable.

(b) *Clinical treatment and attention*

C:9.5 The custody officer must make sure a detainee receives appropriate clinical attention as ★**A–65** soon as reasonably practicable if the person:

(a) appears to be suffering from physical illness; or

(b) is injured; or

(c) appears to be suffering from a mental disorder; or

(d) appears to need clinical attention.

C:9.5A This applies even if the detainee makes no request for clinical attention and whether or not they have already received clinical attention elsewhere. If the need for attention appears urgent, *e.g.* when indicated as in Annex H, the nearest available healthcare professional or an ambulance must be called immediately.

C:9.5B The custody officer must also consider the need for clinical attention as set out in *Note for Guidance 9C* in relation to those suffering the effects of alcohol or drugs.

C:9.6 Paragraph 9.5 is not meant to prevent or delay the transfer to a hospital if necessary of a person detained under the *Mental Health Act* 1983, s.136. See *Note 9D*. When an assessment under that Act is to take place at a police station, see paragraph 3.16, the custody officer must consider whether an appropriate healthcare professional should be called to conduct an initial clinical check on the detainee. This applies particularly when there is likely to be any significant delay in the arrival of a suitably qualified medical practitioner.

C:9.7 If it appears to the custody officer, or they are told, that a person brought to a station under arrest may be suffering from an infectious disease or condition, the custody officer must take reasonable steps to safeguard the health of the detainee and others at the station. In deciding what action to take, advice must be sought from an appropriate healthcare professional. See *Note 9E*. The custody officer has discretion to isolate the person and their property until clinical directions have been obtained.

★**A–66**

C:9.8 If a detainee requests a clinical examination, an appropriate healthcare professional must be called as soon as practicable to assess the detainee's clinical needs. If a safe and appropriate care plan cannot be provided, the appropriate healthcare professional's advice must be sought. The detainee may also be examined by a medical practitioner of their choice at their expense.

C:9.9 If a detainee is required to take or apply any medication in compliance with clinical directions prescribed before their detention, the custody officer must consult the appropriate healthcare professional before the use of the medication. Subject to the restrictions in paragraph 9.10, the custody officer is responsible for the safekeeping of any medication and for making sure the detainee is given the opportunity to take or apply prescribed or approved medication. Any such consultation and its outcome shall be noted in the custody record.

C:9.10 No police officer may administer or supervise the self-administration of medically prescribed controlled drugs of the types and forms listed in the *Misuse of Drugs Regulations* 2001, Sched. 2 or 3. A detainee may only self-administer such drugs under the personal supervision of the registered medical practitioner authorising their use or other appropriate healthcare professional. The custody officer may supervise the self-administration of, or authorise other custody staff to supervise the self-administration of, drugs listed in Schedule 4 or 5 for self-administration if the officer has consulted the appropriate healthcare professional authorising their use and both are satisfied self-administration will not expose the detainee, police officers or anyone else to the risk of harm or injury.

C:9.11 When appropriate healthcare professionals administer drugs or authorise the use of other medications, supervise their self-administration or consult with the custody officer about allowing self-administration of drugs listed in Schedule 4 or 5, it must be within current medicines legislation and the scope of practice as determined by their relevant statutory regulatory body.

C:9.12 If a detainee has in their possession, or claims to need, medication relating to a heart condition, diabetes, epilepsy or a condition of comparable potential seriousness then, even though paragraph 9.5 may not apply, the advice of the appropriate healthcare professional must be obtained.

C:9.13 Whenever the appropriate healthcare professional is called in accordance with this section to examine or treat a detainee, the custody officer shall ask for their opinion about:

- any risks or problems which police need to take into account when making decisions about the detainee's continued detention;
- when to carry out an interview if applicable; and
- the need for safeguards.

C:9.14 When clinical directions are given by the appropriate healthcare professional, whether orally or in writing, and the custody officer has any doubts or is in any way uncertain about any aspect of the directions, the custody officer shall ask for clarification. It is particularly important that directions concerning the frequency of visits are clear, precise and capable of being implemented. See *Note 9F*.

(c) *Documentation*

C:9.15 A record must be made in the custody record of: ★**A–67**

    (a) the arrangements made for an examination by an appropriate healthcare professional under paragraph 9.2 and of any complaint reported under that paragraph together with any relevant remarks by the custody officer;

    (b) any arrangements made in accordance with paragraph 9.5;

    (c) any request for a clinical examination under paragraph 9.8 and any arrangements made in response;

    (d) the injury, ailment, condition or other reason which made it necessary to make the arrangements in (a) to (c); see *Note 9G*;

    (e) any clinical directions and advice, including any further clarifications, given to police by a healthcare professional concerning the care and treatment of the detainee in connection with any of the arrangements made in (a) to (c); see *Notes E* and *9F*;

    (f) if applicable, the responses received when attempting to rouse a person using the procedure in Annex H. See *Note 9H*.

C:9.16 If a healthcare professional does not record their clinical findings in the custody record, the record must show where they are recorded. See *Note 9G*. However, information which is necessary to custody staff to ensure the effective ongoing care and well-being of the detainee must be recorded openly in the custody record, see paragraph 3.8 and Annex G, paragraph 7.

C:9.17 Subject to the requirements of section 4, the custody record shall include:

    • a record of all medication a detainee has in their possession on arrival at the police station;

    • a note of any such medication they claim to need but do not have with them.

Notes for guidance

C:9A *A "healthcare professional" means a clinically qualified person working within the scope of practice* ★**A–68** *as determined by their relevant statutory regulatory body. Whether a healthcare professional is "appropriate" depends on the circumstances of the duties they carry out at the time.*

C:9B *Whenever possible juveniles and mentally vulnerable detainees should be visited more frequently.*

C:9C *A detainee who appears drunk or behaves abnormally may be suffering from illness, the effects of drugs or may have sustained injury, particularly a head injury which is not apparent. A detainee needing or dependent on certain drugs, including alcohol, may experience harmful effects within a short time of being deprived of their supply. In these circumstances, when there is any doubt, police should always act urgently to call an appropriate healthcare professional or an ambulance. Paragraph 9.5 does not apply to minor ailments or injuries which do not need attention. However, all such ailments or injuries must be recorded in the custody record and any doubt must be resolved in favour of calling the appropriate healthcare professional.*

C:9CA *Paragraph 9.3 would apply to a person in police custody by order of a magistrates' court under the* Criminal Justice Act *1988, s.152 (as amended by the* Drugs Act *2005, s.8) to facilitate the recovery of evidence after being charged with drug possession or drug trafficking and suspected of having swallowed drugs. In the case of the healthcare needs of a person who has swallowed drugs, the custody officer subject to any clinical directions, should consider the necessity for rousing every half hour. This does not negate the need for regular visiting of the suspect in the cell.*

C:9D *Whenever practicable, arrangements should be made for persons detained for assessment under the* Mental Health Act *1983, s.136 to be taken to a hospital. Chapter 10 of the Mental Health Act 1983 Code of Practice (as revised) provides more detailed guidance about arranging assessments under section 136 and transferring detainees from police stations to other places of safety.*

C:9E *It is important to respect a person's right to privacy and information about their health must be kept confidential and only disclosed with their consent or in accordance with clinical advice when it is necessary to protect the detainee's health or that of others who come into contact with them.*

C:9F *The custody officer should always seek to clarify directions that the detainee requires constant observation or supervision and should ask the appropriate healthcare professional to explain precisely what action needs to be taken to implement such directions.*

C:9G *Paragraphs 9.15 and 9.16 do not require any information about the cause of any injury, ailment or condition to be recorded on the custody record if it appears capable of providing evidence of an offence.*

C:9H *The purpose of recording a person's responses when attempting to rouse them using the procedure in Annex H is to enable any change in the individual's consciousness level to be noted and clinical treatment arranged if appropriate.*

C:10 Cautions

(a) *When a caution must be given*

★A–69   **C:**10.1 A person whom there are grounds to suspect of an offence, see *Note 10A*, must be cautioned before any questions about an offence, or further questions if the answers provide the grounds for suspicion, are put to them if either the suspect's answers or silence (*i.e.* failure or refusal to answer or answer satisfactorily) may be given in evidence to a court in a prosecution. A person need not be cautioned if questions are for other necessary purposes, *e.g.*:

> (a) solely to establish their identity or ownership of any vehicle;
>
> (b) to obtain information in accordance with any relevant statutory requirement, see paragraph 10.9;
>
> (c) in furtherance of the proper and effective conduct of a search, *e.g.* to determine the need to search in the exercise of powers of stop and search or to seek co-operation while carrying out a search;
>
> (d) to seek verification of a written record as in paragraph 11.13.

C:10.2 Whenever a person not under arrest is initially cautioned, or reminded they are under caution, that person must at the same time be told they are not under arrest and informed of the provisions of paragraph 3.21 which explain how they may obtain legal advice according to whether they are at a police station or elsewhere. See *Note 10C*.

C:10.3 A person who is arrested, or further arrested, must be informed at the time if practicable, or if not, as soon as it becomes practicable thereafter, that they are under arrest and of the grounds and reasons for their arrest, see paragraph 3.4, *Note 10B* and Code G, paragraphs 2.2 and 4.3.

C:10.4 As required by Code G, section 3, a person who is arrested, or further arrested, must also be cautioned unless:

> (a) it is impracticable to do so by reason of their condition or behaviour at the time;
>
> (b) they have already been cautioned immediately prior to arrest as in paragraph 10.1.

(b) *Terms of the cautions*

C:10.5 The caution which must be given on:

> (a) arrest;
>
> (b) all other occasions before a person is charged or informed they may be prosecuted; see section 16,

should, unless the restriction on drawing adverse inferences from silence applies, see Annex C, be in the following terms:

> "*You do not have to say anything. But it may harm your defence if you do not mention when questioned something which you later rely on in court. Anything you do say may be given in evidence.*".

Where the use of the Welsh language is appropriate, a constable may provide the caution directly in Welsh in the following terms:

> "*Does dim rhaid i chi ddweud dim byd. Ond gall niweidio eich amddiffyniad os na fyddwch chiâ n sôn, wrth gael eich holi, am rywbeth y byddwch chiâ n dibynnu arno nes ymlaen yn y llys. Gall unrhyw beth yr ydych yn ei ddweud gael ei roi fel tystiolaeth.*".

See *Note 10G*.

★A–70   **C:**10.6 Annex C, paragraph 2, sets out the alternative terms of the caution to be used when the restriction on drawing adverse inferences from silence applies.

C:10.7 Minor deviations from the words of any caution given in accordance with this code do not constitute a breach of this code, provided the sense of the relevant caution is preserved. See *Note 10D*.

C:10.8 After any break in questioning under caution, the person being questioned must be made aware they remain under caution. If there is any doubt the relevant caution should be given again in full when the interview resumes. See *Note 10E*.

C:10.9 When, despite being cautioned, a person fails to co-operate or to answer particular questions which may affect their immediate treatment, the person should be informed of any relevant consequences and that those consequences are not affected by the caution. Examples are when a person's refusal to provide:

> ● their name and address when charged may make them liable to detention;
>
> ● particulars and information in accordance with a statutory requirement, *e.g.* under the

Road Traffic Act 1988, may amount to an offence or may make the person liable to a further arrest.

(c) *Special warnings under the Criminal Justice and Public Order Act 1994, ss.36 and 37*

C:10.10 When a suspect interviewed at a police station or authorised place of detention after   ★**A–71**
arrest fails or refuses to answer certain questions, or to answer satisfactorily, after due warning,
see *Note 10F*, a court or jury may draw such inferences as appear proper under the *Criminal Justice
and Public Order Act* 1994, ss.36 and 37. Such inferences may only be drawn when:

(a) the restriction on drawing adverse inferences from silence, see Annex C, does not apply; and

(b) the suspect is arrested by a constable and fails or refuses to account for any objects, marks or substances, or marks on such objects found:

- on their person;
- in or on their clothing or footwear;
- otherwise in their possession; or
- in the place they were arrested;

(c) the arrested suspect was found by a constable at a place at or about the time the offence for which that officer has arrested them is alleged to have been committed, and the suspect fails or refuses to account for their presence there.

When the restriction on drawing adverse inferences from silence applies, the suspect may still be
asked to account for any of the matters in (b) or (c) but the special warning described in paragraph
10.11 will not apply and must not be given.

C:10.11 For an inference to be drawn when a suspect fails or refuses to answer a question
about one of these matters or to answer it satisfactorily, the suspect must first be told in ordinary
language:

(a) what offence is being investigated;

(b) what fact they are being asked to account for;

(c) this fact may be due to them taking part in the commission of the offence;

(d) a court may draw a proper inference if they fail or refuse to account for this fact;

(e) a record is being made of the interview and it may be given in evidence if they are brought to trial.

(d) *Juveniles and persons who are mentally disordered or otherwise mentally vulnerable*

C:10.11A The information required in paragraph 10.11 must not be given to a suspect who is
a juvenile or who is mentally disordered or otherwise mentally vulnerable unless the appropriate
adult is present.

C:10.12 If a juvenile or a person who is mentally disordered or otherwise mentally vulnerable
is cautioned in the absence of the appropriate adult, the caution must be repeated in the adult's
presence.

(e) *Documentation*

C:10.13 A record shall be made when a caution is given under this section, either in
the interviewer's pocket book or in the interview record.

Notes for guidance

C:10A *There must be some reasonable, objective grounds for the suspicion, based on known facts or infor-*   ★**A–72**
*mation which are relevant to the likelihood the offence has been committed and the person to be questioned
committed it.*

C:10B *An arrested person must be given sufficient information to enable them to understand that they
have been deprived of their liberty and the reason they have been arrested, e.g. when a person is arrested on
suspicion of committing an offence they must be informed of the suspected offence's nature, when and where it
was committed. The suspect must also be informed of the reason or reasons why the arrest is considered
necessary. Vague or technical language should be avoided.*

C:10C *The restriction on drawing inferences from silence, see Annex C, paragraph 1, does not apply to a
person who has not been detained and who therefore cannot be prevented from seeking legal advice if they
want, see paragraph 3.21.*

C:10D *If it appears a person does not understand the caution, the person giving it should explain it in
their own words.*

C:10E *It may be necessary to show to the court that nothing occurred during an interview break or be-*

tween interviews which influenced the suspect's recorded evidence. After a break in an interview or at the beginning of a subsequent interview, the interviewing officer should summarise the reason for the break and confirm this with the suspect.

C:10F *The* Criminal Justice and Public Order Act *1994, ss.36 and 37, apply only to suspects who have been arrested by a constable or an officer of Revenue and Customs and are given the relevant warning by the police or Revenue and Customs officer who made the arrest or who is investigating the offence. They do not apply to any interviews with suspects who have not been arrested.*

C:10G *Nothing in this code requires a caution to be given or repeated when informing a person not under arrest they may be prosecuted for an offence. However, a court will not be able to draw any inferences under the* Criminal Justice and Public Order Act *1994, s.34, if the person was not cautioned.*

C:11 Interviews—general

(a) *Action*

C:11.1A An interview is the questioning of a person regarding their involvement or suspected involvement in a criminal offence or offences which, under paragraph 10.1, must be carried out under caution. Whenever a person is interviewed they must be informed of the nature of the offence, or further offence. Procedures under the *Road Traffic Act* 1988, s.7, or the *Transport and Works Act* 1992, s.31, do not constitute interviewing for the purpose of this code.

C:11.1 Following a decision to arrest a suspect, they must not be interviewed about the relevant offence except at a police station or other authorised place of detention, unless the consequent delay would be likely to:

(a) lead to:

- interference with, or harm to, evidence connected with an offence;
- interference with, or physical harm to, other people; or
- serious loss of, or damage to, property;

(b) lead to alerting other people suspected of committing an offence but not yet arrested for it; or

(c) hinder the recovery of property obtained in consequence of the commission of an offence.

Interviewing in any of these circumstances shall cease once the relevant risk has been averted or the necessary questions have been put in order to attempt to avert that risk.

C:11.2 Immediately prior to the commencement or re-commencement of any interview at a police station or other authorised place of detention, the interviewer should remind the suspect of their entitlement to free legal advice and that the interview can be delayed for legal advice to be obtained, unless one of the exceptions in paragraph 6.6 applies. It is the interviewer's responsibility to make sure all reminders are recorded in the interview record.

C:11.3 [*Not used.*]

C:11.4 At the beginning of an interview the interviewer, after cautioning the suspect, see section 10, shall put to them any significant statement or silence which occurred in the presence and hearing of a police officer or other police staff before the start of the interview and which have not been put to the suspect in the course of a previous interview. See *Note 11A*. The interviewer shall ask the suspect whether they confirm or deny that earlier statement or silence and if they want to add anything.

C:11.4A A significant statement is one which appears capable of being used in evidence against the suspect, in particular a direct admission of guilt. A significant silence is a failure or refusal to answer a question or answer satisfactorily when under caution, which might, allowing for the restriction on drawing adverse inferences from silence, see Annex C, give rise to an inference under the *Criminal Justice and Public Order Act* 1994, Pt III.

C:11.5 No interviewer may try to obtain answers or elicit a statement by the use of oppression. Except as in paragraph 10.9, no interviewer shall indicate, except to answer a direct question, what action will be taken by the police if the person being questioned answers questions, makes a statement or refuses to do either. If the person asks directly what action will be taken if they answer questions, make a statement or refuse to do either, the interviewer may inform them what action the police propose to take provided that action is itself proper and warranted.

C:11.6 The interview or further interview of a person about an offence with which that person has not been charged or for which they have not been informed they may be prosecuted, must cease when:

(a) the officer in charge of the investigation is satisfied all the questions they consider relevant to obtaining accurate and reliable information about the offence have been put to the suspect, this includes allowing the suspect an opportunity to give an innocent explanation and asking questions to test if the explanation is accurate and reliable, *e.g.* to clear up ambiguities or clarify what the suspect said;

(b) the officer in charge of the investigation has taken account of any other available evidence; and

(c) the officer in charge of the investigation, or in the case of a detained suspect, the custody officer, see paragraph 16.1, reasonably believes there is sufficient evidence to provide a realistic prospect of conviction for that offence. See *Note 11B*.

This paragraph does not prevent officers in revenue cases or acting under the confiscation provisions of the *Criminal Justice Act* 1988 or the *Drug Trafficking Act* 1994 from inviting suspects to complete a formal question and answer record after the interview is concluded.

(b) *Interview records*

C:11.7 (a) An accurate record must be made of each interview, whether or not the interview ★**A–74** takes place at a police station.

(b) The record must state the place of interview, the time it begins and ends, any interview breaks and, subject to paragraph 2.6A, the names of all those present; and must be made on the forms provided for this purpose or in the interviewer's pocket book or in accordance with the Codes of Practice E or F.

(c) Any written record must be made and completed during the interview, unless this would not be practicable or would interfere with the conduct of the interview, and must constitute either a verbatim record of what has been said or, failing this, an account of the interview which adequately and accurately summarises it.

C:11.8 If a written record is not made during the interview it must be made as soon as practicable after its completion.

C:11.9 Written interview records must be timed and signed by the maker.

C:11.10 If a written record is not completed during the interview the reason must be recorded in the interview record.

C:11.11 Unless it is impracticable, the person interviewed shall be given the opportunity to read the interview record and to sign it as correct or to indicate how they consider it inaccurate. If the person interviewed cannot read or refuses to read the record or sign it, the senior interviewer present shall read it to them and ask whether they would like to sign it as correct or make their mark or to indicate how they consider it inaccurate. The interviewer shall certify on the interview record itself what has occurred. See *Note 11E*.

C:11.12 If the appropriate adult or the person's solicitor is present during the interview, they should also be given an opportunity to read and sign the interview record or any written statement taken down during the interview.

C:11.13 A written record shall be made of any comments made by a suspect, including unsolicited comments, which are outside the context of an interview but which might be relevant to the offence. Any such record must be timed and signed by the maker. When practicable the suspect shall be given the opportunity to read that record and to sign it as correct or to indicate how they consider it inaccurate. See *Note 11E*.

C:11.14 Any refusal by a person to sign an interview record when asked in accordance with this code must itself be recorded.

(c) *Juveniles and mentally disordered or otherwise mentally vulnerable people*

C:11.15 A juvenile or person who is mentally disordered or otherwise mentally vulnerable ★**A–75** must not be interviewed regarding their involvement or suspected involvement in a criminal offence or offences, or asked to provide or sign a written statement under caution or record of interview, in the absence of the appropriate adult unless paragraphs 11.1, 11.18 to 11.20 apply. See *Note 11C*.

C:11.16 Juveniles may only be interviewed at their place of education in exceptional circumstances and only when the principal or their nominee agrees. Every effort should be made to notify the parent(s) or other person responsible for the juvenile's welfare and the appropriate adult, if this is a different person, that the police want to interview the juvenile and reasonable time should be allowed to enable the appropriate adult to be present at the interview. If awaiting the appropriate adult would cause unreasonable delay, and unless the juvenile is suspected of an offence against the educational establishment, the principal or their nominee can act as the appropriate adult for the purposes of the interview.

C:11.17 If an appropriate adult is present at an interview, they shall be informed:

- they are not expected to act simply as an observer; and
- the purpose of their presence is to:
  - ~ advise the person being interviewed;
  - ~ observe whether the interview is being conducted properly and fairly;
  - ~ facilitate communication with the person being interviewed.

(d) *Vulnerable suspects—urgent interviews at police stations*

C:11.18 The following persons may not be interviewed unless an officer of superintendent rank or above considers delay will lead to the consequences in paragraph 11.1(a) to (c), and is satisfied the interview would not significantly harm the person's physical or mental state (see Annex G):

(a) a juvenile or person who is mentally disordered or otherwise mentally vulnerable if at the time of the interview the appropriate adult is not present;

(b) anyone other than in (a) who at the time of the interview appears unable to:
- appreciate the significance of questions and their answers; or
- understand what is happening because of the effects of drink, drugs or any illness, ailment or condition;

(c) a person who has difficulty understanding English or has a hearing disability, if at the time of the interview an interpreter is not present.

C:11.19 These interviews may not continue once sufficient information has been obtained to avert the consequences in paragraph 11.1(a) to (c).

C:11.20 A record shall be made of the grounds for any decision to interview a person under paragraph 11.18.

Notes for guidance

★**A–76**   **C:**11A *Paragraph 11.4 does not prevent the interviewer from putting significant statements and silences to a suspect again at a later stage or a further interview.*

C:11B *The* Criminal Procedure and Investigations Act *1996 code of practice, paragraph 3.5 states "In conducting an investigation, the investigator should pursue all reasonable lines of enquiry, whether these point towards or away from the suspect. What is reasonable will depend on the particular circumstances." Interviewers should keep this in mind when deciding what questions to ask in an interview.*

C:11C *Although juveniles or people who are mentally disordered or otherwise mentally vulnerable are often capable of providing reliable evidence, they may, without knowing or wishing to do so, be particularly prone in certain circumstances to provide information that may be unreliable, misleading or self-incriminating. Special care should always be taken when questioning such a person, and the appropriate adult should be involved if there is any doubt about a person's age, mental state or capacity. Because of the risk of unreliable evidence it is also important to obtain corroboration of any facts admitted whenever possible.*

C:11D *Juveniles should not be arrested at their place of education unless this is unavoidable. When a juvenile is arrested at their place of education, the principal or their nominee must be informed.*

C:11E *Significant statements described in paragraph 11.4 will always be relevant to the offence and must be recorded. When a suspect agrees to read records of interviews and other comments and sign them as correct, they should be asked to endorse the record with, e.g. "I agree that this is a correct record of what was said" and add their signature. If the suspect does not agree with the record, the interviewer should record the details of any disagreement and ask the suspect to read these details and sign them to the effect that they accurately reflect their disagreement. Any refusal to sign should be recorded.*

C:12 Interviews in police stations

(a) *Action*

★**A–77**   **C:**12.1 If a police officer wants to interview or conduct enquiries which require the presence of a detainee, the custody officer is responsible for deciding whether to deliver the detainee into the officer's custody. An investigating officer who is given custody of a detainee takes over responsibility for the detainee's care and safe custody for the purposes of this code until they return the detainee to the custody officer when they must report the manner in which they complied with the code whilst having custody of the detainee.

C:12.2 Except as below, in any period of 24 hours a detainee must be allowed a continuous period of at least 8 hours for rest, free from questioning, travel or any interruption in connection with the investigation concerned. This period should normally be at night or other appropriate time which takes account of when the detainee last slept or rested. If a detainee is arrested at a police station after going there voluntarily, the period of 24 hours runs from the time of their arrest and not the time of arrival at the police station. The period may not be interrupted or delayed, except:

  (a) when there are reasonable grounds for believing not delaying or interrupting the period would:

   (i) involve a risk of harm to people or serious loss of, or damage to, property;

   (ii) delay unnecessarily the person's release from custody;

   (iii) otherwise prejudice the outcome of the investigation;

  (b) at the request of the detainee, their appropriate adult or legal representative;

  (c) when a delay or interruption is necessary in order to:

   (i) comply with the legal obligations and duties arising under section 15;

   (ii) to take action required under section 9 or in accordance with medical advice.

If the period is interrupted in accordance with (a), a fresh period must be allowed. Interruptions under (b) and (c), do not require a fresh period to be allowed.

C:12.3 Before a detainee is interviewed the custody officer, in consultation with the officer in charge of the investigation and appropriate healthcare professionals as necessary, shall assess whether the detainee is fit enough to be interviewed. This means determining and considering the risks to the detainee's physical and mental state if the interview took place and determining what safeguards are needed to allow the interview to take place. See Annex G. The custody officer shall not allow a detainee to be interviewed if the custody officer considers it would cause significant harm to the detainee's physical or mental state. Vulnerable suspects listed at paragraph 11.18 shall be treated as always being at some risk during an interview and these persons may not be interviewed except in accordance with paragraphs 11.18 to 11.20.

C:12.4 As far as practicable interviews shall take place in interview rooms which are adequately heated, lit and ventilated.

C:12.5 A suspect whose detention without charge has been authorised under *PACE*, because the detention is necessary for an interview to obtain evidence of the offence for which they have been arrested, may choose not to answer questions but police do not require the suspect's consent or agreement to interview them for this purpose. If a suspect takes steps to prevent themselves being questioned or further questioned, *e.g.* by refusing to leave their cell to go to a suitable interview room or by trying to leave the interview room, they shall be advised their consent or agreement to interview is not required. The suspect shall be cautioned as in section 10, and informed if they fail or refuse to co-operate, the interview may take place in the cell and that their failure or refusal to co-operate may be given in evidence. The suspect shall then be invited to co-operate and go into the interview room.

C:12.6 People being questioned or making statements shall not be required to stand.

C:12.7 Before the interview commences each interviewer shall, subject to paragraph 2.6A, ★A–78 identify themselves and any other persons present to the interviewee.

C:12.8 Breaks from interviewing should be made at recognised meal times or at other times that take account of when an interviewee last had a meal. Short refreshment breaks shall be provided at approximately two hour intervals, subject to the interviewer's discretion to delay a break if there are reasonable grounds for believing it would:

  (i) involve a:

   • risk of harm to people;

   • serious loss of, or damage to, property;

  (ii) unnecessarily delay the detainee's release;

  (iii) otherwise prejudice the outcome of the investigation.

See *Note 12B*.

C:12.9 If during the interview a complaint is made by or on behalf of the interviewee concerning the provisions of any of the codes, or it comes to the interviewer's notice that the interviewee may have been treated improperly, the interviewer should:

  (i) record the matter in the interview record;

  (ii) inform the custody officer, who is then responsible for dealing with it as in section 9.

(b) *Documentation*

C:12.10 A record must be made of the: ★A–79

  • time a detainee is not in the custody of the custody officer, and why;

● reason for any refusal to deliver the detainee out of that custody.

C:12.11 A record shall be made of:

(a) the reasons it was not practicable to use an interview room; and

(b) any action taken as in paragraph 12.5.

The record shall be made on the custody record or in the interview record for action taken whilst an interview record is being kept, with a brief reference to this effect in the custody record.

C:12.12 Any decision to delay a break in an interview must be recorded, with reasons, in the interview record.

C:12.13 All written statements made at police stations under caution shall be written on forms provided for the purpose.

C:12.14 All written statements made under caution shall be taken in accordance with Annex D. Before a person makes a written statement under caution at a police station they shall be reminded about the right to legal advice. See *Note 12A.*

Notes for guidance

★**A-80** **C:**12A *It is not normally necessary to ask for a written statement if the interview was recorded in writing and the record signed in accordance with paragraph 11.11 or audibly or visually recorded in accordance with Code E or F. Statements under caution should normally be taken in these circumstances only at the person's express wish. A person may however be asked if they want to make such a statement.*

C:12B *Meal breaks should normally last at least 45 minutes and shorter breaks after two hours should last at least 15 minutes. If the interviewer delays a break in accordance with paragraph 12.8 and prolongs the interview, a longer break should be provided. If there is a short interview, and another short interview is contemplated, the length of the break may be reduced if there are reasonable grounds to believe this is necessary to avoid any of the consequences in paragraph 12.8(i) to (iii).*

C:13 Interpreters

(a) *General*

★**A-81** **C:**13.1 Chief officers are responsible for making sure appropriate arrangements are in place for provision of suitably qualified interpreters for people who:

● are deaf;

● do not understand English.

See *Note 13A.*

(b) *Foreign languages*

C:13.2 Unless paragraphs 11.1, 11.18 to 11.20 apply, a person must not be interviewed in the absence of a person capable of interpreting if:

(a) they have difficulty understanding English;

(b) the interviewer cannot speak the person's own language;

(c) the person wants an interpreter present.

C:13.3 The interviewer shall make sure the interpreter makes a note of the interview at the time in the person's language for use in the event of the interpreter being called to give evidence, and certifies its accuracy. The interviewer should allow sufficient time for the interpreter to note each question and answer after each is put, given and interpreted. The person should be allowed to read the record or have it read to them and sign it as correct or indicate the respects in which they consider it inaccurate. If the interview is audibly recorded or visually recorded, the arrangements in Code E or F apply.

C:13.4 In the case of a person making a statement to a police officer or other police staff other than in English:

(a) the interpreter shall record the statement in the language it is made;

(b) the person shall be invited to sign it;

(c) an official English translation shall be made in due course.

(c) *Deaf people and people with speech difficulties*

★**A-82** **C:**13.5 If a person appears to be deaf or there is doubt about their hearing or speaking ability, they must not be interviewed in the absence of an interpreter unless they agree in writing to being interviewed without one or paragraphs 11.1, 11.18 to 11.20 apply.

C:13.6 An interpreter should also be called if a juvenile is interviewed and the parent or guardian present as the appropriate adult appears to be deaf or there is doubt about their hearing or speaking ability, unless they agree in writing to the interview proceeding without one or paragraphs 11.1, 11.18 to 11.20 apply.

C:13.7 The interviewer shall make sure the interpreter is allowed to read the interview record and certify its accuracy in the event of the interpreter being called to give evidence. If the interview is audibly recorded or visually recorded, the arrangements in Code E or F apply.

(d) *Additional rules for detained persons*

C:13.8 All reasonable attempts should be made to make the detainee understand that interpreters will be provided at public expense.

C:13.9 If paragraph 6.1 applies and the detainee cannot communicate with the solicitor because of language, hearing or speech difficulties, an interpreter must be called. The interpreter may not be a police officer or any other police staff when interpretation is needed for the purposes of obtaining legal advice. In all other cases a police officer or other police staff may only interpret if the detainee and the appropriate adult, if applicable, give their agreement in writing or if the interview is audibly recorded or visually recorded as in Code E or F.

C:13.10 When the custody officer cannot establish effective communication with a person charged with an offence who appears deaf or there is doubt about their ability to hear, speak or to understand English, arrangements must be made as soon as practicable for an interpreter to explain the offence and any other information given by the custody officer.

(e) *Documentation*

C:13.11 Action taken to call an interpreter under this section and any agreement to be interviewed in the absence of an interpreter must be recorded.

Note for guidance

C:13A *Whenever possible, interpreters should be provided in accordance with national arrangements approved or prescribed by the Secretary of State.*

C:14 Questioning—special restrictions

C:14.1 If a person is arrested by one police force on behalf of another and the lawful period of detention in respect of that offence has not yet commenced in accordance with *PACE*, s.41, no questions may be put to them about the offence while they are in transit between the forces except to clarify any voluntary statement they make. ★**A–83**

C:14.2 If a person is in police detention at a hospital they may not be questioned without the agreement of a responsible doctor. See *Note 14A*.

Note for guidance

C:14A *If questioning takes place at a hospital under paragraph 14.2, or on the way to or from a hospital, the period of questioning concerned counts towards the total period of detention permitted.* ★**A–84**

C:15 Reviews and extensions of detention

(a) *Persons detained under PACE*

C:15.1 The review officer is responsible under *PACE*, s.40, for periodically determining if a person's detention, before or after charge, continues to be necessary. This requirement continues throughout the detention period and except as in paragraph 15.10, the review officer must be present at the police station holding the detainee. See *Notes 15A and 15B*. ★**A–85**

C:15.2 Under *PACE*, s.42, an officer of superintendent rank or above who is responsible for the station holding the detainee may give authority any time after the second review to extend the maximum period the person may be detained without charge by up to 12 hours. Further detention without charge may be authorised only by a magistrates' court in accordance with *PACE*, ss.43 and 44. See *Notes 15C, 15D* and *15E*.

C:15.2A An authorisation under section 42(1) of *PACE* extends the maximum period of detention permitted before charge for indictable offences from 24 hours to 36 hours. Detaining a juvenile or mentally vulnerable person for longer than 24 hours will be dependent on the circumstances of the case and with regard to the person's:

(a) special vulnerability;

(b) the legal obligation to provide an opportunity for representations to be made prior to a decision about extending detention;

    (c) the need to consult and consider the views of any appropriate adult; and

    (d) any alternatives to police custody.

C:15.3 Before deciding whether to authorise continued detention the officer responsible under paragraph 15.1 or 15.2 shall give an opportunity to make representations about the detention to:

    (a) the detainee, unless in the case of a review as in paragraph 15.1, the detainee is asleep;

    (b) the detainee's solicitor if available at the time; and

    (c) the appropriate adult if available at the time.

See *Note 15CA.*

C:15.3A Other people having an interest in the detainee's welfare may also make representations at the authorising officer's discretion.

C:15.3B Subject to paragraph 15.10, the representations may be made orally in person or by telephone or in writing. The authorising officer may, however, refuse to hear oral representations from the detainee if the officer considers them unfit to make representations because of their condition or behaviour. See *Note 15C.*

C:15.3C The decision on whether the review takes place in person or by telephone or by video conferencing (see *Note 15G*) is a matter for the review officer. In determining the form the review may take, the review officer must always take full account of the needs of the person in custody. The benefits of carrying out a review in person should always be considered, based on the individual circumstances of each case with specific additional consideration if the person is:

    (a) a juvenile (and the age of the juvenile); or

    (b) suspected of being mentally vulnerable; or

    (c) in need of medical attention for other than routine minor ailments; or

    (d) subject to presentational or community issues around their detention.

★**A–86**   **C:15.4** Before conducting a review or determining whether to extend the maximum period of detention without charge, the officer responsible must make sure the detainee is reminded of their entitlement to free legal advice, see paragraph 6.5, unless in the case of a review the person is asleep.

C:15.5 If, after considering any representations, the review officer under paragraph 15.1 decides to keep the detainee in detention or the superintendent under paragraph 15.2 extends the maximum period for which they may be detained without charge, then any comment made by the detainee shall be recorded. If applicable, the officer shall be informed of the comment as soon as practicable. See also paragraphs 11.4 and 11.13.

C:15.6 No officer shall put specific questions to the detainee:

    • regarding their involvement in any offence; or

    • in respect of any comments they may make:

       ~ when given the opportunity to make representations; or

       ~ in response to a decision to keep them in detention or extend the maximum period of detention.

Such an exchange could constitute an interview as in paragraph 11.1A and would be subject to the associated safeguards in section 11 and, in respect of a person who has been charged, paragraph 16.5. See also paragraph 11.13.

C:15.7 A detainee who is asleep at a review, see paragraph 15.1, and whose continued detention is authorised must be informed about the decision and reason as soon as practicable after waking.

C:15.8 [*Not used.*]

(b) *Review of detention by telephone and video conferencing facilities*

★**A–87**   **C:15.9** *PACE*, s.40A, provides that the officer responsible under section 40 for reviewing the detention of a person who has not been charged, need not attend the police station holding the detainee and may carry out the review by telephone.

C:15.9A *PACE*, s.45A(2), provides that the officer responsible under section 40 for reviewing the detention of a person who has not been charged, need not attend the police station holding the detainee and may carry out the review by video conferencing facilities. (See *Note 15G.*)

C:15.9B A telephone review is not permitted where facilities for review by video conferencing exist and it is practicable to use them.

C:15.9C The review officer can decide at any stage that a telephone review or review by video conferencing should be terminated and that the review will be conducted in person. The reasons for doing so should be noted in the custody record. See *Note 15F*.

C:15.10 When a review is carried out by telephone or by video conferencing facilities, an officer at the station holding the detainee shall be required by the review officer to fulfil that officer's obligations under *PACE*, s.40, and this code by:

    (a) making any record connected with the review in the detainee's custody record;

    (b) if applicable, making the record in (a) in the presence of the detainee; and

    (c) for a review by telephone, giving the detainee information about the review.

C:15.11 When a review is carried out by telephone or by video conferencing facilities, the requirement in paragraph 15.3 will be satisfied:

    (a) if facilities exist for the immediate transmission of written representations to the review officer, *e.g.* fax or email message, by allowing those who are given the opportunity to make representations, to make their representations:

        (i) orally by telephone or (as the case may be) by means of the video conferencing facilities; or

        (ii) in writing using the facilities for the immediate transmission of written representations; and

    (b) in all other cases, by allowing those who are given the opportunity to make representations, to make their representations orally by telephone or by means of the video conferencing facilities.

(c) Documentation

C:15.12 It is the officer's responsibility to make sure all reminders given under paragraph 15.4 are noted in the custody record.

C:15.13 The grounds for, and extent of, any delay in conducting a review shall be recorded.

C:15.14 When a review is carried out by telephone or video conferencing facilities, a record shall be made of:

    (a) the reason the review officer did not attend the station holding the detainee;

    (b) the place the review officer was;

    (c) the method representations, oral or written, were made to the review officer, see paragraph 15.11.

C:15.15 Any written representations shall be retained.

C:15.16 A record shall be made as soon as practicable of:

    (a) the outcome of each review of detention before or after charge, and if paragraph 15.7 applies, of when the person was informed and by whom;

    (b) the outcome of any determination under *PACE*, s.42, by a superintendent whether to extend the maximum period of detention without charge beyond 24 hours from the relevant time; if an authorisation is given, the record shall state the number of hours and minutes by which the detention period is extended or further extended;

    (c) the outcome of each application under *PACE*, s.43, for a warrant of further detention or under section 44, for an extension or further extension of that warrant; if a warrant for further detention is granted under section 43 or extended or further extended under 44, the record shall state the detention period authorised by the warrant and the date and time it was granted or (as the case may be) the period by which the warrant is extended or further extended.

Note: any period during which a person is released on bail does not count towards the maximum period of detention without charge allowed under *PACE*, ss.41 to 44.

Notes for guidance

C:15A *Review officer for the purposes of:*   ★**A–88**

    • *PACE, ss.40, 40A and 45A means, in the case of a person arrested but not charged, an officer of at least inspector rank not directly involved in the investigation and, if a person has been arrested and charged, the custody officer.*

C:15B *The detention of persons in police custody not subject to the statutory review requirement in paragraph 15.1 should still be reviewed periodically as a matter of good practice. Such reviews can be carried out by an officer of the rank of sergeant or above. The purpose of such reviews is to check the particular power under which a detainee is held continues to apply, any associated conditions are complied with and to make sure appropriate action is taken to deal with any changes. This includes the detainee's prompt release when* the power no longer applies, or their transfer if the power requires the detainee be taken elsewhere as soon as the necessary arrangements are made. Examples include persons:

    (a) *arrested on warrant because they failed to answer bail to appear at court;*

    (b) *arrested under the* Bail Act 1976, s.7(3), *for breaching a condition of bail granted after charge;*

    (c) *in police custody for specific purposes and periods under the* Crime (Sentences) Act 1997, Sched. 1;

    (d) *convicted, or remand prisoners, held in police stations on behalf of the Prison Service under the* Imprisonment (Temporary Provisions) Act 1980, s.6;

    (e) *being detained to prevent them causing a breach of the peace;*

    (f) *detained at police stations on behalf of the Immigration Service;*

    (g) *detained by order of a magistrates' court under the* Criminal Justice Act 1988, s.152 *(as amended by the* Drugs Act 2005, s.8) *to facilitate the recovery of evidence after being charged with drug possession or drug trafficking and suspected of having swallowed drugs.*

    The detention of persons remanded into police detention by order of a court under the Magistrates' Courts Act 1980, s.128, *is subject to a statutory requirement to review that detention. This is to make sure the detainee is taken back to court no later than the end of the period authorised by the court or when the need for their detention by police ceases, whichever is the sooner.*

    C:15C *In the case of a review of detention, but not an extension, the detainee need not be woken for the review. However, if the detainee is likely to be asleep, e.g. during a period of rest allowed as in paragraph 12.2, at the latest time a review or authorisation to extend detention may take place, the officer should, if the legal obligations and time constraints permit, bring forward the procedure to allow the detainee to make representations. A detainee not asleep during the review must be present when the grounds for their continued detention are recorded and must at the same time be informed of those grounds unless the review officer considers the person is incapable of understanding what is said, violent or likely to become violent or in urgent need of medical attention.*

    C:15CA *In paragraph 15.3(b) and (c), "available" includes being contactable in time to enable them to make representations remotely by telephone or other electronic means or in person by attending the station. Reasonable efforts should therefore be made to give the solicitor and appropriate adult sufficient notice of the time the decision is expected to be made so that they can make themselves available.*

    C:15D *An application to a magistrates' court under* PACE, s.43 *or* 44, *for a warrant of further detention or its extension should be made between 10am and 9pm, and if possible during normal court hours. It will not usually be practicable to arrange for a court to sit specially outside the hours of 10am to 9pm. If it appears a special sitting may be needed outside normal court hours but between 10am and 9pm, the clerk to the justices should be given notice and informed of this possibility, while the court is sitting if possible.*

    C:15E *In paragraph 15.2, the officer responsible for the station holding the detainee includes a superintendent or above who, in accordance with their force operational policy or police regulations, is given that responsibility on a temporary basis whilst the appointed long-term holder is off duty or otherwise unavailable.*

    C:15F *The provisions of* PACE, s.40A, *allowing telephone reviews do not apply to reviews of detention after charge by the custody officer. When video conferencing is not required, they allow the use of a telephone to carry out a review of detention before charge. The procedure under* PACE, s.42, *must be done in person.*

    C:15G *Video conferencing facilities means any facilities (whether a live television link or other facilities) by means of which the review can be carried out with the review officer, the detainee concerned and the detainee's solicitor all being able to both see and to hear each other. The use of video conferencing facilities for decisions about detention under section 45A of* PACE *is subject to regulations made by the Secretary of State being in force.*

C:16 Charging detained persons

(a) *Action*

★A–89

    C:16.1 When the officer in charge of the investigation reasonably believes there is sufficient evidence to provide a realistic prospect of conviction for the offence (see paragraph 11.6), they shall without delay, and subject to the following qualification, inform the custody officer who will be responsible for considering whether the detainee should be charged. See *Notes 11B* and *16A*. When a person is detained in respect of more than one offence it is permissible to delay informing the custody officer until the above conditions are satisfied in respect of all the offences, but see paragraph 11.6. If the detainee is a juvenile, mentally disordered or otherwise mentally vulnerable, any resulting action shall be taken in the presence of the appropriate adult if they are present at the time. See *Notes 16B* and *16C*.

    C:16.1A Where guidance issued by the Director of Public Prosecutions under *PACE*, s.37A, is in force the custody officer must comply with that guidance in deciding how to act in dealing with the detainee. See *Notes 16AA* and *16AB*.

C:16.1B Where in compliance with the DPP's guidance the custody officer decides that the case should be immediately referred to the CPS to make the charging decision, consultation should take place with a crown prosecutor as soon as is reasonably practicable. Where the crown prosecutor is unable to make the charging decision on the information available at that time, the detainee may be released without charge and on bail (with conditions if necessary) under section 37(7)(a). In such circumstances, the detainee should be informed that they are being released to enable the Director of Public Prosecutions to make a decision under section 37B.

C:16.2 When a detainee is charged with or informed they may be prosecuted for an offence, see *Note 16B,* they shall, unless the restriction on drawing adverse inferences from silence applies, see Annex C, be cautioned as follows:

"You do not have to say anything. But it may harm your defence if you do not mention now something which you later rely on in court. Anything you do say may be given in evidence.".

Where the use of the Welsh language is appropriate, a constable may provide the caution directly in Welsh in the following terms:

"Does dim rhaid i chi ddweud dim byd. Ond gall niweidio eich amddiffyniad os na fyddwch chiâ n sôn, yn awr, am rywbeth y byddwch chiâ n dibynnu arno nes ymlaen yn y llys. Gall unrhyw beth yr ydych yn ei ddweud gael ei roi fel tystiolaeth.".

Annex C, paragraph 2, sets out the alternative terms of the caution to be used when the restriction on drawing adverse inferences from silence applies.

C:16.3 When a detainee is charged they shall be given a written notice showing particulars of the offence and, subject to paragraph 2.6A, the officer's name and the case reference number. As far as possible the particulars of the charge shall be stated in simple terms, but they shall also show the precise offence in law with which the detainee is charged. The notice shall begin:

"You are charged with the offence(s) shown below." Followed by the caution.

If the detainee is a juvenile, mentally disordered or otherwise mentally vulnerable, a copy of the notice should also be given to the appropriate adult.

C:16.4 If, after a detainee has been charged with or informed they may be prosecuted for an offence, an officer wants to tell them about any written statement or interview with another person relating to such an offence, the detainee shall either be handed a true copy of the written statement or the content of the interview record brought to their attention. Nothing shall be done to invite any reply or comment except to:

(a) caution the detainee, *"You do not have to say anything, but anything you do say may be given in evidence.";*

where the use of the Welsh Language is appropriate, caution the detainee in the following terms:

"Does dim rhaid i chi ddweud dim byd, ond gall unrhyw beth yr ydych yn ei ddweud gael ei roi fel tystiolaeth.";

and

(b) remind the detainee about their right to legal advice.

C:16.4A If the detainee:

● cannot read, the document may be read to them;

● is a juvenile, mentally disordered or otherwise mentally vulnerable, the appropriate adult shall also be given a copy, or the interview record shall be brought to their attention.

C:16.5 A detainee may not be interviewed about an offence after they have been charged with, **★A–90** or informed they may be prosecuted for it, unless the interview is necessary:

● to prevent or minimise harm or loss to some other person, or the public;

● to clear up an ambiguity in a previous answer or statement;

● in the interests of justice for the detainee to have put to them, and have an opportunity to comment on, information concerning the offence which has come to light since they were charged or informed they might be prosecuted.

Before any such interview, the interviewer shall:

(a) caution the detainee, *"You do not have to say anything, but anything you do say may be given in evidence.";*

where the use of the Welsh language is appropriate, the interviewer shall caution the detainee: *"Does dim rhaid i chi ddweud dim byd, ond gall unrhyw beth yr ydych yn ei ddweud gael ei roi fel tystiolaeth.";*

(b) remind the detainee about their right to legal advice.

See *Note 16B*.

C:16.6 The provisions of paragraphs 16.2 to 16.5 must be complied with in the appropriate adult's presence if they are already at the police station. If they are not at the police station then these provisions must be complied with again in their presence when they arrive unless the detainee has been released. See *Note 16C*.

C:16.7 When a juvenile is charged with an offence and the custody officer authorises their continued detention after charge, the custody officer must make arrangements for the juvenile to be taken into the care of a local authority to be detained pending appearance in court unless the custody officer certifies in accordance with *PACE*, s.38(6), that:

> (a) for any juvenile, it is impracticable to do so; or
>
> (b) in the case of a juvenile of at least 12 years old, no secure accommodation is available and other accommodation would not be adequate to protect the public from serious harm from that juvenile. See *Note 16D*.

(b) *Documentation*

C:16.8 A record shall be made of anything a detainee says when charged.

C:16.9 Any questions put in an interview after charge and answers given relating to the offence shall be recorded in full during the interview on forms for that purpose and the record signed by the detainee or, if they refuse, by the interviewer and any third parties present. If the questions are audibly recorded or visually recorded the arrangements in Code E or F apply.

C:16.10 If arrangements for a juvenile's transfer into local authority care as in paragraph 16.7 are not made, the custody officer must record the reasons in a certificate which must be produced before the court with the juvenile. See *Note 16D*.

Notes for guidance

★**A–91**   **C:**16A *The custody officer must take into account alternatives to prosecution under the* Crime and Disorder Act 1998, *reprimands and warning applicable to persons under 18, and in national guidance on the cautioning of offenders, for persons aged 18 and over.*

C:16AA *When a person is arrested under the provisions of the* Criminal Justice Act 2003 *which allow a person to be re-tried after being acquitted of a serious offence which is a qualifying offence specified in Schedule 5 to that Act and not precluded from further prosecution by virtue of section 75(3) of that Act the detention provisions of PACE are modified and make an officer of the rank of superintendent or above who has not been directly involved in the investigation responsible for determining whether the evidence is sufficient to charge.*

C:16AB *Where guidance issued by the Director of Public Prosecutions under section 37B is in force, a custody officer who determines in accordance with that guidance that there is sufficient evidence to charge the detainee, may detain that person for no longer than is reasonably necessary to decide how that person is to be dealt with under PACE, s.37(7)(a) to (d), including, where appropriate, consultation with the duty prosecutor. The period is subject to the maximum period of detention before charge determined by PACE, ss.41 to 44. Where in accordance with the guidance the case is referred to the CPS for decision, the custody officer should ensure that an officer involved in the investigation sends to the CPS such information as is specified in the guidance.*

C:16B *The giving of a warning or the service of the notice of intended prosecution required by the* Road Traffic Offenders Act 1988, *s.1 does not amount to informing a detainee they may be prosecuted for an offence and so does not preclude further questioning in relation to that offence.*

C:16C *There is no power under PACE to detain a person and delay action under paragraphs 16.2 to 16.5 solely to await the arrival of the appropriate adult. Reasonable efforts should therefore be made to give the appropriate adult sufficient notice of the time the decision (charge etc.) is to be implemented so that they can be present. If the appropriate adult is not, or cannot be, present at that time, the detainee should be released on bail to return for the decision to be implemented when the adult is present, unless the custody officer determines that the absence of the appropriate adult makes the detainee unsuitable for bail for this purpose. After charge, bail cannot be refused, or release on bail delayed, simply because an appropriate adult is not available, unless the absence of that adult provides the custody officer with the necessary grounds to authorise detention after charge under PACE, s.38.*

C:16D *Except as in paragraph 16.7, neither a juvenile's behaviour nor the nature of the offence provides grounds for the custody officer to decide it is impracticable to arrange the juvenile's transfer to local authority care. Impracticability concerns the transport and travel requirements and the lack of secure accommodation which is provided for the purposes of restricting liberty does not make it impracticable to transfer the juvenile. The availability of secure accommodation is only a factor in relation to a juvenile aged 12 or over when other local authority accommodation would not be adequate to protect the public from serious harm from them. The* *obligation to transfer a juvenile to local authority accommodation applies as much to a juvenile charged during the daytime as to a juvenile to be held overnight, subject to a requirement to bring the juvenile before a court under PACE, s.46.*

C:17 Testing persons for the presence of specified Class A drugs

(a) *Action*

C:17.1 This section of Code C applies only in selected police stations in police areas where the ★**A–91a** provisions for drug testing under section 63B of *PACE* (as amended by section 5 of the *Criminal Justice Act* 2003 and section 7 of the *Drugs Act* 2005) are in force and in respect of which the Secretary of State has given a notification to the relevant chief officer of police that arrangements for the taking of samples have been made. Such a notification will cover either a police area as a whole or particular stations within a police area. The notification indicates whether the testing applies to those arrested or charged or under the age of 18 as the case may be and testing can only take place in respect of the persons so indicated in the notification. Testing cannot be carried out unless the relevant notification has been given and has not been withdrawn. See *Note 17F.*

C:17.2 A sample of urine or a non-intimate sample may be taken from a person in police detention for the purpose of ascertaining whether they have any specified Class A drug in their body only where they have been brought before the custody officer and:

(a) either the arrest condition, see paragraph 17.3, or the charge condition, see paragraph 17.4 is met;

(b) the age condition, see paragraph 17.5, is met;

(c) the notification condition is met in relation to the arrest condition, the charge condition, or the age condition, as the case may be (testing on charge and/or arrest must be specifically provided for in the notification for the power to apply; in addition, the fact that testing of under 18s is authorised must be expressly provided for in the notification before the power to test such persons applies); see paragraph 17.1; and

(d) a police officer has requested the person concerned to give the sample (the request condition).

C:17.3 The arrest condition is met where the detainee:

(a) has been arrested for a trigger offence, see *Note 17E*, but not charged with that offence; or

(b) has been arrested for any other offence but not charged with that offence and a police officer of inspector rank or above, who has reasonable grounds for suspecting that their misuse of any specified Class A drug caused or contributed to the offence, has authorised the sample to be taken.

C:17.4 The charge condition is met where the detainee:

(a) has been charged with a trigger offence; or

(b) has been charged with any other offence and a police officer of inspector rank or above, who has reasonable grounds for suspecting that the detainee's misuse of any specified Class A drug caused or contributed to the offence, has authorised the sample to be taken.

C:17.5 The age condition is met where:

(a) in the case of a detainee who has been arrested but not charged as in paragraph 17.3, they are aged 18 or over;

(b) in the case of a detainee who has been charged as in paragraph 17.4, they are aged 14 or over.

C:17.6 Before requesting a sample from the person concerned, an officer must:

(a) inform them that the purpose of taking the sample is for drug testing under *PACE*; this is to ascertain whether they have a specified Class A drug present in their body;

(b) warn them that if, when so requested, they fail without good cause to provide a sample they may be liable to prosecution;

(c) where the taking of the sample has been authorised by an inspector or above in accordance with paragraph 17.3(b) or 17.4(b) above, inform them that the authorisation has been given and the grounds for giving it;

(d) remind them of the following rights, which may be exercised at any stage during the period in custody:

(i) the right to have someone informed of their arrest [see section 5];

(ii) the right to consult privately with a solicitor and that free independent legal advice is available [see section 6]; and

(iii) the right to consult these codes of practice [see section 3].

C:17.7 In the case of a person who has not attained the age of 17—

(a) the making of the request for a sample under paragraph 17.2(d) above;

(b) the giving of the warning and the information under paragraph 17.6 above; and

(c) the taking of the sample,

may not take place except in the presence of an appropriate adult. See *Note 17G*.

C:17.8 Authorisation by an officer of the rank of inspector or above within paragraph 17.3(b) or 17.4(b) may be given orally or in writing but, if it is given orally, it must be confirmed in writing as soon as practicable.

C:17.9 If a sample is taken from a detainee who has been arrested for an offence but not charged with that offence as in paragraph 17.3, no further sample may be taken during the same continuous period of detention. If during that same period the charge condition is also met in respect of that detainee, the sample which has been taken shall be treated as being taken by virtue of the charge condition, see paragraph 17.4, being met.

C:17.10 A detainee from whom a sample may be taken may be detained for up to six hours from the time of charge if the custody officer reasonably believes the detention is necessary to enable a sample to be taken. Where the arrest condition is met, a detainee whom the custody officer has decided to release on bail without charge may continue to be detained, but not beyond 24 hours from the relevant time (as defined in section 41(2) of *PACE*), to enable a sample to be taken.

C:17.11 A detainee in respect of whom the arrest condition is met, but not the charge condition, see paragraphs 17.3 and 17.4, and whose release would be required before a sample can be taken had they not continued to be detained as a result of being arrested for a further offence which does not satisfy the arrest condition, may have a sample taken at any time within 24 hours after the arrest for the offence that satisfies the arrest condition.

(b) *Documentation*

C:17.12 The following must be recorded in the custody record:

(a) if a sample is taken following authorisation by an officer of the rank of inspector or above, the authorisation and the grounds for suspicion;

(b) the giving of a warning of the consequences of failure to provide a sample;

(c) the time at which the sample was given; and

(d) the time of charge or, where the arrest condition is being relied upon, the time of arrest and, where applicable, the fact that a sample taken after arrest but before charge is to be treated as being taken by virtue of the charge condition, where that is met in the same period of continuous detention. See paragraph 17.9.

(c) *General*

C:17.13 A sample may only be taken by a prescribed person. See *Note 17C*.

C:17.14 Force may not be used to take any sample for the purpose of drug testing.

C:17.15 The terms "Class A drug" and "misuse" have the same meanings as in the *Misuse of Drugs Act* 1971. "Specified" (in relation to a Class A drug) and "trigger offence" have the same meanings as in Part III of the *Criminal Justice and Court Services Act* 2000.

C:17.16 Any sample taken:

(a) may not be used for any purpose other than to ascertain whether the person concerned has a specified Class A drug present in his body; and

(b) can be disposed of as clinical waste unless it is to be sent for further analysis in cases where the test result is disputed at the point when the result is known, including on the basis that medication has been taken, or for quality assurance purposes.

(d) *Assessment of misuse of drugs*

C:17.17 Under the provisions of Part 3 of the *Drugs Act* 2005, where a detainee has tested positive for a specified Class A drug under section 63B of *PACE* a police officer may, at any time before the person's release from the police station, impose a requirement on the detainee to attend an initial assessment of their drug misuse by a suitably qualified person and to remain for its duration. Where such a requirement is imposed, the officer must, at the same time, impose a second requirement on the detainee to attend and remain for a follow-up assessment. The officer must inform the detainee that the second requirement will cease to have effect if, at the initial assessment they are informed that a follow-up assessment is not necessary. These requirements may only be imposed on a person if:

(a) they have reached the age of 18;

(b) notification has been given by the Secretary of State to the relevant chief officer of police that arrangements for conducting initial and follow-up assessments have been made for those from whom samples for testing have been taken at the police station where the detainee is in custody.

C:17.18 When imposing a requirement to attend an initial assessment and a follow-up assessment the police officer must:

(a) inform the person of the time and place at which the initial assessment is to take place;

(b) explain that this information will be confirmed in writing; and

(c) warn the person that they may be liable to prosecution if they fail without good cause to attend the initial assessment and remain for its duration and if they fail to attend the follow-up assessment and remain for its duration (if so required).

C:17.19 Where a police officer has imposed a requirement to attend an initial assessment and a follow-up assessment in accordance with paragraph 17.17, he must, before the person is released from detention, give the person notice in writing which:

(a) confirms their requirement to attend and remain for the duration of the assessments; and

(b) confirms the information and repeats the warning referred to in paragraph 17.18.

C:17.20 The following must be recorded in the custody record:

(a) that the requirement to attend an initial assessment and a follow-up assessment has been imposed; and

(b) the information, explanation, warning and notice given in accordance with paragraphs 17.17 and 17.19.

C:17.21 Where a notice is given in accordance with paragraph 17.19, a police officer can give the person a further notice in writing which informs the person of any change to the time or place at which the initial assessment is to take place and which repeats the warning referred to in paragraph 17.18(c).

C:17.22 Part 3 of the *Drugs Act* 2005 also requires police officers to have regard to any guidance issued by the Secretary of State in respect of the assessment provisions.

Notes for guidance

C:17A *When warning a person who is asked to provide a urine or non-intimate sample in accordance with paragraph 17.6(b), the following form of words may be used:*

"You do not have to provide a sample, but I must warn you that if you fail or refuse without good cause to do so, you will commit an offence for which you may be imprisoned, or fined, or both".

Where the Welsh language is appropriate, the following form of words may be used:

"Does dim rhaid i chi roi sampl, ond mae'n rhaid i mi eich rhybuddio y byddwch chi'n cyflawni trosedd os byddwch chi'n methu neu yn gwrthod gwneud hynny heb reswm da, ac y gellir, oherwydd hynny, eich car-charu, eich dirwyo, neu'r ddau."

C:17B *A sample has to be sufficient and suitable. A sufficient sample is sufficient in quantity and quality to enable drug-testing analysis to take place. A suitable sample is one which by its nature, is suitable for a particular form of drug analysis.*

C:17C *A prescribed person in paragraph 17.13 is one who is prescribed in regulations made by the Secretary of State under section 63B(6) of the* Police and Criminal Evidence Act *1984. [The regulations are currently contained in regulation S.I. 2001 No. 2645, the* Police and Criminal Evidence Act 1984 (Drug Testing Persons in Police Detention) (Prescribed Persons) Regulations *2001.]*

C:17D *Samples, and the information derived from them, may not be subsequently used in the investigation of any offence or in evidence against the persons from whom they were taken.*

C:17E *Trigger offences are:*

1. *Offences under the following provisions of the* Theft Act *1968:*

   section 1   *(theft)*

   section 8   *(robbery)*

   section 9   *(burglary)*

   section 10   *(aggravated burglary)*

   section 12   *(taking a motor vehicle or other conveyance without authority)*

   section 12A   *(aggravated vehicle-taking)*

section 22   *(handling stolen goods)*

section 25   *(going equipped for stealing, etc.).*

2.   *Offences under the following provisions of the* Misuse of Drugs Act *1971, if committed in respect of a specified Class A drug:*

section 4   *(restriction on production and supply of controlled drugs)*

section 5(2)   *(possession of a controlled drug)*

section 5(3)   *(possession of a controlled drug with intent to supply).*

3.   *Offences under the following provisions of the* Fraud Act 2006:

section 1   *(fraud)*

section 6   *(possession etc. of articles for use in frauds)*

section 7   *(making or supplying articles for use in frauds).*

3A. *An offence under section 1(1) of the* Criminal Attempts Act *1981 if committed in respect of an offence under:*

(a) *any of the following provisions of the* Theft Act *1968:*

section 1   *(theft)*

section 8   *(robbery)*

section 9   *(burglary)*

section 22   *(handling stolen goods)*

(b) *section 1 of the* Fraud Act *2006 (fraud).*

4.   *Offences under the following provisions of the* Vagrancy Act *1824:*

section 3   *(begging)*

section 4   *(persistent begging).*

C:17F *The power to take samples is subject to notification by the Secretary of State that appropriate arrangements for the taking of samples have been made for the police area as a whole or for the particular police station concerned for whichever of the following is specified in the notification:*

(a) *persons in respect of whom the arrest condition is met;*

(b) *persons in respect of whom the charge condition is met;*

(c) *persons who have not attained the age of 18.*

Note: notification is treated as having been given for the purposes of the charge condition in relation to a police area, if testing (on charge) under section 63B(2) of PACE *was in force immediately before section 7 of the* Drugs Act *2005 was brought into force; and for the purposes of the age condition, in relation to a police area or police station, if immediately before that day, notification that arrangements had been made for the taking of samples from persons under the age of 18 (those aged 14–17) had been given and had not been withdrawn.*

C:17G *Appropriate adult in paragraph 17.7 means the person's—*

(a) *parent or guardian or, if they are in the care of a local authority or voluntary organisation, a person representing that authority or organisation; or*

(b) *a social worker of a local authority; or*

(c) *if no person falling within (a) or (b) above is available, any responsible person aged 18 or over who is not a police officer or a person employed by the police.*

ANNEX A

Intimate and strip searches

A *Intimate search*

★**A–92**   **C:1.** An intimate search consists of the physical examination of a person's body orifices other than the mouth. The intrusive nature of such searches means the actual and potential risks associated with intimate searches must never be underestimated.

(a) *Action*

★**A–93**   **C:2.** Body orifices other than the mouth may be searched only:

(a) if authorised by an officer of inspector rank or above who has reasonable grounds for believing that the person may have concealed on themselves:

    (i) anything which they could and might use to cause physical injury to themselves or others at the station; or

    (ii) a Class A drug which they intended to supply to another or to export;

    and the officer has reasonable grounds for believing that an intimate search is the only means of removing those items; and

  (b) if the search is under paragraph 2(a)(ii) (a drug offence search), the detainee's appropriate consent has been given in writing.

C:2A. Before the search begins, a police officer or designated detention officer, must tell the detainee:

  (a) that the authority to carry out the search has been given;

  (b) the grounds for giving the authorisation and for believing that the article cannot be removed without an intimate search.

C:2B. Before a detainee is asked to give appropriate consent to a search under paragraph 2(a)(ii) (a drug offence search) they must be warned that if they refuse without good cause their refusal may harm their case if it comes to trial, see *Note A6*. This warning may be given by a police officer or member of police staff. In the case of juveniles, mentally vulnerable or mentally disordered suspects the seeking and giving of consent must take place in the presence of the appropriate adult. A juvenile's consent is only valid if their parent's or guardian's consent is also obtained unless the juvenile is under 14, when their parent's or guardian's consent is sufficient in its own right. A detainee who is not legally represented must be reminded of their entitlement to have free legal advice, see Code C, paragraph 6.5, and the reminder noted in the custody record.

C:3. An intimate search may only be carried out by a registered medical practitioner or registered nurse, unless an officer of at least inspector rank considers this is not practicable and the search is to take place under paragraph 2(a)(i), in which case a police officer may carry out the search. See *Notes A1 to A5*.

C:3A. Any proposal for a search under paragraph 2(a)(i) to be carried out by someone other than a registered medical practitioner or registered nurse must only be considered as a last resort and when the authorising officer is satisfied the risks associated with allowing the item to remain with the detainee outweigh the risks associated with removing it. See *Notes A1 to A5*.

C:4. An intimate search under:

- paragraph 2(a)(i) may take place only at a hospital, surgery, other medical premises or police station;

- paragraph 2(a)(ii) may take place only at a hospital, surgery or other medical premises and must be carried out by a registered medical practitioner or a registered nurse.

C:5. An intimate search at a police station of a juvenile or mentally disordered or otherwise mentally vulnerable person may take place only in the presence of an appropriate adult of the same sex (see Annex L), unless the detainee specifically requests a particular adult of the opposite sex who is readily available. In the case of a juvenile the search may take place in the absence of the appropriate adult only if the juvenile signifies in the presence of the appropriate adult they do not want the adult present during the search and the adult agrees. A record shall be made of the juvenile's decision and signed by the appropriate adult.

C:6. When an intimate search under paragraph 2(a)(i) is carried out by a police officer, the officer must be of the same sex as the detainee (see Annex L). A minimum of two people, other than the detainee, must be present during the search. Subject to paragraph 5, no person of the opposite sex who is not a medical practitioner or nurse shall be present, nor shall anyone whose presence is unnecessary. The search shall be conducted with proper regard to the sensitivity and vulnerability of the detainee.

(b) *Documentation*

C:7. In the case of an intimate search, the following shall be recorded as soon as practicable, **★A–94** in the detainee's custody record:

  (a) for searches under paragraphs 2(a)(i) and (ii);

- the authorisation to carry out the search;

- the grounds for giving the authorisation;

- the grounds for believing the article could not be removed without an intimate search;

- which parts of the detainee's body were searched;

- who carried out the search;

- who was present;
- the result;

(b) for searches under paragraph 2(a)(ii):

- the giving of the warning required by paragraph 2B;
- the fact that the appropriate consent was given or (as the case may be) refused, and if refused, the reason given for the refusal (if any).

C:8. If an intimate search is carried out by a police officer, the reason why it was impracticable for a registered medical practitioner or registered nurse to conduct it must be recorded.

B *Strip search*

★**A–95**   **C:9.** A strip search is a search involving the removal of more than outer clothing. In this code, outer clothing includes shoes and socks.

(a) *Action*

★**A–96**   **C:10.** A strip search may take place only if it is considered necessary to remove an article which a detainee would not be allowed to keep, and the officer reasonably considers the detainee might have concealed such an article. Strip searches shall not be routinely carried out if there is no reason to consider that articles are concealed.

The conduct of strip searches

C:11. When strip searches are conducted:

(a) a police officer carrying out a strip search must be the same sex as the detainee (see Annex L);

(b) the search shall take place in an area where the detainee cannot be seen by anyone who does not need to be present, nor by a member of the opposite sex (see Annex L) except an appropriate adult who has been specifically requested by the detainee;

(c) except in cases of urgency, where there is risk of serious harm to the detainee or to others, whenever a strip search involves exposure of intimate body parts, there must be at least two people present other than the detainee, and if the search is of a juvenile or mentally disordered or otherwise mentally vulnerable person, one of the people must be the appropriate adult; except in urgent cases as above, a search of a juvenile may take place in the absence of the appropriate adult only if the juvenile signifies in the presence of the appropriate adult that they do not want the adult to be present during the search and the adult agrees; a record shall be made of the juvenile's decision and signed by the appropriate adult; the presence of more than two people, other than an appropriate adult, shall be permitted only in the most exceptional circumstances;

(d) the search shall be conducted with proper regard to the sensitivity and vulnerability of the detainee in these circumstances and every reasonable effort shall be made to secure the detainee's co-operation and minimise embarrassment; detainees who are searched shall not normally be required to remove all their clothes at the same time, *e.g.* a person should be allowed to remove clothing above the waist and redress before removing further clothing;

(e) if necessary to assist the search, the detainee may be required to hold their arms in the air or to stand with their legs apart and bend forward so a visual examination may be made of the genital and anal areas provided no physical contact is made with any body orifice;

(f) if articles are found, the detainee shall be asked to hand them over; if articles are found within any body orifice other than the mouth, and the detainee refuses to hand them over, their removal would constitute an intimate search, which must be carried out as in Part A;

(g) a strip search shall be conducted as quickly as possible, and the detainee allowed to dress as soon as the procedure is complete.

(b) *Documentation*

★**A–97**   **C:12.** A record shall be made on the custody record of a strip search including the reason it was considered necessary, those present and any result.

Notes for guidance

C:A1 *Before authorising any intimate search, the authorising officer must make every reasonable effort to*   ★**A–98**
persuade the detainee to hand the article over without a search. If the detainee agrees, a registered medical
practitioner or registered nurse should whenever possible be asked to assess the risks involved and, if neces-
sary, attend to assist the detainee.

C:A2 *If the detainee does not agree to hand the article over without a search, the authorising officer must*
carefully review all the relevant factors before authorising an intimate search. In particular, the officer must
consider whether the grounds for believing an article may be concealed are reasonable.

C:A3 *If authority is given for a search under paragraph 2(a)(i), a registered medical practitioner or*
registered nurse shall be consulted whenever possible. The presumption should be that the search will be
conducted by the registered medical practitioner or registered nurse and the authorising officer must make
every reasonable effort to persuade the detainee to allow the medical practitioner or nurse to conduct the
search.

C:A4 *A constable should only be authorised to carry out a search as a last resort and when all other ap-*
proaches have failed. In these circumstances, the authorising officer must be satisfied the detainee might use
the article for one or more of the purposes in paragraph 2(a)(i) and the physical injury likely to be caused is
sufficiently severe to justify authorising a constable to carry out the search.

C:A5 *If an officer has any doubts whether to authorise an intimate search by a constable, the officer should*
seek advice from an officer of superintendent rank or above.

C:A6 *In warning a detainee who is asked to consent to an intimate drug offence search, as in paragraph*
2B, the following form of words may be used:

"You do not have to allow yourself to be searched, but I must warn you that if you refuse without good
cause, your refusal may harm your case if it comes to trial.".

Where the use of the Welsh language is appropriate, the following form of words may be used:

"Nid oes rhaid i chi roi caniatâd i gael eich archwilio, ond mae'n rhaid i mi eich rhybuddio os gwrthod-
wch heb reswm da, y gallai eich penderfyniad i wrthod wneud niwed i'ch achos pe bai'n dod gerbron llys.".

ANNEX B

Delay in notifying arrest or allowing access to legal advice

A *Persons detained under PACE*

C:1. The exercise of the rights in section 5 or section 6, or both, may be delayed if the person   ★**A–99**
is in police detention, as in *PACE*, section 118(2), in connection with an indictable offence, has not
yet been charged with an offence and an officer of superintendent rank or above, or inspector rank
or above only for the rights in section 5, has reasonable grounds for believing their exercise will:

    (i) lead to:

        • interference with, or harm to, evidence connected with an indictable offence; or

        • interference with, or physical harm to, other people; or

    (ii) lead to alerting other people suspected of having committed an indictable offence but not
        yet arrested for it; or

    (iii) hinder the recovery of property obtained in consequence of the commission of such an
        offence.

C:2. These rights may also be delayed if the officer has reasonable grounds to believe that:

    (i) the person detained for an indictable offence has benefited from their criminal conduct
        (decided in accordance with Part 2 of the *Proceeds of Crime Act* 2002); and

    (ii) the recovery of the value of the property constituting that benefit will be hindered by the
        exercise of either right.

C:3. Authority to delay a detainee's right to consult privately with a solicitor may be given only
if the authorising officer has reasonable grounds to believe the solicitor the detainee wants to
consult will, inadvertently or otherwise, pass on a message from the detainee or act in some other
way which will have any of the consequences specified under paragraphs 1 or 2. In these circumstances the detainee must be allowed to choose another solicitor. See *Note B3*.

C:4. If the detainee wishes to see a solicitor, access to that solicitor may not be delayed on the
grounds they might advise the detainee not to answer questions or the solicitor was initially
asked to attend the police station by someone else. In the latter case the detainee must be told
the solicitor has come to the police station at another person's request, and must be asked to sign
the custody record to signify whether they want to see the solicitor.

C:5. The fact the grounds for delaying notification of arrest may be satisfied does not automatically mean the grounds for delaying access to legal advice will also be satisfied.

C:6. These rights may be delayed only for as long as grounds exist and in no case beyond 36 hours after the relevant time as in *PACE*, s.41. If the grounds cease to apply within this time, the detainee must, as soon as practicable, be asked if they want to exercise either right, the custody record must be noted accordingly, and action taken in accordance with the relevant section of the code.

C:7. A detained person must be permitted to consult a solicitor for a reasonable time before any court hearing.

B   *[Not used.]*

C *Documentation*

★**A–100**   **C:**13. The grounds for action under this annex shall be recorded and the detainee informed of them as soon as practicable.

C:14. Any reply given by a detainee under paragraphs 6 or 11 must be recorded and the detainee asked to endorse the record in relation to whether they want to receive legal advice at this point.

D *Cautions and special warnings*

C:15. When a suspect detained at a police station is interviewed during any period for which access to legal advice has been delayed under this annex, the court or jury may not draw adverse inferences from their silence.

Notes for guidance

★**A–101**   **C:**B1 *Even if Annex B applies in the case of a juvenile, or a person who is mentally disordered or otherwise mentally vulnerable, action to inform the appropriate adult and the person responsible for a juvenile's welfare if that is a different person, must nevertheless be taken as in paragraph 3.13 and 3.15.*

C:B2 *In the case of Commonwealth citizens and foreign nationals, see Note 7A.*

C:B3 *A decision to delay access to a specific solicitor is likely to be a rare occurrence and only when it can be shown the suspect is capable of misleading that particular solicitor and there is more than a substantial risk that the suspect will succeed in causing information to be conveyed which will lead to one or more of the specified consequences.*

ANNEX C

Restriction on drawing adverse inferences from silence and terms of the caution when the restriction applies

(a) *The restriction on drawing adverse inferences from silence*

★**A–102**   **C:**1. The *Criminal Justice and Public Order Act* 1994, ss.34, 36 and 37 as amended by the *Youth Justice and Criminal Evidence Act* 1999, s.58 describe the conditions under which adverse inferences may be drawn from a person's failure or refusal to say anything about their involvement in the offence when interviewed, after being charged or informed they may be prosecuted. These provisions are subject to an overriding restriction on the ability of a court or jury to draw adverse inferences from a person's silence. This restriction applies:

(a) to any detainee at a police station, see *Note 10C*, who, before being interviewed, see section 11, or being charged or informed they may be prosecuted, see section 16, has:

(i) asked for legal advice, see section 6, paragraph 6.1;

(ii) not been allowed an opportunity to consult a solicitor, including the duty solicitor, as in this code; and

(iii) not changed their mind about wanting legal advice, see section 6, paragraph 6.6(d);

– [note the condition in (ii) will

– apply when a detainee who has asked for legal advice is interviewed before speaking to a solicitor as in section 6, paragraph 6.6(a) or (b);

– not apply if the detained person declines to ask for the duty solicitor, see section 6, paragraphs 6.6(c) and (d)];

   (b) to any person charged with, or informed they may be prosecuted for, an offence who:

      (i) has had brought to their notice a written statement made by another person or the content of an interview with another person which relates to that offence, see section 16, paragraph 16.4;

      (ii) is interviewed about that offence, see section 16, paragraph 16.5; or

      (iii) makes a written statement about that offence, see Annex D paragraphs 4 and 9.

(b) *Terms of the caution when the restriction applies*

C:2. When a requirement to caution arises at a time when the restriction on drawing adverse inferences from silence applies, the caution shall be:

   "You do not have to say anything, but anything you do say may be given in evidence.".

Where the use of the Welsh language is appropriate, the caution may be used directly in Welsh in the following terms:

   "Does dim rhaid i chi ddweud dim byd, ond gall unrhyw beth yr ydych chi'n ei ddweud gael ei roi fel tystiolaeth.".

C:3. Whenever the restriction either begins to apply or ceases to apply after a caution has already been given, the person shall be re-cautioned in the appropriate terms. The changed position on drawing inferences and that the previous caution no longer applies shall also be explained to the detainee in ordinary language. See *Note C2.*

Notes for guidance

C:C1 *The restriction on drawing inferences from silence does not apply to a person who has not been detained and who therefore cannot be prevented from seeking legal advice if they want to, see paragraphs 10.2 and 3.15.*

C:C2 *The following is suggested as a framework to help explain changes in the position on drawing adverse inferences if the restriction on drawing adverse inferences from silence:*

   (a) begins to apply:

   "The caution you were previously given no longer applies. This is because after that caution:

   (i) you asked to speak to a solicitor but have not yet been allowed an opportunity to speak to a solicitor;" see paragraph 1(a); or

   "(ii) you have been charged with/informed you may be prosecuted." See paragraph 1(b).

   "This means that from now on, adverse inferences cannot be drawn at court and your defence will not be harmed just because you choose to say nothing. Please listen carefully to the caution I am about to give you because it will apply from now on. You will see that it does not say anything about your defence being harmed.";

   (b) ceases to apply before or at the time the person is charged or informed they may be prosecuted, see paragraph 1(a);

   "The caution you were previously given no longer applies. This is because after that caution you have been allowed an opportunity to speak to a solicitor. Please listen carefully to the caution I am about to give you because it will apply from now on. It explains how your defence at court may be affected if you choose to say nothing.".

ANNEX D

Written statements under caution

(a) *Written by a person under caution*

C:1. A person shall always be invited to write down what they want to say.   ★**A–103**

C:2. A person who has not been charged with, or informed they may be prosecuted for, any offence to which the statement they want to write relates, shall:

   (a) unless the statement is made at a time when the restriction on drawing adverse inferences from silence applies, see Annex C, be asked to write out and sign the following before writing what they want to say:

      "I make this statement of my own free will. I understand that I do not have to say anything but that it may harm my defence if I do not mention when questioned something which I later rely on in court. This statement may be given in evidence.";

   (b) if the statement is made at a time when the restriction on drawing adverse inferences from silence applies, be asked to write out and sign the following before writing what they want to say;

> "*I make this statement of my own free will. I understand that I do not have to say anything. This statement may be given in evidence.*".

C:3. When a person, on the occasion of being charged with or informed they may be prosecuted for any offence, asks to make a statement which relates to any such offence and wants to write it they shall:

(a) unless the restriction on drawing adverse inferences from silence, see Annex C, applied when they were so charged or informed they may be prosecuted, be asked to write out and sign the following before writing what they want to say:

> "*I make this statement of my own free will. I understand that I do not have to say anything but that it may harm my defence if I do not mention when questioned something which I later rely on in court. This statement may be given in evidence.*";

(b) if the restriction on drawing adverse inferences from silence applied when they were so charged or informed they may be prosecuted, be asked to write out and sign the following before writing what they want to say:

> "*I make this statement of my own free will. I understand that I do not have to say anything. This statement may be given in evidence.*".

C:4. When a person, who has already been charged with or informed they may be prosecuted for any offence, asks to make a statement which relates to any such offence and wants to write it they shall be asked to write out and sign the following before writing what they want to say:

> "*I make this statement of my own free will. I understand that I do not have to say anything. This statement may be given in evidence.*".

C:5. Any person writing their own statement shall be allowed to do so without any prompting except a police officer or police staff may indicate to them which matters are material or question any ambiguity in the statement.

(b) *Written by a police officer or other police staff*

★**A–104**   **C:6.** If a person says they would like someone to write the statement for them, a police officer, or other police staff shall write the statement.

C:7. If the person has not been charged with, or informed they may be prosecuted for, any offence to which the statement they want to make relates they shall, before starting, be asked to sign, or make their mark, to the following:

(a) unless the statement is made at a time when the restriction on drawing adverse inferences from silence applies, see Annex C:

> "*I,...................., wish to make a statement. I want someone to write down what I say. I understand that I do not have to say anything but that it may harm my defence if I do not mention when questioned something which I later rely on in court. This statement may be given in evidence.*";

(b) if the statement is made at a time when the restriction on drawing adverse inferences from silence applies:

> "*I,...................., wish to make a statement. I want someone to write down what I say. I understand that I do not have to say anything. This statement may be given in evidence.*".

C:8. If, on the occasion of being charged with or informed they may be prosecuted for any offence, the person asks to make a statement which relates to any such offence they shall before starting be asked to sign, or make their mark to, the following:

(a) unless the restriction on drawing adverse inferences from silence applied, see Annex C, when they were so charged or informed they may be prosecuted:

> "*I,...................., wish to make a statement. I want someone to write down what I say. I understand that I do not have to say anything but that it may harm my defence if I do not mention when questioned something which I later rely on in court. This statement may be given in evidence.*";

(b) if the restriction on drawing adverse inferences from silence applied when they were so charged or informed they may be prosecuted:

> "*I,...................., wish to make a statement. I want someone to write down what I say. I understand that I do not have to say anything. This statement may be given in evidence.*".

C:9. If, having already been charged with or informed they may be prosecuted for any offence, a person asks to make a statement which relates to any such offence they shall before starting, be asked to sign, or make their mark to:

"I,....................., wish to make a statement. I want someone to write down what I say. I understand that I do not have to say anything. This statement may be given in evidence.".

C:10. The person writing the statement must take down the exact words spoken by the person making it and must not edit or paraphrase it. Any questions that are necessary, *e.g.* to make it more intelligible, and the answers given must be recorded at the same time on the statement form.

C:11. When the writing of a statement is finished the person making it shall be asked to read it and to make any corrections, alterations or additions they want. When they have finished reading they shall be asked to write and sign or make their mark on the following certificate at the end of the statement:

"I have read the above statement, and I have been able to correct, alter or add anything I wish. This statement is true. I have made it of my own free will.".

C:12. If the person making the statement cannot read, or refuses to read it, or to write the above mentioned certificate at the end of it or to sign it, the person taking the statement shall read it to them and ask them if they would like to correct, alter or add anything and to put their signature or make their mark at the end. The person taking the statement shall certify on the statement itself what has occurred.

ANNEX E

Summary of provisions relating to mentally disordered and otherwise mentally vulnerable people

C:1. If an officer has any suspicion, or is told in good faith, that a person of any age may be   **★A–105** mentally disordered or otherwise mentally vulnerable, or mentally incapable of understanding the significance of questions or their replies that person shall be treated as mentally disordered or otherwise mentally vulnerable for the purposes of this code. See paragraph 1.4 and *Note E4.*

C:2. In the case of a person who is mentally disordered or otherwise mentally vulnerable, "the appropriate adult" means:

  (a) a relative, guardian or other person responsible for their care or custody;
  (b) someone experienced in dealing with mentally disordered or mentally vulnerable people but who is not a police officer or employed by the police;
  (c) failing these, some other responsible adult aged 18 or over who is not a police officer or employed by the police.

See paragraph 1.7(b) and *Note 1D.*

C:3. If the custody officer authorises the detention of a person who is mentally vulnerable or appears to be suffering from a mental disorder, the custody officer must as soon as practicable inform the appropriate adult of the grounds for detention and the person's whereabouts, and ask the adult to come to the police station to see them. If the appropriate adult:

  • is already at the station when information is given as in paragraphs 3.1 to 3.5 the information must be given in their presence;
  • is not at the station when the provisions of paragraph 3.1 to 3.5 are complied with these provisions must be complied with again in their presence once they arrive.

See paragraphs 3.15 to 3.17.

C:4. If the appropriate adult, having been informed of the right to legal advice, considers legal advice should be taken, the provisions of section 6 apply as if the mentally disordered or otherwise mentally vulnerable person had requested access to legal advice. See paragraph 3.19 and *Note E1.*

C:5. The custody officer must make sure a person receives appropriate clinical attention as soon as reasonably practicable if the person appears to be suffering from a mental disorder or in urgent cases immediately call the nearest appropriate healthcare professional or an ambulance. It is not intended these provisions delay the transfer of a detainee to a place of safety under the *Mental Health Act* 1983, s.136, if that is applicable. If an assessment under that Act is to take place at a police station, the custody officer must consider whether an appropriate healthcare professional should be called to conduct an initial clinical check on the detainee. See paragraph 9.5 and 9.6.

C:6. It is imperative a mentally disordered or otherwise mentally vulnerable person detained under the *Mental Health Act* 1983, s.136, be assessed as soon as possible. A police station should only be used as a place of safety as a last resort but if that assessment is to take place at the police station, an approved social worker and registered medical practitioner shall be called to the station as soon as possible to carry it out. Once the detainee has been assessed and suitable arrangements been made for their treatment or care, they can no longer be detained under section 136. A detainee should be immediately discharged from detention if a registered medical practitioner having examined them, concludes they are not mentally disordered within the meaning of the Act. See paragraph 3.16.

C:7. If a mentally disordered or otherwise mentally vulnerable person is cautioned in the absence of the appropriate adult, the caution must be repeated in the appropriate adult's presence. See paragraph 10.12.

C:8. A mentally disordered or otherwise mentally vulnerable person must not be interviewed or asked to provide or sign a written statement in the absence of the appropriate adult unless the provisions of paragraphs 11.1 or 11.18 to 11.20 apply. Questioning in these circumstances may not continue in the absence of the appropriate adult once sufficient information to avert the risk has been obtained. A record shall be made of the grounds for any decision to begin an interview in these circumstances. See paragraphs 11.1, 11.15 and 11.18 to 11.20.

C:9. If the appropriate adult is present at an interview, they shall be informed they are not expected to act simply as an observer and the purposes of their presence are to:

- advise the interviewee;
- observe whether or not the interview is being conducted properly and fairly;
- facilitate communication with the interviewee.

See paragraph 11.17.

★**A–106**   **C:**10. If the detention of a mentally disordered or otherwise mentally vulnerable person is reviewed by a review officer or a superintendent, the appropriate adult must, if available at the time, be given an opportunity to make representations to the officer about the need for continuing detention. See paragraph 15.3.

C:11. If the custody officer charges a mentally disordered or otherwise mentally vulnerable person with an offence or takes such other action as is appropriate when there is sufficient evidence for a prosecution this must be carried out in the presence of the appropriate adult if they are at the police station. A copy of the written notice embodying any charge must also be given to the appropriate adult. See paragraphs 16.1 to 16.4A.

C:12. An intimate or strip search of a mentally disordered or otherwise mentally vulnerable person may take place only in the presence of the appropriate adult of the same sex, unless the detainee specifically requests the presence of a particular adult of the opposite sex. A strip search may take place in the absence of an appropriate adult only in cases of urgency when there is a risk of serious harm to the detainee or others. See Annex A, paragraphs 5 and 11(c).

C:13. Particular care must be taken when deciding whether to use any form of approved restraints on a mentally disordered or otherwise mentally vulnerable person in a locked cell. See paragraph 8.2.

Notes for guidance

★**A–107**   **C:**E1 *The purpose of the provision at paragraph 3.19 is to protect the rights of a mentally disordered or otherwise mentally vulnerable detained person who does not understand the significance of what is said to them. If the detained person wants to exercise the right to legal advice, the appropriate action should be taken and not delayed until the appropriate adult arrives. A mentally disordered or otherwise mentally vulnerable detained person should always be given an opportunity, when an appropriate adult is called to the police station, to consult privately with a solicitor in the absence of the appropriate adult if they want.*

C:E2 *Although people who are mentally disordered or otherwise mentally vulnerable are often capable of providing reliable evidence, they may, without knowing or wanting to do so, be particularly prone in certain circumstances to provide information that may be unreliable, misleading or self-incriminating. Special care should always be taken when questioning such a person, and the appropriate adult should be involved if there is any doubt about a person's mental state or capacity. Because of the risk of unreliable evidence, it is important to obtain corroboration of any facts admitted whenever possible.*

C:E3 *Because of the risks referred to in Note E2, which the presence of the appropriate adult is intended to minimise, officers of superintendent rank or above should exercise their discretion to authorise the commencement of an interview in the appropriate adult's absence only in exceptional cases, if it is necessary to avert an immediate risk of serious harm. See paragraphs 11.1, 11.18 to 11.20.*

C:E4 *There is no requirement for an appropriate adult to be present if a person is detained under section 136 of the* Mental Health Act 1983 *for assessment.*

ANNEX F

★**A–108**   [*Not used.*]

ANNEX G

Fitness to be interviewed

★**A–109**   **C:**1. This annex contains general guidance to help police officers and health care professionals assess whether a detainee might be at risk in an interview.

C:2. A detainee may be at risk in an interview if it is considered that:

    (a) conducting the interview could significantly harm the detainee's physical or mental state;

    (b) anything the detainee says in the interview about their involvement or suspected involvement in the offence about which they are being interviewed **might** be considered unreliable in subsequent court proceedings because of their physical or mental state.

C:3. In assessing whether the detainee should be interviewed, the following must be considered:

    (a) how the detainee's physical or mental state might affect their ability to understand the nature and purpose of the interview, to comprehend what is being asked and to appreciate the significance of any answers given and make rational decisions about whether they want to say anything;

    (b) the extent to which the detainee's replies may be affected by their physical or mental condition rather than representing a rational and accurate explanation of their involvement in the offence;

    (c) how the nature of the interview, which could include particularly probing questions, might affect the detainee.

C:4. It is essential health care professionals who are consulted consider the functional ability of   ★**A–110**
the detainee rather than simply relying on a medical diagnosis, *e.g.* it is possible for a person with severe mental illness to be fit for interview.

C:5. Health care professionals should advise on the need for an appropriate adult to be present, whether reassessment of the person's fitness for interview may be necessary if the interview lasts beyond a specified time, and whether a further specialist opinion may be required.

C:6. When health care professionals identify risks they should be asked to quantify the risks. They should inform the custody officer:

- whether the person's condition:
  - is likely to improve;
  - will require or be amenable to treatment; and
- indicate how long it may take for such improvement to take effect.

C:7. The role of the health care professional is to consider the risks and advise the custody officer of the outcome of that consideration. The health care professional's determination and any advice or recommendations should be made in writing and form part of the custody record.

C:8. Once the health care professional has provided that information, it is a matter for the custody officer to decide whether or not to allow the interview to go ahead and if the interview is to proceed, to determine what safeguards are needed. Nothing prevents safeguards being provided in addition to those required under the code. An example might be to have an appropriate health care professional present during the interview, in addition to an appropriate adult, in order constantly to monitor the person's condition and how it is being affected by the interview.

ANNEX H

Detained person: observation list

C:1. If any detainee fails to meet any of the following criteria, an appropriate health care   ★**A–111**
professional or an ambulance must be called.

C:2. When assessing the level of rousability, consider:

    Rousability—can they be woken?

- go into the cell
- call their name
- shake gently

    Response to questions—can they give appropriate answers to questions such as:

- What's your name?
- Where do you live?
- Where do you think you are?

    Response to commands—can they respond appropriately to commands such as:

- Open your eyes!
- Lift one arm, now the other arm!

C:3. Remember to take into account the possibility or presence of other illnesses, injury, or mental condition, a person who is drowsy and smells of alcohol may also have the following:

- Diabetes
- Epilepsy
- Head injury
- Drug intoxication or overdose
- Stroke

ANNEX I
  [*Not used.*]

ANNEX J
  [*Not used.*]

ANNEX K

X-rays and ultrasound scans

(a) *Action*

★**A–111a**   **C:**1. *PACE*, s.55A allows a person who has been arrested and is in police detention to have an x-ray taken of them or an ultrasound scan to be carried out on them (or both) if:

  (a) authorised by an officer of inspector rank or above who has reasonably grounds for believing that the detainee:
    (i) may have swallowed a Class A drug; and
    (ii) was in possession of that Class A drug with the intention of supplying it to another or to export; and
  (b) the detainee's appropriate consent has been given in writing.

  C:2. Before an x-ray is taken or an ultrasound scan carried out, a police officer, designated detention officer or staff custody officer must tell the detainee:

  (a) that the authority has been given; and
  (b) the grounds for giving the authorisation.

  C:3. Before a detainee is asked to give appropriate consent to an x-ray or an ultrasound scan, they must be warned that if they refuse without good cause their refusal may harm their case if it comes to trial, see *Notes K1* and *K2*. This warning may be given by a police officer or member of police staff. In the case of juveniles, mentally vulnerable or mentally disordered suspects the seeking and giving of consent must take place in the presence of the appropriate adult. A juvenile's consent is only valid if their parent's or guardian's consent is also obtained unless the juvenile is under 14, when their parent's or guardian's consent is sufficient in its own right. A detainee who is not legally represented must be reminded of their entitlement to have free legal advice, see Code C, paragraph 6.5, and the reminder noted in the custody record.

  C:4. An x-ray may be taken, or an ultrasound scan may be carried out, only by a registered medical practitioner or registered nurse, and only at a hospital, surgery or other medical premises.

(b) *Documentation*

  C:5. The following shall be recorded as soon as practicable in the detainee's custody record:

  (a) the authorisation to take the x-ray or carry out the ultrasound scan (or both);
  (b) the grounds for giving the authorisation;
  (c) the giving of the warning required by paragraph 3; and
  (d) the fact that the appropriate consent was given or (as the case may be) refused, and if refused, the reason given for the refusal (if any); and
  (e) if an x-ray is taken or an ultrasound scan carried out:
    - where it was taken or carried out;
    - who took it or carried it out;
    - who was present;

● the result.

C:6. Paragraphs 1.4–1.7 of this code apply and an appropriate adult should be present when consent is sought to any procedure under this annex.

Notes for guidance

C:K1 *If authority is given for an x-ray to be taken or an ultrasound scan to be carried out (or both), consideration should be given to asking a registered medical practitioner or registered nurse to explain to the detainee what is involved and to allay any concerns the detainee might have about the effect which taking an x-ray or carrying out an ultrasound scan might have on them. If appropriate consent is not given, evidence of the explanation may, if the case comes to trial, be relevant to determining whether the detainee had a good cause for refusing.*   ★**A–111b**

C:K2 *In warning a detainee who is asked to consent to an x-ray being taken or an ultrasound scan being carried out (or both), as in paragraph 3, the following form of words may be used:*

"You do not have to allow an x-ray of you to be taken or an ultrasound scan to be carried out on you, but I must warn you that if you refuse without good cause, your refusal may harm your case if it comes to trial.".

Where the use of the Welsh language is appropriate, the following form of words may be provided in Welsh:

"Does dim rhaid i chi ganiatáu cymryd sgan uwchsain neu belydr-x (neu'r ddau) arnoch, ond mae'n rhaid i mi eich rhybuddio os byddwch chi'n gwrthod gwneud hynny heb reswm da, fe allai hynny niweidio eich achos pe bai'n dod gerbron llys.".

ANNEX L

Establishing Gender of Persons for the Purpose of Searching

C:1. 1. Certain provisions of this and other *PACE* codes explicitly state that searches and other procedures may only be carried out by, or in the presence of, persons of the same sex as the person subject to the search or other procedure. See *Note L1*.   ★**A–111c**

C:2. All searches and procedures must be carried out with courtesy, consideration and respect for the person concerned. Police officers should show particular sensitivity when dealing with transgender individuals (including transsexual persons) and transvestite persons (see *Notes L2, L3* and *L4*).

(a) *Consideration*

C:3. In law, the gender (and accordingly the sex) of an individual is their gender as registered at birth unless they have been issued with a gender recognition certificate (GRC) under the *Gender Recognition Act* 2004 (*GRA*), in which case the person's gender is their acquired gender. This means that if the acquired gender is the male gender, the person's sex becomes that of a man and, if it is the female gender, the person's sex becomes that of a woman and they must be treated as their acquired gender.   ★**A–111d**

C:4. When establishing whether the person concerned should be treated as being male or female for the purposes of these searches and procedures, the following approach which is designed to minimise embarrassment and secure the person's co-operation should be followed:

  (a) the person must not be asked whether they have a GRC (see paragraph 8);

  (b) if there is no doubt as to as to whether the person concerned should be treated as being male or female, they should be dealt with as being of that sex;

  (c) if at any time (including during the search or carrying out the procedure) there is doubt as to whether the person should be treated, or continue to be treated, as being male or female:

   (i) the person should be asked what gender they consider themselves to be; if they express a preference to be dealt with as a particular gender, they should be asked to indicate and confirm their preference by signing the custody record or, if a custody record has not been opened, the search record or the officer's notebook; subject to (ii) below, the person should be treated according to their preference;

   (ii) if there are grounds to doubt that the preference in (i) accurately reflects the person's predominant lifestyle, for example, if they ask to be treated as a woman but documents and other information make it clear that they live predominantly as a man, or vice versa, they should be treated according to what appears to be their predominant lifestyle and not their stated preference;

(iii) if the person is unwilling to express a preference as in (i) above, efforts should be made to determine their predominant lifestyle and they should be treated as such; for example, if they appear to live predominantly as a woman, they should be treated as being female; or

(iv) if none of the above apply, the person should be dealt with according to what reasonably appears to have been their sex as registered at birth.

C:5. Once a decision has been made about which gender an individual is to be treated as, each officer responsible for the search or procedure should where possible be advised before the search or procedure starts of any doubts as to the person's gender and the person informed that the doubts have been disclosed. This is important so as to maintain the dignity of the person and any officers concerned.

(b) *Documentation*

★**A–111e**   C:6. The person's gender as established under paragraph 4(c)(i) to (iv) above must be recorded in the person's custody record, or if a custody record has not been opened, on the search record or in the officer's notebook.

C:7. Where the person elects which gender they consider themselves to be under paragraph 4(b)(i) but following 4(b)(ii) is not treated in accordance with their preference, the reason must be recorded in the search record, in the officer's notebook or, if applicable, in the person's custody record.

(c) *Disclosure of information*

★**A–111f**   C:8. Section 22 of the *GRA* defines any information relating to a person's application for a GRC or to a successful applicant's gender before it became their acquired gender as "protected information". Nothing in this annex is to be read as authorising or permitting any police officer or any police staff who has acquired such information when acting in their official capacity to disclose that information to any other person in contravention of the *GRA*. Disclosure includes making a record of "protected information" which is read by others.

Notes for Guidance

★**A–111g**   C:L1 *Provisions to which paragraph 1 applies include:*

- *in Code C; paragraph 4.1 and Annex A, paragraphs 5, 6 and 11 (searches, strip and intimate searches of detainees under sections 54 and 55 of* PACE);
- *in Code A; paragraphs 2.8 and 3.6 and Note 4;*
- *in Code D; paragraph 5.5 and Note 5F (searches, examinations and photographing of detainees under section 54A of* PACE) *and paragraph 6.9 (taking samples);*
- *in Code H; paragraph 4.1 and Annex A, paragraphs 6, 7 and 12 (searches, strip and intimate searches under sections 54 and 55 of* PACE *of persons arrested under section 41 of the* Terrorism Act 2000).

C:L2 *While there is no agreed definition of transgender (or trans), it is generally used as an umbrella term to describe people whose gender identity (self-identification as being a woman, man, neither or both) differs from the sex they were registered as at birth. The term includes, but is not limited to, transsexual people.*

C:L3 *Transsexual means a person who is proposing to undergo, is undergoing or has undergone a process (or part of a process) for the purpose of gender reassignment which is a protected characteristic under the* Equality Act 2010 *(see paragraph 1.0) by changing physiological or other attributes of their sex. This includes aspects of gender such as dress and title. It would apply to a woman making the transition to being a man and a man making the transition to being a woman as well as to a person who has only just started out on the process of gender reassignment and to a person who has completed the process. Both would share the characteristic of gender reassignment with each having the characteristics of one sex, but with certain characteristics of the other sex.*

C:L4 *Transvestite means a person of one gender who dresses in the clothes of a person of the opposite gender. However, a transvestite does not live permanently in the gender opposite to their birth sex.*

C:L5 *Chief officers are responsible for providing corresponding operational guidance and instructions for the deployment of transgender officers and staff under their direction and control to duties which involve carrying out, or being present at, any of the searches and procedures described in paragraph 1. The guidance and instructions must comply with the* Equality Act 2010 *and should therefore complement the approach in this annex.*

(5) Identification

The text that follows is of the version of the code that came into force on March 7, 2011 **A–112**
see *ante*, Appendix A–1.

In connection with Code D, see also §§ 14–29 *et seq.* (application of code), §§ 14–33 *et seq.*
(identification parades), § 14–39 (group identification, confrontation and video identification), §§ 14–40 *et seq.* (effect of breaches), §§ 14–43 *et seq.* (photographs), §§ 14–46 *et seq.*
(video recordings), and § 15–179 (photographs) in the main work.

D. Code of Practice for the Identification of Persons by Police Officers
Commencement—Transitional arrangements

This code has effect in relation to any identification procedure carried out after midnight, twenty- **A–113**
one days after the day on which the *Police and Criminal Evidence Act 1984 (Codes of Practice) (Revision of Codes A, B and D) Order* 2010 [*sic*] is made.

D:1 Introduction

D:1.1 This code of practice concerns the principal methods used by police to identify people **A–114**
in connection with the investigation of offences and the keeping of accurate and reliable criminal
records. The powers and procedures in this code must be used fairly, responsibly, with respect
for the people to whom they apply and without unlawful discrimination. The *Equality Act* 2010
makes it unlawful for police officers to discriminate against, harass or victimise any person on the
grounds of the "protected characteristics" of age, disability, gender reassignment, race, religion or
belief, sex and sexual orientation, marriage and civil partnership, pregnancy and maternity when using their powers. When police forces are carrying out their functions they also have a duty to have
regard to the need to eliminate unlawful discrimination, harassment and victimisation and to take
steps to foster good relations.

D:1.2 In this code, identification by an eye-witness arises when a witness who has seen the offender committing the crime and is given an opportunity to identify a person suspected of
involvement in the offence in a video identification, identification parade or similar procedure.
These eyewitness identification procedures (see Part A of section 3 below) are designed to:

- test the witness's ability to identify the suspect as the person they saw on a previous occasion;
- provide safeguards against mistaken identification.

While this code concentrates on visual identification procedures, it does not preclude the police making use of aural identification procedures such as a "voice identification parade", where they judge
that appropriate.

D:1.2A In this code, separate provisions in Part B of section 3 below apply when any person,
including a police officer, is asked if they recognise anyone they see in an image as being someone they know and to test their claim that they recognise that person as someone who is known
to them. Except where stated, these separate provisions are not subject to the eye-witnesses
identification procedures described in paragraph 1.2.

D:1.3 Identification by fingerprints applies when a person's fingerprints are taken to:

- compare with fingerprints found at the scene of a crime;
- check and prove convictions;
- help to ascertain a person's identity.

D:1.3A Identification using footwear impressions applies when a person's footwear impressions are taken to compare with impressions found at the scene of a crime.

D:1.4 Identification by body samples and impressions includes taking samples such as blood
or hair to generate a DNA profile for comparison with material obtained from the scene of a
crime, or a victim.

D:1.5 Taking photographs of arrested people applies to recording and checking identity and
locating and tracing persons who:

- are wanted for offences;
- fail to answer their bail.

D:1.6 Another method of identification involves searching and examining detained suspects to
find, *e.g.*, marks such as tattoos or scars which may help establish their identity or whether they have
been involved in committing an offence.

D:1.7 The provisions of the *Police and Criminal Evidence Act* 1984 (*PACE*) and this code are designed to make sure fingerprints, samples, impressions and photographs are taken, used and retained, and identification procedures carried out, only when justified and necessary for preventing, detecting or investigating crime. If these provisions are not observed, the application of the relevant procedures in particular cases may be open to question.

D:2 General

D:2.1 This code must be readily available at all police stations for consultation by:

- police officers and police staff;
- detained persons;
- members of the public.

D:2.2 The provisions of this code:

- include the Annexes;
- do not include the *Notes for guidance.*

D:2.3 Code C, paragraph 1.4, regarding a person who may be mentally disordered or otherwise mentally vulnerable and the *Notes for guidance* applicable to those provisions apply to this code.

D:2.4 Code C, paragraph 1.5, regarding a person who appears to be under the age of 17 applies to this code.

D:2.5 Code C, paragraph 1.6, regarding a person who appears to be blind, seriously visually impaired, deaf, unable to read or speak or has difficulty communicating orally because of a speech impediment applies to this code.

D:2.6 In this code:

- "appropriate adult" means the same as in Code C, paragraph 1.7;
- "solicitor" means the same as in Code C, paragraph 6.12;
  and the *Notes for guidance* applicable to those provisions apply to this code;
- where a search or other procedure under this code may only be carried out or observed by a person of the same sex as the person to whom the search or procedure applies, the gender of the detainee and other persons present should be established and recorded in line with Annex F of Code A.

D:2.7 References to custody officers include those performing the functions of custody officer, see paragraph 1.9 of Code C.

D:2.8 When a record of any action requiring the authority of an officer of a specified rank is made under this code, subject to paragraph 2.18, the officer's name and rank must be recorded.

D:2.9 When this code requires the prior authority or agreement of an officer of at least inspector or superintendent rank, that authority may be given by a sergeant or chief inspector who has been authorised to perform the functions of the higher rank under *PACE*, s.107.

D:2.10 Subject to paragraph 2.18, all records must be timed and signed by the maker.

D:2.11 Records must be made in the custody record, unless otherwise specified. References to "pocket book" include any official report book issued to police officers or police staff.

D:2.12 If any procedure in this code requires a person's consent, the consent of a:

- mentally disordered or otherwise mentally vulnerable person is only valid if given in the presence of the appropriate adult;
- juvenile is only valid if their parent's or guardian's consent is also obtained unless the juvenile is under 14, when their parent's or guardian's consent is sufficient in its own right. If the only obstacle to an identification procedure in section 3 is that a juvenile's parent or guardian refuses consent or reasonable efforts to obtain it have failed, the identification officer may apply the provisions of paragraph 3.21. See *Note 2A.*

D:2.13 If a person is blind, seriously visually impaired or unable to read, the custody officer or identification officer shall make sure their solicitor, relative, appropriate adult or some other person likely to take an interest in them and not involved in the investigation is available to help check any documentation. When this code requires written consent or signing, the person assisting may be asked to sign instead, if the detainee prefers. This paragraph does not require an appropriate adult to be called solely to assist in checking and signing documentation for a person who is not a juvenile, or mentally disordered or otherwise mentally vulnerable (see *Note 2B* and Code C, paragraph 3.15).

D:2.14 If any procedure in this code requires information to be given to or sought from a suspect, it must be given or sought in the appropriate adult's presence if the suspect is mentally disordered, otherwise mentally vulnerable or a juvenile. If the appropriate adult is not present when the information is first given or sought, the procedure must be repeated in the presence of the appropriate adult when they arrive. If the suspect appears deaf or there is doubt about their hearing or speaking ability or ability to understand English, and effective communication cannot be established, the information must be given or sought through an interpreter.

D:2.15 Any procedure in this code involving the participation of a suspect who is mentally disordered, otherwise mentally vulnerable or a juvenile must take place in the presence of the appropriate adult. See Code C, paragraph 1.4.

D:2.15A Any procedure in this code involving the participation of a witness who is or appears to be mentally disordered, otherwise mentally vulnerable or a juvenile should take place in the presence of a pre-trial support person unless the witness states that they do not want a support person to be present. A support person must not be allowed to prompt any identification of a suspect by a witness. See *Note 2AB*.

D:2.16 References to:

- "taking a photograph", include the use of any process to produce a single, still or moving, visual image;
- "photographing a person", should be construed accordingly;
- "photographs", "films", "negatives" and "copies" include relevant visual images recorded, stored, or reproduced through any medium;
- "destruction" includes the deletion of computer data relating to such images or making access to that data impossible.

D:2.17 Except as described, nothing in this code affects the powers and procedures:

(i) for requiring and taking samples of breath, blood and urine in relation to driving offences, etc, when under the influence of drink, drugs or excess alcohol under the:
- *Road Traffic Act* 1988, ss.4 to 11;
- *Road Traffic Offenders Act* 1988, ss.15 and 16;
- *Transport and Works Act* 1992, ss.26 to 38;

(ii) under the *Immigration Act* 1971, Sched. 2, para. 18, for taking photographs and fingerprints from persons detained under that Act, Schedule 2, paragraph 16 (administrative controls as to control on entry etc.); for taking fingerprints in accordance with the *Immigration and Asylum Act* 1999, ss.141 and 142(3), or other methods for collecting information about a person's external physical characteristics provided for by regulations made under that Act, section 144;

(iii) under the *Terrorism Act* 2000, Sched. 8, for taking photographs, fingerprints, skin impressions, body samples or impressions from people:
- arrested under that Act, section 41,
- detained for the purposes of examination under that Act, Schedule 7, and to whom the code of practice issued under that Act, Schedule 14, paragraph 6, applies ("the terrorism provisions"); see *Note 2C*;

(iv) for taking photographs, fingerprints, skin impressions, body samples or impressions from people who have been:
- arrested on warrants issued in Scotland, by officers exercising powers under the *Criminal Justice and Public Order Act* 1994, s.136(2);
- arrested or detained without warrant by officers from a police force in Scotland exercising their powers of arrest or detention under the *Criminal Justice and Public Order Act* 1994, s.137(2) (cross border powers of arrest etc.).

Note: in these cases, police powers and duties and the person's rights and entitlements whilst at a police station in England and Wales are the same as if the person had been arrested in Scotland by a Scottish police officer.

2.18 Nothing in this code requires the identity of officers or police staff to be recorded or disclosed:

(a) in the case of enquiries linked to the investigation of terrorism;
(b) if the officers or police staff reasonably believe recording or disclosing their names might put them in danger.

In these cases, they shall use warrant or other identification numbers and the name of their police station. *See Note 2D*.

A-118

D:2.19 In this code:

(a) "designated person" means a person other than a police officer, designated under the *Police Reform Act* 2002, Pt 4, who has specified powers and duties of police officers conferred or imposed on them;

(b) any reference to a police officer includes a designated person acting in the exercise or performance of the powers and duties conferred or imposed on them by their designation.

D:2.20 If a power conferred on a designated person:

(a) allows reasonable force to be used when exercised by a police officer, a designated person exercising that power has the same entitlement to use force;

(b) includes power to use force to enter any premises, that power is not exercisable by that designated person except:

(i) in the company, and under the supervision, of a police officer; or

(ii) for the purpose of:

- saving life or limb; or

- preventing serious damage to property.

D:2.21 Nothing in this code prevents the custody officer, or other officer given custody of the detainee, from allowing police staff who are not designated persons to carry out individual procedures or tasks at the police station if the law allows. However, the officer remains responsible for making sure the procedures and tasks are carried out correctly in accordance with the codes of practice. Any such person must be:

(a) a person employed by a police authority maintaining a police force and under the control and direction of the chief officer of that force;

(b) employed by a person with whom a police authority has a contract for the provision of services relating to persons arrested or otherwise in custody.

D:2.22 Designated persons and other police staff must have regard to any relevant provisions of the codes of practice.

Notes for guidance

A-119

D:2A *For the purposes of paragraph 2.12, the consent required from a parent or guardian may, for a juvenile in the care of a local authority or voluntary organisation, be given by that authority or organisation. In the case of a juvenile, nothing in paragraph 2.12 requires the parent, guardian or representative of a local authority or voluntary organisation to be present to give their consent, unless they are acting as the appropriate adult under paragraphs 2.14 or 2.15. However, it is important that a parent or guardian not present is fully informed before being asked to consent. They must be given the same information about the procedure and the juvenile's suspected involvement in the offence as the juvenile and appropriate adult. The parent or guardian must also be allowed to speak to the juvenile and the appropriate adult if they wish. Provided the consent is fully informed and is not withdrawn, it may be obtained at any time before the procedure takes place.*

D:2AB *The* Youth Justice and Criminal Evidence Act *1999 guidance "Achieving Best Evidence in Criminal Proceedings" indicates that a pre-trial support person should accompany a vulnerable witness during any identification procedure unless the witness states that they do not want a support person to be present. It states that this support person should not be (or not be likely to be) a witness in the investigation.*

D:2B *People who are seriously visually impaired or unable to read may be unwilling to sign police documents. The alternative, i.e. their representative signing on their behalf, seeks to protect the interests of both police and suspects.*

D:2C *Photographs, fingerprints, samples and impressions may be taken from a person detained under the terrorism provisions to help determine whether they are, or have been, involved in terrorism, as well as when there are reasonable grounds for suspecting their involvement in a particular offence.*

D:2D *The purpose of paragraph 2.18(b) is to protect those involved in serious organised crime investigations or arrests of particularly violent suspects when there is reliable information that those arrested or their associates may threaten or cause harm to the officers. In cases of doubt, an officer of inspector rank or above should be consulted.*

D:3 Identification and recognition of suspects

(A) *Identification of a suspect by an eye-witness*

A-120

D:3.0 This part applies when an eye-witness has seen the offender committing the crime or in any other circumstances which tend to prove or disprove the involvement of the person they saw in the crime, for example, close to the scene of the crime, immediately before or immediately after it was committed. It sets out the procedures to be used to test the ability of that eye-witness to identify a person suspected of involvement in the offence as the person they saw on the previous occasion. Except where stated, this part does not apply to the procedures described in Part B and *Note 3AA*.

D:3.1 A record shall be made of the suspect's description as first given by a potential witness. This record must:

    (a) be made and kept in a form which enables details of that description to be accurately produced from it, in a visible and legible form, which can be given to the suspect or the suspect's solicitor in accordance with this code; and

    (b) unless otherwise specified, be made before the witness takes part in any identification procedures under paragraphs 3.5 to 3.10, 3.21 or 3.23.

A copy of the record shall where practicable, be given to the suspect or their solicitor before any procedures under paragraphs 3.5 to 3.10, 3.21 or 3.23 are carried out. See *Note 3E*.

(a) *Cases when the suspect's identity is not known*

D:3.2 In cases when the suspect's identity is not known, a witness may be taken to a particular neighbourhood or place to see whether they can identify the person they saw on a previous occasion. Although the number, age, sex, race, general description and style of clothing of other people present at the location and the way in which any identification is made cannot be controlled, the principles applicable to the formal procedures under paragraphs 3.5 to 3.10 shall be followed as far as practicable. For example:

    (a) where it is practicable to do so, a record should be made of the witness's description of the suspect, as in paragraph 3.1(a), before asking the witness to make an identification;

    (b) care must be taken not to direct the witness's attention to any individual unless, taking into account all the circumstances, this cannot be avoided; however, this does not prevent a witness being asked to look carefully at the people around at the time or to look towards a group or in a particular direction, if this appears necessary to make sure that the witness does not overlook a possible suspect simply because the witness is looking in the opposite direction and also to enable the witness to make comparisons between any suspect and others who are in the area; see *Note 3F*;

    (c) where there is more than one witness, every effort should be made to keep them separate and witnesses should be taken to see whether they can identify a person independently;

    (d) once there is sufficient information to justify the arrest of a particular individual for suspected involvement in the offence, *e.g.*, after a witness makes a positive identification, the provisions set out from paragraph 3.4 onwards shall apply for any other witnesses in relation to that individual;

    (e) the officer or police staff accompanying the witness must record, in their pocket book, the action taken as soon as, and in as much detail, as possible. The record should include: the date, time and place of the relevant occasion the witness claims to have previously seen the suspect; where any identification was made; how it was made and the conditions at the time (*e.g.* the distance the witness was from the suspect, the weather and light); if the witness's attention was drawn to the suspect; the reason for this; and anything said by the witness or the suspect about the identification or the conduct of the procedure.

D:3.3 A witness must not be shown photographs, computerised or artist's composite likenesses or similar likenesses or pictures (including "E-fit" images) if the identity of the suspect is known to the police and the suspect is available to take part in a video identification, an identification parade or a group identification. If the suspect's identity is not known, the showing of such images to a witness to obtain identification evidence must be done in accordance with Annex E.

(b) *Cases when the suspect is known and available*

D:3.4 If the suspect's identity is known to the police and they are available, the identification   **A–121** procedures set out in paragraphs 3.5 to 3.10 may be used. References in this section to a suspect being "known" mean there is sufficient information known to the police to justify the arrest of a particular person for suspected involvement in the offence. A suspect being "available" means they are immediately available or will be within a reasonably short time and willing to take an effective part in at least one of the following which it is practicable to arrange:

    • video identification;

    • identification parade; or

    • group identification.

Video identification

D:3.5 A "video identification" is when the witness is shown moving images of a known suspect, together with similar images of others who resemble the suspect. Moving images must be used unless:

- the suspect is known but not available (see paragraph 3.21 of this code); or
- in accordance with paragraph 2A of Annex A of this code, the identification officer does not consider that replication of a physical feature can be achieved or that it is not possible to conceal the location of the feature on the image of the suspect.

The identification officer may then decide to make use of video identification but using **still** images.

D:3.6 Video identifications must be carried out in accordance with Annex A.

Identification parade

D:3.7 An "identification parade" is when the witness sees the suspect in a line of others who resemble the suspect.

D:3.8 Identification parades must be carried out in accordance with Annex B.

Group identification

D:3.9 A "group identification" is when the witness sees the suspect in an informal group of people.

D:3.10 Group identifications must be carried out in accordance with Annex C.

Arranging identification procedures

D:3.11 Except for the provisions in paragraph 3.19, the arrangements for, and conduct of, the identification procedures in paragraphs 3.5 to 3.10 and circumstances in which an identification procedure must be held shall be the responsibility of an officer not below inspector rank who is not involved with the investigation, "the identification officer". Unless otherwise specified, the identification officer may allow another officer or police staff, see paragraph 2.21, to make arrangements for, and conduct, any of these identification procedures. In delegating these procedures, the identification officer must be able to supervise effectively and either intervene or be contacted for advice. No officer or any other person involved with the investigation of the case against the suspect, beyond the extent required by these procedures, may take any part in these procedures or act as the identification officer. This does not prevent the identification officer from consulting the officer in charge of the investigation to determine which procedure to use. When an identification procedure is required, in the interest of fairness to suspects and witnesses, it must be held as soon as practicable.

Circumstances in which an eye-witness identification procedure must be held

A–122   **D:**3.12 Whenever:

    (i) an eye witness has identified a suspect or purported to have identified them prior to any identification procedure set out in paragraphs 3.5 to 3.10 having been held; or

    (ii) there is a witness available who expresses an ability to identify the suspect, or where there is a reasonable chance of the witness being able to do so, and they have not been given an opportunity to identify the suspect in any of the procedures set out in paragraphs 3.5 to 3.10,

and the suspect disputes being the person the witness claims to have seen, an identification procedure shall be held unless it is not practicable or it would serve no useful purpose in proving or disproving whether the suspect was involved in committing the offence, for example:

- where the suspect admits being at the scene of the crime and gives an account of what took place and the eye-witness does not see anything which contradicts that;
- when it is not disputed that the suspect is already known to the witness who claims to have recognised them when seeing them commit the crime.

D:3.13 An eye-witness identification procedure may also be held if the officer in charge of the investigation considers it would be useful.

Selecting an identification procedure

D:3.14 If, because of paragraph 3.12, an identification procedure is to be held, the suspect shall initially be offered a video identification unless:

    (a) a video identification is not practicable; or

    (b) an identification parade is both practicable and more suitable than a video identification; or

    (c) paragraph 3.16 applies.

The identification officer and the officer in charge of the investigation shall consult each other to determine which option is to be offered. An identification parade may not be practicable because of factors relating to the witnesses, such as their number, state of health, availability and travelling requirements. A video identification would normally be more suitable if it could be arranged and completed sooner than an identification parade. Before an option is offered the suspect must also be reminded of their entitlement to have free legal advice, see Code C, paragraph 6.5.

D:3.15 A suspect who refuses the identification procedure first offered shall be asked to state their reason for refusing and may get advice from their solicitor and/or if present, their appropriate adult. The suspect, solicitor and/or appropriate adult shall be allowed to make representations about why another procedure should be used. A record should be made of the reasons for refusal and any representations made. After considering any reasons given, and representations made, the identification officer shall, if appropriate, arrange for the suspect to be offered an alternative which the officer considers suitable and practicable. If the officer decides it is not suitable and practicable to offer an alternative identification procedure, the reasons for that decision shall be recorded.

D:3.16 A group identification may initially be offered if the officer in charge of the investigation considers it is more suitable than a video identification or an identification parade and the identification officer considers it practicable to arrange.

Notice to suspect

D:3.17 Unless paragraph 3.20 applies, before a video identification, an identification parade　　**A–123** or group identification is arranged, the following shall be explained to the suspect:

    (i) the purposes of the video identification, identification parade or group identification;

    (ii) their entitlement to free legal advice; see Code C, paragraph 6.5;

    (iii) the procedures for holding it, including their right to have a solicitor or friend present;

    (iv) that they do not have to consent to or co-operate in a video identification, identification parade or group identification;

    (v) that if they do not consent to, and co-operate in, a video identification, identification parade or group identification, their refusal may be given in evidence in any subsequent trial and police may proceed covertly without their consent or make other arrangements to test whether a witness can identify them, see paragraph 3.21;

    (vi) whether, for the purposes of the video identification procedure, images of them have previously been obtained, see paragraph 3.20, and if so, that they may co-operate in providing further, suitable images to be used instead;

    (vii) if appropriate, the special arrangements for juveniles;

    (viii) if appropriate, the special arrangements for mentally disordered or otherwise mentally vulnerable people;

    (ix) that if they significantly alter their appearance between being offered an identification procedure and any attempt to hold an identification procedure, this may be given in evidence if the case comes to trial, and the identification officer may then consider other forms of identification, see paragraph 3.21 and *Note 3C*;

    (x) that a moving image or photograph may be taken of them when they attend for any identification procedure;

    (xi) whether, before their identity became known, the witness was shown photographs, a computerised or artist's composite likeness or similar likeness or image by the police, see *Note 3B*;

    (xii) that if they change their appearance before an identification parade, it may not be practicable to arrange one on the day or subsequently and, because of the appearance change, the identification officer may consider alternative methods of identification, see *Note 3C*;

    (xiii) that they or their solicitor will be provided with details of the description of the suspect as first given by any witnesses who are to attend the video identification, identification parade, group identification or confrontation, see paragraph 3.1.

D:3.18 This information must also be recorded in a written notice handed to the suspect. The suspect must be given a reasonable opportunity to read the notice, after which, they should be asked to sign a second copy to indicate if they are willing to co-operate with the making of a video or take part in the identification parade or group identification. The signed copy shall be retained by the identification officer.

D:3.19 The duties of the identification officer under paragraphs 3.17 and 3.18 may be performed by the custody officer or other officer not involved in the investigation if:

(a) it is proposed to release the suspect in order that an identification procedure can be arranged and carried out and an inspector is not available to act as the identification officer, see paragraph 3.11, before the suspect leaves the station; or

(b) it is proposed to keep the suspect in police detention whilst the procedure is arranged and carried out and waiting for an inspector to act as the identification officer, see paragraph 3.11, would cause unreasonable delay to the investigation.

The officer concerned shall inform the identification officer of the action taken and give them the signed copy of the notice. See *Note 3C*.

D:3.20 If the identification officer and officer in charge of the investigation suspect, on reasonable grounds that if the suspect was given the information and notice as in paragraphs 3.17 and 3.18, they would then take steps to avoid being seen by a witness in any identification procedure, the identification officer may arrange for images of the suspect suitable for use in a video identification procedure to be obtained before giving the information and notice. If suspect's [*sic*] images are obtained in these circumstances, the suspect may, for the purposes of a video identification procedure, co-operate in providing new images which if suitable, would be used instead, see paragraph 3.17(vi).

(c) *Cases when the suspect is known but not available*

A–124

D:3.21 When a known suspect is not available or has ceased to be available, see paragraph 3.4, the identification officer may make arrangements for a video identification (see Annex A). If necessary, the identification officer may follow the video identification procedures but using still images. Any suitable moving or still images may be used and these may be obtained covertly if necessary. Alternatively, the identification officer may make arrangements for a group identification. See *Note 3D*. These provisions may also be applied to juveniles where the consent of their parent or guardian is either refused or reasonable efforts to obtain that consent have failed (see paragraph 2.12).

D:3.22 Any covert activity should be strictly limited to that necessary to test the ability of the witness to identify the suspect.

D:3.23 The identification officer may arrange for the suspect to be confronted by the witness if none of the options referred to in paragraphs 3.5 to 3.10 or 3.21 are practicable. A "confrontation" is when the suspect is directly confronted by the witness. A confrontation does not require the suspect's consent. Confrontations must be carried out in accordance with Annex D.

D:3.24 Requirements for information to be given to, or sought from, a suspect or for the suspect to be given an opportunity to view images before they are shown to a witness, do not apply if the suspect's lack of co-operation prevents the necessary action.

(d) *Documentation*

A–125

D:3.25 A record shall be made of the video identification, identification parade, group identification or confrontation on forms provided for the purpose.

D:3.26 If the identification officer considers it is not practicable to hold a video identification or identification parade requested by the suspect, the reasons shall be recorded and explained to the suspect.

D:3.27 A record shall be made of a person's failure or refusal to co-operate in a video identification, identification parade or group identification and, if applicable, of the grounds for obtaining images in accordance with paragraph 3.20.

(e) *Showing films and photographs of incidents and information released to the media*

A–126

D:3.28 Nothing in this code inhibits showing films, photographs or other images to the public through the national or local media, or to police officers for the purposes of recognition and tracing suspects. However, when such material is shown to obtain evidence of recognition, the procedures in Part B will apply. See *Note 3AA*.

D:3.29 When a broadcast or publication is made, see paragraph 3.28, a copy of the relevant material released to the media for the purposes of recognising or tracing the suspect, shall be kept. The suspect or their solicitor shall be allowed to view such material before any eye-witness identification procedures under paragraphs 3.5 to 3.10, 3.21 or 3.23 of Part A are carried out, provided it is practicable and would not unreasonably delay the investigation. Each eye-witness involved in the procedure shall be asked, after they have taken part, whether they have seen any film, photograph or image relating to the offence or any description of the suspect which has been broadcast or published in any national or local media or on any social networking site and if they have, they should be asked to give details of the circumstances, such as the date and place as relevant. Their replies shall be recorded. This paragraph does not affect any separate requirement under the *Criminal Procedure and Investigations Act* 1996 to retain material in connection with criminal investigations.

(f) *Destruction and retention of photographs taken or used in eye-witness identification procedures*

D:3.30 *PACE*, s.64A, see paragraph 5.12, provides powers to take photographs of suspects and allows these photographs to be used or disclosed only for purposes related to the prevention or detection of crime, the investigation of offences or the conduct of prosecutions by, or on behalf of, police or other law enforcement and prosecuting authorities inside and outside the United Kingdom or the enforcement of a sentence. After being so used or disclosed, they may be retained but can only be used or disclosed for the same purposes.

D:3.31 Subject to paragraph 3.33, the photographs (and all negatives and copies), of suspects not taken in accordance with the provisions in paragraph 5.12 which are taken for the purposes of, or in connection with, the identification procedures in paragraphs 3.5 to 3.10, 3.21 or 3.23 must be destroyed unless the suspect:

    (a) is charged with, or informed they may be prosecuted for, a recordable offence;

    (b) is prosecuted for a recordable offence;

    (c) is cautioned for a recordable offence or given a warning or reprimand in accordance with the *Crime and Disorder Act* 1998 for a recordable offence; or

    (d) gives informed consent, in writing, for the photograph or images to be retained for purposes described in paragraph 3.30.

D:3.32 When paragraph 3.31 requires the destruction of any photograph, the person must be given an opportunity to witness the destruction or to have a certificate confirming the destruction if they request one within five days of being informed that the destruction is required.

D:3.33 Nothing in paragraph 3.31 affects any separate requirement under the *Criminal Procedure and Investigations Act* 1996 to retain material in connection with criminal investigations.

(B) *Evidence of recognition by showing films, photographs and other images*

D:3.34 This part of this section applies when, for the purposes of obtaining evidence of recognition, any person, including a police officer: **A–126a**

    (a) views the image of an individual in a film, photograph or any other visual medium; and

    (b) is asked whether they recognise that individual as someone who is known to them.

See *Notes 3AA* and *3G*.

D:3.35 The films, photographs and other images shall be shown on an individual basis to avoid any possibility of collusion and to provide safeguards against mistaken recognition (see *Note 3G*), the showing shall as far as possible follow the principles for video identification if the suspect is known, see Annex A, or identification by photographs if the suspect is not known, see Annex E.

D:3.36 A record of the circumstances and conditions under which the person is given an opportunity to recognise the individual must be made and the record must include:

    (a) whether the person knew or was given information concerning the name or identity of any suspect;

    (b) what the person has been told *before* the viewing about the offence, the person(s) depicted in the images or the offender and by whom;

    (c) how and by whom the witness was asked to view the image or look at the individual;

    (d) whether the viewing was alone or with others and if with others, the reason for it;

    (e) the arrangements under which the person viewed the film or saw the individual and by whom those arrangements were made;

    (f) whether the viewing of any images was arranged as part of a mass circulation to police and the public or for selected persons;

    (g) the date time and place images were viewed or further viewed or the individual was seen;

    (h) the times between which the images were viewed or the individual was seen;

    (i) how the viewing of images or sighting of the individual was controlled and by whom;

    (j) whether the person was familiar with the location shown in any images or the place where they saw the individual and if so, why;

    (k) whether or not on this occasion, the person claims to recognise any image shown, or any individual seen, as being someone known to them, and if they do:

        (i) the reason;

(ii) the words of recognition;

(iii) any expressions of doubt;

(iv) what features of the image or the individual triggered the recognition.

D:3.37 The record under paragraph 3.36 may be made by:

- the person who views the image or sees the individual and makes the recognition;
- the officer or police staff in charge of showing the images to the person or in charge of the conditions under which the person sees the individual.

Notes for guidance

D:3AA *The eye-witness identification procedures in Part A should not be used to test whether a witness can recognise a person as someone they know and would be able to give evidence of recognition along the lines that "On (describe date, time location) I saw an image of an individual who I recognised as AB." In these cases, the procedures in Part B shall apply.*

D:3A *Except for the provisions of Annex E, paragraph 1, a police officer who is a witness for the purposes of this part of the code is subject to the same principles and procedures as a civilian witness.*

D:3B *When a witness attending an identification procedure has previously been shown photographs, or been shown or provided with computerised or artist's composite likenesses, or similar likenesses or pictures, it is the officer in charge of the investigation's responsibility to make the identification officer aware of this.*

D:3C *The purpose of paragraph 3.19 is to avoid or reduce delay in arranging identification procedures by enabling the required information and warnings, see sub-paragraphs 3.17(ix) and 3.17(xii), to be given at the earliest opportunity.*

D:3D *Paragraph 3.21 would apply when a known suspect deliberately makes themselves "unavailable" in order to delay or frustrate arrangements for obtaining identification evidence. It also applies when a suspect refuses or fails to take part in a video identification, an identification parade or a group identification, or refuses or fails to take part in the only practicable options from that list. It enables any suitable images of the suspect, moving or still, which are available or can be obtained, to be used in an identification procedure. Examples include images from custody and other CCTV systems and from visually recorded interview records, see Code F, Note for Guidance 2D.*

D:3E *When it is proposed to show photographs to a witness in accordance with Annex E, it is the responsibility of the officer in charge of the investigation to confirm to the officer responsible for supervising and directing the showing, that the first description of the suspect given by that witness has been recorded. If this description has not been recorded, the procedure under Annex E must be postponed. See Annex E, paragraph 2.*

D:3F *The admissibility and value of identification evidence obtained when carrying out the procedure under paragraph 3.2 may be compromised if:*

(a) before a person is identified, the witness's attention is specifically drawn to that person; or

(b) the suspect's identity becomes known before the procedure.

D:3G *The admissibility and value of evidence of recognition obtained when carrying out the procedures in Part B may be compromised if before the person is recognised, the witness who has claimed to know them is given or is made, or becomes aware of, information about the person which was not previously known to them personally but which they have purported to rely on to support their claim that the person is in fact known to them.*

D:4 Identification by fingerprints and footwear impressions

(A) *Taking fingerprints in connection with a criminal investigation*

(a) *General*

D:4.1 References to "fingerprints" means any record, produced by any method, of the skin pattern and other physical characteristics or features of a person's:

(i) fingers; or

(ii) palms.

(b) *Action*

D:4.2 A person's fingerprints may be taken in connection with the investigation of an offence only with their consent or if paragraph 4.3 applies. If the person is at a police station consent must be in writing.

D:4.3 *PACE*, s.61, provides powers to take fingerprints without consent from any person over the age of ten years:

(a) under section 61(3), from a person detained at a police station in consequence of being arrested for a recordable offence, see *Note 4A*, if they have not had their fingerprints taken in the course of the investigation of the offence unless those previously taken fingerprints are not a complete set or some or all of those fingerprints are not of sufficient quality to allow satisfactory analysis, comparison or matching;

(b) under section 61(4), from a person detained at a police station who has been charged with a recordable offence, see *Note 4A*, or informed they will be reported for such an offence if they have not had their fingerprints taken in the course of the investigation of the offence unless those previously taken fingerprints are not a complete set or some or all of those fingerprints are not of sufficient quality to allow satisfactory analysis, comparison or matching;

(c) under section 61(4A), from a person who has been bailed to appear at a court or police station if the person:

(i) has answered to bail for a person whose fingerprints were taken previously and there are reasonable grounds for believing they are not the same person; or

(ii) who has answered to bail claims to be a different person from a person whose fingerprints were previously taken;

and in either case, the court or an officer of inspector rank or above, authorises the fingerprints to be taken at the court or police station (an inspector's authority may be given in writing or orally and confirmed in writing, as soon as practicable);

(ca) under section 61(5A) from a person who has been arrested for a recordable offence and released if the person:

(i) is on bail and has not had their fingerprints taken in the course of the investigation of the offence; or

(ii) has had their fingerprints taken in the course of the investigation of the offence, but they do not constitute a complete set or some, or all, of the fingerprints are not of sufficient quality to allow satisfactory analysis, comparison or matching;

(cb) under section 61(5B) from a person not detained at a police station who has been charged with a recordable offence or informed they will be reported for such an offence if they have not had their fingerprints taken in the course of the investigation or their fingerprints have been taken in the course of the investigation of the offence, but they do not constitute a complete set or some, or all, of the fingerprints are not of sufficient quality to allow satisfactory analysis, comparison or matching;

(d) under section 61(6), from a person who has been:

(i) convicted of a recordable offence;

(ii) given a caution in respect of a recordable offence which, at the time of the caution, the person admitted; or

(iii) warned or reprimanded under the *Crime and Disorder Act* 1998, s.65, for a recordable offence, if, since their conviction, caution, warning or reprimand their fingerprints have not been taken or their fingerprints which have been taken since then do not constitute a complete set or some, or all, of the fingerprints are not of sufficient quality to allow satisfactory analysis, comparison or matching, and in either case, an officer of inspector rank or above, is satisfied that taking the fingerprints is necessary to assist in the prevention or detection of crime and authorises the taking;

(e) under section 61(6A) from a person a constable reasonably suspects is committing or attempting to commit, or has committed or attempted to commit, any offence if either:

● the person's name is unknown and cannot be readily ascertained by the constable; or

● the constable has reasonable grounds for doubting whether a name given by the person is their real name; note: fingerprints taken under this power are not regarded as having been taken in the course of the investigation of an offence; [see *Note 4C*];

(f) under section 61(6D) from a person who has been convicted outside England and Wales of an offence which if committed in England and Wales would be a qualifying offence as defined by *PACE*, s.65A [see *Note 4AB*] if:

(i) the person's fingerprints have not been taken previously under this power or their fingerprints have been so taken on a previous occasion but they do not constitute a complete set or some, or all, of the fingerprints are not of sufficient quality to allow satisfactory analysis, comparison or matching; and

(ii) a police officer of inspector rank or above is satisfied that taking fingerprints is necessary to assist in the prevention or detection of crime and authorises them to be taken.

461

D:4.4 *PACE*, s.63A(4), and Sched. 2A, provide powers to:

(a) make a requirement (in accordance with Annex G) for a person to attend a police station to have their fingerprints taken in the exercise of certain powers in paragraph 4.3 above when that power applies at the time the fingerprints would be taken in accordance with the requirement; those powers are:

(i) section 61(5A)—persons arrested for a recordable offence and released, see paragraph 4.3(ca): the requirement may not be made more than six months from the day the investigating officer was informed that the fingerprints previously taken were incomplete or below standard;

(ii) section 61(5B)—persons charged etc. with a recordable offence, see paragraph 4.3(cb): the requirement may not be made more than six months from:

- the day the person was charged or reported if fingerprints have not been taken since then; or
- the day the investigating officer was informed that the fingerprints previously taken were incomplete or below standard;

(iii) section 61(6)—person convicted, cautioned, warned or reprimanded for a recordable offence in England and Wales, see paragraph 4.3(d): where the offence for which the person was convicted etc is also a qualifying offence (see *Note 4AB*), there is no time limit for the exercise of this power; where the conviction etc. is for a recordable offence which is <u>not</u> a qualifying offence, the requirement may not be made more than two years from:

- the day the person was convicted, cautioned, warned or reprimanded, or the day Schedule 2A comes into force (if later), if fingerprints have not been taken since then; or
- the day an officer from the force investigating the offence was informed that the fingerprints previously taken were incomplete or below standard or the day Schedule 2A comes into force (if later);

(v) [*sic*] section 61(6D)—a person who has been convicted of a qualifying offence (see *Note 4AB*) outside England and Wales, see paragraph 4.3(g): there is no time limit for making the requirement;

note: a person who has had their fingerprints taken under any of the powers in section 61 mentioned in paragraph 4.3 on two occasions in relation to any offence may not be required under Schedule 2A to attend a police station for their fingerprints to be taken again under section 61 in relation to that offence, unless authorised by an officer of inspector rank or above; the fact of the authorisation and the reasons for giving it must be recorded as soon as practicable;

(b) arrest, without warrant, a person who fails to comply with the requirement.

D:4.5 A person's fingerprints may be taken, as above, electronically.

D:4.6 Reasonable force may be used, if necessary, to take a person's fingerprints without their consent under the powers as in paragraphs 4.3 and 4.4.

D:4.7 Before any fingerprints are taken:

(a) without consent under any power mentioned in paragraphs 4.3 and 4.4 above, the person must be informed of:

(i) the reason their fingerprints are to be taken;

(ii) the power under which they are to be taken; and

(iii) the fact that the relevant authority has been given if any power mentioned in paragraph 4.3(c), (d) or (f) applies;

(b) with or without consent at a police station or elsewhere, the person must be informed:

(i) that their fingerprints may be subject of a speculative search against other fingerprints, see *Note 4B*; and

(ii) that their fingerprints may be retained in accordance with Annex F, Part (a) unless they were taken under the power mentioned in paragraph 4.3(e) when they must be destroyed after they have being [*sic*] checked (see *Note 4C*).

(c) *Documentation*

D:4.8A A record must be made as soon as practicable after the fingerprints are taken, of:

- the matters in paragraph 4.7(a)(i) to (iii) and the fact that the person has been informed of those matters; and

● the fact that the person has been informed of the matters in paragraph 4.7(b)(i) and (ii).
The record must be made in the person's custody record if they are detained at a police station when the fingerprints are taken.

D:4.8 If force is used, a record shall be made of the circumstances and those present.

D:4.9 *Not used.*

(B) *Taking fingerprints in connection with immigration enquiries*

Action

D:4.10 A person's fingerprints may be taken and retained for the purposes of immigration law **A–129** enforcement and control in accordance with powers and procedures other than under *PACE* and for which the UK Border Agency (not the police) are responsible. Details of these powers and procedures which are under the *Immigration Act* 1971, Sched. 2 and *Immigration and Asylum Act* 1999, s.141, including modifications to the *PACE* Codes of Practice are contained in Chapter 24 of the operational instructions and guidance manual which is published by the UK Border Agency (see *Note 4D*).

D:4.11 *Not used.*

D:4.12 *Not used.*

D:4.13 *Not used.*

D:4.14 *Not used.*

D:4.15 *Not used.*

(C) *Taking footwear impressions in connection with a criminal investigation*

(a) *Action*

D:4.16 Impressions of a person's footwear may be taken in connection with the investigation of an offence only with their consent or if paragraph 4.17 applies. If the person is at a police station consent must be in writing.

D:4.17 *PACE*, s.61A, provides power for a police officer to take footwear impressions without consent from any person over the age of ten years who is detained at a police station:

(a) in consequence of being arrested for a recordable offence, see *Note 4A*; or if the detainee has been charged with a recordable offence, or informed they will be reported for such an offence; and

(b) the detainee has not had an impression of their footwear taken in the course of the investigation of the offence unless the previously taken impression is not complete or is not of sufficient quality to allow satisfactory analysis, comparison or matching (whether in the case in question or generally).

D:4.18 Reasonable force may be used, if necessary, to take a footwear impression from a detainee without consent under the power in paragraph 4.17.

D:4.19 Before any footwear impression is taken with, or without, consent as above, the person must be informed:

(a) of the reason the impression is to be taken;

(b) that the impression may be retained and may be subject of a speculative search against other impressions, see *Note 4B*, unless destruction of the impression is required in accordance with Annex F, Part (a); and

(c) that if their footwear impressions are required to be destroyed, they may witness their destruction as provided for in Annex F, Part (a).

(b) *Documentation*

D:4.20 A record must be made as soon as possible, of the reason for taking a person's footwear impressions without consent. If force is used, a record shall be made of the circumstances and those present.

D:4.21 A record shall be made when a person has been informed under the terms of paragraph 4.19(b), of the possibility that their footwear impressions may be subject of a speculative search.

Notes for guidance

D:4A *References to "recordable offences" in this code relate to those offences for which convictions, cautions, reprimands and warnings may be recorded in national police records: see* PACE, s.27(4). *The recordable offences current at the time when this code was prepared, are any offences which carry a sentence of imprisonment on conviction (irrespective of the period, or the age of the offender or actual sentence passed) as well as the non-imprisonable offences under the* Vagrancy Act 1824, ss.3 and 4 (begging and persistent begging), *the* Street Offences Act 1959, s.1 (loitering or soliciting for purposes of prostitution), *the* Road Traffic Act 1988, s.25 (tampering with motor vehicles), *the* Criminal Justice and Public Order Act 1994, s.167 (touting for car hire services) *and others listed in the* National Police Records (Recordable Offences) Regulations 2000 *as amended.*

D:4AB *A qualifying offence is one of the offences specified in* PACE, s.65A. *These indictable offences which concern the use or threat of violence or unlawful force against persons, sexual offences and offences against children include, for example, murder, manslaughter, false imprisonment, kidnapping and other offences such as:*

- *sections 4, 16, 18, 20 to 24 or 47 of the* Offences Against the Person Act *1861;*
- *sections 16 to 18 of the* Firearms Act *1968;*
- *sections 9 or 10 of the* Theft Act *1968 or under section 12A of that Act involving an accident which caused a person's death;*
- *section 1 of the* Criminal Damage Act *1971 required to be charged as arson;*
- *section 1 of the* Protection of Children Act *1978 and;*
- *sections 1 to 19, 25, 26, 30 to 41, 47 to 50, 52, 53, 57 to 59, 61 to 67, 69 and 70 of the* Sexual Offences Act *2003.*

D:4B *Fingerprints, footwear impressions or a DNA sample (and the information derived from it) taken from a person arrested on suspicion of being involved in a recordable offence, or charged with such an offence, or informed they will be reported for such an offence, may be subject of a speculative search. This means the fingerprints, footwear impressions or DNA sample may be checked against other fingerprints, footwear impressions and DNA records held by, or on behalf of, the police and other law enforcement authorities in, or outside, the UK, or held in connection with, or as a result of, an investigation of an offence inside or outside the UK. Fingerprints, footwear impressions and samples taken from a person suspected of committing a recordable offence but not arrested, charged or informed they will be reported for it, may be subject to a speculative search only if the person consents in writing. The following is an example of a basic form of words:*

> "*I consent to my fingerprints, footwear impressions and DNA sample and information derived from it being retained and used only for purposes related to the prevention and detection of a crime, the investigation of an offence or the conduct of a prosecution either nationally or internationally.*
>
> *I understand that my fingerprints, footwear impressions or DNA sample may be checked against other fingerprint, footwear impressions and DNA records held by or on behalf of relevant law enforcement authorities, either nationally or internationally.*
>
> *I understand that once I have given my consent for my fingerprints, footwear impressions or DNA sample to be retained and used I cannot withdraw this consent.*"

See Annex F regarding the retention and use of fingerprints and footwear impressions taken with consent for elimination purposes.

D:4C *The power under section 61(6A) of* PACE *described in paragraph 4.3(e) allows fingerprints of a suspect who has not been arrested to be taken in connection with any offence (whether recordable or not) using a mobile device and then checked on the street against the database containing the national fingerprint collection. Fingerprints taken under this power cannot be retained after they have been checked. The results may make an arrest for the suspected offence based on the name condition unnecessary (see code G, paragraph 2.9(a)) and enable the offence to be disposed of without arrest, for example, by summons/charging by post, penalty notice or words of advice. If arrest for a non-recordable offence is necessary for any other reasons, this power may also be exercised at the station. Before the power is exercised, the officer should:*

- *inform the person of the nature of the suspected offence and why they are suspected of committing it;*
- *give them a reasonable opportunity to establish their real name before deciding that their name is unknown and cannot be readily ascertained or that there are reasonable grounds to doubt that a name they have given is their real name;*
- *as applicable, inform the person of the reason why their name is not known and cannot be readily ascertained or of the grounds for doubting that a name they have given is their real name, including, for example, the reason why a particular document the person has produced to verify their real name, is not sufficient.*

D:4D *Powers to take fingerprints without consent for immigration purposes are given to police and immigration officers under the:*

    (a) Immigration Act *1971, Sched. 2, para. 18(2), when it is reasonably necessary for the purposes of identifying a person detained under the* Immigration Act *1971, Sched. 2, para. 16 (detention of person liable to examination or removal), and*

    (b) Immigration and Asylum Act *1999, s.141(7) when a person:*

        ● *fails without reasonable excuse to produce, on arrival, a valid passport with a photograph or some other document satisfactorily establishing their identity and nationality;*

        ● *is refused entry to the UK but is temporarily admitted if an immigration officer reasonably suspects the person might break a residence or reporting condition;*

        ● *is subject to directions for removal from the UK;*

        ● *has been arrested under the* Immigration Act *1971, Sched. 2, para. 17;*

        ● *has made a claim for asylum;*

        ● *is a dependant of any of the above.*

The Immigration and Asylum Act *1999, s.142(3), also gives police and immigration officers power to arrest without warrant a person who fails to comply with a requirement imposed by the Secretary of State to attend a specified place for fingerprinting.*

D:5 Examinations to establish identity and the taking of photographs

(A) *Detainees at police stations*

(a) *Searching or examination of detainees at police stations*

  D:5.1 *PACE*, s.54A(1), allows a detainee at a police station to be searched or examined or both, to establish: **A–130**

    (a) whether they have any marks, features or injuries that would tend to identify them as a person involved in the commission of an offence and to photograph any identifying marks, see paragraph 5.5; or

    (b) their identity, see *Note 5A.*

A person detained at a police station to be searched under a stop and search power, see Code A, is not a detainee for the purposes of these powers.

  D:5.2 A search and/or examination to find marks under section 54A(1)(a) may be carried out without the detainee's consent, see paragraph 2.12, only if authorised by an officer of at least inspector rank when consent has been withheld or it is not practicable to obtain consent, see *Note 5D.*

  D:5.3 A search or examination to establish a suspect's identity under section 54A(1)(b) may be carried out without the detainee's consent, see paragraph 2.12, only if authorised by an officer of at least inspector rank when the detainee has refused to identify themselves or the authorising officer has reasonable grounds for suspecting the person is not who they claim to be.

  D:5.4 Any marks that assist in establishing the detainee's identity, or their identification as a person involved in the commission of an offence, are identifying marks. Such marks may be photographed with the detainee's consent, see paragraph 2.12; or without their consent if it is withheld or it is not practicable to obtain it, see *Note 5D.*

  D:5.5 A detainee may only be searched, examined and photographed under section 54A, by a police officer of the same sex.

  D:5.6 Any photographs of identifying marks, taken under section 54A, may be used or disclosed only for purposes related to the prevention or detection of crime, the investigation of offences or the conduct of prosecutions by, or on behalf of, police or other law enforcement and prosecuting authorities inside, and outside, the UK. After being so used or disclosed, the photograph may be retained but must not be used or disclosed except for these purposes, see *Note 5B.*

  D:5.7 The powers, as in paragraph 5.1, do not affect any separate requirement under the *Criminal Procedure and Investigations Act* 1996 to retain material in connection with criminal investigations.

  D:5.8 Authority for the search and/or examination for the purposes of paragraphs 5.2 and 5.3 may be given orally or in writing. If given orally, the authorising officer must confirm it in writing as soon as practicable. A separate authority is required for each purpose which applies.

  D:5.9 If it is established a person is unwilling to co-operate sufficiently to enable a search and/or examination to take place or a suitable photograph to be taken, an officer may use reasonable force to:

> (a) search and/or examine a detainee without their consent; and
>
> (b) photograph any identifying marks without their consent.

D:5.10 The thoroughness and extent of any search or examination carried out in accordance with the powers in section 54A must be no more than the officer considers necessary to achieve the required purpose. Any search or examination which involves the removal of more than the person's outer clothing shall be conducted in accordance with Code C, Annex A, paragraph 11.

D:5.11 An intimate search may not be carried out under the powers in section 54A.

(b) *Photographing detainees at police stations and other persons elsewhere than at a police station*

A–131   **D:5.12** Under *PACE*, s.64A, an officer may photograph:

> (a) any person whilst they are detained at a police station; and
>
> (b) any person who is elsewhere than at a police station and who has been:
>
> > (i) arrested by a constable for an offence;
> >
> > (ii) taken into custody by a constable after being arrested for an offence by a person other than a constable;
> >
> > (iii) made subject to a requirement to wait with a community support officer under paragraph 2(3) or (3B) of Schedule 4 to the *Police Reform Act* 2002;
> >
> > (iiia) given a direction by a constable under section 27 of the *Violent Crime Reduction Act* 2006.
> >
> > (iv) given a penalty notice by a constable in uniform under Chapter 1 of Part 1 of the *Criminal Justice and Police Act* 2001, a penalty notice by a constable under section 444A of the *Education Act* 1996, or a fixed penalty notice by a constable in uniform under section 54 of the *Road Traffic Offenders Act* 1988;
> >
> > (v) given a notice in relation to a relevant fixed penalty offence (within the meaning of paragraph 1 of Schedule 4 to the *Police Reform Act* 2002) by a community support officer by virtue of a designation applying that paragraph to him;
> >
> > (vi) given a notice in relation to a relevant fixed penalty offence (within the meaning of paragraph 1 of Schedule 5 to the *Police Reform Act* 2002) by an accredited person by virtue of accreditation specifying that that paragraph applies to him; or
> >
> > (vii) given a direction to leave and not return to a specified location for up to 48 hours by a police constable (under section 27 of the *Violent Crime Reduction Act* 2006).

D:5.12A Photographs taken under *PACE*, s.64A:

> (a) may be taken with the person's consent, or without their consent if consent is withheld or it is not practicable to obtain their consent, see *Note 5E*; and
>
> (b) may be used or disclosed only for purposes related to the prevention or detection of crime, the investigation of offences or the conduct of prosecutions by, or on behalf of, police or other law enforcement and prosecuting authorities inside and outside the United Kingdom or the enforcement of any sentence or order made by a court when dealing with an offence. After being so used or disclosed, they may be retained but can only be used or disclosed for the same purposes. See *Note 5B*.

D:5.13 The officer proposing to take a detainee's photograph may, for this purpose, require the person to remove any item or substance worn on, or over, all, or any part of, their head or face. If they do not comply with such a requirement, the officer may remove the item or substance.

D:5.14 If it is established the detainee is unwilling to co-operate sufficiently to enable a suitable photograph to be taken and it is not reasonably practicable to take the photograph covertly, an officer may use reasonable force, see *Note 5F*:

> (a) to take their photograph without their consent; and
>
> (b) for the purpose of taking the photograph, remove any item or substance worn on, or over, all, or any part of, the person's head or face which they have failed to remove when asked.

D:5.15 For the purposes of this code, a photograph may be obtained without the person's consent by making a copy of an image of them taken at any time on a camera system installed anywhere in the police station.

(c) *Information to be given*

D:5.16 When a person is searched, examined or photographed under the provisions as in **A–132**
paragraph 5.1 and 5.12, or their photograph obtained as in paragraph 5.15, they must be
informed of the:

(a) purpose of the search, examination or photograph;

(b) grounds on which the relevant authority, if applicable, has been given; and

(c) purposes for which the photograph may be used, disclosed or retained.

This information must be given before the search or examination commences or the photograph is
taken, except if the photograph is:

(i) to be taken covertly;

(ii) obtained as in paragraph 5.15, in which case the person must be informed as soon as
practicable after the photograph is taken or obtained.

(d) *Documentation*

D:5.17 A record must be made when a detainee is searched, examined, or a photograph of
the person, or any identifying marks found on them, are [*sic*] taken. The record must include the:

(a) identity, subject to paragraph 2.18, of the officer carrying out the search, examination or
taking the photograph;

(b) purpose of the search, examination or photograph and the outcome;

(c) detainee's consent to the search, examination or photograph, or the reason the person
was searched, examined or photographed without consent;

(d) giving of any authority as in paragraphs 5.2 and 5.3, the grounds for giving it and the
authorising officer.

D:5.18 If force is used when searching, examining or taking a photograph in accordance with
this section, a record shall be made of the circumstances and those present.

(B) *Persons at police stations not detained*

D:5.19 When there are reasonable grounds for suspecting the involvement of a person in a **A–133**
criminal offence, but that person is at a police station **voluntarily** and not detained, the provisions of paragraphs 5.1 to 5.18 should apply, subject to the modifications in the following
paragraphs.

D:5.20 References to the "person being detained" and to the powers mentioned in paragraph
5.1 which apply only to detainees at police stations shall be omitted.

D:5.21 Force may not be used to:

(a) search and/or examine the person to:

(i) discover whether they have any marks that would tend to identify them as a person
involved in the commission of an offence; or

(ii) establish their identity, see *Note 5A*;

(b) take photographs of any identifying marks, see paragraph 5.4; or

(c) take a photograph of the person.

D:5.22 Subject to paragraph 5.24, the photographs of persons or of their identifying marks
which are not taken in accordance with the provisions mentioned in paragraphs 5.1 or 5.12,
must be destroyed (together with any negatives and copies) unless the person:

(a) is charged with, or informed they may be prosecuted for, a recordable offence;

(b) is prosecuted for a recordable offence;

(c) is cautioned for a recordable offence or given a warning or reprimand in accordance
with the *Crime and Disorder Act* 1998 for a recordable offence; or

(d) gives informed consent, in writing, for the photograph or image to be retained as in
paragraph 5.6.

D:5.23 When paragraph 5.22 requires the destruction of any photograph, the person must be
given an opportunity to witness the destruction or to have a certificate confirming the destruction
provided they so request the certificate within five days of being informed the destruction is
required.

D:5.24 Nothing in paragraph 5.22 affects any separate requirement under the *Criminal Procedure and Investigations Act* 1996 to retain material in connection with criminal investigations.

Notes for guidance

A–134   **D:5A** *The conditions under which fingerprints may be taken to assist in establishing a person's identity, are described in section 4.*

D:5B *Examples of purposes related to the prevention or detection of crime, the investigation of offences or the conduct of prosecutions include:*

(a) *checking the photograph against other photographs held in records or in connection with, or as a result of, an investigation of an offence to establish whether the person is liable to arrest for other offences;*

(b) *when the person is arrested at the same time as other people, or at a time when it is likely that other people will be arrested, using the photograph to help establish who was arrested, at what time and where;*

(c) *when the real identity of the person is not known and cannot be readily ascertained or there are reasonable grounds for doubting a name and other personal details given by the person are their real name and personal details; in these circumstances, using or disclosing the photograph to help to establish or verify their real identity or determine whether they are liable to arrest for some other offence, e.g. by checking it against other photographs held in records or in connection with, or as a result of, an investigation of an offence;*

(d) *when it appears any identification procedure in section 3 may need to be arranged for which the person's photograph would assist;*

(e) *when the person's release without charge may be required, and if the release is:*

(i) *on bail to appear at a police station, using the photograph to help verify the person's identity when they answer their bail and if the person does not answer their bail, to assist in arresting them; or*

(ii) *without bail, using the photograph to help verify their identity or assist in locating them for the purposes of serving them with a summons to appear at court in criminal proceedings;*

(f) *when the person has answered to bail at a police station and there are reasonable grounds for doubting they are the person who was previously granted bail, using the photograph to help establish or verify their identity;*

(g) *when the person arrested on a warrant claims to be a different person from the person named on the warrant and a photograph would help to confirm or disprove their claim;*

(h) *when the person has been charged with, reported for, or convicted of, a recordable offence and their photograph is not already on record as a result of (a) to (f) or their photograph is on record but their appearance has changed since it was taken and the person has not yet been released or brought before a court.*

D:5C *There is no power to arrest a person convicted of a recordable offence solely to take their photograph. The power to take photographs in this section applies only where the person is in custody as a result of the exercise of another power, e.g. arrest for fingerprinting under PACE, s.27.*

D:5D *Examples of when it would not be practicable to obtain a detainee's consent, see paragraph 2.12, to a search, examination or the taking of a photograph of an identifying mark include:*

(a) *when the person is drunk or otherwise unfit to give consent;*

(b) *when there are reasonable grounds to suspect that if the person became aware a search or examination was to take place or an identifying mark was to be photographed, they would take steps to prevent this happening, e.g. by violently resisting, covering or concealing the mark etc and it would not otherwise be possible to carry out the search or examination or to photograph any identifying mark;*

(c) *in the case of a juvenile, if the parent or guardian cannot be contacted in sufficient time to allow the search or examination to be carried out or the photograph to be taken.*

D:5E *Examples of when it would not be practicable to obtain the person's consent, see paragraph 2.12, to a photograph being taken include:*

(a) *when the person is drunk or otherwise unfit to give consent;*

(b) *when there are reasonable grounds to suspect that if the person became aware a photograph, suitable to be used or disclosed for the use and disclosure described in paragraph 5.6, was to be taken, they would take steps to prevent it being taken, e.g. by violently resisting, covering or distorting their face etc, and it would not otherwise be possible to take a suitable photograph;*

(c) *when, in order to obtain a suitable photograph, it is necessary to take it covertly; and*

(d) *in the case of a juvenile, if the parent or guardian cannot be contacted in sufficient time to allow the photograph to be taken.*

D:5F *The use of reasonable force to take the photograph of a suspect elsewhere than at a police station* *must be carefully considered. In order to obtain a suspect's consent and co-operation to remove an item of religious headwear to take their photograph, a constable should consider whether in the circumstances of the situation the removal of the headwear and the taking of the photograph should be by an officer of the same sex as the person. It would be appropriate for these actions to be conducted out of public view.*

D:6 Identification by body samples and impressions

(A) *General*

D:6.1 References to:

    (a) an "intimate sample" mean a dental impression or sample of blood, semen or any other tissue fluid, urine, or pubic hair, or a swab taken from any part of a person's genitals or from a person's body orifice other than the mouth;

    (b) a "non-intimate sample" means:

        (i) a sample of hair, other than pubic hair, which includes hair plucked with the root, see *Note 6A*;

        (ii) a sample taken from a nail or from under a nail;

        (iii) a swab taken from any part of a person's body other than a part from which a swab taken would be an intimate sample;

        (iv) saliva;

        (v) a skin impression which means any record, other than a fingerprint, which is a record, in any form and produced by any method, of the skin pattern and other physical characteristics or features of the whole, or any part of, a person's foot or of any other part of their body.

(B) *Action*

(a) *Intimate samples*

D:6.2 *PACE*, s.62, provides that intimate samples may be taken under:

    (a) section 62(1), from a person in police detention only:

        (i) if a police officer of inspector rank or above has reasonable grounds to believe such an impression or sample will tend to confirm or disprove the suspect's involvement in a recordable offence, see *Note 4A*, and gives authorisation for a sample to be taken; and

        (ii) with the suspect's written consent;

    (b) section 62(1A), from a person not in police detention but from whom two or more non-intimate samples have been taken in the course of an investigation of an offence and the samples, though suitable, have proved insufficient if:

        (i) a police officer of inspector rank or above authorises it to be taken; and

        (ii) the person concerned gives their written consent; see *Notes 6B* and *6C*;

    (c) section 62(2A), from a person convicted outside England and Wales of an offence which if committed in England and Wales would be qualifying offence [*sic*] as defined by *PACE*, s.65A (see *Note 4AB*) from whom two or more non-intimate samples taken under section 63(3E) (see paragraph 6.6(h)) have proved insufficient if:

        (i) a police officer of inspector rank or above is satisfied that taking the sample is necessary to assist in the prevention or detection of crime and authorises it to be taken; and

        (ii) the person concerned gives their written consent.

D:6.2A *PACE*, s.63A(4), and Sched. 2A, provide powers [*sic*] to:

    (a) [*sic*] make a requirement (in accordance with Annex G) for a person to attend a police station to have an intimate sample taken in the exercise of one of the following powers in paragraph 6.2 when that power applies at the time the sample is to be taken in accordance with the requirement or after the person's arrest if they fail to comply with the requirement:

        (i) section 62(1A)—persons from whom two or more non-intimate samples have been taken and proved to be insufficient, see paragraph 6.2(b); there is no time limit for making the requirement;

        (ii) section 62(2A)—persons convicted outside England and Wales from whom two or more non-intimate samples taken under section 63(3E) (see paragraph 6.6(h)) have proved insufficient, see paragraph 6.2(c); there is no time limit for making the requirement.

D:6.3 Before a suspect is asked to provide an intimate sample, they must be:

(a) informed:

(i) of the reason, including the nature of the suspected offence (except if taken under paragraph 6.2(c) from a person convicted outside England and Wales;

(ii) that authorisation has been given and the provisions under which given;

(iii) that a sample taken at a police station may be subject of a speculative search;

(b) warned that if they refuse without good cause their refusal may harm their case if it comes to trial, see *Note 6D*. If the suspect is in police detention and not legally represented, they must also be reminded of their entitlement to have free legal advice, see Code C, paragraph 6.5, and the reminder noted in the custody record. If paragraph 6.2(b) applies and the person is attending a station voluntarily, their entitlement to free legal advice as in Code C, paragraph 3.21 shall be explained to them.

D:6.4 Dental impressions may only be taken by a registered dentist. Other intimate samples, except for samples of urine, may only be taken by a registered medical practitioner or registered nurse or registered paramedic.

(b) *Non-intimate samples*

A–137   **D:6.5** A non-intimate sample may be taken from a detainee only with their written consent or if paragraph 6.6 applies.

D:6.6 A non-intimate sample may be taken from a person without the appropriate consent in the following circumstances:

(a) under section 63(2A) from a person who is in police detention as a consequence of being arrested for a recordable offence and who has not had a non-intimate sample of the same type and from the same part of the body taken in the course of the investigation of the offence by the police or they have had such a sample taken but it proved insufficient;

(b) under section 63(3) from a person who is being held in custody by the police on the authority of a court if an officer of at least the rank of inspector authorises it to be taken; an authorisation may be given:

(i) if the authorising officer has reasonable grounds for suspecting the person of involvement in a recordable offence and for believing that the sample will tend to confirm or disprove that involvement; and

(ii) in writing or orally and confirmed in writing, as soon as practicable;

but an authorisation may not be given to take from the same part of the body a further non-intimate sample consisting of a skin impression unless the previously taken impression proved insufficient;

(c) under section 63(3ZA) from a person who has been arrested for a recordable offence and released if the person:

(i) is on bail and has not had a sample of the same type and from the same part of the body taken in the course of the investigation of the offence; or

(ii) has had such a sample taken in the course of the investigation of the offence, but it proved unsuitable or insufficient;

(d) under section 63(3A), from a person (whether or not in police detention or held in custody by the police on the authority of a court) who has been charged with a recordable offence or informed they will be reported for such an offence if the person:

(i) has not had a non-intimate sample taken from them in the course of the investigation of the offence;

(ii) has had a sample so taken, but it proved unsuitable or insufficient, see *Note 6B*; or

(iii) has had a sample taken in the course of the investigation of the offence and the sample has been destroyed and in proceedings relating to that offence there is a dispute as to whether a DNA profile relevant to the proceedings was derived from the destroyed sample;

(e) under section 63(3B), from a person who has been:

(i) convicted of a recordable offence;

(ii) given a caution in respect of a recordable offence which, at the time of the caution, the person admitted; or

(iii) warned or reprimanded under the *Crime and Disorder Act* 1998, s.65, for a recordable offence, if, since their conviction, caution, warning or reprimand a non-intimate sample has not been taken from them or a sample which has been taken since then has proved to be unsuitable or insufficient and in either case, an officer of inspector rank or above, is satisfied that taking the fingerprints [*sic*] is necessary to assist in the prevention or detection of crime and authorises the taking;

  (f) under section 63(3C) from a person to whom section 2 of the *Criminal Evidence (Amendment) Act* 1997 applies (persons detained following acquittal on grounds of insanity or finding of unfitness to plead);

  (g) under section 63(3E) from a person who has been convicted outside England and Wales of an offence which if committed in England and Wales would be a qualifying offence as defined by *PACE*, s.65A (see *Note 4AB*) if:

    (i) a non-intimate sample has not been taken previously under this power or unless a sample was so taken but was unsuitable or insufficient; and

    (ii) a police officer of inspector rank or above is satisfied that taking a sample is necessary to assist in the prevention or detection of crime and authorises it to be taken.

D:6.6A *PACE*, s.63A(4), and Sched. 2A, provide powers to:

  (a) make a requirement (in accordance with Annex G) for a person to attend a police station to have a non-intimate sample taken in the exercise of one of the following powers in paragraph 6.6 when that power applies at the time the sample would be taken in accordance with the requirement:

    (i) section 63(3ZA)—persons arrested for a recordable offence and released, see paragraph 6.6(c); the requirement may not be made more than six months from the day the investigating officer was informed that the sample previously taken was unsuitable or insufficient;

    (ii) section 63(3A)—persons charged etc. with a recordable offence, see paragraph 6.6(d); the requirement may not be made more than six months from:

      ● the day the person was charged or reported if a sample has not been taken since then; or

      ● the day the investigating officer was informed that the sample previously taken was unsuitable or insufficient;

    (iii) section 63(3B)—person convicted, cautioned, warned or reprimanded for a recordable offence in England and Wales, see paragraph 6.6(e); where the offence for which the person was convicted etc is also a qualifying offence (see *Note 4AB*), there is no time limit for the exercise of this power; where the conviction etc was for a recordable offence that is not a qualifying offence, the requirement may not be made more than two years from:

      ● the day the person was convicted, cautioned, warned or reprimanded, or the day Schedule 2A comes into force (if later), if a samples [*sic*] has not been taken since then; or

      ● the day an officer from the force investigating the offence was informed that the sample previously taken was unsuitable or insufficient or the day Schedule 2A comes into force (if later);

    (iv) section 63(3E)—a person who has been convicted of qualifying offence (see *Note 4AB*) outside England and Wales, see paragraph 6.6(h); there is no time limit for making the requirement;

    note: a person who has had a non-intimate sample taken under any of the powers in section 63 mentioned in paragraph 6.6 on two occasions in relation to any offence may not be required under Schedule 2A to attend a police station for a sample to be taken again under section 63 in relation to that offence, unless authorised by an officer of inspector rank or above; the fact of the authorisation and the reasons for giving it must be recorded as soon as practicable;

  (b) arrest, without warrant, a person who fails to comply with the requirement.

D:6.7 Reasonable force may be used, if necessary, to take a non-intimate sample from a person without their consent under the powers mentioned in paragraph 6.6.

D:6.8 Before any non-intimate sample is taken:

  (a) without consent under any power mentioned in paragraphs 6.6 and 6.6A, the person must be informed of:

    (i) the reason for taking the sample;

>   (ii) the power under which the sample is to be taken;
>   (iii) the fact that the relevant authority has been given if any power mentioned in paragraph 6.6(b), (e) or (h) applies;
>   (b) with or without consent at a police station or elsewhere, the person must be informed:
>   (i) that their sample or information derived from it may be subject of a speculative search against other samples and information derived from them, see *Note 6E*; and
>   (ii) that their sample and the information derived from it may be retained in accordance with Annex F, Part (a).

(c) *Removal of clothing*

D:6.9 When clothing needs to be removed in circumstances likely to cause embarrassment to the person, no person of the opposite sex who is not a registered medical practitioner or registered health care professional shall be present (unless in the case of a juvenile, mentally disordered or mentally vulnerable person, that person specifically requests the presence of an appropriate adult of the opposite sex who is readily available), nor shall anyone whose presence is unnecessary. However, in the case of a juvenile, this is subject to the overriding proviso that such a removal of clothing may take place in the absence of the appropriate adult only if the juvenile signifies in their presence, that they prefer the adult's absence and they agree.

(c) *Documentation*

D:6.10 A record must be made as soon as practicable after the sample is taken of:
  - the matters in paragraph 6.8(a)(i) to (iii) and the fact that the person has been informed of those matters; and
  - the fact that the person has been informed of the matters in paragraph 6.8(b)(i) and (ii).

D:6.10A If force is used, a record shall be made of the circumstances and those present.

D:6.11 A record must be made of a warning given as required by paragraph 6.3.

Notes for guidance

A–138

D:6A *When hair samples are taken for the purpose of DNA analysis (rather than for other purposes such as making a visual match), the suspect should be permitted a reasonable choice as to what part of the body the hairs are taken from. When hairs are plucked, they should be plucked individually, unless the suspect prefers otherwise and no more should be plucked than the person taking them reasonably considers necessary for a sufficient sample.*

>   (a) *An insufficient sample is one which is not sufficient either in quantity or quality to provide information for a particular form of analysis, such as DNA analysis. A sample may also be insufficient if enough information cannot be obtained from it by analysis because of loss, destruction, damage or contamination of the sample or as a result of an earlier, unsuccessful attempt at analysis.*

>   (b) *An unsuitable sample is one which, by its nature, is not suitable for a particular form of analysis.*

D:6C *Nothing in paragraph 6.2 prevents intimate samples being taken for elimination purposes with the consent of the person concerned but the provisions of paragraph 2.12 relating to the role of the appropriate adult, should be applied. Paragraph 6.2(b) does not, however, apply where the non-intimate samples were previously taken under the Terrorism Act 2000, Sched. 8, para. 10.*

D:6D *In warning a person who is asked to provide an intimate sample as in paragraph 6.3, the following form of words may be used:*

>   *"You do not have to provide this sample/allow this swab or impression to be taken, but I must warn you that if you refuse without good cause, your refusal may harm your case if it comes to trial."*

D:6E *Fingerprints or a DNA sample and the information derived from it taken from a person arrested on suspicion of being involved in a recordable offence, or charged with such an offence, or informed they will be reported for such an offence, may be subject of a speculative search. This means they may be checked against other fingerprints and DNA records held by, or on behalf of, the police and other law enforcement authorities in or outside the UK or held in connection with, or as a result of, an investigation of an offence inside or outside the UK. Fingerprints and samples taken from any other person, e.g. a person suspected of committing a recordable offence but who has not been arrested, charged or informed they will be reported for it, may be subject to a speculative search only if the person consents in writing to their fingerprints being subject of such a search. The following is an example of a basic form of words:*

>   *"I consent to my fingerprints/DNA sample and information derived from it being retained and used only for purposes related to the prevention and detection of a crime, the investigation of an offence or the conduct of a prosecution either nationally or internationally.*

I understand that this sample may be checked against other fingerprint/DNA records held by or on behalf of relevant law enforcement authorities, either nationally or internationally.

I understand that once I have given my consent for the sample to be retained and used I cannot withdraw this consent."

See Annex F regarding the retention and use of fingerprints and samples taken with consent for elimination purposes.

D:6F *Samples of urine and non-intimate samples taken in accordance with sections 63B and 63C of PACE may not be used for identification purposes in accordance with this code. See Code C note for guidance 17D.*

ANNEX A

Video identification

(a) *General*

D:1 The arrangements for obtaining and ensuring the availability of a suitable set of images to be used in a video identification must be the responsibility of an identification officer, who has no direct involvement with the case.   **A–139**

D:2 The set of images must include the suspect and at least eight other people who, so far as possible, resemble the suspect in age, general appearance and position in life. Only one suspect shall appear in any set unless there are two suspects of roughly similar appearance, in which case they may be shown together with at least twelve other people.

D:2A If the suspect has an unusual physical feature, *e.g.* a facial scar, tattoo or distinctive hairstyle or hair colour which does not appear on the images of the other people that are available to be used, steps may be taken to:

    (a) conceal the location of the feature on the images of the suspect and the other people; or

    (b) replicate that feature on the images of the other people.

For these purposes, the feature may be concealed or replicated electronically or by any other method which it is practicable to use to ensure that the images of the suspect and other people resemble each other. The identification officer has discretion to choose whether to conceal or replicate the feature and the method to be used. If an unusual physical feature has been described by the witness, the identification officer should, if practicable, have that feature replicated. If it has not been described, concealment may be more appropriate.

D:2B If the identification officer decides that a feature should be concealed or replicated, the reason for the decision and whether the feature was concealed or replicated in the images shown to any witness shall be recorded.

D:2C If the witness requests to view an image where an unusual physical feature has been concealed or replicated without the feature being concealed or replicated, the witness may be allowed to do so.

D:3 The images used to conduct a video identification shall, as far as possible, show the suspect and other people in the same positions or carrying out the same sequence of movements. They shall also show the suspect and other people under identical conditions unless the identification officer reasonably believes:

    (a) because of the suspect's failure or refusal to co-operate or other reasons, it is not practicable for the conditions to be identical; and

    (b) any difference in the conditions would not direct a witness's attention to any individual image.

D:4 The reasons identical conditions are not practicable shall be recorded on forms provided for the purpose.

D:5 Provision must be made for each person shown to be identified by number.

D:6 If police officers are shown, any numerals or other identifying badges must be concealed. If a prison inmate is shown, either as a suspect or not, then either all, or none of, the people shown should be in prison clothing.

D:7 The suspect or their solicitor, friend, or appropriate adult must be given a reasonable opportunity to see the complete set of images before it is shown to any witness. If the suspect has a reasonable objection to the set of images or any of the participants, the suspect shall be asked to state the reasons for the objection. Steps shall, if practicable, be taken to remove the grounds for objection. If this is not practicable, the suspect and/or their representative shall be told why their   **A–140**

objections cannot be met and the objection, the reason given for it and why it cannot be met shall be recorded on forms provided for the purpose.

D:8 Before the images are shown in accordance with paragraph 7, the suspect or their solicitor shall be provided with details of the first description of the suspect by any witnesses who are to attend the video identification. When a broadcast or publication is made, as in paragraph 3.28, the suspect or their solicitor must also be allowed to view any material released to the media by the police for the purpose of recognising or tracing the suspect, provided it is practicable and would not unreasonably delay the investigation.

D:9 The suspect's solicitor, if practicable, shall be given reasonable notification of the time and place the video identification is to be conducted so a representative may attend on behalf of the suspect. The suspect may not be present when the images are shown to the witness(es). In the absence of the suspect's solicitor, the viewing itself shall be recorded on video. No unauthorised people may be present.

(b) *Conducting the video identification*

A–141

D:10 The identification officer is responsible for making the appropriate arrangements to make sure, before they see the set of images, witnesses are not able to communicate with each other about the case, see any of the images which are to be shown, see, or be reminded of, any photograph or description of the suspect or be given any other indication as to the suspect's identity, or overhear a witness who has already seen the material. There must be no discussion with the witness about the composition of the set of images and they must not be told whether a previous witness has made any identification.

D:11 Only one witness may see the set of images at a time. Immediately before the images are shown, the witness shall be told that the person they saw on a specified earlier occasion may, or may not, appear in the images they are shown and that if they cannot make a positive identification, they should say so. The witness shall be advised that at any point, they may ask to see a particular part of the set of images or to have a particular image frozen for them to study. Furthermore, it should be pointed out to the witness that there is no limit on how many times they can view the whole set of images or any part of them. However, they should be asked not to make any decision as to whether the person they saw is on the set of images until they have seen the whole set at least twice.

D:12 Once the witness has seen the whole set of images at least twice and has indicated that they do not want to view the images, or any part of them, again, the witness shall be asked to say whether the individual they saw in person on a specified earlier occasion has been shown and, if so, to identify them by number of the image. The witness will then be shown that image to confirm the identification, see paragraph 17.

D:13 Care must be taken not to direct the witness's attention to any one individual image or give any indication of the suspect's identity. Where a witness has previously made an identification by photographs, or a computerised or artist's composite or similar likeness, the witness must not be reminded of such a photograph or composite likeness once a suspect is available for identification by other means in accordance with this code. Nor must the witness be reminded of any description of the suspect.

D:14 After the procedure, each witness shall be asked whether they have seen any broadcast or published films or photographs, or any descriptions of suspects relating to the offence and their reply shall be recorded.

(c) *Image security and destruction*

D:15 Arrangements shall be made for all relevant material containing sets of images used for specific identification procedures to be kept securely and their movements accounted for. In particular, no-one involved in the investigation shall be permitted to view the material prior to it being shown to any witness.

D:16 As appropriate, paragraph 3.30 or 3.31 applies to the destruction or retention of relevant sets of images.

(d) *Documentation*

D:17 A record must be made of all those participating in, or seeing, the set of images whose names are known to the police.

D:18 A record of the conduct of the video identification must be made on forms provided for the purpose. This shall include anything said by the witness about any identifications or the conduct of the procedure and any reasons it was not practicable to comply with any of the provisions of this code governing the conduct of video identifications.

ANNEX B

Identification parades

(a) *General*

D:1　A suspect must be given a reasonable opportunity to have a solicitor or friend present, and the suspect shall be asked to indicate on a second copy of the notice whether or not they wish to do so.　**A–142**

D:2　An identification parade may take place either in a normal room or one equipped with a screen permitting witnesses to see members of the identification parade without being seen. The procedures for the composition and conduct of the identification parade are the same in both cases, subject to paragraph 8 (except that an identification parade involving a screen may take place only when the suspect's solicitor, friend or appropriate adult is present or the identification parade is recorded on video).

D:3　Before the identification parade takes place, the suspect or their solicitor shall be provided with details of the first description of the suspect by any witnesses who are attending the identification parade. When a broadcast or publication is made as in paragraph 3.28, the suspect or their solicitor should also be allowed to view any material released to the media by the police for the purpose of recognising or tracing the suspect, provided it is practicable to do so and would not unreasonably delay the investigation.

(b) *Identification parades involving prison inmates*

D:4　If a prison inmate is required for identification, and there are no security problems about the person leaving the establishment, they may be asked to participate in an identification parade or video identification.

D:5　An identification parade may be held in a Prison Department establishment but shall be conducted, as far as practicable under normal identification parade rules. Members of the public shall make up the identification parade unless there are serious security, or control, objections to their admission to the establishment. In such cases, or if a group or video identification is arranged within the establishment, other inmates may participate. If an inmate is the suspect, they are not required to wear prison clothing for the identification parade unless the other people taking part are other inmates in similar clothing, or are members of the public who are prepared to wear prison clothing for the occasion.

(c) *Conduct of the identification parade*

D:6　Immediately before the identification parade, the suspect must be reminded of the procedures governing its conduct and cautioned in the terms of Code C, paragraphs 10.5 or 10.6, as appropriate.　**A–143**

D:7　All unauthorised people must be excluded from the place where the identification parade is held.

D:8　Once the identification parade has been formed, everything afterwards, in respect of it, shall take place in the presence and hearing of the suspect and any interpreter, solicitor, friend or appropriate adult who is present (unless the identification parade involves a screen, in which case everything said to, or by, any witness at the place where the identification parade is held, must be said in the hearing and presence of the suspect's solicitor, friend or appropriate adult or be recorded on video).

D:9　The identification parade shall consist of at least eight people (in addition to the suspect) who, so far as possible, resemble the suspect in age, height, general appearance and position in life. Only one suspect shall be included in an identification parade unless there are two suspects of roughly similar appearance, in which case they may be paraded together with at least twelve other people. In no circumstances shall more than two suspects be included in one identification parade and where there are separate identification parades, they shall be made up of different people.

D:10　If the suspect has an unusual physical feature, *e.g.*, a facial scar, tattoo or distinctive hairstyle or hair colour which cannot be replicated on other members of the identification parade, steps may be taken to conceal the location of that feature on the suspect and the other members of the identification parade if the suspect and their solicitor, or appropriate adult, agree. For example, by use of a plaster or a hat, so that all members of the identification parade resemble each other in general appearance.

D:11 When all members of a similar group are possible suspects, separate identification parades shall be held for each unless there are two suspects of similar appearance when they may appear on the same identification parade with at least twelve other members of the group who are not suspects. When police officers in uniform form an identification parade any numerals or other identifying badges shall be concealed.

D:12 When the suspect is brought to the place where the identification parade is to be held, they shall be asked if they have any objection to the arrangements for the identification parade or to any of the other participants in it and to state the reasons for the objection. The suspect may obtain advice from their solicitor or friend, if present, before the identification parade proceeds. If the suspect has a reasonable objection to the arrangements or any of the participants, steps shall, if practicable, be taken to remove the grounds for objection. When it is not practicable to do so, the suspect shall be told why their objections cannot be met and the objection, the reason given for it and why it cannot be met, shall be recorded on forms provided for the purpose.

D:13 The suspect may select their own position in the line, but may not otherwise interfere with the order of the people forming the line. When there is more than one witness, the suspect must be told, after each witness has left the room, that they can, if they wish, change position in the line. Each position in the line must be clearly numbered, whether by means of a number laid on the floor in front of each identification parade member or by other means.

A–144   **D:**14 Appropriate arrangements must be made to make sure, before witnesses attend the identification parade, they are not able to:

> (i) communicate with each other about the case or overhear a witness who has already seen the identification parade;
>
> (ii) see any member of the identification parade;
>
> (iii) see, or be reminded of, any photograph or description of the suspect or be given any other indication as to the suspect's identity; or
>
> (iv) see the suspect before or after the identification parade.

D:15 The person conducting a witness to an identification parade must not discuss with them the composition of the identification parade and, in particular, must not disclose whether a previous witness has made any identification.

D:16 Witnesses shall be brought in one at a time. Immediately before the witness inspects the identification parade, they shall be told the person they saw on a specified earlier occasion may, or may not, be present and if they cannot make a positive identification, they should say so. The witness must also be told they should not make any decision about whether the person they saw is on the identification parade until they have looked at each member at least twice.

D:17 When the officer or police staff (see paragraph 3.11) conducting the identification procedure is satisfied the witness has properly looked at each member of the identification parade, they shall ask the witness whether the person they saw on a specified earlier occasion is on the identification parade and, if so, to indicate the number of the person concerned, see paragraph 28.

D:18 If the witness wishes to hear any identification parade member speak, adopt any specified posture or move, they shall first be asked whether they can identify any person(s) on the identification parade on the basis of appearance only. When the request is to hear members of the identification parade speak, the witness shall be reminded that the participants in the identification parade have been chosen on the basis of physical appearance only. Members of the identification parade may then be asked to comply with the witness's request to hear them speak, see them move or adopt any specified posture.

A–145   **D:**19 If the witness requests that the person they have indicated remove anything used for the purposes of paragraph 10 to conceal the location of an unusual physical feature, that person may be asked to remove it.

D:20 If the witness makes an identification after the identification parade has ended, the suspect and, if present, their solicitor, interpreter or friend shall be informed. When this occurs, consideration should be given to allowing the witness a second opportunity to identify the suspect.

D:21 After the procedure, each witness shall be asked whether they have seen any broadcast or published films or photographs or any descriptions of suspects relating to the offence and their reply shall be recorded.

D:22 When the last witness has left, the suspect shall be asked whether they wish to make any comments on the conduct of the identification parade.

(d) *Documentation*

D:23 A video recording must normally be taken of the identification parade. If that is impracticable, a colour photograph must be taken. A copy of the video recording or photograph shall be supplied, on request, to the suspect or their solicitor within a reasonable time.

D:24 As appropriate, paragraph 3.30 or 3.31, should apply to any photograph or video taken as in paragraph 23.

D:25 If any person is asked to leave an identification parade because they are interfering with its conduct, the circumstances shall be recorded.

D:26 A record must be made of all those present at an identification parade whose names are known to the police.

D:27 If prison inmates make up an identification parade, the circumstances must be recorded.

D:28 A record of the conduct of any identification parade must be made on forms provided for the purpose. This shall include anything said by the witness or the suspect about any identifications or the conduct of the procedure, and any reasons it was not practicable to comply with any of this code's provisions.

ANNEX C

Group identification

(a) *General*

D:1 The purpose of this annex is to make sure, as far as possible, group identifications follow **A–146** the principles and procedures for identification parades so the conditions are fair to the suspect in the way they test the witness's ability to make an identification.

D:2 Group identifications may take place either with the suspect's consent and co-operation or covertly without their consent.

D:3 The location of the group identification is a matter for the identification officer, although the officer may take into account any representations made by the suspect, appropriate adult, their solicitor or friend.

D:4 The place where the group identification is held should be one where other people are either passing by or waiting around informally, in groups such that the suspect is able to join them and be capable of being seen by the witness at the same time as others in the group. For example people leaving an escalator, pedestrians walking through a shopping centre, passengers on railway and bus stations, waiting in queues or groups or where people are standing or sitting in groups in other public places.

D:5 If the group identification is to be held covertly, the choice of locations will be limited by the places where the suspect can be found and the number of other people present at that time. In these cases, suitable locations might be along regular routes travelled by the suspect, including buses or trains or public places frequented by the suspect.

D:6 Although the number, age, sex, race and general description and style of clothing of other **A–147** people present at the location cannot be controlled by the identification officer, in selecting the location the officer must consider the general appearance and numbers of people likely to be present. In particular, the officer must reasonably expect that over the period the witness observes the group, they will be able to see, from time to time, a number of others whose appearance is broadly similar to that of the suspect.

D:7 A group identification need not be held if the identification officer believes, because of the unusual appearance of the suspect, none of the locations it would be practicable to use, satisfy the requirements of paragraph 6 necessary to make the identification fair.

D:8 Immediately after a group identification procedure has taken place (with or without the suspect's consent), a colour photograph or video should be taken of the general scene, if practicable, to give a general impression of the scene and the number of people present. Alternatively, if it is practicable, the group identification may be video recorded.

D:9 If it is not practicable to take the photograph or video in accordance with paragraph 8, a photograph or film of the scene should be taken later at a time determined by the identification officer if the officer considers it practicable to do so.

D:10 An identification carried out in accordance with this code remains a group identification even though, at the time of being seen by the witness, the suspect was on their own rather than in a group.

D:11 Before the group identification takes place, the suspect or their solicitor shall be provided with details of the first description of the suspect by any witnesses who are to attend the identification. When a broadcast or publication is made, as in paragraph 3.28, the suspect or their solicitor should also be allowed to view any material released by the police to the media for the purposes of recognising or tracing the suspect, provided that it is practicable and would not unreasonably delay the investigation.

D:12 After the procedure, each witness shall be asked whether they have seen any broadcast or published films or photographs or any descriptions of suspects relating to the offence and their reply recorded.

(b) *Identification with the consent of the suspect*

A-148   **D:**13 A suspect must be given a reasonable opportunity to have a solicitor or friend present. They shall be asked to indicate on a second copy of the notice whether or not they wish to do so.

D:14 The witness, the person carrying out the procedure and the suspect's solicitor, appropriate adult, friend or any interpreter for the witness, may be concealed from the sight of the individuals in the group they are observing, if the person carrying out the procedure considers this assists the conduct of the identification.

D:15 The person conducting a witness to a group identification must not discuss with them the forthcoming group identification and, in particular, must not disclose whether a previous witness has made any identification.

D:16 Anything said to, or by, the witness during the procedure about the identification should be said in the presence and hearing of those present at the procedure.

D:17 Appropriate arrangements must be made to make sure, before witnesses attend the group identification, they are not able to:

> (i) communicate with each other about the case or overhear a witness who has already been given an opportunity to see the suspect in the group;

> (ii) see the suspect; or

> (iii) see, or be reminded of, any photographs or description of the suspect or be given any other indication of the suspect's identity.

D:18 Witnesses shall be brought one at a time to the place where they are to observe the group. Immediately before the witness is asked to look at the group, the person conducting the procedure shall tell them that the person they saw may, or may not, be in the group and that if they cannot make a positive identification, they should say so. The witness shall be asked to observe the group in which the suspect is to appear. The way in which the witness should do this will depend on whether the group is moving or stationary.

Moving group

A-149   **D:**19 When the group in which the suspect is to appear is moving, *e.g.* leaving an escalator, the provisions of paragraphs 20 to 24 should be followed.

D:20 If two or more suspects consent to a group identification, each should be the subject of separate identification procedures. These may be conducted consecutively on the same occasion.

D:21 The person conducting the procedure shall tell the witness to observe the group and ask them to point out any person they think they saw on the specified earlier occasion.

D:22 Once the witness has been informed as in paragraph 21 the suspect should be allowed to take whatever position in the group they wish.

D:23 When the witness points out a person as in paragraph 21 they shall, if practicable, be asked to take a closer look at the person to confirm the identification. If this is not practicable, or they cannot confirm the identification, they shall be asked how sure they are that the person they have indicated is the relevant person.

D:24 The witness should continue to observe the group for the period which the person conducting the procedure reasonably believes is necessary in the circumstances for them to be able to make comparisons between the suspect and other individuals of broadly similar appearance to the suspect as in paragraph 6.

Stationary groups

A-150   **D:**25 When the group in which the suspect is to appear is stationary, *e.g.* people waiting in a queue, the provisions of paragraphs 26 to 29 should be followed.

D:26 If two or more suspects consent to a group identification, each should be subject to separate identification procedures unless they are of broadly similar appearance when they may appear in the same group. When separate group identifications are held, the groups must be made up of different people.

D:27 The suspect may take whatever position in the group they wish. If there is more than one witness, the suspect must be told, out of the sight and hearing of any witness, that they can, if they wish, change their position in the group.

D:28 The witness shall be asked to pass along, or amongst, the group and to look at each person in the group at least twice, taking as much care and time as possible according to the circumstances, before making an identification. Once the witness has done this, they shall be asked whether the person they saw on the specified earlier occasion is in the group and to indicate any such person by whatever means the person conducting the procedure considers appropriate in the circumstances. If this is not practicable, the witness shall be asked to point out any person they think they saw on the earlier occasion.

D:29 When the witness makes an indication as in paragraph 28, arrangements shall be made, if practicable, for the witness to take a closer look at the person to confirm the identification. If this is not practicable, or the witness is unable to confirm the identification, they shall be asked how sure they are that the person they have indicated is the relevant person.

All cases

D:30 If the suspect unreasonably delays joining the group, or having joined the group, **A–151** deliberately conceals themselves [*sic*] from the sight of the witness, this may be treated as a refusal to co-operate in a group identification.

D:31 If the witness identifies a person other than the suspect, that person should be informed what has happened and asked if they are prepared to give their name and address. There is no obligation upon any member of the public to give these details. There shall be no duty to record any details of any other member of the public present in the group or at the place where the procedure is conducted.

D:32 When the group identification has been completed, the suspect shall be asked whether they wish to make any comments on the conduct of the procedure.

D:33 If the suspect has not been previously informed, they shall be told of any identifications made by the witnesses.

(c) *Identification without the suspect's consent*

D:34 Group identifications held covertly without the suspect's consent should, as far as **A–152** practicable, follow the rules for conduct of group identification by consent.

D:35 A suspect has no right to have a solicitor, appropriate adult or friend present as the identification will take place without the knowledge of the suspect.

D:36 Any number of suspects may be identified at the same time.

(d) *Identifications in police stations*

D:37 Group identifications should only take place in police stations for reasons of safety, security or because it is not practicable to hold them elsewhere.

D:38 The group identification may take place either in a room equipped with a screen permitting witnesses to see members of the group without being seen, or anywhere else in the police station that the identification officer considers appropriate.

D:39 Any of the additional safeguards applicable to identification parades should be followed if the identification officer considers it is practicable to do so in the circumstances.

(e) *Identifications involving prison inmates*

D:40 A group identification involving a prison inmate may only be arranged in the prison or **A–153** at a police station.

D:41 When a group identification takes place involving a prison inmate, whether in a prison or in a police station, the arrangements should follow those in paragraphs 37 to 39. If a group identification takes place within a prison, other inmates may participate. If an inmate is the suspect, they do not have to wear prison clothing for the group identification unless the other participants are wearing the same clothing.

(f) *Documentation*

D:42 When a photograph or video is taken as in paragraph 8 or 9, a copy of the photograph or video shall be supplied on request to the suspect or their solicitor within a reasonable time.

D:43 Paragraph 3.30 or 3.31, as appropriate, shall apply when the photograph or film taken in accordance with paragraph 8 or 9 includes the suspect.

D:44 A record of the conduct of any group identification must be made on forms provided for the purpose. This shall include anything said by the witness or suspect about any identifications or the conduct of the procedure and any reasons why it was not practicable to comply with any of the provisions of this code governing the conduct of group identifications.

ANNEX D

Confrontation by a witness

A–154   **D:**1 Before the confrontation takes place, the witness must be told that the person they saw may, or may not, be the person they are to confront and that if they are not that person, then the witness should say so.

D:2 Before the confrontation takes place the suspect or their solicitor shall be provided with details of the first description of the suspect given by any witness who is to attend. When a broadcast or publication is made, as in paragraph 3.28, the suspect or their solicitor should also be allowed to view any material released to the media for the purposes of recognising or tracing the suspect, provided it is practicable to do so and would not unreasonably delay the investigation.

D:3 Force may not be used to make the suspect's face visible to the witness.

D:4 Confrontation must take place in the presence of the suspect's solicitor, interpreter or friend unless this would cause unreasonable delay.

D:5 The suspect shall be confronted independently by each witness, who shall be asked "Is this the person?". If the witness identifies the person but is unable to confirm the identification, they shall be asked how sure they are that the person is the one they saw on the earlier occasion.

D:6 The confrontation should normally take place in the police station, either in a normal room or one equipped with a screen permitting a witness to see the suspect without being seen. In both cases, the procedures are the same except that a room equipped with a screen may be used only when the suspect's solicitor, friend or appropriate adult is present or the confrontation is recorded on video.

D:7 After the procedure, each witness shall be asked whether they have seen any broadcast or published films or photographs or any descriptions of suspects relating to the offence and their reply shall be recorded.

ANNEX E

Showing photographs

(a) *Action*

A–155   **D:**1 An officer of sergeant rank or above shall be responsible for supervising and directing the showing of photographs. The actual showing may be done by another officer or police staff, see paragraph 3.11.

D:2 The supervising officer must confirm the first description of the suspect given by the witness has been recorded before they are shown the photographs. If the supervising officer is unable to confirm the description has been recorded they shall postpone showing the photographs.

D:3 Only one witness shall be shown photographs at any one time. Each witness shall be given as much privacy as practicable and shall not be allowed to communicate with any other witness in the case.

D:4 The witness shall be shown not less than twelve photographs at a time, which shall, as far as possible, all be of a similar type.

D:5 When the witness is shown the photographs, they shall be told the photograph of the person they saw may, or may not, be amongst them and if they cannot make a positive identification, they should say so. The witness shall also be told they should not make a decision until they have viewed at least twelve photographs. The witness shall not be prompted or guided in any way but shall be left to make any selection without help.

D:6 If a witness makes a positive identification from photographs, unless the person identified is otherwise eliminated from enquiries or is not available, other witnesses shall not be shown photographs. But both they, and the witness who has made the identification, shall be asked to attend a video identification, an identification parade or group identification unless there is no dispute about the suspect's identification.

A–156   **D:**7 If the witness makes a selection but is unable to confirm the identification, the person showing the photographs shall ask them how sure they are that the photograph they have indicated is the person they saw on the specified earlier occasion.

D:8 When the use of a computerised or artist's composite or similar likeness has led to there being a known suspect who can be asked to participate in a video identification, appear on an identification parade or participate in a group identification, that likeness shall not be shown to other potential witnesses.

D:9 When a witness attending a video identification, an identification parade or group identification has previously been shown photographs or computerised or artist's composite or similar likeness (and it is the responsibility of the officer in charge of the investigation to make the identification officer aware that this is the case), the suspect and their solicitor must be informed of this fact before the identification procedure takes place.

D:10 None of the photographs shown shall be destroyed, whether or not an identification is made, since they may be required for production in court. The photographs shall be numbered and a separate photograph taken of the frame or part of the album from which the witness made an identification as an aid to reconstituting it.

(b) *Documentation*

D:11. Whether or not an identification is made, a record shall be kept of the showing of **A–157** photographs on forms provided for the purpose. This shall include anything said by the witness about any identification or the conduct of the procedure, any reasons it was not practicable to comply with any of the provisions of this code governing the showing of photographs and the name and rank of the supervising officer.

D:12 The supervising officer shall inspect and sign the record as soon as practicable.

ANNEX F

Fingerprints, footwear impressions and samples—destruction and speculative searches

(a) *Fingerprints, footwear impressions and samples taken in connection with a criminal investigation from a person suspected of committing the offence under investigation*
D:1 The retention and destruction of fingerprints, footwear impressions and samples taken in **A–158** connection with a criminal investigation from a person suspected of committing the offence under investigation is subject to *PACE*, s.64.

(b) *Fingerprints, footwear impressions and samples taken in connection with a criminal investigation from a person not suspected of committing the offence under investigation*
D:2 When fingerprints, footwear impressions or DNA samples are taken from a person in connection with an investigation and the person is not suspected of having committed the offence, see *Note F1*, they must be destroyed as soon as they have fulfilled the purpose for which they were taken unless:

    (a) they were taken for the purposes of an investigation of an offence for which a person has been convicted; and

    (b) fingerprints, footwear impressions or samples were also taken from the convicted person for the purposes of that investigation.

However, subject to paragraph 2, the fingerprints, footwear impressions and samples, and the information derived from samples, may not be used in the investigation of any offence or in evidence against the person who is, or would be, entitled to the destruction of the fingerprints, footwear impressions and samples, see *Note F2*.

D:3 The requirement to destroy fingerprints, footwear impressions and DNA samples, and information derived from samples, and restrictions on their retention and use in paragraph 1 do not apply if the person gives their written consent for their fingerprints, footwear impressions or sample to be retained and used after they have fulfilled the purpose for which they were taken, see *Note F1*.

D:4 When a person's fingerprints, footwear impressions or sample are to be destroyed:

    (a) any copies of the fingerprints and footwear impressions must also be destroyed;

    (b) the person may witness the destruction of their fingerprints, footwear impressions or copies if they ask to do so within five days of being informed destruction is required;

    (c) access to relevant computer fingerprint data shall be made impossible as soon as it is practicable to do so and the person shall be given a certificate to this effect within three months of asking; and

(d) neither the fingerprints, footwear impressions, the sample, or any information derived from the sample, may be used in the investigation of any offence or in evidence against the person who is, or would be, entitled to its destruction.

D:5 Fingerprints, footwear impressions or samples, and the information derived from samples, taken in connection with the investigation of an offence which are not required to be destroyed, may be retained after they have fulfilled the purposes for which they were taken but may be used only for purposes related to the prevention or detection of crime, the investigation of an offence or the conduct of a prosecution in, as well as outside, the UK and may also be subject to a speculative search. This includes checking them against other fingerprints, footwear impressions and DNA records held by, or on behalf of, the police and other law enforcement authorities in, as well as outside, the UK.

(b) [*sic*] *Fingerprints taken in connection with Immigration Service enquiries*

A–159   **D:**6 See paragraph 4.10.

Notes for guidance

A–160   **D:**F1 *Fingerprints, footwear impressions and samples given voluntarily for the purposes of elimination play an important part in many police investigations. It is, therefore, important to make sure innocent volunteers are not deterred from participating and their consent to their fingerprints, footwear impressions and DNA being used for the purposes of a specific investigation is fully informed and voluntary. If the police or volunteer seek to have the fingerprints, footwear impressions or samples retained for use after the specific investigation ends, it is important the volunteer's consent to this is also fully informed and voluntary.*

Examples of consent for:

- *DNA/fingerprints/footwear impressions—to be used only for the purposes of a specific investigation;*
- *DNA/fingerprints/footwear impressions—to be used in the specific investigation **and** retained by the police for future use.*

*To minimise the risk of confusion, each consent should be physically separate and the volunteer should be asked to sign **each consent**.*

(a) DNA:

(i) DNA sample taken for the purposes of elimination or as part of an intelligence-led screening and to be used only for the purposes of that investigation and destroyed afterwards:

"*I consent to my DNA/mouth swab being taken for forensic analysis. I understand that the sample will be destroyed at the end of the case and that my profile will only be compared to the crime stain profile from this enquiry. I have been advised that the person taking the sample may be required to give evidence and/or provide a written statement to the police in relation to the taking of it.*".

(ii) DNA sample to be retained on the National DNA database and used in the future:

"*I consent to my DNA sample and information derived from it being retained and used only for purposes related to the prevention and detection of a crime, the investigation of an offence or the conduct of a prosecution either nationally or internationally.*

I understand that this sample may be checked against other DNA records held by, or on behalf of, relevant law enforcement authorities, either nationally or internationally.

I understand that once I have given my consent for the sample to be retained and used I cannot withdraw this consent.".

(b) Fingerprints:

(i) Fingerprints taken for the purposes of elimination or as part of an intelligence-led screening and to be used only for the purposes of that investigation and destroyed afterwards:

"*I consent to my fingerprints being taken for elimination purposes. I understand that the fingerprints will be destroyed at the end of the case and that my fingerprints will only be compared to the fingerprints from this enquiry. I have been advised that the person taking the fingerprints may be required to give evidence and/or provide a written statement to the police in relation to the taking of it.*".

(ii) Fingerprints to be retained for future use:

"*I consent to my fingerprints being retained and used only for purposes related to the prevention and detection of a crime, the investigation of an offence or the conduct of a prosecution either nationally or internationally.*

I understand that my fingerprints may be checked against other records held by, or on behalf of, relevant law enforcement authorities, either nationally or internationally.

I understand that once I have given my consent for my fingerprints to be retained and used I cannot withdraw this consent.".

(c) Footwear impressions:

(i) Footwear impressions taken for the purposes of elimination or as part of an intelligence-led screening and to be used only for the purposes of that investigation and destroyed afterwards:

"I consent to my footwear impressions being taken for elimination purposes. I understand that the footwear impressions will be destroyed at the end of the case and that my footwear impressions will only be compared to the footwear impressions from this enquiry. I have been advised that the person taking the footwear impressions may be required to give evidence and/or provide a writtens statement to the police in relation to the taking of it.".

(ii) Footwear impressions to be retained for future use:

"I consent to my footwear impressions being retained and used only for purposes related to the prevention and detection of a crime, the investigation of an offence or the conduct of a prosecution, either nationally or internationally.

I understand that my footwear impressions may be checked against other records held by, or on behalf of, relevant law enforcement authorities, either nationally or internationally.

I understand that once I have given my consent for my footwear impressions to be retained and used I cannot withdraw this consent.".

D:F2 *The provisions for the retention of fingerprints, footwear impressions and samples in paragraph 1* **A–161** *allow for all fingerprints, footwear impressions and samples in a case to be available for any subsequent miscarriage of justice investigation.*

ANNEX G

Requirement for a person to attend a police station for fingerprints and samples

D:1 A requirement under Schedule 2A for a person to attend a police station to have **A–161a** fingerprints or samples taken:

    (a) must give the person a period of at least seven days within which to attend the police station; and

    (b) may direct them to attend at a specified time of day or between specified times of day.

D:2 When specifying the period and times of attendance, the officer making the requirements must consider whether the fingerprints or samples could reasonably be taken at a time when the person is required to attend the police station for any other reason. See *Note G1*.

D:3 An officer of the rank of inspector or above may authorise a period shorter than 7 days if there is an urgent need for person's fingerprints or sample for the purposes of the investigation of an offence. The fact of the authorisation and the reasons for giving it must be recorded as soon as practicable.

D:4 The constable making a requirement and the person to whom it applies may agree to vary it so as to specify any period within which, or date or time at which, the person is to attend. However, variation shall not have effect for the purposes of enforcement, unless it is confirmed by the constable in writing.

Notes for guidance

    D:G1 *The specified period within which the person is to attend need not fall within the period allowed (if* **A–161b** *applicable) for making the requirement.*

    D:G2 *To justify the arrest without warrant of a person who fails to comply with a requirement, (see paragraph 4.4(b) above), the officer making the requirement, or confirming a variation, should be prepared to explain how, when and where the requirement was made or the variation was confirmed and what steps were taken to ensure the person understood what to do and the consequences of not complying with the requirement.*

(6) Tape-recording of interviews

The text that follows is of the version of the code that came into force on May 1, 2010: **A–162** see *ante*, Appendix A–1.

For further details of the application of the code, and as to commencement of the governing legislation, see § 15–174, *ante*.

E. Code of Practice on Audio Recording Interviews with Suspects

Commencement—Transitional arrangements

A–162a   This code applies to interviews carried out after midnight on 1 May 2010, notwithstanding that the interview may have commenced before that time.

E:1 General

A–163   E:1.1 This code of practice must be readily available for consultation by:

- police officers;
- police staff;
- detained persons;
- members of the public.

E:1.2 The *Notes for Guidance* included are not provisions of this code.

E:1.3 Nothing in this code shall detract from the requirements of Code C, the code of practice for the detention, treatment and questioning of persons by police officers.

E:1.4 This code does not apply to those people listed in Code C, paragraph 1.12.

E:1.5 The term:

- "appropriate adult" has the same meaning as in Code C, paragraph 1.7;
- "solicitor" has the same meaning as in Code C, paragraph 6.12.

E:1.5A Recording of interviews shall be carried out openly to instil confidence in its reliability as an impartial and accurate record of the interview.

A–164   E:1.6 In this code:

(aa) "recording media" means any removable, physical audio recording medium (such as magnetic tape, optical disc or solid state memory) which can be played and copied;

(a) "designated person" means a person other than a police officer, designated under the *Police Reform Act* 2002, Pt 4, who has specified powers and duties of police officers conferred or imposed on them;

(b) any reference to a police officer includes a designated person acting in the exercise or performance of the powers and duties conferred or imposed on them by their designation;

(c) "secure digital network" is a computer network system which enables an original interview recording to be stored as a digital multi media file or a series of such files, on a secure file server which is accredited by the National Accreditor for Police Information Systems in the National Police Improvement Agency (NPIA) in accordance with the UK Government Protective Marking Scheme (see section 7 of this code).

E:1.7 Sections 2 to 6 of this code set out the procedures and requirements which apply to all interviews together with the provisions which apply only to interviews recorded using removable media. Section 7 sets out the provisions which apply to interviews recorded using a secure digital network and specifies the provisions in sections 2 to 6 which do not apply to secure digital network recording.

A–165   E:1.8 Nothing in this code prevents the custody officer, or other officer given custody of the detainee, from allowing police staff who are not designated persons to carry out individual procedures or tasks at the police station if the law allows. However, the officer remains responsible for making sure the procedures and tasks are carried out correctly in accordance with this code. Any such police staff must be:

(a) a person employed by a police authority maintaining a police force and under the control and direction of the chief officer of that force; or

(b) employed by a person with whom a police authority has a contract for the provision of services relating to persons arrested or otherwise in custody.

E:1.9 Designated persons and other police staff must have regard to any relevant provisions of the codes of practice.

E:1.10 References to pocket book [*sic*] include any official report book issued to police officers or police staff.

E:1.11 References to a custody officer include those performing the functions of a custody officer as in paragraph 1.9 of Code C.

E:2 Recording and sealing master recordings

E:2.1 [*Not used.*]

E:2.2 One recording, the master recording, will be sealed in the suspect's presence. A second recording will be used as a working copy. The master recording is either of the two recordings used in a twin deck/drive machine or the only recording in a single deck/drive machine. The working copy is either the second/third recording used in a twin/triple deck/drive machine or a copy of the master recording made by a single deck/drive machine. See *Notes 2A* and *2B*. [*This paragraph does not apply to interviews recorded using a secure digital network, see paragraphs 7.4 to 7.6.*]

E:2.3 Nothing in this code requires the identity of officers or police staff conducting interviews to be recorded or disclosed:

    (a) in the case of enquiries linked to the investigation of terrorism (see paragraph 3.2); or

    (b) if the interviewer reasonably believes recording or disclosing their name might put them in danger.

In these cases interviewers should use warrant or other identification numbers and the name of their police station. See *Note 2C*.

Notes for guidance

E:2A *The purpose of sealing the master recording in the suspect's presence is to show the recording's integ-*   *rity is preserved. If a single deck/drive machine is used the working copy of the master recording must be made in the suspect's presence and without the master recording leaving their sight. The working copy shall be used for making further copies if needed.*

E:2B [*Not used.*]

E:2C *The purpose of paragraph 2.3(b) is to protect those involved in serious organised crime investigations or arrests of particularly violent suspects when there is reliable information that those arrested or their associates may threaten or cause harm to those involved. In cases of doubt, an officer of inspector rank or above should be consulted.*

E:3 Interviews to be audio recorded

E:3.1 Subject to paragraphs 3.3 and 3.4, audio recording shall be used at police stations for   any interview:

    (a) with a person cautioned under Code C, section 10 in respect of any indictable offence, including an offence triable either way, see *Note 3A*;

    (b) which takes place as a result of an interviewer exceptionally putting further questions to a suspect about an offence described in paragraph 3.1(a) after they have been charged with, or told they may be prosecuted for, that offence, see Code C, paragraph 16.5;

    (c) when an interviewer wants to tell a person, after they have been charged with, or informed they may be prosecuted for, an offence described in paragraph 3.1(a), about any written statement or interview with another person, see Code C, paragraph 16.4.

E:3.2 The *Terrorism Act* 2000 makes separate provision for a code of practice for the audio recording of interviews of those arrested under section 41 of, or detained under Schedule 7 to, the Act. The provisions of this code do not apply to such interviews. See *Note 3C*.

E:3.3 The custody officer may authorise the interviewer not to audio record the interview when it is:

    (a) not reasonably practicable because of equipment failure or the unavailability of a suitable interview room or recording equipment and the authorising officer considers, on reasonable grounds, that the interview should not be delayed; or

    (b) clear from the outset there will not be a prosecution.

Note: in these cases the interview should be recorded in writing in accordance with Code C, section 11. In all cases the custody officer shall record the specific reasons for not audio recording. See *Note 3B*.

E:3.4 If a person refuses to go into or remain in a suitable interview room, see Code C, paragraph 12.5, and the custody officer considers, on reasonable grounds, that the interview should not be delayed the interview may, at the custody officer's discretion, be conducted in a cell using portable recording equipment or, if none is available, recorded in writing as in Code C, section 11. The reasons for this shall be recorded.

E:3.5 The whole of each interview shall be audio recorded, including the taking and reading back of any statement.

E:3.6 A sign or indicator which is visible to the suspect must show when the recording equipment is recording.

Notes for guidance

A–169   **E:3A** *Nothing in this code is intended to preclude audio recording at police discretion of interviews at police stations with people cautioned in respect of offences not covered by paragraph 3.1, or responses made by
persons after they have been charged with, or told they may be prosecuted for, an offence, provided this code is
complied with.*

E:3B *A decision not to audio record an interview for any reason may be the subject of comment in court.
The authorising officer should be prepared to justify that decision.*

E:3C *If, during the course of an interview under this code, it becomes apparent that the interview should
be conducted under one of the terrorism codes for recording of interviews the interview should only continue
in accordance with the relevant code.*

E:4 The interview

(a) *General*

A–170   **E:4.1** The provisions of Code C:

- sections 10 and 11, and the applicable *Notes for Guidance* apply to the conduct of
  interviews to which this code applies;
- paragraphs 11.7 to 11.14 apply only when a written record is needed.

E:4.2 Code C, paragraphs 10.10, 10.11 and Annex C describe the restriction on drawing
adverse inferences from a suspect's failure or refusal to say anything about their involvement in
the offence when interviewed or after being charged or informed they may be prosecuted, and
how it affects the terms of the caution and determines if and by whom a special warning under
sections 36 and 37 of the *Criminal Justice and Public Order Act* 1994 can be given.

(b) *Commencement of interviews*

E:4.3 When the suspect is brought into the interview room the interviewer shall, without delay
but in the suspect's sight, load the recorder with new recording media and set it to record. The
recording media must be unwrapped or opened in the suspect's presence. [*This paragraph does not
apply to interviews recorded using a secure digital network, see paragraphs 7.4 and 7.5*].

E:4.4 The interviewer should tell the suspect about the recording process and point out the
sign or indicator which shows that the recording equipment is activated and recording. See
paragraph 3.6. The interviewer shall:

(a) say the interview is being audibly recorded;
(b) subject to paragraph 2.3, give their name and rank and that of any other interviewer
    present;
(c) ask the suspect and any other party present, *e.g.* a solicitor, to identify themselves;
(d) state the date, time of commencement and place of the interview;
(e) state the suspect will be given a notice about what will happen to the copies of the
    recording. [*This sub-paragraph does not apply to interviews recorded using a secure digital
    network, see paragraphs 7.4 and 7.6 to 7.7.*]

See *Note 4A.*

E:4.5 The interviewer shall:

- caution the suspect, see Code C, section 10;
- remind the suspect of their entitlement to free legal advice, see Code C, paragraph 11.2.

E:4.6 The interviewer shall put to the suspect any significant statement or silence, see Code C,
paragraph 11.4.

(c) *Interviews with deaf persons*

A–171   **E:4.7** If the suspect is deaf or is suspected of having impaired hearing, the interviewer shall
make a written note of the interview in accordance with Code C, at the same time as audio recording it in accordance with this code. See *Notes 4B and 4C*.

(d) *Objections and complaints by the suspect*

E:4.8 If the suspect objects to the interview being audibly recorded at the outset, during the
interview or during a break, the interviewer shall explain that the interview is being audibly recorded and that this code requires the suspect's objections to be recorded on the audio recording.
When any objections have been audibly recorded or the suspect has refused to have their objections recorded, the interviewer shall say they are turning off the recorder, give their reasons and
turn it off. The interviewer shall then make a written record of the interview as in Code C, sec-

tion 11. If, however, the interviewer reasonably considers they may proceed to question the suspect with the audio recording still on, the interviewer may do so. This procedure also applies in cases where the suspect has previously objected to the interview being visually recorded, see Code F 4.8, and the investigating officer has decided to audibly record the interview. See *Note 4D.*

E:4.9 If in the course of an interview a complaint is made by or on behalf of the person being questioned concerning the provisions of this code or Code C, the interviewer shall act as in Code C, paragraph 12.9. See *Notes 4E* and *4F.*

E:4.10 If the suspect indicates they want to tell the interviewer about matters not directly connected with the offence and they are unwilling for these matters to be audio recorded, the suspect should be given the opportunity to tell the interviewer at the end of the formal interview.

(e) *Changing recording media*

E:4.11 When the recorder shows the recording media only has a short time left, the interviewer shall tell the suspect the recording media are coming to an end and round off that part of the interview. If the interviewer leaves the room for a second set of recording media, the suspect shall not be left unattended. The interviewer will remove the recording media from the recorder and insert the new recording media which shall be unwrapped or opened in the suspect's presence. The recorder should be set to record on the new media. To avoid confusion between the recording media, the interviewer shall mark the media with an identification number immediately after they are removed from the recorder. [*This paragraph does not apply to interviews recorded using a secure digital network as this does not use removable media, see paragraphs 1.6(c), 7.4 and 7.14 to 7.15.*]

(f) *Taking a break during interview*

E:4.12 When a break is taken, the fact that a break is to be taken, the reason for it and the time shall be recorded on the audio recording. **A–172**

E:4.12A When the break is taken and the interview room vacated by the suspect, the recording media shall be removed from the recorder and the procedures for the conclusion of an interview followed, see paragraph 4.18.

E:4.13 When a break is a short one and both the suspect and an interviewer remain in the interview room, the recording may be stopped. There is no need to remove the recording media and when the interview recommences the recording should continue on the same recording media. The time the interview recommences shall be recorded on the audio recording.

E:4.14 After any break in the interview the interviewer must, before resuming the interview, remind the person being questioned that they remain under caution or, if there is any doubt, give the caution in full again. See *Note 4G.*

[*Paragraphs 4.12 to 4.14 do not apply to interviews recorded using a secure digital network, see paragraphs 7.4 and 7.8 to 7.10.*]

(g) *Failure of recording equipment*

E:4.15 If there is an equipment failure which can be rectified quickly, *e.g.* by inserting new recording media, the interviewer shall follow the appropriate procedures as in paragraph 4.11. When the recording is resumed the interviewer shall explain what happened and record the time the interview recommences. If, however, it will not be possible to continue recording on that recorder and no replacement recorder is readily available, the interview may continue without being audibly recorded. If this happens, the interviewer shall seek the custody officer's authority as in paragraph 3.3. See *Note 4H.* [*This paragraph does not apply to interviews recorded using a secure digital network, see paragraphs 7.4 and 7.11.*]

(h) *Removing recording media from the recorder*

E:4.16 When recording media is removed from the recorder during the interview, they shall be retained and the procedures in paragraph 4.18 followed. [*This paragraph does not apply to interviews recorded using a secure digital network as this does not use removable media, see 1.6(c), 7.4 and 7.14 to 7.15.*]

(i) *Conclusion of interview*

E:4.17 At the conclusion of the interview, the suspect shall be offered the opportunity to clarify anything he or she has said and asked if there is anything they want to add.

E:4.18 At the conclusion of the interview, including the taking and reading back of any written statement, the time shall be recorded and the recording shall be stopped. The interviewer shall seal the master recording with a master recording label and treat it as an exhibit in accordance with force standing orders. The interviewer shall sign the label and ask the suspect and any third party present during the interview to sign it. If the suspect or third party refuse to sign the label an officer of at least inspector rank, or if not available the custody officer, shall be called into the interview room and asked, subject to paragraph 2.3, to sign it.

E:4.19 The suspect shall be handed a notice which explains:

- how the audio recording will be used;
- the arrangements for access to it;
- that if the person is charged or informed they will be prosecuted, a copy of the audio recording will be supplied as soon as practicable or as otherwise agreed between the suspect and the police or on the order of the court.

[*Paragraphs 4.17 to 4.19 do not apply to interviews recorded using a secure digital network, see paragraphs 7.4 and 7.12 to 7.13.*]

Notes for guidance

A–173

E:4A *For the purpose of voice identification the interviewer should ask the suspect and any other people present to identify themselves.*

E:4B *This provision is to give a person who is deaf or has impaired hearing equivalent rights of access to the full interview record as far as this is possible using audio recording.*

E:4C *The provisions of Code C, section 13 on interpreters for deaf persons or for interviews with suspects who have difficulty understanding English continue to apply.*

E:4D *The interviewer should remember that a decision to continue recording against the wishes of the suspect may be the subject of comment in court.*

E:4E *If the custody officer is called to deal with the complaint, the recorder should, if possible, be left on until the custody officer has entered the room and spoken to the person being interviewed. Continuation or termination of the interview should be at the interviewer's discretion pending action by an inspector under Code C, paragraph 9.2.*

A–174

E:4F *If the complaint is about a matter not connected with this code or Code C, the decision to continue is at the interviewer's discretion. When the interviewer decides to continue the interview, they shall tell the suspect the complaint will be brought to the custody officer's attention at the conclusion of the interview. When the interview is concluded the interviewer must, as soon as practicable, inform the custody officer about the existence and nature of the complaint made.*

E:4G *The interviewer should remember that it may be necessary to show to the court that nothing occurred during a break or between interviews which influenced the suspect's recorded evidence. After a break or at the beginning of a subsequent interview, the interviewer should consider summarising on the record the reason for the break and confirming this with the suspect.*

E:4H *Where the interview is being recorded and the media or the recording equipment fails the officer conducting the interview should stop the interview immediately. Where part of the interview is unaffected by the error and is still accessible on the media, that media shall be copied and sealed in the suspect's presence and the interview recommenced using new equipment/media as required. Where the content of the interview has been lost in its entirety the media should be sealed in the suspect's presence and the interview begun again. If the recording equipment cannot be fixed or no replacement is immediately available the interview should be recorded in accordance with Code C, section 11.*

E:5 After the interview

A–175

E:5.1 The interviewer shall make a note in their pocket book that the interview has taken place, was audibly recorded, its time, duration and date and the master recording's identification number.

E:5.2 If no proceedings follow in respect of the person whose interview was recorded, the recording media must be kept securely as in paragraph 6.1 and *Note 6A*.

[*This section (paragraphs 5.1, 5.2 and Note 5A) does not apply to interviews recorded using a secure digital network, see paragraphs 7.4 and 7.14 to 7.15.*]

Note for guidance

A–176

E:5A *Any written record of an audibly recorded interview should be made in accordance with national guidelines approved by the Secretary of State, and with regard to the advice contained in the Manual of Guidance for the preparation, processing and submission of prosecution files.*

E:6 Media security

E:6.1 The officer in charge of each police station at which interviews with suspects are re-   **A–177**
corded shall make arrangements for master recordings to be kept securely and their movements
accounted for on the same basis as material which may be used for evidential purposes, in accordance with force standing orders. See *Note 6A.*

E:6.2 A police officer has no authority to break the seal on a master recording required for
criminal trial or appeal proceedings. If it is necessary to gain access to the master recording, the
police officer shall arrange for its seal to be broken in the presence of a representative of the
Crown Prosecution Service. The defendant or their legal adviser should be informed and given a
reasonable opportunity to be present. If the defendant or their legal representative is present
they shall be invited to reseal and sign the master recording. If either refuses or neither is present this should be done by the representative of the Crown Prosecution Service. See *Notes 6B* and
6C.

E:6.3 If no criminal proceedings result or the criminal trial and, if applicable, appeal proceedings to which the interview relates have been concluded, the chief officer of police is responsible
for establishing arrangements for breaking the seal on the master recording, if necessary.

E:6.4 When the master recording seal is broken, a record must be made of the procedure followed, including the date, time, place and persons present.

[*This section (paragraphs 6.1 to 6.4 and Notes 6A to 6C) does not apply to interviews recorded using a
secure digital network, see paragraphs 7.4 and 7.14 to 7.15.*]

Notes for guidance
E:6A *This section is concerned with the security of the master recording sealed at the conclusion of the*   **A–178**
*interview. Care must be taken of working copies of recordings because their loss or destruction may lead to the
need to access master recordings.*

E:6B *If the recording has been delivered to the Crown Court for their keeping after committal for trial the
crown prosecutor will apply to the chief clerk of the Crown Court centre for the release of the recording for
unsealing by the crown prosecutor.*

E:6C *Reference to the Crown Prosecution Service or to the crown prosecutor in this part of the code*   **A–179**
*should be taken to include any other body or person with a statutory responsibility for prosecution for whom
the police conduct any audibly recorded interviews.*

E:7 Recording of interviews by secure digital network

E:7.1 A secure digital network does not use removable media and this section specifies the   **A–179a**
provisions which will apply when a secure digital network is used.

E:7.2 [*Not used.*]

E:7.3 The following requirements are solely applicable to the use of a secure digital network
for the recording of interviews.

(a) *Application of sections 1 to 6 of Code E*
E:7.4 Sections 1 to 6 of Code E above apply except for the following paragraphs: **A–179b**

- paragraph 2.2 under "Recording and sealing of master recordings"
- paragraph 4.3 under "(b) Commencement of interviews"
- paragraph 4.4 (e) under "(b) Commencement of interviews"
- paragraphs 4.11 – 4.19 under "(e) Changing recording media", "(f) Taking a break during interview", "(g) Failure of recording equipment", "(h) Removing recording media
  from the recorder" and (i) "Conclusion of the interview"
- paragraphs 6.1 – 6.4 and Notes 6A to 6C under "Media security".

(b) *Commencement of interview*
E:7.5 When the suspect is brought into the interview room, the interviewer shall without delay   **A–179c**
and in the sight of the suspect, switch on the recording equipment and enter the information
necessary to log on to the secure network and start recording.

E:7.6 The interviewer must then provide inform the suspect that the interview is being recorded using a secure digital network and that recording has commenced.

E:7.7 In addition to the requirements of paragraph 4.4(a) – (d) above, the interviewer must
inform the person that:

- they will be given access to the recording of the interview in the event that they are charged or informed that they will be prosecuted but if they are not charged or informed that they will be prosecuted they will only be given access as agreed with the police or on the order of a court; and

- they will be given a written notice at the end of the interview setting out their rights to access the recording and what will happen to the recording.

(c) *Taking a break during interview*

A–179d   E:7.8 When a break is taken, the fact that a break is to be taken, the reason for it and the time shall be recorded on the audio recording. The recording shall be stopped and the procedures in paragraphs 7.12 and 7.13 for the conclusion of an interview followed.

E:7.9 When the interview recommences the procedures in paragraphs 7.5 to 7.7 for commencing an interview shall be followed to create a new file to record the continuation of the interview. The time the interview recommences shall be recorded on the audio recording.

E:7.10 After any break in the interview the interviewer must, before resuming the interview, remind the person being questioned that they remain under caution or, if there is any doubt, give the caution in full again. See *Note 4G.*

(d) *Failure of recording equipment*

A–179e   E:7.11 If there is an equipment failure which can be rectified quickly, *e.g.* by commencing a new secure digital network recording, the interviewer shall follow the appropriate procedures as in paragraphs 7.8 to 7.10. When the recording is resumed the interviewer shall explain what happened and record the time the interview recommences. If, however, it is not possible to continue recording on the secure digital network the interview should be recorded on removable media as in paragraph 4.3 unless the necessary equipment is not available. If this happens the interview may continue without being audibly recorded and the interviewer shall seek the custody officer's authority as in paragraph 3.3. See *Note 4H.*

(e) *Conclusion of interview*

A–179f   E:7.12 At the conclusion of the interview, the suspect shall be offered the opportunity to clarify anything he or she has said and asked if there is anything they want to add.

E:7.13 At the conclusion of the interview, including the taking and reading back of any written statement:

    (a) the time shall be orally recorded;

    (b) the suspect shall be handed a notice which explains:

- how the audio recording will be used,
- the arrangements for access to it,
- that if they are charged or informed that they will be prosecuted, they will be given access to the recording of the interview either electronically or by being given a copy on removable recording media, but if they are not charged or informed that they will prosecuted, they will only be given access as agreed with the police or on the order of a court; see *Note 7A;*

    (c) the suspect must be asked to confirm that he or she has received a copy of the notice at paragraph 7.13(b) above; if the suspect fails to accept or to acknowledge receipt of the notice, the interviewer will state for the recording that a copy of the notice has been provided to the suspect and that he or she has refused to take a copy of the notice or has refused to acknowledge receipt;

    (d) the time shall be recorded and the interviewer shall notify the suspect that the recording is being saved to the secure network. The interviewer must save the recording in the presence of the suspect. The suspect should then be informed that the interview is terminated.

(f) *After the interview*

E:7.14 The interviewer shall make a note in their pocket book that the interview has taken place, was audibly recorded, its time, duration and date and the original recording's identification number.

E:7.15 If no proceedings follow in respect of the person whose interview was recorded, the recordings must be kept securely as in paragraphs 7.16 and 7.17. See *Note 5A.*

(g) *Security of secure digital network interview records*

E:7.16 Interview record files are stored in read only format on non-removable storage devices, for example, hard disk drives, to ensure their integrity. The recordings are first saved locally to a secure non-removable device before being transferred to the remote network device. If for any reason the network connection fails, the recording remains on the local device and will be transferred when the network connections are restored.

E:7.17 Access to interview recordings, including copying to removable media, must be strictly controlled and monitored to ensure that access is restricted to those who have been given specific permission to access for specified purposes when this is necessary. For example, police officers and CPS lawyers involved in the preparation of any prosecution case, persons interviewed if they have been charged or informed they may be prosecuted and their legal representatives.

Note for guidance

E:7A *The notice at paragraph 7.13 above should provide a brief explanation of the secure digital network* **A–179g** *and how access is strictly limited to the recording. The notice should also explain the access rights of the suspect, his or her legal representative, the police and the prosecutor to the recording of the interview. Space should be provided on the form to insert the date and the file reference number for the interview.*

(7) **Visual recording of interviews**

The text that follows is of the version of the code that came into force on May 1, 2010: **A–180** see *ante*, Appendix A–1.

The *Police and Criminal Evidence Act 1984 (Visual Recording of Interviews) (Certain Police Areas) Order* 2002 (S.I. 2002 No. 1069) (made under s.60A(1)(b) and (2)) required the visual recording of interviews held by police officers at Basingstoke, Portsmouth, Southampton, Chatham, Gravesend, Tonbridge, Bromley, Colindale, Edmonton, Redditch, Telford and Worcester police stations and commencing after midnight on May 7, 2002.

The *Police and Criminal Evidence Act 1984 (Visual Recording of Interviews) (Certain Police Areas) (No. 2) Order* 2002 (S.I. 2002 No. 2527) (made under s.60A(1)(b) and (2)) required the visual recording of interviews held by police officers at Harlow, Colchester, and Southend police stations and commencing after midnight on October 29, 2002.

The *Police and Criminal Evidence Act 1984 (Visual Recording of Interviews) (Certain Police Areas) Order* 2003 (S.I. 2003 No. 2463) revoked S.I. 2002 No. 1069 and S.I. 2002 No. 2527 (*ante*) as from November 1, 2003, so that visual recording of interviews in the police areas specified in those orders was no longer mandatory.

As at June 22, 2012, there was no requirement on any police force to make visual recordings of interviews, but police officers who choose to make such recordings will still be required to have regard to the provisions of this code.

F. Code of Practice on Visual Recordings With Sound Of Interviews With Suspects

Commencement—Transitional arrangements

The contents of this code should be considered if an interviewing officer decides to make a visual **A–180a** recording with sound of an interview with a suspect after midnight on 1 May 2010. There is no statutory requirement under *PACE* to visually record interviews.

F:1. General

F:1.1 This code of practice must be readily available for consultation by police officers and **A–181** other police staff, detained persons and members of the public.

F:1.2 The notes for guidance included are not provisions of this code. They form guidance to police officers and others about its application and interpretation.

F:1.3 Nothing in this code shall be taken as detracting in any way from the requirements of the Code of Practice for the Detention, Treatment and Questioning of Persons by Police Officers (Code C). [See *Note 1A.*]

F:1.4 The interviews to which this code applies are set out in paragraphs 3.1–3.3.

F:1.5 In this code, the term "appropriate adult", "solicitor" and "interview" have the same meaning as those set out in Code C. The corresponding provisions and Notes for Guidance in Code C applicable to those terms shall also apply where appropriate.

F:1.5A The visual recording of interviews shall be carried out openly to instil confidence in its reliability as an impartial and accurate record of the interview.

F:1.6 Any reference in this code to visual recording shall be taken to mean visual recording with sound and in this code:

(aa) "recording media" means any removable, physical audio recording medium (such as magnetic tape, optical disc or solid state memory) which can be played and copied;

(a) "designated person" means a person other than a police officer, designated under the *Police Reform Act* 2002, Pt 4, who has specified powers and duties of police officers conferred or imposed on them;

(b) any reference to a police officer includes a designated person acting in the exercise or performance of the powers and duties conferred or imposed on them by their designation;

(c) "secure digital network" is a computer network system which enables an original interview recording to be stored as a digital multi media file or a series of such files, on a secure file server which is accredited by the National Accreditor for Police Information Systems in the National Police Improvement Agency (NPIA) in accordance with the UK Government Protective Marking Scheme (see section 7 of this code).

F:1.7 References to "pocket book" in this code include any official report book issued to police officers.

Note for guidance

F:1A *As in paragraph 1.9 of Code C, references to custody officers include those carrying out the functions of a custody officer.*

F:2. Recording and sealing of master recordings

A–182   **F:2.1** [*Not used.*]

F:2.2 The camera(s) shall be placed in the interview room so as to ensure coverage of as much of the room as is practicably possible whilst the interviews are taking place. [See *Note 2A.*]

F:2.3 The certified recording medium will be of a high quality, new and previously unused. When the certified recording medium is placed in the recorder and switched on to record, the correct date and time, in hours, minutes and seconds will be superimposed automatically, second by second, during the whole recording. [See *Note 2B.*] See section 7 regarding the use of a secure digital network to record the interview.

F:2.4 One copy of the certified recording medium, referred to in this code as the master copy, will be sealed before it leaves the presence of the suspect. A second copy will be used as a working copy. [See *Notes 2C* and *2D.*]

F:2.5 Nothing in this code requires the identity of an officer to be recorded or disclosed if:

(a) the interview or record relates to a person detained under the *Terrorism Act* 2000 (see paragraph 3.2); or

(b) otherwise where the officer reasonably believes that recording or disclosing their name might put them in danger.

In these cases, the officer will have their back to the camera and shall use their warrant or other identification number and the name of the police station to which they are attached. Such instances and the reasons for them shall be recorded in the custody record. [See *Note 2E.*]

Notes for guidance

A–183   **F:2A** *Interviewing officers will wish to arrange that, as far as possible, visual recording arrangements are unobtrusive. It must be clear to the suspect, however, that there is no opportunity to interfere with the recording equipment or the recording media.*

F:2B *In this context, the certified recording media should be capable of having an image of the date and time superimposed upon them as they record the interview.*

F:2C *The purpose of sealing the master copy before it leaves the presence of the suspect is to establish their confidence that the integrity of the copy is preserved.*

F:2D *The recording of the interview may be used for identification procedures in accordance with paragraph 3.21 or Annex E of Code D.*

F:2E *The purpose of the [sic] paragraph 2.5(b) is to protect police officers and others involved in the investigation of serious organised crime or the arrest of particularly violent suspects when there is reliable information that those arrested or their associates may threaten or cause harm to the officers, their families or their personal property.*

F:3. Interviews to be visually recorded

F:3.1 Subject to paragraph 3.2 below, if an interviewing officer decides to make a visual re- **A–184** cording, these are the areas where it might be appropriate:

    (a) with a suspect in respect of an indictable offence (including an offence triable either way) [see *Notes 3A* and *3B*];

    (b) which takes place as a result of an interviewer exceptionally putting further questions to a suspect about an offence described in sub-paragraph (a) above after they have been charged with, or informed they may be prosecuted for, that offence [see *Note 3C*];

    (c) in which an interviewer wishes to bring to the notice of a person, after that person has been charged with, or informed they may be prosecuted for an offence described in sub-paragraph (a) above, any written statement made by another person, or the content of an interview with another person [see *Note 3D*];

    (d) with, or in the presence of, a deaf or deaf/blind or speech impaired person who uses sign language to communicate;

    (e) with, or in the presence of anyone who requires an "appropriate adult"; or

    (f) in any case where the suspect or their representative requests that the interview be recorded visually.

F:3.2 The *Terrorism Act* 2000 makes separate provision for a code of practice for the video re- **A–185** cording of interviews in a police station of those detained under Schedule 7 or section 41 of the Act. The provisions of this code do not therefore apply to such interviews [see *Note 3E*].

F:3.3 The custody officer may authorise the interviewing officer not to record the interview visually:

    (a) where it is not reasonably practicable to do so because of failure of the equipment, or the non-availability of a suitable interview room, or recorder and the authorising officer considers on reasonable grounds that the interview should not be delayed until the failure has been rectified or a suitable room or recorder becomes available; in such cases the custody officer may authorise the interviewing officer to audio record the interview in accordance with the guidance set out in Code E;

    (b) where it is clear from the outset that no prosecution will ensue; or

    (c) where it is not practicable to do so because at the time the person resists being taken to a suitable interview room or other location which would enable the interview to be recorded, or otherwise fails or refuses to go into such a room or location, and the authorising officer considers on reasonable grounds that the interview should not be delayed until these conditions cease to apply.

In all cases the custody officer shall make a note in the custody records [*sic*] of the reasons for not taking a visual record. [See *Note 3F*.]

F:3.4 When a person who is voluntarily attending the police station is required to be cautioned in accordance with Code C prior to being interviewed, the subsequent interview shall be recorded, unless the custody officer gives authority in accordance with the provisions of paragraph 3.3 above for the interview not to be so recorded.

F:3.5 The whole of each interview shall be recorded visually, including the taking and reading back of any statement.

F:3.6 A sign or indicator which is visible to the suspect must show when the visual recording equipment is recording.

Notes for guidance

F:3A *Nothing in the code is intended to preclude visual recording at police discretion of interviews at po-* **A–186** *lice stations with people cautioned in respect of offences not covered by paragraph 3.1, or responses made by interviewees after they have been charged with or informed they may be prosecuted for, an offence, provided that this code is complied with.*

F:3B *Attention is drawn to the provisions set out in Code C about the matters to be considered when deciding whether a detained person is fit to be interviewed.*

F:3C *Code C sets out the circumstances in which a suspect may be questioned about an offence after being charged with it.*

F:3D *Code C sets out the procedures to be followed when a person's attention is drawn after charge, to a statement made by another person. One method of bringing the content of an interview with another person to the notice of a suspect may be to play him a recording of that interview.*

F:3E *If, during the course of an interview under this code, it becomes apparent that the interview should be conducted under one of the terrorism codes for video recording of interviews the interview should only continue in accordance with the relevant code.*

F:3F *A decision not to record an interview visually for any reason may be the subject of comment in court. The authorising officer should therefore be prepared to justify their decision in each case.*

F:4. The interview

(a) *General*

A–187   F:4.1 The provisions of Code C in relation to cautions and interviews and the Notes for Guidance applicable to those provisions shall apply to the conduct of interviews to which this code applies.

F:4.2 Particular attention is drawn to those parts of Code C that describe the restrictions on drawing adverse inferences from a suspect's failure or refusal to say anything about their involvement in the offence when interviewed, or after being charged or informed they may be prosecuted and how those restrictions affect the terms of the caution and determine 'whether a special warning under sections 36 and 37 of the *Criminal Justice and Public Order Act* 1994 can be given.

(b) *Commencement of interviews*

A–188   F:4.3 When the suspect is brought into the interview room the interviewer shall without delay, but in sight of the suspect, load the recording equipment and set it to record. The recording media must be unwrapped or otherwise opened in the presence of the suspect. [See *Note 4A*.]

F:4.4 The interviewer shall then tell the suspect formally about the visual recording and point out the sign or indicator which shows that the recording equipment is activated and recording. See paragraph 3.6. The interviewer shall:

    (a) explain the interview is being visually recorded;

    (b) subject to paragraph 2.5, give his or her name and rank, and that of any other interviewer present;

    (c) ask the suspect and any other party present (*e.g.* his solicitor) to identify themselves;

    (d) state the date, time of commencement and place of the interview; and

    (e) state that the suspect will be given a notice about what will happen to the recording.

F:4.5 The interviewer shall then caution the suspect, which should follow that set out in Code C, and remind the suspect of their entitlement to free and independent legal advice and that they can speak to a solicitor on the telephone.

F:4.6 The interviewer shall then put to the suspect any significant statement or silence (*i.e.* failure or refusal to answer a question or to answer it satisfactorily) which occurred before the start of the interview, and shall ask the suspect whether they wish to confirm or deny that earlier statement or silence or whether they wish to add anything. The definition of a "significant" statement or silence is the same as that set out in Code C.

(c) *Interviews with the deaf*

A–189   F:4.7 If the suspect is deaf or there is doubt about their hearing ability, the provisions of Code C on interpreters for the deaf or for interviews with suspects who have difficulty in understanding English continue to apply.

(d) *Objections and complaints by the suspect*

A–190   F:4.8 If the suspect raises objections to the interview being visually recorded either at the outset or during the interview or during a break in the interview, the interviewer shall explain the fact that the interview is being visually recorded and that the provisions of this code require that the suspect's objections shall be recorded on the visual recording. When any objections have been visually recorded or the suspect has refused to have their objections recorded, the interviewer shall say that they are turning off the recording equipment, give their reasons and turn it off. If a separate audio recording is being maintained, the officer shall ask the person to record the reasons for refusing to agree to visual recording of the interview. Paragraph 4.8 of Code E will apply if the person objects to audio recording of the interview. The officer shall then make a written record of the interview. If the interviewer reasonably considers they may proceed to question the suspect with the visual recording still on, the interviewer may do so. See *Note 4G*.

F:4.9 If in the course of an interview a complaint is made by the person being questioned, or on their behalf, concerning the provisions of this code or of Code C, then the interviewer shall act in accordance with Code C, record it in the interview record and inform the custody officer. [See *Notes 4B* and *4C*.]

F:4.10 If the suspect indicates that they wish to tell the interviewer about matters not directly connected with the offence of which they are suspected and that they are unwilling for these matters to be recorded, the suspect shall be given the opportunity to tell the interviewer about these matters after the conclusion of the formal interview.

(e) *Changing the recording media*

F:4.11 In instances where the recording medium is not of sufficient length to record all of the **A–191** interview with the suspect, further certified recording medium will be used. When the recording equipment indicates that the recording medium has only a short time left to run, the interviewer shall advise the suspect and round off that part of the interview. If the interviewer wishes to continue the interview but does not already have further certified recording media with him, they shall obtain a set. The suspect should not be left unattended in the interview room. The interviewer will remove the recording media from the recording equipment and insert the new ones which have been unwrapped or otherwise opened in the suspect's presence. The recording equipment shall then be set to record. Care must be taken, particularly when a number of sets of recording media have been used, to ensure that there is no confusion between them. This could be achieved by marking the sets of recording media with consecutive identification numbers.

(f) *Taking a break during the interview*

F:4.12 When a break is to be taken during the course of an interview and the interview room **A–192** is to be vacated by the suspect, the fact that a break is to be taken, the reason for it and the time shall be recorded. The recording equipment must be turned off and the recording media removed. The procedures for the conclusion of an interview set out in paragraph 4.19, below, should be followed.

F:4.13 When a break is to be a short one, and both the suspect and a police officer are to remain in the interview room, the fact that a break is to be taken, the reasons for it and the time shall be recorded on the recording media. The recording equipment may be turned off, but there is no need to remove the recording media. When the interview is recommenced the recording shall continue on the same recording media and the time at which the interview recommences shall be recorded.

F:4.14 When there is a break in questioning under caution, the interviewing officer must ensure that the person being questioned is aware that they remain under caution. If there is any doubt the caution must be given again in full when the interview resumes. [See *Notes 4D* and *4E*.]

(g) *Failure of recording equipment*

F:4.15 If there is a failure of equipment which can be rectified quickly, the appropriate **A–193** procedures set out in paragraph 4.12 shall be followed. When the recording is resumed the interviewer shall explain what has happened and record the time the interview recommences. If, however, it is not possible to continue recording on that particular recorder and no alternative equipment is readily available, the interview may continue without being recorded visually. In such circumstances, the procedures set out in paragraph 3.3 of this code for seeking the authority of the custody officer will be followed. [See *Note 4F*.]

(h) *Removing used recording media from recording equipment*

F:4.16 Where used recording media are removed from the recording equipment during the **A–194** course of an interview, they shall be retained and the procedures set out in paragraph 4.18 below followed.

(i) *Conclusion of interview*

F:4.17 Before the conclusion of the interview, the suspect shall be offered the opportunity to **A–195** clarify anything he or she has said and asked if there is anything that they wish to add.

F:4.18 At the conclusion of the interview, including the taking and reading back of any written statement, the time shall be recorded and the recording equipment switched off. The master recording shall be removed from the recording equipment, sealed with a master recording label and treated as an exhibit in accordance with the force standing orders. The interviewer shall sign the label and also ask the suspect and any third party present during the interview to sign it. If the suspect or third party refuses to sign the label, an officer of at least the rank of inspector, or if one is not available, the custody officer, shall be called into the interview room and asked, subject to paragraph 2.5, to sign it.

F:4.19 The suspect shall be handed a notice which explains the use which will be made of the recording and the arrangements for access to it. The notice will also advise the suspect that a copy of the tape shall be supplied as soon as practicable if the person is charged or informed that he will be prosecuted.

Notes for guidance

F:4A *The interviewer should attempt to estimate the likely length of the interview and ensure that an appropriate quantity of certified recording media and labels with which to seal the master copies are available in the interview room.*

F:4B *Where the custody officer is called immediately to deal with the complaint, wherever possible the recording equipment should be left to run until the custody officer has entered the interview room and spoken to the person being interviewed. Continuation or termination of the interview should be at the discretion of the interviewing officer pending action by an inspector as set out in Code C.*

F:4C *Where the complaint is about a matter not connected with this code of practice or Code C, the decision to continue with the interview is at the discretion of the interviewing officer. Where the interviewing officer decides to continue with the interview, the person being interviewed shall be told that the complaint will be brought to the attention of the custody officer at the conclusion of the interview. When the interview is concluded, the interviewing officer must, as soon as practicable, inform the custody officer of the existence and nature of the complaint made.*

F:4D *In considering whether to caution again after a break, the officer should bear in mind that he may have to satisfy a court that the person understood that he was still under caution when the interview resumed.*

F:4E *The officer should bear in mind that it may be necessary to satisfy the court that nothing occurred during a break in an interview or between interviews which influenced the suspect's recorded evidence. On the re-commencement of an interview, the officer should consider summarising on the record the reason for the break and confirming this with the suspect.*

F:4F *If any part of the recording media breaks or is otherwise damaged during the interview, it should be sealed as a master copy in the presence of the suspect and the interview resumed where it left off. The undamaged part should be copied and the original sealed as a master tape in the suspect's presence, if necessary after the interview. If equipment for copying is not readily available, both parts should be sealed in the suspect's presence and the interview begun again.*

F:4G *The interviewer should be aware that a decision to continue recording against the wishes of the suspect may be the subject of comment in court.*

F:5. After the interview

F:5.1 The interviewer shall make a note in his or her pocket book of the fact that the interview has taken place and has been recorded, its time, duration and date and the identification number of the master copy of the recording media.

F:5.2 Where no proceedings follow in respect of the person whose interview was recorded, the recording media must nevertheless be kept securely in accordance with paragraph 6.1 and *Note 6A.*

Note for guidance

F:5A *Any written record of a recorded interview shall be made in accordance with national guidelines approved by the Secretary of State, and with regard to the advice contained in the Manual of Guidance for the preparation, processing and submission of files.*

F:6. Master copy security

(a) *General*

F:6.1 The officer in charge of the police station at which interviews with suspects are recorded shall make arrangements for the master copies to be kept securely and their movements accounted for on the same basis as other material which may be used for evidential purposes, in accordance with force standing orders. [See *Note 6A.*]

(b) *Breaking master copy seal for criminal proceedings*

F:6.2 A police officer has no authority to break the seal on a master copy which is required for criminal trial or appeal proceedings. If it is necessary to gain access to the master copy, the police officer shall arrange for its seal to be broken in the presence of a representative of the Crown Prosecution Service. The defendant or their legal adviser shall be informed and given a reasonable opportunity to be present. If the defendant or their legal representative is present they shall be invited to reseal and sign the master copy. If either refuses or neither is present, this shall be done by the representative of the Crown Prosecution Service. [See *Notes 6B* and *6C.*]

(c) *Breaking master copy seal: other cases*

F:6.3 The chief officer of police is responsible for establishing arrangements for breaking the seal of the master copy where no criminal proceedings result, or the criminal proceedings, to which the interview relates, have been concluded and it becomes necessary to break the seal. These arrangements should be those which the chief officer considers are reasonably necessary to demonstrate to the person interviewed and any other party who may wish to use or refer to the interview record that the master copy has not been tampered with and that the interview record remains accurate. [See *Note 6D.*]

F:6.4 Subject to paragraph 6.6, a representative of each party must be given a reasonable opportunity to be present when the seal is broken, the master copy copied and re-sealed.

F:6.5 If one or more of the parties is not present when the master copy seal is broken because they cannot be contacted or refuse to attend or paragraph 6.6 applies, arrangements should be made for an independent person such as a custody visitor, to be present. Alternatively, or as an additional safeguard, arrangement should be made for a film or photographs to be taken of the procedure.

F:6.6 Paragraph 6.5 does not require a person to be given an opportunity to be present when:

(a) it is necessary to break the master copy seal for the proper and effective further investigation of the original offence or the investigation of some other offence; and

(b) the officer in charge of the investigation has reasonable grounds to suspect that allowing an opportunity might prejudice any such an investigation or criminal proceedings which may be brought as a result or endanger any person. [See *Note 6E.*]

(e) *Documentation*

F:6.7 When the master copy seal is broken, copied and re-sealed, a record must be made of **A-201** the procedure followed, including the date time and place and persons present.

Notes for guidance

F:6A *This section is concerned with the security of the master copy which will have been sealed at the* **A-202** *conclusion of the interview. Care should, however, be taken of working copies since their loss or destruction may lead unnecessarily to the need to have access to master copies.*

F:6B *If the master copy has been delivered to the Crown Court for their keeping after committal for trial the crown prosecutor will apply to the chief clerk of the Crown Court centre for its release for unsealing by the crown prosecutor.*

F:6C *Reference to the Crown Prosecution Service or to the crown prosecutor in this part of the code shall be taken to include any other body or person with a statutory responsibility for prosecution for whom the police conduct any recorded interviews.*

F:6D *The most common reasons for needing access to master copies that are not required for criminal proceedings arise from civil actions and complaints against police and civil actions between individuals arising out of allegations of crime investigated by police.*

F:6E *Paragraph 6.6 could apply, for example, when one or more of the outcomes or likely outcomes of the investigation might be: (i) the prosecution of one or more of the original suspects; (ii) the prosecution of someone previously not suspected, including someone who was originally a witness; and (iii) any original suspect being treated as a prosecution witness and when premature disclosure of any police action, particularly through contact with any parties involved, could lead to a real risk of compromising the investigation and endangering witnesses.*

F:7. Visual recording of interviews by secure digital network

F:7.1 This section applies if an officer wishes to make a visual recording with sound of an **A-202a** interview mentioned in section 3 of this code using a secure digital network which does not use removable media (see paragraph 1.6(c) above).

F:7.3 [*sic*] The provisions of sections 1 to 6 of this code which relate or apply only to removable media will not apply to a secure digital network recording.

F:7.4 The statutory requirement and provisions for the audio recording of interviews using a secure digital network set out in section 7 of Code E should be applied to the visual recording with sound of interviews mentioned in section 3 of this code as if references to audio recordings of interviews include visual recordings with sound.

(8) Statutory power of arrest

The first version of Code G came into force on January 1, 2006, to coincide with the commencement of the substantial changes to the provisions of the *PACE Act* 1984 relating to the powers of arrest of police constables. As from that date, all offences became arrestable offences, but the lawfulness of an arrest by a constable for an offence became dependent **A-203** on the constable having "reasonable grounds for believing that for any of the reasons mentioned in subsection (5) [of section 24] it is necessary to arrest the person in question". For the substituted section 24, see § 15–131 in the main work.

As to the content of this code, paragraph 2.1 significantly over-simplifies the requirements of a lawful arrest, and there is an error in paragraph 2.3. This states that a constable may arrest without warrant "in relation to any offence, except for the single exception [*sic*] listed in Note for Guidance 1". That note recites the powers of arrest for offences under the *CLA* 1967, ss.4(1) and 5(1) (assisting offenders/concealment of evidence) require that the offences to which they relate must carry a maximum term of at least five years' imprisonment. This, however, is to confuse the ingredients of the offence and the power of arrest.

★ A revised code G is anticipated to come into force on November 12, 2012 (see *ante*, A–1). The text of the new code will be included in the first supplement to the 2013 edition to be published on November 15, 2012.

G. Code of Practice for the Statutory Power of Arrest by Police Officers

Commencement

A–203a This code applies to any arrest made by a police officer after midnight on 31 December 2005.

G:1 Introduction

A–204 **G:**1.1 This code of practice deals with statutory power of police to arrest persons suspected of involvement in a criminal offence.

G:1.2 The right to liberty is a key principle of the *Human Rights Act* 1998. The exercise of the power of arrest represents an obvious and significant interference with that right.

G:1.3 The use of the power must be fully justified and officers exercising the power should consider if the necessary objectives can be met by other, less intrusive means. Arrest must never be used simply because it can be used. Absence of justification for exercising the powers of arrest may lead to challenges should the case proceed to court. When the power of arrest is exercised it is essential that it is exercised in a non-discriminatory and proportionate manner.

G:1.4 Section 24 of the *Police and Criminal Evidence Act* 1984 (as substituted by section 110 of the *Serious Organised Crime and Police Act* 2005) provides the statutory power of arrest. If the provisions of the Act and this code are not observed, both the arrest and the conduct of any subsequent investigation may be open to question.

G:1.5 This code of practice must be readily available at all police stations for consultation by police officers and police staff, detained persons and members of the public.

G:1.6 The notes for guidance are not provisions of this code.

G:2 Elements of arrest under section 24 PACE

A–205 **G:**2.1 A lawful arrest requires two elements:

> A person's involvement or suspected involvement or attempted involvement in the commission of a criminal offence;

AND

> reasonable grounds for believing that the person's arrest is necessary.

G:2.2 Arresting officers are required to inform the person arrested that they have been arrested, even if this fact is obvious, and of the relevant circumstances of the arrest in relation to both elements and to inform the custody officer of these on arrival at the police station. See Code C, paragraph 3.4.

Involvement in the commission of an offence

A–206 **G:**2.3 A constable may arrest without warrant in relation to any offence, except for the single exception listed in *Note for Guidance* 1. A constable may arrest anyone:

- who is about to commit an offence or is in the act of committing an offence;
- whom the officer has reasonable grounds for suspecting is about to commit an offence or to be committing an offence;
- whom the officer has reasonable grounds to suspect of being guilty of an offence which he or she has reasonable grounds for suspecting has been committed;
- anyone [*sic*] who is guilty of an offence which has been committed or anyone whom the officer has reasonable grounds for suspecting to be guilty of that offence.

Necessity criteria

G:2.4 The power of arrest is only exercisable if the constable has reasonable grounds for **A–207**
believing that it is necessary to arrest the person. The criteria for what may constitute necessity
are set out in paragraph 2.9. It remains an operational decision at the discretion of the arresting
officer as to:

- what action he or she may take at the point of contact with the individual;
- the necessity criterion or criteria (if any) which applies to the individual; and
- whether to arrest, report for summons, grant street bail, issue a fixed penalty notice or
  take any other action that is open to the officer.

G:2.5 In applying the criteria, the arresting officer has to be satisfied that at least one of the
reasons supporting the need for arrest is satisfied.

G:2.6 Extending the power of arrest to all offences provides a constable with the ability to use
that power to deal with any situation. However, applying the necessity criteria requires the constable to examine and justify the reason or reasons why a person needs to be taken to a police
station for the custody officer to decide whether the person should be placed in police detention.

G:2.7 The criteria below are set out in section 24 of *PACE* as substituted by section 110 of the
Serious Organised Crime and Police Act 2005. The criteria are exhaustive. However, the circumstances
that may satisfy those criteria remain a matter for the operational discretion of individual officers.
Some examples are given below of what those circumstances may be.

G:2.8 In considering the individual circumstances, the constable must take into account the
situation of the victim, the nature of the offence, the circumstances of the suspect and the needs
of the investigative process.

G:2.9 The criteria are that the arrest is necessary: **A–208**

- (a) to enable the name of the person in question to be ascertained (in the case where the
  constable does not know, and cannot readily ascertain, the person's name, or has reasonable grounds for doubting whether a name given by the person as his name is his real
  name);
- (b) correspondingly as regards the person's address;

  an address is a satisfactory address for service of summons if the person will be at it
  for a sufficiently long period for it to be possible to serve him or her with a summons;
  or, that some other person at that address specified by the person will accept service
  of the summons on their behalf;
- (c) to prevent the person in question—
  - (i) causing physical injury to himself or any other person;
  - (ii) suffering physical injury;
  - (iii) causing loss or damage to property;
  - (iv) committing an offence against public decency (only applies where members of the
    public going about their normal business cannot reasonably be expected to avoid the
    person in question); or
  - (v) causing an unlawful obstruction of the highway;
- (d) to protect a child or other vulnerable person from the person in question;
- (e) to allow the prompt and effective investigation of the offence or of the conduct of the
  person in question;

  this may include cases such as:
  - (i) where there are reasonable grounds to believe that the person:
    - has made false statements;
    - has made statements which cannot be readily verified;
    - has presented false evidence;
    - may steal or destroy evidence;
    - may make contact with co-suspects or conspirators;
    - may intimidate or threaten or make contact with witnesses;
    - where it is necessary to obtain evidence by questioning [*sic*]; or
  - (ii) when considering arrest in connection with an indictable offence, there is a need to:
    - enter and search any premises occupied or controlled by a person;
    - search the person;

> • prevent contact with others;
> • take fingerprints, footwear impressions, samples or photographs of the suspect;

> (iii) ensuring compliance with statutory drug testing requirements;
> (f) to prevent any prosecution for the offence from being hindered by the disappearance of the person in question;
>> this may arise if there are reasonable grounds for believing that:
>> • if the person is not arrested he or she will fail to attend court;
>> • street bail after arrest would be insufficient to deter the suspect from trying to evade prosecution.

G:3 Information to be given on arrest

(a) Cautions—when a caution must be given (taken from Code C section 10)

A–209   G:3.1 A person whom there are grounds to suspect of an offence (see *Note 2*) must be cautioned before any questions about an offence, or further questions if the answers provide the grounds for suspicion, are put to them if either the suspect's answers or silence (*i.e.* failure or refusal to answer or answer satisfactorily) may be given in evidence to a court in a prosecution. A person need not be cautioned if questions are for other necessary purposes, *e.g.*:

> (a) solely to establish their identify or ownership of any vehicle;
> (b) to obtain information in accordance with any relevant statutory requirement;
> (c) in furtherance of the proper and effective conduct of a search, *e.g.* to determine the need to search in the exercise of powers to stop and search or to seek co-operation while carrying out a search;
> (d) to seek verification of a written record as in Code C, paragraph 11.13;
> (e) when examining a person in accordance with the *Terrorism Act* 2000, Sched. 7 and the Code of Practice for Examining Officers issued under that Act, Schedule 14, paragraph 6.

G:3.2 Whenever a person not under arrest is initally cautioned, or reminded they are under caution, that person must at the same time be told they are not under arrest and are free to leave if they want to.

G:3.3 A person who is arrested, or further arrested, must be informed at the time, or as soon as practicable thereafter, that they are under arrest and the grounds for their arrest, see *Note 3*.

G:3.4 A person who is arrested, or further arrested, must also be cautioned unless:

> (a) it is impracticable to do so by reason of their condition or behaviour at the time;
> (b) they have already been cautioned immediately prior to arrest as in paragraph 3.1.

(c) [sic] Terms of the caution (taken from Code C section 10)

A–210   G:3.5 The caution, which must be given on arrest, should be in the following terms:
"You do not have to say anything. But it may harm your defence if you do not mention when questioned something which you later rely on in court. Anything you do say may be given in evidence.".

See *Note 5*.

G:3.6 Minor deviations from the words of any caution given in accordance with this code do not constitute a breach of this code, provided the sense of the relevant caution is preserved. See *Note 6*.

G:3.7 When, despite being cautioned, a person fails to co-operate or to answer particular questions which may affect their immediate treatment, the person should be informed of any relevant consequences and that those consequences are not affected by the caution. Examples are when aperson's refusal to provide:

> • their name and address when charged may make them liable to detention;
> • particulars and information in accordance with a statutory requirement, *e.g.* under the *Road Traffic Act* 1988, may amount to an offence or may make the person liable to a further arrest.

G:4 Records of arrest

(a) General

A–211   G:4.1 The arresting officer is required to record in his pocket book or by other methods used for recording information:

> • the nature and cirumstances of the offence leading to the arrest;

- the reason or reasons why arrest was necessary;
- the giving of the caution;
- anything said by the person at the time of the arrest.

G:4.2 Such a record should be made at the time of the arrest unless impracticable to do. If not made at that time, the record should then be completed as soon as possible thereafter.

G:4.3 On arrival at the police station, the custody officer shall open the custody record (see paragraph 1.1A and section 2 of Code C). The information given by the arresting officer on the circumstances and reason or reasons for arrest shall be recorded as part of the custody record. Alternatively, a copy of the record made by the officer in accordance with paragraph 4.1 above shall be attached as part of the custody record. See paragraph 2.2 and Code C, paragraphs 3.4 and 10.3.

G:4.4 The custody record will serve as a record of the arrest. Copies of the custody record will be provided in accordance with paragraphs 2.4 and 2.4A of Code C and access for inspection of the original record in accordance with paragraph 2.5 of Code C.

(b) *Interviews and arrests*

G:4.5 Records of interviews, significant statements or silences will be treated in the same way as set out in sections 10 and 11 of Code C and in Code E (audio recording of interviews).

Notes for guidance

G:1 *The powers of arrest for offences under section 4(1) and 5(1) of the* Criminal Law Act *1967 require* **A–212** *that the offences to which they relate must carry a sentence fixed by law or one which a first time offender aged 18 or over could be sentenced to 5 years or more imprisonment.*

G:2 *There must be some reasonable, objective grounds for the suspicion, based on known facts or information which are relevant to the likelihood the offence has been committed and the person to be questioned committed it.*

G:3 *An arrested person must be given sufficient information to enable them to understand they have been deprived of their liberty and the reason they have been arrested, e.g. when a person is arrested on suspicion of committing an offence they must be informed of the suspected offence's nature, when and where it was committed. The suspect must also be informed of the reason or reasons why arrest is considered necessary. Vague or technical language should be avoided.*

G:4 *Nothing in this code requires a caution to be given or repeated when informing a person not under arrest they may be prosecuted for an offence. However, a court will not be able to draw any inferences under the* Criminal Justice and Public Order Act *1994, s.34, if the person was not cautioned.*

G:5 *If it appears a person does not understand the caution, the people giving it should explain it in their own words.*

G:6 *The powers available to an officer as the result of an arrest – for example, entry and search of premises, holding a person incommunicado, setting up road blocks – are only available in respect of indictable offences and are subject to the specific requirements on authorisation as set out in the 1984 Act and relevant PACE code of practice.*

(9) Detention treatment and questioning of terrorist suspects

The *Police and Criminal Evidence Act 1984 (Code of Practice C and Code of Practice H) Or-* **A–213** *der* 2006 (S.I. 2006 No. 1938) provided for a revised Code C (*ante*, A–38 *et seq.*), and for a new Code H (on detention, treatment and questioning by police officers of persons under section 41 of, and Schedule 8 to, the *Terrorism Act* 2000), to come into operation on July 25, 2006. The new codes were consequential upon the commencement of the provisions of the *Terrorism Act* 2006, which were concerned with the 28-day detention of those arrested under section 41 of the 2000 Act. Whereas Code C had previously regulated those detained following arrest under section 41, this is now regulated by Code H. Code C was revised so as to remove references to detention under the 2000 Act. The new Code H largely mirrored the provisions of Code C, but with various differences.

The text that follows is the text of the revised Code H laid before Parliament in May 2012 ★ (but see *ante*, A–1), and anticipated to come into force in early July, 2012 (see *ante*, A–1).

H. Code of Practice in Connection with the Detention, Treatment and Questioning by Police Officers of Persons under Section 41 of, and Schedule 8 to, the Terrorism Act 2000

Commencement—Transitional Arrangements

★**A–214**   This code applies to:

- people in police detention after midnight on the day the *Police and Criminal Evidence Act 1984 (Codes of Practice) (Revision of Codes C, G and H) Order 2012* comes into force, following their arrest under section 41 of the *Terrorism Act* 2000, even though they may have been arrested before that time; and
- persons in respect of whom an authorisation under section 22 of the *Counter-Terrorism Act* 2008 has been given after midnight on the day the *Counter Terrorism Act 2008 (Code of Practice for the Video Recording with Sound of Post-Charge Questioning) Order 2012* comes into force.

H:1 General

★**A–214a**   **H:**1.0 [*Identical to C:1.0.*]

H:1.1 This code of practice applies to, and only to:

(a) persons in police detention after being arrested under section 41 of the *Terrorism Act* 2000 (*TACT*) and detained under section 41 of, or Schedule 8 to that Act and not charged; and

(b) detained persons in respect of whom an authorisation has been given under section 22 of the *Counter-Terrorism Act* 2008 (post-charge questioning of terrorist suspects) to interview them in which case, section 15 of this code will apply.

H:1.2 The provisions in *PACE* Code C apply when a person:

(a) is in custody otherwise than as a result of being arrested section 41 of *TACT* or detained for examination under Schedule 7 to *TACT* (see paragraph 1.4);

(b) is charged with an offence; or

(c) is being questioned about any offence after being charged with that offence without an authorisation being given under section 22 of the *Counter-Terrorism Act* 2008.

See *Note 1N*.

H:1.3 In this code references to an offence and to a person's involvement or suspected involvement in an offence where the person has not been charged with an offence, include being concerned, or suspected of being concerned, in the commission, preparation or instigation of acts of terrorism.

H:1.4 The code of practice issued under paragraph 6 of Schedule 14 to *TACT* applies to a person detained for examination under Schedule 7 to *TACT*. See *Note 1N*.

H:1.5 All persons in custody must be dealt with expeditiously, and released as soon as the need for detention no longer applies.

H:1.6 There is no provision for bail under *TACT* before or after charge. See *Note 1N*.

H:1.7 An officer must perform the assigned duties in this code as soon as practicable. An officer will not be in breach of this code if delay is justifiable and reasonable steps are taken to prevent unnecessary delay. The custody record shall show when a delay has occurred and the reason. See *Note 1H*.

H:1.8–1.10 [*Identical to C:1.2 to C:1.4, respectively.*]

H:1.11 For the purposes of this code, a juvenile is any person under the age of 17. If anyone appears to be under 17, and there is no clear evidence that they are 17 or over, they shall be treated as a juvenile for the purposes of this code.

H:1.12 [*Identical to C:1.6.*]

H:1.13 "The appropriate adult" means, in the case of a:

(a) juvenile:

(i) the parent, guardian or, if the juvenile is in the care of a local authority or voluntary organisation, or is otherwise being looked after under the *Children Act* 1989, a person representing that authority or organisation;

(ii) a social worker of a local authority social services department;

(iii) failing these, some other responsible adult aged 18 or over who is not a police officer or employed by the police;

(b) person who is mentally disordered or mentally vulnerable (see *Note 1D*):

(i) a relative, guardian or other person responsible for their care or custody;

(ii) someone experienced in dealing with mentally disordered or mentally vulnerable people but who is not a police officer or employed by the police;

(iii) failing these, some other responsible adult aged 18 or over who is not a police officer or employed by the police.

H:1.14 [*Identical to C:1.8.*]

H:1.15 [*Identical to C:1.9.*]

H:1.16 When this code requires the prior authority or agreement of an officer of at least inspector or superintendent rank, that authority may be given by a sergeant or chief inspector authorised by section 107 of *PACE* to perform the functions of the higher rank under *TACT*.

H:1.17 In this code:

(a) "designated person" means a person other than a police officer, designated under the *Police Reform Act* 2002, Pt 4, who has specified powers and duties of police officers conferred or imposed on them;

(b) reference to a police officer includes a designated person acting in the exercise or performance of the powers and duties conferred or imposed on them by their designation;

(c) where a search or other procedure to which this code applies may only be carried out or observed by a person of the same sex as the detainee, the gender of the detainee and other parties present should be established and recorded in line with Annex I of this code.

H:1.18 [*Identical to C:1.14.*]

H:1.19 [*Identical to C.1.15.*]

H:1.20 Designated persons and other police staff must have regard to any relevant provisions of this code.

H:1.21 [*Identical to C:1.17.*]

Notes for guidance

H:1A [*Identical to C:1A.*]   ★**A–214b**

H:1B *A person, including a parent or guardian, should not be an appropriate adult if they:*

- *are:*
  - *suspected of involvement in the offence or involvement in the commission, preparation or instigation of acts of terrorism;*
  - *the victim;*
  - *a witness;*
  - *involved in the investigation;*
- *received admissions prior to attending to act as the appropriate adult.*

Note: if a juvenile's parent is estranged from the juvenile, they should not be asked to act as the appropriate adult if the juvenile expressly and specifically objects to their presence.

H:1C–1G [*Identical to C:1C to C:1G, respectively.*]

H:1H *Paragraph 1.7 is intended to cover delays which may occur in processing detainees e.g if:*

- *a large number of suspects are brought into the station simultaneously to be placed in custody;*
- *interview rooms are all being used;*
- *there are difficulties contacting an appropriate adult, solicitor or interpreter.*

H:1I–1K [*Identical to C:1I to C:1K, respectively.*]

H:1L *If a person is moved from a police station to receive medical treatment, or for any other reason, the period of detention is still calculated from the time of arrest under section 41 of TACT (or, if a person was being detained under TACT, Sched. 7, when arrested, from the time at which the examination under Schedule 7 began).*

H:1M *Under paragraph 1 of Schedule 8 to TACT, all police stations are designated for detention of persons arrested under section 41 of TACT. Paragraph 4 of Schedule 8 requires that the constable who arrests a person under section 41 takes him as soon as practicable to the police station which the officer considers is "most appropriate".*

H:1N *The powers under Part IV of PACE to detain and release on bail (before or after charge) a person arrested under section 24 of PACE for any offence (see PACE Code G (Arrest)) do not apply to persons whilst they are detained under the terrorism powers following their arrest/detention under section 41 of, or Schedule 7 to, TACT. If when the grounds for detention under these powers cease the person is arrested under section 24 of PACE for a specific offence, the detention and bail provisions of PACE will apply and must be considered from the time of that arrest.*

H:2 Custody records

★**A–215**   H:2.1 When a person is:

- brought to a police station following arrest under *TACT*, s.41;
- arrested under *TACT*, s.41 at a police station having attended there voluntarily;
- brought to a police station and there detained to be questioned in accordance with an authorisation under section 22 of the *Counter-Terrorism Act* 2008 (post-charge questioning) (see *Notes 15A* and *15B*); or
- at a police station and there detained when authority for post-charge questioning is given under section 22 of the *Counter-Terrorism Act* 2008 (see *Notes 15A* and *15B*),

they should be brought before the custody officer as soon as practicable after their arrival at the station or, if appropriate, following the authorisation of post-charge questioning or following arrest after attending the police station voluntarily: see *Note 3H*. A person is deemed to be "at a police station" for these purposes if they are within the boundary of any building or enclosed yard which forms part of that police station.

H:2.2 A separate custody record must be opened as soon as practicable for each person described in paragraph 2.1. All information recorded under this code must be recorded as soon as practicable in the custody record unless otherwise specified. Any audio or video recording made in the custody area is not part of the custody record.

H:2.3 If any action requires the authority of an officer of a specified rank, this must be noted in the custody record, subject to paragraph 2.8.

H:2.4 *[Identical to C:2.3.]*

H:2.3A *[sic]* If a person is arrested under *TACT*, s.41, and taken to a police station as a result of a search in the exercise of any stop and search power to which *PACE* Code A (stop and search) or the "search powers code" issued under *TACT* applies, the officer carrying out the search is responsible for ensuring that the record of that stop and search is made as part of the person's custody record. The custody officer must then ensure that the person is asked if they want a copy of the search record and if they do, that they are given a copy as soon as practicable. The person's entitlement to a copy of the search record which is made as part of their custody record is in addition to, and does not affect, their entitlement to a copy of their custody record or any other provisions of section 2 (custody records) of this code. See Code A, paragraph 4.2B, and the *TACT* search powers code paragraph 5.3.5.

H:2.5 A solicitor or appropriate adult must be permitted to consult a detainee's custody record as soon as practicable after their arrival at the station and at any other time whilst the person is detained. Arrangements for this access must be agreed with the custody officer and may not unreasonably interfere with the custody officer's duties or the justifiable needs of the investigation.

H:2.6 *[Identical to C:2.4A.]*

H:2.7 The detainee, appropriate adult or legal representative shall be permitted to inspect the original custody record once the detained person is no longer being held under the provisions of *TACT*, s.41, and Sched. 8, or being questioned after charge as authorised under section 22 of the *Counter-Terrorism Act* 2008 (see section 15), provided they give reasonable notice of their request. Any such inspection shall be noted in the custody record.

H:2.8 All entries in custody records must be timed and identified by the maker. Nothing in this code requires the identity of officers or other police staff to be recorded or disclosed in the case of enquiries linked to the investigation of terrorism. In these cases, they shall use their warrant or other identification numbers and the name of their police station: see *Note 2A*. If records are entered on computer these shall also be timed and contain the operator's identification.

H:2.9 *[Identical to C:2.7.]*

Note for guidance

★**A–215a**   H:2A *The purpose of paragraph 2.8 is to protect those involved in terrorist investigations or arrests of terrorist suspects from the possibility that those arrested, their associates or other individuals or groups may threaten or cause harm to those involved.*

H:3 Initial action

(a) *Detained persons—normal procedure*

★**A–215b**   H:3.1 When a person to whom paragraph 2.1 applies is at a police station, the custody officer must make sure the person is told clearly about the following continuing rights which may be exercised at any stage during the period in custody:

(i) the right to have someone informed of their arrest as in section 5;
(ii) the right to consult privately with a solicitor and that free independent legal advice is available;
(iii) the right to consult this code of practice. See *Note 3D*.

H:3.2 *[Identical to C:3.2, save for reference to "paragraph 2.6" in lieu of reference to "paragraph 2.4A".]*

H:3.3 *[Identical to C:3.3.]*

H:3.4 The custody officer shall:

- record that the person was arrested under section 41 of *TACT* and the reason(s) for the arrest on the custody record [see paragraph 10.2 and *Note for Guidance 3G*];
- note on the custody record any comment the detainee makes in relation to the arresting officer's account but shall not invite comment; if the arresting officer is not physically present when the detainee is brought to a police station, the arresting officer's account must be made available to the custody officer remotely or by a third party on the arresting officer's behalf;
- note any comment the detainee makes in respect of the decision to detain them but shall not invite comment;
- not put specific questions to the detainee regarding their involvement in any offence, nor in respect of any comments they may make in response to the arresting officer's account or the decision to place them in detention [see paragraphs 14.1 and 14.2 and *Notes for Guidance 3H, 14A and 14B*]. Such an exchange is likely to constitute an interview as in paragraph 11.1 and require the associated safeguards in section 11.

See paragraph 11.8A in respect of unsolicited comments.

If the first review of detention is carried out at this time, see paragraphs 14.1 and 14.2, and Part II of Schedule 8 to the *Terrorism Act* 2000 in respect of action by the review officer.

H:3.5 The custody officer or other custody staff as directed by the custody officer shall:

(a) ask the detainee, whether at this time, they:
　(i) would like legal advice, see paragraph 6.4;
　(ii) want someone informed of their detention, see section 5;

(b) ask the detainee to sign the custody record to confirm their decisions in respect of (a);

(c) determine whether the detainee:
　(i) is, or might be, in need of medical treatment or attention, see section 9;
　(ii) requires:
　　- an appropriate adult;
　　- help to check documentation;
　　- an interpreter;

(d) record the decision in respect of (c).

Where any duties under this paragraph have been carried out by custody staff at the direction of the custody officer, the outcomes shall, as soon as practicable, be reported to the custody officer who retains overall responsibility for the detainee's care and safe custody and ensuring it complies with this code. See *Note 3I*.

H:3.6 When these needs are determined, the custody officer is responsible for initiating an assessment to consider whether the detainee is likely to present specific risks to custody staff, any individual who may have contact with the detainee (*e.g.* legal advisers, medical staff), or themselves. Such assessments should always include a check on the Police National Computer, to be carried out as soon as practicable, to identify any risks highlighted in relation to the detainee. Although such assessments are primarily the custody officer's responsibility, it will be necessary to obtain information from other sources, especially the investigation team (see *Note 3E*), the arresting officer or an appropriate healthcare professional (see paragraph 9.15). Reasons for delaying the initiation or completion of the assessment must be recorded.

H:3.7 *[Identical to C:3.7.]*

H:3.8 Risk assessments must follow a structured process which clearly defines the categories of risk to be considered and the results must be incorporated in the detainee's custody record. The custody officer is responsible for making sure those responsible for the detainee's custody are appropriately briefed about the risks. The content of any risk assessment and any analysis of the level of risk relating to the person's detention is not required to be shown or provided to the detainee or any person acting on behalf of the detainee. If no specific risks are identified by the assessment, that should be noted in the custody record. See *Note 3F* and paragraph 9.15.

H:3.9 Custody officers are responsible for implementing the response to any specific risk assessment, which should include for example:

- reducing opportunities for self harm;
- calling a health care professional;
- increasing levels of monitoring or observation;
- reducing the risk to those who come into contact with the detainee.

See *Note 3F.*

H:3.10, 3.11 *[Identical to C:3.10 and C:3.11, respectively.]*

H:3.12 A constable, prison officer or other person authorised by the Secretary of State may take any steps which are reasonably necessary for—

(a) photographing the detained person,

(b) measuring the person, or

(c) identifying the person.

H:3.13 Paragraph 3.12 concerns the power in *TACT*, Sched. 8, para. 2. The power in *TACT*, Sched. 8, para. 2, does not cover the taking of fingerprints, intimate samples or non-intimate samples, which is covered in *TACT*, Sched. 8, paras 10–15.

(b) *Detained persons—special groups*

H:3.14–3.16 *[Identical to C:3.12 to C:3.14, respectively.]*

H:3.17 *[Identical to C:3.15, save for reference to "paragraph 3.15" in lieu of reference to "paragraph 3.13".]*

H:3.18–3.20 *[Identical to C:3.17 to C:3.19, respectively.]*

H:3.21 *[Identical to C:3.20, save for reference to "paragraph 3.17" in lieu of reference to "paragraph 3.15".]*

(c) *Documentation*

H:3.22 The grounds for a person's detention shall be recorded, in the person's presence if practicable.

H:3.23 Action taken under paragraphs 3.14 to 3.22 shall be recorded.

Notes for guidance

★**A–216**   **H:**3A *The notice of entitlements should:*

- *list the entitlements in this code, including:*
  - *visits and contact with outside parties where practicable, including special provisions for Commonwealth citizens and foreign nationals;*
  - *reasonable standards of physical comfort;*
  - *adequate food and drink;*
  - *access to toilets and washing facilities, clothing, medical attention, and exercise when practicable;*
- *mention the:*
  - *provisions relating to the conduct of interviews;*
  - *circumstances in which an appropriate adult should be available to assist the detainee and their statutory rights to make representation whenever the period of their detention is reviewed.*

H:3B, 3C *[Identical to C:3B and C:3C, respectively.]*

H:3D *The right to consult this or other relevant codes of practice does not entitle the person concerned to delay unreasonably any necessary investigative or administrative action whilst they do so. Examples of action which need not be delayed unreasonably include:*

- *searching detainees at the police station;*
- *taking fingerprints or non-intimate samples without consent for evidential purposes.*

H:3E *The investigation team will include any officer involved in questioning a suspect, gathering or analysing evidence in relation to the offences of which the detainee is suspected of having committed. Should a custody officer require information from the investigation team, the first point of contact should be the officer in charge of the investigation.*

H:3F *Home Office Circular 32/2000 provides more detailed guidance on risk assessments and identifies key risk areas which should always be considered.*

H:3G *Arrests under TACT, s.41, can only be made where an officer has reasonable grounds to suspect* that the individual concerned is a "terrorist". This differs from the PACE *power of arrest in that it need not be linked to a specific offence. There may also be circumstances where an arrest under* TACT *is made on the grounds of sensitive information which cannot be disclosed. In such circumstances, the grounds for arrest may be given in terms of the interpretation of a "terrorist" set out in* TACT, *s.40(1)(a) or (b).*

H:3H *For the purpose of arrests under* TACT, *s.41, the review officer is responsible for authorising detention (see paragraphs 14.1 and 14.2, and Notes for Guidance 14A and 14B). The review officer's role is explained in* TACT, *Sched. 8, Pt II. A person may be detained after arrest pending the first review, which must take place as soon as practicable after the person's arrest.*

H:3I *A custody officer or other officer who, in accordance with this code, allows or directs the carrying out of any task or action relating to a detainee's care, treatment, rights and entitlements by another officer or any police staff must be satisfied that the officer or police staff concerned are suitable, trained and competent to carry out the task or action in question.*

H:4 Detainee's property

(a) *Action*

H:4.1 The custody officer is responsible for: ★**A–216a**

    (a) ascertaining what property a detainee:

        (i) has with them when they come to the police station, either on first arrival at the police station or any subsequent arrivals at a police station in connection with that detention;

        (ii) might have acquired for an unlawful or harmful purpose while in custody;

    (b) the safekeeping of any property taken from a detainee which remains at the police station.

The custody officer may search the detainee or authorise their being searched to the extent they consider necessary, provided a search of intimate parts of the body or involving the removal of more than outer clothing is only made as in Annex A. A search may only be carried out by an officer of the same sex as the detainee. See *Note 4A* and Annex I.

H:4.2, 4.3 *[Identical to C:4.2 and C:4.3, respectively.]*

(b) *Documentation*

H:4.4 It is a matter for the custody officer to determine whether a record should be made of the property a detained person has with him or had taken from him on arrest [see *Note 4D*]. Any record made is not required to be kept as part of the custody record but the custody record should be noted as to where such a record exists. Whenever a record is made the detainee shall be allowed to check and sign the record of property as correct. Any refusal to sign shall be recorded.

H:4.5 *[Identical to C:4.5.]*

Notes for guidance

H:4A–4C *[Identical to C:4A to C:4C, respectively.]*   ★**A–216b**

H:4D *Section 43(2) of* TACT *allows a constable to search a person who has been arrested under section 41 to discover whether they have anything in their possession that may constitute evidence that they are a terrorist.*

H:5 Right not to be held incommunicado

(a) *Action*

H:5.1 Any person to whom this code applies who is held in custody at a police station or other   ★**A–217** premises may, on request, have one named person who is a friend, relative or a person known to them who is likely to take an interest in their welfare informed at public expense of their whereabouts as soon as practicable. If the person cannot be contacted the detainee may choose up to two alternatives. If they cannot be contacted, the person in charge of detention or the investigation has discretion to allow further attempts until the information has been conveyed. See *Notes 5D and 5E.*

H:5.2 *[Identical to C:5.2.]*

H:5.3 The above right may be exercised each time a detainee is taken to another police station or returned to a police station having been previously transferred to prison. This code does not afford such a right to a person on transfer to a prison, where a detainee's rights will be governed by prison rules [see paragraph 14.8].

H:5.4 If the detainee agrees, they may at the custody officer's discretion receive visits from friends, family or others likely to take an interest in their welfare, or in whose welfare the detainee has an interest. Custody officers should liaise closely with the investigation team [see *Note 3E*] to allow risk assessments to be made where particular visitors have been requested by the detainee or identified themselves to police. In circumstances where the nature of the investigation means that such requests cannot be met, consideration should be given, in conjunction with a representative of the relevant scheme, to increasing the frequency of visits from independent visitor schemes. See *Notes 5B* and *5C*.

H:5.5 [*Identical to C:5.5, save for reference to "Note 5E" in lieu of reference to "Note 5D".*]

H:5.6 The detainee shall be given writing materials, on request, and allowed to telephone one person for a reasonable time, see *Notes 5A* and *5F*. Either or both these privileges may be denied or delayed if an officer of inspector rank or above considers sending a letter or making a telephone call may result in any of the consequences in Annex B, paras 1 and 2, particularly in relation to the making of a telephone call in a language which an officer listening to the call [see paragraph 5.7] does not understand. See *Note 5G*.

Nothing in this paragraph permits the restriction or denial of the rights in paragraphs 5.1 and 6.1.

H:5.7 Before any letter or message is sent, or telephone call made, the detainee shall be informed that what they say in any letter, call or message (other than in a communication to a solicitor) may be read or listened to and may be given in evidence. A telephone call may be terminated if it is being abused [see *Note 5G*]. The costs can be at public expense at the custody officer's discretion.

H:5.8 [*Identical to C:5.7A.*]

(b) *Documentation*

H:5.9 A record must be kept of any:

(a) request made under this section and the action taken;

(b) letters, messages or telephone calls made or received or visit received;

(c) refusal by the detainee to have information about them given to an outside enquirer, or any refusal to see a visitor. The detainee must be asked to countersign the record accordingly and any refusal recorded.

Notes for guidance

★**A–217a**   **H:5A** *A person may request an interpreter to interpret a telephone call or translate a letter.*

H:5B *At the custody officer's discretion (and subject to the detainee's consent), visits should be allowed when possible, subject to sufficient personnel being available to supervise a visit and any possible hindrance to the investigation. Custody officers should bear in mind the exceptional nature of prolonged TACT detention and consider the potential benefits that visits may bring to the health and welfare of detainees who are held for extended periods.*

H:5C *Official visitors should be given access following consultation with the officer who has overall responsibility for the investigation provided the detainee consents, and they do not compromise safety or security or unduly delay or interfere with the progress of an investigation. Official visitors should still be required to provide appropriate identification and subject to any screening process in place at the place of detention. Official visitors may include:*

- *an accredited faith representative;*
- *Members of either House of Parliament;*
- *public officials needing to interview the prisoner in the course of their duties;*
- *other persons visiting with the approval of the officer who has overall responsibility for the investigation;*
- *consular officials visiting a detainee who is a national of the country they represent subject to section 7 of this code.*

Visits from appropriate members of the Independent Custody Visitors Scheme should be dealt with in accordance with the separate Code of Practice on Independent Custody Visiting.

H:5D *If the detainee does not know anyone to contact for advice or support or cannot contact a friend or relative, the custody officer should bear in mind any local voluntary bodies or other organisations that might be able to help. Paragraph 6.1 applies if legal advice is required.*

H:5E *In some circumstances it may not be appropriate to use the telephone to disclose information under paragraphs 5.1 and 5.5.*

H:5F *The telephone call at paragraph 5.6 is in addition to any communication under paragraphs 5.1 and 6.1. Further calls may be made at the custody officer's discretion.*

H:5G *The nature of terrorism investigations means that officers should have particular regard to the possibility of suspects attempting to pass information which may be detrimental to public safety, or to an investigation.*

H:6 Right to legal advice

(a) *Action*

H:6.1 Unless Annex B applies, all detainees must be informed that they may at any time ★**A–217b**
consult and communicate privately with a solicitor, whether in person, in writing or by telephone,
and that free independent legal advice is available from the duty solicitor. Where an appropriate
adult is in attendance, they must also be informed of this right. See paragraph 3.1, *Note 11, Notes
6B* and *6J*.

H:6.2 A poster advertising the right to legal advice must be prominently displayed in the
charging area of every police station. See *Note 6G*.

H:6.3 [*Identical to C:6.4.*]

H:6.4 The exercise of the right of access to legal advice may be delayed exceptionally only as
in Annex B. Whenever legal advice is requested, and unless Annex B applies, the custody officer
must act without delay to secure the provision of such advice. If, on being informed or reminded
of this right, the detainee declines to speak to a solicitor in person, the officer should point out
that the right includes the right to speak with a solicitor on the telephone [see paragraph 5.6]. If
the detainee continues to waive this right the officer should ask them why and any reasons
should be recorded on the custody record or the interview record as appropriate. Reminders of
the right to legal advice must be given as in paragraphs 3.5, 11.3, and *PACE* Code D on the
Identification of Persons by Police Officers, paragraphs 3.17(ii) and 6.3. Once it is clear a detainee
does not want to speak to a solicitor in person or by telephone they should cease to be asked their
reasons. See *Note 6J*.

H:6.5 An officer of the rank of commander or assistant chief constable may give a direction
under *TACT*, Sched. 8, para. 9, that a detainee may only consult a solicitor within the sight and
hearing of a qualified officer. Such a direction may only be given if the officer has reasonable
grounds to believe that if it were not, it may result in one of the consequences set out in *TACT*,
Sched. 8, para. 8(4) or (5)(c). See Annex B, para. 3, and *Note 6I*. A "qualified officer" means a police
officer who:

    (a) is at least the rank of inspector;

    (b) is of the uniformed branch of the force of which the officer giving the direction is a
    member; and

    (c) in the opinion of the officer giving the direction, has no connection with the detained
    person's case.

Officers considering the use of this power should first refer to Home Office Circular 40/2003.

H:6.6 [*Identical to C:6.5A.*]

H:6.7 A detainee who wants legal advice may not be interviewed or continue to be interviewed
until they have received such advice unless:

    (a) [*identical to C:6.6(a)*];

    (b) [*identical to C:6.6(b)*];

    (c) [*identical to C:6.6(c)*];

    (d) the detainee changes their mind, about wanting legal advice or (as the case may be)
    about wanting a solicitor present at the interview, and states that they no longer wish to
    speak to a solicitor; in these circumstances the interview may be started or continued
    without delay provided that:

      (i) an officer of inspector rank or above:

        ● speaks to the detainee to enquire about the reasons for their change of mind (see
        Note 6J); and

        ● makes, or directs the making of, reasonable efforts to ascertain the solicitor's
        expected time of arrival and to inform the solicitor that the suspect has stated that
        they wish to change their mind and the reason (if given);

      (ii) the detainee's reason for their change of mind (if given) and the outcome of the ac-
      tion in (i) are recorded in the custody record;

      (iii) the detainee, after being informed of the outcome of the action in (i) above, confirms
      in writing that they want the interview to proceed without speaking or further speak-
      ing to a solicitor or (as the case may be) without a solicitor being present and do not
      wish to wait for a solicitor by signing an entry to this effect in the custody record;

      (iv) an officer of inspector rank or above is satisfied that it is proper for the interview to
      proceed in these circumstances and:

- gives authority in writing for the interview to proceed and if the authority is not recorded in the custody record, the officer must ensure that the custody record shows the date and time of authority and where it is recorded; and

- takes or directs the taking of, reasonable steps to inform the solicitor that the authority has been given and the time when the interview is expected to commence and records or causes to be recorded, the outcome of this action in the custody record;

(v) when the interview starts and the interviewer reminds the suspect of their right to legal advice (see paragraph 11.3) and the code of practice issued under paragraph 3 of Schedule 8 to the *Terrorism Act* 2000 for the video recording with sound of interviews, the interviewer shall then ensure that the following is recorded in the interview record made in accordance with that code:

- confirmation that the detainee has changed their mind about wanting legal advice or (as the case may be) about wanting a solicitor present and the reasons for it if given;

- the fact that authority for the interview to proceed has been given and, subject to paragraph 2.8, the name of the authorising officer;

- that if the solicitor arrives at the station before the interview is completed, the detainee will be so informed without delay and a break will be taken to allow them to speak to the solicitor if they wish, unless paragraph 6.7(a) applies; and

- that at any time during the interview, the detainee may again ask for legal advice and that if they do, a break will be taken to allow them to speak to the solicitor, unless paragraph 6.7(a), (b) or (c) applies.

Note: in these circumstances the restriction on drawing adverse inferences from silence in Annex C will not apply because the detainee is allowed an opportunity to consult a solicitor if they wish.

H:6.8 If paragraph 6.7(a) applies, where the reason for authorising the delay ceases to apply, there may be no further delay in permitting the exercise of the right in the absence of a further authorisation unless paragraph 6.7(b), (c) or (d) applies. If paragraph 6.7(b)(i) applies, once sufficient information has been obtained to avert the risk, questioning must cease until the detainee has received legal advice unless paragraph 6.7(a), (b)(ii), (c) or (d) applies.

H:6.9 [*Identical to C:6.8, save for reference to "paragraph 6.7" in lieu of reference to "paragraph 6.6".*]

H:6.10 The solicitor may only be required to leave the interview if their conduct is such that the interviewer is unable properly to put questions to the suspect. See *Notes 6C* and *6D*.

H:6.11 [*Identical to C:6.10, save for reference to "Note 6D" in lieu of reference to "Note 6E".*]

H:6.12 [*Identical to C:6.11.*]

H:6.13 [*Identical to C:6.12.*]

H:6.14 [*Identical to C:6.12A, save for references to "Note 6C" and to "paragraphs 6.7 to 6.11" in lieu of references to "Note 6D" and "paragraphs 6.6. to 6.10".*]

H:6.15 In exercising their discretion under paragraph 6.14, the officer should take into account in particular:

- whether:
  - the identity and status of an accredited or probationary representative have been satisfactorily established;
  - they are of suitable character to provide legal advice,

- any other matters in any written letter of authorisation provided by the solicitor on whose behalf the person is attending the police station. See *Note 6E*.

H:6.16 If the inspector refuses access to an accredited or probationary representative or a decision is taken that such a person should not be permitted to remain at an interview, the inspector must notify the solicitor on whose behalf the representative was acting and give them an opportunity to make alternative arrangements. The detainee must be informed and the custody record noted.

H:6.17 If a solicitor arrives at the station to see a particular person, that person must, unless Annex B applies, be so informed whether or not they are being interviewed and asked if they would like to see the solicitor. This applies even if the detainee has declined legal advice or, having requested it, subsequently agreed to be interviewed without receiving advice. The solicitor's attendance and the detainee's decision must be noted in the custody record.

(b) *Documentation*

H:6.18, 6.19 *[Identical to C:6.16 and C:6.17, respectively.]*

Notes for guidance

H:6ZA *No police officer or police staff shall indicate to any suspect, except to answer a direct question, that* ★**A–218**
period for which they are liable to be detained, or the time taken to complete the interview, might be reduced:

- *if they do not ask for legal advice or do not want a solicitor present when they are interviewed; or*
- *if after asking for legal advice, they change their mind about wanting it or (as the case may be) wanting a solicitor present when they are interviewed and agree to be interviewed without waiting for a solicitor.*

H:6A *In considering if paragraph 6.7(b) applies, the officer should, if practicable, ask the solicitor for an estimate of how long it will take to come to the station and relate this to the time detention is permitted, the time of day (i.e. whether the rest period under paragraph 12.2 is imminent) and the requirements of other investigations. If the solicitor is on their way or is to set off immediately, it will not normally be appropriate to begin an interview before they arrive. If it appears necessary to begin an interview before the solicitor's arrival, they should be given an indication of how long the police would be able to wait so there is an opportunity to make arrangements for someone else to provide legal advice. Nothing within this section is intended to prevent police from ascertaining immediately after the arrest of an individual whether a threat to public safety exists (see paragraph 11.2).*

H:6B *A detainee has a right to free legal advice and to be represented by a solicitor. This note for guidance explains the arrangements which enable detainees to whom this code applies to obtain legal advice. An outline of these arrangements is also included in the Notice of Rights and Entitlements given to detainees in accordance with paragraph 3.2.*

The detainee can ask for free advice from a solicitor they know or if they do not know a solicitor or the solicitor they know cannot be contacted, from the duty solicitor.

To arrange free legal advice, the police should telephone the Defence Solicitor Call Centre (DSCC). The call centre will contact either the duty solicitor or the solicitor requested by the detainee as appropriate.

When a detainee wants to pay for legal advice themselves:

- *the DSCC will contact a solicitor of their choice on their behalf;*
- *they should be given an opportunity to consult a specific solicitor or another solicitor from that solicitor's firm; if this solicitor is not available, they may choose up to two alternatives; if these alternatives are not available, the custody officer has discretion to allow further attempts until a solicitor has been contacted and agreed to provide advice;*
- *they are entitled to a private consultation with their chosen solicitor on the telephone or the solicitor may decide to come to the police station;*
- *if their chosen solicitor cannot be contacted, the DSCC may still be called to arrange free legal advice.*

Apart from carrying out duties necessary to implement these arrangements, an officer must not advise the suspect about any particular firm of solicitors.

H:6C *[Identical to C:6D.]*

H:6D *[Identical to C:6E.]*

H:6E *[Identical to C:6F.]*

H:6F *[Identical to C:6G, save for reference to "paragraph 6.7(b)" in lieu of reference to "paragraph 6.6(b)".]*

H:6G *[Identical to C:6H.]*

H:6H *[Not used.]*

H:6I *Whenever a detainee exercises their right to legal advice by consulting or communicating with a solicitor, they must be allowed to do so in private. This right to consult or communicate in private is fundamental. Except as allowed by the Terrorism Act 2000, Sched. 8, para. 9, if the requirement for privacy is compromised because what is said or written by the detainee or solicitor for the purpose of giving and receiving legal advice is overheard, listened to, or read by others without the informed consent of the detainee, the right will effectively have been denied. When a detainee speaks to a solicitor on the telephone, they should be allowed to do so in private unless a direction under Schedule 8, paragraph 9 of the Terrorism Act 2000 has been given or this is impractical because of the design and layout of the custody area, or the location of telephones. However, the normal expectation should be that facilities will be available, unless they are being used, at all police stations to enable detainees to speak in private to a solicitor either face to face or over the telephone.*

H:6J *[Identical to C:6K.]*

H:7 Citizens of independent Commonwealth countries or foreign nationals

★**A–218a**   [*Identical to C:7.*]

H:8 Conditions of detention

(a) *Action*

★**A–218b**   **H:**8.1, 8.2 [*Identical to C:8.1, save for omission of reference to Note 8C, and C:8.2, respectively.*]

H:8.3 [*Identical to C:8.3, save for omission of reference to Note 8A.*]

H:8.4, 8.5 [*Identical to C:8.4 and C:8.5, respectively.*]

H:8.6 At least two light meals and one main meal should be offered in any 24 hour period. See *Note 8B.* Drinks should be provided at meal times and upon reasonable request between meals. Whenever necessary, advice shall be sought from the appropriate health care professional, see *Note 9A*, on medical and dietary matters. As far as practicable, meals provided shall offer a varied diet and meet any specific dietary needs or religious beliefs the detainee may have. Detainees should also be made aware that the meals offered meet such needs. The detainee may, at the custody officer's discretion, have meals supplied by their family or friends at their expense. See *Note 8A.*

H:8.7 Brief outdoor exercise shall be offered daily if practicable. Where facilities exist, indoor exercise shall be offered as an alternative if outside conditions are such that a detainee cannot be reasonably expected to take outdoor exercise (*e.g.*, in cold or wet weather) or if requested by the detainee or for reasons of security. See *Note 8C.*

H:8.8 Where practicable, provision should be made for detainees to practice [*sic*] religious observance. Consideration should be given to providing a separate room which can be used as a prayer room. The supply of appropriate food and clothing, and suitable provision for prayer facilities, such as uncontaminated copies of religious books, should also be considered. See *Note 8D.*

H:8.9 A juvenile shall not be placed in a cell unless no other secure accommodation is available and the custody officer considers it is not practicable to supervise them if they are not placed in a cell or that a cell provides more comfortable accommodation than other secure accommodation in the station. A juvenile may not be placed in a cell with a detained adult.

H:8.10 Police stations should keep a reasonable supply of reading material available for detainees, including but not limited to, the main religious texts. See *Note 8D.* Detainees should be made aware that such material is available and reasonable requests for such material should be met as soon as practicable unless to do so would:

> (i) interfere with the investigation; or

> (ii) prevent or delay an officer from discharging his statutory duties, or those in this code.

If such a request is refused on the grounds of (i) or (ii) above, this should be noted in the custody record and met as soon as possible after those grounds cease to apply.

(b) *Documentation*

H:8.11, 8.12 [*Identical to C:8.9 and C:8.11, respectively.*]

Notes for guidance

★**A–219**   **H:**8A *In deciding whether to allow meals to be supplied by family or friends, the custody officer is entitled to take account of the risk of items being concealed in any food or package and the officer's duties and responsibilities under food handling legislation. If an officer needs to examine food or other items supplied by family and friends before deciding whether they can be given to the detainee, he should inform the person who has brought the item to the police station of this and the reasons for doing so.*

H:8B [*Identical to C:8B.*]

H:8C *In light of the potential for detaining individuals for extended periods of time, the overriding principle should be to accommodate a period of exercise, except where to do so would hinder the investigation, delay the detainee's release or charge, or it is declined by the detainee.*

H:8D *Police forces should consult with representatives of the main religious communities to ensure the provision for religious observance is adequate, and to seek advice on the appropriate storage and handling of religious texts or other religious items.*

H:9 Care and treatment of detained persons

(a) *General*

H:9.1 Notwithstanding other requirements for medical attention as set out in this section, detainees who are held for more than 96 hours must be visited by an appropriate healthcare professional at least once every 24 hours. ★**A–219a**

H:9.2, 9.3 [*Identical to C:9.1, save for omission of reference to Note 8C, and C:9.2, respectively.*]

H:9.4 [*Identical to C:9.3, save for references to "Note 9C", "paragraph 9.15" and "Note 9G" in lieu of references to "Note 9CA", "paragraph 9.13" and "Note 9H", respectively.*]

H:9.5 [*Identical to C:9.4.*]

(b) *Clinical treatment and attention*

H:9.6, 9.7, 9.8 [*Identical to C:9.5, C:9.5A and C: 9.5B, respectively.*]

H:9.9 [*Identical to C:9.7, save for reference to "Note 9D" in lieu of reference to "Note 9E".*]

H:9.10 [*Identical to C:9.8.*]

H:9.11 [*Identical to C:9.9, save for reference to "paragraph 9.12" in lieu of reference to "paragraph 9.10".*]

H:9.12 No police officer may administer or supervise the self-administration of medically prescribed controlled drugs of the types and forms listed in the *Misuse of Drugs Regulations* 2001, Sched. 2 or 3. A detainee may only self-administer such drugs under the personal supervision of the registered medical practitioner authorising their use or other appropriate healthcare professional. The custody officer may supervise the self-administration of, or authorise other custody staff to supervise the self-administration of, drugs listed in Schedule 4 or 5 [*sic*] the officer has consulted the appropriate healthcare professional authorising their use and both are satisfied self-administration will not expose the detainee, police officers or anyone else to the risk of harm or injury.

H:9.13 When appropriate healthcare professionals administer drugs or authorise the use of other medications, or consult with the custody officer about allowing self-administration of drugs listed in Schedule 4 or 5, it must be within current medicines legislation and the scope of practice as determined by their relevant regulatory body.

H:9.14 [*Identical to C:9.12, save for reference to "paragraph 9.6" in lieu of reference to "paragraph 9.5".*]

H:9.15 [*Identical to C:9.13.*]

H:9.16 [*Identical to C:9.14, save for reference to "Note 9E" in lieu of reference to "Note 9F".*]

(c) *Documentation*

H:9.17 [*Identical to C:9.15, save for references to "paragraph 9.3", "paragraph 9.6", "paragraph 9.10", "Note 9F", "Note 9E" and "Note 9G" in lieu of references to "paragraph 9.2", "paragraph 9.5", "paragraph 9.8", "Note 9G", Note 9F" and "Note 9H", respectively.*]

H:9.18 [*Identical to C.9.16, save for reference to "Note 9F" in lieu of reference to "Note 9G".*]

H:9.19 [*Identical to C.9.17.*]

Notes for guidance

H:9A, 9B [*Identical to C:9A and C:9B, respectively.*] ★**A–219b**

H:9C [*Identical to C:9C, save for reference to "Paragraph 9.6" in lieu of reference to "Paragraph 9.5".*]

H:9D, 9E [*Identical to C:9E and C:9F, respectively.*]

H:9F [*Identical to C:9G, save for reference to "Paragraphs 9.17 and 9.18" in lieu of reference to "Paragraphs 9.15 and 9.16".*]

H:9G [*Identical to C:9H.*]

H:10 Cautions

(a) *When a caution must be given*

H:10.1 A person whom there are grounds to suspect of an offence, see *Note 10A*, must be cautioned before any questions about an offence, or further questions if the answers provide the grounds for suspicion, are put to them if either the suspect's answers or silence (*i.e.* failure or refusal to answer or answer satisfactorily) may be given in evidence to a court in a prosecution. ★**A–220**

H:10.2 A person who is arrested, or further arrested, must be informed at the time if practicable, or if not, as soon as it becomes practicable thereafter, that they are under arrest and of the grounds and reasons for their arrest, see paragraph 3.4, *Note 3G* and *Note 10B*.

H:10.3 [*Effectively identical to C:10.4.*]

(b) *Terms of the cautions*

H:10.4 The caution which must be given:

- (a) on arrest;
- (b) on all other occasions before a person is charged or informed they may be prosecuted; see *PACE*, Code C, section 16; and
- (c) before post-charge questioning under section 22 of the *Counter-Terrorism Act* 2008 (see section 15.9);

should, unless the restriction on drawing adverse inferences from silence applies, see Annex C, be in the following terms:

> "You do not have to say anything. But it may harm your defence if you do not mention when questioned something which you later rely on in court. Anything you do say may be given in evidence.".

Where the use of the Welsh language is appropriate, a constable may provide the caution directly in Welsh in the following terms:

> "Does dim rhaid i chi ddweud dim byd. Ond gall niweidio eich amddiffyniad os na fyddwch chiâ n sôn, wrth gael eich holi, am rywbeth y byddwch chiâ n dibynnu arno nes ymlaen yn y llys. Gall unrhyw beth yr ydych yn ei ddweud gael ei roi fel tystiolaeth.".

See *Note 10F.*

H:10.5 [*Identical to C:10.6.*]

H:10.6 [*Identical to C:10.7, save for reference to "Note 10C" in lieu of reference to "Note 10D".*]

H:10.7 [*Identical to C:10.8, save for reference to "Note 10D" in lieu of reference to "Note 10E".*]

H:10.8 [*Identical to C.10.9, but the words following "statutory requirement" have been omitted.*]

(c) *Special warnings under the Criminal Justice and Public Order Act 1994, sections 36 and 37*

H:10.9 [*Identical to C.10.10, save for references to "Note 10E" and "paragraph 10.10" in lieu of references to "Note 10F" and "paragraph 10.11", respectively.*]

H:10.10 [*Identical to C.10.11.*]

(d) *Juveniles and persons who are mentally disordered or otherwise mentally vulnerable*

H:10.10A [*Identical to C:10.11A.*]

H:10.11 [*Identical to C.10.12.*]

(e) *Documentation*

H:10.12 [*Identical to C.10.13.*]

Notes for guidance

H:10A [*Identical to C:10A.*]

H:10B [*Identical to C:10B, save for inclusion of reference to "Note 3G" after the word "committed".*]

H:10C–10F [*Identical to C:10D to C:10G.*]

Interviews—general

(a) *Action*

H:11.1 An interview in this code is the questioning of a person arrested on suspicion of being a terrorist which, under paragraph 10.1, must be carried out under caution. Whenever a person is interviewed they must be informed of the grounds for arrest (see *Note 3G*).

H:11.2 Following the arrest of a person under section 41 *TACT*, that person must not be interviewed about the relevant offence except at a place designated for detention under Schedule 8, paragraph 1, of the *Terrorism Act* 2000, unless the consequent delay would be likely to:

- (a) lead to:
  - interference with, or harm to, evidence connected with an offence;
  - interference with, or physical harm to, other people; or
  - serious loss of, or damage to, property;
- (b) lead to alerting other people suspected of committing an offence but not yet arrested for it; or
- (c) hinder the recovery of property obtained in consequence of the commission of an offence.

Interviewing in any of these circumstances shall cease once the relevant risk has been averted or the necessary questions have been put in order to attempt to avert that risk.

H:11.3 Immediately prior to the commencement or re-commencement of any interview at a designated place of detention, the interviewer should remind the suspect of their entitlement to free legal advice and that the interview can be delayed for legal advice to be obtained, unless one of the exceptions in paragraph 6.7 applies. It is the interviewer's responsibility to make sure all reminders are recorded in the interview record.

H:11.4, 11.5 [*Identical to C:11.4 and C:11.4A.*]

H:11.6 [*Identical to C.11.5, save for reference "paragraph 10.8" in lieu of reference to "paragraph 10.9".*]

H:11.7 [*Identical to C.11.6, but with the omission of the final sub-paragraph of that paragraph.*]

(b) *Interview records*

H:11.8 Interviews of a person detained under section 41 of, or Schedule 8 to, *TACT* must be video recorded with sound in accordance with the code of practice issued under paragraph 3 of Schedule 8 to the *Terrorism Act* 2000, or in the case of post-charge questioning authorised under section 22 of the *Counter-Terrorism Act* 2008, the code of practice issued under section 25 of that Act.

H:11.8A [*Identical to C:11.13.*]

(c) *Juveniles and mentally disordered or otherwise mentally vulnerable people*

H:11.9 [*Identical to C:11.15, save for reference to "paragraphs 11.2, 11.11 to 11.13" in lieu of reference to "paragraphs 11.1, 11.18 to 11.20".*]

H:11.10 If an appropriate adult is present at an interview, they shall be informed:

- they are not expected to act simply as an observer; and
- the purpose of their presence is to:
  - advise the person being interviewed;
  - observe whether the interview is being conducted properly and fairly;
  - facilitate communication with the person being interviewed.

The appropriate adult may be required to leave the interview if their conduct is such that the interviewer is unable properly to put questions to the suspect. This will include situations where the appropriate adult's approach or conduct prevents or unreasonably obstructs proper questions being put to the suspect or the suspect's responses being recorded. If the interviewer considers an appropriate adult is acting in such a way, they will stop the interview and consult an officer not below superintendent rank, if one is readily available, and otherwise an officer not below inspector rank not connected with the investigation. After speaking to the appropriate adult, the officer consulted will decide if the interview should continue without the attendance of that appropriate adult. If they decide it should not, another appropriate adult should be obtained before the interview continues, unless the provisions of paragraph 11.11 below apply.

(d) *Vulnerable suspects—urgent interviews at police stations*

H:11.11–11.13 [*Identical to C:11.18 to C:11.20, save for references to "paragraph 11.2(a) to (c)" and "paragraph 11.11" in lieu of references to "paragraph 11.1(a) to (c)" and "paragraph 11.18", respectively.*]

Notes for guidance

H:11A–11C [*Identical to C:11A (save for erroneous reference to para. 3.4 of code of conduct under 1996 Act) to C:11C, respectively.*] **★A–221**

H:11D *Consideration should be given to the effect of extended detention on a detainee and any subsequent information they provide, especially if it relates to information on matters that they have failed to provide previously in response to similar questioning: see Annex G.*

H:11E [*Identical to C:11E.*]

H:12 Interviews in police stations

(a) *Action*

H:12.1 If a police officer wants to interview or conduct enquiries which require the presence of a detainee, the custody officer is responsible for deciding whether to deliver the detainee into the officer's custody. An investigating officer who is given custody of a detainee takes over responsibility for the detainee's care and treatment for the purposes of this code until they return the detainee to the custody officer when they must report the manner in which they complied with the code whilst having custody of the detainee. **★A–221a**

H:12.2 Except as below, in any period of 24 hours a detainee must be allowed a continuous period of at least 8 hours for rest, free from questioning, travel or any interruption in connection with the investigation concerned. This period should normally be at night or other appropriate time which takes account of when the detainee last slept or rested. If a detainee is arrested at a police station after going there voluntarily, the period of 24 hours runs from the time of their arrest (or, if a person was being detained under *TACT*, Sched. 7, when arrested, from the time at which the examination under Schedule 7 began) and not the time of arrival at the police station. The period may not be interrupted or delayed, except:

    (a) when there are reasonable grounds for believing not delaying or interrupting the period would:

        (i) involve a risk of harm to people or serious loss of, or damage to, property;

        (ii) delay unnecessarily the person's release from custody;

        (iii) otherwise prejudice the outcome of the investigation;

    (b) at the request of the detainee, their appropriate adult or legal representative;

    (c) when a delay or interruption is necessary in order to:

        (i) comply with the legal obligations and duties arising under section 14;

        (ii) to take action required under section 9 or in accordance with medical advice.

If the period is interrupted in accordance with (a), a fresh period must be allowed. Interruptions under (b) and (c), do not require a fresh period to be allowed.

H:12.3 [*Identical to C:12.3, save that there is no reference to "Annex G" and the references to "paragraph 11.18" and "paragraphs 11.18 to 11.20" are replaced by references to "paragraph 11.11" and "paragraphs 11.11 to 11.13".*]

H:12.4 [*Identical to C:12.4.*]

H:12.5 A suspect whose detention without charge has been authorised under *TACT*, Sched. 8, because the detention is necessary for an interview to obtain evidence of the offence for which they have been arrested, may choose not to answer questions but police do not require the suspect's consent or agreement to interview them for this purpose. If a suspect takes steps to prevent themselves being questioned or further questioned, *e.g.* by refusing to leave their cell to go to a suitable interview room or by trying to leave the interview room, they shall be advised their consent or agreement to interview is not required. The suspect shall be cautioned as in section 10, and informed if they fail or refuse to co-operate, the interview may take place in the cell and that their failure or refusal to co-operate may be given in evidence. The suspect shall then be invited to co-operate and go into the interview room.

H:12.6 People being questioned or making statements shall not be required to stand.

H:12.7 Before the interview commences each interviewer shall, subject to the qualification at paragraph 2.8, identify themselves and any other persons present to the interviewee.

H:12.8 [*Identical to C:12.8.*]

H:12.9 During extended periods where no interviews take place, because of the need to gather further evidence or analyse existing evidence, detainees and their legal representative shall be informed that the investigation into the relevant offence remains ongoing. If practicable, the detainee and legal representative should also be made aware in general terms of any reasons for long gaps between interviews. Consideration should be given to allowing visits, more frequent exercise, or for reading or writing materials to be offered: see paragraph 5.4, section 8 and *Note 12C*.

H:12.10 [*Identical to C:12.9.*]

(b) *Documentation*

    H:12.11–12.15 [*Identical to C:12.10 to C:12.14, respectively.*]

Notes for guidance

★**A–221b**   **H:**12A *It is not normally necessary to ask for a written statement if the interview was recorded in accordance with the code of practice issued under* TACT, *Sched. 8, para. 3. Statements under caution should normally be taken in these circumstances only at the person's express wish. A person may however be asked if they want to make such a statement.*

    H:12B [*Identical to C:12B.*]

    H:12C *Consideration should be given to the matters referred to in paragraph 12.9 after a period of over 24 hours without questioning. This is to ensure that extended periods of detention without an indication that the investigation remains ongoing do not contribute to a deterioration of the detainee's well-being.*

H:13 Interpreters

(a) *General*

H:13.1 *[Identical to C:13.1.]*

(b) *Foreign languages*

H:13.2 *[Identical to C:13.2, save for reference to "paragraphs 11.2, 11.11 to 11.13" in lieu of reference to "paragraph 11.1, 11.18 to 11.20".]*

H:13.3 *[Not used.]*

H:13.4 *[Identical to C:13.4.]*

(c) *Deaf people and people with speech difficulties*

H:13.5, 13.6 *[Identical to C:13.5 and C:13.6, respectively, save for references to "paragraphs 11.2, 11.11 to 11.13" in lieu of references to "paragraph 11.1, 11.18 to 11.20".]*

H:13.7 *[Not used.]*

(d) *Additional rules for detained persons*

H:13.8 All reasonable attempts should be made to make the detainee understand that interpreters will be provided at public expense.

H:13.9 If paragraph 6.1 applies and the detainee cannot communicate with the solicitor because of language, hearing or speech difficulties, an interpreter must be called. The interpreter may not be a police officer or any other police staff when interpretation is needed for the purposes of obtaining legal advice. In all other cases a police officer or other police staff may only interpret if the detainee and the appropriate adult, if applicable, give their agreement in writing or if the interview is audibly recorded or visually recorded as in the code of practice issued under *TACT*, Sched. 8, para. 3.

H:13.10 *[Identical to C:13.10.]*

(e) *Documentation*

H:13.11 *[Identical to C:13.11.]*

Note for guidance

H:13A *[Identical to C:13A.]*

H:14 Reviews and extensions of detention under the Terrorism Act 2000

(a) *General*

H:14.1 The powers and duties of the review officer are in the *Terrorism Act* 2000, Sched. 8, Pt **★A–222**
II. See *Notes 14A* and *14B*. A review officer should carry out their duties at the police station where the detainee is held, and be allowed such access to the detainee as is necessary to exercise those duties.

H:14.2 For the purposes of reviewing a person's detention, no officer shall put specific questions to the detainee:

- regarding their involvement in any offence; or
- in respect of any comments they may make:
  - when given the opportunity to make representations; or
  - in response to a decision to keep them in detention or extend the maximum period of detention.

Such an exchange could constitute an interview as in paragraph 11.1 and would be subject to the associated safeguards in section 11.

H:14.3 If detention is necessary for longer than 48 hours from the time of arrest (or if a person was being detained under *TACT*, Sched. 7, from the time at which the examination under Schedule 7 began), a police officer of at least superintendent rank, or a crown prosecutor may apply for a warrant of further detention or for an extension or further extension of such a warrant under paragraph 29 or (as the case may be) 36 of Part III of Schedule 8 to the *Terrorism Act* 2000. See *Note 14C*.

H:14.4 When an application is made for a warrant as described in paragraph 14.3, the detained person and their representative must be informed of their rights in respect of the application. These include:

(i) the right to a written notice of the application; see *Note 14G*;

    (ii) the right to make oral or written representations to the judicial authority/High Court judge about the application;

    (iii) the right to be present and legally represented at the hearing of the application, unless specifically excluded by the judicial authority/High Court judge;

    (iv) their right to free legal advice (see section 6 of this code).

(b) *Transfer of persons detained for more than 14 days to prison*

H:14.5 If the *Detention of Terrorists Suspects (Temporary Extension) Bill* is enacted and in force, a High Court judge may extend or further extend a warrant of further detention to authorise a person to be detained beyond a period of 14 days from the time of their arrest (or if they were being detained under *TACT*, Sched. 7, from the time at which their examination under Schedule 7 began). The provisions of Annex J will apply when a warrant of further detention is so extended or further extended.

    H:14.6–14.10 [*Not used.*]

(c) *Documentation*

H:14.11 It is the responsibility of the officer who gives any reminders as at paragraph 14.4, to ensure that these are noted in the custody record, as well any comments made by the detained person upon being told of those rights.

    H:14.12 The grounds for, and extent of, any delay in conducting a review shall be recorded.

    H:14.13 Any written representations shall be retained.

    H:14.14 A record shall be made as soon as practicable about the outcome of each review and, if applicable, the grounds on which the review officer authorises continued detention. A record shall also be made as soon as practicable about the outcome of an application for a warrant of further detention or its extension.

Notes for guidance

★**A–222a**   **H:**14A *TACT, Sched. 8, Pt II, sets out the procedures for review of detention up to 48 hours from the time of arrest under TACT, s.41 (or if a person was being detained under TACT, Sched. 7, from the time at which the examination under Schedule 7 began). These include provisions for the requirement to review detention, postponing a review, grounds for continued detention, designating a review officer, representations, rights of the detained person and keeping a record. The review officer's role ends after a warrant has been issued for extension of detention under Part III of Schedule 8.*

    H:14B *A review officer may authorise a person's continued detention if satisfied that detention is necessary—*

    (a) *to obtain relevant evidence whether by questioning the person or otherwise;*

    (b) *to preserve relevant evidence;*

    (c) *while awaiting the result of an examination or analysis of relevant evidence;*

    (d) *for the examination or analysis of anything with a view to obtaining relevant evidence;*

    (e) *pending a decision to apply to the Secretary of State for a deportation notice to be served on the detainee, the making of any such application, or the consideration of any such application by the Secretary of State;*

    (f) *pending a decision to charge the detainee with an offence.*

    H:14C *Applications for warrants to extend detention beyond 48 hours, may be made for periods of 7 days at a time (initially under TACT, Sched. 8, para. 29, and extensions thereafter under TACT, Sched. 8, para. 36), up to a maximum period of 14 days (or 28 days if the Detention of Terrorists Suspects (Temporary Extension) Bill is enacted and in force) from the time of their arrest (or if they were being detained under TACT, Sched. 7, from the time at which their examination under Schedule 7 began). Applications may be made for shorter periods than 7 days, which must be specified. The judicial authority or High Court judge may also substitute a shorter period if they feel a period of 7 days is inappropriate.*

    H:14D *Unless Note 14F applies, applications for warrants that would take the total period of detention up to 14 days or less should be made to a judicial authority, meaning a District Judge (Magistrates' Court) designated by the Lord Chief Justice to hear such applications.*

    H:14E *If by virtue of the relevant provisions described in Note 14C being enacted the maximum period of detention is extended to 28 days, any application for a warrant which would take the period of detention beyond 14 days from the time of arrest (or if a person was being detained under TACT, Sched. 7, from the time at which the examination under Schedule 7 began), must be made to a High Court Judge.*

    H:14F *If, when the Detention of Terrorists Suspects (Temporary Extension) Bill is enacted and in force, an application is made to a High Court judge for a warrant which would take detention beyond 14* *days and the High Court judge instead issues a warrant for a period of time which would not take detention beyond 14 days, further applications for extension of detention must also be made to a High Court judge, regardless of the period of time to which they refer.*

H:14G *TACT, Sched. 8, para. 31 requires a notice to be given to the detained person if a warrant is sought for further detention. This must be provided before the judicial hearing of the application for that warrant and must include:*

(a) *notification that the application for a warrant has been made;*

(b) *the time at which the application was made;*

(c) *the time at which the application is to be heard;*

(d) *the grounds on which further detention is sought.*

A notice must also be provided each time an application is made to extend or further extend an existing warrant.

H:14H *An officer applying for an order under TACT , Sched. 8, para. 34, to withhold specified information on which he intends to rely when applying for a warrant of further detention or the extension or further extension of such a warrant, may make the application for the order orally or in writing. The most appropriate method of application will depend on the circumstances of the case and the need to ensure fairness to the detainee.*

H:14I *After hearing any representations by or on behalf of the detainee and the applicant, the judicial authority or High Court judge may direct that the hearing relating to the extension of detention under Part III of Schedule 8 is to take place using video conferencing facilities. However, if the judicial authority requires the detained person to be physically present at any hearing, this should be complied with as soon as practicable. Paragraph 33(4) to (9) of TACT, Sched. 8, govern the hearing of applications via video-link or other means.*

H:15 Charging and post-charge questioning in terrorism cases

(a) *Charging*

H:15.1 Charging of detained persons is covered by *PACE* and guidance issued under *PACE* by the Director of Public Prosecutions. Decisions to charge persons to whom this code (H) applies, the charging process and related matters are subject to section 16 of *PACE* Code C. ★**A-222b**

(b) *Post-charge questioning*

H:15.2 Under section 22 of the *Counter-Terrorism Act* 2008, a judge of the Crown Court may authorise the questioning of a person about an offence for which they have been charged, informed that they may be prosecuted or sent for trial, if the offence: ★**A-222c**

● is a terrorism offence as set out in section 27 of the *Counter-Terrorism Act* 2008; or

● is an offence which appears to the judge to have a terrorist connection (see *Note 15C*).

The decision on whether to apply for such questioning will be based on the needs of the investigation. There is no power to detain a person solely for the purposes of post-charge questioning. A person can only be detained whilst being so questioned (whether at a police station or in prison) if they are already there in lawful custody under some existing power. If at a police station the contents of sections 8 and 9 of this code must be considered the minimum standards of treatment for such detainees.

H:15.3 The Crown Court judge may authorise the questioning if they are satisfied that:

● further questioning is necessary in the interests of justice;

● the investigation for the purposes of which the further questioning is being proposed is being conducted diligently and expeditiously; and

● the questioning would not interfere unduly with the preparation of the person's defence to the charge or any other criminal charge that they may be facing.

See *Note 15E*.

H:15.4 The judge authorising questioning may specify the location of the questioning.

H:15.5 The judge may only authorise a period up to a maximum of 48 hours before further authorisation must be sought. The 48 hour period would run continuously from the commencement of questioning. This period must include breaks in questioning in accordance with paragraphs 8.6 and 12.2 of this code (see *Note 15B*).

H:15.6 Nothing in this code shall be taken to prevent a suspect seeking a voluntary interview with the police at any time.

H:15.7 For the purposes of this section, any reference in sections 6, 10, 11, 12 and 13 of this code to:

● "suspect" means the person in respect of whom an authorisation has been given under section 22 of the *Counter-Terrorism Act* 2008 (post-charge questioning of terrorist suspects) to interview them;

- "interview" means post-charge questioning authorised under section 22 of the *Counter-Terrorism Act* 2008;
- "offence" means an offence for which the person has been charged, informed that they may be prosecuted or sent for trial and about which the person is being questioned; and
- "place of detention" means the location of the questioning specified by the judge (see paragraph 15.4),

and the provisions of those sections apply (as appropriate), to such questioning (whether at a police station or in prison) subject to the further modifications in the following paragraphs:

Right to legal advice

H:15.8 In section 6 of this code, for the purposes of post-charge questioning:

- access to a solicitor may not be delayed under Annex B; and
- paragraph 6.5 (direction that a detainee may only consult a solicitor within the sight and hearing of a qualified officer) does not apply.

Cautions

H:15.9 In section 10 of this code, unless the restriction on drawing adverse inferences from silence applies (see paragraph 15.10), for the purposes of post-charge questioning, the caution must be given in the following terms before any such questions are asked:

> "You do not have to say anything. But it may harm your defence if you do not mention when questioned something which you later rely on in court. Anything you do say may be given in evidence.".

Where the use of the Welsh language is appropriate, a constable may provide the caution directly in Welsh in the following terms:

> "Does dim rhaid i chi ddweud dim byd. Ond gall niweidio eich amddiffyniad os na fyddwch chiâ n sôn, wrth gael eich holi, am rywbeth y byddwch chiâ n dibynnu arno nes ymlaen yn y llys. Gall unrhyw beth yr ydych yn ei ddweud gael ei roi fel tystiolaeth.".

H:15.10 The only restriction on drawing adverse inferences from silence, see Annex C, applies in those situations where a person has asked for legal advice and is questioned before receiving such advice in accordance with paragraph 6.7(b).

Interviews

H:15.11 In section 11, for the purposes of post-charge questioning, whenever a person is questioned, they must be informed of the offence for which they have been charged or informed that they may be prosecuted, or that they have been sent for trial and about which they are being questioned.

H:15.12 Paragraph 11.2 (place where questioning may take place) does not apply to post-charge questioning.

Recording post-charge questioning

H:15.13 All interviews must be video recorded with sound in accordance with the separate code of practice issued under section 25 of the *Counter-Terrorism Act* 2008 for the video recording with sound of post-charge questioning authorised under section 22 of the *Counter-Terrorism Act* 2008 (see paragraph 11.8).

Notes for guidance

★**A–222d**

H:15A *If a person is detained at a police station for the purposes of post-charge questioning, a custody record must be opened in accordance with section 2 of this code. The custody record must note the power under which the person is being detained, the time at which the person was transferred into police custody, their time of arrival at the police station and their time of being presented to the custody officer.*

H:15B *The custody record must note the time at which the interview process commences. This shall be regarded as the relevant time for any period of questioning in accordance with paragraph 15.5 of this code.*

H:15C *Where reference is made to "terrorist connection" in paragraph 15.2, this is determined in accordance with section 30 of the* Counter-Terrorism Act 2008. *Under section 30 of that Act a court must in certain circumstances determine whether an offence has a terrorist connection. These are offences under general criminal law which may be prosecuted in terrorism cases (for example explosives-related offences and conspiracy to murder). An offence has a terrorist connection if the offence is, or takes place in the course of, an* *act of terrorism or is committed for the purposes of terrorism (section 98 of the Act). Normally the court will make the determination during the sentencing process, however for the purposes of post-charge questioning, a Crown Court judge must determine whether the offence could have a terrorist connection.*

H:15D *The powers under section 22 of the* Counter-Terrorism Act 2008 *are separate from and additional to the normal questioning procedures within this code. Their overall purpose is to enable the further questioning of a terrorist suspect after charge. They should not therefore be used to replace or circumvent the normal powers for dealing with routine questioning.*

H:15E *Post-charge questioning has been created because it is acknowledged that terrorist investigations can be large and complex and that a great deal of evidence can come to light following the charge of a terrorism suspect. This can occur, for instance, from the translation of material or as the result of additional investigation. When considering an application for post-charge questioning, the police must "satisfy" the judge on all three points under paragraph 15.3. This means that the judge will either authorise or refuse an application on the balance of whether the conditions in paragraph 15.3 are all met. It is important therefore, when making the application, to consider the following questions:*

- *What further evidence is the questioning expected to provide?*
- *Why was it not possible to obtain this evidence before charge?*
- *How and why was the need to question after charge first recognised?*
- *How is the questioning expected to contribute further to the case?*
- *To what extent could the time and place for further questioning interfere with the preparation of the person's defence (for example if authorisation is sought close to the time of a trial)?*
- *What steps will be taken to minimise any risk that questioning might interfere with the preparation of the person's defence?*

This list is not exhaustive but outlines the type of questions that could be relevant to any asked by a judge in considering an application.

H:16 Testing persons for the presence of specified Class A drugs

H:16.1 The provisions for drug testing under section 63B of *PACE* (as amended by section 5 of the *Criminal Justice Act* 2003 and section 7 of the *Drugs Act* 2005), do not apply to persons to whom this code applies. Guidance on these provisions can be found in section 17 of *PACE* Code C. ★**A–223**

ANNEX A

Intimate and strip searches

A *Intimate search*

H:1. *[Identical to Code C, Annex A, para. 1.]* ★**A–223a**

(a) *Action*

H:2. Body orifices other than the mouth may be searched if authorised by an officer of inspector rank or above who has reasonable grounds for believing that the person may have concealed on themselves anything which they could and might use to cause physical injury to themselves or others at the station and the officer has reasonable grounds for believing that an intimate search is the only means of removing those items.

H:3. *[Identical to Code C, Annex A, para. 2A.]*

H:4. An intimate search may only be carried out by a registered medical practitioner or registered nurse, unless an officer of at least inspector rank considers this is not practicable, in which case a police officer may carry out the search. See *Notes A1 to A5.*

H:5. Any proposal for a search under paragraph 2 to be carried out by someone other than a registered medical practitioner or registered nurse must only be considered as a last resort and when the authorising officer is satisfied the risks associated with allowing the item to remain with the detainee outweigh the risks associated with removing it. See *Notes A1 to A5.*

H:6. An intimate search at a police station of a juvenile or mentally disordered or otherwise mentally vulnerable person may take place only in the presence of an appropriate adult of the same sex (see Annex I), unless the detainee specifically requests a particular adult of the opposite sex who is readily available. In the case of a juvenile the search may take place in the absence of the appropriate adult only if the juvenile signifies in the presence of the appropriate adult they do not want the adult present during the search and the adult agrees. A record shall be made of the juvenile's decision and signed by the appropriate adult.

H:7. When an intimate search under paragraph 2 is carried out by a police officer, the officer must be of the same sex as the detainee (see Annex I). A minimum of two people, other than the detainee, must be present during the search. Subject to paragraph 6, no person of the opposite sex who is not a medical practitioner or nurse shall be present, nor shall anyone whose presence is unnecessary. The search shall be conducted with proper regard to the sensitivity and vulnerability of the detainee.

(b) *Documentation*

H:8. In the case of an intimate search under paragraph 2, the following shall be recorded as soon as practicable, in the detainee's custody record:

- the authorisation to carry out the search;
- the grounds for giving the authorisation;
- the grounds for believing the article could not be removed without an intimate search;
- which parts of the detainee's body were searched;
- who carried out the search;
- who was present;
- the result.

H:9. [*Identical to Code C, Annex A, para. 8.*]

B *Strip search*

H:10. [*Identical to Code C, Annex A, para. 9.*]

(a) *Action*

H:11. [*Identical to Code C, Annex A, para. 10.*]

The conduct of strip searches

H:12. [*Identical to Code C, Annex A, para. 11, save for references to "Annex I" in lieu of references to "Annex L".*]

(b) *Documentation*

H:13. [*Identical to Code C, Annex A, para. 12.*]

Notes for guidance

H:A1 [*Identical to Code C, Annex A, A1.*]

H:A2 [*Identical to Code C, Annex A, A2.*]

H:A3 [*Identical to Code C, Annex A, A3, save for reference to "paragraph 2" in lieu of reference to "paragraph 2(a)(i)".*]

H:A4 [*Identical to Code C, Annex A, A4, save for reference to "paragraph 2" in lieu of reference to "paragraph 2(a)(i)".*]

H:A5 [*Identical to Code C, Annex A, A5.*]

ANNEX B

Delay in notifying arrest or allowing access to legal advice for persons detained under the Terrorism Act 2000

H:1. The rights as in sections 5 or 6, may be delayed if the person is detained under the *Terrorism Act* 2000, s.41, has not yet been charged with an offence and an officer of superintendent rank or above has reasonable grounds for believing the exercise of either right will have one of the following consequences:

- (a) interference with or harm to evidence of a serious offence;
- (b) interference with or physical injury to any person;
- (c) the alerting of persons who are suspected of having committed a serious offence but who have not been arrested for it;
- (d) the hindering of the recovery of property obtained as a result of a serious offence or in respect of which a forfeiture order could be made under section 23;

(e) interference with the gathering of information about the commission, preparation or instigation of acts of terrorism;

(f) the alerting of a person and thereby making it more difficult to prevent an act of terrorism; or

(g) the alerting of a person and thereby making it more difficult to secure a person's apprehension, prosecution or conviction in connection with the commission, preparation or instigation of an act of terrorism.

H:2. These rights may also be delayed if the officer has reasonable grounds for believing that:

(a) the detained person has benefited from his criminal conduct (to be decided in accordance with Part 2 of the *Proceeds of Crime Act* 2002); and

(b) the recovery of the value of the property constituting the benefit will be hindered by—

(i) informing the named person of the detained person's detention (in the case of an authorisation under paragraph 8(1)(a) of Schedule 8 to *TACT*); or

(ii) the exercise of the right under paragraph 7 (in the case of an authorisation under paragraph 8(1)(b) of Schedule 8 to *TACT*).

H:3. Authority to delay a detainee's right to consult privately with a solicitor may be given only if the authorising officer has reasonable grounds to believe the solicitor the detainee wants to consult will, inadvertently or otherwise, pass on a message from the detainee or act in some other way which will have any of the consequences specified under paragraph 8 of Schedule 8 to the *Terrorism Act* 2000. In these circumstances the detainee must be allowed to choose another solicitor. See *Note B3*.

H:4. [*Identical to Code C, Annex B, para. 4.*]

H:5. [*Identical to Code C, Annex B, para. 5.*]

H:6. These rights may be delayed only for as long as is necessary but not beyond 48 hours from the time of arrest (or if a person was being detained under *TACT*, Sched. 7, from the time at which the examination under Schedule 7 began). If the above grounds cease to apply within this time the detainee must as soon as practicable be asked if they wish to exercise either right, the custody record noted accordingly, and action taken in accordance with the relevant section of this code.

H:7. A person must be allowed to consult a solicitor for a reasonable time before any court hearing.

Documentation

H:8. [*Identical to Code C, Annex B, para. 13.*]

H:9. [*Identical to Code C, Annex B, para. 14, save for reference to "paragraph 6" in lieu of reference to "paragraphs 6 or 11".*]

Cautions and special warnings

H:10. [*Identical to Code C, Annex B, para. 15.*]

Notes for guidance

H:B1 [*Identical to Code C, Annex B, B1, save for reference to "paragraph 3.15 and 3.17" in lieu of* ★**A–224a** reference to "paragraph 3.13 and 3.15".*]

H:B2 [*Identical to Code C, Annex B, B2.*]

H:B3 [*Identical to Code C, Annex B, B3.*]

ANNEX C

Restriction on drawing adverse inferences from silence and terms of the caution when the restriction applies

(a) *The restriction on drawing adverse inferences from silence*

H:1. The *Criminal Justice and Public Order Act* 1994, ss.34, 36 and 37 as amended by the *Youth* ★**A–224b** *Justice and Criminal Evidence Act* 1999, s.58 describe the conditions under which adverse inferences may be drawn from a person's failure or refusal to say anything about their involvement in the offence when interviewed, after being charged or informed they may be prosecuted. These provisions are subject to an overriding restriction on the ability of a court or jury to draw adverse inferences from a person's silence. This restriction applies:

  (a) to any detainee at a police station who, before being interviewed, see section 11 or being charged or informed they may be prosecuted, see section 15, has:

   (i) asked for legal advice, see section 6, paragraph 6.1;

   (ii) not been allowed an opportunity to consult a solicitor, including the duty solicitor, as in this code; and

   (iii) not changed their mind about wanting legal advice, see section 6, paragraph 6.7(d);

   Note the condition in (ii) will:

   – apply when a detainee who has asked for legal advice is interviewed before speaking to a solicitor as in section 6, paragraph 6.6(a) or (b);

   – not apply if the detained person declines to ask for the duty solicitor, see section 6, paragraphs 6.7(b) and (c);

  (b) to any person who has been charged with, or informed they may be prosecuted for, an offence who:

   (i) has had brought to their notice a written statement made by another person or the content of an interview with another person which relates to that offence, see *PACE* Code C, section 16, paragraph 16.4;

   (ii) is interviewed about that offence, see *PACE* Code C, section 16, paragraph 16.5; or

   (iii) makes a written statement about that offence, see Annex D, paragraphs 4 and 9,

   unless post-charge questioning has been authorised in accordance with section 22 of the *Counter-Terrorism Act* 2008, in which case the restriction will apply only if the person has asked for legal advice, see section 6, paragraph 6.1, and is questioned before receiving such advice in accordance with paragraph 6.7(b). See paragraph 15.11.

(b) *Terms of the caution when the restriction applies*

   H:2. [*Identical to Code C, Annex C, para. 2.*]

   H:3. [*Identical to Code C, Annex C, para. 3, save for reference to "Note C1" in lieu of reference to "Note C2".*]

Notes for guidance

★**A–225**   H:C1 [*Identical to Code C, Annex C, C2.*]

ANNEX D

Written statements under caution

★**A–225a**   [*Identical to Annex D to Code C.*]

ANNEX E

Summary of provisions relating to mentally disordered and otherwise mentally vulnerable people

★**A–225b**   H:1. [*Identical to Code C, Annex E, para. 1, save for reference to "paragraph 1.10" in lieu of reference to "paragraph 1.4" and absence of any reference to Note E4.*]

   H:2. [*Identical to Code C, Annex E, para. 2, save for reference to "paragraph 1.13(b)" in lieu of reference to "paragraph 1.7(b)".*]

   H:3. If the detention of a person who is mentally vulnerable or appears to be suffering from a mental disorder is authorised by the review officer (see paragraphs 14.1 and 14.2 and *Notes for Guidance 14A and 14B*), the custody officer must as soon as practicable inform the appropriate adult of the grounds for detention and the person's whereabouts, and ask the adult to come to the police station to see them. If the appropriate adult:

   ● is already at the station when information is given as in paragraphs 3.1 to 3.5 the information must be given in their presence

   ● is not at the station when the provisions of paragraph 3.1 to 3.5 are complied with these provisions must be complied with again in their presence once they arrive.

   See paragraphs 3.15 to 3.16.

   H:4. [*Identical to Code C, Annex E, para. 4, save for reference to "paragraph 3.20" in lieu of reference to "paragraph 3.19".*]

H:5. [*Identical to Code C, Annex E, para. 5, save for reference to "paragraph 9.6 and 9.8" in lieu of reference to "paragraph 9.5 and 9.6".*]

H:6. If a mentally disordered or otherwise mentally vulnerable person is cautioned in the absence of the appropriate adult, the caution must be repeated in the appropriate adult's presence. See paragraph 10.11.

H:7. A mentally disordered or otherwise mentally vulnerable person must not be interviewed or asked to provide or sign a written statement in the absence of the appropriate adult unless the provisions of paragraphs 11.2 or 11.11 to 11.13 apply. Questioning in these circumstances may not continue in the absence of the appropriate adult once sufficient information to avert the risk has been obtained. A record shall be made of the grounds for any decision to begin an interview in these circumstances. See paragraphs 11.2, 11.9 and 11.11 to 11.13.

H:8. If the appropriate adult is present at an interview, they shall be informed they are not expected to act simply as an observer and the purposes of their presence are to:

● advise the interviewee;

● observe whether or not the interview is being conducted properly and fairly;

● facilitate communication with the interviewee.

See paragraph 11.10.

H:9. If the custody officer charges a mentally disordered or otherwise mentally vulnerable person with an offence or takes such other action as is appropriate when there is sufficient evidence for a prosecution this must be carried out in the presence of the appropriate adult if they are at the police station. A copy of the written notice embodying any charge must be given to the appropriate adult. See *PACE* Code C, section 16.

H:10. [*Identical to Code C, Annex E, para. 12, save for reference to "paragraphs 6 and 12(c)" in lieu of reference to "paragraphs 5 and 11(c)".*]

H:11. [*Identical to Code C, Annex E, para. 13.*]

Notes for guidance

H:E1 [*Identical to Code C, Annex E, E1, save for reference to "paragraph 3.20" in lieu of reference to "paragraph 3.19".*] ★**A–226**

H:E2 [*Identical to Code C, Annex E, E2.*]

H:E3 [*Identical to Code C, Annex E, E3, save for reference to "paragraphs 11.2, 11.11 to 11.13" in lieu of reference to "paragraphs 11.1, 11.18 to 11.20".*]

ANNEX F

[*Not used.*] ★**A–226a**

ANNEX G

Fitness to be interviewed

[*Identical to Annex G to Code C.*] ★**A–226b**

ANNEX H

Detained person: observation list

[*Identical to Annex H to Code C.*] ★**A–227**

ANNEX I

Establishing gender of persons for the purpose of searching

[*Identical to Annex L to Code C, save that the references to notes are to Note I1, I2 and so on, rather than to Note L1, L2 and so on.*] ★**A–228**

ANNEX J

Transfer of persons detained for more than 14 days to prison

H:1. When a warrant of further detention is extended or further extended by a High Court ★**A–229**

judge to authorise a person's detention beyond a period of 14 days from the time of their arrest (or if they were being detained under *TACT*, Sched. 7, from the time at which their examination under Schedule 7 began), the person must be transferred from detention in a police station to detention in a designated prison as soon as is practicable after the warrant is issued, unless:

>   (a) the detainee specifically requests to remain in detention at a police station and that request can be accommodated; or

>   (b) there are reasonable grounds to believe that transferring the detainee to a prison would:

>>   (i) significantly hinder a terrorism investigation;

>>   (ii) delay charging of the detainee or their release from custody; or

>>   (iii) otherwise prevent the investigation from being conducted diligently and expeditiously.

Any grounds in (b)(i) to (iii) above which are relied upon for not transferring the detainee to prison must be presented to the senior judge as part of the application for the extension or further extension of the warrant. See *Note J1*.

H:2 If at any time during which a person remains in detention at a police station under the warrant, the grounds at (b)(i) to (iii) cease to apply, the person must be transferred to a prison as soon as practicable.

H:3 Police should maintain an agreement with the National Offender Management Service (NOMS) that stipulates named prisons to which individuals may be transferred under this paragraph. This should be made with regard to ensuring detainees are moved to the most suitable prison for the purposes of the investigation and their welfare, and should include provision for the transfer of male, female and juvenile detainees. Police should ensure that the governor of a prison to which they intend to transfer a detainee is given reasonable notice of this. Where practicable, this should be no later than the point at which a warrant is applied for that would take the period of detention beyond 14 days.

H:4 Following a detainee's transfer to a designated prison, their detention will be governed by the terms of Schedule 8 to *TACT* 2000 and the *Prison Rules* and this code of practice will not apply during any period that the person remains in prison detention. The code will once more apply if the person is transferred back from prison detention to police detention. In order to enable the governor to arrange for the production of the detainee back into police custody, police should give notice to the governor of the relevant prison as soon as possible of any decision to transfer a detainee from prison back to a police station. Any transfer between a prison and a police station should be conducted by police and this code will be applicable during the period of transit. See *Note 2J*. A detainee should only remain in police custody having been transferred back from a prison, for as long as is necessary for the purpose of the investigation.

H:5 The investigating team and custody officer should provide as much information as necessary to enable the relevant prison authorities to provide appropriate facilities to detain an individual. This should include, but not be limited to:

>   (i) medical assessments;

>   (ii) security and risk assessments;

>   (iii) details of the detained person's legal representatives;

>   (iv) details of any individuals from whom the detained person has requested visits, or who have requested to visit the detained person.

H:6 Where a detainee is to be transferred to prison, the custody officer should inform the detainee's legal adviser beforehand that the transfer is to take place (including the name of the prison). The custody officer should also make all reasonable attempts to inform:

>   • family or friends who have been informed previously of the detainee's detention; and

>   • the person who was initially informed of the detainee's detention in accordance with paragraph 5.1.

H:7 Any decision not to transfer a detained person to a designated prison under paragraph 1, must be recorded, along with the reasons for this decision. If a request under paragraph 1(a) is not accommodated, the reasons for this should also be recorded.

Notes for guidance

★A–230   **H:J1** *Transfer to prison is intended to ensure that individuals who are detained for extended periods of time are held in a place designed for longer periods of detention than police stations. Prison will provide detainees with a greater range of facilities more appropriate to longer detention periods.*

H:J2 *This code will only apply as is appropriate to the conditions of detention during the period of transit. There is obviously no requirement to provide such things as bed linen or reading materials for the journey between prison and police station.*

B. Under the Criminal Procedure and Investigations Act 1996

(1) As to the recording and retention by the police of material obtained during an investigation and its supply to the prosecutor

Introduction

Pursuant to sections 23 and 25 of the 1996 Act (§§ 12–73, 12–74 in the main work), the   **A–231**
Secretary of State has prepared and published two codes of practice governing the action
the police must take in recording and retaining material obtained in the course of a criminal investigation and regulating its supply to the prosecutor for a decision on disclosure.

The first code came into force on the day appointed for the purpose of Part I of the 1996
Act, namely April 1, 1997 (S.I. 1997 No. 1033). The revised code (set out *post*) came into
force on April 4, 2005: *Criminal Procedure and Investigations Act 1996 (Code of Practice) Order*
2005 (S.I. 2005 No. 985).

In connection with this code, see also § 12–72 in the main work (meaning of
"investigation").

As to the significance of the code of practice in relation to material held overseas, outside
the European Union, by entities not subject to the jurisdiction of the United Kingdom, see
R. v. Flook [2010] 1 Cr.App.R. 30, CA (*ante*, § 12–77).

**CRIMINAL PROCEDURE AND INVESTIGATIONS ACT 1996
CODE OF PRACTICE UNDER PART II**

Preamble

This code of practice is issued under Part II of the *Criminal Procedure and Investigations Act* 1996   **A–232**
("the Act"). It sets out the manner in which police officers are to record, retain and reveal to the
prosecutor material obtained in a criminal investigation and which may be relevant to the investigation, and related matters.

Introduction

1.1 This code of practice applies in respect of criminal investigations conducted by police officers   **A–232a**
which begin on or after the day on which this code comes into effect. Persons other than police officers who are charged with the duty of conducting an investigation as defined in the Act are to have
regard to the relevant provisions of the code, and should take these into account in applying their
own operating procedures.

1.2 This code does not apply to persons who are not charged with the duty of conducting an
investigation as defined in the Act.

1.3 Nothing in this code applies to material intercepted in obedience to a warrant issued under
section 2 of the *Interception of Communications Act* 1985 or section 5 of the *Regulation of Investigatory
Powers Act* 2000, or to any copy of that material as defined in section 10 of the 1985 Act or section 15
of the 2000 Act.

1.4 This code extends only to England and Wales.

Definitions

2.1 In this code: **A–233**

— a *criminal investigation* is an investigation conducted by police officers with a view to it being ascertained whether a person should be charged with an offence, or whether a
person charged with an offence is guilty of it. This will include:

— investigations into crimes that have been committed;

— investigations whose purpose is to ascertain whether a crime has been committed,
with a view to the possible institution of criminal proceedings; and

— investigations which begin in the belief that a crime may be committed, for example

527

when the police keep premises or individuals under observation for a period of time, with a view to the possible institution of criminal proceedings;

— charging a person with an offence includes prosecution by way of summons;

— an *investigator* is any police officer involved in the conduct of a criminal investigation. All investigators have a responsibility for carrying out the duties imposed on them under this code, including in particular recording information, and retaining records of information and other material;

— the *officer in charge of an investigation* is the police officer responsible for directing a criminal investigation. He is also responsible for ensuring that proper procedures are in place for recording information, and retaining records of information and other material, in the investigation;

— the *disclosure officer* is the person responsible for examining material retained by the police during the investigation; revealing material to the prosecutor during the investigation and any criminal proceedings resulting from it, and certifying that he has done this; and disclosing material to the accused at the request of the prosecutor;

— the *prosecutor* is the authority responsible for the conduct, on behalf of the Crown, of criminal proceedings resulting from a specific criminal investigation;

— *material* is material of any kind, including information and objects, which is obtained in the course of a criminal investigation and which may be relevant to the investigation. This includes not only material coming into the possession of the investigator (such as documents seized in the course of searching premises) but also material generated by him (such as interview records);

— material may be *relevant to the investigation* if it appears to an investigator, or to the officer in charge of an investigation, or to the disclosure officer, that it has some bearing on any offence under investigation or any person being investigated, or on the surrounding circumstances of the case, unless it is incapable of having any impact on the case;

— *sensitive material* is material, the disclosure of which, the disclosure officer believes, would give rise to a real risk of serious prejudice to an important public interest;

— references to *prosecution disclosure* are to the duty of the prosecutor under sections 3 and 7A of the Act to disclose material which is in his possession or which he has inspected in pursuance of this code, and which might reasonably be considered capable of undermining the case against the accused, or of assisting the case for the accused;

— references to the disclosure of material to a person accused of an offence include references to the disclosure of material to his legal representative;

— references to police officers and to the chief officer of police include those employed in a police force as defined in section 3(3) of the *Prosecution of Offences Act* 1985.

As to the meaning of "criminal investigation", see *DPP v. Metten*, unreported, January 22, 1999, DC (§ 12–72 in the main work).

General responsibilities

A–234   3.1 The functions of the investigator, the officer in charge of an investigation and the disclosure officer are separate. Whether they are undertaken by one, two or more persons will depend on the complexity of the case and the administrative arrangements within each police force. Where they are undertaken by more than one person, close consultation between them is essential to the effective performance of the duties imposed by this code.

3.2 In any criminal investigation, one or more deputy disclosure officers may be appointed to assist the disclosure officer, and a deputy disclosure officer may perform any function of a disclosure officer as defined in paragraph 2.1.

3.3 The chief officer of police for each police force is responsible for putting in place arrangements to ensure that in every investigation the identity of the officer in charge of an investigation and the disclosure officer is recorded. The chief officer of police for each police force shall ensure that disclosure officers and deputy disclosure officers have sufficient skills and authority, commensurate with the complexity of the investigation, to discharge their functions effectively. An individual must not be appointed as disclosure officer, or continue in that role, if that is likely to result in a conflict of interest, for instance, if the disclosure officer is the victim of the alleged crime which is the subject of the investigation. The advice of a more senior officer must always be sought if there is doubt as to whether a conflict of interest precludes an individual acting as disclosure officer. If thereafter the doubt remains, the advice of a prosecutor should be sought.

3.4 The officer in charge of an investigation may delegate tasks to another investigator, to civilians employed by the police force, or to other persons participating in the investigation under arrangements for joint investigations, but he remains responsible for ensuring that these have been carried out and for accounting for any general policies followed in the investigation. In particular, it is an essential part of his duties to ensure that all material which may be relevant to an investigation is retained, and either made available to the disclosure officer or (in exceptional circumstances) revealed directly to the prosecutor.

3.5 In conducting an investigation, the investigator should pursue all reasonable lines of inquiry, whether these point towards or away from the suspect. What is reasonable in each case will depend on the particular circumstances. For example, where material is held on computer, it is a matter for the investigator to decide which material on the computer it is reasonable to inquire into, and in what manner.

3.6 If the officer in charge of an investigation believes that other persons may be in possession of material that may be relevant to the investigation, and if this has not been obtained under paragraph 3.5 above, he should ask the disclosure officer to inform them of the existence of the investigation and to invite them to retain the material in case they receive a request for its disclosure. The disclosure officer should inform the prosecutor that they may have such material. However, the officer in charge of an investigation is not required to make speculative enquiries of other persons; there must be some reason to believe that they may have relevant material. That reason may come from information provided to the police by the accused or from other inquiries made or from some other source.

3.7 If, during a criminal investigation, the officer in charge of an investigation or disclosure officer for any reason no longer has responsibility for the functions falling to him, either his supervisor or the police officer in charge of criminal investigations for the police force concerned must assign someone else to assume that responsibility. That person's identity must be recorded, as with those initially responsible for these functions in each investigation.

As to the meaning of "criminal investigation", see *DPP v. Metten*, unreported, January 22, 1999, DC (§ 12–72 in the main work).

Where, in the run-up to an election, there was an arrangement that a local electoral office would notify the police of any suspected fraudulent applications for postal votes, where that office submitted 1,600 suspected fraudulent applications to the police (out of a total of 10,000 applications), where the criminal investigation that ensued resulted in the prosecution of the appellants for conspiracy to defraud the electoral officer, and where complaint was made about the non-disclosure of the 8,400 postal vote applications that had been examined by the electoral office, but had not been submitted to the police, there was no duty of disclosure on the electoral office as either a delegate of the investigator or as a joint investigator within paragraph 3.4; the role of the electoral office was in the nature of an examination by a complainant of suspicious documents subsequently handed to the police, comparable to that of a bank handing over suspicious cheques to the police: *R. v. Khan* [2011] L.S. Gazette, October 20, 23, CA ([2011] EWCA Crim. 2240).

Recording of information

4.1 If material which may be relevant to the investigation consists of information which is not re- **A–235** corded in any form, the officer in charge of an investigation must ensure that it is recorded in a durable or retrievable form (whether in writing, on video or audio tape, or on computer disk).

4.2 Where it is not practicable to retain the initial record of information because it forms part of a larger record which is to be destroyed, its contents should be transferred as a true record to a durable and more easily-stored form before that happens.

4.3 Negative information is often relevant to an investigation. If it may be relevant it must be recorded. An example might be a number of people present in a particular place at a particular time who state that they saw nothing unusual.

4.4 Where information which may be relevant is obtained, it must be recorded at the time it is obtained or as soon as practicable after that time. This includes, for example, information obtained in house-to-house enquiries, although the requirement to record information promptly does not require an investigator to take a statement from a potential witness where it would not otherwise be taken.

Retention of material

(a) *Duty to retain material*

5.1 The investigator must retain material obtained in a criminal investigation which may be relevant to the investigation. Material may be photographed, video-recorded, captured digitally or otherwise retained in the form of a copy rather than the original at any time, if the original is perishable; the original was supplied to the investigator rather than generated by him and is to be returned to its owner; or the retention of a copy rather than the original is reasonable in all the circumstances.

5.2 Where material has been seized in the exercise of the powers of seizure conferred by the *Police and Criminal Evidence Act* 1984, the duty to retain it under this code is subject to the provisions on the retention of seized material in section 22 of that Act.

5.3 If the officer in charge of an investigation becomes aware as a result of developments in the case that material previously examined but not retained (because it was not thought to be relevant) may now be relevant to the investigation, he should, wherever practicable, take steps to obtain it or ensure that it is retained for further inspection or for production in court if required.

5.4 The duty to retain material includes in particular the duty to retain material falling into the following categories, where it may be relevant to the investigation:

— crime reports (including crime report forms, relevant parts of incident report books or police officer's notebooks);

— custody records;

— records which are derived from tapes of telephone messages (for example, 999 calls) containing descriptions of an alleged offence or offender;

— final versions of witness statements (and draft versions where their content differs from the final version), including any exhibits mentioned (unless these have been returned to their owner on the understanding that they will be produced in court if required);

— interview records (written records, or audio or video tapes, of interviews with actual or potential witnesses or suspects);

— communications between the police and experts such as forensic scientists, reports of work carried out by experts, and schedules of scientific material prepared by the expert for the investigator, for the purposes of criminal proceedings;

— records of the first description of a suspect by each potential witness who purports to identify or describe the suspect, whether or not the description differs from that of subsequent descriptions by that or other witnesses;

— any material casting doubt on the reliability of a witness.

5.5 The duty to retain material, where it may be relevant to the investigation, also includes in particular the duty to retain material which may satisfy the test for prosecution disclosure in the Act, such as:

— information provided by an accused person which indicates an explanation for the offence with which he has been charged;

— any material casting doubt on the reliability of a confession;

— any material casting doubt on the reliability of a prosecution witness.

5.6 The duty to retain material falling into these categories does not extend to items which are purely ancillary to such material and possess no independent significance (for example, duplicate copies of records or reports).

(b) *Length of time for which material is to be retained*

5.7 All material which may be relevant to the investigation must be retained until a decision is taken whether to institute proceedings against a person for an offence.

5.8 If a criminal investigation results in proceedings being instituted, all material which may be relevant must be retained at least until the accused is acquitted or convicted or the prosecutor decides not to proceed with the case.

5.9 Where the accused is convicted, all material which may be relevant must be retained at least until:

— the convicted person is released from custody, or discharged from hospital, in cases where the court imposes a custodial sentence or a hospital order;

— six months from the date of conviction, in all other cases.

If the court imposes a custodial sentence or hospital order and the convicted person is released from custody or discharged from hospital earlier than six months from the date of conviction, all material which may be relevant must be retained at least until six months from the date of conviction.

5.10 If an appeal against conviction is in progress when the release or discharge occurs, or at the end of the period of six months specified in paragraph 5.9, all material which may be relevant must be retained until the appeal is determined. Similarly, if the Criminal Cases Review Commission is considering an application at that point in time, all material which may be relevant must be retained at least until the Commission decides not to refer the case to the Court.

Preparation of material for prosecutor

(a) *Introduction*

6.1 The officer in charge of the investigation, the disclosure officer or an investigator may seek **A–237** advice from the prosecutor about whether any particular item of material may be relevant to the investigation.

6.2 Material which may be relevant to an investigation, which has been retained in accordance with this code, and which the disclosure officer believes will not form part of the prosecution case, must be listed on a schedule.

6.3 Material which the disclosure officer does not believe is sensitive must be listed on a schedule of non-sensitive material. The schedule must include a statement that the disclosure officer does not believe the material is sensitive.

6.4 Any material which is believed to be sensitive must be either listed on a schedule of sensitive material or, in exceptional circumstances, revealed to the prosecutor separately. If there is no sensitive material, the disclosure officer must record this fact on a schedule of sensitive material.

6.5 Paragraphs 6.6 to 6.11 below apply to both sensitive and non-sensitive material. Paragraphs 6.12 to 6.14 apply to sensitive material only.

(b) *Circumstances in which a schedule is to be prepared*

6.6 The disclosure officer must ensure that a schedule is prepared in the following circumstances:
— the accused is charged with an offence which is triable only on indictment;
— the accused is charged with an offence which is triable either way, and it is considered either that the case is likely to be tried on indictment or that the accused is likely to plead not guilty at a summary trial;
— the accused is charged with a summary offence, and it is considered that he is likely to plead not guilty.

6.7 In respect of either way and summary offences, a schedule may not be needed if a person has admitted the offence, or if a police officer witnessed the offence and that person has not denied it.

6.8 If it is believed that the accused is likely to plead guilty at a summary trial, it is not necessary to prepare a schedule in advance. If, contrary to this belief, the accused pleads not guilty at a summary trial, or the offence is to be tried on indictment, the disclosure officer must ensure that a schedule is prepared as soon as is reasonably practicable after that happens.

(c) *Way in which material is to be listed on schedule*

6.9 The disclosure officer should ensure that each item of material is listed separately on the schedule, and is numbered consecutively. The description of each item should make clear the nature of the item and should contain sufficient detail to enable the prosecutor to decide whether he needs to inspect the material before deciding whether or not it should be disclosed.

6.10 In some enquiries it may not be practicable to list each item of material separately. For example, there may be many items of a similar or repetitive nature. These may be listed in a block and described by quantity and generic title.

6.11 Even if some material is listed in a block, the disclosure officer must ensure that any items among that material which might satisfy the test for prosecution disclosure are listed and described individually.

(d) *Treatment of sensitive material*

6.12 Subject to paragraph 6.13 below, the disclosure officer must list on a sensitive schedule any material, the disclosure of which he believes would give rise to a real risk of serious prejudice to an important public interest, and the reason for that belief. The schedule must include a statement that the disclosure officer believes the material is sensitive. Depending on the circumstances, examples of such material may include the following among others:

  — material relating to national security;

  — material received from the intelligence and security agencies;

  — material relating to intelligence from foreign sources which reveals sensitive intelligence gathering methods;

  — material given in confidence;

  — material relating to the identity or activities of informants, or undercover police officers, or witnesses, or other persons supplying information to the police who may be in danger if their identities are revealed;

  — material revealing the location of any premises or other place used for police surveillance, or the identity of any person allowing a police officer to use them for surveillance;

  — material revealing, either directly or indirectly, techniques and methods relied upon by a police officer in the course of a criminal investigation, for example covert surveillance techniques, or other methods of detecting crime;

  — material whose disclosure might facilitate the commission of other offences or hinder the prevention and detection of crime;

  — material upon the strength of which search warrants were obtained;

  — material containing details of persons taking part in identification parades;

  — material supplied to an investigator during a criminal investigation which has been generated by an official of a body concerned with the regulation or supervision of bodies corporate or of persons engaged in financial activities, or which has been generated by a person retained by such a body;

  — material supplied to an investigator during a criminal investigation which relates to a child or young person and which has been generated by a local authority social services department, an Area Child Protection Committee or other party contacted by an investigator during the investigation;

  — material relating to the private life of a witness.

6.13 In exceptional circumstances, where an investigator considers that material is so sensitive that its revelation to the prosecutor by means of an entry on the sensitive schedule is inappropriate, the existence of the material must be revealed to the prosecutor separately. This will apply only where compromising the material would be likely to lead directly to the loss of life, or directly threaten national security.

6.14 In such circumstances, the responsibility for informing the prosecutor lies with the investigator who knows the detail of the sensitive material. The investigator should act as soon as is reasonably practicable after the file containing the prosecution case is sent to the prosecutor. The investigator must also ensure that the prosecutor is able to inspect the material so that he can assess whether it is disclosable and, if so, whether it needs to be brought before a court for a ruling on disclosure.

Revelation of material to prosecutor

A–238   7.1 The disclosure officer must give the schedules to the prosecutor. Wherever practicable this should be at the same time as he gives him the file containing the material for the prosecution case (or as soon as is reasonably practicable after the decision on mode of trial or the plea, in cases to which paragraph 6.8 applies).

7.2 The disclosure officer should draw the attention of the prosecutor to any material an investigator has retained (including material to which paragraph 6.13 applies) which may satisfy the test for prosecution disclosure in the Act, and should explain why he has come to that view.

7.3 At the same time as complying with the duties in paragraphs 7.1 and 7.2, the disclosure officer must give the prosecutor a copy of any material which falls into the following categories (unless such material has already been given to the prosecutor as part of the file containing the material for the prosecution case):

  — information provided by an accused person which indicates an explanation for the offence with which he has been charged;

  — any material casting doubt on the reliability of a confession;

  — any material casting doubt on the reliability of a prosecution witness;

  — any other material which the investigator believes may satisfy the test for prosecution disclosure in the Act;

  — any other material which the investigator believes may fall within the test for primary prosecution disclosure in the Act.

7.4 If the prosecutor asks to inspect material which has not already been copied to him, the disclosure officer must allow him to inspect it. If the prosecutor asks for a copy of material which has not already been copied to him, the disclosure officer must give him a copy. However, this does not apply where the disclosure officer believes, having consulted the officer in charge of the investigation, that the material is too sensitive to be copied and can only be inspected.

7.5 If material consists of information which is recorded other than in writing, whether it should be given to the prosecutor in its original form as a whole, or by way of relevant extracts recorded in the same form, or in the form of a transcript, is a matter for agreement between the disclosure officer and the prosecutor.

Subsequent action by disclosure officer

8.1 At the time a schedule of non-sensitive material is prepared, the disclosure officer may not **A–239** know exactly what material will form the case against the accused, and the prosecutor may not have given advice about the likely relevance of particular items of material. Once these matters have been determined, the disclosure officer must give the prosecutor, where necessary, an amended schedule listing any additional material:

— which may be relevant to the investigation;
— which does not form part of the case against the accused;
— which is not already listed on the schedule; and
— which he believes is not sensitive,

unless he is informed in writing by the prosecutor that the prosecutor intends to disclose the material to the defence.

8.2 Section 7A of the Act imposes a continuing duty on the prosecutor, for the duration of criminal proceedings against the accused, to disclose material which satisfies the test for disclosure (subject to public interest considerations). To enable him to do this, any new material coming to light should be treated in the same way as the earlier material.

8.3 In particular, after a defence statement has been given, the disclosure officer must look again at the material which has been retained and must draw the attention of the prosecutor to any material which might reasonably be considered capable of undermining the case for the prosecution against the accused or of assisting the case for the accused; and he must reveal it to him in accordance with paragraphs 7.4 and 7.5 above.

Certification by disclosure officer

9.1 The disclosure officer must certify to the prosecutor that to the best of his knowledge and **A–240** belief, all relevant material which has been retained and made available to him has been revealed to the prosecutor in accordance with this code. He must sign and date the certificate. It will be necessary to certify not only at the time when the schedule and accompanying material is submitted to the prosecutor, and when relevant material which has been retained is reconsidered after the accused has given a defence statement, but also whenever a schedule is otherwise given or material is otherwise revealed to the prosecutor.

Disclosure of material to accused

10.1 If material has not already been copied to the prosecutor, and he requests its disclosure to **A–241** the accused on the ground that:

— it satisfies the test for prosecution disclosure; or
— it satisfies the test for prosecution disclosure; or

the disclosure officer must disclose it to the accused.

10.2 If material has been copied to the prosecutor, and it is to be disclosed, whether it is disclosed by the prosecutor or the disclosure officer is a matter of agreement between the two of them.

10.3 The disclosure officer must disclose material to the accused either by giving him a copy or by allowing him to inspect it. If the accused person asks for a copy of any material which he has been allowed to inspect, the disclosure officer must give it to him, unless in the opinion of the disclosure officer that is either not practicable (for example because the material consists of an object which cannot be copied, or because the volume of material is so great), or not desirable (for example because the material is a statement by a child witness in relation to a sexual offence).

10.4 If material which the accused has been allowed to inspect consists of information which is recorded other than in writing, whether it should be given to the accused in its original form or in the form of a transcript is matter for the discretion of the disclosure officer. If the material is transcribed, the disclosure officer must ensure that the transcript is certified to the accused as a true record of the material which has been transcribed.

10.5 If a court concludes that an item of sensitive material satisfies the prosecution disclosure test and that the interests of the defence outweigh the public interest in withholding disclosure, it will be necessary to disclose the material if the case is to proceed. This does not mean that sensitive documents must always be disclosed in their original form: for example, the court may agree that sensitive details still requiring protection should be blocked out, or that documents may be summarised, or that the prosecutor may make an admission about the substance of the material under section 10 of the *Criminal Justice Act* 1967.

(2) As to the practice for arranging and conducting interviews of witnesses notified by the accused

Introduction

A–241a   As from May 1, 2010, a new code of practice entitled "Code of Practice for Arranging and Conducting Interviews of Witnesses Notified by the Accused", which was prepared under section 21A of the *CPIA* 1996, was brought into force by the *Criminal Procedure and Investigations Act 1996 (Code of Practice for Interviews of Witnesses Notified by Accused) Order* 2010 (S.I. 2010 No. 1223).

CODE OF PRACTICE FOR ARRANGING AND CONDUCTING INTERVIEWS OF WITNESSES NOTIFIED BY THE ACCUSED

Preamble

A–241b   This code of practice is issued under section 21A of the *Criminal Procedure and Investigations Act* 1996 ("the Act"). It sets out guidance that police officers and other persons charged with investigating offences must follow if they arrange or conduct interviews of proposed witnesses whose details are disclosed to the prosecution by an accused person pursuant to the disclosure provisions in Part I of the Act.

Introduction

A–241c   1.1 Part I of the Act sets out rules governing disclosure of information in the course of criminal proceedings by both the prosecution and persons accused of offences to which that Part of the Act applies.

1.2. Sections 5 and 6 of the Act provide for accused persons to give defence statements to the prosecution and to the court and section 6A sets out what those defence statements must contain. Section 6A(2) requires that any defence statement that discloses an alibi must give particulars of it, including prescribed details of any witness who the accused believes is able to give evidence in support of the alibi and any information the accused has which may assist in identifying or finding such a witness.

1.3. Section 6C of the Act requires the accused to give to the prosecutor and the court a notice indicating whether he intends to call any witnesses at trial and giving details of those witnesses.

1.4. This code of practice sets out guidance that police officers and other persons charged with investigating offences must have regard to when they are arranging and conducting interviews of proposed witnesses identified in a defence statement given under section 6A(2) of the Act or a notice given under section 6C of the Act.

Definitions

A–241d   2. In this code:—
    - *the accused* means a person mentioned in section 1(1) or (2) of the Act;
    - *an appropriate person* means:
        (a) in the case of a witness under the age of 18:
            (i)   the parent, guardian or, if the witness is in local authority or voluntary organisa-

tion care, or is otherwise being looked after under the *Children Act* 1989, a
person representing that authority or organisation; or

 (ii) a social worker of a local authority; or

 (iii) failing these, some other responsible person aged 18 or over who is not a police
officer or employed by the police; and

 (b) in the case of a witness who is mentally disordered or mentally vulnerable:

  (i) a relative, guardian or other person responsible for the witness's care or custody;
or

  (ii) someone experienced in dealing with mentally disordered or mentally vulnerable people but who is not a police officer or employed by the police; or

  (iii) failing these, some other responsible person aged 18 or over who is not a police
officer or employed by the police.

 - *an investigator* is a police officer or any other person charged with the duty of investigating
offences.

 - *a witness* is a potential witness identified by an accused person either:

  - in a defence statement under section 6A(2) of the Act as being a witness that he
believes is able to give evidence in support of an alibi disclosed in the statement; or

  - in a notice given to the court and the prosecutor under section 6C of the Act as being a person that he intends to call as a witness at his trial.

Arrangement of the interview

Information to be provided to the witness before any interview may take place

3.1. If an investigator wishes to interview a witness, the witness must be asked whether he   **A–241e**
consents to being interviewed and informed that:

- an interview is being requested following his identification by the accused as a proposed
witness under section 6A(2) or section 6C of the Act;

- he is not obliged to attend the proposed interview;

- he is entitled to be accompanied by a solicitor at the interview (but nothing in this code
of practice creates any duty on the part of the Legal Services Commission to provide
funding for any such attendance); and

- a record will be made of the interview and he will subsequently be sent a copy of the
record.

3.2. If the witness consents to being interviewed, the witness must be asked:

- whether he wishes to have a solicitor present at the interview;

- whether he consents to a solicitor attending the interview on behalf of the accused, as an
observer; and

- whether he consents to a copy of the record being sent to the accused. If he does not
consent, the witness must be informed that the effect of disclosure requirements in criminal proceedings may nevertheless require the prosecution to disclose the record to the
accused (and any co-accused) in the course of the proceedings.

Information to be provided to the accused before any interview may take place

4.1. The investigator must notify the accused or, if the accused is legally represented in the   **A–241f**
proceedings, the accused's representatives:

- that the investigator requested an interview with the witness;

- whether the witness consented to the interview; and

- if the witness consented to the interview, whether the witness also consented to a solicitor
attending the interview on behalf of the accused, as an observer.

4.2. If the accused is not legally represented in the proceedings, and if the witness consents to a
solicitor attending the interview on behalf of the accused, the accused must be offered the opportunity, a reasonable time before the interview is held, to appoint a solicitor to attend it.

Identification of the date, time and venue for the interview

5. The investigator must nominate a reasonable date, time and venue for the interview and notify   **A–241g**
the witness of them and any subsequent changes to them.

Notification to the accused's solicitor of the date, time and venue of the interview

A–241h   6. If the witness has consented to the presence of the accused's solicitor, the accused's solicitor must be notified that the interview is taking place, invited to observe, and provided with reasonable notice of the date, time and venue of the interview and any subsequent changes.

Conduct of the interview

The investigator conducting the interview

A–241i   7. The identity of the investigator conducting the interview must be recorded. That person must have sufficient skills and authority, commensurate with the complexity of the investigation, to discharge his functions effectively. That person must not conduct the interview if that is likely to result in a conflict of interest, for instance, if that person is the victim of the alleged crime which is the subject of the proceedings. The advice of a more senior officer must always be sought if there is doubt as to whether a conflict of interest precludes an individual conducting the interview. If thereafter the doubt remains, the advice of a prosecutor must be sought.

Attendance of the accused's solicitor

A–241j   8.1. The accused's solicitor may only attend the interview if the witness has consented to his presence as an observer. Provided that the accused's solicitor was given reasonable notice of the date, time and place of the interview, the fact that the accused's solicitor is not present will not prevent the interview from being conducted. If the witness at any time withdraws consent to the accused's solicitor being present at the interview, the interview may continue without the presence of the accused's solicitor.

8.2. The accused's solicitor may attend only as an observer.

Attendance of the witness's solicitor

A–241k   9. Where a witness has indicated that he wishes to appoint a solicitor to be present, that solicitor must be permitted to attend the interview.

Attendance of any other appropriate person

A–241l   10. A witness under the age of 18 or a witness who is mentally disordered or otherwise mentally vulnerable must be interviewed in the presence of an appropriate person.

Recording of the interview

A–241m   11.1. An accurate record must be made of the interview, whether it takes place at a police station or elsewhere. The record must be made, where practicable, by audio recording or by visual recording with sound, or otherwise in writing. Any written record must be made and completed during the interview, unless this would not be practicable or would interfere with the conduct of the interview, and must constitute either a verbatim record of what has been said or, failing this, an account of the interview which adequately and accurately summarises it. If a written record is not made during the interview it must be made as soon as practicable after its completion. Written interview records must be timed and signed by the maker.

11.2 A copy of the record must be given, within a reasonable time of the interview, to:

   (a) the witness; and

   (b) if the witness consents, to the accused or the accused's solicitor.

II. ATTORNEY-GENERAL'S GUIDELINES

A. DISCLOSURE

Introduction

A–242   In April, 2005, the Attorney-General issued new guidelines on the disclosure of unused material in criminal proceedings in light of the abolition of the distinction between primary and secondary disclosure, and the introduction of a single test for disclosure of material that "might reasonably be considered capable of undermining the prosecution case or assisting the case for the accused". Much of the content followed the 2000 guidelines closely; but there is a strong emphasis on the need for all concerned in the criminal process to apply the provisions of the 1996 Act in a rigorous fashion. The new guidelines were to be adopted with immediate effect in relation to all cases submitted to prosecuting authorities in receipt of the guidelines, save where they specifically refer to provisions of the *CJA* 2003 or the new code of practice on disclosure (*ante*, § A–231 *et seq.*) that did not yet apply to the particular case.

As to the significance of the guidelines in relation to material held overseas, outside the European Union, by entities not subject to the jurisdiction of the United Kingdom, see *R. v. Flook* [2010] 1 Cr.App.R. 30, CA (*ante*, § 12–77).

Foreword

Disclosure is one of the most important issues in the criminal justice system and the application of **A–242a** proper and fair disclosure is a vital component of a fair criminal justice system. The "golden rule" is that fairness requires full disclosure should be made of all material held by the prosecution that weakens its case or strengthens that of the defence.

This amounts to no more and no less than a proper application of the *Criminal Procedure and Investigations Act* 1996 (*CPIA*) recently amended by the *Criminal Justice Act* 2003. The amendments in the *Criminal Justice Act* 2003 abolished the concept of "primary" and "secondary" disclosure, and introduced an amalgamated test for disclosure of material that "might reasonably be considered capable of undermining the prosecution case or assisting the case for accused". It also introduced a new code of practice. In the light of these, other new provisions and case law I conducted a review of the Attorney General's Guidelines issued in November 2000.

Concerns had previously been expressed about the operation of the then existing provisions by judges, prosecutors, and defence practitioners. It seems to me that we must all make a concerted effort to comply with the CPIA disclosure regime robustly in a consistent way in order to regain the trust and confidence of all those involved in the criminal justice system. The House of Lords in *R v H & C* made it clear that so long as the current disclosure system was operated with scrupulous attention, in accordance with the law and with proper regard to the interests of the defendant, it was entirely compatible with Article 6 of the European Convention on Human Rights (ECHR).

It is vital that everybody in the criminal justice system operates these procedures properly and fairly to ensure we protect the integrity of the criminal justice system whilst at the same time ensuring that a just and fair disclosure process is not abused so that it becomes unwieldy, bureaucratic and effectively unworkable. This means that all those involved must play their role.

Investigators must provide detailed and proper schedules. Prosecutors must not abrogate their duties under the *CPIA* by making wholesale disclosure in order to avoid carrying out the disclosure exercise themselves. Likewise, defence practitioners should avoid fishing expeditions and where disclosure is not provided using this as an excuse for an abuse of process application. I hope also that the courts will apply the legal regime set out under the *CPIA* rather than ordering disclosure because either it is easier or it would not "do any harm".

This disclosure regime must be made to work and it can only work if there is trust and confidence in the system and everyone plays their role in it. If this is achieved applications for a stay of proceedings on the grounds of non disclosure will only be made exceedingly sparingly and never on a speculative basis. Likewise such applications are only likely to succeed in extreme cases and certainly not where the alleged disclosure is in relation to speculative requests for material.

I have therefore revised the Guidelines to take account of developments and to start the process of ensuring that everyone works to achieve consistency of approach to *CPIA* disclosure. The amalgamated test should introduce a more streamlined process which is more objective and should therefore deal with some of the concerns about inconsistency in the application of the disclosure regime by prosecutors.

A draft set of these revised Guidelines went out for consultation, and resulted in many thoughtful and detailed responses from practitioners, including members of the judiciary, who have to work with the scheme on a daily basis. The Group that was established to advise me on the revision of the Guidelines has taken account of the results of the consultation exercise. I give my warm thanks to all who have offered responses on the consultation and assisted in the revision of these Guidelines.

I am publishing today the revised Guidelines that, if properly, applied will contribute to ensuring that the disclosure regime operates effectively, fairly and justly - which is vitally important to the integrity of the criminal justice system and the way in which it is perceived by the general public.

Disclosure of information in criminal proceedings

Introduction

1. Every accused person has a right to a fair trial, a right long embodied in our law and guaranteed **A–243**

under Article 6 of the European Convention on Human Rights (ECHR). A fair trial is the proper object and expectation of all participants in the trial process. Fair disclosure to an accused is an inseparable part of a fair trial.

2. What must be clear is that a fair trial consists of an examination not just of all the evidence the parties wish to rely on but also all other relevant subject matter. A fair trial should not require consideration of irrelevant material and should not involve spurious applications or arguments which serve to divert the trial process from examining the real issues before the court.

3. The scheme set out in the *Criminal Procedure and Investigations Act* 1996 (as amended by the *Criminal Justice Act* 2003) (the Act) is designed to ensure that there is fair disclosure of material which may be relevant to an investigation and which does not form part of the prosecution case. Disclosure under the Act should assist the accused in the timely preparation and presentation of their case and assist the court to focus on all the relevant issues in the trial. Disclosure which does not meet these objectives risks preventing a fair trial taking place.

4. This means that the disclosure regime set out in the Act must be scrupulously followed. These Guidelines build upon the existing law to help to ensure that the legislation is operated more effectively, consistently and fairly.

5. Disclosure must not be an open ended trawl of unused material. A critical element to fair and proper disclosure is that the defence play their role to ensure that the prosecution are directed to material which might reasonably be considered capable of undermining the prosecution case or assisting the case for the accused. This process is key to ensuring prosecutors make informed determinations about disclosure of unused material.

6. Fairness does recognise that there are other interests that need to be protected, including those of victims and witnesses who might otherwise be exposed to harm. The scheme of the Act protects those interests. It should also ensure that material is not disclosed which overburdens the participants in the trial process, diverts attention from the relevant issues, leads to unjustifiable delay, and is wasteful of resources.

7. Whilst it is acknowledged that these Guidelines have been drafted with a focus on Crown Court proceedings the spirit of the Guidelines must be followed where they apply to proceedings in the magistrates' court.

General principles

A-244   8. Disclosure refers to providing the defence with copies of, or access to, any material which might reasonably be considered capable of undermining the case for the prosecution against the accused, or of assisting the case for the accused, and which has not previously been disclosed.

9. Prosecutors will only be expected to anticipate what material might weaken their case or strengthen the defence in the light of information available at the time of the disclosure decision, and this may include information revealed during questioning.

10. Generally, material which can reasonably be considered capable of undermining the prosecution case against the accused or assisting the defence case will include anything that tends to show a fact inconsistent with the elements of the case that must be proved by the prosecution. Material can fulfil the disclosure test:

  (a) by the use to be made of it in cross-examination; or

  (b) by its capacity to support submissions that could lead to:

    (i) the exclusion of evidence; or

    (ii) a stay of proceedings; or

    (iii) a court or tribunal finding that any public authority had acted incompatibly with the accused 's rights under the ECHR; or

  (c) by its capacity to suggest an explanation or partial explanation of the accused's actions.

11. In deciding whether material may fall to be disclosed under paragraph 10, especially (b)(ii), prosecutors must consider whether disclosure is required in order for a proper application to be made. The purpose of this paragraph is not to allow enquiries to support speculative arguments or for the manufacture of defences.

12. Examples of material that might reasonably be considered capable of undermining the prosecution case or of assisting the case for the accused are:

  i. Any material casting doubt upon the accuracy of any prosecution evidence.

  ii. Any material which may point to another person, whether charged or not (including a co-accused) having involvement in the commission of the offence.

  iii. Any material which may cast doubt upon the reliability of a confession.

  iv. Any material that might go to the credibility of a prosecution witness.

  v. Any material that might support a defence that is either raised by the defence or apparent from the prosecution papers.

vi. Any material which may have a bearing on the admissibility of any prosecution evidence.

13. It should also be borne in mind that while items of material viewed in isolation may not be reasonably considered to be capable of undermining the prosecution case or assisting the accused, several items together can have that effect.

14. Material relating to the accused's mental or physical health, intellectual capacity, or to any ill treatment which the accused may have suffered when in the investigator's custody is likely to fall within the test for disclosure set out in paragraph 8 above.

Defence statements

15. A defence statement must comply with the requirements of section 6A of the Act. A **A–245** comprehensive defence statement assists the participants in the trial to ensure that it is fair. The trial process is not well served if the defence make general and unspecified allegations and then seek far-reaching disclosure in the hope that material may turn up to make them good. The more detail a defence statement contains the more likely it is that the prosecutor will make an informed decision about whether any remaining undisclosed material might reasonably be considered capable of undermining the prosecution case or of assisting the case for the accused, or whether to advise the investigator to undertake further enquiries. It also helps in the management of the trial by narrowing down and focussing on the issues in dispute. It may result in the prosecution discontinuing the case. Defence practitioners should be aware of these considerations when advising their clients.

16. Whenever a defence solicitor provides a defence statement on behalf of the accused it will be deemed to be given with the authority of the solicitor's client.

Continuing duty of prosecutor to disclose

17. Section 7A of the Act imposes a continuing duty upon the prosecutor to keep under review at **A–246** all times the question of whether there is any unused material which might reasonably be considered capable of undermining the prosecution case against the accused or assisting the case for the accused and which has not previously been disclosed. This duty arises after the prosecutor has complied with the duty of initial disclosure or purported to comply with it and before the accused is acquitted or convicted or the prosecutor decides not to proceed with the case. If such material is identified, then the prosecutor must disclose it to the accused as soon as is reasonably practicable.

18. As part of their continuing duty of disclosure, prosecutors should be open, alert and promptly responsive to requests for disclosure of material supported by a comprehensive defence statement. Conversely, if no defence statement has been served or if the prosecutor considers that the defence statement is lacking specificity or otherwise does not meet the requirements of section 6A of the Act, a letter should be sent to the defence indicating this. If the position is not resolved satisfactorily, the prosecutor should consider raising the issue at a hearing for directions to enable the court to give a warning or appropriate directions.

19. When defence practitioners are dissatisfied with disclosure decisions by the prosecution and consider that they are entitled to further disclosure, applications to the court should be made pursuant to section 8 of the Act and in accordance with the procedures set out in the *Criminal Procedure Rules*. Applications for further disclosure should not be made as ad hoc applications but dealt with under the proper procedures.

Applications for non-disclosure in the public interest

20. Before making an application to the court to withhold material which would otherwise fall to **A–247** be disclosed, on the basis that to disclose would give rise to a real risk of serious prejudice to an important public interest, prosecutors should aim to disclose as much of the material as they properly can (for example, by giving the defence redacted or edited copies or summaries). Neutral material or material damaging to the defendant need <u>not</u> be disclosed and must not be brought to the attention of the court. It is only in truly borderline cases that the prosecution should seek a judicial ruling on the disclosability of material in its possession.

21. Prior to or at the hearing, the court must be provided with full and accurate information. Prior to the hearing the prosecutor and the prosecution advocate must examine all material, which is the subject matter of the application and make any necessary enquiries of the investigator. The prosecutor (or representative) and/or investigator should attend such applications.

22. The principles set out at paragraph 36 of *R v H & C* should be rigorously applied firstly by the prosecutor and then by the court considering the material. It is essential that these principles are scrupulously attended to to ensure that the procedure for examination of material in the absence of the accused is compliant with Article 6 of ECHR.

Responsibilities

Investigators and disclosure officers

23. Investigators and disclosure officers must be fair and objective and must work together with **A–248**

prosecutors to ensure that disclosure obligations are met. A failure to take action leading to inadequate disclosure may result in a wrongful conviction. It may alternatively lead to a successful abuse of process argument, an acquittal against the weight of the evidence or the appellate courts may find that a conviction is unsafe and quash it.

24. Officers appointed as disclosure officers must have the requisite experience, skills, competence and resources to undertake their vital role. In discharging their obligations under the Act, code, common law and any operational instructions, investigators should always err on the side of recording and retaining material where they have any doubt as to whether it may be relevant.

25. An individual must not be appointed as disclosure officer, or continue in that role, if that is likely to result in a conflict of interest, for instance, if the disclosure officer is the victim of the alleged crime which is the subject of investigation. The advice of a more senior investigator must always be sought if there is doubt as to whether a conflict of interest precludes an individual acting as the disclosure officer. If thereafter a doubt remains, the advice of a prosecutor should be sought.

26. There may be a number of disclosure officers, especially in large and complex cases. However, there must be a lead disclosure officer who is the focus for enquiries and whose responsibility it is to ensure that the investigator's disclosure obligations are complied with. Disclosure officers, or their deputies, must inspect, view or listen to all relevant material that has been retained by the investigator, and the disclosure officer must provide a personal declaration to the effect that this task has been undertaken.

27. Generally this will mean that such material must be examined in detail by the disclosure officer or the deputy, but exceptionally the extent and manner of inspecting, viewing or listening will depend on the nature of material and its form. For example, it might be reasonable to examine digital material by using software search tools, or to establish the contents of large volumes of material by dip sampling. If such material is not examined in detail, it must nonetheless be described on the disclosure schedules accurately and as clearly as possible. The extent and manner of its examination must also be described together with justification for such action.

28. Investigators must retain material that may be relevant to the investigation. However, it may become apparent to the investigator that some material obtained in the course of an investigation because it was considered potentially relevant, is in fact incapable of impact. It need not then be retained or dealt with in accordance with these Guidelines, although the investigator should err on the side of caution in coming to this conclusion and seek the advice of the prosecutor as appropriate.

29. In meeting the obligations in paragraph 6.9 and 8.1 of the Code, it is crucial that descriptions by disclosure officers in non-sensitive schedules are detailed, clear and accurate. The descriptions may require a summary of the contents of the retained material to assist the prosecutor to make an informed decision on disclosure. Sensitive schedules must contain sufficient information to enable the prosecutor to make an informed decision as to whether or not the material itself should be viewed, to the extent possible without compromising the confidentiality of the information.

30. Disclosure officers must specifically draw material to the attention of the prosecutor for consideration where they have any doubt as to whether it might reasonably be considered capable of undermining the prosecution case or of assisting the case for the accused.

31. Disclosure officers must seek the advice and assistance of prosecutors when in doubt as to their responsibility as early as possible. They must deal expeditiously with requests by the prosecutor for further information on material, which may lead to disclosure.

Prosecutors

A-249

32. Prosecutors must do all that they can to facilitate proper disclosure, as part of their general and personal professional responsibility to act fairly and impartially, in the interests of justice and in accordance with the law. Prosecutors must also be alert to the need to provide advice to, and where necessary probe actions taken by, disclosure officers to ensure that disclosure obligations are met.

33. Prosecutors must review schedules prepared by disclosure officers thoroughly and must be alert to the possibility that relevant material may exist which has not been revealed to them or material included which should not have been. If no schedules have been provided, or there are apparent omissions from the schedules, or documents or other items are inadequately described or are unclear, the prosecutor must at once take action to obtain properly completed schedules. Likewise schedules should be returned for amendment if irrelevant items are included. If prosecutors remain dissatisfied with the quality or content of the schedules they must raise the matter with a senior investigator, and if necessary, persist, with a view to resolving the matter satisfactorily.

34. Where prosecutors have reason to believe that the disclosure officer has not discharged the obligation in paragraph 26 to inspect, view or listen to relevant material, they must at once raise the matter with the disclosure officer and, if it is believed that the officer has not inspected, viewed or listened to the material, request that it be done.

35. When prosecutors or disclosure officers believe that material might reasonably be considered capable of undermining the prosecution case or assisting the case for the accused, prosecutors must always inspect, view or listen to the material and satisfy themselves that the prosecution can properly be continued having regard to the disclosability of the material reviewed. Their judgement as to what other material to inspect, view or listen to will depend on the circumstances of each case.

36. Prosecutors should copy the defence statement to the disclosure officer and investigator as soon as reasonably practicable and prosecutors should advise the investigator if, in their view, reasonable and relevant lines of further enquiry should be pursued.

37. Prosecutors cannot comment upon, or invite inferences to be drawn from, failures in defence disclosure otherwise than in accordance with section 11 of the Act. Prosecutors may cross-examine the accused on differences between the defence case put at trial and that set out in his or her defence statement. In doing so, it may be appropriate to apply to the judge under section 6E of the Act for copies of the statement to be given to a jury, edited if necessary to remove inadmissible material. Prosecutors should examine the defence statement to see whether it points to other lines of enquiry. If the defence statement does point to other reasonable lines of inquiry further investigation is required and evidence obtained as a result of these enquiries may be used as part of the prosecution case or to rebut the defence.

38. Once initial disclosure is completed and a defence statement has been served requests for disclosure should ordinarily only be answered if the request is in accordance with and relevant to the defence statement. If it is not, then a further or amended defence statement should be sought and obtained before considering the request for further disclosure.

39. Prosecutors must ensure that they record in writing all actions and decisions they make in discharging their disclosure responsibilities, and this information is to be made available to the prosecution advocate if requested or if relevant to an issue.

40. If the material does not fulfil the disclosure test there is no requirement to disclose it. For this purpose, the parties' respective cases should not be restrictively analysed but must be carefully analysed to ascertain the specific facts the prosecution seek to establish and the specific grounds on which the charges are resisted. Neutral material or material damaging to the defendant need not be disclosed and must not be brought to the attention of the court. Only in truly borderline cases should the prosecution seek a judicial ruling on the disclosability of material in its hands.

41. If prosecutors are satisfied that a fair trial cannot take place where material which satisfies the disclosure test cannot be disclosed, and that this cannot or will not be remedied including by, for example, making formal admissions, amending the charges or presenting the case in a different way so as to ensure fairness or in other ways, they must not continue with the case.

Prosecution advocates

42. Prosecution advocates should ensure that all material that ought to be disclosed under the Act **A–250** is disclosed to the defence. However, prosecution advocates cannot be expected to disclose material if they are not aware of its existence. As far as is possible, prosecution advocates must place themselves in a fully informed position to enable them to make decisions on disclosure.

43. Upon receipt of instructions, prosecution advocates should consider as a priority all the information provided regarding disclosure of material. Prosecution advocates should consider, in every case, whether they can be satisfied that they are in possession of all relevant documentation and that they have been instructed fully regarding disclosure matters. Decisions already made regarding disclosure should be reviewed. If as a result, the advocate considers that further information or action is required, written advice should be promptly provided setting out the aspects that need clarification or action. Prosecution advocates must advise on disclosure in accordance with the Act. If necessary and where appropriate a conference should be held to determine what is required.

44. The prosecution advocate must keep decisions regarding disclosure under review until the conclusion of the trial. The prosecution advocate must in every case specifically consider whether he or she can satisfactorily discharge the duty of continuing review on the basis of the material supplied already, or whether it is necessary to inspect further material or to reconsider material already inspected. Prosecution advocates must not abrogate their responsibility under the Act by disclosing material which could not be considered capable of undermining the prosecution case or of assisting the case for the accused.

45. Prior to the commencement of a trial, the prosecuting advocate should always make decisions on disclosure in consultation with those instructing him or her and the disclosure officer. After a trial has started, it is recognised that in practice consultation on disclosure issues may not be practicable; it continues to be desirable, however, whenever this can be achieved without affecting unduly the conduct of the trial.

46. There is no basis in law or practice for disclosure on a "counsel to counsel" basis.

Involvement of other agencies

Material held by government departments or other Crown bodies

A–251   47. Where it appears to an investigator, disclosure officer or prosecutor that a Government department or other Crown body has material that may be relevant to an issue in the case, reasonable steps should be taken to identify and consider such material. Although what is reasonable will vary from case to case, the prosecution should inform the department or other body of the nature of its case and of relevant issues in the case in respect of which the department or body might possess material, and ask whether it has any such material.

48. It should be remembered that investigators, disclosure officers and prosecutors cannot be regarded to be in constructive possession of material held by Government departments or Crown bodies simply by virtue of their status as Government departments or Crown bodies.

49. Departments in England and Wales should have identified personnel as established Enquiry Points to deal with issues concerning the disclosure of information in criminal proceedings.

50. Where, after reasonable steps have been taken to secure access to such material, access is denied the investigator, disclosure officer or prosecutor should consider what if any further steps might be taken to obtain the material or inform the defence.

Material held by other agencies

A–252   51. There may be cases where the investigator, disclosure officer or prosecutor believes that a third party (for example, a local authority, a social services department, a hospital, a doctor, a school, a provider of forensic services) has material or information which might be relevant to the prosecution case. In such cases, if the material or information might reasonably be considered capable of undermining the prosecution case or of assisting the case for the accused prosecutors should take what steps they regard as appropriate in the particular case to obtain it.

52. If the investigator, disclosure officer or prosecutor seeks access to the material or information but the third party declines or refuses to allow access to it, the matter should not be left. If despite any reasons offered by the third party it is still believed that it is reasonable to seek production of the material or information, and the requirements of section 2 of the *Criminal Procedure (Attendance of Witnesses) Act* 1965 or as appropriate section 97 of the *Magistrates Courts Act* 1980 are satisfied, then the prosecutor or investigator should apply for a witness summons causing a representative of the third party to produce the material to the Court.

53. Relevant information which comes to the knowledge of investigators or prosecutors as a result of liaison with third parties should be recorded by the investigator or prosecutor in a durable or retrievable form (for example potentially relevant information revealed in discussions at a child protection conference attended by police officers).

54. Where information comes into the possession of the prosecution in the circumstances set out in paragraphs 51–53 above, consultation with the other agency should take place before disclosure is made: there may be public interest reasons which justify withholding disclosure and which would require the issue of disclosure of the information to be placed before the court.

Other disclosure

Disclosure prior to initial disclosure

A–253   55. Investigators must always be alive to the potential need to reveal and prosecutors to the potential need to disclose material, in the interests of justice and fairness in the particular circumstances of any case, after the commencement of proceedings but before their duty arises under the Act. For instance, disclosure ought to be made of significant information that might affect a bail decision or that might enable the defence to contest the committal proceedings.

56. Where the need for such disclosure is not apparent to the prosecutor, any disclosure will depend on what the accused chooses to reveal about the defence. Clearly, such disclosure will not exceed that which is obtainable after the statutory duties of disclosure arise.

Summary trial

A–254   57. The prosecutor should, in addition to complying with the obligations under the Act, provide to the defence all evidence upon which the Crown proposes to rely in a summary trial. Such provision should allow the accused and their legal advisers sufficient time properly to consider the evidence before it is called.

Material relevant to sentence

A–255   58. In all cases the prosecutor must consider disclosing in the interests of justice any material, which is relevant to sentence (*e.g.* information which might mitigate the seriousness of the offence or assist the accused to lay blame in part upon a co-accused or another person).

Post conviction

59. The interests of justice will also mean that where material comes to light after the conclusion of the proceedings, which might cast doubt upon the safety of the conviction, there is a duty to consider disclosure. Any such material should be brought immediately to the attention of line management.

A–256

60. Disclosure of any material that is made outside the ambit of Act will attract confidentiality by virtue of *Taylor v SFO* [1998].

Applicability of these guidelines

61. Although the relevant obligations in relation to unused material and disclosure imposed on the prosecutor and the accused are determined by the date on which the investigation began, these Guidelines should be adopted with immediate effect in relation to all cases submitted to the prosecuting authorities in receipt of these guidelines save where they specifically refer to the statutory or code provisions of the *Criminal Justice Act* 2003 that do not yet apply to the particular case.

A–257

Digitally-stored material

The Attorney-General has issued guidelines on the disclosure of digitally-stored material. They supplement the 2005 guidelines (*ante*) on the disclosure of unused material to the defence, specifically paragraph 27 (responsibilities of a disclosure officer when examining material retained by the investigator). The objective is to set out how digital material satisfying the test for disclosure can best be identified and disclosed to the defence without imposing unrealistic or disproportionate demands on the investigator or prosecutor. Paragraphs 6 and 7 describe two types of digital material, *viz.* material that is created within an electronic environment (*e.g.* e-mail), and material that that has been digitised from an analogue form (*e.g.* scanned copy of a document). General principles for investigators in handling and examining digital material are set out in paragraphs 8 and 9. Paragraphs 10 and 11 introduce, generally, the topics of seizure, relevance and retention. The legal obligations relating to these are to be found in the *PACE Act* 1984, the *CJPA* 2001, and the *CPIA* 1996; but the guidelines also apply to digital material seized or imaged under other statutory provisions. Paragraphs 12 to 22 concern seizure, with particular attention to seizure under the 1984 Act (paras 16–18) and the 2001 Act (paras 19–22). Digital material must not be seized if an investigator has reasonable grounds for believing it is subject to legal professional privilege, other than where sections 50 and 51 of the 2001 Act (§§ 15–103 *et seq.* in the main work) apply. Retention is dealt with in paragraphs 23 to 27. Digital material that is (or is reasonably believed to be) subject to legal professional privilege is covered by paragraphs 28 to 35, and similar principles apply to excluded or special procedure material (para. 36). When seized, material subject to legal professional privilege, and material suspected to be such, must be isolated from other material seized, and reviewed by a person independent of the investigation to determine whether the material may attract legal professional privilege. Material identified as potentially subject to legal professional privilege must be reviewed by an independent lawyer. Material subject to legal professional privilege may only be retained in accordance with section 54 of the 2001 Act (§ 15–107 in the main work), otherwise it must be returned as soon as practicable without waiting for the whole examination of the seized material. Paragraphs 37 and 38 concern encryption. The procedure the prosecution should follow when sifting through and examining digital material is described in paragraphs 39 to 45. Where there is an enormous volume of material, it is perfectly proper for the investigator or disclosure officer to search it by sample, key words, or other appropriate search tools or analytical techniques, to locate relevant passages, phrases and identifiers. It will usually be appropriate to invite the accused and his legal representative to suggest further reasonable search terms. Paragraphs 46 to 49 concern record keeping, and paragraphs 50 to 53, the scheduling of unused material. Finally, paragraphs 55 to 63 cover material held by a third party, both within the United Kingdom (paras 55–57) and outside it (paras 58–63).

A–258

Disclosure of digitally-stored material

A-259   1. The guidelines are intended to supplement the Attorney General's Guidelines on Disclosure (reissued in April 2005) and specifically paragraph 27. Paragraph 27 explains that the disclosure officer's obligation to inspect retained material may be fulfilled in relation to digitally stored material by using search terms or dip sampling methods, so long as the material is described on the schedules as clearly as possible and the manner and extent of the inspection is recorded along with the justification for adopting that approach.

2. As a result of the number of cases now involving digitally stored material and the scale of the digital material that may be involved, more detailed guidance is considered to be needed. The objective of these guidelines is to set out how material satisfying the tests for disclosure can best be identified and disclosed to the defence without imposing unrealistic or disproportionate demands on the investigator and prosecutor.

3. The approach set out in these guidelines is in line with existing best practice, in that:

(i) investigating and prosecuting agencies, especially in large and complex cases, will apply their respective case management and disclosure strategies and policies and be transparent with the defence and the courts about how the prosecution has approached complying with its disclosure obligations in the context of the individual case;

(ii) the defence will be expected to play their part in defining the real issues in the case. In this context, the defence will be invited to participate in defining the scope of the reasonable searches that may be made of digitally stored material by the investigator to identify material that might reasonably be expected to undermine the prosecution case or assist the defence.

4. If this approach is followed the courts will be in a good position to use their case management powers effectively and to determine applications for disclosure fairly.

5. The Attorney General's guidelines are not detailed operational guidelines. They are intended to set out a common approach to be adopted in the context of digitally stored material.

Types of digital material

A-260   6. Digital material falls into two categories: the first category is material which is created natively within an electronic environment (*e.g.* email, office files, system files, digital photographs, audio etc.); the second category is material which has been digitised from an analogue form (*e.g.* scanned copy of a document, scanned photograph, a faxed document). Irrespective of the way in which technology changes, the categorisation of digital material will remain the same.

7. Digital material is usually held on one of the three types of media. Optical media (*e.g.* CD, DVD, Blu-ray) and solid-state media (*e.g.* removable memory cards, solid state music players or mobile devices etc.) cater for usually lower volume storage. Magnetic media (*e.g.* disk drives and back up tapes) usually cater for the high volume storage.

General principles for investigators

A-261   8. The general principles[1] to be followed by investigators in handling and examining digital material are:

(i) no action taken by investigators or their agents should change data held on a computer or storage media which may subsequently be relied upon in court;

(ii) in circumstances where a person finds it necessary to access original data held on computer or storage media, that person must be competent to do so and be able to give evidence explaining the relevance and implications of their actions;

(iii) an audit trail or other record of all processes applied to computerbased electronic evidence should be created and preserved; an independent third party should be able to examine those processes (see further the sections headed "Record keeping" and "Scheduling" below); and

(iv) the person in charge of the investigation has overall responsibility for ensuring that the law and these principles are followed.

9. Where an investigator has reasonable grounds for believing that digital material may contain material subject to legal professional privilege, very strong legal constraints apply. No digital material may be seized which an investigator has reasonable grounds for believing to be subject to legal privilege, other than where the provisions of the *Criminal Justice and Police Act* 2001 apply. Strict controls need to be applied where privileged material is seized. See the more detailed section on legal professional privilege starting at paragraph 27 below.

Seizure, relevance and retention

A-262   10. The legal obligations are to be found in a combination of the *Police and Criminal Evidence Act* 1984 (*PACE*), the *Criminal Justice and Police Act* 2001 (*CJPA* 2001) and the *Criminal Procedure and Investigations Act* 1996 (the *CPIA* 1996).

11. These guidelines also apply to digital material seized or imaged under other statutory provisions. For example, the Serious Fraud Office has distinct powers of seizure under warrant obtained under section 2(4) of the *Criminal Justice Act* 1987. And in cases concerning obscene material special provisions apply to the handling, storage and copying of such material. Practitioners should refer to specific guidance on the application of those provisions.

Seizure

12. Before searching a suspect's premises where digital evidence is likely to be found, consideration must be given to what sort of evidence is likely to be found and in what volume, whether it is likely to be possible to view and copy, if relevant, the material at the location — it is not uncommon with the advent of cloud computing for digital material to be hosted by a third party — and to what should be seized. Business and commercial premises will often have very substantial amounts of digital material stored on computers and other media. Investigators will need to consider the practicalities of seizing computer hard drives and other media, the effect this may have on the business and, where it is not feasible to obtain an image of digital material, the likely timescale for returning seized items.

A–263

13. In deciding whether to seize and retain digital material it is important that the investigator either complies with the procedure under the relevant statutory authority, relying either on statutory powers or a search warrant, or obtains the owner's consent. In particular, investigators need to be aware of the strong constraints applying to legally privileged material.

14. A computer hard drive or single item of media, such as a back up tape, is a single storage entity. This means that if any digital material found on the hard drive or other media can lawfully be seized the computer hard drive or single item of media may, if appropriate, be seized or imaged. In some circumstances investigators may wish to image specific folders, files or categories of data where it is feasible to do so without seizing the hard drive or other media, or instead of taking an image of all data on the hard drive or other media. In practice, the configuration of most systems means that data may be contained across a number of hard drives and more than one hard drive or item of media may be required in order to access the information sought.

15. Digital material must not be seized if an investigator has reasonable grounds for believing it is subject to legal professional privilege, other than where sections 50 or 51 of the *Criminal Justice and Police Act* 2001 apply. If such material is seized it must be isolated from other seized material and any other investigation material in the possession of the investigating authority.

The Police and Criminal Evidence Act 1984

16. *PACE* 1984 provides powers to seize and retain anything for which the search has been authorised or after arrest, other than items attracting legal professional privilege.[2] In addition, there is a general power to seize anything which is on the premises if there are reasonable grounds to believe that it has been obtained in the commission of an offence, or that it is evidence and that it is necessary to seize it to prevent it being concealed, lost, altered or destroyed.[3] There is another related power to require information which is stored in any electronic form and is accessible from the premises to be produced in a form in which it can be taken away and in which it is visible and legible or from which it can readily be produced in a visible and legible form.[4]

A–264

17. An image (a forensically sound copy) of the digital material may be taken at the location of the search. Where the investigator makes an image of the digital material at the location, the original need not be seized. Alternatively, when originals are taken, investigators must be prepared to copy or image the material for the owners when reasonably practicable in accordance with *PACE* 1984, Code B:7.17.

18. Where it is not possible or reasonably practicable to image the computer or hard drive, it will need to be removed from the location or premises for examination elsewhere. This allows the investigator to seize and sift material for the purpose of identifying that which meets the tests for retention in accordance with the 1984 Act.[5]

The Criminal Justice and Police Act 2001

19. The additional powers of seizure in sections 50 and 51 of the *CJPA* 2001 Act only extend the scope of existing powers of search and seizure under the 1984 Act and other specified statutory authority[6] where the relevant conditions and circumstances apply.

A–265

20. Investigators must be careful only to exercise powers under the *CJPA* when it is necessary and not to remove any more material than is justified. The removal of large volumes of material, much of which may not ultimately be retainable, may have serious consequences for the owner of the material, particularly when they are involved in business or other commercial activities.

21. A written notice must be given to the occupier of the premises where items are seized under sections 50 and 51.[7]

22. Until material seized under the *CJPA* 2001 has been examined, it must be kept securely and separately from any material seized under other powers. Any such material must be examined as soon as reasonably practicable to determine which elements may be retained and which should be returned. Regard must be had to the desirability of allowing the person from whom the property was seized, or a person with an interest in the property, an opportunity of being present or represented at the examination.

Retention

A–266

23. Where material is seized under the powers conferred by *PACE* 1984 the duty to retain it under the code of practice issued under the *CPIA* 1996 is subject to the provisions on retention under section 22 of the 1984 Act. Material seized under sections 50 and 51 of the *CJPA* 2001 may be retained or returned in accordance with sections 53–58 of that Act.

24. Retention is limited to evidence and relevant material (as defined in the code of practice issued under the *CPIA* 1996). Where either evidence or relevant material is inextricably linked to non-relevant material which is not reasonably practicable to separate, that material can also be retained. Inextricably linked material is material that is not reasonably practicable to separate from other linked material without prejudicing the use of that other material in any investigation or proceedings.

25. However, inextricably linked material must not be examined, imaged, copied or used for any purpose other than for providing the source of or the integrity of the linked material.

26. There are four categories of material that may be retained:

(i) material that is evidence or potential evidence in the case; where material is retained for evidential purposes there will be a strong argument that the whole thing (or an authenticated image or copy) should be retained for the purpose of proving provenance and continuity;

(ii) where evidential material has been retained, inextricably linked nonrelevant material which is not reasonably practicable to separate can also be retained (*PACE* Code B, para. 7);

(iii) an investigator should retain material that is relevant to the investigation and required to be scheduled as unused material; this is broader than but includes the duty to retain material which may satisfy the test for prosecution disclosure; the general duty to retain relevant material is set out in the *CPIA* code at paragraph 5;

(iv) material which is inextricably linked to relevant unused material which of itself may not be relevant material; such material should be retained (*PACE* Code B, para. 7).

27. The balance of any digital material should be returned in accordance with sections 53–55 of the 2001 Act and also note paragraph 28 of the Attorney General's Guidelines on Disclosure.

Legal professional privilege (LPP)

A–267

28. No digital material may be seized which an investigator has reasonable grounds for believing to be subject to legal privilege, other than under the additional powers of seizure in the *CJPA* 2001.

29. The *CJPA* 2001 enables an investigator to seize relevant items which contain LPP material where it is not reasonably practicable on the search premises to separate LPP material from non-LPP material.

30. Where LPP material or material suspected of containing LPP is seized it must be isolated from the other material which has been seized in the investigation. The mechanics of securing property vary according to the circumstances; "bagging up", *i.e.* placing materials in sealed bags or containers, and strict subsequent control of access, is the appropriate procedure in many cases.

31. Examination of material may be undertaken by a person independent of the investigation, who may be employed within an investigative body so long as he or she is not one of the investigators or anyone connected with the investigation, to determine whether material may attract LPP.

32. Where material has been identified as potentially containing LPP it must be reviewed by an independent lawyer. No member of the investigative or prosecution team involved in either the current investigation or, if the LPP material relates to other criminal proceedings, in those proceedings should have sight of or access to the LPP material.

33. If the material is voluminous, search terms or other filters may have to be used to identify the LPP material. If so this will also have to be done by someone independent and not connected with the investigation.

34. It is essential that anyone dealing with LPP material maintains proper records showing the way in which the material has been handled and those who have had access to it as well as decisions taken in relation to that material.

35. LPP material can only be retained in specific circumstances in accordance with section 54 of

the *CJPA* 2001, *i.e.* where the property which comprises the LPP material has been lawfully seized and it is not reasonably practicable for the item to be separated from the rest of the property without prejudicing the use of the rest of the property. LPP material which cannot be retained must be returned as soon as practicable after the seizure without waiting for the whole examination of the seized material.

Excluded and special procedure material

36. Similar principles to those that apply to LPP material apply to excluded or special procedure **A–268** material, as set out in section 55 of the *CJPA* 2001.[8]

Encryption

37. Part III of the *Regulation of Investigatory Powers Act* 2000 (*RIPA*) and the Investigation of **A–269** Protected Electronic Information code of practice govern encryption. See the CPS's Guidance *RIPA*, Part III.

38. *RIPA* enables specified law enforcement agencies to compel individuals or companies to provide passwords or encryption keys for the purpose of rendering protected material readable. Failure to comply with *RIPA*, Part III orders is a criminal offence. The code of practice provides guidance when exercising powers under *RIPA*, to require disclosure of protected electronic data in an intelligible form or to acquire the means by which protected electronic data may be accessed or put in an intelligible form.

Sifting/examination

39. In complying with its duty of disclosure, the prosecution should follow the procedure as **A–270** outlined below.

40. Where digital material is examined, the extent and manner of inspecting, viewing or listening will depend on the nature of the material and its form.

41. It is important for investigators and prosecutors to remember that the duty under the 1996 Act code of practice is to "pursue all reasonable lines of enquiry including those that point away from the suspect". Lines of enquiry, of whatever kind, should be pursued only if they are reasonable in the context of the individual case. It is not the duty of the prosecution to comb through all the material in its possession — *e.g.* every word or byte of computer material — on the look out for anything which might conceivably or speculatively assist the defence. The duty of the prosecution is to disclose material which might reasonably be considered capable of undermining its case or assisting the case for the accused which they become aware of, or to which their attention is drawn.

42. In some cases the sift may be conducted by an investigator/disclosure officer manually assessing the content of the computer or other digital material from its directory and determining which files are relevant and should be retained for evidence or unused material.

43. In other cases such an approach may not be feasible. Where there is an enormous volume of material it is perfectly proper for the investigator/disclosure officer to search it by sample, key words, or other appropriate search tools or analytical techniques to locate relevant passages, phrases and identifiers.

44. In cases involving very large quantities of data, the person in charge of the investigation will develop a strategy setting out how the material should be analysed or searched to identify categories of data. Where search tools are used to examine digital material it will usually be appropriate to provide the accused and his or her legal representative with a copy of reasonable search terms used, or to be used, and invite them to suggest any further reasonable search terms. If search terms are suggested which the investigator or prosecutor believes will not be productive — for example because of the use of common words that are likely to identify a mass of irrelevant material, the investigator or prosecutor is entitled to open a dialogue with the defence representative with a view to agreeing sensible refinements. The purpose of this dialogue is to ensure that reasonable and proportionate searches can be carried out.

45. It may be necessary to carry out sampling and searches on more than one occasion, especially as there is a duty on the prosecutor to keep duties of disclosure under review. To comply with this duty it may be appropriate (and should be considered) where further evidence or unused material is obtained in the course of the investigation; the defence statement is served on the prosecutor; the defendant makes an application under section 8 of the *CPIA* for disclosure; or the defendant requests that further sampling or searches be carried out (provided it is a reasonable line of enquiry).

Record keeping

46. A record or log must be made of all digital material seized or imaged and subsequently **A–271** retained as relevant to the investigation.

47. In cases involving very large quantities of data where the person in charge of the investigation has developed a strategy setting out how the material should be analysed or searched to identify categories of data, a record should be made of the strategy and the analytical techniques used to search the data. The record should include details of the person who has carried out the process and the date and time it was carried out. In such cases the strategy should record the reasons why certain categories have been searched for (such as names, companies, dates etc).

48. In any case it is important that any searching or analytical processing of digital material, as well as the data identified by that process, is properly recorded. So far as practicable, what is required is a record of the terms of the searches or processing that has been carried out. This means that in principle the following details may be recorded:

(i) a record of all searches carried out, including the date of each search and the person(s) who conducted it;

(ii) a record of all search words or terms used on each search; however where it is impracticable to record each word or terms (such as where Boolean searches or search strings or conceptual searches are used) it will usually be sufficient to record each broad category of search;

(iii) a log of the key judgements made while refining the search strategy in the light of what is found, or deciding not to carry out further searches;

(iv) where material relating to a "hit" is not examined, the decision not to examine should be explained in the record of examination or in a statement. For instance, a large number of "hits" may be obtained in relation to a particular search word or term, but material relating to the "hits" is not examined because they do not appear to be relevant to the investigation. Any subsequent refinement of the search terms and further hits should also be noted and explained as above.

49. Just as it is not necessary for the investigator or prosecutor to produce records of every search made of hard copy material, it is not necessary to produce records of what may be many hundreds of searches or analyses that have been carried out on digitally stored material, simply to demonstrate that these have been done. It should be sufficient for the prosecution to explain how the disclosure exercise has been approached and to give the accused or suspect's legal representative an opportunity to participate in defining the reasonable searches to be made, as described in the section on sifting/examination.

Scheduling

A–272
50. The disclosure officer should ensure that scheduling of relevant material is carried out in accordance with the 1996 Act code of practice. This requires each item of unused material to be listed separately on the unused material schedule and numbered consecutively. The description of each item should make clear the nature of the item and should contain sufficient detail to enable the prosecutor to decide whether he needs to inspect the material before deciding whether or not it should be disclosed (see paragraph 24).

51. In some enquiries it may not be practicable to list each item of material separately. If so, these may be listed in a block and described by quantity and generic title. Even if the material is listed in a block, the search terms used and any items of material which might satisfy the disclosure test are listed and described separately. In practical terms this will mean, where appropriate, cross referencing the schedules to your disclosure management document.

52. The remainder of any computer hard drive/media containing material which is not responsive to search terms or other analytical technique or not identified by any "hits", and material identified by "hits" but not examined, is unused material and should be recorded (if appropriate by a generic description) and retained.

53. Where continuation sheets of the unused material schedule are used, or additional schedules are sent subsequently, the item numbering must be sequential to all other items on earlier schedules.

Third party material

A–273
54. Third party material is material held by a person, organisation, or government department other than the investigator and prosecutor within the U.K. or outside the U.K.

Within the U.K.

A–274
55. The *CPIA* code and the AG's Guidelines makes clear the obligation on the prosecution to pursue all reasonable lines of enquiry in relation to material held by third parties within the U.K.

56. If as a result of the duty to pursue all reasonable lines of enquiry, the investigator or prosecutor obtains or receives the material from the third party, then it must be dealt with in accordance with the *CPIA* 1996, *i.e.* the prosecutor must disclose material if it meets the disclosure tests, subject to any public interest immunity claim. The person who has an interest in the material (the third party) may make representations to the court concerning public interest immunity (see s.16 of the *CPIA* 1996).

57. Material not in the possession of an investigator or prosecutor falls outside the *CPIA* 1996. In such cases the Attorney General's Guidelines on Disclosure prescribe the approach to be taken to disclosure of material held by third parties (paras 51–54) as does the judicial disclosure protocol (paras 52–62).

Outside the U.K.

58. The obligation on the investigator and prosecutor under the *CPIA* code and the Attorney- **A–275** General's Guidelines to pursue all reasonable lines of enquiry also applies to material held overseas.

59. Where it appears that there is relevant material, the prosecution must take reasonable steps to obtain it, either informally or making use of the powers contained in the *Crime (International Co-operation) Act* 2003 and any E.U. and international conventions. See CPS Guidance Obtaining Evidence and Information from Abroad.

60. There may be cases where a foreign state or a foreign court refuses to make the material available to the investigator or prosecutor. There may be other cases where the foreign state, though willing to show the material to investigators will not allow the material to be copied or otherwise made available and the courts of the foreign state will not order its provision.

61. It is for these reasons that there is no absolute duty on the prosecutor to disclose relevant material held overseas by entities not subject to the jurisdiction of the courts in England and Wales.

62. The obligation on the investigator and prosecutor under the *CPIA* 1996 is to take reasonable steps. Where investigators are allowed to examine files of a foreign state but are not allowed to take copies or notes or list the documents held, there is no breach by the prosecution in its duty of disclosure by reason of its failure to obtain such material, provided reasonable steps have been taken to try and obtain the material. Whether the prosecution has complied with its duty is for the court to judge in each case.

63. In these circumstances it is important that the position is clearly set out in writing so that the court and the defence know what the position is. Investigators and prosecutors must record and explain the situation and set out, insofar as they are permitted by the foreign state, such information as they can and the steps they have taken.

---

[1] Based on: Association of Chief Police Officers: Good Practice Guide for Computer Based Electronic Evidence version 4.

[2] By warrant under section 8 and Schedule 1 and section 18 of the 1984 Act.

[3] S.19 of the 1984 Act.

[4] S.20 of the 1984 Act.

[5] Special provisions exist for the investigations conducted by Her Majesty's Revenue and Customs in the application of their powers under the 1984 Act — see s.114(2)(b) — and the 2001 Act.

[6] Sched. 1 to the 2001 Act.

[7] S.52 of the 2001 Act.

[8] Special provisions exist for investigations conducted by Her Majesty's Revenue and Customs in the application of the powers under the 1984 Act — see s.114(2)(b) — and the 2001 Act.

B. ACCEPTANCE OF PLEAS

Introduction

The Attorney-General has issued revised guidelines on the acceptance of pleas, which **A–276** came into force on December 1, 2009. The new guidelines take into account the amendments to paragraph IV.45 of the *Practice Direction (Criminal Proceedings: Consolidation)* [2002] 1 W.L.R. 2870 (since reissued, but not re-published, in a new consolidation), effected by *Practice Direction (Criminal Proceedings: Substituted and Additional Provisions)* [2009] 1 W.L.R. 1396, which deals with pleas of guilty in the Crown Court (as to which, see §§ 4–109 and 5–91 *et seq.* in the main work, and *post*, A–281 *et seq.*). The principal changes are made to Part C (basis of plea). Paragraph C.1 now makes it clear that in multi-handed cases, the bases of plea must be factually consistent with each other. Paragraph C.2 now states that a defence advocate must reduce an acceptable basis of plea to writing in all cases save for those in which the defendant has indicated that the guilty plea has been or will be tendered on the basis of the prosecution case (previously this was not necessary in cases where the issue was "simple"). Paragraph C.4 now additionally provides that, where the basis of plea differs in its implications for sentencing or the making of ancillary orders from the case originally outlined by the prosecution, the prosecution advocate must ensure that such differences are accurately reflected in the written record prior to showing it to the prosecuting authority. New paragraph C.6 provides that in all cases where it is likely to assist the court where the sentencing issues are complex or unfamiliar, the prosecution must add to the written outline of the case served upon the court a summary of the key considerations, taking the form of brief notes on (a) any statutory limitations, (b) any relevant sentencing authorities or guidelines, (c) the scope for any ancillary orders, and (d) the age of the defendant and information regarding any outstanding offences. Paragraph C.7 is new and clarifies that the prosecution are able to provide further written information where they think that it is likely to assist the judge or where the judge requests it. Old paragraph C.7 becomes new paragraph C.8, and is amended to ensure that the procedure to be followed where the prosecution advocate takes issue with all or part of the written basis of plea is in line with the consolidated criminal practice direction. Old paragraph C.8 is now paragraph C.11.

Attorney-General's Guidelines on the Acceptance of Pleas and the Prosecutor's Role in the Sentencing Exercise

A. Foreword

A–277   **A:**1. Prosecutors have an important role in protecting the victim's interests in the criminal justice process, not least in the acceptance of pleas and the sentencing exercise. The basis of plea, particularly in a case that is not contested, is the vehicle through which the victim's voice is heard. Factual inaccuracies in pleas in mitigation cause distress and offence to victims, the families of victims and witnesses. This can take many forms but may be most acutely felt when the victim is dead and the family hears inaccurate assertions about the victim's character or lifestyle. Prosecution advocates are reminded that they are required to adhere to the standards set out in the Victim's Charter, which places the needs of the victim at the heart of the criminal justice process, and that they are subject to a similar obligation in respect of the Code of Practice for Victims of Crime.

    A:2. The principle of fairness is central to the administration of justice. The implementation of *Human Rights Act* 1998 [*sic*] in October 2000 incorporated into domestic law the principle of fairness to the accused articulated in the European Convention on Human Rights. Accuracy and reasonableness of plea plays an important part in ensuring fairness both to the accused and to the victim.

    A:3. The Attorney General's Guidelines on the Acceptance of Pleas issued on December 7, 2000 highlighted the importance of transparency in the conduct of justice. The basis of plea agreed by the parties in a criminal trial is central to the sentencing process. An illogical or unsupported basis of plea can lead to an unduly lenient sentence being passed and has a consequential effect where consideration arises as to whether to refer the sentence to the Court of Appeal under section 36 of the *Criminal Justice Act* 1988.

    A:4. These Guidelines, which replace the Guidelines issued in October 2005, give guidance on how prosecutors should meet these objectives of protection of victims' interests and of securing fairness and transparency in the process. They take into account paragraphs IV.45.4 and following of the consolidated criminal practice direction, amended May 2009, and the guidance issued by the Court of Appeal (Criminal) Division [*sic*] in *R. v. Beswick* [1996] 1 Cr.App.R. 343, *R. v. Tolera* [1999] 1 Cr.App.R. 25 and *R. v. Underwood* [2005] 1 Cr.App.R 13. They complement the Bar Council Guidance on Written Standards for the Conduct of Professional Work issued with the 7th edition of the Code of Conduct for the Bar of England and Wales and the Law Society's Professional Conduct Rules. When considering the acceptance of a guilty plea prosecution advocates are also reminded of the need to apply "The Farquharson Guidelines on The Role and Responsibilities of the Prosecution Advocate".

    A:5. The Guidelines should be followed by all prosecutors and those persons designated under section 7 of the *Prosecution of Offences Act* 1985 (designated caseworkers) and apply to prosecutions conducted in England and Wales.

B. General Principles

A–278   **B:**1. Justice in this jurisdiction, save in the most exceptional circumstances, is conducted in public. This includes the acceptance of pleas by the prosecution and sentencing.

    B:2. The Code for Crown Prosecutors governs the prosecutor's decision-making prior to the commencement of the trial hearing and sets out the circumstances in which pleas to a reduced number of charges, or less serious charges, can be accepted.

B:3. When a case is listed for trial and the prosecution form the view that the appropriate course is to accept a plea before the proceedings commence or continue, or to offer no evidence on the indictment or any part of it, the prosecution should whenever practicable speak to the victim or the victim's family, so that the position can be explained. The views of the victim or the family may assist in informing the prosecutor's decision as to whether it is the [*sic*] public interest, as defined by the Code for Crown Prosecutors, to accept or reject the plea. The victim or victim's family should then be kept informed and decisions explained once they are made at court.

B:4. The appropriate disposal of a criminal case after conviction is as much a part of the criminal justice process as the trial of guilt or innocence. The prosecution advocate represents the public interest, and should be ready to assist the court to reach its decision as to the appropriate sentence. This will include drawing the court's attention to:

— any victim personal statement or other information available to the prosecution advocate as to the impact of the offence on the victim;
— where appropriate, to any evidence of the impact of the offending on a community;
— any statutory provisions relevant to the offender and the offences under consideration;
— any relevant sentencing guidelines and guideline cases; and
— the aggravating and mitigating factors of the offence under consideration.

The prosecution advocate may also offer assistance to the court by making submissions, in the light of all these factors, as to the appropriate sentencing range.

In all cases, it is the prosecution advocate's duty to apply for appropriate ancillary orders, such as anti-social behaviour orders and confiscation orders. When considering which ancillary orders to apply for, prosecution advocates must always have regard to the victim's needs, including the question of his or her future protection.

C.   The Basis of Plea

C:1. The basis of a guilty plea must not be agreed on a misleading or untrue set of facts and   **A–279** must take proper account of the victim's interests. An illogical or insupportable basis of plea will inevitably result in the imposition of an inappropriate sentence and is capable of damaging public confidence in the criminal justice system. In cases involving multiple defendants the bases of plea for each defendant must be factually consistent with each other.

C:2. When the defendant indicates an acceptable plea, the defence advocate should reduce the basis of the plea to writing. This must be done in all cases save for those in which the defendant has indicated that the guilty plea has been or will be tendered on the basis of the prosecution case.

C:3. The written basis of plea must be considered with great care, taking account of the position of any other relevant defendant where appropriate. The prosecution should not lend itself to any agreement whereby a case is presented to the sentencing judge on a misleading or untrue set of facts or on a basis that is detrimental to the victim's interests. There will be cases where a defendant seeks to mitigate on the basis of assertions of fact which are outside the scope of the prosecution's knowledge. A typical example concerns the defendant's state of mind. If a defendant wishes to be sentenced on this basis, the prosecution advocate should invite the judge not to accept the defendant's version unless he or she gives evidence on oath to be tested in cross-examination. Paragraph IV.45.14 of the consolidated criminal practice direction states that in such circumstances the defence advocate should be prepared to call the defendant and, if the defendant is not willing to testify, subject to any explanation that may be given, the judge may draw such inferences as appear appropriate.

C:4. The prosecution advocate should show the prosecuting authority any written record relating to the plea and agree with them the basis on which the case will be opened to the court. If, as may well be the case, the basis of plea differs in its implications for sentencing or the making of ancillary orders from the case originally outlined by the prosecution, the prosecution advocate must ensure that such differences are accurately reflected in the written record prior to showing it to the prosecuting authority.

C:5. It is the responsibility of the prosecution advocate thereafter to ensure that the defence advocate is aware of the basis on which the plea is accepted by the prosecution and the way in which the prosecution case will be opened to the court.

C:6. In all cases where it is likely to assist the court where the sentencing issues are complex or unfamiliar the prosecution must add to the written outline of the case which is served upon the court a summary of the key considerations. This should take the form of very brief notes on:

— any relevant statutory limitations;

— the names of any relevant sentencing authorities or guidelines;

— the scope for any ancillary orders (*e.g.* concerning anti-social behaviour, confiscation or deportation will need to be considered.

The outline should also include the age of the defendant and information regarding any outstanding offences.

C:7. It remains open to the prosecutor to provide further written information (for example to supplement and update the analysis at later stages of the case) where he or she thought that likely to assist the court, or if the judge requests it.

C:8. When the prosecution advocate has agreed the written basis of plea submitted by the defence advocate, he or she should endorse the document accordingly. If the prosecution advocate takes issue with all or part of the written basis of plea, the procedure set out in the consolidated criminal practice direction (and in Part 37.10(5) of the *Criminal Procedure Rules*) should be followed. The defendant's basis of plea must be set out in writing identifying what is in dispute; the court may invite the parties to make representations about whether the dispute is material to sentence; and if the court decides that it is a material dispute, the court will invite further representations or evidence as it may require and decide the dispute in accordance with the principles set out in *R. v. Newton*, 77 Cr.App.R.13, CA. The signed original document setting out the disputed factual matters should be made available to the trial judge and thereafter lodged with the court papers, as it will form part of the record of the hearing.

C:9. Where the basis of plea cannot be agreed and the discrepancy between the two accounts is such as to have a potentially significant effect on the level of sentence, it is the duty of the defence advocate so to inform the court before the sentencing process begins. There remains an overriding duty on the prosecution advocate to ensure that the sentencing judge is made aware of the discrepancy and of the consideration which must be given to holding a *Newton* hearing to resolve the issue. The court should be told where a derogatory reference to a victim, witness or third party is not accepted, even though there may be no effect on sentence.

C:10. As emphasised in paragraph IV.45.10 of the consolidated criminal practice direction, whenever an agreement as to the basis of plea is made between the prosecution and defence, any such agreement will be subject to the approval of the trial judge, who may of his or her own motion disregard the agreement and direct that a *Newton* hearing should be held to determine the proper basis on which sentence should be passed.

C:11. Where a defendant declines to admit an offence that he or she previously indicated should be taken into consideration, the prosecution advocate should indicate to the defence advocate and the court that, subject to further review, the offence may now form the basis of a new prosecution.

D. Sentence Indications

D:1. Only in the Crown Court may sentence indications be sought. Advocates there are reminded that indications as to sentence should not be sought from the trial judge unless issues between the prosecution and defence have been addressed and resolved. Therefore, in difficult or complicated cases, no less than seven days notice in writing of an intention to seek an indication should normally be given to the prosecution and the court. When deciding whether the circumstances of a case require such notice to be given, defence advocates are reminded that prosecutors should not agree a basis of plea unless and until the necessary consultation has taken place first with the victim and/or the victim's family and second, in the case of an independent prosecution advocate, with the prosecuting authority.

D:2. If there is no final agreement about the plea to the indictment, or the basis of plea, and the defence nevertheless proceeds to seek an indication of sentence, which the judge appears minded to give, the prosecution advocate should remind him or her of the guidance given in *R. v. Goodyear (Karl)* [2005] EWCA 888 [*sic*] that normally speaking an indication of sentence should not be given until the basis of the plea has been agreed or the judge has concluded that he or she can properly deal with the case without the need for a trial of the issue.

D:3. If an indication is sought, the prosecution advocate should normally enquire whether the judge is in possession of or has access to all the evidence relied on by the prosecution, including any victim personal statement, as well as any information about relevant previous convictions recorded against the defendant.

D:4. Before the judge gives the indication, the prosecution advocate should draw the judge's attention to any minimum or mandatory statutory sentencing requirements. Where the prosecution advocate would be expected to offer the judge assistance with relevant guideline cases or the views of the Sentencing Guidelines Council, he or she should invite the judge to allow them to do so. Where it applies, the prosecution advocate should remind the judge that the position [*sic*] of the Attorney General to refer any sentencing decision as unduly lenient is unaffected. In any event, the prosecution advocate should not say anything which may create the impression that the sentence indication has the support or approval of the Crown.

E. Pleas in Mitigation

E:1. The prosecution advocate must challenge any assertion by the defence in mitigation **A–281** which is derogatory to a person's character (for instance, because it suggests that his or her conduct is or has been criminal, immoral or improper) and which is either false or irrelevant to proper sentencing considerations. If the defence advocate persists in that assertion, the prosecution advocate should invite the court to consider holding a *Newton* hearing to determine the issue.

E:2. The defence advocate must not submit in mitigation anything that is derogatory to a person's character without giving advance notice in writing so as to afford the prosecution advocate the opportunity to consider their position under paragraph E:1. When the prosecution advocate is so notified they must take all reasonable steps to establish whether the assertions are true. Reasonable steps will include seeking the views of the victim. This will involve seeking the views of the victim's family if the victim is deceased, and the victim's parents or legal guardian where the victim is a child. Reasonable steps may also include seeking the views of the police or other law enforcement authority, as appropriate. An assertion which is derogatory to a person's character will rarely amount to mitigation unless it has a causal connection to the circumstances of the offence or is otherwise relevant to proper sentencing considerations.

E:3. Where notice has not been given in accordance with paragraph E:2, the prosecution advocate must not acquiesce in permitting mitigation which is derogatory to a person's character. In such circumstances, the prosecution advocate should draw the attention of the court to the failure to give advance notice and seek time, and if necessary, an adjournment to investigate the assertion in the same way as if proper notice had been given. Where, in the opinion of the prosecution advocate, there are substantial grounds for believing that such an assertion is false or irrelevant to sentence, he or she should inform the court of their opinion and invite the court to consider making an order under section 58(8) of the *Criminal Procedure and Investigations Act* 1996, preventing publication of the assertion.

E:4. Where the prosecution advocate considers that the assertion is, if true, relevant to sentence, or the court has so indicated, he or she should seek time, and if necessary an adjournment, to establish whether the assertion is true. If the matter cannot be resolved to the satisfaction of the parties, the prosecution advocate should invite the court to consider holding a *Newton* hearing to determine the issue.

C. Jury Checks

Introduction

For the background to these guidelines, see § 4–275 in the main work. **A–282**

Attorney-General's Guidelines: Jury checks, 88 Cr.App.R. 123 at 124

1. The principles which are generally to be observed are: **A–283**
   (a) that members of a jury should be selected at random from the panel;
   (b) the *Juries Act* 1974 together with the *Juries Disqualification Act* 1984 identified those classes of persons who alone are disqualified from or ineligible for service on a jury. No other class of person may be treated as disqualified or ineligible;
   (c) the correct way for the Crown to seek to exclude a member of the panel from sitting as a juror is by the exercise in open court of the right to request a stand by or, if necessary, to challenge for cause.

2. Parliament has provided safeguards against jurors who may be corrupt or biased. In addition to the provision for majority verdicts, there is the sanction of a criminal offence for a disqualified person to serve on a jury. The omission of a disqualified person from the panel is a matter for the police as the only authority able to carry out such a search as part of their usual function of preventing the commission of offences. The recommendations of the Association of Chief Police Officers respecting checks on criminal records for disqualified persons are annexed to these guidelines.

3. There are however certain exceptional types of case of public importance for which the provisions as to majority verdicts and the disqualification of jurors may not be sufficient to ensure the **A–284**

proper administration of justice. In such cases it is in the interests both of justice and the public that there should be further safeguards against the possibility of bias and in such cases checks which go beyond the investigation of criminal records may be necessary.

    4. These classes of case may be defined broadly as:

        (a) cases in which national security is involved and part of the evidence is likely to be heard *in camera*;

        (b) terrorist cases.

    5. The particular aspects of these cases which may make it desirable to seek extra precautions are:

        (a) in security cases a danger that a juror, either voluntarily or under pressure, may make an improper use of evidence which, because of its sensitivity has been given *in camera*;

        (b) in both security and terrorist cases the danger that a juror's political beliefs are so biased as to go beyond normally reflecting the broad spectrum of views and interests in the community to reflect the extreme views of sectarian interest or pressure group to a degree which might interfere with his fair assessment of the facts of the case or lead him to exert improper pressure on his fellow jurors.

A–285   6. In order to ascertain whether in exceptional cases of the above nature either of these factors might seriously influence a potential juror's impartial performance of his duties or his respecting the secrecy of evidence given *in camera*, it may be necessary to conduct a limited investigation of the panel. In general, such further investigation beyond one of criminal records made for disqualifications may only be made with the records of Police Special Branches. However, in cases falling under paragraph 4(a) above, (security cases), the investigation may, additionally, involve the security services. No checks other than on these sources and no general enquiries are to be made save to the limited extent that they may be needed to confirm the identity of a juror about whom the initial check has raised serious doubts.

    7. No further investigation, as described in paragraph 6 above, should be made save with the personal authority of the Attorney-General on the application of the Director of Public Prosecutions and such checks are hereafter referred to as "authorised checks." When a Chief Officer of Police has reason to believe that it is likely that an authorised check may be desirable and proper in accordance with these guidelines he should refer the matter to the Director of Public Prosecutions with a view to his having the conduct of the prosecution from an early stage. The Director will make any appropriate application to the Attorney-General.

    8. The result of any authorised check will be sent to the Director of Public Prosecutions. The Director will then decide, having regard to the matters set out in paragraph 5 above, what information ought to be brought to the attention of prosecuting counsel.

    9. No right of stand by should be exercised by Counsel for the Crown on the basis of information obtained as a result of an authorised check save with the personal authority of the Attorney-General and unless the information is such as, having regard to the facts of the case and the offences charged, to afford strong reason for believing that a particular juror might be a security risk, be susceptible to improper approaches or be influenced in arriving at a verdict for the reasons given above.

A–286   10. Where a potential juror is asked to stand by for the Crown, there is no duty to disclose to the defence the information upon which it was founded; but counsel may use his discretion to disclose it if its nature and source permit it.

    11. When information revealed in the course of an authorised check is not such as to cause counsel for the Crown to ask for a juror to stand by, but does give reason to believe that he may be biased against the accused, the defence should be given, at least, an indication of why that potential juror may be inimical to their interests; but because of its nature and source it may not be possible to give the defence more than a general indication.

    12. A record is to be kept by the Director of Public Prosecutions of the use made by counsel of the information passed to him and of the jurors stood by or challenged by the parties to the proceedings. A copy of this record is to be forwarded to the Attorney-General for the sole purpose of enabling him to monitor the operation of these guidelines.

    13. No use of the information obtained as a result of an authorised check is to be made except as may be necessary in direct relation to or arising out of the trial for which the check was authorised.

Annex to the Attorney-General's Guidelines on Jury Checks;
Recommendations of the Association of Chief Police Officers,
88 Cr.App.R. 123 at 125

A–287   1. The Association of Chief Police Officers recommends that in the light of observations made in *Mason*, 71 Cr.App.R. 157 the police should undertake a check of the names of potential jurors against records of previous convictions in any case when the Director of Public Prosecutions or a chief constable considers that in all the circumstances it would be in the interests of justice so to do, namely:

    (i) in any case in which there is reason to believe that attempts are being made to circumvent the statutory provisions excluding disqualified persons from service on a jury, including any case when there is reason to believe that a particular juror may be disqualified;

    (ii) in any case in which it is believed that in a previous related abortive trial an attempt was made to interfere with a juror or jurors;

    (iii) in any other case in which in the opinion of the Director of Public Prosecutions or the chief constable it is particularly important to ensure that no disqualified person serves on the jury.

2. The association also recommends that no further checks should be made unless authorised by the Attorney-General under his guidelines and no inquiries carried out save to the limited extent that they may be needed to confirm the identity of a juror about whom the initial check has raised serious doubts.

3. The Association of Chief Police Officers further recommends that chief constables should agree to undertake checks of jurors, on behalf of the defence only if requested to do so by the Director of Public Prosecutions acting on behalf of the Attorney-General. Accordingly if the police are approached directly with such a request they will refer it to the Director.

4. When, as a result of any checks of criminal records, information is obtained which suggests that, although not disqualified under the terms of the *Juries Act* 1974 a person may be unsuitable to sit as a member of a particular jury the police or the Director may pass the relevant information to prosecuting counsel, who will decide what use to make of it.

D. Prosecution's Right of Stand By

For the background to these guidelines, see §§ 4–304, 4–305 in the main work.   **A–288**

Attorney-General's Guidelines on the Exercise by the Crown of its Right of Stand By, 88 Cr.App.R. 123

1. Although the law has long recognised the right of the Crown to exclude a member of a jury   **A–289** panel from sitting as a juror by the exercise in open court of the right to request a stand by or, if necessary, by challenge for cause, it has been customary for those instructed to prosecute on behalf of the Crown to assert that right only sparingly and in exceptional circumstances. It is generally accepted that the prosecution should not use its right in order to influence the overall composition of a jury or with a view to tactical advantage.

2. The approach outlined above is founded on the principles that:

    (a) the members of a jury should be selected at random from the panel subject to any rule of law as to right of challenge by the defence; and

    (b) the *Juries Act* 1974 together with the *Juries Disqualification Act* 1984 identified those classes of persons who alone are disqualified from or ineligible for service on a jury. No other class of person may be treated as disqualified or ineligible.

3. The enactment by Parliament of section 118 of the *Criminal Justice Act* 1988 abolishing the right of defendants to remove jurors by means of peremptory challenge makes it appropriate that the Crown should assert its right to stand by only on the basis of clearly defined and restrictive criteria. Derogation from the principle that members of a jury should be selected at random should be permitted only where it is essential.

4. Primary responsibility for ensuring that an individual does not serve on a jury if he is not competent to discharge properly the duties of a juror rests with the appropriate court officer and, ultimately, the trial judge. Current legislation provides, in sections 9 and 10 of the *Juries Act* 1974, fairly wide discretions to excuse or discharge jurors either at the person's own request, where he offers "good reason why he should be excused," or where the judge determines that "on account of physical For "disability"substitute infirmity or insufficient understanding of English there is doubt as to his capacity to act effectively as a juror. ..."

5. The circumstances in which it would be proper for the Crown to exercise its right to stand by a member of a jury panel are:

    (a) where a jury check authorised in accordance with the Attorney-General's Guidelines on Jury Checks reveals information justifying exercise of the right to stand by in accordance with paragraph 9 of the guidelines and the Attorney-General personally authorises the exercise of the right to stand by; or

    (b) where a person is about to be sworn as a juror who is manifestly unsuitable and the defence agree that, accordingly, the exercise by the prosecution of the right to stand by would be appropriate. An example of the sort of *exceptional* circumstances which might justify stand by is where it becomes apparent that, despite the provisions mentioned in paragraph 4 above, a juror selected for service to try a complex case is in fact illiterate.

E. Conspiracy To Defraud

A–290   The Attorney-General has issued guidance to prosecuting authorities in relation to charging a common law conspiracy to defraud instead of a substantive offence, contrary to the *Fraud Act* 2006, or a statutory conspiracy to commit a substantive offence, contrary to section 1 of the *CLA* 1977 (§ 33–2 in the main work); the prosecutor should consider (i) whether the conduct alleged falls within the ambit of a statutory offence, and (ii) whether such a charge or charges would adequately reflect the gravity of the alleged offending; as to (i), non-exhaustive examples of circumstances falling outside of the range of statutory offences, but within the ambit of the common law offence, are: (a) the dishonest obtaining of land or other property which cannot be stolen; (b) the dishonest infringement of another's right (*e.g.* the dishonest exploitation of another's patent); (c) an agreement involving an intention that the final offence be committed by someone outside the conspiracy; and (d) an agreement where the conspirators cannot be proved to have had the necessary degree of knowledge for the substantive offence to be perpetrated; as to (ii), prosecution for the common law offence may be more effective where the interests of justice can only be served by presenting an overall picture which could not be achieved by charging a series of substantive offences or statutory conspiracies (because of a large number of counts and/or the possibility of severed trials and evidence on one count being deemed inadmissible on another); where a case lawyer proposes to charge the common law offence, he must consider, and set out in the review note, how much such a charge would add to the amount of evidence likely to be called by the parties, the justification for using the charge, and why specific statutory offences are inadequate or otherwise inappropriate; a supervising lawyer experienced in fraud cases must also specifically approve the charge: *Attorney-General's guidance on the use of the common law offence of conspiracy to defraud*, unreported, January 9, 2007.

F. Prosecutor's Role in Applications for Witness Anonymity Orders

A–291   On July 21, 2008, the Attorney-General issued guidelines on the overarching principles which a prosecutor must consider when deciding whether to apply for witness anonymity orders under the *Criminal Evidence (Witness Anonymity) Act* 2008 (now the *Coroners and Justice Act* 2009, ss.86–97 (§§ 8–151 *et seq.* in the main work)).

    The guidance is in four parts (Part A (foreword), Part B (prosecutor's duties), Part C (applications by defendants) and Part D (appointment and role of special counsel)), and, to a large extent, highlights various provisions of the Act and restates elementary aspects of fairness at trial. Paragraph A2 makes clear that, given that the defendant's right to confront and challenge those who accuse him is an important aspect of a fair trial, making a witness anonymity order is a serious step which must only be taken where there are genuine grounds to believe that the conditions set out in the Act have been satisfied, which must be evaluated with care on the facts of each case. Paragraph B3 sets out the prosecutor's role, which prosecutors must approach in light of their overriding duties to be fair, independent and objective, and which includes a duty: (a) to examine with care and probe where appropriate, the material provided in support of the application and the evidential basis for it, and (b) to put before the court and to disclose to the defendant all material relevant to the application and the defence, including material which may undermine or qualify the prosecution case. Any such material is particularly relevant if credibility is in issue, for example, if there is a known link between the witness and defendant or a co-accused. Paragraph B4 explains that applications should only be authorised by prosecutors of an appropriately senior level. Paragraph D5 explains that a prosecutor making an application for an order must always be prepared to assist the court to consider whether the circumstances are such that exceptionally the appointment of special counsel may be called for, and, where appropriate, should draw to the attention of the court any aspect of the application which may be relevant to such appointment. Where the court decides to invite the Attorney-General to appoint special counsel, the prosecutor should (regardless of any steps taken by the court or any defendant) ensure that the Attorney-General's office is promptly notified and receives all information needed to take a decision as to whether to make such appointment. If special counsel is appointed, the prosecutor should then provide special counsel with open material made available to the accused regarding the application, and any other open material requested by special counsel. Closed or unredacted material which has been provided to the court should only be given to special counsel after open material has been provided and after special counsel has subsequently sought instructions from the defendant and his legal representative.

G. Plea Discussions in Cases of Serious or Complex Fraud

(1) Guidelines

On March 18, 2009, the Attorney-General issued guidelines setting out the process by which a prosecutor may discuss allegations of serious or complex fraud with a person whom he is prosecuting or expecting to prosecute. **A–292**

Attorney General's Guidelines on Plea Discussions in Cases of Serious or Complex Fraud

A. Foreword

A:1 These guidelines set out a process by which a prosecutor may discuss an allegation of serious or complex fraud with a person who he or she is prosecuting or expects to prosecute, or with that person's legal representative. They come into force on the 5th day of May 2009 and apply to plea discussions initiated on or after that date. **A–293**

A:2 The guidelines will be followed by all prosecutors in England and Wales when conducting plea discussions in cases of serious or complex fraud. For the purposes of the guidelines, fraud means any financial, fiscal or commercial misconduct or corruption which is contrary to the criminal law. Fraud may be serious or complex if at least two of the following factors are present:

- the amount obtained or intended to be obtained is alleged to exceed £500,000;
- there is a significant international dimension;
- the case requires specialised knowledge of financial, commercial, fiscal or regulatory matters such as the operation of markets, banking systems, trusts or tax regimes;
- the case involves allegations of fraudulent activity against numerous victims;
- the case involves an allegation of substantial and significant fraud on a public body;
- the case is likely to be of widespread public concern;
- the alleged misconduct endangered the economic well-being of the United Kingdom, for example by undermining confidence in financial markets.

Taking account of these matters, it is for the prosecutor to decide whether or not a case is one of fraud, and whether or not it is serious or complex.

A:3 The decision whether a person should be charged with a criminal offence rests with the prosecutor. In selecting the appropriate charge or charges, the prosecutor applies principles set out in the Code for Crown Prosecutors ("the code"). Charges should reflect the seriousness and extent of the offending, give the court adequate sentencing powers and enable the case to be presented in a clear and simple way. The code also states that prosecutors should not go ahead with more charges to encourage a defendant to plead guilty to a few; equally, prosecutors should not charge a more serious offence to encourage a defendant to plead to a less serious one.

A:4 Once proceedings are instituted, the accused may plead guilty to all of the charges selected. If the defendant will plead guilty to some, but not all, of the charges or to a different, possibly less serious charge, the code states that a prosecutor is entitled to accept such pleas if he or she assesses that the court could still pass an adequate sentence. In taking these decisions the prosecutor also applies the Attorney General's Guidelines on the Acceptance of Pleas and the Prosecutor's Role in the Sentencing Exercise ("the acceptance of pleas guidelines") [*ante*, A–259 *et seq.*].

A:5 The purpose of plea discussions is to narrow the issues in the case with a view to reaching a just outcome at the earliest possible time, including the possibility of reaching an agreement about acceptable pleas of guilty and preparing a joint submission as to sentence.

A:6 The potential benefits of plea discussions are that:

- early resolution of the case may reduce the anxiety and uncertainty for victims and witnesses, and provide earlier clarity for accused persons who admit their guilt (subject to the court's power to reject the agreement);
- the issues in dispute may be narrowed so that even if the case proceeds to trial, it can be managed more efficiently in accordance with rule 3.2 of the *Criminal Procedure Rules* 2005. If pleas are agreed, litigation can be kept to a minimum.

A:7 Where plea discussions take place prior to the commencement of proceedings, the charges brought by the prosecutor will reflect those agreed, rather than those that the prosecutor would necessarily have preferred if no agreement had been reached. Also, any criminal investigation may not be complete when these discussions take place. For these reasons it is important that the procedures followed should command public and judicial confidence; that any agreement reached is reasonable, fair and just; that there are safeguards to ensure that defendants are not under improper pressure to make admissions; and that there are proper records of discussions that have taken place.

A:8 The guidelines are not intended to prevent or discourage existing practices by which prosecutors and prosecuting advocates discuss cases with defence legal representatives after charge, in order to narrow the issues or to agree a basis of plea. Neither do they affect the existing practice of judicial sentence indications at the plea and case management hearing or later in accordance with the guidance in *R. v. Goodyear* [2005] 2 Cr.App.R. 20 (§ 5–110 in the main work) (see also the acceptance of pleas guidelines). They complement, and do not detract from or replace, the code and the acceptance of pleas guidelines, or any other relevant guidance such as the Prosecutor's Pledge, the Victim's Charter and the Code of Practice for Victims of Crime.

A:9 Where a plea agreement is reached, it remains entirely a matter for the court to decide how to deal with the case.

B. General Principles

A–294   **B:1** In conducting plea discussions and presenting a plea agreement to the court, the prosecutor must act openly, fairly and in the interests of justice.

B:2 Acting in the interests of justice means ensuring that the plea agreement reflects the seriousness and extent of the offending, gives the court adequate sentencing powers, and enables the court, the public and the victims to have confidence in the outcome. The prosecutor must consider carefully the impact of a proposed plea or basis of plea on the community and the victim, and on the prospects of successfully prosecuting any other person implicated in the offending. The prosecutor must not agree to a reduced basis of plea which is misleading, untrue or illogical.

B:3 Acting fairly means respecting the rights of the defendant and of any other person who is being or may be prosecuted in relation to the offending. The prosecutor must not put improper pressure on a defendant in the course of plea discussions, for example by exaggerating the strength of the case in order to persuade the defendant to plead guilty, or to plead guilty on a particular basis.

B:4 Acting openly means being transparent with the defendant, the victim and the court. The prosecutor must:

- ensure that a full and accurate record of the plea discussions is prepared and retained;
- ensure that the defendant has sufficient information to enable him or her to play an informed part in the plea discussions;
- communicate with the victim before accepting a reduced basis of plea, wherever it is practicable to do so, so that the position can be explained; and
- ensure that the plea agreement placed before the court fully and fairly reflects the matters agreed. The prosecutor must not agree additional matters with the defendant which are not recorded in the plea agreement and made known to the court.

C. Initiating Plea Discussions

When and with whom discussions should be initiated and conducted

C:1 Where he or she believes it advantageous to do so, the prosecutor may initiate plea discussions with any person who is being prosecuted or investigated with a view to prosecution in connection with a serious or complex fraud, and who is legally represented. The prosecutor will not
initiate plea discussions with a defendant who is not legally represented. If the prosecutor
receives an approach from such a defendant, he or she may enter into discussions if satisfied that
it is appropriate to do so.

C:2 Where proceedings have not yet been instituted, the prosecutor should not initiate plea
discussions until he or she and the investigating officer are satisfied that the suspect's criminality
is known. This will not usually be the case until after the suspect has been interviewed under
caution.

C:3 The prosecutor should be alert to any attempt by the defendant to use plea discussions as
a means of delaying the investigation or prosecution, and should not initiate or continue discussions where the defendant's commitment to the process is in doubt. The prosecutor should
ensure that the position is preserved during plea discussions by, for example, restraining assets
in anticipation of the making of a confiscation order. Where a defendant declines to take part in
plea discussions, the prosecutor should not make a second approach unless there is a material
change in circumstances.

Invitation letter

C:4 In order to initiate the plea discussions, the prosecutor will send the defendant's
representatives a letter which:

- asks whether the defence wish to enter into discussions in accordance with these
  guidelines; and
- sets a deadline for a response from the defence.

Terms and conditions letter

C:5 Where the defence agree to engage in plea discussions, the prosecutor should send them
a letter setting out the way in which the discussions will be conducted. This letter should deal
with:

- the confidentiality of information provided by the prosecutor and defendant in the
  course of the plea discussions;
- the use which may be made by the prosecutor of information provided by the defendant;
  and
- the practical means by which the discussions will be conducted.

Confidentiality and use of information

C:6 In relation to confidentiality, the prosecutor will indicate that he or she intends to provide
an undertaking to the effect that the fact that the defendant has taken part in the plea discussions, and any information provided by the defence in the course of the plea discussions will be
treated as confidential and will not be disclosed to any other party other than for the purposes of
the plea discussions and plea agreement (applying these guidelines), or as required by law. The
undertaking will make it clear that the law in relation to the disclosure of unused material may
require the prosecutor to provide information about the plea discussions to another defendant in
criminal proceedings.

C:7 The prosecutor will require the defendant's legal representative to provide an undertaking to the effect that information provided by the prosecutor in the course of the plea discussions
will be treated as confidential and will not be disclosed to any other party, other than for the
purposes of the plea discussion and plea agreement or as required by law.

C:8 In relation to the use of information, the prosecutor will indicate that he or she intends to
undertake not to rely upon the fact that the defendant has taken part in the plea discussions, or
any information provided by the defendant in the course of the discussions, as evidence in any
prosecution of that defendant for the offences under investigation, should the discussions fail.
However, this undertaking will make it clear that the prosecutor is not prevented from:

- relying upon a concluded and signed plea agreement as confession evidence or as admissions;

- relying upon any evidence obtained from enquiries made as a result of the provision of information by the defendant;
- relying upon information provided by the defendant as evidence against him or her in any prosecution for an offence other than the fraud which is the subject of the plea discussion and any offence which is consequent upon it, such as money laundering; and
- relying upon information provided by the defendant in a prosecution of any other person for any offence (so far as the rules of evidence allow).

C:9 In exceptional circumstances the prosecutor may agree to different terms regarding the confidentiality and use of information. However, the prosecutor must not surrender the ability to rely upon a concluded and signed plea agreement as evidence against the defendant. The prosecutor may reserve the right to bring other charges (additional to those to which the defendant has indicated a willingness to plead guilty) in specific circumstances, for example if substantial new information comes to light at a later stage, the plea agreement is rejected by the court, or the defendant fails to honour the agreement.

C:10 Until the issues of confidentiality and use of information have been agreed to the satisfaction of both parties, and the agreement reflected in signed undertakings, the prosecutor must not continue with the substantive plea discussions.

D. Conducting Plea Discussions

Statement of case

A–296

D:1 Where plea discussions take place prior to proceedings being instituted, the prosecutor will provide a statement of case to the defence. This is a written summary of the nature of the allegation against the suspect and the evidence which has been obtained, or is expected to be obtained, to support it. The statement of case should include a list of the proposed charges. Material in support of the statement of case may also be provided, whether or not in the form of admissible evidence. However, the prosecutor is not obliged to reveal to the suspect all of the information or evidence supporting his case, provided that this does not mislead the suspect to his or her prejudice.

D:2 Where plea discussions are initiated after proceedings have been commenced, but before the prosecutor has provided the defence with a case summary or opening note, the prosecutor may provide a statement of case to assist the defendant in understanding the evidence and identifying the issues.

Unused material

D:3 These guidelines do not affect the prosecutor's existing duties in relation to the disclosure of unused material. Where plea discussions take place prior to the institution of proceedings, the prosecutor should ensure that the suspect is not misled as to the strength of the prosecution case. It will not usually be necessary to provide copies of unused material in order to do this.

Conducting and recording the discussions

D:4 Having provided the defence with the statement of case and supporting material, the parties will then be in a position to conduct the plea discussion proper. Whether this is done by correspondence, by face-to-face meetings or by a combination of the two is a matter for the parties to decide in the individual case.

D:5 It is essential that a full written record is kept of every key action and event in the discussion process, including details of every offer or concession made by each party, and the reasons for every decision taken by the prosecutor. Meetings between the parties should be minuted and the minutes agreed and signed. Particular care should be taken where the defendant is not legally represented. The prosecutor should only meet with a defendant who is not legally represented if the defendant agrees to the meeting being recorded, or to the presence of an independent third party.

Queen's evidence

D:6 If the defendant offers at any stage to provide information, or to give evidence about the criminal activities of others, any such offer will be dealt with in accordance with sections 71 to 75 of the *Serious Organised Crime and Police Act* 2005 ("*SOCPA*"), the judgment of the Court of Appeal in *R. v P.*; *R v Blackburn* [2008] 2 Cr.App.R.(S.) 5 (§ 5–136 in the main work) and the guidance agreed and issued by the Director of Public Prosecutions, the Director of the Serious Fraud Office and the Director of Revenue and Customs Prosecutions.

Discussion of pleas

D:7 In deciding whether or not to accept an offer by the defendant to plead guilty, the prosecutor will follow sections 7 and 10 of the code relating to the selection of charges and the acceptance of guilty pleas. The prosecutor should ensure that:

- the charges reflect the seriousness and extent of the offending;
- they give the court adequate powers to sentence and impose appropriate post-conviction orders;
- they enable the case to be presented in a clear and simple way (bearing in mind that many cases of fraud are necessarily complex);
- the basis of plea enables the court to pass a sentence that matches the seriousness of the offending, particularly if there are aggravating features;
- the interests of the victim, and where possible any views expressed by the victim, are taken into account when deciding whether it is in the public interest to accept the plea; and
- the investigating officer is fully appraised of developments in the plea discussions and his or her views are taken into account.

D:8 In reaching an agreement on pleas, the parties should resolve any factual issues necessary to allow the court to sentence the defendant on a clear, fair and accurate basis. Before agreeing to proposed pleas, the prosecutor should satisfy him or herself that the full code test as set out in the code will be made out in respect of each charge. In considering whether the evidential stage of the test will be met, the prosecutor should assume that the offender will sign a plea agreement amounting to an admission to the charge.

Discussion of sentence

D:9 Where agreement is reached as to pleas, the parties should discuss the appropriate sentence with a view to presenting a joint written submission to the court. This document should list the aggravating and mitigating features arising from the agreed facts, set out any personal mitigation available to the defendant, and refer to any relevant sentencing guidelines or authorities. In the light of all of these factors, it should make submissions as to the applicable sentencing range in the relevant guideline. The prosecutor must ensure that the submissions are realistic, taking full account of all relevant material and considerations.

D:10 The prosecutor should bear in mind all of the powers of the court, and seek to include in the joint submission any relevant ancillary orders. It is particularly desirable that measures should be included that achieve redress for victims (such as compensation orders) and protection for the public (such as directors' disqualification orders, serious crime prevention orders or financial reporting orders).

D:11 Due regard should be had to the court's asset recovery powers and the desirability of using these powers both as a deterrent to others and as a means of preventing the defendant from benefiting from the proceeds of crime or funding future offending. The *Proceeds of Crime Act* 2002 requires the Crown Court to proceed to the making of a confiscation order against a convicted defendant who has benefited from his criminal conduct where the prosecutor asks the court to do so, or the court believes that it is appropriate to do so. Fraud is an acquisitive crime, and the expectation in a fraud case should be that a confiscation order will be sought by the prosecutor reflecting the full benefit to the defendant. However, in doing so it is open to the prosecutor to take a realistic view of the likely approach of the court to the determination of any points in dispute (such as the interest of a third party in any property).

D:12 In the course of the plea discussions the prosecutor must make it clear to the defence that the joint submission as to sentence (including confiscation) is not binding on the court.

Liaison with another prosecutor or regulator

D:13 The prosecutor may become aware that another prosecuting authority or regulatory body (either in England and Wales or elsewhere) has an interest in the defendant. The prosecutor should liaise with the other agency, in accordance with the Prosecutors' Convention and any other relevant agreement or guidance. The other agency may wish to take part in the plea discussions, or they may authorise the prosecutor to discuss with the defendant the matters which they are interested in, with a view to resolving all matters in one plea agreement. The prosecutor should warn the defendant that a plea agreement will not bind any other agency which is not a party to it.

E. The Written Plea Agreement

E:1 All matters agreed between the prosecutor and the defence must be reduced to writing as **A-297** a plea agreement and signed by both parties. The plea agreement will include:

- a list of the charges;

- a statement of the facts; and

- a declaration, signed by the defendant personally, to the effect that he or she accepts the stated facts and admits he or she is guilty of the agreed charges.

E:2 Any agreement under the *SOCPA* regarding the giving of assistance to the prosecutor by the defendant should be in a separate document accompanying the plea agreement.

E:3 Once a plea agreement is signed in a case where proceedings have not yet been commenced, the prosecutor will review the case in accordance with the code and, assuming the evidential stage of the full code test is satisfied on the basis of the signed plea agreement and the other available evidence, will arrange for proceedings to be instituted by summons or charge.

E:4 In advance of the defendant's first appearance in the Crown Court, the prosecutor should send the court sufficient material to allow the judge to understand the facts of the case and the history of the plea discussions, to assess whether the plea agreement is fair and in the interests of justice, and to decide the appropriate sentence. This will include:

- the signed plea agreement;

- a joint submission as to sentence and sentencing considerations;

- any relevant sentencing guidelines or authorities;

- all of the material provided by the prosecution to the defendant in the course of the plea discussions;

- any material provided by the defendant to the prosecution, such as documents relating to personal mitigation; and

- the minutes of any meetings between the parties and any correspondence generated in the plea discussions.

E:5 It will then be for the court to decide how to deal with the plea agreement. In particular, the court retains an absolute discretion as to whether or not it sentences in accordance with the joint submission from the parties.

F. Failure of Plea Discussions

A–298　　**F:1** There are several circumstances in which plea discussions may result in an outcome other than the defendant pleading guilty in accordance with a plea agreement. The prosecutor or the defendant may break off the discussions. They may be unable to reach an agreement. They may reach an agreement, but intervening events may lead the prosecutor to decide that proceedings should not be instituted. Proceedings may be instituted but the court may reject the plea agreement. The defendant may decline to plead guilty in accordance with the plea agreement, either as a result of a sentence indication given under the procedure set out in *R. v. Goodyear*, or for some other reason.

F:2 If any of these situations arises, the prosecutor may wish for further enquiries to be made with a view to bringing or completing proceedings against the defendant. If proceedings have already been instituted, the prosecutor will use the appropriate means to delay them – either discontinuing under section 23 or 23A of the *Prosecution of Offences Act* 1985 or (if the indictment has already been preferred) applying for an adjournment or stay of the proceedings. The prosecutor and the defendant's representatives will continue to be bound by the preliminary undertakings made in relation to the confidentiality and use of information provided in the course of the plea discussions.

F:3 Where plea discussions have broken down for any reason, it will be rare that the prosecutor will wish to re-open them, but he or she may do so if there is a material change in circumstances which warrants it.

(2) Practice

A–299　　Paragraphs IV.45.18 to IV.45.28 of the consolidated criminal practice direction, as inserted by *Practice Direction (Criminal proceedings: substituted and additional provisions)* [2009] 1 W.L.R. 1396, Supreme Court, with effect from May 14, 2009, make provision as to the practice to be followed where a plea agreement has been reached and a joint sentencing submission is to be placed before the court.

**Practice Direction (Criminal Proceedings: Consolidation), paras IV.45.18–IV.45.28 (as inserted by
Practice Direction (Criminal proceedings: substituted and additional provisions)
[2009] 1 W.L.R. 1396)**

IV.45.18 In this part—   **A–300**

(a) "a plea agreement" means a written basis of plea agreed between the prosecution and
defendant(s) in accordance with the principles set out in *R v Underwood* [see § 5–90 in the
main work and *ante*], supported by admissible documentary evidence or admissions under
section 10 of the *Criminal Justice Act* 1967;

(b) "a sentencing submission" means sentencing submissions made jointly by the prosecution
and defence as to the appropriate sentencing authorities and applicable sentencing range in
the relevant sentencing guideline relating to the plea agreement;

(c) "serious or complex fraud" includes, but is not limited to, allegations of fraud where two or
more of the following are present [list as per the guidelines, *ante*, A–293]:

Procedure

IV.45.19 The procedure regarding agreed bases of plea outlined in paragraphs IV.45.10 to   **A–301**
IV.45.12, above [§§ 5–91 *et seq.* in the main work], applies with equal rigour to the acceptance of
pleas under this procedure. However, because under this procedure the parties will have been
discussing the plea agreement and the charges from a much earlier stage, it is vital that the judge is
fully informed of all relevant background to the discussions, charges and the eventual basis of plea.

IV.45.20 Where the defendant has not yet appeared before the Crown Court, the prosecutor
must send full details of the plea agreement and sentencing submission(s) to the court, at least 7 days
in advance of the defendant's first appearance. Where the defendant has already appeared before
the Crown Court, the prosecutor must notify the court as soon as is reasonably practicable that a
plea agreement and sentencing submissions under the Attorney-General's Plea Discussion Guidelines
are to be submitted. The court should set a date for the matter to be heard, and the prosecutor must
send full details of the plea agreement and sentencing submission(s) to the court as soon as
practicable, or in accordance with the directions of the court.

IV.45.21 The provision to the judge of full details of the plea agreement requires sufficient information to be provided to allow the judge to understand the facts of the case and the history of the
plea discussions, to assess whether the plea agreement is fair and in the interests of justice, and to
decide the appropriate sentence. This will include, but is not limited to: (i) the plea agreement; (ii)
the sentencing submission(s); (iii) all of the material provided by the prosecution to the defendant in
the course of the plea discussions; (iv) relevant material provided by the defendant, for example
documents relating to personal mitigation; and (v) the minutes of any meetings between the parties
and any correspondence generated in the plea discussions. The parties should be prepared to
provide additional material at the request of the court.

IV.45.22 The court should at all times have regard to the length of time that has elapsed since
the date of the occurrence of the events giving rise to the plea discussions, the time taken to
interview the defendant, the date of charge and the prospective trial date (if the matter were to
proceed to trial) so as to ensure that its consideration of the plea agreement and sentencing submissions does not cause any unnecessary further delay.

Status of plea agreement and joint sentencing submissions

IV.45.23 Where a plea agreement and joint sentencing submissions are submitted, it remains   **A–302**
entirely a matter for the court to decide how to deal with the case. The judge retains the absolute
discretion to refuse to accept the plea agreement and to sentence otherwise than in accordance with
the sentencing submissions made under the Attorney-General's Plea Discussion Guidelines.

IV.45.24 Sentencing submissions should draw the court's attention to any applicable range in
any relevant guideline, and to any ancillary orders that may be applicable. Sentencing submissions
should not include a specific sentence or agreed range other than the ranges set out in sentencing
guidelines or authorities.

IV.45.25 Prior to pleading guilty in accordance with the plea agreement, the defendant(s) may
apply to the court for an indication of the likely maximum sentence [in accordance with *R. v. Goood-
year*, as to which, see § 5–110 in the main work].

IV.45.26 In the event that the judge indicates a sentence or passes a sentence which is not within
the submissions made on sentencing, the plea agreement remains binding.

IV.45.27 If the defendant does not plead guilty in accordance with the plea agreement or if a defendant who has pleaded guilty in accordance with a plea agreement successfully applies to withdraw
his plea under rule 39.3 of the *Criminal Procedure Rules*, the signed plea agreement may be treated

as confession evidence, and may be used against the defendant at a later stage in these or any other proceedings. Any credit for a timely guilty plea may be lost. The court may exercise its discretion under section 78 of the *Police and Criminal Evidence Act* 1984 to exclude any such evidence ... .

IV.45.28 Where a defendant has failed to plead guilty in accordance with a plea agreement, for example in the circumstances set out in paragraph IV.45.27, above, the case is unlikely to be ready for trial immediately. The prosecution may have been commenced earlier than it otherwise would have been, in reliance upon the defendant's agreement to plead guilty. This is likely to be a relevant consideration for the court in deciding whether or not to grant an application to adjourn or stay the proceedings to allow the matter to be prepared for trial in accordance with the protocol on the Control and Management of Heavy Fraud and other Complex Criminal Cases, or as required.

(3) Authorities

A–303   As to the limitations on prosecuting authorities' power to enter into agreements (with overseas authorities or a potential accused) as to how a case should be disposed of, see *R. v. Innospec Ltd*, § 1–369 in the main work. As to this case, see also § 5–804 in the main work.

In *R. v. Dougall* [2011] 1 Cr.App.R.(S.) 37, CA, it was said that a joint submission as to sentence pursuant to the Attorney-General's Guidelines on Plea Discussions in Cases of Serious or Complex Fraud, *ante*, should recognise that it is the court alone that decides on sentence, should avoid advocacy of a particular outcome, and should confine itself to the appropriate range within which it is said the sentence should fall. As to this case, see also § 5–138 in the main work.

H. Asset Recovery Powers of Prosecuting Authorities

A–304   The Attorney-General and the Home Secretary have issued joint guidance under section 2A of the *PCA* 2002 to the Serious Organised Crime Agency, the DPP, the Director of Revenue and Customs Prosecutions, the Director of the Serious Fraud Office and the DPP for Northern Ireland directing them to consider using their civil asset recovery powers under the 2002 Act wherever proceeds of crime have been identified but it is not feasible to secure a conviction, or a conviction has been secured but no confiscation order made (para. 2). They must also consider whether the public interest might be better served by using these powers, rather than by instituting a criminal investigation or prosecution, whilst applying the principle that a criminal disposal will generally make the best contribution to the reduction of crime (para. 3). Paragraph 4 states that the factors listed in the Code for Crown Prosecutors (*post*, Appendix E–6) as being relevant to the question whether a prosecution would be in the public interest might also be relevant when considering at any stage whether or not the civil recovery powers should be used; but it is emphasised that a potential defendant should not be able to escape an appropriate prosecution by the simple device of agreeing to a civil recovery order. Paragraph 5 contains a nonexhaustive list of circumstances in which use of the powers might be appropriate because it is not feasible to secure a conviction and paragraph 6 contains an equivalent list for where a conviction is feasible but where the public interest might be better served by use of these powers. Paragraph 8 sets out the ways in which the relevant authorities should seek to minimise any potential prejudice to a related or potential criminal investigation or proceedings, including through the disclosure of relevant information. Paragraph 9 confirms that the guidance does not prohibit (i) a criminal investigation being carried out by a law enforcement authority at the same time as a civil recovery and/ or a tax investigation; (ii) civil recovery and/ or tax proceedings being instituted where a criminal investigation by a law enforcement authority is being carried out at the same time into unrelated criminality (subject to the duty set out in para. 8, *ante*); or (iii) criminal proceedings being instituted or carried on by a prosecuting authority at the same time as a civil recovery and/ or tax investigation is being carried out. However, paragraph 10 prohibits in all circumstances criminal and civil/ tax proceedings being carried on at the same time in relation to the same criminality. Where criminal proceedings have been stayed by a court, or cannot progress (*e.g.* because the defendant has absconded), they are not being "carried on" for the purposes of this prohibition. Paragraph 11 sets out the circumstances in which a relevant authority may agree to accept a reduced sum in satisfaction of a civil recovery claim.For the full text of the guidance, see http://www.attorneygeneral.gov.uk/Publications/Pages/AttorneyGeneralsGuidelines.aspx.

APPENDIX B

Interpretation Act 1978

General provisions as to enactment and operation

Words of enactment
1. Every section of an Act takes effect as a substantive enactment without introductory words.

B–1

Amendment or repeal in same Session
2. Any Act may be amended or repealed in the Session of Parliament in which it is passed.

B–2

Judicial notice
3. Every Act is a public Act to be judicially noticed as such, unless the contrary is expressly provided by the Act.

B–3

Time of commencement
4. An Act or provision of an Act comes into force—
    (a) where provision is made for it to come into force on a particular day, at the beginning of that day;
    (b) where no provision is made for its coming into force, at the beginning of the day on which the Act receives the Royal Assent.

B–4

Interpretation and construction

Definitions
5. In any Act, unless the contrary intention appears, words and expressions listed in Schedule 1 to this Act are to be construed according to that Schedule.

B–5

Gender and number
6. In any Act, unless the contrary intention appears,—
    (a) words importing the masculine gender include the feminine;
    (b) words importing the feminine gender include the masculine;
    (c) words in the singular include the plural and words in the plural include the singular.

B–6

References to service by post
7. Where an Act authorises or requires any document to be served by post (whether the expression "serve" or the expression "give" or "send" or any other expression is used) then, unless the contrary intention appears, the service is deemed to be effected by properly addressing, prepaying and posting a letter containing the document and, unless the contrary is proved, to have been effected at the time at which the letter would be delivered in the ordinary course of post.

B–7

References to distance
8. In the measurement of any distance for the purposes of an Act, that distance shall, unless the contrary intention appears, be measured in a straight line on a horizontal plane.

B–8

References to time of day
9. Subject to section 3 of the *Summer Time Act* 1972 (construction of references to points of time during the period of summer time), whenever an expression of time occurs in an Act, the time referred to shall, unless it is otherwise specifically stated, be held to be Greenwich mean time.

B–9

References to Sovereign
10. In any Act a reference to the Sovereign reigning at the time of the passing of the Act is to be construed, unless the contrary intention appears, as a reference to the Sovereign for the time being.

B–10

Construction of subordinate legislation
11. Where an Act confers power to make subordinate legislation, expressions used in that legislation have, unless the contrary intention appears, the meaning which they bear in the Act.

B–11

B–12 *Archbold's Criminal Pleading—2012 ed.*

Statutory powers and duties

Continuity of powers and duties

B–12   **12.**—(1) Where an Act confers a power or imposes a duty it is implied, unless the contrary intention appears, that the power may be exercised, or the duty is to be performed, from time to time as occasion requires.

(2) Where an Act confers a power or imposes a duty on the holder of an office as such, it is implied, unless the contrary intention appears, that the power may be exercised, or the duty is to be performed, by the holder for the time being of the office.

Anticipatory exercise of powers

B–13   **13.** Where an Act which (or any provision of which) does not come into force immediately on its passing confers power to make subordinate legislation, or to make appointments, give notices, prescribe forms or do any other thing for the purposes of the Act, then, unless the contrary intention appears, the power may be exercised, and any instrument made thereunder may be made so as to come into force, at any time after the passing of the Act so far as may be necessary or expedient for the purpose—

    (a) of bringing the Act or any provision of the Act into force; or

    (b) of giving full effect to that Act or any such provision at or after the time when it comes into force.

Implied power to amend

B–14   **14.** Where an Act confers power to make—

    (a) rules, regulations or byelaws; or

    (b) Orders in Council, orders or other subordinate legislation to be made by statutory instrument,

it implies, unless the contrary intention appears, a power exercisable in the same manner and subject to the same conditions or limitations, to revoke, amend or re-enact any instrument made under the power.

Repealing enactments

Repeal of repeal

B–15   **15.** Where an Act repeals a repealing enactment, the repeal does not revive any enactment previously repealed unless words are added reviving it.

General savings

B–16   **16.**—(1) Without prejudice to section 15, where an Act repeals an enactment, the repeal does not, unless the contrary intention appears,—

    (a) revive anything not in force or existing at the time at which the repeal takes effect;

    (b) affect the previous operation of the enactment repealed or anything duly done or suffered under that enactment;

    (c) affect any right, privilege, obligation or liability acquired, accrued or incurred under that enactment;

    (d) affect any penalty, forfeiture or punishment incurred in respect of any offence committed against that enactment;

    (e) affect any investigation, legal proceeding or remedy in respect of any such right, privilege, obligation, liability, penalty, forfeiture or punishment;

and any such investigation, legal proceeding or remedy may be instituted, continued or enforced, and any such penalty, forfeiture or punishment may be imposed, as if the repealing Act had not been passed.

(2) This section applies to the expiry of a temporary enactment as if it were repealed by an Act.

[Considered in *R. v. West London Stipendiary Magistrate, ex p. Simeon* [1983] A.C. 234, HL. See also *Hough v. Windus* (1884) 12 Q.B.D. 224, and *R. v. Fisher (Charles)* [1969] 1 W.L.R. 8, CA.]

Repeal and re-enactment

B–17   **17.**—(1) Where an Act repeals a previous enactment and substitutes provisions for the enactment repealed, the repealed enactment remains in force until the substitute provisions come into force.

(2) Where an Act repeals and re-enacts, with or without modification, a previous enactment then, unless the contrary intention appears,—

(a) any reference in any other enactment to the enactment so repealed shall be construed as a reference to the provision re-enacted;

(b) in so far as any subordinate legislation made or other thing done under the enactment so repealed, or having effect as if so made or done, could have been made or done under the provision re-enacted, it shall have effect as if made or done under that provision.

Miscellaneous

Duplicated offences

18. Where an act or omission constitutes an offence under two or more Acts, or both under an Act and at common law, the offender shall, unless the contrary intention appears, be liable to be prosecuted and punished under either or any of those Acts or at common law, but shall not be liable to be punished more than once for the same offence.

B–18

See in the main work, § 4–189.

Citation of other Acts

19. Where an Act cites another Act by year, statute, session or chapter, or a section or other portion of another Act by number or letter, the reference shall, unless the contrary intention appears, be read as referring—

B–19

(a) in the case of Acts included in any revised edition of the statutes printed by authority, to that edition;

(b) in the case of Acts not so included but included in the edition prepared under the direction of the Record Commission, to that edition;

(c) in any other case, to the Acts printed by the Queen's Printer, or under the superintendence or authority of Her Majesty's Stationery Office.

(2) An Act may continue to be cited by the short title authorised by any enactment notwithstanding the repeal of that enactment.

References to other enactments

20.—(1) Where an Act describes or cites a portion of an enactment by referring to words, sections or other parts from or to which or from and to which the portion extends, the portion described or cited includes the words, sections or other parts referred to unless the contrary intention appears.

B–20

(2) Where an Act refers to an enactment, the reference unless the contrary intention appears, is a reference to that enactment as amended, and includes a reference thereto as extended or applied, by or under any other enactment, including any other provision of that Act.

References to EU instruments

20A. Where an Act passed after the commencement of this section refers to a EU instrument that has been amended, extended or applied by another such instrument, the reference, unless the contrary intention appears, is a reference to that instrument as so amended, extended or applied.

B–20a

[This section was inserted by the *Legislative and Regulatory Reform Act* 2006, s.25(1). It is printed as amended by the *European Union (Amendment) Act* 2008, s.3, and Sched., Pt 2.]

Supplementary

Interpretation, etc.

21.—(1) In this Act "Act" includes a local and personal or private Act; and "subordinate legislation" means Orders in Council, orders, rules, regulations, schemes, warrants, byelaws and other instruments made or to be made under any Act.

B–21

(2) This Act binds the Crown.

Application to Acts and Measures

22.—(1) This Act applies to itself, to any Act passed after the commencement of this Act

B–22

(subject, in the case of section 20A, to the provision made in that section) and, to the extent specified in Part I of Schedule 2, to Acts passed before the commencement of this Act.

(2) In any of the foregoing provisions of this Act a reference to an Act is a reference to an Act to which that provision applies; but this does not affect the generality of references to enactments or of the references in section 19(1) to other Acts.

(3) This Act applies to Measures of the General Synod of the Church of England (and, so far as it relates to Acts passed before the commencement of this Act, to Measures of the Church Assembly passed after May 28, 1925) as it applies to Acts.

[This section is printed as amended by the *Legislative and Regulatory Reform Act* 2006, s.25(2).]

Application to other instruments

B–23   **23.**—(1) The provisions of this Act, except sections 1 to 3 and 4(b), apply, so far as applicable and unless the contrary intention appears, to subordinate legislation made after the commencement of this Act and, to the extent specified in Part II of Schedule 2, to subordinate legislation made before the commencement of this Act, as they apply to Acts.

(2) In the application of this Act to Acts passed or subordinate legislation made after the commencement of this Act, all references to an enactment include an enactment comprised in subordinate legislation whenever made, and references to the passing or repeal of an enactment are to be construed accordingly.

(3) Sections 9 and 19(1) also apply to deeds and other instruments and documents as they apply to Acts and subordinate legislation; and in the application of section 17(2)(a) to Acts passed or subordinate legislation made after the commencement of this Act, the reference to any other enactment includes any deed or other instrument or document.

(4) Subsections (1) and (2) of this section do not apply to Orders in Council made under section 5 of the *Statutory Instruments Act* 1946, section 1(3) of the *Northern Ireland (Temporary Provisions) Act* 1972 or Schedule 1 to the *Northern Ireland Act* 1974.

B–23a   **23A.** [*Acts of the Scottish Parliament, etc.*]
B–23b   **23B.** [*Measures and Acts of the National Assembly for Wales, etc.*]
B–24   **24.** [*Application to Northern Ireland.*]

Repeals and savings

B–25   **25.**—(1) The enactments described in Schedule 3 are repealed to the extent specified in the third column of that Schedule.

(2) Without prejudice to section 17(2)(a), a reference to the *Interpretation Act* 1889, to any provision of that Act or to any other enactment repealed by this Act whether occurring in another Act, in subordinate legislation, in Northern Ireland legislation or in any deed or other instrument or document, shall be construed as referring to this Act, or to the corresponding provision of this Act, as it applies to Acts passed at the time of the reference.

(3) The provisions of this Act relating to Acts passed after any particular time do not affect the construction of Acts passed before that time, though continued or amended by Acts passed thereafter.

B–26   **26.** [*Commencement.*]
B–27   **27.** [*Short title.*]

SCHEDULES

SCHEDULE 1

Words and Expressions Defined

B–28   *Note*: The years or dates which follow certain entries in this Schedule are relevant for the purposes of paragraph 4 of Schedule 2 (application to existing enactments).

Definitions

.... .

"Bank of England" means, as the context requires, the Governor and Company of the Bank of England or the bank of the Governor and Company of the Bank of England.

.... .

"British Islands" means the United Kingdom, the Channel Islands and the Isle of Man. [1889]
"British possession" means any part of Her Majesty's dominions outside the United Kingdom; and

where parts of such dominions are under both a central and local legislature, all parts under the central legislature are deemed, for the purposes of this definition, to be one British possession. [1889]

... .

"Central funds", in an enactment providing in relation to England and Wales for the payment of costs out of central funds, means money provided by Parliament.

... .

"Civil partnership" means a civil partnership which exists under or by virtue of the *Civil Partnership Act* 2004 (and any reference to a civil partner is to be read accordingly).

[This definition is inserted by the *Civil Partnership Act* 2004, s.261(1), and Sched. 27, para. 59.]

"Colonial legislature", and "legislature" in relation to a British possession, mean the authority, other than the Parliament of the United Kingdom or Her Majesty in Council, competent to make laws for the possession. [1889]

"Colony" means any part of Her Majesty's dominions outside the British Islands except—

    (a) countries having fully responsible status within the Commonwealth;

    (b) territories for whose external relations a country other than the United Kingdom is responsible;

    (c) associated states; and where parts of such dominions are under both a central and a local legislature, all parts under the central legislature are deemed for the purposes of this definition to be one colony. [1889]

"Commencement", in relation to an Act or enactment, means the time when the Act or enactment comes into force.

"Committed for trial" means—

    (a) *in relation to England and Wales, committed in custody or on bail by a magistrates' court pursuant to section 6 of the* Magistrates' Courts Act *1980 , or by any judge or other authority having power to do so, with a view to trial before a judge and jury;* [1989]

    (b) [*Northern Ireland*].

[This definition is printed as amended by the *MCA* 1980, s.154 and Sched. 7, para. 169. ★ Paragraph (a) is repealed as from a day to be appointed: *CJA* 2003, ss.41 and 332, Sched. 3, para.49(a), and Sched. 37, Pt 4. This amendment came into force on June 18, 2012 (*Criminal Justice Act 2003 (Commencement No. 28 and Saving Provisions) Order* 2012 (S.I. 2012 No. 1320)) in certain areas (as to which, see *ante*, § 1–88). There are associated saving provisions, as to which, see article 5 of the order (*ante*, § 1–88).]

"The EU", or "the EU Treaties" and other expressions defined by section 1 of and Schedule 1 to the *European Communities Act* 1972 have the meanings prescribed by that Act.

[This definition is printed as amended by the *European Union (Amendment) Act* 2008, s.3, and Sched., Pt 2.]

... .

"Consular officer" has the meaning assigned by Article 1 of the Vienna Convention set out in Schedule 1 to the *Consular Relations Act* 1968.

... .

"County Court" means—

    (a) in relation to England and Wales, a court held for a district under the *County Courts Act* 1984;

    (b) [*Northern Ireland*].

[This definition is printed as amended by the *County Courts Act* 1984, Sched. 2.]

"Court of Appeal" means—

    (a) in relation to England and Wales, Her Majesty's Court of Appeal in England;

    (b) in relation to Northern Ireland, Her Majesty's Court of Appeal in Northern Ireland.

"Court of summary jurisdiction", "summary conviction" and "Summary Jurisdiction Acts", in relation to Northern Ireland, have the same meanings as in Measures of the Northern Ireland Assembly and Acts of the Parliament of Northern Ireland.

"Crown Court" means—

> (a) in relation to England and Wales, the Crown Court constituted by section 4 of the *Courts Act* 1971;
>
> (b) [*Northern Ireland*].

. . . .

"EEA agreement" means the agreement on the European Economic Area signed at Oporto on 2nd May 1992, together with the Protocol adjusting that Agreement signed at Brussels on 17th March 1993, as modified or supplemented from time to time. [The date of the coming into force of this paragraph.]

"EEA state", in relation to any time, means—

> (a) a state which at that time is a member State; or
>
> (b) any other state which at that time is a party to the EEA agreement. [The date of the coming into force of this paragraph.]

[These two definitions were inserted, as from January 8, 2007, by the *Legislative and Regulatory Reform Act* 2006, s.26(1).]

"England" means, subject to any alteration of boundaries under Part IV of the *Local Government Act* 1972, the area consisting of the counties established by section 1 of that Act, Greater London and the Isles of Scilly. [1st April 1974]

. . . .

"Governor-General" includes any person who for the time being has the powers of the Governor-General, and "Governor", in relation to any British possession, includes the officer for the time being administering the government of that possession. [1889]

"Her Majesty's Revenue and Customs" has the meaning given by section 4 of the *Commissioners for Revenue and Customs Act* 2005.

[This definition was inserted by the *Commissioners for Revenue and Customs Act* 2005, s.4(3).]

"High Court" means—

> (a) in relation to England and Wales, Her Majesty's High Court of Justice in England;
>
> (b) in relation to Northern Ireland, Her Majesty's High Court of Justice in Northern Ireland.

. . . .

"Land" includes buildings and other structures, land covered with water, and any estate, interest, easement, servitude or right in or over land. [1st January 1979]

. . . .

["Local policing body" has the meaning given by section 101(1) of the *Police Act* 1996.]

[This definition is inserted, as from a day to be appointed, by the *Police Reform and Social Responsibility Act* 2011, s.97(1) and (2).]

"London borough" means a borough described in Schedule 1 to the *London Government Act* 1963, "inner London borough" means one of the boroughs so described and numbered from 1 to 12 and "outer London borough" means one of the boroughs so described and numbered 13 to 32, subject (in each case) to any alterations made under Part IV of the *Local Government Act* 1972 or Part II of the *Local Government Act* 1992.

[This definition is printed as amended by the *Local Government Act* 1992, s.27(1), and Sched. 3, para. 21.]

"Lord Chancellor" means the Lord High Chancellor of Great Britain.

"Magistrates' court" has the meaning assigned to it—

> (a) in relation to England and Wales, by section 148 of the *Magistrates' Courts Act* 1980;
>
> (b) [*Northern Ireland*].

[This definition is printed as amended by the *MCA* 1980, s.154, and Sched. 7, para. 169.]

"Month" means calendar month. [1850]

. . . .

"Oath" and "affidavit" include affirmation and declaration, and "swear" includes affirm and
declare.
"Officer of Revenue and Customs" has the meaning given by section 2(1) of the *Commissioners for
Revenue and Customs Act* 2005.

[This definition was inserted by the *Commissioners for Revenue and Customs Act* 2005,
s.2(7).]

"Ordnance Map" means a map made under powers conferred by the *Ordnance Survey Act* 1841 or
the *Boundary Survey (Ireland) Act* 1854.
"Parliamentary Election" means the election of a Member to serve in Parliament for a constituency.
[1889]
"Person" includes a body of persons corporate or unincorporate. [1889]
["Police and crime commissioner" means a police and crime commissioner established under section 1 of the *Police Reform and Social Responsibility Act* 2011.]

[This definition is inserted, as from a day to be appointed, by the *Police Reform and Social
Responsibility Act* 2011, s.97(1) and (3).]

"Police area", "*police authority*" and other expressions relating to the police have the meaning or
effect described—
    (a) in relation to England and Wales, by section 101(1) of the *Police Act* 1996;
    (b) [*Scotland*].

[This definition is printed as amended by the *Police Act* 1996, Sched. 7, para. 32; and as
amended, as from a day to be appointed, by the *Police Reform and Social Responsibility Act*
2011, s.97(1) and (4) (omission of italicised words and preceding comma).]

["Police authority", in relation to Scotland, has the meaning or effect described by sections 50 and
51(4) of the *Police (Scotland) Act* 1967.]

[This definition is inserted, as from a day to be appointed, by the *Police Reform and Social
Responsibility Act* 2011, s.97(1) and (5).]

"The Privy Council" means the Lords and others of Her Majesty's Most Honourable Privy Council.
"Registered" in relation to nurses, midwives and health visitors, means registered in the register
maintained by the United Kingdom Central Council for Nursing, Midwifery and Health
Visiting by virtue of qualifications in nursing, midwifery or health visiting, as the case may be.

[This definition was inserted by the *Nurses, Midwives and Health Visitors Act* 1979, s.23(4),
and Sched. 7, para. 30.]

"Registered medical practitioner" means a fully registered person within the meaning of the *Medical Act* 1983 who holds a licence to practise under that Act. [1st January 1979]

[This definition is printed as amended by the *Medical Act* 1983, s.56(1), and Sched. 5,
para. 18; and the *Medical Act 1983 (Amendment) Order* 2002 (S.I 2002 No. 3135), Sched.1,
para. 10.]

"Rules of Court" in relation to any court means rules made by the authority having power to
make rules or orders regulating the practice and procedure of that court, and in Scotland
includes Acts of Adjournal and Acts of Sederunt; and the power of the authority to make
rules of court (as above defined) includes power to make such rules for the purpose of any
Act which directs or authorises anything to be done by rules of court. [1889]
"Secretary of State" means one of Her Majesty's Principal Secretaries of State.
"Senior Courts" means the Senior Courts of England and Wales.

[This definition was inserted by the *Constitutional Reform Act* 2005, s.59(5), and Sched. 11,
para. 24.]

["Sent for trial" means, in relation to England and Wales, sent by a magistrates' court to the
Crown Court for trial pursuant to section 51 or 51A of the *Crime and Disorder Act* 1998.]

[This definition is inserted, as from a day to be appointed, by the *CJA* 2003, s.41, and ★

Sched. 3, para. 49(b). This insertion took effect on June 18, 2012 (*Criminal Justice Act 2003 (Commencement No. 28 and Saving Provisions) Order* 2012 (S.I. 2012 No. 1320)) in certain areas (as to which, see *ante*, § 1–88). There are associated saving provisions, as to which, see article 5 of the order (*ante*, § 1–88).]

... .

"Sheriff", in relation to Scotland, includes sheriff principal. [1889]
"The standard scale", with reference to a fine or penalty for an offence triable only summarily,—
>   (a) in relation to England and Wales, has the meaning given by section 37 of the *Criminal Justice Act* 1982;
>   (b) [*Scotland*];
>   (c) [*Northern Ireland*].

[This definition was inserted by the *CJA* 1988, s.170(1), and Sched. 15, para. 58(a). (For s.37 of the 1982 Act, see the main work, § 5–683.)]

"Statutory declaration" means a declaration made by virtue of the *Statutory Declarations Act* 1835.
"Statutory maximum", with reference to a fine or penalty on summary conviction for an offence—
>   (a) in relation to England and Wales, means the prescribed sum within the meaning of section 32 of the *Magistrates' Courts Act* 1980;
>   (b) [*Scotland*]; and
>   (c) [*Northern Ireland*].

[This definition was inserted by the *CJA* 1988, s.170(1), and Sched. 15, para. 58(b). (For s.32 of the 1980 Act, see the main work, § 1–123.)]

"Supreme Court" means the Supreme Court of the United Kingdom.

[This definition is printed as amended by the *Constitutional Reform Act* 2005, s.59(5), and Sched. 11, para. 24.]

"The Treasury" means the Commissioners of Her Majesty's Treasury.
"United Kingdom" means Great Britain and Northern Ireland. [12th April 1927]
"Wales" means the combined area of the counties which were created by section 20 of the *Local Government Act* 1972, as originally enacted, but subject to any alteration made under section 73 of that Act (consequential alteration of boundary following alteration of watercourse) [1st April 1974]

[This definition was substituted by the *Local Government (Wales) Act* 1994, Sched. 2, para. 9.]

... .

"Writing" includes typing, printing, lithography, photography and other modes of representing or reproducing words in avisible form, and expressions referring to writing are construed accordingly.

Construction of certain expressions relating to offences

In relation to England and Wales—
>   (a) "indictable offence" means an offence which, if committed by an adult, is triable on indictment, whether it is exclusively so triable or triable either way;
>   (b) "summary offence" means an offence which, if committed by an adult, is triable only summarily;
>   (c) "offence triable either way" means an offence, other than an offence triable on indictment only by virtue of Part V of the *Criminal Justice Act* 1988 which, if committed by an adult, is triable either on indictment or summarily;
and the terms "indictable", "summary" and "triable either way", in their application to offences are to be construed accordingly.
In the above definitions references to the way or ways in which an offence is triable are to be construed without regard to the effect, if any, of section 22 of the *Magistrates' Courts Act* 1980 on the mode of trial in a particular case.

[This para. is printed as amended by the *MCA* 1980, Sched. 7; and the *CJA* 1988, Sched. 15, para. 59.]

Construction of certain references to relationships

In relation to England and Wales—

(a) references (however expressed) to any relationship between two persons;

(b) references to a person whose father and mother were or were not married to each other at the time of his birth; and

(c) references cognate with references falling within paragraph (b) above,

shall be construed in accordance with section 1 of the *Family Law Reform Act* 1987. [The date of the coming into force of that section.]

[This para. was added by Schedule 2 to the *Family Law Reform Act* 1987.]

NOTE: the definitions of the following expressions have been omitted: "Associated state", "Bank of Ireland", "Building regulations", "Charity Commissioners", "Comptroller and Auditor General", "Consular officer", "The Corporation Tax Acts", "Crown Estate Commissioners", "Financial year", "The Income Tax Acts", "Lands Clauses Act", "National Debt Commissioners", "Northern Ireland legislation", "Sewerage undertaker", "The Tax Acts" and "Water undertaker".

SCHEDULE 2

APPLICATION OF ACT TO EXISTING ENACTMENTS

PART I

ACTS

1. The following provisions of this Act apply to Acts whenever passed:—   **B–29**

    Section 6(a) and (c) so far as applicable to enactments relating to offences punishable on indictment or on summary conviction

    Section 9

    Section 10

    Section 11 so far as it relates to subordinate legislation made after the year 1889

    Section 18

    Section 19(2).

2. The following apply to Acts passed after the year 1850:—

    Section 1

    Section 2

    Section 3

    Section 6(a) and (c) so far as not applicable to such Acts by virtue of paragraph 1

    Section 15

    Section 17(1).

3. The following apply to Acts passed after the year 1889:—

    Section 4

    Section 7

    Section 8

    Section 12

    Section 13

    Section 14 so far as it relates to rules, regulations or byelaws

    Section 16(1)

    Section 17(2)(a)

    Section 19(1)

    Section 20(1).

4.—(1) Subject to the following provisions of this paragraph—

(a) paragraphs of Schedule 1 at the end of which a year or date is specified or described apply, so far as applicable, to Acts passed on or after the date, or after the year, so specified or described; and

(b) paragraphs of that Schedule at the end of which no year or date is specified or described apply, so far as applicable, to Acts passed at any time.

(2) The definition of "British Islands", in its application to Acts passed after the establishment of the Irish Free State but before the commencement of this Act, includes the Republic of Ireland.

(3) The definition of "colony", in its application to an Act passed at any time before the commencement of this Act, includes—

(a) any colony within the meaning of section 18(3) of the *Interpretation Act* 1889 which was excluded, but in relation only to Acts passed at a later time, by any enactment repealed by this Act;

(b) any country or territory which ceased after that time to be part of Her Majesty's dominions but subject to a provision for the continuation of existing law as if it had not so ceased;

and paragraph (b) of the definition does not apply.

(4) The definition of "Lord Chancellor" does not apply to Acts passed before 1st October 1921 in which that expression was used in relation to Ireland only.

(5) The definition of "person", so far as it includes bodies corporate, applies to any provision of an Act whenever passed relating to an offence punishable on indictment or on summary conviction.

(6) This paragraph applies to the *National Health Service Reorganisation Act* 1973 and the *Water Act* 1973 as if they were passed after 1st April 1974.

[Para. 4 is printed as amended by the *Family Law Reform Act* 1987, Scheds 2 and 4.]

5. The following definitions shall be treated as included in Schedule 1 for the purposes specified in this paragraph—

(a) in any Act passed before 1st April 1974, a reference to England includes Berwick upon Tweed and Monmouthshire and, in the case of an Act passed before the *Welsh Language Act* 1967, Wales;

(b) in any Act passed before the commencement of this Act and after the year 1850, "land" includes messuages, tenements and hereditaments, houses and buildings of any tenure;

(c) [*Scotland*].

PART II

SUBORDINATE LEGISLATION

B–30

6. Sections 4(a), 9 and 19(1), and so much of Schedule 1 as defines the following expressions, namely—

England;

Local land charges register and appropriate local land charges register;

Police area (and related expressions) in relation to Scotland;

United Kingdom;

Wales;

apply to subordinate legislation made at any time before the commencement of this Act as they apply to Acts passed at that time.

[Para. 6 is printed as repealed in part by the *British Nationality Act* 1981, Sched. 9.]

7. The definition in Schedule 1 of "county court", in relation to England and Wales, applies to Orders in Council made after the year 1846.

APPENDIX C

The Duties of Advocates

I. CODE OF CONDUCT

The eighth edition of the *Code of Conduct for the Bar of England and Wales* came into force   **C–1**
on October 31, 2004.

CODE OF CONDUCT FOR THE BAR OF ENGLAND AND WALES

Table of contents

Those provisions marked with an asterisk (*) are set out in full below.   **C–2**

Table of Annexes

PART I—PRELIMINARY

C–3   **101** The Eighth Edition of the Code was adopted by the Bar Council on 18 September 2004 and came into force on 31st October 2004.

102 This Code includes the Annexes.

103 Amendments and additions to this Code may be made by Resolution of the Bar Council which shall be operative upon such date as the Resolution shall appoint or if no such date is appointed on the later of:

(a) the date of the Resolution; and

(b) the date when approval of the amendment or addition, if required, is given under Schedule 4 of the Act.

Amendments and additions will be published from time to time in such manner as the Bar Council may determine.

General purpose of the Code

C–4   **104** The general purpose of this Code is to provide the requirements for practice as a barrister and the rules and standards of conduct applicable to barristers which are appropriate in the interests of justice and in particular:

(a) in relation to self-employed barristers to provide common and enforceable rules and standards which require them:

(i) to be completely independent in conduct and in professional standing as sole practitioners;

  (ii) to act only as consultants instructed by solicitors and other approved persons (save where instructions can properly be dispensed with);

  (iii) to acknowledge a public obligation based on the paramount need for access to justice to act for any client in cases within their field of practice;

(b) to make appropriate provision for employed barristers taking into account the fact that such barristers are employed to provide legal services to or on behalf of their employer.

PART III—FUNDAMENTAL PRINCIPLES

Applicable to all barristers

301 A barrister must have regard to paragraph 104 and must not: **C–5**

  (a) engage in conduct whether in pursuit of his profession or otherwise which is:

    (i) dishonest or otherwise discreditable to a barrister;

    (ii) prejudicial to the administration of justice; or

    (iii) likely to diminish public confidence in the legal profession or the administration of justice or otherwise bring the legal profession into disrepute;

  (b) engage directly or indirectly in any occupation if his association with that occupation may adversely affect the reputation of the Bar or in the case of a practising barrister prejudice his ability to attend properly to his practice.

Applicable to practising barristers

302 A barrister has an overriding duty to the Court to act with independence in the interests of **C–6** justice: he must assist the Court in the administration of justice and must not deceive or knowingly or recklessly mislead the Court.

303 A barrister:

  (a) must promote and protect fearlessly and by all proper and lawful means the lay client's best interests and do so without regard to his own interests or to any consequences to himself or to any other person (including any professional client or other intermediary or another barrister);

  (b) owes his primary duty as between the lay client and any professional client or other intermediary to the lay client and must not permit the intermediary to limit his discretion as to how the interests of the lay client can best be served;

  (c) when supplying legal services funded by the Legal Services Commission as part of the Community Legal Service or the Criminal Defence Service owes his primary duty to the lay client subject only to compliance with paragraph 304.

304 A barrister who supplies legal services funded by the Legal Services Commission as part of the Community Legal Service or the Criminal Defence Service must in connection with the supply of such services comply with any duty imposed on him by or under the *Access to Justice Act* 1999 or any regulations or code in effect under that Act and in particular with the duties set out in Annex E.

305.1 A barrister must not in relation to any other person (including a client or another barrister or a pupil or a student member of an Inn of Court) discriminate directly or indirectly or victimise because of race, colour, ethnic or national origin, nationality, citizenship, sex, sexual orientation, marital status, disability, religion or political persuasion.

305.2 A barrister must not in relation to any offer of a pupillage or tenancy discriminate directly or indirectly against a person on grounds of age, save where such discrimination can be shown to be objectively and reasonably justifiable.

306 A barrister is individually and personally responsible for his own conduct and for his professional work: he must exercise his own personal judgment in all his professional activities.

307 A barrister must not:

  (a) permit his absolute independence integrity and freedom from external pressures to be compromised;

  (b) do anything (for example accept a present) in such circumstances as may lead to any inference that his independence may be compromised;

  (c) compromise his professional standards in order to please his client the Court or a third party, including any mediator;

(d) give a commission or present or lend any money for any professional purpose to or (save as a remuneration in accordance with the provisions of this Code) accept any money by way of loan or otherwise from any client or any person entitled to instruct him as an intermediary;

(e) make any payment (other than a payment for advertising or publicity permitted by this Code or in the case of a barrister in independent practice remuneration paid to any clerk or other employee or staff of his chambers) to any person for the purpose of procuring professional instructions;

(f) receive or handle client money securities or other assets other than by receiving payment of remuneration or (in the case of an employed barrister) where the money or other asset belongs to his employer.

PART IV—SELF-EMPLOYED BARRISTERS

Instructions

401 A self-employed barrister whether or not he is acting for a fee:

(a) may supply legal services only if appointed by the Court or is instructed:

  (i) by a professional client;

  (ii) by a licensed access client, in which case he must comply with the Licensed Access Rules (reproduced in Annex F1); or

  (iii) subject to paragraph 204(c), by or on behalf of any other lay client, in which cased he must comply with the Public Access Rules (reproduced in Annex F2); or

(b) must not in the course of his practice:

  (i) undertake the management administration or general conduct of a lay client's affairs;

  (ii) conduct litigation or *inter-partes* work (for example the conduct of correspondence with an opposite party, instructing any expert witness or other person on behalf of his lay client or accepting personal liability for the payment of any such person);

  (iii) investigate or collect evidence for use in any Court;

  (iv) except as permitted by paragraph 707, or by the Public Access Rules, take any proof of evidence in any criminal case;

  (v) attend at a police station without the presence of a solicitor to advise a suspect or interviewee as to the handling and conduct of police interviews;

  (vi) act as a supervisor for the purposes of section 84(2) of the *Immigration and Asylum Act* 1999.

Fees and remuneration

405 Subject to paragraph 307 a barrister in independent practice may charge for any work undertaken by him (whether or not it involves an appearance in Court) on any basis or by any method he thinks fit provided that such basis or method:

(a) is permitted by law;

(b) does not involve the payment of a wage or salary.

406.1 A self-employed barrister who receives fees in respect of work done by another barrister must himself and without delegating the responsibility to anyone else pay forthwith the whole of the fee in respect of that work to that other barrister.

406.2 Subject to paragraph 805 a self-employed barrister who arranges for another barrister to undertake work for him (other than a pupil or a person who has asked to do the work in order to increase his own skill or experience) must himself and without delegating the responsibility to anyone else:

(a) pay proper financial remuneration for the work done;

(b) make payment within a reasonable time and in any event within three months after the work has been done unless otherwise agreed in advance with the other barrister.

PART VI—ACCEPTANCE AND RETURN OF INSTRUCTIONS

Acceptance of instructions and the "Cab-rank rule"

601 A barrister who supplies advocacy services must not withhold those services:

   (a) on the ground that the nature of the case is objectionable to him or to any section of the
public;

   (b) on the ground that the conduct opinions or beliefs of the prospective client are unacceptable to him or to any section of the public;

   (c) on any ground relating to the source of any financial support which may properly be
given to the prospective client for the proceedings in question (for example, on the
ground that such support will be available as part of the Community Legal Service or
Criminal Defence Service).

602 A self-employed barrister must comply with the "Cab-rank rule" and accordingly except only
as otherwise provided in paragraphs 603, 604, 605 and 606 he must in any field in which he
professes to practise in relation to work appropriate to his experience and seniority and irrespective
of whether his client is paying privately or is publicly funded:

   (a) accept any brief to appear before a Court in which he professes to practise;

   (b) accept any instructions;

   (c) act for any person on whose behalf he is instructed;

and do so irrespective of (i) the party on whose behalf he is instructed (ii) the nature of the case and
(iii) any belief or opinion which he may have formed as to the character reputation cause conduct
guilt or innocence of that person.

603 A barrister must not accept any instructions if to do so would cause him to be professionally
embarrassed and for this purpose a barrister will be professionally embarrassed:

   (a) if he lacks sufficient experience or competence to handle the matter;

   (b) if having regard to his other professional commitments he will be unable to do or will not
have adequate time and opportunity to prepare that which he is required to do;

   (c) if the instructions seek to limit the ordinary authority or discretion of a barrister in the
conduct of proceedings in Court or to require a barrister to act otherwise than in
conformity with law or with the provisions of this Code;

   (d) if the matter is one in which he has reason to believe that he is likely to be a witness or in
which whether by reason of any connection with the client or with the Court or a member
of it or otherwise it will be difficult for him to maintain professional independence or the
administration of justice might be or appear to be prejudiced;

   (e) if there is or appears to be a conflict or risk of conflict either between the interests of the
barrister and some other person or between the interests of any one or more clients (unless all relevant persons consent to the barrister accepting the instructions);

   (f) if there is a significant risk that information confidential to another client or former client
might be communicated to or used for the benefit of anyone other than that client or former client without their consent;

   (g) if he is a self-employed barrister where the instructions are delivered by a solicitor or
firm of solicitors in respect of whom a Withdrawal of Credit Direction has been issued by
the Chairman of the Bar pursuant to the Terms of Work on which Barristers Offer their
Services to Solicitors and the Withdrawal of Credit Scheme 1988 as amended and in
force from time to time (reproduced in Annex G1) unless his fees are paid directly by the
Legal Services Commission or the instructions are accompanied by payment of an agreed
fee or the barrister agrees in advance to accept no fee for such work or has obtained the
consent of the Chairman of the Bar;

   (h) if the barrister is instructed by or on behalf of a lay client who has not also instructed a
solicitor or other professional client, and if the barrister is satisfied that it is in the
interests of the client or in the interests of justice for the lay client to instruct a solicitor
or other professional client.

604 Subject to paragraph 601 a self-employed barrister is not obliged to accept instructions:

   (a) requiring him to do anything other than during the course of his ordinary working year;

   (b) other than at a fee which is proper having regard to:

     (i) the complexity length and difficulty of the case;

     (ii) his ability experience and seniority; and

     (iii) the expenses which he will incur;

     and any instructions in a matter funded by the Legal Services Commission as part of the
Community Legal Service or the Criminal Defence Service for which the amount or rate
of the barrister's remuneration is prescribed by regulation or subject to assessment shall

for this purpose unless the Bar Council or the Bar in general meeting otherwise determines (either in a particular case or in any class or classes of case or generally) be deemed to be at a proper professional fee;

(c) to do any work under a conditional fee agreement;

(d) save in a matter funded by the Legal Services Commission as part of the Community Legal Service or the Criminal Defence Service:

(i) unless and until his fees are agreed;

(ii) if having required his fees to be paid before he accepts the instructions those fees are not paid;

(e) from anyone other than a professional client who accepts liability for the barrister's fees;

(f) in a matter where the lay client is also the professional client;

(g) to do any work under the Contractual Terms on which Barristers offer their Services to Solicitors 2001 as amended and in force from time to time (reproduced in Appendix G2) or on any other contractual terms.

605 A self-employed Queen's Counsel is not obliged to accept instructions:

(a) to settle alone any document of a kind generally settled only by or in conjunction with a junior;

(b) to act without a junior if he considers that the interests of the lay client require that a junior should also be instructed.

606.1 A barrister (whether he is instructed on his own or with another advocate) must in the case of all instructions consider whether consistently with the proper and efficient administration of justice and having regard to:

(a) the circumstances (including in particular the gravity complexity and likely cost) of the case;

(b) the nature of his practice;

(c) his ability experience and seniority; and

(d) his relationship with the client;

the best interests of the client would be served by instructing or continuing to instruct him in that matter.

606.2 Where a barrister is instructed in any matter with another advocate or advocates the barrister must in particular consider whether it would be in the best interests of the client to instruct only one advocate or fewer advocates.

606.3 A barrister who in any matter is instructed either directly by the lay client or by an intermediary who is not a solicitor or other authorised litigator should consider whether it would be in the interests of the lay client or the interests of justice to instruct a solicitor or other authorised litigator or other appropriate intermediary either together with or in place of the barrister.

606.4 In cases involving several parties, a barrister must on receipt of instructions and further in the event of any change of circumstances consider whether, having regard to all the circumstances including any actual or potential conflict of interest, any client ought to be separately represented or advised or whether it would be in the best interests of any client to be jointly represented or advised with another party.

607 If at any time in any matter a barrister considers that it would be in the best interests of any client to have different representation, he must immediately so advise the client.

Withdrawal from a case and return to instructions

608 A barrister must cease to act and if he is a self-employed barrister must return any instructions:

(a) if continuing to act would cause him to be professionally embarrassed within the meaning of paragraph 603 provided that if he would be professionally embarrassed only because it appears to him that he is likely to be a witness on a material question of fact he may retire or withdraw only if he can do so without jeopardising the client's interests;

(b) if having accepted instructions on behalf of more than one client there is or appears to be:

(i) a conflict or risk of conflict between the interests of any one or more of such clients; or

(ii) risk of a breach of confidence;

and the clients do not all consent to him continuing to act;

(c) if in any case funded by the Legal Services Commission as part of the Community Legal Service or Criminal Defence Service it has become apparent to him that such funding has been wrongly obtained by false or inaccurate information and action to remedy the situation is not immediately taken by the client;

(d) if the client refuses to authorise him to make some disclosure to the Court which his duty to the Court requires him to make;

(e) if having become aware during the course of a case of the existence of a document which should have been but has not been disclosed on discovery the client fails forthwith to disclose it;

(f) if having come into possession of a document belonging to another party by some means other than the normal and proper channels and having read it before he realises that it ought to have been returned unread to the person entitled to possession of it he would thereby be embarrassed in the discharge of his duties by his knowledge of the contents of the document provided that he may retire or withdraw only if he can do so without jeopardising the client's interests.

609 Subject to paragraph 610 a barrister may withdraw from a case where he is satisfied that:

(a) his instructions have been withdrawn;

(b) his professional conduct is being impugned;

(c) advice which he has given in accordance with paragraph 607 or 703 had not been heeded; or

(d) there is some other substantial reason for so doing.

610 A barrister must not:

(a) cease to act or return instructions without having first explained to the client his reasons for doing so;

(b) return instructions to another barrister without the consent of the client;

(c) return a brief which he has accepted and for which a fixed date has been obtained or (except with the consent of the lay client and where appropriate the Court) break any other engagement to supply legal services in the course of his practice so as to enable him to attend or fulfil an engagement (including a social or non-professional engagement) of any other kind;

(d) except as provided in paragraph 608 return any instructions or withdraw from a case in such a way or in such circumstances that the client may be unable to find other legal assistance in time to prevent prejudice being suffered by the client.

PART VII—CONDUCT OF WORK BY PRACTISING BARRISTERS

General

701 A barrister: C–11

(a) must in all his professional activities be courteous and act promptly conscientiously diligently and with reasonable competence and take all reasonable and practicable steps to avoid unnecessary expense or waste of the Court's time and to ensure that professional engagements are fulfilled;

(b) must not undertake any task which:

(i) he knows or ought to know he is not competent to handle;

(ii) he does not have adequate time and opportunity to prepare for or perform; or

(iii) he cannot discharge within the time requested or otherwise within a reasonable time having regard to the pressure of other work.

(c) must read all instructions delivered to him expeditiously;

(d) must have regard to any relevant Written Standards for the conduct of Professional Work issued by the Bar Council;

(e) must inform his client forthwith and subject to paragraph 610 return the instructions to the client or to another barrister acceptable to the client:

(i) if it becomes apparent to him that he will not be able to do the work within the time requested or within a reasonable time after receipt of instructions;

(ii) if there is an appreciable risk that he may not be able to undertake a brief or fulfil any other professional engagement which he has accepted;

(f) must ensure that adequate records supporting the fees charged or claimed in a case are kept at least until the last of the following: his fees have been paid, any taxation or determination or assessment of costs in the case has been completed, or the time for lodging an appeal against assessment or the determination of that appeal, has expired, and must provide his professional or licensed access client or other intermediary or the lay client with such records or details of the work done as may reasonably be required.

Confidentiality

C–12   702 Whether or not the relation of counsel and client continues a barrister must preserve the confidentiality of the lay client's affairs and must not without the prior consent of the lay client or as permitted by law lend or reveal the contents of the papers in any instructions to or communicate to any third person (other than another barrister, a pupil, in the case of a Registered European Lawyer, the person with whom he is acting in conjunction for the purposes of paragraph 5(3) of the Registered European Lawyers Rules or any other person who needs to know it for the performance of their duties) information which has been entrusted to him in confidence or use such information to the lay client's detriment or to his own or another client's advantage.

Conflicts between lay clients and intermediaries

C–13   703 If a self-employed barrister forms the view that there is a conflict of interest between his lay client and a professional client or other intermediary (for example because he considers that the intermediary may have been negligent) he must consider whether it would be in the lay client's interest to instruct another professional adviser or representative and, if he considers that it would be, the barrister must so advise and take such steps as he considers necessary to ensure that his advice is communicated to the lay client (if necessary by sending a copy of his advice in writing directly to the lay client as well as to the intermediary).

Drafting documents

C–14   704 A barrister must not devise facts which will assist in advancing the lay client's case and must not draft any statement of case, witness statement, affidavit, notice of appeal or other document containing:

    (a) any statement of fact or contention which is not supported by the lay client or by his instructions;

    (b) any contention which he does not consider to be properly arguable;

    (c) any allegation of fraud unless he has clear instructions to make such allegation and has before him reasonably credible material which as it stands establishes a prima facie case of fraud;

    (d) in the case of a witness statement or affidavit any statement of fact other than the evidence which in substance according to his instructions the barrister reasonably believes the witness would give if the evidence contained in the witness statement or affidavit were being given in oral examination;

provided that nothing in this paragraph shall prevent a barrister drafting a document containing specific factual statements or contentions included by the barrister subject to confirmation of their accuracy by the lay client or witness.

Contact with witnesses

C–15   705 A barrister must not:

    (a) rehearse practise or coach a witness in relation to his evidence;

    (b) encourage a witness to give evidence which is untruthful or which is not the whole truth;

    (c) except with the consent of the representative for the opposing side or of the court, communicate directly or indirectly about a case with any witness, whether or not the witness is his lay client, once that witness has begun to give evidence until the evidence of that witness has been concluded.

Attendance of professional client

C–16   706 A self-employed barrister who is instructed by a professional client should not conduct a case in court in the absence of his professional client or a representative of his professional client unless the court rules that it is appropriate or he is satisfied that the interests of the lay client and the interests of justice will not be prejudiced.

707 A self-employed barrister who attends court in order to conduct a case in circumstances where no professional client or representative of a professional client is present may if necessary interview witnesses and take proofs of evidence.

Conduct in court

708 A barrister when conducting proceedings in court: **C–17**

(a) is personally responsible for the conduct and presentation of his case and must exercise personal judgment upon the substance and purpose of statements made and questions asked;

(b) must not unless invited to do so by the court or when appearing before a tribunal where it is his duty to do so assert a personal opinion of the facts or the law;

(c) must ensure that the court is informed of all relevant decisions and legislative provisions of which he is aware whether the effect is favourable or unfavourable towards the contention for which he argues;

(d) must bring any procedural irregularity to the attention of the court during the hearing and not reserve such matter to be raised on appeal;

(e) must not adduce evidence obtained otherwise than from or through the client or devise facts which will assist in advancing the lay client's case;

(f) must not make a submission which he does not consider to be properly arguable;

(g) must not make statements or ask questions which are merely scandalous or intended or calculated only to vilify insult or annoy either a witness or some other person;

(h) must if possible avoid the naming in open court of third parties whose character would thereby be impugned;

(i) must not by assertion in a speech impugn a witness whom he has had an opportunity to cross-examine unless in cross-examination he has given the witness an opportunity to answer the allegation;

(j) must not suggest that a victim, witness or other person is guilty of crime, fraud or misconduct or make any defamatory aspersion on the conduct of any other person or attribute to another person the crime or conduct of which his lay client is accused unless such allegations go to a matter in issue (including the credibility of the witness) which is material to the lay client's case and appear to him to be supported by reasonable grounds.

Media comment

709.1 A barrister must not in relation to any anticipated or current proceedings or mediation **C–18** in which he is briefed or expects to appear or has appeared as an advocate express a personal opinion to or in the press or other media upon the facts of or the issues arising in the proceedings.

709.2 Paragraph 709.1 shall not prevent the expression of such an opinion on an issue in an educational or academic context.

Advertising and publicity

710.1 Subject to paragraph 710.2 a barrister may engage in any advertising or promotion in con- **C–19** nection with his practice which conforms to the British Codes of Advertising and Sales Promotion and such advertising or promotion may include:

(a) photographs or other illustrations of the barrister;

(b) statements of rates and methods of charging;

(c) statements about the nature and extent of the barrister's services;

(d) information about any case in which the barrister has appeared (including the name of any client for whom the barrister acted) where such information has already become publicly available or, where it has not already become publicly available, with the express prior written consent of the lay client.

710.2 Advertising or promotion must not:

(a) be inaccurate or likely to mislead;

(b) be likely to diminish public confidence in the legal profession or the administration of justice or otherwise bring the legal profession into disrepute;

(c) make direct comparisons in terms of quality with or criticisms of other identifiable person (whether they be barristers or members of any other profession);

(d) include statements about the barrister's success rate;

(e) indicate or imply any willingness to accept instructions or any intention to restrict the persons from whom instructions may be accepted otherwise than in accordance with this Code;

(f) be so frequent or obtrusive as to cause annoyance to those to whom it is directed.

II. BAR COUNCIL GUIDANCE

Written standards of work

C–20   The following standards have been issued by the Bar Council together with the eighth edition of the *Code of Conduct*. They do not form part of the code. Paragraph 701(d) of the code (*ante*, C–11) does, however, oblige a barrister to "have regard to any relevant Written Standards".

WRITTEN STANDARDS FOR THE CONDUCT OF PROFESSIONAL WORK

GENERAL STANDARDS

1 Introduction

C–21   **1.1** These Standards are intended as a guide to the way in which a barrister should carry out his work. They consist in part of matters which are dealt with expressly in the Code of Conduct and in part of statements of good practice. They must therefore be read in conjunction with the Code of Conduct, and are to be taken into account in determining whether or not a barrister has committed a disciplinary offence. They apply to employed barristers as well as to barristers in independent practice, except where this would be inappropriate. In addition to these General Standards, there are Standards which apply specifically to the conduct of criminal cases.

2 General

C–22   **2.1** The work which is within the ordinary scope of a barrister's practice consists of advocacy, drafting pleadings and other legal documents and advising on questions of law. A barrister acts only on the instructions of a professional client, and does not carry out any work by way of the management, administration or general conduct of a lay client's affairs, nor the management, administration or general conduct of litigation nor the receipt or handling of clients' money.

2.2 It is a fundamental principle which applies to all work undertaken by a barrister that a barrister is under a duty to act for any client (whether legally aided or not) in cases within his field of practice. The rules which embody this principle and the exceptions to it are set out in paragraphs 303, 601, 602, 603, 604 and 605 of the Code of Conduct.

3 Acceptance of work

C–23   **3.1** As soon as practicable after receipt of any brief or instructions a barrister should satisfy himself that there is no reason why he ought to decline to accept it.

3.2 A barrister is not considered to have accepted a brief or instructions unless he has had an opportunity to consider it and has expressly accepted it.

3.3 A barrister should always be alert to the possibility of a conflict of interests. If the conflict is between the interests of his lay client and his professional client, the conflict must be resolved in favour of the lay client. Where there is a conflict between the lay client and the Legal Aid Fund, the conflict must be resolved in favour of the lay client, subject only to compliance with the provisions of the Legal Aid Regulations.

3.4 If after a barrister has accepted a brief or instructions on behalf of more than one lay client, there is or appears to be a conflict or a significant risk of a conflict between the interests of any one or more of such clients, he must not continue to act for any client unless all such clients give their consent to his so acting.

3.5 Even if there is no conflict of interest, when a barrister has accepted a brief or instructions for any party in any proceedings, he should not accept a brief or instructions in respect of an appeal or further stage of the proceedings for any other party without obtaining the prior consent of the original client.

3.6 A barrister must not accept any brief or instructions if the matter is one in which he has reason to believe that he is likely to be a witness. If, however, having accepted a brief or instructions, it later appears that he is likely to be a witness in the case on a material question of fact, he may retire or withdraw only if he can do so without jeopardising his client's interests.

3.7 A barrister should not appear as a barrister:

(a) in any matter in which he is a party or has a significant pecuniary interest;

(b) either for or against any local authority, firm or organisation of which he is a member or in which he has directly or indirectly a significant pecuniary interest;

(c) either for or against any company of which he is a director, secretary or officer or in which he has directly or indirectly a significant pecuniary interest.

3.8 Apart from cases in which there is a conflict of interests, a barrister must not accept any brief or instructions if to do so would cause him to be otherwise professionally embarrassed: paragraph 603 of the Code of Conduct sets out the general principles applicable to such situations.

4 Withdrawal from a case and return of brief or instructions

4.1 When a barrister has accepted a brief for the defence of a person charged with a serious criminal offence, he should so far as reasonably practicable ensure that the risk of a conflicting professional engagement does not arise. **C–24**

4.2 The circumstances in which a barrister must withdraw from a case or return his brief or instructions are set out in paragraph 608 of the Code of Conduct; the circumstances in which he is permitted to do so are set out in paragraph 609 the circumstances in which he must not do so are set out in paragraph 610.

5 Conduct of work

5.1 A barrister must at all times promote and protect fearlessly and by all proper and lawful means his lay client's best interests. **C–25**

5.2 A barrister must assist the court in the administration of justice and, as part of this obligation and the obligation to use only proper and lawful means to promote and protect the interests of his client, must not deceive or knowingly or recklessly mislead the court.

5.3 A barrister is at all times individually and personally responsible for his own conduct and for his professional work both in court and out of court.

5.4 A barrister must in all his professional activities act promptly, conscientiously, diligently and with reasonable competence and must take all reasonable and practicable steps to ensure that professional engagements are fulfilled. He must not undertake any task which:

(a) he knows or ought to know he is not competent to handle;

(b) he does not have adequate time and opportunity to prepare for or perform; or

(c) he cannot discharge within a reasonable time having regard to the pressure of other work.

5.5 A barrister must at all times be courteous to the court and to all those with whom he has professional dealings.

5.6 In relation to instructions to advise or draft documents, a barrister should ensure that the advice or document is provided within such time as has been agreed with the professional client, or otherwise within a reasonable time after receipt of the relevant instructions. If it becomes apparent to the barrister that he will not be able to do the work within that time, he must inform his professional client forthwith.

5.7 Generally, a barrister should ensure that advice which he gives is practical, appropriate to the needs and circumstances of the particular client, and clearly and comprehensibly expressed.

5.8 A barrister must exercise his own personal judgment upon the substance and purpose of any advice he gives or any document he drafts. He must not devise facts which will assist in advancing his lay client's case and must not draft any originating process, pleading, affidavit, witness statement or notice of appeal containing:

(a) any statement of fact or contention (as the case may be) which is not supported by his lay client or by his brief or instructions;

(b) any contention which he does not consider to be properly arguable;

(c) any allegation of fraud unless he has clear instructions to make such an allegation and has before him reasonably credible material which as it stands establishes a prima facia case of fraud; or

(d) in the case of an affidavit or witness statement, any statement of fact other than the evidence which in substance according to his instructions, the barrister reasonably believes the witness would give if the evidence contained in the affidavit or witness statement were being given *viva voce*.

5.9 A barrister should be available on reasonable notice for a conference prior to the day of hearing of any case in which he is briefed; and if no such conference takes place then the barrister should be available for a conference on the day of the hearing. The venue of a conference is a matter for agreement between the barrister and his professional clients.

5.10 A barrister when conducting proceedings at court:

(a) is personally responsible for the conduct and presentation of his case and must exercise personal judgment upon the substance and purpose of statements made and questions asked;

(b) must not, unless asked to do so by the court or when appearing before a tribunal where it his duty to do so, assert a personal opinion of the facts or the law;

(c) must ensure that the court is informed of all relevant decisions and legislative provisions of which he is aware, whether the effect is favourable or unfavourable towards the contention for which he argues, and must bring any procedural irregularity to the attention of the court during the hearing and not reserve such matter to be raised on appeal;

(d) must not adduce evidence obtained otherwise than from or through his professional client or devise facts which will assist in advancing his lay client's case;

(e) must not make statements or ask questions which are merely scandalous or intended or calculated only to vilify, insult or annoy either a witness or some other person;

(f) must if possible avoid the naming in open court of third parties whose character would thereby be impugned;

(g) must not by assertion in a speech impugn a witness whom he has had an opportunity to cross-examine unless in cross-examination he has given the witness an opportunity to answer the allegation;

(h) must not suggest that a victim, witness or other person is guilty of crime, fraud or misconduct or make any defamatory aspersion on the conduct of any other person or attribute to another person the crime or conduct of which his lay client is accused unless such allegations go to a matter in issue (including the credibility of the witness) which is material to his lay client's case, and which appear to him to be supported by reasonable grounds.

5.11 A barrister must take all reasonable and practicable steps to avoid unnecessary expense or waste of the court's time. He should, when asked, inform the court of the probable length of his case; and he should also inform the court of any developments which affect information already provided.

5.12 In court a barrister's personal appearance should be decorous, and his dress, when robes are worn, should be compatible with them.

6.1 Witnesses

C–26   **6.1.1** The rules which define and regulate the barrister's functions in relation to the preparation of evidence and contact with witnesses are set out in paragraphs 704, 705, 706, 707 and 708 of the Code of Conduct.

6.1.2 There is no longer any rule which prevents a barrister from having contact with any witness.

6.1.3 In particular, there is no longer any rule in any case (including contested cases in the Crown Court) which prevents a barrister from having contact with a witness whom he may expect to call and examine in chief, with a view to introducing himself to the witness, explaining the court's procedure (and in particular the procedure for giving evidence), and answering any questions on procedure which the witness may have.

6.1.4 It is a responsibility of a barrister, especially when the witness is nervous, vulnerable or apparently the victim of criminal or similar conduct, to ensure that those facing unfamiliar court procedures are put as much at ease as possible.

6.1.5 Unless otherwise directed by the court or with the consent of the representative for the opposing side or of the court, a barrister should not communicate directly or indirectly about the case with any witness, whether or not the witness is his lay client, once that witness has begun to give evidence until it has been concluded.

6.2 Discussing the evidence with witnesses

6.2.1 Different considerations apply in relation to contact with witnesses for the purpose of **C–27** interviewing them or discussing with them (either individually or together) the substance of their evidence or the evidence of other witnesses.

6.2.2 Although there is no longer any rule which prevents a barrister from having contact with witnesses for such purposes a barrister should exercise his discretion and consider very carefully whether and to what extent such contact is appropriate, bearing in mind in particular that it is not the barrister's function (but that of his professional client) to investigate and collect evidence.

6.2.3 The guiding principle must be the obligation of counsel to promote and protect his lay client's best interests so far as that is consistent with the law and with counsel's overriding duty to the court (Code of Conduct paragraphs 302, 303).

6.2.4 A barrister should be alert to the risks that any discussion of the substance of a case with a witness may lead to suspicions of coaching, and thus tend to diminish the value of the witness's evidence in the eyes of the court, or may place the barrister in a position of professional embarrassment, for example if he thereby becomes himself a witness in the case. These dangers are most likely to occur if such discussion takes place:

(a) before the barrister has been supplied with a proof of the witness's evidence; or

(b) in the absence of the barrister's professional client or his representative.

A barrister should also be alert to the fact that, even in the absence of any wish or intention to do so, authority figures do subconsciously influence lay witnesses. Discussion of the substance of the case may unwittingly contaminate the witness's evidence.

6.2.5 There is particular danger where such discussions:

(a) take place in the presence of more than one witness of fact; or

(b) involve the disclosure to one witness of fact of the factual evidence of another witness.

These practices have been strongly deprecated by the courts as tending inevitably to encourage the rehearsal or coaching of witnesses and to increase the risk of fabrication or contamination of evidence: *R. v. Arif* (1993) May 26; *Smith New Court Securities Ltd v. Scrimgeour Vickers (Asset Management) Ltd* [1992] B.C.L.C. 1104, [1994] 1 W.L.R. 1271.

That is not to suggest that it is always inappropriate to disclose one witness' evidence to another. If the witness is one to be called by the other party, it is almost inevitable that a witness' attention must be drawn to discrepancies between the two statements. Discretion is, however, required, especially where the evidence of independent witnesses is involved.

6.2.6 Whilst there is no rule that any longer prevents a barrister from taking a witness statement in civil cases (for cases in the Crown Court see below), there is a distinction between the settling of a witness statement and taking a witness statement. It is not appropriate for a barrister who has taken witness statements, as opposed to settling witness statements prepared by others, to act as counsel unless he is a junior member of the team of counsel and will not be examining the witness or there are exceptional circumstances, because it risks undermining the independence of the barrister as an advocate. Exceptional circumstances would include:

(a) the witness is a minor one;

(b) counsel has no choice but to take a proof and this is the only practical course in the interests of justice—this would apply, for instance, where a witness appears unexpectedly at court and there is no one else competent to take the statement.

The Cab-rank Rule does not require a barrister to agree to undertake the task of taking witness statements.

6.2.7 There is no rule which prevents a barrister from exchanging common courtesies with the other side's witnesses. However, a barrister should not discuss the substance of the case or any evidence with the other side's witnesses except in rare and exceptional circumstances and then only with the prior knowledge of his opponent.

6.3 Criminal cases in the Crown Court

6.3.1 Contested criminal cases in the Crown Court present peculiar difficulties and may expose **C–28** both barristers and witnesses to special pressures. As a general principle, therefore, with the exception of the lay client, character and expert witnesses, subject to 6.3.2 it is wholly inappropriate for a barrister in such a case to interview any potential witness. Interviewing includes discussing with any such witness the substance of his evidence or the evidence of other such witnesses.

6.3.2 Prosecution counsel may, if instructed to do so, interview potential witnesses for the purposes of, and in accordance with, the practice set out in the Code for Pre-Trial Witness Interviews.

6.3.3 There may be extraordinary circumstances in which a departure from the general principles set out in paragraphs 6.3.1 and 6.3.2 is unavoidable. An example of such circumstances is afforded by the decision in *Fergus* (1994) 98 Cr.App.R. 313.

6.3.4 Where any barrister has interviewed any potential witness or any such witness has been interviewed by another barrister, that fact shall be disclosed to all other parties in the case before the witness is called. A written record must also be made of the substance of the interview and the reason for it.

7 Documents

C–29

7.1 A barrister should not obtain or seek to obtain a document, or knowledge of the contents of a document, belonging to another party other than by means of the normal and proper channels for obtaining such documents or such knowledge.

7.2 If a barrister comes into possession of a document belonging to another party by some means other than the normal and proper channels (for example, if the document has come into his possession in consequence of a mistake or inadvertence by another person or if the document appears to belong to another party, or to be a copy of such a document, and to be privileged from discovery or otherwise to be one which ought not to be in the possession of his professional or lay client) he should:

(a) where appropriate make enquiries of his professional client in order to ascertain the circumstances in which the document was obtained by his professional or lay client; and

(b) unless satisfied that the document has been properly obtained in the ordinary course of events at once return the document unread to the person entitled to possession of it.

7.3.1 If having come into possession of such document the barrister reads it before he realises that he ought not to, and would be embarrassed in the discharge of his duties by his knowledge of the contents of the document, then provided he can do so without prejudice to his lay client he must return his brief or instructions and explain to his professional client why he has done so.

7.3.2 If, however, to return his brief or instructions would prejudice his lay client (for example, by reason of the proximity of the trial) he should not return his brief or instructions and should, unless the court otherwise orders, make such use of the document as will be in his client's interests. He should inform his opponent of his knowledge of the document and of the circumstances, so far as known to him, in which the document was obtained and of his intention to use it. In the event of objection to the use of such document it is for the court to determine what use, if any, may be made of it.

7.4 If during the course of a case a barrister becomes aware of the existence of a document which should have been but has not been disclosed on discovery he should advise his professional client to disclose it forthwith; and if it is not then disclosed, he must withdraw from the case.

8 Administration of practice

C–30

8.1 A barrister must ensure that his practice is properly and efficiently administered in accordance with the provisions of paragraph 304 of the Code of Conduct.

8.2 A barrister should ensure that he is able to provide his professional client with full and proper details of and appropriate justification for fees which have been incurred, and a proper assessment of any work to be done, so that both the lay client and the professional client are able to determine the level of any financial commitment which has been incurred or may be incurred.

[The next paragraph is C–32.]

STANDARDS APPLICABLE TO CRIMINAL CASES

9 Introduction

C–32

9.1 These standards are to be read together with the General Standards and the Code of Conduct. They are intended as a guide to those matters which specifically relate to practice in the criminal courts. They are not an alternative to the General Standards, which apply to all work carried out by a barrister. Particular reference is made to those paragraphs in the General Standards relating to the general conduct of a case (5.8), conduct in court (5.10), discussion with witnesses (6.1, 6.2) and the use of documents belonging to other parties (7.1, 7.2, 7.3), which are not repeated in these standards.

10 Responsibilities of prosecuting counsel

10A The Standards and principles contained in this paragraph apply as appropriate to all practising barristers, whether in independent practice or employed and whether appearing as counsel in any given case or exercising any other professional capacity in connection with it. **C–33**

10.1 Prosecuting counsel should not attempt to obtain a conviction by all means at his command. He should not regard himself as appearing for a party. He should lay before the court fairly and impartially the whole of the facts which comprise the case for the prosecution and should assist the court on all matters of law applicable to the case.

10.2 Prosecuting counsel should bear in mind at all times whilst he is instructed:

    (i) that he is responsible for the presentation and general conduct of the case;

    (ii) that he should use his best endeavours to ensure that all evidence or material that ought properly to be made available is either presented by the prosecution or disclosed to the defence.

10.3 Prosecuting counsel should, when instructions are delivered to him, read them expeditiously and, where instructed to do so, advise or confer on all aspects of the case well before its commencement.

10.4 In relation to cases tried in the Crown Court, prosecuting counsel:

    (a) should ensure, if he is instructed to settle an indictment, that he does so promptly and within due time, and should bear in mind the desirability of not overloading an indictment with either too many defendants or too many counts, in order to present the prosecution case as simply and as concisely as possible;

    (b) should ask, if the indictment is being settled by some other person, to see a copy of the indictment and should then check it;

    (c) should decide whether any additional evidence is required and, if it is, should advise in writing and set out precisely what additional evidence is required with a view to serving it on the defence as soon as possible;

    (d) should consider whether all witness statements in the possession of the prosecution have been properly served on the defendant in accordance with the Attorney-General's Guidelines;

    (e) should eliminate all unnecessary material in the case so as to ensure an efficient and fair trial, and in particular should consider the need for particular witnesses and exhibits and draft appropriate admissions for service on the defence;

    (f) should in all Class 1 and Class 2 cases and in other cases of complexity draft a case summary for transmission to the court.

10.5 Paragraphs 6 to 6.3.4 of the Written Standards for the Conduct of Professional Work refer.

10.6 Prosecuting counsel should at all times have regard to the report of Mr Justice Farquharson's Committee on the role of Prosecuting Counsel which is set out in *Archbold*. In particular, he should have regard to the following recommendations of the Farquharson Committee:

    (a) where counsel has taken a decision on a matter of policy with which his professional client has not agreed, it would be appropriate for him to submit to the Attorney-General a written report of all the circumstances, including his reasons for disagreeing with those who instructed him;

    (b) when counsel has had an opportunity to prepare his brief and to confer with those instructing him, but at the last moment before trial unexpectedly advises that the case should not proceed or that pleas to lesser offences should be accepted, and his professional client does not accept such advice, counsel should apply for an adjournment if instructed to do so;

    (c) subject to the above, it is for prosecuting counsel to decide whether to offer no evidence on a particular count or on the indictment as a whole and whether to accept pleas to a lesser count or counts.

10.7 It is the duty of prosecuting counsel to assist the court at the conclusion of the summing-up by drawing attention to any apparent errors or omissions of fact or law.

10.8 In relation to sentence, prosecuting counsel:

    (a) should not attempt by advocacy to influence the court with regard to sentence: if, however, a defendant is unrepresented it is proper to inform the court of any mitigating circumstances about which counsel is instructed;

(b) should be in a position to assist the court if requested as to any statutory provisions relevant to the offence or the offender and as to any relevant guidelines as to sentence laid down by the Court of Appeal;

(c) should bring any such matters as are referred to in (b) above to the attention of the court if in the opinion of prosecuting counsel the court has erred;

(d) should bring to the attention of the court any appropriate compensation, forfeiture and restitution matters which may arise on conviction, for example pursuant to sections 35–42 of the *Powers of Criminal Courts Act* 1973 and the *Drug Trafficking Offences Act* 1986;

(e) should draw the attention of the defence to any assertion of material fact made in mitigation which the prosecution believes to be untrue: if the defence persist in that assertion, prosecuting counsel should invite the Court to consider requiring the issue to be determined by the calling of evidence in accordance with the decision of the Court of Appeal in *R. v. Newton* (1983) 77 Crim.App.R. 13.

11 Responsibilities of defence counsel

C–34   **11.1** When defending a client on a criminal charge, a barrister must endeavour to protect his client from conviction except by a competent tribunal and upon legally admissible evidence sufficient to support a conviction for the offence charged.

11.2 A barrister acting for the defence:

(a) should satisfy himself, if he is briefed to represent more than one defendant, that no conflict of interest is likely to arise;

(b) should arrange a conference and if necessary a series of conferences with his professional and lay clients;

(c) should consider whether any enquiries or further enquiries are necessary and, if so, should advise in writing as soon as possible;

(d) should consider whether any witnesses for the defence are required and, if so, which;

(e) should consider whether a notice of alibi is required and, if so, should draft an appropriate notice;

(f) should consider whether it would be appropriate to call expert evidence for the defence and, if so, have regard to the rules of the Crown Court in relation to notifying the prosecution of the contents of the evidence to be given;

(g) should ensure that he has sufficient instructions for the purpose of deciding which prosecution witnesses should be cross-examined, and should then ensure that no other witnesses remain fully bound at the request of the defendant and request his professional client to inform the Crown Prosecution Service of those who can be conditionally bound;

(h) should consider whether any admissions can be made with a view to saving time and expense at trial, with the aim of admitting as much evidence as can properly be admitted in accordance with the barrister's duty to his client;

(i) should consider what admissions can properly be requested from the prosecution;

(j) should decide what exhibits, if any, which have not been or cannot be copied he wishes to examine, and should ensure that appropriate arrangements are made to examine them as promptly as possible so that there is no undue delay in the trial.

(k) should as to anything which he is instructed to submit in mitigation which casts aspersions on the conduct or character of a victim or witness in the case, notify the prosecution in advance so as to give prosecuting counsel sufficient opportunity to consider his position under paragraph 10.8(e).

11.3 A barrister acting for a defendant should advise his lay client generally about his plea. In doing so he may, if necessary, express his advice in strong terms. He must, however, make it clear that the client has complete freedom of choice and that the responsibility for the plea is the client's.

11.4 A barrister acting for a defendant should advise his client as to whether or not to give evidence in his own defence but the decision must be taken by the client himself.

11.5.1 Where a defendant tells his counsel that he did not commit the offence with which he is charged but nevertheless insists on pleading guilty to it for reasons of his own, counsel should:

(a) advise the defendant that, if he is not guilty, he should plead not guilty but that the deci-

sion is one for the defendant; counsel must continue to represent him but only after he
has advised what the consequences will be and that what can be submitted in mitigation
can only be on the basis that the client is guilty;

(b) explore with the defendant why he wishes to plead guilty to a charge which he says he
did not commit and whether any steps could be taken which would enable him to enter a
plea of not guilty in accordance with his profession of innocence.

11.5.2 If the client maintains his wish to plead guilty, he should be further advised:

(a) what the consequences will be, in particular in gaining or adding to a criminal record
and that it is unlikely that a conviction based on such a plea would be overturned on appeal;

(b) that what can be submitted on his behalf in mitigation can only be on the basis that he is
guilty and will otherwise be strictly limited so that, for instance, counsel will not be able
to assert that the defendant has shown remorse through his guilty plea.

11.5.3 If, following all of the above advice, the defendant persists in his decision to plead guilty

(a) counsel may continue to represent him if he is satisfied that it is proper to do so;

(b) before a plea of guilty is entered counsel or a representative of his professional client
who is present should record in writing the reasons for the plea;

(c) the defendant should be invited to endorse a declaration that he has given unequivocal
instructions of his own free will that he intends to plead guilty even though he maintains
that he did not commit the offence(s) and that he understands the advice given by
counsel and in particular the restrictions placed on counsel in mitigating and the consequences to himself; the defendant should also be advised that he is under no obligation
to sign; and

(d) if no such declaration is signed, counsel should make a contemporaneous note of his
advice.

12 Confessions of guilt

12.1 In considering the duty of counsel retained to defend a person charged with an offence who   **C–35**
confesses to his counsel that he did commit the offence charged, it is essential to bear the following
points clearly in mind:

(a) that every punishable crime is a breach of common or statute law committed by a person
of sound mind and understanding;

(b) that the issue in a criminal trial is always whether the defendant is guilty of the offence
charged, never whether he is innocent;

(c) that the burden of proof rests on the prosecution.

12.2 It follows that the mere fact that a person charged with a crime has confessed to his counsel
that he did commit the offence charged is no bar to that barrister appearing or continuing to appear
in his defence, nor indeed does such a confession release the barrister from his imperative duty to
do all that he honourably can for his client.

12.3 Such a confession, however, imposes very strict limitations on the conduct of the defence, a
barrister must not assert as true that which he knows to be false. He must not connive at, much less
attempt to substantiate, a fraud.

12.4 While, therefore, it would be right to take any objections to the competency of the court, to
the form of the indictment, to the admissibility of any evidence or to the evidence admitted, it would
be wrong to suggest that some other person had committed the offence charged, or to call any evidence which the barrister must know to be false having regard to the confession, such, for instance,
as evidence in support of an alibi. In other words, a barrister must not (whether by calling the defendant or otherwise) set up an affirmative case inconsistent with the confession made to him.

12.5 A more difficult question is within what limits may counsel attack the evidence for the prosecution either by cross-examination or in his speech to the tribunal charged with the decision of the
facts. No clearer rule can be laid down than this, that he is entitled to test the evidence given by each
individual witness and to argue that the evidence taken as a whole is insufficient to amount to proof
that the defendant is guilty of the offence charged. Further than this he ought not to go.

12.6 The foregoing is based on the assumption that the defendant has made a clear confession
that he did commit the offence charged, and does not profess to deal with the very difficult questions
which may present themselves to a barrister when a series of inconsistent statements are made to
him by the defendant before or during the proceedings; nor does it deal with the questions which
may arise where statements are made by the defendant which point almost irresistibly to the conclu-

sion that the defendant is guilty but do not amount to a clear confession. Statements of this kind may inhibit the defence, but questions arising on them can only be answered after careful consideration of the actual circumstances of the particular case.

13 General

C–36   **13.1** Both prosecuting and defence counsel:

(a) should ensure that the listing officer receives in good time their best estimate of the likely length of the trial (including whether or not there is to be a plea of guilty) and should ensure that the listing officer is given early notice of any change of such estimate or possible adjournment;

(b) should take all reasonable and practicable steps to ensure that the case is properly prepared and ready for trial by the time that it is first listed;

(c) should ensure that arrangements have been made in adequate time for witnesses to attend court as and when required and should plan, so far as possible, for sufficient witnesses to be available to occupy the full court day;

(d) should, if a witness (for example a doctor) can only attend court at a certain time during the trial without great inconvenience to himself, try to arrange for that witness to be accommodated by raising the matter with the trial judge and with his opponent;

(e) should take all necessary steps to comply with the *Practice Direction (Crime: Tape Recording of Police Interviews)* [1989] 1 W.L.R. 631.

13.2 If properly remunerated (paragraph 502 of the Code), the barrister originally briefed in a case should attend all plea and directions hearings. If this is not possible, he must take all reasonable steps to ensure that the barrister who does appear is conversant with the case and is prepared to make informed decisions affecting the trial.

14 Video recordings

C–37   **14.1** When a barrister instructed and acting for the prosecution or the defence of an accused has in his possession a copy of a video recording of a child witness which has been identified as having been prepared to be admitted in evidence at a criminal trial in accordance with section 54 of the *Criminal Justice Act* 1991, he must have regard to the following duties and obligations:

(a) Upon receipt of the recording, a written record of the date and time and from whom the recording was received must be made and a receipt must be given.

(b) The recording and its contents must be used only for the proper preparation of the prosecution or defence case or of an appeal against conviction and/or sentence, as the case may be, and the barrister must not make or permit any disclosure of the recording or its contents to any person except when, in his opinion, it is in the interests of his proper preparation of that case.

(c) The barrister must not make or permit any other person to make a copy of the recording, nor release the recording to the accused, and must ensure that:

(i) when not in transit or in use, the recording is always kept in a locked or secure place, and;

(ii) when in transit, the recording is kept safe and secure at all times and is not left unattended, especially in vehicles or otherwise.

(d) Proper preparation of the case may involve viewing the recording in the presence of the accused. If this is the case, viewing should be done:

(i) if the accused is in custody, only in the prison or other custodial institution where he is being held, in the presence of the barrister and/or his instructing solicitor;

(ii) if the accused is on bail, at the solicitor's office or in counsel's chambers or elsewhere in the presence of the barrister and/or his instructing solicitor.

(e) The recording must be returned to the solicitor as soon as practicable after the conclusion of the barrister's role in the case. A written record of the date and time despatched and to whom the recording was delivered for despatch must be made.

15 Attendance of counsel at court

C–38   **15.1** Prosecuting counsel should be present throughout the trial, including the summing-up and the return of the jury. He may not absent himself without leave of the court; but, if two or more barristers appear for the prosecution, the attendance of one is sufficient.

15.2.1 Defence counsel should ensure that the defendant is never left unrepresented at any stage of his trial.

15.2.2 Where a defendant is represented by one barrister, that barrister should normally be present throughout the trial and should only absent himself in exceptional circumstances which he could not reasonably be expected to foresee and provided that:

    (a) he has obtained the consent of the professional client (or his representative) and the lay client; and

    (b) a competent deputy takes his place.

15.2.3 Where a defendant is represented by two barristers, neither may absent himself except for good reason and then only when the consent of the professional client (or his representative) and of the lay client has been obtained, or when the case is legally aided and the barrister thinks it necessary to do so in order to avoid unnecessary public expense.

15.2.4 These rules are subject to modification in respect of lengthy trials involving numerous defendants. In such trials, where after the conclusion of the opening speech by the prosecution defending counsel is satisfied that during a specific part of the trial there is no serious possibility that events will occur which will relate to his client, he may with the consent of the professional client (or his representative) and of the lay client absent himself for that part of the trial. He should also inform the judge. In this event it is his duty:

    (a) to arrange for other defending counsel to guard the interests of his client;

    (b) to keep himself informed throughout of the progress of the trial and in particular of any development which could affect his client; and

    (c) not to accept any other commitment which would render it impracticable for him to make himself available at reasonable notice if the interests of his client so require.

15.3.1 If during the course of a criminal trial and prior to final sentence the defendant voluntarily absconds and the barrister's professional client, in accordance with the ruling of the Law Society, withdraws from the case, then the barrister too should withdraw. If the trial judge requests the barrister to remain to assist the court, the barrister has an absolute discretion whether to do so or not. If he does remain, he should act on the basis that his instructions are withdrawn and he will not be entitled to use any material contained in this brief save for such part as has already been established in evidence before the court. He should request the trial judge to instruct the jury that this is the basis on which he is prepared to assist the court.

15.3.2 If for any reason the barrister's professional client does not withdraw from the case, the barrister retains an absolute discretion whether to continue to act. If he does continue, he should conduct the case as if his client were still present in court but had decided not to give evidence and on the basis of any instruction he has received. He will be free to use any material contained in his brief and may cross-examine witnesses called for the prosecution and call witnesses for the defence.

16 Appeals

16.1.1 Attention is drawn to the Guide to Proceedings in the Court of Appeal Criminal Division   **C–39** ("the Guide") which is set out in full [in Appendix J, *post*].

16.1.2 In particular when advising after a client pleads guilty or is convicted, defence counsel is encouraged to follow the procedures set out at paragraphs 1.2 and 1.4 of the Guide.

16.2 If his client pleads guilty or is convicted, defence counsel should see his client after he has been sentenced in the presence of his professional client or his representative. He should then proceed as follows:

    (a) if he is satisfied that there are no reasonable grounds of appeal he should so advise orally and certify in writing. Counsel is encouraged to certify using the form set out in Appendix 1 to the Guide. No further advice is necessary unless it is reasonable for a written advice to be given because the client reasonably requires it or because it is necessary e.g. in the light of the circumstances of the conviction, any particular difficulties at trial, the length and nature of the sentence passed, the effect thereof on the defendant or the lack of impact which oral advice given immediately after the trial may have on the particular defendant's mind.

    (b) If he is satisfied that there are more reasonable grounds of appeal or if his view is a provisional one or if he requires more time to consider the prospects of a successful appeal he should so advise orally and certify in writing. Counsel is encouraged to certify using the form set out in Appendix 1 to the Guide. Counsel should then furnish written advice to the professional client as soon as he can and in any event within 14 days.

16.3 Counsel should not settle grounds of appeal unless he considers that such grounds are properly arguable, and in that event he should provide a reasoned written opinion in support of such grounds.

16.4 In certain cases counsel may not be able to perfect grounds of appeal without a transcript or other further information. In this event the grounds of appeal should be accompanied by a note to the Registrar setting out the matters on which assistance is required. Once such transcript or other information is available, counsel should ensure that the grounds of appeal are perfected by the inclusion of all necessary references.

16.5 Grounds of appeal must be settled with sufficient particularity to enable the Registrar and subsequently the court to identify clearly the matters relied upon.

16.6 If at any stage counsel is of the view that the appeal should be abandoned, he should at once set out his reasons in writing and send them to his professional client.

Service standards on returned briefs agreed with the CPS

C–40   The following standards agreed in 1996 have been issued by the Bar Council. They do not form part of the *Code of Conduct.*

SERVICE STANDARDS ON RETURNED BRIEFS AGREED WITH THE CPS

SERVICE STANDARD ON RETURNED BRIEFS

1 PRINCIPLE

C–41   **1.1** This Standard applies to all advocates instructed to prosecute on behalf of the CPS.

1.2 The fundamental principle upon which the Standard is based is that the advocate initially instructed should conduct the case.

1.3 This applies to all cases irrespective of whether or not they are contested.

1.4 For the purpose of this Standard a return means a brief which is passed to another advocate because the advocate instructed is unable to appear to represent the prosecution at any hearing, subject to the exceptions for interlocutory hearings referred to in paragraphs 1.13–1.15 below.

1.5 There is a need for positive action to be taken by all advocates, acting in conjunction with the CPS, to minimise the level of returns in order to ensure that the best possible service is provided. Such action will include ensuring that the advocate's availability is considered when cases are being fixed and that efforts are made to take this into account.

1.6 Whatever positive action is taken to reduce the level of returns, it is recognised that there will always be some briefs which are returned.

1.7 The impact of a return is dependent upon the nature of the case and the timing of its return.

1.8 There will be some degree of flexibility in uncontested cases in that the acceptability of the return will be influenced by the nature, complexity and seriousness of the case and the degree of involvement of the advocate before committal or transfer.

1.9 Where a return is unavoidable, the advocate will be responsible for ensuring that immediate notice is given to enable the CPS to choose and instruct another advocate and for that advocate fully to prepare the case.

1.10 Special attention must be paid to retrials, sensitive cases or those involving vulnerable witnesses, especially children, and those cases in which the advocate has settled the indictment, provided a substantive advice, attended a conference or been present at an *ex parte* hearing.

1.11 The advocate prosecuting a case in which the brief has been returned should not, without good reason and prior consultation with the CPS, reverse a decision previously taken by the advocate originally instructed. This is especially important in cases involving child witnesses and video evidence.

1.12 Whenever a brief is returned, the choice of an alternative advocate will always be a matter for the CPS. Where counsel has been instructed, the availability of alternative counsel in the chambers holding the brief will not be the determining factor in selecting a new advocate. Counsel's clerk will be expected to make realistic proposals as to an alternative advocate, whether or not within the same chambers, and consideration will be given to them.

1.13 When the CPS instructs an advocate to appear at an interlocutory hearing, including plea and directions hearings (PDH), bail applications, applications to make or break fixtures and mentions, the advocate instructed in the case will, wherever practicable, be expected to attend. If the advocate instructed is not available, an alternative advocate may be instructed provided that advocate is acceptable to the CPS and following consultation with the CPS.

1.14 If an advocate is unable to attend a PDH as a result of work commitments elsewhere, a returned brief will not be treated as a return for the purpose of monitoring compliance with this Standard, unless the advocate's clerk was consulted about, and had confirmed, the advocate's availability for the PDH before the brief was delivered.

1.15 In the case of other interlocutory hearings, which may be potentially difficult or sensitive, the CPS will, whenever possible, consult the advocate's clerk about the advocate's availability before the date of hearing is arranged. Unless such consultation has taken place, a returned brief will not be counted as a return for the purpose of monitoring compliance with this Standard.

1.16 Following any interlocutory hearing, the brief will revert to the advocate originally instructed, subject to the CPS exercising its discretion to depart from this practice in any particular case.

1.17 In any case in which a brief is returned, and whatever the nature of the hearing, it will be the responsibility of the advocate holding the brief to ensure that the advocate to whom the brief is returned is fully informed of all matters relating to that hearing and, *where practicable*, to endorse the brief accordingly.

1.18 Notwithstanding the responsibility resting with the advocate returning the brief, the advocate accepting the brief also has a duty to be fully prepared to deal with any matter likely to arise at the hearing.

1.19 Subject to any other agreement negotiated with the CPS on the transfer of papers between advocates, whenever a brief is returned it will be the responsibility of the advocate or the advocate's clerk holding the brief to make arrangements to transfer the brief promptly to the agreed alternative advocate.

1.20 Neither the advocate nor the advocate's clerk should permit the number of briefs held by a single advocate to reach a point where returns are inevitable. The CPS must be informed if it appears that this situation might arise.

1.21 The CPS will make arrangements for the distribution of work to individual advocates so as to minimise the possibility of this happening.

2 GUIDANCE

2.1 Recommendations and guidance on counsel's responsibilities in relation to returned briefs **C–42** have been given in the following reports:

Seabrook Report on the Efficient Disposal of Business in the Crown Court—June 1992.

- Counsel should ensure that the CPS is notified as soon as he or his clerk knows he might have to return a brief due to other professional commitments.
- Counsel should ensure that immediate steps are taken to return a brief to another barrister acceptable to the CPS as soon as he or his clerk becomes aware that he will not be able to conduct the case.

Bar Standards Review Body Report—Blueprint for the Bar—September 1994.

- Counsel should provide written reasons upon request as to why a brief is returned.
- Counsel returning a brief should do so with as little disruption to the conduct of the case as practicable. This involves the provision of information to counsel taking on the case.

2.2 It is against this background that the procedures which follow have been developed.

3 PROCEDURE

Categorisation of cases

3.1 For the purpose of setting standards aimed at reducing the level of returns cases will fall **C–43** within 3 categories.

3.2 Category A will comprise the following:

- cases in which the fees will be assessed *ex post facto*;
- pre-marked cases in which a Grade 4 Advocate or Special List Advocate (London and South Eastern Circuit) is instructed;
- cases in which Leading Counsel (including a Leading Junior) has been instructed by the CPS;
- cases falling within classes 1 and 2 of the Lord Chief Justice's Practice Direction classifying business within the Crown Court.

3.3 In category A cases no return of the brief is acceptable save where the following applies:

- the advocate is unable to attend court because of illness, accident, childbirth or unexpected incapacity;

- attending court would cause the advocate grave personal hardship as, for example, following a bereavement;
- subject to paragraph 3.8 below, circumstances have arisen outside the advocate's, or the advocate's clerk's, control which are such as to make a return inevitable;
- the case has been fixed for trial by the court in the knowledge that the advocate instructed will not be available.

3.4 Where a case has been so fixed, the CPS will decide whether to apply to the court to change the fixed date or to instruct a different advocate.

3.5 Category B will comprise cases in which the brief has been pre-marked and which do not fall within category A, and standard fee cases in which a fixed trial date has been allocated.

3.6 If a trial date has been fixed, no return of the trial brief is acceptable except as in 3.3 above.

3.7 If a trial date has been fixed before the brief is delivered, or has been fixed regardless of the advocate's availability, immediate steps will be taken by the CPS in liaison with the advocate or the advocate's clerk, to identify an appropriate advocate who will be available on the fixed date. Once the brief has been delivered or reallocated, no return is acceptable.

3.8 The advocate's involvement in a part-heard trial will not in itself justify a return in a category A or B case, unless the part-heard trial has been prolonged by unforeseeable circumstances. Where the advocate is involved in a part-heard trial, the position must be kept under constant review, and the CPS kept fully informed, so that an early decision can be made by the CPS as to whether to require a brief to be returned.

3.9 If a brief in a category A or B case is returned, the advocate will, upon CPS request, provide a written explanation as to why the return was unavoidable.

3.10 Category C will comprise standard fee cases which have not been given fixed trial dates.

3.11 It is recognised that, for cases which attract standard fees, a higher return rate is more difficult to avoid.

3.12 Subject to the requirements of Bar/CPS Standard 2 on pre-trial preparation having been carried out, if the advocate originally instructed in a category C case is not available, the CPS will agree to the brief being returned to another advocate of appropriate experience, who has adequate time to prepare for the hearing.

General procedural matters

C–44

3.13 If a case appears in a warned list or firm date list and the advocate instructed will not be available, the advocate or the advocate's clerk must notify the CPS immediately.

3.14 The CPS will then decide whether to make representations to the court to take the case out of the list, or to allow the brief to be returned to another advocate.

3.15 Where a case has appeared in a reserve list, or where a system of overnight listing operates within the warned list, it is accepted that some returns will be inevitable.

3.16 The advocate or the advocate's clerk should give as much notice as possible of returns in these instances and should aim to give the CPS **two working days notice**. This situation could apply, for example, when an advocate becomes committed part way through the week to a case expected to last several days.

3.17 Where a system of firm dates operates within the warned list period, the CPS must be notified if it appears likely that the advocate may be unavailable, so that an early decision can be made on whether to instruct another advocate or whether to defer the decision.

3.18 The timing of the decision whether to instruct another advocate will always be a matter for the CPS and will be influenced by the nature of the case as well as the information provided by the advocate or the advocate's clerk.

August 1996

Criticism of previous counsel

C–45

In consequence of observations made by the Court of Appeal in *R. v. Clarke and Jones, The Times*, August 19, 1994, and *R. v. Bowler, The Times*, May 9, 1995, the following guidance has been approved by Lord Taylor C.J. and the Bar Council.

1. Allegations against former counsel may receive substantial publicity whether accepted or rejected by the court. Counsel should not settle or sign grounds of appeal unless he is satisfied that they are reasonable, have some real prospect of success and are such that he is prepared to argue before the court (Guide to Proceedings in the

Court of Appeal Criminal Division, para. A2–6 [*post*, Appendix J–5]). When such allegations are properly made however, in accordance with the Code of Conduct counsel newly instructed must promote and protect fearlessly by all proper and lawful means his lay client's best interests without regard to others, including fellow members of the legal profession (Code, para. 303(a)).

2. When counsel newly instructed is satisfied that such allegations are made, and a waiver of privilege is necessary, he should advise the lay client fully about the consequences of waiver and should obtain a waiver of privilege in writing signed by the lay client relating to communications with, instructions given to and advice given by former counsel. The allegations should be set out in the Grounds of Application for Leave of Appeal. Both waiver and grounds should be lodged without delay; the grounds may be perfected if necessary in due course.

3. On receipt of the waiver and grounds, the registrar of Criminal Appeals will send both to former counsel with an invitation on behalf of the court to respond to the allegations made.

4. If former counsel wishes to respond and considers the time for doing so insufficient, he should ask the Registrar for further time. The court will be anxious to have full information and to give counsel adequate time to respond.

5. The response should be sent to the Registrar. On receipt, he will send it to counsel newly instructed who may reply to it. The grounds and the responses will go before the single judge.

6. The Registrar may have received grounds of appeal direct from the applicant, and obtained a waiver of privilege before fresh counsel is assigned. In those circumstances, when assigning counsel, the Registrar will provide copies of the waiver, the grounds of appeal and any response from former counsel.

7. This guidance covers the formal procedures to be followed. It is perfectly proper for counsel newly instructed to speak to former counsel as a matter of courtesy before grounds are lodged to inform him of the position.

As to the need to follow the Bar Council's guidance, see *R. v. Nasser*, *The Times*, February 19, 1998, CA.

Preparation of defence statements

On September 24, 1997, the Professional Conduct and Complaints Committee of the Bar **C–46** Council approved guidance as to the duties of counsel in relation to the preparation of defence statements pursuant to the *CPIA* 1996. The guidance (as revised by the Bar Standards Board in January, 2011) is set out in full in the main work at § 12–98.

III. MISCELLANEOUS AUTHORITIES ON DUTIES OF ADVOCATES

(1) Return of brief or instructions

Members of the criminal bar have a personal responsibility for compliance with provi- **C–47** sions of the Code of Conduct relating to the return of instructions, of which their clerks should be aware. It is open to a court concerned with a problem caused by a late return of a brief to send a complaint to the Professional Conduct Committee of the Bar Council: *R. v. Sutton JJ., ex p. DPP*, 95 Cr.App.R. 180, DC, *per* Brooke J., at p. 186 (decided in relation to paragraphs 507 and 508 of the fifth edition of the Code of Conduct).

The absence of what counsel would regard as sufficient time for preparation does not constitute an exception to the cab-rank rule requiring him to act for his client: see *R. v. Ulcay* (§ 4–67 in the main work).

(2) Duty not to accept certain instructions

C–48   Counsel should not appear for the prosecution in a case where the defendant is a person he has previously represented; para. 501(f) of the Code of Conduct for the Bar (6th ed.) referred to the risk that the barrister might have considential information or special knowledge disadvantageous to the defendant, his former client; it is contrary to the spirit of the code that a barrister should put himself in a position where such a risk might be perceived: *R. v. Dann* [1997] Crim.L.R. 46, CA. As to *Dann*, see further *Re T. and A. (Children) (Risk of Disclosure)* [2002] 1 F.L.R. 859, CA (Civ.Div.).

(3) Duty in relation to the giving of advice and taking of instructions

C–48a   Although not laid down in prescriptive form in the codes of conduct governing barristers and solicitors, solicitors and counsel should make a brief note of the advice given and the instructions received in conference on important issues as to the conduct of the defence (such as discussions relating to strategy, including as to whether the defendant should give evidence); such a note would be to the benefit of the client, in that it will serve to ensure that he has been given the appropriate advice; it would also serve to protect the advocate and his instructing solicitors from criticism based on assertions made after the event by a dissatisfied client: *R. v. Anderson, The Times*, December 23, 2010, CA.

(4) Duty of counsel to acquaint themselves with the terms of the indictment

C–49   See *R. v. Peckham*, 25 Cr.App.R. 125, CCA (prosecution), and *R. v. Olivo*, 28 Cr.App.R. 173, CCA (defence).

(5) Duty concerning recent legislation

C–50   In *R. v. Isaacs, The Times*, February 9, 1990, the Court of Appeal said that when presenting cases at first instance or in appellate courts, counsel have a positive duty to inform the court of all relevant commencement dates of recent legislation.

(6) Duty of counsel to inform themselves of the sentencing powers of the court

C–51   The Court of Appeal has repeatedly emphasised the duty of both counsel to inform themselves before the commencement of proceedings in the Crown Court of the sentencing powers of the court, including powers in relation to ancillary orders, such as costs, compensation, etc. The starting point is *R. v. Clarke (R.W.W.)*, 59 Cr.App.R. 298, CA. Lawton L.J. concluded the judgment of the court with the following general observations and guidance. His Lordship's remarks are even more apposite today than when they were made: legislation in relation to sentence has become ever more complex. Sections 28 and 29 of the *MCA* 1952 were replaced by sections 37 and 38 respectively of the *MCA* 1980, which have themselves since been subject to extensive amendment. Section 37 was eventually repealed by the *CDA* 1998, and section 38 was repealed and replaced by section 3 of the *PCC(S)A* 2000.

> "We adjudge that counsel as a matter of professional duty to the Court, and in the case of defending counsel to their client, should always before starting a criminal case satisfy themselves as to what the maximum sentence is. There can be no excuse for counsel not doing this and they should remember that the performance of this duty is particularly important in a case where a man has been committed to the Crown Court for sentencing pursuant to the provisions of sections 28 and 29 of the *Magistrates' Courts Act* 1952, and section 56 of the *Criminal Justice Act* 1967. Those statutory provisions are pregnant with dangers for court and for counsel and above all for accused persons...
>
> Secondly, those who administer the Crown Court should act as follows. Before the Crown Court came into existence..., it was the practice of many clerks of assize and many clerks of the peace to make a note on the documents put before the trial judge of the maximum sentence which could be passed and of the paragraphs in *Archbold's Criminal Pleading, Evidence and Practice* which dealt with the offence. In some Crown Courts this former practice has been followed. On the other hand it is clear from this case and from inquiries which we have made that it is not always followed. It should

be; and it is particularly important that it should be when judges are asked to deal with cases committed for sentence under the statutory provisions to which I have already referred" (at pp. 301–302).

A reminder of the duty of counsel for both sides to ensure that sentences imposed, and orders made, are within the powers of the court, and to invite the court to vary a sentence if on subsequent consideration it appears to be unlawful, was given in *R. v. Komsta and Murphy*, 12 Cr.App.R.(S.) 63. Turner J. commented that it could not be too clearly understood that there was positive obligation on counsel, both for the prosecution and the defence, to ensure that no order was made that the court had no power to make. The *PCC(S)A* 2000, s.155(1) (see § 5–1289 in the main work) allowed the Crown Court to alter or vary any sentence or order, within the period of 28 [now 56] days of the making of the order. If it appeared to either counsel that the order was one which the court had no power to make, counsel should not hesitate to invite the court to exercise such powers.

See also *R. v. Richards, The Times*, April 1, 1993, CA, *R. v. Hartrey* [1993] Crim.L.R. 230, CA, *R. v. Johnstone (D.), The Times*, June 18, 1996, CA, *R. v. Bruley* [1996] Crim.L.R. 913, CA, *R. v. McDonnell* [1996] Crim.L.R. 914, CA, *R. v. Street*, 161 J.P. 28, CA, *R. v. Blight* [1999] Crim.L.R. 426, CA and, most recently, *R. v. Cain* [2007] 2 Cr.App.R.(S.) 25, CA. In *Blight*, it was said that counsel do not discharge their duty simply by having a copy of *Archbold* "to hand"; it is the duty of both counsel to be aware in advance of the powers of the court so that any error may be recited immediately; as to the defence counsel, it was said to be very difficult to see how mitigation can be done properly without having in the very front of the mind the powers within which the judge must exercise his duty. In *R. v. Cain*, it was said that defence advocates should ascertain and be prepared to assist the judge with any relevant legal restrictions on sentence, and the prosecution advocate should ensure that the sentencer does not, through inadvertence, impose an unlawful sentence; in particular, prosecution advocates should always be ready to assist the court by drawing attention to any statutory provisions that govern the court's sentencing powers and to any sentencing guidelines or guideline decisions of the Court of Appeal.

In *R. v. Reynolds* [2007] 2 Cr.App.R.(S.) 87, CA, it was said that prosecuting and defence **C–52** advocates must ensure that they are fully aware of the potential impact of the provisions of the dangerous offender provisions in Chapter 5 of Part 12 of the *CJA* 2003 (§§ 5–494 *et seq.* in the main work), that they are able to assist the sentencer in that respect and are alert to any mistakes made in passing sentence so that any problem can be resolved before it is too late.

(7) Defendant absconding

See *R. v. Shaw*, 70 Cr.App.R. 313, CA, see § 3–200 in the main work, and for relevant **C–53** provisions of the 8th edition of the Code of Conduct, see *ante*, C–1 in this supplement.

(8) Defendant not giving evidence

In *R. v. Bevan*, 98 Cr.App.R. 354, CA, it was held that where a defendant decides not to **C–54** give evidence, it should be the invariable practice of counsel to record that decision and to cause the defendant to sign that record, indicating clearly first, that he has, of his own free will, decided not to give evidence and, secondly, that he has so decided bearing in mind the advice given to him by counsel. In the light of section 35 of the *CJPOA* 1994 (§ 4–377 in the main work), the advice of the Court of Appeal in *Bevan* is likely to become of greater importance than at the time of the decision. As to this, see also *Ebanks (Kurt) v. The Queen* [2006] 1 W.L.R. 1827, PC (§ 4–382 in the mainwork).

(9) Duties in relation to cross-examination

See §§ 8–216, 8–219 *et seq.* in the main work and, in relation to defence counsel's duty **C–55** when cross-examining a co-defendant, see *R. v. Fenlon*, 71 Cr.App.R. 307, CA, see § 8–297 in the main work.

(10) Duties in relation to the summing up

C–56   See §§ 4–433 *et seq.* in the main work.

(11) Duties in relation to appeal

C–57   As to the duty to advise in relation to the possibility of an appeal against conviction or sentence, see §§ 7–166 *et seq.* in the main work, and *ante*, C–39, C–45.

As to counsel's general duty in relation to the drafting of grounds of appeal, see § 7–168 in the main work. As to criticism of former counsel, see § 7–83 in the main work, and § C–45, *ante*.

As to the duty of counsel for the prosecution, see § 7–201 in the main work.

The duty of a barrister to present his client's case before the Court of Appeal could not extend to advancing the client's assertion, unsubstantiated by any evidence, that the trial judge was corrupt or biased. A barrister's duty in such circumstances is either to decline to comply with the instructions or to withdraw from the case: *Thatcher v. Douglas, The Times,* January 8, 1996, CA (Civ. Div.).

(12) Duties of prosecuting counsel

C–58   Apart from the matters mentioned above, see also (a) *The Role and Responsibilities of the Prosecution Advocate, post,* E–15 *et seq.*; (b) *R. v. Herbert,* 94 Cr.App.R. 230, CA (§ 4–173 in the main work) and *R. v. Richards and Stober,* 96 Cr.App.R. 258, CA (§ 19–87 in the main work), in relation to "plea–bargaining" and the acceptance of pleas, with particular reference to cases where there are two or more defendants; (c) §§ 4–342 *et seq.* in the main work, in relation to the opening of a case generally, and *R. v. Hobstaff,* 14 Cr.App.R.(S.) 605, CA, in relation to opening the facts on a plea of guilty; and (d) the Attorney-General's guidelines on the acceptance of pleas and the prosecutor's role in the sentencing exercise (*ante,* Appendix A–276 *et seq.*).

(13) Advocate as witness

C–59   In *R. v. Jacquith (or Jaquith) and Emode* [1989] Crim.L.R. 508 and 563, CA, junior counsel for one defendant has been called on his behalf to rebut a suggestion of recent invention made against him. The Court of Appeal said that the evidence on this point was admissible but it was very undesirable for counsel to give evidence on this point in court. In addition to the effect on the jury it caused embarrassment and difficulty to other members of the Bar who had to set about cross-examining a colleague.

May L.J. said that the suggestion had been made that the court givesome indication of its views concerning evidence given by counsel and also where a client alleged an attempt to pervert the court of justice by a co-defendant. their Lordships considered, however, that the right course would be to list points for consideration by the Bar Council and the Law Society. It was not sought to lay these maters down as ones of principle; their Lordships merely thought they deserved consideration.

1. No advocate should ever give evidence if that could possibly be avoided. 2. Where it was not possible for an advocate to avoid giving evidence, he should take no further part in the case. It necessarily followed that, if he was not being led, the trial must stop and a retrial be ordered. 3. There was a duty on counsel to anticipate circumstances in which he might be called upon to give evidence. Experienced counsel ought to be able to anticipate whether such a situation might arise. Where such a situation was anticipated, or envisaged even as a possibility, he should withdraw from the case. 4. Where it came to the notice of a legal adviser, through an accused person, that one of his co-defendants had attempted to pervert the court of justice, there was a duty on the legal adviser, usually the instructing solicitor, to take a detailed proof at once to provide a record and for further investigation. 5. Where the giving of evidence by an advocate caused real embarrassment or inhibition or difficulty regarding cross-examination by other advocates, the judge should exercise his discretion to discharge the jury and order a retrial.

For relevant provisions of the 8th edition of the Code of Conduct, see *ante*, in this supplement.

(14) Co-habiting counsel

It is generally undesirable for husband and wife, or other partners living together, to ap- **C–60** pear as counsel on opposite sides in the same criminal matter since it might give rise to an apprehension that the proper conduct of the case had been in some way affected by that personal relationship: *R. v. Batt, The Times*, May 30, 1996, CA. See also *Re L. (Minors) (Care Proceedings: Solicitors)* [2001] 1 W.L.R. 100, Fam D. (Wilson J.).

APPENDIX D

Forms for use at Preliminary Hearings and Plea and Case Management Hearings

CROWN COURT

CASE PROGRESSION

PRELIMINARY HEARING

Date of hearing: /   /   Judge:

Prosecution advocate:		
D1	[bail][custody] represented by:	
D2	[bail][custody] represented by:	
D3	[bail][custody] represented by:	
D4	[bail][custody] represented by:	
D5	[bail][custody] represented by:	

No. of case in Crown Court: [   ]   URN: [   ]

Has the defendant been advised about credit for pleading guilty?

D1	D2	D3	D4	D5

**Has the defendant been warned that if he is on bail and fails to
attend, the proceedings may continue in his absence?**

1) TRIAL JUDGE

**Should the future management of the case be under the supervision of the trial judge or a
nominated judge?**   YES/NO

2) PLEA

a.   **Is it likely that the case can be concluded by the
defendant pleading guilty?**

D1	D2	D3	D4	D5

b.   If yes and if the defendant cannot be sentenced at the preliminary hearing, go to 3) and/or
4) as appropriate

3) LIKELY GUILTY PLEA

a.   *The defendant will be sentenced on: /   /   or at the plea and case management hearing*

b.   *The directions made by the magistrates' court when the case was sent shall apply subject to
the following amendments:*

c.   *The pre-sentence report (if required) to be received by the Crown Court and made
available to the defence and the prosecution by:*

d.   *The defence to serve any material which it wishes the court to consider when sentencing
by:*

e.   **Does the defence intend to make "derogatory assertions"
against a person's character in the course of mitigation?**

D1	D2	D3	D4	D5

f.   *If yes, the court orders:*

g.   Are there any other matters against a defendant which should be dealt with at the same time as the proceedings in this case (other offences/TIC's)?

D1	D2	D3	D4	D5

h.   If yes, give brief details:

i.   *If there are other matters, the court orders:*

j.   *Further orders (e.g. orders re medical, psychiatric reports, confiscation proceedings or Newton hearings):*

4) DIRECTIONS FOR PLEA AND CASE MANAGEMENT HEARING

    a. *The directions made by the Magistrates' Court when the case was sent shall apply subject to the following amendments:*

    b. *Further orders:*

5) EXPERT EVIDENCE

    a. Is this a case in which the parties will rely on expert evidence?

P	D1	D2	D3	D4	D5

    b. *If yes, the court orders:*

6) TRIAL

    a. Can the date of the trial or the period during which the trial will take place be fixed now?   YES/NO

    b. *If yes, the trial will take place on:*
       or within the period of:
       and it is estimated that it will last:

CROWN COURT

CASE PROGRESSION

PRELIMINARY HEARING

<u>GUIDANCE NOTES</u>

General notes

These notes accompany the preliminary hearing form.

The parties must ensure that the Court has a copy of the "CASE SENT TO THE CROWN COURT UNDER SECTION 51 OF THE CRIME AND DISORDER ACT 1998" form completed in the Magistrates' Court.

The answers to the questions in bold must be filled in before the hearing. The proposed italicised orders should be filled in before the hearing, if possible (if there are more than five defendants, a further form should be filled in only so far as necessary).

Except where otherwise required, a direction in the form to "serve" material means serve on the other party(ies) and file with the Crown Court.

Notes relevant to specific sections

1) TRIAL JUDGE OR NOMINATED JUDGE

If the case is due to last for more than 4 weeks or if it seems likely that a preparatory hearing will be ordered, the future case management should normally be under the supervision of the trial judge or a nominated judge. It may also be desirable for the future case management to be under the supervision of the trial judge or a nominated judge in other cases where, for example there are difficult issues of law to be considered or where the prosecution intends to make a public interest immunity application.

If the case fits into this category, the court should normally make the necessary directions for the plea and case management hearing and then direct that the case be considered by the Resident Judge.

2) PLEA

If it is likely that the case can be concluded by all the defendants pleading guilty then 3) should be completed and there should be no need to make any orders under 4). Otherwise any appropriate orders under 3) should be made in respect of those defendants likely to plead guilty and 4) should be completed.

3) LIKELY GUILTY PLEA

3b.The Crown Court has a greater power to vary the time limits than the magistrates' court.

3c. A pre-sentence report will not be required in every case.

3e. Advance notice of the fact that such an assertion is going to be made should be given to the prosecution to enable it to decide whether to challenge the assertion and to enable the sentencing court to consider whether to make an order restricting the publication of the assertion under sections 58-61 of the Criminal Procedure and Investigations Act 1996 ("CPIA").

3i. If the defendant is facing charges in other courts give brief details of offence, court and court number.

4) DIRECTIONS FOR PLEA AND CASE MANAGEMENT HEARING

4a. The Crown Court has a greater power to vary the time limits than the Magistrates' Court.

5) EXPERT EVIDENCE

The court should identify any issues in relation to which it is appropriate to call expert evidence and set a timetable for obtaining, serving, and (if possible) agreeing such evidence or identifying the issues in dispute. See also paragraph 15 of the guidance notes to the PCMH form.

The parties should consider whether orders being considered by the court will involve costs being incurred which may not be met by the Legal Services Commission.

7) TRIAL

The court should consider whether it is possible and desirable to set the trial date or period because, for example, of the health, vulnerability or availability of a witness or the defendant or because the defendant falls within the definition of a persistent young offender, or because experts and/or leading counsel may have to be instructed and, before any such instructions can be expected, it is necessary to know the date.

The Crown Court	Plea and Case Management Hearing

Advocates' Questionnaire

CC Case Number	D1	
Date of trial		
Fixed	☐	
Warned	☐	

■ Parties must complete this form.
■ This form is to be used at all Crown Court Centres, without local variation.
There is an electronic version of the form on the Ministry of Justice website, at:
http://www.justice.gov.uk/guidance/courts-and-tribunals/courts/procedure-rules/criminal/formspage.htm

---

PART ONE
(Questions 1 to 15 are to be completed in all cases, together with question 37 'Witness List')

1   Date of trial and custody time limits

1.1   Date of PCMH   PTI URN

       Judge   Estimated length of trial

1.2   What are the custody time limit expiry dates as agreed between the parties? *(If different custody time limits attach to different offences or defendants, please give details.)*

1.3   Can an application to extend any custody time limit be made today?   ☐ No   ☐ Yes

2   Parties

Parties' names	Age	Remand status	Instructed Advocate	PCMH Advocate (if not the Instructed Advocate)
P				
D1		C ☐ B ☐		

3   Contact details

3.1   Parties

P	Office	Name		Phone	
		Email			

	Advocate	Name		Phone	
		Email			

D1	Solicitor	Name		Phone	
		Email			

	Advocate	Name		Phone	
		Email			

3.2   Case progression officers

P		Name		Phone	
		Email			

D1		Name		Phone	
		Email			

Court		Name		Phone	
		Email			

4   Which, if any, of the orders made at the magistrates' court have not been complied with?

5

D1   Has the defendant been advised that he or she will receive credit for a guilty plea?   ☐ No ☐ Yes

6

D1   Has the defendant been warned that the case may proceed in his or her absence?   ☐ No ☐ Yes

7   What plea(s) is / are the defendant(s) offering?

D1

8   Should the case be referred to the Resident Judge for a trial judge to be allocated?   ☐ No ☐ Yes

9 Give details of any issues relating to the fitness to plead or to stand trial.

D1

10 **Disclosure, the defence statement and notification of defence witnesses**

10.1 Has the prosecution made statutory disclosure?

P

D1

10.2 Has a defence statement been served?

D1

10.3 Does it comply with the statutory requirements?

P

10.4 If not clear from the defence statement, what are the real issues?

D1

10.5
D1 Has / will the defence made / make an application in writing under section 8 of the Criminal Procedure and Investigations Act 1996? ☐ No ☐ Yes

10.6
D1 Has the time limit for the notification of defence witnesses expired?

☐ No ☐ Yes

If yes, give particulars (preferably on the relevant from of Notice).

If no, can any orders be made even at this stage?

☐ No ☐ Yes

Details of any proposed order(s)

11 **Further evidence**
What further evidence is to be served by the prosecution? By when is it reasonably practicable to serve this?

P

12   **Expert evidence**

12.1   Give details of any expert evidence likely to be relied upon, including why it is required and by when it is reasonably practicable to serve this.

P

D1

12.2   Is a note of agreement / disagreement required?

13   **Witnesses**

13.1   Have the parties completed the Witness List (see **37**)?   ☐ No ☐ Yes

13.2   Are the parties satisfied that all the listed witnesses are needed (see **37**)?   ☐ No ☐ Yes
If 'no', give details.

13.3   Are the parties satisfied that the time estimates for questioning witnesses are realistic (see **37**)?   ☐ No ☐ Yes
If 'no', give details.

13.4   Is any witness summons necessary?   ☐ No ☐ Yes
If 'yes', give particulars:

13.5   Can a timetable be fixed now for the calling of witnesses?   ☐ No ☐ Yes
If 'no', why not?

14   **Timetabling of the trial**

14.1   Are there matters which need to be determined at the start of the trial, which may affect the timetable?   ☐ No ☐ Yes

If so, when will (1) the jury and (2) the witnesses be required?

14.2 What timetable can now be set for the conduct of the trial (see rule 3.10)?

15 The indictment

15.1 Has the indictment been signed and dated as required by Part 14 of the CrimPR? ☐ No ☐ Yes

15.2 Is any amendment of the indictment required? ☐ No ☐ Yes

> **PART TWO question 37 (Witness list) is to be completed in every case**
>
> *Answer the remaining questions only where relevant*

16 Admissions and agreed facts

What matters can usefully be admitted or put into schedules, diagrams, visual aids etc.?

17 Case summary

P Is it proposed to serve a case summary or note of opening? ☐ No ☐ Yes

18 Measures to assist witnesses and defendants in giving evidence

18A **Measures to assist a witness in giving evidence.**

Each of these issues must be addressed separately in respect of each young vulnerable or intimidated witness who is or may be required to give evidence in person. (If completed electronically, the form will expand to deal with each separate witness separately. If completed manually, attach separate sheets if necessary.)

Name and age of witness:

name: age:

What arrangements have been made for a pre-trial visit?		
What arrangements have been made to ensure that the witness sees the video of their evidence BEFORE the trial (i.e. not immediately before giving their evidence over the live link)?		
Has the witness been offered a 'supporter'? If 'yes', give particulars:	☐ No	☐ Yes
Does the witness need an intermediary? If 'yes', give particulars:	☐ No	☐ Yes
What arrangements have been made for the witness to access the court building other than by the main public entrance?		
What are the arrangements to ensure that this witness can give evidence without waiting or at least by reducing waiting to a minimum *(e.g. by ensuring that the opening and any preliminary points will be finished before the time appointed for the witness to attend or by agreeing and fixing a timed witness order in advance)*?		
Have the views of the witness been sought and, if so, has s/he expressed any particular view or concerns? If 'yes', give particulars:	☐ No	☐ Yes
If views not sought, why not?		
What material (if any) needs to be available to the witness in the video suite?		

18B **Defendant's evidence direction**

Is any defendant's evidence direction to be sought?	☐ No	☐ Yes
If so, has the necessary application been made, complying with Section 4 of CrimPR Part 29?	☐ No	☐ Yes

Plea and Case Management Hearing, Criminal Procedure Rules 2011 – July 2011   6

If so, give details

18C Witness anonymity order

Is any witness anonymity order sought / to be made?	☐ No ☐ Yes
If so, has an application been made, complying with Section 5 of CrimPR Part 29?	☐ No ☐ Yes

If so give details (subject to the restrictions in Section 5 of CrimPR Part 29).

19 Young or vulnerable defendants

Are any other arrangements needed for any young or vulnerable defendants?

D1

20 Reporting restrictions

State type and grounds of any reporting restriction sought.

P

D1

21 Third party material

21. Is any application to be made for the production of third party material? ☐ No ☐ Yes

22 Defendant's interview(s)

22.1 Specify any issue relating to the admissibility of all or any part of the defendant's interview(s). Can the issue be resolved now ? If not, when ? Are skeleton arguments needed and, if so, when ?

22.2 By how much can the interview(s) be shortened by editing / summary for trial ? Give a timetable for the service of any proposed summary by the prosecution and agreement / counter-proposal by the defence.

22.3   Specify any other issues concerning the defendant's interview(s).

23   Witnesses giving evidence by video or DVD interview

23.1   Is there video or DVD evidence of any young / vulnerable / intimidated witness yet to be served?

23.2   Has each video been transcribed?

23.3   Is there an issue in relation to the accuracy / admissibility / quality / length of any video or transcript?

24   Witness interview(s)

24.1   Are there any videos / audio tapes of witness interviews which, if they meet the disclosure test, are yet to be disclosed as unused material?

24.2   If so, is any application made for that video / audio tape to be transcribed and, if so, why?

25   CCTV evidence

25.1   Are there any outstanding issues in relation to service or disclosure of CCTV footage? *If the material is in the possession of a third party, complete **21** instead.*

25.2   Is an edited version to be served / used?

26 Electronic equipment

26.1   Give details of any special equipment (e.g. CCTV, live link, audio recordings, DVD) required in the trial courtroom.

P

D1

26.2   Is the evidence in its present form compatible with the equipment in court?

27 Cross-examination on sexual history

If an application has not already been made, does the defence intend to make an application under section 41 of the Youth Justice and Criminal Evidence Act 1999 to cross-examine a witness about his or her sexual history?

D1

28 Bad character

Are any directions necessary in relation to bad character applications? Are there to be any further applications?

P

D1

29   Hearsay

Are any directions necessary in relation to hearsay applications? Are there to be any further applications?

P

D1

30   Admissibility and legal issues

What points on admissibility / other legal issues are to be taken? Is it necessary for any to be resolved before trial?

P

D1

31   Public interest immunity

Is any 'on notice' public interest immunity application to be made?

P

32   Jury bundle

What proposals do the prosecution make for a jury bundle?

P

33   Concurrent family proceedings

Give details of any concurrent family proceedings.

Plea and Case Management Hearing, Criminal Procedure Rules 2011 – July 2011   10

34 **Other special arrangements**

Give details of any special arrangements (e.g., interpreter, intermediary, wheelchair access, hearing loop system, breaks) needed for anyone attending the trial.

35 **Linked criminal proceedings**

Are there other criminal proceedings against the defendant or otherwise linked?

36 **Additional orders**

Are any additional orders required?

37 **Witness List** (see table for completion, over page)

37   Witness List

The parties should indicate here which prosecution witnesses are required to give evidence at trial. The attendance of any witness is subject to the judge's direction.

Name of witness	Page No.	Required by	What is the relevant, disputed issue?	Estimated time for questioning	
				Chief	**X - exam**

Plea and Case Management Hearing Form: Guidance Notes

The need for an effective PCMH

i.   The public, and all those concerned in or affected by a criminal case, have a right to expect that the business of the courts will be conducted fairly but also efficiently and effectively. Delays cost money and adversely impact on the quality of justice. The Plea and Case Management Hearing offers the best, and often the only, opportunity for the judge properly and effectively to manage the case before it is listed for trial. Other hearings – formerly called 'mentions' – are expensive and should actively be discouraged; nearly everything formerly done at a 'mention' can – and should – be done in some other way (usually by telephone or on paper or by an exchange of email, as permitted by CrimPR 3.5(2)(d)). An effective PCMH is therefore vital.

ii.   Advocates should attend the hearing fully prepared to deal with the issues that are likely to arise, and the listing officer should consider reasonable requests to list the PCMH to enable trial counsel to attend.

iii.   Since an effective PCMH can only take place after the defence have had a proper opportunity to consider the papers, it is suggested that at least four weeks should elapse between the service of the prosecution case papers and listing of the PCMH.

iv.   The short guidance given here is intended to be followed in every case but, of course, it is not possible to cover exhaustively all the situations which may be relevant to achieving an effective PCMH. See also Consolidated Criminal Practice Direction (CCPD), paragraph IV.41, Management of Cases to be Heard in the Crown Court; and paragraph V.56, Case Management in Magistrates' Courts.

How to use the form

v.   The parties should complete only one form for each case. **The form should be used in every Crown Court centre, without any local exception or variation**.

vi.   The form may be completed in manuscript or electronically.

vii.   Questions 1 to 15 (in Part I) must be answered in every case.

viii.   Questions 16-36 (in Part II) need only be answered if they are relevant.

ix.   Question 37, at the end of the form, (the witness list) must be completed in every case.

x.   The advocate may be asked by the court to expand upon or explain an entry, or to account for the absence of an entry, where one is required. The judge will record on the judicial orders template, or on the PCMH form, any orders made and, if practicable, issue a copy to the parties before the hearing ends. The parties must obtain a copy of that record and comply with the orders made by the date given.

Accessing the form

xi.   The current version of the form is available on the Ministry of Justice website at www.justice.gov.uk/guidance/courts-and-tribunals/courts/procedure-rules/criminal/formspage.htm

Transmitting the form

xii.   If you complete the form on the screen, it can still be printed off and used in hard copy. Alternatively, it can be emailed as an attachment.

Contents of the form

(The following commentary is to assist with the completion of the questions so numbered on the PCMH form.)

1 Date of trial and custody time limits

The date of trial should normally be fixed at the PCMH (or before). Any application to extend the Custody Time Limit is best dealt with at the PCMH, when the reasons for fixing a case beyond the time limits will be clear; otherwise there will be the avoidable expense of another hearing.

2 and 3 Details of case and parties

This section must be fully completed. The parties must be able to contact one another as must case progression officers and the court. Any change in the details must immediately be notified to the other parties and to the court. See CrimPR 3.4.

4 Compliance with the directions given by magistrates' courts

The standard / specific directions given by magistrates' courts should be complied with (CrimPR 3.5(3)). The court will need to know which orders have not been complied with, and why.

5 Credit for guilty plea

Defendants are entitled to be given the advice that credit is given for guilty pleas and the earlier the plea is entered, the greater is the credit given. The judge needs to know that this advice has been given.

6 Trial in absence

Defendants need to be warned that if they waive their right to attend, the trial may proceed in their absence. No one can engineer an adjournment simply by absconding. Those who claim to be ill must support that claim by medical evidence to the effect that they are unfit to attend their trial; it is unlikely that a medical certificate merely suggesting that they are unfit to work will be sufficient. See CCPD, I.13; CrimPR 3.8(2)(a).

7 The pleas which the defendant is offering

Recording in writing pleas offered to alternative offences which the prosecution are initially unwilling to accept will be advantageous to the defendant if the prosecution subsequently

Revised 2011   2

changes its position. In such circumstances, it will be easier for a defendant to claim maximum credit if that offer has been recorded. Pleas offered to counts on the indictment must similarly be recorded before credit is claimed.

8 Allocation of the case

Most courts have a system to identify before the PCMH those cases which require allocation to a particular judge; this question is intended to seek out those cases which have been missed.

9 Fitness to plead

This is self explanatory, but the judge will need assistance to fix a timetable for the service of experts' reports and for the issue to be tried.

10 Disclosure, the defence statement and notification of defence witnesses

The parties must identify any outstanding disclosure points. See Part 22 of The Criminal Procedure Rules 2010. The defence must serve a detailed defence statement setting out the issues in the trial; any failure to do so may be the subject of adverse comment at the trial and the judge may issue a warning to this effect, under section 11(3) of the Criminal Procedure and Investigations Act 1996. Pending service of a defence statement, question 10.4 allows the defence to give some notification of the defence. The practice of appending long 'shopping lists' to vague and unspecific defence statements has no legal foundation; any application for further disclosure should be made by way of formal application under section 8 of the Criminal Procedure and Investigations Act 1996 (as amended). The judge will expect compliance with the relevant Practice Directions, Guidelines and Protocols.

Pursuant to section 6C of the Criminal Procedure and Investigations Act 1996, the defence must notify the prosecution and the court whether he intends to call any witnesses at trial, and if so, give their names, addresses and dates of birth. The Practice Direction sets out a form for use by the defence when giving this notice (see rule 22.4). It may be that the time limit for notification has not expired when the PCMH is held but even so the defence might usefully be reminded of their responsibilities under that provision; if even as early as the PCMH the defence can comply, then they should be encouraged to do so.

11 and 12 Timetable of further evidence and expert evidence

Advocates should have available proper information as to what remains to be served, together with a realistic timetable for compliance. Parties should be prepared to provide realistic time estimates and not rely on a standard time period of, for example, 28 days if this has little bearing on the true amount of time likely to be required. The court needs detailed and accurate information as to when the evidence will be available. These enquiries should be made before the hearing. Failure to do so is likely to cause unnecessary adjournments. Consideration should be given to CrimPR 33.6 and whether (now or later) the experts should be asked to confer, to identify the real areas of dispute.

13 (and 37) Witness list

The mere fact of warning a witness to attend may cause him or her anxiety. Furthermore, the warning of witnesses is time consuming and expensive. When completing the witness list at paragraph 37, it is important to identify the relevant disputed issues to which the evidence of any particular witness is necessary, so that the judge can decide whether their attendance is necessary. The court may decline to order the attendance of witnesses unless their presence is really necessary. Consideration should therefore also be given to those witnesses in respect of whom a summons is required. See CrimPR Part 28 for rules on witness summonses. Thought should always be given to the staggering of witnesses to eliminate or reduce waiting times. The witnesses' availability must be known at the PCMH to ensure that the trial date is convenient.

14 Timetabling of the trial

Part 3.10 CrimPR requires the judge to consider timetabling in every case, with a view to improving efficiency; these matters require consideration throughout the trial; it may be possible to make some orders even at the PCMH.

If there are to be preliminary points taken, then consideration must be given to when a jury will be required and arrangements made to stagger the attendance of witnesses. No one should be asked to attend for a 10.30 am start only to find that there is a lengthy legal argument before the case can even be opened.

15 The Indictment

CrimPR 14.1(3)(a) requires the indictment to be signed by the court officer. Any amendment to the indictment must be ordered by the court.

16 Admissions and agreed facts

Admissions, sometimes more accurately called agreed facts, take time to draft but they can save a great deal of court time and thereby reduce costs. This applies not only to formal evidence (for example of continuity or of the captions to photographs) but also to many other types of evidence, of which these are but examples: lengthy police interviews are often better summarised and agreed; witness statements which are agreed to be read can often be summarised; expert evidence, including medical evidence, is often easier to understand if it is summarised by way of agreement rather than being read; this applies with particular force to evidence of telephone traffic and to cell site analysis; bad character evidence, if admissible, is also often better agreed.

17 Case Summary

Case Summaries should have been provided before the PCMH in all Class 1 cases and in any other case of complexity, but they may be needed in other cases as well.

18 Measures to assist witnesses and defendants in giving evidence

In accordance with CrimPR Part 29, special measures applications should have been made by the parties and considered by the court before the PCMH. This question addresses other points:

> **Question 18A** serves to remind advocates and judges of the needs of vulnerable and intimidated witnesses and of the measures which now exist to assist them in giving evidence;

> **Question 18B** serves a similar purpose in relation to defendants, who may require assistance in giving evidence;

> **Question 18C** alerts the judge to applications to be made in relation to anonymous witnesses, which are likely to require a separate hearing, ideally before the trial judge.

Revised 2011

4

19 Young or vulnerable defendants

Question 18B addresses the assistance which a defendant may need to facilitate giving evidence. This question seeks to identify any other needs of defendants who are children or young people or adults who are 'vulnerable' in that they suffer from a mental disorder or from some other significant impairment of intelligence or social function and for whom special arrangements must be made so that they can effectively understand and participate in the proceedings (as to which see generally paragraph III.30 of the CCPD).

20 Reporting restrictions

Reporting restrictions need to be carefully considered and balanced against the rights of the press and other interested parties. The judge is likely to require assistance before making any order. See CCPD I.3. and the JSB and Society of Editors publication, *Reporting Restrictions in the Criminal Courts*, url
hhtp://www.judiciary.gov.uk/Resources/JCO/Documents/crown court reporting restrictions 021009.pdf.)

21 Third party material

Such applications must comply with CrimPR Part 28. Careful thought needs to go into identifying the witness to be served, the material sought and the reason that it is said to be relevant to an issue in the case. Any person whose right of confidentiality might be adversely affected must also be identified and information provided as to how and by whom they are to be notified, how they are to be permitted to make representations and when and by whom any rulings are to be made. It is important that such applications are made no later than the PCMH to avoid adjournments at a later stage arising out of delayed applications. Any such application is better made using the appropriate form set out in the Practice Direction for use in connection with an application under Part 28, which directs the applicant and the judge to the relevant criteria.

22 Defendant's interviews

Inaccuracies within transcriptions and likely submissions as to admissibility must be identified. Furthermore, the police may interview suspects at length, producing bundles of transcripts, the volume of which may make them unsuitable to put before a jury. The parties must consider producing summaries. The production of the first draft is primarily the responsibility of the advocate for the prosecution. If practicable, interviews should be available in electronic form, so that editing, pagination and copying can be done without delay. Further guidance is given in CCPD IV.43.

23 Witnesses giving evidence by video or DVD interview

These questions, each of which raises a separate point, are self-explanatory but failure to address them is a frequent source of adjournments. The quality of the recording, the accuracy of the transcript and the admissibility of the interview (or any particular part or parts of it) are separate points, each of which needs to be addressed at the PCMH.

Any editing of the tape (or disc) takes time. Particular care must be taken to ensure that any editing of the tapes has not diminished its sound quality and that any editing of the tape is precisely reflected in editing to the transcript; again this takes time. It should not be done on the morning of the trial or the day beforehand.

Only if these issues are addressed in advance can young and vulnerable witnesses be called as soon as they arrive at court. It is unacceptable to prolong the anxiety of young and vulnerable witnesses simply because these issues have not been resolved at PCMH. See also CrimPR Part 29 for rules on special measures directions; and CCPD IV.40.

Furthermore, the extreme and unnecessary length of many of these interviews is becoming a matter of great concern. Judges have a responsibility to eliminate undue repetition and may require interviews to be reduced in length, so as to reduce the burden on the jury, and on the witness, whilst not disadvantaging the defendant.

24 Witness interviews

The issues raised in this question differ from those raised in question 23. There is a growing practice of recording interviews with witnesses before setting out their evidence in a written witness statement. If this is done, then, subject to the disclosure test, the video or audio recording should be disclosed as unused material. The prosecution advocate therefore needs to know if any witness was interviewed in this way (which may not be clear from the papers served). It will normally suffice for the video or audio recording itself to be disclosed. Transcripts are expensive and any claim for a transcript needs to be justified.

25 and 26 CCTV evidence and electronic equipment

Subject to the duties of the prosecution properly to investigate the case under the relevant Guidelines, the prosecution only have duties to consider disclosure of CCTV footage in their possession. If the defence seek footage from third parties, it is for them to do so, rather than the prosecution. Furthermore, much CCTV footage is in a format (e.g. multiplex) which is unsuitable for showing in court without adaptation or editing. This must be sorted out before the trial. Many courts have simple VHS video and DVD playback facilities and the parties must ensure that the material which they want to play is compatible with the court equipment (if not, they must provide their own).

27 Cross-examination on sexual history

Section 41 of the Youth Justice and Criminal Evidence Act 1999 enacts an important principle and compliance with its requirements is vital to ensure that those who complain that they are victims of rape (and other sexual offences) receive the protection which the law affords to them. In accordance with CrimPR Part 36, applications should be made and considered – by the trial judge if possible – at or before the PCMH. Applications made on the day of the trial are strongly to be discouraged.

28 and 29 Bad character and hearsay

CrimPR at Parts 34 (Hearsay) and 35 (Evidence of bad character) provide for detailed applications to be made in the prescribed forms. Questions 28 and 29 therefore only seek to identify any outstanding issues (or potential future applications).

30 Admissibility and legal issues

Issues of admissibility and legal issues should, where possible, be identified before the trial, so that the parties can exchange skeleton arguments and the judge can properly prepare for the hearing. See also section 7 of the Criminal Justice Act 1987; and sections 31 and 40 of the Criminal Procedure and Investigations Act 1996.

31 Public Interest Immunity claims

If a claim is to be made on notice, then the necessary arrangements must be made. See CrimPR 22.3.

32 Jury bundle

If a jury bundle will be needed at the trial, then its content will need to be agreed before the trial. Any outstanding issues need to be identified.

33 Concurrent family proceedings

It is important to identify those cases where there are concurrent family proceedings, so that the Designated Family Judge can be alerted.

34 Special arrangements

Any requirements for an interpreter or for those with a disability must be identified in advance, so that proper arrangements can be made. See CrimPR 10.5(1)(h) and 12.1(1)(e).

35 Linked criminal proceedings

These need to be identified, if possible with the court reference numbers.

36 Additional orders

It is important to identify additional orders which may be required.

37 Witness List

See the note in paragraph 13, above.

Revised 2011   7

Forms for use in cases with two or more defendants

Expanded versions of the plea and case management hearing form, for use in connection **★D–3** with cases involving two to 10 defendants are available on the Ministry of Justice website (http://www.justice.gov.uk/courts/procedure-rules/criminal/formspage).

APPENDIX E

Crown Prosecution Service

I. CODE FOR CROWN PROSECUTORS

A. Introduction

The Crown Prosecution Service is the principal public prosecuting authority for England   **E–1** and Wales and is headed by the Director of Public Prosecutions, who is to discharge his functions under the superintendence of the Attorney-General (*Prosecution of Offences Act* 1985, s.3(1)). The Attorney-General is accountable to Parliament for the Service.

The Crown Prosecution Service is a national organisation consisting of 42 areas. Each area is headed by a Chief Crown Prosecutor and corresponds to a single police force area, with one for London. It was set up in 1986 to prosecute cases investigated by the police.

Although the Crown Prosecution Service works closely with the police, it is independent of them. The independence of crown prosecutors is of fundamental constitutional importance. Casework decisions taken with fairness, impartiality and integrity help deliver justice for victims, witnesses, defendants and the public.

The Crown Prosecution Service co-operates with the investigating and prosecuting agencies of other jurisdictions.

The Director of Public Prosecutions is responsible for issuing a Code for Crown Prosecutors under section 10 of the *Prosecution of Offences Act* 1985, giving guidance on the general principles to be applied when making decisions about prosecutions. This is the sixth edition of the code and replaces all earlier versions. It was issued on February 22, 2010. It applies to all prosecutors (including members of the Revenue and Customs Prosecutions Office, the Director of Public Prosecutions now also being Director of Revenue and Customs Prosecutions), associate prosecutors and police officers when making charging decisions.

B. The Code

1. Introduction

1.1 The Crown Prosecution Service (CPS) is the principal public prosecution service for England   **E–2** and Wales. In January 2010, it merged with the Revenue and Customs Prosecutions Office (RCPO). The service is headed by the Director of Public Prosecutions (DPP) who is also the Director of Revenue and Customs Prosecutions. The DPP exercises his functions independently, subject to the superintendence of the Attorney General who is accountable to Parliament for the work of the prosecution service.

1.2 The DPP is responsible for issuing the Code for Crown Prosecutors (the code) under section 10 of the *Prosecution of Offences Act* 1985. The code gives guidance to prosecutors on the general principles to be applied when making decisions about prosecutions. This is the sixth edition of the code and replaces all earlier versions.

1.3 In this code, the term "prosecutors" is used to describe members of the prosecution service who are designated as crown prosecutors; prosecutors who are members of the RCPO; associate prosecutors who are designated under section 7A of the *Prosecution of Offences Act* 1985 and who exercise their powers in accordance with the instructions issued by the DPP; and other members of the RCPO who are designated by the DPP in his capacity as the Director of the Revenue and Customs Prosecutions under section 39 of the *Commissioners for Revenue and Customs Act* 2005.

1.4 In this code, the expression "police or other investigators" is used to describe members of all those investigative agencies, including the Serious Organised Crime Agency and the UK Border Agency, who prepare and present cases to the prosecution service.

1.5 Although the prosecution service works closely with the police and other investigators, it is independent of them. The independence of prosecutors is of fundamental constitutional importance.

1.6 The prosecution service co-operates with the investigating and prosecuting agencies of other jurisdictions to facilitate enquiries and prosecutions both in England and Wales and abroad.

1.7 In accordance with section 36(2) of the *Commissioners for Revenue and Customs Act* 2005, prosecutors from the RCPO who are acting in that capacity must have regard to the Code for Crown Prosecutors issued by the DPP.

1.8 In this code, the term "suspect" is used to describe a person who is not yet the subject of formal criminal proceedings; the term "defendant" is used to describe a person who has been charged or summonsed; and the term "offender" is used to describe a person who has admitted his or her guilt to a police officer or other investigator or prosecutor, or who has been found guilty in a court of law.

1.9 The code is one of two key published and publicly available documents that explain the purpose and work of the prosecution service. The second is the Core Quality Standards booklet. Only the code is issued by law.

1.10 Together, they let the public know what prosecutors do; how they take their decisions; and the level of service that the prosecution service is committed to providing in every key aspect of its work.

1.11 The code and the Core Quality Standards booklet are available from the contact points listed on the back cover of this booklet.

2. GENERAL PRINCIPLES

E–3   2.1 The decision to prosecute or to offer an individual an out-of-court disposal is a serious step. Fair and effective prosecution is essential to the maintenance of law and order. It is the duty of prosecutors to make sure that the right person is prosecuted for the right offence and to bring offenders to justice wherever possible. Casework decisions taken fairly, impartially and with integrity help to deliver justice for victims, witnesses, defendants and the public.

2.2 It is the duty of prosecutors to review, to advise on and to prosecute cases or to offer an appropriate out-of-court disposal to the offender. Prosecutors must ensure that the law is properly applied; that all relevant evidence is put before the court; and that obligations of disclosure are complied with, in accordance with the principles set out in this code.

2.3 Although each case must be considered on its own facts and on its own merits, there are general principles that apply to the way in which prosecutors must approach every case.

2.4 Prosecutors must be fair, independent and objective. They must not let any personal views about the ethnic or national origin, gender, disability, age, religion or belief, political views, sexual orientation, or gender identity of the suspect, victim or any witness influence their decisions. Neither must prosecutors be affected by improper or undue pressure from any source. Prosecutors must always act in the interests of justice and not solely for the purpose of obtaining a conviction.

2.5 The prosecution service is a public authority for the purposes of current, relevant equality legislation. Prosecutors are bound by the duties set out in this legislation.

2.6 The prosecution service is also a public authority for the purposes of the *Human Rights Act* 1998. Prosecutors must apply the principles of the European Convention on Human Rights, in accordance with the *Human Rights Act*, at each stage of a case. Prosecutors must also comply with any guidelines issued by the Attorney General and with the policies of the prosecution service issued on behalf of the DPP. They must also comply with the *Criminal Procedure Rules* currently in force.

3. THE DECISION WHETHER TO PROSECUTE

E–4   3.1 In more serious or complex cases, prosecutors decide whether a person should be charged with a criminal offence, and, if so, what that offence should be. They make their decisions in accordance with this code and the DPP's Guidance on Charging. The police apply the same principles in deciding whether to charge or summons a person in those cases for which they are responsible.

3.2 The police and other investigators are responsible for conducting enquiries into an allegation that a crime may have been committed. Every case that prosecutors receive from the police or other investigators is reviewed. Prosecutors must ensure that they have all the information they need to make an informed decision about how best to deal with the case. This will often involve prosecutors providing guidance and advice to the police and other investigators about lines of inquiry, evidential requirements, and assistance in any pre-charge procedures throughout the investigative and prosecuting process. However, prosecutors cannot direct the police or other investigators.

3.3 Prosecutors should identify and, where possible, seek to rectify evidential weaknesses, but, subject to the threshold test (see section 5), they should swiftly stop cases which do not meet the evidential stage of the full code test (see section 4) and which cannot be strengthened by further investigation, or where the public interest clearly does not require a prosecution (see section 4). Although the prosecutor primarily considers the evidence and information supplied by the police and other investigators, the suspect or those acting on his or her behalf may also submit evidence or information to the prosecutor via the police or other investigators, prior to charge, to help to inform the prosecutor's decision.

3.4 Prosecutors must only start or continue a prosecution when the case has passed both stages of the full code test (see section 4). The exception is when the threshold test (see section 5) may be applied where it is proposed to apply to the court to keep the suspect in custody after charge, and the evidence required to apply the full code test is not yet available.

3.5 Prosecutors must make sure that they do not allow a prosecution to start or continue where to do so would be seen by the courts as oppressive or unfair so as to amount to an abuse of the process of the court.

3.6 Review is a continuing process and prosecutors must take account of any change in circumstances that occurs as the case develops. Wherever possible, they should talk to the investigator first if they are thinking about changing the charges or stopping the case. Prosecutors and investigators work closely together, but the final responsibility for the decision whether or not a case should go ahead rests with the prosecution service.

3.7 Parliament has decided that a limited number of very serious or sensitive offences should only be taken to court with the agreement of the DPP. These are called "consent" cases. In such cases, the DPP or prosecutors acting on his behalf apply the code in deciding whether to give consent to a prosecution.

4. THE FULL CODE TEST

4.1 The full code test has two stages: (i) the evidential stage; followed by (ii) the public interest **E–5** stage.

4.2 In the vast majority of cases, prosecutors should only decide whether to prosecute after the investigation has been completed and after all the available evidence has been reviewed. However, there will be cases where it is clear, prior to the collection and consideration of all the likely evidence, that the public interest does not require a prosecution. In these rare instances, prosecutors may decide that the case should not proceed further.

4.3 Prosecutors should only take such a decision when they are satisfied that the broad extent of the criminality has been determined and that they are able to make a fully informed assessment of the public interest. If prosecutors do not have sufficient information to take such a decision, the investigation should proceed and a decision taken later in accordance with the full code test set out in this section.

4.4 Prosecutors must follow any guidance issued by the DPP to ensure that decisions in these cases are appropriate and correct.

The evidential stage

4.5 Prosecutors must be satisfied that there is sufficient evidence to provide a realistic prospect of **E–5a** conviction against each suspect on each charge. They must consider what the defence case may be, and how it is likely to affect the prospects of conviction. A case which does not pass the evidential stage must not proceed, no matter how serious or sensitive it may be.

4.6 A realistic prospect of conviction is an objective test based solely upon the prosecutor's assessment of the evidence and any information that he or she has about the defence that might be put forward by the suspect. It means that an objective, impartial and reasonable jury or bench of magistrates or judge hearing a case alone, properly directed and acting in accordance with the law, is more likely than not to convict the defendant of the charge alleged. This is a different test from the one that the criminal courts themselves must apply. A court may only convict if it is sure that the defendant is guilty.

4.7 When deciding whether there is sufficient evidence to prosecute, prosecutors must consider whether the evidence can be used and whether it is reliable. There will be many cases in which the evidence does not give any cause for concern. But there will also be cases in which the evidence may not be as strong as it first appears. In particular, prosecutors will need to consider the following issues.

Can the evidence be used in court?

  a. Is it likely that the evidence will be excluded by the court? There are legal rules that might mean that evidence which seems relevant cannot be given at a trial. For example, is it likely that the evidence will be excluded because of the way in which it was obtained?

  b. Is the evidence hearsay? If so, is the court likely to allow it to be presented under any of the exceptions which permit such evidence to be given in court?

  c. Does the evidence relate to the bad character of the suspect? If so, is the court likely to allow it to be presented?

Is the evidence reliable?

  d. What explanation has the suspect given? Is a court likely to find it credible in the light of the evidence as a whole? Does the evidence support an innocent explanation?

  e. Is there evidence which might support or detract from the reliability of a confession? Is its reliability affected by factors such as the suspect's level of understanding?

  f. Is the identification of the suspect likely to be questioned? Is the evidence of his or her identity strong enough? Have the appropriate identification procedures been carried out? If not, why not? Will any failure to hold the appropriate identification procedures lead to the evidence of identification being excluded?

  g. Are there concerns over the accuracy, reliability or credibility of the evidence of any witness?

  h. Is there further evidence which the police or other investigators should reasonably be asked to find which may support or undermine the account of the witness?

  i. Does any witness have any motive that may affect his or her attitude to the case?

  j. Does any witness have a relevant previous conviction or out-of-court disposal which may affect his or her credibility?

  k. Is there any further evidence that could be obtained that would support the integrity of evidence already obtained?

4.8 Where it is considered that it would be helpful in assessing the reliability of a witness' evidence or in better understanding complex evidence, an appropriately trained and authorised prosecutor should conduct a pre-trial interview with the witness in accordance with the relevant code of practice.

4.9 Prosecutors should not ignore evidence because they are not sure that it can be used or is reliable. But they should look closely at it when deciding if there is a realistic prospect of conviction.

The public interest stage

E–6　　4.10 In 1951, Sir Hartley Shawcross, who was then Attorney General, made the classic statement on public interest: "[i]t has never been the rule in this country—I hope it never will be—that suspected criminal offences must automatically be the subject of prosecution". He added that there should be a prosecution: "wherever it appears that the offence or the circumstances of its commission is or are of such a character that a prosecution in respect thereof is required in the public interest" (House of Commons Debates, Volume 483, 29 January 1951). This approach has been endorsed by Attorneys General ever since.

4.11 Accordingly, where there is sufficient evidence to justify a prosecution or to offer an out-of-court disposal, prosecutors must go on to consider whether a prosecution is required in the public interest.

4.12 A prosecution will usually take place unless the prosecutor is sure that there are public interest factors tending against prosecution which outweigh those tending in favour, or unless the prosecutor is satisfied that the public interest may be properly served, in the first instance, by offering the offender the opportunity to have the matter dealt with by an out-of-court disposal (see section 7). The more serious the offence or the offender's record of criminal behaviour, the more likely it is that a prosecution will be required in the public interest.

4.13 Assessing the public interest is not simply a matter of adding up the number of factors on each side and seeing which side has the greater number. Each case must be considered on its own facts and on its own merits. Prosecutors must decide the importance of each public interest factor in the circumstances of each case and go on to make an overall assessment. It is quite possible that one factor alone may outweigh a number of other factors which tend in the opposite direction. Although there may be public interest factors tending against prosecution in a particular case, prosecutors should consider whether nonetheless a prosecution should go ahead and for those factors to be put to the court for consideration when sentence is passed.

4.14 The absence of a factor does not necessarily mean that it should be taken as a factor tending in the opposite direction. For example, just because the offence was not "carried out by a group" does not transform the "factor tending in favour of a prosecution" into a "factor tending against prosecution".

4.15 Some common public interest factors which should be considered when deciding on the most appropriate course of action to take are listed below. The following lists of public interest factors are not exhaustive and each case must be considered on its own facts and on its own merits.

Some common public interest factors tending in favour of prosecution

4.16 A prosecution is more likely to be required if:

    a. a conviction is likely to result in a significant sentence;

    b. a conviction is likely to result in an order of the court in excess of that which a prosecutor is able to secure through a conditional caution;

    c. the offence involved the use of a weapon or the threat of violence;

    d. the offence was committed against a person serving the public (for example, a member of the emergency services; a police or prison officer; a health or social welfare professional; or a provider of public transport);

    e. the offence was premeditated;

    f. the offence was carried out by a group;

    g. the offence was committed in the presence of, or in close proximity to, a child;

    h. the offence was motivated by any form of discrimination against the victim's ethnic or national origin, gender, disability, age, religion or belief, political views, sexual orientation or gender identity; or the suspect demonstrated hostility towards the victim based on any of those characteristics;

    i. the offence was committed in order to facilitate more serious offending;

    j. the victim of the offence was in a vulnerable situation and the suspect took advantage of this;

    k. there was an element of corruption of the victim in the way the offence was committed;

    l. there was a marked difference in the ages of the suspect and the victim and the suspect took advantage of this;

    m. there was a marked difference in the levels of understanding of the suspect and the victim and the suspect took advantage of this;

    n. the suspect was in a position of authority or trust and he or she took advantage of this;

    o. the suspect was a ringleader or an organiser of the offence;

    p. the suspect's previous convictions or the previous out-of-court disposals which he or she has received are relevant to the present offence;

    q. the suspect is alleged to have committed the offence in breach of an order of the court;

    r. a prosecution would have a significant positive impact on maintaining community confidence;

    s. there are grounds for believing that the offence is likely to be continued or repeated.

Some common public interest factors tending against prosecution

4.17 A prosecution is less likely to be required if:

    a. the court is likely to impose a nominal penalty;

    b. the seriousness and the consequences of the offending can be appropriately dealt with by an out-of-court disposal which the suspect accepts and with which he or she complies (see section 7);

    c. the suspect has been subject to any appropriate regulatory proceedings, or any punitive or relevant civil penalty which remains in place or which has been satisfactorily discharged, which adequately addresses the seriousness of the offending and any breach of trust involved;

   d. the offence was committed as a result of a genuine mistake or misunderstanding;

   e. the loss or harm can be described as minor and was the result of a single incident, particularly if it was caused by a misjudgement;

   f. there has been a long delay between the offence taking place and the date of the trial, unless:

- the offence is serious;
- the delay has been caused wholly or in part by the suspect;
- the offence has only recently come to light;
- the complexity of the offence has meant that there has been a long investigation; or
- new investigative techniques have been used to re-examine previously unsolved crimes and, as a result, a suspect has been identified;

   g. a prosecution is likely to have an adverse effect on the victim's physical or mental health, always bearing in mind the seriousness of the offence and the views of the victim about the effect of a prosecution on his or her physical or mental health;

   h. the suspect played a minor role in the commission of the offence;

   i. the suspect has put right the loss or harm that was caused (but a suspect must not avoid prosecution or an out-of-court disposal solely because he or she pays compensation or repays the sum of money he or she unlawfully obtained);

   j. the suspect is, or was at the time of the offence, suffering from significant mental or physical ill health, unless the offence is serious or there is a real possibility that it may be repeated. Prosecutors apply Home Office guidelines about how to deal with mentally disordered offenders and must balance a suspect's mental or physical ill health with the need to safeguard the public or those providing care services to such persons;

   k. a prosecution may require details to be made public that could harm sources of information, international relations or national security.

The views of victims or their families

E-6a   4.18 In deciding whether a prosecution is required in the public interest, prosecutors should take into account any views expressed by the victim regarding the impact that the offence has had. In appropriate cases, for example, a case of homicide or where the victim is a child or an adult who lacks capacity as defined by the *Mental Capacity Act* 2005, prosecutors should take into account any views expressed by the victim's family.

    4.19 However, the prosecution service does not act for victims or their families in the same way as solicitors act for their clients, and prosecutors must form an overall view of the public interest.

    4.20 Where prosecutors have a responsibility to explain their decision to the victim, for example, when they stop a case or substantially alter the charge in a case, they must comply with the Code of Practice for Victims of Crime and all relevant CPS Guidance. Prosecutors must follow any agreed procedures, including abiding by any time period within which such decisions should be notified to the victim.

5. THE THRESHOLD TEST

E-7   5.1 Prosecutors will apply the full code test wherever possible. However, there will be cases where the suspect presents a substantial bail risk if released and not all the evidence is available at the time when he or she must be released from custody unless charged.

    5.2 In such cases, prosecutors may apply the threshold test in order to make a charging decision.

When the threshold test may be applied

E-7a   5.3 The threshold test may only be applied where the prosecutor is satisfied that all the following four conditions are met:

   a. there is insufficient evidence currently available to apply the evidential stage of the full code test; and

   b. there are reasonable grounds for believing that further evidence will become available within a reasonable period; and

   c. the seriousness or the circumstances of the case justifies the making of an immediate charging decision; and

> d. there are continuing substantial grounds to object to bail in accordance with the *Bail Act*
> 1976 and in all the circumstances of the case an application to withhold bail may properly
> be made.

5.4 Where any of the above conditions is not met, the threshold test cannot be applied and the suspect cannot be charged. Such cases must be referred back to the custody officer who will determine whether the person may continue to be detained or released on bail, with or without conditions.

5.5 There are two parts to the evidential consideration of the threshold test.

The first part of the threshold test—is there reasonable suspicion?

5.6 First, the prosecutor must be satisfied that there is at least a reasonable suspicion that the person to be charged has committed the offence.

5.7 In determining whether reasonable suspicion exists, the prosecutor must consider the evidence which is currently available. This may take the form of witness statements, material or other information, provided the prosecutor is satisfied that:

> a. it is relevant; and
> b. it is capable of being put into an admissible format for presentation in court; and
> c. it would be used in the case.

5.8 If this part of the threshold test is satisfied, the prosecutor should proceed to the second part of the threshold test.

The second part of the threshold test—will there be a realistic prospect of conviction?

5.9 Secondly, the prosecutor must be satisfied that there are reasonable grounds for believing that the continuing investigation will provide further evidence, within a reasonable period of time, so that all the evidence taken together is capable of establishing a realistic prospect of conviction in accordance with the full code test.

5.10 The further evidence must be identifiable and not merely speculative.

5.11 In reaching a decision under this second part of the threshold test, the prosecutor must consider:

> a. the nature, extent and admissibility of any likely further evidence and the impact it will
> have on the case;
> b. the charges that all the evidence will support;
> c. the reasons why the evidence is not already available;
> d. the time required to obtain the further evidence and whether any consequential delay is
> reasonable in all the circumstances.

5.12 If both parts of the threshold test are satisfied, prosecutors must apply the public interest stage of the full code test based on the information available at that time.

Reviewing the threshold test

5.13 A decision to charge under the threshold test must be kept under review. The evidence must **E–8** be regularly assessed to ensure that the charge is still appropriate and that continued objection to the granting of bail is justified. The full code test must be applied as soon as is reasonably practicable and in any event before the expiry of any applicable custody time limit or extended custody time limit.

6. SELECTION OF CHARGES

6.1 Prosecutors should select charges which: **E–9**

> a. reflect the seriousness and extent of the offending supported by the evidence;
> b. give the court adequate powers to sentence and impose appropriate post-conviction
> orders; and
> c. enable the case to be presented in a clear and simple way.

6.2 This means that prosecutors may not always choose or continue with the most serious charge where there is a choice.

6.3 Prosecutors should never go ahead with more charges than are necessary just to encourage a defendant to plead guilty to a few. In the same way, they should never go ahead with a more serious charge just to encourage a defendant to plead guilty to a less serious one.

6.4 Prosecutors should not change the charge simply because of the decision made by the court or the defendant about where the case will be heard.

6.5 Prosecutors must take account of any relevant change in circumstances as the case progresses after charge.

7. OUT-OF-COURT DISPOSALS

E–10
7.1 The prosecution service is responsible for deciding whether to offer an offender a conditional caution in certain cases. In such cases, the full code test must be met. Prosecutors will offer a conditional caution where it is a proportionate response to the seriousness and the consequences of the offending and where the conditions offered meet the aims of rehabilitation, reparation or punishment within the terms of the *Criminal Justice Act* 2003.

7.2 A conditional caution is not a criminal conviction but it forms part of the offender's criminal record and may be cited in court in any subsequent proceedings. It may also be taken into consideration by prosecutors if the offender re-offends. Prosecutors may offer a conditional caution where, having taken into account the views of the victim, they consider that it is in the interests of the suspect, victim or community to do so.

7.3 Prosecutors must follow the relevant code of practice and the DPP's Guidance on Conditional Cautioning when deciding whether to offer an offender a conditional caution.

7.4 The offer of a conditional caution which is accepted and complied with takes the place of a prosecution. If the offer of a conditional caution is refused or the suspect does not make the required admission of guilt to the person who seeks to administer the conditional caution, a prosecution must follow for the original offence. If the terms of the conditional caution are not complied with, the prosecutor will reconsider the public interest and decide whether to charge the offender. Usually, a prosecution should be brought for the original offence.

7.5 Only prosecutors can decide whether to authorise the offer of a simple caution to an offender for an offence that may only be heard in the Crown Court. The occasions when this will be an appropriate disposal will be exceptional.

7.6 In all other cases, prosecutors may direct that a simple caution be offered in accordance with CPS and Home Office guidance, or suggest, for example, the issue of a penalty notice for disorder. The issue of a penalty notice for disorder is, however, a decision for the police.

7.7 Prosecutors must be satisfied that the full code test is met and that there is a clear admission of guilt by the offender in any case in which they authorise or direct a simple caution to be offered by the police.

7.8 The acceptance of a simple caution or other out-of-court disposal which is complied with takes the place of a prosecution. If the offer of a simple caution is refused, a prosecution must follow for the original offence. If any other out-of-court disposal is not accepted, prosecutors will apply the full code test, upon receipt of the case from the police or other investigators, and decide whether to prosecute the offender.

8. YOUTHS

E–11
8.1 For the purposes of the criminal law, a youth is a person under 18 years of age.

8.2 Prosecutors must bear in mind in all cases involving youths that the United Kingdom is a signatory to the United Nations 1989 Convention on the Rights of the Child and the United Nations 1985 Standard Minimum Rules for the Administration of Juvenile Justice. In addition, prosecutors must have regard to the principal aim of the youth justice system which is to prevent offending by children and young people. Prosecutors must consider the interests of the youth when deciding whether it is in the public interest to prosecute.

8.3 Prosecutors should not avoid a decision to prosecute simply because of the suspect's age. The seriousness of the offence or the youth's past behaviour is very important.

8.4 Cases involving youths are usually only referred to the prosecution service for prosecution if the youth has already received a reprimand and final warning, unless the offence is so serious that neither is appropriate or the child or young person does not admit committing the offence.

8.5 Reprimands, final warnings and conditional cautions (see section 7) are intended to prevent re-offending and the fact that a further offence has occurred may indicate that those previous disposals have not been effective. The public interest will usually require a prosecution in such cases.

9. MODE OF TRIAL

E–11a
9.1 Prosecutors must have regard to the current Magistrates' Court Sentencing Guidelines and

the relevant practice direction when making submissions to the court about where the defendant should be tried.

9.2 Speed must never be the only reason for asking for a case to stay in the magistrates' courts. But prosecutors should consider the effect of any likely delay if a case is committed or sent to the Crown Court, and the possible effect on any victim or witness if the case is delayed.

Venue for trial in cases involving youths

9.3 Generally, prosecutors must bear in mind that youths should be tried in the youth court, wherever possible. It is the court which is best designed to meet their specific needs. A trial of a youth in the Crown Court should be reserved for the most serious cases or where the interests of justice require a youth to be jointly tried with an adult.

10. Accepting Guilty Pleas

10.1 Defendants may want to plead guilty to some, but not all, of the charges. Alternatively, they **E–12** may want to plead guilty to a different, possibly less serious, charge because they are admitting only part of the crime.

10.2 Prosecutors should only accept the defendant's plea if they think the court is able to pass a sentence that matches the seriousness of the offending, particularly where there are aggravating features. Prosecutors must never accept a guilty plea just because it is convenient.

10.3 In considering whether the pleas offered are acceptable, prosecutors should ensure that the interests and, where possible, the views of the victim, or in appropriate cases the views of the victim's family, are taken into account when deciding whether it is in the public interest to accept the plea. However, the decision rests with the prosecutor.

10.4 It must be made clear to the court on what basis any plea is advanced and accepted. In cases where a defendant pleads guilty to the charges but on the basis of facts that are different from the prosecution case, and where this may significantly affect sentence, the court should be invited to hear evidence to determine what happened, and then sentence on that basis.

10.5 Where a defendant has previously indicated that he or she will ask the court to take an offence into consideration when sentencing, but then declines to admit that offence at court, prosecutors will consider whether a prosecution is required for that offence. Prosecutors should explain to the defence advocate and the court that the prosecution of that offence may be subject to further review.

10.6 Particular care must be taken when considering pleas which would enable the defendant to avoid the imposition of a mandatory minimum sentence. When pleas are offered, prosecutors also must bear in mind the fact that ancillary orders can be made with some offences but not with others.

10.7 Prosecutors must comply with the "Attorney General's Guidelines on the Acceptance of Pleas and the Prosecutor's Role in the Sentencing Exercise" which set out in greater detail the extent of prosecutors' duties and role in the acceptance of guilty pleas.

11. The Prosecutor's Role in Sentencing

11.1 Sentencing is a decision for the court, but prosecutors have a duty to offer assistance to the **E–12a** sentencing court in reaching its decision as to the appropriate sentence by drawing the court's attention to the following factors:

  a. any aggravating or mitigating factors disclosed by the prosecution case;

  b. any victim personal statement;

  c. where appropriate, evidence of the impact of the offending on a community;

  d. any statutory provisions, sentencing guidelines, or guideline cases which may assist; and

  e. any relevant statutory provisions relating to ancillary orders (such as anti-social behaviour orders).

11.2 Prosecutors may also offer assistance to the court by making submissions, in the light of all the above factors, as to the sentencing range within which the current offence falls.

11.3 In all complex cases or where there is the potential for misunderstanding, the prosecutor must set out in writing the aggravating and mitigating factors that he or she will outline when informing the court of the case in the sentencing hearing. In all other cases, this approach should be considered and undertaken if it will be of benefit to the court or the public to understand the case.

11.4 It is the duty of the prosecutor to apply for compensation and ancillary orders, such as anti-social behaviour orders and confiscation orders, in all appropriate cases. When considering which ancillary orders to apply for, the prosecutor must always have regard to the victim's needs, including the question of their future protection.

11.5 Prosecutors should challenge any assertion made by the defence in mitigation that is inaccurate, misleading or derogatory. If the defence persist in the assertion, and it appears relevant to the sentence, the court should be invited to hear evidence to determine the facts and sentence accordingly.

11.6 Prosecutors must comply with the "Attorney General's Guidelines on the Acceptance of Pleas and the Prosecutor's Role in the Sentencing Exercise" which set out in greater detail the extent of prosecutors' duties and role in the sentencing process.

12. Re-Considering a Prosecution Decision

E–12b   12.1 People should be able to rely on decisions taken by the prosecution service. Normally, if the prosecution service tells a suspect or defendant that there will not be a prosecution, or that the prosecution has been stopped, the case will not start again. But occasionally there are special reasons why the prosecution service will overturn a decision not to prosecute or to deal with the case by way of an out-of-court disposal or when it will re-start the prosecution, particularly if the case is serious.

12.2 These reasons include:

    a. rare cases where a new look at the original decision shows that it was wrong and, in order to maintain confidence in the criminal justice system, a prosecution should be brought despite the earlier decision;

    b. cases which are stopped so that more evidence which is likely to become available in the fairly near future can be collected and prepared. In these cases, the prosecutor will tell the defendant that the prosecution may well start again;

    c. cases which are stopped because of a lack of evidence but where more significant evidence is discovered later; and

    d. cases involving a death in which a review following the findings of an inquest concludes that a prosecution should be brought, notwithstanding any earlier decision not to prosecute.

12.3 There may also be exceptional cases in which, following an acquittal of a serious offence, a prosecutor may, with the written consent of the DPP, apply to the Court of Appeal for an order quashing the acquittal and requiring the defendant to be retried.

© Crown Copyright 2010

C. Authorities

Charging of youths

E–12c   Whereas the code for crown prosecutors requires consideration to be given to the interests of a child or young person when deciding whether it is in the public interest to prosecute (see para. 8.8, *ante*, E–10), there is no requirement that a crown prosecutor should obtain a risk assessment from the youth offending services or that he should contact the potential defendant's school: *R. (A.) v. South Yorkshire Police and CPS*, 171 J.P. 465, DC.

In *D. and B. v. Commr of Police for the Metropolis, CPS, Croydon JJ.* [2008] A.C.D. 47, DC, it was held that it was permissible for a crown prosecutor to decide that the combination of the seriousness of an offence and the public interest warranted prosecution, despite the fact that the particular circumstances of the offence would normally, in accordance with the guidance issued under section 65 of the *CDA* 1998, be such as to justify only a final warning. As to this case, see also § 4–93 in the main work.

Charging victims of human trafficking

E–12d   Where it is possible that a defendant or potential defendant is a victim of human trafficking, a prosecutor should take cognisance of the CPS guidance on (i) the prosecution of defendants charged with immigration offences who might be victims of trafficking, and (ii) the prosecution of young offenders charged with offences who might be such victims; in particular, under (i), when deciding whether to prosecute, or to continue to prosecute, a "credible trafficked victim" for immigration offences, prosecutors should consider whether this would serve the public interest; and under (ii), a case should be discontinued on evidential grounds where there is clear evidence that a youth has a credible defence of duress, but, if the evidence is less certain, further details should be sought from the police and youth offender teams; the defence, on the other hand, should make inquiries wherever there is credible material showing that the defendant might have been a trafficked victim, especially if the client is young; as a signatory to the Council of Europe Convention on Action against Trafficking in Human Beings, the United Kingdom is required to identify and protect victims of trafficking, and, whereas the CPS guidance supports the purpose of the convention, a trial which had failed to have proper regard to it was not fair, either under the principles of the common law or under the principles enshrined in the ECHR: *R. v. O.*, *The Times*, October 2, 2008, CA ([2008] EWCA Crim. 2835).

The court referred to two "protocols" as being among the measures taken by the United Kingdom government in support of the purpose of the convention to which it refers (which was signed by the government on March 23, 2007, ratified on December 17, 2008, and came into force on April 1, 2009), the first of which was said to deal with the matters set out in (i), *ante*, and the second in (ii), *ante*. The court went on to say that these two protocols had been incorporated into the code for crown prosecutors. Yet, the protocols supposedly issued by the United Kingdom do not appear to exist (the only protocols in point being an informal CPS protocol, as to which, see *post*, and the United Nations Protocol to Prevent, Suppress and Punish Trafficking in Persons, especially Women and Children supplementing the United Nations Convention Against Transnational Organised Crime, signed by the United Kingdom on December 14, 2000, and ratified on February 9, 2006), and (as with the current code, *ante*) the then extant code contained no reference to either "human trafficking" or to any such protocols.

What the court appears to have done is to confuse the code (which was only ever intended to deal with general principles) with the various pieces of internal "legal guidance" issued by the CPS in respect of specific categories of offences (as to which, see *post*). Under a number of these, the information highlighted in the judgment in respect of defendants who might be trafficked victims was at that time set out in detail, based on an internal CPS Policy Bulletin (PB 126 2007—Human Trafficking—where victims of human trafficking may be charged with criminal offences). In particular, the legal guidance in relation to immigration offences contained two sections with the same titles as (i) and (ii), *ante*. The legal guidance has since been reorganised, with that relating to a defendant of any age appearing in the section dealing with immigration offences and that relating to young persons (whatever the alleged offence) being in the section dealing with "young people".

R. v. O. and the issues arising from it were further considered in *R. v. M. (L.), B. (M.) and G. (D.)*; *R. v. Tabot*; *R. v. Tijani* [2011] 1 Cr.App.R. 12, CA. It was held that one way in which the duty under article 26 of the Council of Europe Convention (to avoid the imposition of penalties on victims of human trafficking for their involvement in unlawful activities to the extent that they were compelled to become so involved) is met in England and Wales, is by means of the guidance given to prosecutors considering whether charges should be brought against those who are or may be victims of trafficking (the court pointed out that whilst the guidance is now set out in the context of immigration offences only *(ante)*, it should be taken to apply whatever the nature of the allegation). The effect of the CPS's guidance, according to the court, is to require of prosecutors a three-stage exercise, asking, first, whether there is reason to believe that the person has been trafficked, secondly, whether there is clear evidence of a common law defence (in which case, any proceedings will be discontinued on evidential grounds) and, thirdly, where there is no such evidence, but the offence may have been committed as a result of compulsion arising from the trafficking, whether the public interest requires a prosecution. It was said that article 26 does not require a blanket immunity from prosecution for trafficked victims, and that there will normally be no reason not to prosecute a victim of trafficking if the offence appears to have been committed outwith any reasonable nexus of compulsion occasioned by the trafficking. The court said that material considerations for the prosecutor when deciding whether to pursue a prosecution will be the gravity of the offence, the degree of continuing compulsion and the alternatives reasonably available to the defendant. As to this case, see also *ante*, §§ 4–90 and 17–119.

★   *R. v. O.* and *R. v. M. (L.), B. (M.) and G. (D.)*; *R. v. Tabot*; *R. v. Tijani* were further considered in *R. v. N. (A.)*; *R. v. Le* [2012] 1 Cr.App.R. 35, CA. It was held that: (i) implementation of article 26 is normally achieved by the proper exercise of the prosecutorial discretion which enables the Crown, however strong the evidence, to decide that it would be inappropriate to prosecute, or to continue with the prosecution of, a defendant who is unable to advance duress as a defence, but who falls within the protective ambit of that article; this requires a judgment to be made in the light of all the available evidence; the responsibility is not that of the court but of the prosecution; but the court may intervene if its process is abused by using the "ultimate sanction" of a stay; the burden of establishing an improper exercise of the discretion rests on the defendant; that the context is the United Kingdom's convention obligation does not involve the creation of any new principles; apart from the specific jurisdiction to stay proceedings, the court may also, in the exercise of its sentencing responsibilities, implement article 26 in the language of the article itself, by discharging the defendant absolutely or conditionally; (ii) the only publication likely to be relevant to an inquiry into an alleged abuse is the CPS's guidance on human trafficking and smuggling as it was in force at the time when the relevant decisions were made; unless it is to be argued that the guidance itself is open to question because it has failed to keep itself regularly updated in light of developing knowledge, for the purposes of the court considering an alleged abuse for which the prosecution are responsible, it is that guidance that should be the starting, and in the overwhelming majority of cases, the finishing point; (iii) expert evidence is unlikely to assist on the issue of the correctness of the decision to prosecute; (iv) a defendant has one opportunity to give his instructions to his legal advisers; it is only most exceptionally that the court would, on appeal, consider it appropriate to allow a defendant to advance fresh instructions about the facts; and there is no special category of exceptionality in the context of article 26; and (v) an abuse argument founded on the convention that is advanced long after conviction is most unlikely to succeed on the basis that subsequent events show that, if the decision whether to prosecute were to be taken now, the result might have been different from the decision actually taken in the light of the standards and guidance existing at the time it was taken.

The full code test/evidential stage

E-12e   When applying the "realistic prospect of conviction" test, a prosecutor should adopt a "merits based" approach, imagining himself to be the fact finder and asking himself, whether, on balance, the evidence is sufficient to merit a conviction, taking into account what he knows about the defence case, rather than a predictive "bookmaker's" approach, based on past experience of similar cases; questions of how a jury are likely to see a case are not relevant at this stage but at a later stage, under the public interest test in paragraphs 5.6 to 5.13 of the code: *R. (F.B.) v. DPP* [2009] 1 Cr.App.R. 38, DC. As to this case, see also §§ 1–337, 16–40a in the main work.

II. LEGAL GUIDANCE AND CHARGING STANDARDS

E-13   Apart from the code for crown prosecutors, the CPS has prepared legal guidance to prosecutors and caseworkers in relation to many criminal offences and procedural issues. It has never been suggested that such guidance has the force of law, or even parity of standing with the code. It is merely, in the words of the CPS website (where it is available to the public), "an aid to guide crown prosecutors and associate prosecutors in the use of their discretion in making decisions in cases", which "does not create any rights enforceable at law, in any legal proceedings", and is subject to the principles as set out in the code for crown prosecutors.

E-14   Incorporated within the guidance are various "charging standards" for various offences or groups of offences, such as offences against the person, driving offences, public order offences and theft. They contain a mixture of propositions of law (as to the ingredients of the various offences, maximum penalties, available alternative verdicts, *etc.*) and guidance as to the various factors that should be taken into consideration in deciding which offence to charge. The standards emphasise that they:

(a) are not to be used in the determination of any pre-charge decision, such as the decision to arrest;

(b) do not override any guidance issued on the use of appropriate alternative forms of disposal short of charge, such as cautioning;

(c) do not override the principles set out in the code for crown prosecutors;

(d) do not override the need for consideration to be given in every case as to whether a charge or prosecution is in the public interest;

(e) do not override particular policy guidance involving hate crimes; and

(f) do not remove the need for each case to be considered on its individual merits or fetter the discretion of the police to charge and the CPS to prosecute the most appropriate offence depending on the particular facts of the case in question.

The following recitation of general charging principles is common to all the standards:

(a) the charge or charges preferred should accurately reflect the extent of the defendant's involvement and responsibility, thereby allowing the courts the discretion to sentence appropriately;

(b) the choice of charges should ensure the clear and simple presentation of the case, particularly where there is more than one defendant;

(c) it is wrong to encourage a defendant to plead guilty to a few charges by selecting more charges than are necessary;

(d) it is wrong to select a more serious charge which is not supported by the evidence in order to encourage a plea of guilty to a lesser allegation.

III. THE ROLE AND RESPONSIBILITIES OF THE PROSECUTION ADVOCATE

Foreword

The Prosecution Advocate plays an important public role and as such may be considered a **E–15** cornerstone of an open and fair criminal justice system. The principles so well articulated by Farquharson L.J. and his committee as to the role of the prosecution advocate have served us well since they were published in 1986. However, the time has come for new guidance which, whilst building on the established principles, reflects the changes that have occurred in the criminal courts, at the Bar and within the Crown Prosecution Service over recent years.

I welcome and commend the new Guidelines which, whilst not legally binding unless expressly approved by the Court of Appeal, nonetheless provide important practical guidance for practitioners involved in the prosecution process.

Lord Woolf C.J.

Introduction

The work undertaken in 1986 by the committee chaired by Farquharson L.J. has, for over 15 **E–16** years, provided valuable guidance as to role [*sic*] of the prosecution advocate and their relationship with the Crown Prosecution Service (CPS).

However, the ever-evolving criminal justice system, changes at the Bar and developments in the CPS brought about by the implementation of Sir Iain Glidewell's Review, mean that the environment in whcih we all operate has radically changed since the original report was published.

Whilst the principles established by Farquharson L.J.'s committee have been enormously helpful and will continue to apply, the time has come for new guidance that reflects the changes and emphasises the new relationship that is developing between CPS Areas and the local Bar.

The new Guidelines have therefore been developed to take account of the changes and are the result of the Bar and CPS working in partnership and in consultation with the judiciary, Bar Council and Law Society.

We commend the Guidelines as providing valuable guidance and a framework within which the Bar and the CPS can work effectively together.

Lord Goldsmith Q.C., Attorney General
David Calvert-Cmith Q.C., Director of Public Prosecutions

1. Pre-trial preparation

Farquharson

E–17   (a) *It is the duty of prosecution counsel to read the Instructions delivered to him expeditiously and to advise or confer with those instructing him on all aspects of the case well before its commencement.*

E–18   1.1 The Crown Prosecution Service (CPS) will deliver instructions at a stage in the proceedings that allows sufficient time for the prosecution advocate adequately to consider, prepare and advise on the evidence before the court hearing or draft/agree the indictment.

1.2 Where a CPS higher court advocate represents the prosecution at a Plea and Directions Hearing (PDH), the CPS will deliver instructions to the trial advocate no later than 10 working days after the date of the PDH.

1.3 The CPS will deliver instructions which:

   i. address the issues in the case including any strategic decisions that have been or may need to be made;

   ii. identify relevant case law;

   iii. explain the basis and rationale of any decision made in relation to the disclosure of unused material;

   iv. where practical, provide specific guidance or indicate parameters on acceptable plea(s); and

   v. where a case is an appeal either to the Crown Court from the magistrates' court or is before the Court of Appeal, Divisional Court or House of Lords, address the issues raised in the notice of appeal, case stated, application for judicial review or petition.

Action on receipt of instructions

E–19   1.4 On receipt of instructions the prosecution advocate will consider the papers and advise the CPS, ordinarily in writing, or orally in cases of urgency where:

   i. the prosecution advocate forms a different view to that expressed by the CPS (or where applicable a previous prosecution advocate) on acceptability of plea;

   ii. the indictment as preferred requires amendment;

   iii. additional evidence is required;

   iv. there is an evidential deficiency (which cannot be addressed by the obtaining of further evidence) and, applying the Code for Crown Prosecutors, there is no longer a realistic prospect of conviction; or the prosecution advocate believes that it is not in the public interest to continue the prosecution;

   v. in order to expedite and simplify proceedings certain formal admissions should be made;

   vi. the prosecution advocate, having reviewed previous disclosure decisions, disagrees with a decision that has been made; or is not satisfied that he or she is in possession of all relevant documentation; or considers that he or she has not been fully instructed regarding disclosure matters;

   vii. a case conference is required (particularly where there is a sensitive issue, *e.g.* informant/ PII/ disclosure etc);

   viii. the presentation of the case to the court requires special preparation of material for the jury or presentational aids.

E–20   1.5 The prosecution advocate will endeavour to respond within five working days of receiving instructions, or within such period as may be specified or agreed where the case is substantial or the issues complex.

1.6 Where the prosecution advocate is to advise on a specific aspect of the case other than 1.4 (i–viii), the advocate should contact the CPS and agree a realistic timescale within which advice is to be provided.

1.7 The prosecution advocate will inform the CPS without delay where the advocate is unlikely to be available to undertake the prosecution or advise within the relevant timescale.

1.8 When returning a brief, the advocate originally instructed must ensure that the case is in good order and should discuss outstanding issues or potential difficulties with the advocate receiving the brief. Where the newly instructed advocate disagrees with a decision or opinion reached by the original advocate, the CPS should be informed so that the matter can be discussed.

Case summaries

1.9 When a draft case summary is prepared by the CPS, the prosecution advocate will consider the summary and either agree the contents or advise the CPS of any proposed amendment. **E-21**

1.10 In cases where the prosecution advocate is instructed to settle the case summary or schedules, the document(s) will be prepared and submitted to the CPS without delay.

Case management plan

1.11 On receipt of a case management plan the prosecution advocate, having considered the papers, will contact the Crown Prosecutor within seven days, or such period as may be specified or agreed where the case is substantial or the issues complex, to discuss and agree the plan. The plan will be maintained and regularly reviewed to reflect the progress of the case. **E-22**

Keeping the prosecution advocate informed

1.12 The CPS will inform the prosecution advocate of developments in the case without delay and, where a decision is required which may materially affect the conduct and presentation of the case, will consult with the prosecution advocate prior to that decision. **E-23**

1.13 Where the CPS is advised by the defence of a plea(s) of guilty or there are developments which suggest that offering no evidence on an indictment or count therein is an appropriate course, the matter should always be discussed with the prosecution advocate without delay unless to do so would be wholly impracticable.

Victims and witnesses

1.14 When a decision whether or not to prosecute is based on the public interest, the CPS will always consider the consequences of that decision for the victim and will take into account any views expressed by the victim or the victim's family. **E-24**

1.15 The prosecution advocate will follow agreed procedures and guidance on the care and treatment of victims and witnesses, particularly those who may be vulnerable or have special needs.

Appeals

1.16 Where the prosecution advocate forms a different view to that expressed by the CPS on the conduct/approach to the appeal, the advocate should advise the CPS within FIVE working days of receiving instructions or such period as may be specified or agreed where the case is substantial or the issues complex. **E-25**

PDH and other preliminary hearings

1.17 The principles and procedures applying to trials as set out in the following paragraphs will be equally applicable where the prosecution advocate is conducting a PDH or other preliminary hearing. **E-26**

2. Withdrawal of instructions

Farquharson

(b) A solicitor who has briefed counsel to prosecute may withdraw his instructions before the commencement of the trial up to the point when it becomes impracticable to do so, if he disagrees with the advice given by Counsel or for any other proper professional reason. **E-27**

2.1 The CPS will consult and take all reasonable steps to resolve any issue or disagreement and will only consider withdrawing instructions from a prosecution advocate as a last resort.

2.2 If the prosecution advocate disagrees with any part of his or her instructions the advocate should contact the responsible Crown Prosecutor to discuss the matter. Until the disagreement has been resolved the matter will remain confidential and must not be discussed by the prosecution advocate with any other party to the proceedings.

"Proper professional reason"

2.3 The prosecution advocate will keep the CPS informed of any personal concerns, reservations **E-28** or ethical issues that the advocate considers have the potential to lead to possible conflict with his or her instructions.

2.4 Where the CPS identifies the potential for professional embarrassment or has concerns about the prosecution advocate's ability or experience to present the case effectively to the court, the CPS reserves the right to withdraw instructions.

Timing

E–29   2.5 It is often difficult to define when, in the course of a prosecution it becomes impracticable to withdraw instructions as circumstances will vary according to the case. The nature of the case, its complexity, witness availability and the view of the court will often be factors that will influence the decision.

2.6 In the majority of prosecutions it will not be practicable to withdraw instructions once the judge has called the case before the court as a preliminary step to the swearing of the jury.

2.7 If instructions are withdrawn, the prosecution advocate will be informed in writing and reasons will be given.

2.8 Instructions may only be withdrawn by or with the consent of the Chief Crown Prosecutor, Assistant Chief Crown Prosecutor, Head of a CPS Trials Unit or, in appropriate cases, Head of a CPS Criminal Justice Unit.

2.9 In relation to cases prosecuted by the CPS Casework Directorate, the decision may only be taken by the Director Casework or Head of Division.

3. Presentation and conduct

Farquharson

E–30   *(c) While he remains instructed it is for counsel to take all necessary decisions in the presentation and general conduct of the prosecution.*

3.1 The statement at 3(c) applies when the prosecution advocate is conducting the trial, PDH or any other preliminary hearing, but is subject to the principles and procedures relating to matters of policy set out in section 4 below.

Disclosure of material

E–31   3.2 Until the conclusion of the trial the prosecution advocate and CPS have a continuing duty to keep under review decisions regarding disclosure. The prosecution advocate should in every case specifically consider whether he or she can satisfactorily discharge the duty of continuing review on the basis of the material supplied already, or whether it is necessary to inspect further material or to reconsider material already inspected.

3.3 Disclosure of material must always follow the established law and procedure. Unless consultation is impracticable or cannot be achieved without a delay to the hearing, it is desirable that the CPS, and where appropriate the disclosure officer are consulted over disclosure decisions.

4. Policy decisions

Farquharson

E–32   *(d) Where matters of policy[1] fall to be decided after the point indicated in (b) above (including offering no evidence on the indictment or on a particular count, or on the acceptance of pleas to lesser counts), it is the duty of Counsel to consult his Instructing Solicitor/Crown Prosecutor whose views at this stage are of crucial importance.*

(e) In the rare case where counsel and his instructing solicitor are unable to agree on a matter of policy, it is, subject to (g) below, for prosecution counsel to make the necessary decisions.

Policy issues arising at trial

E–33   4.1 The prosecution advocate should alert the CPS at the first opportunity if a matter of policy is likely to arise.

4.2 The prosecution advocate must not give an indication or undertaking which binds the prosecution without first discussing the issue with the CPS.

CPS representation at Crown Court

E–34   4.3 Whenever possible, an experienced Crown Prosecutor will be available at the Crown Court to discuss and agree any issue involving the conduct or progress of the case.

4.4 When it is not possible to provide a Crown Prosecutor at court, an experienced caseworker will attend and facilitate communication between the prosecution advocate and the Crown Prosecutor having responsibility for the case.

4.5 In exceptional circumstances where it is not possible to contact a Crown Prosecutor, the prosecution advocate should ask the court to adjourn the hearing for a realistic period in order to consult with the CPS. Where an adjournment is refused, the prosecution advocate may make the decision but should record his or her reasons in writing.

Referral to senior CPS representative

4.6 Where an issue remains unresolved following consultation with a Crown Prosecutor; or where   **E–35** the case/issue under consideration is substantial, sensitive or complex; or the prosecution advocate disagrees with the advice of the Crown Prosecutor, the matter may be referred to the Chief Crown Prosecutor, the Director Casework or to a senior Crown Prosecutor with delegated authority to act on their behalf.

4.7 In order to ensure consultation takes place at the highest level appropriate to the circumstances and nature of the case, the court should be asked to adjourn if necessary. When an adjournment is sought, the facts leading to the application should be placed before the court only in so far as they are relevant to that application.

4.8 Where a Chief Crown Prosecutor has been directly involved in the decision making process and the issue remains unresolved, the matter may be referred to the Director of Public Prosecutions.

Farquharson

(f) Where counsel has taken a decision on a matter of policy with which his Instructing Solicitor has not   **E–36** *agreed, then it would be appropriate for the Attorney General to require Counsel to submit to him a written report of all the circumstances, including his reasons for disagreeing with those who instruct him.*

4.9 It will only be in exceptional circumstances that the Attorney General will require a written report. The prosecution advocate will first discuss the decision with the Chief Crown Prosecutor or the Director, Casework. Where, by agreement, the issue remains one that either party considers should be drawn to the attention of the Director of Public Prosecutions the prosecution advocate will, on request, provide a written report for submission to the Director of Public Prosecutions. If he considers it appropriate to do so, the Director of Public Prosecutions may refer the matter to the Attorney General.

4.10 Where there has been a disagreement on a matter of policy, provided that the CPS is satisfied that the prosecution advocate followed the principles set out in this document, the professional codes of conduct and was not *Wednesbury* unreasonable, the CPS will not apply sanctions in respect of any future work solely as a result of the decision in a particular case.

5. Change of advice

Farquharson

(g) When counsel has had the opportunity to prepare his brief and to confer with those instructing him, but   **E–37** *at the last moment before trial unexpectedly advises that the case should not proceed or that pleas to lesser offences should be accepted, and his Instructing Solicitor does not accept such advice, counsel should apply for an adjournment if instructed so to do.*

5.1 The CPS and the prosecution advocate should agree a period of adjournment that would al-   **E–38** low a newly instructed advocate to prepare for trial. The period should be realistic and acknowledge that in such circumstances a case conference will usually be required.

5.2 The facts leading to the application for the adjournment should be placed before the court only in so far as they are relevant to that application.

6. Prosecution advocate's role in decision making at trial

Farquharson

(h) Subject to the above, it is for prosecution counsel to decide whether to offer no evidence on a particular   **E–39** *count or on the indictment as a whole and whether to accept pleas to a lesser count or counts.*

6.1 The prosecution advocate may ask the defence advocate as to whether a plea will be forthcoming but at this initial stage should not suggest or indicate a plea that might be considered acceptable to the prosecution before a plea is offered.

6.2 Where the defence advocate subsequently offers details of a plea, the prosecution advocate may discuss the matter with a view to establishing an acceptable plea that reflects the defendant's criminality and provides the court with sufficient powers to sentence appropriately.

Responsibility of prosecution advocate to consult

E–40   6.3 Where the prosecution advocate forms the view that the appropriate course is to accept a plea before proceedings commence or continue, or to offer no evidence on the indictment or any part of it, the prosecution advocate should:

  i. whenever practicable, speak with the victim or victim's family attending court to explain the position;

  ii. ensure that the interests of the victim or any views expressed by the victim or victim's family are taken into account as part of the decision making process; and

  iii. keep the victim or victim's family attending court informed and explain decisions as they are made.

6.4 Where appropriate the prosecution advocate may seek an adjournment of the court hearing in order to facilitate discussion with the victim or victim's family.

6.5 The prosecution advocate should always comply with paragraph 6.3 and, where practicable, discuss the matter with the CPS before informing the defence advocate or the court that a plea is acceptable.

6.6 Where the defendant indicates an acceptable plea, unless the issue is simple, the defence should reduce the basis of the plea to writing. The prosecution advocate should show the CPS any written record relating to the plea and agree with the CPS the basis on which the case will be opened to the court.

6.7 It is the responsibility of the prosecution advocate to ensure that the defence advocate is aware of the basis on which the plea is accepted by the prosecution and the way in which the prosecution case will be opened to the court.

6.8 It will not be necessary for the prosecution advocate to consult the CPS where the plea or course of action accords with the written instructions received from the CPS, although paragraph 6.3 may still apply.

Prosecution advocate's role in sentencing

E–41   6.9 The prosecution advocate should always draw the court's attention to any matters, including aggravating or mitigating features, that might affect sentence. Additionally, the advocate should be in a position to assist the court, if requested, with any statutory provisions or sentencing guidelines and should always draw attention to potential sentencing errors.

6.10 Where a discussion on plea and sentence takes place, the prosecution advocate must adhere to the Attorney General's Guidelines on the Acceptance of Pleas published on 7 December 2000.

7. Seeking judicial approval

Farquharson

E–42   *(i) If prosecution counsel invites the Judge to approve the course he is proposing to take, then he must abide by the judge's decision.*

7.1 A discussion with the judge about the acceptability of a plea or conduct of the case should be held in the presence of the defendant unless exceptional circumstances apply.[2]

7.2 In exceptional circumstances, where the prosecution advocate considers it appropriate to communicate with the judge or seek the judge's view in chambers, the CPS should be consulted before such a step is taken.

7.3 Where discussions take place in chambers it is the responsibility of the prosecution advocate to remind the judge, if necessary, that an independent record must always be kept.

7.4 The prosecution advocate should also make a full note of such an event, recording all decisions and comments. This note should be made available to the CPS.

Farquharson

E–43   *(j) If prosecution counsel does not invite the judge's approval of his decision it is open to the judge to express his dissent with the course proposed and invite counsel to reconsider the matter with those instructing him, but having done so, the final decision remains with counsel.*

7.5 Where a judge expresses a view based on the evidence or public interest, the CPS will carry out a further review of the case.

7.6 The prosecution advocate will inform the CPS in a case where the judge has expressed a dissenting view and will agree the action to be taken. Where there is no CPS representative at court, the prosecution advocate will provide a note of the judge's comments.

7.7 The prosecution advocate will ensure that the judge is aware of all factors that have a bearing on the prosecution decision to adopt a particular course. Where there is a difference of opinion between the prosecution advocate and the CPS the judge will be informed as to the nature of the disagreement.

Farquharson

(k) In an extreme case where the judge is of the opinion that the course proposed by counsel would lead to   **E-44**
serious injustice, he may decline to proceed with the case until counsel has consulted with either the Director or the Attorney General as may be appropriate.

7.8 As a preliminary step, the prosecution advocate will discuss the judge's observations with the Chief Crown Prosecutor in an attempt to resolve the issue. Where the issue remains unresolved the Director of Public Prosecutions will be consulted. In exceptional circumstances the Director of Public Prosecutions may consult the Attorney General.

Note: These Guidelines are subject to the Code of Conduct of the Bar of England and Wales   **E-45**
(barrister advocates) and The Law Society's The Guide to the Professional Conduct of Solicitors (solicitor advocates). Whilst reference is made in the guidelines to the CPS and levels of authority within the Service, the guidelines may be adopted as best practice, with consequential amendments to levels of authority, by other prosecuting authorities.

These Guidelines may be amended at any time and copyright is waived.

These Guidelines are also available on the CPS Website: www.cps.gov.uk.

Footnotes

1. (See Farquharson (d)), "'policy' decisions should be understood as referring to non-evidential   **E-46**
decisions on: the acceptance of pleas of guilty to lesser counts or groups of counts or available alternatives; offering no evidence on particular counts; consideration of a retrial; whether to lodge an appeal; certification of a point of law; and the withdrawal of the prosecution as a whole."

2. (See para. 7.1.), "For the purposes of these guidelines, 'exceptional circumstances' would include the following:

(i) Where there is material or information which should not be made public, e.g. a police text, or for some other compelling reason such as a defendant or witness suffering, unkown to them, from a serious or terminal illness; or

(ii) There are sensitivities surrounding a prosecution decision or proposed action which need to be explained in chambers with a view to obtaining judicial approval. Such approval may be given in open court where it is necessary to explain a prosecution decision or action in order to maintain public confidence in the criminal justice system."

APPENDIX F

The Channel Tunnel

Introduction

The starting point is the Treaty between the United Kingdom of Great Britain and **F–1** Northern Ireland and the French Republic concerning the Construction and Operation by Private Concessionaires of a Channel Fixed Link (the "Treaty of Canterbury") (T.S. No. 15 (1992) (Cm 1827)). It is only necessary to set out Article 1 thereof, which contains definitions. These are incorporated in Article 1(1) of Schedule 2 to the *Channel Tunnel (International Arrangements) Order* 1993 (S.I. 1993 No. 1813) (*post*).

The *Channel Tunnel Act* 1987 provided, *inter alia*, for the construction and operation of the tunnel system, for the incorporation of part of the tunnel system into the United Kingdom and for the application and enforcement of law in relation to, and otherwise for the regulation of, that system and matters connected with it.

S.I. 1993 No. 1813, *ante*, is made under section 11 of the 1987 Act. It makes detailed provision in relation, *inter alia*, to the application of the criminal law outside the United Kingdom and in relation to the powers of constables and other officers. Article 1 provides for it to come into force on a date to be notified in the London, Edinburgh and Belfast *Gazettes*. The date notified was August 2, 1993 (*London Gazette*, August 6, 1993).

In relation to rail traffic between the United Kingdom and Belgium, there is a further agreement and a further order. The agreement is the Agreement between the Government of the Kingdom of Belgium, the Government of the French Republic and the Government of the United Kingdom of Great Britain and Northern Ireland Concerning Rail Traffic between Belgium and the United Kingdom Using the Channel Fixed Link. This agreement came into force on December 1, 1997.

The further order is the *Channel Tunnel (Miscellaneous Provisions) Order* 1994 (S.I. 1994 No. 1405). Apart from certain amending provisions, which came into force on July 1, 1994, this order came into force simultaneously with the agreement.

S.I. 1994 No. 1405 is made under section 11 of the *Channel Tunnel Act* 1987. It gives qualified effect in United Kingdom law to material provisions (the "tripartite articles" set out in Schedule 2) of the agreement.

The tripartite articles are by article 3(1) given the force of law within, and for the purposes specified in article 2(2) outside, the control zones accorded to Belgium ("the Belgian control zone") and to France by the tripartite articles; article 3(2) affirms that Belgian, and French, officers may to the extent specified in the tripartite articles go about their business in the United Kingdom, and article 3(3) ensures that Belgian officers can be provided with the required facilities. Article 4(1) performs the corresponding operation for British officers working in Belgium or France.

Article 5(1) to (3) extends English criminal jurisdiction to conduct in a United Kingdom control zone which, if taking place in England, would constitute an offence under a frontier control enactment as defined in Schedule 1. Article 5(4) creates a presumption as to jurisdiction where it is uncertain in which of the three states an offence not of that kind was committed.

Treaty between the United Kingdom of Great Britain and Northern Ireland and the French Republic Concerning The Construction and Operation by Private Concessionaires of a Channel Fixed Link (T.S. No. 15 (1992) (Cm. 1827))

ARTICLE 1

Object and Definitions

(1) The High Contracting Parties undertake to permit the construction and operation by private **F–2** concessionaires (hereinafter referred to as "the Concessionaires") of a Channel fixed link in accordance with the provisions of this Treaty, of its supplementary Protocols and arrangements and of a concession between the two Governments and the Concessionaires (hereinafter referred to as "the Concession"). The Channel fixed link shall be financed without recourse to government funds or to government guarantees of a financial or commercial nature.

(2) The Channel fixed link (hereinafter referred to as "the Fixed Link"), which shall be more

particularly described in the Concession, means a twin bored tunnel rail link, with associated service tunnel under the English Channel between Cheriton in Kent and Fréthun in the Pas-de-Calais, together with the terminal areas for control of access to, and egress from, the tunnels, and shall include any freight or other facility, and any road link between the United Kingdom and France, which may hereafter be agreed between the High Contracting Parties to form part of the Fixed Link.

Channel Tunnel Act 1987, s.1(1), (3)–(10)

Construction and operation of a tunnel rail link between the United Kingdom and France

F–3   **1.**—(1) The primary purpose of this Act is to provide for the construction and operation of a tunnel rail link (together with associated works, facilities and installations) under the English Channel between the United Kingdom and France, in accordance with—

> (a) the Treaty between the United Kingdom of Great Britain and Northern Ireland and the French Republic concerning the Construction and Operation by Private Concessionaires of a Channel Fixed Link, signed at Canterbury on 12th February 1986, together with its supplementary protocols and arrangements; and
>
> (b) the Concession between Her Majesty's Government in the United Kingdom and the Government of the French Republic on the one hand and private Concessionaires on the other hand which, in accordance with Article 1 of that Treaty, regulates, together with that Treaty, the construction and operation of the Channel fixed link referred to in that Article.

(3) Subject to section 3 of this Act, the expressions defined below in this section have the meanings there given for the purposes of this Act.

(4) "The Treaty" means the Treaty mentioned in paragraph (a) of subsection (1) above, including its supplementary protocols and arrangements, and "the Concession" means the Concession mentioned in paragraph (b) of that subsection.

(5) "Concession agreement" means any agreement or arrangement which for the time being constitutes, or is included among the agreements or arrangements which together for the time being constitute, the Concession.

(6) "Concession lease" means any lease granted by the Secretary of State to the Concessionaires in pursuance of the Concession, and references to a Concession lease include any provisions of a Concession agreement providing for the grant of a lease of any land by the Secretary of State to the Concessionaires.

(7) "The tunnel system" means the tunnel rail link, together with its associated works, facilities and installations, to be constructed in pursuance of the Treaty, and incorporating—

> (a) tunnels under the English Channel between Cheriton, Folkestone, in Kent and Fréthun in the Pas de Calais, comprising two main tunnels capable of carrying both road traffic on shuttle trains and rail traffic, and an associated service tunnel;
>
> (b) two terminal areas, for controlling access to and egress from the tunnels, located at the portals of the tunnels in the vicinity of Cheriton, Folkestone and Fréthun respectively;
>
> (c) a service and maintenance area at the Old Dover Colliery site;
>
> (d) an inland clearance depot at Ashford, in Kent, for the accommodation, in connection with the application to them of customs and other controls, of freight vehicles which have been or are to be conveyed through the tunnels on shuttle services;
>
> (e) necessary links with the road and rail networks of each country; and
>
> (f) the fixed and movable equipment needed for the operation of the tunnels and the associated works, facilities and installations mentioned in paragraphs (b) to (e) above or for the operation of shuttle services using the tunnels.

(8) "The Concessionaires" means the person or persons who, under the Concession, have for the time being the function of constructing and operating or (as the case may be) of operating the tunnel system.

(9) "Shuttle train" means a train designed for the purpose of carrying road traffic between Cheriton, Folkestone and Fréthun by way of the tunnels and "shuttle service" means a service operated by means of a shuttle train.

(10) Where the Concessionaires for the time being are two or more persons, any provision of this Act conferring or imposing upon them any right, power, liability or duty shall have effect (except where the context otherwise requires) so as to confer or impose it upon them jointly; but anything done by or in relation to any one of them which purports to be done by or in relation to both or all of them shall have effect for the purposes of this Act as if done by or in relation to them jointly.

Channel Tunnel Act 1987, s.10(1)

Incorporation of part of the tunnel into the United Kingdom and general application of law

10.—(1) The land compromising the tunnel system as far as the frontier, so far as not forming   **F–4**
part of the United Kingdom before the passing of this Act, shall, as it becomes occupied by or on
behalf of the Concessionaires working from England, together with so much of the surrounding
subsoil as is necessary for the security of the part of the system so occupied, be incorporated into
England and form part of the district of Dover in the county of Kent, and the law of England
shall apply accordingly.

Channel Tunnel Act 1987, s.11(1), (3), (4)

Regulation of the tunnel system: application and enforcement of law, etc.

11.—(1) The appropriate Minister may by order make such provision as appears to him to be   **F–5**
necessary or expedient—

  (a) for the purpose of implementing the international arrangements, or enabling those arrangements to be implemented.

  (b) [*transfer of property*];

  (c) in relation to the construction, operation or use of the tunnel system or any part of the tunnel system, so far as relates to activities carried on, persons employed or engaged in work, things done or omitted or other matters arising anywhere within the system (whether in England or in France), including in particular (without prejudice to the generality of the preceding provision) provision with respect to controls in relation to persons or goods within the system;

  (d) for the purpose of applying any provisions of the law of England (with or without modifications), or excluding or modifying any of those provisions, in relation to things done or omitted or other matters arising anywhere within the tunnel system (whether in England or France);

  (e) with respect to controls in relation to persons or goods—

    (i) on trains engaged on international services; or

    (ii) at authorised terminal control points for such services; outside the tunnel system (whether in the United Kingdom or elsewhere);

  (f) in relation to persons employed or engaged on work outside the tunnel system (whether in the United Kingdom or elsewhere)—

    (i) on any train engaged on an international service, in or for the purposes of or in connection with the operation of that service; or

    (ii) in or for the purposes of or in connection with the exercise, on any such train or at any authorised terminal control point for such service, of any controls in relation to persons or goods as are mentioned in paragraph (e) above;

  (g) for the purpose of dealing with any matters arising out of or connected with any provision within the powers conferred by any of paragraphs (a) to (f) above (whether or not those matters arise within the tunnel system, on any such train or at any such control point); or

  (h) otherwise in relation to, or for regulating any matters arising out of or connected with, the tunnel system.

  (3) Without prejudice to the generality of subsection (1) above, the kind of provision that may be
made by an order under this section includes the following—

  (a) provision creating new criminal offences punishable as may be provided by the order or imposing penalties otherwise than in respect of criminal offences;

  (b) [*fees and charges*];

  (c) provision conferring power on any Minister of the Crown or Government department to make orders, rules, regulations or other subordinate instruments of a legislative character;

  (d) provision for, or authorising any such order, rule, regulation or other subordinate instrument to provide for, the delegation of any functions conferred or imposed by or in pursuance of any order under this section or by any enactment;

  (e) provision, subject to subsection (4) below, for or in connection with the enforcement or execution outside the United Kingdom of any provision of the law of England or within the United Kingdom of any provision of the law of any other country, including in particular—

    (i) provision conferring powers on any officer belonging to the United Kingdom to arrest and detain outside the United Kingdom persons suspected of having committed offences under the law of England and bring them to lawful custody in England;

(ii) provision conferring powers on any such officer to arrest and detain within the United Kingdom persons suspected of having committed offences under the law of any other country and surrender them to the custody of officers belonging to that country without the authority of any order or a court in any part of the United Kingdom; and

(iii) provision for or in connection with the exercise in the United Kingdom by officers belonging to any other country of powers corresponding to those mentioned in sub-paragraph (i) above; and

(f) provision conferring jurisdiction on courts or tribunals in any part of the United Kingdom or limiting the jurisdiction otherwise exercisable by any such courts or tribunals.

(4) An order under this section may not make provision for or in connection with the exercise of powers by officers belonging to one country in any other country except—

(a) within the tunnel system;

(b) on trains engaged on international services; or

(c) at authorised terminal control points for such services.

Channel Tunnel Act 1987, s.12

Controls on board trains engaged on international services

F–6   **12.**—(1) It shall be duty of the appropriate Minister to secure that, where this subsection applies, controls exercisable in relation to—

(a) passengers carried on a train engaged on an international service on a journey beginning or intended to end at a place in Great Britain other than London or Cheriton, Folkestone or any place between those places; or

(b) things contained in the baggage of such passengers;

shall be exercised on the train.

(2) Subject to subsection (3) below, subsection (1) above applies where—

(a) the person operating the service has made a request to the appropriate Minister that the controls in question should be exercised on trains engaged on the service in question;

(b) the appropriate Minister has approved as satisfactory arrangements made by that person for the provision of facilities to enable the controls in question to be exercised on such trains;

(c) facilities enabling the exercise of the controls in question are provided on the train in question in accordance with such approved arrangements; and

(d) the controls are exercised by customs officers or immigration officers.

(3) Subsection (1) above does not apply—

(a) in the case of passengers carried on a particular train or part of a particular train, or things contained in the baggage of such passengers, if in the opinion of a customs officer or immigration officer exercising the controls it is not reasonably practicable effectively to exercise the controls in question on the train or part of a train; and

(b) in the case of any particular passenger or things contained in the baggage of any particular passenger, if in the opinion of any such officer it is not reasonably practicable effectively to exercise the controls in question in relation to the passenger or his baggage on the train.

(4) [*Fees and charges.*]

(5) In this section—

"customs officer" means an officer or other person acting under the authority of the Commissioners of Customs and Excise; and

"immigration officer" means an immigration officer appointed for the purposes of the *Immigration Act* 1971.

Channel Tunnel Act 1987, s.13

Provisions supplementary to sections 11 and 12

F–7   **13.**—(1) Subject to subsection (2) below, in sections 11 and 12 of this Act "the appropriate Minister" means, in relation to any matter, the Minister in charge of any Government department concerned with that matter or, where more than one such department is concerned with that matter, the Ministers in charge of those departments, acting jointly.

(2) Where the Commissioners of Customs and Excise or the Forestry Commissioners are concerned with any matter (whether alone or together with any other Government department) subsection (1) above shall apply as if the references to the Minister or Ministers in charge of any

Government department or departments concerned with that matter were or included references to those Commissioners.

(3) The validity of any order purporting to be made under section 11 of this Act shall not be affected by any question whether or not the order fell by virtue of subsection (1) above to be made by the Minister or department (or any of the Ministers or departments) purporting to make it.

(4) In sections 11 and 12 of this Act "controls" means prohibitions, restrictions or requirements of any descriptions, and any reference to the exercise of controls is a reference to the exercise or performance of any functions conferred or imposed by any enactment, or otherwise under any lawful authority, for or in connection with the enforcement of prohibitions, restrictions or requirements of any description.

(5) For the purposes of those sections a train is engaged on an international service at any time when the whole or any part of the train is being used in the operation of such a service and a place is an authorised terminal control point for international services if it is designated as such in accordance with the international arrangements.

(6) In those sections and this section—

"the international arrangements" includes any agreements or arrangements between Her Majesty's Government in the United Kingdom and the Government of any country on the Continent of Europe other than France which for the time being apply for regulating any matters arising out of or connected with the operation of international services; and

"international service" means any service (including a shuttle service) for the carriage of passengers or goods by way of the tunnel system.

Policing of tunnel system

This is to be undertaken by constables under the direction of the Chief Constable of Kent **F–8** constabulary: *Channel Tunnel Act* 1987, s.14(1). The Railways Board may, on the application of the Chief Constable, provide constables or other assistance for the policing of the tunnel system.

Channel Tunnel Act 1987, s.23

Control of traffic within the tunnel system

23.—(1) Subject to the following provisions of this section, the enactments relating to road traf- **F–9** fic shall apply in relation to any tunnel system road to which the public does not have access as they apply in relation to a road which the public does have access.

(2) Those enactments shall apply in relation to any tunnel system road subject to such exceptions and modifications as the Secretary of State may by order specify.

(3) An order under subsection (2) above may, in particular, confer on the Concessionaires functions exercisable under those enactments by a highway authority or a local authority.

(4) The Secretary of State may by order provide that those enactments shall not apply in relation to any tunnel system road specified in the order and may require the Concessionaires to indicate any such road in a manner so specified.

(5) Those enactments shall not, in the case of any tunnel system road, apply in relation to it until such date as the Secretary of State may by order specify.

(6) Before making an order under this section, the Secretary of State shall consult the Concessionaires.

(7) In this section, "tunnel system road" means any length of road comprised in the tunnel system.

Channel Tunnel Act 1987, s.49(1)

Interpretation

49.—(1) In this Act, except where the context otherwise requires— **F–10**

"enactment" includes an enactment contained in this Act or in any Act passed on or after the date on which this Act is passed, and any subordinate legislation within meaning of the *Interpretation Act* 1978;

"footpath" has the same meaning as in the *Highways Act* 1980;

"frontier" means the frontier between the United Kingdom and France fixed by the Treaty;

"functions" includes powers, duties and obligations;

"goods" includes vehicles (notwithstanding that they may be being used for the carriage of other goods or of persons), animals, plants and any other creature, substance or thing capable of being transported;

"the Intergovernmental Commission" means the Intergovernmental Commission established by the Treaty;

"the international arrangements" means—

(a) the Treaty and the Concession; and

(b) any other agreements or arrangements between Her Majesty's Government in the United Kingdom and the Government of the French Republic which for the time being apply for regulating any matters arising out of or connected with the tunnel system;

"land" includes buildings and other structures, land covered with water, and any estate, interest, easement, servitude or right in or over land;

"modification" includes addition, omission and alteration, and related expressions shall be construed accordingly;

"the Railways Board" has the meaning given by section 5(3);

"the Safety Authority" means the Safety Authority established by the Treaty;

"shuttle service" and "shuttle train" have the meanings given by section 1(9);

"substance" means any natural or artificial substance, whether in solid or liquid form or in the form of a gas or vapour;

"train" includes any locomotive and railway rolling stock of any description;

"the Treaty" has the meaning given by section 1(4);

"the tunnel system" has the meaning given by section 1(7); and

"vehicle" includes a railway vehicle.

F–11 The definitions of the following words and expressions have been omitted from this subsection: "A20 improvement works", "the appropriate authority", "the arbitral tribunal", "bridleway", "deposited plans", "deposited sections", "Dover Harbour", "limits of deviation" and "nature conservation". Subsections (2) to (9) contain further interpretative provisions.

S.I. 1993 No. 1813, art. 1

Citation and commencement

F–12 **1.** This Order may be cited as the *Channel Tunnel (International Arrangements) Order* 1993 and shall come into force on the date on which the Protocol between the Government of the United Kingdom of Great Britain and Northern Ireland and the Government of the French Republic Concerning Frontier Controls and Policing, Co-operation in Criminal Justice, Public Safety and Mutual Assistance Relating to the Channel Fixed Link enters into force. That date will be notified in the London, Edinburgh and Belfast *Gazettes*.

[The commencement date was August 2, 1993: see *ante*, Appendix F–1.]

S.I. 1993 No. 1813, arts 2–7

Interpretation

F–13 **2.**—(1) In this Order, except for the purpose of construing the international articles or the supplementary articles [or the 2012 Agreement], and in any enactment as applied by it with modifications, any expression for which there is an entry in the first column ofSchedule 1 has the meaning given against it in the second column.

(2) In this Order "the authorised purposes" means—

(a) purposes for which provision is authorised by any of paragraphs (a), (d) and (g), and

(b) purposes connected with any matter in relation to or with respect to or for regulating which provision is authorised by any of paragraphs (c), (e), (f) and (h), of section 11(1) of the *Channel Tunnel Act* 1987.

(3) In this Order "the international articles" means the provisions set out in Schedule 2 (being Articles or parts of Articles of the Protocol mentioned in article 1 above); and in the international articles the expression "the Fixed Link" shall for the purposes of this Order be taken to have the same meaning as is given to "the tunnel system" by section 1(7) of the *Channel Tunnel Act* 1987.

(4) In this Order "the supplementary articles" means the provisions set out in Schedule 2A (being Articles of the Additional Protocol between the Government of the United Kingdom of Great Britain

and Nothern Ireland and the Government of the French Republic and amendments to those Articles made by the amending instrument), and in the supplementary articles "the Protocol signed at Sangatte" and "the Sangatte Protocol" mean the Protocol mentioned in article 1 above.

(5) In paragraph (4) and in the supplementary articles, "Additional Protocol" means the Additional Protocol to the Sangatte Protocol on the Establishment of Bureaux Responsible for Controls on Persons Travelling by Train between France and the United Kingdom, signed at Brussels on 29th May 2000.

(6) In paragraph (4) "the amending instrument" means the Agreement between the Government of the United Kingdom of Great Britain and Northern Ireland and the Government of the French Republic making amendments to the Additional Protocol to the Sangatte Protocol on the Establishment of Bureaux responsible for controls on persons travelling by train between the United Kingdom and France, and to the Agreement concerning the carrying of service weapons by French officers on the territory of the United Kingdom of Great Britain and Northern Ireland, signed in Paris on 18th June 2007.

[(7) In this order, the "2012 Agreement" means the Agreement between the Government of the United Kingdom of Great Britain and Northern Ireland and the Government of the Republic of France on Implementation of the Cyclamen Device in the French Terminal of the Channel Tunnel Situated in Coquelles signed in London on 10th May 2012.]

[This article is printed as amended by the *Channel Tunnel (International Arrangements)* ★ *(Amendment No. 3) Order* 2001 (S.I. 2001 No. 1544); and the *Channel Tunnel (International Arrangements) (Amendment) Order* 2007 (S.I. 2007 No. 2907); and as amended, as from the day after the day on which an agreement between the United Kingdom and France regarding security checks within the Channel Tunnel system comes into force (such date to be notified in the London, Edinburgh and Belfast Gazettes), by the *Channel Tunnel (International Arrangements) (Amendment) Order* 2012 (S.I. 2012 No. 1264) (insertion of words in square brackets).]

Application of international articles
   3.—(1) The international articles shall have the force of law in the United Kingdom—
   (a) within the tunnel system,
   (b) within a control zone, and
   (c) elsewhere for the authorised purposes only.

   (2) Without prejudice to paragraph (1) officers belonging to the French Republic shall to the extent specified in the international articles have rights and obligations and powers to carry out functions in the United Kingdom.

   (3) For the purpose of giving full effect to Article 34 of the international articles (accommodation etc., for authorities of adjoining State) the appropriate Minister may by written notice require any occupier or person concerned with the management of a terminal control point to provide free of charge such accommodation, installations and equipment as may be necessary to satisfy requirements determined under Article 33 of the Protocol mentioned in article 1 above (which requires the competent authorities of the two States to determine their respective requirements in consultation with one another).

[This article is printed as amended by the *Channel Tunnel (International Arrangements) (Amendment No. 4) Order* 2001 (S.I. 2001 No. 3707).]

Application of supplementary articles
   3A.—(1) The supplementary articles shall have the force of law in the United Kingdom within a supplementary control zone.

   (2) Subject to paragraph (4), without prejudice to paragraph (1), officers belonging to the French Republic who are responsible for immigration controls shall to the extent specified in the supplementary articles have rights and obligations and powers to carry out functions in the United Kingdom.

   (3) Subject to paragraph (4), for the purpose of enabling the authorities of the French Republic to make use in the United Kingdom of the accommodation, installations and equipment necessary for the performance of their functions under the supplementary articles, the Secretary of State for the Home Department may by written notice require any occupier or person concerned with the management of a terminal control point to provide free of charge such accommodation, installations and equipment as may be necessary to satisfy requirements determined by the authorities of the French Republic in consultation with the authorities of the United Kingdom.

(4) Nothing in this article implies the existence of a supplementary control zone in the station of London-Waterloo on British Territory.

[This article was inserted by the *Channel Tunnel (International Arrangements) (Amendment No. 3) Order* 2001 (S.I. 2001 No. 1544). It is printed as amended by the *Channel Tunnel (International Arrangements) (Amendment No. 4) Order* 2001 (S.I. 2001 No. 3707); and the *Channel Tunnel (International Arrangements) (Amendment) Order* 2007 (S.I. 2007 No. 2907).]

Application of enactments
4.—(1) All frontier control enactments except those relating to transport and road traffic controls shall for the purpose of enabling officers belonging to the United Kingdom to carry out frontier controls extend to France within a control zone.

(1A) All frontier control enactments relating to transport and road traffic controls shall for the purpose of enabling officers belonging to the United Kingdom to carry out such controls extend to France within the control zone in France within the tunnel system.

[(1AA) All security control enactments shall for the purpose of enabling officers belonging to the United Kingdom to carry out security controls extend to France within the tunnel system.]

(1B) All immigration control enactments shall, for the purpose of enabling immigration officers to carry out immigration controls, extend to France within a supplementary control zone.

(1C) The *Race Relations Act* 1976 shall apply to the carrying out by immigration officers of their functions in a control zone or a supplementary control zone outside the United Kingdom as it applies to the carrying out of their functions within the United Kingdom.

(2), (3) [*Application of Data Protection Act* 1984.]

★   [This article is printed as amended by the *Channel Tunnel (International Arrangements) (Amendment) Order* 1996 (S.I. 1996 No. 2283); the *Channel Tunnel (International Arrangements) (Amendment No. 3) Order* 2001 (S.I. 2001 No. 1544); and the *Channel Tunnel (International Arrangements) (Amendment No. 4) Order* 2001 (S.I. 2001 No. 3707); and as prospectively amended (insertion of para. (1AA), and of sub-para. (c) in para. (2)) by S.I. 2012 No. 1264 (as to which, see the annotation to article 2, *ante*).]

The *Data Protection Act* 1984 is repealed and replaced by the *Data Protection Act* 1998.

Application of criminal law
5.—(1) Any act or omission which—
(a) takes place outside the United Kingdom in a control zone, and
(b) would, if taking place in England, constitute an offence under a frontier control enactment,
or any act or omission which—
(c) takes place outside the United Kingdom in a supplementary control zone, and
(d) would, if taking place in England, constitute an offence under an immigration control enactment
shall be treated for the purposes of that enactment as taking place in England.

(1A) Summary proceedings for anything that is by virtue of paragraph (1) an offence triable summarily or triable either way may be taken, and the offence may for all incidental purposes be treated as having been committed, in the county of Kent or in the inner London area as defined in section 2(1)(a) of the *Justices of the Peace Act* 1979.

(2) Any jurisdiction conferred by virtue of paragraphs (1) and (1A) on any court is without prejudice to any jurisdiction exercisable apart from this article by that or any other court.

(3) Where it is proposed to institute proceedings in respect of an alleged offence in any court and a question as to the court's jurisdiction arises under Article 38(2)(a) of the international articles, it shall be presumed, unless the contrary is proved, that the court has jurisdiction by virtue of that Article.

[This article is printed as amended by the *Channel Tunnel (Miscellaneous Provisions) Order* 1994 (S.I. 1994 No. 1405); and the *Channel Tunnel (International Arrangements) (Amendment No. 3) Order* 2001 (S.I. 2001 No. 1544).]

Persons boarding a through train
5A. For the purposes of the exercise of any power of an immigration officer in a supplementary control zone in France, any person who seeks to board a through train shall be deemed to

be seeking to arrive in the United Kingdom through the tunnel system.

[This article was inserted by the *Channel Tunnel (International Arrangements) (Amendment No. 3) Order* 2001 (S.I. 2001 No. 1544).

Powers of officers and supplementary controls

6. Schedule 3 (which contains in Part I provision as to powers exercisable by constables and other officers and in Part II provision for meeting obligations under Article 25 of the Protocol mentioned in article 1 above concerning the prevention of animals from straying into the Fixed Link) shall have effect. **F–13a**

Enactments modified

7.—(1) Without prejudice to the generality of articles 4(1), 4(1B) and 5(1), the frontier control enactments mentioned in Schedule 4 shall—

    (a) in their application to France by virtue of article 4(1) or article 4(1B), and

    (b) in their application to the United Kingdom—

        (i) within the tunnel system, and

        (ii) elsewhere for the authorised purposes,

have effect with the modifications set out in Schedule 4.

(1A) Nothing in paragraph (1)(b)(ii) implies the existence of a supplementary control zone in the station of London-Waterloo on British Territory.

(2) Subject to paragraph (3), within a control zone or a supplementary control zone and on trains within the tunnel system section 54(3) of the *Firearms Act* 1968 (application to Crown Servants) shall have effect as if the reference to a member of a police force included a reference to an officer belonging to the French Republic exercising functions as mentioned in Article 28(2) of the international articles or functions under Article 3 of the supplementary articles.

(3) As respects officers exercising their functions in a control zone paragraph (2) applies only to the agreed number of specified officers mentioned in Article 28(2)(b) of the international articles.

(4) The frontier control enactments relating to transport and road traffic controls in their application to France within the control zone in France within the tunnel system by virtue of Article 4(1A) shall have effect as if any reference therein to a "public road" or "road" were a reference to any part of that control zone.

[This paragraph is printed as amended by S.I. 1996 No. 2283, *ante*; S.I. 2001 No. 1544, *ante*; and S.I. 2007 No. 2907, *ante*.]

Amendment and repeals

Articles 8 and 9 give effect to Schedules 5 and 6, amendments and repeals respectively. **F–14**

S.I. 1993 No. 1813, Sched. 1

Article 2(1)   SCHEDULE 1

EXPRESSIONS DEFINED

Expression	*Meaning*	**F–15**
["2012 Agreement"]	[The meaning given by article 2(7).]	
"The Concessionaires"	The meaning given by section 1(8) (read with section 3(3)) of the *Channel Tunnel Act* 1987.	
"Control zone"	A control zone within the meaning of the international articles.	
"Frontier controls"	So far as they constitute frontier controls within the meaning of the international articles and are controls in relation to persons or goods, police, immigration, customs, health, veterinary and phytosanitary, and transport and road traffic controls.	
"Frontier control enactment"	An Act, or an instrument made under an Act, for the time being in force, which contains provision relating to frontier controls.	

Expression	*Meaning*
"Immigration control enactment"	An Act, or an instrument made under an Act, for the time being in force, which contains provision relating to immigration controls.
"Immigration officer"	The same meaning as in the *Immigration Act* 1971.
"The international articles"	The meaning given by article 2(3) above.
"International service"	The meaning given in section 13(6) of the *Channel Tunnel Act* 1987.
["Security control enactment"]	[An Act, or an instrument made under an Act, for the time being in force, which contains provision relating to security controls.]
["Security controls"]	[Controls in relation to customs carried out for the purposes of the 2012 Agreement.]
"Shuttle train"	The meaning given in section 1(9) of the *Channel Tunnel Act* 1987.
"State of arrival"	The meaning given by the supplementary articles.
"State of departure"	The meaning given by the supplementary articles.
"The supplementary articles"	The meaning given by article 2(4) above.
"Supplementary control zone"	The part of the territory of the State of departure, determined by mutual agreement between the Governments of the State of departure and the State of arrival but excluding the station of London–Waterloo on British territory, within which the officers of the State of arrival are empowered to effect controls under the supplementary articles.
"Terminal control point"	A place which is an authorised terminal control point for international services for the purposes of sections 11 and 12 of the *Channel Tunnel Act* 1987.
"Through train"	A train, other than a shuttle train, which for the purposes of sections 11 and 12 of the *Channel Tunnel Act* 1987 is engaged on an international service.
"Train manager"	In relation to a through train or shuttle train, the person designated as train manager by the person operating the international service on which the train is engaged.
"The tunnel system"	The meaning given by section 1(7) of the *Channel Tunnel Act* 1987.

★   [This Schedule is printed as amended by S.I. 1996 No. 2283; S.I. 2001 No. 1544; S.I. 2001 No. 3707; and S.I. 2007 No. 2907 (*ante*, F–13); and as prospectively amended (insertion of definitions in square brackets) by S.I. 2012 No. 1264 (as to which, see the annotation to article 2, *ante*, F–13).]

S.I. 1993 No. 1813, Sched. 2

Article 2(3)   SCHEDULE 2

INTERNATIONAL ARTICLES

ARTICLE 1

Definitions

F–16   (1) Any term defined in the Treaty shall have the same meaning in this Protocol.

(2) Otherwise for the purposes of this Protocol the expression:

    (a) "frontier controls" means police, immigration, customs, health, veterinary and phytosanitary, consumer protection, and transport and road traffic controls, as well as any other controls provided for in national or European Community laws and regulations;

    (b) "host State" means the State in whose territory the controls of the other State are effected;

(c) "adjoining State" means the other State;

(d) "officers" means persons responsible for policing and frontier controls who are under the command of the persons or authorities designated in accordance with Article 2(1);

(e) "rescue services" means the authorities and organisations whose functions are provided for in the emergency arrangements referred to in Part VII of this Protocol who are under the command of the persons or authorities designated in accordance with Article 2(1);

(f) [...]

(g) "control zone" means the part of the territory of the host State determined by the mutual agreement between the two Governments within which the officers of the adjoining State are empowered to effect controls;

(h) "restricted zone" means the part of the Fixed Link situated in each State subject to special protective security measures;

(i) "through trains" means trains travelling the Fixed Link but originating and terminating outside it, as opposed to "shuttle trains" which are trains travelling solely within the Fixed Link.

PART I

AUTHORITIES AND GENERAL PRINCIPLES OF CO-OPERATION

ARTICLE 2

(1) Each of the Governments shall designate the authorities or the persons having charge of the **F–16a** services which in its territory have responsibility for the exercise of frontier controls, the maintenance of law and order and fire fighting and rescue within the Fixed Link.

. . . .

PART II

FRONTIER CONTROLS AND POLICE: GENERAL

ARTICLE 5

(1) In order to simplify and speed up the formalities relating to entry into the State of arrival and **F–16b** exit from the State of departure, the two Governments agree to establish juxtaposed national control bureaux in the terminal installations situated at Fréthun in French territory and at Folkestone in British territory. These bureaux shall be so arranged that, for each direction of travel, the frontier controls shall be carried out in the terminal in the State of departure.

(2) Supplementary frontier controls may exceptionally be carried out in the Fixed Link by officers of the State of arrival on its own territory.

ARTICLE 6

The competence of those juxtaposed national control bureaux shall extend to all cross-frontier movements with the exception of customs clearance of commercial traffic.

ARTICLE 7

(1) For through trains, each state may carry out its frontier controls during the journey and may authorise the officers of the other State to carry out their frontier controls in its territory.

(2) The two States may agree to an extension of the control zones for through trains, as far as London and Paris, respectively.

ARTICLE 8

Within the Fixed Link, each Government shall permit officers of the other State to carry out their functions in its own territory in application of their powers relating to frontier controls.

ARTICLE 9

The laws and regulations to frontier controls of the adjoining State shall be applicable in the control zone situated in the host State and shall be put into effect by the officers of the adjoining State in the same way as in their own territory.

ARTICLE 10

(1) The officers of the adjoining State shall, in exercise of their national powers, be permitted in the control zone situated in the host State to detain or arrest persons in accordance with the laws

and regulations relating to frontier controls of the adjoining State or persons sought by the authorities of the adjoining State. These officers shall also be permitted to conduct such persons to the territory of the adjoining State.

(2) However, except in exceptional circumstances, no person may be held more than 24 hours in the areas reserved, in the host State, for the frontier controls of the adjoining State. Any such detention shall be subject to the requirements and procedures laid down by the legislation of the adjoining State.

(3) In exceptional circumstances the 24 hour period of detention may be extended for a further period of 24 hours in accordance with the legislation of the adjoining State. The extension of the period of detention shall be notified to the authorities of the host State.

ARTICLE 11

Breaches of the laws and regulations relating to frontier controls of the adjoining State which are detected in the control zone situated in the host State shall be subject to the laws and regulations of the adjoining State, as if the breaches had occurred in the latter's own territory.

ARTICLE 12

(1) The frontier controls of the State of departure shall normally be effected before those of the State of arrival.

(2) The officers of the State of arrival are not authorised to carry out such controls before the end of controls of the State of departure. Any form of relinquishment of such controls shall be considered as a control.

(3) The officers of the State of departure may no longer carry out their controls when the officers of the State of arrival have begun their own operations except with the consent of the competent officers of the State of arrival.

(4) If exceptionally, in the course of the frontier controls, the sequence of operations provided for inparagraph (1) of this Article is modified, the officers of the State of arrival may not proceed to detentions, arrests or seizures until the frontier controls of the State of departure are completed. In such a case, these officers shall escort the persons, vehicles, merchandise, animals or other goods, for which the frontier controls of the State of departure are not yet completed, to the officers of that State. If these latter then wish to proceed to detentions, arrests or seizures, they shall have priority.

ARTICLE 14

The detailed plans for the Fixed Link and its means of access, shall, in accordance with the relevant provisions of the Concession, delimit among other things:

    (a) the control zones;

    (b) the restricted zones and their sub-divisions;

    (c) railway lines and their means of access included in the control zones;

    (d) the area of the frontier control installations and their means of access.

ARTICLE 16

Where investigations and proceedings concern offences committed in the Fixed Link or having a connection with the Fixed Link, the authorities of the host State shall, at the request of the authorities of the adjoining State, undertake official enquiries, the examination of witnesses and experts and the notification to accused persons of summonses and administrative decisions.

ARTICLE 17

The assistance provided for in Article 16 shall be furnished in accordance with the laws, regulations and procedures in force in the State providing the assistance, and with international agreements to which that State is a party.

ARTICLE 18

If the State of arrival refuses admission to persons, vehicles, animals or goods, or if persons decide not to pass through the frontier controls of the State of arrival, or send or take back any vehicles, animals or goods which are accompanying them, the authorities of the State of departure may not refuse to accept back such persons, vehicles, animals or goods. However, the authorities of the State of departure may take any measures to deal with them in accordance with national law and in a way which does not impose obligations on the other State.

ARTICLE 19

(2) In an emergency, the local representatives of the authorities concerned may by mutual agreement, provisionally bring into effect alterations to the delimitation of the control zones which may prove necessary. Any arrangement so reached shall come into effect immediately.

PART III

HEALTH, VETERINARY AND PHYTOSANITARY CONTROLS

[*Articles 20–24*]

PART IV

OFFICERS

ARTICLE 26

Officers of both States shall be permitted to circulate freely in the whole of the Fixed Link for official purposes. In carrying out their functions they shall be authorised to pass through the frontier controls simply by producing appropriate evidence of their identity and status. **F–16c**

. . . .

ARTICLE 28

(1) Officers of the adjoining State may wear their national uniform or visible distinctive insignia in the host State.

(2) In accordance with the laws, regulations and procedures governing the carriage and use of firearms in the host State, the competent authorities of that State will issue permanent licences to carry arms:

    (a) to officers of the adjoining State exercising their official functions on board trains within the Fixed Link; and

    (b) to an agreed number of specified officers of the adjoining State exercising their functions within the control zone of the host State.

ARTICLE 29

(1) The authorities of the host State shall grant the same protection and assistance to officers of the adjoining State, in the exercise of their functions, as they grant to their own officers.

(2) The provisions of the criminal law in force in the host State for the protection of officers in the exercise of their functions shall be equally applicable to the punishment of offences committed against officers of the adjoining State in the exercise of their functions.

ARTICLE 30

(1) Without prejudice to the application of the provisions of Article 46, claims for compensation for loss, injury or damage caused by or to officers of the adjoining State in the exercise of their functions in the host State shall be subject to the law and jurisdiction of the adjoining State as if the circumstances giving rise to the claim had occurred in that State.

(2) Officers of the adjoining State may not be prosecuted by authorities of the host State for any acts performed in the control zone or within the Fixed Link whilst in the exercise of their functions. In such a case, they shall come under the jurisdiction of the adjoining State, as if the act had been committed in that State.

(3) The judicial authorities or the police of the host State, having taken steps to record the complaint and to assemble the facts relating thereto, shall communicate all the particulars and evidence thereof to the competent authorities of the other State for the purposes of a possible prosecution according to the laws in force in the latter.

ARTICLE 31

(1) Officers of the adjoining State shall be permitted freely to transfer to that State sums of money levied on behalf of their Government in the control zone situated in the host State, as well as merchandise and other goods seized there.

(2) They may equally sell such merchandise and other goods in the host State in conformity with the provisions in force in the host State, and transfer the proceeds to the adjoining State.

PART V

FACILITIES

ARTICLE 34

F–16d   The authorities of the adjoining State shall be able to make use in the host State of the accommodation, installations and equipment necessary for the performance of their functions.

ARTICLE 35

(1) The officers of the adjoining State are empowered to keep order within the accommodation appointed for their exclusive use in the host State.

(2) The officers of the host State shall not have access to such accommodation, except at the request of the officers of the adjoining State or in accordance with the laws of the host State applicable to entry into and searches of private premises.

ARTICLE 36

All goods which are necessary to enable the officers of the adjoining State to carry out their functions in the host State shall be exempt from all taxes and dues on entry and exit.

ARTICLE 37

(1) The officers of the adjoining State whilst exercising their functions in the host State shall be authorised to communicate with their national authorities.

. . . .

PART VI

CO-OPERATION IN CRIMINAL JUSTICE

ARTICLE 38

F–16e   (1) Without prejudice to the provisions of Articles 11 and 30(2), when an offence is committed in the territory of one of the two States, including that lying within the Fixed Link up to its frontier, that State shall have jurisdiction.

(2)

(a) Within the Fixed Link, each State shall have jurisdiction and shall apply its own law:

(i) when it cannot be ascertained with certainty where an offence has been committed; or

(ii) when an offence committed in the territory of one State is related to an offence committed on the territory of the other State; or

(iii) when an offence has begun in or has been continued into its own territory;

(b) however, the State which first receives the person suspected of having committed such an offence (in this Article referred to as "the receiving State") shall have priority in exercising jurisdiction.

(3) When the receiving State decides not to exercise its priority jurisdiction under paragraph (2) of this Article it shall inform the other State without delay. If the latter decides not to exercise its jurisdiction, the receiving State shall be obliged to exercise its jurisdiction in accordance with its own national law.

ARTICLE 39

Where an arrest has been made for an offence in respect of which a State has jurisdiction under Article 38, that arrest shall not be affected by the fact that it continues in the territory of the other State.

ARTICLE 40

Without prejudice to the application of Article 3 of the Treaty and Part II of this Protocol, the police and customs officers of one State may in accordance with their own national laws make arrests on the territory of the other State in cases where a person is found committing, attempting to commit, or just having committed an offence:

(a) on board any train which has commenced its journey from one State to the other and is within the Fixed Link; or

(b) within any tunnel described in Article 1(2) of the Treaty.

ARTICLE 41

In the case of arrests covered by Articles 39 and 40:

    (a) the person arrested shall be presented without delay to the competent authorities of the State of arrival for that State to be responsible for determining the exercise of jurisdiction as required by Article 38; and

    (b) where jurisdiction shall be exercised by the other State in accordance with Article 38, the person arrested may be transferred to the territory of that State. However, any such transfer shall take place within 48 hours of the presentation under paragraph (a) of this Article. Moreover, each State reserves the right not to transfer its nationals.

PART VII

PUBLIC SAFETY AND RESCUE

[*Articles 42–44*]

PART VIII

FINAL CLAUSES

[*Articles 46, 47*]

S.I. 1993 No. 1813, Sched. 2A

Article 2(4)   SCHEDULE 2A

SUPPLEMENTARY ARTICLES

ARTICLE 1

Any terms defined in Article 1 of the Protocol signed at Sangatte have the same meaning in this **F–16f** Additional Protocol. For the purposes of this Additional Protocol, the following definitions shall be added:

"State of departure" means the State in which the persons boards the train;

"State of arrival" means the State in which the persons alight from the train.

ARTICLE 2

The authorities of the two States shall jointly put in place control bureaux, for persons using through trains and wishing to travel to the State of arrival, in the stations of London-Waterloo, London-St Pancras and Ashford on British territory, and the stations of Paris-Gare du Nord, Calais and Lille-Europe on French territory.

The provisions of the Protocol signed at Sangatte concerning the officers of the adjoining State shall be applicable, under the same conditions, to the officers of the State of arrival who are on duty in the stations mentioned in the preceeding paragraph.

Amendments to Article 2

In addition to the stations referred to in Article 2, control bureaux shall also be established at the station of Ebbsfleet International on British Territory.

The provisions of the Additional Protocol apply to the station of Ebbsfleet International under the same conditions and in accordance with the same procedures as they apply to the stations referred to in the said Article 2.

ARTICLE 3

The purpose of the controls carried out by the authorities of the State of departure shall be to check whether the person can leave its territory.

The purpose of the controls carried out by the authorities of the State of arrival shall be to check whether the person is in possession of the necessary travel documents and fulfils the other conditions for entry to its territory. If this is not the case, the person shall be immediately handed over to the authorities of the State of departure who shall apply their domestic law procedures.

The authorities of the State of departure and of the State of arrival shall carry out their controls in accordance with this Additional Protocol, with their laws and regulations and with their international obligations.

The controls mentioned in the preceeding paragraphs are without prejudice to customs and security controls.

ARTICLE 4

Notwithstanding the third paragraph of Article 3 of this Additional Protocol, when a person submits a request for refugee status or any other kind of protection provided for in international law or in the domestic law of the State of departure during a control carried out at the station of the State of departure by the officers of the State of arrival, this request shall be examined by the authorities of the State of departure in accordance with the rules and procedures of its domestic law.

The same provisions shall be applicable when the request is submitted after the person has passed through this control and before the train doors close at the last scheduled stop at a station located in the territory of the State of departure. If such a request is made after the train doors have closed, it shall be processed by the State of arrival in accordance with the rules and procedures of its domestic law.

ARTICLE 5

The controls referred to in Article 3 of this Additional Protocol shall be carried out in accordance with Article 12 of the Sangatte Protocol.

ARTICLE 6

The procedures for the implementation of this Additional Protocol may, as far as necessary, be the subject of technical or administrative arrangements between the competent authorities of the two States.

[Sched. 2A was inserted by S.I. 2001 No. 1544 (*ante*, F–13). It is printed as amended by the *Channel Tunnel (International Arrangements) (Amendment) Order* 2007 (S.I. 2007 No. 2907).]

S.I. 1993 No. 1813, Sched. 3

Article 6   SCHEDULE 3

PART I

POWERS OF OFFICERS

Power to assist French authorities

F–17   1.—(1) Where—

　　(a) an officer belonging to the French Republic has in a control zone in the United Kingdom or in a supplementary control zone in the United Kingdom arrested or detained a person as permitted by Article 10(1) of the international articles and Article 2 of the supplementary articles, and

　　(b) such an officer so requests,

a constable or an officer commissioned by the Commissioners of Customs and Excise under section 6(3) of the *Customs and Excise Management Act* 1979 (in this Schedule referred to as a "customs officer") may make arrangements for the person to be taken into temporary custody.

　　(2) A person taken into temporary custody under sub-paragraph (1)—

　　(a) shall be treated for all purposes as being in lawful custody, and

　　(b) may be taken to a police station or such other place as may be appropriate in the circumstances, and shall in that case be treated as being a person in whose case sections 36(7) and (8), 54 to 56 and 58 of the *Police and Criminal Evidence Act* 1984 (in this Schedule referred to as "the 1984 Act"), and in the case of a child or young person section 34(2) to (7), (8) and (9) of the *Children and Young Persons Act* 1933, apply, and

　　(c) must be returned, before the end of the period for which he could in the circumstances be detained in the United Kingdom under Article 10 of the international articles or Article 2 of the supplementary articles, to a place where detention under that Article could be resumed.

　　(3) Where a person falls to be treated as mentioned in sub-paragraph (2)(b) section 56 of the 1984 Act shall be taken to apply as if he were detained for a serious arrestable offence.

[This paragraph is printed as amended by the *Channel Tunnel (Miscellaneous Provisions) Order* 1994 (S.I. 1994 No. 1405); and the *Channel Tunnel (International Arrangements) (Amendment No. 3) Order* 2001 (S.I. 2001 No. 1544).]

Powers of arrest outside United Kingdom

★F–17a   2.—(1) A constable may in a control zone in France—

(a) exercise any power of arrest conferred by a frontier control enactment or conferred by the 1984 Act in respect of an offence under such an enactment,

(b) make any arrest authorised by a warrant issued by a court in the United Kingdom, and

(c) arrest any person whose name or description or both, together with particulars of an indictable offence of which there are reasonable grounds for suspecting him to be guilty, have been made available by a chief officer of police to other such officers.

(2) For the purposes of sub-paragraph (1)(a) the reference in sub-paragraph (1) to a constable shall be construed—

(a) in relation to the powers of arrest conferred by section 28A(1) and (3) of and paragraph 17(1) of Schedule 2 to the *Immigration Act* 1971, as including a reference both—

(i) to an immigration officer appointed for the purposes of that Act under paragraph 1 of that Schedule, and

(ii) to an officer of customs and excise who is the subject of arrangements for the employment of such officers as immigration officers made under that paragraph by the Secretary of State,

and where this sub-paragraph applies, the reference in sub-paragraph (1) [*sic*] to a control zone in France shall be construed as including a reference to a supplementary control zone in France.

(b) in relation to the power of arrest conferred by paragraph 6(4) of Schedule 5 to the *Prevention of Terrorism (Temporary Provisions) Act* 1989, as including a reference to any person who by virtue of paragraph 1(1) of that Schedule is an examining officer for the purposes of that Act, and

(c) in relation to any arrest that may be made by a customs officer by virtue of section 138 of the *Customs and Excise Management Act* 1979 and an arrest for a drug trafficking offence as defined in section 38(1) of the *Drug Trafficking Offences Act* 1986, as including a reference to a customs officer.

(3) A customs officer may[—

(a)] in a control zone in France arrest any person whose name or description or both, together with particulars of an arrestable offence (within the meaning of section 24 of the 1984 Act) which is an offence in relation to an assigned matter as defined in section 1(1) of the *Customs and Excise Management Act* 1979 and of which there are reasonable grounds for suspecting him to be guilty, have been made available to customs officers generally under the authority of the Commissioners for Her Majesty's Revenue and Customs[;

(b) within the tunnel system exercise any power of arrest conferred by a security control enactment in connection with the carrying out of security controls].

(4) For the purpose of enabling constables to make arrests in France in the cases described in Article 40 of the international articles sections 24 and 25 of the 1984 Act shall extend to France.

(5) Where—

(a) an arrest has been made for an offence of the kind mentioned in Article 39 of the international articles, and

(b) it falls to the competent authorities in France to determine the exercise of jurisdiction in accordance with Article 38,

the person arrested shall be treated as continuing to be under arrest while in France until he is presented to those authorities as required by Article 41(a).

(6) Where—

(a) an arrest falling within sub-paragraph (4) or (5) above has been made, and

(b) the competent authorities in France determine under Article 41 of the international articles that jurisdiction is to be exercised by the United Kingdom,

the person arrested shall be treated as having continued to be under arrest throughout, even if he was for some period in the custody of those authorities, and sections 30 and 41 of the 1984 Act shall apply accordingly.

(7) Any power conferred by an enactment to search an arrested person may be exercised following an arrest authorised by this paragraph as if the person had been arrested in the United Kingdom.

[This paragraph is printed as amended by the *Channel Tunnel (International Arrangements) (Amendment No. 3) Order* 2001 (S.I. 2001 No. 1544); the *Serious Organised Crime and Police Act 2005 (Powers of Arrest) (Consequential Amendments) Order* 2005 (S.I. 2005 No. 3389) and the *Commissioners for Revenue and Customs Act* 2005, s.50(1); and as prospectively amended (insertion of text in square brackets) by S.I. 2012 No. 1264 (as to which, see the annotation to article 2, *ante*, F–13).] ★

Arrested persons held in France

★F–17b   3.—(1) Where—

    (a) an arrest of any kind authorised by paragraph 2 above has been made in a control zone in France or in a supplementary control zone in France; or

    (b) an arrest of any such kind has been made in the United Kingdom and the person arrested enters such a control zone while under arrest,

the person arrested may be held in France for a period of not more than 24 hours and, if there are exceptional circumstances and an officer belonging to the French Republic is notified of the extension, for a further period.

    (2) Subject to sub-paragraphs (3) and (4), the person arrested shall be treated as if the place where he is held were for the purposes of the provisions mentioned in paragraph 1(2)(b) above and those of sections 61 to 63 of the 1984 Act a police station, or where the arrest was made by a customs officer, a customs office, in England, not being a police station or customs office designated under section 35 of the 1984 Act.

    (3) Where—

    (a) an arrest falling within paragraph 2(1)(a) or (3)[(a) or (b)] above has been made by a customs officer, and

    (b) the person arrested is held in France in a place within the tunnel system which would if it were in England be a customs office within the meaning of the 1984 Act,

sections 34(1) to (5), 36, 37, 39 to 42, 50, 54, 55, 56(1) to (9), 58(1) to (11), 62, 63 and 64(1) to (6) of the 1984 Act and in the case of a child or young person section 34(2) to (7), (8) and (9) of the *Children and Young Persons Act* 1933, shall apply as if the place where he is held were a customs office in England designated under section 35 of the 1984 Act.

    (4) Where the power of arrest mentioned in paragraph 2(2)(b) has been exercised any detention in France of the person arrested shall be treated for all purposes as being detention under paragraph 6(1) of Schedule 5 to the *Prevention of Terrorism (Temporary Provisions) Act* 1989, and section 16(2) of that Act, sections 51(b), 56 and 58 of the 1984 Act and section 34 of the *Children and Young Persons Act* 1933 as applying accordingly.

★   [This paragraph is printed as amended by the *Channel Tunnel (International Arrangements) (Amendment No. 3) Order* 2001 (S.I. 2001 No. 1544); and as prospectively amended (insertion of text in square brackets in para. (3)(a)) by S.I. 2012 No. 1264 (as to which, see the annotation to article 2, *ante*, F–13).]

Arrested persons arriving in the United Kingdom

F–17c   4.—(1) Where—

    (a) an arrest falling within Article 39 or 40 of the international articles has been made, and

    (b) the person arrested enters the United Kingdom while under arrest,

the person arrested shall be taken to a police station.

    (2) The custody officer at the police station to which the person is taken shall determine—

    (a) whether the offence is one over which the United Kingdom has jurisdiction by virtue of Article 38(1), and

    (b) if he determines that it is not, whether it is one over which the United Kingdom may exercise jurisdiction by virtue of Article 38(2) and if so whether jurisdiction is to be exercised,

and may for the purpose of determining those questions detain the person at the police station for not longer than the permitted period.

    (3) The permitted period is the period of 48 hours beginning at the time at which the person arrives at the police station.

    (4) Subject to sub-paragraph (6), the person shall be treated—

    (a) as not being detained at the police station for the purposes of section 37 of the 1984 Act, and

    (b) as not being in police detention for the purposes of sections 40 to 43 of the 1984 Act.

    (5) Where the custody officer determines that the United Kingdom does not have jurisdiction by virtue of Article 38(1) and—

    (a) that jurisdiction is not exercisable by virtue of Article 38(2), or

    (b) that jurisdiction is exercisable by virtue of Article 38(2) but is not to be exercised,

he shall immediately inform the competent French authorities of his determination and shall arrange for the person to be transferred to France within the permitted period.

    (6) Where the custody officer determines that the United Kingdom has jurisdiction by virtue of Article 38(1) or that jurisdiction is exercisable by virtue of Article 38(2) and is to be exercised—

(a) he shall immediately inform the person of his determination,

(b) the person shall be treated as being in police detention for all purposes of Part IV of the 1984 Act, and

(c) that Part shall have effect in relation to him as if the relevant time mentioned in section 41(1) were the time at which he is informed of the determination.

(7) Where the police station to which the person is taken is not a police station designated under section 35 of the 1984 Act, references in this paragraph to the custody officer are to be construed as references to an officer not below the rank of sergeant.

[The heading of paragraph 4 and sub-paragraph (1) were substituted by the *Channel Tunnel (Miscellaneous Provisions) Order* 1994: S.I. 1994 No. 1405, art. 8 and Sched. 4, with effect from July 1, 1994: *ibid.*, art. 1(2).]

Arrests of French officers

5.—(1) This paragraph applies where an officer belonging to the French Republic ("the officer") is **F–17d** arrested for an act performed in the United Kingdom in the tunnel system or a control zone or supplementary control zone.

(2) If the officer enters France while under arrest—

(a) he shall without delay be handed over for custody to the competent French authorities and shall be treated as continuing to be under arrest until he has been handed over, and

(b) if after consultation with those authorities it is then determined that the act was not performed by the officer whilst in the exercise of his functions and he accordingly does not by virtue of Article 30(2) of the international articles come under French jurisdiction, he shall be treated as having continued to be under arrest until sub-paragraph (3) has been complied with.

(3) Where—

(a) sub-paragraph (2)(b) applies, or

(b) the officer does not enter France while under arrest,

he shall be taken to a police station designated under section 35 of the 1984 Act.

(4) Sub-paragraphs (5) to (9) apply in a case falling within sub-paragraph (3)(b).

(5) The custody officer at the police station to which the officer is taken shall after consultation with the competent French authorities determine whether the act was performed by the officer whilst in the exercise of his functions, and may for the purpose of determining that question detain the officer at the police station for not longer than the permitted period.

(6) The permitted period is the period of 48 hours beginning at the time at which the officer arrives at the police station.

(7) Subject to sub-paragraph (9), the officer shall be treated—

(a) as not being detained at the police station for the purposes of section 37 of the 1984 Act, and

(b) as not being in police detention for the purposes of sections 40 to 43 of the 1984 Act.

(8) Where the custody officer determines that the act was performed by the officer whilst in the exercise of his functions and the officer accordingly comes under French jurisdiction by virtue of Article 30(2), he shall immediately inform the competent French authorities and shall arrange for the officer to be transferred to France within the permitted period.

(9) In any other case—

(a) the custody officer shall immediately inform the officer of his determination,

(b) the officer shall be treated as being in police detention for all purposes of Part IV of the 1984 Act, and

(c) that Part shall have effect in relation to him as if the relevant time mentioned in section 41(1) were the time at which he is informed of the determination.

[This paragraph is printed as amended by the *Channel Tunnel (International Arrangements) (Amendment No. 3) Order* 2001 (S.I. 2001 No. 1544).]

Arrests of United Kingdom officers

6.—(1) This paragraph applies where an officer belonging to the United Kingdom ("the officer") is **F–17e** arrested for an act performed in France in the tunnel system or a control zone or supplementary control zone.

(2) If—

(a) the officer does not enter the United Kingdom while under arrest, and

(b) the competent French authorities determine that the act was performed by the officer

whilst in the exercise of his functions and he accordingly comes under United Kingdom
jurisdiction by virtue of Article 30(2) of the international articles,
he shall on being handed over by those authorities to a constable be treated as having been arrested by the constable.

(3) Where—

    (a) sub-paragraph (2)(b) applies, or

    (b) the officer enters the United Kingdom while under the original arrest,

he shall be taken to a police station designated under section 35 of the 1984 Act.

(4) Sub-paragraphs (5) to (9) apply in a case falling within sub-paragraph (3)(b).

(5) The custody officer at the police station to which the officer is taken shall—

    (a) immediately invite the competent French authorities to determine whether the act was
performed by the officer whilst in the exercise of his functions, and

    (b) afford those authorities any assistance they may require in determining that question,

and may for the purpose of enabling that question to be determined detain the officer at the police station for not longer than the permitted period.

(6) The permitted period is the period of 48 hours beginning at the time at which the officer arrives at the police station.

(7) Subject to sub-paragraph (9), the officer shall be treated—

    (a) as not being detained at the police station for the purposes of section 37 of the 1984 Act,
and

    (b) as not being in police detention for the purposes of sections 40 to 43 of the 1984 Act.

(8) Where the competent French authorities determine that the act was not performed by the officer whilst in the exercise of his functions and the officer accordingly does not by virtue of Article
30(2) come under United Kingdom jurisdiction, the custody officer shall arrange for the officer to be
transferred to France within the permitted period.

(9) In any other case—

    (a) the custody officer shall immediately inform the officer of the determination,

    (b) the officer shall be treated as being in police detention for all purposes of Part IV of the
1984 Act, and

    (c) that Part shall have effect in relation to him as if the relevant time mentioned in section
41(1) were the time at which he is informed of the determination.

[This paragraph is printed as amended by the *Channel Tunnel (International Arrangements)
(Amendment No. 3) Order* 2001 (S.I. 2001 No. 1544).]

Supplementary controls over animals

F–18   Part II, consisting of eight paragraphs, imposes controls for the purpose of preventing
the spread of the rabies virus through the tunnel to the United Kingdom. Failure by the
Concessionaires to carry out the duties imposed is made an offence triable either way
(maximum penalty on conviction on indictment is a fine). It is also an offence, punishable in
the same way, for any person to interfere with any anti-rabies installation, or to do any act
which might impair the effectiveness of any anti-rabies measure, or to obstruct a person
authorised to enforce the provisions of this Part.

Enactments modified

F–19   As to Schedule 4, see article 7, *ante*, F–13a. The enactments modified which fall within the
compass of this work are the *Immigration Act* 1971 (as to which, see § 25–233 in the main
work) and the *Terrorism Act* 2000 (as to which, see *ante*, §§ 25–136a, 25–141).

Amendments, repeals, revocations

F–20   Relevant entries in Schedules 5 (amendments) and 6 (repeals and revocations) are noted
at the appropriate place elsewhere in this work.

S.I. 1994 No. 1405, art. 1

Citation and commencement

F–21   1.—(1) This Order may be cited as the *Channel Tunnel (Miscellaneous Provisions) Order* 1994 and, except as provided in paragraphs (2) and (3) below, shall come into force on the date on which the Agreement between the Government of the Kingdom of Belgium, the Government of the French Republic and the Government of the United Kingdom and Great Britain and Northern Ireland Concerning Rail Traffic between Belgium and the United Kingdom Using the Channel Fixed Link enters into force. That date will be notified in the London, Edinburgh and Belfast *Gazettes*.

(2) Article 8 shall, to the extent necessary to give effect to those of the amendments specified in Schedule 4 that are mentioned in paragraph (3) below, come into force on 1st July 1994.

(3) The amendments are—

(a) those specified in paragraphs 6, 8(b), 9, 10 and 12 of Schedule 4, and

(b) those specified in paragraph 11 of Schedule 4 except the amendments to paragraphs 1(11)(d) and 3(b) of Schedule 4 to the 1993 Order.

S.I. 1994 No. 1405, arts 2–8

Interpretation

2.—(1) In this Order, except for the purpose of construing the tripartite articles, and in any **F-22** enactment as applied by it with modifications, any expression for which there is an entry in the first column of Schedule 1 has the meaning given against it in the second column.

(2) In this Order "the authorised purposes" means—

(a) purposes for which provision is authorised by any of paragraphs (a), (d) and (g), and

(b) purposes connected with any matter in relation to or with respect to or for regulating which provision is authorised by any of paragraphs (c), (e), (f) and (h),

of section 11(1) of the *Channel Tunnel Act* 1987.

(3) In this Order "the tripartite articles" means the provisions set out—

(a) in Part I of Schedule 2 (being Articles or parts of Articles of the Agreement mentioned in article 1 above), and

(b) in Part II of Schedule 2 (being Articles or parts of Articles of the Protocol attached to and forming part of that Agreement);

(c) in Part III of Schedule 2 (being Articles or parts of Articles of the Protocol attached to and forming part of the Agreement, as applied by the Administrative Arrangement to immigration controls upon person travelling on international trains making a commercial stop);

and in the tripartite articles the expression "the Fixed Link" shall for the purposes of this Order be taken to have the same meaning as is given to "the tunnel system" by section 1(7) of the *Channel Tunnel Act* 1987.

[This article is printed as amended by the *Channel Tunnel (Miscellaneous Provisions) (Amendment) Order* 2004 (S.I. 2004 No. 2589).]

Application of tripartite articles

3.—(1) The tripartite articles shall have the force of law in the United Kingdom—

(a) within a control zone, and

(b) elsewhere for the authorised purposes only.

(2) Subject to paragraph (4), without prejudice to paragraph (1) officers belonging to the Kingdom of Belgium and officers belonging to the French Republic shall to the extent specified in the tripartite articles have rights and obligations and powers to carry out functions in the United Kingdom.

(3) Subject to paragraph (4), for the purpose of giving full effect to Article 17 of the Part II provisions and to Article 17 of the Part III provisions (accommodation, etc., for Belgian authorities) the appropriate Minister may by written notice require any occupier or person concerned with the management of a terminal control point to provide such accommodation, installations and equipment as may be necessary to satisfy requirements determined under Article 16 of the Protocol mentioned in article 2(3)(b) above and under that Article as applied by Article 3 of the Administrative Arrangement (which requires the competent authorities of the Kingdom of Belgium and of the United Kingdom to determine their respective requirements in consultation with one another).

(4) Nothing in this article implies the existence of a control zone in the station of London-Waterloo on British Territory.

[This article is printed as amended by the *Channel Tunnel (Miscellaneous Provisions) (Amendment) Order* 2004 (S.I. 2004 No. 2589); and the *Channel Tunnel (Miscellaneous Provisions) (Amendment) Order* 2007 (S.I. 2007 No. 2908).]

Application of enactments

4.—(1) All frontier enactments shall for the purpose of enabling officers belonging to the United Kingdom to carry out frontier controls extend—

    (a) to France within a control zone, and

    (b) to Belgium within a control zone.

    (1A) The *Race Relations Act* 1976 shall apply to the carrying out by immigration officers of their functions in a control zone outside the United Kingdom as it applies to the carrying out of their functions within the United Kingdom.

    (2), (3) [*Application of Data Protection Act* 1984.]

[This article is printed as amended by S.I. 2007 No. 2908 (*ante*).]

Application of criminal law

    5.—(1) Any act or omission which—

    (a) takes place outside the United Kingdom in a control zone, and

    (b) would, if taking place in England, constitute an offence under a frontier control enactment, shall be treated for the purposes of that enactment as taking place in England.

    (2) Summary proceedings for anything that is by virtue of paragraph (1) an offence triable summarily or triable either way may be taken, and the offence may for all incidental purposes be treated as having been committed, in the county of Kent or in the inner London area as defined in section 2(1)(a) of the *Justices of the Peace Act* 1979.

    (3) Any jurisdiction conferred by virtue of paragraphs (1) and (2) on any court is without prejudice to any jurisdiction exercisable apart from this article by that or any other court.

    (4) Where it is proposed to institute proceedings in respect of an alleged offence in any court and a question as to the court's jurisdiction arises under Article 11(2) of the Part I provisions, it shall be presumed, unless the contrary is proved, that the court has jurisdiction by virtue of that Article.

Powers of officers

    6. Schedule 3 (which contains provision as to powers exercisable by constables and other officers) shall have effect.

Enactments modified

    7.—(1) Without prejudice to the generality of articles 4(1) and 5(1), the enactments specified in paragraph (2) shall—

    (a) in their application to France and Belgium by virtue of article 4(1), and

    (b) in their application to the United Kingdom for the authorised purposes, have effect with modifications the same as those set out in Schedule 4 to the 1993 Order.

    (2) Nothing in paragraph (1)(b) implies the existence of a control zone in the station of London-Waterloo on British Territory.

    (2) The enactments are—

    (a) *Immigration Act* 1971;

    (b) *Public Health (Control of Disease) Act* 1984;

    (c) *Immigration and Asylum Act* 1999;

    (d) *Terrorism Act* 2000; and

    (e) *Immigration, Asylum and Nationality Act* 2006.

[This article is printed as amended by the *Channel Tunnel (Miscellaneous Provisions) (Amendment) Order* 2006 (S.I. 2006 No. 2627); S.I. 2007 No. 2908 (*ante*); and the *Channel Tunnel (International Arrangements and Miscellaneous Provisions) (Amendment) Order* 2007 (S.I. 2007 No. 3579) (insertion of second para. (2)).]

Amendments of instruments

    8. The instruments mentioned in Schedule 4 shall have effect with the amendments there specified.

Article 2(1)   SCHEDULE 1

EXPRESSIONS DEFINED

Expression	*Meaning*	**F–23**
"Administrative arrangement"	The Administrative Arrangement made between the Secretary of State for the Home Department of the United Kingdom of Great Britain and Northern Ireland, the Vice Prime Minister, Minister of Home Affairs of the Kingdom of Belgium, and the Minister of the Interior, of Internal Security and Local Freedoms of the French Republic, concerning the exercise of Immigration Controls by British Officials at the Gare du Midi in Brussels and by Belgian Officials at Waterloo International Staton in London and Ashford International dated 1st October 2004.	
"Control zone"	A control zone defined under Article 1(6) of the Part I provisions but excluding the station of London-Waterloo on British territory.	
"Frontier controls"	So far as they constitute frontier controls as defined in Article 1(1) of the Part I provisions and are controls in relation to persons or goods, police, immigration, customs, health, veterinary and phytosanitary controls.	
"Immigration controls"	The controls carried out by the authorities of the State of arrival to check whether passengers making a journey between Belgium and the United Kingdom are in possession of the necessary travel documents and fulfil the other conditions for entry to its territory.	
"International service"	The meaning given in section 13(6) of the *Channel Tunnel Act* 1987.	
"Officers"	Persons responsible for authorising departure from or entry to the State of arrival.	
"The 1993 Order"	The *Channel Tunnel (International Arrangements) Order* 1993.	
"The Part I provisions"	The provisions set out in Part I of Schedule 2.	
"The Part II provisions"	The provisions set out inPart II of Schedule 2.	
"The Part III provisions"	The Provisions set out in Part III of Schedule 2.	
"Through train"	A train, other than a shuttle train as defined in section 1(9) of the *Channel Tunnel Act* 1987, which for the purposes of sections 11 and 12 of that Act is engaged on an international service.	

[The definitions of "Administrative arrangement", "Immigration controls", "Officers", and "The Part III provisions" were inserted by the *Channel Tunnel (Miscellaneous Provisions) (Amendment) Order* 2004 (S.I. 2004 No. 2589). In addition to the above definitions, the Schedule also contains definitions of the following expressions, which are identical to those contained in Schedule 1 to the 1993 Order (*ante*, F–15): "Frontier control enactment", "Terminal control point", "Train manager" and "The tunnel system". The definition of "control zone" is printed as amended by the *Channel Tunnel (Miscellaneous Provisions) (Amendment) Order* 2007 (S.I. 2007 No. 2908).]

Article 2(3)   SCHEDULE 2

<small>TRIPARTITE ARTICLES</small>

<small>PART I</small>

<small>AGREEMENT</small>

<small>PART I</small>

General provisions

<small>ARTICLE 1</small>

Definitions

F–24   (1) "Frontier controls" means police, immigration, customs, health, veterinary and phytosanitary, consumer protection, and transport controls, as well as any other controls provided for in national or European Community laws and regulations.

(2) "Fixed Link" means the Channel Fixed Link defined in Article 1 of the Treaty done at Canterbury on 12 February 1986.

(3) "Trains" means international trains travelling between Belgium and British territory, using the Fixed Link and passing through French territory.

(4) "Non-stop trains" means international trains travelling between Belgian and British territory, using the Fixed Link and crossing French territory without making a commercial stop, except for technical stops.

(5) "Officers" means persons responsible for policing and frontier controls who are under the command of the persons or authorities designated in accordance with Article 3(2).

(6) "Control Zone" means that part of the territory of the host State and the non-stop trains, within which the officers of the other States are empowered to effect controls. Each control zone shall be defined by mutual agreement between the host State and the State whose officers will be operating in the said zone; however, in the case of non-stop trains, the control zone in French territory shall be determined jointly by the three Governments.

(7) "Host State" means the State in whose territory the controls of the other States are effected.

<small>ARTICLE 2</small>

Scope

(1) This Agreement shall apply to rail traffic between the United Kingdom and Belgium travelling via the Fixed Link and passing through French territory.

. . . .

(3) A Protocol concerning frontier controls and policing on non-stop trains between the United Kingdom and Belgium via the Fixed Link is attached as an annex to this Agreement and shall form an integral part thereof.

<small>PART II</small>

Authorities and General Principles of Co-operation

<small>ARTICLE 3</small>

F–24a   . . . .

(2) Each of the Governments shall designate the authorities or persons having charge of the services which in its territory have responsibility for the exercise of frontier controls and the maintenance of law and order.

. . . .

<small>ARTICLE 4</small>

On non-stop trains, British officers may exercise frontier controls in Belgian and French territory, and Belgian officers in British and French territory.

ARTICLE 5

It is agreed that the frontier controls relating to non-stop trains shall in principle be effected under the exclusive responsibility of the British and Belgian authorities.

ARTICLE 9

The officers of the three States shall be authorised to circulate freely over the whole of the route between London and Brussels for official purposes simply by producing appropriate evidence of their identity and status.

PART III

Co-operation in Criminal Justice

ARTICLE 11

(1) Without prejudice to the provisions of Articles 4 and 14(2) of the Protocol attached as an an- **F–24b** nex to this Agreement, when an offence is committed on the territory of one of the three States that State shall have jurisdiction.

(2) When it cannot be ascertained where such an offence has been committed, the State of arrival shall have jurisdiction.

ARTICLE 12

Where an arrest is made for an offence in respect of which one State has jurisdiction under Article 11, that arrest shall not be affected by the fact that its effects continue in the territory of the other States.

ARTICLE 13

Persons who are found committing, attempting to commit, or just having committed an offence and who are apprehended on the train during the journey shall be handed over as soon as possible to the empowered officers of the State which has jurisdiction under Article 11.

ARTICLE 14

(1) In the event that a person is found committing, attempting to commit or just having committed on board a train in the territory of a State one of the following offences: homicide, rape, arson, armed robbery, kidnapping and hostage taking, or use of explosives, the train must be stopped in order to enable the competent authorities of that State to take any measures relevant to their investigations and, where appropriate, detain the person suspected of having committed the offence.

(2) If the train cannot be stopped because it is within the Fixed Link or because it is about to leave the territory of the State in which one of the offences referred to in the preceding paragraph has been committed, authorised officers who are present must take all appropriate interim measures to ensure that, when the train arrives, the officers of the State which has jurisdiction under Article 11 are able to interview witnesses, take evidence or receive information relevant to their investigations and, where appropriate, take charge of the person suspected of having committed the offence.

ARTICLE 15

(1) When a person is arrested in a manner covered by Articles 6, 12, 13 and 14(2) of this Agreement, the arrest shall be notified without delay to the authorities of the State of arrival. The person arrested may be transferred to the territory of the State which has jurisdiction under Article 11.

(2) However, any such transfer shall take place within no more than 24 hours of the notification under the preceding paragraph. Moreover, each State reserves the right not to authorise the transfer of its nationals.

PART V

Co-operation Between the Competent Authorities

ARTICLE 23

(1) Each State shall waive any claim which it may have against the other States for compensation **F–24c** in respect of damage caused to its officers or its property.

(2) The provisions of this Article shall not affect in any way the rights of third parties under the laws of each State.

Part VI

Final Clauses

Article 24

F–24d In addition to the arrangements provided for under Article 20, the procedures for the implementation of this Agreement and its Protocol may, as far as necessary, be the subject of technical or administrative arrangements between the competent authorities of the three States.

Part II

Protocol

Article 1

F–24e This Protocol shall apply to non-stop rail traffic between the United Kingdom and Belgium travelling via the Fixed Link and passing through French territory.

Article 2

(1) The laws and regulations relating to frontier controls of one State shall be applicable in the control zone situated in the other States and shall be put into effect by the officers of that State in the same way as in their own territory.

(2) The officers of each State shall be subject to the legislation of that State on the protection of individuals with regard to automated processing of personal data when using their automated data files and equipment in the control zone situated in either of the other States.

Article 3

(1) The officers of the other States shall, in exercise of their national powers, be permitted in the control zone situated in the host State to detain or arrest persons in accordance with the laws and regulations relating to frontier controls of their own State or persons sought by the authorities of their own State. These officers shall also be permitted to conduct such persons to the territory of their own State.

(2) However, no person may be held for more than 24 hours in the areas reserved for frontier controls in the host State. Any such detention shall be subject to the requirements and procedures laid down by the legislation of the State of the officers who have made the detention or arrest.

Article 4

Breaches of the laws and regulations relating to frontier controls of other States which are detected in the control zone situated in the host State shall be subject to the laws and regulations of those other States, as if the breaches had occurred in the territory of the latter.

Article 5

(1) The frontier controls of the State of departure shall normally be effected before those of the State of arrival.

(2) The officers of the State of arrival are not authorised to begin to carry out such controls before the end of the controls of the State of departure. Any form of relinquishment of such controls shall be considered as a control.

(3) The officers of the State of departure may no longer carry out their controls when the officers of the State of arrival have begun their own operations, except with the consent of the competent officers of the State of arrival.

(4) If exceptionally, in the course of the frontier controls, the sequence of operations provided for in paragraph (1) of this Article is modified, the officers of the State of arrival may not proceed to detentions, arrests or seizures until the frontier controls of the State of departure are completed. In such a case, these officers shall escort the persons, vehicles, merchandise, animals or other goods, for which the frontier controls of the State of departure are not yet completed, to the officers of that State. If these latter then wish to proceed to detentions, arrests or seizure, they shall have priority.

ARTICLE 6

If the State of arrival refuses admission to persons, vehicles, animals or goods, or if persons refuse to submit to the frontier controls of the State of arrival, or send or take back any vehicles, animals or goods which are accompanying them, the authorities of the State of departure may not refuse to accept back such persons, vehicles, animals or goods. However, the authorities of the State of departure may take any measures to deal with them in accordance with the law applicable in that State and in a way which does not impose obligations either on the State of transit or on the State of arrival.

ARTICLE 7

. . . .

(2) In an emergency, the local representatives of the authorities concerned may by mutual agreement provisionally bring into effect alterations to the delimitation of the control zones which may prove necessary. Any arrangements so reached shall come into effect immediately.

ARTICLES 8–11

[Health, veterinary and phytosanitary controls]

ARTICLES 12

Officers of the other States may wear their national uniform or visible distinctive insignia in the host State.

ARTICLE 13

(1) The authorities of the host State shall grant the same protection and assistance to officers of the other States, in the exercise of their functions, as they grant to their own officers.

(2) The provisions of the criminal law in force in the host State for the protection of officers in the exercise of their functions shall be equally applicable to the punishment of offences committed against officers of the other States in the exercise of their functions.

ARTICLE 14

(1) Without prejudice to the application of the provisions of Article 23 of the Agreement, claims for compensation for loss, injury or damage caused by or to officers of the other States in the exercise of their functions in the host State shall be subject to the law and jurisdiction of the State to which those officers belong as if the circumstance giving rise to the claim had occurred in that State.

(2) Officers of the other States may not be prosecuted by authorities of the host State for any acts performed in the control zone whilst in the exercise of their functions. In such a case, they shall come under the jurisdiction of their own State as if the act had been committed in that State.

(3) The judicial authorities or police of the host State who take steps to record the complaint and assemble the facts relating thereto shall communicate all the particulars and evidence thereof to the competent authorities of the State to which the accused officer belongs for the purposes of a possible prosecution according to the laws in force in that State.

ARTICLE 15

(1) Officers of the other States shall be permitted freely to transfer to their own States sums of money levied on behalf of their Governments in the control zone situated in the host State, as well as merchandise and other goods seized there.

(2) They may equally sell such merchandise and other goods in the host State in conformity with the provisions in force in the host State and transfer the proceeds to their own State.

ARTICLE 17

The authorities of the Kingdom of Belgium and of the United Kingdom shall use their best endeavours to ensure that the authorities of the other Party are able to make use in the host State of the accommodation, installations and equipment necessary for the performance of their functions.

ARTICLE 18

(1) The officers of the other States are empowered to keep order within the accommodation appointed for their exclusive use in the host State.

(2) The officers of the host State shall not have access to such accommodation, except at the request of the officers of the State concerned or in accordance with the laws of the host State applicable to entry into and searches of private premises.

ARTICLE 19

All goods which are necessary to enable the officers of the other States to carry out their functions in the host State shall be exempt from all taxes and dues on entry and exit.

ARTICLE 20

(1) The officers of the other States whilst exercising their functions in the host State shall be authorised to communicate with their national authorities.

....

PART III

Articles or parts of Articles of the Protocol attached to and forming part of the Agreement, as applied by the Administrative Arrangement to immigration controls upon passengers travelling on international trains making a commercial stop

ARTICLE 1

F–24f   This Protocol shall apply to rail traffic between the United Kingdom and Belgium travelling via the Fixed Link and making a commercial stop in French territory.

ARTICLE 2

(1) The laws and regulations relating to immigration controls of one State shall be applicable in the control zone situated in the other States and shall be put into effect by the officers of that State in the same way as in their own territory.

(2) The officers of each State shall be subject to the legislation of that State on the protection of individuals with regard to automated processing of personal data when using their automated data files and equipment in the control zone situated in either of the other States.

ARTICLE 3

(1) The officers of the other States shall, in exercise of their national powers, be permitted in the control zone situated in the host state to detain or arrest persons in accordance with the laws relating to immigration control of their own State. These officers shall also be permitted to conduct such persons to the territory of their own State.

(2) However, no person may be held for more than 24 hours in the areas reserved for immigration controls in the host State. Any such detention shall be subject to the requirements and procedures laid down by the legislation of the State of the officers who have made the detention or arrest.

ARTICLE 4

Breaches of the laws and regulations relating to immigration controls of the other States which are detected in the control zone situated in the host State shall be subject to the laws and regulations of those other States, as if the breaches had occurred in the territory of the latter.

ARTICLE 5

(1) The immigration controls of the State of departure shall normally be effected before those of the state of arrival.

(2) The officers of the State of arrival are not authorised to begin to carry out such controls before the end of the controls of the State of departure. Any form of relinquishment of such controls shall be considered as a control.

(3) The officers of the State of departure may no longer carry out their immigration controls when the officers of the State of arrival have begun their own operations, except with the consent of the competent officers of the State of arrival.

(4) If exceptionally, in the course of the immigration controls, the sequence of operations provided for in paragraph (1) of this Article is modified, the officers of the State of arrival may not proceed to

detentions, arrests or seizures until the immigration controls of the State of departure are completed. In such a case, these officers shall escort any persons and goods for which the immigration controls of the State of departure are not yet completed, to the officers of that State. If these latter then wish to proceed to detentions, arrests or seizures, they shall have priority.

ARTICLE 6

If the state of arrival refuses admission to persons or goods or if the persons refuse to submit to the immigration controls of the State of arrival, or send or take back any goods which are accompanying them, the authorities of the State of departure may not refuse to accept back such persons or goods. However, the authorities of the State of departure may take any measures to deal with them in accordance with the law applicable in that State and in a way which does not impose obligations either on the State of transit or on the State of arrival.

ARTICLE 7

In an emergency, the local representatives of the authorities concerned may by mutual agreement provisionally bring into effect alterations to the delimitation of the control zones which may prove necessary. Any arrangements so reached shall come into effect immediately.

ARTICLE 8

Immigration controls on persons for the purpose of safeguarding public health shall be carried out in the control zones situated in the host State by the competent authorities of the State of arrival in conformity with the regulations applicable in that State.

ARTICLE 12

Officers of the other States may wear their national uniform or visible distinctive insignia in the host State.

ARTICLE 13

(1) The authorities of the host State shall grant the same protection and assistance to officers of the other States, in the exercise of their functions, as they grant to their own officers.

(2) The provisions of the criminal law in force in the host State for the protection of officers in the exercise of their functions shall be equally applicable to the punishment of offences committed against officers of the other States in the exercise of their functions.

ARTICLE 14

(1) Without prejudice to the application of the provisions of Article 23 of the Agreement, claims for compensation for loss, injury or damage caused by or to officers of the other States in the exercise of their functions in the host State shall be subject to the law and jurisdiction of the State to which those officers belong as if the circumstance giving rise to the claim had occurred there.

(2) Officers of the other States may not be prosecuted by the authorities of the host State for any acts performed in the control zone whilst in the exercise of their functions. In such a case, they shall come under the jurisdiction of their own State as if the act had been committed there.

(3) The judicial authorities or police of the host State who take steps to record the complaint and assemble the facts relating thereto shall communicate all the particulars and evidence thereof to the competent authorities of the State to which the officer belongs for the purposes of a possible prosecution according to the laws in force in that State.

ARTICLE 17

The authorities of the Kingdom of Belgium and of the United Kingdom shall use their best endeavours to ensure that the authorities of the other party are able to make use in the host State of the accommodation, installations and equipment necessary for the performance of their functions.

ARTICLE 18

(1) The officers of the other State are empowered to keep order within the accommodation appointed for their exclusive use in the host State.

(2) The officers of the host State shall not have access to such accommodation except at the request of the officers of the State concerned or in accordance with the laws of the host State applicable to entry into and searches of private premises.

ARTICLE 19

All goods which are necessary to enable the officers of the other State to carry out their functions in the host State shall be exempt from all taxes and duty on entry and exit.

ARTICLE 20

The officers of the other State whilst exercising their functions in the host State shall be authorised to communicate with their national authorities.

[Part III of this schedule was inserted by the *Channel Tunnel (Miscellaneous Provisions) Order* 2004 (S.I. 2004 No. 2589).]

Powers of officers

F–25   Paragraph 1 of Schedule 3 to S.I. 1994 No. 1405 provides that Part I of Schedule 3 to the 1993 Order (*ante*, F–17) shall, with the variations set out in paragraphs 2 to 7, be taken to apply as if it were contained in the 1994 Order. Part I of Schedule 3 to the 1993 Order, *as so varied*, is set out below.

S.I. 1993 No. 1813, Sched. 3, Pt I (as varied by S.I. 1994 No. 1405, Sched. 3)

SCHEDULE 3

PART I

POWERS OF OFFICERS

Powers of arrest outside United Kingdom

F–26   2.—(1) A constable may in a control zone in France or Belgium—

    (a) exercise any power of arrest conferred by a frontier control enactment or conferred by the *Police and Criminal Evidence Act* 1984 (in this Schedule referred to as "the 1984 Act") in respect of an offence under such an enactment,

    (b) make any arrest authorised by a warrant issued by a court in the United Kingdom, and

    (c) arrest any person whose name or description or both, together with particulars of an arrestable offence (within the meaning of section 24 of the 1984 Act) of which there are reasonable grounds for suspecting him to be guilty, have been made available by a chief officer of police to other such officers.

(2) For the purposes of sub-paragraph (1)(a) the reference in sub-paragraph (1) to a constable shall be construed—

    (a) in relation to the powers of arrest conferred by section 25(3) of and paragraph 17(1) of Schedule 2 to the *Immigration Act* 1971, as including a reference both—

        (i) to an immigration officer appointed for the purposes of that Act under paragraph 1 of that Schedule, and

        (ii) to an officer of customs and excise who is the subject of arrangements for the employment of such officers as immigration officers made under that paragraph by the Secretary of State.

    (b) in relation to the power of arrest conferred by paragraph 6(4) of Schedule 5 to the *Prevention of Terrorism (Temporary Provisions) Act* 1989, as including a reference to any person who by virtue of paragraph 1(1) of that Schedule is an examining officer for the purposes of that Act, and

    (c) in relation to any arrest that may be made by a customs officer by virtue of section 138 of the *Customs and Excise Management Act* 1979 and an arrest for a drug trafficking offence as defined in section 38(1) of the *Drug Trafficking Offences Act* 1986, as including a reference to a customs officer.

(3) A customs officer may in a control zone in France or Belgium arrest any person whose name or description or both, together with particulars of an arrestable offence (within the meaning of section 24 of the 1984 Act) which is an offence in relation to an assigned matter as defined in section 1(1) of the *Customs and Excise Management Act* 1979 and of which there are reasonable grounds for suspecting him to be guilty, have been made available to customs officers generally under the authority of the Commissioners of Customs and Excise.

(4) Sub-paragraph (5) applies where—

(a) an arrest has been made for an offence of the kind mentioned in Article 12 of the Part I provisions, and

(b) the person arrested enters France or Belgium ("the State of arrival") while under arrest.

(5) If jurisdiction is not asserted by the State of arrival, the person arrested shall be treated as having continued to be under arrest throughout, notwithstanding any intervening transfer of Custody to a person other than the person who arrested him, and sections 30 and 41 of the 1984 Act shall apply accordingly.

(6) [*Not printed in this work.*]

(7) Any power conferred by an enactment to search an arrested person may be exercised following an arrest authorised by this paragraph as if the person had been arrested in the United Kingdom.

3.—(1) Where—

(a) an arrest of any kind authorised by paragraph 2 above has been made in a control zone in France or Belgium; or

(b) an arrest of any such kind has been made in the United Kingdom and the person arrested enters such a control zone while under arrest,

the person arrested may be held in France or, as the case may be, Belgium for a period of not more than 24 hours.

(2) Subject to sub-paragraph (4), the person arrested shall be treated as if the place where he is held were for the purposes of sections 36(7) and (8), 54 to 56, 58 and 61 to 63 of the 1984 Act and in the case of a child or young person section 34(2) to (7), (8) and (9) of the *Children and Young Persons Act* 1933 a police station, or where the arrest was made by a customs officer, a customs office, in England, not being a police station or customs office designated under section 35 of the 1984 Act.

(4) Where the power of arrest mentioned in paragraph 2(2)(b) has been exercised any detention in France or Belgium of the persons arrested shall be treated for all purposes as being detention under paragraph 6(1) of Schedule 5 to the *Prevention of Terrorism (Temporary Provisions) Act* 1989, and section 16(2) of that Act, sections 51(b), 56 and 58 of the 1984 Act and section 34 of the *Children and Young Persons Act* 1933 as applying accordingly.

Arrested persons arriving in the United Kingdom

4.—(1) Where a constable is satisfied that an arrest made outside the United Kingdom on a **F–26a** through train was one falling within Article 13 or 14 of the Part I provisions (persons found committing, attempting to commit or just having committed an offence) he may arrange for the person arrested to be taken into temporary custody.

(2) A person taken into temporary custody under sub-paragraph (1)—

(a) shall be treated for all purposes as being in lawful custody, and

(b) may be taken to a police station or such other place as may be appropriate in the circumstances, and shall in that case be treated as being a person in whose case sections 36(7) and (8), 54 to 56 and 58 of the 1984 Act, and in the case of a child or young person section 34(2) to (7), (8) and (9) of the *Children and Young Persons Act* 1933, apply;

and arrangements must be made for him to be transferred within 24 hours from the time at which he was taken into custody to the State having jurisdiction by virtue of Article 11(1) of the Part I provisions.

(2A) Where an arrest has been made for an offence in respect of which the United Kingdom may have jurisdiction as the State of arrival by virtue of Article 11(2) of the Part I provisions the person arrested shall be taken to a police station.

(2B) The custody officer at the police station to which the person is taken shall consider whether the offence is one in respect of which the United Kingdom has jurisdiction by virtue of Article 11(2) of the Part I provisions and may for that purpose detain the person at the police station for not longer than the permitted period.

(3) The permitted period is the period of 24 hours beginning at the time at which the person arrives at the police station.

(4) Subject to sub-paragraph (6), the person shall be treated—

(a) as not being detained at the police station for the purposes of section 37 of the 1984 Act, and

(b) as not being in police detention for the purposes of sections 40 to 43 of the 1984 Act.

(5) Where the custody officer reaches the conclusion that the United Kingdom does not have jurisdiction by virtue of Article 11(2) he shall immediately inform the competent authorities of the State appearing to him to have jurisdiction by virtue of Article 11(1) that he has reached that conclusion and shall arrange for the person to be transferred to that State within the permitted period.

(6) Where the custody officer reaches the conclusion that the United Kingdom has jurisdiction by virtue of Article 11(2)—

(a) he shall immediately inform the person of his conclusion,

(b) the person shall be treated as being in police detention for all purposes of Part IV of the 1984 Act, and

(c) that Part shall have effect in relation to him as if the relevant time mentioned in section 41(1) were the time at which he is informed of the conclusion.

(7) Where the police station to which the person is taken is not a police station designated under section 34 of the 1984 Act, references in this paragraph to the custody officer are to be construed as references to an officer not below the rank of sergeant.

Arrests of French officers

F–26b   5.—(1) This paragraph applies where an officer belonging to the French Republic or to the Kingdom of Belgium ("the officer") is arrested for an act performed in the United Kingdom in a control zone.

(2) If the officer enters the State to which he belongs ("the home State") while under arrest—

(a) he shall without delay be handed over for custody to the competent authorities of the home State and shall be treated as continuing to be under arrest until he has been handed over, and

(b) if after consultation with those authorities it is then determined that the act was not performed by the officer whilst in the exercise of his functions and he accordingly does not by virtue of Article 14(2) of the Part II provisions come under the jurisdiction of the home State, he shall be treated as having continued to be under arrest until sub-paragraph (3) has been complied with.

(3) Where—

(a) sub-paragraph (2)(b) applies, or

(b) the officer does not leave the United Kingdom whilst under arrest,

he shall be taken to a police station designated under section 35 of the 1984 Act.

(4) Sub-paragraphs (5) to (9) apply in a case falling within sub-paragraph (3)(b).

(5) The custody officer at the police station to which the officer is taken shall after consultation with the competent authorities of the home State determine whether the act was performed by the officer whilst in the exercise of his functions, and may for the purpose of determining that question detain the officer at the police station for not longer than the permitted period.

(6) The permitted period is the period of 24 hours beginning at the time at which the officer arrives at the police station.

(7) Subject to sub-paragraph (9), the officer shall be treated—

(a) as not being detained at the police station for the purposes of section 37 of the 1984 Act, and

(b) as not being in police detention for the purposes of sections 40 to 43 of the 1984 Act.

(8) Where the custody officer determines that the act was performed by the officer whilst in the exercise of his functions and the officer accordingly comes under the jurisdiction of the home State by virtue of Article 14(2), he shall immediately inform the competent authorities of the home State and shall arrange for the officer to be transferred to the home State within the permitted period.

(9) In any other case—

(a) the custody officer shall immediately inform the officer of his determination,

(b) the officer shall be treated as being in police detention for all purposes of Part IV of the 1984 Act, and

(c) that Part shall have effect in relation to him as if the relevant time mentioned in section 41(1) were the time at which he is informed of the determination.

Arrests of United Kingdom officers

F–26c   6.—(1) This paragraph applies where an officer belonging to the United Kingdom ("the officer") is arrested for an act performed in France or Belgium in a control zone.

(2) If—

(a) the officer does not enter the United Kingdom while under arrest, and

(b) the competent authorities of the State in which the act was performed ("the State concerned") determine that the act was performed by the officer whilst in the exercise of his functions and he accordingly comes under United Kingdom jurisdiction by virtue of Article 14(2) of the Part II provisions,

he shall on being handed over by those authorities to a constable be treated as having been arrested by the constable.

(3) Where—

(a) sub-paragraph (2)(b) applies, or

(b) the officer enters the United Kingdom while under the original arrest,

he shall be taken to a police station designated under section 35 of the 1984 Act.

(4) Sub-paragraphs (5) to (9) apply in a case falling within sub-paragraph (3)(b).

(5) The custody officer at the police station to which the officer is taken shall—

(a) immediately invite the competent authorities of the State concerned to determine whether the act was performed by the officer whilst in the exercise of his functions, and

(b) afford those authorities any assistance they may require in determining that question

and may for the purpose of enabling that question to be determined detain the officer at the police station for not longer than the permitted period.

(6) The permitted period is the period of 24 hours beginning at the time at which the officer arrives at the police station.

(7) Subject to sub-paragraph (9), the officer shall be treated—

(a) as not being detained at the police station for the purposes of section 37 of the 1984 Act, and

(b) as not being in police detention for the purposes of sections 40 to 43 of the 1984 Act.

(8) Where the competent authorities of the State concerned determine that the act was not performed by the officer whilst in the exercise of his functions and the officer accordingly does not by virtue of Article 14(2) come under United Kingdom jurisdiction, the custody officer shall arrange for the officer to be transferred to the State concerned within the permitted period.

(9) In any other case—

(a) the custody officer shall immediately inform the officer of the determination,

(b) the officer shall be treated as being in police detention for all purposes of Part IV of the 1984 Act, and

(c) that Part shall have effect in relation to him as if the relevant time mentioned in section 41(1) were the time at which he is informed of the determination.

Amendments

Relevant entries in Schedule 4 are noted at the appropriate place elsewhere in this work. **F–27**

APPENDIX G

Guidelines on Claims for Fees under a Crown Court Representation Order and in the Court of Appeal

A. Summary of Source Material

Legislation

As from April 2, 2001 the relevant provisions of the *Legal Aid in Criminal and Care*   **G–1**
Proceedings (Costs) Regulations 1989 (S.I. 1989 No. 343), as amended, were superseded,
virtually unamended, by the *Criminal Defence Service (Funding) Order* 2001 (S.I. 2001 No.
855) ("the *Funding Order* 2001"). This was significantly amended by the *Criminal Defence
Service (Funding) (Amendment) (No. 3) Order* 2001 (S.I. 2001 No. 3341) which came into
force on October 29, 2001, the *Criminal Defence Service (Funding) (Amendment) Order* 2004
(S.I. 2004 No. 2045) which came into force on August 2, 2004, and the *Criminal Defence Service (Funding) (Amendment) Order* 2005 (S.I. 2005 No. 2621) which came into effect on
October 3, 2005, and applied in respect of proceedings in which a representation order was
made on or after that date and to appeals to a costs judge made on or after that date. The
amendments modified and extended graduated fees to cover trials estimated to last up to 30
days, and introduced and later amended a new regime for Very High Cost Cases. In relation to representation orders granted on or after April 30, 2007, the *Funding Order* 2001
was revoked and replaced by the *Criminal Defence Service (Funding) Order* 2007 (S.I. 2007
No. 1174) ("the *Funding Order* 2007") (see art. 4 of the 2007 order for the transitional
provisions).

The 2007 order was first amended by the *Criminal Defence Service (Funding) (Amendment)
Order* 2007 (S.I. 2007 No. 3552). This made minor changes to Schedule 1 (the advocates'
graduated fee scheme), disapplied the principal order to very high costs cases and
introduced a graduated fee scheme for litigators in the Crown Court. The amendments apply to proceedings in which a representation order was granted on or after January 14,
2008, and to proceedings which the Legal Services Commission classified as a very high
costs case on or after that date.

The 2007 order was further amended by the *Criminal Defence Service (Funding) (Amendment) Order* 2008 (S.I. 2008 No. 957) with effect from April 24, 2008. The effect of the
amendments was: (i) that the principal order would apply to a Very High Cost Case where
a litigator instructed an advocate who was not a member of a Very High Cost Case (Crime)
Panel in accordance with the Very High Cost Case contract for panel members dated April
2, 2008, (ii) that in such a case the litigator would claim payment from the Legal Services
Commission in respect of work undertaken by the advocate and authorised in accordance
with the contract, and (iii) that where such a claim was made, the Legal Services Commission would pay the litigator at rates no higher than the rates specified.

The third set of amendments to the 2007 order was made by the *Criminal Defence Service
(Funding) (Amendment No. 2) Order* 2008 (S.I. 2008 No. 2930). The effect was (i) to increase
the maximum payments which the Legal Services Commission could make in very high cost
criminal cases in which an advocate was instructed who was not a member of a panel for

such cases, and (ii) in such cases, to provide for the payment of travelling and accommodation expenses incurred by the advocate where it considered there were exceptional circumstances.

The 2007 order was next amended by the *Criminal Defence Service (Funding) (Amendment) Order* 2009 (S.I. 2009 No. 1843) so as (i) to clarify the situations in which a case (including a Very High Cost Case) is or is not transferred and make other provision relating to cases which cease to be Very High Cost Cases; (ii) to introduce a cap on the number of pages of prosecution evidence where the number of pages is used to determine certain fees for litigators, but to provide for a special preparation fee where the cap is exceeded; (iii) to provide for the fees to be payable where a case is transferred between litigators before sentence (including after retrial); (iv) to introduce a new fixed fee for hearings subsequent to sentence under the *CDA* 1998, s.1CA (variation and discharge of anti-social behaviour orders under s.1C) (§ 5–1206 in the main work), the *PCC(S)A* 2000, s.155 (alteration of Crown Court sentence) (§ 5–1289 in the main work) or the *SOCPA* 2005, s.74 (assistance by defendant: review of sentence) (§ 5–133 in the main work); (v) to extend the fee for proceedings relating to breaches of Crown Court orders to all litigators, whether or not they represented the defendant in the earlier proceedings; (vi) to increase the fixed fees relating to appeals against sentence, appeals against conviction and committals for sentence; and (vii) to make other minor changes. These amendments apply to proceedings in which a representation order was granted on or after August 3, 2009, but the 2007 order continues to apply as if this order had not been made in respect of proceedings in which a representation order was granted before that date.

The *Criminal Defence Service (Funding) (Amendment No. 2) Order* 2009 (S.I. 2009 No. 2086) amended paragraph 11 of Schedule 1 to the 2007 order so as to provide for a mixture of fixed and graduated fees to be payable to defence advocates appearing in publicly funded confiscation proceedings. Where the proceedings attract a graduated fee (which will be dependent on the page count for the purposes of the proceedings, as to which see the new para. 11(3)), the fee payable will be greater than that payable under the former regime. This order came into force on August 21, 2009, and applies to hearings which are concluded on or after that day.

The *Criminal Defence Service (Funding) (Amendment) Order* 2010 (S.I. 2010 No. 679) amended the 2007 order so as to provide for a fixed fee (£318) to be payable to a litigator who acts for a defendant in committal proceedings and in subsequent Crown Court proceedings resulting from those committal proceedings. This fee would be one element of the overall fee payable under Schedule 2 to the 2007 order (litigators' graduated fee scheme). To achieve this, articles 3(1) and 10 were revoked, articles 2, 3(2) and paragraph 10 of Schedule 2 were amended, and a new article 12A, a new paragraph 12B of that schedule and a new entry in the table following paragraph 14 of that schedule were inserted. This order came into force on April 6, 2010. As to this, see also *post*.

The *Criminal Defence Service (Funding) (Amendment No. 2) Order* 2010 (S.I. 2010 No. 1181) further amended the 2007 order so as to introduce a phased reduction in fees payable to advocates under the advocates' graduated fee scheme. The reduced levels of fees took effect in relation to representation orders made on or after April 27, 2010, and April 1, 2011. A further phased reduction was due to take effect on April 1, 2012, but this has now been superseded (*post*).

The *Criminal Defence Service (Funding) (Amendment) Order* 2011 (S.I. 2011 No. 2065) further amended the 2007 order so as: (i) to revoke the third phased reduction in fees payable to advocates that was to have come into force on April 1, 2012 (*ante*), and to introduce a new phased reduction which took effect in relation to representation orders granted on or after October 3, 2011, and April 1, 2012 (ii) to reduce graduated fees for cracked trials and guilty pleas by 25 per cent (except in relation to a cracked trial or guilty plea where a case is committed to the Crown Court for trial at the election of the defendant, as to which see *post*); (iii) to align the fees payable for murder and manslaughter cases (Class A) with those payable for rape and other serious sexual offences (Class J); (iv) to align the fees payable for all offences of dishonesty where the value is less than £100,000 (Class G) with those payable for offences of dishonesty where the value is less than £30,000 (Class F); (v) to omit the definitions of "Very High Cost Case contract" and "Very High Cost Case (Crime) Panel" from the 2007 order as they no longer exist; (vi) to provide for fixed fees for the provision of funded services in proceedings in magistrates' courts by the insertion of a new article 4A and new Schedule 5; (vii) to provide for the fixed fees and hourly rates, as set out in new Schedule 6, for expert services in magistrates' courts and the Crown Court by the insertion of a new article 15A; (viii) to vary the definition of "pages of prosecution evidence" to include a document which has existed in a paper form and which the prosecution have converted into digital form to enable service by means of electronic communication; (ix) to introduce fixed fees for a cracked trial or guilty plea where a case is committed to the Crown Court for trial at the election of the defendant by inserting new paragraphs 7A and 7B in Schedule 1 and new paragraphs 8A and 8B in Schedule 2; and (x) to remove sentence hearings from the list of hearings for which a fixed fee is payable and include them instead under standard appearances.

S.I. 2011 No. 2065 also amended the 2007 order so as to remove the fixed fee of £318 ★ payable to litigators acting under a representation order for committal proceedings which resulted in the defendant being committed to the Crown Court, and which was introduced by S.I. 2010 No. 679 (*ante*). A challenge to the lawfulness of this amendment was rejected in *R. (Law Society of England and Wales) v. Lord Chancellor* [2012] L.S. Gazette, April 13, 13, DC ([2012] EWHC 794 (Admin.)). For critical comment on some of the court's reasoning, see CLW/12/15/35.

The *Criminal Defence Service (Funding) (Amendment) Order* 2012 (S.I. 2012 No. 750) came ★ into force on April 1, 2012. It applies to proceedings in which a representation order is granted on or after that date. Articles 6(2) (claims for fees and disbursements by litigators in the Crown Court) and 14(1) (interim payment of disbursements) of the 2007 order are amended to extend their application to disbursements incurred in proceedings in a magistrates' court that are subsequently committed to the Crown Court, and there are consequential amendments to article 3(2) and (3) (scope).

There are various amendments to Schedule 1 (advocates' graduated fee scheme). The definition of "standard appearance" in paragraph 1(1) is amended so that a sentencing hearing falling under paragraph 29 (mitigation of sentence) is excluded, and so that a preliminary hearing and a hearing relating to breach of bail, failure to surrender to bail or execution of a bench warrant are included. New paragraphs 1(2) to (2C) replace paragraphs 1(2) and (2A), with the effect that, while a document served by the prosecution in electronic form is generally included in the number of pages of prosecution evidence, a documentary or pictorial exhibit that has been served by the prosecution in electronic form and has never existed in paper form is not included unless the appropriate officer decides that it would be appropriate so to include it. An error in paragraph 2 is corrected by omitting the second sub-paragraph (5). Paragraph 14 (fees for special preparation) is amended as a consequence of the amendments relating to pages of prosecution evidence (*ante*) so as to allow for a special preparation fee in respect of time spent on documentary or pictorial exhibits served by the prosecution in electronic form which have never existed in paper form, which have not been included in the page count, but in respect of which the appropriate officer considers it reasonable to make a payment. In the table of fixed fees following paragraph 19, the entry for "cracked trial or guilty plea (at the election of the defendant)" is omitted, and an entry for "hearing for mitigation of sentence" is inserted (and paragraph 29 is amended accordingly). Finally, there are amendments to the entries relating to a junior acting alone in the table of fees for trials lasting over 40 days (para. 25) (bringing the fees for Class G offences into line with those for Class F offences). The amendments to the tables following paragraphs 19 and 25 are to those tables as amended by the *Criminal Defence Service (Funding) (Amendment) Order* 2011 (S.I. 2011 No. 2065) in relation to representation orders granted on or after April 1, 2012 (as to which see *post*, G–57, G–63).

The amendments relating to pages of prosecution evidence made to Schedule 1 are replicated in Schedule 2 (litigators' graduated fee scheme) (paras 1 and 15). The table relating to retrials and transfers (Sched. 2, para. 10) is amended with a view to clarifying the proportion of the graduated fee that is payable to the original litigator and the new litigator where a case has been transferred between litigators after a trial or guilty plea and before the sentencing hearing or after a retrial or cracked retrial and before the sentencing hearing. Finally, in Schedule 5 (magistrates' courts rates), the categories "category 1 (either way)" and "category 1 (summary only)" in the table of higher and lower standard fees are replaced by "category 1A" and "category 1B", and new paragraphs 1(3) to (6) are inserted to describe what cases are included in each of categories 1A, 1B, 2 and 3

★   The *Criminal Defence Service (Funding) (Amendment No. 2) Order* 2012 (S.I. 2012 No. 1343) amends the 2007 order in light of the *Criminal Justice Act 2003 (Commencement No. 28 and Saving Provisions) Order* 2012 (S.I. 2012 No. 1320), and, in particular, to reflect the fact that, with the taking effect of that order, in certain local justice areas (as to which, see *ante*, § 1–88), offences triable either way will be sent from a magistrates' court to the Crown Court, rather than reaching the Crown Court by way of committal proceedings.

The relevant provisions of the *Legal Aid in Criminal and Care Proceedings (General) Regulations* 1989 (S.I. 1989 No. 344) were also replaced, again with little amendment, by the *Criminal Defence Service (General) (No. 2) Regulations* (S.I. 2001 No. 1437) (the "General Regulations"). Any reference hereafter to a regulation is a reference to the General Regulations. Any reference to an article or a schedule, is a reference to the *Funding Order* 2007. The General Regulations together with details of all amendments are set out *in extenso* in the main work at §§ 6–152 *et seq.* The *Funding Order* 2007 is set out in full, *post*, G–6 *et seq.*

The current regimes

G–2   Apart from a handful of historical cases which will be governed by the former provisions for *ex post facto* taxation (as to which see Appendix G–200 *et seq.* in the supplements to the 2010 edition of this work), advocates' fees in the Crown Court effectively fall into one of two regimes:

(i) *Graduated fees.* These were introduced in 1997 for trials lasting up to 10 days, appeals and other minor Crown Court business: *Legal Aid in Criminal and Care Proceedings (Costs) Regulations* 1989 (S.I. 1989 No. 343), Sched. 3. The scheme was then extended to cover trials of up to 25 days and, as from 2005, of trials up to 40 days. As from April 30, 2007, it is intended that the scheme will cover all Crown Court work save for those cases contracted under the Very High Costs Case provisions: *Funding Order* 2007, art. 3(6A), and Sched. 1, para. 2(1). The new scheme is sometimes referred to as the Revised Advocacy Graduated Fee Scheme (RAGFS). The details are now contained in Schedule 1 to the *Funding Order* 2007, which replaces Schedule 4 to the *Funding Order* 2001.

(ii) *Very High Cost Cases (VHCC).* This regime came into effect on October 29, 2001. All cases estimated to last more than 24 days are capable of being subject to a VHCC contract. As to the current VHCC regime, see *post*, G–181 *et seq.*

Notes for guidance

(a) *Graduated fees*

G–3   The Ministry of Justice's *Graduated Fee Scheme Guidance (GFSG)* is updated at regular intervals. In addition, guidance notes in respect of the *Funding Order* 2007, and RAGFS have been issued by the Criminal Bar Association, and are available on both the Criminal Bar Association's and the Courts Service's National Taxing Team's websites. The *GFSG* includes references to costs judges' decisions which are given and commonly referred to and indexed by their "X" references. For convenience these references are used hereafter. The guidance may be cited by advocates when asking for a re-determination: *GFSG, Preface.* However, while interesting and instructive, it is simply the department's gloss on the wording of the regulations, and does not bind costs judges: *R. v. Phillips*, X1, SCTO 594/97.

The Bar Council has also introduced a *Graduated Fee Payment Protocol.* This is an essential part of the mechanism by which advocates will be remunerated in future, and sets out arrangements to ensure that substitute advocates are paid by instructed advocates. The protocol falls outside the immediate scope of this work. It is available on both the Bar Council's and the Criminal Bar Association's websites.

(b) *Very High Cost Cases*

Very High Cost Cases are governed by the *Very High Cost (Crime) Cases Arrangements* 2010 **G–4**
(see *post*, G–181 *et seq.*). Additional guidance is contained in the 2010 VHCC Guidance (Issue 1, published by the Legal Services Commission, dated August 19, 2010).

Contract Appeals Committee decisions

Summaries of decisions of the Contract Appeals Committee (which heard appeals in re- **G–5**
spect of disputes arising under the VHCC regimes which operated before July 14, 2010)
have been collated and appear on the website of the Complex Crime Unit of the Legal Services Commission. These are meant to be updated regularly. It is understood that summaries of decisions of the VHCC Appeals Panel (which will hear appeals in respect of
disputes arising under the VHCC regime which began operating on July 14, 2010 (see *post*,
G–181 *et seq.*)) will be made available at the same location (as to which, see *post*, G–279).

B. The Funding Order (2007)

Criminal Defence Service (Funding) Order 2007
(S.I. 2007 No. 1174)

Citation and commencement

1. This Order may be cited as the *Criminal Defence Service (Funding) Order* 2007 and shall come **G–6**
into force on 30th April 2007.

Interpretation

2. In this Order— **G–7**

"the Act" means the *Access to Justice Act* 1999;

"advocate" means a barrister, a solicitor advocate or a solicitor who is exercising their automatic
rights of audience in the Crown Court;

"appropriate officer" means —

(a) in the case of proceedings in the civil division of the Court of Appeal, the head of the
civil appeals office;

(b) in the case of proceedings in the criminal division of the Court of Appeal, the registrar;

(c) in the case of proceedings in the Crown Court, the Commission;

(d) in respect of advice or assistance as to an appeal from the Crown Court to the Court
of Appeal (except in the case of an appeal under section 9(11) of the *Criminal Justice
Act* 1987 (preparatory hearings)), where, on the advice of any representative
instructed, notice of appeal is given, or application for leave to appeal is made,
whether or not such appeal is later abandoned, the registrar;

(e) in respect of advice or assistance as to an appeal to the Courts-Martial Appeal Court,
the registrar;

(f) in respect of advice or assistance as to an appeal from the Court of Appeal to the
Supreme Court, where the appeal is not lodged with the Supreme Court, the registrar; and

(g) in any other case, the Commission,

and, in any case, includes an officer designated by the appropriate officer to act on his behalf
for the purposes of this Order;

"assisted person" means a person in receipt of funded services;

"CDS Regulations" means the *Criminal Defence Service (General) (No.2) Regulations* 2001;

"class 1 offence", "class 2 offence" and "class 3 offence" have the meanings given in paragraph
III.21.1 of the *Practice Direction (Criminal Proceedings: Consolidation)*;

"the Commission" means the Legal Services Commission established under section 1 of the Act;

"committal proceedings" means proceedings in a magistrates' court up to and including a hearing at which an assisted person is committed to the Crown Court for trial under section 6(1)
or (2) of the *Magistrates' Courts Act* 1980;

"fee earner" means a litigator, or person employed by a litigator, who undertakes work on a
case;

"funded services" means services which are provided directly for an individual and funded for that individual as part of the Criminal Defence Service under sections 12 to 18 of the Act;

"instructed advocate" means

    (a) where a representation order provides for a single advocate, the first barrister or solicitor advocate instructed in the case, who has primary responsibility for the case; or

    (b) where a representation order provides for more than one advocate, each of—

        (i) the leading instructed advocate; and

        (ii) the led instructed advocate;

"leading instructed advocate" means the first leading barrister or solicitor advocate instructed in the case, who has primary responsibility for those aspects of a case undertaken by a leading advocate;

"led instructed advocate" means the first led barrister or solicitor advocate instructed in the case, who has primary responsibility for those aspects of the case undertaken by a led advocate;

"litigator" means the person named on the representation order as representing an assisted person, being a solicitor, firm of solicitors or other appropriately qualified person;

"registrar" means the registrar of criminal appeals;

"related proceedings" means —

    (a) two or more sets of proceedings involving the same defendant which are prepared, heard or dealt with together; or

    (b) proceedings involving more than one defendant which arise out of the same incident, so that the defendants are charged, tried or disposed of together;

"representation order" means a document granting a right to representation;

"representative" means a litigator or an advocate, including, where appropriate, an instructed advocate;

"senior solicitor" means a solicitor who, in the judgement of the appropriate officer, has the skill, knowledge and experience to deal with the most difficult and complex cases;

"solicitor advocate" means a solicitor who has obtained a higher courts advocacy qualification in accordance with regulations and rules of conduct of the Law Society;

"solicitor, legal executive or fee earner of equivalent experience" means a solicitor, Fellow of the Institute of Legal Executives or equivalent senior fee earner who, in the judgement of the appropriate officer, has good knowledge and experience of the conduct of criminal cases;

"trainee solicitor or fee earner of equivalent experience" means a trainee solicitor or other fee earner who is not a Fellow of the Institute of Legal Executives, who, in the judgement of the appropriate officer, carries out the routine work on a case; and

"Very High Cost Case" means a case in which a representation order has been granted and which the Commission classifies as a Very High Cost Case on the grounds that—

    (a) in relation to fees claimed by litigators—

        (i) if the case were to proceed to trial, the trial would in the opinion of the Commission be likely to last for more than 40 days, and the Commission considers that there are no exceptional circumstances which make it unsuitable to be dealt with under its contractual arrangements for Very High Cost Cases; or

        (ii) if the case were to proceed to trial, the trial would in the opinion of the Commission be likely to last no fewer than 25 and no more than 40 days and the Commission considers that there are circumstances which make it suitable to be dealt with under its contractual arrangements for Very High Cases;

    (b) in relation to fees claimed by advocates, if the case were to proceed to trial, the trial would in the opinion of the Commission be likely to last for more than 60 days, and the Commission considers that there are no exceptional circumstances which make it unsuitable to be dealt with under its contractual arrangements for Very High Cost Cases,

[This article is printed as amended by S.I. 2007 No. 3552 (*ante*, G–1); the *Constitutional Reform Act 2005 (Consequential Amendments) Order* 2009 (S.I. 2009 No. 2468)); S.I. 2010 No. 679 (*ante*, G–1); S.I. 2010 No. 1181 (*ante*, G–1) (substituting a new definition of "Very High Cost Case" from July 14, 2010); and S.I. 2011 No. 2065 (*ante*, G–1).

Scope

★G–8   **3.**—(1A) Article 4A applies to proceedings in magistrates' courts only.

(2) Articles 6(2), 12, 12A, 14(1) and 15A of this Order apply to proceedings in magistrates' courts and to proceedings in the Crown Court.

(3) Articles 5, 6(1) and (3) to (8), 14(2) to (8), 15 to 24, and 29 to 31 of, and Schedules 1 and 2 to, this Order apply to proceedings in the Crown Court only.

(4) Articles 4, 11, 13, 25 to 28 and 32 of this Order apply to proceedings in the Crown Court and to proceedings in the Court of Appeal.

(5) Article 8 of, and Schedule 4 to, this Order apply to proceedings in the Court of Appeal only.

(6) Article 9 of this Order applies to proceedings in the Supreme Court only.

(6A) This order does not apply to Very High Costs Case.

(7) For the purpose of this Order any reference to the Court of Appeal includes a reference to—

    (a) the criminal division of the Court of Appeal;

    (b) the civil division of the Court of Appeal;

    (c) the Courts-Martial Appeal Court; and

    (d) a Divisional Court of the High Court.

[This article is printed as amended by S.I. 2007 No. 3552 (*ante*, G–1); S.I. 2008 No. 957 (*ante*, G–1); S.I. 2009 No. 2468 (*ante*, G–7); S.I. 2010 No. 679 (*ante*, G–1); S.I. 2011 No. 2065 (*ante*, G–1); and S.I. 2012 No. 750 (*ante*, G–1).]

Funding of services

4.—(1) Where a representation order is granted on or after 30th April 2007 for proceedings in   **G–9** the Crown Court or Court of Appeal—

    (a) the Commission must fund representation in accordance with its duty under section 14(1) of the Act; and

    (b) the provisions of this Order apply.

(2) Where a representation order is granted on or after 1st April 2003, but before 30th April 2007 for proceedings in the Crown Court or the Court of Appeal—

    (a) the Commission must fund representation in accordance with its duty under section 14(1) of the Act; and

    (b) the provisions of the *Criminal Defence Service (Funding) Order* 2001 apply.

(3) Where a representation order is granted before 1st April 2003 for—

    (a) criminal proceedings in the Supreme Court;

    (b) proceedings in the Court of Appeal; or

    (c) proceedings in the Crown Court,

the duty of the Commission under section 14(1) of the Act has effect as a duty of the Lord Chancellor and the provisions of the *Criminal Defence Service (Funding) Order* 2001 apply.

(4) Where a representation order is granted before 1st April 2003 for—

    (a) any proceedings in the Crown Court which are prescribed under section 12(2)(g) of the Act;

    (b) any Very High Cost Case which is the subject of an individual contract for the provision of funded services; or

    (c) any proceedings in which representation is provided by a person employed by the Commission for that purpose,

the Commission must fund representation in accordance with its duty under section 14(1) of the Act and the provisions of the *Criminal Defence Service (Funding) Order* 2001 apply.

[This article is printed as amended by S.I. 2009 No. 2468 (*ante*, G–7).]

Funding of services in the magistrates' court

4A. Where a representation order is granted for proceedings in the magistrates' court—   **G–9a**

    (a) any contract for the provision of representation must provide for the payment by the Commission at the fees and hourly rates set out in Schedule 5; and

    (b) claims for the payment of expert services must be determined in accordance with article 15A.

[This article was inserted by S.I. 2011 No. 2065 (*ante*, G–1).]

Claims for fees by advocates—Crown Court

5.—(1) Claims for fees by an instructed advocate in proceedings in the Crown Court must be   **G–10** made and determined in accordance with the provisions of Schedule 1 to this Order.

(2) A claim for fees under this article and Schedule 1 must be made by each instructed advocate.

(3) Subject to article 32, a claim by an instructed advocate for fees in respect of work done under

a representation order must not be entertained unless he submits it within three months of the conclusion of the proceedings to which it relates.

(4) An instructed advocate must submit a claim for fees to the appropriate officer in such form and manner as he may direct.

(5) An instructed advocate must supply such further information and documents as the appropriate officer may require.

(6) Where a confiscation hearing under Part 2 of the *Proceeds of Crime Act* 2002 (Confiscation: England and Wales), section 2 of the *Drug Trafficking Act* 1994 (confiscation orders) or section 71 of the *Criminal Justice Act* 1988 (confiscation orders) is to be held more than 28 days after—

(a) the conclusion of the trial to which the representation order relates; or

(b) the entering of a guilty plea,

an instructed advocate may submit any claim for fees in respect of the trial or guilty plea as soon as the trial has concluded or the guilty plea has been entered.

(7) Where a representation order provides for representation by—

(a) a single advocate other than a QC, and a QC agrees to appear as the single advocate; or

(b) two or more advocates other than QC, and a QC agrees to appear as a leading junior,

that QC must be treated for all the purposes of this Order as having been instructed under that representation order, and his remuneration must be determined as if he were not a QC.

[This article is printed as amended by S.I. 2007 No. 3552 (*ante*, G–1).]

Claims for fees and disbursements by litigators—Crown Court

★**G–11**   **6.**—(1) Claims for fees by litigators in proceedings in the Crown Court must be made and determined in accordance with the provisions of Schedule 2 to this Order.

(2) Claims for disbursements by litigators in proceedings in the Crown Court or in proceedings in a magistrates' court which are subsequently committed or sent for trial to the Crown Court must be made and determined in accordance with the provisions of articles 14 to 16.

(3) Subject to article 32, a claim by a litigator for fees in respect of work done under a representation order must not be entertained unless he submits it within three months of the conclusion of the proceedings to which it relates.

(4) Subject to paragraph (5), a claim for fees in proceedings in the Crown Court must be submitted to the appropriate officer in such form and manner as he may direct and must be accompanied by the representation order and any receipts or other documents in support of any disbursement claimed.

(5) A claim under paragraph 15 or 21 of Schedule 2 to this order must—

(a) summarise the items of work done by a fee earner in respect of which fees are claimed according to the classes specified in paragraph 2(1) of Schedule 2;

(b) state, where appropriate, the dates on which the items of work were done, the time taken, the sums claimed and whether the work was done for more than one assisted person;

(c) specify, where appropriate, the level of fee earner who undertook each of the items of work claimed; and

(d) give particulars of any work done in relation to more than one indictment or a retrial.

(6) Where the litigator claims that paragraph 24 of Schedule 2 applies in relation to an item of work, he must give full particulars in support of his claim.

(7) The litigator must specify any special circumstances which the litigator considers should be drawn to the attention of the appropriate officer.

(8) The litigator must supply such further information and documents as the appropriate officer may require.

[This article is printed as amended by S.I. 2007 No. 3552 (*ante*, G–1); S.I. 2009 No. 1843 (*ante*, G–1); S.I. 2012 No. 750 (*ante*, G–1); and S.I. 2012 No. 1343 (*ante*, G–1).]

Very High Cost Cases

G–12   **7.** [*Revoked by S.I. 2007 No. 3552, ante, G–1.*]

Proceedings in the Court of Appeal

G–13   **8.** Claims for fees by representatives in proceedings in the Court of Appeal must be made and determined in accordance with the provisions of Schedule 4 to this Order.

Proceedings in the Supreme Court

G–14   **9.**—(1) In proceedings in the Supreme Court, the fees payable to a representative under sections 13 or 14 of the Act must be determined by such officer as may be prescribed by order of the Supreme Court.

(2) Subject to paragraph (1), this Order does not apply to proceedings in the Supreme Court.

[This article is printed as amended by S.I. 2009 No. 2468 (*ante*, G–7).]

The Unified Contract (Crime)
10. [*Revoked by S.I. 2010 No. 679, ante, G–1.*]   **G–15**

Payments from other sources
11. Where a representation order has been made in respect of any proceedings, the represen-   **G–16**
tative, whether acting under a representation order or otherwise, must not receive or be a party to the making of any payment for work done in connection with those proceedings, except such payments as may be made—

    (a) by the Lord Chancellor or the Commission; or

    (b) in respect of any expenses or fees incurred in—

        (i) preparing, obtaining or considering any report, opinion or further evidence, whether provided by an expert witness or otherwise; or

        (ii) obtaining any transcripts or recordings,

    where an application under CDS Regulations for an authority to incur such fees or expenses has been refused by a committee appointed under arrangements made by the Commission to deal with, amongst other things, appeals of, or review of, assessment of costs.

Cases sent for trial to the Crown Court
12.—(1) Where a case is sent for trial to the Crown Court ..., the payment in relation to work   **★G–17**
carried out in the magistrates' court is included within the applicable fee payable under Schedule 1 or Schedule 2.

(2) Paragraph (1) does not apply where the case is remitted to a magistrates' court.

[This article is printed as amended by S.I. 2007 No. 3552 (*ante*, G–1); and S.I. 2012 No. 1343 (*ante*, G–1).]

Either way offences
12A.—(1) The Commission may remunerate a litigator for work done in relation to committal   **G–17a**
proceedings only in accordance with this article.

(2) Where a litigator represents an assisted person in the Crown Court who was committed for trial, the fee payable to that litigator for work done in relation to the committal proceedings, including attending any hearing in the magistrates' court, is included within the fixed fee payable for such proceedings under Part 3 of Schedule 2.

(3) The Commission may remunerate a litigator for work done in relation to committal proceedings only where—

    (a) that litigator acted for the assisted person in relation to those proceedings; and

    (b) a representation order provides for that litigator to represent the assisted person in the Crown Court.

(4) Where—

    (a) a litigator represents more than one assisted person in relation to related proceedings; and

    (b) any or all of those assisted persons are committed for trial at the same hearing,

the Commission may pay only a single fixed fee in remuneration for representing all those assisted persons in the committal proceedings.

[This article was inserted by S.I. 2010 No. 679 (*ante*, G–1).]

As to this article, see *R. (Law Society of England and Wales) v. Lord Chancellor, ante,* G–1,   **★**
and the commentary at CLW/12/18/35.

13. Where representation is provided in proceedings referred to in section 12(2)(f) of the Act   **G–18**
(proceedings for contempt in the face of a court), the Commission may only fund services as part of the Criminal Defence Service under section 13(2)(b) or 14(2)(b) of the Act in accordance with Schedules 1, 2 and 4.

[This article is printed as substituted by S.I. 2007 No. 3552.]

Interim payment of disbursements

★**G–19**
14.—(1) A litigator may submit a claim to the appropriate officer for payment of a disbursement for which he has incurred liability in proceedings in the Crown Court or in proceedings in a magistrates' court which are subsequently committed or sent for trial to the Crown Court in accordance with the provisions of this article.

(2) A claim for payment under paragraph (1) may be made where—

(a) a litigator has obtained prior authority to incur expenditure of £100 or more under CDS Regulations; and

(b) he has incurred such a liability.

(3) Without prejudice to articles 16(4) and 16(5) a claim for payment under paragraph (1) must not exceed the maximum amount authorised under the prior authority.

(4) A claim for payment under paragraph (1) may be made at any time before the litigator submits a claim for fees under article 6.

(5) A claim for payment under paragraph (1) must be submitted to the appropriate officer in such form and manner as he may direct and must be accompanied by the authority to incur expenditure and any invoices or other documents in support of the claim.

(6) Subject to article 15A, the appropriate officer must allow the disbursement subject to the limit in paragraph (3) if it appears to have been reasonably incurred in accordance with the prior authority.

(6A) The appropriate officer must notify the litigator and, where the disbursement claimed includes the fees or charges of any person, may notify that person, of his decision.

(7) Where the appropriate officer allows the disbursement, he must notify the litigator and, where the disbursement includes the fees or charges of any person, may notify that person, of the amount payable, and must authorise payment to the litigator accordingly.

(8) Articles 29 to 31 do not apply to a payment under this article.

[This article is printed as amended by S.I. 2007 No. 3552; S.I. 2009 No. 1843 (*ante*, G–1); S.I. 2011 No. 2065 (*ante*, G–1); S.I. 2012 No. 750 (*ante*, G–1); and S.I. 2012 No. 1343 (*ante*, G–1).]

Interim disbursements and final determination of fees

G–20
15.—(1) On a final determination of fees, articles 6(2) and 16 apply notwithstanding that a payment has been made under article 14.

(2) Where the amount found to be due under article 16 in respect of a disbursement is less than the amount paid under article 14 ("the interim payment"), the appropriate officer must deduct the difference from the sum otherwise payable to the litigator on the determination of fees, and where the amount due under article 16 exceeds the interim payment, the appropriate officer must add the difference to the amount otherwise payable to the litigator.

Expert services

G–20a
15A.—(1) Subject to paragraph (2), the Commission may provide for the payment of expert services only at the fixed fees or at rates not exceeding the rates set out in Schedule 6.

(2) The appropriate officer may, in relation to a specific claim, increase the fixed fees or rates set out in Schedule 6 if that officer considers it reasonable to do so in exceptional circumstances as defined in paragraph (3).

(3) For the purposes of paragraph (2), exceptional circumstances are where the expert's evidence is key to the client's case and either—

(i) the complexity of the material is such that an expert with a high level of seniority is required; or

(ii) the material is of such a specialised and unusual nature that only very few experts are available to provide the necessary evidence.

[This article was inserted by S.I. 2011 No. 2065 (*ante*, G–1).]

Determination of litigators' disbursements

G–21
16.—(1) Subject to paragraphs (2) to (5), the appropriate officer must allow such disbursements claimed under article 6(2) as appear to him to have been reasonably incurred.

(2) If the disbursements claimed are abnormally large by reason of the distance of the court or the assisted person's residence or both from the litigator's place of business, the appropriate officer may limit reimbursement of the disbursements to what otherwise would, having regard to all the circumstances, be a reasonable amount.

(3) No question as to the propriety of any step or act in relation to which prior authority has been obtained under CDS Regulations may be raised on any determination of disbursements, unless the litigator knew or ought reasonably to have known that the purpose for which the authority was given had failed or had become irrelevant or unnecessary before the disbursements were incurred.

(4) Where disbursements are reasonably incurred in accordance with and subject to the limit imposed by a prior authority given under CDS Regulations, no question may be raised on any determination of fees as to the amount of the payment to be allowed for the step or act in relation to which the authority was given.

(5) Where disbursements are incurred in taking any steps or doing any act for which authority may be given under CDS Regulations, without such authority having been given or in excess of any fee so authorised, payment in respect of those disbursements may nevertheless be allowed on a determination of disbursements payable under article 6.

(6) Paragraph (7) applies where the Commission receives a request for funding of an expert service of a type not listed in Schedule 6.

(7) In considering the rate at which to fund the expert service the Commission—

(a) must have regard to the rates set out in Schedule 6; and

(b) may require more than one quotation for provision of the service to be submitted to the Commission.

[This article is printed as amended by S.I. 2011 No. 2065 (*ante*, G–1).]

Interim payments in cases awaiting determination of fees

17.—(1) The appropriate officer must make an interim payment in respect of a claim for fees **G–22** in proceedings in the Crown Court in accordance with this article.

(2) Entitlement to a payment arises in respect of a claim for fees by an instructed advocate, where—

(a) the graduated fee claimed in accordance with Schedule 1 is £4,000 or more (exclusive of VAT); and

(c) the claim for fees is for less than the amounts mentioned in (a) but is related to any claim for fees falling under (a).

(3) For the purposes of this article, the following claims for fees are related to each other—

(a) the claims of instructed advocates acting in the same proceedings for a defendant; and

(b) the claims of any instructed advocate acting for any assisted person in related proceedings.

(4) Entitlement to a payment under paragraph (1) does not arise until three months have elapsed from the earlier of—

(a) the date on which the claim for fees is received by the appropriate officer for determination, except that where there are related claims for fees, the date on which the last claim is received by the appropriate officer; or

(b) three months after the conclusion of the last of any related proceedings.

(5) ... an instructed advocate may submit a claim for an interim payment under this article where—

(a) no payment has been made under paragraph (1); and

(b) six months have elapsed from the conclusion of the proceedings against the assisted person.

(6) Subject to article 32, payment must not be made under this article unless the instructed advocate has submitted a claim for fees in accordance with article 5(3).

[This article is printed as amended by S.I. 2007 No. 3552 (*ante*, G–1).]

Amount of interim payments in cases awaiting determination of fees

18.—(1) Where entitlement to an interim payment arises under article 17, the amount payable **G–23** is 40 per cent of the total claim for fees, less any sum already paid.

(2) Articles 29 to 31 do not apply to an interim payment under this article.

Staged payments in long Crown Court proceedings

19.—(1) ... an instructed advocate may submit a claim to the appropriate officer for a staged **G–24** payment of his fees in relation to proceedings in the Crown Court.

(2) Where a claim is submitted in accordance with this article, a staged payment must be allowed where the appropriate officer is satisfied—

(a) that the claim relates to fees for a period of preparation of 100 hours or more, for which the ... instructed advocate will, subject to final determination of the fees payable, be entitled to be paid in accordance with Schedule 1; and

    (b) that the period from committal, transfer or sending for trial (or from the date of the representation order, if later) to the conclusion of the Crown Court proceedings is likely to exceed 12 months, having regard, amongst other matters, to the number of defendants, the anticipated pleas and the weight and complexity of the case.

  (3) In this article "preparation" means—

    (a) reading the papers in the case;

    (b) contact with prosecutors;

    (c) written or oral advice on plea;

    (d) researching the law, preparation for examination of witnesses and preparation of oral submissions;

    (e) viewing exhibits or undisclosed material at police stations;

    (f) written advice on evidence;

    (g) preparation of written submissions, notices or other documents for use at the trial; and

    (h) attendance at views at the scene of the alleged offence;

and is limited to preparation done before the trial, except in proceedings in which a preparatory hearing has been ordered under section 8 of the *Criminal Justice Act* 1987 (commencement of trial and arraignment), in which case it is limited to preparation done before the date on which the jury is sworn (or on which it became certain, by reason of pleas of guilty or otherwise, that the matter would not proceed to trial).

  (4) The amount allowed for preparation falling within paragraph (3) must be computed by reference to the number of hours of preparation which it appears to the appropriate officer, without prejudice to the final determination of the fees payable, has been reasonably done, multiplied by the hourly rate for special preparation as set out in the table following paragraph 19 of Schedule 1, as appropriate to the category of advocate.

  (6) A claim for staged payment of fees under this article must be made to the appropriate officer in such form and manner as he may direct, including such case plan as he may require for the purposes of paragraph (2)(a).

  (7) An instructed advocate may claim further staged payments in accordance with this article in respect of further periods of preparation exceeding 100 hours which were not included in an earlier claim.

  (8) Articles 29 to 31 do not apply to a payment under this article.

[This article is printed as amended by S.I. 2007 No. 3552 (*ante*, G–1).]

G–25   **20.** [*Revoked by S.I. 2007 No. 3552, ante, G–1.*]

Hardship payments

G–26   **21.**—(1) Subject to paragraphs (4) and (5), the appropriate officer may allow a hardship payment to a representative in the circumstances set out in paragraph (2).

  (2) Those circumstances are that the representative—

    (a) represents the assisted person in proceedings in the Crown Court;

    (b) applies for such payment, in such form and manner as the appropriate officer may direct, not less than six months after he was first instructed in those proceedings, or in related proceedings if he was instructed in those proceedings earlier than in the proceedings to which the application relates;

    (c) is unlikely to receive final payment in respect of the proceedings, as determined under Schedules 1 or 2, within the three months following the application for the hardship payment; and

    (d) satisfies the appropriate officer that, by reason of the circumstance in sub-paragraph (c), he is likely to suffer financial hardship.

  (3) Every application for a hardship payment by an advocate must be accompanied by such information and documents as the appropriate officer may require as evidence of—

    (a) the work done by the advocate in relation to the proceedings up to the date of the application; and

    (b) the likelihood of financial hardship.

  (3A) Every application for a hardship payment by a litigator must be accompanied by such information and documents as the appropriate officer may require as evidence of—

    (a) the Class of Offence with which the assisted person is charged, in accordance with Part 6 of Schedule 1;

    (b) the length of trial, where appropriate;

(c) the number of pages of prosecution evidence, calculated in accordance with paragraph 1(2) of Schedule 2;

(d) the total number of defendants in the proceedings who are represented by the litigator;

(e) the likelihood of financial hardship.

(4) The amount of any hardship payment is at the discretion of the appropriate officer, but must not exceed such sum as would be reasonable remuneration for the work done by the representative in the proceedings up to the date of the application.

(5) A hardship payment must not be made if it appears to the appropriate officer that the sum which would be reasonable remuneration for the representative, or the sum required to relieve his financial hardship, is less than £5,000 (excluding VAT).

(6) Where the appropriate officer allows a hardship payment under paragraph (1), he must authorise payment accordingly.

(7) Where the application for a hardship payment is made by an advocate other than an instructed advocate, and the appropriate officer allows a hardship payment under paragraph (1)—

(a) payment must be made to the leading instructed advocate or the led instructed advocate, as appropriate; and

(b) the appropriate officer must notify the advocate who made the application that payment has been made to the instructed advocate.

[This article is printed as amended by S.I. 2007 No. 3552 (*ante*, G–1).]

Computation of final claim where an interim payment has been made

22.—(1) At the conclusion of a case in which one or more payments have been made to an **G–27** instructed advocate or a litigator under articles 17 to 21, he must submit a claim under article 5 or 6 for the determination of his overall remuneration, whether or not such a claim will result in any payment additional to those already made.

(2) In the determination of the amount payable to an instructed advocate or litigator under article 5 or 6—

(a) the appropriate officer must deduct the amount of any payment made under articles 17 to 21 in respect of the same case from the amount that would otherwise be payable; and

(b) if the amount of the interim payment is greater than the amount that would otherwise be payable, the appropriate officer may recover the amount of the difference, either by way of repayment by the instructed advocate or litigator or by way of deduction from any other amount that may be due to him.

Payment of fees to advocates—Crown Court

23.—(1) Having determined the fees payable to each instructed advocate, in accordance with **G–28** Schedule 1, the appropriate officer must notify each instructed advocate of the fees payable and authorise payment accordingly.

(2) Where, as a result of any redetermination or appeal made or brought pursuant to articles 29 to 31—

(a) the fees payable under paragraph (1) are increased, the appropriate officer must authorise payment of the increase; or

(b) the fees payable under paragraph (1) are decreased, the instructed advocate must repay the amount of such decrease.

(3) Where the payment of any fees of an instructed advocate is ordered under article 30(12) or article 31(8), the appropriate officer must authorise payment.

[This article is printed as amended by S.I. 2007 No. 3552 (*ante*, G–1).]

Payment of fees to litigators—Crown Court

24.—(1) Having determined the fees payable to a litigator in accordance with Schedule 2, the **G–29** appropriate officer must authorise payment accordingly.

(1A) Where the appropriate officer determines that the fees payable under paragraph (1) are greater than or less than the amount claimed by the litigator under article 6(1), he must notify the litigator of the amount he has determined to be payable.

(2) Where, as a result of any redetermination or appeal made or brought pursuant to articles 29 to 31—

(a) the fees payable under paragraph (1) are increased, the appropriate officer must authorise payment of the increase; or

(b) the fees payable under paragraph (1) are decreased, the litigator must repay the amount of such decrease.

(3) Where the payment of any fees of the litigator is ordered under article 30(12) or article 31(8), the appropriate officer must authorise payment.

[This article is printed as amended by S.I. 2007 No. 3552 (*ante*, G–1).]

Notification of fees

G–30   **25.** For the purposes of an order which is made under section 17 of the Act, except where the proceedings are in a magistrates' court only, having determined the fees payable to a representative in accordance with this Order, the appropriate officer must notify the court before which the proceedings are heard of the amount determined.

Recovery of overpayments

G–31   **26.**—(1) This article applies where a representative is entitled to be paid a certain sum ("the amount due") by virtue of the provisions of Schedules 1, 2 or 4 and, for whatever reason, he is paid an amount greater than that sum.

(2) Where this article applies, the appropriate officer may—

> (a) require immediate repayment of the amount in excess of the amount due ("the excess amount") and the representative must repay the excess amount to the appropriate officer; or
>
> (b) deduct the excess amount from any other sum which is or becomes payable to the representative by virtue of the provisions of Schedules 1, 2 or 4.

(3) The appropriate officer may proceed under paragraph (2)(b) without first proceeding under paragraph (2)(a).

(4) Paragraph (2) applies notwithstanding that the representative to whom the excess amount was paid is exercising, or may exercise, a right under articles 29 to 31.

Adverse observations

G–32   **27.**—(1) Where in any proceedings to which Schedule 1, 2 or 4 applies, the court makes adverse observations concerning a representative's conduct of the proceedings, the appropriate officer may reduce any fee which would otherwise be payable in accordance with Schedule 1, 2 or 4 by such proportion as he considers reasonable.

(2) Before reducing the fee payable to a representative in accordance with the provisions of paragraph (1), the appropriate officer must give the representative the opportunity to make representations about whether it is appropriate to reduce the fee and the extent to which the fee should be reduced.

[This article is printed as amended by S.I. 2007 No. 3552 (*ante*, G–1).]

Wasted costs orders

G–33   **28.**—(1) Subject to paragraph (2), where the court has disallowed the whole or any part of any wasted costs under section 19A of the *Prosecution of Offences Act* 1985 (costs against legal representatives etc.), the appropriate officer, in determining fees in respect of work done by the representative against whom the wasted costs order was made, may deduct the amount in the wasted costs order from the amount otherwise payable in accordance with this Order.

(2) Where the appropriate officer, in accordance with this article, is minded to disallow any amount of a claim for work done to which the wasted costs order relates, he must disallow that amount or the amount of the wasted costs order, whichever is the greater.

Redetermination of fees by appropriate officer

G–34   **29.**—(1) Where—

> (a) an advocate in proceedings in the Crown Court is dissatisfied with the decision not to allow any of the following fees, or with the number of hours allowed in the calculation of such a fee, namely—
>
> > (i) a special preparation fee under paragraph 14 of Schedule 1; or
> >
> > (ii) a wasted preparation fee under paragraph 15 of Schedule 1; or
>
> (b) an instructed advocate in proceedings in the Crown Court is dissatisfied with—
>
> > (i) the decision not to allow an hourly fee in respect of attendance at conferences or views at the scene of the alleged offence under paragraph 16 of Schedule 1, or with the number of hours allowed in the calculation of such a fee;
> >
> > (ii) the calculation by the appropriate officer of the fee payable to the instructed advocate in accordance with Schedule 1; or

   (iii) the decision of the appropriate officer under paragraph 3(3) of Schedule 1 (reclassification of an offence not specifically listed in the relevant Table of Offences and so deemed to fall within Class H); or

(c) a litigator is dissatisfied with—

   (i) the calculation by the appropriate officer of the fee payable to the litigator in accordance with Schedule 2 (except for paragraph 10(5)(a) of that Schedule); or

   (ii) the decision of the appropriate officer under paragraph 3(3) of Schedule 2 (reclassification of an offence not specifically listed in the relevant Table of Offences and so deemed to fall within Class H);

the advocate, instructed advocate or litigator, as the case may be, may apply to the appropriate officer to redetermine those fees, to review that decision or to reclassify the offence, as appropriate.

(2) An application under paragraph (1) may not challenge the quantum of any of the fees set out in Schedule 1 and Schedule 2.

(3) Subject to article 32, an application under paragraph (1), or paragraph 15(1) of Schedule 4, must be made—

(a) within 21 days of the receipt of the fees payable under article 23, article 24 or paragraph 15 of Schedule 4, as appropriate;

(b) by giving notice in writing to the appropriate officer, specifying the matters in respect of which the application is made and the grounds of objection; and

(c) in such form and manner as the appropriate officer may direct.

(4) The notice of application must be accompanied by the information and documents supplied under article 5, article 6 or Schedule 4, as appropriate.

(5) The notice of application must state whether the applicant wishes to appear or to be represented and, if the applicant so wishes, the appropriate officer must notify the applicant of the hearing date and time.

(6) The applicant must supply such further information and documents as the appropriate officer may require.

(7) The appropriate officer must, in the light of the objections made by the applicant or on his behalf—

(a) redetermine the fees, whether by way of confirmation, or increase or decrease in the amount previously determined;

(c) confirm the classification of the offence within Class H; or

(d) reclassify the offence,

as the case may be, and must notify the applicant of his decision.

(8) Where the applicant so requests, the appropriate officer must give reasons in writing for his decision.

(9) Subject to article 32, any request under paragraph (8) must be made within 21 days of receiving notification of the appropriate officer's decision under paragraph (7).

[This article is printed as amended by S.I. 2007 No. 3552; and S.I. 2009 No. 1843 (*ante*, G–1).]

Appeals to a Costs Judge

30.—(1) Where the appropriate officer has given his reasons for his decision under article **G–35** 29(8), a representative who is dissatisfied with that decision may appeal to a Costs Judge.

(2) Subject to article 32, an appeal under paragraph (1) or paragraph 15(2) of Schedule 4 must be instituted within 21 days of the receipt of the appropriate officer's reasons, by giving notice in writing to the Senior Costs Judge.

(3) The appellant must send a copy of any notice of appeal given under paragraph (2) to the appropriate officer.

(4) The notice of appeal must be accompanied by—

(a) a copy of any written representations given under article 29(3);

(b) the appropriate officer's reasons for his decision given under article 29(8); and

(c) the information and documents supplied to the appropriate officer under article 29.

(5) The notice of appeal must—

(a) be in such form as the Senior Costs Judge may direct—

(b) specify separately each item appealed against, showing (where appropriate) the amount claimed for the item, the amount determined and the grounds of the objection to the determination; and

(c) state whether the appellant wishes to appear or to be represented or whether he will accept a decision given in his absence.

(6) The Senior Costs Judge may, and if so directed by the Lord Chancellor either generally or in a particular case must, send to the Lord Chancellor a copy of the notice of appeal together with copies of such other documents as the Lord Chancellor may require.

(7) With a view to ensuring that the public interest is taken into account, the Lord Chancellor may arrange for written or oral representations to be made on his behalf and, if he intends to do so, he must inform the Senior Costs Judge and the appellant.

(8) Any written representations made on behalf of the Lord Chancellor under paragraph (7) must be sent to the Senior Costs Judge and the appellant and, in the case of oral representations, the Senior Costs Judge and the appellant must be informed of the grounds on which such representations will be made.

(9) The appellant must be permitted a reasonable opportunity to make representations in reply.

(10) The Costs Judge must inform the appellant (or the person representing him) and the Lord Chancellor, where representations have been or are to be made on his behalf, of the date of any hearing and, subject to the provisions of this article, may give directions as to the conduct of the appeal.

(11) The Costs Judge may consult the trial judge or the appropriate officer and may require the appellant to provide any further information which he requires for the purpose of the appeal and, unless the Costs Judge otherwise directs, no further evidence may be received on the hearing of the appeal and no ground of objection may be raised which was not raised under article 29.

(12) The Costs Judge has the same powers as the appropriate officer under this Order and, in the exercise of such powers, may alter the redetermination of the appropriate officer in respect of any sum allowed, whether by increase or decrease, as he thinks fit.

(13) The Costs Judge must communicate his decision and the reasons for it in writing to the appellant, the Lord Chancellor and the appropriate officer.

(14) Where he increases the sums redetermined under article 29, the Costs Judge may allow the appellant a sum in respect of part or all of any reasonable costs incurred by him in connection with the appeal (including any fee payable in respect of an appeal).

[This article is printed as amended by S.I. 2007 No. 3552 (*ante*, G–1).]

Appeals to the High Court

G–36   **31.**—(1) A representative who is dissatisfied with the decision of a Costs Judge on an appeal under article 30 may apply to a Costs Judge to certify a point of principle of general importance.

(2) Subject to article 32, an application under paragraph (1) or paragraph 15(3) of Schedule 4 must be made within 21 days of receiving notification of a Costs Judge's decision under article 30(13).

(3) Where a Costs Judge certifies a point of principle of general importance the appellant may appeal to the High Court against the decision of a Costs Judge on an appeal under article 30, and the Lord Chancellor must be a respondent to such an appeal.

(4) Subject to article 32, an appeal under paragraph (3) must be instituted within 21 days of receiving notification of a Costs Judge's certificate under paragraph (1).

(5) Where the Lord Chancellor is dissatisfied with the decision of a Costs Judge on an appeal under article 30, he may, if no appeal has been made by an appellant under paragraph (3), appeal to the High Court against that decision, and the appellant must be a respondent to the appeal.

(6) Subject to article 32, an appeal under paragraph (5) must be instituted within 21 days of receiving notification of the Costs Judge's decision under article 30(13).

(7) An appeal under paragraph (3) or (5) must—

(a) be brought in the Queen's Bench Division;

(b) subject to paragraph (4), follow the procedure set out in Part 52 of the *Civil Procedure Rules 1998*; and

(c) be heard and determined by a single judge whose decision will be final.

(8) The judge has the same powers as the appropriate officer and a Costs Judge under this Order and may reverse, affirm or amend the decision appealed against or make such other order as he thinks fit.

Time limits

G–37   **32.**—(1) Subject to paragraph (2), the time limit within which any act is required or authorised to be done under this Order may, for good reason, be extended—

(a) in the case of acts required or authorised to be done under article 30 or 31, by a Costs Judge or the High Court as the case may be; and

(b) in the case of acts required or authorised to be done by a representative under any other article, by the appropriate officer.

(2) Where a representative without good reason has failed (or, if an extension were not granted, would fail) to comply with a time limit, the appropriate officer, a Costs Judge or the High Court, as the case may be, may, in exceptional circumstances, extend the time limit and must consider whether it is reasonable in the circumstances to reduce the fees payable to the representative under articles 5, 6 or 8, provided that the fees must not be reduced unless the representative has been allowed a reasonable opportunity to show cause orally or in writing why the fees should not be reduced.

(3) A representative may appeal to a Costs Judge against a decision made under this article by an appropriate officer and such an appeal must be instituted within 21 days of the decision being given by giving notice in writing to the Senior Costs Judge specifying the grounds of appeal.

In connection with this article, see *post*, G–269.

Revocation

33. Subject to article 4, the *Criminal Defence Service (Funding) Order* 2001 is revoked.   **G–38**

Article 5(1)   SCHEDULE 1

ADVOCATES' GRADUATED FEE SCHEME

PART 1

DEFINITIONS AND SCOPE

Interpretation

1.—(1) In this Schedule—   **★G–39**

"case" means proceedings in the Crown Court against any one assisted person—

    (a) on one or more counts of a single indictment;

    (b) arising out of a single notice of appeal against conviction or sentence, or a single committal for sentence, whether on one or more charges; or

    (c) arising out of a single alleged breach of an order of the Crown Court,

and a case falling within paragraph (c) must be treated as a separate case from the proceedings in which the order was made;

"cracked trial" means a case on indictment in which—

    (a) a plea and case management hearing takes place and—

        (i) the case does not proceed to trial (whether by reason of pleas of guilty or for other reasons) or the prosecution offers no evidence; and

        (ii) either—

            (aa) in respect of one or more counts to which the assisted person pleaded guilty, he did not so plead at the plea and case management hearing; or

            (bb) in respect of one or more counts which did not proceed, the prosecution did not, before or at the plea and case management hearing, declare an intention of not proceeding with them; or

    (b) the case is listed for trial without a plea and case management hearing taking place;

"guilty plea" means a case on indictment which—

    (a) is disposed of without a trial because the assisted person pleaded guilty to one or more counts; and

    (b) is not a cracked trial;

"main hearing" means —

    (a) in relation to a case which goes to trial, the trial;

    (b) in relation to a guilty plea, the hearing at which pleas are taken or, where there is more than one such hearing, the last such hearing;

    (c) in relation to a cracked trial, the hearing at which—

        (i) the case becomes a cracked trial by meeting the conditions in the definition of a cracked trial, whether or not any pleas were taken at that hearing; or

        (ii) a formal verdict of not guilty was entered as a result of the prosecution offering no evidence, whether or not the parties attended the hearing;

    (d) in relation to an appeal against conviction or sentence in the Crown Court, the hearing of the appeal;

(e) in relation to proceedings arising out of a committal for sentence in the Crown Court, the sentencing hearing; and

(f) in relation to proceedings arising out of an alleged breach of an order of the Crown Court, the hearing at which those proceedings are determined;

"*Newton* Hearing" means a hearing at which evidence is heard for the purpose of determining the sentence of a convicted person in accordance with the principles of *R. v. Newton* (1982) 77 Cr.App.R. 13;

"standard appearance" means an appearance by the trial advocate or substitute advocate in any of the following hearings which do not form part of the main hearing—

(a) a plea and case management hearing, except the first plea and case management hearing;

(b) a pre-trial review;

(c) the hearing of a case listed for plea which is adjourned for trial;

(d) any hearing (except a trial, a plea and case management hearing, a pre-trial review or a hearing referred to in paragraph 2(1)(b)) which is listed but cannot proceed because of the failure of the assisted person or a witness to attend, the unavailability of a pre-sentence report or other good reason;

(e) custody time limit applications;

(f) bail and other applications (except where any such applications take place in the course of a hearing referred to in paragraph 2(1)(b));

(g) the hearing of the case listed for mention only, including applications relating to the date of the trial (except where an application takes place in the course of a hearing referred to in paragraph 2(1)(b)),

(h) a sentencing hearing other than one falling within paragraph 2(1)(b)(ii), paragraph 12(1) or paragraph 29,

(i) a preliminary hearing; or

(j) a hearing, whether contested or not, relating to breach of bail, failure to surrender to bail or execution of a bench warrant,

provided that a fee is not payable elsewhere under this Schedule in respect of the hearing;

"substitute advocate" means an advocate who is not an instructed advocate or the trial advocate but who undertakes work on the case; and

"trial advocate" means an advocate instructed in accordance with a representation order to represent the assisted person at the main hearing in any case, including a QC or a leading junior advocate so instructed after the hearing at which pleas are taken.

(2) For the purposes of this Schedule, the number of pages of prosecution evidence served on the court shall be determined in accordance with paragraphs (2A) to (2C).

(2A) The number of pages of prosecution evidence includes all—

(a) witness statements;

(b) documentary and pictorial exhibits;

(c) records of interviews with the assisted person; and

(d) records of interviews with other defendants,

which form part of the committal or served prosecution documents or which are included in any notice of additional evidence.

(2B) Subject to paragraph (2C), a document served by the prosecution in electronic form is included in the number of pages of prosecution evidence.

(2C) A documentary or pictorial exhibit which—

(a) has been served by the prosecution in electronic form; and

(b) has never existed in paper form,

is not included within the number of pages of prosecution evidence unless the appropriate officer decides that it would be appropriate to include it in the pages of prosecution evidence taking into account the nature of the document and any other relevant circumstances.

(3) In proceedings on indictment in the Crown Court initiated otherwise than by committal for trial, the appropriate officer must determine the number of pages of prosecution evidence in accordance with sub-paragraph (2) or as nearly in accordance with sub-paragraph (2) as possible as the nature of the case permits.

(4) A reference to the Table of Offences in this Schedule is to the Table of Offences in Part 6 and a reference to a Class of Offence in this Schedule is to the Class in which that offence is listed in the Table of Offences.

[This paragraph is printed as amended by S.I. 2007 No. 3552 (*ante*, G–1); S.I. 2011 No. 2065 (*ante*, G–1); and S.I. 2012 No. 750 (*ante*, G–1).]

Application

2.—(1) Subject to sub-paragraphs (3) to (8), this Schedule applies to—   ★G–40

(a) every case on indictment; and

(b) the following proceedings in the Crown Court—

(i) an appeal against conviction or sentence;

(ii) a sentencing hearing following a committal for sentence to the Crown Court; and

(iii) proceedings arising out of an alleged breach of an order of the Crown Court (whether or not this Schedule applies to the proceedings in which the order was made).

(3) Sub-paragraphs (4) and (4A) apply where, following a trial, an order is made for a new trial and the same trial advocate appears at both trials where—

(i) the defendant is an assisted person at both trials; or

(ii) the defendant is an assisted person at the new trial only; or

(iii) the new trial is a cracked trial or guilty plea.

(4) Subject to sub-paragraph (4A), in respect of a new trial, or if he so elects, in respect of the first trial, the trial advocate will receive a graduated fee calculated in accordance with Part 2 or Part 3, as appropriate, except that the fee will be reduced by—

(a) 30 percent, where the new trial started within one month of the conclusion of the first trial;

(b) 20 percent, where the new trial did not start within one month of the conclusion of the first trial;

(c) 40 percent where the new trial becomes a cracked trial or guilty plea within one month of the conclusion of the first trial; or

(d) 25 percent where the new trial becomes a cracked trial or guilty plea more than one month after the conclusion of the first trial.

(4A) Where—

(a) in relation to the first trial, the case was committed or sent for trial to the Crown Court on the election of a defendant where the magistrates' court had determined the case to be suitable for summary trial; and

(b) the new trial becomes a cracked trial or guilty plea,

the trial advocate will receive a graduated fee, calculated in accordance with Part 2, in respect of the first trial and the fixed fee set out in paragraph 7B in respect of the new trial.

(4B) Sub-paragraphs (5) and (5A) apply in the circumstances set out in sub-paragraph (3) but where a different trial advocate appears for the assisted person at each trial.

(5) Subject to sub-paragraph (5A), in respect of each trial the trial advocate will receive a graduated fee calculated in accordance with Part 2 or Part 3 as appropriate.

(5A) Where—

(a) in relation to the first trial, the case was committed or sent for trial to the Crown Court on the election of a defendant where the magistrates' court had determined the case to be suitable for summary trial; and

(b) the new trial becomes a cracked trial or guilty plea,

the trial advocate at the first trial will receive a graduated fee, calculated in accordance with Part 2 and the trial advocate at the new trial will receive the fixed fee set out in paragraph 7B.

(6) Where following a case on indictment a *Newton* hearing takes place—

(a) for the purposes of this Schedule the case will be treated as having gone to trial;

(b) the length of the trial will be taken to be the combined length of the main hearing and the *Newton* hearing;

(c) the provisions of this Schedule relating to cracked trials and guilty pleas will not apply; and

(d) no fee will be payable under paragraph 12 in respect of the *Newton* hearing.

(7) Sub-paragraph (8) applies where proceedings are—

(a) sent for trial to the Crown Court ...; or

(b) transferred to the Crown Court under—

(i) section 4 of the *Criminal Justice Act* 1987 (transfer of serious fraud cases); or

(ii) section 53 of the *Criminal Justice Act* 1991 (transfer of certain cases involving children).

(8) Where, at any time after proceedings are sent or transferred to the Crown Court as referred to in sub-paragraph (7), they are—

(a) discontinued by a notice served under section 23A of the *Prosecution of Offences Act* 1985 (discontinuance of proceedings after accused has been sent for trial); or

(b) dismissed pursuant to—

    (i) paragraph 2 of Schedule 3 to the *Crime and Disorder Act* 1998 (applications for dismissal);

    (ii) section 6 of the *Criminal Justice Act* 1987 (applications for dismissal); or

    (iii) paragraph 5 of Schedule 6 to the *Criminal Justice Act* 1991 (applications for dismissal),

the provisions of paragraph 18 apply.

(9) For the purposes of this Schedule, a case on indictment which discontinues at or before the plea and case management hearing otherwise than—

    (a) by reason of a plea of guilty being entered, or

    (b) in accordance with paragraph 2 (8),

must be treated as a guilty plea.

[This paragraph is printed as amended by S.I. 2007 No. 3552 (*ante*, G–1); S.I. 2011 No. 2065 (*ante*, G–1); S.I. 2012 No. 750 (*ante*, G–1); and S.I. 2012 No. 1343 (*ante*, G–1).]

Class of offences

G–41   3.—(1) For the purposes of this Schedule—

    (a) every indictable offence falls within the Class under which it is listed in the Table of Offences and, subject to sub-paragraph (2), indictable offences not specifically so listed will be deemed to fall within Class H;

    (b) conspiracy to commit an indictable offence contrary to section 1 of the *Criminal Law Act* 1977 (the offence of conspiracy), incitement to commit an indictable offence and attempts to commit an indictable offence contrary to section 1 of the *Criminal Attempts Act* 1981 (attempting to commit an offence), fall within the same Class as the substantive offence to which they relate;

    (c) where the Table of Offences specifies that the Class within which an offence falls depends on whether the value involved exceeds a stated limit, the value must be presumed not to exceed that limit unless the advocate making the claim under article 5 proves otherwise to the satisfaction of the appropriate officer;

    (d) where more than one count of the indictment is for an offence in relation to which the Class depends on the value involved, that value must be taken to be the total value involved in all those offences, but where two or more counts relate to the same property, the value of that property must be taken into account once only;

    (e) where an entry in the Table of Offences specifies an offence as being contrary to a statutory provision, then subject to any express limitation in the entry that entry will include every offence contrary to that statutory provision whether or not the words of description in the entry are appropriate to cover all such offences;

    (f) where in a case on indictment there is a hearing to determine the question of whether an assisted person is unfit to plead or unfit to stand trial, the trial advocate must elect whether that hearing falls within the same Class as the indictable offence to which it relates or within Class D; and

    (g) where in a case on indictment a restriction order is made under section 41 of the *Mental Health Act* 1983 (power of higher courts to restrict discharge from hospital), the offence falls within Class A, regardless of the Class under which the offence would be listed in the Table of Offences but for this paragraph.

(2) Where an advocate in proceedings in the Crown Court is dissatisfied with the classification within Class H of an indictable offence not listed in the Table of Offences, he may apply to the appropriate officer when lodging his claim for fees to reclassify the offence.

(3) The appropriate officer must, in light of the objections made by the advocate—

    (a) confirm the classification of the offence within Class H; or

    (b) reclassify the offence,

and must notify the advocate of his decision.

PART 2

GRADUATED FEES FOR TRIAL

Calculation of graduated fees

G–42   4.—(1) The amount of the graduated fee for a single trial advocate representing one assisted person being tried on one indictment in the Crown Court in a trial lasting one to 40 days must be calculated in accordance with the following formula—

$$G = B + (d \times D) + (e \times E) + (w \times W)$$

(2) In the formula in sub-paragraph (1)—

G is the amount of the graduated fee;

B is the basic fee specified in the Table following paragraph 5 as appropriate to the offence for which the assisted person is tried and the category of trial advocate;

d is the number of days or parts of a day on which the advocate attends at court by which the trial exceeds 2 days but does not exceed 40 days;

D is the fee payable in respect of daily attendance at court for the number of days by which the trial exceeds two days but does not exceed 40 days, as appropriate to the offence for which the assisted person is tried and the category of trial advocate;

e is the number of pages of prosecution evidence excluding the first 50, up to a maximum of 10,000;

E is the evidence uplift specified in the Table following paragraph 5 as appropriate to the offence for which the assisted person is tried and the category of trial advocate;

w is the number of prosecution witnesses excluding the first 10;

W is the witness uplift specified in the Table following paragraph 5 as appropriate to the offence for which the assisted person is tried and the category of trial advocate.

Table of fees

5. For the purposes of paragraph 4 the basic fee (B), the daily attendance fee (D), the evidence **G–43** uplift (E) and the witness uplift (W) appropriate to any offence will be those specified in the Table following this paragraph in accordance with the Class within which that offence falls.

TABLE OF FEES AND UPLIFTS

Class of Offence	Basic Fee (B)	Daily attendance fee (D)	Evidence uplift (E)	Witness uplift (W)
QC				
A.	2,856	979	1.63	6.53
B	2,529	857	1.63	6.53
C	1,968	816	1.63	6.53
D	2,284	816	1.63	6.53
E	1,514	612	1.63	6.53
F	1,514	612	1.63	6.53
G	1,514	612	1.63	6.53
H	1,903	816	1.63	6.53
I	2,122	816	1.63	6.53
J	2,856	979	1.63	6.53
K	2,856	979	1.63	6.53
Leading Junior				
A	2,142	734	1.23	4.9
B	1,897	643	1.23	4.9
C	1,476	612	1.23	4.9
D	1,714	612	1.23	4.9
E	1,136	459	1.23	4.9
F	1,136	459	1.23	4.9
G	1,136	459	1.23	4.9
H	1,427	612	1.23	4.9
I	1,592	612	1.23	4.9
J	2,142	734	1.23	4.9
K	2,142	734	1.23	4.9
Led Junior				
A	1,632	490	0.81	3.26
B	1,265	428	0.81	3.26
C	898	408	0.81	3.26
D	1,125	408	0.81	3.26

Class of Offence	Basic Fee (B)	Daily attendance fee (D)	Evidence uplift (E)	Witness uplift (W)
E	694	306	0.81	3.26
F	694	306	0.81	3.26
G	694	306	0.81	3.26
H	816	408	0.81	3.26
I	979	408	0.81	3.26
J	1,632	490	0.81	3.26
K	1,428	490	0.81	3.26
Junior alone				
A	1,632	530	0.98	4.9
B	1,305	469	0.98	4.9
C	898	408	0.98	4.9
D	1,125	408	0.98	4.9
E	653	326	0.98	4.9
F	694	326	0.98	4.9
G	694	326	0.98	4.9
H	816	408	0.98	4.9
I	979	408	0.98	4.9
J	1,632	530	0.98	4.9
K	1,632	530	0.98	4.9

[This table is printed as substituted by S.I. 2010 No. 1181 (*ante*, G–1) in relation to representation orders granted on or after April 1, 2011; and as amended by S.I. 2011 No. 2065 (*ante*, G–1) in relation to representation orders granted on or after April 1, 2012.]

PART 3

GRADUATED FEES FOR GUILTY PLEAS AND CRACKED TRIALS

Scope of Part 3

★G–44   5A. Subject to paragraph 18, this Part does not apply to a case committed or sent for trial to the Crown Court on the election of a defendant where the magistrates' court has determined the case to be suitable for summary trial.

[This paragraph was inserted by S.I. 2011 No. 2065 (*ante*, G–1); and is printed as amended by S.I. 2012 No. 1343 (*ante*, G–1).]

Calculation of graduated fees in guilty pleas and cracked trials—

G–44a   6. The amount of the graduated fee for a single trial advocate representing one assisted person in a guilty plea or cracked trial is—

    (a) the basic fee specified in the table following paragraph 7 as appropriate to the offence with which the assisted person is charged, the category of trial advocate and whether the case is a guilty plea or a cracked trial; and

    (b) the evidence uplift, as appropriate to the number of pages of prosecution evidence, calculated in accordance with the table following paragraph 7.

Tables of fees

G–45   7.—(1) Subject to sub-paragraphs (2) and (3), for the purposes of paragraph 6 the basic fee and evidence uplift appropriate to any offence are specified in the Tables following this paragraph in accordance with the class within which that offence falls.

    (2) Where—

    (a) the trial of a case does not commence on the date first fixed; or

    (b) the case is not taken and disposed of from the first warned list in which it is entered,
the basic fee and evidence uplift for the offence are specified for the last third in the Table referred to in sub-paragraph (1).

    (3) In this paragraph, and in the Tables following this paragraph, references to the first, second and last third are references to the first, second and last third—

(a) where a case is first listed for trial on a fixed date, of the period of time beginning after the date on which the case is so listed and ending before the date so fixed,

(b) where the case is first placed in a warned list, of the period of time beginning after the date on which the case is so placed and ending before the date of the start of that warned list, and

where the number of days in this period of time cannot be divided by three equally, any days remaining after such division must be added to the last third.

(4) Where a graduated fee is calculated in accordance with this Part for the purposes of paragraph 2(4), the fee must be calculated as if the trial had cracked in the final third.

TABLE A

FEES AND UPLIFTS IN GUILTY PLEAS AND TRIALS WHICH CRACK IN THE FIRST THIRD

Class of Offence	Basic fee	Evidence uplift per page of prose-cution evidence (pages 1 to 1,000)	Evidence uplift per page of prose-cution evidence (1,001 to 10,000)
QC			
A	1,714	2.85	1.43
B	1,305	1.8	0.9
C	1,224	1.28	0.64
D	1,305	2.85	1.43
E	1,081	0.92	0.46
F	1,081	1.2	0.61
G	1,081	1.2	0.61
H	1,224	1.65	0.82
I	1,224	1.61	0.8
J	1,714	2.85	1.43
K	1,714	1.59	0.8
Leading Junior			
A	1,285	2.15	1.07
B	979	1.35	0.67
C	918	0.96	0.48
D	979	2.15	1.07
E	811	0.69	0.35
F	811	0.9	0.46
G	811	0.9	0.46
H	918	1.24	0.61
I	918	1.21	0.6
J	1,285	2.15	1.07
K	1,285	1.19	0.6
Led Junior			
A	857	1.43	0.72
B	653	0.9	0.45
C	612	0.64	0.32
D	653	1.43	0.72
E	541	0.46	0.23
F	541	0.61	0.3
G	541	0.61	0.3
H	612	0.83	0.42
I	612	0.8	0.4
J	857	1.43	0.72
K	857	0.8	0.4
Junior Alone			
A	979	1.19	0.59

Class of Offence	Basic fee	Evidence uplift per page of prosecution evidence (pages 1 to 1,000)	Evidence uplift per page of prosecution evidence (1,001 to 10,000)
B	694	0.81	0.41
C	449	0.6	0.3
D	694	1.19	0.59
E	408	0.35	0.17
F	408	0.54	0.27
G	408	0.54	0.27
H	490	0.54	0.28
I	571	0.42	0.22
J	979	1.19	0.59
K	979	1.02	0.51

[This table is printed as substituted by S.I. 2010 No. 1181 (*ante*, G–1) in relation to representation orders granted on or after April 1, 2011; and as amended by S.I. 2011 No. 2065 (*ante*, G–1) in relation to representation orders granted on or after April 1, 2012.]

TABLE B

FEES AND UPLIFTS IN TRIALS WHICH CRACK IN THE SECOND OR FINAL THIRD

Class of Offence	Basic Fee	Evidence uplift per page of prosecution evidence (pages 1 to 250)	Evidence up lift per page of prosecution evidence (pages 251–1000)	Evidence uplift per page of prosecution evidence (pages 1,001 to 10,000)
QC				
A	2,324	5.07	1.27	1.68
B	1,743	3.2	0.8	1.06
C	1,520	2.27	0.57	0.75
D	1,743	5.07	1.27	1.68
E	1,232	1.63	0.41	0.54
F	1,232	2.14	0.54	0.71
G	1,232	2.14	0.54	0.71
H	1,540	2.93	0.73	0.96
I	1,598	2.87	0.71	0.94
J	2,324	5.07	1.27	1.68
K	2,324	2.83	0.71	0.94
Leading Junior				
A	1,744	3.8	0.95	1.26
B	1,307	2.4	0.6	0.8
C	1,140	1.7	0.43	0.56
D	1,307	3.8	0.95	1.26
E	924	1.22	0.31	0.41
F	924	1.6	0.41	0.53
G	924	1.6	0.41	0.53
H	1,155	2.2	0.54	0.72
I	1,198	2.14	0.53	0.71
J	1,744	3.8	0.95	1.26
K	1,744	2.13	0.53	0.71

Class of Offence	Basic Fee	Evidence uplift per page of prosecution evidence (pages 1 to 250)	Evidence up lift per page of prosecution evidence (pages 251–1000)	Evidence uplift per page of prosecution evidence (pages 1,001 to 10,000)
Led Junior				
A	1162	2.54	0.64	0.84
B	871	1.6	0.4	0.53
C	760	1.14	0.28	0.37
D	871	2.54	0.64	0.84
E	616	0.82	0.2	0.27
F	616	1.07	0.27	0.36
G	616	1.07	0.27	0.36
H	770	1.46	0.37	0.48
I	798	1.43	0.36	0.48
J	1162	2.54	0.64	0.84
K	1162	1.42	0.36	0.47
Junior alone				
A	1307	4.52	2.1	0.69
B	908	3.11	1.45	0.48
C	581	2.31	1.07	0.36
D	808	4.52	2.1	0.69
E	508	1.34	0.63	0.2
F	508	2.08	0.96	0.32
G	508	2.08	0.96	0.32
H	618	2.08	0.97	0.32
I	726	1.63	0.76	0.25
J	1307	4.52	2.1	0.69
K	1234	3.91	1.82	0.60

[This table is printed as substituted by S.I. 2011 No. 2065 (*ante*, G–1) in relation to representation orders granted on or after October 3, 2011; and as amended by that order in relation to representation orders granted on or after April 1, 2012.]

PART 3A

FIXED FEE FOR GUILTY PLEAS AND CRACKED TRIALS

Scope of Part 3A

7A. This Part applies to a case committed or sent for trial to the Crown Court on the election of a **★G–46** defendant where the magistrates' court has determined the case to be suitable for summary trial.

Fixed fee for guilty pleas or cracked trials

7B. The fee payable to an advocate in relation to a guilty plea or cracked trial to which this Part applies must be £203 per proceedings.

[Part 3A was inserted by S.I. 2011 No. 2065 (*ante*, G–1). In relation to representation orders granted on or after April 1, 2012, that order substitutes "£194" for "£203" in para. 7B. Paragraph 7A is printed as amended by S.I. 2012 No. 1343 (*ante*, G–1).]

PART 4

FIXED FEES

General provisions

8.—(1) All work undertaken by an advocate in a case to which Part 3A applies is included within **G–46a** the fee set out in paragraph 7B except for attendance at a confiscation hearing to which paragraph 11 applies.

(2) Except as provided under this Part, all work undertaken by an advocate in a case to which Part 3 applies is included within the basic fee (B) specified in the Table following paragraph 5, or that following paragraph 7, as appropriate to—

    (a) the offence for which the assisted person is tried;

    (b) the category of advocate; and

    (c) whether the case is a cracked trial, guilty plea or trial.

[This paragraph is printed as substituted by S.I. 2011 No. 2065 (*ante*, G–1).]

Fees for plea and case management hearings and standard appearances

G–47   9.—(1) The fee payable in respect of—

    (a) an appearance by the trial advocate or substitute advocate at the first plea and case management hearing or pre-trial review; and

    (b) up to four standard appearances by the trial advocate or substitute advocate,

is included within the basic fee (B) specified in paragraph 5 or 7 as appropriate to the offence for which the assisted person is tried and the category of trial advocate.

(2) The fee payable in respect of an appearance by the trial advocate or substitute advocate at a plea and case management hearing or standard appearance not included in sub-paragraph (1) is specified in the Table following paragraph 19 as appropriate to the category of trial advocate or substitute advocate.

(3) The fee payable for preparing and filing the plea and case management questionnaire where no oral hearing takes place is specified in the Table following paragraph 19 as appropriate to the category of trial advocate or substitute advocate.

(4) This paragraph does not apply to a standard appearance which is or forms part of the main hearing in a case or to a hearing for which a fee is payable elsewhere under this Schedule.

[This paragraph is printed as amended by S.I. 2009 No. 1843 (*ante*, G–1).]

Fees for abuse of process, disclosure, admissibility and withdrawal of plea hearings

G–48   10.—(1) This paragraph applies to—

    (a) the hearing of an application to stay the case on indictment or any count on the ground that the proceedings constitute an abuse of the process of the court;

    (b) any hearing relating to the question of whether any material should be disclosed by the prosecution to the defence or the defence to the prosecution (whether or not any claim to public interest immunity is made);

    (c) the hearing of an application under section 2(1) of the *Criminal Procedure (Attendance of Witnesses) Act* 1965 (issue of witness summons on application to Crown Court) for disclosure of material held by third parties;

    (d) any hearing relating to the question of the admissibility as evidence of any material; and

    (e) the hearing of an application to withdraw a plea of guilty where the application is—

        (i) made by an advocate other than the advocate who appeared at the hearing at which the plea of guilty was entered; and

        (ii) unsuccessful.

(2) Where a hearing to which this paragraph applies is held on any day of the main hearing of a case on indictment, no separate fee is payable in respect of attendance at the hearing, but the hearing is included in the length of the main hearing for the purpose of calculating the fees payable.

(3) Where a hearing to which this paragraph applies is held prior to the first or only day of the main hearing, it is not included in the length of the main hearing for the purpose of calculating the fees payable and the trial advocate or substitute advocate must be remunerated for attendance at such a hearing—

    (a) in respect of any day where the hearing begins before and ends after the luncheon adjournment, at the daily rate set out in the Table following paragraph 19 as appropriate to the category of trial advocate or substitute advocate; or

    (b) in respect of any day where the hearing begins and ends before the luncheon adjournment, or begins after the luncheon adjournment, at the half-daily rate set out in the Table following paragraph 19 as appropriate to the category of trial advocate or substitute advocate.

Fees for confiscation hearings

G–49   11.—(1) This paragraph applies to—

    (a) a hearing under Part 2 of the *Proceeds of Crime Act* 2002 (confiscation: England and Wales);

(b) a hearing under section 2 of the *Drug Trafficking Act* 1994 (confiscation orders); and

(c) a hearing under section 71 of the *Criminal Justice Act* 1988 (confiscation orders).

(2) A hearing to which this paragraph applies is not included in the length of the main hearing or of any sentencing hearing for the purpose of calculating the fees payable, and the trial advocate or substitute advocate must be remunerated in respect of such a hearing—

(a) where the number of pages of evidence is fewer than 51, for attendance—

(i) in respect of any day when the hearing begins before and ends after the luncheon adjournment, at the daily rate set out in the first section of the table following this sub-paragraph; or

(ii) in respect of any day when the hearing begins and ends before the luncheon adjournment, or begins after the luncheon adjournment, at the half-daily rate set out in the first section of that table,

as appropriate to the category of trial advocate or substitute advocate;

(b) where the number of pages of evidence is between 51 and 1000—

(i) at the rates for the relevant number of pages set out in the second section of the table following this sub-paragraph; and

(ii) where the hearing lasts for more than one day, for attendance on subsequent days or half-days at the daily rate or half-daily rate set out in the first section of that table,

as appropriate to the category of trial advocate or substitute advocate; or

(c) where the number of pages of evidence exceeds 1000—

(i) at the rates for 751 to 1000 pages set out in the second section of the table following this sub-paragraph;

(ii) with such fee as the appropriate officer considers reasonable for preparation in respect of the pages in excess of 1000, at the hourly rates for preparation set out in the third section of that table; and

(iii) where the hearing lasts for more than one day, for attendance on subsequent days or half-days at the daily rate or half-daily rate set out in the first section of that table,

as appropriate to the category of trial advocate or substitute advocate.

Fees for confiscation hearings				
	Fee for QC	Fee for leading junior	Fee for junior alone	Fee for led junior
1 – Daily and half-daily rates				
Half-daily rate	260	195	130	130
Daily rate	497	346	238	238
2 – Pages of evidence				
51–250	649	541	433	324
251–500	973	811	649	486
501–750	1,298	1,081	865	649
751–1000	1,946	1,622	1,298	973
3 – Preparation				
Hourly rates	74	56	39	39

(3) In sub-paragraph (2) "evidence" means—

(a) the statement of information served under section 16 of the *Proceeds of Crime Act* 2002 and relied on by the prosecution for the purposes of a hearing under Part 2 of that Act, or a similar statement served and so relied on for the purposes of a hearing under section 2 of the *Drug Trafficking Act* 1994 or under section 71 of the *Criminal Justice Act* 1988 and, in each case, any attached annexes and exhibits;

(b) any other document which—

(i) is served as a statement or an exhibit for the purposes of the trial;

(ii) is specifically referred to in, but not served with, a statement mentioned in paragraph (a); and

(iii) the prosecution state that they intend to rely on in the hearing; and

    (c) any written report of an expert obtained with the prior authority of the Commission under CDS Regulations or allowed by the appropriate officer under this Order, and any attached annexes and exhibits, other than documents contained in such annexes or exhibits which have also been served under paragraph (a) or (b) or which consist of financial records or similar data.

[This paragraph is printed as amended by S.I. 2009 No. 2086 (*ante*, G–1). The fees in the table are printed as substituted by S.I. 2011 No. 2065 (*ante*, G–1). The revised fees apply in relation to representation orders made on or after April 1, 2012.]

Fees for sentencing hearings

G–50   12.—(1) This paragraph applies to a sentencing hearing following a case on indictment to which this Schedule applies, where sentence has been deferred under section 1 of the *Powers of Criminal Courts (Sentencing) Act* 2000 (deferment of sentence).

    (2) The fee payable to an advocate for appearing at a hearing to which this paragraph applies is that set out in the Table following paragraph 19 as appropriate to the category of trial advocate or substitute advocate and the circumstances of the hearing.

[This paragraph is printed as amended by S.I. 2011 No. 2065 (*ante*, G–1).]

Fees for ineffective trials

G–51   13. The fee set out in the Table following paragraph 19 as appropriate to the category of trial advocate will be payable in respect of each day on which the case was listed for trial but did not proceed on the day for which it was listed, for whatever reason.

Fees for special preparation

★**G–52**   14.—(1) This paragraph applies where, in any case on indictment in the Crown Court in respect of which a graduated fee is payable under Part 2 or Part 3—

        (a) it has been necessary for an advocate to do work by way of preparation substantially in excess of the amount normally done for cases of the same type because the case involves a very unusual or novel point of law or factual issue;

        (b) the number of pages of prosecution evidence, as defined in paragraph 1(2), exceeds 10,000 and the appropriate officer considers it reasonable to make a payment in excess of the graduated fee payable under this Schedule; or

        (c) a documentary or pictorial exhibit is served by the prosecution in electronic form where—

            (i) the exhibit has never existed in paper form; and

            (ii) the appropriate officer—

                (aa) does not consider it appropriate to include the exhibit in the pages of prosecution evidence; and

                (bb) considers it reasonable to make a payment in respect of the exhibit in excess of the graduated fee.

    (2) Where this paragraph applies, a special preparation fee may be paid, in addition to the graduated fee payable under Part 2 or Part 3.

    (3) The amount of the special preparation fee must be calculated—

        (a) where sub-paragraph (1)(a) applies, from the number of hours preparation in excess of the amount the appropriate officer considers reasonable for cases of the same type;

        (b) where sub-paragraph (1)(b) applies, from the number of hours which the appropriate officer considers reasonable to read the excess pages; and

        (c) where sub-paragraph (1)(c) applies, from the number of hours which the appropriate officer considers reasonable to view the prosecution evidence,

and in each case using the rates of hourly fees set out in the table following paragraph 19 as appropriate to the category of trial advocate.

    (4) Any claim for a special preparation fee under this paragraph must be made by an instructed advocate, whether or not he did the work claimed for.

    (5) An instructed advocate claiming a special preparation fee must supply such information and documents as may be required by the appropriate officer in support of the claim.

    (6) In determining a claim under this paragraph, the appropriate officer must take into account all the relevant circumstances of the case, including, where special preparation work has been undertaken by more than one advocate, the benefit of such work to the trial advocate.

[This paragraph is printed as amended by S.I. 2011 No. 2065 (*ante*, G–1); and S.I. 2012 No. 750 (*ante*, G–1).]

Fees for wasted preparation

G–53   15.—(1) A wasted preparation fee may be claimed where a trial advocate in any case to which this paragraph applies is prevented from representing the assisted person in the main hearing by any of the following circumstances—

    (a) the trial advocate is instructed to appear in other proceedings at the same time as the main hearing in the case and has been unable to secure a change of date for either the main hearing or the other proceedings;

    (b) the date fixed for the main hearing is changed by the court despite the trial advocate's objection;

    (c) the trial advocate has withdrawn from the case with the leave of the court because of his professional code of conduct or to avoid embarrassment in the exercise of his profession;

    (d) the trial advocate has been dismissed by the assisted person or the litigator; or

    (e) the trial advocate is obliged to attend at any place by reason of a judicial office held by him or other public duty.

(2) This paragraph applies to every case on indictment to which this Schedule applies provided that—

    (a) the case goes to trial, and the trial lasts for five days or more; or

    (b) the case is a cracked trial, and the number of pages of prosecution evidence exceeds 150.

(3) The amount of the wasted preparation fee must be calculated from the number of hours of preparation reasonably carried out by the trial advocate, using the rates for hourly fees set out in the Table following paragraph 19 as appropriate to the category of trial advocate, but no such fee is payable unless the number of hours of preparation is eight or more.

(4) Any claim for a wasted preparation fee under this paragraph must be made by an instructed advocate, whether or not he did the work claimed for.

(5) An instructed advocate claiming a wasted preparation fee must supply such information and documents as may be required by the appropriate officer as proof of the circumstances in which he was prevented from representing the assisted person and of the number of hours of preparation.

Fees for conferences and views

16.—(1) This paragraph applies to the following types of work—

    (a) attendance by the trial advocate at pre-trial conferences with prospective or actual expert witnesses not held at court;

    (b) attendance by the trial advocate at views at the scene of the alleged offence;

    (c) attendance by the trial advocate at pre-trial conferences with the assisted person not held at court;

    (d) reasonable travelling time by the trial advocate for the purpose of attending a view at the scene of the alleged offence; or

    (e) reasonable travelling time by the trial advocate for the purpose of attending a pre-trial conference with the assisted person or prospective or actual expert witness, where the appropriate officer is satisfied that the assisted person or prospective or actual expert witness was unable or could not reasonably have been expected to attend a conference at the trial advocate's chambers or office.

(2) The fees payable in respect of attendance at the first three pre-trial conferences or views, as set out in sub-paragraph (1)(a) to (c), are included in the basic fee (B) specified in the Table following paragraph 5 or paragraph 7, as appropriate to the offence for which the assisted person is tried, the category of trial advocate and whether the case is a guilty plea, cracked trial or trial, provided that the trial advocate satisfies the appropriate officer that the work was reasonably necessary.

(3) The fee specified in the Table following paragraph 19 as appropriate to the category of trial advocate will be payable in the following circumstances, provided that the trial advocate satisfies the appropriate officer that the work was reasonably necessary—

    (a) for trials lasting not less than 21 and not more than 25 days, and cracked trials where it was accepted by the court at the plea and case management hearing that the trial would last not less than 21 days and not more than 25 days, one further pre-trial conference or view not exceeding two hours;

    (b) for trials lasting not less than 26 and not more than 35 days, and cracked trials where it was accepted by the court at the plea and case management hearing that the trial would last not less than 26 days and not more than 35 days, two further pre-trial conferences or views each not exceeding two hours; and

    (c) for trials lasting not less than 36 days, and cracked trials where it was accepted by the court at the plea and case management hearing that the trial would last not less than 36 days and not more than 40 days, three further pre-trial conferences or views each not exceeding two hours.

(4) Travel expenses must be paid for all conferences and views set out in sub-paragraph (1)(a) to

G–54

(c), provided that the trial advocate satisfies the appropriate officer that they were reasonably incurred.

(5) Travelling time must be paid for all conferences and views set out in sub-paragraph (1)(a) to (c), provided that the trial advocate satisfies the appropriate officer that it was reasonable.

Fees for appeals, committals for sentence and breach hearings

G–55
17.—(1) Subject to sub-paragraphs (4) and (5) and paragraph 21 the fee payable to a trial advocate in any of the hearings referred to in paragraph 2(1)(b) is the fixed fee specified in the Table following paragraph 19.

(2) Where a hearing referred to in paragraph 2(1)(b) is listed but cannot proceed because of the failure of the assisted person or a witness to attend, the unavailability of a pre-sentence report, or other good reason, the fee payable to the advocate is the fixed fee specified in the Table following paragraph 19.

(3) Where—

    (a) a bail application;

    (b) a mention hearing; or

    (c) any other application

takes place in the course of a hearing referred to in paragraph 2(1)(b), the fee payable to the advocate is the fixed fee specified in the Table following paragraph 19.

(4) Where it appears to the appropriate officer that the fixed fee allowed under sub-paragraph (1) would be inappropriate taking into account all of the relevant circumstances of the case he may instead allow fees in such amounts as appear to him to be reasonable remuneration for the relevant work in accordance with sub-paragraph (5).

(5) The appropriate officer may allow any of the following classes of fees to an advocate in respect of work allowed by him under this paragraph—

    (a) a fee for preparation including, where appropriate, the first day of the hearing including, where they took place on that day—

        (i) short conferences;

        (ii) consultations;

        (iii) applications and appearances (including bail applications);

        (iv) views at the scene of the alleged offence; and

        (v) any other preparation;

    (b) a refresher fee for any day or part of a day for which a hearing continued, including, where they took place on that day—

        (i) short conferences;

        (ii) consultations;

        (iii) applications and appearances (including bail applications);

        (iv) views at the scene of the alleged offence; and

        (v) any other preparation; and

    (c) subsidiary fees for—

        (i) attendance at conferences, consultations and views at the scene of the alleged offence not covered by paragraph (a) or (b);

        (ii) written advice on evidence, plea, appeal, case stated or other written work; and

        (iii) attendance at applications and appearances (including bail applications and adjournments for sentence) not covered by paragraph (a) or (b).

Fees for contempt proceedings

G–55a
17A.—(1) Subject to sub-paragraph (2), remuneration for advocates in proceedings referred to in section 12(2)(f) of the Act in the Crown Court must be at the rates specified in the table following this sub-paragraph.

Category of advocate	Payment rates (£ per day)
QC	300
Leading junior	225
Led junior or junior acting alone	150

(2) Where an advocate and a litigator are instructed in proceedings referred to in section 12(2)(f) of the Act, remuneration must be at the rates specified in the table following this sub-paragraph, as appropriate to the category of advocate.

Category of advocate	Payment rates (£ per day)
QC	175
Leading junior	125
Led junior or junior acting alone	100

[This paragraph was inserted by S.I. 2007 No. 3552 (*ante*, G–1).]

Discontinuance or dismissal of sent or transferred proceedings

18.—(1) This paragraph applies to proceedings which are—   ★**G–56**
   (a) sent for trial to the Crown Court ...; or
   (b) transferred to the Crown Court under—
       (i) section 4 of the *Criminal Justice Act* 1987 (transfer of serious fraud cases); or
       (ii) section 53 of the *Criminal Justice Act* 1991 (transfer of certain cases involving children).

(2) Where proceedings referred to in sub-paragraph (1) are discontinued by a notice served under section 23A of the *Prosecution of Offences Act* 1985 (discontinuance of proceedings after accused has been sent for trial) at any time before the prosecution serves its evidence in accordance with the *Crime and Disorder Act 1998 (Service of Prosecution Evidence) Regulations* 2005 the advocate must be paid 50 per cent of the basic fee (B) for a guilty plea, as specified in the Table following paragraph 7 as appropriate to the offence for which the assisted person is charged and the category of advocate.

(3) Where proceedings referred to in sub-paragraph (1) are discontinued by a notice served under section 23A of the *Prosecution of Offences Act* 1985 (discontinuance of proceedings after accused has been sent for trial) at any time after the prosecution serves its evidence in accordance with the *Crime and Disorder Act 1998 (Service of Prosecution Evidence) Regulations* 2005, the advocate must be paid a graduated fee calculated in accordance with paragraph 6, as appropriate for representing an assisted person in a guilty plea.

(4) Sub-paragraph (4A) applies to—
   (a) a plea and case management hearing that takes place after the prosecution serves its evidence; and
   (b) any other hearing that takes place before a plea and case management hearing has taken place but after the prosecution has served its evidence.

(4A) Where, at a hearing to which this sub-paragraph applies—
   (a) the prosecution offers no evidence and the assisted person is discharged; or
   (b) the case is remitted to the magistrates' court in accordance with paragraph 10(3)(a), 13(2) or 15(3)(a) of Schedule 3 to the *Crime and Disorder Act* 1998,
the advocate instructed in the proceedings must be paid a graduated fee calculated in accordance with paragraph 6, as appropriate for representing an assisted person in a guilty plea.

(5) Where an application for dismissal is made under paragraph 2 of Schedule 3 to the *Crime and Disorder Act* 1998 (applications for dismissal), section 6 of the *Criminal Justice Act* 1987 (applications for dismissal) or paragraph 5 of Schedule 6 to the *Criminal Justice Act* 1991 (applications for dismissal), the advocate must be remunerated for attendance at the hearing of the application for dismissal—
   (a) in respect of any day where the hearing begins before and ends after the luncheon adjournment, at the daily rate set out in the Table following paragraph 19 as appropriate to the category of advocate; or
   (b) in respect of any day where the hearing begins and ends before the luncheon adjournment, or begins after the luncheon adjournment, at the half-daily rate set out in that Table as appropriate to the category of advocate,
provided that a fee is not payable elsewhere under this Schedule in respect of any day of the hearing.

(6) Where an application for dismissal is made under paragraph 2 of Schedule 3 to the *Crime and Disorder Act* 1998, section 6 of the *Criminal Justice Act* 1987 or paragraph 5 of Schedule 6 to the *Criminal Justice Act* 1991, and—
   (a) the charge, or charges, are dismissed and the assisted person is discharged; or
   (b) the case is remitted to the magistrates' court in accordance with paragraph 10(3)(a), 13(2) or 15(3)(a) of Schedule 3 to the *Crime and Disorder Act* 1998,
in respect of the first day of the hearing of the application to dismiss, the advocate instructed in the proceedings must be paid a graduated fee calculated in accordance with paragraph 6, as appropriate for representing an assisted person in a guilty plea.

G–56 — *Archbold's Criminal Pleading—2012 ed.*

(7) Where an advocate represents more than one assisted person in proceedings referred to in sub-paragraph (1), the advocate must be paid a fixed fee of 20 per cent of—

    (a) the fee specified in sub-paragraph (2) where that sub-paragraph applies; or

    (b) the basic fee (B) specified in the Table following paragraph 7 where sub-paragraph (3), (4) or (5) applies, as appropriate for the circumstances set out in the relevant sub-paragraph,

in respect of each additional assisted person he represents.

[This paragraph is printed as amended by S.I. 2007 No. 3552 (*ante*, G–1); and S.I. 2012 No. 1343 (*ante*, G–1).]

Noting brief fees

G–57 19. The fee payable to an advocate retained solely for the purpose of making a note of any hearing must be the daily fee set out in the table following this paragraph.

FIXED FEES

Category of work	Paragraph providing for fee	Fee for QC £	Fee for leading junior £	Fee for led junior or junior alone £
Standard appearance	9(2)	173 per day	130 per day	87 per day
Paper plea and case management hearing	9(3)	26 per case	26 per case	26 per case
Abuse of process hearing	10(1)(a)	260 Half day	195 Half day	130 Half day
		497 Full day	346 Full day	238 Full day
Hearings relating to disclosure	10(1)(b) and (c)	260 Half day	195 Half day	130 Half day
		497 Full day	346 Full day	238 Full day
Hearings relating to the admissibility of evidence	10(1)(d)	260 Half day	195 Half day	130 Half day
		497 Full day	346 Full day	238 Full day
Hearings on withdrawal of guilty plea	10(1)(e)	260 Half day	195 Half day	130 Half day
		497 Full day	346 Full day	238 Full day
Deferred sentencing hearing	12(1)(a)	324 per day	238 per day	173 per day
Ineffective trial payment	13	281 per day	195 per day	130 per day
Special preparation	14	74 per hour	56 per hour	39 per hour
Wasted preparation	15	74 per hour	56 per hour	39 per hour
Conferences and views	16	74 per hour	56 per hour	39 per hour

Category of work	Paragraph providing for fee	Fee for QC £	Fee for leading junior £	Fee for led junior or junior alone £
Appeals to the Crown Court against conviction	17(1)	260 per day	195 per day	130 per day
Appeals to the Crown Court against sentence	17(1)	216 per day	151 per day	108 per day
Proceedings relating to breach of an order of the Crown Court	17(1)	216 per day	151 per day	108 per day
Committal for sentence	17(1)	260 per day	195 per day	130 per day
Adjourned appeals, committals for sentence and breach hearings	17(2)	173 per day	130 per day	87 per day
Bail applications, mentions and other applications in appeals, committals for sentence and breach hearings	17(3)	173 per day	130 per day	87 per day
Second and subsequent days of an application to dismiss	18(6)	260 Half day	195 Half day	130 Half day
		497 Full day	346 Full day	238 Full day
Noting brief	19	—	—	108 per day
Hearing for mitigation of sentence	29	£260 per day	£173 per day	£108 per day

[This table is printed as amended by S.I. 2009 No. 2086 (*ante*, G–1); S.I. 2011 No. 2065 ★ (*ante*, G–1) (revision of fees in relation to representation orders made on or after April 1, 2012); and S.I. 2012 No. 750 (*ante*, G–1).]

PART 5

MISCELLANEOUS

Identity of instructed advocate

20.—(1) Where an instructed advocate is appointed before the plea and case management hear-   **G–58**
ing, he must notify the Court in writing as soon as he is appointed and, where appropriate, he must
confirm whether he is the leading instructed advocate or the led instructed advocate.

(2) Where the representation order provides for a single advocate and no instructed advocate has
been notified to the Court in accordance with sub-paragraph (1)—

    (a) the barrister or solicitor advocate who attends the plea and case management hearing will
        be deemed to be the instructed advocate; and

    (b) the Court will make a written record of this fact.

(3) Where the representation order provides for a single advocate and no barrister or solicitor
advocate attends the plea and case management hearing—

    (a) the barrister or solicitor advocate who attends the next hearing in the case will be deemed
        to be the instructed advocate; and

    (b) the Court will make a written record of this fact.

(4) Where the representation order provides for more than one advocate, and no leading
instructed advocate has been notified to the Court in accordance with sub-paragraph (1), the leading
advocate who attends—

    (a) the plea and case management hearing; or

    (b) where no leading advocate attends the plea and case management hearing, the next hear-
        ing in the case attended by a leading advocate

will be deemed to be the leading instructed advocate, and the Court will make a written record of this fact.

(5) Where the representation order provides for more than one advocate, and no led instructed advocate has been notified to the Court in accordance with sub-paragraph (1), the led advocate who attends—

    (a) the plea and case management hearing; or

    (b) where no led advocate attends the plea and case management hearing, the next hearing in the case attended by a led advocate

will be deemed to be the led instructed advocate, the Court will make a written record of this fact.

(6) Where a representation order is amended after the plea and case management hearing to provide for more than one advocate—

    (a) the additional instructed advocate must notify the Court in writing of his appointment within 7 days of the date on which the representation order is amended; and

    (b) each instructed advocate must notify the Court whether he is the leading instructed advocate or the led instructed advocate.

(7) Where no additional instructed advocate has been notified to the Court in accordance with sub-paragraph (6)(a), the advocate who attends the next hearing in the case will be deemed to be an instructed advocate and the Court will record in writing whether he is the leading instructed advocate or the led instructed advocate, as appropriate to the circumstances of the case.

(7A) Where—

    (a) a case ceases to be a Very High Cost Case (in relation to fees claimed by advocates), and

    (b) none of sub-paragraphs (1) to (7) applies,

the instructed advocate must notify the Court in writing of his appointment within 7 days of the case ceasing to be a Very High Cost Case (in relation to fees claimed by advocates).

(8) The Court will attach—

    (a) any notice received under sub-paragraph (1), (6) or (7A); and

    (b) any record made by it under sub-paragraph (2), (3), (4), (5) or (7)

to the representation order.

(9) An instructed advocate must remain as instructed advocate at all times, except where—

    (a) a date for trial is fixed at or before the plea and case management hearing and the instructed advocate is unable to conduct the trial due to his other pre-existing commitments;

    (b) he is dismissed by the assisted person or the litigator; or

    (c) he is required to withdraw because of his professional code of conduct.

(10) Where, in accordance with sub-paragraph (9), an instructed advocate withdraws, he must—

    (a) immediately notify the court of his withdrawal—

        (i) in writing; or

        (ii) where the withdrawal takes place at a plea and case management hearing, orally; and

    (b) within 7 days of the date of his withdrawal, notify the court in writing of the identity of a replacement instructed advocate, who must fulfil all the functions of an instructed advocate in accordance with this Order.

(11) This paragraph does not apply to a claim for fees under paragraph 27, 28 or 29.

[This paragraph is printed as amended by S.I. 2009 No. 1843 (*ante*, G–1); and (in relation to proceedings in which a representation order is granted on or after July 14, 2010) S.I. 2010 No. 1181 (*ante*, G–1).]

Payment of fees to instructed advocate

G–59   21.—(1) In accordance with article 23 the appropriate officer must notify each instructed advocate of the total fees payable and authorise payment to him accordingly.

(2) Payment of the fees in accordance with sub-paragraph (1) must be made to each instructed advocate.

(3) Where the representation order provides for a single advocate, the instructed advocate is responsible for arranging payment of fees to the trial advocate and any substitute advocate who has undertaken work on the case.

(4) Where there are two instructed advocates for an assisted person, payment must be made to each instructed advocate individually, and—

    (a) the leading instructed advocate is responsible for arranging payment of fees to the trial advocate and any substitute advocate who have undertaken work on the case of a type for which a leading advocate is responsible; and

    (b) the led instructed advocate is responsible for arranging payment of fees to the trial advocate and any substitute advocate who have undertaken work on the case of a type for which a led advocate is responsible.

(5) This paragraph does not apply to a claim for fees under paragraph 27, 28 or 29.

Additional charges and additional cases

22.—(1) Where an assisted person is charged with more than one offence on one indictment, the **G–60** fee payable to the trial advocate under this Schedule will be based on whichever of those offences the trial advocate selects.

(2) Where two or more cases to which this Schedule applies involving the same trial advocate are heard concurrently (whether involving the same or different assisted persons)—

(a) the trial advocate must select one case ("the principal case"), which must be treated for the purposes of remuneration in accordance with this Schedule;

(b) in respect of the main hearing in each of the other cases the trial advocate must be paid a fixed fee of 20 per cent of—

(i) the basic fee (B) specified in the Table following paragraph 5 or paragraph 7, as appropriate, for the principal case, where that is a case falling within paragraph 2(1)(a), or

(ii) the fixed fee for the principal case, where that is a case falling within paragraph 2(1)(b) or paragraph 7B.

(2A) Nothing in sub-paragraphs (3) to (5) permits a fixed fee under Part 4, other than one to which paragraph 11 applies, to be paid in a case to which Part 3A applies.

(3) Where a trial advocate or substitute advocate appears at a hearing specified in paragraph 9, 10, 11, 12 or 13, forming part of two or more cases involving different assisted persons, he must be paid—

(a) in respect of the first such case, the fixed fee for that hearing specified in the Table following paragraph 19; and

(b) in respect of each of the other cases, 20 per cent of that fee.

(4) Subject to sub-paragraphs (1) to (3), where a trial advocate or substitute advocate appears at a hearing forming part of two or more cases, he must be paid the fixed fee for that hearing specified in the Table following paragraph 19 in respect of one such case, without any increase in respect of the other cases.

(5) Where a trial advocate selects—

(a) one offence, in preference to another offence, under sub-paragraph (1); or

(b) one case as the principal case, in preference to another case, under sub-paragraph (2),

that selection does not affect his right to claim any of the fees set out in the Table following paragraph 19 to which he would otherwise have been entitled.

[This paragraph is printed as amended by S.I. 2011 No. 2065 (*ante*, G–1).]

Multiple advocates

23.—(1) Where a representation order provides for three advocates in a case the provisions of this **G–61** Schedule will apply, and the fees payable to the led juniors in accordance with Part 2 or Part 3 will be payable to each led junior who is instructed in the case.

[This paragraph is printed as amended by S.I. 2007 No. 3552 (*ante*, G–1).]

Non-local appearances

24. Where an advocate is instructed to appear in a court which is not within 40 kilometres of his **G–62** office or chambers, the appropriate officer may allow an amount for travelling and other expenses incidental to that appearance, provided that the amount must not be greater than the amount, if any, which would be payable to a trial advocate from the nearest local Bar or the nearest advocate's office (whichever is the nearer) unless the advocate instructed to appear has obtained prior approval under CDS Regulations for the incurring of such expenses or can justify his attendance having regard to all the relevant circumstances of the case.

Trials lasting over 40 days

25. Where a trial exceeds 40 days, the trial advocate must be paid a fee as set out in the Table fol- **G–63** lowing this paragraph, as appropriate to the category of trial advocate and the class of offence, for each day by which the trial exceeds 40 days on which the trial advocate attends court.

[This paragraph is printed as amended by S.I. 2007 No. 3552 (*ante*, G–1).]

DAILY RATES PAYABLE WHERE A TRIAL LASTS OVER 40 DAYS

Class of Offence	Daily rate payable for days 41 to 50	Daily rate payable for days 51 and over
QC		
A–K	387	414

Class of Offence	Daily rate payable for days 41 to 50	Daily rate payable for days 51 and over
Leading Junior		
A–K	331	356
Led Junior		
A–K	221	237
Junior Acting Alone		
A	266	285
B	247	265
C	247	265
D	266	285
E	225	241
F	225	241
G	225	241
H	247	265
I	247	265
J	266	285
K	266	285

★ [This table is printed as substituted by S.I. 2010 No. 1181 (*ante*, G–1) in relation to representation orders granted on or after April 1, 2011; as amended by S.I. 2011 No. 2065 (*ante*, G–1) in relation to representation orders granted on or after October 3, 2011; and as further amended by the latter order (and by S.I. 2012 No. 750 (*ante*, G–1)) in relation to representation orders granted on or after April 1, 2012.]

Assisted person unfit to plead or stand trial

G–64
26. Where in any case a hearing is held to determine the question of whether the assisted person is unfit to plead or to stand trial (a "fitness hearing")—

    (a) if a trial on indictment is held, or continues, at any time thereafter, the length of the fitness hearing is included in determining the length of the trial for the calculation of the graduated fee in accordance with Part 2 or Part 3;

    (b) if a trial on indictment is not held, or does not continue, thereafter by reason of the assisted person being found unfit to plead or to stand trial, the trial advocate must be paid—

        (i) a graduated fee calculated in accordance with paragraph 4 as appropriate to the combined length of—

            (aa) the fitness hearing; and

            (bb) any hearing under section 4A of the *Criminal Procedure (Insanity) Act* 1964 (finding that the accused did the act or made the omission charged against him); or

        (ii) a graduated fee calculated in accordance with paragraph 6 as appropriate for representing an assisted person in a cracked trial,

    whichever the trial advocate elects; and

    (c) if at any time the assisted person pleads guilty to the indictable offence, the trial advocate must be paid either—

        (i) a graduated fee calculated in accordance with paragraph 4 as appropriate to the length of the fitness hearing; or

        (ii) a graduated fee calculated in accordance with paragraph 6 as appropriate for representing an assisted person in a guilty plea,

    whichever the trial advocate elects.

Cross examination of witness

G–65
27.—(1) Where in any case on indictment an advocate is retained solely for the purpose of cross-examining a witness under section 38 of the *Youth Justice and Criminal Evidence Act* 1999 (defence representation for purposes of cross-examination), he must be paid a graduated fee calculated in accordance with paragraph 4.

(2) For the purposes of this paragraph the daily attendance fee (D) is as set out in the Table following paragraph 5 as appropriate to the number of days of attendance at court by the advocate.

Provision of written or oral advice

28.—(1) Where in any case on indictment an advocate is assigned under a representation order **G–66**
solely for the purpose of providing written or oral advice, he will be paid for the reasonable number
of hours of preparation for that advice using the rates of hourly fees for special preparation set out
in the table following paragraph 19 as appropriate to the category of trial advocate.

(2) An advocate claiming a fee for advice under this paragraph may apply to the appropriate officer to redetermine the fee under article 29 and he must supply such information and documents as
may be required by the appropriate officer as proof of the number of hours of preparation.

Mitigation of sentence

29.—(1) Where in any case on indictment an advocate is assigned under a representation order to **★G–67**
appear at a sentencing hearing solely for the purpose of applying to the court to mitigate the assisted person's sentence, he must be paid in respect of that appearance the fee specified in the Table
following paragraph 19 together with a fee calculated from the reasonable number of hours of preparation for that appearance using the rates of hourly fees for special preparation set out in the table
following paragraph 19 as appropriate to the category of trial advocate.

(2) An advocate claiming an hourly preparation fee under this paragraph may apply to the appropriate officer to redetermine such hourly fee under article 29 and he must supply such information and documents as may be required by the appropriate officer as proof of the number of hours
of preparation.

[This paragraph is printed as amended by S.I. 2012 No. 750 (*ante*, G–1).]

Table of offences

At the end of Schedule 1 to the 2007 order, there is a table of offences. For the effect **G–68**
thereof, see *post*, G–168 *et seq.*

Article 6(1)   SCHEDULE 2

LITIGATORS' GRADUATED FEE SCHEME

PART 1

DEFINITION AND SCOPE

Interpretation

1.—(1) In this Schedule—   **★G–69**
"case" means proceedings in the Crown Court against any one assisted person—
    (a) on one or more counts of a single indictment;
    (b) arising out of a single notice of appeal against conviction or sentence, or a single
        committal for sentence, whether on one or more charges; or
    (c) arising out of a single alleged breach of an order of the Crown Court,
and a case falling within paragraph (c) must be treated as a separate case from the proceedings in
which the order was made;
"cracked trial" means a case on indictment in which—
    (a) a plea and case management hearing takes place and—
        (i) the case does not proceed to trial (whether by reason of pleas of guilty or for
           other reasons) or the prosecution offers no evidence; and
        (ii) either—
           (aa) in respect of one or more counts to which the assisted person pleaded guilty,
               he did not so plead at the plea and case management hearing; or
           (bb) in respect of one or more counts which did not proceed, the prosecution did
               not, before or at the plea and case management hearing, declare an inten-
               tion of not proceeding with them; or
    (b) the case is listed for trial without a plea and case management hearing taking place;
"guilty plea" means a case on indictment which—
    (a) is disposed of without a trial because the assisted person pleaded guilty to one or
        more counts; and
    (b) is not a cracked trial;
"main hearing" means —
    (a) in relation to a case which goes to trial, the trial;

(b) in relation to a guilty plea, the hearing at which pleas are taken or, where there is more than one such hearing, the last such hearing;

(c) in relation to a cracked trial, the hearing at which—

(i) the case becomes a cracked trial by meeting the conditions in the definition of a cracked trial, whether or not any pleas were taken at that hearing; or

(ii) a formal verdict of not guilty was entered as a result of the prosecution offering no evidence, whether or not the parties attended the hearing;

(d) in relation to an appeal against conviction or sentence in the Crown Court, the hearing of the appeal;

(e) in relation to proceedings arising out of a committal for sentence in the Crown Court, the sentencing hearing;

(f) in relation to proceedings arising out of an alleged breach of an order of the Crown Court, the hearing at which those proceedings are determined;

"*Newton* hearing" means a hearing at which evidence is heard for the purpose of determining the sentence of a convicted person in accordance with the principles of *R. v. Newton* (1982) 77 Cr.App.R. 13;

"PPE Cut-off" means the minimum number of pages of prosecution evidence for use in calculating the fee payable to a litigator under this Schedule, as set out in the tables following paragraphs 4(1) and 4(2).

(2) For the purposes of this Schedule, the number of pages of prosecution evidence served on the court shall be determined in accordance with paragraphs (2A) to (2C).

(2A) The number of pages of prosecution evidence includes all—

(a) witness statements;

(b) documentary and pictorial exhibits;

(c) records of interviews with the assisted person; and

(d) records of interviews with other defendants,

which form part of the committal or served prosecution documents or which are included in any notice of additional evidence.

(2B) Subject to paragraph (2C), a document served by the prosecution in electronic form is included in the number of pages of prosecution evidence.

(2C) A documentary or pictorial exhibit which—

(a) has been served by the prosecution in electronic form; and

(b) has never existed in paper form,

is not included within the number of pages of prosecution evidence unless the appropriate officer decides that it would be appropriate to include it in the pages of prosecution evidence taking into account the nature of the document and any other relevant circumstances.

(3) In proceedings on indictment in the Crown Court initiated otherwise than by committal for trial, the appropriate officer must determine the number of pages of prosecution evidence in accordance with sub-paragraph (2) or as nearly in accordance with sub-paragraph (2) as possible as the nature of the case permits.

(4) A reference to the Table of Offences in this Schedule is to the Table in Part 6 of Schedule 1 and a reference to a Class of Offence in this Schedule refers to the Class in which that offence is listed in the Table of Offences.

[This paragraph is printed as amended by S.I. 2011 No. 2065 (*ante*, G–1); and S.I. 2012 No. 750 (*ante*, G–1).]

Application

★**G–69a**   2.—(1) Subject to sub-paragraphs (2) to (3), this Schedule applies to—

(a) every case on indictment;

(b) the following proceedings in the Crown Court—

(i) an appeal against conviction or sentence from the magistrates' court;

(ii) a sentencing hearing following a committal for sentence to the Crown Court;

(iii) proceedings arising out of an alleged breach of an order of the Crown Court (whether or not this Schedule applies to the proceedings in which the order was made); ...

(d) a sentencing hearing following a case on indictment to which this Schedule applies, where sentence has been deferred under section 1 of the *Powers of Criminal Courts (Sentencing) Act* 2000 (deferment of sentence);

(e) any other post-sentence hearing.

(2) Sub-paragraph (3) applies where proceedings are—

    (a) sent for trial to the Crown Court ...; or

    (b) transferred to the Crown Court under—

        (i) section 4 of the *Criminal Justice Act* 1987 (transfer of serious fraud cases); or

        (ii) section 53 of the *Criminal Justice Act* 1991 (transfer of certain cases involving children).

(3) Where, at any time after proceedings are sent or transferred to the Crown Court as referred to in sub-paragraph (2), they are—

    (a) discontinued by a notice served under section 23A of the *Prosecution of Offences Act* 1985 (discontinuance of proceedings after accused has been sent for trial); or

    (b) dismissed pursuant to—

        (i) paragraph 2 of Schedule 3 to the *Crime and Disorder Act* 1998 (applications for dismissal);

        (ii) section 6 of the *Criminal Justice Act* 1987 (applications for dismissal); or

        (iii) paragraph 5 of Schedule 6 to the *Criminal Justice Act* 1991 (applications for dismissal,

the provisions of paragraphs 16 and 17 apply.

(4) Where, following a case on indictment, a *Newton* hearing takes place—

    (a) for the purposes of this Schedule the case will be treated as having gone to trial;

    (b) the length of the trial will be taken to be the combined length of the main hearing and the *Newton* hearing;

    (c) the provisions of this Schedule relating to cracked trials and guilty pleas will not apply.

(5) For the purposes of this Schedule, a case on indictment which discontinues at or before the plea and case management hearing otherwise than—

    (a) by reason of a plea of guilty being entered, or

    (b) in accordance with sub-paragraph (3) of this paragraph,

must be treated as a guilty plea.

(6) For the purposes of this Schedule, where a trial that is not a Very High Cost Case (in relation to fees claimed by litigators) lasts over 200 days, it must be treated as if it had lasted 200 days.

(7) For the purposes of this Schedule, where the number of pages of prosecution evidence in a case which is not a Very High Cost Case exceeds (in relation to fees claimed by litigators)—

    (a) the PPE Cut-off figure specified in the table following paragraph 4(2) as appropriate to the offence for which the assisted person is to be tried and the length of trial, and

    (b) 10,000,

the case must be treated as though it had 10,000 pages of prosecution evidence.

[This paragraph is printed as amended by S.I. 2009 No. 1843 (*ante*, G–1); S.I. 2010 No. 1181 (*ante*, G–1); and S.I. 2012 No. 1343 (*ante*, G–1).]

Class of offences

3.—(1) For the purposes of this Schedule—   **G–70**

    (a) every indictable offence falls within the Class under which it is listed in the Table of Offences and, subject to sub-paragraph (2), indictable offences not specifically so listed will be deemed to fall within Class H;

    (b) conspiracy to commit an indictable offence contrary to section 1 of the *Criminal Law Act* 1977 (the offence of conspiracy), incitement to commit an indictable offence and attempts to commit an indictable offence contrary to section 1 of the *Criminal Attempts Act* 1981 (attempting to commit an offence), fall within the same Class as the substantive offence to which they relate;

    (c) where the Table of Offences specifies that the Class within which an offence falls depends on whether the value involved exceeds a stated limit, the value must be presumed not to exceed that limit unless the litigator making the claim under article 6 proves otherwise to the satisfaction of the appropriate officer;

    (d) where more than one count of the indictment is for an offence in relation to which the Class depends on the value involved, that value must be taken to be the total value involved in all those offences, but where two or more counts relate to the same property, the value of that property must be taken into account once only;

    (e) where an entry in the Table of Offences specifies an offence as being contrary to a statutory provision, then subject to any express limitation in the entry that entry will include every offence contrary to that statutory provision whether or not the words of description in the entry are appropriate to cover all such offences;

(f) where in a case on indictment there is a hearing to determine the question of whether an assisted person is unfit to plead or unfit to stand trial, the litigator must elect whether that hearing falls within the same Class as the indictable offence to which it relates or within Class D;

(g) where in a case on indictment a restriction order is made under section 41 of the *Mental Health Act* 1983 (power of higher courts to restrict discharge from hospital), the offence falls within Class A, regardless of the Class under which the offence would be listed in the Table of Offences, but for this paragraph.

(2) Where a litigator in proceedings in the Crown Court is dissatisfied with the classification within Class H of an indictable offence not listed in the Table of Offences, he may apply to the appropriate officer, when lodging his claim for fees, to reclassify the offence.

(3) The appropriate officer must, in light of the objections made by the litigator—

(a) confirm the classification of the offence within Class H; or

(b) reclassify the offence

and must notify the litigator of his decision.

PART 2

GRADUATED FEES FOR GUILTY PLEAS, CRACKED TRIALS AND TRIALS

Scope of Part 2

★**G–70a**   3A. Subject to paragraph 16, this Part does not apply to a guilty plea or cracked trial in a case committed or sent for trial to the Crown Court on the election of a defendant where the magistrates' court has determined the case to be suitable for summary trial.

[This paragraph was inserted by S.I. 2011 No. 2065 (*ante*, G–1); and it is printed as amended by S.I. 2012 No. 1343 (*ante*, G–1).]

Pages of prosecution evidence

G–70b   4.—(1) For the purposes of this Part, the PPE Cut-off figures in a cracked trial or guilty plea are specified in the table following this sub-paragraph, as appropriate to the offence with which the assisted person is charged.

PPE CUT-OFF FIGURES IN CRACKED TRIALS AND GUILTY PLEAS

	Class of offence										
Type of case	*A*	*B*	*C*	*D*	*E*	*F*	*G*	*H*	*I*	*J*	*K*
Cracked trial or guilty plea	80	70	40	80	40	50	50	40	40	80	120

(2) For the purposes of this Part, the PPE Cut-off figures in a trial are specified in the table following this sub-paragraph, as appropriate to the offence for which the assisted person is tried, and the length of trial.

PPE Cut-off figures in trials

Trial length in days	PPE Cut off A	PPE Cut off B	PPE Cut off C	PPE Cut off D	PPE Cut off E	PPE Cut off F	PPE Cut off G	PPE Cut off H	PPE Cut off I	PPE Cut off J	PPE Cut off K
1	80	70	40	80	40	50	50	40	40	80	120
2	80	70	40	80	40	50	50	40	40	80	120
3	95	105	81	95	120	138	138	122	134	95	186
4	126	139	120	126	158	173	173	157	185	126	252
5	156	170	157	156	195	206	206	191	232	156	314
6	186	203	193	186	229	240	240	225	281	186	372
7	218	238	230	218	265	276	276	260	329	218	433
8	257	274	267	257	301	310	310	301	376	257	495
9	293	306	301	293	333	342	342	338	420	293	550
10	330	338	339	330	365	373	373	374	464	330	606
11	367	370	378	367	399	405	405	412	509	367	663
12	404	402	417	404	433	437	437	449	554	404	721
13	440	434	455	440	467	470	470	486	598	440	779
14	477	465	493	477	500	501	501	523	642	477	836
15	514	497	531	514	532	533	533	559	686	514	894
16	551	535	569	551	565	564	564	596	730	551	951
17	587	573	607	587	598	596	596	637	774	587	1,007
18	624	611	646	624	646	627	627	687	818	624	1,063
19	661	649	684	661	696	659	659	736	862	661	1,119
20	697	687	722	697	746	690	690	786	907	697	1,174
21	742	722	753	742	787	720	720	826	943	742	1,230
22	786	757	785	786	828	752	752	867	980	786	1,286
23	830	792	819	830	868	784	784	908	1,017	830	1,341
24	874	826	857	874	908	816	816	948	1,053	874	1,396
25	917	860	894	917	948	848	848	988	1,088	917	1,451
26	961	895	931	961	988	880	880	1,028	1,124	961	1,505
27	1,005	935	967	1,005	1,028	912	912	1,068	1,160	1,005	1,560
28	1,049	975	1,004	1,049	1,068	944	944	1,107	1,196	1,049	1,615
29	1,099	1,016	1,041	1,099	1,108	976	976	1,147	1,231	1,099	1,670

Trial length in days	PPE Cut off A	PPE Cut off B	PPE Cut off C	PPE Cut off D	PPE Cut off E	PPE Cut off F	PPE Cut off G	PPE Cut off H	PPE Cut off I	PPE Cut off J	PPE Cut off K
30	1,150	1,057	1,077	1,150	1,148	1,007	1,007	1,187	1,267	1,150	1,725
31	1,200	1,098	1,114	1,200	1,188	1,039	1,039	1,226	1,303	1,200	1,780
32	1,251	1,138	1,151	1,251	1,228	1,070	1,070	1,266	1,349	1,251	1,835
33	1,301	1,179	1,187	1,301	1,268	1,102	1,102	1,307	1,394	1,301	1,889
34	1,352	1,220	1,224	1,352	1,308	1,133	1,133	1,357	1,439	1,352	1,944
35	1,402	1,261	1,262	1,402	1,347	1,165	1,165	1,407	1,485	1,402	1,999
36	1,453	1,302	1,303	1,453	1,435	1,196	1,196	1,457	1,530	1,453	2,054
37	1,503	1,348	1,345	1,503	1,526	1,228	1,228	1,507	1,575	1,503	2,109
38	1,554	1,395	1,386	1,554	1,617	1,259	1,259	1,557	1,621	1,554	2,164
39	1,604	1,441	1,428	1,604	1,708	1,291	1,291	1,607	1,666	1,604	2,219
40	1,652	1,484	1,444	1,652	1,745	1,314	1,314	1,629	1,704	1,652	2,271
41	1,700	1,527	1,461	1,700	1,782	1,338	1,338	1,651	1,742	1,700	2,324
42	1,748	1,570	1,477	1,748	1,820	1,361	1,361	1,673	1,780	1,748	2,377
43	1,796	1,613	1,494	1,796	1,857	1,384	1,384	1,695	1,818	1,796	2,430
44	1,844	1,656	1,511	1,844	1,895	1,410	1,410	1,716	1,856	1,844	2,483
45	1,892	1,699	1,527	1,892	1,932	1,440	1,440	1,738	1,894	1,892	2,536
46	1,939	1,742	1,544	1,939	1,970	1,470	1,470	1,760	1,932	1,939	2,589
47	1,987	1,785	1,560	1,987	2,007	1,501	1,501	1,782	1,970	1,987	2,642
48	2,039	1,828	1,577	2,039	2,045	1,531	1,531	1,804	2,008	2,039	2,695
49	2,091	1,871	1,594	2,091	2,082	1,561	1,561	1,826	2,046	2,091	2,749
50	2,144	1,914	1,610	2,144	2,120	1,591	1,591	1,848	2,084	2,144	2,802
51	2,196	1,957	1,627	2,196	2,158	1,622	1,622	1,870	2,122	2,196	2,855
52	2,249	2,000	1,644	2,249	2,195	1,652	1,652	1,892	2,160	2,249	2,908
53	2,301	2,043	1,660	2,301	2,233	1,682	1,682	1,914	2,198	2,301	2,962
54	2,354	2,086	1,677	2,354	2,271	1,712	1,712	1,936	2,236	2,354	3,015
55	2,406	2,129	1,694	2,406	2,308	1,743	1,743	1,958	2,275	2,406	3,068
56	2,459	2,172	1,710	2,459	2,346	1,773	1,773	1,980	2,313	2,459	3,121
57	2,512	2,215	1,727	2,512	2,384	1,803	1,803	2,002	2,351	2,512	3,175
58	2,564	2,258	1,744	2,564	2,422	1,833	1,833	2,024	2,389	2,564	3,228
59	2,617	2,301	1,760	2,617	2,459	1,864	1,864	2,046	2,427	2,617	3,281

Trial length in days	PPE Cut off A	PPE Cut off B	PPE Cut off C	PPE Cut off D	PPE Cut off E	PPE Cut off F	PPE Cut off G	PPE Cut off H	PPE Cut off I	PPE Cut off J	PPE Cut off K
60	2,669	2,345	1,777	2,669	2,497	1,894	1,894	2,068	2,465	2,669	3,335
61	2,722	2,388	1,794	2,722	2,535	1,924	1,924	2,090	2,503	2,722	3,388
62	2,775	2,431	1,811	2,775	2,572	1,959	1,959	2,112	2,542	2,775	3,442
63	2,827	2,474	1,827	2,827	2,610	2,020	2,020	2,134	2,580	2,827	3,495
64	2,880	2,517	1,844	2,880	2,648	2,081	2,081	2,156	2,618	2,880	3,549
65	2,933	2,561	1,861	2,933	2,686	2,141	2,141	2,178	2,656	2,933	3,602
66	2,985	2,604	1,877	2,985	2,723	2,202	2,202	2,200	2,694	2,985	3,656
67	3,038	2,647	1,894	3,038	2,761	2,263	2,263	2,222	2,776	3,038	3,709
68	3,091	2,690	1,911	3,091	2,799	2,323	2,323	2,244	2,865	3,091	3,763
69	3,144	2,734	1,927	3,144	2,836	2,384	2,384	2,266	2,954	3,144	3,816
70	3,196	2,777	1,944	3,196	2,874	2,445	2,445	2,288	3,043	3,196	3,870
71	3,249	2,820	1,961	3,249	2,912	2,506	2,506	2,310	3,132	3,249	3,923
72	3,302	2,864	1,978	3,302	2,950	2,566	2,566	2,332	3,221	3,302	3,977
73	3,355	2,907	1,994	3,355	2,987	2,627	2,627	2,354	3,310	3,355	4,031
74	3,407	2,950	2,016	3,407	3,025	2,688	2,688	2,376	3,399	3,407	4,084
75	3,460	2,994	2,040	3,460	3,063	2,749	2,749	2,398	3,488	3,460	4,138
76	3,513	3,037	2,064	3,513	3,101	2,809	2,809	2,420	3,577	3,513	4,192
77	3,566	3,080	2,089	3,566	3,138	2,870	2,870	2,442	3,666	3,566	4,245
78	3,619	3,124	2,113	3,619	3,176	2,931	2,931	2,464	3,755	3,619	4,299
79	3,672	3,167	2,137	3,672	3,214	2,992	2,992	2,486	3,844	3,672	4,353
80	3,724	3,211	2,161	3,724	3,251	3,052	3,052	2,508	3,933	3,724	4,406
81	3,777	3,254	2,185	3,777	3,289	3,113	3,113	2,530	4,023	3,777	4,460
82	3,830	3,297	2,210	3,830	3,327	3,174	3,174	2,552	4,112	3,830	4,514
83	3,883	3,341	2,234	3,883	3,365	3,235	3,235	2,575	4,201	3,883	4,568
84	3,936	3,384	2,258	3,936	3,402	3,295	3,295	2,597	4,290	3,936	4,622
85	3,989	3,428	2,282	3,989	3,440	3,356	3,356	2,619	4,379	3,989	4,675
86	4,042	3,471	2,307	4,042	3,478	3,417	3,417	2,641	4,469	4,042	4,729
87	4,095	3,515	2,331	4,095	3,516	3,478	3,478	2,663	4,558	4,095	4,783
88	4,148	3,558	2,355	4,148	3,553	3,539	3,539	2,685	4,647	4,148	4,837
89	4,201	3,602	2,379	4,201	3,591	3,599	3,599	2,707	4,737	4,201	4,891

Trial length in days	PPE Cut off A	PPE Cut off B	PPE Cut off C	PPE Cut off D	PPE Cut off E	PPE Cut off F	PPE Cut off G	PPE Cut off H	PPE Cut off I	PPE Cut off J	PPE Cut off K
90	4,254	3,645	2,404	4,254	3,629	3,660	3,660	2,729	4,826	4,254	4,945
91	4,307	3,689	2,428	4,307	3,666	3,721	3,721	2,751	4,915	4,307	4,999
92	4,360	3,733	2,452	4,360	3,704	3,782	3,782	2,774	5,005	4,360	5,053
93	4,413	3,776	2,477	4,413	3,742	3,843	3,843	2,796	5,094	4,413	5,107
94	4,466	3,820	2,501	4,466	3,780	3,903	3,903	2,818	5,183	4,466	5,161
95	4,519	3,863	2,525	4,519	3,817	3,964	3,964	2,840	5,273	4,519	5,215
96	4,572	3,907	2,549	4,572	3,855	4,025	4,025	2,862	5,362	4,572	5,269
97	4,625	3,951	2,574	4,625	3,893	4,086	4,086	2,884	5,452	4,625	5,323
98	4,679	3,994	2,598	4,679	3,930	4,147	4,147	2,906	5,541	4,679	5,377
99	4,732	4,038	2,622	4,732	3,968	4,207	4,207	2,929	5,631	4,732	5,431
100	4,785	4,082	2,647	4,785	4,006	4,268	4,268	2,951	5,720	4,785	5,485
101	4,838	4,125	2,671	4,838	4,044	4,329	4,329	2,973	5,810	4,838	5,539
102	4,891	4,169	2,695	4,891	4,081	4,390	4,390	2,995	5,899	4,891	5,593
103	4,944	4,213	2,720	4,944	4,119	4,451	4,451	3,032	5,989	4,944	5,647
104	4,997	4,257	2,744	4,997	4,157	4,512	4,512	3,073	6,079	4,997	5,702
105	5,051	4,300	2,768	5,051	4,195	4,573	4,573	3,114	6,168	5,051	5,756
106	5,104	4,344	2,793	5,104	4,232	4,633	4,633	3,155	6,258	5,104	5,810
107	5,157	4,388	2,817	5,157	4,270	4,694	4,694	3,196	6,348	5,157	5,864
108	5,210	4,432	2,841	5,210	4,308	4,755	4,755	3,237	6,437	5,210	5,918
109	5,264	4,475	2,866	5,264	4,345	4,816	4,816	3,278	6,527	5,264	5,973
110	5,317	4,519	2,890	5,317	4,383	4,877	4,877	3,319	6,617	5,317	6,027
111	5,370	4,563	2,914	5,370	4,421	4,938	4,938	3,361	6,706	5,370	6,081
112	5,423	4,607	2,939	5,423	4,459	4,999	4,999	3,402	6,796	5,423	6,135
113	5,477	4,650	2,963	5,477	4,496	5,059	5,059	3,443	6,886	5,477	6,189
114	5,530	4,694	2,987	5,530	4,534	5,120	5,120	3,484	6,976	5,530	6,244
115	5,583	4,738	3,012	5,583	4,572	5,181	5,181	3,525	7,066	5,583	6,298
116	5,637	4,782	3,036	5,637	4,610	5,242	5,242	3,566	7,155	5,637	6,352
117	5,690	4,826	3,060	5,690	4,647	5,303	5,303	3,607	7,245	5,690	6,406
118	5,743	4,869	3,085	5,743	4,685	5,364	5,364	3,648	7,335	5,743	6,460
119	5,797	4,913	3,109	5,797	4,723	5,425	5,425	3,689	7,425	5,797	6,514

Trial length in days	PPE Cut off A	PPE Cut off B	PPE Cut off C	PPE Cut off D	PPE Cut off E	PPE Cut off F	PPE Cut off G	PPE Cut off H	PPE Cut off I	PPE Cut off J	PPE Cut off K
120	5,850	4,957	3,133	5,850	4,760	5,486	5,486	3,730	7,515	5,850	6,569
121	5,904	5,001	3,158	5,904	4,798	5,547	5,547	3,771	7,605	5,904	6,623
122	5,956	5,044	3,182	5,956	4,836	5,607	5,607	3,812	7,693	5,956	6,677
123	6,009	5,088	3,206	6,009	4,874	5,668	5,668	3,853	7,782	6,009	6,731
124	6,061	5,131	3,230	6,061	4,911	5,729	5,729	3,895	7,871	6,061	6,785
125	6,114	5,175	3,254	6,114	4,949	5,789	5,789	3,936	7,959	6,114	6,839
126	6,167	5,218	3,278	6,167	4,987	5,850	5,850	3,977	8,048	6,167	6,892
127	6,219	5,261	3,302	6,219	5,025	5,911	5,911	4,017	8,137	6,219	6,945
128	6,272	5,304	3,326	6,272	5,062	5,971	5,971	4,058	8,225	6,272	6,999
129	6,324	5,347	3,350	6,324	5,100	6,032	6,032	4,098	8,314	6,324	7,052
130	6,377	5,390	3,374	6,377	5,138	6,093	6,093	4,139	8,403	6,377	7,106
131	6,430	5,433	3,398	6,430	5,175	6,153	6,153	4,179	8,491	6,430	7,159
132	6,482	5,476	3,422	6,482	5,213	6,214	6,214	4,219	8,580	6,482	7,212
133	6,535	5,520	3,446	6,535	5,251	6,274	6,274	4,260	8,669	6,535	7,266
134	6,588	5,563	3,470	6,588	5,289	6,335	6,335	4,300	8,757	6,588	7,319
135	6,640	5,606	3,494	6,640	5,326	6,396	6,396	4,341	8,846	6,640	7,373
136	6,693	5,649	3,518	6,693	5,364	6,456	6,456	4,381	8,935	6,693	7,426
137	6,745	5,692	3,542	6,745	5,402	6,517	6,517	4,422	9,023	6,745	7,479
138	6,798	5,735	3,566	6,798	5,439	6,578	6,578	4,462	9,112	6,798	7,533
139	6,851	5,778	3,590	6,851	5,477	6,638	6,638	4,503	9,201	6,851	7,586
140	6,903	5,821	3,614	6,903	5,515	6,699	6,699	4,543	9,289	6,903	7,639
141	6,956	5,864	3,638	6,956	5,553	6,760	6,760	4,584	9,378	6,956	7,693
142	7,008	5,908	3,662	7,008	5,590	6,820	6,820	4,624	9,467	7,008	7,746
143	7,061	5,951	3,686	7,061	5,628	6,881	6,881	4,664	9,555	7,061	7,800
144	7,114	5,994	3,709	7,114	5,666	6,942	6,942	4,705	9,644	7,114	7,853
145	7,166	6,037	3,733	7,166	5,704	7,002	7,002	4,745	9,733	7,166	7,906
146	7,219	6,080	3,757	7,219	5,741	7,063	7,063	4,786	9,821	7,219	7,960
147	7,272	6,123	3,781	7,272	5,779	7,124	7,124	4,826	9,910	7,272	8,013
148	7,324	6,166	3,805	7,324	5,817	7,184	7,184	4,867	9,999	7,324	8,067
149	7,377	6,209	3,829	7,377	5,854	7,245	7,245	4,907	10,087	7,377	8,120

Trial length in days	PPE Cut off A	PPE Cut off B	PPE Cut off C	PPE Cut off D	PPE Cut off E	PPE Cut off F	PPE Cut off G	PPE Cut off H	PPE Cut off I	PPE Cut off J	PPE Cut off K
150	7,429	6,252	3,853	7,429	5,892	7,305	7,305	4,948	10,176	7,429	8,173
151	7,482	6,296	3,877	7,482	5,930	7,366	7,366	4,988	10,265	7,482	8,227
152	7,535	6,339	3,901	7,535	5,968	7,427	7,427	5,029	10,353	7,535	8,280
153	7,587	6,382	3,925	7,587	6,005	7,487	7,487	5,069	10,442	7,587	8,333
154	7,640	6,425	3,949	7,640	6,043	7,548	7,548	5,110	10,531	7,640	8,387
155	7,692	6,468	3,973	7,692	6,081	7,609	7,609	5,150	10,619	7,692	8,440
156	7,745	6,511	3,997	7,745	6,119	7,669	7,669	5,190	10,708	7,745	8,494
157	7,798	6,554	4,021	7,798	6,156	7,730	7,730	5,231	10,797	7,798	8,547
158	7,850	6,597	4,045	7,850	6,194	7,791	7,791	5,271	10,885	7,850	8,600
159	7,903	6,641	4,069	7,903	6,232	7,851	7,851	5,312	10,974	7,903	8,654
160	7,956	6,684	4,093	7,956	6,269	7,912	7,912	5,352	11,063	7,956	8,707
161	8,008	6,727	4,117	8,008	6,307	7,973	7,973	5,393	11,151	8,008	8,760
162	8,061	6,770	4,141	8,061	6,345	8,033	8,033	5,433	11,240	8,061	8,814
163	8,113	6,813	4,165	8,113	6,383	8,094	8,094	5,474	11,329	8,113	8,867
164	8,166	6,856	4,189	8,166	6,420	8,155	8,155	5,514	11,417	8,166	8,921
165	8,219	6,899	4,213	8,219	6,458	8,215	8,215	5,555	11,506	8,219	8,974
166	8,271	6,942	4,237	8,271	6,496	8,276	8,276	5,595	11,595	8,271	9,027
167	8,324	6,985	4,261	8,324	6,534	8,337	8,337	5,636	11,683	8,324	9,081
168	8,376	7,029	4,285	8,376	6,571	8,397	8,397	5,676	11,772	8,376	9,134
169	8,429	7,072	4,309	8,429	6,609	8,458	8,458	5,716	11,861	8,429	9,188
170	8,482	7,115	4,333	8,482	6,647	8,518	8,518	5,757	11,949	8,482	9,241
171	8,534	7,158	4,357	8,534	6,684	8,579	8,579	5,797	12,038	8,534	9,294
172	8,587	7,201	4,380	8,587	6,722	8,640	8,640	5,838	12,127	8,587	9,348
173	8,639	7,244	4,404	8,639	6,760	8,700	8,700	5,878	12,215	8,639	9,401
174	8,692	7,287	4,428	8,692	6,798	8,761	8,761	5,919	12,304	8,692	9,454
175	8,745	7,330	4,452	8,745	6,835	8,822	8,822	5,959	12,393	8,745	9,508
176	8,797	7,373	4,476	8,797	6,873	8,882	8,882	6,000	12,481	8,797	9,561
177	8,850	7,417	4,500	8,850	6,911	8,943	8,943	6,040	12,570	8,850	9,615
178	8,903	7,460	4,524	8,903	6,948	9,004	9,004	6,081	12,659	8,903	9,668
179	8,955	7,503	4,548	8,955	6,986	9,064	9,064	6,121	12,747	8,955	9,721

Trial length in days	PPE Cut off A	PPE Cut off B	PPE Cut off C	PPE Cut off D	PPE Cut off E	PPE Cut off F	PPE Cut off G	PPE Cut off H	PPE Cut off I	PPE Cut off I	PPE Cut off K
180	9,008	7,546	4,572	9,008	7,024	9,125	9,125	6,162	12,836	9,008	9,775
181	9,060	7,589	4,596	9,060	7,062	9,186	9,186	6,202	12,925	9,060	9,828
182	9,113	7,632	4,620	9,113	7,099	9,246	9,246	6,242	13,013	9,113	9,881
183	9,166	7,675	4,644	9,166	7,137	9,307	9,307	6,283	13,102	9,166	9,935
184	9,218	7,718	4,668	9,218	7,174	9,368	9,368	6,323	13,191	9,218	9,988
185	9,271	7,762	4,692	9,271	7,211	9,428	9,428	6,364	13,279	9,271	10,042
186	9,323	7,805	4,716	9,323	7,248	9,489	9,489	6,404	13,368	9,323	10,095
187	9,376	7,848	4,740	9,376	7,285	9,549	9,549	6,445	13,457	9,376	10,148
188	9,429	7,891	4,764	9,429	7,322	9,610	9,610	6,485	13,545	9,429	10,202
189	9,481	7,934	4,788	9,481	7,360	9,671	9,671	6,526	13,634	9,481	10,255
190	9,534	7,977	4,812	9,534	7,397	9,731	9,731	6,566	13,723	9,534	10,309
191	9,587	8,020	4,836	9,587	7,434	9,792	9,792	6,607	13,811	9,587	10,362
192	9,639	8,063	4,860	9,639	7,471	9,853	9,853	6,647	13,900	9,639	10,415
193	9,692	8,106	4,884	9,692	7,508	9,913	9,913	6,687	13,988	9,692	10,469
194	9,744	8,150	4,908	9,744	7,545	9,974	9,974	6,728	14,077	9,744	10,522
195	9,797	8,193	4,932	9,797	7,582	10,035	10,035	6,768	14,166	9,797	10,575
196	9,850	8,236	4,956	9,850	7,620	10,095	10,095	6,809	14,254	9,850	10,629
197	9,902	8,279	4,980	9,902	7,657	10,156	10,156	6,849	14,343	9,902	10,682
198	9,955	8,322	5,004	9,955	7,694	10,217	10,217	6,890	14,432	9,955	10,736
199	10,007	8,365	5,028	10,007	7,731	10,277	10,277	6,930	14,520	10,007	10,789
200	10,060	8,408	5,051	10,060	7,768	10,338	10,338	6,971	14,609	10,060	10,842

[The tables in this paragraph are printed as amended by S.I. 2011 No. 2065 (*ante*, G–1).]

Cracked trial or guilty plea where the number of pages of prosecution evidence is less than or equal to the PPE Cut-off

G–71   5.—(1) Where in a cracked trial or guilty plea the number of pages of prosecution evidence is less than or equal to the PPE Cut-off specified in the table following paragraph 4(1) as appropriate to the class of offence with which the assisted person is charged, the total fee payable to the litigator will be—

(a) the basic fee, calculated in accordance with the table following sub-paragraph (2) of this paragraph;

(b) the defendant uplift, if any, calculated in accordance with the table following paragraph 9; and

(c) the adjustment for transfers and retrials, if any, calculated in accordance with paragraph 10.

(2) For the purposes of sub-paragraph (1), the basic fee appropriate to a cracked trial or a guilty plea is specified in the table following this sub-paragraph, in accordance with the type of case and Class of offence with which the assisted person is charged.

| Type of case | *Class of Offence* | | | | | | | | | | |
	A	*B*	*C*	*D*	*E*	*F*	*G*	*H*	*I*	*J*	*K*
Cracked trial	991.32	775.15	575.16	941.75	255.38	245.73	254.73	259.73	277.99	991.32	848.07
Guilty plea	745.63	609.44	485.38	708.34	202.41	214.59	214.59	209.28	191.34	745.63	702.29

[The table in this paragraph is printed as amended by S.I. 2011 No. 2065.]

Trial where the number of pages of prosecution evidence is less than or equal to the PPE Cut-off

G–71a   6.—(1) Where in a trial the number of pages of prosecution evidence is less than or equal to the PPE Cut-off specified in the table following paragraph 4(2) as appropriate to the offence for which the assisted person is tried and the length of trial, the total fee payable to the litigator will be—

(a) the basic fee, calculated in accordance with the table following sub-paragraph (2) of this paragraph;

(b) the length of trial proxy, if any, calculated in accordance with the table following sub-paragraph (3);

(c) the defendant uplift, if any, calculated in accordance with the table following paragraph 9; and

(d) the adjustment for transfers and retrials, if any, calculated in accordance with paragraph 10.

(2) For the purposes of sub-paragraph (1), the basic fee appropriate to a trial is specified in the table following this sub-paragraph, in accordance with the offence for which the assisted person is tried.

BASIC FEES FOR TRIALS (£)

| Type of case | *Class of Offence* | | | | | | | | | | |
	A	*B*	*C*	*D*	*E*	*F*	*G*	*H*	*I*	*J*	*K*
Trial	1608.31	1202.92	810.51	1527.89	386.54	391.89	391.89	392.05	391.72	1608.31	1130.76

(3) For the purposes of sub-paragraph (1), the length of trial proxy is specified in the table below, in accordance with the offence for which the assisted person is tried and the length of trial.

Archbold paragraph numbers

LENGTH OF TRIAL PROXY

Trial Length in Days	Trial length proxy A	Trial length proxy B	Trial length proxy C	Trial length proxy D	Trial length proxy E	Trial length proxy F	Trial length proxy G	Trial length proxy H	Trial length proxy I	Trial length proxy J	Trial length proxy K
1	0.00	0.00	0.00	0.00	0.00	0.00	0.00	0.00	0.00	0.00	0.00
2	0.00	0.00	0.00	0.00	0.00	0.00	0.00	0.00	0.00	0.00	0.00
3	276.76	496.31	473.98	262.93	785.29	597.73	597.73	771.17	945.08	276.76	276.76
4	843.60	964.00	924.20	801.42	1,132.77	1,187.50	1,187.50	1,106.66	1,447.59	843.60	843.60
5	1,382.09	1,408.31	1,351.90	1,312.99	1,462.86	1,747.80	1,747.80	1,425.36	1,924.97	1,382.09	1,382.09
6	1,930.05	1,858.61	1,776.66	1,833.56	1,772.17	2,270.67	2,270.67	1,741.43	2,411.61	1,930.05	1,930.05
7	2,469.99	2,303.80	2,203.87	2,346.50	2,099.12	2,824.77	2,824.77	2,059.74	2,890.57	2,469.99	2,469.99
8	3,009.93	2,748.97	2,631.09	2,859.44	2,426.07	3,378.86	3,378.86	2,378.05	3,369.53	3,009.93	3,009.93
9	3,518.82	3,149.63	3,015.57	3,342.88	2,720.32	3,877.54	3,877.54	2,664.53	3,806.50	3,518.82	3,518.82
10	4,027.71	3,550.30	3,400.07	3,826.32	3,014.59	4,376.22	4,376.22	2,951.00	4,243.47	4,027.71	4,027.71
11	4,540.38	3,951.50	3,794.99	4,313.36	3,322.37	4,897.29	4,897.29	3,245.35	4,689.34	4,540.38	4,540.38
12	5,049.58	4,352.20	4,190.10	4,797.10	3,630.24	5,418.70	5,418.70	3,539.33	5,135.58	5,049.58	5,049.58
13	5,558.78	4,752.90	4,576.22	5,280.84	3,937.70	5,940.11	5,940.11	3,826.93	5,574.00	5,558.78	5,558.78
14	6,067.98	5,153.61	4,962.33	5,764.59	4,235.69	6,461.49	6,461.49	4,114.53	6,012.41	6,067.98	6,067.98
15	6,577.18	5,554.31	5,348.45	6,248.32	4,532.77	6,982.85	6,982.85	4,402.14	6,450.82	6,577.18	6,577.18
16	7,086.38	5,955.02	5,734.56	6,732.06	4,829.87	7,503.38	7,503.38	4,689.74	6,889.23	7,086.38	7,086.38
17	7,595.57	6,355.73	6,120.68	7,215.80	5,126.96	8,010.04	8,010.04	4,977.34	7,327.64	7,595.57	7,595.57
18	8,104.77	6,756.43	6,506.79	7,699.54	5,424.05	8,516.70	8,516.70	5,264.94	7,766.05	8,104.77	8,104.77
19	8,613.97	7,157.13	6,892.90	8,183.28	5,721.14	9,023.36	9,023.36	5,552.54	8,204.46	8,613.97	8,613.97
20	9,123.17	7,557.84	7,279.02	8,667.02	6,018.23	9,530.02	9,530.02	5,840.14	8,642.88	9,123.17	9,123.17
21	9,642.08	7,927.97	7,596.29	9,159.97	6,263.74	10,036.68	10,036.68	6,076.67	9,003.14	9,642.08	9,642.08
22	10,160.89	8,298.07	7,913.63	9,652.84	6,509.26	10,543.34	10,543.34	6,313.31	9,363.42	10,160.89	10,160.89
23	10,670.92	8,668.15	8,231.00	10,137.38	6,747.46	11,050.01	11,050.01	6,549.95	9,723.73	10,670.92	10,670.92
24	11,180.95	9,029.83	8,548.37	10,621.91	6,985.68	11,556.66	11,556.66	6,786.59	10,080.08	11,180.95	11,180.95
25	11,691.00	9,391.50	8,864.09	11,106.44	7,223.89	12,063.32	12,063.32	7,019.41	10,431.95	11,691.00	11,691.00
26	12,201.03	9,753.17	9,174.28	11,590.99	7,462.10	12,569.98	12,569.98	7,250.40	10,783.83	12,201.03	12,201.03
27	12,711.06	10,114.85	9,484.49	12,075.51	7,700.31	13,076.64	13,076.64	7,481.38	11,135.70	12,711.06	12,711.06
28	13,221.10	10,476.53	9,794.68	12,560.05	7,938.53	13,583.31	13,583.31	7,712.37	11,487.57	13,221.10	13,221.10

Trial Length in Days	Trial length proxy A	Trial length proxy B	Trial length proxy C	Trial length proxy D	Trial length proxy E	Trial length proxy F	Trial length proxy G	Trial length proxy H	Trial length proxy I	Trial length proxy J	Trial length proxy K
29	13,731.14	10,838.20	10,104.88	13,044.58	8,176.73	14,089.97	14,089.97	7,943.34	11,839.46	13,731.14	13,731.14
30	14,241.17	11,199.87	10,415.07	13,529.11	8,414.94	14,596.63	14,596.63	8,174.32	12,191.33	14,241.17	14,241.17
31	14,751.21	11,561.55	10,725.27	14,013.65	8,653.16	15,103.29	15,103.29	8,405.31	12,543.20	14,751.21	14,751.21
32	15,261.24	11,923.23	11,035.47	14,498.18	8,891.37	15,609.95	15,609.95	8,636.29	12,895.08	15,261.24	15,261.24
33	15,771.29	12,284.90	11,345.67	14,982.72	9,129.58	16,116.60	16,116.60	8,867.28	13,246.95	15,771.29	15,771.29
34	16,281.32	12,646.57	11,655.86	15,467.26	9,367.79	16,623.27	16,623.27	9,098.26	13,598.83	16,281.32	16,281.32
35	16,791.35	13,008.25	11,966.06	15,951.79	9,606.00	17,129.93	17,129.93	9,329.24	13,950.71	16,791.35	16,791.35
36	17,301.39	13,369.92	12,276.26	16,436.32	9,844.21	17,636.59	17,636.59	9,560.22	14,302.58	17,301.39	17,301.39
37	17,811.43	13,731.60	12,586.46	16,920.86	10,082.43	18,143.25	18,143.25	9,791.21	14,654.45	17,811.43	17,811.43
38	18,321.46	14,093.27	12,896.66	17,405.39	10,320.64	18,649.91	18,649.91	10,022.19	15,006.33	18,321.46	18,321.46
39	18,831.50	14,454.94	13,206.85	17,889.92	10,558.84	19,156.57	19,156.57	10,253.17	15,358.20	18,831.50	18,831.50
40	19,312.20	14,785.90	13,329.94	18,346.59	10,654.34	19,641.20	19,641.20	10,353.05	15,651.51	19,312.20	19,312.20
41	19,795.51	15,119.38	13,454.39	18,805.74	10,752.37	20,129.41	20,129.41	10,454.14	15,946.54	19,795.51	19,795.51
42	20,278.95	15,452.95	13,578.88	19,265.01	10,850.45	20,617.80	20,617.80	10,555.27	16,241.65	20,278.95	20,278.95
43	20,762.51	15,786.64	13,703.38	19,724.39	10,948.58	21,106.33	21,106.33	10,656.41	16,536.81	20,762.51	20,762.51
44	21,246.19	16,120.43	13,827.90	20,183.88	11,046.75	21,595.04	21,595.04	10,757.57	16,832.03	21,246.19	21,246.19
45	21,729.98	16,454.31	13,952.45	20,643.48	11,144.95	22,083.91	22,083.91	10,858.77	17,127.33	21,729.98	21,729.98
46	22,213.90	16,788.30	14,077.02	21,103.21	11,243.21	22,572.94	22,572.94	10,959.97	17,422.67	22,213.90	22,213.90
47	22,697.92	17,122.39	14,201.62	21,563.03	11,341.51	23,062.14	23,062.14	11,061.21	17,718.09	22,697.92	22,697.92
48	23,182.08	17,456.59	14,326.24	22,022.98	11,439.86	23,551.50	23,551.50	11,162.47	18,013.57	23,182.08	23,182.08
49	23,666.34	17,790.89	14,450.89	22,483.03	11,538.24	24,041.02	24,041.02	11,263.74	18,309.10	23,666.34	23,666.34
50	24,150.72	18,125.29	14,575.55	22,943.19	11,636.66	24,530.71	24,530.71	11,365.05	18,604.70	24,150.72	24,150.72
51	24,635.23	18,459.79	14,700.25	23,403.47	11,735.14	25,020.57	25,020.57	11,466.37	18,900.37	24,635.23	24,635.23
52	25,119.85	18,794.39	14,824.96	23,863.86	11,833.66	25,510.58	25,510.58	11,567.72	19,196.09	25,119.85	25,119.85
53	25,604.59	19,129.10	14,949.70	24,324.37	11,932.22	26,000.76	26,000.76	11,669.09	19,491.87	25,604.59	25,604.59
54	26,089.45	19,463.91	15,074.46	24,784.97	12,030.83	26,491.11	26,491.11	11,770.48	19,787.72	26,089.45	26,089.45
55	26,574.42	19,798.82	15,199.24	25,245.69	12,129.47	26,981.61	26,981.61	11,871.89	20,083.63	26,574.42	26,574.42
56	27,059.51	20,133.84	15,324.06	25,706.54	12,228.16	27,472.28	27,472.28	11,973.33	20,379.61	27,059.51	27,059.51
57	27,544.72	20,468.95	15,448.89	26,167.49	12,326.89	27,963.11	27,963.11	12,074.78	20,675.64	27,544.72	27,544.72

Trial Length in Days	Trial length proxy A	Trial length proxy B	Trial length proxy C	Trial length proxy D	Trial length proxy E	Trial length proxy F	Trial length proxy G	Trial length proxy H	Trial length proxy I	Trial length proxy J	Trial length proxy K
58	28,030.05	20,804.17	15,573.74	26,628.55	12,425.63	28,454.11	28,454.11	12,176.26	20,971.74	28,030.05	28,030.05
59	28,515.50	21,139.50	15,698.63	27,089.73	12,524.37	28,945.28	28,945.28	12,277.77	21,267.90	28,515.50	28,515.50
60	29,001.06	21,474.92	15,823.53	27,551.00	12,623.11	29,436.60	29,436.60	12,379.29	21,564.12	29,001.06	29,001.06
61	29,486.75	21,810.44	15,948.46	28,012.41	12,721.86	29,928.09	29,928.09	12,480.84	21,860.41	29,486.75	29,486.75
62	29,972.54	22,146.08	16,073.41	28,473.92	12,820.60	30,419.74	30,419.74	12,582.42	22,156.76	29,972.54	29,972.54
63	30,458.47	22,481.80	16,198.38	28,935.55	12,919.34	30,911.56	30,911.56	12,684.01	22,453.17	30,458.47	30,458.47
64	30,944.50	22,817.64	16,323.39	29,397.28	13,018.08	31,403.54	31,403.54	12,785.63	22,749.63	30,944.50	30,944.50
65	31,430.66	23,153.57	16,448.41	29,859.12	13,116.82	31,895.69	31,895.69	12,887.26	23,046.17	31,430.66	31,430.66
66	31,916.93	23,489.62	16,573.46	30,321.09	13,215.56	32,387.99	32,387.99	12,988.92	23,342.77	31,916.93	31,916.93
67	32,403.32	23,825.76	16,698.52	30,783.16	13,314.30	32,880.47	32,880.47	13,090.60	23,639.42	32,403.32	32,403.32
68	32,889.83	24,162.01	16,823.62	31,245.34	13,413.04	33,373.11	33,373.11	13,192.31	23,936.14	32,889.83	32,889.83
69	33,376.46	24,498.35	16,948.73	31,707.63	13,511.78	33,865.90	33,865.90	13,294.04	24,232.93	33,376.46	33,376.46
70	33,863.20	24,834.80	17,073.87	32,170.04	13,610.52	34,358.87	34,358.87	13,395.79	24,529.77	33,863.20	33,863.20
71	34,350.07	25,171.35	17,199.04	32,632.57	13,709.26	34,851.99	34,851.99	13,497.57	24,826.68	34,350.07	34,350.07
72	34,837.05	25,508.01	17,324.22	33,095.20	13,808.00	35,345.28	35,345.28	13,599.36	25,123.65	34,837.05	34,837.05
73	35,324.14	25,844.77	17,449.44	33,557.95	13,906.74	35,838.74	35,838.74	13,701.17	25,420.68	35,324.14	35,324.14
74	35,811.36	26,181.63	17,574.67	34,020.80	14,005.48	36,332.36	36,332.36	13,803.02	25,717.78	35,811.36	35,811.36
75	36,298.70	26,518.59	17,699.93	34,483.76	14,104.22	36,826.14	36,826.14	13,904.89	26,014.94	36,298.70	36,298.70
76	36,786.15	26,855.65	17,825.21	34,946.85	14,202.96	37,320.09	37,320.09	14,006.77	26,312.15	36,786.15	36,786.15
77	37,273.73	27,192.82	17,950.52	35,410.04	14,301.70	37,814.19	37,814.19	14,108.67	26,609.43	37,273.73	37,273.73
78	37,761.41	27,530.09	18,075.85	35,873.35	14,400.44	38,308.47	38,308.47	14,210.60	26,906.77	37,761.41	37,761.41
79	38,249.23	27,867.46	18,201.20	36,336.77	14,499.18	38,802.91	38,802.91	14,312.56	27,204.19	38,249.23	38,249.23
80	38,737.15	28,204.93	18,326.58	36,800.29	14,597.92	39,297.51	39,297.51	14,414.54	27,501.65	38,737.15	38,737.15
81	39,225.19	28,542.51	18,451.97	37,263.94	14,696.66	39,792.27	39,792.27	14,516.54	27,799.18	39,225.19	39,225.19
82	39,713.35	28,880.19	18,577.40	37,727.69	14,795.40	40,287.21	40,287.21	14,618.55	28,096.77	39,713.35	39,713.35
83	40,201.63	29,217.97	18,702.85	38,191.56	14,894.14	40,782.29	40,782.29	14,720.60	28,394.43	40,201.63	40,201.63
84	40,690.03	29,555.86	18,828.31	38,655.53	14,992.89	41,277.55	41,277.55	14,822.66	28,692.14	40,690.03	40,690.03
85	41,178.54	29,893.84	18,953.81	39,119.62	15,091.63	41,772.98	41,772.98	14,924.75	28,989.92	41,178.54	41,178.54
86	41,667.18	30,231.93	19,079.34	39,583.83	15,190.37	42,268.55	42,268.55	15,026.86	29,287.77	41,667.18	41,667.18

Trial Length in Days	Trial length proxy A	Trial length proxy B	Trial length proxy C	Trial length proxy D	Trial length proxy E	Trial length proxy F	Trial length proxy G	Trial length proxy H	Trial length proxy I	Trial length proxy J	Trial length proxy K
87	42,155.93	30,570.12	19,204.88	40,048.14	15,289.11	42,764.31	42,764.31	15,129.00	29,585.68	42,155.93	42,155.93
88	42,644.81	30,908.42	19,330.44	40,512.57	15,387.85	43,260.22	43,260.22	15,231.15	29,883.64	42,644.81	42,644.81
89	43,133.80	31,246.81	19,456.03	40,977.11	15,486.59	43,756.29	43,756.29	15,333.33	30,181.67	43,133.80	43,133.80
90	43,622.90	31,585.31	19,581.64	41,441.75	15,585.33	44,252.53	44,252.53	15,435.52	30,479.76	43,622.90	43,622.90
91	44,112.13	31,923.91	19,707.28	41,906.52	15,684.07	44,748.94	44,748.94	15,537.75	30,777.91	44,112.13	44,112.13
92	44,601.46	32,262.61	19,832.94	42,371.40	15,782.81	45,245.50	45,245.50	15,639.99	31,076.13	44,601.46	44,601.46
93	45,090.93	32,601.42	19,958.62	42,836.38	15,881.55	45,742.23	45,742.23	15,742.26	31,374.41	45,090.93	45,090.93
94	45,580.50	32,940.33	20,084.33	43,301.48	15,980.29	46,239.13	46,239.13	15,844.55	31,672.75	45,580.50	45,580.50
95	46,070.20	33,279.34	20,210.06	43,766.69	16,079.03	46,736.19	46,736.19	15,946.87	31,971.15	46,070.20	46,070.20
96	46,560.02	33,618.46	20,335.82	44,232.02	16,177.77	47,233.40	47,233.40	16,049.19	32,269.62	46,560.02	46,560.02
97	47,049.95	33,957.68	20,461.60	44,697.46	16,276.51	47,730.79	47,730.79	16,151.51	32,568.14	47,049.95	47,049.95
98	47,540.00	34,297.00	20,587.40	45,163.00	16,375.25	48,228.34	48,228.34	16,253.84	32,866.73	47,540.00	47,540.00
99	48,030.17	34,636.42	20,713.23	45,628.66	16,473.99	48,726.06	48,726.06	16,356.16	33,165.39	48,030.17	48,030.17
100	48,520.45	34,975.94	20,839.07	46,094.43	16,572.73	49,223.93	49,223.93	16,458.49	33,464.09	48,520.45	48,520.45
101	49,010.86	35,315.57	20,964.94	46,560.32	16,671.47	49,721.97	49,721.97	16,560.81	33,762.88	49,010.86	49,010.86
102	49,501.38	35,655.29	21,090.84	47,026.31	16,770.21	50,220.18	50,220.18	16,663.13	34,061.71	49,501.38	49,501.38
103	49,992.03	35,995.12	21,216.77	47,492.43	16,868.95	50,718.54	50,718.54	16,765.46	34,360.61	49,992.03	49,992.03
104	50,482.78	36,335.06	21,342.70	47,958.65	16,967.69	51,217.08	51,217.08	16,867.78	34,659.57	50,482.78	50,482.78
105	50,973.66	36,675.10	21,468.63	48,424.97	17,066.43	51,715.78	51,715.78	16,970.10	34,958.60	50,973.66	50,973.66
106	51,464.66	37,015.23	21,594.56	48,891.42	17,165.17	52,214.52	52,214.52	17,072.43	35,257.69	51,464.66	51,464.66
107	51,955.77	37,355.44	21,720.49	49,357.97	17,263.91	52,713.27	52,713.27	17,174.75	35,556.84	51,955.77	51,955.77
108	52,447.00	37,695.64	21,846.43	49,824.66	17,362.66	53,212.02	53,212.02	17,277.07	35,856.05	52,447.00	52,447.00
109	52,938.35	38,035.85	21,972.36	50,291.43	17,461.40	53,710.76	53,710.76	17,379.40	36,155.33	52,938.35	52,938.35
110	53,429.81	38,376.05	22,098.29	50,758.32	17,560.14	54,209.51	54,209.51	17,481.72	36,454.66	53,429.81	53,429.81
111	53,921.40	38,716.26	22,224.22	51,225.34	17,658.88	54,708.26	54,708.26	17,584.04	36,754.06	53,921.40	53,921.40
112	54,413.10	39,056.46	22,350.15	51,692.45	17,757.62	55,207.00	55,207.00	17,686.37	37,053.52	54,413.10	54,413.10
113	54,904.92	39,396.66	22,476.09	52,159.69	17,856.36	55,705.74	55,705.74	17,788.69	37,353.05	54,904.92	54,904.92
114	55,396.86	39,736.87	22,602.02	52,627.02	17,955.10	56,204.49	56,204.49	17,891.01	37,652.64	55,396.86	55,396.86
115	55,888.92	40,077.07	22,727.95	53,094.47	18,053.84	56,703.23	56,703.23	17,993.34	37,952.28	55,888.92	55,888.92

Trial Length in Days	Trial length proxy A	Trial length proxy B	Trial length proxy C	Trial length proxy D	Trial length proxy E	Trial length proxy F	Trial length proxy G	Trial length proxy H	Trial length proxy I	Trial length proxy J	Trial length proxy K
116	56,381.10	40,417.28	22,853.88	53,562.04	18,152.58	57,201.98	57,201.98	18,095.66	38,251.99	56,381.10	56,381.10
117	56,873.39	40,757.48	22,979.81	54,029.72	18,251.32	57,700.72	57,700.72	18,197.98	38,551.77	56,873.39	56,873.39
118	57,365.80	41,097.69	23,105.74	54,497.51	18,350.06	58,199.47	58,199.47	18,300.31	38,851.60	57,365.80	57,365.80
119	57,858.33	41,437.89	23,231.68	54,965.41	18,448.80	58,698.22	58,698.22	18,402.63	39,151.50	57,858.33	57,858.33
120	58,350.98	41,778.09	23,357.61	55,433.43	18,547.54	59,196.96	59,196.96	18,504.95	39,451.46	58,350.98	58,350.98
121	58,843.74	42,118.30	23,483.54	55,901.56	18,646.28	59,695.71	59,695.71	18,607.28	39,751.48	58,843.74	58,843.74
122	59,329.22	42,458.50	23,609.47	56,362.76	18,745.02	60,194.46	60,194.46	18,709.60	40,047.31	59,329.22	59,329.22
123	59,814.69	42,798.71	23,735.40	56,823.97	18,843.76	60,693.20	60,693.20	18,811.92	40,343.13	59,814.69	59,814.69
124	60,300.17	43,134.92	23,859.50	57,285.16	18,942.50	61,190.98	61,190.98	18,914.25	40,638.96	60,300.17	60,300.17
125	60,785.64	43,470.02	23,983.54	57,746.36	19,041.24	61,682.25	61,682.25	19,016.57	40,934.79	60,785.64	60,785.64
126	61,271.11	43,805.11	24,107.58	58,207.57	19,139.98	62,173.51	62,173.51	19,118.83	41,230.61	61,271.11	61,271.11
127	61,756.60	44,140.22	24,231.63	58,668.77	19,238.72	62,664.77	62,664.77	19,219.63	41,526.44	61,756.60	61,756.60
128	62,242.07	44,475.32	24,355.67	59,129.97	19,337.46	63,156.04	63,156.04	19,320.42	41,822.27	62,242.07	62,242.07
129	62,727.54	44,810.42	24,479.71	59,591.17	19,436.20	63,647.30	63,647.30	19,421.20	42,118.09	62,727.54	62,727.54
130	63,213.02	45,145.52	24,603.75	60,052.37	19,534.94	64,138.57	64,138.57	19,521.99	42,413.92	63,213.02	63,213.02
131	63,698.49	45,480.62	24,727.80	60,513.57	19,633.69	64,629.84	64,629.84	19,622.78	42,709.75	63,698.49	63,698.49
132	64,183.97	45,815.73	24,851.84	60,974.77	19,732.43	65,121.10	65,121.10	19,723.57	43,005.57	64,183.97	64,183.97
133	64,669.45	46,150.83	24,975.88	61,435.97	19,831.17	65,612.37	65,612.37	19,824.36	43,301.40	64,669.45	64,669.45
134	65,154.92	46,485.92	25,099.92	61,897.17	19,929.91	66,103.63	66,103.63	19,925.15	43,597.23	65,154.92	65,154.92
135	65,640.39	46,821.03	25,223.97	62,358.37	20,028.65	66,594.89	66,594.89	20,025.93	43,893.06	65,640.39	65,640.39
136	66,125.87	47,156.13	25,348.02	62,819.57	20,127.39	67,086.16	67,086.16	20,126.72	44,188.89	66,125.87	66,125.87
137	66,611.34	47,491.23	25,472.06	63,280.77	20,226.13	67,577.42	67,577.42	20,227.51	44,484.71	66,611.34	66,611.34
138	67,096.82	47,826.33	25,596.10	63,741.98	20,324.87	68,068.69	68,068.69	20,328.30	44,780.54	67,096.82	67,096.82
139	67,582.29	48,161.43	25,720.14	64,203.18	20,423.61	68,559.96	68,559.96	20,429.09	45,076.37	67,582.29	67,582.29
140	68,067.77	48,496.54	25,844.19	64,664.38	20,522.35	69,051.22	69,051.22	20,529.88	45,372.20	68,067.77	68,067.77
141	68,553.24	48,831.63	25,968.23	65,125.58	20,621.09	69,542.49	69,542.49	20,630.66	45,668.02	68,553.24	68,553.24
142	69,038.71	49,166.74	26,092.27	65,586.78	20,719.83	70,033.75	70,033.75	20,731.46	45,963.85	69,038.71	69,038.71
143	69,524.20	49,501.84	26,216.31	66,047.99	20,818.57	70,525.01	70,525.01	20,832.25	46,259.68	69,524.20	69,524.20
144	70,009.67	49,836.94	26,340.36	66,509.19	20,917.31	71,016.28	71,016.28	20,933.03	46,555.50	70,009.67	70,009.67

Trial Length in Days	Trial length proxy A	Trial length proxy B	Trial length proxy C	Trial length proxy D	Trial length proxy E	Trial length proxy F	Trial length proxy G	Trial length proxy H	Trial length proxy I	Trial length proxy J	Trial length proxy K
145	70,495.14	50,172.04	26,464.40	66,970.38	21,016.05	71,507.55	71,507.55	21,033.82	46,851.33	70,495.14	70,495.14
146	70,980.62	50,507.14	26,588.44	67,431.59	21,114.79	71,998.81	71,998.81	21,134.60	47,147.16	70,980.62	70,980.62
147	71,466.09	50,842.25	26,712.49	67,892.79	21,213.53	72,490.07	72,490.07	21,235.40	47,442.98	71,466.09	71,466.09
148	71,951.57	51,177.34	26,836.53	68,354.00	21,312.27	72,981.34	72,981.34	21,336.19	47,738.81	71,951.57	71,951.57
149	72,437.05	51,512.44	26,960.57	68,815.19	21,411.01	73,472.60	73,472.60	21,436.97	48,034.64	72,437.05	72,437.05
150	72,922.52	51,847.55	27,084.61	69,276.39	21,509.75	73,963.86	73,963.86	21,537.76	48,330.46	72,922.52	72,922.52
151	73,407.99	52,182.65	27,208.66	69,737.60	21,608.49	74,455.13	74,455.13	21,638.55	48,626.29	73,407.99	73,407.99
152	73,893.47	52,517.74	27,332.70	70,198.80	21,707.23	74,946.39	74,946.39	21,739.34	48,922.12	73,893.47	73,893.47
153	74,378.94	52,852.85	27,456.74	70,660.00	21,805.97	75,437.66	75,437.66	21,840.13	49,217.94	74,378.94	74,378.94
154	74,864.42	53,187.95	27,580.78	71,121.20	21,904.71	75,928.92	75,928.92	21,940.92	49,513.77	74,864.42	74,864.42
155	75,349.90	53,523.06	27,704.83	71,582.40	22,003.46	76,420.19	76,420.19	22,041.70	49,809.60	75,349.90	75,349.90
156	75,835.37	53,858.15	27,828.87	72,043.61	22,102.20	76,911.46	76,911.46	22,142.49	50,105.42	75,835.37	75,835.37
157	76,320.84	54,193.25	27,952.91	72,504.80	22,200.94	77,402.71	77,402.71	22,243.29	50,401.25	76,320.84	76,320.84
158	76,806.32	54,528.36	28,076.95	72,966.01	22,299.68	77,893.98	77,893.98	22,344.07	50,697.08	76,806.32	76,806.32
159	77,291.80	54,863.46	28,201.00	73,427.21	22,398.42	78,385.25	78,385.25	22,444.86	50,992.90	77,291.80	77,291.80
160	77,777.27	55,198.56	28,325.05	73,888.41	22,497.16	78,876.51	78,876.51	22,545.65	51,288.73	77,777.27	77,777.27
161	78,262.75	55,533.66	28,449.09	74,349.61	22,595.90	79,367.78	79,367.78	22,646.43	51,584.56	78,262.75	78,262.75
162	78,748.22	55,868.76	28,573.13	74,810.81	22,694.64	79,859.05	79,859.05	22,747.23	51,880.38	78,748.22	78,748.22
163	79,233.69	56,203.86	28,697.17	75,272.02	22,793.38	80,350.31	80,350.31	22,848.02	52,176.21	79,233.69	79,233.69
164	79,719.17	56,538.96	28,821.22	75,733.22	22,892.12	80,841.57	80,841.57	22,948.80	52,472.04	79,719.17	79,719.17
165	80,204.65	56,874.07	28,945.26	76,194.41	22,990.86	81,332.84	81,332.84	23,049.59	52,767.86	80,204.65	80,204.65
166	80,690.12	57,209.17	29,069.30	76,655.62	23,089.60	81,824.10	81,824.10	23,150.38	53,063.69	80,690.12	80,690.12
167	81,175.59	57,544.26	29,193.34	77,116.82	23,188.34	82,315.37	82,315.37	23,251.17	53,359.52	81,175.59	81,175.59
168	81,661.07	57,879.37	29,317.39	77,578.03	23,287.08	82,806.64	82,806.64	23,351.96	53,655.34	81,661.07	81,661.07
169	82,146.54	58,214.47	29,441.43	78,039.22	23,385.82	83,297.90	83,297.90	23,452.75	53,951.17	82,146.54	82,146.54
170	82,632.02	58,549.57	29,565.47	78,500.42	23,484.56	83,789.17	83,789.17	23,553.53	54,247.00	82,632.02	82,632.02
171	83,117.50	58,884.67	29,689.51	78,961.63	23,583.30	84,280.43	84,280.43	23,654.32	54,542.83	83,117.50	83,117.50
172	83,602.97	59,219.77	29,813.56	79,422.83	23,682.04	84,771.69	84,771.69	23,755.11	54,838.66	83,602.97	83,602.97
173	84,088.44	59,554.88	29,937.60	79,884.03	23,780.78	85,262.95	85,262.95	23,855.90	55,134.49	84,088.44	84,088.44

Trial Length in Days	Trial length proxy A	Trial length proxy B	Trial length proxy C	Trial length proxy D	Trial length proxy E	Trial length proxy F	Trial length proxy G	Trial length proxy H	Trial length proxy I	Trial length proxy J	Trial length proxy K
174	84,573.92	59,889.97	30,061.64	80,345.23	23,879.52	85,754.22	85,754.22	23,956.69	55,430.31	84,573.92	84,573.92
175	85,059.40	60,225.07	30,185.69	80,806.43	23,978.26	86,245.48	86,245.48	24,057.47	55,726.14	85,059.40	85,059.40
176	85,544.87	60,560.18	30,309.73	81,267.63	24,077.00	86,736.75	86,736.75	24,158.26	56,021.97	85,544.87	85,544.87
177	86,030.35	60,895.28	30,433.77	81,728.83	24,175.74	87,228.01	87,228.01	24,259.06	56,317.79	86,030.35	86,030.35
178	86,515.82	61,230.38	30,557.81	82,190.03	24,274.49	87,719.28	87,719.28	24,359.84	56,613.62	86,515.82	86,515.82
179	87,001.29	61,565.48	30,681.86	82,651.23	24,373.23	88,210.54	88,210.54	24,460.63	56,909.45	87,001.29	87,001.29
180	87,486.77	61,900.58	30,805.90	83,112.43	24,471.97	88,701.80	88,701.80	24,561.42	57,205.27	87,486.77	87,486.77
181	87,972.25	62,235.69	30,929.95	83,573.63	24,570.71	89,193.07	89,193.07	24,662.20	57,501.10	87,972.25	87,972.25
182	88,457.72	62,570.78	31,053.99	84,034.83	24,669.45	89,684.34	89,684.34	24,763.00	57,796.93	88,457.72	88,457.72
183	88,943.20	62,905.89	31,178.03	84,496.04	24,766.77	90,175.60	90,175.60	24,863.79	58,092.75	88,943.20	88,943.20
184	89,428.67	63,240.99	31,302.08	84,957.24	24,864.03	90,666.87	90,666.87	24,964.57	58,388.58	89,428.67	89,428.67
185	89,914.14	63,576.09	31,426.12	85,418.43	24,961.29	91,158.14	91,158.14	25,065.36	58,684.41	89,914.14	89,914.14
186	90,399.63	63,911.19	31,550.16	85,879.64	25,058.55	91,649.40	91,649.40	25,166.15	58,980.23	90,399.63	90,399.63
187	90,885.10	64,246.29	31,674.20	86,340.84	25,155.81	92,140.66	92,140.66	25,266.94	59,276.06	90,885.10	90,885.10
188	91,370.57	64,581.39	31,798.25	86,802.05	25,253.07	92,631.93	92,631.93	25,367.73	59,571.89	91,370.57	91,370.57
189	91,856.04	64,916.49	31,922.29	87,263.24	25,350.33	93,123.19	93,123.19	25,468.52	59,867.71	91,856.04	91,856.04
190	92,341.52	65,251.59	32,046.33	87,724.44	25,447.59	93,614.46	93,614.46	25,569.30	60,163.54	92,341.52	92,341.52
191	92,827.00	65,586.70	32,170.37	88,185.65	25,544.85	94,105.73	94,105.73	25,670.09	60,459.37	92,827.00	92,827.00
192	93,312.47	65,921.80	32,294.42	88,646.85	25,642.11	94,596.99	94,596.99	25,770.89	60,755.19	93,312.47	93,312.47
193	93,797.95	66,256.89	32,418.46	89,108.05	25,739.37	95,088.26	95,088.26	25,871.67	61,051.02	93,797.95	93,797.95
194	94,283.42	66,592.00	32,542.50	89,569.25	25,836.63	95,579.52	95,579.52	25,972.46	61,346.85	94,283.42	94,283.42
195	94,768.89	66,927.10	32,666.54	90,030.45	25,933.89	96,070.78	96,070.78	26,073.25	61,642.67	94,768.89	94,768.89
196	95,254.37	67,262.20	32,790.59	90,491.66	26,031.15	96,562.05	96,562.05	26,174.03	61,938.50	95,254.37	95,254.37
197	95,739.85	67,597.30	32,914.63	90,952.85	26,128.41	97,053.30	97,053.30	26,274.83	62,234.33	95,739.85	95,739.85
198	96,225.32	67,932.40	33,038.67	91,414.06	26,225.67	97,544.57	97,544.57	26,375.62	62,530.15	96,225.32	96,225.32
199	96,710.80	68,267.51	33,162.71	91,875.26	26,322.93	98,035.84	98,035.84	26,476.40	62,825.98	96,710.80	96,710.80
200	97,196.27	68,602.60	33,286.76	92,336.46	26,420.19	98,527.10	98,527.10	26,577.19	63,121.81	97,196.27	97,196.27

[The tables in this paragraph are printed as amended by S.I. 2011 No. 2065 (*ante*, G–1).]

Cracked trials and guilty pleas where the number of pages of prosecution evidence exceeds the PPE Cut-off

7.—(1) Where in a cracked trial or guilty plea the number of pages of prosecution evidence exceeds the PPE Cut-off specified in the tables following paragraph 4(1) as appropriate to the offence with which the assisted person is charged, the total fee payable to the litigator will be—

(a) the final fee, calculated in accordance with sub-paragraph (2) of this paragraph;

(b) the defendant uplift, if any, calculated in accordance with the table following paragraph 9; and

(c) the adjustment for transfers and retrials, if any, calculated in accordance with paragraph 10.

(2) For the purposes of sub-paragraph (1), the final fee payable to a litigator in a cracked trial or guilty plea will be calculated in accordance with the following formula—

$$F = I + (D \times i)$$

(3) In the formula in sub-paragraph (2)—

F is the amount of the final fee;

I is the initial fee specified in the tables following this paragraph, as appropriate to the type of case, the offence with which the assisted person is charged and the number of pages of prosecution evidence;

D is the difference between—

(a) the number of pages of prosecution evidence in the case; and

(b) the lower number in the PPE range as specified in the tables following this paragraph, as appropriate to the type of case, the offence with which the assisted person is charged and the number of pages of prosecution evidence in the case;

i is the incremental fee per page of prosecution evidence specified in the tables following this paragraph, as appropriate to the type of case, the offence with which the assisted person is charged and the number of pages of prosecution evidence in the case.

TABLE OF FINAL FEES IN CRACKED TRIALS

Class of Offence	*PPE Range*	*Initial fee (£)*	*Incremental fee per page of prosecution evidence (£)*
A and J	0–79	991.32	0
A and J	80–249	991.32	11.7216
A and J	250–999	2,983.99	7.3571
A and J	1000–2799	8,501.81	4.3001
A and J	2800–4599	16,241.92	4.3001
A and J	4600–6399	23,982.04	3.4135
A and J	6400–8199	30,126.41	3.4135
A and J	8200–9999	36,270.78	3.4135
A and J	10,000	42,411.74	0.0000
B	0–69	771.15	0
B	70–249	771.15	8.5755
B	250–999	2,320.73	4.0137
B	1000–2799	5,331.02	2.6733
B	2800–4599	10,143.02	2.6733
B	4600–6399	14,995.02	2.2478
B	6400–8199	19,001.08	2.2478

Class of Offence	PPE Range	Initial fee (£)	Incremental fee per page of prosecution evidence (£)
B	8200–9999	23,047.12	2.2478
B	10,000	27,090.92	0.0000
C	0–39	575.17	0
C	40–249	575.17	4.2997
C	250–999	1,478.10	2.4611
C	1000–2799	3,323.90	1.5674
C	2800–4599	6,145.18	1.5674
C	4600–6399	8,966.46	1.5674
C	6400–8199	11,787.74	1.5674
C	8200–9999	14,609.03	1.5674
C	10,000	17,428.74	0.0000
D	0–79	941.75	0
D	80–249	941.75	11.1082
D	250–999	2,830.14	6.6941
D	1000–2799	7,850.70	3.9525
D	2800–4599	14,965.19	3.9525
D	4600–6399	22,079.68	3.2433
D	6400–8199	27,917.58	3.2433
D	8200–9999	33,755.47	3.2433
D	10,000	39,590.12	0.0000
E	0–39	255.38	0
E	40–249	255.38	5.0432
E	250–999	1,314.44	1.5958
E	1000–2799	2,511.28	0.6689
E	2800–4599	3,715.35	0.6689
E	4600–6399	4,919.42	0.6689
E	6400–8199	6,123.50	0.6689
E	8200–9999	7,327.57	0.6689
E	10,000	8,530.97	0.0000
F and G	0–49	245.72	0
F and G	50–249	245.72	4.8400
F and G	250–999	1,213.73	1.9622
F and G	1000–2799	2,685.36	0.7636
F and G	2800–4599	4,059.91	0.7636

Class of Offence	PPE Range	Initial fee (£)	Incremental fee per page of prosecution evidence (£)
F and G	4600–6399	5,434.46	0.7636
F and G	6400–8199	6,809.00	0.7636
F and G	8200–9999	8,183.55	0.7636
F and G	10,000	9,557.33	0.0000
H	0–39	259.73	0
H	40–249	259.73	4.6685
H	250–999	1,240.12	1.7046
H	1000–2799	2,518.58	0.7626
H	2800–4599	3,891.28	0.7626
H	4600–6399	5,263.97	0.7626
H	6400–8199	6,636.67	0.7626
H	8200–9999	8,009.37	0.7626
H	10,000	9,381.30	0.0000
I	0–39	278.00	0
I	40–249	278.00	6.4873
I	250–999	1,640.33	2.5353
I	1000–2799	3,541.82	0.9835
I	2800–4599	5,312.17	0.9835
I	4600–6399	7,082.51	0.9835
I	6400–8199	8,852.85	0.9835
I	8200–9999	10,623.20	0.9835
I	10,000	12,392.55	0.0000
K	0–119	848.07	0
K	120–249	848.07	7.1738
K	250–999	1,780.66	5.5001
K	1000–2799	5,905.73	4.8159
K	2800–4599	14,574.29	4.8159
K	4600–6399	23,242.87	4.1067
K	6400–8199	30,634.84	4.1067
K	8200–9999	38,026.81	4.1066
K	10,000	45,414.67	0.0000

[This table is printed as substituted by S.I. 2011 No. 2065 (*ante*, G–1).]

TABLE OF FINAL FEES IN GUILTY PLEAS

Class of Offence	PPE Range	Initial fee (£)	Incremental fee per page of prosecution evidence (£)
A and J	0–79	745.63	0
A and J	80–399	745.63	6.1572
A and J	400–999	2,715.93	3.2471
A and J	1000–2799	4,664.21	2.0766
A and J	2800–4599	8,402.07	2.0766
A and J	4600–6399	12,139.92	1.2255
A and J	6400–8199	14,345.86	1.2255
A and J	8200–9999	16,551.81	1.2255
A and J	10,000	18,756.53	0.0000
B	0–69	609.44	0
B	70–399	609.44	4.9497
B	400–999	2,242.84	2.4934
B	1000–2799	3,738.90	1.5916
B	2800–4599	6,603.75	1.5916
B	4600–6399	9,468.61	1.1661
B	6400–8199	11,567.51	1.1661
B	8200–9999	13,666.41	1.1661
B	10,000	15,764.14	0.0000
C	0–39	485.38	0
C	40–399	485.38	2.9193
C	400–999	1,536.31	1.5971
C	1000–2799	2,494.54	0.8668
C	2800–4599	4,054.72	0.8668
C	4600–6399	5,614.91	0.8668
C	6400–8199	7,175.10	0.8668
C	8200–9999	8,735.29	0.8668
C	10,000	10,294.60	0.0000
D	0–79	708.34	0
D	80–399	708.34	5.7339
D	400–999	2,543.19	3.0095
D	1000–2799	4,348.90	1.8739
D	2800–4599	7,721.86	1.8739

Class of Offence	PPE Range	Initial fee (£)	Incremental fee per page of prosecution evidence (£)
D	4600–6399	11,094.83	1.1647
D	6400–8199	13,191.21	1.1646
D	8200–9999	15,287.57	1.1647
D	10,000	17,382.78	0.0000
E	0–39	202.41	0
E	40–399	202.41	3.2041
E	400–999	1,355.88	1.3732
E	1000–2799	2,179.80	0.5057
E	2800–4599	3,090.08	0.5057
E	4600–6399	4,000.36	0.5057
E	6400–8199	4,910.64	0.5057
E	8200–9999	5,820.92	0.5057
E	10,000	6,730.69	0.0000
F and G	0–49	214.59	0
F and G	50–399	214.59	3.1058
F and G	400–999	1,301.62	1.0840
F and G	1000–2799	1,952.01	0.3488
F and G	2800–4599	2,579.80	0.3488
F and G	4600–6399	3,207.59	0.3488
F and G	6400–8199	3,835.38	0.3488
F and G	8200–9999	4,463.17	0.3488
F and G	10,000	5,090.61	0.0000
H	0–39	209.28	0
H	40–399	209.28	3.0613
H	400–999	1,311.33	1.0852
H	1000–2799	1,962.46	0.3465
H	2800–4599	2,586.14	0.3465
H	4600–6399	3,209.84	0.3465
H	6400–8199	3,833.53	0.3465
H	8200–9999	4,457.23	0.3465
H	10,000	5,080.55	0.0000
I	0–39	191.34	0
I	40–399	191.34	3.4214
I	400–999	1,423.04	1.4936

Class of Offence	PPE Range	Initial fee (£)	Incremental fee per page of prosecution evidence (£)
I	1000–2799	2,319.22	0.5581
I	2800–4599	3,323.86	0.5581
I	4600–6399	4,328.49	0.5581
I	6400–8199	5,333.13	0.5581
I	8200–9999	6,337.78	0.5581
I	10,000	7,341.86	0.0000
K	0–119	702.29	0
K	120–399	702.29	5.7624
K	400–999	2,315.76	3.2075
K	1000–2799	4,240.26	2.9871
K	2800–4599	9,617.04	2.9871
K	4600–6399	14,993.82	2.2779
K	6400–8199	19,094.01	2.2779
K	8200–9999	23,194.20	2.2779
K	10,000	27,292.10	0.0000

[This table is printed as substituted by S.I. 2011 No. 2065 (*ante*, G–1).]

Trials where the number of pages of prosecution evidence exceeds the PPE Cut-off

8.—(1) Where in a trial the number of pages of prosecution evidence exceeds the PPE Cut-off **G–72a** figure specified in the table following paragraph 4(2) as appropriate to the offence for which the assisted person is tried and the length of trial, the total fee payable to the litigator will be—

    (a) the final fee, calculated in accordance with sub-paragraph (2) of this paragraph;

    (b) the defendant uplift, if any, calculated in accordance with the table following paragraph 9; and

    (c) the adjustment for transfers and retrials, if any, calculated in accordance with paragraph 10.

(2) For the purposes of sub-paragraph (1), the final fee will be calculated in accordance with the following formula—

$$F = I + (D \times i)$$

(3) In the formula in sub-paragraph (2)—

    F is the amount of the final fee;

    I is the initial fee specified in the table following this paragraph, as appropriate to the offence for which the assisted person is tried and the number of pages of prosecution evidence;

    D is the difference between—

    (a) the number of pages of prosecution evidence in the case; and

(b) the lower number in the PPE range as specified in the table following this paragraph, as appropriate to the offence for which the assisted person is tried and the number of pages of prosecution evidence in the case;

i is the incremental fee per page of prosecution evidence specified in the table following this paragraph, as appropriate to the offence for which the assisted person is tried and the number of pages of prosecution evidence in the case.

TABLE OF FINAL FEES IN TRIALS

Offence Class	PPE Range	Initial Fee	Incremental fee per page
B	0–69	1,202.92	0
B	70–199	1,202.92	14.0353
B	200–499	3,027.51	12.5398
B	500–899	6,789.46	10.5557
B	900–1299	11,011.74	8.8680
B	1300–1999	14,558.94	7.7722
B	2000–3299	19,999.46	7.7722
B	3300–4999	30,103.28	7.7722
B	5000–5999	43,315.97	7.7722
B	6000–7999	51,088.14	7.7722
B	8000–8999	66,632.48	7.7722
B	9000–9999	74,404.65	7.7722
B	10000	82,169.05	0
C	0–39	810.51	0
C	40–299	810.51	11.5783
C	300–799	3,820.87	10.1155
C	800–1249	8,878.62	8.4660
C	1250–1999	12,688.32	7.4854
C	2000–3199	18,302.39	5.1761
C	3200–4559	24,513.74	5.1761
C	4560–5919	31,553.29	5.1761
C	5920–7279	38,592.83	5.1761
C	7280–8639	45,632.37	5.1761
C	8640–9999	52,671.91	5.1762
C	10000	59,706.30	0
D	0–79	1,527.89	0
D	80–209	1,527.89	17.2578
D	210–699	3,771.41	13.1781
D	700–1049	10,228.68	11.0609
D	1050–1999	14,100.00	9.5912
D	2000–3599	23,211.67	8.7658
D	3600–5199	37,236.90	8.7658
D	5200–6799	51,262.14	8.7658
D	6800–8399	65,287.39	8.7658
D	8400–9999	79,312.63	8.7658
D	10000	93,329.10	0
E	0–39	386.54	0
E	40–69	386.54	10.4287
E	70–129	699.40	9.3950
E	130–599	1,263.10	9.0869
E	600–1349	5,533.96	5.9649
E	1350–2999	10,007.63	2.6174

Offence Class	PPE Range	Initial Fee	Incremental fee per page
E	3000–4749	14,326.32	2.6174
E	4750–6499	18,906.75	2.6174
E	6500–8249	23,487.17	2.6174
E	8250–9999	28,067.60	2.6174
E	10000	32,645.40	0
F and G	0–49	391.89	0
F and G	50–229	391.89	8.0098
F and G	230–699	1,833.66	7.6326
F and G	700–1399	5,420.98	6.1357
F and G	1400–1949	9,715.95	4.7354
F and G	1950–3549	12,320.41	2.3624
F and G	3550–5149	16,100.18	2.3624
F and G	5150–6749	19,879.95	2.3624
F and G	6750–8349	23,659.72	2.3624
F and G	8350–9999	27,439.49	2.3624
F and G	10000	31,335.02	0
H	0–39	392.05	0
H	40–249	392.05	9.4203
H	250–619	2,370.32	7.8338
H	620–1299	5,268.81	5.8194
H	1300–2999	9,226.02	4.6188
H	3000–4999	17,077.91	2.4911
H	5000–5999	22,060.10	2.4910
H	6000–6999	24,551.12	2.4911
H	7000–7999	27,042.22	2.4911
H	8000–8999	29,533.32	2.4911
H	9000–9999	32,024.42	2.4911
H	10000	34,513.02	0
I	0–39	391.72	0
I	40–369	391.72	10.0165
I	370–799	3,697.16	9.9618
I	800–1299	7,980.75	9.8555
I	1300–2699	12,908.52	7.7641
I	2700–4199	23,778.23	3.3365
I	4200–5359	28,783.04	3.3365
I	5360–6519	32,653.42	3.3365
I	6520–7679	36,523.80	3.3366
I	7680–8839	40,394.20	3.3365
I	8840–9999	44,264.58	3.3365
I	10000	48,131.63	0
J and A	0–79	1,608.31	0
J and A	80–209	1,608.31	18.1662
J and A	210–699	3,969.91	13.8717
J and A	700–1049	10,767.03	11.6431
J and A	1050–1999	14,842.10	10.0960
J and A	2000–3599	24,433.34	9.2271
J and A	3600–5199	39,196.75	9.2271
J and A	5200–6799	53,960.15	9.2271

Offence Class	PPE Range	Initial Fee	Incremental fee per page
J and A	6800–8399	68,723.57	9.2271
J and A	8400–9999	83,486.98	9.2271
J and A	10000	98,241.16	0
K	0–119	1,130.76	0
K	120–734	1,130.76	9.4875
K	735–1289	6,965.55	9.5522
K	1290–2399	12,267.04	9.7237
K	2400–4499	23,060.31	9.6873
K	4500–7999	43,403.55	9.6873
K	8000–8399	77,308.93	9.6872
K	8400–8799	81,183.82	9.6872
K	8800–9199	85,058.72	9.6873
K	9200–9599	88,933.63	9.6872
K	9600–9999	92,808.53	9.6872
K	10000	96,673.74	0

[This table is printed as amended by S.I. 2009 No. 1843 (*ante*, G–1); and S.I. 2011 No. 2065 (*ante*, G–1).]

PART 2A

FIXED FEE FOR GUILTY PLEAS AND CRACKED TRIALS

Scope of Part 2A

★G–73   8A. This Part applies to a guilty plea or cracked trial in a case committed or sent for trial to the Crown Court on the election of a defendant where the magistrates' court has determined the case to be suitable for summary trial.

8B. The fee payable to a litigator in relation to a guilty plea or cracked trial to which this Part applies must be £362 per proceedings.

[This Part was inserted by S.I. 2011 No. 2065 (*ante*, G–1). Paragraph 8A is printed as amended by S.I. 2012 No. 1343 (*ante*, G–1).]

PART 2B

DEFENDANT UPLIFTS, RETRIALS AND TRANSFERS

Defendant uplifts

G–73a   9.—(1) The defendant uplift payable to a litigator will be calculated in accordance with the table following sub-paragraph (3).

(2) Only one defendant uplift will be payable in each case.

(3) In the table following this paragraph, the total fee means—

    (a) in a cracked trial or guilty plea where the number of pages of prosecution evidence does not exceed the PPE Cut-off specified in the table following paragraph 4(1), the basic fee specified in the table following paragraph 5(2);

    (b) in a trial where the number of pages of prosecution evidence does not exceed the PPE Cut-off specified in the table following paragraph 4(2), the basic fee specified in the table following paragraph 6(2) plus the length of trial proxy specified in the table following paragraph 6(3);

    (c) in a cracked trial or guilty plea where the number of pages of prosecution evidence exceeds the PPE Cut-off specified in the table following paragraph 4(1), the final fee, as calculated in accordance with paragraph 7(2); and

    (d) in a trial where the number of pages of prosecution evidence exceeds the PPE Cut-off specified in the table following paragraph 4(2), the final fee, as calculated in accordance with paragraph 8(2);

    (e) where appropriate the fee set out in paragraph 8B.

(4) In a case where the representation of one defendant would attract a fixed fee under Part 2A and the representation of one or more of the other defendants would attract a graduated fee under Part 2, the total fee is the fee falling within whichever of sub-paragraphs (3)(a) to (d) is appropriate.

Defendant uplifts

Total number of defendants represented by litigator	Percentage uplift to total fee
2–4	20%
5+	30%

[Paragraph 9 is printed as amended by S.I. 2011 No. 2065 (*ante*, G–1).]

Retrials and transfers

10.—(1) Where following a trial an order is made for a retrial and the same litigator acts for the   **G–73b**
assisted person at both trials that litigator will receive—

    (a) in respect of the first trial, a fee calculated in accordance with the provisions of this Schedule; and

    (b) in respect of the retrial, 25% of the fee, as appropriate to the circumstances and timing of the retrial, in accordance with the provisions of this Schedule.

  (2) Where—

    (a) a case is transferred to a new litigator; or

    (b) a retrial is ordered and a new litigator acts for the assisted person at the retrial,

the original litigator and the new litigator must receive a percentage of the total fee, in accordance with the table following this paragraph, as appropriate to the circumstances and timing of the retrial, transfer or withdrawal of the representation order.

  (3) In sub-paragraph (2), "transfer" includes the grant of a representation order to an individual who, immediately before the grant of the order—

    (a) had represented himself; or

    (b) had been represented (otherwise than under a representation order) by the litigator named in the order,

and for the purposes of that sub-paragraph the litigator shall be treated as a new litigator.

  (4) For the purposes of sub-paragraph (2), a case is not transferred to a new litigator where—

    (a) a firm of solicitors is named as litigator in the representation order and the solicitor or other appropriately qualified person with responsibility for the case moves to another firm;

    (b) a firm of solicitors is named as litigator in the representation order and the firm changes (whether by merger or acquisition or in some other way), but so that the new firm remains closely related to the firm named in the order; or

    (c) a solicitor or other appropriately qualified person is named as litigator in the representation order and responsibility for the case is transferred to another solicitor or appropriately qualified person in the same firm or a closely related firm.

  (5) For the purposes of sub-paragraph (2), where a case which has been transferred to a new litigator is transferred again, that new litigator—

    (a) shall be treated as the original litigator, where the transfer takes place at any time before the trial or any retrial;

    (b) shall be treated as a new litigator, where the transfer takes place during the trial or any retrial; and

    (c) shall not receive any fee, where the transfer takes place after the trial or any retrial but before the sentencing hearing.

  (6) Where a representation order is withdrawn before the case ends, a litigator must receive a percentage of the total fee, in accordance with the table following this paragraph, as appropriate to the circumstances and timing of a transfer.

  (7) In the table following this paragraph, the total fee means—

    (a) in a cracked trial or guilty plea in a case to which Part 2 applies, where the number of pages of prosecution evidence is less than or equal to the PPE Cut-off specified in the table following paragraph 4(1), the basic fee as set out in the table following paragraph 5(2);

    (b) in a trial where the number of pages of prosecution evidence is less than or equal to the PPE Cut-off specified in the table following paragraph 4(2), the basic fee specified in the table following paragraph 6(2) plus the length of trial proxy specified in the table following paragraph 6(3);

    (c) in a cracked trial or guilty plea in a case to which Part 2 applies, where the number of pages of prosecution evidence exceeds the PPE Cut-off specified in the table following paragraph 4(1), the final fee as calculated in accordance with paragraph 7(2);

(d) in a trial where the number of pages of prosecution evidence exceeds the PPE Cut-off specified in the table following paragraph 4(2), the final fee, as calculated in accordance with paragraph 8(2);

(e) in a cracked trial or guilty plea in a case to which Part 2A applies, the fixed fee set out in paragraph 8B.

(8) Where a case becomes a Very High Cost Case after a representation order has been granted and is transferred from the litigator named on the representation order to a new litigator—

(a) the original litigator will be remunerated in accordance with the individual Very High Cost Case contract entered into by that litigator; and

(b) the new litigator will be remunerated in accordance with the individual Very High Cost Case contract entered into by that litigator.

(9) Where a case becomes a Very High Cost Case after a representation order has been granted and the representation order is withdrawn before the end of the case, the litigator will be remunerated in accordance with the table following this paragraph as appropriate to the circumstances and timing of the withdrawal.

(10) Sub-paragraph (11) applies where—

(a) the case is a case to which Part 2A would apply if it resulted in a cracked trial or guilty plea; and

(b) at the time the case is transferred to a new litigator in accordance with sub-paragraph (2) it is not known whether the case would result in a cracked trial or guilty plea or whether it would proceed to trial.

(11) Where this sub-paragraph applies—

(a) for the purpose of a claim by the original litigator at the time of the transfer of the case, "total fee" in the table following this paragraph, means the fixed fee set out in paragraph 8B;

(b) the original litigator may, if the case proceeds to trial, claim the difference between the payment received at the time of transfer of the case and the payment that would have been due at that time if that payment had been based on the case proceeding to trial.

(12) A litigator may not be treated both as an original litigator and as a new litigator in a case.

[This paragraph is printed as substituted by S.I. 2011 No. 2065 (*ante*, G–1). It is open to question whether the drafting of sub-para. (8)(a) reflects what was intended.]

RETRIALS AND TRANSFERS

Scenario	Percentage of the total fee	Case type used to determine total fee	Claim period
Cracked trial before retrial, where there is no change of litigator	25%	Cracked trial	—
Retrial, where there is no change of litigator	25%	Trial	—
Up to and including plea and case management hearing transfer (original litigator)	25%	Cracked trial	—
Up to and including plea and case management hearing transfer — guilty plea (new litigator)	100%	Guilty plea	—
Up to and including plea and case management hearing transfer — cracked trial (new litigator)	100%	Cracked trial	—
Up to and including plea and case management hearing transfer — trial (new litigator)	100%	Trial	—
Before trial transfer (original litigator)	75%	Cracked trial	—
Before trial transfer — cracked trial (new litigator)	100%	Cracked trial	—

Scenario	Percentage of the total fee	Case type used to determine total fee	Claim period
Before trial transfer — trial (new litigator)	100%	Trial	—
During trial transfer (original litigator)	100%	Trial	Claim up to and including the day before the transfer
During trial transfer (new litigator)	50%	Trial	Claim for the full trial length
Transfer after trial or guilty plea and before sentencing hearing (original litigator)	100%	Trial, cracked trial or guilty plea as appropriate	Claim for the full trial length, excluding the length of the sentencing hearing
Transfer after trial or guilty plea and before sentencing hearing (new litigator)	10%	Trial	Claim for one day, or for the length of the sentencing hearing if longer than one day
Transfer before retrial (original litigator)	25%	Cracked trial	—
Transfer before cracked retrial (new litigator)	50%	Cracked trial	
Transfer before retrial (new litigator)	50%	Trial	Claim for the full retrial length
Transfer during retrial (original litigator)	25%	Trial	Claim up to and including the day before the transfer
Transfer during retrial (new litigator)	50%	Trial	Claim for the full retrial length
Transfer after retrial or cracked retrial and before sentencing hearing (original litigator)	25%	Trial or cracked trial as appropriate	Claim for the full retrial length, excluding the length of the sentencing hearing
Transfer after retrial or cracked retrial and before sentencing hearing (new litigator)	10%	Trial	Claim for one day, or for the length of the sentencing hearing if longer than one day

[This table is printed as amended by S.I. 2009 No. 1843 (*ante*, G–1); and S.I. 2012 No. 750 (*ante*, G–1).] ★

PART 3

FIXED FEES

General provisions

11.—(1) All work undertaken by a litigator in a case to which Part 2A applies is included within the fee set out in paragraph 8B except for a defendant uplift as provided for in paragraph 17.   **G–74**

(2) Except as provided under this Part, remuneration for all work undertaken by a litigator in a case to which Part 2 applies is included within the fee set out in Part 2 of this schedule as appropriate to—

    (a) the offence for which the assisted person is charged or tried;

    (b) whether the case is a cracked trial, guilty plea or trial; and

    (c) the number of pages of prosecution evidence.

[This paragraph is printed as substituted by S.I. 2011 No. 2065 (*ante*, G–1).]

Fees for appeals and committals for sentence hearings

12. The fee payable to a litigator instructed in—   **G–74a**

(a) an appeal against sentence from a magistrates' court;

(b) an appeal against conviction from a magistrates' court;

(c) a sentencing hearing following a committal for sentence to the Crown Court.

is that set out in the table following paragraph 14.

Fees for hearing subsequent to sentence

G–74b   12A. The fee payable to a litigator instructed in relation to a hearing under an enactment listed in sub-paragraph (2) is that set out in the table following paragraph 14.

(2) The enactments are—

(a) section 1CA of the *Crime and Disorder Act* 1998 (variation and discharge of orders under section 1C);

(b) section 155 of the *Powers of Criminal Courts (Sentencing) Act* 2000 (alteration of Crown Court sentence);

(c) section 74 of the *Serious Organised Crime and Police Act* 2005 (assistance by defendant: review of sentence).

[This paragraph was inserted by S.I. 2009 No. 1843 (*ante*, G–1.]

Fees for contempt proceedings

G–75   13. This paragraph applies to proceedings referred to in section 12(2)(f) of the Act in the Crown Court.

(2) Where, in proceedings to which this paragraph applies, the contempt is alleged to have been committed by a person other than a defendant in a case to which this Schedule applies, remuneration for litigators must be at the rate set out in the table following paragraph 14.

(3) Where, in proceedings to which this paragraph applies, the contempt is alleged to have been committed by the defendant in a case to which this Schedule applies, all work undertaken by the litigator is included within—

(a) the fee payable under Part 2 of this Schedule, or

(b) in proceedings under paragraph 12 or 14, the fixed fee set out in the table following paragraph 14.

Fees for alleged breaches of a Crown Court order

G–75a   14.—(1) This paragraph applies to proceedings in the Crown Court against one assisted person arising out of a single alleged breach of an order of the Crown Court.

(3) ... the fee payable to the litigator in respect of the proceedings to which this paragraph applies is that set out in the table following this sub-paragraph.

[This paragraph is printed as amended by S.I. 2009 No. 1843 (*ante*, G–1.]

FIXED FEES

Type of proceedings	*Paragraph providing for fee*	*Fee payable (£ per proceedings)*
Appeal against sentence from a magistrates' Court	12	170.21
Appeal against conviction from a magistrates' Court	12	382.98
Committal for sentence	12	255.32
Hearing subsequent to sentence	12A	170.21
Contempt proceedings (where contempt is alleged to have been committed by a person other than the defendant)	13(2)	127.66
Alleged breach of a Crown Court order	14(2)	85.11

[This table is printed as amended by S.I. 2009 No. 1843 (*ante*, G–1); S.I 2010 No. 679 (*ante*, G–1); and S.I. 2011 No. 2065 (*ante*, G–1).]

Fees for special preparation

★G–76   15.—(1) This paragraph applies in any case on indictment in the Crown Court—.

(a) where a documentary or pictorial exhibit is served by the prosecution in electronic form and—

(i) the exhibit has never existed in paper form; and

(ii) the appropriate officer does not consider it appropriate to include the exhibit in the pages of prosecution evidence;

(b) in respect of which a fee is payable under Part 2 (other than paragraph 6), where the number of pages of prosecution evidence, as so defined, exceeds 10,000, and the appropriate officer considers it reasonable to make a payment in excess of the fee payable under Part 2.

(2) Where this paragraph applies, a special preparation fee may be paid, in addition to the fee payable under Part 2.

(3) The amount of the special preparation fee must be calculated from the number of hours which the appropriate officer considers reasonable—.

(a) where sub-paragraph (1)(a) applies, to view the prosecution evidence; and

(b) where sub-paragraph (1)(b) applies, to read the excess pages,

and in each case using the rates specified in the table following paragraph 22.

(4) A litigator claiming a special preparation fee must supply such information and documents as may be required by the appropriate officer in support of the claim.

(5) In determining a claim under this paragraph, the appropriate officer must take into account all the relevant circumstances of the case.

[This paragraph is printed as amended by S.I. 2009 No. 1843 (*ante*, G–1); S.I. 2011 No. 2065 (*ante*, G–1); S.I. 2012 No. 750 (*ante*, G–1); and S.I. 2012 No. 1343 (*ante*, G–1).]

As to claims for special preparation fees, see *post*, G–157.

Discontinuance or dismissal of sent or transferred proceedings

16.—(1) This paragraph applies to proceedings which are— ★**G–76a**

(a) sent for trial to the Crown Court ...; or

(b) transferred to the Crown Court under—

    (i) section 4 of the *Criminal Justice Act* 1987 (transfer of serious fraud cases); or

    (ii) section 53 of the *Criminal Justice Act* 1991 (transfer of certain cases involving children).

(2) Where proceedings to which this paragraph applies are discontinued by a notice served under section 23A of the *Prosecution of Offences Act* 1985 (discontinuance of proceedings after accused has been sent for trial) at any time before the prosecution serves its evidence in accordance with the *Crime and Disorder Act 1998 (Service of Prosecution Evidence) Regulations* 2005 the litigator must be paid 50 percent of the Basic fee for a guilty plea, as specified in the table following paragraph 5, as appropriate to the offence for which the assisted person is charged.

(3) Where proceedings to which this paragraph applies are discontinued by a notice served under section 23A of the *Prosecution of Offences Act* 1985 (discontinuance of proceedings after accused has been sent for trial) at any time after the prosecution serves its evidence in accordance with the *Crime and Disorder Act 1998 (Service of Prosecution Evidence) Regulations* 2005, the litigator must be paid a fee calculated in accordance with paragraph 5, or, where appropriate, paragraph 7, as appropriate for representing an assisted person in a guilty plea.

(4) Where an application for dismissal is made under paragraph 2 of Schedule 3 to the *Crime and Disorder Act* 1998, section 6 of the *Criminal Justice Act* 1987 or paragraph 5 of Schedule 6 to the *Criminal Justice Act* 1991, and—

(a) the charge, or charges are dismissed and the assisted person is discharged; or

(b) the case is remitted to the magistrates' court in accordance with paragraph 10(3)(a), 13(2) or 15(3)(a) of Schedule 3 to the *Crime and Disorder Act* 1998,

the litigator instructed in the proceedings must be paid a fee calculated in accordance with paragraph 5, or where appropriate, paragraph 7, as appropriate for representing an assisted person in a guilty plea.

(5) Sub-paragraph (6) applies to—

(a) a plea and case management hearing that takes place after the prosecution serves its evidence; and

(b) any other hearing that takes place before a plea and case management hearing has taken place, but after the prosecution has served its evidence.

(6) Where, at a hearing to which this paragraph applies—

(a) the prosecution offers no evidence and the assisted person is discharged; or

(b) the case is remitted to the magistrates' court in accordance with paragraph 10(3)(a), 13(2) or 15(3)(a) of Schedule 3 to the *Crime and Disorder Act* 1998,

the litigator must be paid a fee calculated in accordance with paragraph 5 or where appropriate paragraph 7, as appropriate for representing an assisted person in a guilty plea.

[This paragraph is printed as amended by S.I. 2012 No. 1343 (*ante*, G–1).]

Defendant uplifts

17.—(1) Where a litigator represents more than one assisted person in proceedings referred to in **G–77**
paragraph 16(2), (3), (4) or (5), a defendant uplift will be payable.

(2) The defendant uplift will be calculated in accordance with the table following this paragraph.

(3) In the table following this paragraph, the total fee means—

(a) the fee specified in sub-paragraph (2) of paragraph 16 where that sub-paragraph applies; or

(b) the basic fee (B) specified in the table following paragraph 5, or, where appropriate, the initial fee specified in paragraph 7, where paragraph 16(3), (4) or (5) applies, as appropriate for the circumstances set out in that sub-paragraph;

(c) where appropriate the fee set out in paragraph 8B.

(4) In a case where the representation of one defendant would attract a fixed fee under Part 2A and the representation of one or more of the other defendants would attract a graduated fee under Part 2, the total fee in the table following this paragraph means the fee falling within sub-paragraph (3)(b).

DEFENDANT UPLIFTS

Total number of defendants represented by litigator	Percentage uplift to total fee
2–4	20%
5+	30%

[Paragraph 17 is printed as amended by S.I. 2011 No. 2065 (*ante*, G–1).]

Warrant for arrest

G–77a 18.—(1) This paragraph applies where—

(a) the assisted person fails to attend a hearing;

(b) at that hearing the court issues a warrant for the arrest of the assisted person, pursuant to section 7(1) of the *Bail Act* 1976 ("the warrant");

(c) the case does not proceed in the absence of the assisted person.

(2) Where in a case on indictment the warrant is not executed within three months of the date on which it was issued, the fee payable to the litigator is—

(a) where the warrant is issued at or before the plea and case management hearing, the fee payable for a guilty plea in accordance with paragraph 5, or where appropriate, paragraph 7;

(b) where the warrant is issued after the plea and case management hearing but before the trial, the fee payable for a cracked trial in accordance with paragraph 5 or where appropriate paragraph 7, as appropriate to the class of offence with which the assisted person is charged;

(c) where the warrant is issued during the trial, and the trial is aborted as a result, the fee payable for a trial as if the trial had ended on the day the warrant was issued.

(3) Where the warrant is issued during the course of proceedings referred to in paragraph 12 or 14 the fee payable to the litigator is the fee set out in the table following paragraph 14, as appropriate to the type of proceedings.

(4) Sub-paragraph (5) applies where—

(a) a fee has been paid, or is payable, to the litigator in accordance with sub-paragraph (2);

(b) the warrant is executed within 15 months of the date on which it was issued;

(c) the case proceeds after the warrant has been executed; and

(d) the litigator submits a claim for fees for the determination of his overall remuneration in the case, in accordance with article 6.

(5) Where this sub-paragraph applies—

(a) the appropriate officer must deduct the amount paid or payable in accordance with sub-paragraph (2) from the amount payable to the litigator on the final determination of fees in the case;

(b) if the fee paid or payable in accordance with sub-paragraph (2) is greater than the amount payable to the litigator on the final determination of fees in the case, the appropriate officer may recover the amount of the difference by way of repayment by the litigator.

PART 4

MISCELLANEOUS

Additional charges

G–78 19.—(1) Where an assisted person is charged with more than one offence on one indictment, the fee payable to the litigator under this Schedule will be based on whichever of those offences the litigator selects.

(2) Where a litigator selects one offence, in preference to another offence, under sub-paragraph (1) that selection does not affect his right to claim any of the fees provided for in Part 3 of this Schedule to which he would otherwise have been entitled.

Assisted person unfit to plead or stand trial

20. Where in any case a hearing is held to determine the question of whether the assisted person is unfit to plead or to stand trial (a "fitness hearing")— **G–78a**

   (a) if a trial on indictment is held, or continues, at any time thereafter, the length of the fitness hearing is included in determining the length of the trial for the calculation of the fee in accordance with Part 2;

   (b) if a trial on indictment is not held, or does not continue, thereafter by reason of the assisted person being found unfit to plead or to stand trial, the litigator must be paid—

      (i) a fee calculated in accordance with paragraph 6 or where appropriate paragraph 8, as appropriate to the combined length of—

         (aa) the fitness hearing; and

         (bb) any hearing under section 4A of the *Criminal Procedure (Insanity) Act* 1964 (finding that the accused did the act or made the omission charged against him); or

      (ii) a fee calculated in accordance with paragraph 5, or where appropriate paragraph 7, as appropriate, for representing an assisted person in a cracked trial,

     whichever the litigator elects; and

   (c) if at any time the assisted person pleads guilty to the indictable offence, the litigator must be paid either—

      (i) a fee calculated in accordance with paragraph 6 or, where appropriate, paragraph 8, as appropriate to the length of the fitness hearing; or

      (ii) a fee calculated in accordance with paragraph 5 or, where appropriate, paragraph 7, as appropriate for representing an assisted person in a guilty plea,

     whichever the litigator elects.

Fees for confiscation proceedings

21.—(1) This paragraph applies to— **G–79**

   (a) proceedings under Part 2 of the *Proceeds of Crime Act* 2002 (confiscation: England and Wales);

   (b) proceedings under section 2 of the *Drug Trafficking Act* 1994 (confiscation orders) and

   (c) proceedings under section 71 of the *Criminal Justice Act* 1988 (confiscation orders).

(2) Where this paragraph applies, the appropriate officer may allow work done in the following classes by a litigator—

   (a) preparation, including taking instructions, interviewing witnesses, ascertaining the prosecution case, preparing and perusing documents, dealing with letters and telephone calls, instructing an advocate and expert witnesses, conferences, consultations and work done in connection with advice on appeal;

   (b) attending at court where an advocate is instructed, including conferences with the advocate at court;

   (c) travelling and waiting;

   (d) writing routine letters and dealing with routine telephone calls.

(3) The appropriate officer must consider the claim, any further particulars, information or documents submitted by the litigator under article 6 and any other relevant information and must allow such work as appears to him to have been reasonably done in the proceedings.

(4) Subject to sub-paragraph (3), the appropriate officer must allow fees under this paragraph in accordance with paragraph 22.

(5) The appropriate officer must allow fees in accordance with paragraphs 22–24 as appropriate to such of the following grades of fee earner as he considers reasonable—

   (a) senior solicitor;

   (b) solicitor, legal executive or fee earner of equivalent experience; or

   (c) trainee or fee earner of equivalent experience.

Prescribed fee rates

22. Subject to paragraphs 23 and 24, for proceedings in the Crown Court to which paragraph 21 applies the appropriate officer must allow fees for work under paragraph 21(2) at the following prescribed rates— **G–80**

TABLE 1

Class of work	Grade of fee earner	Rate	Variations
Preparation	Senior solicitor	£53.00 per hour	£55.75 per hour for a fee earner whose office is situated within the London region of the Commission
	Solicitor, legal executive or fee earner of equivalent experience	£45.00 per hour	£47.25 per hour for a fee earner whose office is situated within the London region of the Commission
	Trainee or fee earner of equivalent experience	£29.75 per hour	£34.00 per hour for a fee earner whose office is situated within the London region of the Commission
Attendance at court where more than one representative instructed	Senior solicitor	£42.25 per hour	—
	Solicitor, legal executive or fee earner of equivalent experience	£34.00 per hour	—
	Trainee or fee earner of equivalent experience	£20.50 per hour	—
Travelling and waiting	Senior solicitor	£24.75 per hour	—
	Solicitor, legal executive or fee earner of equivalent experience	£24.75 per hour	—
	Trainee or fee earner of equivalent experience	£12.50 per hour	—
Writing routine letters and dealing with routine telephone calls		£3.45 per item	£3.60 per item for a fee earner whose office is situated within the London region of the Commission

Allowing fees at less than the prescribed rates

G–81   23. In respect of any item of work, the appropriate officer may allow fees at less than the relevant prescribed rate specified in paragraph 22 where it appears to him reasonable to do so having regard to the competence and despatch with which the work was done.

Allowing fees at more than the prescribed rates

G–81a   24.—(1) Upon a determination the appropriate officer may, subject to the provisions of this paragraph, allow fees at more than the relevant prescribed rate specified in paragraph 22 for preparation, attendance at court where more than one representative is instructed, routine letters written and routine telephone calls, in respect of offences in Class A, B, C, D, G, I, J or K in the Table of Offences.

(2) The appropriate officer may allow fees at more than the prescribed rate where it appears to him, taking into account all the relevant circumstances of the case, that—

    (a) the work was done with exceptional competence, skill or expertise;

    (b) the work was done with exceptional despatch; or

    (c) the case involved exceptional complexity or other exceptional circumstances.

(3) Paragraph 3 of Schedule 1 applies to litigators in respect of proceedings in the Crown Court as it applies to advocates.

(4) Where the appropriate officer considers that any item or class of work should be allowed at

more than the prescribed rate, he must apply to that item or class of work a percentage enhancement in accordance with the following provisions of this paragraph.

(5) In determining the percentage by which fees should be enhanced above the prescribed rate the appropriate officer must have regard to—

    (a) the degree of responsibility accepted by the fee earner;

    (b) the care, speed and economy with which the case was prepared; and

    (c) the novelty, weight and complexity of the case.

(6) The percentage above the relevant prescribed rate by which fees for work may be enhanced must not exceed 100 per cent.

(7) The appropriate officer may have regard to the generality of proceedings to which this Order applies in determining what is exceptional within the meaning of this paragraph.

In *R. v. Farrell and Selby* [2007] Costs L.R. 495, it was held in relation to the provisions of **G–81b** paragraph 4 of Part 1 of Schedule 2 to the *Criminal Defence Service (Funding) Order* 2001 (S.I. 2001 No. 855) for paying enhanced rates to solicitors, (i) it was open to a determining officer to apply different rates of enhancement to different items of work; since a determining officer was required, in deciding on the rate of enhancement, to have regard, *inter alia*, to the "degree of responsibility accepted by the solicitor and his staff", it was permissible for a determining officer to apply a lesser rate of enhancement to work of a routine nature done by Grade B fee earners than that applied to the senior fee earners to whom they reported; (ii) when enhancement was appropriate, a determining officer should first assess what enhanced rate would have been applied if legal aid had been granted prior to October 1, 1994 (the date of commencement of the revised rules as to enhancement introduced by the *Legal Aid in Criminal and Care Proceedings (Costs) (Amendment) (No. 3) Regulations* 1994 (S.I. 1994 No. 2218)), *viz.* the hourly broad average direct cost rate plus an appropriate uplift for care and conduct, and then he should adjust the resulting figure upwards to allow for subsequent inflation; he should then decide on a rate of enhancement such as would match this figure; where, however, the figure exceeded the maximum enhanced rate under the 2001 order, then the determining officer should apply the maximum enhanced rate. Since the provisions under consideration corresponded to those of paragraph 6 of Schedule 2 to the 2007 order (prior to amendment), it could safely be taken that this decision carried across to the current order (prior to amendment) with the effect—as in this case—that, wherever enhanced rates are appropriate, the rate of enhancement is always going to be 100 per cent because the 1994 hourly direct cost plus uplift for care and attention, plus uplift for inflation is always going to exceed twice the current hourly rates, which have remained unchanged for many years. This was confirmed in *R. v. Bowles* [2007] Costs L.R. 514. Whilst the provision for payment at enhanced rates under the 2007 order (as amended) relates only to fees payable under paragraph 21, the provisions of paragraph 24 correspond to paragraph 6 of the unamended Schedule 2, and it would appear that the decision in *Farrell and Selby* will carry across to this paragraph in the same way that it carried across to paragraph 6.

Article 8 SCHEDULE 4

PROCEEDINGS IN THE COURT OF APPEAL

General provisions

1.—(1) The provisions of this Schedule apply to proceedings in the Court of Appeal. **G–82**

(2) In determining fees the appropriate officer must, subject to the provisions of this Schedule—

    (a) take into account all the relevant circumstances of the case including the nature, importance, complexity or difficulty of the work and the time involved; and

    (b) allow a reasonable amount in respect of all work actually and reasonably done.

Claims for fees and disbursements by litigators

2.—(1) Subject to article 32, no claim by a litigator for fees and disbursements in respect of work done in proceedings in the Court of Appeal under a representation order must be entertained unless he submits it within three months of the conclusion of the proceedings to which it relates.

(2) Subject to sub-paragraph (3), a claim for fees in proceedings in the Court of Appeal must be submitted to the appropriate officer in such form and manner as he may direct and must be accompanied by the representation order and any receipts or other documents in support of any disbursement claimed.

(3) A claim must—

    (a) summarise the items of work done by a fee earner in respect of which fees are claimed according to the classes specified in paragraph 3(1);

    (b) state, where appropriate, the dates on which the items of work were done, the time taken, the sums claimed and whether the work was done for more than one assisted person;

    (c) specify, where appropriate, the level of fee earner who undertook each of the items of work claimed;

    (d) give particulars of any work done in relation to more than one indictment or a retrial; and

    (e) specify any disbursements claimed, the circumstances in which they were incurred and the amounts claimed in respect of them.

(4) Where the litigator claims that paragraph 9(1) applies in relation to an item of work, he must give full particulars in support of his claim.

(5) The litigator must specify any special circumstances which the litigator considers should be drawn to the attention of the appropriate officer.

(6) The litigator must supply such further information and documents as the appropriate officer may require.

(7) Where a retrospective representation order has been made under regulation 10(6) of the *Criminal Defence Service (General) (No. 2) Regulations* 2001 in respect of any proceedings where an appellant has been successful on appeal and granted a defendant's costs order under section 16(4) of the *Prosecution of Offences Act* 1985 (defence costs), the litigator must certify that no claim for fees incurred before the retrospective representation order was made has been or will be made from central funds in relation to that work.

Determination of litigators' fees

G–83

3.—(1) The appropriate officer may allow work done in the following classes by fee earners—

    (a) preparation, including taking instructions, interviewing witnesses, ascertaining the prosecution case, advising on plea and mode of trial, preparing and perusing documents, dealing with letters and telephone calls which are not routine, preparing for advocacy, instructing an advocate and expert witnesses, conferences, consultations, views and work done in connection with advice on appeal;

    (b) advocacy, including applications for bail and other applications to the court;

    (c) attending at court where an advocate is assigned, including conferences with the advocate at court;

    (d) travelling and waiting; and

    (e) writing routine letters and dealing with routine telephone calls.

(2) The appropriate officer must consider the claim, any further information or documents submitted by the fee earner under paragraph 2 and any other relevant information and must allow—

    (a) such work as appears to him to have been reasonably done under the representation order (including any representation or advice which is deemed to be work done under that order) by a fee earner, classifying such work according to the classes specified in sub-paragraph (1) as he considers appropriate; and

    (b) such time in each class of work allowed by him (other than routine letters written and routine telephone calls) as he considers reasonable.

(3) The fees allowed in accordance with this Schedule are those appropriate to such of the following grades of litigator as the appropriate officer considers reasonable—

    (a) senior solicitor;

    (b) solicitor, legal executive or fee earner of equivalent experience; or

    (c) trainee or fee earner of equivalent experience.

Determination of litigators' disbursements

G–84

4. The appropriate officer must allow such disbursements claimed under paragraph 2 as appear to him to have been reasonably incurred, provided that—

    (a) if they are abnormally large by reason of the distance of the court or the assisted person's residence or both from the litigator's place of business, the appropriate officer may limit reimbursement of the disbursements to what otherwise would, having regard to all the circumstances, be a reasonable amount; and

(b) the cost of a transcript, or any part thereof, of the proceedings in the court from which the appeal lies obtained otherwise than through the registrar must not be allowed except where the appropriate officer considers that it is reasonable in all the circumstances for such disbursement to be allowed.

Claims for fees by advocates

5.—(1) Subject to article 32, a claim by an advocate for fees for work done in proceedings in the Court of Appeal under a representation order must not be entertained unless he submits it within three months of the conclusion of the proceedings to which the representation order relates.

(2) Where the advocate claims that paragraph 13 applies in relation to an item of work he must give full particulars in support of his claim.

(3) Subject to sub-paragraph (4), a claim for fees by an advocate in proceedings in the Court of Appeal must be submitted to the appropriate officer in such form and manner as he may direct.

(4) A claim must—

(a) summarise the items of work done by an advocate in respect of which fees are claimed according to the classes specified in paragraph 6(2);

(b) state, where appropriate, the dates on which the items of work were done, the time taken, the sums claimed and whether the work was done for more than one assisted person;

(c) give particulars of any work done in relation to more than one indictment or a retrial.

(5) The advocate must specify any special circumstances which the advocate considers should be drawn to the attention of the appropriate officer.

(6) The advocate must supply such further information and documents as the appropriate officer may require.

Determination of advocate's fees

6.—(1) The appropriate officer must consider the claim, any further particulars and information **G–85** submitted by an advocate under paragraph 5 and any other relevant information and must allow such work as appears to him to have been reasonably done.

(2) The appropriate officer may allow any of the following classes of fee to an advocate in respect of work allowed by him under this paragraph—

(a) a basic fee for preparation including preparation for a pre-trial review and, where appropriate, the first day's hearing including, where they took place on that day, short conferences, consultations, applications and appearances (including bail applications), views and any other preparation;

(b) a refresher fee for any day or part of a day during which a hearing continued, including, where they took place on that day, short conferences, consultations, applications and appearances (including bail applications), views at the scene of the alleged offence and any other preparation;

(c) subsidiary fees for—

(i) attendance at conferences, consultations and views at the scene of the alleged offence not covered by paragraph (a) or (b);

(ii) written advice on evidence, plea or appeal or other written work; and

(iii) attendance at pre-trial reviews, applications and appearances (including bail applications and adjournments for sentence) not covered by paragraph (a) or (b).

(3) Where a representation order provides for representation by—

(a) a single advocate other than a QC and a QC agrees to appear as the single advocate; or

(b) two advocates other than QC, and a QC agrees to appear as a leading junior,

that QC must be treated for all the purposes of this Schedule as having been instructed under that representation order, and his remuneration must be determined as if he were not a QC.

In connection with this paragraph, see *R. v. Bromige, post,* G–160.

Litigators' fees for proceedings in the Court of Appeal

7. For proceedings in the Court of Appeal the appropriate officer must allow fees for work by litigators at the following prescribed rates— **G–86**

Class of work	Grade of fee earner	Rate	Variations
Preparation	Senior solicitor	£53.00 per hour	£55.75 per hour for a litigator whose office is situated within the London region of the Commission
	Solicitor, legal executive or fee earner of equivalent experience	£45.00 per hour	£47.25 per hour for a litigator whose office is situated within the London region of the Commission
	Trainee or fee earner of equivalent experience	£29.75 per hour	£34.00 per hour for a litigator whose office is situated within the London region of the Commission
Advocacy	Senior solicitor	£64.00 per hour	
	Solicitor	£56.00 per hour	
Attendance at court where more than one representative assigned	Senior solicitor	£42.25 per hour	
	Solicitor, legal executive or fee earner of equivalent experience	£34.00 per hour	
	Trainee or fee earner of equivalent experience	£20.50 per hour	
Travelling and waiting	Senior solicitor	£24.75 per hour	
	Solicitor, legal executive or fee earner of equivalent experience	£24. 75 per hour	
	Trainee or fee earner of equivalent experience	£12.50 per hour	
Routine letters written and routine telephone calls		£3.45 per item	£3.60 per item for a fee earner whose office is situated within the London region of the Commission

G–87

8. In respect of any item of work, the appropriate officer may allow fees at less than the relevant prescribed rate specified in paragraph 7 where it appears to him reasonable to do so having regard to the competence and despatch with which the work was done.

9.—(1) Upon a determination of fees the appropriate officer may, subject to the provisions of this paragraph, allow fees at more than the relevant prescribed rate specified in paragraph 7 for preparation, advocacy, attendance at court where more than one representative is assigned, routine letters written and routine telephone calls, in respect of offences in Class A, B, C, D, G, I, J or K in the Table of Offences in Part 6 of Schedule 1.

(2) The appropriate officer may allow fees at more than the prescribed rate where it appears to him, taking into account all the relevant circumstances of the case, that—

(a) the work was done with exceptional competence, skill or expertise;

(b) the work was done with exceptional despatch; or

(c) the case involved exceptional complexity or other exceptional circumstances.

(3) Paragraph 3 of Schedule 1 applies to litigators in respect of proceedings in the Court of Appeal as it applies to advocates.

(4) Where the appropriate officer considers that any item or class of work should be allowed at more than the prescribed rate, he must apply to that item or class of work a percentage enhancement in accordance with the following provisions of this paragraph.

(5) In determining the percentage by which fees should be enhanced above the prescribed rate the appropriate officer may have regard to—

    (a) the degree of responsibility accepted by the fee earner;

    (b) the care, speed and economy with which the case was prepared; and

    (c) the novelty, weight and complexity of the case.

  (6) The percentage above the relevant prescribed rate by which fees for work may be enhanced must not exceed 100 per cent.

  (7) The appropriate officer may have regard to the generality of proceedings to which this Order applies in determining what is exceptional within the meaning of this paragraph.

Advocates' fees for proceedings in the Court of Appeal

  10. Subject to paragraph 13, for proceedings in the Court of Appeal the appropriate officer must **G–88** allow fees for work by advocates at the following prescribed rates—

JUNIOR COUNSEL

Type of proceedings	Basic fee	Full day refresher	Subsidiary fees		
			Attendance at consultation, conferences and views	Written work	Attendance at pre-trial reviews, applications and other appearances
All appeals	Maximum amount: £545.00 per case	Maximum amount: £178.75 per day	£33.50 per hour, minimum amount: £16.75	Maximum amount: £58.25 per item	Maximum amount: £110 per appearance

QC

Type of proceedings	Basic fee	Full day refresher	Subsidiary fees		
			Attendance at consultation, conferences and views	Written work	Attendance at pre-trial reviews, applications and other appearances
All appeals	Maximum amount: £5,400.00 per case	Maximum amount: £330.50 per day	£62.50 per hour, minimum amount: £32.00	Maximum amount: £119.50 per item	Maximum amount: £257.50 per appearance

  11. Where an hourly rate is specified in the Table following paragraph 10, the appropriate officer **G–89** must determine any fee for such work in accordance with that hourly rate; provided that the fee determined must not be less than the minimum amount specified.

  12. Where a refresher fee is claimed in respect of less than a full day, the appropriate officer must allow such fee as appears to him reasonable having regard to the fee which would be allowable for a full day.

  13. Where it appears to the appropriate officer, taking into account all the relevant circumstances **G–90** of the case, that owing to the exceptional circumstances of the case the amount payable by way of fees in accordance with the Table following paragraph 10 would not provide reasonable remuneration for some or all of the work he has allowed, he may allow such amounts as appear to him to be reasonable remuneration for the relevant work.

Payment of fees

  14.—(1) Having determined the fees payable to a representative in accordance with the terms of **G–91** this Schedule, the appropriate officer must notify the representative of the fees payable and authorise payment accordingly.

  (2) Where, as a result of any redetermination or appeal made or brought pursuant to paragraph 15—

    (a) the fees payable under sub-paragraph (1) are increased, the appropriate officer must authorise payment of the increase; and

(b) the fees payable under sub-paragraph (1) are decreased, the representative must repay the amount of such decrease.

(3) Where the payment of any fees of the representative is ordered under article 30(12) or article 31(8), the appropriate officer must authorise payment.

[This paragraph is printed as amended by S.I. 2007 No. 3552 (*ante*, G–1).]

Redeterminations and appeals

G–92   15.—(1) Where a representative is dissatisfied with—

(a) the fees determined in accordance with the provisions of this Schedule; or

(b) the decision of the appropriate officer under paragraph 3(3) of Schedule 1

he may apply to the appropriate officer to redetermine those fees or reclassify the offence, in accordance with the provisions of article 29(3) to (9).

(2) Where—

(a) a representative has made an application to the appropriate officer under sub-paragraph (1); and

(b) the appropriate officer has given his reasons for a decision under article 29(7)

a representative who is dissatisfied with that decision may appeal to a Costs Judge, in accordance with the provisions of article 30(2) to (14).

(3) A representative who is dissatisfied with the decision of a Costs Judge on an appeal under sub-paragraph (2) may apply to a Costs Judge to certify a point of principle of general importance, and the provisions of article 31(2) to (8) will apply.

Article 4A   SCHEDULE 5

MAGISTRATES' COURTS RATES

Interpretation of this Schedule

★**G–92a**   1.—(1) Words and expressions used in this Schedule have the same meaning as in the 2010 Standard Crime Contract. The fees and rates in this Schedule are exclusive of value added tax.

(2) "2010 Standard Crime Contract" means the contract so named between the Commission and a provider for the provision of funded services, including the contract for signature, the standard terms, the schedule and the specification.

(3) The reference to "Category 1A" cases is a reference to the following proceedings—

(a) either way guilty pleas;

(b) indictable only cases heard in the youth court;

(c) proceedings (other than committal proceedings) relating to either way offences which are discontinued or withdrawn or where the prosecution offer no evidence; and

(d) proceedings (other than committal proceedings) relating to either way offences which result in a bind over.

(4) The reference to "Category 1B" cases is a reference to the following proceedings—

(a) summary only guilty pleas;

(b) uncontested proceedings arising out of a breach of an order of a magistrates' courts [*sic*] (including proceedings in a magistrates' court relating to a breach of a Crown Court community rehabilitation order, community punishment order or suspended sentence);

(c) proceedings (other than committal proceedings) relating to summary offences which are discontinued or withdrawn or where the prosecution offer no evidence;

(d) proceedings (other than committal proceedings) relating to summary offences which result in a bind over;

(e) proceedings arising out of a deferment of sentence (including any subsequent sentence hearing) under section 1 of the *Powers of Criminal Courts (Sentencing) Act* 2000;

(f) proceedings prescribed under regulation 3(2) of the *Criminal Defence Service (General) (No. 2) Regulations* 2001, except where the case was listed and fully prepared for a contested hearing to decide whether an order should be made; and

(g) proceedings relating to either-way offences which must be tried in a magistrates' court in accordance with section 22 of the *Magistrates' Courts Act* 1980.

(5) The reference to "Category 2" cases is a reference to—

(a) contested trials;

(b) proceedings which were listed and fully prepared for trial in a magistrates' court but are disposed of by a guilty plea on the day of trial before the opening of the prosecution case;

(c) proceedings which were listed and fully prepared for trial in a magistrates' court but are discontinued or withdrawn or where the prosecution offers no evidence or which result in a bind over on the day of trial before the opening of the prosecution case;

(d) contested proceedings relating to a breach of an order of a magistrates' court (including proceedings relating to a breach of a Crown Court community rehabilitation order, community punishment order or suspended sentence);

(e) proceedings where mixed pleas are entered; and

(f) proceedings prescribed under regulation 3(2) of the *Criminal Defence Service (General) (No. 2) Regulations* 2001 where the case was listed and fully prepared for a contested hearing to decide whether an order should be made.

(6) The reference to "Category 3" cases is a reference to committal proceedings which are discontinued or withdrawn.

HIGHER AND LOWER STANDARD FEES TABLE

Column header	Lower Standard Fee	Lower Standard Fee Limit	Higher Standard Fee	Higher Standard Fee Limit
Designated Area Standard Fees				
Category 1A	272.56	298.45	517.05	517.10
Category 1B	221.59	298.45	477.41	517.10
Category 2	378.46	512.70	792.71	854.40
Category 3	357.87	452.20	734.56	789.50
Undesignated Area Standard Fees				
Category 1A	213.35	298.45	451.84	517.10
Category 1B	173.45	298.45	417.20	517.10
Category 2	306.25	512.70	702.40	854.40
Category 3	276.50	452.20	626.50	789.50

REPRESENTATION IN THE MAGISTRATES' COURT

Hourly rates (for recording time and to determine whether the Lower or Higher Standard Fee Limit has been reached, and for claiming costs in cases which fall outside the Standard Fee payment scheme).

	All Areas
Routine letters written and telephone calls per item	£3.90
Preparation hourly rate	£49.70
Advocacy hourly rate (including applications for bail and other applications to the court)	£62.35
Attendance at court where counsel is assigned (including conferences with counsel at court) hourly rate	£34.00
Travelling and waiting hourly rate (only claimable where the Undesignated Area fees apply)	£26.30

[Schedule 5 was inserted by S.I. 2011 No. 2065. It is printed as amended by S.I. 2012 No. 750 (*ante*, G–1).]

Article 15A   SCHEDULE 6

EXPERTS' FEES AND RATES

Expert	Non-London Hourly Rate or fixed fee	London Hourly Rate or fixed fee	Comments	**G–92b**
A&E consultant	£126	£135		

G–92b

Expert	Non-London Hourly Rate or fixed fee	London Hourly Rate or fixed fee	Comments
Accident reconstruction	£90	£68	
Accountant	£50 – £144	£50 – £144	Partner £144, Manager £108, Accountant £80, General staff £50.
Anaesthetist	£135	£90	
Architect	£99	£90	
Back calculations	£180 fixed fee	£189 fixed fee	
Benefit expert	£90	£90	
Cardiologist	£144	£90	
Cell telephone site analysis	£90	£90	
Child psychiatrist	£135	£90	
Child psychologist	£126	£90	
Computer expert	£90	£90	
Consultant engineer	£90	£68	
Dentist	£117	£90	
Dermatologist	£108	£90	
Disability consultant	£68	£68	
DNA (per person) –testing of sample	£315 per test	£315 per test	
DNA (per person) –preparation of report	£90	£90	
Doctor (GP)	£99	£90	
Drug expert	£90	£90	
Employment consultant	£68	£68	
Enquiry agent	£32	£23	
ENT surgeon	£126	£90	
Facial mapping	£135	£90	
Fingerprint expert	£90	£47	
Fire investigation	£90	£68	
Firearm expert	£90	£90	
Forensic scientist	£113	£90	
General surgeon	£135	£90	
Geneticist	£108	£90	
GP (records report)	£63 fixed fee	£90 fixed fee	
Gynaecologist	£135	£90	
Haematologist	£122	£90	
Handwriting expert	£90	£90	
Interpreter	£32	£25	
Lip reader / Signer	£72	£41	
Mediator	£126	£126	
Medical Consultant	£135	£90	
Medical microbiologist	£135	£90	
Medical Report	£99	£90	
Meteorologist	£126	£180 fixed fee	

Expert	Non-London Hourly Rate or fixed fee	London Hourly Rate or fixed fee	Comments
Midwife	£90	£90	
Neonatologist	£135	£90	
Neurologist	£153	£90	
Neuropsychiatrist	£158	£90	
Neuroradiologist	£171	£90	
Neurosurgeon	£171	£90	
Nursing expert	£81	£81	
Obstetrician	£135	£90	
Occupational Therapist	£68	£68	
Oncologist	£140	£90	
Orthopaedic surgeon	£144	£90	
Paediatrician	£135	£90	
Pathologist	£153	£540 fixed fee	
Pharmacologist	£122	£90	
Photographer	£32	£23	
Physiotherapist	£81	£81	
Plastic surgeon	£135	£90	
Process server	£32	£23	
Psychiatrist	£135	£90	
Psychologist	£117	£90	
Radiologist	£135	£90	
Rheumatologist	£135	£90	
Risk assessment expert	£63	£63	
Speech therapist	£99	£90	
Surgeon	£135	£90	
Surveyor	£50	£50	
Telecoms expert	£90	£90	
Toxicologist	£135	£90	
Urologist	£135	£90	
Vet	£90	£90	
Voice recognition	£117	£90	

[Schedule 6 was inserted by S.I. 2011 No. 2065.]

C. Representation Orders

Representatives are entitled to claim and be remunerated only for work done in respect of Crown Court proceedings in accordance with the provisions of the schedules to the funding order: *Funding Order* 2007, arts 4, 5, 6 and 11.   **G–93**

Existence of a valid representation order

Payment can only be made for work done under a representation order. There is no power under the legislation to make a payment in respect of work actually and reasonably undertaken by counsel in the genuine but mistaken belief that the appropriate order was in existence.   **G–94**

Solicitors are obliged to enclose a copy of the representation order with counsel's instructions, and to inform counsel of any subsequent amendments: *General Criminal Contract:*

Archbold
paragraph
numbers

Contract Specification, Part B, para. 5.4. It is, however, incumbent upon counsel to check whether the appropriate order exists. If it is not with his instructions, then it is his duty, if he seeks to look to the Criminal Defence Service (CDS) thereafter for remuneration, to see that the appropriate authority is obtained and supplied to him: *Hunt v. East Dorset Health Authority* [1992] 1 W.L.R. 785 at 788 (Hobhouse J.); and *R. v. Welsby* [1998] 1 Cr.App.R. 197, Crown Court (Ebsworth J.) (counsel has a professional duty to ensure that he is covered by appropriate certificate).

Determining the effective date of a representation order

G–95   The effective date of a representation order for the purposes of determining which regulations apply is the date upon which representation was first granted to counsel's instructing solicitors and not the date of the later representation order under which they instructed counsel: *R. v. Hadley* [2005] Costs L.R. 548.

Orders made ultra vires

G–96   Representation orders assigning solicitors or counsel which are made *ultra vires* are invalid, and work done under such an order cannot be remunerated. However, where it is possible to construe an order as *intra vires*, that construction should be adopted: *R. v. O'Brien and Oliffe*, 81 Cr.App.R. 25 at 30 (Hobhouse J.). There is no power to backdate a representation order: *R. v. Welsby, ante*; followed in *R. v. Conroy* [2004] Costs L.R. 182 in respect of the current regulations.

Orders for two or more advocates

G–97   The instruction of more than one advocate must be specifically authorised by the court. A representation order may be amended to provide for the services of: (i) Queen's Counsel alone; (ii) two advocates, one of whom must be a Queen's Counsel or junior advocate and the other of whom must be a junior advocate or noting junior; or (iii) in the case of a Serious Fraud Office prosecution, three advocates, the additional advocate being a junior or noting junior: reg. 14(2), (6). Regulation 14 (wherein "junior advocate" means any advocate other than Queen's Counsel: reg. 14(2)) provides the criteria for making or amending the appropriate representation order. A two advocate order or an order for Queen's Counsel can only be made in the course of a trial, preliminary hearing, or pleas and directions hearing by a specified judge: reg. 14(13). As to orders made by magistrates, see *post*, G–98.

It is submitted that a leading junior would not be entitled to any remuneration where he acts under a certificate granted for Queen's Counsel. A leading junior who acted under an unamended legal aid certificate granted to cover Queen's Counsel was not covered by the certificate and could not be remunerated under the order or by a defendant's costs order under section 16 of the *Prosecution of Offences Act* 1985: *R. v. Liverpool Crown Court, ex p. The Lord Chancellor, The Times*, April 22, 1993, DC. However, a Queen's Counsel must be remunerated at the appropriate rate for junior counsel where he agrees to act as a sole advocate or as a leading junior: *Funding Order* 2007, art. 5(7).

In every case where the services of more than one advocate are provided, it is the duty of each legal representative to keep under review the need for the number of advocates provided for in the representation order, and for Queen's Counsel to keep under review whether he could act alone. Where the legal representative is of the opinion that the representation order should be amended to reduce the number of advocates instructed, he is under a duty so to notify the court and the other legal representatives in writing: reg. 14(16), (17).

[The next paragraph is G–99.]

Orders for advocate acting without a solicitor

G–99   A representation order may be granted by a court for an advocate alone, without a solicitor, in respect of contempt proceedings, appeals to the Court of Appeal, or in cases or urgency where it appears to the court that there is no time to instruct a solicitor: reg. 15.

Orders for Queen's Counsel acting alone

Where prior authority has been obtained to instruct a Queen's Counsel alone, the **G–100** propriety of the order may not be challenged on the determination of Queen's Counsel's fees unless the solicitor knew or ought reasonably to have known that the purpose for which the authority had been given had failed or become irrelevant or unnecessary before the fees were incurred: *Funding Order* 2007, art. 16(3).

Work done under the order

The work claimed for must have been done under the order. Work done before the date **G–101** of commencement of the representation order cannot be claimed or allowed: *R. v. Clarke* (1991) Costs L.R. 496. An order cannot be backdated in respect of proceedings in the Crown Court: *R. v. North Staffordshire JJ., ex p. O'Hara* [1994] C.O.D. 248, DC; *R. v. Welsby* [1998] 1 Cr.App.R. 197, Crown Court (Ebsworth J.).

"Topping up"

An assisted person's solicitor or advocate is prohibited from receiving or being party to **G–102** the making of any payment for work done in connection with the proceedings in respect of which the representation order was made other than payments by the Lord Chancellor or the Legal Services Commission or in respect of various specified disbursements: reg. 22 (§ 6–176 in the main work). These provisions are designed to prevent "topping" up of fees, rather than to prevent counsel from receiving payment for private fees incurred before the representation order was granted or *ex gratia* payments from solicitors who wrongly instructed counsel in the mistaken belief that he was covered by a representation order. However, once a representation order has been granted, the prohibition applies to all solicitors and advocates and not merely those persons acting under the representation order: *R. v. Grant* [2006] Costs L.R. 173.

D. Reasonable Remuneration

The basic principle of remuneration under the former *ex post facto* regime was that **G–103** counsel should receive reasonable remuneration for work actually and reasonably undertaken by him. Assessment of the work undertaken and the remuneration claimed was made in each case after the event by experienced officers appointed by the Lord Chancellor's department and subject to the appellate and expert supervision of costs judges and the High Court.

Graduated fees are calculated by reference to pre-determined fixed fees. Although allow- **G–104** ances are made for different classes of case and for the length and size of each case, the scheme necessarily embraces a "swings and roundabouts" principle. Save in exceptional cases, graduated fees draw no distinction between straightforward and complex cases of the same length, class and size.

When they were introduced in 1997, it was intended that they would be cost neutral. The extension of fees to cover 25 to 40 day cases represented a diminution in fees for defence work, balanced by an increase in the fees of prosecution counsel who are now subject to a similar scheme. The further extension of the scheme under the *Funding Order* 2007 to all trials on indictment save for those covered by VHCC contracts is a far remove from its original ambit, and may give rise to some serious underfunding of cases or aspects of cases.

Very High Cost Cases are remunerated by an hourly preparation fee and refreshers which fall within prescribed bands. The categorisation of the class of case, rates of remuneration, refresher and the number of hours of preparation allowed to counsel must be agreed before the work is undertaken. The Very High Costs Cases regime represents a significant diminution in the individual fees considered to be reasonable under the former *ex post facto* regime.

E. INTERIM FEES AND OTHER PRE-ASSESSMENT PAYMENTS

(1) Staged payments for preparation in long cases

G–105   Where the period from committal, transfer or sending to the Crown Court and the conclusion of the proceedings is likely to exceed 12 months, a legal representative may apply for staged payments (*i.e.* interim fees for the preparation of a case) in respect of each period of preparation of 100 hours or more undertaken before trial or, in serious fraud cases, before the empanelling of a jury. Preparation in this context is widely defined and includes, *inter alia*, conferences with the defendant, written advice on evidence or plea, legal research and preparation for oral or written submissions: *Funding Order* 2007, art. 19.

[The next paragraph is G–110.]

(2) Interim payment of expenses

G–110   A litigator may make a claim for an interim payment of disbursements in accordance with the provisions of article 14 of the *Funding Order* 2007 (*ante*, G–19).

(3) Interim payment pending determination

Entitlement

G–111   In certain circumstances, an advocate may claim an interim payment of 40 per cent of the total claim less any sum already paid: *Funding Order* 2007, art. 18(1). Such payments may only be made where, (a) the basic fee claimed by counsel, or the total costs claimed by a solicitor in a related claim, or the basic fee claimed by counsel in a related claim, exceeds £4,000 (exclusive of VAT); and (b) three months have elapsed from either the date on which the bill is ready to tax or, if earlier, three months after the conclusion of the last of any related proceedings. A bill is deemed to be ready to tax on the date of receipt of the last bill in a related claim. Related claims are claims for costs of solicitors and counsel in the same proceedings acting for the same defendant or acting in related proceedings. Related proceedings are those involving the same defendant which are prepared, heard, or dealt with together, or proceedings involving more than one defendant arising out of the same incident so that the defendants are charged, tried, or disposed of together: *Funding Order* 2007, art. 17.

There is no right of re-determination or appeal against the interim award: *Funding Order* 2007, art. 18(2).

Claims

G–112   An advocate may submit a claim for interim payment where, (a) he is entitled to such payment; (b) no payment has been made; (c) six months have elapsed since the conclusion of the proceedings against the defendant he represented; and (d) counsel has submitted a proper claim under regulation 8(1) (three-month time limit for the submission of claims): *Funding Order* 2007, art. 17(2)(a), (4)–(6).

(4) Hardship payments

G–113   A discretionary hardship payment may be made on proof of the likelihood of financial hardship. The proof required is left to the discretion of taxing officers. Counsel are advised to contact their circuit representative, before submitting a claim, to determine the form of proof likely to be acceptable. The sum paid cannot exceed the amount which is likely to be eventually paid, but payment will not be made for sums less than £5,000. Claims may only be made, (a) at least six months after the legal representative was first instructed, and (b) where final payment is unlikely to be made within the next three months by reason of which the applicant is likely to suffer financial hardship: *Funding Order* 2007, art. 21.

(5) Obligations to submit claims

Any person who has received a staged, interim or hardship payment must submit a claim **G–114** under the appropriate regulation for final determination of his overall remuneration: *Funding Order* 2007, art. 22(1). Any such payment will be set off against the overall remuneration on final determination and excess payments can be recovered: *ibid.*, art. 22(2).

F. Graduated Fees

(1) Introduction

Graduated fees were introduced into the *Legal Aid in Criminal and Care Proceedings (Costs)* **G–115** *Regulations* 1989 (S.I. 1989 No. 343) (see *ante*, G–1) by the *Legal Aid in Criminal and Care Proceedings (Costs) (Amendment) (No. 2) Regulations* 1996 (S.I. 1996 No. 2655) which came into effect on January 1, 1997: reg. 3(1). Those provisions were incorporated *seriatim* as Schedule 4 to the *Funding Order* 2001 although amendments were introduced by the *Criminal Defence Service (Funding) (Amendment) (No. 3) Order* (S.I. 2001 No. 3341) and the *Criminal Defence Service (Funding) (Amendment) Order* 2004 (S.I. 2004 No. 2045) which came into force on October 29, 2001, and August 2, 2004, respectively. Those amendments extended the ambit of graduated fees to cover trials estimated to last up to 25 days and then to 40 days. The *Funding Order* 2007 applied a new scheme, the *Revised Advocacy Graduated Fee Scheme* (RAGFS) in respect of representation orders made on or after April 30, 2007. The RAGFS applies to all trials on indictment save for those contracted under the VHCC scheme: *Funding Order* 2007, art. 3(6A), and Sched. 1, para. 2.

The scheme determines the taxation and payment of fees for advocacy and preparation in something of a mechanistic or formulaic way: *Meeke and Taylor v. Secretary of State for Constitutional Affairs* [2006] Costs L.R. 1. It is a comprehensive scheme which must be applied by examining the particular wording of the legislation: *R. v. Kemp*, X15 363/99. There is no "equity" in the regulations; they have to be construed and given effect however hard the result might be: *R. v. Riddell*, X3, SCCO 319/98, even where payment is morally due: see *R. v. Dhaliwal* [2004] Costs L.R. 689. Conversely, as was pointed out in *R. v. Chubb* [2002] Costs L.R. 333:

> "As has often been said, when the graduated fee system was introduced, it was on a principle which was expressed as being 'swings and roundabouts'. It is perfectly reasonable where the system operates against the Lord Chancellor's Department, that an appeal should be launched. There are many occasions, in my experience, when the graduated fee system has operated very much to the disadvantage of members of the bar and there is no reason why the bar should not take advantage when it operates in their favour."

References within this section to paragraphs are references to paragraphs in Schedule 1 to the *Funding Order* 2007.

[The next paragraph is G–118.]

(2) Cases on indictment

Scheduled offences

A "case" includes proceedings in the Crown Court against any one assisted person on one **G–118** or more counts of a single indictment: *Funding Order* 2007, Sched. 1, para. 1(1). Where counts or defendants are severed and dealt with separately, then each separate indictment is a separate case. Conversely, indictments which are joined should be treated as one case: *GFSG*: A1, A2: *R. v. Chubb* [2002] Costs L.R. 333. A "case" should not be confused with a trial; there may be two trials in one case: *R. v. Bond* [2005] Costs L.R. 533.

All cases on indictment now fall within the scheme unless specifically excluded: *Funding Order* 2007, Sched. 1, para. 2. As to pre-indictment hearings, see *post*, G–121a.

In *R. v. Hussain* [2011] Costs L.R. 689, after one defendant was committed for trial and a plea and case management hearing was conducted in relation to a single-count indictment, a second defendant was committed for trial, as a result of which a second indictment was preferred which included the allegation against the first defendant in the single-count indictment, and the defendants were in due course tried on the second indictment. It was held that: (i) whereas paragraph 1(1) of Schedule 2 to the *Funding Order* 2007 (*ante*, G–69) provides that "'case' means proceedings in the Crown Court against any one assisted person—(a) on one or more counts of a single indictment ...", there were two "cases"; (ii) in respect of the second indictment, the solicitors were entitled to a graduated fee for trial, together with the appropriate uplift for representing more than one defendant; and (iii) in respect of the first indictment, they were entitled to a graduated fee for a cracked trial. The costs judge observed that whilst it might be thought that the solicitors had obtained something of a windfall for, in layman's terms, this was really only one case, the regulations must be applied mechanically.

Table of offences

G–119   The table of offences in Schedule 1 to the *Funding Order* 2007 contains offences listed by statute with a description set out only for convenience. The statutory reference includes every offence contrary to that reference, whether or not the description of the offence is apt to describe the offence actually charged: *Funding Order* 2007, Sched. 1, para. 3(1)(e). Cases which do not appear in the table of offences are deemed to fall within Class H: *Funding Order* 2007, Sched. 1, para. 3 (1)(a). An advocate who is dissatisfied with that deemed classification may apply to the appropriate officer to reclassify the offence: *Funding Order* 2007, Sched. 1, para. 3(2).

The offences are divided into the following classes:

Class A	Homicide and related grave offences
Class B	Offences involving serious damage and serious drug offences
Class C	Lesser offences involving violence or damage, and less serious drug offences
Class D	Sexual offences and offences against children
Class E	Burglary and going equipped
Class F	Other offences of dishonesty including those where the value does not exceed £30,000
Class G	Other more serious offences of dishonesty including those where the value exceeds £30,000 but does not exceed £100,000
Class H	Miscellaneous lesser offences
Class I	Offences against public justice and similar offences
Class J	Serious sexual offences
Class K	The most serious offences of dishonesty and other offences where the value exceeds £100,000

Where counts of differing classes appear in the same indictment, the fee is based upon the class selected by the advocate: *Funding Order* 2007, Sched. 1, para. 22(1). Once counsel has chosen which count to use as the basis of a claim, that choice is irrevocable: *R. v. Buoniauto*, X25, SCCO 483/2000. Where two or more advocates appear for the same defendant, the grounds of each claim must be the same: *R. v. Powell*, X8, SCTO 336/98.

The offences are summarised and listed alphabetically by statute: *post*, G–168 *et seq.*

Conspiracy, incitement or attempt to commit an offence fall within the same class as the **G–120**
substantive offence: *Funding Order* 2007, Sched. 1, para. 3 (1)(b). Conspiracy to defraud at
common law does not appear in the table of offences. Under the 2007 order, conspiracy
to defraud will fall within Class F, G or K depending on the value of the fraud. Where
the appropriate class depends upon a value, the lower value is presumed unless the
claimant "proves otherwise to the satisfaction of the appropriate authority": *Funding Order* 2007, Sched. 1, para. 3(1)(c). This may be done by extracts from the indictment or
witness statements. Values relating to offences taken into consideration should be
excluded from the computation: *GFSG*: E10.

In *R. v. O'Donnell and Fawley* [2012] Costs L.R. 431, it was held that the scheme under ★
Schedule 1 to the *Funding Order* 2007 is mechanistic and that there is no discretion for the
court to say that, because the defendants may have been shown to have committed offences in a different class, which would attract a higher fee, it is permissible to reclassify
the offence actually charged accordingly.

The calculation of values

The property values of each count falling within the same class may be aggregated, **G–121**
provided the same property is not counted twice: *Funding Order* 2007, Sched. 1, para.
3(1)(d). However, offences taken into consideration are excluded from the calculation,
even where it is agreed that the counts on the indictment are to be treated merely as
sample counts: *R. v. Knight*, X35, SCCO 34/2003.

In *R. v. Wei* [2010] Costs L.R. 846, it was held that "value", for the purposes of paragraph
3 of Schedule 2 to the *Funding Order* 2007 and the table of offences in Part 6 of Schedule
1 (*ante*, G–68, G–70; *post* G–168 *et seq.*), must, in the context of an offence of dishonesty,
such as possession of articles for use in fraud, mean the value of the dishonest enterprise,
and not the value of the particular articles. The court said that the obvious intention of the
2007 order is to provide greater remuneration for more complex and lengthy cases within
the confines of the formulaic graduated fee system.

In *Lord Chancellor v. Shapiro* [2010] Costs L.R. 769, QBD (Sweeney J.), it was held that **G–121a**
for a first hearing in the Crown Court of a case sent for trial under section 51 of the *CDA*
1998 (§ 1–24 in the main work) to fall within the graduated fee scheme under the *Funding Order* 2007 there must be an indictment in existence at the time. It was said that since
the order makes no specific provision for such hearings, it follows that they fall to be
remunerated as part of the basic fee if there is an indictment in existence at the time,
and, if there is not, there is no provision for payment; in particular, the order making no
provision for *ex post facto* taxation (except in strictly limited circumstances), there is no
power to make a payment on an *ex post facto* basis. For criticism of this decision, see the
commentary in CLW/10/38/8.

Pleas and directions hearings and pre-trial reviews

Pleas and directions hearings are not defined under the *Funding Order* 2007. Accordingly **G–122**
if a matter is listed as a pleas and directions hearing, it will be so treated. There is nothing to prevent a pleas and directions hearing from being adjourned, or there being more
than one or even a series of such hearings: *R. v. Beecham*, X11, QBD (Ebsworth J.).
However, the listing of the case is not necessarily determinative. For example, although a
case may be listed as a pleas and directions hearing, if a defendant pleads at that hearing
and is sentenced, it cannot be said that a pleas and directions hearing has taken place: *R. v.
Johnson*, SCCO 51/06. Pleas and directions hearings (other than those which form part of
the main hearing) and pre-trial reviews are payable at a fixed rate. Any pre-trial hearings to
determine, for example, the admissibility of evidence, fall outside the main hearing and are
remunerated as standard appearance fees: *R. v. Rahman*, X21, SCCO 119/2000; *R. v. Carter*, X18, SCCO 384/99. As to section 51 hearings under the *CDA* 1998, see *ante*, G–121a.

Under the *Funding Order* 2007 fees are payable for preparing and filing a plea and case
management questionnaire where no oral hearing takes place: Sched. 1, para. 9(3). Fees
for oral hearings which fall within the definition of a standard appearance are deemed to

be included in the basic fee: see *post*, G–129. Plea and case management hearings which are not standard appearances are remunerated according to the fees set out in the table following paragraph 19: *Funding Order* 2007, Sched. 1, para. 9(2). As to standard appearances, see *post*, G–129.

The start of the main hearing

G–123   In *Lord Chancellor v. Ian Henery Solicitors Ltd* [2012] Costs L.R. 205, QBD (Spencer J.), it was held that when considering the question whether, and if so on what date, a case has proceeded to trial, the following principles apply: (i) whether or not a jury have been sworn is not conclusive; (ii) there can be no doubt that a trial will have begun if the jury have been sworn, the case has been opened, and evidence has been called; (iii) a trial will also have begun if the jury have been sworn and the case has been opened to any extent, even if only for a few minutes (*Meeke and Taylor v. Secretary of State for Constitutional Affairs* [2006] Costs L.R. 1, QBD (David Clarke J.)); (iv) a trial will not have begun, even if the jury have been sworn (and whether or not the defendant has been put in the charge of the jury), if there has been no trial in a meaningful sense, *e.g.* because, before the case can be opened, the defendant pleads guilty (*R. v. Brook* [2004] Costs L.R. 178, *R. v. Baker and Fowler* [2004] Costs L.R. 693, and *R. v. Sanghera* [2008] Costs L.R. 823); (v) a trial will have begun, even if there has been no empanelment of a jury, if submissions have begun in a continuous process resulting in the empanelling of a jury, the opening of the case, and the leading of evidence (considering *R. v. Wembo* [2011] Costs L.R. 926, *R. v. Bullingham* [2011] Costs L.R. 1078, and an unreported decision of Mitting J. in December, 2005, in the case of *R. v. Smith*); (vi) if, in accordance with modern practice in long cases, a jury have been selected but not sworn, then provided the court is dealing with substantial matters of case management it may well be that the trial has begun in a meaningful sense; and (vii) where there is likely to be any difficulty in deciding whether a trial has begun, and if so when it began, the judge should be prepared, upon request, to indicate his view on the matter for the benefit of the parties and the determining officer, in the light of these principles.

In *R. v. Budai* [2011] Costs L.R. 1073, the costs judge acknowledged the principle in (v), *ante*, but held that this did not cover a case where, on the day listed for trial, all that was done was that interpreters were sworn, a potential panel of 18 jurors was selected (prior to their being sent away until the following day to assess their availability for a lengthy trial) and there was a direction made regarding the amendment of the indictment. On the other side of the line are *R. v. Wembo*, *ante* (where, immediately prior to a jury being empanelled, counsel had attended two days of hearings that related to a witness anonymity order, those days had formed part of the trial for the purposes of calculating the graduated fee); and *R. v. Bullingham*, *ante* (where a jury had not been empanelled, but the judge directed that there should be a *voire dire* to determine the admissibility of evidence which the prosecution wanted to open to the jury, and there was such a *voire dire* at which evidence was called, the trial started with the giving of that direction even though the effect of the ruling on the *voire dire* was that the prosecution decided to accept pleas to lesser offences in consequence of which the defendant pleaded guilty and there was no requirement for a jury). The reasoning in *Bullingham* was expressly approved in *Lord Chancellor v. Ian Henery Solicitors Ltd*, *ante*, but it is submitted that the result is difficult to justify, not least for its failure to give effect to the obvious purpose of paragraph 10 of Schedule 1 (*ante*, § G–46), which the costs judge did not even refer to. Sub-paragraph (1)(d) expressly contemplates that a hearing as to the admissibility of evidence may take place before the main hearing of a case (trial or cracked trial), and if it does, it is to be remunerated in accordance with that paragraph. The decision of the costs judge effectively emasculates this by converting the admissibility hearing into the main hearing. See also the commentary in CLW/12/01/14.

The start of a preparatory hearing is the commencement of the trial for the purposes of the regulations: *R. v. Jones*, X17, SCCO 527/99: *GFSG*: B8, B8A.

Calculating the length of the main hearing

G–124   Length of the main hearing means the number of days of the main hearing together with the number of days of any *Newton* hearing in relation to the assisted person whose trial is under consideration: *Funding Order* 2007, Sched. 1, paras 1(1) and 2(6). Thus, where counsel successfully submits that there is no case to answer, the main hearing ceases, despite the fact that the trial may continue against the co-defendants: *Secretary of State for Constitutional Affairs v. Stork, The Times*, October 7, 2005, QBD (Gray J.). This can lead to harsh anomalies, as where a defendant pleads guilty shortly after a jury have been sworn during an estimated three-week trial; despite preparation for a three-week trial, counsel will be remunerated as for a one day trial: *Meeke and Taylor v. Secretary of State for Constitutional Affairs, ante.* Non-sitting days cannot be included: *R. v. Nassir*, X13, SCCO 703/98. Where a jury are sworn, but discharged the same day for some reason other than the private or professional convenience of counsel, with a new jury sworn the following day, there may be sufficient continuity to conclude that the trial did in fact proceed, and start of the trial is the date on which the first jury were sworn: *R. v. Gussman*, X14, SCTO 40/99, but part of a day counts as a whole day: *Funding Order* 2007, Sched. 1, para. 4(2). Applications relating to abuse of process, disclosure and witness summonses are to be treated as part of the main hearing where they are heard during the main hearing: *Funding Order* 2007, Sched. 1, para. 10(2). The length of a fitness hearing which precedes a trial on indictment must also be included in determining the length of the trial: *Funding Order* 2007, Sched. 1, para. 26(a). Confiscation proceedings are excluded from the computation: *Funding Order* 2007, Sched. 1, para. 11(2).

Where, during the currency of a trial, there had been a day when one juror could not attend, but the judge had directed all counsel to attend in order that agreement should be reached as to how to reduce one section of the evidence, counsel was not entitled to count that day as a day of the trial; although the judge had indicated he would be available in case there was some issue on which agreement could not be reached, it had not been necessary to involve the judge and the case had not been called on in court; counsel was, however, entitled to a non-effective hearing fee for that day (under Sched. 1, para. 13 (*ante*, G–51)); the case was listed for that day, counsel had been obliged to attend, but in fact the trial did not proceed on that day: *R. v. Budai, ante.*

Fees for contested trials

The calculation of any graduated fee involves arcane formulae: *Funding Order* 2007, **G–125** Sched. 1, para. 4. To calculate the correct fee, the appropriate figures should be substituted from the tables of fees and uplifts: *Funding Order* 2007, Sched. 1, para. 5.

[**The next paragraph is G–129.**]

Standard appearances

Standard appearances are defined in the *Funding Order* 2007 as appearances which do **★G–129** not form part of the main hearing, and constitute (i) plea and case management hearings (other than the first such hearing); (ii) pre-trial reviews; (iii) the hearing of a case listed for plea which is adjourned for trial; (iv) custody time limit, bail and other applications; (v) mentions, including applications relating to the date of trial; (vi) a sentencing hearing other than one following a committal for sentence to the Crown Court, or one where sentence has been deferred under the *PCC(S)A* 2000, s.1, or one where the advocate has been instructed solely for the purposes of entering a plea in mitigation under paragraph 29 of Schedule 1; (vii) a hearing, whether contested or not, relating to breach of bail, failure to surrender to bail or execution of a bench warrant ; and (viii) any hearing (except a trial, plea and case management hearing, appeal against conviction or sentence, sentencing hearing following a committal for sentence to the Crown Court, or proceedings arising out of an alleged breach of an order of the Crown Court) which is listed but cannot proceed because of the failure of the assisted person or a witness to attend, the unavailability of a pre-sentence report or other good reason: Sched. 1, para. 1(1). Under the *Funding Order* 2007, an advocate's fees payable for the first plea and case management hearing or pre-trial review and up to four standard appearances are deemed to be included in the basic fee and are not subject to separate remuneration: Sched. 1, para. 9 (*ante*, G–47). The fifth and subsequent standard appearances are remunerated as set out in the table following paragraph 19: *ibid.*, para. 9(2).

Where an advocate made three appearances at non-effective hearings, the first two of which had been listed as a plea and case management hearing and the third of which had been listed for an anticipated plea of guilty to be taken, where the third hearing was ineffective because the defendant had absconded, and where a bench warrant had been issued which remained outstanding, paragraph 9(1) did not apply as no basic fee had become payable (and thus it did not prevent payment in respect of the three appearances); payment could be made under paragraph 9(2); there was no authority in the 2007 order for a statement in the graduated fee scheme guidance that suggested that no fee could be paid so long as a bench warrant was outstanding: *R. v. Metcalf* [2010] Costs L.R. 646.

Trial of Bail Act offences

G–130   The trial of any *Bail Act* 1976 offence in the Crown Court entitles counsel who attends to apply for a new "trial" fee for the contested trial or plea: *R. v. Shaw* [2005] Costs L.R. 326; *R. v. Despres* [2005] Costs L.R. 750.

Sendings and transfers to the Crown Court

G–131   Where cases are sent or transferred to the Crown Court under the *CDA* 1998, s.51, the *CJA* 1987, s.4 (serious fraud cases) or the *CJA* 1991, s.53 (transfer of certain cases involving children), and are discontinued before the prosecution serve their evidence (cases sent for trial), the advocate is entitled to 50 per cent of the fee calculated on the basis of a guilty plea: *Funding Order* 2007, Sched. 1, para. 18(2), together with an additional 20 per cent of that fee for each additional person represented: para. 18(7)(a). Once the prosecution have served their evidence, discontinuance, the offering of no evidence at a pleas and case management hearing, or the remitting of the case to the magistrates' court at such hearing because the indictment contains no indictable offence, is treated for the purposes of calculating the relevant fee as if each was a guilty plea: *ibid.*, para. 18(3) and (4). An advocate representing more than one person in the latter circumstances is entitled to 20 per cent of the appropriate basic fee for each additional person he represents: para. 18(7)(b).

Dismissal hearings

G–132   Where a successful application for dismissal is made under the *CDA* 1998, Sched. 3, para. 2, the *CJA* 1987, s.6, or the *CJA* 1991, Sched. 6, para. 5, with the result that the case is dismissed or remitted back to the magistrates' court, the fee is calculated as if the matter had been disposed of by a guilty plea, together with an attendance fee based upon the total number of days and half days occupied by the hearing: *Funding Order* 2007, Sched. 1, para. 18(5) and (6). A full day's hearing is any court day which begins before and ends after the luncheon adjournment: para. 18(5)(a). An advocate representing more than one person in such circumstances is entitled to 20 per cent of the appropriate basic fee for each additional person he represents: para. 18(7)(b).

Transfers

G–133   In *R. v. Rayan* [2010] Costs L.R. 969, it was held that, for the purposes of paragraph 10(2) of Schedule 2 to the *Funding Order* 2007 (*ante*, G–73a), which provides that where a case is transferred from one litigator to another, the original litigator is entitled to 25 per cent of the cracked trial fee where the transfer took place "up to and including plea and case management hearing" or a fee of 75 per cent of the cracked trial fee for a "before trial transfer", the reference to a "plea and case management hearing" must be taken to be a reference to an effective such hearing. An effective hearing, it was held, requires there to have been a plea, and for case management directions of sufficient substance to have been made such that the hearing could be described as a plea and case management hearing.

Retrials

(a) *Under representation orders made on or after April 30, 2007*

A standard graduated fee is paid for retrials, where the same advocate appears, subject to   **G–134** the following discounts based upon the time elapsed from the conclusion of the first trial to the start of the retrial: *Funding Order* 2007, para. 2(4):

30 per cent	retrial starts within one month
20 per cent	retrial starts after one month
40 per cent	retrial is cracked or becomes a guilty plea within one month
25 per cent	retrial is cracked or becomes a guilty plea after one month.

No discounts are applied where the advocate who conducts the retrial is not the advocate who conducted the original trial: *ibid.*, para. 2(5).

Where the case was committed to the Crown Court on the election of the defendant where the magistrates' court had determined the case to be suitable for summary trial, and the new trial becomes a cracked trial or guilty plea, the advocate will receive a graduated fee for the first trial and a fixed fee for the second trial: *Funding Order* 2007, Sched. 1, para. 2(4A). This also applies where the trial advocate is different at the second trial: *Funding Order* 2007, Sched. 1, para. 2(5) and (5A).

(b) *Under representation orders made before or after April 30, 2007*

Where a defence advocate was initially retained privately but, the jury at the first trial   **G–134a** having been unable to agree on a verdict, was then instructed for the retrial under a representation order, the defendant having run out of money, and where the defendant was acquitted at the retrial with a defendant's costs order being made in his favour, no payment could be made under the defendant's costs order out of central funds in respect of work done in preparation for the retrial between the date of the first trial and the grant of the representation order; the graduated fee payable for a retrial under the *Funding Order* 2001 was intended to allow for all preparation carried out for that retrial; to have authorised the payment would have resulted in a double payment out of public funds effectively in respect of the same work: *R. v. Long* [2009] Costs L.R. 151. The result would be the same under the *Funding Order* 2007.

In *Lord Chancellor v. Purnell and McCarthy* [2010] Costs L.R. 81, QBD (Sir Christopher Holland), where a full trial had been conducted in which the jury had acquitted the defendant on the main charge of murder, but had been unable to agree on an alternative charge of manslaughter and on another count of violent disorder, where a date for a retrial had been fixed, where the prosecution eventually decided to offer no evidence, and where it was clear that counsel had not, meanwhile, been standing by awaiting a decision by the prosecution whether to proceed (it was not the case that the matter had been adjourned after trial to allow the prosecution time to decide whether they intended to proceed further) but, on the contrary, had begun preparing for the retrial, it was held that counsel were entitled to a graduated fee for a "cracked trial" under paragraph 9 of Schedule 4 to the *Funding Order* 2001. They had every reason to expect and prepare for a retrial, as the case was serious and had so far featured a finding by at least three jurors that manslaughter had been proved against the defendant to the criminal standard. Under the 2001 order, there was no provision for any percentage reduction of the fee in such cases. This, however, has been remedied in the *Funding Order* 2007: see Sched. 1, para. 2(3) and (4) (*ante*, G–40).

In *R. v. Seivwright* [2011] Costs L.R. 327, it was held that paragraph 10(1) of Schedule 2 to the *Funding Order* 2007 (*ante*, G–73a) applies only where the retrial follows a trial and an order has been made for a retrial following appeal or where a jury have failed to reach a verdict, and that "retrial" for this purpose means a new trial which is not part of the same procedural and temporal matrix as the first trial. It was said that whilst this conclusion might be thought to conflict with the Litigator Graduated Fee Scheme Guidance published

by the Legal Services Commission, that was merely guidance and not a source of law that
was binding. On the facts, it was held that where the trial had commenced on a Monday,
the jury had been discharged on the Thursday, the matter was listed for mention on the
Friday when it was agreed that a new jury would be empanelled on the following Monday,
and where they were so empanelled, there was but one trial.

Guilty pleas

G–135   The *Funding Order* 2007 defines a guilty plea as a case on indictment which is disposed
of without trial because of the guilty plea, and is not a cracked trial: Sched. 1, para.
1(1)(b). Cases which result in a *Newton* hearing are excluded: *Funding Order* 2007, Sched.
1, para. 2(6)(c); and see *post*, G–147.

The graduated fee for guilty pleas is calculated by reference to the basic fee, together
with the appropriate evidence uplift per page as set out in the table of fees and uplifts:
Funding Order 2007, Sched. 1, paras 6 and 7 (and Table A).

Graduated fees for guilty pleas under Part 3 of Schedule 1 to the *Funding Order* 2007 no
longer apply to cases committed to the Crown Court on the election of the defendant
where the magistrates' court determined that the case was suitable for summary trial:
Funding Order 2007, Sched. 1, para. 5A.

In *R. v. Agbobu* [2009] Costs L.R. 374, it was held that even though a case may not be a
"guilty plea" within the definition in paragraph 1(1) of Schedule 2 to the *Funding Order*
2007 (*ante*, G–69), paragraph 16(4) of Part 3 of that schedule (*ante*, G–76a) nevertheless
provides that "where an application for dismissal is made ... and—(a) the charge, or charges
are dismissed and the assisted person is discharged; ... the litigator instructed in the
proceedings must be paid a fee calculated in accordance with paragraph 5, or where appropriate, paragraph 7, as appropriate for representing an assisted person in a guilty plea".
Accordingly, the fee payable for a litigator representing a defendant against whom charges
were dismissed was that payable for a guilty plea and not a cracked trial.

Cracked trials

G–136   A cracked trial is a case on indictment in which (a) a plea and case management hearing
takes place and (i) the case does not proceed to trial (whether by reason of pleas of guilty or
for other reasons) or the prosecution offer no evidence; and (ii) either (aa) in respect of one
or more counts to which the assisted person pleaded guilty, he did not so plead at the plea
and case management hearing; or (bb) in respect of one or more counts which did not
proceed, the prosecution did not, before or at the plea and case management hearing, declare an intention of not proceeding with them; or (b) the case is listed for trial without a
plea and case management hearing taking place: *Funding Order* 2007, Sched. 1, para. 1(1)
(the definition is defective in that in (b) there is no reference to the case not proceeding
to trial (read literally it would cover cases that go to trial where no plea and case management hearing took place)). The rationale for the cracked trial fee is that it provides some
element of compensation for the loss of refreshers and trial length increments which
otherwise would have been payable: *R. v. Frampton* [2005] Costs L.R. 527. Graduated fees
for guilty pleas under Part 3 of Schedule 1 to the *Funding Order* 2007 no longer apply to
cases committed to the Crown Court on the election of the defendant where the magistrates' court determined that the case was suitable for summary trial: *Funding Order* 2007,
Sched. 1, para. 5A.

The essence of a cracked trial is that after the conclusion of a pleas and directions hearing
there are still counts on which the prosecution and defence do not agree so that a trial
remains a real possibility: *R. v. Minster*, X23, SCTO 647/99; *R. v. Mohammed*, X27, SCCO
210/2000. A case listed for a plea and directions hearing is ultimately defined by what actually happens at that hearing. If a defendant pleads guilty at what is listed as a plea and
directions hearing, the plea obviates the need for such a hearing. Accordingly, an advocate
is entitled to a fee for a cracked trial: *R. v. Johnson* [2006] Costs L.R. 852 (*sed quaere*, as this
flies in the face of the definition of a "cracked trial": see (a), *ante*). Where an indictment
containing two counts was listed for trial following a pleas and directions hearing, but the

defendant pleaded guilty to one count, which was acceptable to the prosecution, whereupon the case was put back for sentence, and where, at the adjourned hearing, a formal not guilty verdict was entered on the other count and where the defendant was represented by different counsel on the two occasions, it was counsel who represented him on the first occasion who was entitled to the "cracked trial" fee as what happened on that occasion came within the definition of a "cracked trial" (*viz.* case was one in which pleas and directions hearing took place, case did not proceed to trial, but guilty plea not entered at that hearing): *R. v. Johnson (Craig)* [2007] Costs L.R. 316. Once a meaningful trial has started, a change of plea cannot convert the trial into a cracked trial: *R. v. Maynard*, X19, SCCO 461/99; *R. v. Karra*, X19A, SCCO 375/99; and *Meeke and Taylor v. Secretary of State for Constitutional Affairs* [2006] Costs L.R. 1, QBD (David Clarke J.). Where a jury were discharged on the second day of a trial on a three count indictment, and on the following working day the prosecution added a new lesser count, and, before a new jury were sworn, the defendant offered sufficient pleas to the indictment, counsel was entitled to a fee for the first (abortive) trial, and a cracked trial fee for the later hearing at which pleas were tendered: *Frampton, ante*.

Cracked trial fees do not apply where a person pleads not guilty at a pleas and directions hearing, but later the same day changes his plea; a guilty plea fee is appropriate: *R. v. Baxter*, X22, SCCO 375/99.

The fee for a cracked trial is calculated by reference to when the case cracked, *i.e.* in the first, second or third part of a period calculated from the date when the court first fixed the date of trial or first ordered that the case should be placed into a warned list, to the date of that first fixture or the date of the start of that warned list. The fact that the fixture might later be broken, or the case moved to another warned list is immaterial and does not affect the calculation. Where the number of days in the period cannot be equally divided by three, the remainder is simply added to the last third of the period: *Funding Order* 2007, Sched. 1, paras 6 and 7. The fee is payable to the advocate who appeared at the hearing where pleas were entered or the last such hearing if there was more than one: *R. v. Faulkner*, X33, SCCO 201/02.

In *R. v. Carty* [2009] Costs L.R. 500, it was held that where the prosecution of one of several defendants was stayed, the case fell within the definition of a "cracked trial" in paragraph 1(1) of Schedule 1 to the *Funding Order* 2007 (*ante*, G–39). The fact that the defendant's advocate had not been present on the occasion of the stay (which had been ordered at a hearing when the principal defendant, being before the court on a separate indictment, had then entered acceptable pleas to the indictment in question) did not preclude payment. Moreover, since 1996, there had been an administrative practice which permitted the prosecution to offer no evidence and an acquittal to be pronounced in open court without the legal representatives being present, and paragraph F.11 of the Graduated Fee Guidance Manual permitted a cracked trial fee to be paid in such circumstances. For this purpose, there was no reason to differentiate between a cracked trial arising from the prosecution offering no evidence and one arising from a stay.

In *R. v. Harris* [2009] Costs L.R. 507, where the defendant had pleaded guilty at a pleas and directions hearing to various offences, but where his "benefit" for the purpose of confiscation proceedings under the *CJA* 1988 had not yet been agreed, and where sentence and those proceedings had therefore been adjourned, the matter was held not to fall within the definition of a "cracked trial" in paragraph 9(3) of Schedule 4 to the *Funding Order* 2001 (which corresponds to the definition in para. 1(1) of Sched. 1 to the *Funding Order* 2007, *ante*, G–39), and the hearing at which the confiscation order was eventually made was said not to fall within the definition of a *Newton* hearing (*R. v. Newton*, 77 Cr.App.R. 13, CA) under paragraph 1(1) (corresponding to the definition in para. 1(1) of Sched. 1 to the 2007 order) for the purposes of paragraph 2(6) (see now para. 2(6) of Sched. 1 to the 2007 order, *ante*, G–40). The prosecution had accepted the basis of the defendant's guilty plea, but in the knowledge that it would take further time, and in all likelihood another hearing, to work out the defendant's benefit. The matter, therefore, fell within the definition of "guilty plea" under paragraph 9(5).

As to the distinction between a "trial" and a "cracked trial", see also *ante*, G–123.

Calculating the pages of prosecution evidence

G–137   Prosecution evidence includes all witness statements, documentary and pictorial exhibits and records of interview with any defendant forming part of the committal documents or included in any notice of additional evidence, and now includes documents served in electronic form, except for a documentary or pictorial exhibit which has never existed in paper form, unless the appropriate officer decides that it would be appropriate to include it in the page count taking into account the nature of the document and any other relevant circumstances: *Funding Order* 2007, Sched. 1, para. 1(2) to (2C), and Sched. 2, para. 1(2) to (2C). The first 50 pages must be excluded for the purposes of the calculation: *Funding Order* 2007, Sched. 1, para. 4(2). Additional documents cannot be included in the computation unless accompanied by a written notice of additional evidence: *R. v. Sturdy*, X9, December 18, 1998, SCTO 714/98; and *R. v. Gkampos* [2011] Costs L.R. 142 (pages of antecedent materials relating to the defendant). Where one or more notices of additional evidence have been served, a page count should include the contents of all such notices, unless all sides are agreed that service of a particular notice was an administrative error; and it is irrelevant when a notice was served, or whether it was requested by the defence or prosecution: *R. v. Taylor* [2005] Costs L.R. 712 (notice served on day jury retired). A prosecution notice of intention to adduce bad character evidence does not fall within the term "any notice of additional evidence": *R. v. McCall* [2011] Costs L.R. 914 (but for a critique of the reasoning, see CLW/11/40/5). Where the Crown have exhibited and served tapes of interview, and defence counsel considers that a transcript of the interview is necessary, the pages of transcript should be included in the computation: *R. v. Brazier*, X5, SCTO 810/97. Taxing officers have been directed to include the fullest transcript produced, together with the version in the transfer bundle (if shorter), and also to include any video evidence transcripts requested by the judge: *GFSG* A4, A4A. Taxing officers have been directed to exclude title and separator pages: *GFSG*: A4A; and any additional edited versions of transcripts placed before a jury: *GFSG*: A5. Fax front sheets which are no more than title pages, duplicate witness statements, whether typed or hand-written, and very short lists of (*e.g.* two) exhibits should not be counted: *R. v. El Treki*, X26, SCCO 431/2000. And nor should pages comprising admissions and a jury bundle consisting of, *inter alia*, an index and details of the defendants: *R. v. Wei* [2010] Costs L.R. 846. No allowance is made for small or large typefaces or for line spacing. Unused material is also excluded.

Whereas paragraph 1(2A) of Schedule 2 to the *Funding Order* 2007 (*ante*, G–69) lists the documents that may be included when calculating the "pages of prosecution evidence" for the purposes of determining a litigator's fee under the graduated fee scheme, the list is to be taken to be exhaustive, notwithstanding that it does not include documents which will have to be read in most cases or even referred to in court (such as the indictment, custody records, correspondence, crime reports, and unused material): *R. v. Tucker* [2010] Costs L.R. 850.

The decisions of the costs judges in *R. v. O'Cuneff* [2010] Costs L.R. 476, *R. v. Burbidge* [2010] Costs L.R. 639, and *R. v. Ibefune*, unreported, June 24, 2010, evidence a conflict as between them and the Legal Services Commission as to the weight to be given to the number of pages of prosecution evidence agreed between the parties and the Crown Court at the end of the case. The commission's stance of not accepting this figure without additional objective evidence has now, however, been fully vindicated by one of the amendments to the consolidated criminal practice direction effected by *Practice Direction (Criminal Proceedings: Listing and Case Management)* [2010] 1 W.L.R. 2333, Senior Courts. This inserts new requirements relating to the pagination and indexing of served evidence (as to which, see § 4–344 in the main work). It was plainly no coincidence that, in doing so, the practice direction adopted the (then) definition of "pages of prosecution evidence" contained in the *Funding Order* 2007. Compliance with the requirements of the new provisions by the prosecution will supply the commission (and costs judges) with an objective measure of the number of pages of prosecution evidence.

In *R. v. Greenwood* [2010] Costs L.R. 268, it was held that whereas paragraph 10(2) of Schedule 2 to the *Funding Order* 2007 (*ante*, G–73b) provides that "where ... a case is transferred to a new litigator ... the original litigator and the new litigator must receive a percentage of the total fee, in accordance with the table following [this paragraph], as appropriate to the circumstances and timing of the ... transfer", and whereas the table provides that where a case is transferred prior to the plea and case management hearing the original litigator should receive 25 per cent of a cracked trial fee, in calculating that fee, the number of pages of prosecution evidence should be taken to be the number of such pages served on the court as at the date of transfer.

Images and photographs

See now paragraphs 1(2) to (2C) of Schedules 1 and 2 to the *Funding Order* 2007 (as   **★G–138** substituted by S.I. 2012 No. 750 (as to which, see *ante*, G–1)). For authorities on the former provision, which will still apply where the representation order was granted before April 1, 2012, see *R. v. Rigelsford* [2006] Costs L.R. 518, and *R. v. Austin* [2006] Costs L.R. 857.

Fees for leading and junior counsel

Under the *Funding Order* 2007, fees payable to Queen's Counsel, leading juniors and   **G–139** led juniors are not directly related, and are calculated from the relevant tables: see, for example, the tables following paragraphs 5 and 7 of Schedule 1. Where two or more led juniors are instructed in the same case, each is paid as if they were the sole junior: Sched. 1, para. 23(1). Where a junior appears alone, but a co-defendant is represented by two counsel, the single junior is paid at the same rate as a led junior, unless his claim is for fees for a Class A offence, when he is paid as a single unled junior: *ibid.*, para. 23(2) and (3).

In *R. v. Newport* [2009] Costs L.R. 983, where two juniors appeared for the defendant   **G–140** when the representation order authorised instruction of junior counsel and Queen's Counsel, it was held that whilst a strict approach would lead to the conclusion that the leading junior was entitled to no payment, such an outcome would be unjust. Justice demanded that some payment should be made, especially given that the representation order had contemplated payment of two counsel. However, it was said that payment should be at the rate applicable to a leading junior. As to this case, see also *post*, G–269.

Advocates instructed for limited purposes

Advocates retained for a limited purpose are remunerated according to the specific provi-   **G–141** sions of the *Funding Order* 2007. The limited purposes are:
   (a) the cross-examination of witnesses under the *YJCEA* 1999, s.38, which is remunerated as if for trial, save that the daily attendance fee is calculated by reference to the number of days the advocate actually attended court, instead of the number of days of the trial itself: *Funding Order* 2007, Sched. 1, para. 27;
   (b) the provision of written or oral advice: see *post*, G–160;
   (c) mitigation of sentence on indictment, which is remunerated as for a sentencing hearing together with a fee based on the fixed hourly special preparation rate according to the "reasonable number of hours" taken: *Funding Order* 2007, Sched. 1, para. 29(1); and an advocate who is discontented with the fee paid may seek a redetermination: paras 30(2) and 29(2) respectively.

[The next paragraph is G–143.]

Instructed and substitute advocates

An instructed advocate is the first advocate instructed in the case who has primary   **G–143** responsibility for the case, or, where a representation order provides for more than one advocate, it means both the first advocate instructed who has primary responsibility for those aspects of a case undertaken by a leading advocate and the first advocate instructed who has primary responsibility for those aspects of a case undertaken by a led advocate: art. 1(1).

The new scheme (RAGFS) places great emphasis on continuity of representation. It seeks to achieve this partly by identifying an "instructed advocate" who is responsible for advocacy services and partly by paying the total fee for advocacy to the instructed advocate. An instructed advocated remains an instructed advocate at all times, although provision is made for the instructed advocate to be changed, where, for example, he is unable to conduct the trial because of a clash of commitments, is dismissed by the client, or professionally embarrassed: see Sched. 1, para. 20(9). If the instructed advocate cannot attend a preliminary hearing, and sends a substitute advocate, he nevertheless remains responsible both for the conduct of the case and the ultimate payment of the substitute advocate.

The *Funding Order* 2007 places great emphasis on identifying the instructed advocate. Instructed advocates appointed before the pleas and directions hearing must in writing inform the court of their appointment as soon as they are appointed, otherwise the advocate who attends the pleas and directions hearing will be deemed to be the instructed advocate. If no advocate attends the plea and directions hearing, the advocate who attends the next hearing will be deemed to be and will be recorded by the court as the instructed advocate: see Sched. 1, para. 20(1)–(6). Where the representation order is amended after a plea and case management hearing to include a second advocate, each advocate must notify the court in writing whether they are the led or leading advocate. Where no additional instructed advocate is notified to the court in writing within seven days of the plea and case management hearing, the advocate to appear at the next hearing is deemed to be the instructed advocate and the court will record in writing whether he is the leading instructed advocate or the led instructed advocate, as appropriate to the circumstances of the case: *ibid.*, para. 20(7).

To give effect to the scheme, emphasise the continuity of representation, and ensure that all substitute advocates are paid for any RAGFS work they undertake, the Bar Council has introduced a *Graduated Fee Payment Protocol*. The protocol is an essential part of the mechanism by which advocates will be remunerated in future, but it falls outside the immediate scope of this work. It is available on both the Bar Council's and the Criminal Bar Association's websites.

Sentencing hearings in cases on indictment

G–144   Any person appearing at a sentencing hearing in a case on indictment is entitled to a fixed fee where sentence has been deferred: *Funding Order* 2007, Sched. 1, para. 12.

A contested application for an anti-social behaviour order at a sentencing hearing does not attract a separate or additional fee: *R. v. Brinkworth* [2006] Costs L.R. 512.

Under the *Funding Order* 2007, an advocate instructed solely for the purpose of mitigation shall be paid the fee payable under paragraph 12 together with a fee calculated by reference to the reasonable number of hours of preparation for that appearance multiplied by the hourly rate set out in the table following paragraph 19 which is appropriate to the category of trial advocate: Sched. 1, para. 29(1). The advocate may apply for redetermination of such fee and shall supply such information and documents as may be required by the appropriate officer as proof of the number of hours of preparation: *ibid.*, para. 29(2).

Fitness hearings

G–145   A fitness hearing is a hearing to determine whether a defendant is fit to plead or stand trial: *Funding Order* 2007, Sched. 1, para. 26. If there is a trial on indictment at any time thereafter, the length of the fitness hearing shall be included in determining the length of the trial: *ibid.*, para. 26(a). Where a person pleads guilty at any time after a fitness hearing is held, the advocate may elect to be paid either as if the fitness hearing was a trial or for the guilty plea: *ibid.*, para. 26(c). Where a person is found to be unfit, the trial advocate may elect to treat the fitness hearing either as a trial or as a cracked trial: *ibid.*, para. 26(b).

Cross-examination of vulnerable witnesses

Where an advocate is retained solely for the purpose of cross-examining a vulnerable wit- **G–146** ness under section 38 of the *YJCEA* 1999, the graduated fee shall be assessed as though the matter was a trial, with the length of trial uplift and refresher calculated by reference to the number of days the advocate attended court: *Funding Order* 2007, Sched. 1, para. 27.

Newton hearings

Where a *Newton* hearing takes place following a trial on indictment the provisions relat- **G–147** ing to cracked trials, guilty pleas and sentencing hearings do not apply. The hearing is remunerated as for a contested trial. For the purposes of computation, the length of the *Newton* hearing is added to the main hearing: *Funding Order* 2007, Sched. 1, para. 2(6). Thus the main hearing starts on the day the plea is entered, even if this occurred during a pleas and directions hearing: *R. v. Gemeskel*, X2, SCTO 180/98. The advocate who attended the main hearing should claim the whole fee and remunerate the other advocate (if any) who attended the *Newton* hearing: *GFSG*: B12, 13.

Where a *Newton* hearing does not take place because the basis of plea was subsequently agreed, the case reverts to a guilty plea or cracked trial as appropriate: *R. v. Riddell*, X3, SCTO 318/98. If the hearing is aborted, the usual rules apply: see *post*, G–162, and *R. v. Ayres* [2002] Costs L.R. 330.

In *R. v. Newton*, 77 Cr.App.R. 13, the Court of Appeal clearly envisaged circumstances in which a sentencing judge could reach a conclusion without hearing evidence. However, the regulations define a *Newton* hearing as one at which evidence is heard for the purpose of determining the sentence of a convicted person in accordance with the *Newton* principles. Accordingly, a *Newton* hearing at which no evidence is called can only be remunerated by a standard appearance fee as it is not a *Newton* hearing for the purposes of the regulations: *R. v. Hunter-Brown*, X29, SCCO, 164/2001.

Where a *Newton* hearing is held on a committal for sentence, the only fee payable under Schedule 2 to the *Funding Order* 2007 is the fixed fee payable for a committal for sentence: *R. v. Holden* [2010] Costs L.R. 851.

Adverse judicial comment and reduction of graduated or fixed fees

Where a trial judge makes adverse observations concerning an advocate's conduct of a **G–148** graduated or fixed fee case, the appropriate authority may reduce the fee by such proportion as it "considers reasonable", having first given the advocate the opportunity to make representations about the extent of the reduction: *Funding Order* 2007, art. 27. See also *post*, G–220.

(3) Additional fees

Confiscation proceedings

Hearings under section 2 of the *DTA* 1994, section 71 of the *CJA* 1988 or Part 2 of the **G–149** *PCA* 2002 are excluded from the length computation of the main hearing and are remunerated separately as work for which a daily or half-daily fee is payable: *Funding Order* 2007, Sched. 1, para. 11(1) and (2). Entitlement to the daily fee arises where the hearing begins before but ends after the luncheon adjournment; a half-daily fee is paid where the hearing ends before or begins after the luncheon adjournment: *Funding Order* 2001, Sched. 4, para. 14; *Funding Order* 2007, Sched. 1, para. 11(2). The appropriate rates are set out in the table following paragraph 19 (*ante*, G–57).

Abuse of process, disclosure and witness summonses' etc.

Applications relating to abuse of process, disclosure or witness summonses heard before **G–150** the main hearing are paid by the same fixed daily fee as that for confiscation hearings:

Funding Order 2007, Sched. 1, para. 10(2), *ante*, G–149. As to remuneration for such applications where they take place as part of the main hearing, see *ante*, G–124. A hearing merely relating to the failure of the prosecution to comply with an earlier disclosure order attracts only a standard appearance fee: *GFSG*: 12.

In respect of representation orders granted on or after April 30, 2007, these provisions were extended to include applications relating to the admissibility of evidence, and an unsuccessful application to withdraw a guilty plea made by an advocate other than the advocate who appeared at the hearing where the plea was tendered: *Funding Order* 2007, Sched. 1, para. 10(1)(d) and (e).

[The next paragraph is G–152.]

Conferences and views

G–152   The first three pre-trial conferences or views are not separately remunerated; the fees are deemed to be included in the basic fee: Sched. 1, para. 16(2). Thereafter, the permitted number of further conferences or views (each not exceeding two hours) is as follows:

1 conference	trials of more than 20 but less than 25 days
2 conferences	trials of more than 25 days but less than 35 days
3 conferences	trials of more than 35 but less than 40 days

The number of further conferences allowed in respect of cracked trials is similar, save that the anticipated length of trial is that accepted by the court at the plea and case management hearing: Sched. 1, para. 16(3).

G–153   Conferences include conferences with expert witnesses: *Funding Order* 2007, Sched. 1, para. 16(1)(a). Travel expenses and the time taken in travelling, including time taken to travel to a conference with a defendant who could not reasonably be expected to attend counsel's chambers, are remunerated at the specified hourly rate: *ibid.*, para. 16(5). Where such fees are allowed, reasonable travelling expenses may also be claimed: *ibid.*, para. 16(4). The local bar rule has no application to such fees: *R. v. Carlyle* [2002] Costs L.R. 192.

[The next paragraph is G–156.]

Special preparation

G–156   Special preparation is preparation substantially in excess of the amount normally done for cases of the type in question and undertaken because the case involves "a very unusual or novel point of law or factual issue": *Funding Order* 2007, Sched. 1, para. 14(1)(a). "Very" qualifies both "unusual" and "novel" and the phrase "very unusual or novel" qualifies both the expressions "point of law" and "factual issue": *Meeke and Taylor v. Secretary of State for Constitutional Affairs* [2006] Costs L.R. 1, QBD (David Clarke J.). Remuneration is calculated at an hourly rate for "the number of hours preparation in excess of the amount the appropriate officer considers reasonable for cases of the same type": *Funding Order* 2007, Sched. 1, para. 14(3)(a); and with no enhancement under paragraph 24: *Lord Chancellor v. McLarty & Co. Solicitors* [2012] Costs L.R. 190, QBD (Burnett J.).

What falls to be compensated is the extra work caused by the unusual or novel point by comparison with the sort of case involved without the unusual or novel point; as the term is used in relation to the quantification of fees, "type" in this context should be defined as an indication of weight; but the exercise does not include any consideration of the reasonableness of the time claimed; thus, once the determining officer has resolved that the case qualifies for a special preparation fee, he must assess the number of hours worked in excess of the norm and compensate for those hours at the prescribed hourly rate: *R. v. Goodwin* [2008] Costs L.R. 497.

R. v. Goodwin, ante, was considered in *R. v. Kholi* [2010] Costs L.R. 982, in which it was held that under paragraph 52(i) of the Guidance Manual for the CPS Graduated Fee Scheme (which is in materially identical terms to para. 14(1)(a) of Sched. 1 to the *Funding Order* 2007 (*ante,* G–53)), it is only those hours of work attributable to the unusual or novel point of law or factual issue which was involved, which fall to be remunerated as special preparation; it is not the case that all time spent by the advocate in preparation over and above the norm for the type of case should be so remunerated.

The concept of "normal preparation" done for a case of the same type is wholly artificial. Other than in routine cases of burglary and theft, in virtually all other crimes in the criminal calendar, the circumstances vary infinitely: *R. v. Briers* [2005] Costs L.R. 146. The test is "What is the normal preparation for this offence?" not "What is the normal preparation for a case exhibiting these particular facts": *Briers, ante; R. v. Ward-Allen* [2005] Costs L.R. 745.

It is for counsel to differentiate between what he considers to be the normal preparation for a case of that type and the actual preparation that he has carried out: *Briers, ante; R. v. Marandola* [2006] Costs L.R. 184.

Very unusual or novel points of law have an obvious meaning, namely a point of law which either has never been raised or decided (novel) or which is outwith the usual professional experience (very unusual): *R. v. Ward-Allen, ante.* Some further assistance can be found in *Perry v. Lord Chancellor, The Times,* May 26, 1994, although it should be noted that that case was not concerned with these regulations.

Very unusual or novel factual issues have a similar meaning, namely a factual issue which either has never been raised or which is outwith the usual professional experience: *R. v. Ward-Allen, ante.* Such issues might cover extremely rare medical conditions, such as Munchausen's Syndrome by Proxy or "pubic symphysitis dysfunction", the exceptional, if not unique, nature of which was held in *R. v. Bishop* [2008] Costs L.R. 808, to justify a special preparation fee where it had contributed to prosecution material of over 600 pages (not served as part of the page count); novel issues might, for example have included DNA fingerprinting when it was introduced, but it would not qualify now. A case involving "shaken baby syndrome" does not necessarily attract a special preparation fee, unless there are additional medical complications: *R. v. Khair* [2005] Costs L.R. 542. A special preparation fee was allowed in *R. v. Thompson* [2006] Costs L.R. 668 where the defendant was accused of murdering her husband 10 years earlier. Counsel had to consider not only pathology and toxicology reports, but also a psychiatric profile on the husband prepared by a psychiatrist who had never met him, and issues arising in diabetology and physiology. Transcripts of the original coroner's inquest and the defendant's previous trials for theft and attempted murder of another husband were also served.

The novelty of the bad character provisions of the *CJA* 2003 did not provide grounds for claiming a special preparation fee; the criminal law is constantly changing: *R. v. Christie* [2010] 4 Costs L.R. 634.

A special preparation fee would be reasonable where counsel had to check a sample of over 33,000 original photographs of which the prosecution had only copied a representative fraction for use at trial: *R. v. Rigelsford* [2006] Costs L.R. 523; and see *ante,* G–138. But the mere fact that preparation properly undertaken for a complex three-week rape trial was "wasted" because the defendant decided to plead guilty during the prosecution opening did not justify a special preparation fee: *Meeke and Taylor v. Secretary of State for Constitutional Affairs, ante.*

A large quantity of unused material does not of itself give rise to a novel or unusual factual issue even where it is accepted that detailed examination of the material was necessary: *R. v. Lawrence* [2007] Costs L.R. 138; and even where the trial judge has extended a representation order to allow two juniors to peruse such material: *R. v. Dhaliwal* [2004] Costs L.R. 689. Such work is not remunerated under the graduated fee scheme or indeed at all: *ibid.* Nor does the mere failure of the scheme to accommodate unused material amount to as breach of the principle of equality of arms: *R. v. Marandola, ante.*

An advocate can also claim a special preparation fee where the prosecution evidence exceeds 10,000 pages and the appropriate officer considers that it is reasonable to make a payment in excess of the graduated fee which would otherwise be payable; the fee is calculated by reference to the number of hours which the appropriate officer considers reasonable to read the excess pages, using the current hourly fee rate: *Funding Order* 2007, Sched. 1, para. 14(1)(b), (2) and (3)(b).

Evidence served electronically

★**G–157**   In respect of representation orders made under the *Funding Order* 2007, a special preparation fee may also be claimed where a documentary or pictorial exhibit, which has never existed in paper form, is served by the prosecution in electronic form, and the appropriate officer does not consider it appropriate to include it in the pages of prosecution evidence; and such fee may be paid if the appropriate officer considers it reasonable to make a payment in excess of the fee otherwise payable under the graduated fee scheme, with the amount of the payment depending on the number of hours which the appropriate officer considers reasonable to view the exhibit: see Sched. 1, para. 14(1)(c) and (2), and Sched. 2, para. 15(1)(a) and (2). The drafting of these provisions in the two schedules is slightly different, but it is submitted that the intent is the same. As to the drafting, this – taken at face value – gives the appropriate officer a discretion whether to make a payment even where he considers it reasonable to do so. It is submitted, however, that the legislation is unlikely to be so construed: if the appropriate officer considers it reasonable to make a payment, then it is likely to be held that he should do so. The revised wording of these provisions (introduced by S.I. 2012 No. 750) was doubtless intended to avoid the difficulties caused by the former wording and which gave rise to a series of decisions, such as *R. v. Rigelsford* [2006] Costs L.R. 518, *R. v. Austin* [2006] Costs L.R. 857, *Lord Chancellor v. Michael J. Reed Ltd* [2010] Costs L.R. 72, QBD (Penry-Davey J.), *Lord Chancellor v. McLarty & Co. Solicitors* [2012] Costs L.R. 190, QBD (Burnett J.), and *R. v. Jones* [2010] Costs L.R. 469. For details of these authorities, which will still have application to cases in which a representation order was granted before April 1, 2012, see previous supplements.

[The next paragraph is G–159.]

Listening to or viewing tapes

G–159   Unlike under the *Funding Order* 2001, there is now no provision for any separate payment for listening to or viewing tapes. These are now treated as being rolled up within the whole of the graduated fee.

Provision of written or oral advice

G–160   Any advocate instructed solely to provide written or oral advice shall be paid a fee calculated from the reasonable number of hours of preparation for that advice using the appropriate hourly rate in the table following paragraph 19 of Schedule 1 to the *Funding Order* 2007: 2007 order, Sched. 1, para. 28(1). The advocate may apply for re-determination of such fee under article 29, and he shall supply such information and documents as may be required by the appropriate officer as proof of the number of hours of preparation: *ibid.*, para. 28(2).

As to whether a solicitor may properly instruct counsel other than counsel who appeared at trial to advise on the question of appeal where trial counsel has advised in the negative, see *R. v. Umezie*, § 7–165 in the main work.

R. v. Umezie was considered in *R. v. Bromige* [2011] Costs L.R. 145, in which it was held that where solicitors, on receipt of trial counsel's negative advice as to the prospects of a successful appeal against sentence, instructed fresh counsel to advise on the question, trial counsel's negative advice (whether written or oral) did not terminate the representation order; paragraph A1-2 of the Guide to Commencing Proceedings in the Court of Appeal (Criminal Division) (*post*, Appendix J–4) did not preclude payment of a fee for subsequent advice given by fresh counsel in relation to the appeal, because that paragraph was only concerned with the amendment of representation orders, and no amendment to the representation order granted by the magistrates' court was necessary to instruct fresh counsel to advise; however, fresh counsel's claim for a fee for his advice could only fall within paragraph 6 of Schedule 4 to the *Criminal Defence Service Funding Order* 2007 (S.I. 2007 No. 1174) (*ante*, G–85), which provides, that upon the determination of an advocate's fees in proceedings in the Court of Appeal, "the appropriate officer must consider the claim … and must allow such work as appears to him to have been reasonably done"; as a general principle it will not be reasonable to obtain advice on a point that has already been the subject of advice, with the obvious exceptions to this principle being if the initial advice is incompetent or ambiguous, or if there is a change in circumstances or if new evidence has come to light; the reason given in this case for seeking further advice, *viz.* that the solicitors were not convinced as to the correctness of the negative oral advice from trial counsel, was not sufficient; therefore the work done by fresh counsel was not reasonably done for the purposes of paragraph 6 because no good reason had been shown for instructing him to give advice on a point that had already been the subject of advice. For the submission that the costs judge's reliance on paragraph 6 of Schedule 4 is unsustainable, see CLW/11/08/45.

(4) Acting for more than one defendant, or in more than one "case"

The definition of "case" in paragraph 1(1) of Schedule 2 (*ante*, G–69) could not possibly **G–161** lead to the conclusion that if a litigator represents more than one defendant charged and tried on the same indictment that litigator is then entitled to be paid on the basis that there are as many cases as there are defendants: *Lord Chancellor v. Eddowes Perry and Osbourne Ltd* [2011] Costs L.R. 498, QBD (Spencer J.). As to this case, see also *post*, G–273.

An uplift of one-fifth for each additional defendant represented may only be claimed where the regulations so provide: *Funding Order* 2007, Sched. 1, para. 22(2). Where an advocate acts for more than one defendant, the advocate must select the case on which remuneration is to be based (the principal case). Claims for such uplifts may be made for pleas and directions hearings, some aborted hearings, main hearings, appeals against conviction, committals for sentence, proceedings for a breach of a Crown Court order, disclosure, abuse and witness summons hearings, and confiscation proceedings: *Funding Order* 2007, Sched. 1, para. 22(3). But no uplifts for these hearings, with the exception of confiscation proceedings, are payable in cases that were committed to the Crown Court on the election of the defendant, where the magistrates' court had determined that the case was suitable for summary trial: *Funding Order* 2007, Sched. 1, para. 22(2A). In respect of a trial, the uplift is limited to one-fifth of the basic fee and not the basic fee enhanced by reference to the prosecution evidence, witnesses and length of trial uplift: *Funding Order* 2007, Sched. 1, para. 22(2)(b), *i.e.* where the main hearing in each case was heard concurrently: *R. v. Fletcher*, X6, SCTO 815/97.

The above provisions also apply where the advocate conducts two or more cases concurrently: *Funding Order* 2007, Sched. 1, para. 22(2). Proceedings arising out of a single notice of appeal against conviction or sentence, or single committal for sentence, constitute a separate "case": para. 1(1) of Schedule 1 to the 2007 order. However, a committal for sentence together with a committal for breach of a community service order constituted two separate "cases" as the latter was a committal for breach of an earlier order: *R. v. Hines*, X24, SCCO 337/2000. As a case means proceedings on one or more counts of a single indictment, it is submitted that two trials arising from a severed indictment give rise to two separate graduated fees, as the trials are not heard concurrently.

In *R. v. Fury* [2011] Costs L.R. 919, it was said that if a hearing deals with one case then another, independently of each other, it will be hearing them consecutively; hearings will be concurrent only if they are combined or conjoined or somehow interlinked; this will be so where the main hearings of a number of cases against the same defendant are listed together and the defendant either pleads guilty or is to be sentenced in all of the cases; the cases will impact on each other either as to the directions that are given for sentencing or as to the sentences that are imposed; they will not be considered independently of each other. For criticism of the actual decision in this case (cases were not heard concurrently where, as part of an agreed package, defendant pleaded guilty to one indictment and prosecution offered no evidence on the other, all counts having originally been in the same indictment), see CLW/11/40/3.

In *R. v. Sturmer and Lewis* [2009] Costs L.R. 364, it was said that the combined effect of paragraph 12 and the table following paragraph 14 of Part 3 of Schedule 2 to the *Funding Order* 2007 (*ante*, Appendix G–74a, G–75a) is that where a litigator is "instructed in ... a sentencing hearing following a committal for sentence to the Crown Court", the "fee payable ... is that set out in the table" (para. 12), *i.e.* "£212.77" per proceedings (the table). "Proceedings" can involve more than one defendant and, if there is only one "proceedings", only one fee will be payable, however many defendants are represented by the litigator.

[**The next paragraph is G–163.**]

(5) Abortive hearings

G–163   The payment of fixed fees for abortive hearings is limited to ineffective trials: see Sched. 1, para. 13. As to this, see *R. v. Budai, ante*, G–124.

(6) Wasted preparation

G–164   Wasted preparation occurs where an advocate does not represent his client because of (a) a clash of listings and the advocate has been unable to secure a change of date for either hearing; or (b) a fixture for a main hearing is altered by the court despite the advocate's objection; or (c) the advocate withdraws with leave of the court because of professional embarrassment; or (d) the advocate is dismissed by the client; or (e) the advocate is obliged to undertake judicial or other public duties: *Funding Order* 2007, Sched. 1, para. 15(1). A representation order replacing a single junior with Queen's Counsel acting alone does not entitle junior counsel to claim a wasted preparation fee in respect of the preparation reasonably and properly undertaken; counsel has no redress under the scheme: *R. v. Schultz*, X10, SCTO 552/98. The hourly fee may be claimed only where eight or more hours of preparation have been undertaken, and (a) the trial lasted for five days or more, or (b) in the case of a cracked trial, there are more than 150 pages of prosecution evidence: *Funding Order* 2007, Sched. 1, para. 15(2). The wasted preparation fee is calculated by reference to the number of hours of preparation reasonably carried out by the advocate, who must supply such information and documents in support of the claim as may be required: *Funding Order* 2007, Sched. 1, para. 15(3) and (5).

The requirements of paragraph 18(1) of Schedule 4 to the *Funding Order* 2001 (see Sched. 1, para. 15(1)(b), to the 2007 order, *ante*, G–53) were satisfied where, following the vacation of the trial date by the trial judge and his proposal of a new date, counsel had written objecting to the new date (on the grounds that he had booked and paid for a holiday abroad that started within 10 days of the new date), but where, despite that objection, the trial had gone ahead on the proposed date, with the result that counsel had had to return the brief: *R. v. Ghaffar* [2009] Costs L.R. 980. The fact that counsel's objection was to the new date, and not to the vacation of the original fixture, was not a valid ground for refusing a wasted preparation fee in respect of the substantial preparation done by counsel prior to the vacation of the original fixture. Changing a fixture is a process and an objection to part of that process is therefore an objection to the change. There was nothing in paragraph 18(1)(b) that restricted it to counsel's professional commitments.

(7) Appeals, pleas before venue, committals and other fees

G–165   Graduated fixed fees are also payable in respect of committals for sentence (which include plea before venue cases), appeals from magistrates' courts and breach of Crown Court orders: *Funding Order* 2007, Sched. 4, para. 17; noting briefs: *Funding Order* 2007, Sched. 4, para. 19; bail and other applications, and mentions when not forming part of a main hearing or other hearing for which a fixed fee is provided: *Funding Order* 2007, Sched. 4, para. 17(3). The appropriate rate is that listed in the table following paragraph 19 in Schedule 1 to the 2007 order. After the Crown Court is seized of a case, any bail applications, or executions of bench warrants made in a magistrates' court are remunerated as if made in the Crown Court: *R. v. Bailey*, X16, 378/99. As to trials of *Bail Act* 1976 offences, see *ante*, G–130.

(8) Contempt proceedings

Remuneration for proceedings for contempt in the face of the court is fixed at discrete daily rates: *Funding Order* 2007, art. 13, and Sched. 1, para. 17A. The fees are fixed and there is no discretion to allow *ex post facto* payment, however regrettable and unfair the result may be: *R. v. Russell* [2006] Costs L.R. 841. Such payments do not fall within the graduated fee scheme and, therefore, such hearings do not form part of the main hearing or the sentencing hearing. **G–166**

(9) Travel expenses

Travel and hotel expenses may be claimed subject to the usual 40 kilometre local bar rule: *Funding Order* 2007, Sched. 1, para. 24 (see generally *post*, G–253). Expenses should not be paid in respect of conferences for which advocates are not entitled to be remunerated, unless the conference was abortive due to circumstances beyond the advocate's control: *R. v. Pickett*, X39. **G–167**

(10) Table of offences

The effect of the table of offences at the end of Schedule 1 to the *Funding Order* 2007 (as amended by the *Bribery Act 2010 (Consequential Amendments) Order* 2011 (S.I. 2011 No. 1441)) is set out in the following paragraphs. Under the 2007 order, offences are divided into those below £30,000, those where the value is £30,000 or more, but less than £100,000, and those where the value involved is £100,000 or more. As to the method of calculation for the purposes of determining value, see *ante*, G–121. As to conspiracy, incitement and attempt, see *ante*, G–120. **G–168**

An "armed robbery" (see the *Theft Act* 1968 entries) arises where the offender was armed with a firearm or imitation firearm, or was thought by the victim to have been so armed, or was armed with an offensive weapon: *R. v. Stables*, X12, SCTO 102/99.

Where a judge proposes to try an offence under the *Bail Act* 1976, s.6, in respect of a defendant who is first brought up before him for non-attendance, then there is a trial or guilty plea under the graduated fee scheme: *R. v. Shaw* [2005] Costs L.R. 326.

As several statutes are listed under more than one class, the following is a list of the statutes and orders featured in the table, with the classes in which they appear— **G–169**

Air Navigation Order 2005 (S.I. 2005 No. 1970)	H
Aviation Security Act 1982	B
Bail Act 1976	H
Bribery Act 2010	I
Child Abduction Act 1984	C
Crime and Disorder Act 1998	B, C, H
Children and Young Persons Act 1933	B, J
Cremation Act 1902	I
Criminal Damage Act 1971	B, C
Criminal Justice Act 1961	C
Criminal Justice Act 1967	I
Criminal Justice Act 1988	H
Criminal Justice Act 1991	B

Criminal Justice (International Co-operation) Act 1990	B
Criminal Justice (Terrorism and Conspiracy) Act 1998	I
Criminal Justice and Public Order Act 1994	I
Criminal Law Act 1967	I
Criminal Law Act 1977	D
Customs and Excise Management Act 1979	B, C, F, G, H, K
Dangerous Dogs Act 1991	C
Disorderly Houses Act 1751	H
Domestic Violence, Crime and Victims Act 2004	B
Drug Trafficking Act 1994	B, I
Drug Trafficking Offences Act 1986	C
European Communities Act 1972	I
Explosive Substances Act 1883	A, B
Firearms Act 1968	B, C
Firearms (Amendment) Act 1988	C
Forgery Act 1861	F, I
Forgery and Counterfeiting Act 1981	F, G, K
Fraud Act 2006	F, G, K
Hallmarking Act 1973	F, G, K
Identity Cards Act 2006	F
Immigration Act 1971	C
Indecency with Children Act 1960	J
Indecent Displays (Control) Act 1981	H
Infant Life (Preservation) Act 1929	A
Infanticide Act 1938	A
Insolvency Act 1986	G
Magistrates' Courts Act 1980	I
Malicious Damage Act 1861	H
Mental Health Act 1983	D
Merchant Shipping Act 1970	H
Misuse of Drugs Act 1971	B, C, H
Nuclear Material (Offences) Act 1983	B
Obscene Publications Act 1959	H
Offences against the Person Act 1861	A, B, C, H
Perjury Act 1911	I
Post Office Act 1953	H
Prevention of Corruption Act 1906	I
Prevention of Crime Act 1953	H
Prison Act 1952	C
Prison Security Act 1992	B
Proceeds of Crime Act 2002	B
Prohibition of Female Circumcision Act 1985	C
Protection from Eviction Act 1977	H
Protection from Harassment Act 1997	H

Protection of Children Act 1978	J
Public Bodies Corrupt Practices Act 1889	I
Public Order Act 1986	B, C, H
Public Passenger Vehicles Act 1981	H
Road Traffic Act 1960	H
Road Traffic Act 1988	B, H
Road Traffic Regulation Act 1984	H
Sexual Offences Act 1956	D, H, J
Sexual Offences Act 1967	D, H, J
Sexual Offences Act 2003	D, J
Sexual Offences (Amendment) Act 2000	D
Stamp Duties Management Act 1891	F, G, K
Submarine Telegraph Act 1885	C
Suicide Act 1961	B
Taking of Hostages Act 1982	B
Terrorism Act 2000	B, C
Theatres Act 1968	H
Theft Act 1968	B, C, E, F, G, H, K
Theft Act 1978	F, G, H, K
Trade Descriptions Act 1968	H, I
Treason Act 1842	C
Value Added Tax Act 1994	F, G, K
Vehicle Excise and Registration Act 1994	H

Class A: homicide and related grave offences

(i) *Common law offences*
   Murder and manslaughter

G–170

(ii) *Offences created by primary or secondary legislation*
   Those contrary to the following provisions:
        Explosive Substances Act 1883, ss.2 and 3;
        Infant Life (Preservation) Act 1929, s.1(1);
        Infanticide Act 1938, s.1(1);
        Offences against the Person Act 1861, s.4.

Class B: offences involving serious violence or damage, and serious drugs offences

(i) *Common law offences*
   Kidnapping and false imprisonment

G–171

(ii) *Offences created by primary or secondary legislation*
   Those contrary to the following provisions:
        Aviation Security Act 1982, s.2(1)(b);
        Crime and Disorder Act 1998, s.30(1);

Children and Young Persons Act 1933, s.1;
Criminal Damage Act 1971, s.1(2) and (where the value exceeds £30,000) s.1(3);
Criminal Justice Act 1991, s.90;
Criminal Justice (International Co-operation) Act 1990, ss.12 and 18;
Customs and Excise Management Act 1979, s.50 (Class A or B drugs), s.85, s.170(2)(b)
  or (c) (in relation to Class A or B drugs);
Domestic Violence, Crime and Victims Act 2004, s.5;
Drug Trafficking Act 1994, ss.49, 50, 51, 52 and 53;
Explosive Substances Act 1883, s.4(1);
Firearms Act 1968, ss.5, 16, 17 and 18;
Misuse of Drugs Act 1971, s.4 (Class A or B drug), s.5(3) (Class A or B drug), ss.6, 8, 9,
  12 and 13;
Nuclear Material (Offences) Act 1983, s.2;
Offences against the Person Act 1861, ss.16, 17, 18, 21, 22, 23, 28, 29, 30, 32, 33, 34
  and 58;
Prison Security Act 1992, s.1;
Proceeds of Crime Act 2002, ss.327, 328, 329, 330, 331, 332, 333, 339(1A);
Public Order Act 1986, ss.1, 2 and 38;
Road Traffic Act 1988, ss.1, 3A and 22A;
Suicide Act 1961, s.2;
Taking of Hostages Act 1982, s.1;
Terrorism Act 2000, ss.11, 12, 13, 15, 16, 17, 18, 39, 54, 56, 57, 58 and 59;
Theft Act 1968, s.8(1) (if "armed"), s.8(2) (if "with weapon"), s.10, s.12A (if resulting
  in death) and 21.

Class C: lesser offences involving violence or damage, and less serious drugs offences

(i) *Common law offences*

G–172   Permitting an escape, rescue, breach of prison and escaping from lawful custody without
force

(ii) *Offences created by primary or secondary legislation*
     Those contrary to the following provisions:
          Child Abduction Act 1984, ss.1 and 2;
          Crime and Disorder Act 1998, ss.29(1) and 30(1);
          Criminal Damage Act 1971, s.1(1) and, where the offence does not also fall within sec-
            tion 1(2) and where the value of the damage is less than £30,000, s.1(3), s.2 and
            s.3;
          Criminal Justice Act 1961, s.22;
          Criminal Law Act 1977, s.51;
          Customs and Excise Management Act 1979, s.50 (in relation to Class C drugs), s.68A(1)
            and (2), s.86, s.170(2)(b), (c) (in relation to Class C drugs);
          Dangerous Dogs Act 1991, s.3;
          Drug Trafficking Offences Act 1986, ss.26B and 26C;
          Firearms Act 1968, ss.1, 2, 3, 4, 19, 20, 21(4), 21(5) and 42;
          Firearms (Amendment) Act 1988, s.6(1);
          Immigration Act 1971, s.25;
          Misuse of Drugs Act 1971, s.4 (Class C drug), s.5(2) (Class A drug), s.5(3) (Class C
            drug);
          Offences against the Person Act 1861, ss.20, 24, 26, 27, 31, 37, 47, 59, 60 and 64;
          Prison Act 1952, s.39;
          Prohibition of Female Circumcision Act 1985, s.1;

Public Order Act 1986, ss.18 to 23;
Submarine Telegraph Act 1885, s.3;
Terrorism Act 2000, s.19;
Theft Act 1968, s.8(1) (other than when "armed");
Treason Act 1842, s.2.

Class D: sexual offences and offences against children

Offences created by primary or secondary legislation
    Those contrary to the following provisions: **G–173**
        Criminal Law Act 1977, s.54;
        Mental Health Act 1983, s.127;
        Sexual Offences Act 1956, s.4, s.9, s.10 (other than by man with girl under 13), s.11,
            s.13 (between male aged 21 or over and male under 16), ss.14, 15, 19, 21, 23, 27,
            29, 30 and 31;
        Sexual Offences Act 1967, s.5;
        Sexual Offences Act 2003, s.3, s.4 (without penetration), ss.11 to 13, 15 to 19, 32, 33,
            36, 37, 40, 41, 52, 53, 61 to 67, 69 and 70;
        Sexual Offences (Amendment) Act 2000, s.3.

Class E: burglary, etc.

Offences created by primary or secondary legislation
    Those contrary to the following provisions: **G–174**
        Theft Act 1968, ss.9 and 25

Classes F, G and K: other offences of dishonesty (offences always in Class F)

Offences created by primary or secondary legislation
    Those contrary to the following provisions: **G–175**
        Forgery Act 1861, ss.36, 37;
        Identity Cards Act 2006, s.25(1), (3) and (5).

Classes F, G and K: other offences of dishonesty (offences always in Class G)

Offences created by primary or secondary legislation
    Those contrary to the following provisions: **G–176**
        Customs and Excise Management Act 1979, s.50 (counterfeit notes or coins), s.170(2)(b)
            or (c) (counterfeit notes or coins);
        Forgery and Counterfeiting Act 1981, ss.14 to 17;
        Insolvency Act 1986, s.360.

Classes F, G and K: other offences of dishonesty (offences in Class G if value exceeds £30,000, in Class K if value exceeds £100,000 and otherwise in Class F)

Offences created by primary or secondary legislation
    Those contrary to the following provisions: **G–177**
        Customs and Excise Management Act 1979, s.50 (to the extent not specified elsewhere),
            s.168, s.170(1)(b), s.170(2)(b), (c) (to the extent not specified elsewhere);
        Forgery and Counterfeiting Act 1981, ss.1 to 5;
        Fraud Act 2006, ss.2, 3, 4, 6, 7, 9 and 11;
        Hallmarking Act 1973, s.6;
        Stamp Duties Management Act 1891, s.13;

Theft Act 1968, ss.1, 11, 13, 15, 16 and 22;
Theft Act 1978, ss.1 and 2;
Value Added Tax Act 1994, s.72(1)–(8).

Class H: miscellaneous other offences

(i) *Common law offences*

G–178   Keeping a disorderly house, outraging public decency

(ii) *Offences created by primary or secondary legislation*
   Those contrary to the following provisions:
   Air Navigation Order 2005 (S.I. 2005 No. 1970), art. 75;
   Bail Act 1976, s.9(1);
   Crime and Disorder Act 1998, ss.1(10), 2(8), 31(1) and 32(1);
   Criminal Justice Act 1988, s.139;
   Customs and Excise Management Act 1979, ss.13 and 16;
   Disorderly Houses Act 1751, s.8;
   Indecent Displays (Control) Act 1981, s.1;
   Malicious Damage Act 1861, s.36;
   Merchant Shipping Act 1970, s.27;
   Misuse of Drugs Act 1971, s.5(2) (Class B or C drug); s.11;
   Obscene Publications Act 1959, ss.1 and 2;
   Offences against the Person Act 1861, ss.35 and 38;
   Post Office Act 1953, s.11;
   Prevention of Crime Act 1953, s.1;
   Protection from Eviction Act 1977, s.1;
   Protection from Harassment Act 1997, ss.3(6), 4(1) and 5(5);
   Public Order Act 1986, s.3;
   Public Passenger Vehicles Act 1981, s.65;
   Road Traffic Act 1960, s.233;
   Road Traffic Act 1988, ss.2 and 173;
   Road Traffic Regulation Act 1984, s.115;
   Sexual Offences Act 1956, ss.2, 3, 12, 13 (other than where one participant over 21
      and the other under 16), 22, 24 and 32;
   Sexual Offences Act 1967, s.4;
   Theatres Act 1968, s.2;
   Theft Act 1968, s.12A (but not where death results);
   Theft Act 1978, s.3;
   Trade Descriptions Act 1968, ss.1, 8, 9, 12, 13 and 14;
   Vehicle Excise and Registration Act 1994, s.44.

Class I: offences against public justice and similar offences

(i) *Common law offences*

G–179   Embracery, fabrication of evidence with intent to mislead tribunal, perverting the course
of justice and personation of jurors

(ii) *Offences created by primary or secondary legislation*
   Those contrary to the following provisions:
   Bribery Act 2010, ss.1, 2 and 6;
   Cremation Act 1902, s.8(2);
   Criminal Justice Act 1967, s.89;

Criminal Justice (Terrorism and Conspiracy) Act 1998, s.5;
Criminal Justice and Public Order Act 1994, ss.51(1) and (2), 75(1) and (2);
Criminal Law Act 1967, ss.4(1) and 5;
Drug Trafficking Act 1994, s.58(1);
European Communities Act 1972, s.11;
Forgery Act 1861, s.34;
Magistrates' Courts Act 1980, s.106;
Perjury Act 1911, ss.1 to 7(2);
Prevention of Corruption Act 1906, s.1;
Public Bodies Corrupt Practices Act 1889, s.1;
Trade Descriptions Act 1968, s.29(2).

Class J: serious sexual offences

Offences created by primary or secondary legislation
   Those contrary to the following provisions: **G–180**
      Children and Young Persons Act 1933, ss.25, 26;
      Indecency with Children Act 1960, s.1(1);
      Protection of Children Act 1978, s.1;
      Sexual Offences Act 1956, ss.1(1), 5, 6, 7, 10, 12 (of person under 16), 16, 17, 20, 25,
        26 and 28;
      Sexual Offences Act 2003, ss.1, 2, 4 (activity involving penetration), 5 to 10, 14, 25, 26,
        30, 31, 34, 35, 38, 39, 47 to 50 and 57 to 59.

G. Very High Cost Cases

Definition

For the definition of a "Very High Cost Case", see article 2 of the *Funding Order* 2007 **G–181**
(*ante*, G–7). Article 3(6) (*ante*, G–8) provides that the order does not apply to Very High
Costs Cases.

Background

Unlike the former scheme for the *ex post facto* taxation of fees (as to which, see Appendix **G–182**
G in the supplements to the 2010 edition of this work) and the graduated fee scheme, the
Very High Cost Case ("VHCC") regime is not concerned with fee assessment after the
completion of a case. VHCCs operate under a contract-based system where litigators' and
advocates' tasks and the time allotted for each task are agreed or determined before the
work is undertaken. They are managed by the Complex Crimes Unit ("CCU") of the Legal
Services Commission. Under the current regime (described in more detail, *post*), litigators
(referred to by the Legal Services Commission as "organisations") are required to notify the
Legal Services Commission of any case which is, or is likely to be, a VHCC (General Regulations, reg. 23). Under the current (post July 13, 2010) arrangements, once a case is classified
by the commission as a VHCC, the organisation is required to become accredited in order
to undertake the case, and, if it is successful, must sign a VHCC contract (for organisations)
with the commission. The current regime differs from the VHCC panel regime that operated between January 14, 2008 and July 13, 2010 in that under the previous regime, a
time-limited "best value" tendering competition took place between supplier law firms for
places on the VHCC Panel, and only organisations which had become members of the
panel were permitted to conduct VHCCs. Under the current regime, organisations may apply for accreditation at any time as and when they need to do so.

Cases where the representation order was granted on or after July 14, 2010, are governed
by the *Very High Cost (Crime) Cases Arrangements 2010* (Version 2 – July 27, 2010), made by
the commission under section 3(4) of the *Access to Justice Act* 1999. Cases where the repre-

sentation order was granted on or after January 14, 2008, but before July 14, 2010, operate under the previous VHCC panel contracting system, which is detailed in the third supplement to the 2010 edition of this work. Cases classified as VHCCs prior to January 14, 2008, are governed by an older individual case contracts regime detailed in the first supplement to the 2008 edition of this work. In multi-handed cases where different defendants have representation orders dated before and after the cut-off dates for the different regimes, the commission will decide which scheme to apply, taking into account the dates of all the representation orders and all the circumstances of the case.

Classification of a case as a Very High Cost Case

G–183   In relation to cases where the representation order is dated on or after July 14, 2010, article 5 of the *Criminal Defence Service (Funding) (Amendment No. 2) Order* 2010 (S.I. 2010 No. 1181) amended article 2 of the *Funding Order* 2007 (*ante*, G–7) so as to substitute a revised definition of a VHCC which differs depending on whether the fee is being claimed by an organisation ("litigator") or by a self-employed advocate (a barrister in independent practice or a solicitor-advocate).

A case will be deemed to be a VHCC in relation to organisations where the representation order is granted on or after July 14, 2010 and, (a) if the case were to proceed to trial, the trial would in the opinion of the Legal Services Commission, be likely to last for more than 40 days, and the commission consider that there are no exceptional circumstances which make the case unsuitable to be dealt with under its contractual arrangements for Very High Cost Cases, or (b) if the case were to proceed to trial, the trial would in the opinion of the commission be likely to last no fewer than 25 and no more than 40 days and the commission consider that there are circumstances which make it suitable to be dealt with as a VHCC. Paragraph 5.4 of the Arrangements provides that the commission will only classify a category (b) case as a VHCC if it is prosecuted by the Serious Fraud Office, is a terrorism case, or if, in the opinion of the commission, exceptional circumstances apply.

A case will be deemed to be a VHCC in relation to advocates where, if the case were to proceed to trial, the trial would in the opinion of the commission be likely to last for more than 60 days, and the commission consider that there are no exceptional circumstances which make it unsuitable for the case to be dealt with under its contractual arrangements for VHCCs.

Once a case is deemed by the commission to be a VHCC, a decision letter is issued to the organisation which notified the commission of the case, and, if applicable, to the self-employed advocate instructed in the case.

Paragraph 10(6) of Schedule 2 (now para. 10(9), *ante*, G–73b) is not to be construed literally; where, therefore (in a case in which the representation order was granted in April, 2009), a very high cost case panel firm was instructed under the representation order prior to the case being classified as a very high cost case, where it continued to act after such classification and where, after the defendant had pleaded guilty and been put back for sentence, the representation order was withdrawn (apparently on the application of the solicitors) by order of the court, solicitors and counsel fell to be remunerated under the very high cost cases regime, not the graduated fee regime; paragraph 10(6) had no application to this situation; rather, it was intended to deal with the remuneration of a non-panel firm where a case is reclassified as a very high cost case whereupon the representation order is withdrawn (rather than being transferred to another litigator, in which case para. 10(5) (now para. 10(8)) is engaged): *Lord Chancellor v. Alexander Johnson & Co. Solicitors and McCarthy* [2011] Costs L.R. 987, QBD (Davis J.).

Notification that a case will be, or is likely to be, a Very High Cost Case

G–184   Under regulation 23(1) of the General Regulations (§ 6–177 in the main work), any litigator (the person named on the representation order as representing an assisted person) who has conduct of a case which is, or is likely to be classified as, a VHCC must notify the Legal Services Commission accordingly, in writing, as soon as is practicable. Notification is effected by submitting a VHCC Notification Request Form, which is available on the commission's website, to the CCU: Arrangements, para 4.3. The notification must be submitted within five business days of (it is presumed, the earlier of) the earliest hearing at which the court sets a trial estimate, or of the organisation identifying the case as being or being likely to be a VHCC. Where an organisation fails to notify the commission on time, the commission may impose any sanction on the organisation in accordance with any contract it has with the organisation, and it may exclude the organisation from undertaking work on the case which was not notified on time. Where an organisation persistently fails to notify the commission of cases which will be, or are likely to be, classified as a VHCC, the commission may exclude the organisation from undertaking future VHCC work, and may refuse any payment to the organisation in relation to the case: Arrangements, paras. 4.1, 4.2.

VHCC accreditation of organisations and advocates

The Legal Services Commission will only enter into a contract for a case classified as a   **G–185** VHCC for organisations, with organisations which have been granted VHCC accreditation. Where a case is classified both as a VHCC for organisations and as a VHCC for advocates, any self-employed advocate instructed on the case must be accredited and must work on the case under the VHCC Contract (for advocates), unless the advocate works on the case *pro bono* or is privately funded. Where a case is classified as a VHCC for organisations but not for advocates, any self-employed advocate instructed on the case will not be required to be accredited, and will be remunerated under the advocates' graduated fee scheme as for any other case.

Organisations may apply for accreditation at any point from July 14, 2010, onwards, via an e-accreditation system, guidance on which is available from the commission's website. Organisations must meet the eligibility criteria contained in Annex A to the Arrangements in order to undertake VHCC work, other than in specified exceptional circumstances, in which case the express written permission of the commission will be required. Previous members of the VHCC Crime Panel do not need to resubmit information which was provided in 2007/8, provided there have been no fundamental changes to their structure.

If an organisation's application is successful, the commission will issue a conditional accreditation notice which confirms that the organisation satisfies criteria 1–16 in Annex A and is effective in relation to each VHCC which the organisation applies to undertake. A full accreditation notice must be granted in relation to each VHCC, and is granted when the commission confirm that criteria 17 and 18 are met, *viz.* that the organisation has a VHCC supervisor in post, and that person meets specified requirements.

If an organisation's application is unsuccessful, it may apply for reassessment and, if again unsuccessful, may not re-apply for accreditation within six months unless, in the opinion of the commission, exceptional circumstances apply. Such an organisation will be instructed to pass the VHCC in respect of which it sought accreditation to an organisation which has been accredited, and a date will be specified by the commission from which no work undertaken on the case will be paid for by the commission.

As at October 2011, it was understood that the Legal Services Commission were proposing to write directly to advocates whom the commission had identified as being regularly instructed on VHCCs, with details of the accreditation process for advocates. Other advocates must apply to the commission for accreditation, when it is proposed that they be instructed on a case which is, or is likely to be, a VHCC. After accreditation for an advocate's first VHCC has been obtained, accreditation will need to be obtained for each subsequent VHCC through a shortened process.

The VHCC Contracts

Once the Legal Services Commission issue a decision letter classifying a case as a VHCC,   **G–186** it will issue a 2010 VHCC Contract (for organisations) to the organisation and, where the case satisfies the definition of a VHCC for advocates and a self-employed advocate has been instructed, a 2010 VHCC Contract (for self-employed advocates) to the self-employed advocate: Arrangements, paras 5.5, 5.6. The organisation and, where applicable, self-employed advocate, must submit a signed copy of the contract within 15 business days from the date of the decision letter: Arrangements, para. 6.1. The terms of any such contract will only apply from the point at which it is signed by both parties, but, from the date of the decision letter, the organisation (and, where applicable, self-employed advocate) may not claim payment for work done otherwise than under the VHCC scheme: 2010 VHCC Guidance (as to which, see *ante*, G–3), para. 2.22. An organisation that fails to submit a signed copy of the contract within 15 business days will be unable to claim any payment for work undertaken on the VHCC after the expiry of the 15-day time limit.

The contractual arrangement between the organisation and the commission is contained in three documents: the 2010 VHCC Contract for Signature (for organisations), including the Annex; the 2010 VHCC Specification (for organisations); and the Standard Terms 2010. Any conflict between the terms of the documents, which is not explicitly dealt with in the documents themselves, is resolved in the order in which the documents are listed in the previous sentence (*i.e.* the Contract for Signature is first in order of priority): clause 12.1 of the Standard Terms, as amended by clause 3.6 of the Contract for Signature. Equivalent contractual documents exist for self-employed advocates, but all references herein to contractual documents are to clauses in the contracts for organisations.

The Contract for Signature contains terms specific to the VHCC which is the subject of the contract, and is the only contractual document which needs to be signed each time an organisation undertakes a new VHCC. Upon sending out the decision letter and contract documents, the CCU will complete case-specific fields in the Contract for Signature, the Annex to which sets out information and terms specific to the organisation and the VHCC. The VHCC Specification contains terms governing the conduct of all VHCCs, and the Standard Terms contain terms applicable to all work undertaken under a contract with the Legal Services Commission.

If for any reason the commission serve notice that they do not intend to enter into a contract with an organisation, or if the organisation does not wish to undertake the case, the organisation must notify the client of his right to select another accredited organisation to undertake the case. The commission will specify a date from which no work undertaken on the case will be paid for.

Remuneration

G–187 Preparatory and advocacy work on a VHCC is remunerated at the rates specified in section 7 of the VHCC Specifications. Once a case is classified as a VHCC, the Legal Services Commission will assign it to one of four categories against the criteria contained in clause 4.22 of the VHCC Specification (see also §§ 4.12 *et seq.* in the VHCC Guidance). For this purpose, the contracted organisation is required to submit a completed VHCC category assessment sheet within 15 business days of the decision letter: Arrangements, para. 6.2(c). The category to which the case is assigned determines the hourly rate payable for preparatory work undertaken by litigators. Advocacy rates are non-category specific.

Self-employed advocates are remunerated directly by the LSC: clause 5.22 of the VHCC Specification (for organisations). Where the VHCC has been classified both as a VHCC for organisations and for advocates, self-employed advocates must claim under their VHCC contract. Where the case is a VHCC for organisations but has not been classified as a VHCC for advocates, any self-employed advocate must claim under the advocates' graduated fee scheme. Employed advocates must claim payment through their organisation, whether under the graduated fee scheme (where the VHCC has not been classified as a VHCC for advocates) or under the VHCC scheme (where the VHCC is a VHCC in relation to both organisations and advocates).

[The next paragraph is G–195.]

H. Preparation and Submission of Claims

(1) The preparation of claims

There is no mandatory graduated fee form. The use of computer-generated forms is   **G–195**
permitted and this allows only the relevant data to be submitted. As to graduated fees generally, see *ante*, G–115 *et seq.*

(2) Time limits for the submission of claims

No claim by an advocate for fees for work done shall be entertained unless submitted   **G–196**
within three months of the conclusion of the proceedings to which it relates: *Funding Order*
2007, art. 5(3). However, where a confiscation hearing under section 2 of the *DTA* 1994,
section 71 of the *CJA* 1988 or Part 2 of the *PCA* 2002 is held more than 28 days after a
person has been found or pleaded guilty, a graduated fee claim can be submitted despite
the fact that the proceedings have not yet been completed: *Funding Order* 2007, art. 5(6).
The time limit may be extended for "good reason": *Funding Order* 2007, art. 32(1); for
example, where the claim is particularly complicated and difficult to prepare, where a co-
defendant's case is awaiting disposal, or because there is a genuine misunderstanding
about the submission of a claim. Extensions should be sought before the time limit
expires.

Where there are no good reasons, the time may be extended in "exceptional circum-   **G–197**
stances", in which case the appropriate authority shall consider whether it is reasonable to
reduce the fee: *Funding Order* 2007, art. 32(2). An advocate should be given a reasonable
opportunity to show cause why his costs should not be reduced (*Funding Order* 2007, art.
32(2)). Any reduction may be challenged by appeal to the taxing master: *post*, G–269. As
to what may constitute "good reason" or "exceptional circumstances", see *post*, G–269.

Notwithstanding that a representation order may be expressed to cover proceedings in
the Crown Court "and in the event of [the defendant] being convicted or sentenced ...,
advice and assistance in regard to the making of an appeal", the legislation is clear as to the
need for a claim in relation to work done in the Crown Court to be submitted within three
months of the conclusion of the proceedings in that court, rather than within three months
of the date on which an application for leave to appeal to the Court of Appeal was refused:
R. v. White [2008] Costs L.R. 479 (decided in relation to a like provision relating to claims
by solicitors under the 2001 order).

(3) Submitting an amended claim

Where a genuine error is made in submitting a graduated fee claim, counsel should not   **G–198**
be precluded for all time from submitting an amended claim where the refusal to permit
him to do so could result in his being deprived of fees to which he would have been entitled
had the claim been advanced correctly in the first place: *R. v. Hann* [2009] Costs L.R. 833.
Where, therefore, counsel, as a result of a genuine error, had submitted a claim for a
cracked trial where the case was disposed of as a guilty plea (albeit there had been a long
delay between plea and sentence, throughout which it had been on the cards that a *Newton*
hearing (*R. v. Newton*, 77 Cr.App.R. 13, CA) would eventually be required), it was held that
counsel (who had been paid the appropriate graduated fee for a guilty plea) should be
granted an extension of time in which to submit an amended claim for a guilty plea plus a
special preparation fee (*Funding Order* 2001, Sched. 4, para. 17). See also *R. v. Lafayette*
[2010] 4 Costs L.R. 650 (there is no good reason why a lawyer who has submitted a claim
should not be permitted to amend it before it has been determined).

[The next paragraph is G–251.]

I. Disbursements and Expenses

(1) Disbursements

G–251   A barrister is not entitled to claim for disbursements or expenses other than those permitted under the *Funding Order* 2007.

(2) Travelling and accommodation expenses

Entitlement under the regulations

G–252   Travel and other expenses incidental to appearance at court may be claimed provided the court is not within 40 kilometres of the advocate's office or chambers. Unless prior approval for the expenditure has been obtained under the regulations, or unless the advocate can justify his attendance having regard to all the relevant circumstances of the case, the amount payable shall not be greater than that, if any, payable to a trial advocate from the nearest local Bar or the nearest advocate's office (whichever is the nearer): *Funding Order* 2007, Sched. 1, para. 24. As to interim payment of travel and accommodation expenses, see *ante*, G–107, G–108.

Local bars

G–253   In *R. v. Comer* [2009] Costs L.R. 972, it was said that in paragraph 24 of Schedule 1 to the *Funding Order* 2007 (*ante*, G–62), the juxtaposition of the phrase "local Bar" with the phrase "advocate's office" suggests that a fairly modest number of practitioners can constitute a local bar. The existence of a bar mess is not a prerequisite, and whether the barristers based in an area constitute a local bar will be a question of feel. In this case, the view of the resident judge that "there is a healthy local bar" was considered to be the best evidence of such a bar. As to this case, see also *post*, G–258.

An advocate may be able to justify his attendance in a distant court which is usually serviced by a local bar where:

   (a) the instruction of local counsel might lead to suspicion of prejudice, lack of independence or lack of objectivity (*e.g.* cases of local notoriety involving public figures or officials);

   (b) there are insufficient local counsel whom instructing solicitors consider are sufficiently experienced to undertake the case in question so as to give the client a reasonable choice;

   (c) the services of an advocate who has specialised experience and knowledge of the type of case of an unusual or technical nature are required;

   (d) the advocate has previously been instructed in related matters which would assist him in the presentation or preparation of the case in question: *R. v. Conboy* (1990) Costs L.R. 493; and see *R. v. Gussman*, X14, SCTO 40/99 (counsel had represented his client seven years earlier on a charge of murder; his knowledge of his client's earlier medical condition was relevant to the current charges of rape, and this amounted to special circumstances justifying his attendance).

It is submitted that a further justification arises where an advocate is forced to follow a particular judge on circuit who is seized of his case and it was not reasonable to instruct another local advocate for that particular hearing. Where an advocate is instructed from outside a local bar for any of the above reasons it is advisable that he obtains a letter from his instructing solicitor explaining why he was instructed, and for his clerk to obtain prior approval for incurring such expenses from the court. This applies also to Queen's Counsel practising off-circuit: *post*, G–256.

[The next paragraph is G–256.]

Queen's Counsel and local bars

G–256   Queen's Counsel should not be regarded as being "local" to any particular bar, even though his chambers are in one particular place. Where Queen's Counsel practises on circuit, he should as a general rule receive an amount in respect of travelling and hotel expenses actually and reasonably incurred and necessarily and exclusively attributable to his attendance at a court on the circuit on which he practises: *R. v. Thomas*; *R. v. Davidson*; *R. v. Hutton* (1985) Costs L.R. 469. Where Queen's Counsel practises outside his circuit, the "local bar" rules apply: *ante*, G–253.

Expenses reasonably incurred

The reasonableness of an advocate's claim for travel and hotel expenses should be judged   **G–257** not by reference to the expenses incurred by other advocates in the same case, but in relation to the demands upon the advocate in putting forward his lay client's case and his own particular circumstances in relation to the conduct of the trial: *R. v. Plews* (1984) Costs L.R. 466; *post*, G–260.

The regulations refer to expenditure "reasonably incurred", whereas earlier regulations referred to expenses "actually and reasonably incurred". In *R. v. Conboy* (1990) Costs L.R. 493, the taxing master observed that the current wording is wider. It is submitted that the alteration acknowledges an advocate's entitlement to recover a reasonable amount in respect of expenses necessarily and exclusively attributable to attendance at court. Thus, where the expense incurred was reasonable, an advocate should recover in full. Where the travel undertaken or accommodation used was reasonable but the cost incurred was excessive, an advocate may only claim for and recover a reasonable amount being a sum no greater than that which he would have incurred had his expenses been reasonable.

Travel to court

In determining what is actually and reasonably incurred the relevant travel is that be-   **G–258** tween court and an advocate's chambers: *R. v. Khan*, January 1989, TC C/13. Actual expenses incurred in travelling from an advocate's home to court will only be allowed if his home is nearer to court than his chambers, otherwise his journey is deemed to start from chambers: *R. v. Slessor* (1984) Costs L.R. 438. And, in such a case, he will only be entitled to travelling expenses actually incurred, *i.e.* from home to court: *R. v. Comer* [2009] Costs L.R. 972 (as to which, see also *ante*, G–253).

(i) *Public transport expenses*

Where expenses are recoverable, travel costs are generally limited to the cost of public   **G–259** transport actually incurred, together with the expense incurred in getting from the starting point to the railhead or coach station and the expense incurred from getting from the terminal to the court: *Slessor, ante.*

(ii) *Car expenses*

Where an advocate chooses to journey by car, the expenses allowed will not exceed the   **G–260** equivalent cost of public transport: *Slessor, ante*; *Conboy, ante*. The expenses of travel by car will be allowed where public transport is not available or is not reasonably convenient. What is "not reasonably convenient" is a matter for the discretion of the taxing officer. What may be convenient in one case may not be convenient in another. The time spent in getting from the starting point to the railhead, and from the terminus to court is always relevant: if it is considerable, the use of a car may be justified. Taxing officers have been urged to adopt a flexible and broad approach to the problem: *Slessor, ante*. Where the case papers are heavy and bulky, an advocate may be justified in using a car (an example given by the taxing officer in argument in *Conboy, ante*). In *R. v. Plews* (1984) Costs L.R. 466, counsel would have had to catch a 7.15 a.m. train from London to allow him to arrive at court in sufficient time to robe, see his client and solicitor, and to hold any pre-hearing discussions. It was therefore reasonable for counsel, bearing in mind that he had to travel from his home to the station and was faced with a full day in court, to travel by car.

(iii) *Expenses for reasonable travel by car*

In *Plews, ante*, counsel's claim, based on a mileage rate less than that prescribed for medi-   **G–261** cal practitioners in regulations then current, was considered reasonable, the taxing master observing that a claim based upon the equivalent rate would have been allowed. The usual means of estimating the expenses of travel by car is the standard mileage rate which is calculated by reference to the average cost of running a motor car, including such matters as depreciation, insurance, maintenance, etc., which are referable to the running of a car of the relevant engine capacity. Although the rate is not a precise measure of the actual cost of a particular form of transport, it is intended to provide a mechanism for reimbursing expenses incurred when travelling by car: *Conboy, ante.* Where it is reasonable to incur the expense of travelling by car it must also be reasonable to incur necessary and consequential costs of car parking (if any).

The Legal Services Commission announced an increase in its rates for civil solicitors from 36p per mile to 45p per mile as from April 2, 2001. It is submitted that it is reasonable that similar rates should apply to criminal advocates.

Accommodation expenses

G–262   Hotel or accommodation expenses cannot be divorced from travelling expenses. They should be paid instead of travelling expenses where an advocate reasonably chooses, or by reason of distance is obliged, to stay near a court distant from his chambers rather than travel daily. If travelling expenses are not payable then neither are hotel or accommodation expenses: *R. v. Khan*, January 1989, TC C/13. Where an advocate claims expenses for overnight accommodation and the cost equals or is less than that of the daily travel for which he would be entitled to be reimbursed, such expenses should be allowed. Where the hotel expenses are more than the cost of daily travel, they should be allowed if, having regard to the demands of the case on an advocate, including the need for conferences after court and overnight preparation, the advocate could not have returned home at a reasonable hour: *Plews, ante.*

Conference travel expenses and travel time

G–263   Travel expenses reasonably incurred and necessarily and exclusively attributable to attending a conference should be reimbursed where an advocate attends a conference in prison where the authorities will only produce the client at the place of detention; the same principle applies when the client is a patient in a psychiatric hospital: *R. v. Hindle* (1987) Costs L.R. 486.

J. Proceedings in the Court of Appeal

General principles

G–264   Payment for proceedings in the Court of Appeal is governed by Schedule 4 to the *Funding Order* 2007 *(ante,* G–82 *et seq.),* which provides for *ex post facto* taxation, the overriding principles being that the appropriate officer should, in determining fees, allow a "reasonable amount" in respect of all work "actually and reasonably done".

Advice on appeal

G–265   As to this, see, in particular, *R. v. Umezie,* § 7–165 in the main work, and *R. v. Bromige, ante,* G–160.

Solicitor advocates

G–266   In *R. v. Mansell* [2011] Costs L.R. 531, it was held that: (i) under the *Funding Order* 2007, the fees of a solicitor advocate in the Court of Appeal fall to be determined under Schedule 4 as if he were an advocate, and not a litigator; (ii) a solicitor advocate is an "advocate" for all proceedings covered by the 2007 order, including in the Court of Appeal (see the definition of "advocate" in art. 2, *ante,* G–7); and (iii) that paragraph 3 of Schedule 4 (determination of litigators' fees (*ante*, G–83)), which permits payment of advocacy by litigators, does not mean that all advocacy by solicitors is payable under that paragraph.

K. Determinations and Appeals

(1) The taxing authorities

Graduated fee claims are determined by Crown Court taxing officers and should usually **G–267** be paid within 10 working days of receipt of the claim.

Applications for re-determination are addressed to the chief clerk of the Crown Court or the regional taxation director as appropriate. The re-determination does not have to be carried out by the original officer, although this is usually the case. Where difficult points of principle arise or large sums are in dispute the matter is referred to the regional taxing director or his assistant. Appeals from re-determinations are heard by costs judges appointed by the Lord Chancellor.

(2) Guide to the process of determination and appeal

A brief outline of the various stages of the determination of an advocate's fees is set out **G–268** below. The articles referred to are those of the *Funding Order* 2007 (*ante*, §§ G–6 *et seq.*). The table below is merely intended as a guide to the relevant procedures.

As to the circumstances in which an advocate or a litigator may apply to the appropriate officer for a redetermination of his fees, for a review of specified decisions or for an offence to be reclassified, see article 29 of the 2007 order (*ante*, G–34).

The references in the last column in the tables below are references to articles of the *Funding Order* 2007.

Stage	Description	art.
Submission of Claim		[14] 5
Time limit	Within 3 months of conclusion of proceedings (see *ante*, G–199)	5(3)
Particulars submitted in all cases	In the form and manner directed by the appropriate officer	5(3)
Interim payments (40% of total claim less any sum paid)		18
Definition	Payable where:	17
	(a) the basic fee claimed by any counsel in any related proceedings exceeds £4,000, and	17(2)
	(b) 3 months have elapsed from the date of the conclusion of related proceedings or the date on which the bill is ready to tax, whichever is earlier.	17(4)
Related proceedings	Proceedings involving the same defendant heard or dealt with together or proceedings involving more than one defendant arising out of the same incident so that defendants are charged, tried or disposed of together.	17(3)
When the bill is ready to tax	Date of receipt of last bill in related proceedings.	17(4)
Entitlement	Where counsel is entitled to an interim payment but no interim payment has been made and counsel has submitted his claim.	17(4), (5)

Stage	Description	art.
Time limit	6 months after the conclusion of proceedings against the defendant represented.	17(5)
Determination and notification of costs; authorisation of payment		
	Costs determined on the basis of work reasonably done.	23(1)
	Counsel notified of costs payable and payment authorised.	23(1)
Re-calculation of graduated fee or re-determination of decision to allow special or wasted preparation fee, or classification of offence		
Time limit	Within 21 days of receipt or notification of costs payable.	29(3)
Particulars to be submitted	(a) Written notice specifying matters in respect of which application is made, grounds of objection and whether counsel wishes to appear or to be represented.	29(3), (5)
	(b) Documents and information supplied with submission of claim.	29(4)
	(c) Further information, particulars and documents as required by the appropriate officer.	29(6)
Re-determination of decision not to allow conference fee (time limit and particulars as above)		29(1)(b)
Re-determination by the appropriate officer		29(7)
Application for written reasons		29(8)
Time limit	21 days of notification of the decision	29(8), (9)
Appeal to costs judge		30(1)
Time limit	21 days of receipt of written reasons.	30(2)
Particulars to be submitted to costs judge and appropriate officer	(a) Copy of written representations on application for re-determination. (b) Appropriate officer's written reasons. (c) All documents supplied hereto.	30(4)
Form of notice of appeal	(a) As directed by the costs judge. (b) Specifying separately each item appealed against, showing amount claimed and determined for each item and the ground of objection. (c) Stating whether appellant wishes to appear or to be represented.	30(5)
Lord Chancellor's written representations	Where the Lord Chancellor makes written representations, counsel shall have a reasonable opportunity to make representations in reply.	30(9)
Notification of hearing	The costs judge shall inform counsel of hearing date and give directions as to conduct of appeal.	30(10)

Stage	Description	art.
No further evidence	Unless costs judge otherwise directs no other evidence shall be raised at the hearing nor objection taken which was not raised at redetermination.	30(11)
Notification of costs judge's decision		30(13)
Costs	Costs may be awarded where the appeal is allowed.	30(14)
Appeals to the High Court		31
Right of appeal	Right of appeal to single QBD judge from costs judge's decision on a point of principle of public importance.	31(7)
Application for costs judge's certificate	Counsel may apply to the costs judge to certify a point of principle of general importance.	31(1)
Time limit for application	Within 21 days of notification of costs judge's decision.	31(2)
Time limit for appeal	Within 21 days from receipt of costs judge's certificate.	
Appeal by Lord Chancellor	Within 21 days of notification of costs judge's decision, the Lord Chancellor may appeal the decision if counsel does not do so.	31(5)

(3) The enforcement and extension of time limits

Time limits may be extended for good reason by the appropriate authority, *i.e.* the ap- **G–269** propriate officer, costs judge, or the High Court: *Funding Order* 2007, art. 32(1). Where for no good reason the time limit is not adhered to, the appropriate authority may in exceptional circumstances extend the time limit and shall consider whether it is reasonable in the circumstances to reduce the costs, subject to granting the advocate a reasonable opportunity to state either orally or in writing why the costs should not be reduced: *Funding Order* 2007, art. 32(2). A decision not to extend time, or to reduce costs for claims out of time may be appealed by notice in writing to the senior costs judge specifying the grounds of appeal. The appeal must be instituted within 21 days of the decision being given: *Funding Order* 2007, art. 32(3); and see *ante*, G–198.

It was held in *R. v. Mahmood* [2008] Costs L.R. 326, that where a 10 per cent penalty was imposed following a delay of over two months in submitting a claim for costs, but where the representative had only received a notice, prior to the case being tried, stating that all late claims would be the subject of a penalty unless there was a good reason, this did not constitute notice to show cause why the claim should not be reduced. The determining officer had clearly not considered the circumstances of the particular case on its own merits.

In *R. v. Roberts* [2008] Costs L.R. 323, the oversight of two fee earners, the holiday of one of those fee-earners (even if well-deserved), and a subsequent systematic firm-wide failure did not constitute "good reason" or "exceptional circumstances" so as to justify an extension of time, following a delay of 17 months in submitting a claim for costs. Nor did previous good character constitute "exceptional circumstances", although it was said that it might amount to mitigating circumstances when considering the extent of any reduction in costs (were an extension to be granted). This was the case despite a general softening in the attitude to the delay.

A misunderstanding of the legislation cannot amount to "good reason", but could amount to "exceptional circumstances" where the evidence was that other bills that had been submitted late for like reason in the past had been accepted: *R. v. White* [2008] Costs L.R. 479. But a simple failure to follow up a case could rarely constitute "good reason" or "exceptional circumstances", and it made no difference that the firm in question had generally had a good record for submitting claims in time: *R. v. Johnson* [2008] Costs L.R. 983.

Neither "mere oversight" on the part of leading counsel nor a mistaken belief on the part of junior counsel that leading counsel's clerk was dealing with their fees could amount to "good reason" for not submitting their claims on time; but disallowance of fees *in toto* may be so disproportionate as to amount to "exceptional circumstances": see *R. v. Lafayette* [2010] 4 Costs L.R. 650.

In *R. v. Griffin* [2008] Costs L.R. 483, leading counsel had been under the mistaken impression that his junior was going to prepare a taxation note to be agreed between them before submission. However, in the event, his junior submitted his own claim independently and sent a copy of his taxation note to his leader, such note making it plain that he had submitted a claim and asserting, mistakenly, that leading counsel had already submitted his own claim. It was held that as this was already seven months out of time, and leading counsel only submitted his own claim after a further two years, neither the misunderstanding as between leader and junior, nor extreme pressure of work plus some personal pressure over the two years that followed discovery of the fact that his junior had submitted his own claim, could amount to "good reason" for the failure to submit the claim within the three-month time limit; nor could they amount to "exceptional circumstances" so as to justify an extension of time despite the absence of good reason. There had been no obligation on the determining officer to remind counsel that his claim was late and the absence, at the time, of published criteria to be applied to the submission of late claims, did not avail counsel. What was critical to the outcome was the fact that two years before his eventual submission of his claim, he had been alerted by his junior's note to the fact that he would need to submit his own claim and he had failed then to take any steps to address the situation.

G–270   In *R. v. Islami* [2009] Costs L.R. 988, following a ruling that total disallowance of a claim by solicitors for £58,060.13 (including disbursements and travelling expenses) due to delay (of three years and nine months) would be so disproportionate (because of the substantial effect that this would have on the firm's profits) as to amount to "exceptional circumstances" and that the claim should be re-submitted, albeit that a five per cent penalty should be applied to the sum ultimately allowed, it was held that the fact that an administrative officer at the firm had then not complied with her instructions to submit the relevant documents for taxation, and the fact that this was only discovered during her ensuing extensive sick leave, did not amount to a "good reason" for a further delay of nine months in re-submitting the claim. In these circumstances, total disallowance of the claim, and the ensuing effect on the firm's profits, was no longer a disproportionate penalty sufficient to constitute "exceptional circumstances". Had the sum been needed with the urgency suggested at the original hearing, the firm would have ensured that the claim was re-submitted immediately and carefully tracked. Instead, the administrative problems identified at the original hearing had clearly not been resolved. However, it was said that this conclusion should be applied only to the profit costs and that the claim, so far as it related to disbursements (which had long since been paid out by the firm), should still be determined (without penalty), provided that the necessary papers were lodged within 14 days.

G–271   In *R. v. Newport* [2009] Costs L.R. 983, it was said that, although it has often been stated that barristers must have suitable systems in place to ensure that claims for fees and requests for redeterminations are made within the relevant time limits, and although the delay in this particular case was significant (over three years after the determining officer had refused payment), "exceptional circumstances" for extending the time to apply for a redetermination had been made out where counsel had trusted his senior clerk to ensure that the claim and any appeal procedure was appropriately and punctually concluded, but where he had been deliberately misled by the clerk, who failed, despite counsel's regular enquiries, to inform counsel that his claim had been refused *in toto*. This was found to be a rare and regrettable situation and not akin to an argument that "pressures of work" constituted exceptional circumstances (which would not be successful).

(4) Re-determinations and appeals

Graduated fees

An advocate may only seek re-determination or appeal in respect of graduated fees **G–272** where, (a) the issue is either whether the graduated fee scheme applied to the relevant proceedings, or (b) complaint is made as to the calculation of the remuneration payable, or (c) where the advocate is dissatisfied with a refusal to allow a special preparation fee or the number of hours allowed in the calculation of such fee; or (d) where the advocate is dissatisfied with the classification of an offence which does not appear in the Table of Offences: *Funding Order* 2007, art. 29(3). Under the 2007 order, a re-determination may also be sought in respect of a decision not to allow an hourly fee in respect of attendance at conferences or views at the scene of the alleged offence, or of the number of hours allowed in the calculation of such a fee: see art. 29(1)(b)(i).

Re-determination

On an application for re-determination an advocate shall specify the grounds of his objec- **G–273** tion to all or any part of the determination (*Funding Order* 2007, art. 29(3)(b)) and may appear in person or through another to make representations: *Funding Order* 2007, art. 29(5). An advocate is not obliged to provide fresh information or material to assist the determining officer in the redetermination. If no additional information is provided, the determining officer has a duty to redetermine on the basis of the information already supplied: *R. v. O'Brien* [2003] Costs L.R. 625. Many appeals which might otherwise have succeeded have failed because the representations made to the appropriate officer have been perfunctory and inexplicit: *R. v. Davies* (1985) Costs L.R. 472.

As from January 1, 1994, the General Council of the Bar has agreed that all requests for fees to be re-determined or for written reasons to be provided should be signed by counsel personally.

Re-determination should, where possible, be carried out by the officer who determined costs. Where cases are cited in support of the re-determination, sufficient references must be given to allow an advocate to identify and look them up: *R. v. Pelepenko*, X27A, SCCO 186/2001.

Where the Legal Services Commission makes a decision to recover an overpayment of fees pursuant to article 26 of the *Funding Order* 2007 (*ante*, G–31) and the litigator requests a review, a subsequent confirmation by the commission of its decision to recoup constitutes a redetermination within the meaning of article 29 (*ante*, G–34), so as to allow the litigator to appeal to a costs judge pursuant to article 30(1) (*ante*, G–35): *Lord Chancellor v. Eddowes Perry and Osbourne Ltd* [2011] Costs L.R. 498, QBD (Spencer J.) (disapproving *R. v. Charlery*; *R. v. Small* [2011] Costs L.R. 331). As to this case, see also *ante*, G–161.

Further evidence on appeal and supplemental written reasons

On appeal before a costs judge no further evidence shall be received and no ground of **G–274** objection shall be valid which was not raised on the application for re-determination unless the costs judge otherwise directs: *Funding Order* 2007, art. 30(11). These provisions are strictly applied. A costs judge will rarely accede to a request to adduce further evidence or allow a fresh objection to be raised. Where written reasons do not address a point raised in the claim, counsel cannot pursue the matter in the appeal. The proper method of dealing with such an omission is to seek supplemental written reasons from the appropriate officer.

Appeals

The right of appeal to a costs judge is effectively limited in that no appeal lies against a **G–275** determination unless the advocate has applied for a re-determination and, thereafter, for written reasons under the *Funding Order* 2007, art. 30(1).

An advocate wishing to appeal must have regard to, and be familiar with, the provisions of Part 5 of the *Practice Direction (Criminal Proceedings: Costs)* [2010] 1 W.L.R. 2351, Senior Courts (§§ 6–112 *et seq.* in the main work).

Representation, costs and expenses of appeal

G–276 For the purposes of an appeal to a costs judge, an advocate is treated as the appellant and can elect to be represented at the hearing. A successful appellant may be awarded a sum in respect of part or all of any reasonable costs incurred in connection with the appeal: *Funding Order* 2007, art. 30(14); and see *R. v. Boswell; R. v. Halliwell* [1987] 1 W.L.R. 705 (Leggatt J.).

A barrister without the intervention of a solicitor may accept a brief or instructions, with or without fee, directly from, and represent, another barrister on that other barrister's appeal as to his fees before a costs judge: see *Code of Conduct*, 8th ed., para. 401 (Appendix C–7, *ante*). A professional fee payable by one barrister to another for conducting the former's appeal is capable of constituting part of the costs incurred by the appellant counsel: *R. v. Boswell; R. v. Halliwell, ante.* In assessing such costs the costs judge is entitled to take account of time and skill expended by the appellant or his counsel in the drawing of grounds and preparation of the appeal, and the conduct of the hearing, and travel and subsidence costs: *ibid.* Costs incurred in instructing other counsel are clearly reasonable where there is some technical question on the applicability of some part of the regulations or other issue which legitimately deserves the attention of specialist costs counsel. Costs are not reasonably incurred if trial counsel is available, could easily have represented himself and the only real issue is the weight of the case or the value of a particular item of work undertaken: *Jackson v. Lord Chancellor* [2003] Costs L.R. 395; and *R. v. Martin* [2007] Costs L.R. 128. A successful appellant will ordinarily be entitled to the return of the fee payable in respect of the appeal.

Appeals to the single judge

G–277 As to appeals from a costs judge to the High Court, see the *Funding Order* 2007, art. 31. The ambit of an appeal is strictly limited to the point of principle certified by the costs judge as being of general importance (such certificate being a pre-condition to an appeal): *Patten v. Lord Chancellor*, 151 N.L.J. 851, QBD (Leveson J.), not following *Harold v. Lord Chancellor* [1999] Costs L.R. 14. Although *Patten* was concerned with the interpretation of regulation 16 of the *Legal Aid in Criminal and Care Proceedings (Costs) Regulations* 1989 (S.I. 1989 No. 343), article 30 of the *Funding Order* 2007 is worded in almost identical terms. A refusal of a costs judge to certify that the matter raises a point of principle of general importance is not susceptible to judicial review: *R. v. Supreme Court Taxing Office, ex p. John Singh & Co* [1997] 1 Costs L.R. 49, CA (Civ. Div). As to the limited scope for a challenge, by way of judicial review, to the substantive decision of a costs judge where a certificate has been refused, see § 6–64 in the main work.

(5) Recovery of overpayment

G–278 Where an advocate receives a sum in excess of his entitlement, the taxing authority may either require immediate repayment of that excess, or deduct the excess from any other sum payable to the advocate under the regulations: *Funding Order* 2007, art. 26. These provisions apply notwithstanding the fact that a re-determination or appeal has been or may be requested: *Funding Order* 2007, art. 26(4).

(6) Appeals under VHCCs

G–279 Under the arrangements that came into force on July 14, 2010 (*ante*, G–181 *et seq.*), both the VHCC Specification for organisations and that for advocates provide for a right of appeal to the VHCC Appeals Panel. The details are set out in paragraph 6 of the specifications, with paragraph 6.4 listing the issues in relation to which there is a right of appeal (*e.g.*

the category to which a case has been assigned) and paragraph 6.5 listing those issues in relation to which there is no right of appeal. The appeal process, including time limits, is provided for by paragraphs 6.6 to 6.30. The appeal will normally be determined by a single adjudicator but may be referred to an appeals committee. The decision of the adjudicator or committee is final (para. 6.28), but is binding only in relation to the particular appeal (para. 6.29). Anonymised versions of decisions will be published on the Legal Services Commission's website (para. 6.30).

APPENDIX H

Sexual Offences (The Law as at April 30, 2004)

A. Introduction

The history of the sexual offences legislation since 1956 is set out in detail at §§ 20–1 *et* **H–1**
seq. in the main work. All the statutory provisions contained in this appendix were repealed
with effect from May 1, 2004, by the *SOA* 2003, but, as stated in the main work, they have
continuing effect in relation to conduct occurring prior to that date. It should be borne
in mind that this appendix states the law as at April 30, 2004, and that, therefore, there
may yet be prosecutions for offences committed prior to even earlier material changes in
the law: see, in particular, the amendments effected by the *SOA* 1985 and the *CJPOA*
1994 (summarised at §§ 20–2, 20–3 in the main work).

B. Sexual Offences Act 1956

(1) Rape

(a) *Introduction*

Section 1 of the 1956 Act made rape an offence. Section 1(1) of the *Sexual Offences (Amend-* **H–2**
ment) Act 1976 provided a statutory definition of rape in terms designed to give effect to the
Report of the Advisory Group on the Law of Rape (Cmnd. 6352) and the views expressed
by the House of Lords in *DPP v. Morgan* [1976] A.C. 182. Section 1(1) was repealed by the
CJPOA 1994, which also substituted a new section 1 in the 1956 Act. The effect of this
was to adopt the 1976 definition, but to extend it so as to cover anal intercourse with a
woman or a man. In addition, the new provision referred simply to "sexual intercourse"
whereas the 1976 Act referred to "unlawful sexual intercourse". The omission of the
word "unlawful" made clear Parliament's adoption of the decision of the House of Lords
in *R. v. R.* [1992] A.C. 599, that a man may rape his wife.

Section 7(2) of the 1976 Act (as amended by the *CJA* 1988, s.158(1) and (6)) provided
that in that Act "a rape offence":

> "means any of the following, namely rape, attempted rape, aiding, abetting, counselling and
> procuring rape or attempted rape, incitement to commit rape, conspiracy to rape and burglary
> with intent to rape."

(b) *Statute*

Sexual Offences Act 1956, s.1

Rape of woman or man
  1.—(1) It is an offence for a man to rape a woman or another man.   **H–3**
  (2) A man commits rape if—
    (a) he has sexual intercourse with a person (whether vaginal or anal) who at the time of the in-
      tercourse does not consent to it; and
    (b) at the time he knows that the person does not consent to the intercourse or is reckless as to
      whether that person consents to it.

(3) A man also commits rape if he induces a married woman to have sexual intercourse with him by impersonating her husband.

(4) Subsection (2) applies for the purposes of any enactment.

[This section is printed as substituted (from November 3, 1994) by the *CJPOA* 1994, s.142.]

Sexual Offences (Amendment) Act 1976, s.1

H–4   **1.**—(1) [*Repealed by* Criminal Justice and Public Order Act *1994, s.168(3) and Sched. 11.*]

(2) It is hereby declared that if at a trial for a rape offence the jury has to consider whether a man believed that a woman or man was consenting to sexual intercourse, the presence or absence of reasonable grounds for such a belief is a matter to which the jury is to have regard, in conjunction with any other relevant matters, in considering whether he so believed.

[Subs. (2) is printed as amended by the *CJPOA* 1994, s.168(2), and Sched. 10, para. 35(1), (2).]

As to the use of the words "man" and "woman", see *post*, H–222. As to the meaning of "a rape offence", see *ante*, H–2.

In the case of a summary trial or a trial by court-martial, the references to the jury in section 1(2) of the 1976 Act are to be construed as references to the court: *ibid.*, s.7(3).

(c) *Anonymity*

H–5   See §§ 20–257 *et seq.* in the main work.

(d) *Indictment*

STATEMENT OF OFFENCE

H–6   *Rape, contrary to section 1(1) of the* Sexual Offences Act *1956.*

PARTICULARS OF OFFENCE

A B on the —— day of ——, 20—, had sexual intercourse with C D who at the time of the said intercourse did not consent to it, the said A B either knowing that the said C D did not so consent or being reckless as to whether she [or he] so consented.

Where the victim is a woman, the intercourse may be vaginal or anal: s.1(1) of the 1956 Act, *ante*, H–3. It is unnecessary to specify in the indictment whether the allegation is of vaginal or anal intercourse, but there will be cases where it is of assistance to do so. This can be done by adding the words "*per vaginam*" or "*per anum*" after the words "sexual intercourse". The addition of these words will be particularly useful where it is alleged that a woman was raped both vaginally and anally; the counts will reflect this and will ensure, in the event of a conviction on one count only, that the court is aware of the basis of the jury's verdict. As to where it is unclear on the evidence whether penetration was of the vagina or the anus, see *R. v. K. (Robert)* [2009] 1 Cr.App.R. 24, CA (§ 20–20 in the main work).

Good practice does not require that, where the prosecution rely on recklessness as an alternative to knowledge, there should be separate counts (alleging respectively knowledge and recklessness): *R. v. Flitter* [2001] Crim.L.R. 328, CA.

Allegation of joint offence

H–7   Where a person has been raped by more than one man on the same occasion, all the accused should be charged in one count of rape, with no mention of aiders and abettors: see the direction of the House of Lords in *DPP v. Merriman* [1973] A.C. 584. This enables the jury to be told that it matters not whether an individual accused physically committed the act of rape, or assisted or encouraged someone else to; thus, several accused may be convicted where the jury is satisfied only that each played a guilty part, but not as to who committed the physical act.

(e) *Class of offence and mode of trial*

This offence and an attempt to commit it are class 2 offences (§ 2–17 in the main work), **H–8** triable on indictment only: *SOA* 1956, s.37(2), and Sched. 2, para. 1.

(f) *Alternative verdicts*

On a count of rape, the accused may be convicted of procurement of a woman by threats **H–9** (s.2) or false pretences (s.3) or of administering drugs to obtain or facilitate intercourse (s.4): *SOA* 1956, s.37(4), and Sched. 2, para. 1.

As to alternative verdicts generally, see §§ 4–524 *et seq.* in the main work. Where the alleged victim was a girl under 16 years of age, then whether or not her age is averred in the indictment, a jury may not convict the accused under section 6(3) of the *CLA* 1967 (§ 4–525 in the main work) of an offence contrary to section 6 of the *SOA* 1956 (unlawful intercourse with a girl under 16): *R. v. Fisher* [1969] 2 Q.B. 114, Assizes (Cusack J.); *R. v. Mochan*, 54 Cr.App.R. 5, Assizes (Cusack J.), approved in *R. v. Hodgson* [1973] Q.B. 565, 57 Cr.App.R. 502, CA.

As every charge of rape contains the essential ingredients of indecent assault (*viz.* an assault and indecency), it follows that where a man is acquitted of rape on the ground of the victim's consent, it is open to the jury to convict him where the victim is under 16, of indecent assault, because the consent which provided a defence to a charge of rape cannot, by virtue of the *SOA* 1956, ss.14(2) and 15(2), provide a defence to a charge of indecent assault. Age is not an ingredient of, nor an essential averment in the framing of a count of indecent assault: *R. v. Hodgson, ante.*

In *R. v. Timmins* [2006] 1 Cr.App.R. 18, CA, it was held that the effect of the decision in *R. v. J.* [2005] 1 A.C. 562, HL (on a true construction of the 1956 Act, it was impermissible to prosecute a charge of indecent assault under section 14(1) (*post*, H–117) in circumstances where the only conduct upon which the charge was based was an act of unlawful sexual intercourse with a girl under the age of 16 in respect of which no prosecution could be commenced under section 6(1) (*post*, H–50) by virtue of the time bar contained in section 37(2) of, and Schedule 2 to, the Act) was not such as to preclude a judge from leaving it to a jury to convict of indecent assault as an alternative to a charge of rape, under section 6(3) of the *CLA* 1967 (*ante*), where they were satisfied as to the act of sexual intercourse and as to the fact that the girl was under 16 at the time, and where they acquitted of rape on the ground that they were not satisfied as to lack of consent, and this was so notwithstanding that the proceedings for rape had been begun over 12 months after the alleged offence; the decision in *J.* had turned on the words of Schedule 2 to the 1956 Act, which provided that "A prosecution may not be commenced more than 12 months after the offence charged."; leaving a possible alternative verdict to a jury could not be described as a "commencement" of proceedings for the offence; but it would be an abuse of process to bring a charge of rape against a person against whom there was no evidence whatever of rape (in particular lack of consent) in order to circumvent a time limit.

In the earlier case of *R. v. Rabbitts* (2005) 149 S.J. 890, CA, it was held that, *R. v. J.* having decided that, as a matter of statutory construction, it was not open to the prosecution to bring a charge of indecent assault where the conduct on which the prosecution was based was an act of consensual sexual intercourse with a girl under 16, and where the purpose was to circumvent the statutory time limit of 12 months on prosecutions for unlawful sexual intercourse with a girl of that age, it made no difference that the count of indecent assault was included in the indictment as an alternative to a charge of rape to cater for the possibility that the jury would not be satisfied as to lack of consent.

In *R. v. Cottrell*; *R. v. Fletcher* [2008] 1 Cr.App.R. 7, CA, it was said that to the extent that *Timmins* and *Rabbitts* were inconsistent, they should be followed as they apply to the facts of the individual case. As to the flawed nature of the decision in *Timmins*, see *Criminal Law Week* 2005/43/4.

(g) *Autrefois acquit and convict*

H–10   For the general principles, see §§ 4–183 *et seq.* in the main work.

An acquittal upon an indictment for rape was held to be no bar to a subsequent indictment on the same facts for a common assault: *R. v. Dungey* (1864) 4 F. & F. 99 (and see now s.6(3A) of the *CLA* 1967 (§ 4–525 in the main work), reversing the effect of *R. v. Mearns* [1991] 1 Q.B. 82, 91 Cr.App.R. 312, CA).

An acquittal on an indictment for rape cannot be successfully pleaded as a bar to a subsequent indictment for assault with intent to commit rape: *R. v. Gisson* (1847) 2 C. & K. 781, or, in certain circumstances, to a subsequent indictment for attempted rape, see *R. v. Hearn* [1970] Crim.L.R. 175, CA (§ 4–203 in the main work).

However, it should be noted that there was (as at April 30, 2004), in all probability, no longer an offence of assault with intent to rape, contrary to common law. It did not survive the creation of an identical statutory offence in the *Offences against the Person Act* 1861, s.38, which was in turn abolished by virtue of section 10 of, and Schedule 3 to, the *Criminal Law Act* 1967: *R. v. P.* [1990] Crim.L.R. 323, Crown Court (Pill J.) (but note the commentary and reference, by Professor J. C. Smith, to the opposite view expressed by Turner J. in *R. v. J.*, unreported, June 9, 1986). *Cf.* section 16 of the 1956 Act (assault with intent to commit buggery), *post*, H–138.

(h) *Sentence*

Maximum

H–11   Rape: life imprisonment—*SOA* 1956, s.37(3), and Sched. 2, para. 1(a).

Attempted rape: life imprisonment—*SOA* 1956, s.37(3), and Sched. 2, para. 1(a) (as amended by the *SOA* 1985, s.3).

Guidelines

H–12   See the guidelines of the Sentencing Guidelines Council, *post*, Appendix K–83 *et seq.*

In *R. v. H.* [2012] 2 Cr.App.R.(S.) 21, CA, it was said that in the search for principle, it is impossible to reconcile all the authorities that purport to provide guidance on sentencing for historic sexual offending; that the following considerations, derived from statute (general provisions about sentencing in the *CJA* 2003, Pt 12, Chap. 1 (ss.142–176), and the *Coroners and Justice Act* 2009, s.125 (sentencing guidelines: duty of court (§ 5–149 in the main work))) and case law, should be treated as guidance; and that reference to earlier decisions (with the exception of *R. v. Millberry*; *R. v. Morgan*; *R. v. Lackenby, post*, Appendix K–83) is unlikely to be helpful and is to be discouraged. First, sentence will be imposed on the basis of the legislative provisions current at the time of sentence, and by measured reference to any definitive sentencing guidelines relevant to the situation revealed by the established facts. Secondly, although sentence must be limited to the maximum permissible at the date when the offence was committed, it is wholly unrealistic to attempt an assessment of sentence by seeking to identify today what the sentence was likely to have been if the offence had come to light at or shortly after its commission. Thirdly, the particular circumstances in which the offence was committed and its seriousness must be the main focus; due allowance for the passage of time may be appropriate; the date may have a considerable bearing on the offender's culpability; for example, if he was young and immature at the time, that remains a continuing feature of the sentencing decision; similarly, if the allegations had come to light many years earlier, and the offender admitted them, but, for whatever reason, the complaint had not been drawn to the attention of, or investigated by, the police, or had been investigated but had not then been pursued to trial, these too would be relevant matters. Fourthly, careful judgment of the harm done to the victim is always a critical feature of the sentencing decision; simultaneously, equal care needs to be taken to assess the true extent of the offender's criminality by reference to what he actually did and the circumstances in which he did it. Fifthly, the passing of the years may demonstrate aggravating features if, for example, the offender has continued to commit sexual crime or he represents a continuing risk to the public; on the other hand, mitigation may be found in an unblemished life over the intervening years, particularly if accompanied by evidence of positive good character. Sixthly, early admissions and a guilty plea are of particular importance in historic cases; given that it is tempting to lie about events long ago, it is greatly to the offender's credit if he makes early admissions; even more powerful mitigation is available to the offender who, out of a sense of guilt and remorse, reports himself to the authorities. The court considered, *inter alia*, *R. v. Bowers* [1999] 2 Cr.App.R.(S.) 97, CA, *R. v. Fowler* [2002] 2 Cr.App.R.(S.) 99, CA, *Att.-Gen.'s References (Nos 37, 38, 44, 54, 51, 53, 35, 40, 43, 45, 41 and 42 of 2003)* [2004] 1 Cr.App.R.(S.) 84, CA, *R. v. McKendrick* [2005] 2 Cr.App.R.(S.) 68, CA, *R. v. Patterson* [2006] 2 Cr.App.R.(S.) 48, CA, *Att.-Gen.'s Reference (No. 39 of 2006) (R. v. J. (Rodney Clive))* [2007] 1 Cr.App.R.(S.) 34, CA, *R. v. Moon* [2011] 1 Cr.App.R.(S.) 34, CA, *R. v. Hartley (Practice Note)* [2012] 1 Cr.App.R. 7, CA, and *Att.-Gen.'s Reference (No. 78 of 2010)* [2011] 2 Cr.App.R.(S.) 109, CA.

(i) *Ingredients of the offence*

A "man"

The common law presumption that a boy under the age of 14 was incapable of sexual intercourse was abolished (for both natural and unnatural intercourse) by the *SOA* 1993, ss.1, 2(2), (3). **H–13**

A woman may be convicted as an aider and abettor: *R. v. Ram* (1893) 17 Cox 609 at 610n.

A man may be convicted of raping his wife: *R. v. R.* [1992] 1 A.C. 599, HL (confirmed by the revised definition of "rape" introduced by the *CJPOA* 1994, *ante*, § H–3).

Sexual intercourse

Where it is necessary to prove sexual intercourse (whether natural or unnatural), it shall not be necessary to prove the completion of the intercourse by the emission of seed, but it shall be deemed complete upon proof of penetration only: *SOA* 1956, s.44 (*post*, § H–219). "Unnatural" intercourse in section 44 means buggery (including bestiality): *R. v. Gaston*, 73 Cr.App.R. 164, CA. **H–14**

The amendment of section 1 of the 1956 Act by the 1994 Act (§ 20–3 in the main work, and *ante*, H–3) did not alter the law (whereunder even the slightest penetration would be sufficient: see *R. v. R'Rue* (1838) 8 C. & P. 641; *R. v. Allen* (1839) 9 C. & P. 31) so as to make penetration of the vagina, properly so-called, an essential ingredient of "vaginal" rape; it is sufficient that there was any degree of penetration by the penis within the labia of the pudendum of the complainant; the word "vaginal" in section 1 is used in comparison with, or in addition to, "anal", and not so as to indicate that the word is being used in the medical sense, rather than the general sense of the female genitalia: *R. v. J.F.*, unreported, December 16, 2002, CA ([2002] EWCA Crim. 2936).

Sexual intercourse is a continuing act; it follows that consensual intercourse will become rape if the woman (or man) ceases to consent during the intercourse, and the man (other man), with the necessary *mens rea*, continues the act: *Kaitamaki v. R.* [1985] A.C. 147, PC (decided on the corresponding New Zealand legislation). It should be noted that these were not the facts in *Kaitamaki*; the facts were that the defendant claimed he only realised the woman was not consenting after intercourse had begun. As to this aspect of the decision, see *post*, H–20. However, the foregoing proposition appears to follow as a matter of logic from the Board's decision on the narrower point.

Absence of consent

General

H–15   It must be proved that the accused had sexual intercourse with the complainant without her or his consent: s.1(2)(a) of the 1956 Act, *ante*, H–3. This applies even where the offence is alleged to have been committed on a person under the age of 16, though sometimes in such a case the prosecution will not need to prove much more than the age of the victim: *R. v. Harling*, 26 Cr.App.R. 127, CCA. It is not, however, necessary to support a charge of rape that there is evidence that the complainant demonstrated her lack of consent or communicated it to the accused; the minimum requirement is evidence of lack of consent in fact, which might take many forms; the most obvious is the complainant's simple assertion, which may or may not be backed up by evidence of force or threats; alternatively, it may consist of evidence that by reason of drink, drugs, sleep, age or mental handicap the complainant was unaware of what was occurring and/or incapable of giving consent; or it may consist of evidence that the complainant was deceived as to the identity of the man with whom she had intercourse: *R. v. Malone* [1998] 2 Cr.App.R. 447, CA. As to intercourse with a woman known to be asleep, see *R. v. Mayers* (1872) 12 Cox 311; *R. v. Young* (1878) 14 Cox 114.

Lack of consent will have been established if the jury are satisfied that although the complainant did not dissent, her understanding and lack of knowledge were such, whether on account of age, the consumption of drink or drugs or mental handicap, that she was incapable of giving consent or of exercising any judgment on the matter: see *R. v. Howard*, 50 Cr.App.R. 56, CCA (age); *R. v. Lang*, 62 Cr.App.R. 50, CA (drink); *R. v. Fletcher* (1859) Bell 63; *R. v. Ryan* (1846) 2 Cox 115; *R. v. Fletcher* (1866) L.R. 1 C.C.R. 39; *R. v. Barratt* (1873) L.R. 2 C.C.R. 81; *R. v. Pressy* (1867) 10 Cox 635, CCR (mental handicap). To the extent that they suggest that where no force, threat or deceit was used, there must be evidence of some resistance on the part of the complainant, *Howard* and *Lang* should no longer be taken to represent the law: *Malone*, *ante*.

Evidence of resistance may, of course, be highly relevant to the separate issue of the defendant's knowledge or recklessness in relation to the lack of consent.

H–16   Although juries should be told that "consent" in the context of the offence of rape is a word which must be given its ordinary meaning, it is sometimes necessary for the judge to go further. For example, he should point out, if necessary, that there is a difference between consent and submission (as to which, see also § 20–10 in the main work). In cases where intercourse took place after threats not involving violence, or the fear of it, a jury should be directed to concentrate on the state of mind of the victim immediately before the act of intercourse. The jury should be reminded too of the wide spectrum of states of mind which consent could comprehend and that where a dividing line had to be drawn between real consent and mere submission they should apply their combined good sense, experience and knowledge of human nature and modern behaviour to all the relevant facts of the case: *R. v. Olugboja*, 73 Cr.App.R. 344, CA (*cf. R. v. McAllister* [1997] Crim.L.R. 233, CA, *post*, H–124). The word "want" should not be used in directing a jury on the issue of consent, there being a clear difference between "wanting" to have intercourse and "consenting" to it: *R. v. T. (D.)* [2000] 7 *Archbold News* 3, CA.

As to evidence about the lack of sexual experience of a complainant, see § 20–11 in the main work.

As to intercourse with a defective, see also the *SOA* 1956, ss.7 and 45 (*post*, H–64, H–68).

Intercourse by false pretences

H–17   The only types of fraud which vitiate consent for the purposes of the law of rape are frauds as to the nature of the act or as to the identity of the person doing the act: *R. v. Linekar* [1995] 2 Cr.App.R. 49, CA. As to frauds as to the nature of the act, see *R. v. Case* (1850) 1 Den. 580, and *R. v. Flattery* (1877) 2 Q.B.D. 410, where the consent was induced by the pretence that the act of intercourse was a form of medical treatment, and *R. v. Williams* [1923] 1 K.B. 340, 17 Cr.App.R. 56, CCA, where a choirmaster pretended to be testing a girl's breathing powers with an instrument. As to fraud as to the identity of the perpetrator of the Act, section 1(3) of the *SOA* 1956 (*ante*, H–3) makes express provision for the case of a man inducing a married woman to have sexual intercourse with him by impersonating her husband. This provision was first introduced by the *Criminal Law Amendment Act* 1885 for the purpose of reversing the decision in *R. v. Barrow* (1868) L.R. 1 C.C.R. 156. As to other instances of impersonation, it is possible that the principle in *Barrow* will still prevail; but it was dissented from in *R. v. Dee* (1884) 15 Cox C.C. 57, and doubt about the correctness of the decision was expressed in *Flattery*. What was said in *Linekar* as to fraud as to identity vitiating consent was *obiter*, the case not concerning mistake as to identity at all, but it is submitted that the view of the Court of Appeal represents the modern and better view.

See also section 3 of the *SOA* 1956 (*post*, H–27) in relation to false pretences of a less fundamental character; and *R. v. Tabassum* [2000] 2 Cr.App.R. 328, CA (*post*, H–124) in which it was held that a deception as to the quality of the act vitiated consent in a case of indecent assault.

Recent complaint

    See § 20–12 in the main work.   **H–18**

Distress of victim

    See § 20–13 in the main work.   **H–19**

Mens rea

General

    It must be proved that at the time of the non-consensual intercourse, the defendant either knew that the victim was not consenting or that he was reckless as to whether she or he was consenting: see s.1(2)(b) of the *SOA* 1956, *ante*, H–3. If the tribunal of fact has to consider whether the defendant believed that a person was consenting to intercourse, the presence or absence of reasonable grounds for such a belief is a matter to which the tribunal is to have regard, in conjunction with any other relevant matters, in considering whether he so believed: *Sexual Offences (Amendment) Act* 1976, s.1(2), *ante*, H–4.   **H–20**

Sexual intercourse is a continuing act, which ends upon withdrawal. If, therefore, a man becomes aware that the other person is not consenting after intercourse has commenced and he does not desist, he will be guilty of rape from the moment that he realises that she or he is not consenting: *Kaitamaki v. R.* [1985] A.C. 147, PC. This case was decided on sections 127 and 128 of the *New Zealand Crimes Act* 1961, which are to the same effect as section 44 of the 1956 Act (*post*, H–219) and section 1 of the 1956 Act (*ante*, H–3). As to the situation where the victim was in fact consenting at the outset, but ceases to consent, see *ante*, H–14. This will also be rape provided that the man was aware of the change or was reckless in respect thereof.

Restlessness

    Substantive offences. In *R. v. Satnam and Kewal*, 78 Cr.App.R. 149, CA, earlier confusion was resolved. The authorities having been reviewed, it was held that any direction as to the definition of rape should be based upon section 1 of the *Sexual Offences (Amendment) Act* 1976 (see now s.1(2) of the *SOA* 1956, *ante*, H–3) and upon *DPP v. Morgan* [1976] A.C. 182, HL (§ 17–10 in the main work). The court suggested that a practical definition of recklessness in sexual cases had been given in *R. v. Kimber*, 77 Cr.App.R. 225, CA (a case of indecent assault), namely if the jury were sure that the defendant had been indifferent to the feelings and wishes of the victim, aptly described colloquially as "couldn't care less" then that in law was "reckless". Thus (see pp. 154–155), in summing up a case of rape which involves the issue of consent, the judge should, in dealing with the state of mind of the defendant, direct the jury that before they can convict, the Crown must have proved either that he knew the woman did not consent to sexual intercourse, or that he was reckless as to whether she consented. If the jury are sure he knew she did not consent, they will find him   **H–21**

guilty of rape knowing there to be no consent. If they are not sure about that, they will go on to consider reckless rape. If he may genuinely have believed that she did consent, even though he was mistaken in that belief he must be acquitted: see s.1(2) of the 1976 Act, *ante*, H–4. In considering whether his belief may have been genuine, the jury should take into account all the relevant circumstances (including presence or absence of reasonable grounds: see s.1(2)). If, after considering them, the jury are sure that the defendant had no genuine belief that the woman consented to have intercourse, then they will convict. He will be guilty because that finding of fact would mean that his mental state was such that either he knew she was not consenting or he was reckless as to whether she was consenting. If the jury are sure that he could not have cared less whether she wanted to have sexual intercourse or not, but pressed on regardless, then he would have been reckless and could not have believed that she wanted to.

In *R. v. Taylor (Robert)*, 80 Cr.App.R. 327, CA, Lord Lane C.J. said (at p.332) that in rape, the defendant is reckless if he does not believe the woman is consenting and could not care less whether she is consenting or not but presses on regardless. *Taylor* was followed and applied in *R. v. Adkins* [2000] 2 All E.R. 185, CA, where it was held to be unnecessary to give a direction as to honest belief in every case where consent is in issue; such a direction is only required when, on the evidence in the case, there is room for the possibility of a genuine mistaken belief that the victim had consented; equally, the question of honest belief does not necessarily arise where reckless rape is in issue, for the defendant might have failed to address his mind to the question whether or not there was consent, or have been indifferent as to whether or not there was consent, in circumstances where, if he had addressed his mind to the question, he could not genuinely have believed that there was consent; where, therefore, the defence case was not merely that the complainant consented but that she actively facilitated intercourse, there was no scope for a genuine, but mistaken, belief as to consent.

H–22   **Attempts.** In *R. v. Khan*, 91 Cr.App.R. 29, the Court of Appeal held that precisely the same analysis can be made of the offence of attempted rape as that of the full offence, namely: (a) the intention of the offender is to have sexual intercourse with another person; (b) the offence is committed if, but only if, the circumstances are that: (i) the other person does not consent; *and* (ii) the defendant knows that he or she is not consenting or is reckless as to that fact.

Drunkenness and mistake of fact

H–23   It is clear from both *DPP v. Majewski* [1977] A.C. 443, HL (§ 17–107 in the main work) and *R. v. Caldwell* [1982] A.C. 341, HL (§ 17–112 in the main work) that "recklessness" as a consequence of voluntarily induced intoxication cannot amount to a defence.

If the accused was, or may have been, genuinely mistaken as to fact (see generally, §§ 17–10 *et seq.* in the main work, and H–21, *ante*), for example, if he thought or may have thought that the complainant was consenting to sexual intercourse, and the jury are sure that that mistake was a consequence of intoxication, what then is the position? It appears to be this: implicit in such a finding is the finding that but for the voluntary consumption of drink the jury are sure that the accused would have known either that the complainant was not consenting or, at the very least, that there was a risk that she was not consenting. Whatever the true scope of the meaning of "reckless" in the context of sexual offences, it is plain (see *ante*, H–21) that to proceed knowing that there was a risk that the complainant was not consenting and not caring whether she consented or not is to act recklessly. It therefore follows that if the jury are sure that by virtue of drink (or drugs) the accused was not alerted, at the very least to the existence of that risk, that in itself constitutes the necessary recklessness for the purposes of the offence, see *Majewski* (§ 17–109 in the main work); and a genuine mistake as to fact in such circumstances constitutes no defence. This approach is borne out by the decision of the Court of Appeal in *R. v. Woods (W.)*, 74 Cr.App.R. 312. It was conceded on behalf of W that, but for section 1(2) of the *Sexual Offences (Amendment) Act 1976* (*ante*, H–4), the principles in *Majewski* and *Caldwell* (as to the relevance of drink to recklessness) would apply and that accordingly a genuine mistake as to fact as a consequence of drink could found no defence. However, it was argued that section 1(2) of the

1976 Act permitted the jury to take into account a defendant's drunken state as a possible reasonable ground for his belief that a woman was consenting to intercourse. The submission was roundly rejected. "Relevant" in that subsection means "*legally* relevant". W's drunkenness was not a matter that the jury were entitled to take into consideration in deciding whether or not reasonable grounds existed for W's belief that the woman consented to intercourse.

The question was considered again in *R. v. Fotheringham*, 88 Cr.App.R. 206, CA, in which the defendant was charged with rape. His defence was that he was so drunk at the time that he believed he was having intercourse with his wife. Applying *Majewski, Caldwell, Woods, ante,* and *R. v. O'Grady* [1987] Q.B. 995, 85 Cr.App.R. 315, CA (§ 17–16 in the main work), the court held that "in rape, self-induced intoxication is no defence, whether the issue be intention, consent or, as here, mistake as to the identity of the victim" (at p.212).

(j) *Liability of accessories*

As to indicting accessories to rape, see *ante*, H–7; and as to their liability to conviction, notwithstanding the acquittal of the alleged principal, see *R. v. Cogan and Leak* [1976] Q.B. 217, 61 Cr.App.R. 217, CA (§ 20–26 in the main work). **H–24**

(k) *Attempts*

See § 20–27 in the main work, and, in relation to the *mens rea* of an attempt, see *ante*, H–22. **H–25**

(2) Procurement of intercourse by threats or false pretences

(a) *Statute*

Sexual Offences Act 1956, ss.2, 3

2.—(1) It is an offence for a person to procure a woman, by threats or intimidation, to have ... sexual intercourse in any part of the world. **H–26**
  (2) [*Repealed by* CJPOA *1994, s.33(1).*]

[Subs. (1) is printed as repealed in part by the *CJPOA* 1994, s.168(1) and (3), and Scheds 9, para. 2, and 11.]

3.—(1) It is an offence for a person to procure a woman, by false pretences or false representations, to have ... sexual intercourse in any part of the world. **H–27**
  (2) [*Repealed by* Criminal Justice and Public Order Act *1994, s.33(1).*]

[Subs. (1) is printed as repealed in part by the *CJPOA* 1994, s.168(1) and (3), and Scheds 9, para. 2, and 11.]

As to the meaning of "sexual intercourse", see *post*, H–219; as to the use of the word "woman", see *post*, H–222.

For anonymity provisions, see §§ 20–257 *et seq.* in the main work.

(b) *Indictment*

STATEMENT OF OFFENCE

Procuration, contrary to section 3(1) of the Sexual Offences Act *1956.* **H–28**

PARTICULARS OF OFFENCE

A B, on the —— day of ——, 20—, procured J N, a woman, to have sexual intercourse with himself [or *with E F, as the case may be*] *by falsely pretending or representing to her that* [state in ordinary language the false pretence or representation].

The false pretences must be set out: *R. v. Field* (1892) 116 CCC Sess.Pap. 1891–1892, 757; but they need not be expressly negatived: *R. v. Clarke*, 59 J.P. 248.

An indictment for an offence contrary to section 2 may easily be framed from the above specimen.

(c) *Class of offence and mode of trial*

H–29   The offence contrary to section 2 and an attempt to commit it are class 3 offences (§ 2–17 in the main work), triable on indictment only: *SOA* 1956, s.37(2), and Sched. 2, para. 7(a), (b).

The offence contrary to section 3 is a class 3 offence (§ 2–17 in the main work), triable on indictment only: *SOA* 1956, s.37(2), and Sched. 2, para. 8.

(d) *Alternative verdicts*

H–30   As to the possibility of a conviction of either of these offences on a charge of rape, see *ante*, H–9.

(e) *Sentence*

H–31   Either offence, or an attempt to commit the offence contrary to section 2: imprisonment not exceeding two years—*SOA* 1956, s.37(3), and Sched. 2, paras 7(a), (b) and 8.

(f) *Ingredients of the offences*

"Procure"

H–32   See *post*, H–171.

False pretences

H–33   Seduction by a married man of a woman under promise of marriage by false representation was held to be within section 3(2) of the *Criminal Law Amendment Act* 1885 (*rep.*), of which section 3(1) of the Act of 1956 was a replacement: *R. v. Williams*, 62 J.P. 310. It is immaterial whether the intercourse was procured with the defendant or with another: *ibid.*, and see *R. v. Jones* [1896] 1 Q.B. 4.

(3) **Administering drugs to obtain or facilitate intercourse**

(a) *Statute*

Sexual Offences Act 1956, s.4

H–34   4.—(1) It is an offence for a person to apply or administer to, or cause to be taken by, a woman any drug, matter or thing with intent to stupefy or overpower her so as thereby to enable any man to have unlawful sexual intercourse with her.

(2) [*Repealed by* Criminal Justice and Public Order Act *1994, s.33(1)*.]

As to the meaning of "sexual intercourse", see *post*, H–219; as to the use of the words "man" and "woman", see *post*, H–222.

For anonymity provisions, see *post*, §§ 20–257 *et seq.* in the main work.

(b) *Class of offence and mode of trial*

This offence is a class 3 offence (§ 2–17 in the main work), triable only on indictment: **H–35**
SOA 1956, s.37(2), and Sched. 2, para. 9.

(c) *Alternative verdicts*

As to the possibility of a conviction of this offence on a charge of rape, see *ante*, H–9. **H–36**

(d) *Sentence*

Imprisonment not exceeding two years: *SOA* 1956, s.37(3), and Sched. 2, para. 9. **H–37**

(e) *Ingredients of the offence*

"Unlawful" sexual intercourse means illicit sexual intercourse, *i.e.* outside the bond of **H–38**
marriage: *R. v. Chapman* [1959] 1 Q.B. 100, 42 Cr.App.R. 257, CCA (considering s.19 of the
1956 Act, *post*, H–148).

The essence of the offence is the administering of the drug. If there has been only one
administration, there can be only one offence, even though the intention of the administration was to enable more than one man to have intercourse with the woman: *R. v. Shilling-
ford and Vanderwall*, 52 Cr.App.R. 188, CA.

(4) Sexual intercourse with girl under 13

(a) *Statute*

Sexual Offences Act 1956, s.5

5. It is an offence for a man to have unlawful sexual intercourse with a girl under the age of **H–39**
thirteen.

[This section is printed as effectively amended by the *CLA* 1967, s.12(5)(a).]

As to the meaning of "sexual intercourse", see *post*, H–219; as to the use of the words
"man" and "girl", see *post*, H–222.

For anonymity provisions, see §§ 20–257 *et seq.* in the main work.

(b) *Indictment*

STATEMENT OF OFFENCE

Sexual intercourse with a girl under 13, contrary to section 5 of the Sexual Offences Act *1956.* **H–40**

PARTICULARS OF OFFENCE

A B, on the —— day of ——, 20—, had sexual intercourse with J N, a girl under the age of 13 years.

(c) *Class of offence and mode of trial*

This offence and an attempt to commit it are class 2 offences (§ 2–17 in the main work), **H–41**
triable only on indictment: *SOA* 1956, s.37(2), and Sched. 2, para. 2(a), (b).

(d) *Alternative verdicts*

H–42   Indecent assault, contrary to section 14(1) of the 1956 Act (*post*, H–117): *R. v. McCormack* [1969] 2 Q.B. 442, 53 Cr.App.R. 514, CA. As to alternative verdicts generally, see §§ 4–524 *et seq.* in the main work.

(e) *Sentence*

H–43   The full offence: life imprisonment—*SOA* 1956, s.37(2), and Sched. 2, para. 2(a).

Attempt: imprisonment not exceeding seven years—*ibid.*, para. 2(b).

Custodial sentences are normally imposed, unless the offender is psychologically abnormal or of limited intelligence (see in particular *Att.-Gen.'s Reference (No. 20 of 1994)*, 16 Cr.App.R.(S.) 578, CA.). Some guidance may be obtained from the guideline of the Sentencing Guidelines Council in relation to offences under the *SOA* 2003 (*post*, Appendix K–83 *et seq.*); and for guidance as to how to sentence historic offences, see *R. v. H.*, *ante*, H–12.

(f) *Ingredients of the offence*

Man

H–44   As to the abolition of the presumption that a boy under 14 is incapable of sexual intercourse, see *ante*, H–13.

Consent immaterial

H–45   The evidence is the same as in rape, with the exception that it is immaterial whether the act was done with or without the consent of the girl. If it was in fact without her consent, an indictment for rape will lie, notwithstanding the age of the child: *R. v. Dicken* (1877) 14 Cox 8; *R. v. Harling*, 26 Cr.App.R. 127, CCA; *R. v. Howard*, 50 Cr.App.R. 56, CCA, *ante*, H–15. So, where the defendant was indicted for an attempt to commit the offence, and the evidence was that he had attempted to have sexual intercourse with the girl, but that she had consented to the attempt, it was held that the fact of her consent was immaterial, and that the defendant was properly convicted: *R. v. Beale* (1865) L.R. 1 C.C.R. 10.

Knowledge of age immaterial

H–46   A mistake as to the age of the girl, even if based on reasonable grounds, will not avail a defendant: *R. v. Prince* (1875) L.R. 2 C.C.R. 154 (*post*, H–161); *R. v. K.* [2002] 1 A.C. 462, HL; and see the specific defence provided by section 6(3) in relation to the less serious offence of intercourse with a girl under 16 (*post*, H–50).

(g) *Evidence*

Recent complaint

H–47   See § 20–12 in the main work.

Distress of victim

H–48   See § 20–13 in the main work.

Age

H–49   The provisions of section 99(2) of the *CYPA* 1933 (§ 19–326 in the main work), as to presumption and determination of age do not apply: see the proviso to Schedule 1 to the 1933 Act (whilst the proviso was repealed by the *SOA* 2003 (see § 19–326 in the main work), its effect in relation to any prosecution for an offence under the 1956 Act will be saved by virtue of the *Interpretation Act* 1978, s.16 (*ante*, Appendix B–16)). The girl must be proved to have been under 13 years of age when the offence was committed. The best way of doing this is to produce a duly certified copy of the certificate of birth, coupled with evidence of identity; but the age may be proved by any other legal means: *R. v. Cox* [1898] 1 Q.B. 179 (age could be proved by persons who had seen the child and by a teacher at an elementary school which the child attended). Where a certificate of birth is put in, there must be evidence of identity as well: see *R. v. Nicholls* (1867) 10 Cox 476; *R. v. Bellis*, 6 Cr.App.R. 283, CCA; *R. v. Rogers*, 10 Cr.App.R. 276, CCA.

In the case of an adopted child, the date of birth may be proved by a certified copy of an entry in the Adopted Children Register: *Adoption and Children Act* 2002, s.77(5).

(5) Sexual intercourse with a girl under 16

(a) *Statute*

Sexual Offences Act 1956, s.6

6.—(1) It is an offence, subject to the exceptions mentioned in this section, for a man to have unlawful sexual intercourse with a girl . . . under the age of sixteen. **H–50**

(2) Where a marriage is invalid under section two of the *Marriage Act* 1949, or section one of the *Age of Marriage Act* 1929 (the wife being a girl under the age of sixteen), the invalidity does not make the husband guilty of an offence under this section because he has sexual intercourse with her, if he believes her to be his wife, and has reasonable cause for the belief.

(3) A man is not guilty of an offence under this section because he has unlawful sexual intercourse with a girl under the age of sixteen, if he is under the age of twenty-four and has not previously been charged with a like offence, and he believes her to be of the age of sixteen or over and has reasonable cause for the belief.

In this subsection "a like offence" means an offence under this section or an attempt to commit one, or an offence under paragraph (1) of section five of the *Criminal Law Amendment Act* 1885 (the provision replaced for England and Wales by this section).

[This section is printed as repealed in part by the *CLA* 1967, s.10(1), and Sched. 2, para. 14.]

As to the meaning of "sexual intercourse", see *post*, H–219; as to the use of the words "man" and "girl", see *post*, H–222.

As to the proof of exceptions, see the *SOA* 1956, s.47, *post*, H–225.

For anonymity provisions, see §§ 20–257 *et seq.* in the main work.

Marriage Act 1949, s.2

Marriages of persons under sixteen

2. A marriage solemnized between persons either of whom is under the age of sixteen shall be void. **H–51**

(b) *Indictment*

Statement of Offence

Sexual intercourse with a girl under 16, contrary to section 6(1) of the Sexual Offences Act *1956.* **H–52**

Particulars of Offence

A B, on the —— day of ——, 20—, had sexual intercourse with J N, a girl under the age of 16 years.

(c) *Class of offence and mode of trial*

H–53   This offence and an attempt to commit it are class 3 offences (§ 2–17 in the main work), triable either way: *MCA* 1980, s.17(1), and Sched. 1 (§ 1–130 in the main work).

(d) *Alternative verdicts*

H–54   Indecent assault, contrary to section 14(1) of the 1956 Act (*post*, H–117): *R. v. McCormack* [1969] 2 Q.B. 442, 53 Cr.App.R. 514, CA. As to alternative verdicts generally, see §§ 4–524 *et seq.* in the main work.

(e) *Time limit on prosecutions*

H–55   Prosecutions for an offence under section 6 or an attempt to commit such offence may not be commenced more than 12 months after the offence charged: *SOA* 1956, s.37(2), and Sched. 2, para. 10(a), (b).

As to what is a commencement of the prosecution, see *R. v. West* [1898] 1 Q.B. 174; *R. v. Wakely* [1920] 1 K.B. 688, 14 Cr.App.R. 121, CCA.

In appropriate circumstances, evidence of prior offences by the defendant against the same girl committed outside the 12 months' time limit will be admissible: *R. v. Shellaker* [1914] 1 K.B. 414, 9 Cr.App.R. 240, CCA; *cf. R. v. Hewitt*, 19 Cr.App.R. 64, CCA; *R. v. Adams*, *The Times*, April 8, 1993, CA.

As to the impropriety of bringing a prosecution for indecent assault, based on an act of consensual sexual intercourse, where a prosecution under section 6 is time barred, see *R. v. J.*, *post*, H–118.

(f) *Sentence*

H–56   The full offence, or an attempt to commit it: imprisonment not exceeding two years' *SOA* 1956, s.37(3), and Sched. 2, para. 10(a), (b). The penalty on summary conviction is governed by section 32 of the *MCA* 1980 (§ 1–125 in the main work).

In *R. v. Taylor*, 64 Cr.App.R. 182, CA, the court laid down guidelines for the sentencing of persons convicted of having unlawful sexual intercourse with a girl under the age of 16. Lawton L.J. distinguished between cases where "virtuous friendship" between young people of about the same age ended in sexual intercourse, and cases where a man in a supervisory capacity set out to seduce a girl under 16 who was in his charge. In the first type of case, sentences of a punitive nature were not required; in the second, sentences near the maximum of two years should be passed.

In *R. v. Bayliss* [2000] 1 Cr.App.R.(S.) 412, CA, it was said that attitudes to teenage prostitution had changed since *Taylor*, and that there was a greater appreciation that this offence and that of taking indecent photographs of children, contrary to the *Protection of Children Act* 1978 (§§ 31–107 *et seq.* in the main work), had been put on the statute book for the protection of children, including against themselves.

(g) *Ingredients of the offence*

Man

H–57   As to the abolition of the presumption that a boy under 14 is incapable of sexual intercourse, see *ante*, H–13.

A girl under 16 cannot be indicted for "abetting" or "inciting" a man to have unlawful sexual intercourse with herself: *R. v. Tyrrell* [1894] 1 Q.B. 710.

As to doctors who prescribe contraceptive pills to girls under 16, see *Gillick v. West Norfolk and Wisbech Area Health Authority* [1986] A.C. 112, HL, *post*, H–196.

Consent immaterial

See *ante*, H–45, and *R. v. Ratcliffe* (1882) 10 Q.B.D. 74.   **H–58**

"Unlawful" sexual intercourse

See *R. v. Chapman*, *ante*, H–38.   **H–59**

(h) *Evidence*

Recent complaint

See § 20–12 in the main work.   **H–60**

Distress of victim

See § 20–13 in the main work.   .**H–61**

Age

See *ante*, H–49, the contents of which apply, *mutatis mutandis*, to the offence under section   **H–62**
6.

(i) *Defences*

In the case of a man under the age of 24, the presence of reasonable cause to believe that   **H–63**
the girl was over the age of 16 years is a valid defence provided that the defendant has not
previously been charged with a like offence: *SOA* 1956, s.6(3) (*ante*, H–50). As to the meaning of the expression "a like offence", see *ibid*. The defence is not incompatible with Article
6 (right to fair trial (§ 16–57 in the main work)) or 14 (prohibition on discrimination (§ 16–
139 in the main work)) of the ECHR as being discriminatory on the grounds that, (a) a
woman who had sexual intercourse with a boy under 16 would, if prosecuted, be charged
with indecent assault, in relation to which she would have a defence, whatever her age, of
genuine belief that the boy was 16 or more, and (b) it was restricted to men under the age
of 24; as to (b), even though the choice of age was arbitrary, it did not introduce an element
of disproportionality into the offence: *R. v. Kirk and Russell* [2002] Crim.L.R. 756, CA.

In *R. v. Rider*, 37 Cr.App.R. 209, Assizes, Streatfeild J. had to construe the wording of the
Criminal Law Amendment Act 1922. The proviso to section 2 of that Act gave a man under 24
years of age a defence to a charge of unlawful sexual intercourse with a girl under 16 years
of age if at the time of the intercourse he had reasonable cause to believe that the girl was
over the age of 16; but the defence was only available "on the first occasion on which he is
charged with" such an offence. It was held that "charged" in this context meant "appeared
before a court with jurisdiction to deal with the matter". The defendant had been committed for trial on two separate occasions in respect of like allegations relating to different girls.
Both allegations were joined in the same indictment and it was held that appearance before
the assize was the first occasion on which he appeared before a court with jurisdiction to
deal with the matter and, therefore, the defence was available in respect of both counts.
Streatfeild J. said, however, that had the magistrates refused to commit for trial in respect of
the first matter, the appearance at the assize on the second matter would have been the
second occasion. This result seems illogical. It should be borne in mind that at the time of
Rider, the offence in question could be tried only on indictment. It is now triable either way
and it is respectfully submitted that the defence should only be available to a person who at
the time of the alleged offence has not been before a court (magistrates' court, whether or
not the matter is to be tried summarily, Crown Court or service court) on a charge of such
an offence. This gives due effect to the actual decision in *Rider* to the revised formulation of
the defence in the 1956 Act and to the changes in the legislation relating to mode of trial. It
is also consistent with the rationale underlying the restriction on the defence, *viz*. that once

the serious nature of such conduct has been brought to the attention of a man, he can legitimately be expected to be more careful about a girl's age.

To constitute a defence under this proviso, where it applies, the defendant must have reasonable cause to believe, and, in fact, must have believed that the girl was over the age of 16 years: *R. v. Banks* [1916] 2 K.B. 621, 12 Cr.App.R. 74, CCA; *R. v. Harrison*, 26 Cr.App.R. 166, CCA. The question of the existence of reasonable cause to believe is one for the jury: *R. v. Forde* [1923] 2 K.B. 400, 17 Cr.App.R. 99, CCA.

The defence is available not only where intercourse has taken place, but also where it has been merely attempted: *R. v. Collier* [1960] Crim.L.R. 204, Assizes (Streatfeild J.).

As to the burden of proof of the "exceptions" (defences) in subsections (2) and (3) of section 6, see section 47 of the 1956 Act, *post*, H–225.

(6) Intercourse with defectives

(a) *Statute*

Sexual Offences Act 1956, ss.7, 9

Intercourse with defective

H–64   **7.**—(1) It is an offence, subject to the exception mentioned in this section, for a man to have unlawful sexual intercourse with a woman who is a defective.

(2) A man is not guilty of an offence under this section because he has unlawful sexual intercourse with a woman if he does not know and has no reason to suspect her to be a defective.

[This section is printed as substituted by the *MHA* 1959, s.127(1)(a).]

Procurement of defective

H–65   **9.**—(1) It is an offence, subject to the exception mentioned in this section, for a person to procure a woman who is a defective to have unlawful sexual intercourse in any part of the world.

(2) A person is not guilty of an offence under this section because he procures a defective to have unlawful sexual intercourse, if he does not know and has no reason to suspect her to be a defective.

As to the meaning of "sexual intercourse", see *post*, H–219 as to the use of the words "man" and "woman", see *post*, H–222; as to the meaning of "defective", see *post*, H–68.

For anonymity provisions, see §§ 20–257 *et seq.* in the main work.

As to the burden of proof in relation to the exception in subsection (2) of both sections, see section 47 of the Act, *post*, H–225.

(b) *Class of offence and mode of trial*

H–66   Offences against sections 7 and 9, and attempts to commit them, are class 3 offences (§ 2–17 in the main work), triable only on indictment: *SOA* 1956, s.37(2), and Sched. 2, paras 11(a), (b), and 13(a), (b).

(c) *Sentence*

H–67   Offences against sections 7 and 9, and attempts to commit them: imprisonment not exceeding two years—*SOA* 1956, s.37(3), and Sched. 2, paras 11(a), (b), and 13(a), (b). For an illustrative example, see *R. v. Adcock* [2000] 1 Cr.App.R.(S.) 563, CA.

(d) *Ingredients of the offences*

"Defective"

Sexual Offences Act 1956, s.45

Meaning of defective

H–68   **45.** In this Act "defective" means a person suffering from a state of arrested or incomplete development of mind which includes severe impairment of intelligence and social functioning.

[This section is printed as substituted by the *MHA* 1959, s.127(1); and as amended by the *Mental Health (Amendment) Act* 1982, Sched. 3.]

The words "severe impairment of intelligence and social functioning" are ordinary English words and not words of art; they were inserted in the definition to protect women, if defectives, from exploitation. Severe impairment is to be measured against the standards of normal persons: *R. v. Hall (J.H.)*, 86 Cr.App.R. 159, CA. The trial judge's direction that it was for them to decide on all the evidence whether the victim was severely impaired within the ordinary meaning of those words was correct.

"Unlawful" sexual intercourse

See *R. v. Chapman, ante*, H–38.　　　　　　　　　　　　　　　　　　　　**H–69**

"Procure"

See *post*, H–171.　　　　　　　　　　　　　　　　　　　　　　　　　　**H–70**

(7) Incest by a man

(a) *Statute*

Sexual Offences Act 1956, s.10

10.—(1) It is an offence for a man to have sexual intercourse with a woman whom he knows to　**H–71**
be his grand-daughter, daughter, sister or mother.

(2) In the foregoing subsection "sister" includes half-sister and for the purposes of that subsection any expression importing a relationship between two people shall be taken to apply notwithstanding that the relationship is not traced through lawful wedlock.

As to the meaning of "sexual intercourse", see *post*, H–219; as to the use of the words "man" and "woman", see *post*, § H–222.
For anonymity provisions, see §§ 20–257 *et seq.* in the main work.

(b) *Indictment*

STATEMENT OF OFFENCE

Incest, contrary to section 10(1) of the Sexual Offences Act *1956.*　　　　　**H–72**

PARTICULARS OF OFFENCE

A B, being a male person, on the —— day of ——, 20—, had sexual intercourse with J N, whom he knew to be his daughter [if under the age of 13, add her age].

An indictment which charged the offence as having been committed "on divers days" between two specified dates was held to be bad for duplicity: *R. v. Thompson* [1914] 2 K.B. 99, 9 Cr.App.R. 252, CCA.

Where a brother and sister were charged in separate counts of the same indictment with committing incest and were tried separately, with the result that the brother was convicted and the sister acquitted, it was held that the acquittal of the sister did not make the conviction of the brother bad: *R. v. Gordon*, 19 Cr.App.R. 20, CCA. As to inconsistent verdicts generally, see §§ 7–70 *et seq.* in the main work.

(c) *Class of offence and mode of trial*

H–73   This offence, and an attempt to commit it, are class 3 offences (unless with a girl under 13, in which case they are class 2 offences) (§ 2–17 in the main work), triable only on indictment: *SOA* 1956, s.37(2), and Sched. 2, para. 14(a), (b).

(d) *Alternative verdicts*

H–74   On a charge of the full offence, unlawful sexual intercourse with a girl under 13 (s.5) or with a girl under 16 (s.6): *SOA* 1956, s.37(4), and Sched. 2, para. 14(a). Where the girl is under 16, indecent assault (whether or not the indictment avers her age): *R. v. Rogina*, 64 Cr.App.R. 79, CA. This possibility arises by virtue of the combination of section 37(5) (*post*, H–226) and the specific provision in Schedule 2 for a conviction of an offence under either section 5 or 6 (indecent assault being an alternative on an indictment charging either of those offences, *ante*, H–42, H–54).

(e) *Restriction on prosecution*

H–75   A prosecution for this offence, or an attempt to commit it, may not be commenced except by or with the consent of the DPP: *SOA* 1956, s.37(2), and Sched. 2, para. 14(a), (b).

(f) *Sentence*

Maximum

H–76   The full offence and an attempt to commit it: if with a girl under 13, and so charged in the indictment, life imprisonment, otherwise imprisonment not exceeding seven years—*SOA* 1956, s.37(3), and Sched. 2, para. 14(a), (b).

Basis of sentence

H–77   See *R. v. Huchison*, 56 Cr.App.R. 307, CA.

Guidelines

H–78   In *Att.-Gen.'s Reference (No. 1 of 1989)*, 90 Cr.App.R. 141, the Court of Appeal laid down guidelines for sentencing in cases of incest by a father against a daughter. The court made the following suggestions "as a broad guide" to the level of sentence for various categories of the crime of incest. All were on the assumption that there had been no plea of guilty. They should be read subject to *Practice Statement (Crime: Sentencing)* [1992] 1 W.L.R. 948. See, in particular, paragraph 10 thereof.

(i) *Girl aged over 16 years*

H–79   A range from three years' imprisonment down to a nominal penalty would be appropriate depending in particular on the one hand whether force was used and the degree of harm if any, to the girl, and, on the other, the desirability where it existed of keeping family disruption to a minimum. The older the girl the greater the possibility that she might have been willing or even the instigating party, a factor which would be reflected in the sentence.

(ii) *Girl aged from 13 to 16 years*

H–80   A sentence between about five years' and three years' imprisonment would be appropriate. Much the same principles would apply as in the case of the girl over 16 years, though the likelihood of corruption increased in inverse proportion to the age of the girl.

(iii) *Girl aged under 13 years*

H–81   It was here that the widest range of sentences was likely to be found. If any case of incest could properly be described as the "ordinary" type of case, it would be one where the sexual relationship between husband and wife had broken down; the father had probably resorted to excessive drinking and the eldest daughter was gradually, by way of familiarities, indecent acts and suggestions made the object of the father's frustrated inclinations. If the girl was not far short of her thirteenth birthday and there were no particularly adverse or favourable features, a term of about six years' imprisonment would seem to be appropriate. The younger the girl when the sexual approach was started, the more likely it would be that the girl's will was overborne and, accordingly, the more serious would be the crime.

(iv) *Aggravating factors*

Whatever the age of the girl, the following, *inter alia*, would aggravate the offence: **H–82**
   (a) physical or psychological suffering from the offence;
   (b) the incest taking place at frequent intervals or over a long period;
   (c) the use of threats or violence, or the girl being otherwise terrified of her father;
   (d) the incest being accompanied by perversions abhorrent to the girl, such as buggery or *fellatio*;
   (e) the girl becoming pregnant; and
   (f) the commission of similar offences against more than one girl.

(v) *Mitigating features*

Possible mitigating features were, *inter alia*:   **H–83**
   (a) a plea of guilty;
   (b) genuine affection on the defendant's part rather than the intention to use the girl simply as an outlet for his sexual inclinations;
   (c) previous sexual experience by the girl; and
   (d) deliberate attempts at seduction by the girl.
   In relation to a plea of guilty, the court said that such a plea was seldom not entered and it should be met by an appropriate discount, depending on the usual considerations, that is, how promptly the defendant confessed, the degree of contrition and so on. The court also said that occasionally a shorter term of imprisonment than would otherwise be imposed might be justified as being of benefit to the victim and the family.
   For cases illustrating the application of these guidelines, see CSP B4–2. For cases of incest by a brother with a sister, see *ibid.*, B4–2.3D; for a case of incest by a mother with her young son, see *ibid.*, B4–2.3E.

(g) *Effect of adoption*

The prohibition contained in section 10(1) applies notwithstanding the adoption of one of   **H–84**
the parties: *Adoption and Children Act* 2002, s.74(1)(b) (whilst this provision was amended to substitute a reference to sections 64 and 65 of the *SOA* 2003 for the references to sections 10 and 11 of the 1956 Act, its previous operation will be saved by virtue of section 16 of the *Interpretation Act* 1978 (*ante*, Appendix B–16)).

(h) *Ingredients of the offence*

If a man makes a genuine mistake as to the identity of the person with whom he has in-   **H–85**
tercourse, he will not commit the offence: *R. v. Baillie-Smith*, 64 Cr.App.R. 76, CA (intercourse with daughter, thinking her to be his wife).
   As to the abolition of the common law presumption that a boy under 14 is incapable of sexual intercourse, see *ante*, H–13.

(i) *Evidence*

H–86   The relationship between the parties may be proved by oral evidence or by certificates of marriage and birth, coupled with identification. An admission by the defendant that the person with whom the offence had been committed was his daughter may be sufficient evidence of the relationship: *R. v. Jones (Evan)*, 24 Cr.App.R. 55, CCA.

Evidence tending to show pre-existent sexual passion between the parties is admissible: *R. v. Ball* [1911] A.C. 47, HL.

The defendant was charged with incest with S, who was alleged to be his daughter. His defence was that he had no knowledge that S *was* his daughter. He desired to give evidence:

  (a) that he had been told by his first wife (the mother of S) that S had been begotten by another man and that he believed that statement to be true;

  (b) that he had told his second wife that he was not the father of S;

  (c) explaining statements which he had made on certain occasions acknowledging S to be his daughter.

It was held (on appeal) that this evidence was relevant to the issue whether the defendant *knew* that S was his daughter and that he was entitled to give any evidence relevant to that issue, including evidence of an admission by his first wife: *R. v. Carmichael* [1940] 1 K.B. 630, 27 Cr.App.R. 183, CCA.

(8) Incitement to incest of girls under 16

H–87   See the *CLA* 1977, s.54, *post*, H–239.

(9) Incest by a woman

(a) *Statute*

Sexual Offences Act 1956, s.11

H–88   **11.**—(1) It is an offence for a woman of the age of sixteen or over to permit a man whom she knows to be her grandfather, father, brother or son to have sexual intercourse with her by her consent.

(2) In the foregoing subsection "brother" includes half-brother, and for the purposes of that subsection any expression importing a relationship between two people shall be taken to apply notwithstanding that the relationship is not traced through lawful wedlock.

As to the meaning of "sexual intercourse", see *post*, H–219; as to the use of the words "woman" and "man", see *post*, H–222.

For anonymity provisions, see §§ 20–257 *et seq.* in the main work.

(b) *Indictment*

STATEMENT OF OFFENCE

H–89   *Incest, contrary to section 11(1) of the Sexual Offences Act 1956.*

PARTICULARS OF OFFENCE

A B, being a female person of the age of 18, on the —— day of ——, 20—, with her consent permitted J N, whom she knew to be her father, to have sexual intercourse with her.

As to the form of the indictment, see also *R. v. Thompson, ante,* H–72.

(c) *Class of offence and mode of trial*

This offence, and an attempt to commit it, are class 3 offences (§ 2–17 in the main work), **H–90** triable only on indictment: *SOA* 1956, s.37(2), and Sched. 2, para. 15(a), (b).

(d) *Restriction on prosecution*

A prosecution for this offence or an attempt to commit it may not be commenced except **H–91** by or with the consent of the DPP: *SOA* 1956, s.37(2), and Sched. 2, para. 15(a), (b).

(e) *Sentence*

The full offence: imprisonment not exceeding seven years—*SOA* 1956, s.37(3), and **H–92** Sched 2, para. 15(a).
Attempt: imprisonment not exceeding two years—*ibid.*, para. 15(b).

(f) *Effect of adoption*

The prohibition contained in section 11(1) applies notwithstanding the adoption of one of **H–93** the parties: *Adoption and Children Act* 2002, s.74(1)(b) (as to which, see *ante*, H–84).

(g) *Ingredients of offence*

The common law presumption as to incapacity in relation to boys under 14 years of age **H–94** (*ante*, H–13) had no application where a woman was charged with committing incest with such a boy: *R. v. Pickford* [1995] 1 Cr.App.R. 420, CA.

(10) Buggery

(a) *Introduction*

The *SOA* 1956 contains two "unnatural offences", namely buggery (with a person or **H–95** with an animal) and gross indecency between men. There are time limits and requirements as to the consent of the DPP in respect of both offences in certain circumstances.

The *SOA* 1967 amended the law by providing, in particular, that consenting men over the age of 21 (reduced to 18 by the *CJPOA* 1994, and to 16 by the *Sexual Offences (Amendment) Act* 2000) who commit buggery or gross indecency in private, do not commit an offence (s.1, *post*, H–97). There are different rules regarding the lawfulness of procuration of buggery and gross indecency (s.4, *post*, H–236). Section 11(3) provides that section 46 of the 1956 Act (use of words "man", "boy" and other expressions) shall apply for the purposes of the provisions of the 1967 Act as it applies for the purposes of the provisions of that Act. For section 46, see *post*, H–222.

The *CJPOA* 1994 effected further changes in the law. Apart from reducing the age of consent for homosexual acts to 18 (*ante*), it redefined the offence of rape to include non-consensual anal intercourse with a man or a woman (*ante*, H–3). Non-consensual buggery should, therefore, be charged as rape. Consensual buggery between two people will not be an offence if the act takes place in private and both parties have achieved the age of 16.

As to the offences of indecent assault on a man and assault with intent to commit buggery, which may be on a man or a woman (categorised in the 1956 Act as "assault" offences rather than as "unnatural offences"), see sections 15, *post*, H–127, and 16, *post*, H–138.

(b) *Statute*

Sexual Offences Act 1956, s.12

H–96   **12.**—(1) It is an offence for a person to commit buggery with another person otherwise than in the circumstances first described in subsection (1A) or (1AA) below or with an animal.

(1A) The circumstances referred to in subsection (1) are that the act of buggery takes place in private and both parties have attained the age of sixteen.

(1AA) The other circumstances so referred to are that the person is under the age of sixteen and the other person has attained that age.

(1B) An act of buggery by one man with another shall not be treated as taking place in private if it takes place—

(a) when more than two persons take part or are present; or

(b) in a lavatory to which the public have or are permitted to have access, whether on payment or otherwise.

(1C) In any proceedings against a person for buggery with another person it shall be for the prosecutor to prove that the act of buggery took place otherwise than in private or that one of the parties to it had not attained the age of sixteen.

(2), (3) [*Repealed by* Police and Criminal Evidence Act *1984, Sched. 7.*]

[Subs. (1) is printed as amended by the *CLA* 1967, s.12(5)(a); the *CJPOA* 1994, s.143(1), (2); and the *Sexual Offences (Amendment) Act* 2000, s.2(1)(a) and (b); subss. (1A), (1B) and (1C) were inserted by the 1994 Act, s.143(1), (3); and are printed as amended by the 2000 Act, s.1(1); subs. (1AA) was inserted by the 2000 Act, s.2(1)(c).]

For anonymity provisions, see §§ 20–257 *et seq.* in the main work.

As to conspiracy or incitement to commit this offence, see *R. v. Boulton* (1871) 12 Cox 87.

Sexual Offences Act 1967, s.1

Amendment of law relating to homosexual acts in private

H–97   **1.**—(1) Notwithstanding any statutory or common law provision, ...

(a) a homosexual act in private shall not be an offence provided that the parties consent thereto and have attained the age of sixteen years; and

(b) a homosexual act by any person shall not be an offence if he is under the age of sixteen and the other party has attained that age.

(2) An act which would otherwise be treated for the purposes of this Act as being done in private shall not be so treated if done—

(a) when more than two persons take part or are present; or

(b) in a lavatory to which the public have or are permitted to have access, whether on payment or otherwise.

(3) A man who is suffering from severe mental handicap cannot in law give any consent which, by virtue of subsection (1) of this section, would prevent a homosexual act from being an offence, but a person shall not be convicted, on account of the incapacity of such a man to consent, of an offence consisting of such an act if he proves that he did not know and had no reason to suspect that man to be suffering from severe mental handicap.

(3A) In subsection (3) of this section "severe mental handicap" means a state of arrested or incomplete development of mind which includes severe impairment of intelligence and social functioning.

(4) Section 128 of the *Mental Health Act* 1959 (prohibition on men on the staff of a hospital, or otherwise having responsibility for mental patients, having sexual intercourse with women patients) shall have effect as if any reference therein to having unlawful sexual intercourse with a woman included a reference to committing buggery or an act of gross indecency with another man.

(5) [*Repealed by* CJPOA *1994, s.168(3) and Sched. 11.*]

(6) It is hereby declared that where in any proceedings it is charged that a homosexual act is an offence the prosecutor shall have the burden of proving that the act was done otherwise than in private or otherwise than with the consent of the parties or that any of the parties had not attained the age of sixteen years.

(7) For the purposes of this section a man shall be treated as doing a homosexual act if, and only if, he commits buggery with another man or commits an act of gross indecency with another man or is a party to the commission by a man of such an act.

[This section is printed as amended and repealed in part by the *Mental Health (Amendment) Act* 1982, s.65(1), (2), and Scheds 3, para. 34, and 4; the *CJPOA* 1994, ss.146(1) and 168(3), and Sched. 11; and the *Sexual Offences (Amendment) Act* 2000, ss.1(2)(a) and 2(3)(a) and (b).]

As to the use of the word "man", see *post*, H–222.
For section 128 of the *MHA* 1959, see *post*, H–228.

(c) *Indictment for buggery with a person*

STATEMENT OF OFFENCE

Buggery, contrary to section 12(1) of the Sexual Offences Act *1956.* **H–98**

PARTICULARS OF OFFENCE

A B, a person of [or over] the age of 21 years, on the —— day of ——, 20—, committed buggery with J N, a person under the age of 18 years.

Because the penalty provisions have the effect of creating a number of separate offences (see *post*, H–103), the particulars should be clear as to which offence is alleged; in the specimen set out above, it is a five year offence that is alleged. Alternative counts may be laid, where appropriate: see *R. v. Reakes* [1974] Crim.L.R. 615, CA.

As to the correct practice where old offences are charged, see *R. v. R.* [1993] Crim.L.R. 541, CA; *R. v. B.*, *ibid*. As to the need for special caution where extremely old offences are alleged, *i.e.* dating back to the period prior to the passing of the *SOA* 1967 (July 27, 1967), see *R. v. D.* [1993] Crim.L.R. 542, CA.

As to the particulars which need to be averred on a charge of attempted buggery, see *R. v. D.*, *ante*. The principles are the same as for the full offence.

(d) *Indictment for buggery with an animal (bestiality)*

STATEMENT OF OFFENCE

Buggery, contrary to section 12(1) of the Sexual Offences Act *1956.* **H–99**

PARTICULARS OF OFFENCE

A B, a person of [or over] the age of 21 years, on the —— day of ——, 20—, committed buggery with a cow [or as the case may be].

(e) *Class of offence and mode of trial*

This offence, and an attempt to commit it, are class 3 offences (§ 2–17 in the main work), **H–100** triable only on indictment: *SOA* 1956, s.37(2), and Sched. 2, para. 3(a), (b).

(f) *Time limits*

Sexual Offences Act 1967, s.7

7.—(1) No proceedings for an offence to which this section applies shall be commenced after **H–101** the expiration of twelve months from the date on which that offence was committed.

(2) This section applies to—

    (a) any offence under section 13 of the Act of 1956 (gross indecency between men);

    (b) [*repealed by* Criminal Law Act *1977, Sched. 13*];

    (c) any offence of buggery by a man with another man not amounting to an assault on that other man and not being an offence by a man with a boy under the age of 16.

For section 13 of the 1956 Act, see *post*, H–107.

Where it was unclear upon the evidence given at the trial whether the offence charged had been committed within the 12 month period prior to the commencement of proceedings for the offence, the court quashed the conviction: *R. v. Lewis*, 68 Cr.App.R. 310, CA. A judge need not in every case to which section 7(1) applies direct the jury that they must be sure the offence was committed within the prescribed period. However, he must do so where an issue under the subsection is raised by the defence, or where it clearly arises on the evidence given at the trial: *ibid.*

(g) *Restriction on prosecutions*

Sexual Offences Act 1967, s.8

H–102   **8.** No proceedings shall be instituted except by or with the consent of the Director of Public Prosecutions against any man for the offence of buggery with, or gross indecency with, another man ... or for aiding, abetting, counselling, procuring or commanding its commission where either of those men was at the time of its commission under the age of sixteen.

[This section is printed as amended by the *Sexual Offences (Amendment) Act* 2000, s.1(2)(b); and as repealed in part by the *Criminal Jurisdiction Act* 1975, s.14(5), and Sched. 6, Pt I; and the *Criminal Attempts Act* 1981, s.10, and Sched., Pt I.]

Failure to obtain the consent of the DPP will lead to the quashing of the conviction: *R. v. Angel*, 52 Cr.App.R. 280, CA; *Secretary of State for Defence v. Warn* [1970] A.C. 394, HL (proceedings before court-martial).

Section 8 does not apply to proceedings under the *Indecency with Children Act* 1960 (*post*, H–230): *CJA* 1972, s.48.

(h) *Sentence*

Maximum

H–103   The full offence, or an attempt to commit it: if with a person under the age of 16 or with an animal, life imprisonment; if the accused is of or over the age of 21 and the other person is under the age of 18, imprisonment not exceeding five years; otherwise, imprisonment not exceeding two years—*SOA* 1956, s.37(3), and Sched. 2, para. 3(a), (b) (as substituted by the *CJPOA* 1994, s.144(1), (2)). (For an offence of non-consensual buggery with a male over 15 committed before the commencement of the amendments effected by the 1994 Act (November 3, 1994), the maximum remains at 10 years: *Att.-Gen.'s Reference (No. 48 of 1994) (R. v. Jeffrey)*, 16 Cr.App.R.(S.) 980, CA.)

The effect of the different penalty provisions is to create distinct offences: see *R. v. Courtie* [1984] A.C. 463, HL.

Absence of consent not being an ingredient of the offence, it is not open to a judge to sentence on the basis that there was lack of consent; if lack of consent is alleged, there should be a charge of rape: *R. v. Davies* [1998] 1 Cr.App.R.(S.) 380, CA; *R. v. D. (Anthony)* [2000] 1 Cr.App.R.(S.) 120, CA.

Guidelines

H–104   The bracket of sentencing in cases of homosexual offences against boys with neither aggravating nor mitigating factors was set out in *R. v. Willis*, 60 Cr.App.R. 146, CA, as being from three to five years. The court in that case also identified the principal aggravating and mitigating features. In *R. v. A. and W.* [2001] 2 Cr.App.R. 18, CA, the court specifically said that the guidelines in *Willis* remained the starting point. In *R. v. Patterson* [2006] 2 Cr.App.R.(S.) 48, however, the Court of Appeal said that sentences in historic cases of buggery should now be determined as if the offence were one of rape in accordance with the guidelines in *R. v. Millberry*; *R. v. Morgan*; *R. v. Lackenby* [2003] 1 Cr.App.R. 25, CA, instead of by reference to the *Willis* guidelines. The court said that it is important that the sentence should reflect the gravity of the offence rather than the particular label attached to it, and since there is no distinction in principle or in essential gravity made in the *Millberry* guidelines between rape of a male and rape of a female, it would be wrong for a sentence of buggery to be imposed on any other basis. This approach was taken further in *R. v. Kearns* [2009] 1 Cr.App.R.(S.) 107, CA, where it was applied to what was apparently a case of consensual buggery of a 15-year-old boy. For criticism of the *Patterson/Kearns* approach, see the commentaries at CLW/06/34/24 and CLW/09/16/8. Whilst this criticism remains valid, sentencers dealing with historic offending should now be guided, as to general principles, by the judgment of the Court of Appeal in *R. v. H.*, *ante*, H–12.

(i) *Ingredients of the offence*

The definition of the offence derives from the common law. It consists of sexual inter-   **H–105**
course (*per anum*—*R. v. Jacobs* (1817) R. & R. 331) by man with man or, in the same manner, by man with woman (*R. v. Wiseman* (1718) Fortescue K.B. 91; Fost. 91), or by man or woman in any manner (*R. v. Bourne*, 36 Cr.App.R. 125, CCA) with beast (also referred to as bestiality): see 1 Hale 669; 1 Hawk. c. 4; 1 East P.C. 480; 1 Russ. Cr., 12th ed., 735. Once penetration is proved, both parties (if consenting) are equally guilty.

Penetration, without emission, is sufficient: *R. v. Reekspear* (1832) 1 Mood. 342.

As to the abolition of the common law presumption that a boy under 14 is incapable of sexual intercourse, see *ante*, H–13.

The offence of bestiality does not depend on consent but on the commission of a particular act: *R. v. Bourne*, *ante* (defendant convicted of aiding and abetting his wife to commit buggery with a dog, it being assumed that she would have been entitled to an acquittal on the ground of duress).

The following direction on the question of privacy (1967 Act, s.1, *ante*) has been approved by the Court of Appeal: "you look at all the circumstances, the time of night, the nature of the place including such matters as lighting and you consider further the likelihood of a third person coming upon the scene": *R. v. Reakes* [1974] Crim.L.R. 615.

In relation to subsection (3A) of section 1 of the 1967 Act, it is open to the prosecution to prove severe mental handicap without calling medical evidence but by inviting the jury to observe the behaviour and reactions of the complainant and to draw what they consider to be an appropriate inference: *R. v. Robbins* [1988] Crim.L.R. 744, CA.

(j) *Evidence*

The rule as to the admissibility of recent complaints was held to apply in the case of bug-   **H–106**
gery with a youth of 19: *R. v. Wannell*, 17 Cr.App.R. 53, CCA.

(11) **Gross indecency**

(a) *Statute*

Sexual Offences Act 1956, s.13

13. It is an offence for a man to commit an act of gross indecency with another man otherwise   **H–107**
than in the circumstances described below, whether in public or private, or to be a party to the commission by a man of an act of gross indecency with another man, or to procure the commission by a man of an act of gross indecency with another man.

The circumstances referred to above are that the man is under the age of sixteen and the other man has attained that age.

[This section is printed as amended by the *Sexual Offences (Amendment) Act* 2000, s.2(2)(a) and (b).]

Gross indecency is no longer an offence where the act takes place in private and both parties consent thereto and both have attained the age of 16: see *SOA* 1967, s.1 (as amended by the *Sexual Offences (Amendment) Act* 2000, s.1(2)(a)), *ante*, H–97.

Furthermore, it is not an offence under this section for a man to procure the commission by another man of an act of gross indecency with himself which by reason of section 1 of the 1967 Act is not an offence under this section: see section 4(3) of the 1967 Act, *post*, H–236. As to procuration of gross indecency, see further H–113, *post*.

As to the use of the word "man", see *post*, H–222.

(b) *Indictment*

STATEMENT OF OFFENCE

H–108   *Gross indecency, contrary to section 13 of the* Sexual Offences Act *1956.*

PARTICULARS OF OFFENCE

A B, on the —— day of ——, 20—, being a male person, committed an act of gross indecency with J N, a male person otherwise than in private [or *with J N, a male person under the age of 18 years, namely, of the age of —— years*].

(c) *Class of offence and mode of trial*

H–109   Offences contrary to section 13, and an attempt to procure the commission by a man of an act of gross indecency with another man, are class 3 offences (§ 2–17 in the main work), triable either way: *MCA* 1980, s.17(1), and Sched. 1 (§ 1–130 in the main work).

(d) *Time limits and restrictions on prosecutions*

H–110   See *ante*, H–101, H–102.

(e) *Sentence*

H–111   Offences contrary to section 13: if by a man of or over the age of 21 with a man under the age of 16, imprisonment not exceeding five years, otherwise two years—*SOA* 1956, s.37(3), and Sched. 2, para. 16(a) (as amended by the *CJPOA* 1994, s.144(1), (3), and the *Sexual Offences (Amendment) Act* 2000, s.1(1)).

An attempt to procure the commission by a man of an act of gross indecency with another man: as for the full offences—*SOA* 1956, s.37(3), and Sched. 2, para. 16(b) (as amended by the *CJPOA* 1994, s.144(1), (3), and the *Sexual Offences (Amendment) Act* 2000, s.1(1)).

Penalties on summary conviction are provided for by the *MCA* 1980, s.32 (§ 1–125 in the main work).

An attempt to commit any other offence than the one specifically provided for by the 1956 Act will be punishable in accordance with the *Criminal Attempts Act* 1981, ss.1 and 4 (§§ 33–120 *et seq.* in the main work).

(f) Ingredients of the offences

Gross indecency

If there is an agreement whereby two male persons act in concert to behave in a grossly **H–112** indecent manner, as, for example, to make a grossly indecent exhibition, the offence is committed even though there has been no actual physical contact: *R. v. Hunt*, 34 Cr.App.R. 135, CCA.

An offence of indecency between men is not committed unless both men participate in the indecency. "With another man" in section 13 cannot be construed as meaning "against" or "directed towards" a person who did not consent: *R. v. Preece and Howells* [1977] Q.B. 370, 63 Cr.App.R. 28, CA, and see *R. v. Hornby and Peaple*, 32 Cr.App.R. 1, CCA, and *R. v. Hunt, ante*.

Where two persons are jointly indicted for an offence under the section, one may be convicted and the other acquitted: *R. v. Jones* [1896] 1 Q.B. 4; *R. v. Pearce*, 35 Cr.App.R. 17, CCA; but see *R. v. Batten, The Times*, March 16, 1990, CA, where two men were charged with committing an act of gross indecency with each other. The jury convicted one defendant, but failed to agree in respect of the other and were discharged. The Court of Appeal quashed the conviction: the issue was the same in the case of both men and it was not a case where there was some evidence such as a confession, implicating one man but not the other. If both are to be convicted, it is important that the jury should be directed that, to establish the offence, it must be proved that there was an act of gross indecency by the one defendant with the other and that the two defendants were acting in concert: *R. v. Hornby and Peaple, ante*.

A conviction for attempting to commit an act of gross indecency may be maintained where one of the persons implicated alone has been charged and the other has not been charged but has been called as a witness for the prosecution and swears that he did not consent to any act of indecency: *R. v. Pearce, ante*.

Procuring gross indecency

It is an offence within section 13 for a male person to procure the commission with **H–113** himself of an act of gross indecency by another male person: *R. v. Jones, ante*; *R. v. Cope*, 16 Cr.App.R. 77, CCA. But, if the act itself is not an offence by virtue of section 1 of the *SOA* 1967, the procuration thereof will not be an offence either: *ibid.*, s.4(3). See *ante*, H–97, and *post*, H–236.

If a male person persuades, or attempts to persuade, a boy to handle him indecently, such person alone may be charged and convicted under this section. In a case where indecent assault may be difficult or impossible to prove, because no threat or hostile act by the defendant towards the boy can easily be established, the proper charge is that of procuring or attempting to procure (as the case may be) an act of gross indecency with the defendant himself: *R. v. Burrows*, 35 Cr.App.R. 180, CCA.

On a charge of incitement to procure an act of gross indecency, it is not necessary that there should be, at the time of the incitement, an ascertained person with whom the act was to be committed: *R. v. Bentley* [1923] 1 K.B. 403, CCA.

As to the meaning of "procure", see also *post*, H–171.

Attempting to procure an act of gross indecency

Procuring the commission of an act of gross indecency under section 13 of the 1956 Act is **H–114** itself a substantive offence. Section 1(4)(b) of the *Criminal Attempts Act* 1981 (§ 33–120 in the main work) does not preclude the charging of an attempt to procure an act of gross indecency under section 1(1) of the 1981 Act because section 1(4)(b) applies in circumstances when the alleged procurement is additional to and not part of the substantive offence: *Chief Constable of Hampshire v. Mace*, 84 Cr.App.R. 40, DC. (The penalty for such attempt is specifically provided for by the 1956 Act: see *ante*, H–111.)

What conduct will be sufficient to constitute an attempt will depend on the application of the formula in section 1(1) of the 1981 Act: was what was done "more than merely preparatory to the commission of the offence"?

Authorities decided prior to the 1981 Act can be no more than illustrative: see *R. v. Cope, ante*; *R. v. Woods*, 22 Cr.App.R. 41, CCA; *R. v. Miskell*, 37 Cr.App.R. 214, Ct-MAC.

(g) *Evidence*

Guilty plea by one defendant

H–115   See *R. v. Mattison* [1990] Crim.L.R. 117, CA (§ 9–90 in the main work).

Recent complaint

H–116   The rule as to admissibility of recent complaints was held not to apply to this offence on the ground that consent of the other male person is immaterial: *R. v. Hoodless*, 64 J.P. 282.

(12) Indecent assault on a woman

(a) *Statute*

Sexual Offences Act 1956, s.14

Indecent assault on a woman

H–117   **14.**—(1) It is an offence, subject to the exception mentioned in subsection (3) of this section, for a person to make an indecent assault on a woman.

(2) A girl under the age of sixteen cannot in law give any consent which would prevent an act being an assault for the purposes of this section.

(3) Where a marriage is invalid under section two of the *Marriage Act* 1949, or section one of the *Age of Marriage Act* 1929 (the wife being a girl under the age of sixteen), the invalidity does not make the husband guilty of any offence under this section by reason of her incapacity to consent while under that age, if he believes her to be his wife and has reasonable cause for the belief.

(4) A woman who is a defective cannot in law give any consent which would prevent an act being an assault for the purposes of this section, but a person is only to be treated as guilty of an indecent assault on a defective by reason of that incapacity to consent, if that person knew or had reason to suspect her to be a defective.

As to the use of the words "woman" and "girl", see *post*, H–222.

As to the meaning of "defective", see *ante*, H–68.

For the *Marriage Act* 1949, s.2, see *ante*, H–51.

For the burden of proof of exceptions, see section 47 of the 1956 Act, *post*, H–225.

For anonymity provisions, see *post*, §§ 20–257 *et seq.* in the main work.

(b) *Indictment*

STATEMENT OF OFFENCE

H–118   *Indecent assault, contrary to section 14(1) of the* Sexual Offences Act *1956.*

PARTICULARS OF OFFENCE

A B, on the —— day of ——, 20—, indecently assaulted J N, a woman.

Age is not an essential ingredient of, nor an essential averment in, the framing of a count under section 14(1): *R. v. Hodgson* [1973] Q.B. 565, 57 Cr.App.R. 502, CA. As to the need, however, to specify the age of the girl in certain old cases, see *post*, H–120.

Where the prosecution case leaves it open to the jury to convict on either of two distinct factual bases, it will be necessary for the judge to direct them as to the need for unanimity as to the basis of any verdict of guilty: see *R. v. Turner* [2000] Crim.L.R. 325, CA, and *R. v. D.* [2001] 1 Cr.App.R. 13, CA.

In *R. v. J.* [2005] 1 A.C. 562, HL, it was held that, on a true construction of the *SOA* 1956, it is impermissible to prosecute a charge of indecent assault under section 14(1) in circumstances where the only conduct upon which that charge was based was an act of unlawful sexual intercourse with a girl under the age of 16 in respect of which no prosecution might be commenced under section 6(1) (*ante*, H–50) by virtue of the time bar of 12 months contained in section 37(2) of, and Schedule 2, para. 10, to, the Act (as to which, see *ante*, H–55). Their Lordships held that the court was under a duty to give effect to a statute which was plain and unambiguous; it must have been intended that the prohibition in paragraph 10 would have some meaningful effect, otherwise there would have been no possible purpose in prohibiting prosecution under section 6 after a lapse of 12 months if exactly the same conduct could thereafter be prosecuted, with exposure to the same penalty (at the time of enactment), under section 14; but this did not prevent a prosecution being properly founded on independent acts other than sexual intercourse itself or conduct inherent in or forming part of it. As to the effect of this decision in relation to indecent assault as a possible alternative verdict on a charge of rape, see the cases cited at H–9, *ante*.

(c) *Class of offence and mode of trial*

This offence is a class 3 offence (§ 2–17 in the main work), triable either way: *MCA* 1980,   **H–119** s.17(1), and Sched. 1 (§ 1–130 in the main work).

(d) *Sentence*

Imprisonment, not exceeding 10 years: *SOA* 1956, s.37, and Sched. 2, para. 17 (as   **H–120** amended by the *SOA* 1985, s.3(3)). The 1985 amendment took effect on September 16, 1985: prior to that, the maximum penalty was two years' imprisonment, save where the girl was under 13 and was so stated in the indictment, in which case the maximum was five years' imprisonment. In relation to cases where the facts date back beyond September 16, 1985, see *R. v. R.* [1993] Crim.L.R. 541, CA; *R. v. B.*, *ibid.*

Where a defendant charged with rape of a girl under 16 is acquitted of rape, but convicted of indecent assault on the basis that consent is no defence, the sentence should not exceed the maximum for an offence of unlawful sexual intercourse with a girl under 16 (as to which, see *ante*, H–56): *R. v. Iles* [1998] 2 Cr.App.R.(S.) 63, CA.

The fact that the victim had been abused on a previous occasion does not reduce, but might increase, the gravity of further offending by an adult thereafter. If, however, by reason of being corrupted or precocious, or both, the victim instigated offences against herself, that was an aspect which the judge was entitled to take into account. But it was mitigation only in a negative sense, namely that the child was not being treated in a way which she was personally resisting or found repugnant: *Att.-Gen.'s Reference (No. 36 of 1995) (R. v. Dawson)* [1996] 2 Cr.App.R.(S.) 50, CA.

There is no sentencing principle which precludes the imposition of a custodial sentence on a first conviction of a persistent indecent assault (on a female on an underground train): *R. v. Townsend*, 16 Cr.App.R.(S.) 553, CA, *R. v. Tanyildiz* [1998] 1 Cr.App.R.(S.) 362, CA, and *R. v. Diallo* [2000] 1 Cr.App.R.(S.) 426, CA (not following *R. v. Neem*, 14 Cr.App.R.(S.) 18, CA).

Cases decided prior to the increase in the statutory maximum effected by the *SOA* 1985 could not be regarded as authoritative in relation to the tariff after the increase; the conclusion in *R. v. Demel* [1997] 2 Cr.App.R.(S.) 5, CA, that the upper end of the tariff for a single incident involving a breach of trust following a trial was in the range of 13 to 18 months' imprisonment should not be followed as the authorities relied on were decided in relation to a different statutory framework or had been decided without apparent appreciation of the effect of the 1985 Act: *R. v. L.* [1999] 1 Cr.App.R. 117, CA (two years' imprisonment following trial for "grave" breach of trust by 52-year-old man on nine-year-old girl upheld; declining to issue guidelines, but observing that in most cases the personal circumstances of the offender would have to take second place to the duty of the court to protect victims). See also *R. v. Wellman* [1999] 2 Cr.App.R.(S.) 162, CA.

For cases of indecent assault, see CSP B4–6.

As to the non-applicability of the Sentencing Guidelines Council's guideline on sexual offences (*post*, Appendix K–83 *et seq.*) to offences under the 1956 Act, see *Att.-Gen.'s Reference (No. 78 of 2010)* [2011] 2 Cr.App.R.(S.) 109, CA (pointing out that offences under the *SOA* 2003 are differently defined and have different (more severe) maximum penalties); but see *R. v. H., ante*, H–12, as to the approach to sentencing for historic offences generally.

(e) *Ingredients of the offence*

General

H–121   For a full exposition of the elements of the offence, see *R. v. Court* [1989] A.C. 28, HL.

   (a) Most indecent assaults will be clearly of a sexual nature. Some may have only sexual undertones. The jury must decide whether "right-minded persons would consider the conduct indecent or not". The test is whether what occurred was so offensive to contemporary standards of modesty and privacy as to be indecent.

   (b) If the circumstances of the assault are *incapable* of being regarded as indecent, then the undisclosed intention of the accused could not make the assault an indecent one: see *R. v. George* [1956] Crim.L.R. 52, Assizes (Streatfeild J.).

   (c) The victim need not be aware of the circumstances of indecency or apprehended indecency.

   (d) Cases which ordinarily present no problem are those in which the facts, *devoid of explanation*, will give rise to the irresistible inference that the defendant intended to assault his victim in a manner which right-minded persons would clearly think was indecent. Where the circumstances are such as only to be *capable* of constituting an indecent assault, in order to determine whether or not right-minded persons might think that the assault was indecent the following factors are relevant:

      (i) the relationship of the defendant to the victim (relative, friend, stranger);

      (ii) how the defendant had come to embark on this conduct and why he was so behaving.

   Such information helps a jury to answer the vital question: are we sure that the defendant not only intended to commit an assault but an assault which was indecent? Any evidence which tends to explain the reason for the defendant's conduct is relevant to establish whether or not he intended to commit not only an assault but an indecent one.

   (e) The prosecution must prove: (i) that the accused intentionally assaulted the victim; (ii) that the assault, or the assault and the circumstances accompanying it, are capable of being considered by right-minded persons as indecent; and (iii) that the accused intended to commit such an assault as is referred to in (ii) above.

The above propositions are founded upon Lord Ackner's speech (at p.36), with which the other members of the House concurred, except Lord Goff, who dissented from the decision. It follows that no offence will be committed where the man believes that the woman is consenting to his conduct, whether his belief is based on reasonable grounds or not: this was the effect of the earlier Court of Appeal decision in *R. v. Kimber*, 77 Cr.App.R. 225.

R. v. Court was considered in *R. v. C.* [1992] Crim.L.R. 642, CA, in which it was held that where an assault was indecent in itself, it was unnecessary to establish a specific indecent intent. In *Court*, the issue of whether or not what had occurred amounted to an indecent assault turned on motive and, therefore, specific intent had been necessary to the verdict. Where there was no question whether what had occurred was indecent or not, the basic intent of assault was sufficient. The law before *Court* remained the law and indecent assault remained an offence of basic intent; self-induced voluntary intoxication is not a defence. See also *DPP v. H.* [1992] C.O.D. 266, an earlier decision of the Divisional Court to the same effect.

Court and *George, ante,* were referred to in *R. v. Price* [2004] 1 Cr.App.R. 12, CA, in which it was held that stroking a woman's legs over trousers and below the knee was capable of amounting to an indecent assault.

In *R. v. Kumar* (2006) 150 S.J. 1053, CA, it was said that whilst *Court* was authority for the proposition that a doctor who obtained sexual satisfaction from a necessary medical examination properly conducted was not guilty of indecent assault where the prosecution case was limited to an allegation that he had carried out a medical examination in appropriate circumstances but in an inappropriate way and as a cloak for his own sexual gratification, where the issue had been as to the manner in which the defendant had carried out the examination (*i.e.* in an appropriate way in the presence of a chaperon or in an inappropriate way in the absence of a chaperon), there had been no need to direct the jury as to the remote theoretical possibility suggested in *Court*.

Person

A woman may be guilty of an offence under this section: *R. v. Hare* [1934] 1 K.B. 354, 24 **H–122** Cr.App.R. 108, CCA.

Assault

As to this, see generally, §§ 19–166 *et seq.* in the main work. **H–123**

In *Fairclough v. Whipp*, 35 Cr.App.R. 138, DC, the respondent exposed himself in the presence of a girl aged nine and invited her to touch his exposed person, which she did. *Held,* an invitation to another person to touch the invitor could not amount to an assault on the invitee, and that therefore there had been no assault and consequently no indecent assault by the respondent: applied in *DPP v. Rogers*, 37 Cr.App.R. 137, DC; but *cf. Beal v. Kelley*, 35 Cr.App.R. 128, DC, and *R. v. Sargeant*, 161 J.P. 127, CA, *post*, H–133. See also *R. v. Sutton*, 66 Cr.App.R. 21, CA, *post*, H–134, and the *Indecency with Children Act* 1960, *post*, H–230 *et seq.*

If a man inserts his finger into the vagina of a girl under 16, this is an indecent assault, however willing or co-operative the girl may be: *R. v. McCormack* [1969] 2 Q.B. 442, 53 Cr.App.R. 514, CA.

Consent

If the person assaulted is under 16, her consent is no defence: *SOA* 1956, s.14(2) (*ante*, **H–124** H–117).

Where the woman's consent was procured by fraud as to the nature (*R. v. Case* (1850) 4 Cox 220) or quality (*R. v. Tabassum* [2000] 2 Cr.App.R. 328, CA) of the act, such consent constitutes no defence. See also § 19–180 in the main work, and *ante*, H–17.

Where a jury asked for the difference between consent and submission to be defined, it was not incumbent on the judge to direct the jury that reluctant acquiescence amounted to consent; it was for the jury to decide whether there was consent and their good sense and experience should lead them to the right conclusion: *R. v. McAllister* [1997] Crim.L.R. 233, CA (*cf. R. v. Olugboja*, 73 Cr.App.R. 344, CA, *ante*, H–16).

Consent cannot be a defence where the indecent assault consists in the infliction of blows intended or likely to cause bodily harm: *R. v. Donovan* [1934] 2 K.B. 498, 25 Cr.App.R. 1, CCA; approved and applied by the House of Lords in *R. v. Brown (Anthony)* [1994] 1 A.C. 212. (As to *Brown*, see also § 19–180 in the main work.) *Donovan* was also referred to in *R. v. Boyea* [1992] Crim.L.R. 574, CA, in which it was held that an assault which was intended or likely to cause bodily harm, and which was accompanied by indecency, constituted the offence of indecent assault regardless of consent, provided that the injury was not "transient or trifling". However, the tribunal of fact must take account of changing social attitudes, particularly in the field of sexual relations between adults. As a generality, the level of vigour in sexual congress which was generally acceptable, and therefore the voluntarily accepted risk of incurring some injury was probably higher now than in 1934, when *Donovan* was decided. It followed that the phrase "transient or trifling" must be understood in the light of current conditions. *Boyea* was approved in *Brown (Anthony)*, *ante*. (See also *R. v. Wilson (A.)* [1996] 2 Cr.App.R. 241, CA (§ 19–182 in the main work).)

Bona fide belief as to age of girl

H–125   Where the complainant was under the age of 16 at the time of the alleged offence, the defendant's genuine belief that she was in fact 16 or over at the time will negative criminal liability if the complainant in fact consented or the defendant genuinely believed that she was consenting: *R. v. K.* [2002] 1 A.C. 462, HL.

Indecent assault within marriage

H–126   A man may be guilty of indecent assault upon his wife: *R. v. Kowalski*, 86 Cr.App.R. 339, CA.

(13) Indecent assault on a man

(a) *Statute*

Sexual Offences Act 1956, s.15

H–127   15.—(1) It is an offence for a person to make an indecent assault on a man.

(2) A boy under the age of sixteen cannot in law give any consent which would prevent an act being an assault for the purposes of this section.

(3) A man who is a defective cannot in law give any consent which would prevent an act being an assault for the purposes of this section, but a person is only to be treated as guilty of an indecent assault on a defective by reason of that incapacity to consent, if that person knew or had reason to suspect him to be a defective.

(4), (5) [*Repealed by* Police and Criminal Evidence Act *1984, Sched. 7.*]

As to the use of the words "man" and "boy", see *post*, H–222.
As to the meaning of "defective", see *ante*, H–68.
For anonymity provisions, see §§ 20–257 *et seq.* in the main work.

(b) *Indictment*

STATEMENT OF OFFENCE

H–128   *Indecent assault on male person, contrary to section 15(1) of the* Sexual Offences Act *1956.*

PARTICULARS OF OFFENCE

A B, on the —— day of ——, 20—, indecently assaulted J N, a male person.

In practice, the age of the alleged victim, if he was under the age of 16, was usually averred.

(c) *Class of offence and mode of trial*

H–129   This offence is a class 3 offence (§ 2–17 in the main work), triable either way: *MCA* 1980, s.17(1), and Sched. 1 (§ 1–130 in the main work).

(d) *Sentence*

Imprisonment not exceeding 10 years: *SOA* 1956, s.37(3), and Sched. 2, para. 18.   **H–130**
As to the approach to sentencing for historic offences, see *R. v. H.*, *ante*, H–12.

(e) *Ingredients of the offence*

General

See *R. v. Court* and *R. v. C.*, *ante*, H–121, which, it is submitted, apply equally to this   **H–131**
offence.

Person

A woman may be guilty of this offence: *R. v. Hare*, *ante*, H–122.   **H–132**

Assault

As to assaults generally, see §§ 19–166 *et seq.* in the main work.   **H–133**
An offence under section 15 is committed when a woman immediately prior to having
sexual intercourse with a 14-year-old boy holds his penis. The act alleged to constitute the
assault is an indecent act, consent is therefore no defence (s.15(2)—see *R. v. Sutton*, 66
Cr.App.R. 21, CA): *Faulkner v. Talbot*, 74 Cr.App.R. 1, DC.
Semble, an allegation of sexual intercourse by a woman with a boy under 16, *per se* connotes an allegation of indecent assault: see *R. v. McCormack* [1969] 2 Q.B. 442, 53 Cr.App.R.
514, CA; *Faulkner v. Talbot*, *ante*.
If there is an assault committed in circumstances of indecency, then there need not be an
indecent touching: see *Beal v. Kelly*, 35 Cr.App.R. 128, DC (when boy refused to touch
defendant's penis when asked to do so, defendant pulled boy towards him, but let him go);
and *R. v. Sargeant*, 161 J.P. 127, CA (grabbed boy, then used threat of further force to
compel boy to masturbate himself). *Cf. Fairclough v. Whipp*, *ante*, H–123.
In order to constitute an assault against a child under 16, the act complained of either   **H–134**
must itself be inherently indecent or it must be one that is hostile or threatening or an act
which the child is demonstrably reluctant to accept (see *DPP v. Rogers*, 37 Cr.App.R. 137,
DC, and *Williams v. Gibbs* [1958] Crim.L.R. 127, DC). Although sections 14(2) and 15(2) of
the 1956 Act bar the child's consent from preventing an act being an indecent assault,
consent does avail to prevent the act being an assault if the act is not inherently indecent.
The proper course where there is an act which could not conceivably be called an assault
but which takes place in an indecent situation, is to prosecute under the *Indecency with Children Act* 1960 (*post*, H–230 *et seq.*): *R. v. Sutton*, 66 Cr.App.R. 21, CA. The defendant
photographed partially clothed and unclothed boys, intending to sell the photographs to
magazines. In order to arrange poses, he touched the boys on the hands, legs and torso; the
actions were not threatening or hostile and the boys consented to them. His convictions
under section 15(1) were quashed: touching merely to indicate a pose was not of itself
indecent and was consented to. Consent did therefore avail to prevent the acts having been
assaults and the question of indecency did not arise.

Consent

Consent is a defence as it negatives the assault: see *R. v. Wollaston* (1872) 12 Cox 180,   **H–135**
CCR. See also *ante*, H–124.
A boy under the age of 16 cannot in law give any consent which would prevent an act being an assault for the purposes of the section: s.15(2), *ante*, H–127; but see the cases cited in
the previous paragraph.

Bona fide belief as to age of boy

See *R. v. K.* [2002] 1 A.C. 462, HL, *ante*, H–125; and *R. v. Fernandez*, *The Times*, June 26,   **H–136**
2002, CA (confirming that the decision of the House of Lords applies equally to this offence).

(f) *Evidence*

H–137   The rule as to the admissibility of recent complaints (§§ 8–207 *et seq.* in the main work) was held to apply in the case of an indecent assault upon a boy of 15: *R. v. Camelleri* [1922] 2 K.B. 122, 16 Cr.App.R. 162, CCA.

(14) Assault with intent to commit buggery

(a) *Statute*

Sexual Offences Act 1956, s.16

H–138   **16.**—(1) It is an offence for a person to assault another person with intent to commit buggery.
(2)–(3) [*Repealed by* Police and Criminal Evidence Act *1984, Sched. 7.*]

As to the offence of buggery, see *ante*, H–96 *et seq.*
As to assault, see generally, §§ 19–166 *et seq.* in the main work.
For anonymity provisions, see §§ 20–257 *et seq.* in the main work.

(b) *Indictment*

STATEMENT OF OFFENCE

H–139   *Assault with intent to commit buggery, contrary to section 16(1) of the* Sexual Offences Act *1956.*

PARTICULARS OF OFFENCE

A B, on the —— day of ——, 20—, assaulted J N with intent to commit buggery with the said J N.

(c) *Class of offence*

H–140   This offence is a class 3 offence (§ 2–17 in the main work), triable only on indictment: *SOA* 1956, s.37(2), and Sched. 2, para. 19.

(d) *Sentence*

H–141   Imprisonment not exceeding 10 years: *SOA* 1956, s.37(3), and Sched. 2, para. 19.

(e) *Effect of Criminal Justice and Public Order Act 1994*

H–142   It seems that no thought could have been given to the effect on this offence of the redefinition of rape to include non-consensual anal intercourse. The logical solution would have been to substitute "rape" for "buggery" at the end of subsection (1). The offence consisting of an assault allied to a specific intent suggests non-consensual buggery, but because of the bizarre nature of the amendments to section 12, not all nonconsensual buggery (*e.g.* both parties over 18 and the act takes place in private) constitutes the *offence* of buggery, although it will always be rape. It is submitted that the proper interpretation is that an offence under section 16 is committed where there is an assault accompanied by the requisite intent regardless of whether or not the act itself, if completed, would constitute the offence of buggery. This does, of course, lead to anomalous results; it would be an offence contrary to this provision to assault a woman intending to have anal intercourse with her but it would not be an offence to do so intending to have vaginal intercourse, although both acts, if completed, would constitute rape. The alternative interpretation would be to confine the offence to the commission of an assault with intent to commit buggery in circumstances which would make the act, if completed, an offence contrary to section 12. Because of the assault ingredient, this would effectively confine the offence to assaults on persons under 18. This seems to be an unwarranted restriction of the scope of the offence; Parliament having, if anything, deemed non-consensual buggery to be a more serious offence than it was previously, it would be an extremely curious result of the legislation if someone who committed an assault with the intention of committing that more serious offence should no longer be guilty of an offence under section 16.

As to whether there was a common law offence of assault with intent to rape, see *ante,* H–10.

(15) Abduction of woman by force or for the sake of her property

(a) *Statute*

Sexual Offences Act 1956, s.17

17.—(1) It is an offence for a person to take away or detain a woman against her will with the **H–143** intention that she shall marry or have unlawful sexual intercourse with that or any other person, if she is so taken away or detained either by force or for the sake of her property or expectations of property.

(2) In the foregoing subsection, the reference to a woman's expectations of property relates only to property of a person to whom she is next of kin or one of the next of kin, and "property" includes any interest in property.

[This section is printed as effectively amended by the *CLA* 1967, s.12(5)(a).]

As to the meaning of "sexual intercourse", see *post,* H–219; as to the use of the word "woman", see *post,* H–222.

(b) *Indictment*

STATEMENT OF OFFENCE

Abduction, contrary to section 17(1) of the Sexual Offences Act *1956.* **H–144**

PARTICULARS OF OFFENCE

A B, on the —— day of ——, 20—, took away [or *detained*] *J N against her will and by force* [or *for the sake of her property or expectations of property*] *with the intention that she should have unlawful sexual intercourse with him the said A B or with another* [or *with the intention that she should marry him the said A B or another*].

(c) *Class of offence and mode of trial*

This offence is a class 3 offence (§ 2–17 in the main work), triable on indictment only: **H–145** *SOA* 1956, s.37(2), and Sched. 2, para. 4.

(d) *Sentence*

Imprisonment not exceeding 14 years: *SOA* 1956, s.37(3), and Sched. 2, para. 4. **H–146**

(e) *Ingredients of the offence*

As to the meaning of "unlawful" sexual intercourse, see *ante,* H–38. **H–147**

If the woman is taken away with her own consent, but afterwards refuses to continue further with the offender, and is forcibly detained by him, this is within the statute: see 1 Hawk. c.41 (*Forcible Marriage*), s.7.

(16) **Abduction of unmarried girl under 18 from parent or guardian**

(a) *Statute*

Sexual Offences Act 1956, s.19

H–148   19.—(1) It is an offence, subject to the exception mentioned in this section, for a person to take an unmarried girl under the age of eighteen out of the possession of her parent or guardian against his will, if she is taken with the intention that she shall have unlawful sexual intercourse with men or with a particular man.

(2) A person is not guilty of an offence under this section because he takes such a girl out of the possession of her parent or guardian as mentioned above, if he believes her to be of the age of eighteen or over and has reasonable cause for the belief.

(3) In this section "guardian" means any person having the parental responsibility for or care of the girl.

[This section is printed as amended by the *Children Act* 1989, s.108(4), and Sched. 12, para. 11.]

As to the meaning of "sexual intercourse", see *post*, H–219; as to the use of the words "girl" and "man", see *post*, H–222; as to the meaning of "parental responsibility", see *post*, H–224.

For the burden of proof of exceptions, see section 47 of the 1956 Act, *post*, H–225.

(b) *Indictment*

STATEMENT OF OFFENCE

H–149   ·   *Abduction of girl, contrary to section 19(1) of the* Sexual Offences Act *1956.*

PARTICULARS OF OFFENCE

A B, on the —— day of ——, 20—, unlawfully took or caused to be taken J N, an unmarried girl under the age of 18, out of the possession and against the will of her father [or mother or of C D then having parental responsibility for or care of her] with an intent unlawfully to have sexual intercourse with her [or that she should have unlawful sexual intercourse with E F or generally].

(c) *Class of offence and mode of trial*

H–150   This offence is a class 3 offence (§ 2–17 in the main work), triable on indictment only: *SOA* 1956, s.37(2), and Sched. 2, para. 20.

(d) *Sentence*

H–151   Imprisonment not exceeding two years: *SOA* 1956, s.37(3), and Sched. 2, para. 20.

(e) *Ingredients of the offence*

H–152   For the evidence necessary to support this indictment, see *post*, H–157 *et seq.*, *mutatis mutandis*.

As to the meaning of "unlawful" sexual intercourse, see *ante*, H–38.

Upon an indictment under this section for taking a girl out of the possession of her father, it was proved that at the time of the commission of the alleged offence she was employed by another person as barmaid at a distance from her father's home. It was held that she was under the lawful charge of her employer and not in the possession of her father, and that therefore the defendant could not be convicted of the offence with which he was charged: *R. v. Henkers* (1886) 16 Cox 257. The age of the girl must be proved by the prosecution, as *ante*, H–49. The presumption of the *CYPA* 1933, s.99, does not apply to this offence: see the proviso to Schedule 1 to the 1933 Act (as to which see *ante*, H–49).

(17) Abduction of unmarried girl under 16 from parent or guardian

(a) *Statute*

Sexual Offences Act 1956, s.20

20.—(1) It is an offence for a person acting without lawful authority or excuse to take an   **H–153**
unmarried girl under the age of sixteen out of the possession of her parent or guardian against his will.

(2) In the foregoing subsection "guardian" means any person having parental responsibility for or care of the girl.

[This section is printed as amended by the *Children Act* 1989, s.108(4), and Sched. 12, para. 12.]

As to the use of the word "girl", see *post*, H–222; as to the meaning of "parental responsibility", see *post*, H–224.

See now section 2 of the *Child Abduction Act* 1984 (§ 19–313 in the main work) which covers much the same ground and is not limited to the abduction of girls.

(b) *Indictment*

STATEMENT OF OFFENCE

Abduction of a girl, contrary to section 20(1) of the Sexual Offences Act *1956.*   **H–154**

PARTICULARS OF OFFENCE

A B, on the —— day of ——, 20—, unlawfully took or caused to be taken J N, an unmarried girl aged 14, out of the possession and against the will of her father [or mother or of E F then having parental responsibility for or care of her].

(c) *Class of offence and mode of trial*

This offence is a class 3 offence (§ 2–17 in the main work), triable on indictment only: **H–155**
SOA 1956, s.37(2), and Sched. 2, para. 21.

(d) *Sentence*

Imprisonment not exceeding two years: *SOA* 1956, s.37(3), and Sched. 2, para. 21.   **H–156**

(e) *Ingredients of the offence*

That the girl was in the possession of her father, etc.

This is a question for the jury: *R. v. Mace*, 50 J.P. 776. A girl will still be in the possession   **H–157**
of her parent/guardian even while she is away from home if she intends to return; and if, when so out of the house, the defendant induces her to run away with him, he is guilty: *R. v. Mycock* (1871) 12 Cox 28. See also *R. v. Baillie* (1859) 8 Cox 238; *R. v. Green* (1862) 3 F. & F. 274; and *R. v. Miller* (1876) 13 Cox 179.

The taking

The taking need not be by force, either actual or constructive, and it is immaterial   **H–158** whether the girl consents or not: *R. v. Manktelow* (1853) 6 Cox 143, and see *R. v. Kipps* (1850) 4 Cox 167; *R. v. Booth* (1872) 12 Cox 231; and *R. v. Robins* (1844) 1 C. & K. 456 (where the girl positively encouraged the defendant).

The words "taking out of the possession and against the will" of the parent mean some conduct amounting to a substantial interference with the possessory relationship of parent and child: *R. v. Jones (J.W.)* [1973] Crim.L.R. 621 (Swanwick J.)—attempt to take girls (aged 10) for a walk with a view to indecently assaulting them held not to constitute an attempt to commit the offence. (*Cf. R. v. Leather*, 98 Cr.App.R. 179, CA, decided on the *Child Abduction Act* 1984 (§ 19–314 in the main work).)

It is no defence that the defendant acted in concert with the girl and had no intention of keeping her away from her home permanently: *R. v. Timmins* (1860) 8 Cox 401; *R. v. Frazer and Norman, ibid.* at 446. See also *R. v. Baillie, ibid.* at 238.

Instead of a taking, it can be shown that a girl left her parent or guardian, in consequence of some persuasion, inducement or blandishment held out to her by the defendant: *R. v. Henkers* (1886) 16 Cox 257, following *R. v. Olifier* (1866) 10 Cox 402.

H–159   Where a man induces a girl, by promise of what he will do for her, to leave her father's house and live with him, he may be convicted, although he is not actually present or assisting her at the time when she leaves her father's roof: *R. v. Robb* (1864) 4 F. & F. 59. If the girl leaves her father, without any persuasion, inducement or blandishment held out to her by the defendant, so that she has got fairly away from home, and then goes to him, although it may be his moral duty to return her to her father's custody, yet his not doing so is no infringement of this statute, for the statute does not say he shall restore, but only that he shall not take her away: *R. v. Olifier, ante*, and this is so even though it be proved that before she so left he had taken her about to places of amusement and had intercourse with her: *R. v. Kauffman*, 68 J.P. 189. If the suggestion to go away with the defendant comes from the girl only, and he takes merely the passive part of yielding to her suggestion, he is entitled to an acquittal: *R. v. Jarvis* (1903) 20 Cox 249. It is submitted that the ruling to the contrary in *R. v. Biswell* (1847) 2 Cox 279 is not law. For a discussion of the authorities, see *R. v. Mackney* (1903) 29 Vict.L.R. 22, where the English cases are considered.

Against the will, etc.

H–160   If the defendant induced the parents, by false and fraudulent representations, to allow him to take the child away, this is an abduction: *R. v. Hopkins* (1842) C. & Mar. 254.

Where the girl's mother had encouraged her in a lax course of life, by permitting her to go out alone at night and dance at public-houses, from one of which she went away with the defendant, Cockburn C.J. ruled that she could not be said to be taken away against her mother's will: *R. v. Primelt* (1858) 1 F. & F. 50.

To prove this element of the offence, it has been said that the parent or guardian must be called: *R. v. Nash, The Times*, July 2, 1903. *Sed quaere.*

Under 16, etc.

H–161   Prove that she was under the age of 16 years and unmarried. As to the power of a court to presume her age from her appearance, see the *CYPA* 1933, s.99(2) (§ 19–326 in the main work) and Sched. 1 (§ 19–322 in the main work (prior to its repeal by the *SOA* 2003, the proviso to Sched. 1 stipulated that s.99(2) did apply to offences under s.20)). It is no defence that the defendant did not know her to be under 16, or might suppose from her appearance that she was older: *R. v. Olifier, ante*; *R. v. Mycock, ante*; *R. v. Booth, ante*; or even that the defendant bona fide believed and had reasonable grounds for believing that she was over 16: *R. v. Prince* (1875) L.R. 2 C.C.R. 154. Doubts about *Prince* were expressed by the House of Lords in *B. (a Minor) v. DPP* [2000] 2 A.C. 428 (*post*, H–235) and *R. v. K.* [2002] 1 A.C. 462 (*ante*, H–125), but its correctness did not fall to be decided upon. Those expressions of doubt are likely to found a challenge to *Prince*, but it is submitted that the express provision of a defence based on mistake as to age in relation to the offence contrary to section 19 (*ante*, H–148) makes it abundantly clear that Parliament intended that there should be no corresponding defence in relation to the abduction of a girl under 16.

Mens rea

The act of abduction is positively prohibited, and therefore the absence of a corrupt mo- **H–162** tive is no answer to the charge: see *R. v. Booth, ante.*

If the defendant, at the time he took the girl away, did not know, and had no reason to know, that she was subject to the parental responsibility and care of her father, mother or some other person, he is not guilty of this offence: *R. v. Hibbert* (1869) L.R. 1 C.C.R. 184.

Without lawful authority or excuse

The defendant must show that he had either lawful authority or a lawful excuse; motive **H–163** is irrelevant: *R. v. Tegerdine*, 75 Cr.App.R. 298, CA (statutory history reviewed). It is submitted that the burden on the defendant is merely an evidential one, which is discharged if there is sufficient evidence to raise an issue on the matter: *cf.* the specific provision in section 47 (*post*, H–225) in relation to "exceptions" under the Act. And see generally, §§ 4–444 *et seq.* in the main work.

(18) Abduction of defective from parent or guardian

(a) *Statute*

Sexual Offences Act 1956, s.21

21.—(1) It is an offence, subject to the exception mentioned in this section, for a person to take **H–164** a woman who is a defective out of the possession of her parent or guardian against his will, if she is so taken with the intention that she shall have unlawful sexual intercourse with men or with a particular man.

(2) A person is not guilty of an offence under this section because he takes such a woman out of the possession of her parent or guardian as mentioned above, if he does not know and has no reason to suspect her to be a defective.

(3) In this section "guardian" means any person having parental responsibility for or care of the woman.

[This section is printed as amended by the *Children Act* 1989, s.108(4), and Sched. 12, para. 13.]

As to the meaning of "sexual intercourse", see *post*, H–219; as to the meaning of "unlawful" sexual intercourse, see *ante*, H–38; as to the use of the words "man" and "woman", see *post*, H–222; as to the meaning of "defective", see *ante*, H–68; as to the meaning of "parental responsibility", see *post*, H–224.

For the burden of proof of exceptions, see section 47 of the 1956 Act, *post*, H–225.

(b) *Class of offence and mode of trial*

This offence is a class 3 offence (§ 2–17 in the main work), triable on indictment only: **H–165** *SOA* 1956, s.37(2), and Sched. 2, para. 22.

(c) *Sentence*

Imprisonment not exceeding two years: *SOA* 1956, s.37(3), and Sched. 2, para. 22. **H–166**

(19) Causing prostitution of women

(a) *Statute*

Sexual Offences Act 1956, s.22

H–167   22.—(1) It is an offence for a person—

(a) to procure a woman to become, in any part of the world, a common prostitute; or

(b) to procure a woman to leave the United Kingdom, intending her to become an inmate of or frequent a brothel elsewhere; or

(c) to procure a woman to leave her usual place of abode in the United Kingdom, intending her to become an inmate of or frequent a brothel in any part of the world for the purposes of prostitution.

(2) [*Repealed by* Criminal Justice and Public Order Act *1994, s.33(1)*.]

As to the use of the word "woman", see *post*, H–222.

(b) *Indictment*

STATEMENT OF OFFENCE

H–168   *Procuring a woman to become a common prostitute, contrary to section 22(1)(a) of the* Sexual Offences Act *1956*.

PARTICULARS OF OFFENCE

A B, on or about the —— day of ——, 20—, at —— procured C D, a woman, to become a common prostitute.

(c) *Class of offence and mode of trial*

H–169   This offence, and an attempt to commit it, are class 3 offences (§ 2–17 in the main work), triable on indictment only: *SOA* 1956, s.37(2), and Sched. 2, para. 23(a), (b).

(d) *Sentence*

H–170   The full offence, and an attempt to commit it: imprisonment not exceeding two years: *SOA* 1956, s.37(3), and Sched. 2, para. 23(a), (b).

(e) *Ingredients of the offence*

"Procure"

H–171   As to the meaning of the word "procure" in general, see §§ 18–22, 18–23 in the main work, and see *Att.-Gen.'s Reference (No. 1 of 1975)* [1975] Q.B. 773, 61 Cr.App.R. 118, CA; *Re Royal Victoria Pavilion, Ramsgate* [1961] Ch. 581, Ch D, and *Blakely v. DPP* [1991] R.T.R. 405, DC. In the first of these authorities, Lord Widgery C.J. said that to procure, "means to produce by endeavour. You procure a thing by setting out to see that it happens and taking the appropriate steps to produce that happening" (at pp.779, 121). In *Re Royal Victoria Pavilion, Ramsgate*, Pennycuick J. (at p.587) defined "to procure" as "to obtain by care and effort" or "to see to it".

In *R. v. Broadfoot*, 64 Cr.App.R. 71, CA, the court described *Att.-Gen's Reference (No. 1 of 1975)*, *ante*, as a useful guide. Whilst saying that the interpretation of the word was a matter of common sense for the jury to determine in the light of the particular facts, the court appears to have approved (see p.74) the suggestion of Shaw L.J., during argument, that it could be regarded as bringing about a course of conduct which the woman in question would not have embarked upon of her own volition. *R. v. Christian* (1913) 23 Cox 541, was distinguished. It was there held that procuration could be negatived by evidence showing the girl was not really procured, because she needed no procuring, and acted of her own free will.

If a woman is already a common prostitute she cannot become one and accordingly cannot be procured to become one. It follows that if there is evidence of procuration but "the woman" is a police officer it is a good defence to a charge of attempting to procure a woman to become a prostitute contrary to section 1(1) of the *Criminal Attempts Act* 1981, that the defendant thought that "the woman" he was attempting to procure was already a prostitute. If he believed (or might have believed) that, it could not be said that he was trying to procure her to become that which he believed she already was. Section 1(3) of the 1981 Act (§ 33–120 in the main work) is concerned with the converse case where the woman is a common prostitute but the defendant believes she is not. In such circumstances, he may be convicted of an attempt even though the commission of the offence is impossible: *R. v. Brown (R.A.),* 80 Cr.App.R. 36, CA.

As to "attempting to do the impossible", see also § 33–129 in the main work.

"Common prostitute"

This includes a woman who offers her body commonly for acts of lewdness for payment **H–172** although there is no act or offer of an act of ordinary sexual intercourse: *R. v. De Munck* [1918] 1 K.B. 635, 13 Cr.App.R. 113, CCA. The word "common" in the term "common prostitute" is not mere surplusage—a common prostitute is any woman who offers herself commonly for lewdness for reward. Whether or not the performance by a woman of a single act of lewdness with a man on one occasion for reward constitutes the woman a prostitute, it plainly does not make her a woman who offers herself commonly for lewdness. That must be someone who is prepared for reward to engage in acts of lewdness with all and sundry or with anyone who may hire her for that purpose: *R. v. Morris-Lowe*, 80 Cr.App.R. 114, CA, applying *R. v. De Munck, ante.*

It is not necessary that she should have submitted to acts of lewdness in a passive way. Active acts of indecency by the woman herself, *e.g.* masturbation by her of clients when acting as a masseuse will fall within the section: *R. v. Webb* [1964] 1 Q.B. 357, 47 Cr.App.R. 265, CCA.

In *R. v. McFarlane* [1994] Q.B. 419, 99 Cr.App.R. 8, CA, it was held in relation to a prosecution under section 30 of the 1956 Act (*post*, H–197) that the essence of prostitution is the making of an offer of sexual services for reward, and that it is immaterial that the person making the offer does not intend to perform them and does not do so. It is obviously desirable that "prostitution" is given the same meaning wherever it appears in a statute; accordingly, this decision is likely to be applied to section 22. For a criticism of this decision, see the 1996 edition of this work.

(20) Procuration of girl under 21

(a) *Statute*

Sexual Offences Act 1956, s.23

23.—(1) It is an offence for a person to procure a girl under the age of twenty-one to have **H–173** unlawful sexual intercourse in any part of the world with a third person.

(2) [*Repealed by* Criminal Justice and Public Order Act *1994, s.33(1)*.]

As to the meaning of "sexual intercourse", see *post*, H–219; as to the use of the word "girl", see *post*, H–222.

(b) *Class of offence and mode of trial*

H–174   This offence, and an attempt to commit it, are class 3 offences (§ 2–17 in the main work), triable on indictment only: *SOA* 1956, s.37(2), and Sched. 2, para. 24(a), (b).

(c) *Sentence*

H–175   The full offence, and an attempt to commit it: imprisonment not exceeding two years; *SOA* 1956, s.37(3), and Sched. 2, para. 24(a), (b).

(d) *Ingredients of the offence*

H–176   As to the meaning of "procure", see *ante*, H–171. As to the meaning of "unlawful" sexual intercourse, see *ante*, H–38.

Before the defendant can be found guilty of an offence contrary to this section, it is necessary to prove that unlawful sexual intercourse did take place; if intercourse is not proved to have taken place but procurement with the intention that it should take place is proved, there may be a conviction of an attempt to commit the full offence: *R. v. Johnson* [1964] 2 Q.B. 404, 48 Cr.App.R. 25, CCA. As to the difference between an attempt and an intention, see *R. v. Landow*, 8 Cr.App.R. 218, CCA. As to conspiracy with the procurer, see *R. v. Mackenzie and Higginson*, 6 Cr.App.R. 64, CCA.

(21) Detention of a woman in brothel or other premises

(a) *Statute*

Sexual Offences Act 1956, s.24

H–177   **24.**—(1) It is an offence for a person to detain a woman against her will on any premises with the intention that she shall have unlawful sexual intercourse with men or with a particular man, or to detain a woman against her will in a brothel.

(2) Where a woman is on any premises for the purpose of having unlawful sexual intercourse or is in a brothel, a person shall be deemed for the purpose of the foregoing subsection to detain her there if, with the intention of compelling or inducing her to remain there, he either withholds from her her clothes or any other property belonging to her or threatens her with legal proceedings in the event of her taking away clothes provided for her by him or on his directions.

(3) A woman shall not be liable to any legal proceedings, whether civil or criminal, for taking away or being found in possession of any clothes she needed to enable her to leave premises on which she was for the purpose of having unlawful sexual intercourse or to leave a brothel.

As to the meaning of "sexual intercourse", see *post*, H–219; as to the use of the words "man" and "woman", see *post*, H–222.

(b) *Indictment*

STATEMENT OF OFFENCE

H–178   *Detaining a woman against her will for unlawful sexual intercourse [or in a brothel], contrary to section 24(1) of the Sexual Offences Act 1956.*

PARTICULARS OF OFFENCE

A B, on or about the —— day of ——, 20—, detained C D, a woman, against her will at —— intending her to have unlawful sexual intercourse with men [or with E F, a man] [or detained C D, a woman, against her will at ——, a brothel].

(c) *Class of offence and mode of trial*

This offence is a class 3 offence (§ 2–17 in the main work), triable on indictment only: **H–179**
SOA 1956, s.37(2), and Sched. 2, para. 25.

(d) *Sentence*

Imprisonment not exceeding two years: *SOA* 1956, s.37(3), and Sched. 2, para. 25.   **H–180**

(e) *Ingredients of offence*

Unlawful sexual intercourse

See *ante*, H–38.   **H–181**

"Brothel"

See §§ 20–233 *et seq.* in the main work.   **H–182**

(f) *Evidence*

See § 20–235 in the main work.   **H–183**

(22) Allowing premises to be used for intercourse

(a) *Statute*

Sexual Offences Act 1956, ss.25, 26, 27

Permitting girl under thirteen to use premises for intercourse
    25. It is an offence for a person who is the owner or occupier of any premises, or who has, or   **H–184**
acts or assists in, the management or control of any premises, to induce or knowingly suffer a girl
under the age of thirteen to resort to or be on those premises for the purpose of having unlawful
sexual intercourse with men or with a particular man.

[This section is printed as effectively amended by the *CLA* 1967, s.12(5)(a).]

Permitting girl between thirteen and sixteen to use premises for intercourse
    26. It is an offence for a person who is the owner or occupier of any premises, or who has, or   **H–185**
acts or assists in, the management or control of any premises, to induce or knowingly suffer a girl
... under the age of sixteen, to resort to or be on those premises for the purpose of having
unlawful sexual intercourse with men or with a particular man.

[The words omitted were repealed by the *CLA* 1967, s.10(1), and Sched. 2, para. 14.
This repeal renders the marginal note misleading.]

Permitting defective to use premises for intercourse
    27.—(1) It is an offence, subject to the exception mentioned in this section, for a person who is   **H–186**
the owner or occupier of any premises, or who has, or acts or assists in, the management or
control of any premises, to induce or knowingly suffer a woman who is a defective to resort to or
be on those premises for the purpose of having unlawful sexual intercourse with men or with a
particular man.
    (2) A person is not guilty of an offence under this section because he induces or knowingly suffers
a defective to resort to or be on any premises for the purpose mentioned, if he does not know and
has no reason to suspect her to be a defective.

As to the meaning of "sexual intercourse", see *post*, H–219; as to the use of the words
"man", "woman" and "girl", see *post*, H–222; as to the meaning of "defective", see *ante*,
H–68.

For the burden of proof of exceptions, see section 47 of the 1956 Act, *post*, H–225.

(b) *Class of offence and mode of trial*

H–187 Section 25—this offence is a class 3 offence (§ 2–17 in the main work), triable only on indictment: *SOA* 1956, s.37(2), and Sched. 2, para. 6.

Section 26—this offence is a class 3 offence (§ 2–17 in the main work), triable either way: *MCA* 1980, s.17(1), and Sched. 1 (§ 1–130 in the main work).

Section 27—this offence is a class 3 offence (§ 2–17 in the main work), triable only on indictment: *SOA* 1956, s.37(2), and Sched. 2, para. 27.

(c) *Sentence*

H–188 Section 25—life imprisonment: *SOA* 1956, s.37(3), and Sched. 2, para. 6.

Section 26—imprisonment not exceeding two years: *SOA* 1956, s.37(3), and Sched. 2, para. 26. The penalty on summary conviction is provided for by the *MCA* 1980, s.32 (§ 1–125 in the main work).

Section 27—imprisonment not exceeding two years: *SOA* 1956, s.37(3), and Sched. 2, para. 27.

(d) *Ingredients of the offences*

"Management", "assists in the management"

H–189 See the following cases, decided in relation to section 33 of the 1956 Act ("assisting in the management of a brothel"): *Abbott v. Smith* [1965] 2 Q.B. 662, DC (meaning of "management"); *Gorman v. Standen*; *Palace-Clark v. Standen* [1964] 1 Q.B. 294, 48 Cr.App.R. 30, DC; *Jones and Wood v. DPP*, 96 Cr.App.R. 130, DC; and *Elliott v. DPP*; *Dublides v. DPP*, *The Times*, January 19, 1989, DC ("assisting in the management"). In the last of these cases, the court appears to have accepted a distinction between assisting in the management of premises and assisting the management of premises.

"Unlawful" sexual intercourse

H–190 See *ante*, H–38.

"Knowingly suffer"

H–191 In *R. v. Webster* (1885) 16 Q.B.D. 134, it was held that the words "knowingly suffer" mean that the defendant knew of the girl's purpose in being on the premises and did not prevent the unlawful sexual intercourse from occurring when it was in his power to do so. The girl was the defendant's daughter, and the premises were her home, where she resided with the defendant. But see *R. v. Merthyr Tydfil JJ.* (1894) 10 T.L.R. 375, where a mother was held not within the section, who for the purposes of obtaining conclusive evidence against a man who had seduced her daughter, permitted him to come to her house to repeat his unlawful intercourse.

(23) Causing or encouraging prostitution, etc.

(a) *Statute*

Sexual Offences Act 1956, ss.28, 29

Causing or encouraging prostitution of, intercourse with, or indecent assault on, girl under sixteen

H–192 **28.**—(1) It is an offence for a person to cause or encourage the prostitution of, or the commission of unlawful sexual intercourse with, or of an indecent assault on, a girl under the age of sixteen for whom he is responsible.

(2) Where a girl has become a prostitute, or has had unlawful sexual intercourse, or has been indecently assaulted, a person shall be deemed for the purposes of this section to have caused or encouraged it, if he knowingly allowed her to consort with, or to enter or continue in the employment of, any prostitute or person of known immoral character.

(3) The persons who are to be treated for the purposes of this section as responsible for a girl are (subject to subsection (4) of this section)—

(a) her parents;

(b) any person who is not a parent of hers but who has parental responsibility for her; and

(c) any person who has care of her.

(4) An individual falling within subsection (3)(a) or (b) of this section is not to be treated as responsible for a girl if—

(a) a residence order under the *Children Act* 1989 is in force with respect to her and he is not named in the order as the person with whom she is to live; *or*

(aa) a special guardianship order under that Act is in force with respect to her and he is not her special guardian; or

(b) a care order under that Act is in force with respect to her.

(5) If, on a charge of an offence against a girl under this section, the girl appears to the court to have been under the age of sixteen at the time of the offence charged, she shall be presumed for the purposes of this section to have been so, unless the contrary is proved.

[This section is printed as amended by the *Children Act* 1989, s.108(4), and Sched. 12, para. 14; and the *Adoption and Children Act* 2002, s.139(1), and Sched. 3, para. 8.]

Causing or encouraging prostitution of defective

29.—(1) It is an offence, subject to the exception mentioned in this section, for a person to **H–193** cause or encourage the prostitution in any part of the world of a woman who is a defective.

(2) A person is not guilty of an offence under this section because he causes or encourages the prostitution of such a woman, if he does not know and has no reason to suspect her to be a defective.

As to the meaning of "sexual intercourse", see *post*, H–219; as to the use of the words "woman" and "girl", see *post*, H–222; as to the meaning of "parental responsibility", see *post*, H–224; as to the meaning of "defective", see *ante*, H–68.

For the burden of proof of exceptions, see section 47 of the 1956 Act, *post*, § H–225.

(b) *Class of offence and mode of trial*

These offences are class 3 offences (§ 2–17 in the main work), triable only on indictment: **H–194** *SOA* 1956, s.37(2), and Sched. 2, paras 28 and 29.

(c) *Sentence*

Sections 28 and 29—imprisonment not exceeding two years: *SOA* 1956, s.37(3), and **H–195** Sched. 2, paras 28 and 29.

(d) *Ingredients of the offences*

As to what constitutes "causing" or "encouraging", see *R. v. Ralphs*, 9 Cr.App.R. 86, CCA; **H–196** *R. v. Chainey* [1914] 1 K.B. 137, 9 Cr.App.R. 175, CCA.

In *R. v. Drury*, 60 Cr.App.R. 195, CA, it was held that there was evidence on which it could be held that a girl (aged 14) was in the care of the defendant where, at the time of the assault by a friend of the defendant, she was babysitting for him. The case was decided on the original wording of section 28(3)(c), *viz.* "any other person who has the custody, charge or care of her". The 1989 amendment (*ante*) would not appear to affect this point. As to encouragement, the court said that there must be encouragement in fact and an intention to encourage.

A doctor who in the exercise of his clinical judgment gives contraceptive advice and treatment to a girl under 16 without her parents' consent does not commit an offence under section 6 or 28 of the 1956 Act, because the bona fide exercise by the doctor of his clinical judgment negates the *mens rea* which is an essential ingredient of those offences: *Gillick v. West Norfolk and Wisbech Area Health Authority* [1986] A.C. 112, HL.

As to the meaning of "unlawful" sexual intercourse, see *ante*, H–38.

(24) Man living on earnings of prostitution

(a) *Statute*

Sexual Offences Act 1956, s.30

H–197   **30.**—(1) It is an offence for a man knowingly to live wholly or in part on the earnings of prostitution.

(2) For the purposes of this section a man who lives with or is habitually in the company of a prostitute, or who exercises control, direction or influence over a prostitute's movements in a way which shows he is aiding, abetting or compelling her prostitution with others, shall be presumed to be knowingly living on the earnings of prostitution, unless he proves the contrary.

As to the use of the word "man", see *post*, H–222.

(b) *Indictment*

STATEMENT OF OFFENCE

H–198   *Living on prostitution, contrary to section 30(1) of the* Sexual Offences Act *1956.*

PARTICULARS OF OFFENCE

A B, being a man, on the —— day of ——, 20—, and on other days between that date and the —— day of ——, 20—, knowingly lived wholly or in part on the earnings of the prostitution of J N.

In an indictment for this offence a person may be charged with having committed the offence on one specified day only: *R. v. Hill*, 10 Cr.App.R. 56, CCA. Evidence is admissible to show what the defendant's relations with the woman in question had been either before or after the day specified in the indictment: *ibid.*

As to the application of the alibi notice provisions to this offence, see *R. v. Hassan*, 54 Cr.App.R. 56, CA (§ 12–57a in the main work).

(c) *Class of offence and mode of trial*

H–199   This offence is a class 3 offence (§ 2–17 in the main work), triable either way: *SOA* 1956, s.37(2), and Sched. 2, para. 30.

(d) *Sentence*

Maximum

H–200   On conviction on indictment, imprisonment not exceeding seven years; on summary conviction, six months, or a fine not exceeding £5,000: *SOA* 1956, s.37(3), and Sched. 2, para. 30 (as amended by the *Street Offences Act* 1959, s.4), and the *MCA* 1980, ss.32, 34(3)(a).

Guidelines

H–201   A sentence exceeding two years should be reserved for cases where there is some evidence of physical or mental coercion of the prostitutes involved, or of corruption. The existence of such coercion or corruption is the crucial sentencing factor: *R. v. Farrugia*, 69 Cr.App.R. 108, CA. See also *R. v. Thomas*, 5 Cr.App.R.(S.) 138, CA; *R. v. El-Gazzar*, 8 Cr.App.R.(S.) 182, CA; *R. v. Malik* [1998] 1 Cr.App.R.(S.) 115, CA; and CSP B5–1.

(e) *Ingredients of the offence*

"Man"

In *R. v. Tan* [1983] Q.B. 1053, 76 Cr.App.R. 300, CA, it was held that a person who was **H–202** born a man and who remained biologically a man was a man for all purposes although he had undergone hormone treatment and surgical treatment consisting of sex-change operations and had become philosophically or psychologically female (applying *Corbett v. Corbett* [1971] P. 83).

Prostitution

As to what constitutes "prostitution", see *ante*, H–172. As to proving that at the material **H–203** time the woman was a prostitute, see § 20–235 in the main work, and *R. v. Wilson (D.T.)*, 78 Cr.App.R. 247, CA, in which *Woodhouse v. Hall*, 72 Cr.App.R. 39, DC, was applied in the context of a prosecution under section 30.

Knowingly living on earnings of prostitution

There are three distinct foundations upon which the prosecution can rely in order to **H–204** raise a presumption that an offence has been committed under section 30(2) (*ante*, H–197):

(a) proof that the accused was at the material time living with the prostitute;

(b) proof that he was habitually at the material time in her company;

(c) proof that he exercised control, direction or influence over her movements in a way which showed him to be aiding or abetting her prostitution.

Once evidence giving rise to the presumption has been led, it then has two facets: (a) it is presumed that he is living on immoral earnings; and (b) it is presumed that he is doing so knowingly: *R. v. Clarke*, 63 Cr.App.R. 16, CA. It is not necessary to prove that he was living with or habitually in the company of such a prostitute in a way which showed that he was aiding, abetting or compelling her prostitution with others: *ibid*. See also *R. v. Lawrence, post*, H–206.

In *R. v. Stewart*, 83 Cr.App.R. 327, CA, the court was referred to *R. v. Silver*, 40 Cr.App.R. **H–205** 32, CCC (Judge Maude); *R. v. Thomas*, 41 Cr.App.R. 121, CCA; *Shaw v. DPP* [1962] A.C. 220, HL; *R. v. Calderhead and Bidney*, 68 Cr.App.R. 37, CA; and *R. v. Wilson (D.T.), ante.* Mustill L.J. said, in giving the court's judgment:

> "What we collect from them is as follows: according to the literal meaning of the section any person who supplies goods or services to a prostitute is in one sense living off the earnings of prostitution: for in part he earns his livelihood from payments which the woman would not be able to make but for her trade. This cannot be the right view. There has to be a closer connection between the receipt of money and the trade before the recipient commits an offence. We doubt whether it is possible to devise a definition of the type and closeness of the necessary connection which will deal with all the circumstances which may arise; and, indeed, it is dangerous to treat words or phrases from judgments delivered in relation to one set of facts, as if they provided a statutory gloss which can be reliably applied to facts of a quite different nature ... .
>
> Subject to this reservation, we believe that an approach which will often be useful is to identify for the jury the flavour of the words 'living off', and then to express this general concept in the shape of guidance more directly referable to the case in hand. In our judgment, the word 'parasite' (to be found in the speech of Lord Reid in *Shaw v. DPP* ...), or some expanded equivalent, provides a useful starting point for this exercise, and does express a concept which accounts for all the reported cases except for *Silver*.
>
> Adopting this general approach, and dealing specifically with a defendant who supplies goods or services to a prostitute, a good working test, sufficient to deal with many cases, is whether the fact of supply means that the supplier and the prostitute were engaged in the business of prostitution together: and 'the fact of supply' will include the scale of supply, the price charged and the

nature of the goods or services. It will be impossible to say in advance that certain categories of supplies must necessarily fall outside the section, any more than that other categories must be within it, but the idea of participation in the prostitute's business will enable the jury to distinguish readily between (say) the supplier of groceries on the one hand and the publisher of prostitutes' advertisements on the other. There will remain a residue of more difficult cases, and these include the situation where premises are let at a market rent with knowledge of the purpose to which they are to be put. We see no room here for any rule of thumb distinction between premises which are or are not let at abnormally high rates. Certainly, the jury will find it easier to infer in the former case that the lessor participates in the woman's earnings. ... We can, however, see no logic in the suggestion that the lessor cannot be convicted unless the rent is exorbitant and indeed the judgment of Ashworth J. in *Shaw v. DPP* (at p.230) and the speech of Lord Simonds in the same case (at p. 265 ... see the words 'whatever the rent') are authority for the view that the presence or absence of this factor is not conclusive. Nor in our opinion is the question whether the premises are occupied or capable of occupation as residential premises to be taken as the touchstone.

Instead, the judge must bear in mind when framing his direction the distinction between the offence under section 30(1), and the offences under sections 34, 35 and 36, and must not allow the jury to believe that knowledge of use to which the premises are put will be sufficient in itself to found a conviction. He must draw the attention of the jury to whatever factors are material to the individual case. These will often include, but not be limited to, the nature and location of the premises, the involvement of the lessor in adapting, furnishing or outfitting the premises for prostitution, the duration of the letting, the hours during which the premises are occupied, the rent at which they are let, the method of payment of rent, the fact that the prostitute does or does not live as well as work at the premises, the presence or absence of a personal relationship between the lessor and the lessee, the steps taken by the lessor to remove the prostitutes from his premises, and the steps taken by the lessor to disguise his relationship with the premises and the persons working there. Having presented the facts to the jury, the judge will invite them to consider whether they are sure that the lessor was involved together with the prostitute in the business of prostitution" (at pp.332–333).

H–206   Mustill L.J. then said that in the opinion of the court, the judge's direction, that where a letting was referable to prostitution and nothing else it was immaterial whether the letting was at a higher than normal rent, was correct, and to the extent that *Silver, ante,* is a decision to the contrary, it should not be followed.

It is essential that a jury should receive a clear and careful direction with regard to this offence and the burden of proof in relation to it. In particular, where the prosecution rely on subsection (2) (*ante,* H–197), the jury's attention should be directed to the various alternatives contained in the subsection, and to any evidence relating to any of those alternatives: *R. v. Lawrence,* 47 Cr.App.R. 72, CCA.

In *R. v. Howard,* 94 Cr.App.R. 89, CA, Lord Lane C.J. said that what is required is a simple direction based primarily on what was said in *Shaw v. DPP, ante,* and *Stewart, ante,* adjusted to the facts of the particular case.

(f) Evidence

H–207   That the defendant knowingly lived wholly or in part on the earnings of prostitution is usually proved by evidence that the prostitute paid the rent of rooms where both were living together, or paid for his food, or supplied him with money, or paid for drink consumed by him in public-houses, or the like. Whether conversation and association with a prostitute amounts to proof that the defendant was habitually in her company is a question of fact for the jury: *R. v. Ptohopoulos,* 52 Cr.App.R. 47, CA.

There need not be proof that the prostitute handed money to the defendant if the evidence establishes that what the defendant received was earned by the prostitute (see *Calvert v. Mayes* [1954] 1 Q.B. 242, approved in *Shaw*). Nor, as was held in *R. v. Ansell* [1975] Q.B. 215, 60 Cr.App.R. 45, CA, if the money comes from the men with whom the prostitutes are dealing and not from the prostitutes themselves, does that fact in law prevent the money being the earnings of prostitution: see, for example, *R. v. Farrugia,* 69 Cr.App.R. 108, CA.

(25) Woman exercising control over prostitute

(a) *Statute*

Sexual Offences Act 1956, s.31

31. It is an offence for a woman for purposes of gain to exercise control, direction or influence **H–208**
over a prostitute's movements in a way which shows she is aiding, abetting or compelling her
prostitution.

As to the use of the word "woman", see *post*, H–222. As to the meaning of "prostitution",
see *ante*, H–172.

(b) *Class of offence and mode of trial*

This offence is a class 3 offence (§ 2–17 in the main work), triable either way: *SOA* 1956, **H–209**
s.37(2), and Sched. 2, para. 31.

(c) *Sentence*

On conviction on indictment, imprisonment not exceeding seven years; on summary **H–210**
conviction, six months, or a fine not exceeding £5,000: *SOA* 1956, s.37(3), and Sched. 2,
para. 31 (as amended by the *Street Offences Act* 1959, s.4), and the *MCA* 1980, ss.32,
34(3)(a).

(26) Solicitation for immoral purposes

(a) *Statute*

Sexual Offences Act 1956, s.32

32. It is an offence for a man persistently to solicit or importune in a public place for immoral **H–211**
purposes.

As to the use of the word "man", see *post*, H–222.

(b) *Class of offence and mode of trial*

This offence is a class 3 offence (§ 2–17 in the main work), triable either way: *SOA* 1956, **H–212**
s.37(2), and Sched. 2, para. 32.

(c) *Sentence*

On conviction on indictment, imprisonment not exceeding two years; on summary convic- **H–213**
tion, six months, or a fine not exceeding £5,000: *SOA* 1956, s.37(3), and Sched. 2, para. 32,
and the *MCA* 1980, ss.32, 34(3)(a).

(d) *Ingredients of the offence*

"persistently"

Two separate acts of importuning within the period named in the information or indict- **H–214**
ment are sufficient to render the importuning persistent: *Dale v. Smith* [1967] 1 W.L.R. 700,
DC (justices entitled to treat the use of the word "Hello" by the defendant to a youth in a
public lavatory as an act of importuning, in view of the fact that the same word had been
used by the defendant to another youth on the previous evening and had been followed by
an undoubted act of importuning, *viz.* an invitation to look at indecent photographs).

"solicit"

H–215   In *Behrendt v. Burridge*, 63 Cr.App.R. 202, DC, the defendant was observed for about 50 minutes sitting on a high stool in the bay window of a house. She sat silent and motionless, dressed in a low cut top and mini-skirt. The bay window was illuminated by a red light. She was charged with soliciting for the purpose of prostitution, contrary to section 1 of the *Street Offences Act* 1959. The Divisional Court said that the fact that her behaviour could be described as an explicit form of advertising was not decisive in her favour: advertising and soliciting are not mutually exclusive. It was clear that she was soliciting in the sense of tempting or allowing prospective customers to come in for the purposes of prostitution.

See also *Horton v. Mead* [1913] 1 K.B. 154, DC, and *Burge v. DPP* [1962] 1 W.L.R. 265, DC.

"importune"

H–216   See *Dale v. Smith, ante,* H–214.

"public place"

H–217   No definition appears in the 1956 Act, but it is a frequently used expression in legislation: see, for example, the *Public Order Act* 1936, s.9 (§ 25–329 in the main work), the *Prevention of Crime Act* 1953, s.1(4) (§ 24–106a in the main work) and the *Firearms Act* 1968, s.57(4) (§ 24–85 in the main work).

"for immoral purposes"

H–218   An immoral purpose within section 32 has to be some kind of sexual activity: *Crook v. Edmondson* [1966] 2 Q.B. 81, DC; *R. v. Kirkup*, 96 Cr.App.R. 352, CA.

Section 32 applies both to heterosexual and homosexual behaviour: *R. v. Goddard*, 92 Cr.App.R. 185, CA.

Although section 1 of the *SOA* 1967 (*ante*, H–97) prevents homosexual practices in private between consenting parties who have attained the age of 16 from being a criminal offence, the 1967 Act did not change the law to the extent of preventing approaches for such purposes from being the offence of persistently importuning for "immoral purposes": *R. v. Ford*, 66 Cr.App.R. 46, CA. The judge correctly ruled that the conduct complained of could amount to an offence and correctly left the jury to decide whether the conduct was or was not immoral.

Similarly, in *R. v. Goddard, ante,* the unchallenged evidence of two young women was that they had had explicit sexual invitations made to them by G. It was held: (a) that it did not matter that the proposed sexual activity may be within the law; and (b) that it was a matter for the jury to decide, whether the invitations were for sexually immoral purposes, considering the circumstances in which the overtures were made and the nature of the overtures. This decision effectively overruled that part of the majority decision in *Crook v. Edmondson, ante,* which had held that "immoral purposes" was to be confined to purposes declared to be offences under other provisions of the 1956 Act.

The correct procedure is for the trial judge to rule whether the acts complained of could amount to an offence and, provided they are so capable, to leave it to the jury to decide whether the conduct, in fact, involved an immoral purpose, applying contemporary standards of morality: *R. v. Goddard, ante.*

(27) Interpretation

(a) *Meaning of "sexual intercourse"*

Sexual Offences Act 1956, s.44

H–219   44. Where, on the trial of any offence under this Act, it is necessary to prove sexual intercourse (whether natural or unnatural), it shall not be necessary to prove the completion of the intercourse by the emission of seed, but the intercourse shall be deemed complete upon proof of penetration only.

See further, *ante*, H–14.

Boys under the age of 14

As to the abolition of the common law presumption that a boy under the age of 14 is   **H–220** incapable of sexual intercourse, see *ante*, H–13. The presumption did not apply to a charge of aiding and abetting the commission of an offence: 1 Hale 630; *R. v. Williams* [1893] 1 Q.B. 320. Nor would it apply where the boy was not the defendant: see *R. v. Pickford* [1995] 1 Cr.App.R. 420, CA (*ante*, H–94).

(b) *Meaning of "defective"*

See section 45 of the *SOA* 1956, *ante*, H–68.   **H–221**

(c) *Use of words "man", "boy", "woman" and "girl"*

Sexual Offences Act 1956, s.46

46. The use in any provision of this Act of the word "man" without the addition of the word   **H–222** "boy", or *vice versa*, shall not prevent the provision applying to any person to whom it would have applied if both words had been used, and similarly with the words "woman" and "girl".

As to the use of the word "man", see *R. v. Tan* [1983] Q.B. 1053, 76 Cr.App.R. 300, CA, *ante*, H–202.

Section 46 applies for the purposes of the provisions of the *SOA* 1967 as it applies for the purposes of the provisions of the 1956 Act: *SOA* 1967, s.11(3). It also has effect as if the reference to the 1956 Act included a reference to the *Sexual Offences (Amendment) Act* 1976: *Sexual Offences (Amendment) Act* 1976, s.7(2).

(d) *Meaning of "parental responsibility"*

Sexual Offences Act 1956, s.46A

46A. In this Act "parental responsibility" has the same meaning as in the *Children Act* 1989.   **H–223**

[This section was inserted by the *Children Act* 1989, s.108(4), and Sched. 12, para. 17.]

Section 105(1) of the Act of 1989 provides that in that Act "parental responsibility" has the meaning given by section 3.

Children Act 1989, s.3

3.—(1) In this Act "parental responsibility" means all the rights, duties, powers, responsibilities   **H–224** and authority which by law a parent of a child has in relation to the child and his property.

(2) It also includes the rights, powers and duties which a guardian of the child's estate (appointed, before the commencement of section 5, to act generally) would have had in relation to the child and his property.

(3) The rights referred to in subsection (2) include, in particular, the right of the guardian to receive or recover in his own name, for the benefit of the child, property of whatever description and wherever situated which the child is entitled to receive or recover.

(4) The fact that a person has, or does not have, parental responsibility for a child shall not affect—

    (a) any obligation which he may have in relation to the child (such as a statutory duty to maintain the child); or

(b) any rights which, in the event of the child's death, he (or any other person) may have in relation to the child's property.

(5) A person who—

(a) does not have parental responsibility for a particular child; but

(b) has care of the child,

may (subject to the provisions of this Act) do what is reasonable in all the circumstances of the case for the purpose of safeguarding or promoting the child's welfare.

Further reference may need to be made to sections 2 (parental responsibility for children) and 12 (residence orders and parental responsibility) of the 1989 Act.

(28) Proof of exceptions

Sexual Offences Act 1956, s.47

H–225 47. Where in any of the foregoing sections the description of an offence is expressed to be subject to exceptions mentioned in the section, proof of the exception is to lie on the person relying on it.

(29) Powers and procedure for dealing with offenders

Sexual Offences Act 1956, s.37

Prosecution and punishment of offences

H–226 37.—(1) The Second Schedule to this Act shall have effect, subject to and in accordance with the following provisions of this section, with respect to the prosecution and punishment of the offences listed in the first column of the Schedule, being the offences under this Act and attempts to commit certain of those offences.

(2) The second column in the Schedule shows, for any offence, if it may be prosecuted on indictment or summarily, or either … and what special restrictions (if any) there are on the commencement of a prosecution.

(3) The third column in the Schedule shows, for any offence, the punishments which may be imposed on conviction on indictment or on summary conviction, a reference to a period giving the maximum term of imprisonment and a reference to a sum of money the maximum fine.

(4) The fourth column in the Schedule contains provisions which are either supplementary to those in the second or third column or enable a person charged on indictment with the offence specified in the first column to be found guilty of another offence if the jury are not satisfied that he is guilty of the offence charged or of an attempt to commit it, but are satisfied that he is guilty of the other offence.

(5) A provision in the fourth column of the Schedule enabling the jury to find the accused guilty of an offence specified in that provision authorises them, if not satisfied that he is guilty of the offence so specified, to find him guilty of any other offence of which they could find him guilty if he had been indicted for the offence so specified.

(6) Where in the Schedule there is used a phrase descriptive of an offence or group of offences followed by a reference to a section by its number only, the reference is to a section of this Act, and the phrase shall be taken as referring to any offence under the section mentioned.

(7) Nothing in this section or in the Second Schedule to this Act shall exclude the application to any of the offences referred to in the first column of the Schedule—

(a) of section 24 of the *Magistrates' Courts Act* 1980 (which relates to the summary trial of young offenders for indictable offences); or

(b) of subsection (5) of section 121 of the *Magistrates' Courts Act* 1980 (which limits the punishment which may be imposed by a magistrates' court sitting in an occasional courthouse); or

(c) of any enactment or rule of law restricting a court's power to imprison; or

(d) of any enactment or rule of law authorising an offender to be dealt with in a way not authorised by the enactments specially relating to his offence; or

(e) of any enactment or rule of law authorising a jury to find a person guilty of an offence other than that with which he is charged.

[This section is printed as amended by the *MCA* 1980, Sched. 7, para. 17; and as repealed in part by the *Courts Act* 1971, s.56(4), and Sched. 11, Pt IV.]

Subsection (5) was considered in *R. v. Rogina*, 64 Cr.App.R. 79, CA, *ante*, H–74.

Attempts

Schedule 2 to the 1956 Act is not set out in this appendix. All relevant provisions thereof **H–227** are referred to in the context of the individual offences, *ante*. Some of the paragraphs in the Schedule specifically refer to an attempt to commit a particular offence (sometimes with a different penalty to the full offence, sometimes with the same penalty). Wherever there is specific reference to an attempt in the schedule, this is referred to in the text in relation to the offence in question; where there is no such reference in the text, this is because there is no separate reference to an attempt in the schedule. In such cases, the *Criminal Attempts Act* 1981 will exclusively determine liability to prosecution and punishment for an attempt: for the 1981 Act, see §§ 33–120 *et seq.* in the main work.

C. Mental Health Act 1959

Mental Health Act 1959, s.128

Sexual intercourse with patients

128.—(1) Without prejudice to section seven of the *Sexual Offences Act* 1956, it shall be an of- **H–228** fence, subject to the exception mentioned in this section,—

(a) for a man who is an officer on the staff of or is otherwise employed in, or is one of the managers of, a hospital independent hospital or care home to have unlawful sexual intercourse with a woman who is for the time being receiving treatment for mental disorder in that hospital or home, or to have such intercourse on the premises of which the hospital or home forms part with a woman who is for the time being receiving such treatment there as an outpatient;

(b) for a man to have unlawful sexual intercourse with a woman who is a mentally disordered patient and who is subject to his guardianship under the *Mental Health Act* 1983 or is otherwise in his custody or care under the *Mental Health Act* 1983 or in pursuance of arrangements under ... Part III of the *National Assistance Act* 1948 ... or the *National Health Service Act* 1977, or as a resident in a care home.

(2) It shall not be an offence under this section for a man to have sexual intercourse with a woman if he does not know and has no reason to suspect her to be a mentally disordered patient.

(3) Any person guilty of an offence under this section shall be liable on conviction on indictment to imprisonment for a term not exceeding two years.

(4) No proceedings shall be instituted for an offence under this section except by or with the consent of the Director of Public Prosecutions.

(5) This section shall be construed as one with the *Sexual Offences Act* 1956; and section 47 of that Act (which relates to the proof of exceptions) shall apply to the exception mentioned in this section.

(6) In this section "independent hospital" and "care home" have the same meaning as in the *Care Standards Act* 2000.

[This section is printed as amended by the *National Health Service Act* 1977, s.129, Sched. 15, para. 29, and Sched. 16; the *MHA* 1983, s.148, and Sched. 3, para. 15; the *Registered Homes Act* 1984, s.57, and Sched. 1, para. 2; and the *Care Standards Act* 2000, s.116, and Sched. 4, para. 2.]

As to the meaning of "sexual intercourse", see *ante*, H–219; as to the meaning of "unlaw- **H–229** ful" sexual intercourse, see *R. v. Chapman*, *ante*, H–38; as to the use of the words "man" and "woman", see *ante*, H–222.

For anonymity provisions, see §§ 20–257 *et seq.* in the main work.

For section 47 of the 1956 Act (burden of proof of exceptions), see *ante*, H–225.

By section 1(4) of the *Sexual Offences Act* 1967, section 128 is to have effect as if any reference therein to having unlawful sexual intercourse with a woman included a reference to committing buggery or an act of gross indecency with another man.

In connection with the offences created by this section, see *R. v. Davies and Poolton* [2000] Crim.L.R. 297, CA (§ 19–282 in the main work), decided in relation to the similarly worded section 127 of the 1959 Act.

D. Indecency With Children Act 1960

(1) Statute

Indecency with Children Act 1960, s.1(1)

H–230   **1.**—(1) Any person who commits an act of gross indecency with or towards a child under the age of sixteen, or who incites a child under that age to such an act with him or another, shall be liable on conviction on indictment to imprisonment for a term not exceeding ten years, or on summary conviction to imprisonment for a term not exceeding six months, to a fine not exceeding the prescribed sum, or to both.

(2) [*Repealed by* Police and Criminal Evidence Act *1984, Sched. 7.*]

(3) References in the *Children and Young Persons Act* 1933 ... to the offences mentioned in the First Schedule to that Act shall include offences under this section.

(4) Offences under this section shall be deemed to be offences against the person for the purpose of section three of the *Visiting Forces Act* 1952 (which restricts the trial by United Kingdom courts of offenders connected with visiting forces).

[Subs. (1) is printed as amended by the *C(S)A* 1997, s.52 (substitution of "ten" for "two"); and the *CJCSA* 2000, s.39 (substitution of "sixteen" for "fourteen"). The first of these amendments took effect on October 1, 1997, but does not apply to offences committed before that date: *Crime (Sentences) Act (Commencement No. 2 and Transitional Provisions) Order* 1997 (S.I. 1997 No. 2200). The second amendment took effect on January 11, 2001: *Criminal Justice and Court Services Act 2000 (Commencement No. 1) Order* 2000 (S.I. 2000 No. 3302).]

As to Schedule 1 to the *CYPA* 1933, see § 19–322 in the main work.

For anonymity provisions, see §§ 20–257 *et seq.* in the main work.

(2) Indictment

Statement of Offence

H–231   *Indecency with a child, contrary to section 1(1) of the* Indecency with Children Act *1960.*

Particulars of Offence

A B, on the —— day of ——, 20—, committed an act of gross indecency with [or *towards*] *J N, a child of the age of 10 years* [or *incited J N, a child of the age of 10 years to commit an act of gross indecency with him the said A B* (or *with Y Z*)].

It is a prerequisite of a conviction contrary to section 1 that the child was under the age of 16 at the time of the act or incitement: the child's age is an ingredient of the offence about which the jury must be satisfied and, unless age is admitted, calls for an appropriate direction from the judge: see *R. v. Goss and Goss*, 90 Cr.App.R. 400, CA, and *R. v. Radcliffe* [1990] Crim.L.R. 524, CA.

As to the propriety of preferring a charge of outraging public decency although the facts are covered by section 1(1), see *R. v. May (J.)*, 91 Cr.App.R. 157, CA (§ 20–238 in the main work).

(3) Class of offence and mode of trial

H–232   This offence is a class 3 offence (§ 2–17 in the main work), triable either way: s.1(1), *ante.*

(4) Sentence

See section 1(1), *ante*. As to "the prescribed sum", see section 32 of the *MCA* 1980 (§ 1– 125 in the main work). **H–233**

(5) Consent of Director of Public Prosecutions

Section 8 of the *SOA* 1967 (no proceedings shall be instituted except by or with the consent of the Director against any man for gross indecency or certain other offences where any person involved is under 21) shall not apply to proceedings under the *Indecency with Children Act* 1960: *CJA* 1972, s.48. **H–234**

(6) Ingredients of the offence

In *R. v. Speck*, 65 Cr.App.R. 161, CA, it was held that section 1 was contravened where S passively permitted a child to keep her hand on his penis for so long (in this case about five minutes) that his inactivity amounted to an invitation to her to continue the activity. If such an invitation could properly be inferred, it would constitute an "act" within section 1(1). Apart from allowing the child's hand to remain where she had placed it, S did nothing to encourage the child. A proper direction to the jury in such circumstances would be that the defendant's conduct might constitute an offence under section 1(1) if it amounted to an invitation from the defendant to the child to continue the activity in question. If they took that view (*i.e.* that there had been an "act") then they should go on to determine whether the act was an act of gross indecency. See also *R. v. B.* [1999] Crim.L.R. 594, CA. **H–235**

Section 1(1) creates one offence of gross indecency, namely, the committing of an act of gross indecency involving a child; that is, "with or towards a child" is to be read as a phrase: *DPP v. Burgess* [1971] Q.B. 432, DC; *R. v. Francis*, 88 Cr.App.R. 127, CA. In *Francis*, the court considered the circumstances in which a man contravened section 1(1) if he masturbated in the presence of a child: the act had to be directed towards the child, the offender at the very least deriving satisfaction from the knowledge that the child was watching what he was doing.

As to the age of the victim being an essential ingredient of the offence, see *ante*, H–220; and it is necessary for the prosecution to prove the absence of a genuine belief on the part of the defendant that the victim was 16 years or above: *B. (a Minor) v. DPP* [2000] 2 A.C. 428, HL. The presence or absence of reasonable grounds for such belief goes only to whether such belief was genuinely held: *ibid.*

E. Sexual Offences Act 1967

(1) Procuring others to commit homosexual acts

Sexual Offences Act 1967, s.4

4.—(1) A man who procures another man to commit with a third man an act of buggery which by reason of section 1 of this Act is not an offence shall be liable on conviction on indictment to imprisonment for a term not exceeding two years. **H–236**

(2) [*Repealed by* Criminal Law Act *1977, Sched.* 13.]

(3) It shall not be an offence under section 13 of the Act of 1956 for a man to procure the commission by another man of an act of gross indecency with the first-mentioned man which by reason of section 1 of this Act is not an offence under the said section 13.

The offence under subsection (1) is triable either way: *MCA* 1980, s.17(1), and Sched. 1 (§ 1–125 in the main work).

As to the use of the word "man", see *ante*, H–222.

As to the offence of buggery, see *ante*, H–95 *et seq.*

For section 13 of the 1956 Act, see *ante*, H–107.

As to "procures", see *ante*, H–171.

(2) Living on earnings of male prostitution

Sexual Offences Act 1967, s.5

H–237   5.—(1) A man or woman who knowingly lives wholly or in part on the earnings of prostitution of another man shall be liable—

(a) on summary conviction to imprisonment for a term not exceeding six months, or

(b) on conviction on indictment to imprisonment for a term not exceeding seven years.

(2) [*Repealed by* Criminal Law Act *1977, Sched. 13.*]

(3) Anyone may arrest without a warrant a person found committing an offence under this section.

H–238   As to the use of the words "man" and "woman", see *ante*, H–222 and—in relation to "man"—see *R. v. Tan* [1983] Q.B. 1053, 76 Cr.App.R. 300, CA, *ante*, H–202.

The offence is a class 3 offence (§ 2–17 in the main work).

Subsection (3) has ceased to have effect by virtue of the *PACE Act* 1984, s.26(1) (§ 15–133 in the main work).

F. Criminal Law Act 1977

Criminal Law Act 1977, s.54

Incitement of girls under 16

H–239   54.—(1) It is an offence for a man to incite to have sexual intercourse with him a girl under the age of sixteen whom he knows to be his grand-daughter, daughter or sister.

(2) In the preceding subsection "man" includes boy, "sister" includes half-sister, and for the purposes of that subsection any expression importing a relationship between two people shall be taken to apply notwithstanding that the relationship is not traced through lawful wedlock.

(3) The following provisions of section 1 of the *Indecency with Children Act* 1960, namely—

...

subsection (3) (references in *Children and Young Persons Act* 1933 to the offences mentioned in Schedule 1 to that Act to include offences under that section);

subsection (4) (offences under that section to be deemed offences against the person for the purpose of section 3 of the *Visiting Forces Act* 1952),

shall apply in relation to offences under this section.

(4) A person guilty of an offence under this section shall be liable—

(a) on summary conviction, to imprisonment for a term not exceeding six months or to a fine not exceeding the prescribed sum or both;

(b) on conviction on indictment to imprisonment for a term not exceeding two years.

[This section is printed as effectively amended by the *MCA* 1980, s.32(2) (substitution of reference to "the prescribed sum"); and as repealed in part by the *PACE Act* 1984, Sched. 7.]

H–240   As to Schedule 1 to the *CYPA* 1933, see § 19–322 in the main work.

As to "the prescribed sum", see the *MCA* 1980, s.32(2) and (9) (§ 1–125 in the main work).

For anonymity provisions, see §§ 20–257 *et seq.* in the main work.

Section 54 filled a *lacuna* in the law, identified in *R. v. Whitehouse* [1977] Q.B. 868, 65 Cr.App.R. 33, CA.

As to incitement at common law, see *ante*, §§ 33–78 *et seq.*

G. Sexual Offences (Amendment) Act 2000

(1) Statute

Sexual Offences (Amendment) Act 2000, ss.3, 4

Abuse of position of trust

3.—(1) Subject to subsections (2) and (3) below, it shall be an offence for a person aged 18 or   **H–241**
over—

    (a) to have sexual intercourse (whether vaginal or anal) with a person under that age; or

    (b) to engage in any other sexual activity with or directed towards such a person,

if (in either case) he is in a position of trust in relation to that person.

(2) Where a person ("A") is charged with an offence under this section of having sexual intercourse with, or engaging in any other sexual activity with or directed towards, another person ("B"), it shall be a defence for A to prove that, at the time of the intercourse or activity—

    (a) he did not know, and could not reasonably have been expected to know, that B was under 18;

    (b) he did not know, and could not reasonably have been expected to know, that B was a person in relation to whom he was in a position of trust; or

    (c) he was lawfully married to B.

(3) It shall not be an offence under this section for a person ("A") to have sexual intercourse with, or engage in any other sexual activity with or directed towards, another person ("B") if immediately before the commencement of this Act—

    (a) A was in a position of trust in relation to B; and

    (b) a sexual relationship existed between them.

(4) A person guilty of an offence under this section shall be liable—

    (a) on summary conviction, to imprisonment for a term not exceeding six months, or to a fine not exceeding the statutory maximum, or to both;

    (b) on conviction on indictment, to imprisonment for a term not exceeding five years, or to a fine, or to both.

(5) In this section, "sexual activity"—

    (a) does not include any activity which a reasonable person would regard as sexual only with knowledge of the intentions, motives or feelings of the parties; but

    (b) subject to that, means any activity which such a person would regard as sexual in all the circumstances.

As to "the commencement of this Act", see the *Sexual Offences (Amendment) Act 2000 (Commencement No. 1) Order* 2000 (S.I. 2000 No. 3303), which brought the Act into force on January 8, 2001.

Meaning of "position of trust"

4.—(1) For the purposes of section 3 above, a person aged 18 or over ("A") is in a position of   **H–242**
trust in relation to a person under that age ("B") if any of the four conditions set out below, or any condition specified in an order made by the Secretary of State by statutory instrument, is fulfilled.

(2) The first condition is that A looks after persons under 18 who are detained in an institution by virtue of an order of a court or under an enactment, and B is so detained in that institution.

(3) The second condition is that A looks after persons under 18 who are resident in a home or other place in which—

    (a) accommodation and maintenance are provided by an authority under section 23(2) of the *Children Act* 1989 or Article 27(2) of the *Children (Northern Ireland) Order* 1995;

    (b) accommodation is provided by a voluntary organisation under section 59(1) of that Act or Article 75(1) of that Order; or

    (c) accommodation is provided by an authority under section 26(1) of the *Children (Scotland) Act* 1995,

and B is resident, and is so provided with accommodation and maintenance or accommodation, in that place.

(4) The third condition is that A looks after persons under 18 who are accommodated and cared for in an institution which is—

    (a) a hospital;

    (b) a residential care home, nursing home, mental nursing home or private hospital;

(c) a community home, voluntary home, children's home or residential establishment; or

(d) a home provided under section 82(5) of the *Children Act* 1989,

and B is accommodated and cared for in that institution.

(5) The fourth condition is that A looks after persons under 18 who are receiving full-time education at an educational institution, and B is receiving such education at that institution.

(6) No order shall be made under subsection (1) above unless a draft of the order has been laid before and approved by a resolution of each House of Parliament.

(7) A person looks after persons under 18 for the purposes of this section if he is regularly involved in caring for, training, supervising or being in sole charge of such persons.

(8) For the purposes of this section a person receives full-time education at an educational institution if—

(a) he is registered or otherwise enrolled as a full-time pupil or student at the institution; or

(b) he receives education at the institution under arrangements with another educational institution at which he is so registered or otherwise enrolled.

(9) In this section, except where the context otherwise requires—

"authority" means—

(a) in relation to Great Britain, a local authority; and

(b) [*Northern Ireland*];

"children's home" has—

(a) in relation to England and Wales, the meaning which would be given by subsection (3) of section 63 of the *Children Act* 1989 if the reference in paragraph (a) of that subsection to more than three children were a reference to one or more children; and

(b) [*Northern Ireland*];

"community home" has the meaning given by section 53(1) of the *Children Act* 1989;

"hospital" has—

(a) in relation to England and Wales, the meaning given by section 128(1) of the *National Health Service Act* 1977;

(b) [*Scotland*]; and

(c) [*Northern Ireland*];

"mental nursing home" has, in relation to England and Wales, the meaning given by section 22(1) of the *Registered Homes Act* 1984

"nursing home"—

(a) in relation to England and Wales, has the meaning given by section 21(1) of the *Registered Homes Act* 1984;

(b) [*Scotland*];

(c) [*Northern Ireland*];

"private hospital" has—

(a) [*Scotland*]; and

(b) [*Northern Ireland*];

"residential care home"—

(a) in relation to England and Wales, has the meaning given by section 1(2) of the *Registered Homes Act* 1984;

(b) [*Scotland*]; and

(c) [*Northern Ireland*];

"residential establishment" has the meaning given by section 93(1) of the *Children (Scotland) Act* 1995 as the meaning of that expression in Scotland;

"voluntary home" has—

(a) in relation to England and Wales, the meaning given by section 60(3) of the *Children Act* 1989; and

(b) [*Northern Ireland*].

(2) Indictment

STATEMENT OF OFFENCE

H–243   *Abuse of a position of trust, contrary to section 3(1)(a) of the* Sexual Offences (Amendment) Act *2000.*

PARTICULARS OF OFFENCE

A B, on the —— day of ——, 20—, being a person of the age of at least 18 years, had sexual intercourse

*with J N, being a person under the age of 18 years, and being at the time in a position of trust in relation to
J N, in that at the time he looked after persons under the age of 18 years who were receiving full-time education at —— school, and J N was at the time in receipt of such education at the aforesaid school.*

(3) Class of offence and mode of trial

This offence is a class 3 offence (§ 2–17 in the main work), triable either way: s.3(4), *ante.*   **H–244**

(4) Sentence

See s.3(4), *ante.*   **H–245**

The setting out of the various positions of trust in section 4(2) to (5) is not to be taken as
indicative of descending seriousness: *R. v. Hubbard* [2002] 2 Cr.App.R.(S.) 101, CA.

APPENDIX J

A Guide to Commencing Proceedings in the Court of Appeal (Criminal Division)

NOTE: the text of the guide that follows has been subjected to some editorial revision (in relation to such matters as punctuation, use of upper and lower case, abbreviations, manner of citation of legislative references and authorities, and in order to correct a small number of obvious, minor errors). None of these revisions has any effect on the sense of the guide.

Foreword by the Lord Chief Justice of England and Wales

In recent years the Court of Appeal Criminal Division has faced increased complexity in appeals, **J-1**
not only against conviction but also against sentence, particularly in the light of the plethora of
recent sentencing legislation. Additionally, the jurisdiction of the court has expanded to encompass a
variety of diverse applications and appeals by the defence, the Crown and other interested parties.

This guide provides invaluable advice as to the initial steps for commencing proceedings in the
Court of Appeal Criminal Division generally and in relation to perhaps unfamiliar provisions.

The first and most important step is, of course, the preparation of the grounds of appeal. The
rules prescribe the form and content of the Notice and Grounds of Appeal. Practitioners are also
required to summarise the facts and outline their arguments concisely. Well drafted grounds of appeal assist the single judge when considering leave and serve to shorten any hearing before the full
court. Ill-prepared and prolix documents necessarily lead to wasted time spent on preparation and
unnecessarily protracted hearings.

It is important that we all take seriously our responsibility to ensure the effective progression of
cases and keep delay to a minimum. Once an application or appeal is commenced, the responsible
officer at the Criminal Appeal Office will be available to assist with any queries on practice or
procedure.

The court could not deal with this volume of work efficiently without the support of the Registrar
and his staff in the Criminal Appeal Office. Their experience and expertise is invaluable and can
always be relied on by those who use the court, not least those who are unfamiliar with its practice
and procedures.

Judge C.J.
October 2008

Introduction

Since the publication of the last Guide to Proceedings in the Court of Appeal (Criminal Division), **J-2**
the court's jurisdiction has increased. It hears appeals not only against conviction and sentence, but
also against various interlocutory rulings, as well as other appeals and applications.

This guide provides practical information about how to commence and conduct proceedings
before the court. Once proceedings are commenced, an application will have its own unique reference number and a case progression officer who can help with any difficulties or queries about
procedure.

The guide is set out as follows:

A. General principles of practice and procedure when applying for leave to appeal conviction and
sentence.

B. Guidance on appeals against rulings made in preparatory hearings.

C. Guidance on prosecution appeals against 'terminating' rulings.

D. Brief guidance on other appeals in bullet point form showing:
   - the type of appeal,
   - the relevant section of the statute
   - the relevant Criminal Procedure Rules
   - who can apply
   - the forms to be used and time limits
   - respondents' notices,
   - whether representation orders are available
   - whether leave to appeal is required

E. Guidance on applications for a retrial for a serious offence.

A list of all up to date forms referred to in this guide may be accessed from the HMCS website at
www.hmcourts-service.gov.uk or the Criminal Procedure Rules Committee website at *www.justice.gov.uk/
criminal/procrules*. Where the *Criminal Procedure Rules* do not provide for a specific form, this guide
indicates the appropriate form to be used.

This guide was prepared under my direction by the staff of the Criminal Appeal Office, but
principally by Ms Alix Beldam and Ms Susan Holdham. It describes the law and practice of the
Court as at 1st October 2008.

Master Venne
Registrar of Criminal Appeals

Terminology

The *Criminal Appeal Act* 1968 refers to "leave to appeal". This is now referred to as "permission to **J-3**
appeal" in the *Criminal Procedure Rules* 2007. This guide keeps to the terminology used by the Act.

Also consistently with the Act, an "appellant" is referred to without distinction, but it should be borne in mind that it is the accepted practice of the Criminal Appeal Office (CAO) to refer to a person who has served notice of appeal but not been granted leave to appeal as an "applicant" and use the term "appellant" to refer to a person who has been granted leave to appeal.

Any reference to counsel should be read as including a solicitor advocate as appropriate.

A. General Principles of Practice and Procedure when Applying for Leave to Appeal Conviction and Sentence

A1 Advice and assistance

J–4   A1–1 Provision for advice or assistance on appeal is included in the trial representation order issued by the Crown Court. Solicitors should not wait to be asked for advice by the defendant. Immediately following the conclusion of the case, the legal representatives should see the defendant and counsel should express orally his final view as to the prospects of a successful appeal (whether against conviction or sentence or both). If there are no reasonable grounds of appeal, that should be confirmed in writing and a copy provided then, or as soon as practicable thereafter, to the defendant by the solicitor. If there are reasonable grounds, grounds of appeal should be drafted, signed and sent to instructing solicitors as soon as possible. Solicitors should immediately send a copy of the documents received from counsel to the defendant.

A1–2 Prior to the lodging of the notice and grounds of appeal by service of Form NG, the Registrar has no power to grant a representation order. Also, the Crown Court can only amend a representation order in favour of fresh legal representatives if advice on appeal has not been given by trial legal representatives and it is necessary and reasonable for another legal representative to be instructed. Where advice on appeal has been given by trial legal representatives, application for funding may only be made to the Legal Services Commission (LSC).

A1–3 Once the Form NG has been lodged, the Registrar is the authority for decisions about representation orders, in accordance with the principle that the court before which there are proceedings is the court with power to grant a right to representation (*Access to Justice Act* 1999, Sched. 3, affirmed by regulation 10 of the *Criminal Defence Service (General) (No. 2) Regulations* 2001 (S.I. 2001 No. 1437)).

A1–4 Where, in order to settle grounds of appeal, work of an exceptional nature is contemplated or where the expense will be great, legal representatives should submit a Form NG with provisional grounds of appeal and with a note to the Registrar requesting a representation order to cover the specific work considered necessary to enable proper grounds of appeal to be settled.

A2 Form NG and grounds of appeal

J–5   A2–1 Where counsel has advised an appeal, solicitors should forward the signed grounds of appeal to the Crown Court accompanied by Form NG and such other forms as may be appropriate. It should be noted that Form NG and grounds of appeal are required to be served within the relevant time limit in all cases, whether or not leave to appeal is required (*e.g.* where a trial judge's certificate has been granted). However, on a reference by the Criminal Cases Review Commission (CCRC), if no Form NG and grounds are served within the required period, then the reference shall be treated as the appeal notice: rule 68.5(2).

A2–2 Grounds must be settled with sufficient particularity to enable the Registrar, and subsequently the court, to identify clearly the matters relied upon. A mere formula such as "the conviction is unsafe" or "the sentence is in all the circumstances too severe" will be ineffective as grounds and time will continue to run against the defendant.

A2–3 Rule 68.3(1) sets out the information that must be contained in the appeal notice. The notice must ... [*see § 7–382 in the main work*].

A2–4 There is now a requirement for the grounds of appeal to set out the relevant facts and nature of the proceedings concisely in one all encompassing document, not separate grounds and advice. The intended readership of this document is the court and not the lay or professional client. Its purpose is to enable the single judge to grasp quickly the facts and issues in the case. In appropriate cases, draft grounds of appeal may be perfected before submission to the single judge (*see further below para. A5*).

A2–5 Any document mentioned in the grounds should be identified clearly, by exhibit number or otherwise. Similarly, if counsel requires an original exhibit or shorthand writer's tape recording, he should say so well in advance of any determination or hearing.

A2–6 Counsel should not settle or sign grounds unless they are reasonable, have some real prospect of success and are such that he is prepared to argue them before the court. Counsel should not settle grounds he cannot support because he is "instructed" to do so by a defendant.

A2–7 Procedure in relation to particular grounds of appeal

A2–7.1 *Applications to call fresh evidence*

A Form W and a statement from the witness in the form prescribed by section 9 of the *CJA* 1967 should be lodged in respect of each witness it is proposed to call. The Form W should indicate whether there is an application for a witness order. The Registrar or the single judge may direct the issue of a witness order, but only the court hearing the appeal may give leave for a witness to be called.

The court will require a cogent explanation for the failure to adduce the evidence at trial. A supporting witness statement or affidavit from the appellant's solicitor should be lodged in this regard (*R. v. Gogana, The Times* July 12, 1999).

If there is to be an application to adduce hearsay and/or evidence of bad character or for special measures, then the appropriate forms should be lodged: rule 68.7(1).

A2–7.2 *Complaints against trial counsel as a ground of appeal*

Where a ground of appeal explicitly criticises trial counsel and/or trial solicitors, the Registrar will institute the "waiver of privilege" procedure. The appellant will be asked to "waive privilege" in respect of instructions to and advice at trial from legal representatives. If he does waive privilege, the grounds of appeal are sent to the appropriate trial representative(s) and they are invited to respond. Any response will be sent to the appellant or his fresh legal representatives for comment. All these documents will be sent to the single judge when considering the application for leave. The single judge may draw inferences from any failure to participate in the process. "Waiver of privilege" is a procedure that should be instigated by the Registrar and not by fresh legal representatives, who should go no further than obtaining a waiver of privilege from the appellant: *R. v. Doherty and McGregor* [1997] 2 Cr.App.R. 218.

A2–7.3 *Insufficient weight given to assistance to prosecution authorities*

Where a ground of appeal against sentence is that the judge has given insufficient weight to the assistance given to the prosecution authorities, the "text" which had been prepared for the sentencing judge is obtained by the Registrar. Grounds of appeal should be drafted in an anodyne form with a note to the Registrar alerting him to the existence of a "text". The single judge will have seen the "text" when considering leave as will the full court before the appeal hearing and it need not be alluded to in open court.

A3 Time limits

A3–1 Notice and grounds should reach the Crown Court within 28 days from the date of the conviction in the case of an application for leave to appeal against conviction and within 28 days from the date of sentence in the case of an application for leave to appeal against sentence [*CAA* 1968, s.18 and rule 68.2(1)]. On a reference by the CCRC, Form NG and grounds should be served on the Registrar not more than 56 days after the Registrar has served notice that the CCRC has referred a conviction and not more than 28 days in the case of a sentence referral: rule 68.2(2).   **J-6**

A3–2 A confiscation order (whether made under the *CJA* 1988, the *DTA* 1994 or the *PCA* 2002) is a sentence [*CAA* 1968, s.50]. Where sentences are passed in separate proceedings on different dates there may be two appeals against sentence. Thus, there may be an appeal against the custodial part of a sentence and an appeal against a confiscation order (*R. v. Neal* [1999] 2 Cr.App.R.(S.) 352).

A3–3 An application for extension of the 28 day period in which to give notice of application for leave to appeal or notice of appeal must always be supported by reasons why the application for leave was not submitted in time. It is not enough merely to tick the relevant box on Form NG.

A3–4 Such an application should be submitted when the application for leave to appeal against either conviction or sentence is made and not in advance. Notwithstanding the terms of section 18(3) of the *CAA* 1968, it has long been the practice of the Registrar to require the extension of time application to be made at the time of service of the notice and grounds of appeal. This practice is now reflected by *Criminal Procedure Rule* 65.4.

A4 Transcript and notes of evidence

A4–1 In conviction cases, transcripts of the summing up and proceedings up to and including   **J-7**
verdict are obtained as a matter of course. Similarly, the transcript of the prosecution opening of

facts on a guilty plea and the judge's observations on passing sentence are usually obtained in sentence cases. There is now an obligation under rule 68.3(2) for counsel to identify any further transcript which counsel considers the court will need and to provide a note of names, dates and times to enable an order to be placed with the shorthand writers. Whether or not any further transcript is required is a matter for the judgment of the Registrar or his staff.

A4–2 Transcript should only be requested if it is essential for the proper conduct of the appeal in the light of the grounds. If the Registrar and counsel are unable to agree the extent of the transcript to be obtained, the Registrar may refer that matter to a judge. In some cases the Registrar may propose that counsel agree a note in place of transcript.

A4–3 In certain circumstances the costs of unnecessary transcript could be ordered to be paid by the appellant. Where transcript is obtained otherwise than through the Registrar, he may disallow the cost on taxation of public funding.

A5 Perfection of grounds of appeal

A5–1 The purpose of perfection is (a) to save valuable judicial time by enabling the court to identify at once the relevant parts of the transcript and (b) to give counsel the opportunity to reconsider his original grounds in the light of the transcript. Perfected grounds should consist of a fresh document which supersedes the original grounds of appeal and contains *inter alia* references by page number and letter (or paragraph number) to all relevant passages in the transcript.

A5–2 In conviction or confiscation cases, the Registrar will almost certainly invite counsel to perfect grounds in the light of the transcript obtained, to assist the single judge or full court. Where counsel indicates a wish to perfect grounds of appeal against sentence, the Registrar will consider the request and will only invite perfection where he considers it necessary for the assistance of the single judge or full court.

A5–3 If perfection is appropriate, counsel will be sent a copy of the transcript and asked to perfect his grounds within 14 days. In the absence of any response from counsel, the existing notice and grounds of appeal will be placed before the single judge or the court without further notice. If counsel does not wish to perfect his grounds, the transcript should be returned with a note to that effect.

A5–4 If, having considered the transcript, counsel is of opinion that there are no valid grounds, he should set out his reasons in a further advice and send it to his instructing solicitors. He should inform the Registrar that he has done so, but should not send him a copy of that advice. Solicitors should send a copy to the appellant and obtain instructions, at the same time explaining that if the appellant persists with his application the court may consider whether to make a loss of time order *(see further below A–13)*.

A6 Respondent's notice

A6–1 The *Criminal Procedure Rules* 2005 provide for the service of a respondent's notice. Under rule 68.6(1) the Registrar may serve the appeal notice on any party directly affected by the appeal (usually the prosecution) and must do so in a CCRC case. That party may then serve a respondent's notice if it wishes to make representations and must do so if the Registrar so directs: rule 68.6(2). The respondent's notice should be served within 14 days (rule 68.6(4)) on the appellant, the Registrar and any other party on whom the Registrar served the appeal notice (rule 68.6(3)). The respondent's notice must be in the specified form [Form RN], in which a respondent should set out the grounds of opposition (rule 68.6(5)) and which must include the information set out in rule 68.6(6).

A6–2 In practice, this procedure primarily applies prior to consideration of leave by the single judge in both conviction and sentence cases. The Attorney General and the Registrar, following consultation with representatives from the Crown Prosecution Service (CPS) and the Revenue and Customs Prosecution Office (RCPO), have agreed guidance on types of cases and/or issues where the Registrar should consider whether to serve an appeal notice and direct or invite a party to serve a respondent's notice before the consideration of leave by the single judge. Examples of when the Registrar might **direct** a respondent's notice include where the grounds concern matters which were the subject of public interest immunity (PII), allegations of jury irregularity, criticism of the conduct of the judge and complex frauds. Cases where it might be appropriate for the Registrar to **invite** a respondent's notice include, for example, homicide offences, serious sexual offences, cases with national profile or high media interest, cases of violence or domestic violence.

A6–3 In conviction cases where leave has been granted or where the application for leave has been referred to the full court, the Crown is briefed to attend the hearing and required to submit a respondent's notice/skeleton argument. In relation to sentence cases where leave has been granted, referred or an appellant is represented on a renewed application, the sentence protocol set out in paragraph II.1 of the consolidated criminal practice direction (§ 7–203 in the main work) will apply. In those cases, a respondent's notice/skeleton argument will have to be served when the Crown indicates a wish to attend or when the Registrar invites or directs the Crown to attend.

A7 Referral by the Registrar

A7–1 Leave to appeal is required in all cases except where the trial judge or sentencing judge has **J–10** certified that the case is fit for appeal (*CAA* 1968, ss.1(2) and 11(1A)) or where the case has been referred by the CCRC. The appellant must obtain leave to pursue grounds not related to the Commission's reasons for referral: *CAA* 1995, s.14(4B).

A7–2 Where leave to appeal is required and the Registrar has obtained the necessary documents, he will refer the application(s) either (a) to a single judge for decision under section 31 of the *CAA* 1968 or (b) directly to the full court, in which case a representation order is usually granted for the hearing. However, the Registrar will not grant a representation order when the presence of counsel is not required, *e.g.* where the application refers solely to an amendment of the number of days to be credited as "remand time" and the figure is agreed by the parties. Where an application is referred to the full court by the Registrar because an unlawful sentence has been passed or other procedural error identified, a representation order will ordinarily be granted, but counsel should be aware that the court may make observations for the attention of the determining officer that a full fee should not be allowed on taxation.

A7–3 Where leave to appeal is not required, *e.g.* on appeal by certificate of the trial judge, the Registrar will usually grant a representation order for the hearing. On a reference from the CCRC, it is the Registrar's usual practice to grant a representation order in the first instance, to solicitors for them to nominate and instruct counsel to settle grounds of appeal. Once counsel's details are known, a further representation order will be granted to cover the preparation (including settling grounds) and presentation of the appeal by counsel and further work by solicitors, as necessary in light of the grounds.

A8 Bail pending appeal

A8–1 Bail may be granted (a) by a single judge or the full court or (b) by a trial or sentencing **J–11** judge who has certified the case fit for appeal. In the latter case, bail can only be granted within 28 days of the conviction or sentence which is the subject of the appeal and may not be granted if an application for bail has already been made to the Court of Appeal.

A8–2 An application to the Court of Appeal for bail must be supported by a completed Form B, whether or not the application is made at the same time as the notice and grounds are served. The completed Form B must be served on the Registrar and the prosecution at least 24 hours before any application is made to enable the Crown to make representations (either written or oral) about the application and any conditions.

A8–3 An application for bail will not be considered by a single judge or the court until notice of application for leave to appeal or notice of appeal has first been given. In practice, judges will also require the relevant transcripts to be available so they may take a view as to the merits of the substantive application.

A8–4 It is the practice of the court, if bail is granted, to require a condition of residence. An application for variation of conditions of bail may be determined by the Registrar (if unopposed) or a single judge.

A9 Consideration of the applications by single judge

A9–1 Normally a single judge will consider the application for leave to appeal together with any **J–12** ancillary applications, *e.g.* for bail or representation order, without hearing oral argument. Counsel may request an oral hearing, but it is only in very rare circumstances that the Registrar would consider it appropriate to grant a representation order for the proceedings before a single judge at an oral hearing, but counsel may appear to argue the applications before the single judge where instructed to do so, usually appearing either *pro bono* or privately funded. Oral applications for leave and bail are usually heard at 9.30 a.m. before the normal court sittings. Counsel appears unrobed. If counsel considers that an application may take longer than 20 minutes, the Registrar must be informed.

A10 Powers of the single judge

A10–1 The single judge may grant the application for leave, refuse it or refer it to the full court. **J–13**

In conviction cases and in sentence cases where appropriate, the single judge may grant limited leave, *i.e.* leave to argue some grounds but not others. If the grounds upon which leave has been refused are to be renewed before the full court, counsel must notify the Registrar within 14 days. In the absence of any notification of renewal, it will be assumed that the grounds upon which leave was refused will not be pursued.

The single judge may also grant, refuse or refer any ancillary application.

A11 Grant of leave or reference to full court

J–14

A11–1 Where the single judge grants leave or refers an application to the court, it is usual to grant a representation order for the preparation and presentation of the appeal. This is usually limited to the services of counsel only, in which event counsel will be assigned by the Registrar. In such a case the Registrar will provide a brief but does not act as an appellant's solicitor. Counsel who settled grounds of appeal will usually be assigned. However, the Registrar may assign one counsel to represent more than one appellant if appropriate. If it is considered that a representation order for two counsel and/or solicitors is required, counsel should notify the Registrar and provide written justification in accordance with the *Criminal Defence Service (General) (No. 2) Regulations* 2001.

A11–2 If solicitors are assigned, it should be noted that by virtue of regulation 13 of the *Criminal Defence Service (General) (No. 2) Regulations* 2001, a representation order can only be issued to a solicitor if he holds a General Criminal Contract (Crime Franchise) with the LSC. A solicitor not holding such a franchise may apply to the LSC for an individual case contract (by virtue of which the solicitor is employed on behalf of the LSC to represent an appellant in a given case). Such a contract is sufficient for the purposes of regulation 13.

A11–3 In some circumstances, the Registrar may refer an application to the full court. This may be because there is a novel point of law or because in a sentence case, the sentence passed is unlawful and regardless of the merits, the sentence should be amended. A representation order for counsel is usually granted. Counsel for the prosecution usually attends a Registrar's referral.

A12 Refusal by the single judge

J–15

A12–1 Where the single judge refuses leave to appeal, the Registrar sends a notification of the refusal, including any observations which the judge may have made, to the appellant, who is informed that he may require the application to be considered by the court by serving a renewal notice [Form SJ-Renewal] upon the Registrar within 14 days from the date on which the notice of refusal was served on him.

A12–2 A refused application which is not renewed within 14 days lapses. An appellant may apply for an extension of time in which to renew his application for leave: *CAA* 1968, s.31, and rule 65.5(2). The Registrar will normally refer such an application to the court to be considered at the same time as the renewed application for leave to appeal. An application for extension for time in which to renew must be supported by cogent reasons.

A12–3 If it is intended that counsel should represent the appellant at the hearing of the renewed application for leave to appeal, whether privately instructed or on a *pro bono* basis, such intention must be communicated to the CAO in writing as soon as that decision has been made. Whilst a representation order is not granted by the Registrar in respect of a renewed application for leave, counsel may apply at the hearing to the court for a representation order to cover that appearance. In practice, this is only granted where the application for leave is successful.

A13 Directions for loss of time

J–16

A13–1 The *CAA* 1968, s. 29, empowers the court to direct that time spent in custody as an appellant shall not count as part of the term of any sentence to which the appellant is for the time being subject. The court will do so where it considers that an application is wholly without merit. Such an order may not be made where leave to appeal or a trial judge's certificate has been granted, on a reference by the CCRC or where an appeal has been abandoned.

A13–2 The mere fact that counsel has advised that there are grounds of appeal will not be a sufficient answer to the question as to whether or not an application has indeed been brought which was wholly without merit: *R. v. Hart; R. v. George; R. v. Clarke; R. v. Brown* [2007] 1 Cr.App.R. 31.

A13–3 The Form SJ, on which the single judge records his decisions, and the reverse of which is used by appellants to indicate their wish to renew, includes:
- a box for the single judge to initial to indicate that that the full court should consider loss of time if the application is renewed and

- a box for the applicant to give reasons why such an order should not be made, whether or not an indication has been given by a single judge.

A14 Abandonment

A14–1 An appeal or application may be abandoned at any time before the hearing without leave **J–17** by completing and lodging Form A. An oral instruction or letter indicating a wish to abandon is insufficient.

A14–2 At the hearing, an application or appeal can only be abandoned with the permission of the court: rule 65.13(2). An appeal or application which is abandoned is treated as having been dismissed or refused by the full court, as the case may be: rule 65.13(4)(c).

A14–3 A notice of abandonment cannot be withdrawn nor can it be conditional. A person who wants to reinstate an application or appeal after abandonment must apply in writing with reasons: rule 65.13(5). The court has power to allow reinstatement only where the purported abandonment can be treated as a nullity (see *R. v. Medway*, 62 Cr.App.R. 85; *R. v. Burt*, *The Independent*, December 3, 2004; *R. v Grant* (2005) 149 S.J. 1186).

A15 Case management duties

A15–1 Rule 65.2 gives the court and parties the same powers and duties of case management as in **J–18** Part 3 of the rules. In accordance with those duties, for each application received, the Registrar nominates a case progression officer (the "responsible officer"). There is also a duty on the parties actively to assist the court to progress cases. Close contact between counsel and solicitors and the responsible officer is encouraged in order to facilitate the efficient preparation and listing of appeals, especially in complex cases and those involving witnesses.

A15–2 Powers exercisable by the single judge and the Registrar are contained in the *CAA* 1968, s.31. These powers include the power to make procedural directions for the efficient and effective preparation of an application or appeal and the power to make an order under section 23(1)(a) of the 1968 Act for the production of evidence *etc.* necessary for the determination of the case.

A15–3 Procedural directions given by the Registrar may be appealed to a single judge. Those given by a single judge, including a single Lord Justice, are final.

B. Interlocutory Appeals against Rulings in Preparatory Hearings

Appeal against a ruling under section 9 of the Criminal Justice Act 1987 or a decision under section 35 of the Criminal Procedure and Investigations Act 1996 [Part 66 Criminal Procedure Rules 2007]

B1 Where a judge has ordered a preparatory hearing, he may make a ruling as to the admissibil- **J–19** ity of evidence; any other question of law relating to the case or any question as to the severance or joinder of charges. (s.9(3)(b), (c) and (d) of the 1987 Act/s.31(3)(a), (b) and (c) of the 1996 Act)

B2 Under section 9(11) of the 1987 Act/section 35(1) of the 1996 Act the defence or the prosecution may appeal to the CACD (and ultimately to the House of Lords) against such a ruling, but only with the leave of the trial judge, single judge or the full court. As to the scope of a judge's powers in relation to a preparatory hearing and thus the extent of appeal rights, see *R. v. H* (§ 7–310 in the main work).

B3 If the trial date is imminent and the application is urgent, the Registrar should be notified so that he may consider referring the application directly to the full court and make arrangements for listing.

B4 If an application for leave to appeal is made to the trial judge, it should be made orally immediately after the ruling, or within two business days by serving a notice of an application on the appropriate officer of the Crown Court and all parties directly affected: rule 66.4. Notice of appeal or application for leave to appeal [Form NG (Prep)] is to be served on the Registrar, the Crown Court and the parties within five business days of the ruling or the trial judge's decision whether to grant leave: rule 66.2.

B5 The notice and grounds of appeal having been served on the other parties, grounds of opposition should be served in a respondent's notice [Form RN (Prep)] within five business days of service of the appeal notice: rule 66.5.

B6 Defence representatives are usually covered by the Crown Court representation order if one is in force (*Access to Justice Act* 1999, Sched. 3, para. 2(2)).

B7 If the relevant time limits are not complied with, the court has power to grant an extension of time, but cogent grounds in support of the application will be required. Where a single judge refuses leave to appeal or an extension of time within which to serve a notice, the application may be renewed for determination by the full court by serving the notice of refusal, appropriately completed, upon the Registrar within five business days of the refusal being served (rule 66.7).

C. Appeals by a Prosecutor Against a "Terminating" Ruling

Criminal Justice Act 2003, s.58 [Part 67 Criminal Procedure Rules 2007]

J–20

C1 Section 58 of the 2003 Act gives the prosecution a right of appeal in relation to a "terminating" ruling: in effect where the prosecution agrees to the defendant's acquittal if the appeal against the ruling is not successful (*R. v. Y.* [2008] 1 Cr.App.R. 34). This is wide enough to encompass a case-management decision (*R. v. Clarke* [2008] 1 Cr.App.R. 33).

C2 There is no right of appeal in respect of a ruling that the jury be discharged or a ruling in respect of which there is a right of appeal to the Court of Appeal by virtue of another enactment (s.57(2)). The prosecution should therefore consider whether there is a right of appeal under section 9 of the *CJA* 1987 or section 35 of the *CPIA* 1996.

C3 The prosecution must inform the court that it intends to appeal or request an adjournment to consider whether to appeal (s.58(4)), which will be until the next business day (rule 67.2(2)). The judge has a discretion to adjourn for longer if there is a real reason for doing so (*R. v. H.* [2008] EWCA Crim 483). The prosecution can then ask the trial judge to grant leave to appeal (rule 67.5), although leave to appeal can be granted by the trial judge, the single judge or the full court. The Crown must give the undertaking (as to the defendant's acquittal if the appeal is abandoned or leave to appeal is not obtained) at the time when it informs the court of its intention to appeal. The failure to give it then is fatal to an application to the Court of Appeal for leave: s.58(8); *R. v. Arnold* [2008] R.T.R. 25.

C4 Whether or not leave is granted, the trial judge must then decide if the appeal is to be expedited and if so, adjourn the case. If he decides that the appeal should not be expedited, then he can adjourn the case or discharge the jury (s.59). Leave should be granted only where the trial judge considers there is a real prospect of success and not in an attempt to speed up the hearing of the appeal (*R. v. J.G.* [2006] EWCA Crim 3276).

C5 Whether the appeal is expedited or not affects the time limits for service of the notice of appeal [Form NG (Pros)] and respondent's notice [Form RN(Pros)]. If expedited, the appeal notice must be served the next business day after the decision, if not expedited, it must be served within five business days. Similar time limits apply to the service of the respondent's notice. Defence representatives are usually covered by the Crown Court representation order if one is in force (such proceedings being considered incidental within the *Access to Justice Act* 1999, Sched. 3, para. 2(2)). If the relevant time limits are not complied with, the court has power to grant an extension of time.

C6 Expedition does not impose time limits on the Registrar or Court of Appeal. However, if leave has not been granted by the trial judge, the application may be referred to the full court by the Registrar to enable the application and appeal to be heard together to ensure that the matter is dealt with quickly.

C7 The Registrar endeavours to list prosecution appeals where a jury has not been discharged as quickly as possible. He is unlikely to be able to list an appeal in less than a week from the ruling because it is necessary for the prosecution to obtain transcripts, papers to be copied and the judges to read their papers. It is of great assistance if it is anticipated that there is to be an appeal against a ruling where the jury has not been discharged, that a telephone call is made to the Registrar or CAO general office (020 7947 6011) notifying the office even before the appeal notice is sent, so that the list office may be put on notice. The listing of an urgent appeal invariably means that other cases have to be removed from the list.

D. Other Appeals

D1 Prosecution appeal against the making of a confiscation order or where the court declines to make one (save on reconsideration of benefit)

J–21

- S.31 of the *PCA* 2002.
- Parts 71 and 72 of the *Criminal Procedure Rules*.
- From April 1, 2008 only the prosecution can appeal.

- Proceedings are commenced by serving a Form PoCA 1 on the defendant and the Crown Court within 28 days of the decision appealed against. [*Proceeds of Crime Act (Appeals under Part 2) Order* 2003, art. 3(2)(a).]
- A respondent's notice PoCA 2 is to be served on the Registrar of Criminal Appeals and the appellant not later than 14 days after receiving PoCA 1.
- An undischarged Crown Court representation order will cover advice and assistance on the merits of opposing the appeal and drafting the respondent's notice, otherwise an application for a representation order can be made to the Registrar [*Access to Justice Act* 1999, ss.12(2)(b), 26]. In any event, where an application for a representation order is made on PoCA 2, the Registrar will consider a representation order for the hearing.
- Leave to appeal can be granted by a single judge or the full court.

D2 Appeal in relation to a restraint order
- S.43 of the *PCA* 2002.   **J–22**
- Parts 71 and 73 of the *Criminal Procedure Rules*.
- The prosecution or an accredited financial investigator can appeal a refusal to make a restraint order. A person who applied for an order or who is affected by the order can apply to the Crown Court to vary or discharge the order and then appeal that decision to the Court of Appeal.
- Proceedings are commenced by serving a form PoCA 3 on the Crown Court within 14 days of the decision being appealed. PoCA 3 must then be served on any respondent, and on any person who holds realisable property to which the appeal relates, or is affected by the appeal, not later than seven days after the form is lodged at the Crown Court. The documents which are to be served with PoCA 3 are set out in rule 73.2(3).
- A respondent's notice PoCA 4 is to be served on the Registrar not later than 14 days after the respondent is notified that the appellant has leave to appeal or notified that the application for leave and any appeal are to be heard together. PoCA 4 is then to be served on the appellant and any other respondent as soon as is practicable and not later than seven days after it was served on the Registrar.
- An application for a restraint order can be made as soon as a criminal investigation has begun. The proposed defendant may not have been charged: *PCA* 2002, s.40. This affects the type of public funding.
- If a defendant has been charged with a criminal offence connected to the restraint order then the restraint proceedings are regarded as incidental to the criminal proceedings and are treated as criminal proceedings for funding purposes [*Criminal Defence Service (General) (No. 2) Regulations* 2001, reg.3(3)(c)] and the Registrar can grant a representation order if a defendant appeals a decision on an application to vary or discharge the restraint order.
- If the prosecution apply for a restraint order in the Crown Court before the subject of the restraint order has been charged with a criminal offence and the subject of that order wishes to appeal a decision on an application to vary or discharge the restraint order then civil legal aid may be available as these proceedings fall within the *Access to Justice Act* 1999, Sched. 2, para. 3. The Legal Services Commission should be contacted for funding within the Community Legal Service scheme.
- Similarly, a person affected by the order who wishes to appeal a decision on an application to vary or discharge the restraint order should apply to the Legal Services Commission for funding within the Community Legal Service scheme.
- Leave to appeal can be granted by a single judge or full court.

D3 Appeal in relation to a receivership order
- S.65 of the *PCA* 2002.   **J–23**
- Parts 71 and 73 of the *Criminal Procedure Rules*.
- An appeal can be brought by:
  - (a) the person who applied for the order,
  - (b) a person who is affected by the order or,
  - (c) the receiver.
  The orders against which an appeal will lie are:
  - (1) the appointment or non-appointment of a receiver,
  - (2) the powers of a receiver,

(3) an order giving a direction to a receiver, and

(4) the variation or discharge of a receivership order.

- Proceedings are commenced by serving a Form PoCA 3 on the Crown Court within 14 days of the decision being appealed. PoCA 3 must then be served on any respondent and on any person who holds realisable property to which the appeal relates, or is affected by the appeal, not later than seven days after the form is lodged at the Crown Court. The documents which are to be served with PoCA 3 are set out in rule 73.2(3).
- A respondent's notice PoCA 4 is to be served on the Registrar not later than 14 days after the respondent is notified that the appellant has leave to appeal or is notified that the application for leave and any appeal are to be heard together. PoCA 4 is then to be served on the appellant and any other respondent as soon as is practicable and not later than seven days after it was served on the Registrar.
- If a defendant has been charged with a criminal offence connected to a receivership order then the receivership proceedings are regarded as incidental to the criminal proceedings and are treated as criminal proceedings for funding purposes [*Criminal Defence Service (General) (No. 2) Regulations* 2001, reg.3(3)(c)] and the Registrar can grant a representation order if a defendant appeals a decision relating to a receivership order.
- If a management receivership order or an application for such an order is made in the Crown Court before a criminal offence has been charged and a person affected by the order (including the proposed defendant) wishes to appeal a decision then civil legal aid may be available as these proceedings fall within *Access to Justice Act* 1999, Sched. 2, para. 3. The Legal Services Commission should be contacted for funding within the Community Legal Service scheme.
- Leave to appeal can be granted by a single judge or the full court.

D4 Appeal against an order of the Crown Court in the exercise of its jurisdiction to punish for contempt – usually a finding of contempt or sentence for contempt

J–24
- S.13 of the *Administration of Justice Act* 1960.
- Part 68 of the *Criminal Procedure Rules*.
- Anyone dealt with by the Crown Court for contempt may appeal.
- Proceedings are commenced by lodging a Form NG at the Crown Court not more than 28 days after the order to be appealed.
- The Registrar may direct a respondent's notice Form RN or the Crown may serve one if they wish to make representations to the court.
- An undischarged Crown Court representation order will cover advice and assistance on appeal. The Registrar will usually grant a representation order for the hearing: *Access to Justice Act* 1999, s.12(2)(b).
- No leave to appeal is required. The appeal is as of right.
- Appeals occur most frequently when an appellant wishes to appeal a sentence for failing to appear at the Crown Court as the failing to appear is dealt with as if it were contempt.

D5 Appeal against a minimum term set or reviewed by a High Court judge

J–25
- Para. 14 of Schedule 22 to the *CJA* 2003
- Part 68 of the *Criminal Procedure Rules*
- A defendant with a mandatory life sentence imposed before December 18, 2003 who has had his minimum term set or reviewed by a High Court judge can appeal.
- Proceedings are commenced by service of Form NG (MT) on the Registrar not more than 28 days after the decision.
- The Registrar may direct a respondent's notice Form RN or the Crown may serve one if they wish to make representations to the court.
- An application for a representation order can be made to the Registrar [*Access to Justice Act* 1999, s.12(2)(b)].
- Leave to appeal is required and can be granted by the full court or a single judge: *Criminal Justice Act 2003 (Mandatory Life Sentences: Appeals in Transitional Cases) Order* 2005 (S.I. 2005 No. 2798), art. 8.

D6 Attorney General's reference of an unduly lenient sentence

J–26
- S.36 of the *CJA* 1988.

- Part 70 of the *Criminal Procedure Rules*.
- The Attorney General can refer sentences only in relation to specific offences or sentences [*CJA* 1988, ss.35, 36, and *Criminal Justice Act 1988 (Reviews of Sentencing) Order* 2006] including a minimum term, set or reviewed by a High Court judge [*CJA* 2003, Sched. 22, para 15].
- Although rule 70.3(1) implies there is a specific form to commence proceedings, in practice a standard letter with supporting documents is sent by the Attorney General's office no more than 28 days after sentence.
- If the defendant wishes to make representations to the court he must serve a respondent's notice within 14 days of the Registrar serving the application upon him. Again, there is no specific form designated.
- Representation orders are not issued to respond to an Attorney General's reference but a defendant who appears by counsel is entitled to his reasonable costs from central funds. The cost of instructing leading counsel in addition to or instead of junior counsel is generally not considered reasonable unless there is a compelling reason. It is advisable to consult with the Registrar before leading counsel is instructed.
- The leave of the Court of Appeal is required.

D7 Attorney General's reference of a point of law on an acquittal
- S.36 of the *CJA* 1972.   **J–27**
- Part 70 of the *Criminal Procedure Rules*.
- The Attorney General can refer a point of law to the Court of Appeal for an opinion on the acquittal on indictment of the defendant.
- Although rule 70.3(1) implies there is a specific form to commence proceedings, there is no such form and rule 70.3 sets out what should be included in the reference. The defendant should not be identified.
- There is no time limit.
- If the defendant wishes to make representations to the court he must serve a respondent's notice within 28 days of the Registrar serving the application upon him. Again there is no specific form.
- Representation orders are not issued to respond to an Attorney General's reference but a defendant who appears by counsel is entitled to his reasonable costs from central funds.
- Leave is not required.

D8 Appeal against a finding of unfitness to plead or a finding that the accused did the act or made the omission charged
- S.15 of the *CAA* 1968.   **J–28**
- Part 68 of the *Criminal Procedure Rules*.
- The accused can appeal (by the person appointed to represent the accused) against
  — a finding of unfitness to plead (but not fitness to plead as the defendant can appeal any subsequent conviction in the usual way on the basis he was not fit to plead) or
  — that he did the act or made the omission charged or
  — both findings.
  The appeal does not lie until both findings have been made.
- Proceedings are commenced by the service of Form NG on the Crown Court not more than 28 days after the finding made which the accused wishes to appeal.
- The Crown should serve a respondent's notice Form RN if directed by the Registrar or if they wish to make representations to the court.
- There does not appear to be any statutory provision empowering the grant of a representation order. The *Prosecution of Offences Act* 1985, s.19, refers to costs from central funds being available to cover the fees of a person appointed by the Crown Court under section 4A of the *Criminal Procedure (Insanity) Act* 1964. In *R. v. Antoine* ([1999] 2 Cr.App.R 225, CA) this was interpreted to include the costs of an appeal. The *Prosecution of Offences Act* 1985, s.16(4) provides that where the Court of Appeal allows an appeal under Part 1 of the *CAA* 1968 against a finding under the *Criminal Procedure (Insanity) Act* 1964 that the appellant is under a disability, or that he did the act or made the omission charged against him the court may make a defendant's costs order in favour of the accused.
- Leave to appeal may be granted by the Crown Court judge, a single judge or the full court.

D9 Appeal against a verdict of not guilty by reason of insanity
- S.12 of the *CAA* 1968.   **J–29**

- Part 68 of the *Criminal Procedure Rules*.
- The defendant can appeal a verdict of not guilty by reason of insanity.
- Proceedings are commenced by the service of Form NG on the Crown Court not more than 28 days after the verdict.
- The Crown should serve a respondent's notice Form RN if directed by the Registrar or if they wish to make representations to the court.
- There does not appear to be any statutory provision empowering the grant of a representation order. The *Prosecution of Offences Act* 1985, s.16(4), provides that where the Court of Appeal allows an appeal then the court may make a defendant's costs order. If the appeal is not allowed costs from central funds should be available on the same basis as was allowed in *Antoine* (*ante*) in the absence of any statutory provision.
- Leave to appeal may be granted by the Crown Court judge, a single judge or the full court.

D10 Appeal against the order following a verdict of not guilty by reason of insanity or a finding of unfitness to plead

J–30
- S.16A of the *CAA* 1968.
- Part 68 of the *Criminal Procedure Rules*.
- An accused who, as a result of a verdict of not guilty by reason of insanity or a finding of fitness to plead has a hospital order, interim hospital order or supervision order made against him may appeal against the order.
- Proceedings are commenced by the service of Form NG on the Crown Court not more than 28 days after the order.
- [As D9, *ante*.]
- [As D9, *ante*.]
- [As D9, *ante*.]

D11 Appeal against review of sentence

J–31
- S.74(8) of the *SOCPA* 2005.
- Part 68 of the *Criminal Procedure Rules*.
- A defendant or specified prosecutor may appeal.
- Proceedings are commenced by serving a Form NG (RD) on the Crown Court not more than 28 days after the review.
- A respondent's notice Form RN should be served if directed by the Registrar or if the respondent wishes to make representations to the Court.
- An application for a representation order can be made to the Registrar: *Access to Justice Act* 1999, s.12(2)(b).
- Leave to appeal can be granted by the single judge or full court [*Serious Organised Crime and Police Act 2005 (Appeals under section 74) Order* 2006 (S.I. 2006 No. 2135)].

D12 Appeal against an order for trial by jury of sample counts

J–32
- S.18 of the *Domestic Violence, Crime and Victims Act* 2004.
- Part 66 of the *Criminal Procedure Rules*.
- The defendant can appeal.
- An application for the jury to try some counts as sample counts and the judge to try the remainder if the jury convict, must be determined at a preparatory hearing and section 18 confers rights of interlocutory appeal. A Form NG (Prep) must be served on the Crown Court, the Registrar and any party directly affected not more than five business days after the order or the Crown Court judge granting or refusing leave. (*For applications to the Crown Court judge, see Part B above.*)
- A respondent's notice Form RN (Prep) should be served if the court directs or the Crown (or any party affected) wants to make representations to the court.
- Defence representatives are usually covered by the Crown Court representation order if one is in force [*Access to Justice Act* 1999, Sched. 3, para. 2(2)].
- The Crown Court Judge, single judge or full court can grant leave to appeal.

D13 Appeal against an order relating to a trial to be conducted without a jury where there is a danger of jury tampering

J–33
- S.9(11) of the *CJA* 1987 and s.35(1) of the *CPIA* 1996.

- Part 66 of the *Criminal Procedure Rules*.
- The prosecution can appeal the refusal to make an order; the defence can appeal the making of an order.
- A Form NG (Prep) must be served on the Crown Court, the Registrar and any party directly affected not more than five business days after the order or the Crown Court judge grants or refuses leave. *(For applications to the Crown Court judge, see Part B above.)*
- A respondent's notice Form RN (Prep) should be served if the court directs or the Crown (or any party affected) wants to make representations to the court.
- Defence representatives are usually covered by the Crown Court representation order if one is in force [*Access to Justice Act* 1999, Sched. 3, para.2 (2)].
- Leave is required. The Crown Court judge, single judge or full court can grant leave to appeal.

D14 Appeal against an order that a trial should continue without a jury or a new trial take place without a jury after jury tampering

- S.47 of the *CJA* 2003.   J–34
- Part 66 of the *Criminal Procedure Rules* (relating to appeals against an order made in a preparatory hearing notwithstanding the ruling will not have been in the context of a preparatory hearing).
- The defendant can appeal.
- As D13, *ante*
- As D13, *ante*
- As D13, *ante*
- As D13, *ante*

D15 Appeal against orders restricting or preventing reports or restricting public access

- S.159 of the *CJA* 1988   J–35
- Part 69 of the *Criminal Procedure Rules*
- A person aggrieved may appeal.
- Applications against orders restricting reporting shall be made within 10 business days after the date on which the order was made by serving Form NG (159) on the Registrar, the Crown Court, the prosecutor and defendant and any other affected person. Applications against orders to restrict public access must be made the next business day after the order was made. If advance notice of an order restricting public access is given, then advance notice of an intention to appeal may be made not more than five business days after the advance notice is displayed.
- A person on whom an appeal notice is served should serve a respondent's notice Form RN (159) within three business days if he wishes to make representations to the court or the court so directs.
- The court may make such order as to costs as it thinks fit (*CJA* 1988, s.159(5)(c)), but not out of central funds – *Holden v. CPS (No. 2)* [1994] 1 A.C. 22, HL.
- A single judge or the full court can grant leave to appeal: *CAA* 1968, s.31(2B).
- Applications for leave to appeal and appeals in relation to reporting restrictions may be heard in private (rule 65.6 (1)). Applications for leave to appeal and appeals relating to restricting public access must be determined without a hearing (rule 65.6(3)).

D16 Appeal against a wasted costs order and appeal against a third party costs order

- Regulation 3C (costs wasted) and 3E (third party costs) of the *Costs in Criminal Cases (General)*   J–36 *Regulations* 1986.
- A legal or other representative against whom a wasted costs order has been made in the Crown Court or a third party against whom a third party costs order has been made may appeal.
- Notice of appeal should be served on the Crown Court within 21 days of the order being made. There is no specific form. The notice should be served on any interested party (including, if appropriate, the Ministry of Justice).
- Any interested party can make representations orally or in writing.
- There is no power to grant a representation order or to order costs out of central funds as these proceedings are civil in nature.
- Leave to appeal is not required.

D17 Appeal relating to serious crime prevention orders

J–37
- S.24 of the *SCA* 2007.
- Part 68 of the *Criminal Procedure Rules*.
- A person subject to the order, an applicant authority or anyone given the opportunity to make representations at the Crown Court about the making, refusal to make, variation or non-variation of an order may appeal.
- Proceedings are commenced by the service of Form NG (SCPO) on the Crown Court not more than 28 days after the order.
- A respondent's notice Form RN (SCPO) should be served if directed by the Registrar or if the respondent wishes to make representations to the court.
- Proceedings before the Crown Court or the Court of Appeal relating to serious crime prevention orders and arising by virtue of section 19, 20, 21 or 24 of the *SCA* 2007 are criminal proceedings for the purposes of section 12(2)(g) of the *Access to Justice Act* 1999 [see the *Criminal Defence Service (General) (No. 2) (Amendment) Regulations* (S.I. 2008 No. 725)]. Accordingly, the Registrar may grant a representation order to a person subject to the order. A person who made representations at the Crown Court can apply to the LSC for funding. The court has discretion to order costs as it thinks fit [*Serious Crime Act 2007 (Appeals under section 24) Order* 2008 (S.I. 2008 No. 1863), Pt 3].
- Leave to appeal can be granted by the Crown Court judge, full court or single judge [S.I. 2008 No. 1863, art. 9].

D18 Appeal against the non-making of a football banning order

J–38
- S.14A(5A) of the *Football Spectators Act* 1989.
- Part 68 of the *Criminal Procedure Rules*.
- The prosecution can appeal.
- The appeal notice should be served on the Crown Court within 28 days of the decision not to make an order. However, there is no designated form.
- A respondent's notice should be served if directed by the Registrar or if the respondent wishes to make representations to the court. However, again there is no designated form.
- An application for a representation order may be made to the Registrar – *Access to Justice Act* 1999, s.12(2)(b).
- Currently, the Court of Appeal has been given no powers to deal with these appeals.

E. APPLICATION FOR A RETRIAL FOR A SERIOUS OFFENCE

E1 Application by a prosecutor to quash an acquittal and seek a retrial for a qualifying offence

S.76(1) of the Criminal Justice Act 2003 [Part 41 of the Criminal Procedure Rules]

J–39
E1–1 There must be new and compelling evidence and it must be in the interests of justice for the acquitted person to be retried for a qualifying offence as listed in the *CJA* 2003, Sched. 5, Pt 1 (*CJA* 2003, ss.78, 79: see *R. v. Dunlop* [2007] 1 Cr.App.R. 8, and *R. v. Miell* [2008] 1 Cr.App.R. 23).

E1–2 Proceedings can begin in one of two ways.

(1) By serving notice of the application under section 76 on the Court of Appeal and within two days serving the notice on the acquitted person (s.80). This notice charges him with the offence. It requires the personal written consent of the Director of Public Prosecutions (DPP) (s.76(3)). If the acquitted person is not in custody the prosecution can ask the Crown Court to issue:
   (i) a summons for the acquitted person to appear before the Court of Appeal for the hearing of the application or
   (ii) a warrant for his arrest (s.89(3)).
   Once arrested on the warrant the acquitted person must be brought before the Crown Court within 48 hours (s.89(6)).

(2) An acquitted person may be charged with the offence before an application under section 76 has been made. This may be after an arrest in an investigation authorised by the DPP (s.85(2)) or where no authorisation has been given, after arrest under a warrant issued by a justice of the peace (s.87(1)). Having been charged, the acquitted person must be brought before the Crown Court to consider bail within 24 hours (s.88(2)). He can then be remanded in custody or on bail for 42 days whilst an application under s.76 is prepared: s.88(6) unless an extension is granted

under subsection (8). Once a notice of application under section 76 has been served, stating that the acquitted person has previously been charged with the offence, the acquitted person must be brought before the Crown Court to consider bail within 48 hours of the notice being given to the Registrar, if the acquitted person is already in custody under secton 88 (*ante*) (s.89(2)).

E1–3 Thus in either case, bail is dealt with largely by the Crown Court. The Court of Appeal only considers bail on the adjournment of the hearing of the application under section 76 (s.90(1)).

E1–4 The notice ["Notice of a s.76 application required by s.80(1) *Criminal Justice Act* 2003"] should where practicable be accompanied by the witness statements which are relied on as the new and compelling evidence, the original witness statements, unused statements, indictment, paper exhibits from the original trial, any relevant transcripts from the original trial and any other documents relied on: rule 41.2(2).

E1–5 An acquitted person who wants to oppose a section 76 application must serve a response ["Response of the acquitted person under s.80 *Criminal Justice Act* 2003"] not more than 28 days after receiving the notice: rule 41.3(2).

E2 Application by a prosecutor for a determination whether a foreign acquittal is a bar to a trial and if so, an order that it not be a bar

S.76(2) of the Criminal Justice Act 2003 [Part 41 of the Criminal Procedure Rules]

E2–1 The prosecution can apply, with the personal written consent of the DPP (s.76(3)) for a de-　**J–40** termination whether an acquittal outside the UK is a bar to the acquitted person being tried in England and Wales and if it is found to be so, an order that the acquittal not be a bar. Proceedings can begin in the same way as for an application under section 76(1).

E3 Application for restrictions on publication relating to an application under section 76

S.82 of the Criminal Justice Act 2003 [Part 41 of the Criminal Procedure Rules]

E3–1 An application can be made by the DPP for reporting restrictions. This can be made after a　**J–41** notice of an application for a retrial has been made and may also be made by the court of its own motion (s.82(5)). An application can also be made by the DPP for reporting restrictions before a notice of an application for a retrial if an investigation has been commenced: s.82(6). The application for reporting restrictions must be served on the Registrar ["Application for restrictions on publication under s.82 *Criminal Justice Act* 2003"] and (usually) the acquitted person (rule 41.8(1)).

E3–2 A party who wants to vary or revoke an order for restrictions onpublication under section 82(7) may apply to the Court of Appeal in writing at any time after the order was made (rule 41.9(1)).

E4 Representation orders

E4–1 The Registrar will usually grant a representation order to the acquitted person for solicitors　**J–42** and counsel to respond to any of the above applications.

APPENDIX K

Guidelines issued by the Sentencing Guidelines Council and by the Sentencing Council for England and Wales

901

I. GUIDELINES

A. Reduction in Sentence for a Guilty Plea

Guideline

Contents

K–1   Foreword

    A   Statutory provisions

    B   Statement of purpose

    C   Application of the reduction principle

    D   Determining the level of reduction

    E   Withholding a reduction

    F   Application to sentencing for murder

    G   Application to other indeterminate sentences

        Annex 1

Foreword

K–2   One of the first guidelines to be issued by the Sentencing Guidelines Council related to the statutory obligation to take account of any guilty plea when determining sentence. As set out in the foreword to that guideline[1], the intention was "to promote consistency in sentencing by providing clarity for courts, court users and victims so that everyone knows exactly what to expect". Prior to that guideline there had been different understandings of the purpose of the reduction and the extent of any reduction given.

Since the guideline was issued, there has been much greater clarity but there still remain concerns about some of the content of the guideline and about the extent to which the guideline has been consistently applied. Accordingly the council has undertaken a review of the guideline (in accordance with the statutory obligation placed upon it to do so from time to time[2]); it has also requested that the Judicial Studies Board consider further ways in which judicial training can incorporate the guideline.

The council is extremely grateful to the Sentencing Advisory Panel for the speed and thoroughness with which it has prepared its advice following extensive consultation. The council has accepted almost all the recommendations of the panel; the issues and arguments are set out fully in the panel's advice (see www.sentencing-guidelines.gov.uk). This revised guideline applies to all cases sentenced on or after 23 July 2007.

The council has agreed with the panel that the general approach of the guideline is correct in setting out clearly the purpose of the reduction for a guilty plea, in settling for a reduction no greater than one third (with lower levels of reduction where a plea is entered other than at the first reasonable opportunity) and in continuing to provide for a special approach when fixing the minimum term for a life sentence imposed following conviction for murder.

The council has agreed with the panel that some discretion should be introduced to the approach where the prosecution case is "overwhelming".

The council has not accepted the panel's recommendation in relation to circumstances where a magistrates' court is sentencing an offender for a number of offences where the overall maximum imprisonment is six months. The council continues to consider that there must be some incentive to plead guilty in such circumstances; this is consistent with other aspects of the guideline.

The council has not accepted the panel's recommendation in relation to the "capping" of the effect of reduction on very large fines. The number of such fines is very low and the council was not convinced that the arguments were strong enough to justify a departure from the general approach in the guideline not to "cap" the effect of the reduction. In addition, the revised guideline provides guidance as to when the "first reasonable opportunity" is likely to occur in relation to indictable only offences; emphasises that remorse and material assistance provided to prosecuting authorities are separate issues from those to which the guideline applies and makes clear that the approach to calculation of the reduction where an indeterminate sentence is imposed (other than that following conviction for murder) should be the same as that for determinate sentences.

Since the guideline was issued in 2004, there have been changes in the statutory provisions governing the reduction for guilty plea and in those relating to sentences for public protection. The review has provided an opportunity to bring the guideline up to date and those changes have been incorporated.

The council published a draft guideline in accordance with section 170(8) of the *Criminal Justice Act* 2003 inviting responses by 14 March 2007. A response has been received from the Home Affairs Committee, a response has been received from the Attorney General and seven other responses have been received. A summary of the responses and the decisions of the council has been published separately.

Chairman of the Council

July 2007

A. Statutory Provisions

Section 144 *Criminal Justice Act* 2003 provides [the guideline here sets out the text of section 144 of the 2003 Act, set out in the main work at § 5–107]. **K–3**

Section 174(2) *Criminal Justice Act* 2003 provides [the guideline here sets out the text of section 174(2)(d) of the 2003 Act, set out in the main work at § 5–165].

1.1 This guideline applies whether a case is dealt with in a magistrates' court or in the Crown Court and whenever practicable in the youth court (taking into account legislative restrictions such as those relevant to the length of detention and training orders).

1.2 The application of this guideline to sentencers when arriving at the appropriate minimum term for the offence of murder is set out in Section F.

1.3 This guideline can also be found at www.sentencing-guidelines.gov.uk or can be obtained from the Council's Secretariat at 4th Floor, 8–10 Great George Street, London SW1P 3AE.

B. Statement of Purpose

2.1 When imposing a custodial sentence, statute requires that a court must impose the shortest term that is commensurate with the seriousness of the offence(s)[4]. Similarly, when imposing a community order, the restrictions on liberty must be commensurate with the seriousness of the offence(s)[5]. Once that decision is made, a court is required to give consideration to the reduction for any guilty plea. As a result, the final sentence after the reduction for a guilty plea will be less than the seriousness of the offence requires. **K–4**

2.2 A reduction in sentence is appropriate because a guilty plea avoids the need for a trial (thus enabling other cases to be disposed of more expeditiously), shortens the gap between charge and sentence, saves considerable cost, and, in the case of an early plea, saves victims and witnesses from the concern about having to give evidence. The reduction principle derives from the need for the effective administration of justice and not as an aspect of mitigation.

2.3 Where a sentencer is in doubt as to whether a custodial sentence is appropriate, the reduction attributable to a guilty plea will be a relevant consideration. Where this is amongst the factors leading to the imposition of a non-custodial sentence, there will be no need to apply a further reduction on account of the guilty plea. A similar approach is appropriate where the reduction for a guilty plea is amongst the factors leading to the imposition of a financial penalty or discharge instead of a community order.

2.4 When deciding the most appropriate length of sentence, the sentencer should address separately the issue of remorse, together with any other mitigating features, before calculating the reduction for the guilty plea. Similarly, assistance to the prosecuting or enforcement authorities is a separate issue which may attract a reduction in sentence under other procedures; care will need to be taken to ensure that there is no "double counting".

2.5 The implications of other offences that an offender has asked to be taken into consideration should be reflected in the sentence before the reduction for guilty plea has been applied.

2.6 A reduction in sentence should only be applied to the punitive elements of a penalty[6]. The guilty plea reduction has no impact on sentencing decisions in relation to ancillary orders, including orders of disqualification from driving.

C. APPLICATION OF THE REDUCTION PRINCIPLE

K–5   3.1 Recommended approach

> The court decides sentence for the offence(s) taking into account aggravating and mitigating factors and any other offences that have been formally admitted (TICs)
>
> ⇩
>
> The court selects the amount of the reduction by reference to the sliding scale
>
> ⇩
>
> The court applies the reduction
>
> ⇩
>
> When pronouncing sentence the court should usually state what the sentence would have been if there had been no reduction as a result of the guilty plea.

D. DETERMINING THE LEVEL OF REDUCTION

K–6   4.1 The level of reduction should be *a proportion of the total sentence* imposed, with the proportion calculated by reference to the circumstances in which the guilty plea was indicated, in particular the stage in the proceedings. The greatest reduction will be given where the plea was indicated at the "first reasonable opportunity".

4.2 Save where section 144(2) of the 2003 Act applies[7], the level of the reduction will be gauged on a *sliding scale* ranging from a recommended *one third* (where the guilty plea was entered at the first reasonable opportunity in relation to the offence for which sentence is being imposed), reducing to a recommended *one quarter* (where a trial date has been set) and to a recommended *one tenth* (for a guilty plea entered at the 'door of the court' or after the trial has begun). *See diagram below.*

4.3 The level of reduction should reflect the stage at which the offender indicated a *willingness to admit guilt* to the offence for which he is eventually sentenced:

(i) the largest recommended reduction will not normally be given unless the offender indicated willingness to admit guilt at the first reasonable opportunity; when this occurs will vary from case to case (see *Annex 1 for illustrative examples*);

(ii) where the admission of guilt comes later than the first reasonable opportunity, the reduction for guilty plea will normally be less than one third;

(iii) where the plea of guilty comes very late, it is still appropriate to give some reduction;

(iv) if after pleading guilty there is a *Newton* hearing and the offender's version of the circumstances of the offence is rejected, this should be taken into account in determining the level of reduction;

(v) if the not guilty plea was entered and maintained for tactical reasons (such as to retain privileges whilst on remand), a late guilty plea should attract very little, if any, discount.

> **In each category, there is a presumption that the recommended reduction will be given unless there are good reasons for a lower amount.**
>
> | First reasonable opportunity | After a trial date is set | Door of the court/ after trial has begun |
> |---|---|---|
> | ======= \| ============= \| ============= \| | | |
> | **recommended 1/3** | **recommended 1/4** | **recommended 1/10** |

E. Witholding a Reduction

On the basis of dangerousness   **K–7**

5.1   Where a sentence for a "dangerous offender" is imposed under the provisions in the *Criminal Justice Act* 2003, whether the sentence requires the calculation of a minimum term or is an extended sentence, the approach will be the same as for any other determinate sentence (see also section G below)[8].

Where the prosecution case is overwhelming

5.2   The purpose of giving credit is to encourage those who are guilty to plead at the earliest opportunity. Any defendant is entitled to put the prosecution to proof and so every defendant who is guilty should be encouraged to indicate that guilt at the first reasonable opportunity.

5.3   Where the prosecution case is overwhelming, it may not be appropriate to give the full reduction that would otherwise be given. Whilst there is a presumption in favour of the full reduction being given where a plea has been indicated at the first reasonable opportunity, the fact that the prosecution case is overwhelming without relying on admissions from the defendant may be a reason justifying departure from the guideline.

5.4   Where a court is satisfied that a lower reduction should be given for this reason, a recommended reduction of 20% is likely to be appropriate where the guilty plea was indicated at the first reasonable opportunity.

5.5   A court departing from a guideline must state the reasons for doing so[9].

Where the maximum penalty for the offence is thought to be too low

5.6   The sentencer is bound to sentence for the offence with which the offender has been charged, and to which he has pleaded guilty. The sentencer cannot remedy perceived defects (for example an inadequate charge or maximum penalty) by refusal of the appropriate discount.

Where jurisdictional issues arise

(i)   Where sentencing powers are limited to six months' imprisonment despite multiple offences

5.7   When the total sentence for both or all of the offences is six months' imprisonment, a court may determine to impose consecutive sentences which, even allowing for a reduction for a guilty plea where appropriate on each offence, would still result in the imposition of the maximum sentence available. In such circumstances, in order to achieve the purpose for which the reduction principle has been established[10], some modest allowance should normally be given against the total sentence for the entry of a guilty plea.

(ii)   Where a maximum sentence might still be imposed

5.8   Despite a guilty plea being entered which would normally attract a reduction in sentence, a magistrates' court may impose a sentence of imprisonment of 6 months for a single either-way offence where, but for the plea, that offence would have been committed to the Crown Court for sentence.

5.9   Similarly, a detention and training order of 24 months may be imposed on an offender aged under 18 if the offence is one which would but for the plea have attracted a sentence of long-term detention in excess of 24 months under the *Powers of Criminal Courts (Sentencing) Act* 2000, s.91.

F.   Application to Sentencing for Murder

6.1   Murder has always been regarded as the most serious criminal offence and the sentence   **K–8** prescribed is different from other sentences. By law, the sentence for murder is imprisonment (detention) for life and an offender will remain subject to the sentence for the rest of his/her life.

6.2   The decision whether to release the offender from custody during this sentence will be taken by the Parole Board which will consider whether it is safe to release the offender on licence. The court that imposes the sentence is required by law to set a minimum term that has to be served before the Parole Board may start to consider whether to authorise release on licence. If an offender is released, the licence continues for the rest of the offender's life and recall to prison is possible at any time.

6.3   Uniquely, Parliament has set starting points[11] (based on the circumstances of the killing) which a court will apply when it fixes the minimum term. Parliament has further prescribed that, having identified the appropriate starting point, the court must then consider whether to increase or reduce it in the light of aggravating or mitigating factors, some of which are listed in statute. Finally, Parliament specifically provides[12] that the obligation to have regard to any guilty plea applies to the fixing of the minimum term, by making the same statutory provisions that apply to other offences apply to murder without limiting the court's discretion (as it did with other sentences under the *Powers of Criminal Courts (Sentencing) Act* 2000).

6.4   There are important differences between the usual fixed term sentence and the minimum term set following the imposition of the mandatory life sentence for murder. The most significant of these, from the sentencer's point of view, is that a reduction for a plea of guilty in the case of murder will have double the effect on time served in custody when compared with a determinate sentence. This is because a determinate sentence will provide (in most circumstances) for the release of the offender[13] on licence half way through the total sentence whereas in the case of murder a minimum term is the period in custody before consideration is given by the Parole Board to whether release is appropriate.

6.5   Given this difference, the special characteristic of the offence of murder and the unique statutory provision of starting points, careful consideration will need to be given to the extent of any reduction and to the need to ensure that the minimum term properly reflects the seriousness of the offence. Whilst the general principles continue to apply (both that a guilty plea should be encouraged and that the extent of any reduction should reduce if the indication of plea is later than the first reasonable opportunity), the process of determining the level of reduction will be different.

6.6 Approach

K–9
1.   Where a court determines that there should be a whole life minimum term, there will be no reduction for a guilty plea.

2.   In other circumstances,

(a) the court will weigh carefully the overall length of the minimum term taking into account other reductions for which the offender may be eligible so as to avoid a combination leading to an inappropriately short sentence;

(b) where it is appropriate to reduce the minimum term having regard to a plea of guilty, the reduction will not exceed one sixth and will never exceed five years;

(c) the sliding scale will apply so that, where it is appropriate to reduce the minimum term on account of a guilty plea, the maximum reduction (one sixth or five years whichever is the less) is only available where there has been an indication of willingness to plead guilty at the first reasonable opportunity, with a recommended 5% for a late guilty plea;

(d) the court should then review the sentence to ensure that the minimum term accurately reflects the seriousness of the offence taking account of the statutory starting point, all aggravating and mitigating factors and any guilty plea entered.

G.   APPLICATION TO OTHER INDETERMINATE SENTENCES

K–10
7.1   There are other circumstances in which an indeterminate sentence will be imposed. This may be a discretionary life sentence or imprisonment for public protection.

7.2   As with the mandatory life sentence imposed following conviction for murder, the court will be obliged to fix a minimum term to be served before the Parole Board is able to consider whether the offender can be safely released.

7.3   However, the process by which that minimum term is fixed is different from that followed in relation to the mandatory life sentence and requires the court first to determine what the equivalent determinate sentence would have been. Accordingly, the approach to the calculation of the reduction for any guilty plea should follow the process and scale adopted in relation to determinate sentences, as set out in section D above.

Annex 1

First reasonable opportunity

K–11
1.   The critical time for determining the maximum reduction for a guilty plea is the first reasonable opportunity for the defendant to have indicated a willingness to plead guilty. This opportunity will vary with a wide range of factors and the court will need to make a judgement on the particular facts of the case before it.

2.   The key principle is that the purpose of giving a reduction is to recognise the benefits that come from a guilty plea not only for those directly involved in the case in question but also in enabling courts more quickly to deal with other outstanding cases.

3.   This Annex seeks to help courts to adopt a consistent approach by giving examples of circumstances where a determination will have to be made:

(a) the first reasonable opportunity may be the first time that a defendant appears before the court and has the opportunity to plead guilty;

(b) but the court may consider that it would be reasonable to have expected an indication of willingness even earlier, perhaps whilst under interview;

Note: For (a) and (b) to apply, the court will need to be satisfied that the defendant (and any legal adviser) would have had sufficient information about the allegations

(c) where an offence triable either way is committed to the Crown Court for trial and the defendant pleads guilty at the first hearing in that court, the reduction will be less than if there had been an indication of a guilty plea given to the magistrates' court (recommended reduction of one third) but more than if the plea had been entered after a trial date had been set (recommended reduction of one quarter), and is likely to be in the region of 30%;

(d) where an offence is triable only on indictment, it may well be that the first reasonable opportunity would have been during the police station stage; where that is not the case, the first reasonable opportunity is likely to be at the first hearing in the Crown Court;

(e) where a defendant is convicted after pleading guilty to an alternative (lesser) charge to that to which he/she had originally pleaded not guilty, the extent of any reduction will be determined by the stage at which the defendant first formally indicated to the court willingness to plead guilty to the lesser charge and the reason why that lesser charge was proceeded with in preference to the original charge.

[The next paragraph is K–13.]

B. Overarching Principles: Seriousness

Guideline

Contents

Foreword

In accordance with the provisions of section 170(9) *Criminal Justice Act* 2003, the Sentencing **K–14** Guidelines Council issues this guideline as a definitive guideline. By virtue of section 172 of the Act, every court must have regard to a relevant guideline.

The Council was created in 2004 in order to frame Guidelines to assist Courts as they deal with criminal cases across the whole of England and Wales.

The Council has stated that it intends to follow a principled approach to the formulation of guidelines to assist sentencers which will include consideration of overarching and general principles relating to the sentencing of offenders. Following the planned implementation of many of the sentencing provisions in the 2003 Act in April 2005, this guideline deals with the general concept of seriousness in the light of those provisions and considers how sentencers should determine when the respective sentencing thresholds have been crossed when applying the provisions of the Act.

This guideline applies only to sentences passed under the sentencing framework applicable to those aged 18 or over although there are some aspects that will assist courts assessing the seriousness of offences committed by those under 18. The Council has commissioned separate advice from the Sentencing Advisory Panel on the sentencing of young offenders.

This is the first time that it has been possible to produce definitive guidelines not only before new provisions come into force but also before much of the training of judiciary and practitioners.

The Council has appreciated greatly the work of the Sentencing Advisory Panel in preparing the advice on which this guideline has been based and for the many organisations and individuals who have responded so thoughtfully to the consultation of both the Panel and the Council. The advice and this guideline are available on www.sentencing-guidelines.gov.uk or from the Sentencing Guidelines Secretariat. A summary of the responses to the Council's consultation also appears on the website.

Chairman of the Council

December 2004

Seriousness

A. Statutory Provision

K–15   1.1   In every case where the offender is aged 18 or over at the time of conviction, the court must have regard to the five purposes of sentencing contained in section 142(1) *Criminal Justice Act* 2003:

(a) the punishment of offenders

(b) the reduction of crime (including its reduction by deterrence)

(c) the reform and rehabilitation of offenders

(d) the protection of the public

(e) the making of reparation by offenders to persons affected by their offence

1.2   The Act does not indicate that any one purpose should be more important than any other and in practice they may all be relevant to a greater or lesser degree in any individual case—the sentencer has the task of determining the manner in which they apply.

1.3   The sentencer must start by considering the seriousness of the offence, the assessment of which will:

- determine which of the sentencing thresholds has been crossed;
- indicate whether a custodial, community or other sentence is the most appropriate;
- be the key factor in deciding the length of a custodial sentence, the onerousness of requirements to be incorporated in a community sentence and the amount of any fine imposed.

1.4   A court is required to pass a sentence that is commensurate with the seriousness of the offence. The seriousness of an offence is determined by two main parameters; the **culpability** of the offender and the **harm** caused or risked being caused by the offence

1.5   Section 143(1) *Criminal Justice Act* 2003 provides [see § 5–67 in the main work].

B. Culpability

K–16   1.6   Four levels of criminal culpability can be identified for sentencing purposes:

1.7   Where the offender;

(i) has the **intention** to cause harm, with the highest culpability when an offence is planned. The worse the harm intended, the greater the seriousness.

(ii) is **reckless** as to whether harm is caused, that is, where the offender appreciates at least some harm would be caused but proceeds giving no thought to the consequences even though the extent of the risk would be obvious to most people.

(iii) has **knowledge** of the specific risks entailed by his actions even though he does not intend to cause the harm that results.

(iv) is guilty of **negligence**.

Note: *There are offences where liability is strict and no culpability need be proved for the purposes of obtaining a conviction, but the degree of culpability is still important when deciding sentence. The extent to which recklessness, knowledge or negligence are involved in a particular offence will vary.*

C. Harm

K–17   1.8   The relevant provision is widely drafted so that it encompasses those offences where harm is caused but also those where neither individuals nor the community suffer harm but a risk of harm is present.

To individual victims

1.9   The types of harm caused or risked by different types of criminal activity are diverse and victims may suffer physical injury, sexual violation, financial loss, damage to health or psychological distress. There are gradations of harm within all of these categories.

1.10   The nature of harm will depend on personal characteristics and circumstances of the victim and the court's assessment of harm will be an effective and important way of taking into consideration the impact of a particular crime on the victim.

1.11   In some cases no actual harm may have resulted and the court will be concerned with assessing the relative dangerousness of the offender's conduct; it will consider the likelihood of harm occurring and the gravity of the harm that could have resulted.

To the community

1.12   Some offences cause harm to the community at large (instead of or as well as to an individual victim) and may include economic loss, harm to public health, or interference with the administration of justice.

Other types of harm

1.13   There are other types of harm that are more difficult to define or categorise. For example, cruelty to animals certainly causes significant harm to the animal but there may also be a human victim who also suffers psychological distress and/or financial loss.

1.14   Some conduct is criminalised purely by reference to public feeling or social mores. In addition, public concern about the damage caused by some behaviour, both to individuals and to society as a whole, can influence public perception of the harm caused, for example, by the supply of prohibited drugs.

D.   The Assessment of Culpability and Harm

1.15   Section 143(1) makes clear that the assessment of the seriousness of any individual offence **K–18** must take account not only of any harm actually caused by the offence, but also of any harm that was intended to be caused or might foreseeably be caused by the offence.

1.16   Assessing seriousness is a difficult task, particularly where there is an imbalance between culpability and harm:

- sometimes the harm that actually results is greater than the harm intended by the offender;
- in other circumstances, the offender's culpability may be at a higher level than the harm resulting from the offence

1.17   Harm must always be judged in the light of culpability. The precise level of culpability will be determined by such factors as motivation, whether the offence was planned or spontaneous or whether the offender was in a position of trust.

Culpability will be greater if:

- an offender deliberately causes more harm than is necessary for the commission of the offence, or
- where an offender targets a vulnerable victim (because of their old age or youth, disability or by virtue of the job they do).

1.18   Where unusually serious harm results and was unintended and beyond the control of the offender, culpability will be significantly influenced by the extent to which the harm could have been foreseen.

1.19   If much **more** harm, or much **less** harm has been caused by the offence than the offender intended or foresaw, the culpability of the offender, depending on the circumstances, may be regarded as carrying greater or lesser weight as appropriate.

The culpability of the offender in the particular circumstances of an individual case should be the initial factor in determining the seriousness of an offence.

(i) Aggravating factors

1.20   Sentencing guidelines for a particular offence will normally include a list of aggravating **K–19** features which, if present in an individual instance of the offence, would indicate *either* a higher than usual level of culpability on the part of the offender, *or* a greater than usual degree of harm caused by the offence (or sometimes both).

1.21   The lists below bring together the most important aggravating features with potential application to more than one offence or class of offences. They include some factors (such as the vulnerability of victims or abuse of trust) which are integral features of certain offences; in such cases, the presence of the aggravating factor is already reflected in the penalty for the offence and **cannot be used as justification for increasing the sentence further**. The lists are not intended to be comprehensive and the aggravating factors are not listed in any particular order of priority. On occasions, two or more of the factors listed will describe the same feature of the offence and care needs to be taken to avoid "double counting". Those factors starred with an asterisk are statutory aggravating factors where the statutory provisions are in force. Those marked with a hash are yet to be brought into force but as factors in an individual case are still relevant and should be taken into account.

1.22 **Factors indicating higher culpability:**
- Offence committed whilst on bail for other offences
- Failure to respond to previous sentences
- Offence was racially or religiously aggravated
- Offence motivated by, or demonstrating, hostility to the victim based on his or her sexual orientation (or presumed sexual orientation)
- Offence motivated by, or demonstrating, hostility based on the victim's disability (or presumed disability)
- Previous conviction(s), particularly where a pattern of repeat offending is disclosed
- Planning of an offence
- An intention to commit more serious harm than actually resulted from the offence
- Offenders operating in groups or gangs
- "Professional" offending
- Commission of the offence for financial gain (where this is not inherent in the offence itself)
- High level of profit from the offence
- An attempt to conceal or dispose of evidence
- Failure to respond to warnings or concerns expressed by others about the offender's behaviour
- Offence committed whilst on licence
- Offence motivated by hostility towards a minority group, or a member or members of it
- Deliberate targeting of vulnerable victim(s)
- Commission of an offence while under the influence of alcohol or drugs
- Use of a weapon to frighten or injure victim
- Deliberate and gratuitous violence or damage to property, over and above what is needed to carry out the offence
- Abuse of power
- Abuse of a position of trust

1.23 **Factors indicating a more than usually serious degree of harm:**
- Multiple victims
- An especially serious physical or psychological effect on the victim, even if unintended
- A sustained assault or repeated assaults on the same victim
- Victim is particularly vulnerable
- Location of the offence (for example, in an isolated place)
- Offence is committed against those working in the public sector or providing a service to the public
- Presence of others *e.g.* relatives, especially children or partner of the victim
- Additional degradation of the victim (*e.g.* taking photographs of a victim as part of a sexual offence)
- In property offences, high value (including sentimental value) of property to the victim, or substantial consequential loss (*e.g.* where the theft of equipment causes serious disruption to a victim's life or business)

(ii) Mitigating factors

K–20   1.24 Some factors may indicate that an offender's culpability is **unusually** low, or that the harm caused by an offence is less than usually serious.

1.25 **Factors indicating significantly lower culpability:**
- A greater degree of provocation than normally expected
- Mental illness or disability
- Youth or age, where it affects the responsibility of the individual defendant

• The fact that the offender played only a minor role in the offence

(iii) Personal mitigation

1.26   Section 166(1) *Criminal Justice Act* 2003 makes provision for a sentencer to take account of   **K–21**
any matters that "in the opinion of the court, are relevant in mitigation of sentence".

1.27   When the court has formed an initial assessment of the seriousness of the offence, then it
should consider any offender mitigation. The issue of remorse should be taken into account at this
point along with other mitigating features such as admissions to the police in interview.

(iv) Reduction for a guilty plea

1.28   Sentencers will normally reduce the severity of a sentence to reflect an early guilty plea. This   **K–22**
subject is covered by a separate guideline and provides a sliding scale reduction with a normal
maximum one-third reduction being given to offenders who enter a guilty plea at the first reasonable
opportunity.

1.29   Credit may also be given for ready co-operation with the authorities. This will depend on
the particular circumstances of the individual case.

E.   The Sentencing Thresholds

1.30   Assessing the seriousness of an offence is only the first step in the process of determining the   **K–23**
appropriate sentence in an individual case. Matching the offence to a type and level of sentence is a
separate and complex exercise assisted by the application of the respective threshold tests for
custodial and community sentences.

The custody threshold

1.31   Section 152(2) *Criminal Justice Act* 2003 provides [see § 5–458 in the main work].   **K–24**

1.32   In applying the threshold test, sentencers should note: the clear intention of the threshold
test is to reserve prison as a punishment for the most serious offences;
  • it is impossible to determine definitively which features of a particular offence make it serious
    enough to merit a custodial sentence;
  • passing the custody threshold does not mean that a custodial sentence should be deemed inevi-
    table, and custody can still be avoided in the light of personal mitigation or where there is a
    suitable intervention in the community which provides sufficient restriction (by way of punish-
    ment) while addressing the rehabilitation of the offender to prevent future crime. For example,
    a prolific offender who currently could expect a short custodial sentence (which, in advance of
    custody plus, would have no provision for supervision on release) might more appropriately
    receive a suitable community sentence.

1.33   The approach to the imposition of a custodial sentence under the new framework should be
as follows:
  (a) has the custody threshold been passed?
  (b) if so, is it unavoidable that a custodial sentence be imposed?
  (c) if so, can that sentence be suspended? (sentencers should be clear that they would have imposed
      a custodial sentence if the power to suspend had not been available)
  (d) if not, can the sentence be served intermittently?
  (e) if not, impose a sentence which takes immediate effect for the term commensurate with the
      seriousness of the offence.

The threshold for community sentences

1.34   Section 148(1) *Criminal Justice Act* 2003 provides [see § 5–248 in the main work].   **K–25**

1.35   In addition, the threshold for a community sentence can be crossed even though the
seriousness criterion is not met. Section 151 *Criminal Justice Act* 2003 provides that, in relation to an
offender aged 16 or over on whom, on three or more previous occasions, sentences had been passed
consisting only of a fine, a community sentence may be imposed (if it is in the interests of justice) despite the fact that the seriousness of the current offence (and others associated with it) might not warrant such a sentence.

1.36   Sentencers should consider all of the disposals available (within or below the threshold
passed) at the time of sentence before reaching the provisional decision to make a community

sentence, so that, even where the threshold for a community sentence has been passed, a financial penalty or discharge may still be an appropriate penalty.

Summary

K-26   1.37   It would not be feasible to provide a form of words or to devise any formula that would provide a general solution to the problem of where the custody threshold lies. Factors vary too widely between offences for this to be done. It is the task of guidelines for individual offences to provide more detailed guidance on what features within that offence point to a custodial sentence, and also to deal with issues such as sentence length, the appropriate requirements for a community sentence or the use of appropriate ancillary orders.

Having assessed the seriousness of an individual offence, sentencers must consult the sentencing guidelines for an offence of that type for guidance on the factors that are likely to indicate whether a custodial sentence or other disposal is most likely to be appropriate.

F.   PREVALENCE

K-27   1.38   The seriousness of an individual case should be judged on its own dimensions of harm and culpability rather than as part of a collective social harm. It is legitimate for the overall approach to sentencing levels for particular offences to be guided by their cumulative effect. However, it would be wrong to further penalise individual offenders by increasing sentence length for committing an individual offence of that type.

1.39   There may be exceptional local circumstances that arise which may lead a court to decide that prevalence should influence sentencing levels. The pivotal issue in such cases will be the harm being caused to the community. It is essential that sentencers both have supporting evidence from an external source (for example the local Criminal Justice Board) to justify claims that a particular crime is prevalent in their area and are satisfied that there is a compelling need to treat the offence more seriously than elsewhere.

The key factor in determining whether sentencing levels should be enhanced in response to prevalence will be the level of harm being caused in the locality. Enhanced sentences should be exceptional and in response to exceptional circumstances. Sentencers must sentence within the sentencing guidelines once the prevalence has been addressed. Having assessed the seriousness of an individual offence, sentencers must consult the sentencing guidelines for an offence of that type for guidance on the factors that are likely to indicate whether a custodial sentence or other disposal is most likely to be appropriate.

Published by the Sentencing Guidelines Secretariat, December 2004

C.   NEW SENTENCES: CRIMINAL JUSTICE ACT 2003

Guideline

FOREWORD

K-28   In accordance with the provisions of section 170(9) *Criminal Justice Act* 2003, the Sentencing Guidelines Council issues this guideline as a definitive guideline. By virtue of section 172 of the Act, every court must have regard to a relevant guideline.

The Council was created in 2004 in order to frame Guidelines to assist Courts as they deal with criminal cases across the whole of England and Wales.

This guideline relates to the new sentencing framework introduced by the *Criminal Justice Act* 2003, which affects the nature of community and custodial sentences. Only those sentences and related provisions which are expected to come into force by April 2005 are dealt with in this guideline. It will be followed by further guidelines in due course. This is an unusual guideline since it covers a range of sentences outside the context of individual offences and does so in readiness for the coming into force of the statutory provisions creating the sentences. It is designed with the object of ensuring a consistent approach when the sentences become available.

This guideline applies only to sentences passed under the sentencing framework applicable to those aged 18 or over.

The guideline is divided into two sections:

- Sections 1 covers the practical aspects of implementing the non-custodial powers namely the new community sentence and the new form of deferred sentence;

- Section 2 deals with the new custodial sentence provisions relating to suspended sentences, prison sentences of 12 months or more, and intermittent custody.[1]

The Act also contains an extensive range of provisions to protect the public from dangerous offenders. These will be dealt with separately.

The Advice of the Sentencing Advisory Panel to the Council (published on 20th September 2004) has been broadly accepted by the Council and forms the basis of this guideline. Further information on the issues covered in this guideline can be found in that Advice or in the discussion document that preceded it. All these documents are available on www.sentencing-guidelines.gov.uk or from the Sentencing Guidelines Secretariat.

Chairman of the Council

December 2004

SECTION 1 PART 1—COMMUNITY SENTENCES

A. STATUTORY PROVISIONS

(i) The thresholds for community sentence

K–30   1.1.1   Seriousness—Section 148 *Criminal Justice Act* 2003 [sets out subsection (1), as to which, see § 5–248 in the main work].

1.1.2   Persistent offenders—Section 151 *Criminal Justice Act* 2003 [sets out subsections (1) and (2), as to which, see § 5–252 in the main work].

(ii) The sentences available

K–31   1.1.3   Meaning of community sentence—Section 147 *Criminal Justice Act* 2003 [sets out subsection (1), as to which, see § 5–247 in the main work].

1.1.4   Offenders aged 16 or over—Section 177 *Criminal Justice Act* 2003 [sets out subsections (1) to (4), as to which, see § 5–253 in the main work].

(iii) Determining which orders to make & requirements to include

K–32   1.1.5   Suitability—Section 148 *Criminal Justice Act* 2003 [sets out subsection (2), as to which see § 5–248 in the main work].

1.1.6   Restrictions on liberty—Section 148 *Criminal Justice Act* 2003 [sets out subsection (1), as to which see § 5–248 in the main work].

1.1.7   Compatibility—Section 177 *Criminal Justice Act* 2003 [sets out subsection (6), as to which see § 5–253 in the main work].

(iv) Electronic monitoring

K–33   1.1.8   Section 177 *Criminal Justice Act* 2003 [sets out subsections (3) and (4), as to which see § 5–253 in the main work].

B. IMPOSING A COMMUNITY SENTENCE—THE APPROACH

K–34   1.1.9   On pages 8 and 9 of the seriousness guideline the two thresholds for the imposition of a community sentence are considered. Sentencers must consider all of the disposals available (within or below the threshold passed) at the time of sentence, and reject them before reaching the provisional decision to make a community sentence, so that even where the threshold for a community sentence has been passed a financial penalty or discharge may still be an appropriate penalty. Where an offender has a low risk of reoffending, particular care needs to be taken in the light of evidence that indicates that there are circumstances where inappropriate intervention can increase the risk of reoffending rather than decrease it. In addition, recent improvements in enforcement of financial penalties make them a more viable sentence in a wider range of cases.

1.1.10   Where an offender is being sentenced for a non-imprisonable offence or offences, great care will be needed in assessing whether a community sentence is appropriate since failure to comply could result in a custodial sentence.

1.1.11   Having decided (in consultation with the Probation Service where appropriate) that a community sentence is justified, the court must decide which requirements should be included in the community order. The requirements or orders imposed will have the effect of restricting the offender's liberty, whilst providing punishment in the community, rehabilitation for the offender, and/or ensuring that the offender engages in reparative activities.

The key issues arising are:
(i) which requirements to impose;
(ii) how to make allowance for time spent on remand; and
(iii) how to deal with breaches.

(i) Requirements

K–35   1.1.12   When deciding which requirements to include, the court must be satisfied on three matters—

(i) that the **restriction on liberty is commensurate with the seriousness** of the offence(s);[2]

(ii) that the **requirements are the most suitable** for the offender;[3] and

(iii) that, where there are two or more requirements included, they are **compatible with each other.**[4]

1.1.13   Sentencers should have the possibility of breach firmly in mind when passing sentence for the original offence. If a court is to reflect the seriousness of an offence, there is little value in setting requirements as part of a community sentence that are not demanding enough for an offender. On the other hand, there is equally little value in imposing requirements that would "set an offender up to fail" and almost inevitably lead to sanctions for a breach.

In community sentences, the guiding principles are proportionality and suitability. Once a court has decided that the offence has crossed the community sentence threshold and that a community sentence is justified, the *initial* **factor in defining which requirements to include in a community sentence should be the seriousness of the offence committed.**

1.1.14   This means that "seriousness" is an important factor in deciding whether the court chooses the low, medium or high range (see below) but, having taken that decision, selection of the content of the order within the range will be determined by a much wider range of factors.

- **Sentencing ranges must remain flexible enough to take account of the suitability of the offender, his or her ability to comply with particular requirements and their availability in the local area.**
- **The justification for imposing a community sentence in response to persistent petty offending is the persistence of the offending behaviour rather than the seriousness of the offences being committed. The requirements imposed should ensure that the restriction on liberty is proportionate to the seriousness of the offending, to reflect the fact that the offences, of themselves, are not sufficiently serious to merit a community sentence.**

(a) Information for sentencers

1.1.15   In many cases, a pre-sentence report[5] will be pivotal in helping a sentencer decide **K-36** whether to impose a custodial sentence or whether to impose a community sentence and, if so, whether particular requirements, or combinations of requirements, are suitable for an individual offender. The court must always ensure (especially where there are multiple requirements) that the restriction on liberty placed on the offender is proportionate to the seriousness of the offence committed.[6] The court must also consider the likely effect of one requirement on another, and that they do not place conflicting demands upon the offender.[7]

1.1.16   The council supports the approach proposed by the panel at paragraph 78 of its Aadvice that, having reached the provisional view that a community sentence is the most appropriate disposal, the sentencer should request a pre-sentence report, indicating which of the three sentencing ranges is relevant and the purpose(s) of sentencing that the package of requirements is required to fulfil. Usually the most helpful way for the court to do this would be to produce a written note for the report writer, copied on the court file. If it is known that the same tribunal and defence advocate will be present at the sentencing hearing and a probation officer is present in court when the request for a report is made, it may not be necessary to commit details of the request to writing. However, events may change during the period of an adjournment and it is good practice to ensure that there is a clear record of the request for the court. These two factors will guide the Probation Service in determining the nature and combination of requirements that may be appropriate and the onerousness and intensity of those requirements. A similar procedure should apply when ordering a pre-sentence report when a custodial sentence is being considered.

1.1.17   There will be occasions when any type of report may be unnecessary despite the intention to pass a community sentence though this is likely to be infrequent. A court could consider dispensing with the need to obtain a pre-sentence report for adult offenders—

- where the offence falls within the LOW range of seriousness (see pp.9–10); and
- where the sentencer was minded to impose a single requirement, such as an exclusion requirement (where the circumstances of the case mean that this would be an appropriate disposal without electronic monitoring); and
- where the sentence will not require the involvement of the Probation Service, for example an electronically monitored curfew (subject to the court being satisfied that there is an appropriate address at which the curfew can operate).

(b) Ranges of sentence within the community sentence band

1.1.18   To enable the court to benefit from the flexibility that community sentences provide and **K-37** also to meet its statutory obligations, any structure governing the use of community requirements must allow the courts to choose the most appropriate sentence for each individual offender.

1.1.19   Sentencers have a statutory obligation to pass sentences that are commensurate with the seriousness of an offence. However, within the range of sentence justified by the seriousness of the offence(s), courts will quite properly consider those factors that heighten the risk of the offender committing further offences or causing further harm with a view to lessening that risk. The extent to which requirements are imposed must be capable of being varied to ensure that the restriction on liberty is commensurate with the seriousness of the offence.

1.1.20   The council recognises that it would be helpful for sentencers to have a framework to help them decide on the most appropriate use of the new community sentence. While there is no single guiding principle, the seriousness of the offence that has been committed is an important factor. Three sentencing ranges (low, medium and high) within the community sentence band can be identified. It is not possible to position particular types of offence at firm points within the three ranges because the seriousness level of an offence is largely dependent upon the culpability of the offender and this is uniquely variable. The difficulty is particularly acute in relation to the medium range where it is clear that requirements will need to be tailored across a relatively wide range of offending behaviour.

1.1.21   In general terms, the lowest range of community sentence would be for those offenders whose offence was relatively minor within the community sentence band and would include persistent petty offenders whose offences only merit a community sentence by virtue of failing to respond to the previous imposition of fines. Such offenders would merit a 'light touch' approach, for example, normally a single requirement such as a short period of unpaid work, or a curfew, or a prohibited activity requirement or an exclusion requirement (where the circumstances of the case mean that this would be an appropriate disposal without electronic monitoring).

1.1.22   The top range would be for those offenders who have only just fallen short of a custodial sentence and for those who have passed the threshold but for whom a community sentence is deemed appropriate.

1.1.23   In all three ranges there must be sufficient flexibility to allow the sentence to be varied to take account of the suitability of particular requirements for the individual offender and whether a particular requirement or package of requirements might be more effective at reducing any identified risk of re-offending. It will fall to the sentencer to ensure that the sentence strikes the right balance between proportionality and suitability.

There should be three sentencing ranges (low, medium and high) within the community sentence band based upon seriousness.

It is not intended that an offender necessarily progress from one range to the next on each sentencing occasion. The decision as to the appropriate range each time is based upon the seriousness of the new offence(s).

The decision on the nature and severity of the requirements to be included in a community sentence should be guided by:

  (i)   the assessment of offence seriousness (low, medium or high);

  (ii)   the purpose(s) of sentencing the court wishes to achieve;

  (iii)   the risk of re-offending;

  (iv)   the ability of the offender to comply, and

  (v)   the availability of requirements in the local area.

The resulting restriction on liberty must be a proportionate response to the offence that was committed.

1.1.24   Below we set out a non-exhaustive description of examples of requirements that might be appropriate in the three sentencing ranges. These examples focus on punishment in the community, although it is recognised that not all packages will necessarily need to include a punitive requirement. There will clearly be other requirements of a rehabilitative nature, such as a treatment requirement or an accredited programme, which may be appropriate depending on the specific needs of the offender and assessment of suitability. Given the intensity of such interventions, it is expected that these would normally only be appropriate at medium and high levels of seriousness, and where assessed as having a medium or high risk of re-offending. In addition, when passing sentence in any one of the three ranges, the court should consider whether a rehabilitative intervention such as a programme requirement, or a restorative justice intervention might be suitable as an additional or alternative part of the sentence.

Low

K–38   1.1.25   For offences only just crossing the community sentence threshold (such as persistent petty offending, some public order offences, some thefts from shops, or interference with a motor vehicle, where the seriousness of the offence or the nature of the offender's record means that a discharge or fine is inappropriate).

1.1.26   Suitable requirements might include:

• 40 to 80 hours of unpaid work; or

• a curfew requirement within the lowest range (*e.g.* up to 12 hours per day for a few weeks); or

• an exclusion requirement (where the circumstances of the case mean that this would be an appropriate disposal without electronic monitoring) lasting a few months; or

• a prohibited activity requirement; or

• an attendance centre requirement (where available).

1.1.27   Since the restriction on liberty must be commensurate with the seriousness of the offence, particular care needs to be taken with this band to ensure that this obligation is complied with. In most cases, only one requirement will be appropriate and the length may be curtailed if additional requirements are necessary.

Medium

1.1.28   For offences that obviously fall within the community sentence band such as handling   **K–39** stolen goods worth less than £1000 acquired for resale or somewhat more valuable goods acquired for the handler's own use, some cases of burglary in commercial premises, some cases of taking a motor vehicle without consent, or some cases of obtaining property by deception.

1.1.29   Suitable requirements might include:

• a greater number (*e.g.* 80 to 150) of hours of unpaid work; or

• an activity requirement in the middle range (20 to 30 days); or

• a curfew requirement within the middle range (*e.g.* up to 12 hours for 2–3 months); or

• an exclusion requirement lasting in the region of six months or

• a prohibited activity requirement.

1.1.30   Since the restriction on liberty must be commensurate with the seriousness of the offence, particular care needs to be taken with this band to ensure that this obligation is complied with.

High

1.1.31   For offences that only just fall below the custody threshold or where the custody threshold   **K–40** is crossed but a community sentence is more appropriate in all the circumstances, for example some cases displaying the features of a standard domestic burglary committed by a first-time offender.

1.1.32   More intensive sentences which combine two or more requirements may be appropriate at this level. Suitable requirements might include an unpaid work order of between 150 and 300 hours; an activity requirement up to the maximum 60 days; an exclusion order lasting in the region of 12 months; a curfew requirement of up to 12 hours a day for 4–6 months.

(c) Electronic monitoring

1.1.33   The court must also consider whether an electronic monitoring requirement[8] should be   **K–41** imposed which is mandatory[9] in some circumstances.

Electronic monitoring should be used with the primary purpose of promoting and monitoring compliance with other requirements, in circumstances where the punishment of the offender and/or the need to safeguard the public and prevent re-offending are the most important concerns.

(d) Recording the sentence imposed

1.1.34   Under the new framework there is only one (generic) community sentence provided by   **K–42** statute. This does not mean that offenders who have completed a community sentence and have then re-offended should be regarded as ineligible for a second community sentence on the basis that this has been tried and failed. Further community sentences, perhaps with different requirements, may well be justified.

1.1.35   Those imposing sentence will wish to be clear about the 'purposes' that the community sentence is designed to achieve when setting the requirements. Sharing those purposes with the offender and Probation Service will enable them to be clear about the goals that are to be achieved.

1.1.36 Any future sentencer must have full information about the requirements that were inserted by the court into the previous community sentence imposed on the offender (including whether it was a low/medium/high level order) and also about the offender's response. This will enable the court to consider the merits of imposing the same or different requirements as part of another community sentence. The requirements should be recorded in such a way as to ensure that they can be made available to another court if another offence is committed.

When an offender is required to serve a community sentence, the court records should be clearly annotated to show which particular requirements have been imposed.

(ii) Time spent on remand

K–43

1.1.37 The court will need to consider whether to give any credit for time spent in custody on remand.[10] (For further detail from the Panel's Advice, see Annex A.)

The court should seek to give credit for time spent on remand (in custody or equivalent status) in all cases. It should make clear, when announcing sentence, whether or not credit for time on remand has been given (bearing in mind that there will be no automatic reduction in sentence once section 67 of the *Criminal Justice Act* 1967 is repealed) and should explain its reasons for not giving credit when it considers either that this is not justified, would not be practical, or would not be in the best interests of the offender.

1.1.38 Where an offender has spent a period of time in custody on remand, there will be occasions where a custodial sentence is warranted but the length of the sentence justified by the seriousness of the offence would mean that the offender would be released immediately. Under the present framework, it may be more appropriate to pass a community sentence since that will ensure supervision on release.

1.1.39 However, given the changes in the content of the second part of a custodial sentence of 12 months or longer, a court in this situation where the custodial sentence would be 12 months or more should, under the new framework, pass a custodial sentence in the knowledge that licence requirements will be imposed on release from custody. This will ensure that the sentence imposed properly reflects the seriousness of the offence.

1.1.40 Recommendations made by the court at the point of sentence will be of particular importance in influencing the content of the licence. This will properly reflect the gravity of the offence(s) committed.

(iii) Breaches

K–44

1.1.41 Where an offender fails, without reasonable excuse, to comply with one or more requirements, the 'responsible officer'[11] can either give a warning or initiate breach proceedings. Where the offender fails to comply without reasonable excuse for the second time within a 12-month period, the 'responsible officer' must initiate proceedings.

1.1.42 In such proceedings the court must[12] either **increase the severity of the existing sentence** (i.e. impose more onerous conditions including requirements aimed at enforcement, such as a curfew or supervision requirement) or **revoke the existing sentence and proceed as though sentencing for the original offence**. The court is required to take account of the circumstances of the breach,[13] which will inevitably have an impact on its response.

1.1.43 In certain circumstances (where an offender has wilfully and persistently failed to comply with an order made in respect of an offence that is not itself punishable by imprisonment), the court can **impose a maximum of 51 weeks custody**.[14]

1.1.44 When increasing the onerousness of requirements, the court must consider the impact on the offender's ability to comply and the possibility of precipitating a custodial sentence for further breach. For that reason, and particularly where the breach occurs towards the end of the sentence, the court should take account of compliance to date and may consider that extending the supervision or operational periods will be more sensible; in other cases it might choose to add punitive or rehabilitative requirements instead. In making these changes the court must be mindful of the legislative restrictions on the overall length of community sentences and on the supervision and operational periods allowed for each type of requirement.

1.1.45 The court dealing with breach of a community sentence should have as its primary objective ensuring that the requirements of the sentence are finished, and this is important if the court is to have regard to the statutory purposes of sentencing. A court that imposes a custodial sentence for breach without giving adequate consideration to alternatives is in danger of imposing a sentence that is not commensurate with the seriousness of the original offence and is solely a punishment for breach. This risks undermining the purposes it has identified as being important. Nonetheless, courts will need to be vigilant to ensure that there is a realistic prospect of the purposes of the order being achieved.

Having decided that a community sentence is commensurate with the seriousness of the offence, the primary objective when sentencing for breach of requirements is to ensure that those requirements are completed.

1.1.46   A court sentencing for breach must take account of the extent to which the offender has complied with the requirements of the community order, the reasons for breach and the point at which the breach has occurred. Where a breach takes place towards the end of the operational period and the court is satisfied that the offender's appearance before the court is likely to be sufficient in itself to ensure future compliance, then given that it is not open to the court to make no order, an approach that the court might wish to adopt could be to re-sentence in a way that enables the original order to be completed properly—for example, a differently constructed community sentence that aims to secure compliance with the purposes of the original sentence.

1.1.47   If the court decides to increase the onerousness of an order, it must give careful consideration, with advice from the Probation Service, to the offender's ability to comply. A custodial sentence should be the last resort, where all reasonable efforts to ensure that an offender completes a community sentence have failed.

- **The Act allows for a custodial sentence to be imposed in response to breach of a community sentence. Custody should be the last resort, reserved for those cases of deliberate and repeated breach where all reasonable efforts to ensure that the offender complies have failed.**
- **Before increasing the onerousness of requirements, sentencers should take account of the offender's ability to comply and should avoid precipitating further breach by overloading the offender with too many or conflicting requirements.**
- **There may be cases where the court will need to consider re-sentencing to a differently constructed community sentence in order to secure compliance with the purposes of the original sentence, perhaps where there has already been partial compliance or where events since the sentence was imposed have shown that a different course of action is likely to be effective.**

SECTION 1 PART 2—DEFERRED SENTENCES

A. Statutory Provisions

1.2.1   Under the existing legislation,[15] a court can defer a sentence for up to six months, provided   **K–45** the offender consents and the court considers that deferring the sentence is in the interests of justice.

1.2.2   The new provisions[16] continue to require the consent of the offender and that the court be satisfied that the making of such a decision is in the interests of justice. However, it is also stated that the power to defer sentence can only be exercised where:

"the offender undertakes to comply with any requirements as to his conduct during the period of the deferment that the court considers it appropriate to impose;".[17]

1.2.3   This enables the court to impose a wide variety of conditions (including a residence requirement).[18] The Act allows the court to appoint the probation service or other responsible person to oversee the offender's conduct during this period and prepare a report for the court at the point of sentence i.e. the end of the deferment period.

1.2.4   As under the existing legislation, if the offender commits another offence during the deferment period the court may have the power to sentence for both the original and the new offence at once. Sentence cannot be deferred for more than six months and, in most circumstances, no more than one period of deferment can be granted.[19]

1.2.5   A significant change is the provision enabling a court to deal with an offender before the end of the period of deferment.[20] For example if the court is satisfied that the offender has failed to comply with one or more requirements imposed in connection with the deferment, the offender can be brought back before the court and the court can proceed to sentence.

B. USE OF DEFERRED SENTENCES

1.2.6   Under the new framework, there is a wider range of sentencing options open to the courts,   **K–46** including the increased availability of suspended sentences, and deferred sentences are likely to be used in very limited circumstances. A deferred sentence enables the court to review the conduct of the defendant before passing sentence, having first prescribed certain requirements. It also provides several opportunities for an offender to have some influence as to the sentence passed—

(a) it tests the commitment of the offender not to re-offend;

(b) it gives the offender an opportunity to do something where progress can be shown within a short period;

(c) it provides the offender with an opportunity to behave or refrain from behaving in a particular way that will be relevant to sentence.

1.2.7   Given the new power to require undertakings and the ability to enforce those undertakings before the end of the period of deferral, the decision to defer sentence should be predominantly for a small group of cases at either the custody threshold or the community sentence threshold where the sentencer feels that there would be particular value in giving the offender the opportunities listed because, if the offender complies with the requirements, a different sentence will be justified at the end of the deferment period. This could be a community sentence instead of a custodial sentence or a fine or discharge instead of a community sentence. It may, rarely, enable a custodial sentence to be suspended rather than imposed immediately.

The use of deferred sentences should be predominantly for a small group of cases close to a significant threshold where, should the defendant be prepared to adapt his behaviour in a way clearly specified by the sentencer, the court may be prepared to impose a lesser sentence.

1.2.8   A court may impose any conditions during the period of deferment that it considers appropriate.[21] These could be specific requirements as set out in the provisions for community sentences,[22] or requirements that are drawn more widely. These should be specific, measurable conditions so that the offender knows exactly what is required and the court can assess compliance; the restriction on liberty should be limited to ensure that the offender has a reasonable expectation of being able to comply whilst maintaining his or her social responsibilities.

1.2.9   Given the need for clarity in the mind of the offender and the possibility of sentence by another court, the court should give a clear indication (and make a written record) of the type of sentence it would be minded to impose if it had not decided to defer and ensure that the offender understands the consequences of failure to comply with the court's wishes during the deferral period.

When deferring sentence, the sentencer must make clear the consequence of not complying with any requirements and should indicate the type of sentence it would be minded to impose. Sentencers should impose specific, measurable conditions that do not involve a serious restriction on liberty.

SECTION 2—CUSTODIAL SENTENCES

PART 1—CUSTODIAL SENTENCES OF 12 MONTHS OR MORE

A. STATUTORY PROVISIONS

K–47

2.1.1   Under existing legislation:

● an adult offender receiving a custodial sentence of at least 12 months and below 4 years will automatically be released at the halfway point and will then be supervised under licence until the three-quarter point of the sentence. [For some, the actual release date may be earlier as a result of release on home detention curfew (HDC).]

● an adult offender receiving a determinate sentence of 4 years or above will be eligible for release from the halfway point and, if not released before, will automatically be released at the two-thirds point. After release, the offender will be supervised under licence until the three-quarter point of the sentence.

2.1.2   Under the new framework, the impact of a custodial sentence will be more severe since the period in custody and under supervision will be for the whole of the sentence term set by the court. Additionally, separate provisions for the protection of the public will be introduced for those offenders designated as "dangerous" under the Act which are designed to ensure that release only occurs when it is considered safe to do so.

2.1.3   Where a prison sentence of 12 months or more is imposed on an offender who is not classi-fied as "dangerous", that offender will be entitled to be released from custody after completing half of the sentence. The whole of the second half of the sentence will be subject to licence requirements. These requirements will be set shortly before release by the Secretary of State (with advice from the Governor responsible for authorising the prisoner's release in consultation with the Probation Ser-vice) but a court will be able to make recommendations at the sentencing stage on the content of those requirements.[23] The conditions that the Secretary of State may attach to a licence are to be prescribed by order.[24]

2.1.4   The Act requires that a custodial sentence for a fixed term should be for the shortest term that is commensurate with the seriousness of the offence.[37]

B. Imposition of custodial sentences of 12 months or more

(i) Length of sentence

2.1.5   The requirement that the second half of a prison sentence will be served in the community subject to conditions imposed prior to release is a major new development and will require offenders to be under supervision for the full duration of the sentence prescribed by the court. The Probation Service will be able to impose a number of complementary requirements on the offender during the second half of a custodial sentence and these are expected to be more demanding and involve a greater restriction on liberty than current licence conditions. **K–48**

2.1.6   As well as restricting liberty to a greater extent, the new requirements will last until the very end of the sentence, rather than to the three-quarter point as at present, potentially making a custodial sentence significantly more demanding than under existing legislation. Breach of these requirements at any stage is likely to result in the offender being returned to custody and this risk continues, therefore, for longer under the new framework than under the existing legislation.

Transitional arrangements

2.1.7   In general, a fixed term custodial sentence of 12 months or more under the new framework will increase the sentence actually served (whether in custody or in the community) since it continues to the end of the term imposed. Existing guidelines issued since 1991 have been based on a different framework and so, in order to maintain consistency between the lengths of sentence under the cur-rent and the new framework, there will need to be some adjustment to the starting points for custodial sentences contained in those guidelines (subject to the special sentences under the 2003 Act where the offender is a "dangerous" offender). **K–49**

2.1.8   This aspect of the guideline will be temporary to overcome the short-term situation where sentencing guidelines (issued since implementation of the reforms to custodial sentences introduced by the *Criminal Justice Act* 1991) are based on a different framework and the new framework has made those sentences more demanding. As new guidelines are issued they will take into account the new framework in providing starting points and ranges of appropriate sentence lengths for offences and an adjustment will not be necessary.

2.1.9   Since there are so many factors that will vary, it is difficult to calculate precisely how much more demanding a sentence under the new framework will be. The Council's conclusion is that the sentencer should seek to achieve the best match between a sentence under the new framework and its equivalent under the old framework so as to maintain the same level of punishment. As a guide, the Council suggests the sentence length should be reduced by in the region of 15%.

2.1.10   The changes in the nature of a custodial sentence will require changes in the way the sentence is announced. Sentencers will need to continue[38] to spell out the practical implications of the sentence being imposed so that offenders, victims and the public alike all understand that the sentence does not end when the offender is released from custody. The fact that a breach of the requirements imposed in the second half of the sentence is likely to result in a return to custody should also be made very clear at the point of sentence.

- **When imposing a fixed term custodial sentence of 12 months or more under the new provi-sions, courts should consider reducing the overall length of the sentence that would have been imposed under the current provisions by in the region of 15%.**
- **When announcing sentence, sentencers should explain the way in which the sentence has been calculated, how it will be served and the implications of non-compliance with licence requirements. In particular, it needs to be stated clearly that the sentence is in two parts, one in custody and one under supervision in the community.**

- **This proposal does not apply to sentences for dangerous offenders, for which separate provision has been made in the Act.**

(ii) Licence conditions

K–50   2.1.11   Under the Act, a court imposing a prison sentence of 12 months or more may recommend conditions that should be imposed by the Secretary of State (with advice from the governor responsible for authorising the prisoner's release in consultation with the Probation Service) on release from custody.[27] Recommendations do not form part of the sentence and they are not binding on the Secretary of State.[28]

2.1.12   When passing such a sentence, the court will not know with any certainty to what extent the offender's behaviour may have been addressed in custody or what the offender's health and other personal circumstances might be on release and so it will be extremely difficult, especially in the case of longer custodial sentences, for sentencers to make an informed judgement about the most appropriate licence conditions to be imposed on release. However, in most cases, it would be extremely helpful for sentencers to indicate areas of an offender's behaviour about which they have the most concern and to make suggestions about the types of intervention whether this, in practice, takes place in prison or in the community.

2.1.13   The involvement of the Probation Service at the pre-sentence stage will clearly be pivotal. A recommendation on the likely post-release requirements included in a presentence report will assist the court with the decision on overall sentence length, although any recommendation would still have to be open to review when release is being considered. A curfew, exclusion requirement or prohibited activity requirement might be suitable conditions to recommend for the licence period. A court might also wish to suggest that the offender should complete a rehabilitation programme, for example for drug abuse, anger management, or improving skills such as literacy and could recommend that this should be considered as a licence requirement if the programme has not been undertaken or completed in custody.

2.1.14   The governor responsible for authorising the prisoner's release, in consultation with the Probation Service, is best placed to make recommendations at the point of release; this is the case at present and continues to be provided for in the Act. Specific court recommendations will only generally be appropriate in the context of relatively short sentences, where it would not be unreasonable for the sentencer to anticipate the relevance of particular requirements at the point of release. Making recommendations in relation to longer sentences (other than suggestions about the types of intervention that might be appropriate at some point during the sentence) would be unrealistic. The governor and Probation Service should have due regard to any recommendations made by the sentencing court and the final recommendation to the Secretary of State on licence conditions will need to build upon any interventions during the custodial period and any other changes in the offender's circumstances.

- **A court may sensibly suggest interventions that could be useful when passing sentence, but should only make specific recommendations about the requirements to be imposed on licence when announcing short sentences and where it is reasonable to anticipate their relevance at the point of release. The governor and Probation Service should have due regard to any recommendations made by the sentencing court but its decision should be contingent upon any changed circumstances during the custodial period.**
- **The court should make it clear, at the point of sentence, that the requirements to be imposed on licence will ultimately be the responsibility of the Governor and Probation Service and that they are entitled to review any recommendations made by the court in the light of any changed circumstances.**

SECTION 2 PART 2—SUSPENDED SENTENCES OF IMPRISONMENT

A. STATUTORY PROVISIONS

K–51   2.2.1   Section 189 *Criminal Justice Act* 2003 [sets out full text of section 189, as to which, see § 5–547 in the main work].

K–52   2.2.2   Imposition of requirements—Section 190 *Criminal Justice Act* 2003 [sets out full text of section 190, as to which, see § 5–556 in the main work].

K–53   2.2.3   Power to provide for review—Section 191 *Criminal Justice Act* 2003 [sets out full text of section 191, as to which, see § 5–551 in the main work].

K–54   2.2.4   Periodic reviews—Section 192 *Criminal Justice Act* 2003 [sets out full text of section 192, as to which, see § 5–552 in the main work].

2.2.5   Breach, revocation or amendment of orders, and effect of further conviction—Section 193   **K–55**
Criminal Justice Act 2003 [sets out full text of section 193, as to which, see § 5–554 in the main work].

B. Imposing a Suspended Sentence

2.2.6   A suspended sentence is a sentence of imprisonment. It is subject to the same criteria as a   **K–56**
sentence of imprisonment which is to commence immediately. In particular, this requires a court to
be satisfied that the custody threshold has been passed and that the length of the term is the shortest
term commensurate with the seriousness of the offence.

2.2.7   A court which passes a prison sentence of less than 12 months may suspend it for between
six months and two years (the operational period).[30] During that period, the court can impose one
or more requirements for the offender to undertake in the community. The requirements are identical to those available for the new community sentence.

2.2.8   The period during which the offender undertakes community requirements is "the supervision period" when the offender will be under the supervision of a "responsible officer"; this period
may be shorter than the operational period. The court may periodically review the progress of the
offender in complying with the requirements and the reviews will be informed by a report from the
responsible officer.

2.2.9   If the offender fails to comply with a requirement during the supervision period, or commits a further offence during the operational period, the suspended sentence can be activated in full
or in part or the terms of the supervision made more onerous. There is a presumption that the
suspended sentence will be activated either in full or in part.

(i) The decision to suspend

2.2.10   There are many similarities between the suspended sentence and the community sentence.   **K–57**
In both cases, requirements can be imposed during the supervision period and the court can respond to breach by sending the offender to custody. The crucial difference is that the suspended
sentence is a prison sentence and is appropriate only for an offence that passes the custody threshold
and for which imprisonment is the only option. A community sentence may also be imposed for an
offence that passes the custody threshold where the court considers that to be appropriate.

2.2.11   The full decision making process for imposition of custodial sentences under the new
framework (including the custody threshold test) is set out in paragraphs 1.31–1.33 of the seriousness guideline. For the purposes of suspended sentences the relevant steps are:

(a) has the custody threshold been passed?

(b) if so, is it unavoidable that a custodial sentence be imposed?

(c) if so, can that sentence be suspended? (sentencers should be clear that they would have imposed
a custodial sentence if the power to suspend had not been available)

(d) if not, can the sentence be served intermittently?

(e) if not, impose a sentence which takes immediate effect for the term commensurate with the
seriousness of the offence.

(ii) Length of sentence

2.2.12   Before making the decision to suspend sentence, the court must already have decided that   **K–58**
a prison sentence is justified and should also have decided the length of sentence that would be the
shortest term commensurate with the seriousness of the offence if it were to be imposed immediately.
The decision to suspend the sentence should not lead to a longer term being imposed than if the
sentence were to take effect immediately.

**A prison sentence that is suspended should be for the same term that would have applied if the
offender were being sentenced to immediate custody.**

2.2.13   When assessing the length of the operational period of a suspended sentence, the court
should have in mind the relatively short length of the sentence being suspended and the advantages
to be gained by retaining the opportunity to extend the operational period at a later stage (see
below).

**The operational period of a suspended sentence should reflect the length of the sentence being
suspended. As an approximate guide, an operational period of up to 12 months might normally**

be appropriate for a suspended sentence of up to 6 months and an operational period of up to 18 months might normally be appropriate for a suspended sentence of up to 12 months.

(iii) Requirements

K–59   2.2.14   The court will set the requirements to be complied with during the supervision period. Whilst the offence for which a suspended sentence is imposed is generally likely to be more serious than one for which a community sentence is imposed, the imposition of the custodial sentence is a clear punishment and deterrent. In order to ensure that the overall terms of the sentence are commensurate with the seriousness of the offence, it is likely that the requirements to be undertaken during the supervision period would be less onerous than if a community sentence had been imposed. These requirements will need to ensure that they properly address those factors that are most likely to reduce the risk of re-offending.

Because of the very clear deterrent threat involved in a suspended sentence, requirements imposed as part of that sentence should generally be less onerous than those imposed as part of a community sentence. A court wishing to impose onerous or intensive requirements on an offender should reconsider its decision to suspend sentence and consider whether a community sentence might be more appropriate.

C. Breaches

K–60   2.2.15   The essence of a suspended sentence is to make it abundantly clear to an offender that failure to comply with the requirements of the order or commission of another offence will almost certainly result in a custodial sentence. Where an offender has breached any of the requirements without reasonable excuse for the first time, the responsible officer must either give a warning or initiate breach proceedings.[31] Where there is a further breach within a twelve-month period, breach proceedings must be initiated.[32]

2.2.16   Where proceedings are brought the court has several options, including extending the operational period. However, the presumption (which also applies where breach is by virtue of the commission of a further offence) is that the suspended prison sentence will be activated (either with its original custodial term or a lesser term) unless the court takes the view that this would, in all the circumstances, be unjust. In reaching that decision, the court may take into account both the extent to which the offender has complied with the requirements and the facts of the new offence.[33]

2.2.17   Where a court considers that the sentence needs to be activated, it may activate it in full or with a reduced term. Again, the extent to which the requirements have been complied with will be very relevant to this decision.

2.2.18   If a court amends the order rather than activating the suspended prison sentence, it must either make the requirements more onerous, or extend the supervision or operational periods (provided that these remain within the limits defined by the Act).[34] In such cases, the court must state its reasons for not activating the prison sentence,[35] which could include the extent to which the offender has complied with requirements or the facts of the subsequent offence.

2.2.19   If an offender near the end of an operational period (having complied with the requirements imposed) commits another offence, it may be more appropriate to amend the order rather than activate it.

2.2.20   If a new offence committed is of a less serious nature than the offence for which the suspended sentence was passed, it may justify activating the sentence with a reduced term or amending the terms of the order.

2.2.21   It is expected that any activated suspended sentence will be consecutive to the sentence imposed for the new offence.

2.2.22   If the new offence is non-imprisonable, the sentencer should consider whether it is appropriate to activate the suspended sentence at all.

Where the court decides to amend a suspended sentence order rather than activate the custodial sentence, it should give serious consideration to extending the supervision or operational periods (within statutory limits) rather than making the requirements more onerous.

A. STATUTORY PROVISIONS

2.3.1   Section 183 *Criminal Justice Act* 2003 [sets out full text of section 183, as to which see § 5– **K–61**
542, *ante*].

2.3.2   Restrictions on power to make orders—Section 184 *Criminal Justice Act* 2003 [sets out full **K–62**
text of section 184, as to which see § 5–543, *ante*].

2.3.3   Licence conditions—Section 185 *Criminal Justice Act* 2003 [sets out full text of section 185, **K–63**
as to which see § 5–544, *ante*].

2.3.4   Further provisions—Section 186 *Criminal Justice Act* 2003 [sets out full text of section 186, **K–64**
which (i) makes provision as to the application of the *Prison Act* 1952, s.21 (expenses of conveyance
to prison), to intermittent custody prisoners, (ii) amends section 49 of that Act (persons unlawfully at
large), (iii) amends section 23 of the *CJA* 1961 (prison rules), and (iv) amends section 1 of the
Prisoners (Return to Custody) Act 1995 (remaining at large after temporary release)].

2.3.5   Revocation or amendment—Section 187 *Criminal Justice Act* 2003 [sets out full text of sec- **K–65**
tion 187, which gives effect to Schedule 10 (revocation and amendment of custody plus orders and
intermittent custody orders) (*ante*, §§ 5–558 *et seq.*)].

B. IMPOSING AN INTERMITTENT CUSTODY ORDER

2.3.6   Intermittent custody must be used only for offences that have crossed the custodial **K–66**
threshold. It is an alternative to immediate full-time custody and so must meet all the criteria that
apply to such a sentence, in particular the need to pass the custody threshold and the need to ensure
that the sentence is for the shortest term commensurate with the seriousness of the offence.

2.3.7   The prison sentence is not continuous but is interspersed by periods when the offender is
released on temporary licence in the community. A court may only impose intermittent custody if the
offender consents to serving the custodial part of the sentence intermittently. The court must also
make sure that the relevant resources are available in the local area and must consult the Probation
Service[36] to confirm that the offender is an appropriate candidate for such a sentence.

2.3.8   This sentence is currently being piloted and this guidance will be reviewed and may need to
be developed further in the light of the outcome.

(i) Circumstances when intermittent custody may be appropriate

2.3.9   Guidance supporting the pilots[37] states that intermittent custody is not intended to be used **K–67**
for sex offenders or those convicted of serious offences of either violence or burglary. There may be
other offences which by their nature would make intermittent custody inappropriate and public
safety should always be the paramount consideration.

2.3.10   The circumstances of the offender are likely to be the determining factor in deciding
whether an intermittent custody order is appropriate. It is only appropriate where the custody
threshold has been crossed and where suspending the custodial sentence or imposing a non-custodial
sentence have been ruled out. Suitable candidates for weekend custody might include offenders who
are: full-time carers; employed; or in education.

2.3.11   The full decision making process for imposition of custodial sentences under the new
framework (including the custody threshold test) is set out in paragraphs 1.31–1.33 of the seriousness guideline. For the purposes of intermittent custody the relevant steps are:

(a) has the custody threshold been passed?
(b) if so, is it unavoidable that a custodial sentence be imposed?
(c) if so, can that sentence be suspended? (sentencers should be clear that they would have imposed
   a custodial sentence if the power to suspend had not been available)
(d) if not, can it be served intermittently?
(e) if not, impose a sentence which takes immediate effect for the term commensurate with the
   seriousness of the offence.

- **Courts must be satisfied that a custodial sentence of less than 12 months is justified and that
  neither a community sentence nor a suspended sentence is appropriate before considering
  whether to make an intermittent custody order.**
- **When imposing a custodial sentence of less than 12 months, the court should always consider**

whether it would be appropriate to sentence an offender to intermittent custody; primary
considerations will be public safety, offender suitability and sentence availability.
● Courts should strive to ensure that the intermittent custody provisions are applied in a way
that limits discrimination and they should, in principle, be considered for all offenders.

(ii) Licence requirements

K–68   2.3.12   As a primary objective of being able to serve a custodial sentence intermittently is to enable
offenders to continue to fulfil existing obligations in the community, and since the time spent in
custody is utilised extensively for activities, experience has so far shown that additional, similar,
requirements to be completed whilst on licence are not practical. However, requirements such as
curfews, prohibited activity and exclusion requirements might be appropriate in a particular case.

**The practical workings of an intermittent custody sentence will effectively rule out the use of
some of the longer or more intensive community requirements. Requirements such as curfews,
prohibited activity and exclusion requirements might be appropriate in a particular case.**

(iii) Sentence length

K–69   2.3.13   The demands made on the offender by this sentence will generally be considerably greater
than for a custodial sentence to be served immediately in full. The disruptive effect on family life, the
psychological impact of going in and out of custody and the responsibility on the offender to travel to
and from the custodial establishment on many occasions all make the sentence more onerous.

**Once a court has decided that an offender should be sent to prison and has determined the
length of the sentence, it should reduce the overall length of the sentence because it is to be
served intermittently.**

ANNEX A

Time spent on remand—Sentencing Advisory Panel's advice

K–70   The Act makes provision for a sentencer to give credit for time spent on remand in custody where
a custodial sentence is passed.[38] It also empowers the court to have regard to time spent on remand
in custody when determining the restrictions on liberty to be imposed by a community order or
youth community order.[39] Where an offender has spent several weeks in custody, this may affect the
nature of the offence that is passed. For example, where the court decides that a custodial sentence is
justified some sentencers may decide to pass a community sentence instead, on the basis that the offender has already completed the equivalent of a punitive element in a sentence. The Panel takes the
view that, given the changes in the content of the second part of a custodial sentence, in such cases it
will be more appropriate to pass a custodial sentence knowing that licence requirements will be
imposed on release from custody (which may be immediate). Recommendations made by the court at
the point of sentence will then be of particular importance in influencing the content of the licence.
This will help to ensure that the record clearly shows the assessment of seriousness of the offending
behaviour.
     Whereas the Act clearly states that time spent on remand is to be regarded as part of a custodial
sentence unless the Court considers it unjust,[40] it states that sentencers passing a community sentence
may have regard to time spent on remand, but no further information is given on how this discretion should be exercised. The Panel recognises that giving credit for time spent on remand is likely
to be easier to apply in relation to punitive requirements rather than the rehabilitative elements of a
community sentence. For example, reducing the number of unpaid work hours could be fairly easy,
whereas reducing the length of a rehabilitation programme might not be appropriate as it could
undermine its effectiveness. Where an offender has been kept on remand, one could take the view
that this action was justified by the bail provisions and that the sentencer should not, therefore, feel
obliged to adjust the terms of the community sentence. However, in principle, the Panel recommends that the court should seek to give credit for time spent on remand in all cases and should
explain its reasons for not doing so when it considers either that this is not justified, would not be
practical, or would not be in the best interests of the offender.
     *The court should seek to give credit for time spent on remand in all cases. It should make clear, when
announcing sentence, whether or not credit for time on remand has been given and should explain its
reasons for not giving credit when it considers either that this is not justified, would not be practical, or
would not be in the best interests of the offender.*

Where, following a period of time spent in custody on remand, the court decides that a custodial sentence is justified then, given the changes in the content of the second part of a custodial sentence, the court should pass a custodial sentence in the knowledge that licence requirements will be imposed on release from custody. Recommendations made by the court at the point of sentence will be of particular importance in influencing the content of the licence.[41]

D. Manslaughter by Reason of Provocation

Guideline

Foreword

In accordance with section 170(9) of the *Criminal Justice Act* 2003, the Sentencing Guidelines **K–71** Council issues this guideline as a definitive guideline. By virtue of section 172 of the Act, every court must have regard to a relevant guideline. This guideline applies to offenders convicted of manslaughter by reason of provocation who are sentenced after 28 November 2005.

This guideline stems from a reference from the Home Secretary for consideration of the issue of sentencing where provocation is argued in cases of homicide, and, in particular, domestic violence homicides. For the purpose of describing "domestic violence", the Home Secretary adopted the Crown Prosecution Service definition.[1] The guideline applies to sentencing of an adult offender for this offence in whatever circumstances it occurs. It identifies the widely varying features of both the provocation and the act of retaliation and sets out the approach to be adopted in deciding both the sentencing range and the starting point within that range.

This guideline is for use where the conviction for manslaughter is clearly founded on provocation alone. There will be additional, different and more complicated matters to be taken into account where the other main partial defence, diminished responsibility, is a factor.

The Council's Guideline *New Sentences: Criminal Justice Act 2003* recognised the potentially more demanding nature of custodial sentences of 12 months or longer imposed under the new framework introduced by the *Criminal Justice Act* 2003. Consequently the sentencing ranges and starting points in this guideline take that principle into account.

Guidelines are created following extensive consultation. The Sentencing Advisory Panel first consults widely on the basis of a thoroughly researched consultation paper, then provides the Council with advice. Having considered the advice, the Council prepares a draft guideline on which there is further consultation with Parliament, with the Home Secretary and with Ministers of other relevant Government Departments. This guideline is the culmination of that process.

The Council has appreciated greatly the work of the Sentencing Advisory Panel in preparing the advice on which this guideline has been based and for those who have responded so thoughtfully to the consultation of both the Panel and the Council.

The advice and this guideline are available on *www.sentencing-guidelines.gov.uk* or from the Sentencing Guidelines Secretariat at 85 Buckingham Gate, London SW1E 6PD. A summary of the responses to the Council's consultation also appears on the website.

SIGNATURE
Chairman of the Council
November 2005

Contents

D Sentence Ranges and Starting Points
   Identifying sentence ranges
   Factors to take into consideration
   Guideline

MANSLAUGHTER BY REASON OF PROVOCATION

A. STATUTORY PROVISION

K–73   1.1 Murder and manslaughter are common law offences and there is no complete statutory definition of either. 'Provocation' is one of the partial defences by which an offence that would otherwise be murder may be reduced to manslaughter.

1.2 Before the issue of provocation can be considered, the Crown must have proved beyond reasonable doubt that all the elements of murder were present, including the necessary intent (*i.e.* the offender must have intended either to kill the victim or to cause grievous bodily harm). The court must then consider section 3 of the *Homicide Act* 1957, which provides:

Where on a charge of murder there is evidence on which the jury can find that the person charged was provoked (whether by things done or by things said or by both together) to lose his self-control, the question whether the provocation was enough to make a reasonable man do as he did shall be left to be determined by the jury; and in determining that question the jury shall take into account everything both done and said according to the effect which, in their opinion, it would have on a reasonable man.

> Although both murder and manslaughter result in death, the difference in the level of culpability creates offences of a distinctively different character. Therefore the approach to sentencing in each should start from a different basis.

B. ESTABLISHING THE BASIS FOR SENTENCING

K–74   2.1 The Court of Appeal in *Attorney General's References (Nos. 74, 95 and 118 of 2002) (Suratan and others)*,[2] set out a number of assumptions that a judge must make in favour of an offender found not guilty of murder but guilty of manslaughter by reason of provocation. The assumptions are required in order to be faithful to the verdict and should be applied equally in all cases whether conviction follows a trial or whether the Crown has accepted a plea of guilty to manslaughter by reason of provocation:

- first, that the offender had, at the time of the killing, lost self-control; mere loss of temper or jealous rage is not sufficient
- second, that the offender was caused to lose self-control by things said or done, normally by the person killed
- third, that the offender's loss of control was reasonable in all the circumstances, even bearing in mind that people are expected to exercise reasonable control over their emotions and that, as society advances, it ought to call for a higher measure of self-control
- fourth, that the circumstances were such as to make the loss of self-control sufficiently excusable to reduce the gravity of the offence from murder to manslaughter.

> Bearing in mind the loss of life caused by manslaughter by reason of provocation, the starting point for sentencing should be a custodial sentence. Only in a very small number of cases involving very exceptional mitigating factors should a judge consider that a on-custodial sentence is justified.
>
> The same general sentencing principles should apply in all cases of manslaughter by reason of provocation irrespective of whether or not the killing takes place in a domestic context.

C. Factors Influencing Sentence

3.1 A number of elements must be considered and balanced by the sentencer. Some of these are common to all types of manslaughter by reason of provocation; others have a particular relevance in cases of manslaughter in a domestic context.

3.2 **The degree of provocation as shown by its nature and duration**—An assessment of the *degree* of the provocation as shown by its nature and duration is the critical factor in the sentencing decision.

(a) In assessing the *degree* of provocation, account should be taken of the following factors:

- if the provocation (which does not have to be a wrongful act) involves gross and extreme conduct on the part of the victim, it is a more significant mitigating factor than conduct which, although significant, is not as extreme
- the fact that the victim presented a threat not only to the offender, but also to children in his or her care
- the offender's previous experiences of abuse and/or domestic violence either by the victim or by other people
- any mental condition which may affect the offender's perception of what amounts to provocation
- the nature of the conduct, the period of time over which it took place and its cumulative effect
- discovery or knowledge of the fact of infidelity on the part of a partner does not necessarily amount to *high* provocation. The gravity of such provocation depends entirely on all attendant circumstances.

(b) Whether the provocation was suffered over a *long or short* period is important to the assessment of gravity. The following factors should be considered:

- the impact of provocative behaviour on an offender can build up over a period of time
- consideration should not be limited to acts of provocation that occurred immediately before the victim was killed. For example, in domestic violence cases, cumulative provocation may eventually become intolerable, the latest incident seeming all the worse because of what went before.

(c) When looking at the *nature* of the provocation the court should consider both the type of provocation and whether, in the particular case, the actions of the victim would have had a particularly marked effect on the offender:

- actual (or anticipated) violence from the victim will <u>generally</u> be regarded as involving a higher degree of provocation than provocation arising from abuse, infidelity or offensive words unless that amounts to psychological bullying
- in cases involving actual or anticipated violence, the culpability of the offender will therefore <u>generally</u> be less than in cases involving verbal provocation
- where the offender's actions were motivated by fear or desperation, rather than by anger, frustration, resentment or a desire for revenge, the offender's culpability will <u>generally</u> be lower.

3.3 **The extent and timing of the retaliation**—It is implicit in the verdict of manslaughter by reason of provocation that the killing was the result of a loss of self-control because of things said and/or done. The intensity, extent and nature of that loss of control must be assessed in the context of the provocation that preceded it.

3.4 The *circumstances of the killing* itself will be relevant to the offender's culpability, and hence to the appropriate sentence:

- in general, the offender's violent response to provocation is likely to be less culpable the shorter the time gap between the provocation (or the last provocation) and the killing—as evidenced, for example, by the use of a weapon that happened to be available rather than by one that was carried for that purpose or prepared for use in advance
- conversely, it is not necessarily the case that greater culpability will be found where there has been a significant lapse of time between the provocation (or the last provocation) and the killing. Where the provocation is cumulative, and particularly in those circumstances where the offender is found to have suffered domestic violence from the victim over a significant period of time, the required loss of self-control may not be sudden as some experience a "slow-burn" reaction and appear calm
- choosing or taking advantage of favourable circumstances for carrying out the killing (so that the victim was unable to resist, such as where the victim was not on guard, or was asleep) may well be an aggravating factor—unless this is mitigated by the circumstances of the offender, resulting in the offender being the weaker or vulnerable party.

3.5 The *context of the relationship* between the offender and the victim must be borne in mind when assessing the nature and degree of the provocation offered by the victim before the crime and the length of time over which the provocation existed. In cases where the parties were still in a relationship at the time of the killing, it will be necessary to examine the balance of power between one party and the other and to consider other family members who may have been drawn into, or been victims of, the provocative behaviour.

> Although there will usually be less culpability when the retaliation to provocation is sudden, it is not always the case that greater culpability will be found where there has been a significant lapse of time between the provocation and the killing.
>
> It is for the sentencer to consider the impact on an offender of provocative behaviour that has built up over a period of time.
>
> An offence should be regarded as aggravated where it is committed in the presence of a child or children or other vulnerable family member, whether or not the offence takes place in a domestic setting.

3.6 **Post-offence behaviour**—The behaviour of the offender after the killing can be relevant to sentence:

- immediate and genuine remorse may be demonstrated by the summoning of medical assistance, remaining at the scene, and co-operation with the authorities
- concealment or attempts to dispose of evidence or dismemberment of the body may aggravate the offence.

> Post-offence behaviour is relevant to the sentence. It may be an aggravating or mitigating factor. When sentencing, the judge should consider the motivation behind the offender's actions.

3.7 *Use of a weapon*

(a) In relation to this offence, as in relation to many different types of offence, the carrying and use of a weapon is an aggravating factor. Courts must consider the type of weapon used and, importantly, whether it was to hand or carried to the scene and who introduced it to the incident.

(b) The use or not of a weapon is a factor heavily influenced by the gender of the offender. Whereas men can and do kill using physical strength alone, women often cannot and thus resort to using a weapon. The issue of key importance is whether the weapon was to hand or carried deliberately to the scene, although the circumstances in which the weapon was brought to the scene will need to be considered carefully.

> The use of a weapon should not necessarily move a case into another sentencing bracket.
>
> In cases of manslaughter by reason of provocation, use of a weapon may reflect the imbalance in strength between the offender and the victim and how that weapon came to hand is likely to be far more important than the use of the weapon itself.
>
> It will be an aggravating factor where the weapon is brought to the scene in contemplation of use *before* the loss of self-control (which may occur some time before the fatal incident).

D. SENTENCE RANGES AND STARTING POINTS

K-77 4.1 **Manslaughter is a "serious offence" for the purposes of the provisions in the *Criminal***

Justice Act 2003[3] **for dealing with dangerous offenders. It is possible that a court will be
required to use the sentences for public protection prescribed in the Act when sentencing an
offender convicted of the offence of manslaughter by reason of provocation. An alternative is a
discretionary life sentence. In accordance with normal practice, when setting the minimum
term to be served within an indeterminate sentence under these provisions, that term will usually be half the equivalent determinate sentence.**

4.2 *Identifying sentence ranges*—The key factor that will be relevant in every case is the nature
and the duration of the provocation.

(a) The process to be followed by the court will be:

identify the sentence range by reference to the degree of provocation

adjust the starting point within the range by reference to the length of time
over which the provocation took place

take into consideration the circumstances of the killing (e.g. the length
of time that had elapsed between the provocation and the retaliation
and the circumstances in which any weapon was used)

(b) This guideline establishes that:

- there are three sentencing ranges defined by the **degree of provocation**—low, substantial and
high
- within the three ranges, the starting point is based on provocation taking place over **a short period of time**.
- the court will move from the starting point (based upon the degree of provocation) by considering the length of time over which the provocation has taken place, and by reference to any **aggravating and mitigating factors**

Manslaughter by Reason of Provocation

Factors to take into consideration

1. The sentences for public protection <u>must</u> be considered in all cases of manslaughter.   **K–78**

2. The presence of any of the general aggravating factors identified in the Council's Guideline
Overarching Principles: Seriousness or any of the additional factors identified in this Guideline will
indicate a sentence above the normal starting point.

3. This offence will not be an initial charge but will arise following a charge of murder. The
Council Guideline *Reduction in Sentence for a Guilty Plea* will need to be applied with this in mind. In
particular, consideration will need to be given to the time at which it was indicated that the defendant would plead guilty to manslaughter by reason of provocation.

4. An assessment of the *degree* of the provocation as shown by its nature and duration is the critical factor in the sentencing decision.

5. The intensity, extent and nature of the loss of control must be assessed in the context of the
provocation that preceded it.

6. Although there will usually be less culpability when the retaliation to provocation is sudden, it
is not always the case that greater culpability will be found where there has been a significant lapse of
time between the provocation and the killing.

7. It is for the sentencer to consider the impact on an offender of provocative behaviour that has
built up over a period of time.

8. The use of a weapon should not necessarily move a case into another sentencing bracket.

9. Use of a weapon may reflect the imbalance in strength between the offender and the victim and
how that weapon came to hand is likely to be far more important than the use of the weapon itself.

10. It will be an aggravating factor where the weapon is brought to the scene in contemplation of use *before* the loss of self-control (which may occur some time before the fatal incident).

11. Post-offence behaviour is relevant to the sentence. It may be an aggravating or mitigating factor. When sentencing, the judge should consider the motivation behind the offender's actions.

Manslaughter by Reason of Provocation

This is a serious offence for the purposes of section 224 of the Criminal Justice Act 2003

K–79   Maximum penalty: **Life imprisonment**

Type/Nature of Activity	Sentence Ranges & Starting Points
Low degree of provocation: A low degree of provocation occurring over a short period	Sentence Range: 10 years – life Starting Point – 12 years custody
Substantial degree of provocation: A substantial degree of provocation occurring over a short period	Sentence Range: 4 – 9 years Starting Point – 8 years custody
High degree of provocation: A high degree of provocation occurring over a short period	Sentence Range: if custody is necessary, up to 4 years Starting Point – 3 years custody

Additional aggravating factors	Additional mitigating factors
1. Concealment or attempts to dispose of evidence*	1. The offender was acting to protect another
2. Dismemberment or mutilation of the body*	2. Spontaneity and lack of premeditation
3. Offence committed in the presence of a child/children or other vulnerable family member	3. Previous experiences of abuse and/or domestic violence
	4. Evidence that the victim presented an ongoing danger to the offender or another
*subject to para 3.6 above.	5. Actual (or reasonably anticipated) violence from the victim

The Council Guideline New Sentences: Criminal Justice Act *2003 recognised the potentially more demanding nature of custodial sentences of 12 months or longer imposed under the new framework introduced by the* Criminal Justice Act *2003. The sentencing ranges and starting points in the above guideline take account of this.*

E. Robbery

K–80   The Sentencing Guidelines Council has issued a definitive guideline on robbery (*Theft Act* 1968, s.8(1) (§ 21–84 in the main work)). It deals with offenders sentenced on or after August 1, 2006. The drafting of the guideline is inconsistent and repetitious. It lacks a coherent structure, and consists, in large part, of a series of lists and bullet points. Accordingly, it is not set out in full here. The following is a summary of its essential contents, but for those wishing to refer to the original, it may be located at www.sentencing-guidelines.gov.uk.

The foreword states that robbery will usually merit a custodial sentence, but that exceptional circumstances may justify a non-custodial penalty for an adult and, more frequently, for a young offender; that the guideline is not, therefore, intended to mark a significant shift in sentencing practice; and that the sentencing ranges and starting points in the guideline take into account the more demanding nature of custodial sentences of 12 months or more under the *CJA* 2003. The guideline only provides guidance in relation to street robberies, robberies of small businesses, and less sophisticated commercial robberies. No guidance is provided in relation to violent personal robberies in the home and professionally planned commercial robberies.

The sentences suggested by the guideline are determined by the identification of one of three levels of seriousness. These are themselves determined by reference to the type of activity which characterises the offence, and the degree of force or threat present. Level 1 involves a threat and/or minimal use of force. Level 2 involves use of a weapon to threaten and/or use of significant force. Level 3 involves use of a weapon and/or significant force, and the causing of serious injury. Where the offence will fall within a particular level is determined by the presence of one or more aggravating features. However, exceptionally serious aggravating features may have the effect of moving the case to the next level. Aggravating factors which are particularly relevant to the assessment of seriousness are:

(a) the nature and degree of any force or violence used or threatened;
(b) the nature of any weapon carried or used, or the use of which is threatened;
(c) the vulnerability of the victim;
(d) the number of offenders involved and their roles;
(e) the value of the property taken;
(f) the fact that the offence was committed at night or in the hours of darkness; and
(g) the wearing of a disguise.

Mitigating factors which are particularly relevant are:

(a) an unplanned or opportunistic offence;
(b) a peripheral involvement in the offence; and
(c) the voluntary return of the property taken.

Where an offence is committed by a young offender, sentencers should additionally take into account age and immaturity and any group pressure under which the offender may have been acting. Further, in relation to such an offender, the guideline requires that where there is evidence that the offence was committed to fund a drug habit and that treatment might help tackle offending behaviour, the court should consider a drug treatment requirement as part of a supervision order or action plan. In all cases, the court should consider making a restitution or compensation order; in cases where a non-custodial order is made, the court may consider making an anti-social behaviour order.

Starting points and sentencing ranges are prescribed depending on whether the offender is an adult or a young offender. In each case, the starting point is based upon a first time offender who has pleaded not guilty, and who has not been assessed as being dangerous for the purposes of the dangerous offender provisions under the *CJA* 2003, Pt 12, Chap. 5 (ss.224 *et seq.*) (§§ 5–495 *et seq.* in the main work). In the case of young offenders, the starting points are based on a 17-year-old. Sentencers are required to consider whether a lower starting point is justified on account of the offender's age or immaturity. In the case of an adult offender, the starting point for a level 1 offence is 12 months' custody and the sentence range is from a community order (in exceptional circumstances, as stated in the foreword) to three years' custody. The starting point for a level 2 offence is four years' custody and the sentence range is two to seven years. The starting point for a level 3 offence is eight years' custody and the sentence range is seven to 12 years. In the case of the notional young offender, the starting point for a level 1 offence is a community order and the sentence range is from a community order to a 12-month detention and training order. The starting point for a level 2 offence is three years' detention and the sentence range is one to six years' detention. The starting point for a level 3 offence is seven years' detention and the sentence range is six to 10 years' detention.

F. Breach of a Protective Order

The Sentencing Guidelines Council has issued a definitive guideline relating to the 　**K–81** sentencing of offenders who have breached either a restraining order under the *Protection from Harassment Act* 1997, s.5 (§ 19–277f in the main work), or a non-molestation order imposed under section 42 of the *Family Law Act* 1996 (breach being made an offence by section 42A, which is inserted, as from a day to be appointed, by the *Domestic Violence, Crime and Victims Act* 2004, s.1). It deals with offenders sentenced on or after December 18, 2006.

Paragraph 2 points out that the facts constituting the breach may amount to a substantive offence in their own right. It advises that in such cases it is desirable that there should be separate counts, and, where necessary, there should be consecutive sentences to reflect the seriousness of the counts and to achieve the appropriate totality. It continues, however, by saying that where there is only the one count, the overall sentence should not generally be affected. If the sole count is the breach, the sentence should reflect the nature of the breach; and if the substantive offence alone has been charged, the fact that it constituted a breach of a court order should be regarded as a matter of aggravation. Where no substantive offence was involved, the sentence should reflect the circumstances of the breach, including whether it was an isolated breach, or part of a course of conduct in breach of the order; whether it was planned or spontaneous; and any consequences of the breach, including psychiatric injury or distress to the person protected by the order.

Paragraph 3 is headed "Factors influencing sentencing". It says that since the order will have been made for the purpose of protecting an individual from harm, the main aim of the sentencer should be to achieve future compliance with the order where that is realistic. The nature of the original conduct or offence is relevant in so far as it allows a judgment to be made on the level of harm caused to the victim by the breach and the extent to which that harm was intended by the offender (para. 3.5). However, sentence following a breach is for the breach alone and must avoid punishing the offender again for the offence or conduct as a result of which the order was made (para. 3.7).

When dealing with a breach, a court will need to consider the extent to which the conduct amounting to the breach put the victim at risk of harm (para. 3.8). Where the order is breached by the use of physical violence, the starting point should normally be a custodial sentence (para. 3.9). Non-violent behaviour and/or indirect contact can also cause (or be intended to cause) a high degree of harm and anxiety. In such circumstances, it is likely that the custody threshold will have been crossed (para. 3.10). Where an order was made in civil proceedings, its purpose may have been to cause the subject of the order to modify behaviour rather than to imply that the conduct was especially serious. If so, it is likely to be disproportionate to impose a custodial sentence for a breach of the order if the breach did not involve threats or violence (para. 3.11). In some cases where a breach might result in a short custodial sentence but the court is satisfied that the offender genuinely intends to reform his behaviour and there is a real prospect of rehabilitation, the court may consider it appropriate to impose a sentence that will allow this. This may mean imposing a suspended sentence order or a community order (where appropriate with a requirement to attend an accredited domestic violence programme) (para. 3.12).

Paragraph 4 deals with matters of aggravation and mitigation. The matters of aggravation mirror those in the guideline on domestic violence (*post*, Appendix K–82), but there is added the fact that the breach was a further breach following previous breach proceedings or that it was committed shortly after the order was made. The matters of mitigation that are listed are that the breach followed a long period of compliance, or that the victim initiated contact.

At the end of the guideline there is a table with suggested starting points. The premise is that the "activity has either been prosecuted separately as an offence or is not of a character sufficient to justify prosecution of it as an offence in its own right". The first column is headed "Nature of activity" and the second column is headed "Starting points". There are five entries in the first column, "Breach (whether one or more) involving significant physical violence and significant physical or psychological harm to the victim", "More than one breach involving some violence and/or significant physical or psychological harm to the victim", "Single breach involving some violence and/or significant physical or psychological harm to the victim", "More than one breach involving no/ minimal contact or some direct contact" and "Single breach involving no/ minimal direct contact". The corresponding entries in the second column are, "More than 12 months. The length of the ... sentence will depend on the nature and seriousness of the breaches.", "26–39 weeks' custody [Medium/

High Custody Plus order] (when the relevant provisions of the *CJA* 2003 are in force)",
"13–26 weeks' custody [Low/Medium Custody Plus order] (when the relevant provisions
of the *CJA* 2003 are in force)", "Medium range community order" and "Low range community order".

G. Domestic Violence

The Sentencing Guidelines Council has issued a definitive guideline for use in all cases   **K–82**
that fall within the Crown Prosecution Service definition of "domestic violence", *viz.* "Any
incident of threatening behaviour, violence or abuse [psychological, physical, sexual,
financial or emotional] between adults who are or have been intimate partners or family
members, regardless of gender or sexuality." It deals with offenders sentenced on or after
December 18, 2006. The guideline makes clear that offences committed in a domestic
context should be regarded as being no less serious than offences committed in a non-
domestic context. Indeed, because an offence has been committed in a domestic context,
there are likely to be aggravating factors present that make it more serious. The foreword,
signed by Lord Phillips C.J., as chairman of the council, states that in many situations of domestic violence, the circumstances require the sentence to demonstrate clearly that the
conduct is unacceptable, but that there will be cases where all parties genuinely and realistically wish the relationship to continue as long as the violence stops. In such cases, and
where the violence is towards the lower end of the scale of seriousness, it is likely to be appropriate for the court to impose a sentence that provides the necessary support.

Paragraph 1 defines "domestic violence" for the purposes of the guideline (*ante*).
Paragraph 2 relates to the assessment of seriousness and says nothing new. Paragraph 3 is
concerned with matters of aggravation and mitigation. By way of preamble it is stated that
the history of the relationship will be relevant to the assessment of seriousness. There follows a non-exhaustive list of aggravating matters, *viz.* abuse of trust or power, that the
victim is particularly vulnerable, the exposure of children to an offence (directly or
indirectly), using contact arrangements with a child to instigate an offence, a proven history
of violence or threats by the offender in a domestic setting, a history of disobedience to
court orders and conduct which has forced the victim to leave home. The two matters of
mitigation that are listed are positive good character and provocation, but, as to the former,
the point is made that the perpetrator of domestic violence may have two personae, and
that good character in relation to conduct outside the home should generally be of no
relevance where there is a proven pattern of behaviour.

Paragraph 4 deals with the relevance of the wishes of the victim to the sentence. As a matter of general principle, the sentence should be determined by the seriousness of the offence, not by the expressed wishes of the victim. The guideline states that it is particularly
important that this principle should be observed in this context, as (a) it is undesirable that
a victim should feel a responsibility for the sentence imposed; (b) there is a risk that a plea
for mercy made by a victim will be induced by threats made by, or by a fear of, the offender; and (c) the risk of such threats will be increased if it is generally believed that the
severity of the sentence may be affected by the wishes of the victim. However, there may be
cases in which the court can properly mitigate a sentence to give effect to the expressed wish
of the victim that the relationship should be permitted to continue. The court must,
however, be confident that such a wish is genuine, and that giving effect to it will not expose
the victim to a real risk of further violence. Up-to-date information in a pre-sentence report
and victim personal statement will be of vital importance. Either the offender or the victim
(or both) may ask the court to take into consideration the interests of any children and to
impose a less severe sentence. The court will wish to have regard not only to the effect on
the children if the relationship is disrupted but also to the likely effect on the children of
any further incidents of domestic violence.

The final section of the guideline is headed "Factors to Take into Consideration". It
contains nothing new, save that it advises that where "the custody threshold is only just
crossed, so that if a custodial sentence is imposed it will be a short sentence, the court will
wish to consider whether the better option is a suspended sentence order or a community

order, including in either case a requirement to attend an accredited domestic violence programme. Such an option will only be appropriate where the court is satisfied that the offender genuinely intends to reform his ... behaviour and that there is a real prospect of rehabilitation being successful. Such a situation is unlikely to arise where there has been a pattern of abuse."

H. Sexual Offences

K–83   The Sentencing Guidelines Council has issued a definitive guideline on sexual offences, which applies to offenders sentenced on or after May 14, 2007. Although its title refers only to the *SOA* 2003, it also deals with offences concerning indecent photographs of children (*Protection of Children Act* 1978, s.1, *CJA* 1988, s.160) and keeping a brothel used for prostitution (*SOA* 1956, s.33A).

The foreword states that guidance from Court of Appeal judgments on offences under the 2003 Act has been incorporated into the guideline; that the guideline uses a starting point of five years for the rape of an adult with no other aggravating or mitigating factors (derived from *R. v. Millberry*; *R. v. Morgan*; *R. v. Lackenby* [2003] 1 Cr.App.R. 25 (and as to the guidelines in *Millberry* being "reinforced" by this guideline, see *Att.-Gen.'s Reference (No. 52 of 2009) (R. v. Tiffany)* [2010] 1 Cr.App.R.(S.) 99, CA)) as the baseline from which all other sentences for offences in the guideline have been calculated; and that the more onerous nature of the release on licence regime under the *CJA* 2003 has been taken into account, such that the transitional arrangements in paragraphs 2.1.7 to 2.1.10 of the "New sentences: *CJA* 2003" guideline (*ante*, K–49) do not apply.

The guideline is in seven parts and is set out across more than 140 pages. The following description sets out the key principles and excludes the recitation of ordinary sentencing principles that will be familiar to sentencers and practitioners. To that end, the description is not intended to be a substitute for the guideline, but a quick reference ("pocket sized") guide to it. The description sets the guidelines out in a tabulated form, accompanied by explanatory text. Starting points and sentencing ranges are set out (here, not in the guideline itself) in the form of x $(y–z)$, with x indicating the starting point and $y–z$ indicating the sentencing range. Unless otherwise indicated, these figures refer to custodial sentences measured in years.

Part 1: General principles

K–84   Part 1 of the guideline sets out various general principles applicable to the imposition of sentences for sexual offences. In particular, save where a distinction is justified by the nature of the offence, the guidelines apply irrespective of the gender of the offender.

Starting points and sentencing ranges

K–85   Except where otherwise indicated, the starting points and sentencing ranges relate to adult offenders of previous good character convicted following a plea of not guilty. Starting points are based on a "basic offence" (*i.e.* one in which the ingredients of the offence as defined are present, and assuming no aggravating or mitigating factors) in the particular category. References to a "non-custodial sentence" are references to a community order or a fine (although, in most cases, the threshold will have been crossed for a community order). The *sentencing range* is the bracket into which the provisional sentence will fall after consideration of aggravating or mitigating factors (although particular circumstances may require a sentence outside of that range). To that end, the suggested starting points and sentencing ranges are not rigid, and movement within and between ranges will depend upon the circumstances of individual cases and, in particular, the aggravating and mitigating factors present. Previous convictions which aggravate the seriousness of the current offence may take the provisional sentence beyond the range given. Likewise personal mitigation and the reduction for a guilty plea may also take a sentence outside of a range indicated.

Aggravating and mitigating factors

K–86   Aggravating and mitigating factors which are particularly relevant to each offence are listed in the individual offence guidelines. These lists are non-exhaustive and the factors are not ranked in any particular order. Where a factor is an ingredient of an offence or is used to identify a starting point, it cannot also be an aggravating factor and care will be necessary to avoid double counting. Since sexual offences often involve some form of violence as an essential element of the offence, this is included in the starting points. However, it will be an aggravating factor if harm was inflicted over and above that necessary to commit the offence. Additionally, regard should be had to the generic list of aggravating and mitigating factors referred to in paragraphs 1.20 to 1.27 of the "Guideline on seriousness" (*ante*, K–19). The foreword states that if an offence is committed in a domestic context, and falls within the definition of "domestic violence", reference should also be made to the additional principles and factors referred to in the "Overarching principles: domestic violence" guideline (*ante*, K–82 *et seq.*). The presence of generic and offence-specific aggravating factors will significantly influence the type and length of sentence imposed.

Young offenders

As to the culpability of young offenders, Part 7 of the guideline deals with the situation where an offence prescribes a different maximum penalty depending on the age of the offender. Such cases apart, youth and immaturity must always be potential mitigating factors to be taken into account (although not necessarily if an offence is particularly serious). Unless specifically stated, the starting points assume that the offender is an adult. **K–87**

Victim personal statements

If a statement has not been produced, the court should enquire whether the victim has had the opportunity to make one. Where there is no statement, it should not be assumed that the offence had no impact on the victim. **K–88**

Pre-sentence reports

A pre-sentence report should normally be prepared before a sentence is passed since it may address the likelihood of re-offending and it will be in the interests of public protection to provide treatment to sex offenders at the earliest opportunity; a psychiatric report may also be appropriate. **K–89**

Community orders

Where a community order is the recommended starting point, the requirements to be imposed are left for the court to decide according to the particular facts of the individual case. Where a community order is the proposed starting point for different levels of seriousness of the same offence or for a second or subsequent offence of the same level of seriousness, this should be reflected by means of the imposition of more onerous requirements. **K–90**

Ancillary orders

The guideline states that notification requirements follow automatically upon conviction of an offence; that it is the duty of a sentencer to consider whether to make a sexual offences prevention order under the *SOA* 2003, s.104, and/ or an order disqualifying the offender from working with children under the *CJCSA* 2000, ss.28 and 29; and that sentencers should also consider whether to make confiscation, deprivation or compensation orders. **K–91**

Treatment programmes

Treatment programmes are not specifically mentioned in the sentence recommendations, but the summary of general principles concludes by stating that a sentencer should always consider whether, in the circumstances of the individual case, and having regard to the profile of the offending behaviour, it would be sensible to require the offender to take part in a programme designed to address sexually deviant behaviour. **K–92**

Part 2: Non-consensual offences (*Sexual Offences Act* 2003)

The same starting points apply to all offences dealt with in this part whatever the relationship between the offender and the victim (*i.e.* in a relationship, acquaintances, strangers, *etc.*). Extreme youth or old age of a victim is an aggravating factor; and if the victim is a child, the greater the disparity in the ages of the offender and victim, the more serious the offence. Youth or immaturity of an offender should also be taken into account. It should be noted that offenders under the age of 18 convicted of offences contrary sections 11 and 12 should be dealt with under Part 7 of the guideline. **K–93**

Parts 2A (rape (ss.1 & 5) and assault by penetration (ss.2 & 6)) and 2B (sexual assault (ss.3 & 7))

The planning of an offence indicates a higher level of culpability than an opportunistic or impulsive offence. Whether an offender's culpability is reduced because the offender and victim had engaged in consensual sexual activity on the same occasion immediately before the offence took place will depend on the nature of the previous activity as compared to the subsequent activity and timing. There may be cases where the seriousness of the non-consensual activity overwhelms any other consideration. As to rape, there is no distinction between starting points for penetration of the vagina, mouth or anus. As to an assault by penetration, brief penetration with fingers, toes or tongue may result in a significantly lower sentence where no physical harm is caused. As to sexual assault, some offences may justify a lesser sentence where the actions were more offensive than threatening and comprised a single act rather then more persistent behaviour. Further, where an offence is being dealt with in a magistrates' court, more detailed guidance will be provided in the Magistrates' Court Sentencing Guidelines.

Part 2C (causing sexual activity without consent (ss.4, 8 & 31))

The same starting points apply whether the activity was caused or incited and whether or not the incited activity took place. Some reduction will generally be appropriate where the incited activity did not in fact take place; but the degree to which the victim may have suffered as a result of knowing or believing that an offence would take place should be taken into account.

Part 2D (other non-consensual offences (ss.11 & 32 and 12 & 33))

Where an offence can be committed by causing or inciting sexual activity, the same starting points apply whether the activity was caused or incited and whether or not the incited activity took place.

Key to table of starting points, *etc.*, for part 2

‡   Denotes that an offence is a "serious offence" for the purposes of the *Criminal Justice Act 2003*, s.224

Aggravating factors.

A1:   Offender ejaculated or caused victim to ejaculate
A2:   Background of intimidation or coercion
A3:   Use of drugs, alcohol or other substance to facilitate the offence
A4:   Threats to prevent victim reporting the incident
A5:   Abduction or detention
A6:   Offender aware that he or she is suffering from a sexually transmitted infection
A7:   Pregnancy or infection results
A8:   Physical harm caused
A9:   Prolonged activity or contact
A10:   Images of violent activity

Mitigating factors

M1:   Victim is aged 16 or over and previously engaged in consensual sexual activity with the offender on the same occasion and immediately before the offence
M2:   Victim is aged under 16 and the sexual activity was mutually agreed and experimental between two children
M3:   Victim is aged under 16 but offender is a young offender and reasonably believed victim to be aged 16 or over
M4:   Penetration is minimal or for a short duration
M5:   Youth and immaturity of offender
M6:   Minimal or fleeting contact

OFFENCE	TYPE/ NATURE OF ACTIVITY	STARTING POINTS (AND SENTENCING RANGES)			AGG. & MIT. FACTORS	GUIDELINE PAGES
		Victim is under 13	Victim 13 or over/ under 16	Victim 16 or over		
Rape 1 (rape) ‡ 5 (rape of a child under 13) ‡	Repeated rape of same victim over a course of time or rape involving multiple victims		15 (13–19)		A1, A2, A3, A4, A5, A6, A7 M1, M2, M3	24–26
	Rape accompanied by any one of the following; abduction or detention; offender aware that he is suffering from a sexually transmitted infection; more than one offender acting together; abuse of trust; offence motivated by prejudice (race, religion, sexual orientation, physical disability); sustained attack	13 (11–17)	10 (8–13)	8 (6–11)		
	Single offence of rape by single offender	10 (8–13)	8 (6–11)	5 (4–8)		
Assault by penetration 2 (assault by penetration) ‡ 6 (assault of a child under 13 by penetration) ‡	Penetration with an object or body part, accompanied by any one of the following; abduction or detention; more than one offender acting together; abuse of trust; offence motivated by prejudice (race, religion, sexual orientation, physical disability); sustained attack	13 (11–17)	10 (8–13)	8 (6–11)	A2, A3, A4, A5, A6, A8, A1 M1, M2, M3, M4	28–30
	Penetration with an object	7 (5–10)	5 (4–8)	3 (2–5)		
	Penetration with a body part where no physical harm sustained by victim	5 (4–8)	4 (3–7)	2 (1–4)		
Sexual assault 3 (sexual assault) ‡ 7 (sexual assault of a child under 13) ‡	Contact between naked genitalia of offender and naked genitalia, face or mouth of the victim	5 (4–8)	3 (2–5)		A1, A2, A3, A4, A5, A6, A8, A9 M1, M2, M3, M5, M6	32–34
	Contact between naked genitalia of offender and another part of victim's body/ Contact with genitalia of victim by offender using part of his or her body other than the genitalia, or an object/ Contact between either the clothed genitalia of offender and naked genitalia of victim or naked genitalia of offender and clothed genitalia of victim	2 (1–4)	12 mths (6–24 mths)			
	Contact between part of offender's body (other than the genitalia) with part of the victim's body (other than the genitalia)	6 mths (4 wks to 18 mths)	Community order (appropriate non-custodial sentence)			

OFFENCE	TYPE/ NATURE OF ACTIVITY	STARTING POINTS (AND SENTENCING RANGES)			AGG. & MIT. FACTORS	GUIDELINE PAGES
		Victim is under 13	Victim 13 or over/ under 16	Victim 16 or over		
Causing sexual activity without consent 4 (causing a person to engage in sexual activity without consent) ‡ 8 (causing or inciting a child under 13 to engage in sexual activity) ‡ 31 (causing or inciting a person, with a mental disorder impeding choice, to engage in sexual activity) ‡ **N.B. For the purposes of the offence contrary to s.31, the starting points applicable are those for victims under the age of 13**	Penetration with any one of the following aggravating factors: abduction or detention; offender aware that he or she is suffering from a sexually transmitted infection; more than one offender acting together; abuse of trust; offence motivated by prejudice (race, religion, sexual orientation, physical disability); sustained attack	13 (11–17)	10 (8–13)	8 (6–11)	A1, A2, A3, A4, A5, A6	38–41
	Single offence of penetration of/ by single offender with no aggravating or mitigating factors	7 (5–10)	5 (4–8)	3 (2–5)		
	Contact between naked genitalia of offender and naked genitalia of victim, or causing two or more victims to engage in such activity with each other, or causing victim to masturbate himself/herself.	5 (4–8)	3 (2–5)			
	Contact between naked genitalia of offender and another part of victim's body/ contact with naked genitalia of victim by offender using part of the body other than the genitalia or an object / contact between either the clothed genitalia of offender and naked genitalia of victim, or naked genitalia of offender and clothed genitalia of victim. (*Or causing two or more victims to engage in such activity with each other*).	2 (1–4)	12 mths (6–24 mths)			
	Contact between part of offender's body (other than the genitalia) with part of the victim's body (other than the genitalia)	6 mths (4 wks to 18 mths)	Community order (appropriate non-custodial sentence)			
Sexual activity in the presence of another person 11 (engaging in sexual activity in the presence of a child) (offender 18 or over)‡ 32 (engaging in sexual activity in the presence of a person with a mental disorder impeding choice) ‡	Consensual intercourse or other forms of consensual penetration	2 (1–4)			A2, A3, A4, A5	44, 45
	Masturbation (of oneself or another person)	18 mths (12–30 mths)				
	Consensual sexual touching involving naked genitalia	12 mths (6–18 mths)				
	Consensual sexual touching of naked body parts but not involving naked genitalia	6 mths (4 wks–18 mths)				

OFFENCE	TYPE/ NATURE OF ACTIVITY	STARTING POINTS (AND SENTENCING RANGES)			AGG. & MIT. FACTORS	GUIDELINE PAGES
		Victim is under 13	Victim 13 or over/ under 16	Victim 16 or over		
Causing or inciting another person to watch a sexual act 12 (causing a child to watch a sexual act) (offender 18 or over) ‡ 33 (causing a person with a mental disorder impeding choice to watch a sexual act) ‡	Live sexual activity	18 mths (12–24 mths)			A2, A3, A4, A5, A10	46, 47
	Moving or still images of people engaged in sexual activity involving penetration	32 wks (26–52 wks)				
	Moving or still images of people engaged in sexual activity other than penetration	Community order (community order to 26 wks' custody)				

Part 3: Offences involving ostensible consent (*Sexual Offences Act* 2003)

K–95   It should be noted that an offender under the age of 18 convicted of an offence contrary to section 9, 10, 25 or 26 should be dealt with under Part 7 of the guideline.

Part 3A (offences involving children (ss.9 & 10, 25 & 26, 16 & 17, 18, 19, 14))

Extreme youth of an offender and close proximity in age between the offender and the victim are both factors that will be relevant. As to sexual activity with a child, the same starting points apply whether the activity was caused or incited (causing or inciting offences). As to familial child sex offences, where the victim is over the age of consent, the starting points assume that the offender is a close relative. Further, where the victim was aged 16 or 17 when the sexual activity was commenced and the relationship was unlawful only because it was in a familial setting (*e.g.* offence involves foster siblings, a lodger or *au pair*) the starting points should be in line with generic breach of trust cases. Evidence that the offender has been "groomed" by the offender will aggravate the seriousness of the offence. As to abuse of trust cases, evidence of serious coercion, threats or trauma should move a sentence well above a starting point. The same starting points apply whether the activity was caused or incited (causing or inciting offences).

Part 3B (offences against vulnerable adults (ss.30, 34 & 35, 38 & 39, 36 & 40, 37 & 41))

The period of time during which the sexual activity has taken place will be relevant in determining the seriousness of an offence; although, depending on the particular circumstances, this could amount to aggravation (repeated exploitative behaviour) or mitigation (longer-term relationship where victim has low-level mental disorder). In general, the same starting points should be applied whether (a) the victim has a mental disorder impeding choice, or a mental disorder making him vulnerable to inducement, threat or deception, and (b) the activity was caused or incited (causing or inciting offences).

Key to table of starting points, *etc.*, for part 3

†   Denotes that an offence is a "specified offence" for the purposes of the *Criminal Justice Act* 2003, s.224

‡   Denotes that an offence is a "serious offence" for the purposes of the *Criminal Justice Act* 2003, s.224

Aggravating factors.

A1:   Offender ejaculated or caused victim to ejaculate

A2:   Background of intimidation or coercion

A3:   Use of drugs, alcohol or other substance to facilitate the offence

A4:   Threats to prevent victim reporting the incident

A5:   Abduction or detention

A6:   Offender aware that he or she is suffering from a sexually transmitted infection

A7:   Pregnancy or infection results

A8:   Physical harm caused

A9:   Prolonged activity or contact

A10:   Images of violent activity

A11:   Closeness of familial relationship

A12:   Number of victims involved

Mitigating factors

M7:   Offender intervenes to prevent incited offence from taking place

M8:   Small disparity in age between victim and offender

M9:   Relationship of genuine affection

M10:   No element of corruption

M11:   Offender had a mental disorder at the time of the offence which significantly affected his or her culpability

OFFENCE	TYPE/ NATURE OF ACTIVITY	STARTING POINTS (AND SENTENCING RANGES)	AGG. & MIT. FACTORS	GUIDELINE PAGES
Sexual activity with a child 9 (sexual activity with a child) (offender 18 or over) ‡ 10 (causing or inciting a child to engage in sexual activity) (offender 18 or over) ‡	Penile penetration of the vagina, anus or mouth or penetration of the vagina or anus with another body part or an object	4 (3–7)	A1, A4, A6 M7, M8	52–54
	Contact between naked genitalia of offender and naked genitalia or another part of victim's body, particularly face or mouth	2 (1–4)		
	Contact between naked genitalia of offender or victim and clothed genitalia of victim or offender or contact with naked genitalia of victim by offender using part of his or her body other than the genitalia or an object	12 months (26 weeks to 24 months)		
	Contact between part of offender's body (other than the genitalia) with part of the victim's body (other than the genitalia)	Community order (appropriate non-custodial sentence)		

OFFENCE	TYPE/ NATURE OF ACTIVITY	STARTING POINTS (AND SENTENCING RANGES)	AGG. & MIT. FACTORS	GUIDELINE PAGES
Familial child sex offences 25 (sexual activity with a child family member) (offender 18 or over) ‡ 26 (inciting a child family member to engage in sexual activity) (offender 18 or over) ‡	**Victim is 13 or over but under 16, regardless of familial relationship with offender/ victim is 16 or 17 but sexual relationship commenced when victim was under 16/ victim is aged 16 or 17 and offender is a blood relative**		A2, A3, A4, A6, A11 M8	56–58
	Penile penetration of the vagina, anus or mouth or penetration of the vagina or anus with another body part or an object	5 (4–8)		
	Contact between naked genitalia of offender and naked genitalia of victim	4 (3–7)		
	Contact between naked genitalia of offender or victim and clothed genitalia of victim or offender	18 months (12 months to 30 months)		
	Contact between naked genitalia of victim by another part of offender's body or an object, or between naked genitalia of offender and another part of victim's body	18 months (12 months to 30 months)		
	Contact between part of offender's body (other than the genitalia) with part of the victim's body (other than the genitalia)	Community order (appropriate non-custodial sentence)		
	Victim was aged 16 or 17 when sexual relationship commenced and relationship was only unlawful because of abuse of trust implicit in relationship			
	Penile penetration of the vagina, anus or mouth or penetration of the vagina or anus with another body part or an object	2 (1–4)		
	Any other form of non-penetrative sexual activity involving naked contact between offender and victim	12 months (6 to 24 months)		
	Contact between clothed part of offender's body (other than genitalia) with clothed part of victim's body (other than the genitalia)	Community order (appropriate non-custodial sentence)		
Abuse of trust: sexual activity with a person under 18 16 (abuse of position of trust: sexual activity with a child) † 17 (abuse of position of trust: causing or inciting child to engage in sexual activity) †	Penile penetration of the vagina, anus or mouth or penetration of the vagina or anus with another body part or an object	18 months (12 months to 30 months)	A2, A1, A3, A6 M8, M9, M10	60, 61
	Other forms of non-penetrative activity	26 weeks (4 weeks to 18 months)		
	Contact between part of offender's body (other than the genitalia) with part of the victim's body (other than the genitalia)	Community order (appropriate non-custodial sentence)		

OFFENCE	TYPE/ NATURE OF ACTIVITY	STARTING POINTS (AND SENTENCING RANGES)	AGG. & MIT. FACTORS	GUIDELINE PAGES
Abuse of trust: sexual activity in the presence of a person under 18 18 (abuse of trust: sexual activity in the presence of a child) †	Consensual intercourse or other forms of consensual penetration	2 (1–4)	A2, A3, A4, A5	62, 63
	Masturbation (of oneself or another person)	18 months (12 months to 30 months)		
	Consensual sexual touching involving naked genitalia	12 months (6 months to 24 months)		
	Consensual sexual touching of naked body parts but not involving naked genitalia	26 weeks (4 weeks to 18 months)		
Abuse of trust: causing a person under 18 to watch a sexual act 19 (abuse of position of trust: causing a child to watch a sexual act) †	Live sexual activity	18 months (12 months to 24 months)	A2, A3, A4, A5, A10	64, 65
	Moving or still images of people engaged in sexual activity involving penetration	32 weeks (26–52 weeks)	M8	
	Moving or still images of people engaged in sexual activity other than penetration	Community order (community order–26 weeks custody)		
Arranging a child sex offence 14 (arranging or facilitating the commission of a child sex offence) ‡	Where the activity is arranged or facilitated as part of a commercial enterprise, even if the offender is under 18	Starting points and sentencing ranges should be increased above those for the relevant substantive offence under sections 9 to 13.	A2, A3, A4, A5, A12	66, 67
	Basic offence assuming no aggravating or mitigating factors	Starting point and sentencing ranges should be commensurate with that for the relevant substantive offence under sections 9 to 13.		

OFFENCE	TYPE/ NATURE OF ACTIVITY	STARTING POINTS (AND SENTENCING RANGES)	AGG. & MIT. FACTORS	GUIDE-LINE PAGES
Sexual activity with a person with a mental disorder 30 (sexual activity with a person with a mental disorder impeding choice)‡ 34 (inducement, threat or deception to procure sexual activity with a person with a mental disorder)‡ 35 (causing a person with a mental disorder to engage in, or agree to engage in, sexual activity by inducement, threat or deception)‡	Penetration with any of the following aggravating factors: abduction or detention; offender aware that he or she is suffering from a sexually transmitted infection; more than one offender acting together; offence motivated by prejudice (race, religion, sexual orientation, physical disability); sustained or repeated activity	13 (11–17)	A2, A1, A3, A4, A5, A6 M9, M11	70–72
	Single offence of penetration of/ by single offender with no aggravating or mitigating factors	10 (8–13)		
	Contact between naked genitalia of offender and naked genitalia of victim	5 (4–8)		
	Contact between naked genitalia of offender and another part of victim's body or naked genitalia of victim by offender using part of his or her body other than the genitalia / Contact between clothed genitalia of offender and naked genitalia of victim or naked genitalia of offender and clothed genitalia of victim	15 months (36 weeks to 3 years)		
	Contact between part of offender's body (other than the genitalia) with parts of victim's body (other than the genitalia)	26 weeks (4 weeks to 18 months)		
Care workers: sexual activity with a person with a mental disorder 38 (care workers: sexual activity with a person with a mental disorder)‡ 39 (care workers: causing or inciting sexual activity)‡	Basic offence of sexual activity involving penetration, assuming no aggravating or mitigating factors	3 (2–5)	A2, A3, A4, A5, A6 M9	74, 75
	Other forms of non-penetrative activity	12 months (6 months to 24 months)		
	Naked contact between part of the offender's body with part of the victim's body	Community order (an appropriate non-custodial sentence)		
Sexual activity in the presence of a person with a mental disorder 36 (engaging in sexual activity in the presence, secured by inducement, threat or deception, of a person with a mental disorder)‡ 40 (care workers: sexual activity in the presence of a person with a mental disorder)‡	Consensual intercourse or other forms of consensual penetration	2 (1–4)	A2, A3, A4, A5	76, 77
	Masturbation (of oneself or another person)	18 months (12 months to 30 months)		
	Consensual sexual touching involving naked genitalia	12 months (6 months to 24 months)		
	Consensual sexual touching of naked body parts but not involving naked genitalia	26 weeks (4 weeks–18 months)		

OFFENCE	TYPE/ NATURE OF ACTIVITY	STARTING POINTS (AND SENTENCING RANGES)	AGG. & MIT. FACTORS	GUIDELINE PAGES
Causing or inciting a person with a mental disorder to watch a sexual act 37 (causing a person with a mental disorder to watch a sexual act by inducement, threat or deception) ‡ 41 (care workers: causing a person with a mental disorder to watch a sexual act) †	Live sexual activity	18 months (12 months to 24 months)	A2, A3, A4, A5, A10	78, 79
	Moving or still images of people engaged in sexual activity involving penetration	32 weeks (26–52 weeks)		
	Moving or still images of people engaged in sexual activity other than penetration	Community order (community order–26 weeks custody)		

Part 4: Preparatory offences (*Sexual Offences Act* 2003, ss.15, 62, 63, 61)

K-97   In addition to the generic aggravating factors, the main factors determining the seriousness of these offences are: the seriousness of the intended offence (which will affect both the
offender's culpability and the degree of risk to which the victim has been exposed); the
degree to which the offence was planned; the sophistication of the grooming (s.15); the determination of the offender; how close the offender came to success; the reason why the offender did not succeed (*i.e.* whether it was a change of mind or whether someone or
something prevented the offender from continuing); and any physical or psychological
injury suffered by the victim.

Key to table of starting points, *etc.*, for part 4

†   Denotes that an offence is a "specified offence" for the purposes of the *Criminal Justice Act* 2003,
          s.224

‡   Denotes that an offence is a "serious offence" for the purposes of the *Criminal Justice Act* 2003, s.224

Aggravating factors.

A2:   Background of intimidation or coercion

A3:   Use of drugs, alcohol or other substance to facilitate the offence

A4:   Threats to prevent victim reporting the incident

A5:   Abduction or detention

A6:   Offender aware that he or she is suffering from a sexually transmitted infection

A13:   Targeting of vulnerable victim

A14:   Significant impact on persons present in the premises

A15:   Targeting of the victim

Mitigating factors

M7:   Offender intervenes to prevent incited offence from taking place

M12:   Offender decides, of his own volition, not to proceed with the intended sexual offence

M13:   Incident of brief duration

OFFENCE	TYPE/ NATURE OF ACTIVITY	STARTING POINTS (AND SENTENCING RANGES)		AGG. & MIT. FACTORS	GUIDELINE PAGES
		Victim is under 13	Victim is 13 or over		
Sexual grooming 15 (meeting a child for sexual grooming, *etc.*) (offender over 18) ‡	Where the intent is to commit an assault by penetration or rape	4 (3–7)	2 (1–4)	A2, A3, A6, A5	82, 83
	Where the intent is to the coerce child into sexual activity	2 (1–4)	18 months (12–30 months)		
Committing another offence with intent 62 (committing an offence with intent to commit a sexual offence) ‡	Any offence committed with intent to commit a sexual offence, *e.g.* assault	Commensurate with that for preliminary offence actually committed, but enhanced to reflect intention to commit a sexual offence (2 years where intent to commit rape or assault by penetration)		A3, A6 M12, M13	84, 85
Trespass with intent 63 (trespass with intent to commit a sexual offence) ‡	Intent to commit an assault by penetration or rape	4 (3–7)		A6, A13, A14 M12	86, 87
	Intent is other sexual offence	2 (1–4)			
Administering a substance with intent 61 (administering a substance with intent) ‡	Intent to commit an assault by penetration or rape	8 (6–9)	6 (4–9)	A4, A5, A6, A15, M7	88, 89
	Intent to commit any other sexual offence	6 (4–9)	4 (3–7)		

Part 5: Other offences (*Sexual Offences Act* 2003, ss.64 & 65, 71, 66, 67, 69, 70)

K–99   As to prohibited adult sexual relationships (ss.64 & 65), the most important issue for the sentencer to consider is the circumstances in which the offence was committed and any harm caused or risked. As to exposure (s.66), voyeurism (s.67), intercourse with an animal (s.69) and sexual penetration of a corpse (s.70), a pre-sentence report will be extremely helpful in determining the most appropriate disposal. Where an offence is being dealt with in a magistrates' court more detailed guidance will be provided in the Magistrates' Court Sentencing Guidelines.

Key to table of starting points, *etc.*, for part 5

†   Denotes that an offence is a "specified offence" for the purposes of the *Criminal Justice Act* 2003, s.224

‡   Denotes that an offence is a "serious offence" for the purposes of the *Criminal Justice Act* 2003, s.224

Aggravating factors.

A2:	Background of intimidation or coercion
A3:	Use of drugs, alcohol or other substance to facilitate the offence
A4:	Threats to prevent victim reporting the incident
A6:	Offender aware that he or she is suffering from a sexually transmitted infection
A16:	Evidence of long-term grooming
A17:	No effort made to avoid pregnancy or sexual transmission of infection
A18:	Intimidating behaviour/ threats of violence to member(s) of the public
A19:	Intimidating behaviour/ threats of violence
A20:	Victim is a child
A21:	Recording activity and circulating pictures/ videos
A22:	Circulating pictures or videos for commercial gain (particularly if victim is vulnerable, *e.g.* a child or person with a mental or physical disorder)
A23:	Distress to victim (*e.g.* where the pictures/ videos are circulated to persons known to the victim)
A24:	Distress caused to relatives or friends of the deceased
A25:	Physical damage caused to body of deceased
A26:	Corpse was that of a child
A27:	Offence committed in funeral home or mortuary

Mitigating factors

M8:	Small disparity in age between victim and offender
M9:	Relationship of genuine affection
M14:	Symptom of isolation rather than depravity

OFFENCE	TYPE/ NATURE OF ACTIVITY	STARTING POINTS (AND SENTENCING RANGES)	AGG. & MIT. FACTORS	GUIDE-LINE PAGES
Prohibited adult sexual relationships: sex with an adult relative: 64 (sex with an adult relative: penetration) †	Evidence of long-term grooming when person being groomed was under 18 (offender over 18)	12 months (26 weeks to 24 months)	A2, A3, A4, A16, A6, A17	92, 93
65 (sex with an adult relative: consenting to penetration) †	Evidence of grooming of one party by the other when both parties were over 18	Community order (appropriate non-custodial sentence)	M8, M9	
	Sexual penetration with no aggravating factors	Community order (appropriate non-custodial sentence)		
Sexual activity in a public lavatory 71 (sexual activity in a public lavatory)	Repeat offending and/ or aggravating factors	Community order (appropriate non-custodial sentence)	A18	94, 95
	Basic offence assuming no aggravating or mitigating factors	Fine (appropriate non-custodial sentence)		
Exposure 66 (exposure) †	Repeat offender	12 weeks (4–26 weeks)	A4, A19, A20	96, 97
	Basic offence assuming no aggravating or mitigating factors, or some offences with aggravating factors	Community order (appropriate non-custodial sentence)		
Voyeurism 67 (voyeurism) †	Offence with serious aggravating factors such as recording sexual activity and placing it on a website or circulating it for commercial gain	12 months (26 weeks to 24 months)	A4, A21, A22, A23	98, 99
	Offence with aggravating factors such as recording sexual activity and showing it to others	26 weeks (4 weeks to 18 months)		
	Basic offence assuming no aggravating or mitigating factors (*e.g.* offender spies through a hole he or she has made in a changing room wall)	Community order (appropriate non-custodial sentence)		
Intercourse with an animal 69 (intercourse with an animal) †	Basic offence assuming no aggravating or mitigating factors	Community order (appropriate non-custodial sentence)	A21, M14	100, 101
Sexual penetration of a corpse 70 (sexual penetration of a corpse) †	Repeat offending and/ or aggravating factors	26 weeks (4 weeks to 18 months)	A24, A25, A26, A27	102, 103
	Basic offence assuming no aggravating or mitigating factors	Community order (appropriate non-custodial sentence)		

Part 6A: Indecent photographs of children

K–101   This part of the guideline (pp.109–114) deals with offences contrary to the *Protection of Children Act* 1978, s.1, and the *CJA* 1988, s.160. It is based on the sentencing levels identified in *R. v. Oliver*; *R. v. Hartrey*; *R. v. Baldwin* [2003] 1 Cr.App.R. 28, CA, which have been "reviewed". Pseudo-photographs should generally be treated as less serious than real photographs, save, for example, where the imagery is particularly grotesque and beyond the scope of normal photography. The presence of any aggravating factors will substantially increase a sentence. Where it cannot be established that a victim was under 13, the sentence should be based on starting points for children aged over 13 but under 16. Inferences should not be drawn as to the status of unknown material; but using devices to destroy or hide material will amount to the generic aggravating factor of "an attempt to conceal or dispose of evidence". Where the material is shown or distributed without the victim's consent, the fact that the victim is over the age of consent has no bearing on sentence levels even if the material was made and possessed with the victim's consent. Any profit for the victim, financial or otherwise, actual or anticipated, should be neutral for sentencing purposes. An offence contrary to the 1978 Act is a serious offence for the purposes of section 224 of the *CJA* 2003, whereas an offence contrary to the 1988 Act is a specified offence.

Where the child depicted is aged 16 or 17, the starting points should reflect the fundamental facts of the case, including that the child is over the legal age of consent. Sentences should be lower than in cases involving children under 16 where the offender possesses only a few photographs, none of which includes sadism or bestiality, and they are retained solely for use of the offender.

Aggravating factors

A2:   Background of intimidation or coercion

A4:   Threats to prevent victim reporting the incident

A28:   Images shown or distributed to others, especially children

A29:   Collection is systematically stored or organised, indicating a sophisticated approach to trading or a high level of personal interest

A30:   Images stored, made available or distributed in such a way that they can be inadvertently accessed by others

A31:   Use of drugs, alcohol or other substance to facilitate the offence of making or taking

A32:   Threats to disclose victim's activity to friends or relatives

A33:   Financial or other gain

Mitigating factors

M15:   Few images held solely for personal use

M16:   Images viewed but not stored

M17:   Few images held solely for personal use and it is established both that the subject was aged 16 or 17 and that he or she was consenting

Levels of seriousness

L1:   Images depicting erotic posing with no sexual activity

L2:   Non-penetrative sexual activity between children, or solo masturbation by a child

L3:   Non-penetrative sexual activity between adults and children

L4:   Penetrative sexual activity involving a child or children, or both children and adults

L5:   Sadism or penetration of, or by, an animal

K–102

TYPE/ NATURE OF ACTIVITY	STARTING POINTS (AND SENTENCING RANGES)
Offender commissioned or encouraged the production of level 4 or 5 images	6 (4–9)
Offender involved in the production of level 4 or 5 images	6 (4–9)

Level 4 or 5 images shown or distributed	3 (2–5)
Offender involved in the production of, or has traded in, material at levels 1–3	2 (1–4)
Possession of a large quantity of level 4 or 5 material for personal use only	12 months (6 months to 24 months)
Large number of level 3 images shown or distributed	12 months (6 months to 24 months)
Possession of a large quantity of level 3 material for personal use	26 weeks (4 weeks to 18 months)
Possession of a small number of images at level 4 or 5	26 weeks (4 weeks to 18 months)
Large number of level 2 images shown or distributed	26 weeks (4 weeks to 18 months)
Small number of level 3 images shown or distributed	26 weeks (4 weeks to 18 months)
Offender in possession of a large amount of material at level 2 or a small amount at level 3	12 weeks (4–26 weeks)
Offender has shown or distributed material at level 1 or 2 on a limited scale	12 weeks (4–26 weeks)
Offender has exchanged images at level 1 or 2 with other collectors, but with no element of financial gain	12 weeks (4–26 weeks)
Possession of a large amount of level 1 material and/or no more than a small amount of level 2, and the material is for personal use and has not been distributed or shown to others	Community order (appropriate non-custodial sentence)

Parts 6B to 6D: Abuse of children through prostitution and pornography (*Sexual Offences Act* 2003, ss.47, 48–50); **exploitation of prostitution** (*Sexual Offences Act* 2003, ss.52, 53, *Sexual Offences Act* 1956, s.33A); **trafficking** (*Sexual Offences Act* 2003, ss.57–59)

As to offences connected with child prostitution and pornography, where a number of   **K–103** children are involved, consecutive sentences may be appropriate leading to cumulative sentences considerably higher than the suggested starting points for individual offences. A more lenient approach may be appropriate where the offender was to a degree also a victim. As to exploitation of prostitution, the degree of coercion (both in terms of recruitment and subsequent control of a prostitute's activities) is highly relevant; as is the harm suffered as a result, the level of involvement of the offender, the scale of the operation and the timescale over which it has been run. Mitigation may be available where the offender had no active involvement in the coercion or control of the victim(s), where the offender acted through fear or intimidation, or where the offender was trying to escape from prostitution. For causing and inciting offences, the starting points are the same whether prostitution was caused or incited, and whether or not the incited activity took place. A fine may be appropriate for minimal involvement. Where the offence is being dealt with in a magistrates' court, more detailed guidance will be provided in the Magistrates' Court Sentencing Guidelines. As to keeping a brothel used for prostitution, the applicable principles are similar to those for offences of exploitation of prostitution. As to trafficking, the factors to be taken into consideration broadly correspond to those that relate to exploitation of prostitution. Additionally, aggravation such as participation in a large-scale commercial operation involving a high degree of planning, organisation or sophistication, financial or other gain, and the coercion and vulnerability of victims should move sentences towards the maximum of 14 years. Where a number of children are involved, consecutive sentences may be appropriate, with total sentences significantly higher than the suggested starting point for individual offences. The court should consider making confiscation and deprivation orders.

Key to table of starting points, *etc.*, for parts 6B to 6D

†   Denotes that an offence is a "specified offence" for the purposes of section 224 of the *Criminal Justice Act* 2003

‡   Denotes that an offence is a "serious offence" for the purposes of section 224 of the *Criminal Justice Act* 2003

Aggravating factors.

A2:   Background of intimidation or coercion

A3:   Use of drugs, alcohol or other substance to facilitate the offence

A4:   Threats to prevent victim reporting the incident

A5:   Abduction or detention

A6:   Offender aware that he or she is suffering from a sexually transmitted disease

A30:   Images stored, made available or distributed in such a way that they can be inadvertently accessed by others

A32:   Threats to disclose victim's activity to friends or relatives

A33:   Financial or other gain

A34:   Use of drugs, alcohol or other substance to secure the victim's compliance

A35:   Large-scale commercial operation

A36:   Induced dependency on drugs

A37:   Forcing a victim to violate another person

A38:   Victim has been manipulated into physical and emotional dependence on the offender

A39:   Images distributed to other children or persons known to the victim

A40:   Substantial gain (in the region of £5,000 and upwards)

A41:   Personal involvement in the prostitution of others

A42:   High degree of planning or sophistication

A43:   Large number of people trafficked

A44:   Fraud

A45:   Financial extortion of the victim

A46:   Deception

A47:   Threats against victim or members of victim's family

A48:   Restriction of victim's liberty

A49:   Inhumane treatment

A50:   Confiscation of victim's passport

A51:   Use of force, threats of force, or other forms of coercion

Mitigating factors

M18:   Offender also being controlled in prostitution or pornography and subject to threats and intimidation

M19:   Using employment as a route out of prostitution and not actively involved in exploitation

M20:   Coercion by a third party

M21:   No evidence of personal gain

M22:   Limited involvement

OFFENCE	TYPE/ NATURE OF ACTIVITY	STARTING POINTS (AND SENTENCING RANGES)			AGG. & MIT. FAC- TORS	GUIDE- LINE PAGES
		Victim under the age of 13	Victim is 13 or over but under 16	Victim is 16 or over		
Paying for sexual services of a child 47 (paying for sexual services of a child) ‡	History of paying for penetrative sex with children under 18	15 (13–19)	7 (5–10)	3 (2–5)	A34, A5, A4, A32, A6	116–118
	Penile penetration of the vagina, anus or mouth/ penetration of the vagina or anus with any other body part or object	12 (10–16)	5 (4–8)	2 (1–4)		
	Sexual touching falling short of penetration	5 (4–8)	4 (3–7)	12 months (6 to 24 months)		
Child prostitution and pornography 48 (causing or inciting child prostitution or pornography) ‡ 49 (controlling a child prostitute or a child involved in pornography) ‡ 50 (arranging or facilitating child prostitution or pornography) ‡	Penetrative activity: organised commercial exploitation	10 (8–13)	8 (6–11)	4 (3–7)	A2, A35, A34, A36, A37, A38, A5, A4, A32, A30, A39, A33 M18	120–123
	Penetrative activity: offender's involvement is minimal and not perpetrated for gain	8 (6–11)	5 (4–8)	2 (1–4)		
	Non-penetrative activity: organised commercial exploitation	8 (6–11)	6 (4–9)	3 (2–5)		
	Non-penetrative activity: offender's involvement is minimal and not perpetrated for gain	6 (4–9)	3 (2–5)	12 months (6 to 24 months)		
Exploitation of prostitution 52 (causing or inciting prostitution for gain) † 53 (controlling prostitution for gain) †	Evidence of physical and/ or mental coercion		3 (2–5)		A2, A35, A40, A34, A36, A5, A4, A32 M18	126, 127
	No coercion or corruption, but offender is closely involved in victim's prostitution	12 months (6 months –24 months)				
	No evidence that victim was physically coerced or corrupted and involvement of offender was minimal	Community order (appropriate non-custodial sentence)				

OFFENCE	TYPE/ NATURE OF ACTIVITY	STARTING POINTS (AND SENTENCING RANGES)			AGG. & MIT. FACTORS	GUIDE-LINE PAGES
		Victim under the age of 13	Victim is 13 or over but under 16	Victim is 16 or over		
Keeping a brothel used for prostitution 33A *SOA* 1956 (keeping a brothel used for prostitution)	Offender is keeper of a brothel and has made substantial profits in the region of £5,000 and upwards		2 (1–4)		A2, A35,	128, 129
	Offender is keeper of a brothel and is personally involved in its management	12 months (6 months 24 months)			A41, A5, A33	
	Involvement of the offender was minimal	Community order (appropriate non-custodial sentence)			M19, M20	
Trafficking 57 (trafficking into the U.K. for sexual exploitation) ‡ 58 (trafficking within the U.K. for sexual exploitation) ‡ 59 (trafficking out of the U.K. for sexual exploitation) ‡	Involvement at any level in any stage of the trafficking operation where the victim was coerced		6 (4–9)		A35, A42, A43, A40, A44, A45, A46, A51, A47, A5, A48, A49, A50	130, 131
	Involvement at any level in any stage of the trafficking operation where there was no coercion of the victim		2 (1–4)		M20, M21, M22	

Part 7: Sentencing young offenders—offences with a lower statutory maximum

The guidelines in this part are intended for cases where the court considers that the facts found by the court justify the involvement of the criminal law, which findings may be different from those on which a decision to prosecute was made. The guidelines relate to sentencing on conviction of a first time offender. Where a young offender pleads guilty to one of the offences dealt with in this part, a youth court may impose an absolute discharge, a mental health disposal, a custodial sentence, or make a referral order. Where a custodial sentence is imposed in the Crown Court, it may be a detention and training order, or detention under section 91 of the *PCC(S)A* 2000 for a period up to the maximum for the offence.

The guideline (as originally drafted) referred to the offences in this part as being contrary to sections 9, 10, 11, 12, 25 and 26 of the 2003 Act. These can be split into two, as slightly different considerations apply to sections 9 to 12 as compared with sections 25 and 26.

As to sections 9 to 12, the guideline was in error in its premise that a person under 18 can commit one of these offences. Each of those offences is defined in such a way that it can only be committed by a person aged 18 or over. If a person under that age does an act proscribed by any of those sections, he does not offend against them. Section 13(1) (not mentioned in the guideline as originally drafted), however, provides that "(1) A person under 18 commits an offence if he does anything which would be an offence under any of sections 9 to 12 if he were aged 18.", and subsection (2) provides for a lesser maximum penalty. A person under 18 who does that which is prohibited by any of those sections would commit an offence under section 13, and should be charged as having committed an offence "contrary to section 13". The guideline has now been corrected in this respect. An offence contrary to section 13 is a specified offence, but not a serious offence for the purposes of Chapter 5 of Part 12 of the *CJA* 2003.

With sections 25 and 26, the position is less clear-cut. It is subsection (1) in each case that creates the offence and age is not an ingredient of the offence; but subsections (4) and (5) contain different penalty provisions according to whether the offender is aged 18 or over or under 18. Where the offender is under 18, the maximum is five years' custody. Taking the section as a whole, it is submitted, on the basis of *R. v. Courtie* [1984] A.C. 463, HL (the effect of the varying penalty provisions in the *SOA* 1956, according to the circumstances of an act of buggery, was to create separate offences), that sections 25 and 26 create distinct offences for those under 18. If this is correct, then these offences are specified offences, but not serious offences, because they carry a maximum of five years' custody and they cannot—by definition—be committed by an 18-year-old. The separate listing of these offences in section 91 of the *PCC(S)A* 2000 (§ 5–610 in the main work) supports this view: an offence under section 25 or 26 committed by an adult carries 14 years' imprisonment and there would have been no need to make special mention of it if there were only one offence.

This view has not been accepted by the Sentencing Guidelines Council as the guideline still shows the offences contrary to sections 25 and 26, when committed by an under 18-year-old, as "serious offences". It is submitted that the better view is that they are "specified", but not "serious" offences.

Key to table of starting points, *etc.*, for parts 6B to 6D

† Denotes that an offence is a "specified offence" for the purposes of section 224 of the *Criminal Justice Act* 2003

‡ Denotes that an offence is a "serious offence" for the purposes of section 224 of the *Criminal Justice Act* 2003

Aggravating factors.

A2:   Background of intimidation or coercion

A3:   Use of drugs, alcohol or other substance to facilitate the offence

A4:   Threats to prevent victim reporting the incident

A5:   Abduction or detention

A6:   Offender aware that he or she is suffering from a sexually transmitted infection

A10:   Images of violent activity

Mitigating factors

M5:   Youth and immaturity of offender

M7:   Offender intervenes to prevent incited offence from taking place

M8:   Small disparity in age between victim and offender

M9:   Relationship of genuine affection

OFFENCE	TYPE/ NATURE OF ACTIVITY	STARTING POINTS (AND SENTENCING RANGES)	AGG. & MIT. FACTORS	GUIDE-LINE PAGES
Sexual activity with a child 13(9) (intentional sexual touching of a person under 16) (offender under 18) †	Offence involving penetration where one or more aggravating factors exist or where there is a substantial age gap between the parties	12-month detention and training order (6- to 24- month detention and training order)	A2, A3, A4, A5, A6	135
	Any form of sexual activity (non-penetrative or penetrative) not involving any aggravating factors	Community order (appropriate non-custodial sentence)	M9, M5	
Causing or inciting a child to engage in sexual activity 13(10) (causing or inciting a child to engage in sexual activity) (offender under 18) †	Offence involving penetration where one or more aggravating factors exist or where there is a substantial age gap between the parties	12-month detention and training order (6- to 24- month detention and training order)	A2, A3, A4, A5, A6	136
	Any form of sexual activity (non-penetrative or penetrative) not involving any aggravating factors	Community order (appropriate non-custodial sentence)	M9, M7, M5	
Engaging in sexual activity in the presence of a child 13(11) (engaging in sexual activity in the presence of a child) (offender under 18) †	Sexual activity involving penetration where one or more aggravating factors exist	12-month detention and training order (6- to 24- month detention and training order)	A2, A3, A4, A5	137
	Any form of sexual activity (non-penetrative or penetrative) not involving any aggravating factors	Community order (appropriate non-custodial sentence)	M5	
Causing a child to watch a sexual act 13(12) (causing a child to watch a sexual act) (offender under 18) †	Live sexual activity	8-month detention and training order (6- to 12- month detention and training order)	A2, A3, A4, A5, A10	138
	Moving or still images of people engaged in sexual acts involving penetration	Community order (appropriate non-custodial sentence)	M5	
	Moving or still images of people engaged in sexual acts other than penetration	Community order (appropriate non-custodial sentence)		

OFFENCE	TYPE/ NATURE OF ACTIVITY	STARTING POINTS (AND SENTENCING RANGES)	AGG. & MIT. FACTORS	GUIDE-LINE PAGES
Sexual activity with a child family member and inciting a child family member to engage in sexual activity 25 (sexual activity with a child family member) (offender under 18) ‡ 26 (inciting a child family member to engage in sexual activity) (offender under 18) ‡ **N.B.: As to whether these offences are "serious offences",** see *ante*.	Offence involving penetration where one or more aggravating factors exist or where there is a substantial age gap between the parties	18-month detention and training order (6- to 24- month detention and training order)	A2, A3, A4, A6 M8, M9, M5	139
	Any form of sexual activity that does not involve any aggravating factors	Community order (appropriate non-custodial sentence)		

I. Failing to Surrender to Bail

The Sentencing Guidelines Council has issued a definitive guideline on failing to surrender to bail (*Bail Act* 1976, s.6(1) and (2) (§ 3–27 in the main work)). It deals with offenders sentenced on or after December 10, 2007, and only relates to the sentencing of those
aged 18 or over.

Assessment of seriousness

The seriousness of an offence is to be determined by: (a) the offender's culpability (in particular, whether the failure to surrender was intended to cause harm and, if so, what level of
harm), and (b) any harm which the offence caused, was intended to cause or might foreseeably have caused (in particular, to what extent the failure to surrender impeded the course
of justice), and "harm" includes not only harm caused to victims and witnesses but also the
consequential drain on the police and the courts and the wider negative impact on public
confidence in the criminal justice system. The same approach to sentencing should be
adopted for offences under both section 6(1) and (2), though the seriousness is likely to be
less for an offence under subsection (2). The assessment of culpability requires consideration
of the immediate reason why the defendant failed to appear, which can range from forgetful-
ness or fear of the outcome of the hearing to a deliberate act, and where the failure to surrender was deliberate, it will be relevant whether it was designed to disrupt the system to
the defendant's advantage or whether the defendant simply gave no thought at all to the
consequences. Failure to surrender will always cause some degree of harm, will inevitably
delay justice, and will almost always waste public money. The circumstances of an offence,
and the harm likely to be caused, will range from failure to appear for a first hearing but
attending shortly afterwards (where the only harm caused is likely to be financial and
procedural), to failure to appear for trial or sentence, especially where the trial does not
proceed in the defendant's absence (where the harm caused may extend to the prevention
of justice). Generally, the same approach should be taken whether the failure to surrender
is to a court or to a police station, but the harm caused is likely to be less in the case of a
police station, and there are also circumstances where the culpability may be less. Where
sentence is passed in advance of the offence in respect of which bail was granted, the
seriousness of that offence should not affect the assessment of seriousness, but the nature of
that offence may affect the degree or likelihood of harm caused, such as where it is a violent
or sexual offence, and an acquittal for that offence will not affect the seriousness of the failure to surrender.

Aggravating factors that are particularly relevant to the assessment of seriousness are: (a)
repeated offences under section 6; (b) the absence of the offender causing a lengthy delay to
the administration of justice; and (c) a determined effort to avoid the jurisdiction of the
court or to undermine the course of justice. Mitigating factors that are particularly relevant
are: (a) prompt voluntary surrender (if initiated by the offender); (b) misunderstanding
(which must be differentiated from a mistake on the part of the offender); (c) a failure to
comprehend the requirements or significance of bail; and (d) caring responsibilities (where
these are the cause of the failure to surrender). The fact that the offender has a disorganised
or chaotic lifestyle (which may be due to dependence on drugs or alcohol) does not mitigate
the seriousness of the offence (though it may amount to personal mitigation).

Procedural issues

As to when to sentence, the key principle is stated to be that a court should deal with a defendant who fails to surrender as soon as it is practicable, even if the trial or other hearing
for the offence in respect of which bail was granted is adjourned. Relevant factors when
deciding what is practicable include: (a) when the proceedings in respect of which bail was
granted are expected to conclude; (b) the seriousness of that offence; and (c) the type of
penalty that might be imposed for that offence and for the failure to surrender. Liability for
the section 6 offence should be determined as soon as possible, since it will be central to the

issue of whether bail should be renewed; accordingly, a trial should be held on the first appearance after arrest or surrender, unless an adjournment is necessary. Occasions on which it may be more appropriate to sentence both offences together include circumstances where the totality of sentence may affect sentence type and where the harm caused cannot be assessed at an earlier stage.

K–110   *As to sentencing*, the alternatives to immediate custody are a community order, including an electronically monitored curfew requirement and, perhaps, a supervision or activity requirement, and, in more serious cases, a suspended sentence. Where custodial sentences are imposed both for the section 6 offence and for the substantive offence, they should normally be consecutive, but should be concurrent where otherwise the overall sentence would be disproportionate to the combined seriousness of the offences.

K–111   *As to trial in the defendant's absence*, where it has proved possible to proceed to trial or conclude proceedings in the absence of the defendant, this should have no bearing on culpability, but may be relevant to the assessment of harm, if the harm caused by the failure to attend has been reduced or avoided by such a course.

Sentencing ranges and starting points

K–112   The sentencing ranges and starting points relate to persons convicted following a plea of not guilty, and who do not have a conviction which, by virtue of the *CJA* 2003, s.143(2) (§ 5–67 in the main work), must be treated as an aggravating factor. A court should identify the description that most nearly matches the facts of the offence and this will identify a starting point, from which a provisional sentence can be reached. The sentencing range is the bracket into which the provisional sentence will fall after consideration of aggravating or mitigating factors (although particular circumstances, particular matters of aggravation or mitigation or the reduction for a guilty plea may require a sentence outside of that range). A court should give reasons for imposing a sentence of a different kind or outside the range provided in the guideline.

For a deliberate failure to attend causing delay and/or interference with the administration of justice, the starting point is 14 days' custody, and the range, in a magistrates' court, should be from a community order (low) to 10 weeks' custody, and in the Crown Court, should be from a community order (medium) to 40 weeks' custody, with the type and degree of harm actually caused affecting where in the range the case falls. For a negligent or non-deliberate failure to attend causing delay and/or interference with the administration of justice, the starting point should be a fine, and the range (regardless of court) should be from a fine to a community order (medium). Where the defendant surrenders late, but the case proceeds as planned, the starting point and the range should be a fine.

J. Assault and Other Offences Against the Person

K–113   The Sentencing Council for England and Wales has issued a definitive guideline on non-fatal offences against the person, applying to all offenders aged 18 or over who are sentenced on or after June 13, 2011, regardless of the date of their offence. The offences covered are: (A) causing grievous bodily harm, or wounding, with intent to do grievous bodily harm (*Offences against the Person Act* 1861, s.18 (§ 19–199 in the main work)), (B) inflicting grievous bodily harm or unlawful wounding (1861 Act, s.20 (*ibid.*, § 19–200)) and racially or religiously aggravated grievous bodily harm or unlawful wounding (*CDA* 1998, s.29 (*ibid.*, § 19–214a)), (C) assault occasioning actual bodily harm (1861 Act, s.47 (*ibid.*, § 19–190)) and racially or religiously aggravated actual bodily harm (1998 Act, s.29), (D) assault with intent to resist arrest (1861 Act, s.38 (*ibid.*, § 19–255)), (E) assault on a police constable in execution of his duty (*Police Act* 1996, s.89), and (F) common assault (*CJA* 1988, s.39) and racially or religiously aggravated common assault (1998 Act, s.29).

K–114   The guideline sets out eight to nine steps to be followed (in order) when sentencing for these offences, which are as follows, subject to any modifications set out in the specific sections relating to each group (*post*).

Step one requires the court to determine within which of three categories reflecting various degrees of seriousness the offence falls. Category 1 requires greater harm and higher culpability, category 2 requires either greater harm and lower culpability or lesser harm and higher culpability, and category 3 requires lesser harm and lower culpability. In determining the offender's culpability and the harm caused (or intended), the court should refer only to the factors indicating harm and culpability set out in the specific sections relating to A to F, *post*, which comprise the principal factual elements of the offence.

Step two requires the court to use the starting point identified for the relevant category (as to which, see also the specific sections relating to A–F, *post*) to reach a sentence within the category range (*post*). The starting point applies to all offenders irrespective of plea or previous convictions. A case of particular gravity, reflected by multiple features of culpability in step one, could merit upward adjustment from the starting point before further adjustment is made for the aggravating or mitigating factors increasing or reducing seriousness or reflecting personal mitigation set out in the specific sections relating to A to F, *post*, which contain a non-exhaustive list of additional factual elements providing the context of the offence and factors relating to the offender. Having considered all these, and other relevant factors, it might be appropriate to move outside the identified category range.

At step three, the court should take into account sections 73 and 74 of the *SOCPA* 2005 (assistance by defendants: reduction or review of sentence (*ibid.*, §§ 5–132, 5–133)), and any other rule of law by virtue of which an offender may receive a discounted sentence in consequence of assistance given (or offered) to the prosecutor or investigator.

At step four, the court should take account of any potential reduction for a guilty plea in accordance with section 144 of the *CJA* 2003 (*ibid.*, § 5–107) and the revised guideline on reductions in sentence for guilty pleas (*ante*, Appendix K–1 *et seq.*).

At step five, which does not apply to the offence in E (assault on a police constable in execution of his duty), the court will consider whether the offender meets the dangerousness criteria for a life sentence or imprisonment for public protection (in respect of those offences which are serious offences within the meaning of the 2003 Act, Ch. 5 (*ibid.*, §§ 5–495 *et seq.*), in which case the notional determinate sentence should be used as the basis for setting the minimum term) or an extended sentence (in respect of those offences which are specified offences within the meaning of the 2003 Act, Ch. 5).

At step six (or five), the court should apply the totality principle, step seven (or six), consider whether to make compensation or other ancillary orders or both, step eight (or seven), give its reasons for, and explain the effect of, the sentence (2003 Act, s.174 (*ibid.*, § 5–165)), and step nine (or eight) take into account any time spent on remand in custody or on bail (2003 Act, ss.240 and 240A (*ibid.*, §§ 5–640, 5–645)).

For offences under the 1998 Act, s.29, only, the court should determine the appropriate sentence for the offence without taking account of the element of aggravation, and then make an addition to the sentence, considering the level of aggravation involved. It may be appropriate to move outside the identified category range, taking into account the increased statutory maximum.

Key to factors indicating greater harm and higher or lower culpability (step one)

Factors indicating greater harm

    a. Injury (which includes disease transmission and/ or psychological harm) which is serious in the context of the offence (must normally be present). **K–115**

    b. Victim is particularly vulnerable because of personal circumstances.

    c. Sustained or repeated assault on the same victim.

    d. Injury or fear of injury which is serious in the context of the offence (must normally be present).

Factors indicating higher culpability

Statutory aggravating factors: **K–116**

    e. Offence racially or religiously aggravated.

    f. Offence motivated by, or demonstrating, hostility to the victim based on his or her sexual orientation (or presumed sexual orientation).

    g. Offence motivated by, or demonstrating, hostility to the victim based on the victim's disability (or presumed disability).

  Other aggravating factors:

    h. A significant degree of premeditation.

    i. Use of weapon or weapon equivalent (*e.g.* shod foot, headbutting, use of acid, use of animal).

    j. Threatened use of weapon or weapon equivalent.

    k. Intention to commit more serious harm than actually resulted from the offence.

    l. Deliberately causes more harm than is necessary for commission of offence.

    m. Deliberate targeting of vulnerable victim.

    n. Leading role in group or gang.

    o. Offence motivated by, or demonstrating, hostility based on the victim's age, sex, gender identity (or presumed gender identity).

Factors indicating lower culpability

K–117   p. Subordinate role in group or gang.

    q. A greater degree of provocation than normally expected.

    r. Lack of premeditation.

    s. Mental disorder or learning disability, where linked to commission of the offence.

    t. Excessive self defence.

Key to factors increasing or reducing seriousness or reflecting personal mitigation (step 2)

Factors increasing seriousness

K–118 Statutory aggravating factors:

    u. Previous convictions (in accordance with the 2003 Act, s.143(2) (§ 5–67 in the main work)).

    v. Offence committed whilst on bail (2003 Act, s.143(3)).

  Other aggravating factors include:

    w. Location of the offence.

    x. Timing of the offence.

    y. Continuing effect upon the victim.

    z. Offence committed against those working in the public sector or providing a service to the public.

    aa. Presence of others including relatives, especially children or partner of the victim.

    bb. Gratuitous degradation of victim.

    cc. In domestic violence cases, victim forced to leave home.

    dd. Failure to comply with current court orders.

    ee. Offence committed whilst on licence.

    ff. An attempt to conceal or dispose of evidence.

    gg. Failure to respond to warnings or concerns expressed by others about the offender's behaviour.

    hh. Commission of offence whilst under the influence of alcohol or drugs.

    ii. Abuse of power and/ or position of trust.

    jj. Exploiting contact arrangements with a child to commit an offence.

    kk. Any steps taken to prevent the victim reporting an incident, obtaining assistance and/ or from assisting or supporting the prosecution.

    ll. Offences taken into consideration.

Factors reducing seriousness or reflecting personal mitigation

K–119   mm. No previous convictions or no relevant/ recent convictions.

nn. Single blow.

oo. Remorse.

pp. Good character and/ or exemplary conduct.

qq. Determination and/ or demonstration of steps taken to address addiction or offending behaviour.

rr. Serious medical conditions requiring urgent, intensive or long-term treatment.

ss. Isolated incident.

tt. Age and/ or lack of maturity where it affects the responsibility of the offender.

uu. Lapse of time since the offence where this is not the fault of the offender.

vv. Mental disorder or learning disability, where not linked to the commission of the offence.

ww. Sole or primary carer for dependent relatives.

Fine bands

Fine band	Starting point (applicableto all offenders)	Category range (applicable to all offenders)
band A	50% of relevant weekly income	25 – 75% of relevant weekly income
band B	100% of relevant weekly income	75 – 125% of relevant weekly income
band C	150% of relevant weekly income	125 – 175% of relevant weekly income

K–120

Community orders

The following table sets out a non-exhaustive description of examples of requirements that might be appropriate for low, medium and high level community orders (respectively). Where two or more requirements are ordered, they must be compatible with each other.

K–121

Low	Medium	High
In general, only one requirement will be appropriate and the length may be curtailed if additional requirements are necessary		More intensive sentences which combine two or more requirements may be appropriate

Low	Medium	High
Suitable requirements might include: • 40 – 80 hours unpaid work • curfew requirement within the lowest range (*e.g.* up to 12 hours per day for a few weeks) • exclusion requirement, without electronic monitoring, for a few months • prohibited activity requirement • attendance centre requirement (where available)	Suitable requirements might include: • greater number of hours of unpaid work (*e.g.* 80 – 150 hours) • an activity requirement in the middle range (20 – 30 days) • curfew requirement within the middle range (*e.g.* up to 12 hours for two – three months) • exclusion requirement, lasting in the region of six months • prohibited activity requirement	Suitable requirements might include: • 150 – 300 hours unpaid work • activity requirement up to the maximum of 60 days • curfew requirement up to 12 hours per day for four – six months • exclusion order lasting in the region of 12 months

A. Causing grievous bodily harm, or wounding, with intent to do grievous bodily harm

K–122   In assessing whether there has been greater harm for the purposes of determining the offence category in respect of these offences, serious injury must normally be present.

Factors indicating harm and culpability (step one)
> Greater harm: a–c
> Lesser harm: injury which is less serious in the context of the offence
> Higher culpability: e–i, k–o
> Lower culpability: p–t

Starting point and category range (step two)

Offence category	Starting point (applicable to all offenders)	Category range (applicable to all offenders)
category 1	12 years' custody	nine – 16 years' custody
category 2	six years' custody	five – nine years' custody
category 3	four years' custody	three – five years' custody

Factors increasing or reducing seriousness or reflecting personal mitigation
> Factors increasing seriousness: u–z, aa–ll
> Factors reducing seriousness or reflecting personal mitigation: mm–ww

B. Inflicting grievous bodily harm or unlawful wounding and racially or religiously aggravated grievous bodily harm or unlawful wounding

K–123   In assessing whether there has been greater harm for the purposes of determining the offence category in respect of these offences, serious injury must normally be present.

Factors indicating harm and culpability (step one)
> Greater harm: a–c

Lesser harm: injury which is less serious in the context of the offence
Higher culpability: f–i, k–o
Lower culpability: p–t

Starting point and category range (step two)

Offence category	Starting point (applicable to all offenders)	Category range (applicable to all offenders)
category 1	three years' custody	30 months' – four years' custody
category 2	18 months' custody	one – three years' custody
category 3	high level community order	low level community order – 51 weeks' custody

When sentencing for category three offences, the court should consider whether the custody threshold has been passed, if so, whether it is unavoidable that a custodial sentence be imposed and, if so, whether that sentence can be suspended.

Factors increasing or reducing seriousness or reflecting personal mitigation
Same as for A, *ante*.

C. Assault occasioning actual bodily harm and racially or religiously aggravated actual bodily harm

In assessing whether there has been "greater harm" for the purposes of determining the　**K–124**
offence category in respect of these offences, serious injury must normally be present.

Factors indicating harm and culpability (step one)
Same as for B, *ante*.

Starting point and category range (step two)

Offence category	Starting point (applicable to all offenders)	Category range (applicable to all offenders)
category 1	18 months' custody	one – three years' custody
category 2	26 weeks' custody	low level community order – 51 weeks' custody
category 3	medium level community order	band A fine – high level community order

When sentencing for category two offences, the court should consider whether the custody threshold has been passed, if so, whether it is unavoidable that a custodial sentence be imposed and, if so, whether that sentence can be suspended; and in sentencing for category three offences, the court should also consider whether the community order threshold has been passed.

Factors increasing or reducing seriousness or reflecting personal mitigation
Same as for A and B, *ante*.

D. Assault with intent to resist arrest

Factors indicating harm and culpability (step one)
Greater harm: c　　　　　　　　　　　　　　　　　　　　　　　　**K–125**
Lesser harm: injury which is less serious in the context of the offence

Higher culpability: e–i, k–l, n, o
Lower culpability: p, r, s

Starting point and category range (step two)

Offence category	Starting point (applicable to all offenders)	Category range (applicable to all offenders)
category 1	26 weeks' custody	12 – 51 weeks' custody
category 2	medium level community order	low level community order – high level community order
category 3	band B fine	band A fine – band C fine

When sentencing for category one offences, the court should consider whether the sentence can be suspended.

Factors increasing or reducing seriousness or reflecting personal mitigation
Factors increasing seriousness: u–y, bb, dd–hh, kk, ll
Factors reducing seriousness or reflecting personal mitigation: mm–tt, vv, ww

E. Assault on a police constable in execution of his duty

Factors indicating harm and culpability (step one)
K–126   Same as for D, *ante*.

Starting point and category range (step two)

Offence category	Starting point (applicable to all offenders)	Category range (applicable to all offenders)
category 1	12 weeks' custody	low level community order – 26 weeks' custody
category 2	medium level community order	low level community order – high level community order
category 3	band B fine	band A fine – band C fine

When sentencing for category one offences, the court should consider whether the custody threshold has been passed, if so, whether it is unavoidable that a custodial sentence be imposed and, if so, whether that sentence can be suspended.

Factors increasing or reducing seriousness or reflecting personal mitigation
Factors increasing seriousness: u–y, bb, dd–hh, kk, ll
Factors reducing seriousness or reflecting personal mitigation: mm–ww

F. Common assault and racially or religiously aggravated common assault

K–127   In assessing whether there has been "greater harm" for the purposes of determining the offence category in respect of these offences, injury or fear of injury must normally be present.

Factors indicating harm and culpability (step one)
Greater harm: b–d
Lesser harm: injury which is less serious in the context of the offence

Higher culpability: f–o
Lower culpability: p–t

Starting point and category range (step two)

Offence category	Starting point (applicable to all offenders)	Category range (applicable to all offenders)
category 1	high level community order	low level community order – 26 weeks' custody
category 2	medium level community order	band A fine – high level community order
category 3	band A fine	discharge – band C fine

When sentencing for category one offences, the court should consider whether the custody threshold has been passed, if so, whether it is unavoidable that a custodial sentence be imposed and, if so, whether that sentence can be suspended. When sentencing for category two offences, the court should consider whether the community order threshold has been crossed.

Factors increasing or reducing seriousness or reflecting personal mitigation
Same as for A, B and C, *ante.*

[The next paragraph is K–131.]

K. ASSAULTS ON CHILDREN AND CRUELTY TO A CHILD

The Sentencing Guidelines Council has issued a definitive guideline (i) supplementing the guideline on assaults and other offences against the person (*ante,* K–113 *et seq.*) by detailing additional principles which apply where the victim of the offence was aged 15 or under and (ii) on the offence of cruelty to a child (*CYPA* 1933, s.1(1)). It deals with offenders sentenced on or after March 3, 2008, and only relates to the sentencing of those aged 18 or over.   **K–131**

Part 1: Assaults on children: general principles

Assessing seriousness

The seriousness of an offence is to be determined by (a) the culpability of the offender and (b) the harm caused, intended or reasonably foreseeable, and guidance on whether sentencing thresholds have been reached is provided by the guideline on seriousness. Where an offender has previous convictions, the court must consider whether it should treat any of them as an aggravating factor, having regard to the nature and relevance of each offence and the time that has elapsed since the conviction. The fact that the victim is a child is likely to aggravate the seriousness of the offence where the offender is an adult.   **K–132**

Aggravation
The fact that the victim of an assault is a child will often mean that the offence involves a particularly vulnerable victim. The most relevant aggravating factors are: (i) the victim is particularly vulnerable; (ii) an abuse of power; (iii) an abuse of a position of trust; (iv) an especially serious physical or psychological effect on the victim, even if unintended; (v) the presence of others, *e.g.* relatives, especially other children; and (vi) additional degradation of the victim. Additional aggravating factors are: (i) sadistic behaviour; (ii) the making of   **K–133**

threats to prevent the victim reporting the offence; (iii) the deliberate concealment of the victim from the authorities; and (iv) a failure to seek medical help. The location and particular circumstances of the offence may also be relevant aggravating factors.

Mitigation

K-134   The defence of lawful chastisement is only available on a charge of common assault, and where that defence is not available or is not made out, sentencing for the offence should normally be approached in the same way as for any other assault, even where an offender held a genuine belief that his actions amounted to no more than a legitimate form of physical punishment. However, if an offender has been charged with assault occasioning actual bodily harm and the court has found that he only intended to administer lawful chastisement to the child, and that the injury that was inflicted was neither intended nor foreseen by him, there should be a substantial reduction in sentence and a custodial sentence should not normally be imposed. Where the injury was neither intended nor foreseen, and was not even reasonably foreseeable, then a discharge might be appropriate.

Other factors relevant to sentencing

Adverse effect of the sentence on the victim

K-135   Imposition of a custodial sentence will often protect a victim from further harm and anguish, and some children will be less traumatised once they are no longer living with an abusive carer, but where imprisonment of the offender deprives a child victim of his sole or main carer (and may result in the child being taken into care), it may punish and re-victimise the child. Imposing a custodial sentence on the offender may be the only option, but where other sentencing options remain open, the court should take into account the impact that a custodial sentence for the offender might have on the victim. The court also needs to be aware of the progress of any concurrent family proceedings.

Offenders who have primary care responsibilities

K-136   Where the offender is the sole or primary carer of the victim or other dependants, this should potentially be taken into account for sentencing purposes, regardless of whether the offender is male or female. In such cases, an immediate custodial sentence may not be appropriate and, subject to a risk assessment, the offender may be able to resume care of or have contact with the victim.

Part 2: Cruelty to a child

Assessing seriousness

K-137   One category of child cruelty is not automatically more serious than another and, in order properly to assess the seriousness of an offence, its precise nature must be established before consideration is given to a range of contingent factors, including the defendant's intent, the length of time over which the cruelty took place, and the degree of physical and psychological harm suffered by the victim.

Culpability

K-138   Culpability should be the initial factor in determining the seriousness of an offence. An offence may be the consequence of a wide range of factors including: (i) sadism; (ii) violence resulting from any number of causes; (iii) a reduced ability to protect a child in the face of aggression from an overbearing partner; (iv) indifference or apathy resulting from low intelligence or induced by alcohol or drug dependence; (v) immaturity or social deprivation resulting in an inability to cope with the pressures of caring for children; and (vi) psychiatric illness. It might also arise as the result of a momentary lack of control by an otherwise responsible and loving carer. The extent to which any of these factors might have contributed to the commission of an offence will be important in determining the culpability of the offender. A court must strike a balance between the need to reflect the serious view which society takes of the ill-treatment of young children and the need to protect those children, and also the pressures upon immature and inadequate parents attempting to cope with the problems of infancy, and the extent to which remorse should influence sentence will always have to be judged in the light of all the circumstances. The normal starting point should be a custodial sentence, the length of which should be influenced by the circumstances surrounding the offence.

Harm

It is helpful if the indictment clearly states the nature of the offender's conduct, but even **K–139** where this is clear, difficulties arise in determining the relative seriousness of the different forms of child cruelty. There is, however, a significant distinction between cases of wilful ill-treatment which usually involve positive acts of abuse and physical violence, and cases of neglect which are typified by the absence of actions. There is also a distinction between cases involving physical injury, whether resulting directly from an assault or ill-treatment or resulting from a period of abandonment or neglect, and cases where the harm occasioned is exposure to the risk of harm or lack of proper care, attention or supervision. In addition, whether one form of cruelty is worse than another will depend not only on the degree to which the victim suffers as a result but also on the motivation and culpability of the offender.

Aggravating and mitigating factors

The guideline refers to the guideline on seriousness for general aggravating and mitigat- **K–140** ing factors. In particular, care should be taken to avoid "double-counting" when an essential element of an offence might, in other circumstances, be an aggravating factor, and the abuse of trust or abuse of power inherent in the offence have been built into the guideline and should not be treated as aggravating factors. Relevant aggravating factors are targeting one particular child from the family and the four additional aggravating factors listed under "Assaults on children: general principles" (*ante*). The sole relevant mitigating factor is seeking medical help or bringing the situation to the notice of the authorities.

Other factors relevant to sentencing

Long-term psychological harm

The starting points have been calculated to reflect the likelihood of psychological harm **K–141** and this cannot be treated as an aggravating factor. Where there is an especially serious physical or psychological effect on the victim, even if unintended, this should result in an increased sentence.

Adverse effect of the sentence on the victim

As in Part 1, *ante*. **K–142**

Offenders who have primary care responsibilities

As in Part 1, *ante*. **K–143**

Personal mitigation

The most relevant areas of personal mitigation are likely to be: (i) mental illness/ depres- **K–144** sion; (ii) inability to cope with the pressures of parenthood; (iii) lack of support; (iv) sleep deprivation; (v) domination of the offender by an abusive or stronger partner; (vi) extreme behavioural difficulties in the child, often coupled with a lack of support; and (vii) inability to secure assistance or support services in spite of every effort having been made by the offender. However, some of these factors could be regarded as an inherent part of caring for children, especially with young children, and so before they are accepted in mitigation, there must be evidence that these factors were present to a high degree and had an identifiable and significant impact on the offender's behaviour.

Factors to take into consideration

K–145   *Dangerous offenders*: the offence is a "specified offence" within the *CJA* 2003, s.224, and so a court must consider the imposition of a sentence for public protection. The guideline only applies to offenders who have not been classed as dangerous.

Categories of offence: the same starting point applies regardless of which of the various ways in which the offence can be committed is in point, and it already assumes an abuse of trust or power and the likelihood of psychological harm, and is designed to reflect the seriousness with which society as a whole regards these offences.

Additional factors: only additional aggravating and mitigating factors specifically relevant to this offence are included in the guideline, and a court must always take into account the full list of factors in the guideline on seriousness.

Sentencing ranges and starting points

K–146   The sentencing ranges and starting points relate to persons convicted following a plea of not guilty, and who do not have a conviction which, by virtue of the 2003 Act, s.143(2) (§ 5–67 in the main work), must be treated as an aggravating factor. A court should identify the description that most nearly matches the facts of the offence and this will identify a starting point, from which a provisional sentence can be reached. The sentencing range is the bracket into which the provisional sentence will fall after consideration of aggravating or mitigating factors (although particular circumstances, particular matters of aggravation or mitigation, or the reduction for a guilty plea may require a sentence outside of that range). The provisional sentence may then be reduced by matters of personal mitigation, which may also take it outside the appropriate sentencing range. A court should give reasons for imposing a sentence of a different kind or outside the range provided in the guideline.

Where there has been (i) serious cruelty over a period of time, (ii) serious long-term neglect, or (iii) a failure to protect a child from either of these, the starting point is six years' custody and the sentencing range is five to nine years' custody.

Where there has been (i) a series of assaults (the more serious the individual assaults and the longer the period over which they are perpetrated, the more serious the offence), (ii) protracted neglect or ill-treatment (the longer the period of ill-treatment or neglect and the longer the period over which it takes place, the more serious the offence), or (iii) a failure to protect a child from either of these, the starting point is three years' custody and the sentencing range is two to five years' custody.

Where there has been (i) an assault resulting in injuries consistent with assault occasioning actual bodily harm, (ii) more than one incident of neglect or ill-treatment (but not amounting to long-term behaviour), (iii) a single incident of long-term abandonment or regular incidents of short-term abandonment (the longer the period of long-term abandonment or the greater the number of incidents of short-term abandonment, the more serious the offence), or (iv) a failure to protect a child from any of these, the starting point is 36 weeks' custody and the sentencing range is 26 weeks' to two years' custody.

Where there has been (i) short-term neglect or ill-treatment, (ii) a single incident of short-term abandonment, or (iii) a failure to protect a child from any of these, the starting point is 12 weeks' custody and the sentencing range is a community order (low) to 26 weeks' custody.

L. Sentencing in Magistrates' Courts

Introduction

K–147   The Sentencing Guidelines Council has issued a guideline on offences for which sentence is frequently imposed in magistrates' courts when dealing with adult offenders, which replaces the guidelines which were effective from January 1, 2004. The foreword and introduction state that they are to apply to all relevant cases appearing for allocation (mode of trial) or for sentence on or after August 4, 2008, not only in magistrates' courts, but also in the Crown Court when dealing with appeals against sentence and when sentencing for summary only offences. The guideline should be consulted when dealing with an either-way offence for which there is no plea or an indication of a not guilty plea, since they will be relevant to the mode of trial decision, and where an offence is included in this guideline, it supersedes the equivalent part of the mode of trial guidelines in Part V.51 of the consolidated criminal practice direction (§ 1–119 in the main work). The guideline will also be relevant to decisions as to committal for sentence.

There have been five updates to these guidelines. An update that took effect on January 5, 2009, made changes to Parts 1 (indices), 3 (offence guidelines) and 5 (explanatory material). The effect of the changes to Part 3 was (i) to include extracts from the guideline on breach of an anti-social behaviour order (*post*, K–196 *et seq.*) and the guideline on theft and burglary in a building other than a dwelling (*post*, K–209 *et seq.*) in these guidelines in the appropriate places, and (ii) to make a clarificatory amendment to the existing guideline for burglary in a dwelling. Consequential amendments were made to the section in Part 5 that relates to ancillary orders, in respect of anti-social behaviour orders, and an amendment was also made to that section in respect of orders disqualifying an offender from driving, to reflect recent case law.

An update implemented on August 4, 2008, made equivalent changes to Part 3 in relation to the guideline on causing death by driving (*post*, K–185 *et seq.*) and modified Part 5 in respect of explanatory material relating to dangerous offenders (to take account of changes made by the *CJIA* 2008).

The third update was published on October 13, 2009. This included new guidelines for statutory offences of fraud (reflective of the guideline for such offences (*post*, K–228 *et seq.*). In addition, supplementary guidance was provided in relation to sentencing for health and safety offences following changes to the maximum penalty for certain offences effected by the *Health and Safety (Offences) Act* 2008 and which came into effect on January 16, 2009.

As from June 13, 2011, a fourth update will apply to all offenders aged 18 or over who are sentenced on or after that date, regardless of the date of their offence, with the effect that the new guideline on offences against the person (as to which, see *ante*, K–113 *et seq.*) is imported, except for those parts dealing with indictable-only offences, with the imposition of sentences which magistrates are not entitled to impose, and with sections 73 and 74 of the *SOCPA* 2005 (§§ 5–132, 5–133 in the main work), since they apply only in the Crown Court.

A fifth update was issued on October 13, 2011, and applies to all offenders aged 18 or over who are sentenced on or after January 16, 2012, regardless of the date of their offence. The effect is to import the guidelines on domestic and non-domestic burglary (but not aggravated burglary, which is an indictable-only offence) (as to which, see *post*, K–259 *et seq.*), except that, at step three, there is no mention of sections 73 and 74 of the *SOCPA* 2005 (§§ 5–132, 5–133 in the main work), since they apply only in the Crown Court. The starting points and category ranges apply to all offenders in all cases, irrespective of plea or previous convictions.

A sixth update was issued on January 24, 2012. This applies to all offenders aged 18 or over who are sentenced on or after February 27, 2012, regardless of the date of their offence. The effect is to import the guidelines on drug offences (*post*, K–271 *et seq.*).

As from June 11, 2012, a seventh update applies to all offenders aged 18 or over who are ★ sentenced on or after that date, regardless of the date of their offence, with the effect that a new definitive guideline on the allocation of offences (see *ante*, § 1–97) and a guideline on offences taken into consideration (*ante*, §§ 5–160 *et seq.*) and totality (*post*, K–280 *et seq.*) are imported. It also corrects an error in one of the drug offence guidelines (importation) issued in the sixth update (this correction has been incorporated into the supplement at K–275, *post*).

As from August 20, 2012, an eighth update will apply to all offenders aged 18 or over ★

who are sentenced on or after that date, regardless of the date of their offence, with the effect that a new definitive guideline on dangerous dog offences (*post*, K–291 *et seq.*) is imported into the guideline.

Recommendations

K-148   The following recommendations are sentence recommendations where the starting points are based on a first time offender who has pleaded not guilty. However, the guideline makes plain that they are to be used by magistrates in making decisions as to whether or not an offender should be tried or sentenced in the magistrates' court or the Crown Court. What is set out below is confined to that which is material to the latter decision. It follows, therefore, that the full range of recommendations is not necessarily set out. For example, in the case of burglary of a dwelling, for a case involving an unforced entry with property of low value being stolen and no aggravating features, the top end of the recommended range is 12 weeks' custody, which is well within the maximum available to a magistrates' court. Any description of offence which is of a less serious nature than the descriptions set out below may, therefore, be taken to be suitable for summary trial.

Whilst the guideline itself lists aggravating and mitigating features for all the offences, these are only set out below where the presence or absence of such features is relevant to the decision as to the appropriate court for trial or sentence.

Burglary in a dwelling

K-149   The guideline recommends —
  (i) a starting point of 12 weeks' custody and a range of sentence from a high level community order to sentence in the Crown Court for a case of forced entry where the goods stolen were not of high value and without aggravating features;
  (ii) sentence in the Crown Court where the goods stolen were of high value and any aggravating feature was present.

K-150   Particular aggravating features mentioned are: (*as indicating higher culpability*) ransacking, professionalism, a victim deliberately targeted, *e.g.* out of spite, the carrying of housebreaking implements or weapons; (*as indicating greater degree of harm*) occupier at home or returning home during burglary, goods stolen being of sentimental value.

As to aggravating features, see *R. v. Saw, post,* § K–441.

For offences for which sentence is passed on or after January 16, 2012, see now the guideline issued by the Sentencing Council for England and Wales, *post*, K–259 *et seq.*

Handling stolen goods

K-151   The guideline recommends —
  (i) a starting point of 12 weeks' custody and a range of sentence from six weeks' custody to sentence in the Crown Court for sophisticated offending or the presence of at least two aggravating features;
  (ii) sentence in the Crown Court where the offence was committed in the context of a business, the offender acts as an organiser/ distributor of the proceeds of crime, the offender makes himself available to other criminals as willing to handle the proceeds of thefts or burglaries, the offending was highly organised or professional, or the original offence was particularly serious, *e.g.* armed robbery.

K-152   Particular aggravating features mentioned are: (*as indicating higher culpability*) closeness of offender to primary offence, which may be geographical (arising from presence at or near the primary offence) or temporal (where offender instigated primary offence or, soon after, provided safe haven or route for disposal), high level of profit made or expected; (*as indicating greater degree of harm*) seriousness of the primary offence, including domestic burglary, high (including sentimental) value of goods; threats of violence or abuse of power by offender over others, such as an adult commissioning criminal activity by children or a drug dealer pressurising addicts to steal to fund their habit.

Going equipped for theft

The guideline recommends a starting point of a high level community order and a range **K–153**
of a medium level community order to sentence in the Crown Court in the case of possession of items for burglary or robbery.

False statements/representations to obtain social security benefits

For offences under the *Social Security Administration Act* 1992, s.111A, see the fraud **K–154**
guideline, *post*, K–228 *et seq.*

Vehicle licence/registration fraud (Vehicle Excise and Registration Act 1994, s.44)

The guideline recommends sentence in the Crown Court in the case of (a) use of number **K–155**
plates from another vehicle, or (b) the forging or altering of licence/ number plates for sale
to another.

Assault occasioning actual bodily harm and racially/religiously aggravated versions

The guideline recommends — **K–156**
(i) a starting point of 24 weeks' custody and a range of 12 weeks' custody to sentence in
the Crown Court for a pre-meditated assault resulting in minor, non-permanent
injury;
(ii) sentence in the Crown Court for a pre-meditated assault either resulting in relatively
serious injury or involving the use of a weapon.

Inflicting grievous bodily harm/wounding and racially/religiously aggravated versions

The guideline recommends — **K–157**
(i) a starting point of 24 weeks' custody and and a range of a high level community order to sentence in the Crown Court for "other assault" where no weapon has been
used;
(ii) a starting point of sentence in the Crown Court and a range of 24 weeks' custody to
sentence in the Crown Court for a pre-meditated assault where no weapon has been
used;
(iii) sentence in the Crown Court for a pre-meditated assault where a weapon has been
used or for any other assault where particularly grave injury results or a weapon has
been used.

Assault with intent to resist arrest

The guideline recommends a starting point of sentence in the Crown Court and a range **K–158**
from 24 weeks' custody to sentence in the Crown Court.

Threats to kill

The guideline recommends sentence in the Crown Court for repeated threats or a threat **K–159**
accompanied by a visible weapon.

Firearm, carrying in public place (Firearms Act 1968, s.19)

The guideline recommends (but note that certain offences under this section are triable **K–160**
only on indictment (not mentioned in the guideline) and certain offences are triable only
summarily, as to which, see § 24–57 in the main work)—
(i) a starting point of a high level community order and a range of a medium level com-

munity order to sentence in the Crown Court for the carrying of an imitation firearm or an unloaded shot gun without ammunition;

(ii) sentence in the Crown Court for the carrying of a loaded shot gun or for the carrying of a shot gun or any other firearm together with ammunition for it.

Bladed article/offensive weapon (possession of)

K–161   The guideline recommends—

(i) a starting point of six weeks' custody and a range of a high level community order to sentence in the Crown Court where the weapon was not used to threaten or cause fear but the offence was committed in dangerous circumstances;

(ii) sentence in the Crown Court where the weapon was used to threaten or cause fear and the offence was committed in dangerous circumstances.

Cruelty to a child

K–162   The guideline recommends —

(i) a starting point of sentence in the Crown Court and a range of 26 weeks' custody to sentence in the Crown Court for an assault (assaults) resulting in injuries consistent with actual bodily harm, more than one incident of neglect or ill-treatment (but not amounting to long-term behaviour), a single incident of long-term abandonment or regular incidents of short-term abandonment (the longer the period of abandonment or the greater the number of incidents of short-term abandonment, the more serious the offence) or failure to protect a child from any of the foregoing;

(ii) sentence in the Crown Court for a series of assaults, protracted neglect or ill-treatment, serious cruelty over a period of time or failure to protect a child from any of the foregoing.

Affray

K–163   The guideline recommends 18 weeks' custody as a starting point and a range of 12 weeks' custody to sentence in the Crown Court in the case of a fight involving a weapon or the throwing of objects or conduct causing risk of serious injury.

Harassment (putting people in fear of violence) (Protection from Harassment Act 1997, s.4), and the racially/religiously aggravated version

K–164   The guideline recommends —

(i) a starting point of 18 weeks' custody and a range of 12 weeks' custody to sentence in the Crown Court for a case involving deliberate threats or persistent action over a longer period or an intention to cause a fear of violence;

(ii) sentence in the Crown Court for "sexual threats, vulnerable person targeted".

Breach of a protective order (other than in a domestic context)

K–165   The guideline recommends —

(i) a starting point of sentence in the Crown Court and a range of 26 weeks' custody to sentence in the Crown Court for more than one breach involving some violence and/or significant physical or psychological harm to the victim;

(ii) sentence in the Crown Court for a breach (one or more) involving significant physical violence and significant physical or psychological harm to the victim.

Witness intimidation

K–166   The guideline recommends —

(i) a starting point of 18 weeks' custody and a range of 12 weeks' custody to sentence in the Crown Court for conduct amounting to a threat, staring at, approaching or following witnesses, talking about the case, trying to alter or stop evidence;

(ii) sentence in the Crown Court for threats of violence to witnesses and/or their families or for deliberately seeking out witnesses.

Sexual assault (Sexual Offences Act 2003, ss.3, 7)

See Part 2 of the sexual offences guideline, *ante*, K–93, and, in particular, the table at K–94. **K–167**

Child prostitution and pornography

The guideline recommends that these offences should normally be dealt with in the Crown Court but that there may be rare cases of non-penetrative activity involving a victim aged 16 or 17 where the offender's involvement is minimal and not for gain in which a custodial sentence within the power of a magistrates' court may be appropriate. **K–168**

Exploitation of prostitution (Sexual Offences Act 2003, ss.52, 53)

See Parts 6B to 6D of the sexual offences guideline, *ante*, K–103, and, in particular, the table at K–104. **K–169**

Exposure (Sexual Offences Act 2003, s.66)

See Part 5 of the sexual offences guideline, *ante*, K–99, and, in particular, the table at K–100. **K–170**

Voyeurism (Sexual Offences Act 2003, s.67)

See Part 5 of the sexual offences guideline, *ante*, K–99, and, in particular, the table at K–100. **K–171**

Keeping a brothel used for prostitution (Sexual Offences Act 1956, s.33A)

See Parts 6B to 6D of the sexual offences guideline, *ante*, K–103, and, in particular, the table at K–104. **K–172**

Indecent photographs of children

See Part 6A of the sexual offences guideline, *ante*, K–101, and, in particular, the table at K–102. **K–173**

Failure to comply with the notification requirements applicable to sex offenders

The guideline recommends a starting point of 18 weeks' custody and a range of six weeks' custody to sentence in the Crown Court for a deliberate failure to comply or the supply of information known to be false accompanied by long-period of non-compliance or attempts to avoid detection. **K–174**

Drugs

See *ante*, K–147; and *post*, K–271 *et seq.* **K–175**

[The next paragraph is K–179.]

Dangerous driving

The guideline recommends sentence in the Crown Court for (a) prolonged bad driving involving deliberate disregard for the safety of others, (b) incidents involving excessive **K–179** speed or showing off, especially on busy roads or in a built up area, by a disqualified driver, or while driver was being pursued by the police.

Aggravated vehicle-taking (damage to property other than the vehicle taken in accident or to the vehicle)

K–180   The guideline recommends sentence in the Crown Court if the vehicle was taken as part of a burglary or from private premises and the damage caused was valued at in excess of £5,000.

Aggravated vehicle-taking (dangerous driving or accident causing injury)

K–181   The guideline recommends sentence in the Crown Court if there was a course of prolonged bad driving involving deliberate disregard for the safety of others.

Arson

K–182   The guideline recommends sentence in the Crown Court in the case of "significant" damage.

Criminal damage (not arson) and racially/religiously aggravated version of offence

K–183   The guideline recommends sentence in the Crown Court if the value of the damage done was in excess of £10,000.

Identity documents (possession of false or of another's improperly obtained) (Identity Cards Act 2006, s.25(5))

K–184   The guideline recommends —
  (i) a starting point of 12 weeks' custody and a range of a six weeks' custody to sentence in the Crown Court for a small number of documents where there is no evidence of dealing;
  (ii) sentence in the Crown Court for "considerable number of documents possessed, evidence of involvement in larger operation".

M. Causing Death by Driving

K–185   The Sentencing Guidelines Council has issued a guideline on the offences of causing death by dangerous driving (*RTA* 1988, s.1), causing death by careless driving when under the influence of drink or drugs or having failed without reasonable excuse either to provide a specimen for analysis or to permit the analysis of a blood sample (*ibid.*, s.3A), causing death by careless or inconsiderate driving (*ibid.*, s.2B) and causing death by driving while unlicensed, disqualified or uninsured (*ibid.*, s.3ZB). The guideline applies to offenders aged 18 or over who are sentenced on or after August 4, 2008, and is based on first-time offenders convicted after trial.

The guideline has an introduction and four parts. Part A sets out factors relating to the assessment of seriousness, Part B relates to ancillary orders, Part C contains explanatory material relating to sentencing ranges and starting points, and a description of the decision making process, and Part D contains the offence guidelines. The introduction also refers to Annex A which sets out the statutory definitions of dangerous driving, careless driving and inconsiderate driving, and gives examples.

The introduction makes plain that since the causing of death is common to all offences covered by the guideline, the factor that is going to have the greatest weight in determining a starting point for any particular offence will be the culpability of the offender and, accordingly, the primary task for the court (apart from s.3ZB cases) will be an evaluation of the quality of the driving involved and the degree of danger that it foreseeably created. The degree of intoxication must also be considered where this is an element of the offence. The introduction further points out that the guideline draws a distinction between those factors of an offence that are intrinsic to the quality of the driving ("determinants of seriousness") and those which, while they aggravate the offence (*e.g.* more than one death), are not.

Part A: Assessing seriousness

Determinants of seriousness

There are five determinants of seriousness, for each of which the guideline sets out **K–186** examples: (i) the offender's awareness of risk (*e.g.* typified by a prolonged, persistent and deliberate course of bad driving), (ii) where the presence of alcohol or drugs is not an element of the offence, the effect of consumption of any alcohol or drugs (which includes a failure to supply a specimen for analysis (unless inherent in the offence or charged separately) and the consumption of legal drugs where this impaired the offender's ability to drive and the offender knew or should have known about the likelihood of impairment), (iii) whether the offender was driving at an inappropriate speed, (iv) whether the offender behaved in a seriously culpable manner, and (v) the identity of the victim (*e.g.* failing to have regard to, and to take extra care when driving near, vulnerable road users such as cyclists, motorcyclists, horse riders, pedestrians and those working in the road).

Examples of (iv), *ante*, are aggressive driving, driving whilst using a hand-held mobile telephone, driving whilst the driver's attention is avoidably distracted (*e.g.* reading or adjusting the controls of electronic equipment), driving when knowingly suffering from a medical or physical condition that significantly impairs the offender's driving skills (including failure to take prescribed medication), driving when knowingly deprived of adequate sleep or rest, particularly where this is caused by commercial concerns, and driving a poorly maintained or dangerously loaded vehicle, again, particularly where this is caused by commercial concerns. A distinction is drawn between ordinary avoidable distractions and gross avoidable distractions (*e.g.* reading or composing a text message over a period of time), but where the degree of impairment is so serious that it is used to determine whether the offence is based on dangerous or careless driving, care must be taken to avoid double counting.

Aggravating and mitigating factors

Once the court has considered the determinants of seriousness, it must then consider **K–187** whether any aggravating or mitigating factors affect culpability so as to increase or decrease the starting point, or move the offence into a different sentencing range. When assessing seriousness, the court should have regard to the full list of aggravating and mitigating factors set out in the guideline on seriousness (*ante*, § K–13) and the particular aggravating and mitigating factors applicable to each offence, a key to which is set out, *post*:

Key to aggravating factors:

1	Previous convictions for motoring offences, particularly offences that involve bad driving or the consumption of excessive alcohol or drugs before driving.	**K–188**
2	Previous convictions for motoring offences, particularly offences that involve bad driving.	
3	Previous convictions for motoring offences, whether involving bad driving or an offence of the same kind that forms part of the present conviction.	
4	More than one person killed as a result of the offence. Where the number of deaths is high and that was reasonably foreseeable, this is likely to provide sufficient justification for moving an offence into the next highest sentencing range.	
5	Serious injury to one or more victims, in addition to the death(s).	

6	Disregard of warnings.
7	Other offences committed at the same time, such as driving other than in accordance with the terms of a valid licence, driving while disqualified, *etc.*
8	Irresponsible behaviour such as failing to stop, falsely claiming that one of the victims was responsible, or trying to throw the victim off the car by swerving in order to escape.
9	Irresponsible behaviour such as failing to stop or falsely claiming that one of the victims was responsible for the collision.
10	Driving off in an attempt to avoid detection or apprehension.

Key to mitigating factors:

K–189	11	Alcohol or drugs consumed unwittingly.
	12	Offender was seriously injured in the collision, but the greater the driver's fault, the less effect this factor should have on mitigation.
	13	The victim was a close friend or relative, but the greater the driver's fault, the less effect this factor should have on mitigation.
	14	Actions of the victim or a third party contributed significantly to the likelihood of a collision occurring and/ or death resulting.
	15	Actions of the victim or a third party contributed to the commission of the offence.
	16	The offender's lack of driving experience contributed significantly to the likelihood of a collision occurring and/ or death resulting.
	17	The offender's lack of driving experience contributed to the commission of the offence.
	18	The driving was in response to a proven and genuine emergency falling short of a defence.
	19	The offender genuinely believed that he or she was insured or licensed to drive.

Personal mitigation

K–190   If the offender can show that he previously had a good driving record, or can demonstrate remorse or that he provided direct and positive assistance to a victim at the scene of the accident, this may justify a reduction in sentence.

Part B: Ancillary orders

K–191   An order disqualifying an offender from driving is usually a mandatory requirement when sentencing for these offences. In principle, the minimum period of disqualification should either equate to the length of the custodial sentence imposed or the relevant statutory minimum disqualification period, whichever results in the longer period of disqualification.

The court may also consider whether to impose an order depriving the offender of property, *e.g.*, a vehicle.

Part D: Offence guidelines

Causing death by dangerous driving

K–192   There are three levels of seriousness which relate predominantly to the standard of driving.

Level 1 (starting point 8 years, sentencing range of 7–14 years): driving that involved a deliberate decision to ignore (or a flagrant disregard for) the rules of the road and an apparent disregard for the great danger being caused to others. Determinants of seriousness (as identified *ante*) that will fix a case at this level include (a) a prolonged, persistent and deliberate course of bad driving, (b) consumption of substantial amounts of alcohol or drugs leading to gross impairment, and/or (c) a group of determinants of seriousness which in isolation or smaller number would place the offence in level 2. The presence of both (a) and (b), particularly if accompanied by aggravating factors will move the offence towards the top of the sentencing range.

Level 2 (starting point 5 years, sentencing range of 4–7 years): driving that created a *substantial* risk of danger. Determinants of seriousness that will fix a case at this level include greatly excessive speed, racing or competitive driving, gross avoidable distraction, driving whilst ability to drive is impaired as a result of consumption of alcohol or drugs, failing to take prescribed medication or a known medical condition, or a group of determinants of seriousness which in isolation or smaller number would place the offence in level 3.

Level 3 (starting point 3 years, sentencing range of 2–5 years): driving that created a *significant* risk of danger. Relevant determinants of seriousness include driving above the speed limit or at a speed that is inappropriate for the prevailing conditions, driving when knowingly deprived of adequate sleep or rest or knowing that the vehicle has a dangerous defect or is poorly maintained or is dangerously loaded, a brief but obvious danger arising from a seriously dangerous manoeuvre, driving whilst avoidably distracted, or failing to have proper regard to vulnerable road users. Where the driving is markedly less serious than this level, reference should be made to the starting point for the most serious level of causing death by careless driving.

Additional aggravating and mitigating factors applicable to sentencing for this offence: 1, 4–8, 10–13, 16, 17 (as to which, see the key, *ante*).

Causing death by careless driving when under the influence of drink or drugs etc.

The legal limit of alcohol is 35µg breath (80mg in blood and 107mg in urine)	Careless/ inconsiderate driving arising from momentary inattention with no aggravating factors	Other cases of careless/ inconsiderate driving	Careless/ inconsiderate driving falling not far short of dangerousness
Level 1 71µg or above of alcohol/ high quantity of drugs OR deliberate non-provision of specimen where evidence of serious impairment	Starting point 6 years Sentencing range 5–10 years	Starting point 7 years Sentencing range 6–12 years	Starting point 8 years Sentencing range 7–14 years
Level 2 51–70µg of alcohol/ moderate quantity of drugs OR deliberate non-provision of specimen	Starting point 4 years Sentencing range 3–7 years	Starting point 5 years Sentencing range 4–8 years	Starting point 6 years Sentencing range 5–9 years
Level 3 35–50µg of alcohol/ minimum quantity of drugs OR test refused because of honestly held but unreasonable belief	Starting point 18 months Sentencing range 26 weeks–4 years	Starting point 3 years Sentencing range 2–5 years	Starting point 4 years Sentencing range 3–6 years

Additional aggravating and mitigating factors applicable to sentencing for this offence: 1, 4, 5, 7, 9, 11–14, 18 (as to which, see the key, *ante*).

Causing death by careless or inconsiderate driving

K–194   There are three levels of seriousness defined by the degree of carelessness involved in the standard of driving. A fine is unlikely to be an appropriate sentence for this offence. The most likely requirements to be included in a community order are unpaid work requirements, activity requirements, programme requirements and curfew requirements.

Level 1 (starting point 15 months, sentencing range of 36 weeks–3 years): careless or inconsiderate driving falling not far short of dangerous driving.

Level 2 (starting point 36 weeks, sentencing range of community order (high)–2 years): other cases of careless or inconsiderate driving.

Level 3 (starting point community order (medium), sentencing range of community order (low)–community order (high)): careless or inconsiderate driving arising from momentary inattention with no aggravating features. Examples include misjudging the speed of a vehicle or turning without seeing an oncoming vehicle because of restricted visibility.

Additional aggravating and mitigating factors applicable to sentencing for this offence: 2, 4, 5, 7, 9, 11, 12, 14, 15, 17 (as to which, see the key, *ante*).

Causing death by driving while unlicensed, disqualified or uninsured

K–195   A fine is unlikely to be an appropriate sentence for this offence.

Level 1 (starting point 12 months, sentencing range of 36 weeks–2 years): (i) the offender was disqualified from driving or (ii) the offender was unlicensed or uninsured and there are two or more aggravating features from the list, *post*.

Level 2 (starting point 26 weeks, sentencing range of community order (high)–36 weeks): the offender was unlicensed or uninsured and there was at least one aggravating factor from the list, *post*.

Level 3 (starting point community order (medium), sentencing range of community order (low)–community order (high)): the offender was unlicensed or uninsured, with no aggravating factors.

Additional aggravating and mitigating factors applicable to sentencing for this offence: 3, 4, 5, 9, 11, 12, 17, 19 (as to which, see the key, *ante*).

N. Breach of an Anti-Social Behaviour Order

Summary

K–196   The Sentencing Guidelines Council has issued a guideline on the sentencing of offenders convicted of breaching an anti-social behaviour order. It applies to the sentencing of adult and young offenders, who are sentenced on or after January 5, 2009, and is based on first-time offenders (*i.e.* in respect of adult offenders, those who do not have a previous conviction for breach of an anti-social behaviour order and, in respect of young offenders, to have its usual meaning) convicted after trial. Since the sentencing framework for offenders under 18 is significantly different from that for older offenders, the guidance for young offenders is in the form of principles (see Part E, *post*). It is noted that regard should also be had to the approach to sentencing for breaches of orders set out in the guideline on new sentences (*ante*, K–28 *et seq.*) and the guideline on breach of a protective order (*ante*, K–81).

The guideline is in five parts. Part A sets out section 1(10), and summarises the effect of section 1(11), of the *CDA* 1998 (§ 5–1199 in the main work), Part B is an introduction, Part C sets out factors relating to the assessment of seriousness, Part D contains explanatory material relating to sentencing ranges and starting points, a description of the decision making process, and the sentencing guideline for adult offenders, and Part E sets out sentencing principles in relation to young offenders.

Part B: introduction

The main aim of sentencing for breach of an order is to achieve the purpose of the   **K–197**
order.When sentencing, the primary consideration should therefore be to reflect the harassment, alarm or distress involved, with the fact that it constituted a breach of a court order
(and the consequent harm caused by the undermining of public confidence in the effective
administration of justice) being a secondary consideration.

Part C: assessing seriousness

This must be assessed by considering the offender's culpability in committing the offence   **K–198**
and the harm which the offence caused, was intended to cause, or might foreseeably have
caused. In order properly to assess the seriousness of a breach, a court needs to be aware of
the purpose of the order and the context in which it was made. To this end, Annex A summarises the key principles and considerations applicable when making an order. Whereas a
breach may be of one or more prohibitions in an order, the approach to sentencing should
be based on an assessment of the seriousness of the harm arising from the breach (or
intended by the offender) rather than the number of prohibitions not complied with.

Culpability and harm

When determining the seriousness of a breach, the court will need to consider (a) the   **K–199**
degree to which the offender intended to breach the order, and (b) the degree to which the
offender intended to cause the harm that resulted (or could have resulted).

Relevance of the originating conduct

As stated in previous guidelines, the original conduct that led to the making of an order   **K–200**
is relevant in so far as it indicates the level of harm caused and whether this was intended.
High culpability and/ or harm may be indicated if the breach continues a pattern of behaviour against an identifiable victim, but the offence may be less serous if there is little connection between the breach and the behaviour that the order was aimed at. The court should
examine the prohibitions of the order itself (particularly those in older orders made without
the benefit of the guidance set out in Annex A), and their necessity and reasonableness in
the circumstances.

Breach of an interim order

Breach of such an order is as serious as breach of a final order, and the same approach to   **K–201**
sentencing should be taken. If the hearing regarding the final order can be brought forward,
this should be done so that the two issues can be considered together, but sentencing for the
interim breach should not be delayed for this purpose and should take place as soon as
possible. The court should also consider the extent to which an urgent need for specific
interim prohibitions was originally demonstrated, or if the interim order was sought
principally in order to obtain additional time to prepare a case for the full hearing.

Breach that also constitutes another criminal offence

If the substantive offence only has been charged, the fact that it also constitutes breach of   **K–202**
an anti-social behaviour order should be treated as an aggravating factor.

If breach of the order only has been charged, the sentence should reflect the full circumstances of the breach, which will include the conduct that could have been charged as a
substantive offence.

Where breach of the order also constitutes another offence with a lower maximum penalty,
that penalty is an element to be considered in the interests of proportionality, although the
court will not be limited by it.

Aggravating and mitigating factors

For ease of reference, Annex B sets out the aggravating and mitigating factors in the   **K–203** guideline on seriousness (*ante*, K–13 *et seq.*) that might increase or mitigate the seriousness of an offence. Additional aggravating and mitigating factors are identified in the guideline (*post*).

Personal mitigation

K–204   This is particularly relevant to breach of an anti-social behaviour order, since compliance depends on an ability to understand its terms and make rational decisions. Sentence may be mitigated where the offender has a lower level of understanding due to mental health issues or learning difficulties, was acting under the influence of an older or more experienced offender or has complied with an individual support order or intervention order imposed at the same time as the anti-social behaviour order.

Part D: sentencing guideline—adult offenders

K–205   There are three levels of seriousness:
  (i) *serious harm caused or intended*: examples may involve the use of violence, significant threats or intimidation, or the targeting of individuals or groups of people in a manner that leads to a fear of violence;
  (ii) *lesser degree of harm intended or likely*: examples may include lesser degrees of threats or intimidation, the use of seriously abusive language or causing more than minor damage to property;
  (iii) *no harm caused or intended*: examples may involve being drunk or begging, the prohibited use of public transport, or entry into a prohibited area, provided there is no evidence that harassment, alarm or distress was caused or intended.

K–206   The suggested starting points, *post*, are based on the assumption that the offender had the highest level of culpability (*i.e.* he intended the breach). Care needs to be taken to ensure that there is no double counting when an element of the breach determines the level of seriousness where it might in other circumstances be an aggravating factor. In the most serious cases involving repeat offending and a breach causing serious harassment, together with the presence of several aggravating factors such as the use of violence, a sentence beyond the highest range will be justified.

A conditional discharge is not available as a sentence for this offence.

Nature of failure and harm	Starting point	Sentencing range
Serious harassment, alarm or distress has been caused or where such harm was intended	26 weeks' custody	Custody threshold–2 years' custody
Lesser degree of harassment, alarm or distress, where such harm was intended, or where it would have been likely if the offender had not been apprehended	6 weeks' custody	Community order (medium)–26 weeks' custody
No harassment, alarm or distress was actually caused by the breach and none was intended by the offender	Community order (low)	Fine (Band B)–community order (medium)

K–207   Additional aggravating factors:
  (i) offender has a history of disobedience to court orders;
  (ii) breach was committed immediately or shortly after the order was made;
  (iii) breach was committed subsequent to earlier breach proceedings arising from the same order;

(iv) targeting of a person the order was made to protect or a witness in the original proceedings.

Additional mitigating factors:

(i) breach occurred after a long period of compliance;

(ii) the prohibition(s) breached was/were not fully understood, especially where an interim order was made without notice.

Part E: sentencing guideline—young offenders

It is noted that the principles covered in Part C apply equally to young offenders. **K–208**

Apart from those cases where the court is bound to make a referral order, in less serious cases, such as where the breach has not involved any harassment, alarm or distress, a fine may be appropriate if it will be paid by the offender; otherwise a reparation order. In most cases, however, the appropriate sentence will be a community sentence. The custody threshold should be set at a significantly higher level than for adults, and will usually not be crossed unless the breach involves serious harassment alarm or distress (as to which, see the levels of seriousness, *ante*). Exceptionally, the custody threshold may also be crossed where a youth is being sentenced for more than one offence of breach (committed on separate occasions within a short period) involving a lesser but substantial degree of harassment, alarm or distress. Even where the custody threshold is crossed, the court should normally impose a community sentence in preference to a detention and training order and custody should be used only as a last resort. Where custody is unavoidable, the starting point for sentencing should be four months' detention, with a range of up to 12 months. Where the youth is being sentenced for more than one breach involving serious harassment, alarm or distress, however, the sentence may go beyond that range.

Factors likely to aggravate or mitigate a breach are the same as the additional factors listed in the guideline for adult offenders (*ante*) and the principles relating to personal mitigation (*ante*) also apply. In addition, peer pressure and lack of parental support may justify mitigation of sentence.

When imposing a community sentence, a court must consider what requirements will best prevent further offending and the individual circumstances of the offender, including his particular stage of intellectual or emotional maturity. Any requirements imposed must be compatible both with each other and with the prohibitions of the anti-social behaviour order, if it remains in force, and the combination of both must not be so onerous as to make further breaches likely.

O. Theft and Burglary in a Building Other Than a Dwelling

Summary

The Sentencing Guidelines Council has issued a guideline on these offences. The **K–209** guideline applies only to the sentencing of offenders aged 18 and over, who are sentenced on or after January 5, 2009, and is based on first-time offenders convicted after trial (but as to offences of burglary for which sentence is to be passed on or after January, 16, 2012, see *post*, K–259 *et seq.*).

The guideline is in five parts. Part A sets out the statutory provisions relating to the offences, Part B sets out factors relating to the assessment of seriousness, Part C relates to ancillary orders, Part D contains explanatory material relating to sentencing ranges and starting points, and a description of the decision making process, and Part E contains the offence guidelines.

Part A: statutory provisions

In addition to setting out the relevant statutory provisions, the mode of trial and the **K–210** maximum penalties, Part A states that (i) in relation to burglary, the guideline relates solely to cases in which an offender enters a building other than a dwelling as a trespasser with intent to steal or, having entered a building as a trespasser, actually goes on to steal, and (ii) the forms of theft covered by the guideline are theft in breach of trust, theft in a dwelling, theft from persons, and theft from shops; but that (iii) the principles in Parts B and C are of general application and likely to be of assistance where a court is sentencing for any other form of theft.

Part B: assessing seriousness

K-211   This must be assessed by considering the offender's culpability in committing the offence and the harm which the offence caused, was intended to cause, or might foreseeably have caused. When assessing the harm caused, the starting point should be the loss suffered by the victim. However, the monetary value might not reflect the full extent of the harm and the court should take into account the impact of the offence on the particular victim (*e.g.* where the value of the loss is high in proportion to the victim's financial circumstances), any harm to a person other than the immediate victim, and any harm in the form of public concern or erosion of public confidence.

Aggravating and mitigating factors which may affect the seriousness of the offence must be considered, including those identified in the guideline on seriousness (*ante*, K–13 *et seq.*) (and set out in Annex A) and the additional factors indentified in each offence guideline. Since the suggested starting points and sentencing ranges are based on the assumption that the offender was motivated by greed or a desire to live beyond his means, in order to avoid double counting, such a motivation should not be treated as a factor that increases culpability. The aggravating factors from the seriousness guideline most relevant to these offences are planning, offenders operating in groups or gangs and deliberate targeting of vulnerable victims, and the most relevant aggravating factors indicating a more than usually serious degree of harm are particularly vulnerable victims, high levels of gain and the high value (including sentimental value) of property to the victim or substantial consequential loss.

The court must also consider the following matters of personal mitigation: return of stolen property (depending on voluntariness and timeliness of return), whether the offender has been motivated by addiction (in which case, while seriousness will not be mitigated, it may be appropriate to impose a drug rehabilitation requirement, alcohol treatment requirement or activity or supervision requirement, as part of a community or suspended sentence order), and whether the offender has been motivated by desperation or need (which may count as personal mitigation in exceptional circumstances).

Part C: ancillary orders

K-212   The ancillary orders which a court must consider are restitution (*PCC(S)A* 2000, s.148 (§ 5–711 in the main work)), compensation (*ibid.*, s.130 (§ 5–691 in the main work)), deprivation (*ibid.*, s.143 (§ 5–726 in the main work)) and confiscation (*PCA* 2002, s.6 (§ 5–805 in the main work)). Neither restitution nor compensation orders should normally impact or influence the choice of sentence. However, where an offender has acted (as opposed to offered) to free assets in order to pay compensation, this is akin to making voluntary restitution and may be regarded as personal mitigation. In making compensation orders, consideration should be given to the wishes of the victim and, where it is difficult to ascertain the full amount of the loss suffered, the making of an order for an amount representing the agreed or likely loss.

Part D: offence guidelines

Theft in breach of trust

K-213   While the seriousness of the offence will generally increase in line with the level of trust breached, the extent to which the nature and degree of trust placed in an offender should be regarded as increasing seriousness will depend on a careful assessment of the circumstances of each individual case, including the type and terms of the relationship between the offender and victim. A court should also consider whether a suspended sentence would be appropriate, particularly where this may allow reparation to be made either to the victim or to the community at large.

Type/ nature of activity	Starting point	Sentencing range
Theft of £125,000 or more **or** theft of £20,000 or more in breach of a high degree of trust	3 years' custody	2–6 years' custody
Theft of £20,000 or more but less than £125,000 **or** theft of £2,000 or more but less than £20,000 in breach of a high degree of trust	2 years' custody	12 months–3 years' custody
Theft of £2,000 or more but less than £20,000 **or** theft of less than £2,000 in breach of a high degree of trust	18 weeks' custody	Community order (high)–12 months' custody
Theft of less than £2,000	Community order (medium)	Fine–26 weeks' custody

Additional aggravating factors: **K–214**
  (i) long course of offending;
  (ii) suspicion deliberately thrown on others;
  (iii) offender motivated by intention to cause harm or out of revenge.
Additional mitigating factors:
  (i) offender has been given inappropriate degree of trust or responsibility;
  (ii) genuine cessation of offending before discovery (particularly where evidence of remorse);
  (iii) offender reports undiscovered offending;
  (iv) other than in the most exceptional of circumstances, loss of employment and any consequential hardship should **not** constitute personal mitigation.

Theft in a dwelling
  It is noted that the guideline does not apply where the offender has been convicted of a **K–215** burglary (for which the authorities on sentencing are discussed at § 21–113 *et seq.* in the main work).
  For the purposes of the table, post, property should generally be regarded as having a high monetary value if it is worth more than £2,000 and a victim is vulnerable if he is targeted by the offender because it is anticipated that he will be unlikely or unable to resist the theft.

Type/ nature of activity	Starting point	Sentencing range
Where the effect on the victim is particularly severe, the stolen property is of high value (see *ante*), or substantial consequential loss (*e.g.* serious disruption to victim's life or business) results, a sentence higher than the range into which the offence otherwise would fall may be appropriate		
Theft from a vulnerable victim (see *ante*) involving intimidation or the use or threat of force (falling short of robbery) or the use of deception	18 months' custody	12 months–3 years' custody

Type/ nature of activity	Starting point	Sentencing range
Theft from a vulnerable victim	18 weeks' custody	Community order (high)–12 months' custody
Theft not involving vulnerable victim	Community order (medium)	Fine–18 weeks' custody

K–216   Additional aggravating factors:
   (i) offender motivated by intention to cause harm or out of revenge;
   (ii) intimidation or face-to-face confrontation with victim (except where this takes the offence into a higher sentencing range);
   (iii) use of force, or threat of force, against victim (not amounting to robbery) (except where this takes the offence into a higher sentencing range);
   (iv) use of deception (except where this takes the offence into a higher sentencing range);
   (v) offender takes steps to prevent the victim from reporting the crime or seeking help.

Theft from the person

K–216a   It is noted that the guideline does not apply where the offender has been convicted of robbery (the guideline for which is set out *ante*, K–80 *et seq.*). As to the approach, to issues of local prevalence, see the seriousness guideline (*ante*, K–27). Issues of national prevalence should **not** be used by sentencers to justify including a deterrent element as this is already taken into account in these and other guidelines.
   For the purposes of the table, post, property should generally be regarded as having a high monetary value if it is worth more than £2,000 and a victim is vulnerable if he is targeted by the offender because it is anticipated that he will be unlikely or unable to resist the theft (*e.g.* because of youth or age or disability).

Type/ nature of activity	Starting point	Sentencing range
Where the effect on the victim is particularly severe, the stolen property is of high value (see *ante*), or substantial consequential loss (*e.g.* serious disruption to victim's life or business) results, a sentence higher than the range into which the offence otherwise would fall may be appropriate		
Theft from a vulnerable victim (see *ante*) involving intimidation or the use or threat of force (falling short of robbery)	18 months' custody	12 months–3 years' custody
Theft from a vulnerable victim	18 weeks' custody	Community order (high)–12 months' custody
Theft not involving vulnerable victim	Community order (medium)	Fine–18 weeks' custody

K–216b   Additional aggravating factors:
   (i) offender motivated by intention to cause harm or out of revenge;
   (ii) intimidation or face-to-face confrontation with victim (except where this takes the offence into a higher sentencing range);
   (iii) use of force, or threat of force, against victim (not amounting to robbery) (except where this takes the offence into a higher sentencing range);
   (iv) high level of inconvenience caused to victim, *e.g.* replacing house keys, credit cards, etc., or where the victim is a tourist.

Theft from a shop

K–217   When assessing the level of harm, the circumstances of the retailer (*e.g.* size) are a proper consideration. However, the seriousness of an individual case must be judged on its own dimension of harm and culpability and the sentence on an individual offender should not be increased to reflect the harm caused to retailers in general by the totality of this type of offending (*e.g.* higher insurance premiums, cost of preventative security measures). Whereas the seriousness guideline requires the value of goods to be taken into account in property offences, where this is associated with other aggravating factors such as the degree of planning and/or operating in a group, care will need to be taken to avoid double counting.

When taking previous convictions into account, if the offender demonstrates a level of persistent or seriously persistent offending, the community and custody thresholds may be crossed even though the other characteristics of the offence would otherwise warrant a lesser sentence.

Type/ nature of activity	Starting point	Sentencing range
Organised gang/ group **and** intimidation or the use or threat of force (short of robbery)	12 months' custody	36 weeks–4 years' custody
Significant intimidation or threats **or** use of force resulting in slight injury **or** very high level of planning **or** significant related damage	6 weeks' custody	Community order (high)–36 weeks' custody
Low level intimidation or threats **or** some planning, *e.g.* a session of stealing on the same day or going equipped **or** some related damage	Community order (low)	Fine—community order (medium)
Little or no planning or sophistication **and** goods stolen of low value	Fine	Conditional discharge–community order (low)

Additional aggravating factors: **K–218**
  (i)   child accompanying offender where child is involved or aware of theft;
  (ii) offender is subject to a banning order that includes the store targeted (care to be taken to avoid double counting where offender also being sentenced for breach of order);
  (iii) offender motivated by intention to cause harm or out of revenge;
  (iv) professional offending;
  (v)   victim particularly vulnerable (*e.g.* small, independent shop);
  (vi) offender targeted high value goods;
  (vii) intimidation, threat or use of force (falling short of robbery) and additional damage to property.

[The next paragraph is K–221.]

P. ATTEMPTED MURDER

The Sentencing Guidelines Council has issued a guideline which applies only to the   **K–221** sentencing of offenders aged 18 and over, who are sentenced on or after July 27, 2009, and is based on first-time offenders convicted after trial. The guideline is not intended to provide for an offence found to be based on a genuine belief that murder would be an act of mercy, although the approach to assessing the seriousness in such cases might be similar.

Part A: Assessing seriousness

K–222   This must be assessed, first, by considering the offender's culpability in committing the offence. While an offender convicted of an offence of attempted murder will have already demonstrated a high level of culpability (intention to kill), the precise level of culpability will vary in line with the circumstances of the offence (*e.g.* whether a weapon was used) and whether it was planned or spontaneous.

Next, the court must consider the harm caused. Since there is a potential imbalance between culpability and harm, the degree of (or lack of) physical or psychological harm suffered by a victim may generally influence sentence, in particular where the degree of harm actually caused to the victim is negligible.

Aggravating and mitigating factors will also affect the seriousness of the offence. The court should consider (i) the specific factors identified in Part D (*post*), which follow those set out in the *CJA* 2003, Sched. 21 (§ 5–425 in the main work), (ii) the factors identified in the guideline on seriousness (*ante*, K–13 *et seq.*), although, here, care needs to be taken to ensure that there is no double counting where an essential element of the offence charged might, in other circumstances, be an aggravating factor, and (iii) the additional statutory aggravating factor introduced by the *Counter-Terrorism Act* 2008, s.30 (§ 25–213 in the main work) and Sched. 2 (offence having a terrorist connection).

Part B: ancillary orders

K–223   A court must consider making a compensation order.

Part C: sentencing ranges and starting points

K–224   Part C contains explanatory material relating to sentencing ranges and starting points, and a description of the decision making process. This is largely repetitious of material that appears in previous guidelines (see, in particular, the guideline on the assessment of seriousness, *ante*, K–13 *et seq.*, and, in relation to sexual offences, *ante*, K–85).

Part D: offence guidelines

K–225

Nature of offence	Starting point	Sentencing range
Level 1		
The most serious offences including those which (if the charge had been murder) would come within the 2003 Act, Sched. 21, paras 4 and 5		
Serious and long term physical or psychological harm	30 years' custody	27–35 years' custody
Some physical or psychological harm	20 years' custody	17–25 years' custody
Little or no physical or psychological harm	15 years' custody	12–20 years' custody
Level 2		
Other planned attempt to kill		
Serious and long term physical or psychological harm	20 years' custody	17–25 years' custody
Some physical or psychological harm	15 years' custody	12–20 years' custody
Little or no physical or psychological harm	10 years' custody	7–15 years' custody
Level 3		

Other spontaneous attempt to kill		
Serious and long term physical or psychological harm	15 years' custody	12–20 years' custody
Some physical or psychological harm	12 years' custody	9–17 years' custody
Little or no physical or psychological harm	9 years' custody	6–14 years' custody

Specific aggravating factors: **K–226**
  (i) the fact that the victim was particularly vulnerable, *e.g.*, because of age or disability;
  (ii) mental or physical suffering inflicted on the victim;
  (iii) the abuse of a position of trust;
  (iv) the use of duress or threats against another person to facilitate the commission of the offence;
  (v) the fact that the victim was providing a public service or performing a public duty.

Specific mitigating factors: **K–227**
  (i) the fact that the offender suffered from any mental disorder or mental disability which lowered his degree of culpability;
  (ii) the fact that the offender was provoked (for example, by prolonged stress);
  (iii) the fact that the offender acted to any extent in self-defence;
  (iv) the age of the offender.

Q. Fraud — Statutory Offences

The Sentencing Guidelines Council has issued a guideline on statutory offences of fraud   **K–228** (*viz. Fraud Act* 2006, ss.1, 6 and 7 (§§ 21–356, 21–390, 21–391 in the main work), *Theft Act* 1968, s.17 (*ibid.*, § 21–226), *Tax Credits Act* 2002, s.35, *Social Security Administration Act* 1992, s.111A, *Value Added Tax Act* 1994 s.72 (*ibid.*, § 25–532), and *CEMA* 1979, ss.50, 170 and 170B (*ibid.*, §§ 25–430, 25–474, 25–505)). It applies only to offenders aged 18 and over, who are sentenced on or after October 26, 2009, and is based on first-time offenders convicted after trial.

The guideline is in six parts and there are two annexes. Annex A contains statutory definitions and the maximum penalties for fraud offences included in the guideline. Annex B sets out in full the aggravating and mitigating factors identified in the guideline on over-arching principles and the assessment of seriousness (*ante*, K–13 *et seq.*).

Part A: statutory provisions and introduction

In addition to listing the offences covered, Part A states that: (i) the guideline aims to pro-   **K–229** duce a coherent and consistent approach to sentencing all forms of fraudulent behaviour; as such it supersedes previous guideline (and other significant) cases; (ii) the guidelines focus on the type of fraud, rather than the specific offence of which the offender has been convicted; (iii) the types of offence covered are confidence fraud, possessing, making or sup-plying articles for use in fraud, banking and insurance fraud, and the obtaining of credit through fraud, benefit fraud and revenue fraud; (iv) as the offence of obtaining services dishonestly (*Fraud Act* 2006, s.11 (§ 21–403 in the main work)) may be committed in cir-cumstances that otherwise could be charged as an offence of fraud or may be more akin to making off without payment, it has not been included specifically within any of the guidelines, the guideline to be applied being determined by the nature of the conduct form-ing the basis of the conviction; and (v) the primary consideration in sentencing is the seriousness of the offending behaviour.

Part B: assessing seriousness

This must be assessed by considering the offender's culpability in committing the offence   **K–230** and the harm which the offence caused, was intended to cause, or might foreseeably have caused. When assessing the harm caused, the primary consideration is the loss to the victim or to the community at large. In some cases, the harm that results may be greater than the harm intended by the offender. In others, the offender may have intended more harm than actually results. In these situations, the harm caused by the offence should be judged in light of the offender's culpability. In general terms, the greater the loss, the more serious the offence. However, the financial value of the loss may not reflect the full extent of the harm caused by the offence, and the court should take into account the impact of the offence on the victim (including relative harm and sentimental value), any harm to persons other than the direct victim, any erosion of public confidence, any physical harm or risk of physical harm to the direct victim or any other person, any difference between the loss intended and the actual result, and any legitimate entitlement to part or all of the amount obtained.

Aggravating and mitigating factors which may affect the seriousness of the offence must be considered, including those identified in the guideline on seriousness. The aggravating factors most likely to be present in offences of fraud are planning, an intention to commit more serious harm than actually resulted, operating in groups or gangs, "professional offending", a high level of profit, any attempt to conceal or dispose of evidence, the deliberate targeting of the vulnerable, abuse of a position of trust, multiple victims and high value (including sentimental value) of property to the victim, or subsequent consequential loss. Factors that are particularly relevant when sentencing for fraud are the number of persons involved and the role of the offender, the period of time over which the offending was carried out, the use of another person's identity, and the offence having a lasting effect on the victim.

Mitigating factors most likely to be present are mental illness or disability, youth or age where it affects responsibility, the fact that the offender played only a minor role, the offender's behaviour not being fraudulent from the outset, and the offender having been given misleading or incomplete advice. Personal mitigation that may be peculiarly relevant includes a voluntary cessation of offending (depending on the reasons and the time elapsed since the last offence), a complete and unprompted disclosure of the extent of the fraud (having regard to the point at which the disclosure is made and the degree of assistance to the authorities), voluntary restitution, and, in exceptional circumstances, financial pressure on the offender, where that pressure is not of the offender's own making.

Part C: other sentencing matters

K–231   In light of the extensive powers available to the court relating to confiscation and to seizure of assets or the proceeds of crime, and of the general powers relating to compensation, forfeiture and confiscation, a court normally should not impose a fine alongside a custodial sentence. Exceptionally, it may be appropriate to do so where: (i) a confiscation order is not being contemplated; (ii) there is no obvious victim in whose favour a compensation order can be made; and (iii) the offender has, or will have, resources from which a fine can be paid. A court must ensure that the overall sentence remains commensurate with the seriousness of the offence and that the size of the fine does not allow wealthier offenders to "buy themselves out of custody".

Part D: ancillary orders

K–232   The ancillary orders which a court must consider or which are most likely to be imposed are compensation (*PCC(S)A* 2000, s.148 (§ 5–691 in the main work)), confiscation (*PCA* 2002, s.6 (*ibid.*, § 5–805)), deprivation (2000 Act, s.143 (*ibid.*, § 5–726)), restitution (2000 Act, s.148 (*ibid.*, § 5–711)), disqualification from acting as a company director (*CDDA* 1986, s.2 (*ibid.*, § 5–1117)), disqualification from driving (2000 Act, ss.146, 147 (*ibid.*, §§ 5–1106 *et seq.*)), financial reporting (*SOCPA* 2005, s.76 (*ibid.*, § 5–1212)) and serious crime prevention (*SCA* 2007, ss.1 and 19 (*ibid.*, §§ 5–1151, 5–1168). Neither restitution nor compensation orders should normally impact or influence the choice of sentence. However, where an offender has acted (as opposed to offered) to free assets in order to pay compensation, this is akin to making voluntary restitution and may be regarded as personal mitigation. In making compensation orders, consideration should be given (i) to the wishes of the victim, and (ii) where it is difficult to ascertain the full amount of the loss suffered, to the making of an order for an amount representing the agreed or likely loss. Disqualification from driving is a punitive sanction and should be taken into account in ensuring that the overall sentence is commensurate with the seriousness of the offence.

Part E: sentencing ranges and starting points

See *ante*, K–224.   **K–233**

Part F: offence guidelines

The maximum penalty for most of the offences covered by this guideline is seven years' **K–234**
imprisonment. Where fraud under the 2006 Act is charged, the maximum penalty is 10 years; and the proposed sentencing ranges leave headroom for offences involving the most serious frauds to be sentenced outside the range and up to that maximum. In all cases where the value of property or consequential loss involved is one of the determinants of seriousness, if the amount the offender intended to obtain cannot be established, the appropriate measure will be the amount that was likely to be achieved in all the circumstances.

Confidence fraud

This type of offending involves a victim transferring money and/or property as a result of **K–235**
being deceived or misled by the offender. It includes advance fee frauds, such as lottery/prize draw and foreign money-making scams and the fraudulent sale of goods (non-existent or worthless) or services (unnecessary, overpriced or never performed).

Nature of offence	Value of property or consequential loss			
	£500,000 or more	£100,000 or more and less than £500,000	£20,000 or more and less than £100,000	Less than £20,000
	Starting point based on:	Starting point based on:	Starting point based on:	Starting point based on:
	£750,000*	£300,000*	£60,000*	£10,000*
Large scale advance fee fraud **or** other confidence fraud involving the deliberate targeting of a large number of vulnerable victims	**Starting point:** 6 years' custody **Range:** 5–8 years' custody	**Starting point:** 5 years' custody **Range:** 4–7 years' custody	**Starting point:** 4 years' custody **Range:** 3–6 years' custody	**Starting point:** 3 years' custody **Range:** 2–5 years' custody
Lower scale advance fee fraud **or** other confidence fraud characterised by a degree of planning and/or multiple transactions	**Starting point:** 5 years' custody **Range:** 4–7 years' custody	**Starting point:** 4 years' custody **Range:** 3–6 years' custody	**Starting point:** 3 years' custody **Range:** 2–5 years' custody	**Starting point:** 18 months' custody **Range:** 26 weeks–3 years' custody

Single fraudulent transaction confidence fraud involving targeting of a vulnerable victim			**Starting point:** 26 weeks' custody **Range:** community order (high)–18 months' custody	**Starting point:** 6 weeks' custody **Range:** community order (medium)–26 weeks' custody
Single fraudulent transaction confidence fraud not targeting a vulnerable victim, and involving no or limited planning			**Starting point:** 12 weeks' custody **Range:** community order (medium) – 3–6 weeks' custody	**Starting point:** community order (medium) **Range:** fine–6 weeks' custody

* Where the actual amount is smaller than the figure on which the starting point is based, that is likely to be one of the factors that will move the sentence within the range.

Possessing, making or supplying articles for use in fraud

K-236   The sentencing range for the most serious category of this type of offence is deliberately wide; most offences will be at the lower end of the range but there are likely to be some offences, possibly but not exclusively those with an international dimension, that will justify a sentence at the top of the range or even higher.

Type of offence		
Nature of offence	Making, adapting, supplying or offering to supply (s.7)	Possessing (s.6)
Article(s) intended for use in an extensive and skilfully planned fraud	**Starting point:** 4 years' custody **Range:** 2–7 years' custody	**Starting point:** 36 weeks' custody **Range:** 6 weeks–2 years' custody
Article(s) intended for use in a less extensive and less skilfully planned fraud	**Starting point:** 26 weeks' custody **Range:** community order (high)–2 years' custody	**Starting point:** community order (medium) **Range:** community order (low)–26 weeks' custody

Banking and insurance fraud, and obtaining credit through fraud

K-237   Use of another person's identity is a feature of nearly all payment card and bank account frauds. Courts should therefore depart from the suggested starting points in all cases of payment card and bank account fraud (and any other case in which it arises) to reflect the presence of this matter of aggravation.

Nature of offence	Amount obtained or intended to be obtained				
	£500,000 or more starting point based on: £750,000*	£100,000 or more and less than £500,000 starting point based on: £300,000*	£20,000 or more and less than £100,000 starting point based on: £60,000*	£5,000 or more and less than £20,000 starting point based on: £12,500*	Less than £5,000 starting point based on: £2,500*
Fraudulent from the outset, professionally planned **and either** fraud carried out over a significant period of time **or** multiple frauds	**Starting point:** 5 years' custody **Range:** 4–7 years' custody	**Starting point:** 4 years' custody **Range:** 3–5 years' custody	**Starting point:** 2 years' custody **Range:** 18 months–3 years' custody		
Fraudulent from the outset **and either** fraud carried out over a significant period of time **or** multiple frauds	**Starting point:** 4 years' custody **Range:** 3–7 years' custody	**Starting point:** 3 years' custody **Range:** 2–4 years' custody	**Starting point:** 15 months' custody **Range:** 18 weeks–30 months' custody	**Starting point:** 12 weeks' custody **Range:** community order (high) –12 months' custody	**Starting point:** community order (high) **Range:** community order (low)–6 weeks' custody
Not fraudulent from the outset **and either** fraud carried out over a significant period of time **or** multiple frauds	**Starting point:** 3 years' custody **Range:** 2–6 years' custody	**Starting point:** 2 years' custody **Range:** 12 months–3 years' custody	**Starting point:** 36 weeks' custody **Range:** 12 weeks–18 months' custody	**Starting point:** 6 weeks custody **Range:** community order (medium)–26 weeks' custody	**Starting point:** community order (medium) **Range:** fine–community order (high)

Single fraudulent transaction, fraudulent from the outset			**Starting point:** 26 weeks' custody	**Starting point:** community order (high)	**Starting point:** community order (low)
			Range: 6 weeks–12 months' custody	**Range:** fine–18 weeks' custody	**Range:** fine–community order (medium)
Single fraudulent transaction, not fraudulent from the outset			**Starting point:** 12 weeks' custody	**Starting point:** community order (medium)	**Starting point:** fine
			Range: community order (medium)–36 weeks' custody	**Range:** fine–6 weeks' custody	**Range:** fine–community order (low)

* Where the actual amount is greater or smaller than the figure on which the starting point is based, that is likely to be one of the factors that will move the sentence within the range.

Benefit fraud

K-238   The fact that sums obtained fraudulently may have been, or are in the process of being, recovered is not relevant to the choice of the type of sentence to be imposed. The guidelines themselves are in identical terms to those for banking and insurance fraud, and obtaining credit through fraud (*ante*).

Revenue fraud

K-239   The guidelines (in identical terms to those for banking and insurance fraud, and obtaining credit through fraud (*ante*)) take as a starting point an offender who acts intentionally. Where the offender acts recklessly courts should adjust the assessment of seriousness to take account of the offender's reduced culpability (this being relevant only to offences under the *Value Added Tax Act* 1994).

R. SENTENCING YOUTHS

K-240   The Sentencing Guidelines Council has now issued a definitive guideline in relation to the sentencing of offenders who are under 18 years of age. It applies to any sentence imposed on or after November 30, 2009. The foreword states that the offence-specific guidelines for youths convicted of offences under the *SOA* 2003 which have a lower maximum penalty when committed by a person under the age of 18 (*ante*, K-83 *et seq.*), and of robbery (*ante*, K-80), continue to apply and are not superseded by these guidelines. As with other guidelines issued by the council, there is a great deal of repetition both within the guideline itself and of material from other guidelines.

General approach

Statutory provisions

K-241   As well as summarising key statutory provisions, this section reminds sentencers that they must be aware of a range of international conventions which emphasise the importance of avoiding "criminalisation" of young people while ensuring that they are held responsible for their actions and, where possible, take part in repairing the damage that they have caused, the intention being to establish responsibility and to promote re-integration rather than to impose retribution.

Sentencing principles

The approach will be individualistic, with the response varying significantly according to   **K–242** the actual age and maturity of the offender. Sentences must remain proportionate (except in the case of dangerous offenders), with particular care needing to be taken where a young person has committed a relatively less serious offence but there is a high risk of re-offending. Whilst a court is sometimes required to treat the seriousness of an offence as aggravated where there are previous convictions (*CJA* 2003, s.143(2) (§ 5–67 in the main work)), a sentence that follows re-offending does not need to be more severe than a previous sentence solely because of the previous conviction.

As to the *CDA* 1998, s.37 (principal aim of the youth justice system is to prevent offending by children and young people (§ 5–63 in the main work)), the guideline points out that, in relation to the offender, this incorporates the need to demonstrate that his conduct is not acceptable in a way that makes an impact on him whilst also identifying and seeking to address any other factors that make offending more likely; and that, for any victim and society as a whole, it incorporates the need to demonstrate that the law is being effectively enforced and to sustain confidence in the rule of law. Overall, the emphasis should be on approaches that seem most likely to be effective in realising the aim set out in section 37.

As to the duty to have regard to the welfare of the offender (*CYPA* 1933, s.44 (§ 5–64 in the main work)), a court should ensure that it is alert to—

   (i) the high incidence of mental health problems and learning difficulties or disabilities amongst young people in the criminal justice system;

   (ii) the effect that speech and language difficulties might have on the ability of the young person (or any adult with them) to communicate with the court, to understand the sanction imposed or to fulfil the obligations resulting from that sanction;

   (iii) the extent to which young people anticipate that they will be discriminated against by those in authority and the effect that it has on the way that they conduct themselves during court proceedings;

   (iv) the vulnerability of young people to self harm, particularly within a custodial environment;

   (v) the extent to which the changes which take place during adolescence can lead to experimentation; and

   (vi) the effect on young people of experiences of loss or abuse.

Effect on sentence of the offender being a young person

There is an expectation that, generally, a youth will be dealt with less severely than an   **K–243** adult, although the distinction diminishes as the offender approaches the age of 18. Factors which govern the approach to the sentencing of young people who offend (compared with the approach for adult offenders), and which will affect the sentence imposed in individual cases, include:

   (i) offending by a young person is frequently a phase which passes fairly rapidly and therefore the reaction to it needs to be kept well balanced in order to avoid alienating the young person from society;

   (ii) a criminal conviction at this stage of a person's life may have a disproportionate impact on the ability of the offender to gain meaningful employment and play a worthwhile role in society;

   (iii) the impact of punishment is felt more heavily by young people in the sense that any sentence will seem far longer in comparison with their relative age than a like sentence imposed on an adult;

(iv) young people may be receptive to changing the way they conduct themselves and should be able to respond more quickly to interventions;

(v) young people should be given greater opportunity to learn from their mistakes; and

(vi) young people will be no less vulnerable than adults to the contaminating influences that can be expected within a custodial context and probably more so.

Having taken account of all relevant considerations, the court should, within a disposal that is no more restrictive of liberty than is proportionate to the seriousness of the offence(s), impose a sentence which:

(i) confronts the young offender with the consequences of the offending (either for the offender himself, his family, the victim(s) or the community), and helps him to develop a sense of personal responsibility;

(ii) tackles the particular factors (personal, family, social, educational or health) that put the young person at risk of offending;

(iii) strengthens those factors that reduce the risk that the young person will continue to offend;

(iv) encourages reparation; and

(v) defines, agrees and reinforces the responsibilities of the parents.

Crossing a significant age threshold between commission of an offence and sentence

K–244   Where an increase in the age of an offender results in the maximum sentence on the date of conviction being greater than that available on the date on which the offence was committed, a court should take as its starting point the sentence likely to have been imposed on the date on which the offence was committed. It would be rare for a court to have to consider passing a sentence more severe than the maximum it would have had jurisdiction to pass at the time the offence was committed even where the offender has subsequently attained the age of 18. However, a sentence at or close to the maximum may be appropriate, especially where a serious offence was committed by an offender close to the age threshold.

Persistent offenders

K–245   Whereas certain sentences are available only where the offender is a "persistent offender", in determining whether a young person is a persistent offender for these purposes a court should consider simply whether he is someone who persists in offending. A finding of persistence may be derived from previous convictions but may also arise from other orders or disposals which require an admission or finding of guilt. A finding of persistence is likely where an offender has been convicted of, or made subject of a pre-court disposal that involved an admission or finding of guilt in relation to, imprisonable offences on at least three occasions in a 12-month period.

Enforcing the responsibilities of parents and guardians

K–246   In considering whether to make a parenting order under the *CDA* 1998, s.8(6) (§ 5–1282 in the main work), a court must consider the strength of familial relationships and any diversity issues, in particular relating to sexual orientation or race, which might impact on the achievement of the purpose of the order.

Particular sentences and orders

Referral orders

K–247   A court should be prepared to use the full range of periods allowed; in general, orders of 10 to 12 months should be made only for more serious offences. Typically, the length of an order should be three to five months, five to seven months or seven to nine months according to whether the court assesses the seriousness of the offending to be relatively low, of medium seriousness or relatively high.

Financial orders

It will rarely be appropriate to take an education maintenance allowance or a similar **K–248** means-related provision into account as a resource from which a young person may pay a financial penalty, especially where the recipient is a young person who is living indepen- dently or as part of a household primarily dependent on state benefit.

Youth rehabilitation orders

From the commencement (on November 30, 2009) of section 1 of the *CJIA* 2008 (§ 5–314 **K–249** in the main work), youth rehabilitation orders have been the sole available community sentence for young offenders. Where a court is considering sentence for an offence for which a custodial sentence is justified, a guilty plea may be one of the factors that persuades a court that it can properly impose a youth rehabilitation order instead, and in those circumstances no further adjustment to that sentence would need to be made in order to fulfil the obligation to give credit for the plea. Where, however, the provisional sentence is already a youth rehabilitation order, the necessary reduction for a guilty plea should apply to those requirements within the order that are primarily punitive rather than those which are primarily rehabilitative.

Determining the requirements and the length of an order: where a court concludes that **K–249a** a youth rehabilitation order is appropriate, taking account of the assessment in the pre- sentence report, the court should consider (i) the requirements that are most suitable for the offender, (ii) what period is necessary to ensure that all requirements may be satisfactorily completed, and (iii) whether the restrictions on liberty that result from those requirements are commensurate with the seriousness of the offence.

Orders with intensive supervision and surveillance: when imposing a youth rehabilita- **K–249b** tion order with intensive supervision and surveillance a court must ensure that the requirements are not so onerous as to make the likelihood of a breach almost inevitable.

Orders with a fostering requirement: it is unlikely that the statutory criteria, contained **K–249c** in Schedule 1, para. 4, to the 2008 Act (§ 5–318 in the main work), will be met in many cases; where they are met and the court is considering making an order, care should be taken to ensure that there is a well developed plan for the care and support of the young person throughout the period of the order and following conclusion of the order.

Breaches: the primary objective when dealing with a breach of an order is to ensure **K–249d** that the young person completes the requirements imposed by the court. Where the fail- ure arises primarily from non-compliance with reporting or other similar obligations, if a sanction is necessary, the most appropriate one is likely to be the inclusion of, or increase in, a primarily punitive requirement. A court must ensure that it has sufficient informa- tion to enable it to understand why the order has been breached and that all steps have been taken by relevant authorities to give the young person appropriate opportunity and support. This will be particularly important if the court is considering imposing a custodial sentence as a result of the breach. Where a court is considering whether a young person has "wilfully and persistently" breached an order, it should apply the same approach as when determining whether an offender is a "persistent offender" (as to which, see *ante*). In particular, a young person almost certainly will have "persistently" breached an order where there have been three breaches (each resulting in an appearance before the court) demonstrating a lack of willingness to comply with the order.

Custodial sentences

Threshold and approach: a pre-sentence report must be considered in all cases before **K–250** a custodial sentence is imposed. Even where the custody threshold (*viz.* that the youth cannot properly be dealt with by a fine alone or by a youth rehabilitation order) has been crossed, a court is not required to impose a custodial sentence. This is likely only to be the case where a custodial sentence will be more effective in preventing offending by children and young persons. The obligation to have regard to the welfare of the offender will require the court to take account of a wide range of issues including those relating to mental health, capability and maturity.

K–250a   **Length of sentence (offenders aged 15, 16 or 17):** where the offender is aged 15, 16 or 17, the court will need to consider the maturity of the offender as well as age. Where there is no offence-specific guideline it may be appropriate, depending on maturity, to consider a starting point from half to three-quarters of that which would have been identified for an adult offender. The closer the offender was to being 18 when the offence was committed, and the greater the maturity of the offender, or the sophistication of the offence, the closer the starting point is likely to be to that appropriate for an adult. For younger offenders, greater flexibility is required to reflect the potentially wider range of culpability. Where an offence shows considerable planning or sophistication, a court may need to adjust this approach upwards; conversely, where an offender is particularly immature, the approach may need to be adjusted downwards. It will be particularly important to consider maturity when the court has to sentence multiple offenders. When the offenders are of different ages, including when one or more is over 18, the court will also need to have proper regard to parity between their sentences.

K–250b   **Length of sentence (offenders aged under 15):** where the offender is under 15, sentence should normally be imposed in a youth court, and the length of sentence will normally be shorter than for an older offender convicted of the same offence. An offender should be sentenced to detention under the *PCC(S)A* 2000, s.91 (§ 5–610 in the main work), only where necessary for the protection of the public, either because of the risk of harm from future offending or the persistence of the offending behaviour, or, exceptionally, because the seriousness of the offence alone warrants such a disposal.

K–250c   **Length of sentence (detention and training orders):** in determining the term of a detention and training order the proper approach to taking account of any period for which the offender has been remanded in custody or on bail subject to a qualifying curfew condition and electronic monitoring (see s.101(8) of the Act of 2000 (*ibid.*, § 5–598)) is to reduce, if possible, the length of the part of the sentence that is to be served in custody from what would otherwise have been appropriate, in order to reflect that period.

Trial and sentencing of cases in the Crown Court

K–251   A youth will appear for trial and sentence in the Crown Court only when charged with homicide, when subject to a statutory minimum sentence, when charged with a "grave crime" and a youth court has determined that, if convicted, its powers of sentence would be insufficient, or when charged together with an adult offender who has been sent to the Crown Court and it has been determined that the cases should be kept together. Where a sentence under the "dangerous offender" provisions is likely to be needed the youth may be committed for trial or for sentence.

"Grave crimes"

K–251a   The power of a youth court to commit a young person charged with a "grave crime" for trial (*MCA* 1980, s.24 (§ 1–110 in the main work)) should be exercised sparingly, since (i) it is the general policy of Parliament that those under 18 should be tried in a youth court wherever possible, (ii) trial in the Crown Court should be reserved for the most serious cases, recognising the greater formality of the proceedings and the greatly increased number of people involved, and (iii) offenders aged under 15 will rarely attract a period of detention under the "grave crimes" provision, and those under 12 even more rarely. A child aged 10 or 11 (or aged 12 to 14 but not a persistent offender) should be committed to the Crown Court only when charged with an offence of such gravity that, despite the normal prohibition on a custodial sentence for a person of that age, a sentence exceeding two years is a realistic possibility. A young person aged 12 to 17 (for whom a detention and training order could have been imposed) should be committed to the Crown Court only when charged with an offence of such gravity that a sentence substantially beyond the two year maximum for a detention and training order is a realistic possibility.

Dangerous offenders

K–251b   A sentence under the dangerous offender provisions of the *CJA* 2003 (§§ 5–497, 5–499 in the main work) may be imposed only where an equivalent determinate sentence of at least four years would have been imposed. Criteria relating to future offending and the risk of serious harm must be assessed in light of the maturity of the offender, the possibility of change in a much shorter time than would apply for an adult, and the wider circumstances of a young person. Where a young person charged with a specified offence would not otherwise be committed or sent to the Crown Court for trial, it is generally preferable for the decision whether to commit under these provisions to be taken after conviction.

Remittal from the Crown Court

Where a child or young person is convicted before the Crown Court of an offence other **K–251c** than homicide there is an obligation to remit to a youth court for sentence unless it would be undesirable to do so. In considering whether remittal is undesirable, a court should balance the need for expertise in the sentencing of young offenders with the benefits of sentence being imposed by the court which has determined guilt. Particular attention should be given to the obligation to remit where a young person appears before the Crown Court only because he was jointly charged with an adult.

For the full text of the guidelines, see www.sentencing-guidelines.gov.uk/guidelines/council/final.html.

S. Corporate Manslaughter and Health and Safety Offences Causing Death

The Sentencing Guidelines Council has issued a definitive guideline in relation to **K–252** corporate manslaughter and health and safety offences causing death. It applies to the sentencing of organisations on or after February 15, 2010.

The guidelines are in nine parts (elements of the offences; factors likely to affect serious- **K–253** ness; financial information — size and nature of the organisation; level of fines; compensation; costs; publicity orders; remedial orders; summary of approach to sentence) and there is an annex (financial information expected to be provided to the court). Part B emphasises that the guideline only applies to corporate manslaughter and to those health and safety offences where the offence is shown to have been a significant cause of the death. The approach to the assessment of seriousness requires the court to consider the foreseeability of serious injury, how far short of the applicable standard the defendant fell, how common the kind of breach in the organisation was, and at what level the organisation was at fault. There is a non-exhaustive list of aggravating factors (more than one death/ grave injury in addition to death/ failure to heed warnings or advice/ cost-cutting/ deliberate failure to obtain or comply with relevant licences/ injury to vulnerable persons), and a similar list of mitigating factors (prompt acceptance of responsibility/ high level of co-operation with investigation beyond that which will always be expected/ genuine efforts to remedy defect/ good record/ responsible attitude). Paragraph 9 states that it is unlikely, in relation to an offence of corporate manslaughter (having regard to the definition of the offence), that the unauthorised act of an employee will significantly reduce the culpability of the defendant, whereas paragraph 10 advises that, where a health and safety offence is established solely by reference to the unauthorised act of an employee, an assessment of the culpability of the organisation itself must be undertaken.

Part C states that there is no direct correlation between size and culpability. Size is, **K–254** however, relevant, as the means of any defendant are relevant to the fine (which is the principal available penalty for organisations) that is to be imposed in any case. Paragraph 14 states that the court should require information about the financial circumstances of the defendant, and that the best practice in such circumstances would be to call for the relevant information for a three year period including the year of the offence, so as to avoid any risk of atypical figures in a single year. The financial information ordinarily expected to be provided to the court is set out in Annex A. A fixed correlation between turnover and fine is not appropriate (para. 15). Paragraph 19 sets out a non-exhaustive list of factors which may or may not be relevant when the court is assessing the financial consequences of a fine. The effect on the employment of the innocent may be relevant; the effect on shareholders, directors or prices will not normally be relevant, save in the case of the prices of a monopoly supplier of public services; the effect on the provision of services to the public will be relevant; liability to pay civil compensation and the cost of meeting any remedial work will ordinarily be irrelevant; whether the fine will have the effect of putting the defendant out of business will be relevant, although in bad cases, this may be an acceptable consequence. Although in the case of a large organisation payment of any fine should be required within 28 days, it is permissible, in the case of a smaller or financially stretched organisation, to require payment to be spread over a much longer period. Where commission of the offence resulted in a broadly quantifiable saving, it will be appropriate to ensure that the fine is such as to remove the profit and impose an additional penalty.

K–255   Part D states that the level of fine will vary considerably, but that any fine must be punitive and sufficient to have an impact on the defendant. For an offence of corporate manslaughter the appropriate fine will seldom be less than £500,000 and may be measured in millions of pounds. For health and safety offences, the range of seriousness is greater, but the appropriate fine will seldom be less than £100,000 and may be measured in hundreds of thousands of pounds or more. Part E states that, in the great majority of cases, the court should conclude that compensation should be dealt with in a civil court, and should say that no order is made for that reason. Part F provides that the defendant ought ordinarily (subject to means) to be ordered to pay the properly incurred costs of the prosecution.

K–256   Part G concerns publicity orders, which are available under the *Corporate Manslaughter and Corporate Homicide Act* 2007, s.10 (§ 19–117i in the main work), and which should ordinarily be imposed in such cases. The order should particularise the matters to be published, the place where the public announcement is to be made, the size of any notice and the number of insertions (if to be made in a newspaper). The prosecution should serve a draft order on the court and the defendant and the judge should personally endorse the final form of the order. The order may stipulate that any comment placed by the defendant alongside the required announcement should be separated from it and clearly identified as such. Since a publicity order is part of the penalty, the cost of compliance should be kept in mind when fixing the fine.

K–257   Part H concerns remedial orders under section 9 of the 2007 Act (§ 19–117h in the main work) and section 42 of the *Health and Safety at Work etc. Act* 1974. Where appropriate remedial action has not already been taken, such an order should be imposed, provided that it can be made sufficiently specific to be enforceable.

K–258   Annex A says that for companies, partnerships and "third sector" organisations, audited accounts should be produced. In the case of the first two, particular attention should be paid to turnover, profit before tax, directors' remuneration (partners' drawings), loan accounts and pension provision, and assets, as disclosed by the balance sheet. Where such information is not produced, an inference may properly be made that the defendant can afford any appropriate fine. For local authorities, police and fire authorities and similar public bodies, it is said that reference should be made to their annual revenue budget. For health trusts, reference should be made to the quarterly reports and annual figures as to their financial strength and stability published by Monitor, their regulator. This will reveal their annual income.

T. Aggravated Burglary and Burglary

K–259   On October 13, 2011, the Sentencing Council for England and Wales issued a definitive guideline on burglary, applying to all offenders aged 18 or over who are sentenced on or after January 16, 2012, regardless of the date of their offence. The offences covered are: (A) aggravated burglary (*Theft Act* 1968, s.10 (§ 21–129 in the main work)), (B) domestic burglary (1968 Act, s.9 (*ibid.*, § 21–108)) and (C) non-domestic burglary (1968 Act, s.9).

The guideline sets out nine steps to be followed (in order) when sentencing for these offences, which correspond to the steps set out in the guideline on assault and other offences against the person (*ante*, K–114), subject to the modifications set out in the specific sections A to C relating to each offence (*post*).

In particular, step one requires the court to determine within which of three categories reflecting various degrees of seriousness the offence falls. Category 1 requires greater harm and higher culpability, category 2 requires either greater harm and lower culpability or lesser harm and higher culpability, and category 3 requires lesser harm and lower culpability. In determining the offender's culpability and the harm caused or intended, the court should refer only to the factors indicating harm and culpability set out in the specific sections relating to A to C, *post*, which comprise the principal factual elements of the offence. Where an offence does not fall squarely into a category, individual factors may require a degree of weighting before making an overall assessment and determining the appropriate offence category.

Step two requires the court to use the starting point identified for the relevant category (as to which, see also the specific sections relating to A–C, *post*) to reach a sentence within the category range (*post*). The starting point applies to all offenders irrespective of plea or previous convictions. A case of particular gravity, reflected by multiple features of culpability in step one, could merit upward adjustment from the starting point before further adjustment is made for the aggravating or mitigating factors increasing or reducing seriousness or reflecting personal mitigation set out in the specific sections A to C, *post*, which contain a non-exhaustive list of additional factual elements providing the context of the offence and factors relating to the offender. In particular, relevant recent convictions are likely to result in an upward adjustment. Having considered all these, and other relevant factors, it might be appropriate to move outside the identified category range.

Fine bands, and a non-exhaustive description of examples of requirements that might be appropriate for low, medium and high level community orders, correspond to those set out in the guideline on assaults and other offences against the person (*ante*), and are set out in the annex to the guideline.

Key to factors indicating greater or lesser harm and higher or lower culpability (step one)

A number of the following factors may apply when determining the offence category for **K–260** aggravated burglary, and domestic and non-domestic burglary. As to which factors may apply to each type of offence, see the specific sections A–C, *post*.

(a) *Factors indicating greater harm*

    i. Theft of/damage to property causing a significant degree of loss to the victim **K–261** (whether economic, sentimental or personal).

    ii. Soiling, ransacking or vandalism of property.

    iii. Occupier and/or victim at home or on the premises (or returns) while offender present.

    iv. Significant physical or psychological injury or other significant trauma to the victim.

    v. Violence used or threatened against victim (particularly, in relation to offences of aggravated burglary, involving a weapon).

    vi. Context of general public disorder.

    vii. Trauma to the victim, beyond the normal inevitable consequence of intrusion and theft.

(b) *Factors indicating lesser harm*

    i. No physical or psychological injury or other significant trauma to the victim. **K–262**

    ii. No violence used or threatened and a weapon is not produced.

    iii. Nothing stolen or only property of very low value to the victim (whether economic, sentimental or personal).

    iv. Limited damage or disturbance to property.

(c) *Factors indicating higher culpability*

    i. Victim or premises deliberately targeted (for example, due to vulnerability or **K–263** hostility based on disability, race, sexual orientation, and, in relation to offences of non-domestic burglary, to include a pharmacy or doctor's surgery).

   ii. A significant degree of planning or organisation.

  iii. Equipped for burglary (for example, implements carried and/or use of vehicle).

  iv. Weapon present on entry.

   v. Member of a group or gang.

  vi. Knife or other weapon carried (where not charged separately).

(d) *Factors indicating lower culpability*

K–264   i. Offender exploited by others.

   ii. Mental disorder or learning disability, where linked to the commission of the offence.

  iii. Offence committed on impulse, with limited intrusion into property.

Key to factors increasing or reducing seriousness or reflecting personal mitigation (step 2)

K–265   A number of the following factors may apply when determining the sentence within the category range for offences of aggravated burglary, and domestic and non-domestic burglary. As to which factors may apply to each type of offence, see the specific sections A–C, *post*.

(e) *Factors increasing seriousness*

K–266   Statutory aggravating factors:

    i. Previous convictions (in accordance with the *Criminal Justice Act* 2003, s.143(2) (*ibid.*, § 5–54)).

   ii. Offence committed whilst on bail (2003 Act, s.143(3)).

Other aggravating factors include:

  iii. Child at home (or returns home) when offence committed.

  iv. Offence committed at night (particularly, in relation to offences of non-domestic burglary, where staff are, or are likely to be, present).

   v. Abuse of power and/or position of trust.

  vi. Gratuitous degradation of victim.

  vii. Any steps taken to prevent the victim reporting the incident or obtaining assistance and/or from assisting or supporting the prosecution.

 viii. Victim compelled to leave home (in particular victims of domestic violence).

  ix. Established evidence of community impact.

   x. Commission of offence whilst under the influence of alcohol or drugs.

  xi. Failure to comply with current court orders.

  xii. Offence committed whilst on licence.

 xiii. Offences taken into consideration.

(f) *Factors reducing seriousness or reflecting personal mitigation*

K–267   i. Subordinate role in a group or gang.

   ii. Injuries caused recklessly.

  iii. Nothing stolen or only property of low value to the victim (whether economic, commercial, sentimental or personal).

  iv. Offender has made voluntary reparation to the victim.

   v. No previous convictions or no relevant/recent convictions.

  vi. Remorse.

  vii. Good character and/or exemplary conduct.

viii. Determination, and/or demonstration of steps taken to address addiction or offending behaviour.
ix. Serious medical condition requiring urgent, intensive or long-term treatment.
x. Age and/or lack of maturity where it affects the responsibility of the offender.
xi. Lapse of time since the offence where this is not the fault of the offender.
xii. Mental disorder or learning disability, where not linked to the commission of the offence.
xiii. Sole or primary carer for dependent relatives.

A. Aggravated burglary

Factors indicating harm and culpability (step one)

Greater harm *list (a)*	i–vi	**K–268**
Lesser harm *list (b)*	i, ii	
Higher culpability *list (c)*	i–iii, v, vi	
Lower culpability *list (d)*	i–iii	

Starting point and category range (step two)

Offence category	Starting point (applicable to all offenders)	Category range (applicable to all offenders)
category 1	10 years' custody	nine – 13 years' custody
category 2	six years' custody	four – nine years' custody
category 3	two years' custody	one – four years' custody

Factors increasing or reducing seriousness or reflecting personal mitigation

Factors increasing seriousness *list (e)*	i–xiii
Factors reducing seriousness or reflecting personal mitigation *list (f)*	i–xiii

B. Domestic burglary

Factors indicating harm and culpability (step one)

Greater harm *list (a)*	i–iii, v–vii	**K–269**
Lesser harm *list (b)*	iii, iv	
Higher culpability *list (c)*	i–iii, v, vi	

Lower culpability *list (d)*	i–iii

Starting point and category range (step two)

Offence category	Starting point (applicable to all offenders)	Category range (applicable to all offenders)
category 1	three years' custody	two – six years' custody
category 2	one year's custody	high level community order – two years' custody
category 3	high level community order	low level community order – 26 weeks' custody

Where the defendant is dependent on, or has a propensity to misuse, drugs and there is sufficient prospect of success, a community order with a drug rehabilitation requirement under section 209 of the 2003 Act (*ibid.*, § 5–145) may be a proper alternative to a short or moderate custodial sentence.

When sentencing for category 2 or 3 offences, the court should consider whether the custody threshold has been passed, if so, whether it is unavoidable that a custodial sentence be imposed and, if so, whether that sentence can be suspended.

Factors increasing or reducing seriousness or reflecting personal mitigation

Factors increasing seriousness *list (e)*	i–iv, vi–xiii
Factors reducing seriousness or reflecting personal mitigation *list (f)*	i, iv–xiii

C. Non-domestic burglary

Factors indicating harm and culpability (step one)

K–270 As for B, *ante*.

Starting point and category range (step two)

Offence category	Starting point (applicable to all offenders)	Category range (applicable to all offenders)
category 1	two years' custody	one – five years' custody
category 2	18 weeks' custody	low level community order – 51 weeks' custody
category 3	medium level community order	band B fine – 18 weeks' custody

Where the defendant is dependent on, or has a propensity to misuse, drugs and there is sufficient prospect of success, a community order with a drug rehabilitation requirement under section 209 of the 2003 Act may be a proper alternative to a short or moderate custodial sentence.

When sentencing for category 2 or 3 offences, the court should consider whether the custody threshold has been passed, if so, whether it is unavoidable that a custodial sentence be imposed and, if so, whether that sentence can be suspended; and in sentencing for category three offences, the court should also consider whether the community order threshold has been passed.

Factors increasing or reducing seriousness or reflecting personal mitigation

Factors increasing seriousness *list (e)*	i, ii, iv–vii, ix–xiii
Factors reducing seriousness or reflecting personal mitigation *list (f)*	i, iv–xiii

U. Drug Offences

On January 24, 2012, the Sentencing Council for England and Wales issued a definitive   **K–271**
guideline, applying to all offenders aged 18 or over who are sentenced on or after February 27, 2012, regardless of the date of their offence. The offences covered are:

I. fraudulent evasion of a prohibition on the importation or exportation of a controlled drug (*CEMA* 1979, s.170(2) (§ 25–474 in the main work));

II. supplying or offering to supply such a drug (*Misuse of Drugs Act* 1971, s.4(3) (*ibid.*, § 27–28)) and possession of such a drug with intent to supply it to another (1971 Act, s.5(3) (*ibid.*, § 27–50));

III. production of such a drug (1971 Act, s.4(2)(a) or (b)) and cultivation of a cannabis plant (1971 Act, s.6(2) (*ibid.*, § 27–79));

IV. permitting premises to be used (1971 Act, s.8 (*ibid.*, § 27–84)); and

V. possession of a controlled drug (1971 Act, s.5(2)).

The guideline sets out eight steps to be followed (in order), which broadly correspond to the steps set out in the guideline on offences against the person (*ante*, Appendix K–113 *et seq.*), except that there is no step requiring the court to consider whether an offender meets the dangerousness criteria.

Step one requires the court to determine the offence category based on varying factors set out in the specific sections I to V (*post*).

Step two requires the court to use the starting point identified for the relevant category (as to which, see also the specific sections relating to I–V, *post*) to reach a sentence within the category range (*post*) dependent on whether the offence in question relates to a Class A, B or C drug. The starting point applies to all offenders. The court should then consider adjustment within the category range for aggravating or mitigating features set out in the specific sections I to V, *post*, which contain a non-exhaustive list of additional factual elements providing the context of the offence and factors relating to the offender. Having considered all these, and other relevant factors, it might be appropriate to move outside the identified category range. In cases where the offender is regarded as being at the very top of a "leading role" (which does not apply to section IV and V offences), it may be justifiable for the court to depart from the guideline. Where the defendant is dependent on, or has a propensity to misuse, drugs and there is a sufficient prospect of success, a community order with a drug rehabilitation requirement under the *CJA* 2003, s.209 (§ 5–275 in the main work), can be a proper alternative to a short or moderate length custodial sentence. As with previous guidelines, the council emphasises that, where appropriate, courts should consider whether community or custodial thresholds have been passed and, if the latter threshold has been passed, whether it is unavoidable that a custodial sentence be imposed and, if so, whether that sentence can be suspended. The guidelines are subject to section 110 of the *PCC(S)A* 2000 (minimum sentences for third drug trafficking offence (*ibid.*, § 5–443)).

In addition to considering whether to make ancillary orders, step six also requires the court, except for section V offences, to consider confiscation where the Crown invokes the process or where it considers it appropriate.

Fine bands, and a non-exhaustive description of examples of requirements that might be appropriate for low, medium and high level community orders, correspond to those in the guideline on offences against the person (*ante*), and are set out in the annex to the guideline.

Key to factors increasing or reducing seriousness or reflecting personal mitigation (step two)

K–272   A number of the following factors may apply when determining the sentence within the category range. As to which factors may apply to each type of offence, see the specific sections I to V, *post*.

(a) *Factors increasing seriousness*

K–273   Statutory aggravating factors:
  (i) Previous convictions (*CJA* 2003, s.143(2) (§ 5–67 in the main work)).
  (ii) Using or permitting a person under 18 to deliver a controlled drug to a third person (1971 Act, s.4A (*ibid.*, § 27–28a)).
  (iii) Supplying or offering to supply a drug on, or in the vicinity of, school premises (1971 Act, s.4A).
  (iv) Offence committed on bail (2003 Act, s.143(3)).

Other aggravating factors include:
  (v) Targeting of any premises to locate vulnerable individuals or supply to such individuals and/ or supply to those under 18.
  (vi) Nature of any likely supply.
  (vii) Level of any profit element.
  (viii) Use of premises accompanied by unlawful access to electricity/ other utility supply.
  (ix) Continuing/ large scale operation as evidenced by presence and nature of specialist equipment.
  (x) Exposure of others to more than usual danger, *e.g.* drugs cut with harmful substances.
  (xi) Length of time over which premises used for drug activity.
  (xii) Volume of drug activity permitted.
  (xiii) Premises adapted to facilitate drug activity.
  (xiv) Location of premises, *e.g.* proximity to school.
  (xv) Attempts to conceal or dispose of evidence, where not charged separately.
  (xvi) Possession of drug in prison or in a school or licensed premises.
  (xvii) Presence of others, especially children and/ or non-users.
  (xviii) Presence of weapon(s), where not charged separately.
  (xix) Charged as importation of a very small amount.
  (xx) High purity or high potential yield.
  (xxi) Failure to comply with current court orders or offence committed on licence.
  (xxii) Established evidence of community impact.

(b) *Factors reducing seriousness or reflecting personal mitigation*

K–274   (i) Involvement due to pressure, intimidation or coercion, except where already taken into account at step one.
  (ii) Supply only of drug to which offender addicted.
  (iii) Mistaken belief as to type of drug, taking into account the reasonableness of such belief.
  (iv) Isolated incident.
  (v) Low purity.
  (vi) No previous convictions **or** no relevant or recent convictions.

(vii) Offender's vulnerability was exploited.

(viii) Remorse.

(ix) Good character and/ or exemplary conduct.

(x) Offender is using cannabis to help with a diagnosed medical condition.

(xi) Determination and/ or demonstration of steps having been taken to address addiction or offending behaviour.

(xii) Serious medical conditions requiring urgent, intensive or long-term treatment.

(xiii) Age and/ or lack of maturity where it affects the responsibility of the offender.

(xiv) Mental disorder or learning disability.

(xv) Sole or primary carer for dependent relatives.

I. Fraudulent evasion of a prohibition on importation or exportation

Determining the offence category (step one)

The court should determine the weight of the drugs involved and the offender's culpabil- **K-275** ity demonstrated by his role, by reference to the tables below. Where there are characteristics present that fall under different role categories, the court should balance them to reach a fair assessment of the offender's culpability.

Culpability demonstrated by offender's role
One or more of these characteristics may demonstrate the offender's role. These lists are not exhaustive.
LEADING role: • directing or organising buying and selling on a commercial scale; • substantial links to, and influence on, others in a chain; • close links to original source; • expectation of substantial financial gain; • use of business as cover; • abuse of a position of trust or responsibility.
SIGNIFICANT role: • operational or management function within a chain; • involvement of others whether by pressure, influence, intimidation or reward; • motivated by financial or other advantage, whether or not operating alone; • some awareness and understanding of scale of operation.
LESSER role: • performance of limited function under direction; • engaged by pressure, coercion, intimidation; • involvement through naïvety/ exploitation; • no influence on those above in a chain; • little, if any, awareness or understanding of the scale of operation; • if own operation, solely for own use (considering reasonableness of account).

Category of harm
Indicative quantity of drug concerned (upon which the starting point is based):
Category 1 - heroin, cocaine - 5 kg; Ecstasy - 10,000 tablets; LSD - 250,000 squares; amphetamine - 20 kg; cannabis - 200 kg; ketamine - 5 kg.
Category 2 - heroin, cocaine - 1 kg; Ecstasy - 2,000 tablets; LSD - 25,000 squares; amphetamine - 4 kg; cannabis - 40 kg; ketamine - 1 kg.
Category 3 - heroin, cocaine - 150g; Ecstasy - 300 tablets; LSD - 2,500 squares; amphetamine - 750g; cannabis - 6 kg; ketamine - 150g.
Category 4 - heroin, cocaine - 5g; Ecstasy - 20 tablets; LSD - 170 squares; amphetamine - 20g; cannabis - 100g; ketamine - 5g.

Where the operation is on the most serious and commercial scale, involving a quantity of drugs significantly higher than category 1, sentences of 20 years and above may be appropriate, depending on the role of the offender.

Starting point and category range (step two)

Class A	Leading role	Significant role	Lesser role
Category 1	**Starting point** 14 years **Category range** 12 – 16 years	**Starting point** 10 years **Category range** 9 – 12 years	**Starting point** 8 years **Category range** 6 – 9 years
Category 2	**Starting point** 11 years **Category range** 9 – 13 years	**Starting point** 8 years **Category range** 6.5 – 10 years	**Starting point** 6 years **Category range** 5 – 7 years
Category 3	**Starting point** 8.5 years **Category range** 6.5 – 10 years	**Starting point** 6 years **Category range** 5 – 7 years	**Starting point** 4.5 years **Category range** 3.5 – 5 years
Category 4	Where the quantity falls below the indicative amount set out for category 4 in the "category of harm" table (*ante*), first identify the role for the importation offence, then refer to the starting point and ranges for possession or supply offences, depending on intent. Where the quantity is significantly larger than the indicative amounts for category 4 but below category 3 amounts, refer to the category 3 ranges above.		

Class B	Leading role	Significant role	Lesser role
Category 1	**Starting point** 8 years **Category range** 7 – 10 years	**Starting point** 5.5 years **Category range** 5 – 7 years	**Starting point** 4 years **Category range** 2.5 – 5 years
Category 2	**Starting point** 6 years **Category range** 4.5 – 8 years	**Starting point** 4 years **Category range** 2.5 – 5 years	**Starting point** 2 years **Category range** 1.5 – 3 years
Category 3	**Starting point** 4 years **Category range** 2.5 – 5 years	**Starting point** 2 years **Category range** 1.5 – 3 years	**Starting point** 1 year **Category range** 12 weeks – 18 months
Category 4	As for "Category 4" Class A offences, *ante*.		

Class C	Leading role	Significant role	Lesser role
Category 1	**Starting point** 5 years **Category range** 4 – 8 years	**Starting point** 3 years **Category range** 2 – 5 years	**Starting point** 1.5 years **Category range** 1 – 3 years

Category 2	**Starting point** 3.5 years **Category range** 2 – 5 years	**Starting point** 1.5 years **Category range** 1 – 3 years	**Starting point** 26 weeks **Category range** 12 weeks – 18 months
Category 3	**Starting point** 1.5 years **Category range** 1 – 3 years	**Starting point** 26 weeks **Category range** 12 weeks – 18 months	**Starting point** high level com- munity order **Category range** medium level com- munity order – 12 weeks
Category 4	As for "Category 4" class A offences, *ante*.		

Factors increasing or reducing seriousness or reflecting personal mitigation

Factors increasing seriousness	i, ii, iv, x, xv, xviii, xx, xxiii
Factors reducing seriousness or reflecting personal mitigation	i, iii–ix, xi–xvi

II. Supplying, offering to supply, possession with intent to supply

Determining the offence category (step one)

The court should determine the weight of the drugs and the offender's culpability demonstrated by his role, by reference to the tables below. Where there are characteristics present that fall under different role categories, the court should balance them to reach a fair assessment of the offender's culpability.   **K–276**

Culpability demonstrated by offender's role One or more of these characteristics may demonstrate the offender's role. These lists are not exhaustive.
LEADING role: As for "Leading role" in section I, *ante*.
SIGNIFICANT role: As for "Significant role" in section I, *ante*, but also: supply, other than by a person in a position of responsibility, to a prisoner for gain without coercion.
LESSER role: As for "Lesser role" in section I, *ante*, save that: if own operation, absence of any financial gain, *e.g.* joint purchase for no profit, or sharing minimal quantity between peers on non-commercial basis.

Category of harm Indicative quantity of drug concerned (upon which the starting point is based):
Category 1 As for "Category 1" in section I, *ante*.
Category 2 As for "Category 2" in section I, *ante*.

| **Category 3** |
| As for "Category 3" in section I, *ante*. |
| OR |
| supplying drugs in prison by a prison employee or "street dealing", *i.e.* selling directly to users (including test purchase officers). |
| **Category 4** |
| As for "Category 4" in section I, *ante*, |

Where the operation is on the most serious and commercial scale, involving a quantity of drugs significantly higher than category 1, sentences of 20 years and above may be appropriate, depending on the role of the offender.

Starting point and category range (step two)

Class A	Leading role	Significant role	Lesser role
Category 1	**Starting point** 14 years	**Starting point** 10 years	**Starting point** 7 years
	Category range 12 – 16 years	**Category range** 9 – 12 years	**Category range** 6 – 9 years
Category 2	**Starting point** 11 years	**Starting point** 8 years	**Starting point** 5 years
	Category range 9 – 13 years	**Category range** 6.5 – 10 years	**Category range** 3.5 – 7 years
Category 3	**Starting point** 8.5 years	**Starting point** 4.5 years	**Starting point** 3 years
	Category range 6.5 – 10 years	**Category range** 3.5 – 7 years	**Category range** 2 – 4.5 years
Category 4	**Starting point** 5.5 years	**Starting point** 3.5 years	**Starting point** 1.5 years
	Category range 4.5 – 7.5 years	**Category range** 2 – 5 years	**Category range** high level community order – 3 years

Class B	Leading role	Significant role	Lesser role
Category 1	**Starting point** 8 years	**Starting point** 5.5 years	**Starting point** 3 years
	Category range 7 – 10 years	**Category range** 5 – 7 years	**Category range** 2.5 – 5 years
Category 2	**Starting point** 6 years	**Starting point** 4 years	**Starting point** 1 year
	Category range 4.5 – 8 years	**Category range** 2.5 – 5 years	**Category range** 26 weeks – 3 years
Category 3	**Starting point** 4 years	**Starting point** 1 year	**Starting point** high level community order
	Category range 2.5 – 5 years	**Category range** 26 weeks – 3 years	**Category range** low level community order – 26 weeks

Category 4	Starting point 1.5 years	Starting point high level community order	Starting point low level community order
	Category range 26 weeks – 3 years	Category range medium level community order – 26 weeks	Category range band B fine – medium level community order

Class C	Leading role	Significant role	Lesser role
Category 1	Starting point 5 years	Starting point 3 years	Starting point 1.5 years
	Category range 4 – 8 years	Category range 2 – 5 years	Category range 1 – 3 years
Category 2	Starting point 3.5 years	Starting point 1.5 years	Starting point 26 weeks
	Category range 2 – 5 years	Category range 1 – 3 years	Category range 12 weeks – 1.5 years
Category 3	Starting point 1.5 years	Starting point 26 weeks	Starting point high level community order
	Category range 1 – 3 years	Category range 12 weeks – 1.5 years	Category range low level community order – 12 weeks
Category 4	Starting point 26 weeks	Starting point high level community order	Starting point low level community order
	Category range high level community order – 1.5 years	Category range low level community order – 12 weeks	Category range band A fine – medium level community order

Factors increasing or reducing seriousness or reflecting personal mitigation

Factors increasing seriousness	i–v, x, xv, xvii–xxii
Factors reducing seriousness or reflecting personal mitigation	i–ix, xi–xv

III. Production of a controlled drug OR cultivation of a cannabis plant

Determining the offence category (step one)

K–277

The court should determine the offender's culpability demonstrated by his role and the output or potential output based on the weight of the product or number of plants/ scale of operation, by reference to the tables below. Where there are characteristics present that fall under different role categories, the court should balance them to reach a fair assessment of the offender's culpability.

Culpability demonstrated by offender's role
One or more of these characteristics may demonstrate the offender's role. These lists are not exhaustive.
LEADING role: As for "Leading role" in section I, *ante*, save that there is no reference here to closeness to the original source.
SIGNIFICANT role: As for "Significant role" in section I, *ante*.
LESSER role: As for "Lesser role" in section I, *ante*.

Category of harm
Indicative quantity of drug concerned (upon which the starting point is based):
Category 1 As for "Category 1" in section I, *ante*, except that the quantity specified for cannabis is an operation capable of producing industrial quantities for commercial use.
Category 2 As for "Category 2" in section I, *ante*, except that the quantity specified for cannabis is an operation capable of producing significant quantities for commercial use.
Category 3 As for "Category 3" in section I, *ante*, except that the quantity specified for cannabis is 28 plants (with an assumed yield of 40g per plant).
Category 4 As for "Category 4" in section I, *ante*, except that the quantity specified for cannabis is nine plants (with an assumed yield of 40g per plant) (domestic operation).

Where the operation is on the most serious and commercial scale, involving a quantity of drugs significantly higher than category 1, sentences of 20 years and above may be appropriate, depending on the role of the offender.

Starting point and category range (step two)
For Class A offences, as for "Class A" in section II, *ante*, except for category 3:

Class A	Leading role	Significant role	Lesser role
Category 3	**Starting point** 8.5 years	**Starting point** 5 years	**Starting point** 3.5 years
	Category range 6.5 – 10 years	**Category range** 3.5 – 7 years	**Category range** 2 – 5 years

For Class B offences, as for "Class B" in section II, *ante*, except for category 4:

Class B	Leading role	Significant role	Lesser role
Category 4	**Starting point** 1 year	**Starting point** high level community order	**Starting point** band C fine
	Category range high level community order – 3 years	**Category range** medium level community order – 26 weeks	**Category range** discharge – medium level community order

Class C	Leading role	Significant role	Lesser role
Category 1	**Starting point** 5 years **Category range** 4 – 8 years	**Starting point** 3 years **Category range** 2 – 5 years	**Starting point** 1.5 years **Category range** 1 – 3 years
Category 2	**Starting point** 3.5 years **Category range** 2 – 5 years	**Starting point** 1.5 years **Category range** 1 – 3 years	**Starting point** 26 weeks **Category range** high level community order – 1.5 years
Category 3	**Starting point** 1.5 years **Category range** 1 – 3 years	**Starting point** 26 weeks **Category range** high level community order – 1.5 years	**Starting point** high level community order **Category range** low level community order – 12 weeks
Category 4	**Starting point** 26 weeks **Category range** high level community order – 1.5 years	**Starting point** high level community order **Category range** low level community order – 12 weeks	**Starting point** band C fine **Category range** discharge – medium level community order

Factors increasing or reducing seriousness or reflecting personal mitigation

Factors increasing seriousness	i, iv, vi–x, xv, xvii, xviii, xx–xxii
Factors reducing seriousness or reflecting personal mitigation	i, iv–ix, xi–xv

IV. Permitting premises to be used

Determining the offence category (step one)

The court should determine into which of three categories the offence falls by reference **K–278** to the offender's culpability and the harm caused (which will be based on the extent of the activity and/ or the quantity of drugs). Category 1 requires greater harm and higher culpability, category 2 requires either greater harm and lower culpability or lesser harm and higher culpability, and category 3 requires lesser harm and lower culpability.

Factors indicating higher culpability (non-exhaustive):
- Premises used primarily for drug activity, *e.g.* crack house.
- Expectation of substantial financial gain.
- Use of legitimate business premises to aid and/ or conceal illegal activity, *e.g.* public house or club.

Factors indicating lower culpability (non-exhaustive):
- Limited or no financial gain.
- No active role in any supply taking place.
- Involvement through naïvety.

Factors indicating greater harm (non-exhaustive):
- Regular drug-related activity.

- Higher quantity of drugs, *e.g.* more than 5g of heroin or cocaine or more than 50g of cannabis.

Factors indicating lesser harm (non-exhaustive):

- Infrequent drug-related activity.
- Lower quantity of drugs.

Starting point and category range (step two)

Class A	Starting point	Category range
Category 1	2.5 years	1.5 – 4 years
Category 2	36 weeks	high level community order – 1.5 years
Category 3	medium level community order	low level community order – high level community order

Class B	Starting point	Category range
Category 1	1 year	26 weeks – 1.5 years
Category 2	high level community order	low level community order – 26 weeks
Category 3	band C fine	band A fine – low level community order

Class C	Starting point	Category range
Category 1	12 weeks	high level community order – 26 weeks (3 months if tried summarily)
Category 2	low level community order	band C fine – high level community order
Category 3	band A fine	discharge – band C fine

Factors increasing or reducing seriousness or reflecting personal mitigation

Factors increasing seriousness	i, iv, xi–xv, xvii, xviii, xx–xxii
Factors reducing seriousness or reflecting personal mitigation	i, iv–ix, xi–xv

V. Possession of a controlled drug

Determining the offence category (step one)

K–279   The court should determine the offence category based on the class of drug involved.

Starting point and category range (step two)

Offence category	Starting point	Category range
Category 1 (Class A)	band C fine	band A fine – 51 weeks

| Category 2 (Class B) | band B fine | discharge – 26 weeks |
| Category 3 (Class C) | band A fine | discharge – medium level community order |

Factors increasing or reducing seriousness or reflecting personal mitigation

| Factors increasing seriousness | i, iv, xv–xvii, xix, xxi, xxii |
| Factors reducing seriousness or reflecting personal mitigation | iv, vi, viii–xv |

V. Offences Taken into Consideration and Totality

The Sentencing Council has issued a guideline on the related topics of taking offences into consideration (TICs) and totality, applying to all offenders whose cases are dealt with on or after June 11, 2012. In addition to setting out the applicable principles to be gleaned from legislation and case-law, the guideline covers the following.   ★K–280

A. Offences taken into consideration

See *ante*, §§ 5–160 *et seq.*   ★K–281

B. Totality

This part of the guideline applies to the sentencing of an offender for multiple offences or when he is serving an existing sentence. The principle of totality comprises two elements: (i) all courts when sentencing for more than a single offence should pass a just and proportionate total sentence that reflects all the offending behaviour, whether the sentences are structured as concurrent or consecutive (in respect of which there is no inflexible rule); (ii) it is usually impossible to arrive at a just and proportionate total sentence simply by adding together notional single sentences - it is necessary to address the offending behaviour, together with the factors personal to the offender, as a whole.   ★K–282

The general approach (as applied to determinate custodial sentences) consists of four steps:

(i) consider the sentence for each individual offence;

(ii) determine whether the case calls for concurrent or consecutive sentences;

(iii) test the overall sentence against the requirement that it should be just and proportionate; and

(iv) consider whether the sentence is structured in a way that will be best understood by all concerned with it.

As to (ii), concurrent sentences will ordinarily be appropriate where the offences arise out of the same incident or facts or where there is a series of offences of the same or similar kind, especially when committed against the same person, with examples of both being set out in the guideline. Consecutive offences will be appropriate where the offences arise out of unrelated facts or incidents, where the offences are of the same or similar kind, but where the overall criminality will not sufficiently be reflected by concurrent sentences, or where one or more offence qualifies for a statutory minimum sentence and concurrent sentences would improperly undermine that minimum. Examples are again set out, including ways in which the court can reach a just and proportionate sentence where this is not achieved by simply aggregating the consecutive sentences (*e.g.* with offences of a similar level of severity, by reducing all of the sentences proportionately or by identifying the most serious principal offence and reducing the remainder proportionately; with offences of differing levels of seriousness, by recording lesser offences as "no separate penalty" or by ordering the lesser sentences to run concurrently).

Tables follow the guideline, setting out the approach to be taken when applying the totality principle in specified circumstances (this is in large part based on existing legislation and case-law).

Determinate custodial sentence to be passed

★**K–283**   a. where the offender is serving an existing custodial determinate sentence: if the new offence was committed before the imposition of that sentence, the court should consider what sentence would have been imposed if the court had dealt with the offences at the same time; if it was committed after that sentence, then generally the sentence will be consecutive;

b. where the offender is serving a custodial determinate sentence, but had been released from custody prior to being recalled, the court should follow *R. v. Costello* [2010] 2 Cr.App.R.(S.) 94, CA (§ 5–669 in the main work);

c. where the offender is liable to be returned to custody under the *PCC(S)A* 2000, s.116 (*ante*, § 5–633), see subsection (6)(c);

d. where the offender is in breach of a suspended sentence, the additional sentence will generally be consecutive to the activated suspended sentence;

Extended sentences

★**K–284**   e. when using multiple offences to calculate the requisite determinate term (in accordance with *R. v. Joyce*; *R. v. Pinnell* [2011] 2 Cr.App.R.(S.) 30, CA (§ 5–523 in the main work)), the custodial period must be adjusted for totality in the same way as determinate sentences would be;

Indeterminate sentences

★**K–285**   f. when imposing multiple indeterminate sentences and using multiple offences to calculate the minimum term for an indeterminate sentence, assess the notional determinate term for all offences (serious, specified or otherwise) in the usual way, adjusting for totality, and then, normally, impose the indeterminate sentence on all serious specified offences concurrently;

g. where the offender is already serving an existing determinate sentence, the court should order the sentence to run concurrently but adjust the minimum term to reflect half of any period still remaining to be served under the existing sentence; where the offender is already serving an existing indeterminate sentence, the court may order the sentence to run consecutively to the existing sentence (*R. v. Hills* [2009] 1 Cr.App.R.(S.) 75, CA (§ 5–523 in the main work)), but the aggregate minimum terms should be adjusted if this is not just and proportionate;

h. when ordering a determinate sentence to run consecutively to an indeterminate sentence, the court should consider the total sentence that the offender will serve before becoming eligible for consideration for release, achieving justice and proportionality, if necessary, by reducing the length of the determinate sentence or, alternatively, ordering the second sentence to be served concurrently;

Multiple fines for non-imprisonable offences

★**K–286**   i. where the offender has been convicted of more than one offence where a fine is appropriate, there are various ways in which the court can achieve a just and proportionate fine if this is not achieved by simply totting up the fines; the court should also consider *R. v. John Pointon & Sons Ltd* [2008] 2 Cr.App.R.(S.) 82, CA (as to the need to avoid double counting);

Fines in combination with other sentences

★**K–287**   j. a fine may be imposed in addition to any other sentence (subject to statutory exceptions), but combining a fine with an immediate custodial sentence is only likely to be justifiable if a confiscation order is not contemplated, there is no obvious victim to receive compensation and the offender has the means to pay;

Community orders

    k. multiple offences that do not individually cross the custody threshold may do so   ★**K–288**
when taken in combination;

    l. where there is more than one offence, with one meriting immediate custody and
one meriting a community order, the custodial sentence should be enhanced by
virtue of the associated offence or no separate penalty should be imposed for the
lesser offence;

    m. where the offender has been convicted of more than one offence where a com-
munity order is appropriate, the court should generally impose a single community order that reflects the overall criminality of the offending behaviour;
where it is necessary to impose more than one community order, these should be
ordered to run concurrently and, for ease of administration, each of the orders
should be identical;

    n. where the offender is convicted of an offence while serving a community order,
the court should consider if the overall seriousness of the offending behaviour
justifies a custodial sentence; if not, it should impose a single community order
reflecting the overall totality of criminality; and it should take into account the
extent to which the offender complied with the requirements of the previous
order;

Disqualifications from driving

    o. where the offender has been convicted of two or more obligatory disqualification   ★**K–289**
offences, the court should take into account all offences when determining the
disqualification periods and should generally impose like periods for each offence
(which have to be concurrent);

    p. where the offender has been convicted of two or more offences and is liable to
disqualification under the "totting up" provisions of the *RTOA* 1988, s.35 (§ 32–
192 in the main work), the guideline simply sets out the effect of subsection (3);

    q. where the offender has otherwise been convicted of two or more offences involv-
ing discretionary disqualification, it is generally desirable for the court to impose a
single disqualification order that reflects the overall criminality of the offending
behaviour;

Compensation orders

    r. a global compensation order should not be made unless the offences were commit-   ★**K–290**
ted against the same victim; where there are competing claims for limited funds,
the amount available should normally be apportioned on a *pro rata* basis;

    s. compensation may be combined with a fine (with priority to compensation), a
confiscation order, a community order, a suspended sentence or an immediate
custodial sentence (where the offender is clearly able to pay or has good prospects of
employment on release).

W. Dangerous Dog Offences

   The Sentencing Council for England and Wales has issued a definitive guideline, apply-   ★**K–291**
ing to all offenders aged 18 or over who are sentenced on or after August 20, 2012, regardless of the date of the offence. The offences covered are: (A) owning or being in charge of a
dog that injures a person whilst dangerously out of control in a public place (*Dangerous
Dogs Act* 1991, s.3(1) (§ 31–35 in the main work)), and allowing a dog to enter a private
place where the dog is not permitted to be, where it then injures any person (1991 Act,
s.3(3)(a)), (B) owning or being in charge of a dog dangerously out of control in a public
place (1991 Act, s.3(1)), and allowing a dog to enter a private place where the dog is not
permitted to be, and, while it is there, there are grounds for reasonable apprehension that
it will injure any person (1991 Act, s.3(3)(b)), and (C) possession of a prohibited dog (1991
Act, s.1(3)), and breeding, selling, exchanging or advertising a prohibited dog (1991 Act,
s.1(2)).

The guideline sets out eight steps to be followed (in order), which broadly correspond to the steps set out in the guideline on offences against the person (*ante*, K–113 *et seq.*), except that there is no step requiring the court to consider whether an offender meets the dangerousness criteria, and consideration of compensation and/ or ancillary orders is step five (as to which, see the specific sections relating to A to C, *post*), preceding consideration of the totality principle (now step six).

Step one requires the court to determine within which of three categories reflecting various degrees of seriousness the offence falls. In determining the offender's culpability and the harm caused (or intended), the court should refer only to the factors indicating harm and culpability set out in the specific sections relating to A to C, *post*, which comprise the principal factual elements of the offence.

Step two requires the court to use the starting point identified for the relevant category (as to which, see also the specific sections relating to A to C, *post*) to reach a sentence within the category range. The starting point applies to all offenders irrespective of plea or previous convictions. The court should then consider adjustment within the category range for aggravating or mitigating features set out in the specific sections A to C, *post*, which contain a non-exhaustive list of additional factual elements providing the context of the offence and factors relating to the offender. Having considered all these, and other relevant factors, it might be appropriate to move outside the identified category range. As with previous guidelines, the council emphasises that, where appropriate, courts should consider whether community or custodial thresholds have been passed and, if the latter threshold has been passed, whether it is unavoidable that a custodial sentence be imposed and, if so, whether that sentence can be suspended.

Fine bands, and a non-exhaustive description of examples of requirements that might be appropriate for low, medium and high level community orders, correspond to those in the guideline on offences against the person (*ante*), and are set out in the annex to the guideline.

Key to factors increasing or reducing seriousness or reflecting personal mitigation (step two)

★K–292   A number of the following factors may apply when determining the sentence within the category range. As to which factors may apply to each type of offence, see the specific sections A to C, *post*.

(a) *Factors increasing seriousness*
    Statutory aggravating factors:
       i. Previous convictions.
      ii. Offence committed on bail.
    Other aggravating factors include:
     iii. Injury to other animal(s).
     iv. Location of offence.
      v. Continuing effect upon victim and/ or others.
     vi. Failure to take adequate precautions to prevent dog escaping.
    vii. Allowing insufficiently experienced or trained person to be in charge of dog.
   viii. Presence of children or others who are vulnerable because of personal circumstances.
     ix. Ill-treatment or failure to ensure welfare needs of dog, where not charged separately.
      x. Dog known to be prohibited.
     xi. Lack or loss of control of dog due to influence of alcohol or drugs.
    xii. Offence committed against those working in the public sector or providing a service to the public.
   xiii. Established evidence of community impact.
   xiv. Failure to comply with current court orders or offence committed on licence.

(b) *Factors reducing seriousness or reflecting personal mitigation*
      i. No previous convictions or no relevant/ recent convictions.

  ii. Isolated incident.

 iii. No previous complaints against, or incidents involving, the dog.

 iv. Unaware that dog was prohibited type despite reasonable efforts to identify type.

  v. Evidence of safety or control measures having been taken by owner.

 vi. Prosecution results from owner notification.

vii. Remorse.

viii. Good character and/ or exemplary conduct.

 ix. Evidence of responsible ownership.

  x. Determination, and/ or demonstration of steps taken, to address addiction or of-
     fending behaviour.

 xi. Serious medical condition requiring urgent, intensive or long-term treatment.

xii. Age and/ or lack of maturity where it affects the responsibility of the offender.

xiii. Lapse of time since the offence where this was not the fault of the offender.

xiv. Mental disorder or learning disability (for offences in sections A and B only, where
     not linked to commission of the offence).

 xv. Sole or primary carer for dependent relatives.

A. Dog dangerously out of control in a public place, injuring any person, or allowing a dog to enter a private place where the dog is not permitted to be, where it then injures any person

Determining the offence category (step one)

   Category 1 requires greater harm and higher culpability, category 2 requires either   **★K–293**
greater harm and lower culpability or lesser harm and higher culpability, and category 3
requires lesser harm and lower culpability.

Factors indicating greater harm
- Serious injury (including disease transmission and/ or psychological harm)
- Sustained or repeated attack
- Victim is a child or otherwise vulnerable because of personal circumstances

Factors indicating lesser harm
- Minor injury

Factors indicating higher culpability
  Statutory aggravating factors:
- Offence racially or religiously aggravated
- Offence motivated by, or demonstrating, hostility to the victim based on sexual orientation or disability (or presumed sexual orientation or disability)

  Other aggravating factors:
- Failure to respond to others' warnings or concerns about dog's behaviour
- Goading, or allowing goading, of dog
- Dog used as weapon to intimidate victim
- Offence motivated by, or demonstrating, hostility to the victim based on age, sex, or (presumed) gender identity

Factors indicating lower culpability
- Attempts made to regain control of dog and/ or intervene
- Provocation of dog without fault of offender
- Evidence of safety or control measures taken
- Mental disorder or disability, where linked to the commission of the offence

Starting point and category range (step two)

Offence category	Starting point (applicable to all offenders)	Category range (applicable to all offenders)
category 1	six months' custody	medium level community order - 18 months' custody
category 2	medium level community order	band B fine - six months' custody
category 3	band B fine	discharge - band C fine

Factors increasing or reducing seriousness or reflecting personal mitigation
> Factors increasing seriousness: i-vii, ix–xiv
> Factors reducing seriousness or reflecting personal mitigation: i–iii, vii–xii, xiv, xv

Compensation and ancillary orders (step five)
    The court should consider whether to make a compensation order and/ or other ancillary orders. The court may disqualify the offender from having custody of a dog, the test being whether the offender is a fit and proper person to have custody of a dog. The court shall make a destruction order (after giving the owner, where not the offender, an opportunity to be present and make representations) unless satisfied that the dog would not constitute a danger to public safety. In reaching a decision, the court should consider the relevant circumstances, which include (i) the incident — what degree of harm was caused by the dog's behaviour, (ii) past behaviour of the dog — whether this was an isolated incident or whether there have been previous warnings or incidents, and (iii) the owner's character — whether the owner is a fit and proper person to own the particular dog. If satisfied that the dog would not constitute a danger to public safety, the court shall make a contingent destruction order imposing certain conditions. Where the court makes a destruction order, it may order the offender to pay reasonable expenses.

B. Dog dangerously out of control in a public place, or allowing a dog to enter a private place where the dog is not permitted to be, where there are grounds for reasonable apprehension that it will injure any person

Determining the offence category (step one)
★**K–294**   Same categories as for A, *ante*.

Factors indicating greater harm
> ● Presence of children or others who are vulnerable because of personal circumstances
> ● Injury to another animal(s)

Factors indicating lesser harm
> ● Low risk to the public

Factors indicating higher culpability
> ● Same as for A, *ante*

Factors indicating lower culpability
> ● Same as for A, *ante*

Starting point and category range (step two)

Offence category	Starting point (applicable to all offenders)	Category range (applicable to all offenders)
category 1	medium level community order	band C fine - six months' custody
category 2	band B fine	band A fine - low level community order
category 3	band A fine	discharge - band B fine

Factors increasing or reducing seriousness or reflecting personal mitigation
    Factors increasing seriousness: i, ii, iv–vii, ix–xiv
    Factors reducing seriousness or reflecting personal mitigation: i–iii, vii–xii, xiv, xv

Compensation and ancillary orders (step five)
    Same as for A, *ante*, except the court is permitted (rather than required) to make a destruction order or contingent destruction order. In reaching a decision, the court should consider the relevant circumstances, which include those set out in section A, *ante*.

C. Possession of a prohibited dog, or breeding, selling, exchanging or advertising a prohibited dog

Determining the offence category (step one)
    Category 1 requires greater harm and higher culpability, category 2 requires either   **★K–295** greater harm or higher culpability, and category 3 requires that there be neither greater harm nor higher culpability.

Factors indicating greater harm
- Injury to person
- Injury to another animal(s)

Factors indicating higher culpability
- Dog known to be prohibited
- Offence committed for gain
- Dog used to threaten or intimidate
- Permitting fighting
- Training and/ or possession of paraphernalia for dog fighting

Starting point and category range (step two)

Offence category	Starting point (applicable to all offenders)	Category range (applicable to all offenders)
category 1	medium level community order	band C fine - six months' custody
category 2	band C fine	band A fine - medium level community order
category 3	band A fine	discharge - band B fine

Factors increasing or reducing seriousness or reflecting personal mitigation
    Factors increasing seriousness: i, ii, viii, ix, xiii, xiv
    Factors reducing seriousness or reflecting personal mitigation: i, iv–xv.

Ancillary orders (step five)

★K–296   The court may disqualify the offender from having custody of a dog, the test being whether the offender is a fit and proper person to have custody of a dog. The court shall make a destruction order unless satisfied that the dog would not constitute a danger to public safety. In reaching a decision, the court should consider the relevant circumstances, which include those set out in section A, *ante*. If the court does not make a destruction order, the court shall make a contingent destruction order providing that unless the dog is exempted from the prohibition within two months it shall be destroyed. Where the offender is the owner of the dog, it would not normally be appropriate to make a contingent destruction order in conjunction with a disqualification order. Further, the court must not transfer ownership of the dog to another. Where the court makes a destruction order, it may order the offender to pay reasonable expenses.

[The next paragraph is K–350.]

II. AUTHORITIES ON OFFICIAL GUIDELINES

A. REDUCTION IN SENTENCE FOR GUILTY PLEA

Introduction

K–350   The purpose of this section of this appendix is to give details of authorities considering particular aspects of final guidelines issued by the Sentencing Guidelines Council and which are set out in full or summarised in the previous section of this appendix. There is, however, a fine line that divides cases specifically on some aspect of a guideline from those considering a statutory provision or some more general aspect of sentencing. Accordingly, practitioners looking for authorities on sentencing in relation to one of the guideline subjects should also make reference to the relevant paragraphs of the main work.

Relevant main work references

K–351   For sentencing guidelines generally, see section 125 of the *Coroners and Justice Act* 2009 (§ 5–149 in the main work); and for the reduction in sentence for a guilty plea, see section 144 of that Act (*ibid.*, § 5–107), and the authorities set out at §§ 5–109 *et seq.*, and, in particular, §§ 5–115, 5–118.

Credit in overwhelming cases

★K–352   Even in overwhelming cases, a plea of guilty was a distinct public benefit and the earlier it was put forward the better it was for everyone; where, therefore, the judge had given no credit for a plea of guilty on the basis that the evidence was such that the offender had had no option but to plead guilty, and where no specific feature of the case required the Sentencing Guidelines Council's guidance on credit for pleas of guilty (*ante*, K–7) to be disapplied, it was appropriate to vary the sentence to allow limited credit; it would be productive ultimately of chaos, and would undermine consistency in sentencing and the value of a guilty plea to the criminal justice system, if an existing guideline could be disregarded, unless it was possible to find that the interests of justice required its disapplication; it was important to underline that part of the advice that would be given to a defendant was that a guilty plea, even in an extreme case, would attract some discount: *R. v. Wilson (Paul), The Times*, March 13, 2012, CA.

[The next paragraph is K–360.]

B. Overarching Principles: Seriousness

Introduction

As to the purpose of this section of this appendix, see *ante*, K–350.   **K–360**

Relevant main work references

For sentencing guidelines generally, see section 125 of the *Coroners and Justice Act* 2009   **K–361**
(§ 5–149 in the main work); and for the determination of the seriousness of an offence, see
section 143 of that Act (*ibid.*, § 5–67).

Vulnerability of victim

It had not been open to the Crown Court to sentence on the basis that the victim of a do-   **K–362**
mestic assault was particularly vulnerable where none of the features of vulnerability
mentioned in paragraph 1.17 of the guideline on overarching principles (*ante*, K–18) or in
paragraph 3 of the domestic violence guideline (*ante*, K–82 *et seq.*) were present, with the
finding instead being based on the complainant's timid demeanour when giving evidence:
Barnard v. DPP [2011] A.C.D. 108, DC.

C. New Sentences: Criminal Justice Act 2003

Introduction

As to the purpose of this section of this appendix, see *ante*, K–350.   **K–370**

Relevant main work references

For sentencing guidelines generally, see section 125 of the *Coroners and Justice Act* 2009   **K–371**
(§ 5–149 in the main work). As to community sentences generally, see § 5–185 *et seq.* in the
main work; as to the restrictions on the imposition of such sentences, see *ibid.*, § 5–248; as to
community orders generally, see *ibid.*, §§ 5–253 *et seq.*; as to the requirements that may be
included in a community order, see *ibid.*, §§ 5–265 *et seq.*; as to the misleading terminology
adopted in this guideline, see *ibid.*, § 5–288.

Transitional arrangements

In *R. v. Whittle* (2007) 151 S.J. 398, CA, it was said that whereas paragraph 2.1.9 suggests   **K–372**
that any sentence of 12 months or more should be reduced by in the region of 15 per cent
to reflect the more onerous nature of the release on licence regime under the *CJA* 2003,
where an offender is sentenced to a term of four years or more, the sentencer may be
entitled not to reduce the sentence to the full extent or at all; in relation to such sentences, the increased onerousness of the licence conditions would be more or less in balance with the fact that the offender would be entitled to release at the half way point
under the new regime instead of at the two-thirds point under the pre-existing regime.

D. Manslaughter by Reason of Provocation

Introduction

As to the purpose of this section of this appendix, see *ante*, K–350.   **K–380**

Relevant main work references

For sentencing guidelines generally, see section 125 of the *Coroners and Justice Act* 2009   **K–381**
(§ 5–149 in the main work); and for provocation as a defence to a charge of murder gener-

ally, see *ante*, §§ 19–61 *et seq.* For "loss of control" as a defence to murder, see §§ 19–50 *et seq.* in the main work. It is submitted that pending the issuing of any new guideline, the existing guideline may be applied to the new defence, with appropriate caution to take account of the differing ingredients of the two defences.

Approach to guideline

K–382   Referring to heightened and justifiable public concern about cases involving the stabbing of one teenager by another, the court in *R. v. Daley* [2008] 2 Cr.App.R.(S.) 95, CA, said that the guideline had not been intended to lay down fixed or rigid boundaries.

In *Att.-Gen.'s Reference (No. 8 of 2011) (R. v. Edwards)* [2012] 1 Cr.App.R.(S.) 53, CA, the court emphasised that the guideline on manslaughter by reason of provocation should be approached with caution. It did not reflect the impact on sentencing for murder of Schedule 21 to the *CJA* 2003 (§§ 5–425 *et seq.* in the main work); and, in a series of cases, it had now been recognised that the upward shift in sentencing for murder required a corresponding upward shift in sentencing for manslaughter (see, in particular, *R. v. Thornley, post*, K–383). The court commented that the apparently higher threshold for the loss of control defence under the *Coroners and Justice Act* 2009 (§§ 19–51, 19–52 in the main work), as compared with the common law defence of provocation, may impact on sentencing both for murder and for manslaughter.

Use of a knife

K–383   Just as sentencing guidelines are not tramlines, nor are they ring-fenced; the interests of justice require that consideration be given to any subsequent thinking of the Court of Appeal and the legislature on sentencing issues which may impact on any definitive guideline; since the guideline on manslaughter by reason of provocation was issued, there had been at least four developments relevant to the sentencing of manslaughter by provocation using a knife (*viz.* (a) the Court of Appeal had, in *R. v. Povey* (§ 24–109 in the main work), addressed the issue of knife crime generally, and the need for the courts to be alert on appropriate occasions to impose deterrent sentences on those who carry knives, (b) the court had come to appreciate the impact of Schedule 21 to the *CJA* 2003 (*ibid.*, §§ 5–425 *et seq.*) on cases of manslaughter because of the need for there to be a proportionate relationship with sentences for murder, (c) a specific provision relating to the use of a knife as a murder weapon had been introduced into Schedule 21, and (d) the entire law on provocation had been changed by legislation); as to (a) and (b), the weight to be attached to decisions of the Court of Appeal on sentencing issues or policy was undiminished by the issue of guidelines; as to (c) and (d), these changes could not be ignored on the basis of a guideline issued in 2005; accordingly, the use of a knife should now be regarded as a more significant feature of aggravation than it was when the guideline was published: *R. v. Thornley* [2011] 2 Cr.App.R.(S.) 62, CA.

E. ROBBERY

Introduction

K–390   As to the purpose of this section of this appendix, see *ante*, K–350.

Relevant main work references

K–391   For sentencing guidelines generally, see section 125 of the *Coroners and Justice Act* 2009 (§ 5–149 in the main work)). As to this guideline, see, in particular, § 21–93 in the main work; as to sentencing for armed robbery, for robbery in the course of burglary and for the hijacking of cars, see *ibid.*, §§ 21–91, 21–92 and 21–94 respectively. For examples of the application of the dangerous offender provisions of the 2003 Act to cases of robbery, see *ibid.*, § 5–520.

Dangerous offenders

K–391a   The guideline is unequivocal (see para. G.1) about its non-applicability to offenders who have been assessed as dangerous. However, since section 227(3) of the *CJA* 2003 (§ 5–498 in the main work) requires the custodial element of an extended sentence to be fixed by reference to the term that would have been passed had the offender not been found to be dangerous, it would seem that the sentencer is bound to have regard to the guideline where an extended sentence is to be imposed: see, for example, *R. v. Greaves* [2009] 2 Cr.App.R.(S.) 88, CA.

"less sophisticated commercial robbery"

In *Att.-Gen.'s References (Nos 32, 33 and 34 of 2007) (R. v. Bate)* [2007] Crim.L.R. 815, **K–392** CA, it was held that for the purposes of the guideline on robbery, (i) the boundary between a "less sophisticated commercial robbery" falling within the guideline and a "professionally planned commercial robbery" falling without the guideline is not a hard and fast one and many cases would properly be regarded as falling on either side of the line; and a judge had been entitled to regard as falling within the guideline (and to regard the case as a level 1 case) two robberies during normal working hours (involving prior reconnaissance or information and the use of a stolen car) in which the three unarmed defendants, wearing masks and using a stolen car, had intercepted unaccompanied lorry drivers making deliveries of cigarettes to shops; and (ii) whereas "vulnerability of the victim" as an aggravating factor is expressly stated to be "targeting the elderly, the young, those with disabilities and persons performing a service to the public, especially outside normal working hours", there was nonetheless a low level of vulnerability (and hence aggravation) where the targets of the robberies were delivery drivers working alone, albeit delivering to shops where there were people to receive them.

Whilst the *CJA* 2003, s.172, required a court to have regard to a relevant sentencing guideline (see now the *Coroners and Justice Act* 2009, s.125 (§ 5–149 in the main work)), a guideline is only a guideline and the guideline on robbery cannot cover each and every category because of the immense variety of circumstances in which offences of robbery are committed, and as such there is a wide spectrum of offences that fall between "less sophisticated commercial robberies" and "professionally-planned commercial robberies", as described in the guideline; where, therefore, four men had "swiftly" robbed the driver of a delivery van in a robbery that was "cynically and callously planned" with one of the men persuading him to drive with them to a secluded place whilst wearing a mask and rubber gloves and being armed with a knife, the case did not fall neatly and cleanly within the category of the "less sophisticated commercial robbery" (which has an indicated starting point of four years' custody) and instead fell within a range of six to 10 years (possibly more for a ring leader); and, in the case of the respondent (40), who acted as the driver of the robbers' vehicle, three years' imprisonment on conviction was unduly lenient given that, although he was not a prime mover and did not wield the knife, it must have been within his contemplation that some degree of threat or force would be used on the victim; taking account, however, of the fact that he suffered from Asperger's syndrome, which made him vulnerable to being manipulated by more sophisticated offenders, the appropriate bracket was six to eight years' imprisonment: *Att.-Gen.'s Reference (No. 147 of 2006) (R. v. Gunner)* [2008] 1 Cr.App.R.(S.) 9(2), CA (substituting six years).

As to there being a category of case that falls between the "less sophisticated commercial robbery" and the "professionally planned commercial robbery", see also *R. v. Eccleston* [2008] 2 Cr.App.R.(S.) 56, CA.

In *R. v. Yarboi* [2010] 2 Cr.App.R.(S.) 40, CA, one of the defendants snatched a cash box containing £11,530 from a security guard who was attempting to deliver it to a cash machine. He ran to a car (the number plates of which had been removed) being driven by another of the defendants and, after half a mile, they abandoned the car and got into a third vehicle driven by a further defendant. The Court of Appeal found that the case did not fit easily within any of the categories within the Sentencing Guidelines Council's guideline (see *ante*, K–80), being close to the border between "less sophisticated commercial robberies" and "professionally planned robberies". The most aggravating feature was that the robbery had been pre-planned, although cases could come within the least serious category even where there had been some pre-planning. The removal of the first car's number plates, and the use of a second "clean" getaway car, however, made the case rather more unusual, and showed a significant degree of planning. On the other hand, the force used was minimal, being only that which was necessary in order to snatch the container from the security guard, there was only a single robber involved at that stage, and there was no intimidation from a group, no weapon, no threat of force, and no disguises were used. The court said that whilst the planning, therefore, might have taken the case out of the least serious category, it was difficult to conclude that it was of such sophistication as to justify a starting point of double the maximum for that category. In all the circumstances, it was decided that the proper starting point was four-and-a-half years.

"vulnerability of the victim"

K–393   See *Att.-Gen.'s References (Nos 32, 33 and 34 of 2007) (R. v. Bate)*, ante, § K–392.

Ranges

K–394   For an example of a sentence that was significantly above the recommended range being upheld on account of "additional aggravating features", albeit that most of them are foreshadowed in the guideline, see *R. v. Sheller* [2010] 1 Cr.App.R.(S.) 107, CA.

F. Breach of a Protective Order

Introduction

K–400   As to the purpose of this section of this appendix, see *ante*, K–350.

Relevant main work references

K–401   For sentencing guidelines generally, see section 125 of the *Coroners and Justice Act* 2009 (§ 5–149 in the main work); for breach of a restraining order under the *Protection from Harassment Act* 1997, see *ibid.*, § 19–277j; and for breach of a sexual offences prevention order, see *ibid.*, § 20–334. As to breach of an anti-social behaviour order, see *ante*, K–196 *et seq.*

G. Domestic Violence

Introduction

K–410   As to the purpose of this section of this appendix, see *ante*, K–350.

Relevant main work references

K–411   For sentencing guidelines generally, see section 125 of the *Coroners and Justice Act* 2009 (§ 5–149 in the main work); and for breach of a restraining order under the *Protection from Harassment Act* 1997, see § 19–277j in the main work.

Attitude of victim

K–412   In *R. v. Fazli*, unreported, April 24, 2009, CA ([2009] EWCA Crim. 939), the court emphasised that the principle (see para. 4 of the guideline) that a sentence should not be determined by the expressed wishes of the victim, was of particular importance in cases of domestic violence. The court said that, in the case with which it was concerned, the victim (the defendant's wife) had been made to feel responsible for his incarceration, and that such feelings on the part of the victim were a familiar consequence of controlling and intimidating behaviour such as that of the offender. The responsibility for what had happened to him lay entirely with him.

Vulnerability of victim

K–413   See *Barnard v. DPP*, ante, K–362.

H. Sexual Offences

Introduction

As to the purpose of this section of this appendix, see *ante*, K–350.   **K–420**

Relevant main work references

For sentencing guidelines generally, see section 125 of the *Coroners and Justice Act* 2009   **K–421**
(§ 5–149 in the main work).

Historic offences

See *R. v. H.*, *ante*, H–12 *et seq.*   **K–421a**

Age of offence/offender

In *Att.-Gen.'s Reference (No. 70 of 2008) (R. v. W.)* [2009] 2 Cr.App.R.(S.) 64, CA, it was   **K–422**
said, without making any reference to the guideline, that in cases of serious sexual assault,
the age of the offender or the age of the offence could be mitigation although, in many
cases, they would not receive much weight, especially if the offender had pressurised his
victims into silence; but they did not cease to be factors which could form part of the mitigation, and they were not always of comparatively little weight.

In *R. v. S.* [2011] 1 Cr.App.R.(S.) 9, CA, the offender (18) went, in 1991, to the 45-year-
old victim's home asking if he could use the lavatory. The victim suffered from cerebral
palsy, had significant communication problems, and used a wheelchair at home. After using
the lavatory, the offender forced the victim onto her bed and raped her, causing heavy
bleeding from the vagina, which required an operation and a blood transfusion. The victim
also suffered bruising and cuts around her vagina and anus compatible with being caused
by a fist or knee. It was not until 2008 that a DNA sample taken from the victim was
matched to a sample provided by the offender in 2005. A sentence of 16-and-a-half years'
imprisonment on a late plea of guilty was quashed and a sentence of nine years' imprisonment substituted. Among the reasons for reducing the sentence was that the offender was
young at the time, and it was said that although the passage of time was not in itself a reason for imposing a lesser sentence, the fact that the offender had not been in trouble since
the offence was committed suggested that he was no longer a danger to women.

In the case of a young offender who fell to be sentenced, following guilty pleas, for five
counts of rape and one count of assault on a child under 13 by penetration, where the
charges arose out of conduct that occurred over a three-year period and which began when
the offender was aged 12, and the victim, his half-sister, was five, the court emphasised the
importance of not losing sight of the need for flexibility and sensitivity to the particular facts
when looking at guidelines that were geared to adults: *R. v. B.* [2011] 2 Cr.App.R.(S.) 57,
CA.

In *R. v. Record* [2011] 2 Cr.App.R.(S.) 83, CA, an 18-year-old had unprotected consensual
sexual intercourse with a friend's sister (11 days short of her 15th birthday) when staying
the night at his friend's house. The court held that the parties' ages were important and
drew particular attention to the fact that the guideline (*ante*, K–87) emphasised that youth
and immaturity of the offender were important in the context of sexual offences. It also held
that, given that the offender was aged just over 18, the judge should have had regard to the
fact that the maximum sentence for an offender under 18 is only five years' detention (2003
Act, s.13(2)(b) (§ 20–79 in the main work)) (compared to 14 years' custody if aged 18 or
over: 2003 Act, s.9 (§ 20–58 in the main work)), and that, in such cases, the guideline
recommends a starting point of a detention and training order of 12 months, and a range
of six to 24 months (compared to a starting point of four years' custody and a range of
three to seven years for an offender aged 18 or over); furthermore, it is a mitigating factor if
the difference in age between complainant and offender is small. To similar effect, see *R. v.
Hoare* [2011] 2 Cr.App.R.(S.) 1, CA.

★   When considering an offence of sexual activity with a child, contrary to section 9 of the *SOA* 2003 (§ 20–58 in the main work), the nearer the offender is to the age of the victim, and the nearer the victim is to the age of consent, the more the starting point and range in the guideline must be adjusted: *R. v. Hines-Randle* [2012] 1 Cr.App.R.(S.) 65, CA.

Gender of victim/offender

K–422a   Sentencing guidelines were put forward on the basis that they should apply irrespective of the gender of the victim or of the offender (see *ante*, K–84), except in specified circumstances where a distinction is justified by the nature of the offence; Parliament did not seek to distinguish between the genders in the legislation and neither should the courts: *Att.-Gen.'s Reference (No. 67 of 2008) (R. v. Edwards)* [2009] 2 Cr.App.R.(S.) 60, CA.

Ranges

K–423   For an illustration of the need for a non-literal approach to the categories provided for in the guidelines, see *R. v. Elliott* [2010] 2 Cr.App.R.(S.) 55, CA.

In *Att.-Gen.'s Reference (No. 79 of 2010) (R. v. Sidaway)* [2011] 2 Cr.App.R.(S.) 56, CA, the court stressed that the ranges set out in the guideline are not rigid, and the presence of aggravating factors can make an offence significantly more serious than the nature of the sexual activity alone might suggest so as to render a sentence unduly lenient, notwithstanding that, on a literal reading of the guideline, the sentence would be in accord with it (15 months' imprisonment on plea of guilty to sexual assault increased to four years where the suggested range was 26 weeks to two years).

In *R. v. Frew* [2009] 1 Cr.App.R.(S.) 17, CA, the court said that the recommended range for the offence in question was three to seven years' imprisonment and that, in terms of gravity, the particular offence was not at the bottom of the range, yet it substituted a sentence that equated to 27 months after a trial. Whilst the court said that the guideline emphasised the need for flexibility and variability, the result suggests that the ranges are considerably wider than those recommended in the guideline. To similar effect, see *R. v. P. (John James)* [2009] 1 Cr.App.R.(S.) 45, CA (assault by penetration of child under 13 came within most serious category, with range of 11 to 17 years; appropriate penalty before discount for plea was seven-and-a-half years). For a case in which the court went above the relevant range without giving reasons, see *R. v. Olawo, post,* K–434b.

For two cases in which the Court of Appeal held the appropriate sentences to be lower than the minimum recommended in the Sentencing Guidelines Council's definitive guideline, see *R. v. Johnson* [2011] 1 Cr.App.R.(S.) 97 (where, on conviction for sexual activity with a person with a mental disorder impeding choice, contrary to section 30 of the *SOA* 2003 (§ 20–125 in the main work), the sentence imposed on appeal was five years' imprisonment, falling outside the 11 to 17 years recommended in the guideline (*ante*, K–96) for this offence), and *R. v. F.B.* [2011] 1 Cr.App.R.(S.) 99 (where, on conviction for sexual assault on a child under 13 by penetration, contrary to section 6 of the *SOA* 2003 (§ 20–50 in the main work), the sentence imposed on appeal was nine years' imprisonment, falling outside the 11 to 17 years recommended in the guideline (*ante*, K–94) for this offence).

For an example of a suspended sentence of six months' imprisonment (on an early plea of guilty) being adjudged lenient, but not unduly so, where the recommended range was three to seven years' custody, see *Att.-Gen.'s Reference (No. 72 of 2009) (R. v. Kent)* [2010] 2 Cr.App.R.(S.) 10, CA (observing that it was unfortunate that the judge had failed to refer to the guideline).

In *R. v. Ayeva* [2010] 2 Cr.App.R.(S.) 22, CA, a 33-year-old approached his 19-year-old victim outside a public library, where she was waiting for her father to collect her, and engaged her in conversation. He asked personal questions and told her he loved her, after which she made excuses and left, but when she returned he reappeared. She went into the library with the offender, hoping her father would have arrived by the time they came back outside. However, he had not, and the offender put his arm around the victim's waist. She

went down an alleyway to escape, but the offender followed her and grabbed her from
behind, at which point he bent her arm behind her back and forced her to take hold of his
erect penis, and, holding his hand around hers, forced her to masturbate him to ejaculation.
The Court of Appeal found there to be a number of aggravating features which took this offence outside the correct sentencing guideline for an offence of causing a person to engage
in sexual activity without consent (contact between the naked genitalia of the offender and
another part of the victim's body (as to which, *see ante*, Appendix K–94)), which has a range
of 26 weeks to two years, with a starting point of 12 months. These were that the unwelcome
conduct was persisted in over a significant period of time, the victim had made it clear that
the offender's attentions were unwelcome, the offender had first grabbed the victim's
breasts, there was not a brief, isolated, touching of the penis, but rather the victim was held
so that she could not escape, the offender ejaculated (which was a significant aggravating
feature), the conduct replicated behaviour which had previously led to him being cautioned,
and he had been less than frank with the police and had effectively denied the offence in an
interview with a probation officer conducted for the purpose of preparing a pre-sentence
report. Thus, it was considered that the appropriate sentence after a trial would have been
30 months' imprisonment. The Court of Appeal, in its judgment, reiterated the need for
the sentencing process for sexual offences, more than for many others, to allow for flexibility
and variability.

Multiple offences

Where the offender fell to be dealt with for two offences and the recommended starting   **K–423a**
point was 10 years' imprisonment for a single offence, the judge's starting point of 12 years
was said to be unimpeachable in *R. v. Clements* [2009] 2 Cr.App.R.(S.) 97, CA.

Rape

As a matter of principle, a court should approach rape within a relationship, including   **K–424**
marriage, as being no less serious than rape by a stranger, although the aggravating features
will be different in the sense that rape within a relationship constitutes a betrayal of trust:
Att.-Gen.'s Reference (No. 1 of 2011) (R. v. A.) [2011] 2 Cr.App.R.(S.) 112, CA.

The appropriate category (*ante*, K–94) was that of "repeated rape of same victim over a
course of time", rather than rape accompanied by a "sustained attack", where the offender,
over a period of four hours, slapped the victim around the face, dragged her across the
floor, inserted his fingers into her vagina twice, forcefully inserted a vibrator into her vagina
four times and into her anus, rammed his penis into her mouth three times, penetrated her
anus with his fingers and twice with his penis, and inserted his penis into her vagina: *R. v.
S. (Charles Derek)* [2011] 1 Cr.App.R.(S.) 83, CA.

For an example of a case in which a planned attack in which the offender used sexual
violence to punish, degrade and humiliate the victim, was considered to have constituted a
"sustained attack" so as to place the offence in the intermediate category (range of six to 11
years) in the guideline (*ante*, K–94), see *R. v. Cadogan* [2011] 1 Cr.App.R.(S.) 53, CA.

The rape of a victim in her own home is a pitiless, life-scarring crime; given that culpability will be at its highest and the harm done to the victim at its most grave, such offences
should be approached as if they are among the most serious offences of their kind; whilst
they are not dealt with directly in the current sentencing guideline, it would, for example,
be wrong in principle for an offence of rape in such circumstances to be treated as a "single
offence of rape by [a] single offender"; dealing with the matter very generally, in a case
where rape has been committed after, or in the course of, burglary in the victim's home,
even if there are no additional features beyond the rape and the burglary, the starting point
should rarely be less than 12 years' imprisonment; and, where there are (as will usually be
the case) aggravating features, the starting point will increase to 15 years' imprisonment and
beyond; the pernicious new habit of criminals taking photographs of their victims, often just
to show off to their friends, often just to add something to the humiliation which the victim
is already suffering, and sometimes as a form of pressure to discourage any complaint (in
that sense a form of blackmail), but also possibly for the purposes of blackmail, should

always be treated as an aggravating feature of any case and, in particular, of any sexual case, where it will usually constitute a seriously aggravating feature: *Att.-Gen.'s References (Nos 73, 75 of 2010, and 03 of 2011) (R. v. Anigbugu)* [2011] 2 Cr.App.R.(S.) 100, CA. As to this case, see also §§ 5–144, 5–514 in the main work.

R. v. Donoghue [2011] 1 Cr.App.R.(S.) 46, CA, was a case of vaginal and oral rape, where the offences were committed in the victim's own home, where the offender was armed with a knife which he repeatedly held against the victim's throat, where he ejaculated into the victim's mouth and he took, or pretended to take, photographs of what he was doing. In upholding a sentence of life imprisonment, the court said that there could be few worse cases of rape.

Rape of a child under 13

K–424a
Actual consent is capable of being a mitigating factor, but careful consideration has to be given in all cases, and particularly where there is a significant difference in age, to the extent to which ostensible consent had been obtained opportunistically, or by means of coercion, which might be subtle, or exploitation, which could be particularly relevant where there may have been an element of grooming; in such cases, ostensible consent might well have little value as mitigation, and in all cases the age difference would be of great significance; as to a reasonable belief that the victim was aged 16 or over, this was capable of being mitigation (even where the offender was aged 18 or over (though the guideline only lists such a mistaken belief as mitigation where the offender is under 18), but the older the offender, the less relevant a mistake as to age would be; in determining the extent to which mitigation relating to consent or a mistaken belief as to age can justify departing from the sentencing bracket (of eight to 13 years), it may be helpful to consider the guideline on penetrative sexual activity with a person under the age of 16, where the offender does not reasonably believe that the other person is 16 or over (contrary to section 9 of the 2003 Act), *viz.* a starting point of four years and a sentencing range of three to seven years; bearing this, and the legislative purpose of creating the absolute offence under section 5 for victims under the age of 13, in mind, four years should be the minimum for an offence under section 5, subject to plea and personal mitigation, in the case of a young adult where there is ostensible consent and a reasonable belief that the victim was 16 or over: *Att.-Gen's References (Nos 74 and 83 of 2007) (R. v. Fenn; R. v. Foster)* [2008] 1 Cr.App.R.(S.) 110, CA.

★
In *R. v. Charles* [2012] 1 Cr.App.R.(S.) 74, CA, it was said that the guideline for this offence was not suitable where young men have consensual sexual activity with girls whom they believe to be over 16; and that the correct approach was set out in the pre-guideline case of *R. v. Corran* [2005] 2 Cr.App.R.(S.) 73, CA, where it was said that a short period of custody is likely to suffice for a teenager where the other party consents; and that, in exceptional cases, a non-custodial sentence may be appropriate for a young defendant.

For a case which did not fit readily within the guideline in relation to rape at all, and where the sentence imposed on appeal (a 12-month detention and training order) fell far below the range in the guideline (eight to 13 years), see *R. v. Mooney* [2010] 2 Cr.App.R.(S.) 97, CA.

Causing or inciting a child under 13 to engage in sexual activity

K–424b
In *Att.-Gen.'s Reference (No. 28 of 2010) (R. v. Charnley)* [2011] 1 Cr.App.R.(S.) 58, CA, the 55-year-old offender had, on 35 occasions, over a period of 10 weeks, contacted adults in the Philippines via the internet and agreed to pay them to abuse children (including by penetration) aged between two and 17, according to his instructions, while he watched the events in real time and then downloaded the images. Increasing the original sentence to a total sentence of 12 years' imprisonment on pleas of guilty to various offences, including five counts under section 8 of the *SOA* 2003 (one of which involved penetration) and 19 counts of making indecent photographs, the court said that the gravity and cruelty of the offences went beyond anything contained in the guidelines or in the previous authority of the court.

Sexual assault

K–426
In *Att.-Gen.'s Reference (No. 26 of 2009) (R. v. Heeney)* [2010] 1 Cr.App.R.(S.) 41, CA,

where the offence took place in the victim's home in the early hours of the morning, it was said that one of the difficulties in applying the guideline (*ante*, K–94) is that individual cases may not slot easily into any particular category. This case was more akin to an offence under section 63 of the 2003 Act (trespass with intent to commit a sexual offence (*ibid.*, § 20–197)) than a straightforward sexual assault.

Exposure

In *R. v. Lam-Callinan* [2010] 1 Cr.App.R.(S.) 49, CA, it was held that, for the purposes of **K–427** the guideline (*ante*, K–100), an offender may be a "repeat offender" though he does not have previous convictions (doubting *R. v. Bell* [2008] 2 Cr.App.R.(S.) 55, CA).

Trafficking

In *R. v. Pacan* [2010] 2 Cr.App.R.(S.) 2, CA, the court pointed out that there is a degree **K–428** of ambiguity in the guideline relating to offences under sections 57 to 59 of the *SOA* 2003 (*ante*, K–103, K–104), in that the bracket for the more serious of the two forms of trafficking (range of four to nine years' custody) assumes coercion, but coercion is further listed as a potentially aggravating factor.

I. Failing to Surrender to Bail

Introduction

As to the purpose of this section of this appendix, see *ante*, K–350. **K–430**

Relevant main work references

For sentencing guidelines generally, see section 125 of the *Coroners and Justice Act* 2009 **K–431** (§ 5–149 in the main work); for paragraph I.13 of the consolidated criminal practice direction (which touches on the same issues), see §§ 3–32 *et seq.* in the main work; and for the prior sentencing authorities, see *ibid.*, §§ 3–31, 3–35. To the extent that there are any differences between the provisions of the practice direction and of the guideline, it may be taken that the guideline will prevail so far as concerns sentencing considerations. As to procedure, it is apparent that the guideline has drawn on the practice direction and is generally consistent therewith.

J. Assault and Other Offences Against the Person

Introduction

As to the purpose of this section of this appendix, see *ante*, K–350. **K–433**

Relevant main work references

For sentencing guidelines generally, see section 125 of the *Coroners and Justice Act* 2009 **K–434** (§ 5–149 in the main work).

Use in case of young offenders

In *R. v. Bowley* [2009] 1 Cr.App.R.(S.) 79, CA, where a 17-year-old pleaded guilty to caus- **K–434a** ing grievous bodily harm with intent after stabbing a rival gang member, the court said (i) that the judge had been entitled to look to this guideline for assistance, even though it does not apply to offenders under 18 and (ii) in making use of it, the judge need not have been unduly constrained by the particular sentencing brackets set out therein, because the case was one where an element of deterrence was an essential ingredient of the sentencing decision.

Ranges

K–434b   In *R. v. Olawo* [2008] 2 Cr.App.R.(S.) 113, a sentence of 12 months' imprisonment was imposed by the Court of Appeal for an offence contrary to section 20 of the *Offences against the Person Act* 1861, for which the recommended range was up to 36 weeks' imprisonment. The court said that the fact that the victim was a certified enforcement officer was a seriously aggravating factor, but this is a factor specifically mentioned in the guideline on seriousness (see K–19, *ante*) and is presumptively allowed for in the range. No reason was given by the court for going outside the range. For a case in which the court went below the relevant range without giving reasons, see *R. v. Frew, ante*, K–423; and for an exceptional case of wounding with intent which the guidelines did not address and in which a suspended sentence was justified, see *Att.-Gen.'s Reference (No. 95 of 2009) (R. v. Blight)* [2010] 2 Cr.App.R.(S.) 83, CA.

As to whether deterrence is a legitimate reason for going outside the recommended bracket, see *R. v. Bowley, ante*, K–434a.

As to the need, when sentencing for an offence of violence to have regard to foreseeable harm, as well as actual or intended harm, when assessing the seriousness of any given case, see *R. v. Abbas* [2010] 1 Cr.App.R.(S.) 47, CA.

Where an offence of assault occasioning actual bodily harm fell within category 2 as being one of lesser harm and greater culpability, the judge had been entitled to go outside the category range where there were present six factors from the non-exhaustive list of 18 factors that are capable of increasing the seriousness of the offence and there was just one factor reducing its seriousness: *R. v. Nelson, The Times*, October 27, 2011, CA.

As to departure from the guidelines when sentencing those convicted of an offence committed during the widespread public disorder of the kind seen in the riots that occurred around the country in August, 2011, and as to the appropriateness of sentences beyond the range set out in those guidelines, see *R. v. Blackshaw, ante*, § 29–9.

Section 18

Use of a knife

K–434c   In *R. v. Osman* [2008] 2 Cr.App.R.(S.) 89, CA, it was said that the need for the courts to take account of legitimate public concern and to deter the premeditated carrying and use of a knife to inflict an intentional wound by the imposition of condign and/or deterrent sentences was all too obvious; and was reflected in the guideline.

Revenge attacks

K–434d   As to a case where, despite the fact that the purpose of an attack was revenge, the circumstances of the case were exceptional and fell outside the scope of the guideline, see *R. v. Hussain (Tokeer) and Hussain (Munir)* [2010] 2 Cr.App.R.(S.) 60, CA. For a more conventional view as to the seriousness of revenge attacks, see *Att.-Gen.'s Reference (No. 102 of 2009) (R. v. Martin)* [2010] 2 Cr.App.R.(S.) 80, CA.

Section 20

K–434e   In *R. v. Abdille* [2010] 1 Cr.App.R.(S.) 18, CA, the court commented on the difficulty of applying the guideline for offences contrary to section 20 of the *Offences against the Person Act* 1861. The case concerned a serious, unprovoked attack on a young girl as she tried to get away from the offender, who was in a drunken, aggressive state. The Court of Appeal found that the punch which he inflicted upon her had not itself been premeditated, but it had caused a serious injury, albeit not one, in the words of the guideline, which was "particularly grave". It was said that, on a literal reading of the guideline, the offence would be in the very bottom range, with a starting point of 24 weeks' custody and a sentencing range of a community order to 36 weeks' custody. However, the court considered that the case had features which took it well outside that range and that, after a trial, it would have merited a sentence of 24 to 30 months' imprisonment. As to this case, see also § 5–584 in the main work.

In *R. v. Williamson* [2010] 1 Cr.App.R.(S.) 16, CA, the offender punched and kicked his girlfriend to the extent that she suffered a broken nose, loose teeth and a fractured cheekbone. On a plea of guilty entered at the earliest opportunity, four years' imprisonment was held to be wrong in principle and manifestly excessive. The court explained that whilst this was a grave offence, and the offender was fortunate not to have been charged with a more serious offence, it would be quite wrong to sentence on the basis that he had been under-charged.

Sections 18 and 20 ("particularly grave injury")

In *R. v. Collins* [2010] 2 Cr.App.R.(S.) 3, CA, it was said that, whilst the guideline (*ante*, K–113 *et seq.*) throws no particular light on what is meant by "particularly grave injury" (bearing in mind that "grievous" bodily harm is by definition serious), bullet wounds to two vital parts of the body, one of which perforated the colon in several places and led to two major operations (a colostomy and a reversal of that colostomy), were on any view particularly grave injuries, and the fact that the victim had made a good recovery did not show otherwise. A non-permanent injury may be particularly grave, and a permanent injury (such as a scar) may not be particularly grave. The Court of Appeal said that where one of the shots had been potentially fatal, since it had been aimed close to both the liver and the kidney, this was also relevant to the overall view of the gravamen of the matter. **K–434f**

In *R. v. Howard* [2010] 1 Cr.App.R.(S.) 88, CA, it was said that a broken hip could not be said to be a "particularly grave injury".

K. Assaults on Children and Cruelty to a Child

Introduction

As to the purpose of this section of this appendix, see *ante*, K–350. **K–436**

Relevant main work references

For sentencing guidelines generally, see section 125 of the *Coroners and Justice Act* 2009 (§ 5–149 in the main work). **K–437**

The four categories of seriousness

In *R. v. S. (Will)* [2009] 1 Cr.App.R.(S.) 40, CA, the offender (30/good character/no previous parenting experience) subjected a "challenging" five-year-old, one of the four children of his (now ex-)partner, to a particularly harsh regime of discipline. She was shouted at, made to feel unwanted, and sent to her room for long periods (sometimes day after day). No violence was used except on one occasion, when the offender put masking tape over her mouth (for which he later expressed regret). At school, it was noticed that the child, from being a relatively happy child, became tearful and unsettled. On pleas of guilty to two counts of "causing cruelty to a child", 30 months' imprisonment was held to be manifestly and grossly excessive. The court found that it was clear that the offender's actions were not those of a gratuitous bully, but of an inexperienced parent, at the end of his tether, who, together with the mother, was doing what he mistakenly believed to be the right thing in respect of what he saw as an ill-behaved child. In particular, it was said that the judge had wrongly identified the case as falling within the second of the four categories of seriousness in the guideline, which, the court noted, should more properly be reserved for cases of actual abuse, either through physical violence or deprivation of food, clothing, shelter or attendance. A community order with a supervision requirement (to include a parenting course) was substituted. **K–438**

It had been open to a judge to place the offender's intense neglect of her child into the category of "protracted" neglect (*ante*, Appendix K–146), where it took place over a period that adults might regard as a relatively short period (a few days): *R. v. Sutherland* [2011] 1 Cr.App.R.(S.) 90, CA.

L. Sentencing in Magistrates' Courts

Introduction

K–439   As to the purpose of this section of this appendix, see *ante*, K–350.

Relevant main work references

K–440   For sentencing guidelines generally, see section 125 of the *Coroners and Justice Act* 2009 (§ 5–149 in the main work); for paragraph V.51 of the consolidated criminal practice direction, which is superseded by this guideline so far as it relates to particular offences dealt with in the guideline, but which also contains general mode of trial considerations, see § 1–119 in the main work.

Burglary in a dwelling

K–441   In *R. v. Saw* [2009] 2 Cr.App.R.(S.) 54, the Court of Appeal observed that when applying the provisions of the guideline relating to dwelling house burglaries, regard should always be had to all the matters of aggravation and mitigation listed in the judgment (as to which, see § 21–114 in the main work).

For offences for which sentence is passed on or after January 16, 2012, see now the guideline issued by the Sentencing Council for England and Wales, *ante*, K–259 *et seq.*

M. Causing Death by Driving

Introduction

K–442   As to the purpose of this section of this appendix, see *ante*, K–350.

Relevant main work references

K–443   For sentencing guidelines generally, see section 125 of the *Coroners and Justice Act* 2009 (§ 5–149 in the main work). For the penalty provisions relating to the offences covered by this guideline, see § 32–6 (causing death by dangerous driving); § 32–47e (causing death by careless or inconsiderate driving); § 32–59 (causing death by careless driving when under the influence of drink or drugs or having failed without reasonable excuse either to provide a specimen for analysis or to permit the analysis of a blood sample) and § 32–63e (causing death by driving while unlicensed, disqualified or uninsured). As to disqualification and endorsement, see §§ 32–167 *et seq.*

Aggravating and mitigating factors

K–444   As to the importance of taking care to ensure that factors which put an offence into a particular category are not then double-counted as matters of aggravation, see *R. v. Watson* [2010] 1 Cr.App.R.(S.) 29, CA.

In *R. v. Lawes* [2010] 2 Cr.App.R.(S.) 43, CA, it was held that the potentially aggravating feature, identified in the guideline, of more than one death was not intended to apply to the case of a pregnant mother and her unborn child.

Borderline between careless and dangerous driving

K–445   For a case of dangerous driving that was close to the borderline with careless driving, see *R. v. Foster* [2010] 1 Cr.App.R.(S.) 36, CA. A 64-year-old man had been driving his wife, who suffered from motor neurone disease, home from the hospital, where she had been told that her condition had deteriorated to the point that her treatment should no longer be continued, when he crossed onto the wrong side of the road and collided with a motorcyclist. The central issue at trial had been whether the defendant had crossed onto the wrong side of the road because he had "blacked out"; in passing sentence, the judge proceeded on the basis that the defendant had convinced himself that that was what had happened. On appeal, the court reduced a sentence of 18 months' imprisonment to 12 months' imprisonment suspended for two years, on the basis that the appellant was distracted for a "matter of seconds at most" and, importantly, when his emotions as a result of the hospital visit must have made him susceptible to distraction. The court pointed out that the guideline on causing death by driving states (see *ante*, K–192) that where the driving is markedly less culpable than for the lowest of the three categories for the offence of causing death by dangerous driving, reference should be made to the starting point for the most serious level of causing death by careless driving (starting point 15 months' imprisonment, range of 36 weeks to three years) and that, having regard to this, and to the other mitigation, in particular the appellant's character and his deep and genuine remorse, that starting point could be reduced. The court concluded that if it be a merciful sentence to suspend the term of imprisonment, this was a proper case for mercy.

In *R. v. Crew* [2010] 2 Cr.App.R.(S.) 23, CA, a 52-year-old, the day after an overnight flight from the United States (where he lived), fell asleep momentarily at the wheel of his car while travelling along a long straight road in daylight hours. It was likely that, on waking, he instinctively over-corrected the car's direction of travel as he was used to driving on the opposite side of the road, and in so doing he collided with an oncoming car. A sentence of 14 months' imprisonment on a plea of guilty, entered at the earliest opportunity, was upheld by the Court of Appeal. It was said that the case fell into the most serious category identified in the Sentencing Guidelines Council's guideline (*ante*, Appendix K–194), and that the carelessness had bordered on dangerous driving. The offender had had no more than five hours' sleep in the previous 24 hours, during which he had twice been disturbed to take his young son to the lavatory, and, as an experienced traveller, he must have known the risk he was taking, so his culpability was accordingly high.

Causing death by careless or inconsiderate driving

In *R. v. Campbell (Karl)* [2010] 2 Cr.App.R.(S.) 28, CA, the court said that whereas the   **K–446**
guideline (*ante*, K–194) identified three categories of case, the most serious being cases where the driving was not far short of dangerous driving and the least serious comprising cases of momentary inattention with no aggravating features, the guideline provided no assistance as to the intermediate category of "other cases", but this could include cases of single misjudgments, such as a failure to see a vehicle approaching from the right when emerging from a minor road and when the visibility permitted the vehicle to have been seen in good time.

Campbell (Karl) was considered in *R. v. Odedara* [2010] 2 Cr.App.R.(S.) 51, CA, in which the court said of a case of momentary inattention with no aggravating features and some mitigating features, that it did not pass the custody threshold on a plea of guilty and probably would not have done so on conviction.

Ranges

In *R. v. Shepherd* [2010] 2 Cr.App.R.(S.) 54, CA, it was pointed out that since the recom-   **K–447**
mended range for the most serious of the three categories of cases of causing death by careless driving stops short (at four years' custody) of the statutory maximum (five years), there must be cases in which a judge will be entitled to go above the recommended range.

Where the offender, despite being aware that the braking system of the coach he was driving was not operating satisfactorily, drove the coach in terrain where there were regular hills, the driving created a "substantial risk of danger" such that the case fell within level 2, rather than a "significant risk of danger" such that the case would fall within level 3, of the guideline relating to causing death by dangerous driving (*ante*, K–192): *R. v. Oughton* [2011] 1 Cr.App.R.(S.) 62, CA.

N. Breach of an Anti-Social Behaviour Order

Introduction

K–450   As to the purpose of this section of this appendix, see *ante*, K–350.

Relevant main work references

K–451   For sentencing guidelines generally, see section 125 of the *Coroners and Justice Act* 2009 (§ 5–149 in the main work). For the power to make an anti-social behaviour order on conviction, see section 1C of the *CDA* 1998 (§ 5–1198 in the main work). For authorities considering the imposition of an anti-social behaviour order, see § 5–1202 in the main work.

Ranges

K–452   In *R. v. Fagan* [2011] 1 Cr.App.R.(S.) 105, CA, the court upheld a sentence that was above the upper bracket for the most serious category in the guideline (*ante*, K–206), even though it was accepted that the case fell within the intermediate category. Referring to the maximum permissible sentence of five years' imprisonment, the court said that it followed that the guideline (which recommended a maximum of two years for a single offence) was not appropriate in the case of a persistent offender such as the appellant.

O. Theft and Burglary in a Building Other Than a Dwelling

Introduction

K–475   As to the purpose of this section of this appendix, see *ante*, K–350.

Relevant main work references

K–476   For sentencing guidelines generally, see section 125 of the *Coroners and Justice Act* 2009 (§ 5–149 in the main work). For previous guidelines in relation to various types of theft, see §§ 21–4c *et seq.* in the main work.

Theft in breach of trust

K–477   In *R. v. Hakimzadeh* [2010] 1 Cr.App.R.(S.) 8, CA, the appellant was a 61-year-old American of Iranian origin, who was an expert on cultural relations between Iran and the western world. He owned an extensive collection of materials relating to that topic and considered his library to be the fourth most significant in the world. Over a substantial period, in order to improve his personal library, he stole maps and illustrations from books and some books themselves from the British and Bodleian libraries. The court said that whilst the guideline did not specifically address such cases, the section on theft in breach of trust provided some relevant basis of comparison; the offender was able to access the books in the manner that he did partly because of his reputation and partly because he was trusted to treat them in the way that scholars should treat such important resources. See also § 5–1267 in the main work.
    R. v. Hakimzadeh, ante, was considered in *R. v. Jacques* [2011] 2 Cr.App.R.(S.) 39, CA, a case that involved the theft of a set of 13 rare books from The Linley, the public library of the Royal Horticultural Society, which were valued at £40,000 for insurance purposes (but could have been sold for £27,000). The offender had gained access using a reader's card under an assumed name and was found to be in possession of a list of 70 other books and their valuations. The court held that the case was wholly different to *R. v. Hakimzadeh, ante,* because none of what was regarded as exceptional mitigation in that case applied here. As to the guideline, it was said that this provided an inadequate foundation for identifying the

appropriate level of sentence in a case such as this; to categorise this case as a breach of trust was a poor guide to the gravity of this type of offending, which constituted a deliberate attack undermining the importance of libraries.

Pickpocketing

In *R. v. De Weever* [2010] 1 Cr.App.R.(S.) 3, CA, the appellant had pushed a woman as she boarded a tube train and stolen a purse from her shoulder bag. The Court of Appeal found that the offence fell into the bottom level of seriousness identified in the Sentencing Guidelines Council's guidelines on theft from the person (see *ante*, K–215). However, they considered that there were a number of grave aggravating factors (*viz.* the offence was clearly planned and was carried out in a highly professional manner, it involved the use of force (a push) short of robbery and resulted in a high level of inconvenience to the victim, the offender had a number of like convictions, albeit from many years ago, and he had failed to respond to his most recent sentences) which took the offence out of the lowest level in the guideline, and to the top of the level above it, where the starting point would be 12 months' imprisonment. **K–478**

Offences occurring in the context of widespread public disorder

As to departure from the guidelines when sentencing those convicted of theft and burglary in the context of widespread public disorder of the kind seen in the riots that occurred around the country in August, 2011, and as to the appropriateness of sentences beyond the range set out in those guidelines, see *R. v. Blackshaw, ante*, § 29–9. **K–479**

P. ATTEMPTED MURDER

Introduction

As to the purpose of this section of this appendix, see *ante*, § K–350. **K–500**

Relevant main work references

For sentencing guidelines generally, see section 125 of the *Coroners and Justice Act* 2009 (§ 5–149 in the main work). For the statutory guidelines on fixing the minimum term in a case of murder, see Schedule 21 to the *CJA* 2003 (§§ 5–425 *et seq.* in the main work). **K–501**

Conspiracy to murder

It was correct for the judge to have considered the Sentencing Guidelines Council's guideline on attempted murder in a case charged as a conspiracy to murder but in which the facts would have supported a charge of attempted murder: *R. v. Jolie* [2011] 1 Cr.App.R.(S.) 87, CA. **K–502**

Ranges

The Sentencing Guidelines Council's guideline had no application to the scale of criminality involved in a "hideous" case where the offender woke the lone female victim at night, stole from her and subjected her to rape, beatings, stabbings and set fire to her clothes and her home after tying her up, see *Att.-Gen.'s Reference (No. 37 of 2011) (R. v. Parsons)* [2012] 1 Cr.App.R.(S.) 84, CA. **★K–503**

Q. FRAUD—STATUTORY OFFENCES

Introduction

As to the purpose of this section of this appendix, see *ante*, K–350. **K–525**

Relevant main work references

K–526   For sentencing guidelines generally, see section 125 of the *Coroners and Justice Act* 2009 (§ 5–149 in the main work). For the *Theft Act* 1968, s.17 (false accounting), see § 21–226; for the *Fraud Act* 2006, s.1 (offence of fraud), see § 21–356; for sections 6 (possession of articles for use in fraud) and 7 (making or supplying articles for use in fraud) of the 2006 Act, see §§ 21–390, 21–391; for the *CEMA* 1979, ss.50 (improper importation of goods), 170 (fraudulent evasion of duty) and 170B (taking preparatory steps for evasion of duty), see §§ 25–430, 25–474, 25–505; and for the *Value Added Tax Act* 1994, s.72, see § 25–532.

Confidence fraud

K–527   For a case in which the confidence fraud guideline was applied where the conduct of the offender was arguably more akin to theft in breach of trust (*ante*, K–213), see *R. v. Lawson* [2010] 2 Cr.App.R.(S.) 71, CA.

Assessing seriousness

K–528   In *R. v. Chaytor* [2011] 2 Cr.App.R.(S.) 114, CA, it was held that whereas paragraph 21 of the guideline (*ante*, K–230) provides that, where an offender may have been entitled to all or part of the money obtained (*e.g.* where claims have been exaggerated), the starting point should be based on the amount to which the offender was not legitimately entitled, it does not follow that, in a case of making fraudulent expenses claims, the calculation of the losses consequent on the dishonesty actually perpetrated falls to be reduced because the defendant might, operating honestly and within the relevant rules, have been able to make legitimate claims for some or all of the amounts claimed.

R. Sentencing Youths

Introduction

K–550   As to the purpose of this section of this appendix, see *ante*, K–350.

Relevant main work references

K–551   As to the aim of the youth justice system, see section 37 of the *CDA* 1998 (§ 5–63 in the main work); as to the requirement for a court to have regard to the welfare of a child or young person, see section 44 of the *CYPA* 1933 (*ibid.*, § 5–64); as to the purposes of sentencing when dealing with young offenders, see section 142A of the *CJA* 2003 (*ibid.*, § 5–66) (not in force as at October 12, 2011); as to youth rehabilitation orders, see §§ 5–314 *et seq.* in the main work; as to the enforcement of such orders, see §§ 5–380 *et seq.* in the main work; as to detention and training orders, see sections 100 to 107 of the *PCC(S)A* 2000 (§§ 5–597 *et seq.* in the main work); and as to the detention of young offenders convicted of certain grave crimes, see section 91 of the 2000 Act (*ibid.*, § 5–610).

    For sentencing guidelines generally, see section 125 of the *Coroners and Justice Act* 2009 (§ 5–149 in the main work).

S. Corporate Manslaughter and Health and Safety Offences Causing Death

Introduction

K–575   As to the purpose of this section of this appendix, see *ante*, K–350.

Relevant main work references

K–576   For sentencing guidelines generally, see section 125 of the *Coroners and Justice Act* 2009 (§ 5–149 in the main work). As to the offence of corporate manslaughter, see §§ 19–117 *et* *seq.* in the main work. For the maximumsentence, for the power to order the taking of remedial action and for the power to order a conviction to be publicised, see sections 1(2), 9 and 10 of the *Corporate Manslaughter and Corporate Homicide Act* 2007 respectively (§§ 19–117, 19–117h, 19–117i in the main work). For decisions of the Courtof Appeal considering the proper approach to determining the amount of a fine, see § 5–688 in the main work.

T. Aggravated Burglary and Burglary

Introduction

As to the purpose of this section of this appendix, see *ante*, K–350.   **K–600**

Relevant main work references

For sentencing guidelines generally, see section 125 of the *Coroners and Justice Act* 2009   **K–601** (§ 5–149 in the main work). For previous guidelines in relation to burglary of a dwelling, see § 21–114 in the main work (and for previous guidelines in relation to burglary otherwise than in a dwelling, see *ante*, K–209 *et seq.*). For section 9 of the *Theft Act* 1968 (burglary), see § 21–108 in the main work; and for section 10 of the 1968 Act (aggravated burglary, see § 21–129 in the main work).

U. Drug Offences

Introduction

As to the purpose of this section of this appendix, see *ante*, K–350.   **K–625**

Relevant main work references

For sentencing guidelines generally, see section 125 of the *Coroners and Justice Act* 2009   **K–626** (§ 5–149). For section 170 of the *CEMA* 1979, see § 25–474; and for the penalty provisions in Schedule 1 to that Act, see § 25–508; for section 4 of the *Misuse of Drugs Act* 1971 (restriction of production and supply of controlled drugs), see § 27–28; for section 4A of the 1971 Act (aggravation of offence of supply of controlled drug), see § 27–28a; for section 5 of the 1971 Act (restriction of possession of controlled drug), see § 27–50; for section 6 of the 1971 Act (restriction of cultivation of cannabis plant), see § 27–79; for section 8 of the 1971 Act (occupiers of premises), see § 27–84; for section 25 of the 1971 Act (prosecution and punishment of offences), see § 27–105; for the sentencing guidelines of the Court of Appeal, see §§ 27–107 *et seq.*; and for the table of maximum penalties under the 1971 Act (and mode of trial provisions), see § 27–130.

V. Offences Taken into Consideration and Totality

Introduction

As to the purpose of this section of this appendix, see *ante*, K–350.   **★K–650**

Relevant main work references

For sentencing guidelines generally, see section 125 of the *Coroners and Justice Act* 2009   **★K–651** (§ 5–149).

As to offences taken into consideration, see §§ 5–160 *et seq.*

As to "totality" and consecutive or concurrent sentences, see the *CJA* 2003, ss.166(3)(b) (§ 5-126) and 265 (§ 5–668); and for the existing case law, see §§ 5–585 *et seq.*

W. Dangerous Dog Offences

Introduction

As to the purpose of this section of this appendix, see *ante*, K–350.   **★K–675**

Relevant main work references

★K-676   For sentencing guidelines generally, see section 125 of the *Coroners and Justice Act* 2009
(§ 5–149). For sections 3, 4 and 4A of the *Dangerous Dogs Act* 1991, see §§ 31–35, 31–38 and
31–38a respectively.

III. COMPENDIUM OF GUIDELINE CASES

K-1000   The Sentencing Guidelines Council has published a compendium of those cases that it
regards as constituting considered guidance and issued over the past 30 years. The list is in
two parts, "Generic sentencing principles" and "Offences". It has been updated five times,
with some cases having been removed from the original list.

In the first list are: *R. v. Martin (Selina)* [2007] 1 Cr.App.R.(S.) 3 (**approach to sentencing**); *Att.-Gen.'s Reference (No. 4 of 1989) (R. v. Brunt)*, 11 Cr.App.R.(S.) 517 (**Attorney-
General's references**); *R. v. Montgomery*, 16 Cr.App.R.(S.) 274 (**contempt**); *R. v. Bernard*
[1997] 1 Cr.App.R.(S.) 135 (**health of the offender**); *R. v. Goodyear* [2005] 3 All E.R. 117; *R.
v. Kulah* [2008] 1 Cr.App.R.(S.) 85 (**indication of sentence**); *R. v. Buckland* [2000] 1 W.L.R.
1262 (**automatic life sentences**); *R. v. Hodgson*, 52 Cr.App.R. 113; *R. v. Chapman* [2000] 1
Cr.App.R. 77; *R. v. McNee, Gunn and Russell* [2008] 1 Cr.App.R.(S.) 24; *R. v. Kehoe* [2009] 1
Cr.App.R.(S.) 9; *R. v. Davies* [2009] 1 Cr.App.R.(S.) 15 (**discretionary life sentences**); *R. v.
M. (Discretionary Life Sentence)*; *R. v. L.* [1999] 1 W.L.R. 485; *R. v. Szczerba* [2002] 2
Cr.App.R.(S.) 86 (**life sentence—specified period**); *R. v. McLean*, 6 Cr.App.R. 26; *R. v. Si-
mons*, 37 Cr.App.R. 120; *R. v. Walsh*, unreported, March 8, 1973 (**taking offences into
consideration**); *Att.-Gen.'s Reference (No. 52 of 2003) (R. v. Webb)* [2004] Crim.L.R. 306
(**prosecution duty**); *R. v. Kelly and Donnelly* [2001] 2 Cr.App.R.(S.) 73; *R. v. McGillivray*
[2005] 2 Cr.App.R.(S.) 60; *R. v. O'Callaghan* [2005] 2 Cr.App.R.(S.) 83 (**racially aggravated
offences**); *R. v. A. and B.* [1999] 1 Cr.App.R.(S.) 52; *R. v. Guy* [1999] 2 Cr.App.R.(S.) 24; *R.
v. X. (No. 2)* [1999] 2 Cr.App.R.(S.) 294; *R. v. R. (Informer: Reduction in sentence), The Times*,
February 18, 2002; *R. v. P.*; *R. v. Blackburn* [2008] 2 Cr.App.R.(S.) 5 (**discount on account
of assistance given to the police**); *R. v. Bird*, 9 Cr.App.R.(S.) 77; *R. v. Tiso*, 12 Cr.App.R.(S.)
122 (**discount on account of lapse of time since offence**); *R. v. Bibi* [1980] 1 W.L.R. 1193;
R. v. Ollerenshaw [1999] 1 Cr.App.R.(S.) 65; *R. v. Kefford* [2002] 2 Cr.App.R.(S.) 106 (**length
of custodial sentences**); *R. v. Nelson* [2002] 1 Cr.App.R.(S.) 134; *R. v. Cornelius* [2002] 2
Cr.App.R.(S.) 69; *R. v. Pepper* [2006] 1 Cr.App.R.(S.) 20 (**length of extended sentences**); *R.
v. Lang* [2006] 2 Cr.App.R.(S.) 3; *R. v. S.*; *R. v. Burt* [2006] 2 Cr.App.R.(S.) 35; *CPS v. South
East Surrey Youth Court* [2006] 2 Cr.App.R.(S.) 26 (**dangerousness**); *R. v. Reynolds* [2007] 2
Cr.App.R.(S.) 87; *R. v. Johnson* [2007] 1 Cr.App.R.(S.) 112; *R. v. O'Brien* [2007] 1
Cr.App.R.(S.) 75; *R. v. O'Halloran*, unreported, November 14, 2006 ([2006] EWCA Crim.
3148) (**dangerousness: imprisonment for public protection**); *R. v. Brown and Butterworth*
[2007] 1 Cr.App.R.(S.) 77; *R. v. Lay* [2007] 2 Cr.App.R.(S.) 4; *R. v. C.*; *R. v. Bartley* [2007] 2
Cr.App.R.(S.) 98 (**dangerousness: extended sentences**); *Att.-Gen.'s Reference (No. 101 of
2006) (R. v. P.)*, unreported, December 8, 2006 ([2006] EWCA Crim. 3335) (**deferment of
sentence**); *R. v. Cain* [2007] 2 Cr.App.R.(S.) 25 (**prosecution and defence duty to assist at
sentencing**); *R. v. Seed*; *R. v. Stark* [2007] 2 Cr.App.R.(S.) 69 (**sentence length: custodial
sentences**); *R. (Stellato) v. Secretary of State for the Home Department* [2007] 2 A.C. 70 (**sentence
length: licence period**); *Att.-Gen.'s Reference (No. 6 of 2006) (R. v. Farish)* [2007] 1
Cr.App.R.(S.) 12 (**sentence length: minimum sentences**); *R. v. Gordon* [2007] 2 All E.R. 768
(**sentence length: time spent in custody on remand**); *R. v. Tyre*, 6 Cr.App.R.(S.) 247
(**sentence length: joint conviction with a juvenile offender**); *R. v. Davies* [2009] 1
Cr.App.R.(S.) 15 (**sentence length: standard of proof**); *R. v. Raza* [2010] 1 Cr.App.R.(S.) 56,
CA (**sentence length: discounts; totality and mandatory minimum sentences**); *R. v. Round*;
R. v. Dunn [2010] 2 Cr.App.R.(S.) 45, CA (**sentence length: early release provisions**); *Att.-
Gen.'s Reference (No. 55 of 2008) (R. v. C.)* [2009] 2 Cr.App.R.(S.) 22, CA (**sentence length:
imprisonment for public protection**); *R. v. Costello* [2010] 2 Cr.App.R.(S.) 94, CA (**sentence
length: offence committed whilst on licence**); *R. v. McGrath* [2005] 2 Cr.App.R.(S.). 85; *R.
v. Morrison* [2006] 1 Cr.App.R.(S.) 85; *R. v. Lamb* [2006] 2 Cr.App.R.(S.) 11 (**anti-social be-

haviour orders); *R. v. P. (Shane Tony)* [2004] 2 Cr.App.R.(S.) 63 (**anti-social behaviour order imposed with custody**); *R. v. Sullivan* [2003] EWCA Crim. 1736 (**compensation with custody**); *R. v. Robinson* [2002] 2 Cr.App.R.(S.) 95; *Att.-Gen.'s Reference (No. 64 of 2003)* [2004] 2 Cr.App.R.(S.) 22; *R. v. Woods and Collins* [2006] 1 Cr.App.R.(S.) 83 (**drug treatment and testing orders**); *R. v. Richards* [2007] 1 Cr.App.R.(S.) 120 (**sexual offences prevention orders**); *R. v. Kidd*; *R. v. Canavan*; *R. v. Shaw (Dennis)* [1998] 1 W.L.R. 604; *R. v. Tovey*; *R. v. Smith* [2005] 2 Cr.App.R.(S.) 100 (**specimen offences**); *R. v. Perks* [2001] 1 Cr.App.R.(S.) 66; *R. v. Ismail* [2005] 2 Cr.App.R.(S.) 88 (**victim's wishes**); *R. v. Danga*, 13 Cr.App.R.(S.) 408 (**age for purpose of sentencing**); *R. (W.) v. Southampton Youth Court*; *R. (K.) v. Wirral Borough Magistrates' Court* [2003] 1 Cr.App.R.(S.) 87 (**venue for trial**); *R. v. Sharma* [2006] 2 Cr.App.R.(S.) 63 (**confiscation orders**); *R. v. Oshungbure and Odewale* [2005] 2 Cr.App.R.(S.) 102 (**confiscation proceedings following sentence**); *R. v. Richards (Michael)* [2005] 2 Cr.App.R.(S.) 97 (**confiscation order: obtaining social security benefits by false representations**); *R. v. Debnath* [2006] 2 Cr.App.R.(S.) 25 (**restraining orders**); *R. v. Lees-Wolfenden* [2007] 1 Cr.App.R.(S.) 119 (**suspended sentence orders**); *R. v. Sheppard* [2008] 2 Cr.App.R.(S.) 93, CA; *R. v. Chalmers*, unreported, August 7, 2009, CA ([2009] EWCA Crim. 1814) (**activation of suspended sentences**).

In the second list are:—

affray—*R. v. Fox and Hicks* [2006] 1 Cr.App.R.(S.) 17;

breach of licence—*R. v. Pick and Dillon* [2006] 1 Cr.App.R.(S.) 61;

burglary (domestic)—*R. v. McInerney*; *R. v. Keating* [2003] 1 All E.R. 1089; *R. v. Saw* [2009] 2 Cr.App.R.(S.) 54, CA;

counterfeiting and forgery—*R. v. Howard*, 7 Cr.App.R.(S.) 320 (dealing in counterfeit currency); *R. v. Crick*, 3 Cr.App.R.(S.) 275 (counterfeiting coins); *R. v. Kolawole* [2005] 2 Cr.App.R.(S.) 14; *R. v. Mutede* [2006] 2 Cr.App.R.(S.) 22; *Att.-Gen.'s Reference (Nos 1 and 6 of 2008) (R. v. Dziruni and Laby)* [2008] 2 Cr.App.R.(S.) 99; *R. v. Mabengo, Lomoka, Salang and Birindwa, The Times*, July 17, 2008, CA; and *R. v. Ovieriakhi* [2009] 2 Cr.App.R.(S.) 91, CA (false passports);

drugs—*R. v. Aramah*, 76 Cr.App.R. 190 (general); *R. v. Aranguren*, 99 Cr.App.R. 347 (importation of Class A); *R. v. Martinez*, 6 Cr.App.R.(S.) 364 (cocaine); *R. v. Bilinski*, 9 Cr.App.R.(S.) 360 (heroin); *R. v. Mashaollahi* [2001] 1 Cr.App.R. 6 (opium); *R. v. Warren and Beeley* [1996] 1 Cr.App.R. 120 (Ecstasy); *R. v. Wijs*; *R. v. Rae*; *R. v. Donaldson*; *R. v. Church*; *R. v. Haller* [1998] 2 Cr.App.R. 436 (importation of amphetamine); *R. v. v. Ronchetti* [1998] 2 Cr.App.R.(S.) 100 (importation of cannabis (prior to reclassification)); *R. v. Maguire* [1997] 1 Cr.App.R.(S.) 130; *R. v. Wagenaar and Pronk* [1997] 1 Cr.App.R.(S.) 178 (in transit on high seas); *R. v. Singh (Satvir)*, 10 Cr.App.R.(S.) 402 (possession of Class A with intent to supply); *R. v. Hurley* [1998] 1 Cr.App.R.(S.) 299 (possession of LSD with intent to supply); *R. v. Morris (Harold Linden)* [2001] 1 Cr.App.R. 25 (purity analysis of Class A); *R. v. Djahit* [1999] 2 Cr.App.R.(S.) 142; *R. v. Twisse* [2001] 2 Cr.App.R.(S.) 9; *R. v. Afonso*; *R. v. Sajid*; *R. v. Andrews* [2005] 1 Cr.App.R.(S.) 99 (supply and dealing in Class A); *R. v. Prince* [1996] 1 Cr.App.R.(S.) 335 (supply to prisoners); *R. v. Herridge* [2006] 1 Cr.App.R.(S.) 45; *R. v. Xu* [2008] 2 Cr.App.R.(S.) 50 (production/cultivation of cannabis);

explosive offences—*R. v. Martin* [1999] 1 Cr.App.R.(S.) 477;

firearms offences—*R. v. Avis*; *R. v. Barton*; *R. v. Thomas*; *R. v. Torrington*; *R. v. Marquez*; *R. v. Goldsmith* [1998] 1 Cr.App.R. 420; *Att.-Gen.'s Reference (No. 43 of 2009) (R. v. Bennett)*; *R. v. Wilkinson* [2010] 1 Cr.App.R.(S.) 100; *R. v. Rehman*; *R. v. Wood* [2006] 1 Cr.App.R.(S.) 77 (exceptional circumstances);

fraud—*R. v. Feld* [1999] 1 Cr.App.R.(S.) 1 (company management); *R. v. Palk and Smith* [1997] 2 Cr.App.R.(S.) 167 (fraudulent trading); *R. v. Roach* [2002] 1 Cr.App.R.(S.) 12 (obtaining money transfer by deception);

handling stolen goods—*R. v. Webbe* [2002] 1 Cr.App.R.(S.) 22;

health and safety offences—*R. v. F. Howe and Son (Engineers) Ltd* [1999] 2 All E.R. 249; *R. v. Rollco Screw and Rivet Co Ltd* [1999] 2 Cr.App.R.(S.) 436; *R. v. Balfour Beatty Infrastructure Ltd* [2007] 1 Cr.App.R.(S.) 65;

immigration—*R. v. Le and Stark* [1999] 1 Cr.App.R.(S.) 422; *R. v. Ai (Lu Zhu)* [2006] 1 Cr.App.R.(S.) 5 (failing to produce an immigration document);

incest—*Att.-Gen.'s Reference (No. 1 of 1989)*, 11 Cr.App.R.(S.) 409;

indecent assault—*Att.-Gen.'s References (Nos 120, 91 and 119 of 2002)* [2003] 2 All E.R. 955 (general); *R. v. Lennon* [1999] 1 Cr.App.R. 117 (on male);

insider dealing—*R. v. McQuoid* [2010] 1 Cr.App.R.(S.) 43, CA;

intimidation of witness—*R. v. Williams* [1997] 2 Cr.App.R.(S.) 221; *R. v. Chinery* [2002] 2 Cr.App.R.(S.) 244(55);

kidnapping—*R. v. Spence and Thomas*, 5 Cr.App.R.(S.) 413;

manslaughter—*R. v. Chambers*, 5 Cr.App.R.(S.) 190 (diminished responsibility); *R. v. Furby* [2006] 2 Cr.App.R.(S.) 8; *Att.-Gen.'s Reference (No. 60 of 2009) (R. v. Appleby)* [2010] 2 Cr.App.R.(S.) 46, CA ("single punch"); *Att.-Gen.'s Reference (No. 111 of 2006) (R. v. Hussain)* [2007] 2 Cr.App.R.(S.) 26 ("motor"); *R. v. Wood* [2010] 1 Cr.App.R.(S.) 2, CA (diminished responsibility);

money laundering—*R. v. Basra* [2002] 2 Cr.App.R.(S.) 100; *R. v. Gonzalez and Sarmineto* [2003] 2 Cr.App.R.(S.) 9 (general); *R. v. El-Delbi* [2003] 7 *Archbold News* 1 (proceeds of drug trafficking);

murder—*R. v. Jones* [2006] 2 Cr.App.R.(S.) 19; *R. v. Barot* [2008] 1 Cr.App.R.(S.) 31; *R. v. McNee, Gunn and Russell* [2008] 1 Cr.App.R.(S.) 24 (conspiracy); *R. v. Davies* [2009] 1 Cr.App.R.(S.) 15 (minimum term); *R. v. Javed* [2008] 2 Cr.App.R.(S.) 12 (soliciting); *R. v. M.; R. v. A.M.; R. v. Kika* [2010] 2 Cr.App.R.(S.) 19, CA (with a knife);

offensive weapons—*R. v. Poulton; R. v. Celaire* [2003] 4 All E.R. 869; *R. v. Povey* [2009] 1 Cr.App.R.(S.) 42;

perjury—*R. v. Archer* [2003] 1 Cr.App.R.(S.) 86;

perverting the course of justice—*R. v. Walsh and Nightingale*, 14 Cr.App.R.(S.) 671; *R. v. Tunney* [2007] 1 Cr.App.R.(S.) 91, CA;

pornography—*R. v. Holloway*, 4 Cr.App.R.(S.) 128 (having obscene articles for publication for gain); *R. v. Nooy and Schyff*, 4 Cr.App.R.(S.) 308 (importation of indecent or obscene publications);

prison breaking (escape)—*R. v. Coughtrey* [1997] 2 Cr.App.R.(S.) 269;

public nuisance—*R. v. Kavanagh* [2008] 2 Cr.App.R.(S.) 86;

riot—*R. v. Najeeb* [2003] 2 Cr.App.R.(S.) 69;

robbery—*R. v. Snowden, The Times*, November 11, 2002 (hijacking of cars);

sex offenders' register—*Att.-Gen.'s Reference (No. 50 of 1997) (R. v. V.)* [1998] 2 Cr.App.R.(S.) 155;

theft—*R. v. Evans* [1996] 1 Cr.App.R.(S.) 105 ("ringing" stolen cars);

trafficking women for prostitution—*Att.-Gen.'s Reference (No. 6 of 2004) (R. v. Plakici)* [2005] 1 Cr.App.R.(S.) 19;

violent disorder—*R. v. Chapman* (2002) 146 S.J. (LB 242);

K–1001   In addition to the compendium of cases (*ante*), the Sentencing Guidelines Council issued a "guide" for practitioners and sentencers concerning the dangerous offender provisions of the *CJA* 2003 in September, 2007. It has now been updated to take account of the amendments effected by the *CJIA* 2008 which apply to everyone sentenced on or after July 14, 2008. The introduction expressly states that the "guide" is not a "guideline" for the purposes of section 172 of the 2003 Act (§ 5–144 in the main work). Its purpose is to set out clearly the statutory requirements that determine whether one (or more) of the new sentences is available, and to summarise the Court of Appeal (and High Court) guidance regarding the application of those requirements. The guide does not apply to protective sentences under the pre-2003 Act regimes.

Parts 2 and 3 of the guide respectively set out the criteria for imposing sentences under the dangerous offender provisions in respect of offenders aged 18 or over and offenders aged under 18. Part 4 sets out matters in connection with the determination of venue where an offender is under the age of 18. Part 5 deals with the giving of a *Goodyear* indication (*R. v. Goodyear (Practice note)* [2005] 2 Cr.App.R. 20, CA (§ 5–110 in the main work)) in relation to offenders charged with serious or specified offences. Part 6 deals with the assessment of dangerousness. Part 7 sets out matters in connection with the imposition of imprisonment (or custody or detention) for life. Part 8 deals with the choice of whether an extended sentence or a sentence for public protection should be imposed in respect of an offender aged under 18. Part 9 deals with the fixing of "minimum terms", and "custodial terms" and "extension periods". Part 10 deals with questions arising where an offender falls to be sentenced for more than one offence and/or is serving an existing custodial sentence. Part 11 deals with the correction of errors and omissions. Part 12 is a glossary.

There are six annexes. Annex A sets out simple flow charts. Annexes B and C purport to list all serious and specified violent offences; and Annexes D and E purport to do the same in respect of sexual offences. Annex F reproduces sections 225 to 229 of the 2003 Act in amended form, including the new Schedule 15A.

Reduction in Sentence: Guilty Pleas

[1] Published December 2004 (K–2).

[2] *Criminal Justice Act* 2003, s.170(4) (K–2).

[4] *Criminal Justice Act* 2003, s.153(2) (K–4).

[5] *Criminal Justice Act* 2003, s.148(2) (K–4).

[6] Where a court imposes an indeterminate sentence for public protection, the reduction principle applies in the normal way to the determination of the minimum term (see para. 5.1, footnote and para. 7 below) but release from custody requires the authorisation of the Parole Board once that minimum term has been served (K–4)).

[7] See section A above (K–6).

[8] There will be some cases arising from offences committed before the commencement of the relevant provisions of the *Criminal Justice Act* 2003 in which a court will determine that a longer than commensurate, extended, or indeterminate sentence is required for the protection of the public. In such a case, the minimum custodial term (but not the protection of public element of the sentence) should be reduced to reflect the plea (K–7).

[9] *Criminal Justice Act* 2003, s.174(2)(a) (K–7).

[10] See section B above on page 4 (K–7).

[11] *Criminal Justice Act* 2003, Schedule 21 (K–8).

[12] *Criminal Justice Act* 2003, Schedule 1, para 12(c) (K–8).

[13] In accordance with the provisions of the *Criminal Justice Act* 2003 (K–8).

New Sentences: *Criminal Justice Act* 2003

[1] References to the Probation Service reflect current roles and responsibilities. By the time these provisions come into force, some or all of those roles and responsibilities may be those of the National Offender Management Service (NOMS) (K–28).

[2] *Criminal Justice Act* 2003 section 148(2)(b) (K–35).

[3] *ibid* section 148(2)(a) (K–35).

[4] *ibid* section 177(6) (K–35).

[5] Under the Act, a pre-sentence report includes a full report following adjournment, a specific sentence report, a short format report or an oral report. The type of report supplied will depend on the level of information requested. Wherever it appears, the term "pre-sentence report" includes all these types of report (K–36).

[6] *Criminal Justice Act* 2003 section 148(2) (K–36).

[7] *ibid* section 177(6) (K–36).

[8] *ibid* section 177(3) and (4) (K–41).

[9] unless the necessary facilities are not available or, in the particular circumstances of the case, the court considers it inappropriate (K–41).

[10] *Criminal Justice Act* 2003 section 149 (K–43).

[11] *Criminal Justice Act* 2003 Schedule 8, paragraphs 5–6 (K–44).

[12] *ibid* paragraphs 9–10 (K–44).

[13] *ibid* paragraph 9(2) (K–44).

[14] *ibid* paragraph 9(1)(c) (K–44).

[15] *Powers of Criminal Courts (Sentencing) Act* 2000 sections 1 and 2 (K–45).

[16] *Criminal Justice Act* 2003 schedule 23 repealing and replacing sections 1 and 2 of the 2000 Act (K–45).

[17] *ibid* new section 1(3)(b) as inserted by Schedule 23 to the *Criminal Justice Act* 2003 (K–45).

[18] *ibid* new section 1A(1) (K–45).

[19] *ibid* new section 1(4) (K–45).

[20] *ibid* new section 1B (K–45).

[21] *ibid* new section 1 (3)(b) as inserted by Schedule 23 to the *Criminal Justice Act* 2003 (K–46).

[22] *Criminal Justice Act* 2003 section 177 (K–46).

[23] *Criminal Justice Act* 2003 section 238(1) (K–47).

[24] *ibid* section 250 (K–47).

[25] *ibid* section 153(2) (K–47).

[26] Having reference to the Consolidated Criminal Practice Direction [2002] 2 Cr App R 533, Annex C, as suitably amended (K–49).

[27] *Criminal Justice Act* 2003 section 238(1) (K–50).

[28] *ibid* section 250 (K–50).

[30] The power to suspend a sentence is expected to come into force earlier than the provisions implementing "custody plus" and transitional provisions are expected to enable any sentence of imprisonment of under 12 months to be suspended. This guideline therefore is written in the language of the expected transitional provisions (K–56).

[31] *Criminal Justice Act* 2003 schedule 12, para. 4 (K–60).

[32] *ibid* para. 5 (K–60).

[33] *ibid* para. 8(4) (K–60).

[34] *ibid* section 189(3) and (4) (K–60).

[35] *ibid* schedule 12, para. 8(3) (K–60).

[36] *Criminal Justice Act* 2003 section 184(2) (K–66).

[37] IC Pilot Project "A Brief Guide to Intermittent Custody" 02/03/04 HMPS (K–67).

[38] *Criminal Justice Act* 2003 section 240 (K–70).

[39] *ibid* section 149 (K–70).

[40] *ibid* section 240 (which will, at a future date, replace *Criminal Justice Act* 1967, section 67, by which such period is now deducted automatically) (K–70).

[41] This recommendation only applies to sentences of 12 months and above pending the implementation of 'custody plus' (K–70).

Manslaughter by Reason of Provocation

[1] "Any criminal offence arising out of physical, sexual, psychological, emotional or financial abuse by one person against a current or former partner in a close relationship, or against a current or former family member." A new definition of domestic violence was agreed in 2004 (and appears in the CPS Policy on Prosecuting cases of Domestic Violence, 2005) "any incident of threatening behaviour, violence or abuse [psychological, physical, sexual, financial or emotional] between adults who are or have been intimate partners or family members, regardless of gender or sexuality" (K–71).

[2] [2003] 2 Cr.App.R.(S.) 42 (K–74).

[3] Sections 224–230 (K–77).

APPENDIX N

Protocols

A. CONTROL AND MANAGEMENT OF HEAVY FRAUD AND OTHER COMPLEX CRIMINAL CASES

A protocol issued by the Lord Chief Justice of England and Wales   **N–1**

22 March 2005

Introduction
The investigation
        The role of the prosecuting authority and the judge
        Interviews
        The prosecution and defence teams
        Initial consideration of the length of a case
        Notification of cases likely to last more than 8 weeks
        Notification of cases likely to last more than 8 weeks
        Venue
Designation of the trial judge
        The assignment of a judge
Case management
        Objectives
        The assignment of a judge
Case management
        Objectives
        Fixing the trial date
        The first hearing for the giving of initial directions
        The first Case Management Hearing
        Further Case Management Hearings
        Consideration of the length of the trial
        The exercise of the powers
        Fixing the trial date
        The first hearing for the giving of initial directions
        The first Case Management Hearing
        Further Case Management Hearings
        Consideration of the length of the trial
        The exercise of the powers
        Expert Evidence
        Surveillance Evidence
Disclosure
Abuse of process
The trial
        The particular hazard of heavy fraud trials
        Judicial mastery of the case
        The order of the evidence

Introduction

N–2   There is a broad consensus that the length of fraud and trials of other complex crimes must be controlled within proper bounds in order:

(i) To enable the jury to retain and assess the evidence which they have heard. If the trial is so long that the jury cannot do this, then the trial is not fair either to the prosecution or the defence.

(ii) To make proper use of limited public resources: see *Jisl* [2004] EWCA Crim 696 at [113]–[121].

There is also a consensus that no trial should be permitted to exceed a given period, save in exceptional circumstances; some favour 3 months, others an outer limit of 6 months. Whatever view is taken, it is essential that the current length of trials is brought back to an acceptable and proper duration.

This Protocol supplements the *Criminal Procedure Rules* and summarises good practice which experience has shown may assist in bringing about some reduction in the length of trials of fraud and other crimes that result in complex trials. Flexibility of application of this Protocol according to the needs of each case is essential; it is designed to inform but not to proscribe.

This Protocol is primarily directed towards cases which are likely to last eight weeks or longer. It should also be followed, however, in all cases estimated to last more than four weeks. This Protocol applies to trials by jury, but many of the principles will be applicable if trials without a jury are permitted under s.43 of the *Criminal Justice Act* 2003.

The best handling technique for a long case is continuous management by an experienced Judge nominated for the purpose.

It is intended that this Protocol be kept up to date; any further practices or techniques found to be successful in the management of complex cases should be notified to the office of the Lord Chief Justice.

1. The investigation

(i) The role of the prosecuting authority and the judge

N–3   (a) Unlike other European countries, a judge in England and Wales does not directly control the investigation process; that is the responsibility of the Investigating Authority, and in turn the Prosecuting Authority and the prosecution advocate. Experience has shown that a prosecution lawyer (who must be of sufficient experience and who will be a member of the team at trial) and the prosecution advocate, if different, should be involved in the investigation as soon as it appears that a heavy fraud trial or other complex criminal trial is likely to ensue. The costs that this early preparation will incur will be saved many times over in the long run.

(b) The judge can and should exert a substantial and beneficial influence by making it clear that, generally speaking, trials should be kept within manageable limits. In most cases 3 months should be the target outer limit, but there will be cases where a duration of 6 months, or in exceptional circumstances, even longer may be inevitable.

(ii) Interviews

   (a) At present many interviews are too long and too unstructured. This has a knock-on effect **N–4** on the length of trials. Interviews should provide an opportunity for suspects to respond to the allegations against them. They should not be an occasion to discuss every document in the case. It should become clear from judicial rulings that interviews of this kind are a waste of resources.

   (b) The suspect must be given sufficient information before or at the interview to enable them to meet the questions fairly and answer them honestly; the information is not provided to give him the opportunity to manufacture a false story which fits undisputable facts.

   (c) It is often helpful if the principal documents are provided either in advance of the interview or shown as the interview progresses; asking detailed questions about events a considerable period in the past without reference to the documents is often not very helpful.

(iii) The prosecution and defence teams

   (a) **The Prosecution Team** **N–5**
While instructed it is for the lead advocate for the prosecution to take all necessary decisions in the presentation and general conduct of the prosecution case. The prosecution lead advocate will be treated by the court as having that responsibility.

However, in relation to policy decisions the lead advocate for the prosecution must not give an indication or undertaking which binds the prosecution without first discussing the issue with Director of the Prosecuting authority or other senior officer.

"Policy" decisions should be understood as referring to non-evidential decisions on: the acceptance of pleas of guilty to lesser counts or groups of counts or available alternatives: offering no evidence on particular counts; consideration of a re-trial; whether to lodge an appeal; certification of a point of law; and the withdrawal of the prosecution as a whole (for further information see the "Farquharson Guidelines" on the role and responsibilities of the prosecution advocate).

   (b) **The Defence Team**
In each case, the lead advocate for the defence will be treated by the court as having responsibility to the court for the presentation and general conduct of the defence case.

   (c) In each case, a case progression officer must be assigned by the court, prosecution and defence from the time of the first hearing when directions are given (as referred to in paragraph 3(iii)) until the conclusion of the trial.

   (d) In each case where there are multiple defendants, the LSC will need to consider carefully the extent and level of representation necessary.

(iv) Initial consideration of the length of a case

If the prosecutor in charge of the case from the Prosecuting Authority or the lead advocate for the **N–6** prosecution consider that the case as formulated is likely to last more than 8 weeks, the case should be referred in accordance with arrangements made by the Prosecuting Authority to a more senior prosecutor. The senior prosecutor will consider whether it is desirable for the case to be prosecuted in that way or whether some steps might be taken to reduce its likely length, whilst at the same time ensuring that the public interest is served.

Any case likely to last 6 months or more must be referred to the Director of the Prosecuting Authority so that similar considerations can take place.

(v) Notification of cases likely to last more than 8 weeks

Special arrangements will be put in place for the early notification by the CPS and other Prosecut- **N–7** ing Authorities, to the LSC and to a single designated officer of the Court in each Region (Circuit) of any case which the CPS or other Prosecuting Authority consider likely to last over 8 weeks.

(vi) Venue

The court will allocate such cases and other complex cases likely to last 4 weeks or more to a **N–8** specific venue suitable for the trial in question, taking into account the convenience to witnesses, the parties, the availability of time at that location, and all other relevant considerations.

2. Designation of the trial judge

The assignment of a judge

N–9
(a) In any complex case which is expected to last more than four weeks, the trial judge will be assigned under the direction of the Presiding Judges at the earliest possible moment.

(b) Thereafter the assigned judge should manage that case "from cradle to grave"; it is essential that the same judge manages the case from the time of his assignment and that arrangements are made for him to be able to do so. It is recognised that in certain court centres with a large turnover of heavy cases (e.g. Southwark) this objective is more difficult to achieve. But in those court centres there are teams of specialist judges, who are more readily able to handle cases which the assigned judge cannot continue with because of unexpected events; even at such courts, there must be no exception to the principle that one judge must handle all the pre-trial hearings until the case is assigned to another judge.

3. Case management

(i) Objectives

N–10
(a) The number, length and organisation of case management hearings will, of course, depend critically on the circumstances and complexity of the individual case. However, thorough, well-prepared and extended case management hearings will save court time and costs overall.

(b) Effective case management of heavy fraud and other complex criminal cases requires the judge to have a much more detailed grasp of the case than may be necessary for many other Plea and Case Management Hearings (PCMHs). Though it is for the judge in each case to decide how much pre-reading time he needs so that the judge is on top of the case, it is not always a sensible use of judicial time to allocate a series of reading days, during which the judge sits alone in his room, working through numerous boxes of ring binders.

See paragraph 3(iv)(e) below

(ii) Fixing the trial date

N–11
Although it is important that the trial date should be fixed as early as possible, this may not always be the right course. There are two principal alternatives:

(a) The trial date should be fixed at the first opportunity—i.e. at the first (and usually short) directions hearing referred to in The first hearing for the giving of initial directions. From then on everyone must work to that date. All orders and pre-trial steps should be time-tabled to fit in with that date. All advocates and the judge should take note of this date, in the expectation that the trial will proceed on the date determined.

(b) The trial date should not be fixed until the issues have been explored at a full case management hearing (referred to in The first Case Management Hearing), after the advocates on both sides have done some serious work on the case. Only then can the length of the trial be estimated.

Which is apposite must depend on the circumstances of each case, but the earlier it is possible to fix a trial date, by reference to a proper estimate and a timetable set by reference to the trial date, the better.

It is generally to be expected that once a trial is fixed on the basis of the estimate provided, that it will not be **increased** if, and only if, the party seeking to extend the time justifies why the original estimate is no longer appropriate.

(iii) The first hearing for the giving of initial directions

N–12
At the first opportunity the assigned judge should hold a short hearing to give initial directions. The directions on this occasion might well include:

(a) That there should be a full case management hearing on, or commencing on, a specified future date by which time the parties will be properly prepared for a meaningful hearing and the defence will have full instructions.

(b) That the prosecution should provide an outline written statement of the prosecution case at least one week in advance of that case management hearing, outlining in simple terms:
(i) the key facts on which it relies;
(ii) the key evidence by which the prosecution seeks to prove the facts.
The statement must be sufficient to permit the judge to understand the case and for the

defence to appreciate the basic elements of its case against each defendant. The prosecution may be invited to highlight the key points of the case orally at the case management hearing by way of a short mini-opening. The outline statement should not be considered binding, but it will serve the essential purpose in telling the judge, and everyone else, what the case is really about and identifying the key issues.

(c) That a core reading list and core bundle for the case management hearing should be delivered at least one week in advance.

(d) Preliminary directions about disclosure: see paragraph 4.

(iv) The first case management hearing

   (a) At the first case management hearing: **N–13**

      (1) the prosecution advocate should be given the opportunity to highlight any points from the prosecution outline statement of case (which will have been delivered at least a week in advance;

      (2) each defence advocate should be asked to outline the defence.

   If the defence advocate is not in a position to say what is in issue and what is not in issue, then the case management hearing can be adjourned for a short and limited time and to a fixed date to enable the advocate to take instructions; such an adjournment should only be necessary in exceptional circumstances, as the defence advocate should be properly instructed by the time of the first case management hearing and in any event is under an obligation to take sufficient instructions to fulfil the obligations contained in sections 33–39 of *Criminal Justice Act* 2003.

   (b) There should then be a real dialogue between the judge and all advocates for the purpose of identifying:

      (i) the focus of the prosecution case;

      (ii) the common ground;

      (iii) the real issues in the case. (Rule 3.2 of the *Criminal Procedure Rules*.)

   (c) The judge will try to generate a spirit of co-operation between the court and the advocates on all sides. The expeditious conduct of the trial and a focussing on the real issues must be in the interests of **all** parties. It cannot be in the interests of any defendant for his good points to become lost in a welter of uncontroversial or irrelevant evidence.

   (d) In many fraud cases the primary facts are not seriously disputed. The real issue is what each defendant knew and whether that defendant was dishonest. Once the judge has identified what is in dispute and what is not in dispute, the judge can then discuss with the advocate how the trial should be structured, what can be dealt with by admissions or agreed facts, what uncontroversial matters should be proved by concise oral evidence, what timetabling can be required under Rule 3.10 *Criminal Procedure Rules*, and other directions.

   (e) In particularly heavy fraud or complex cases the judge may possibly consider it necessary to allocate a whole week for a case management hearing. If that week is used wisely, many further weeks of trial time can be saved. In the gaps which will inevitably arise during that week (for example while the advocates are exploring matters raised by the judge) the judge can do a substantial amount of informed reading. The case has come "alive" at this stage. Indeed, in a really heavy fraud case, if the judge fixes one or more case management hearings on this scale, there will be need for fewer formal reading days. Moreover a huge amount can be achieved in the pre-trial stage, if all trial advocates are gathered in the same place, focussing on the case **at the same time**, for several days consecutively.

   (f) Requiring the defence to serve proper case statements may enable the court to identify

      (i) what is common ground and

      (ii) the real issues.

   It is therefore important that proper defence case statements be provided as required by the *Criminal Procedure Rules*; judges will use the powers contained in ss.28–34 of the *Criminal Proceedings and Evidence Act* 1996 [*sic*] (and the corresponding provisions of the *CJA* 1987, ss.33 and following of the *Criminal Justice Act* 2003) and the *Criminal Procedure Rules* to ensure that realistic defence case statements are provided.

   (g) Likewise this objective may be achieved by requiring the prosecution to serve draft admissions by a specified date and by requiring the defence to respond within a specified number of weeks.

(v) Further case management hearings

   (a) The date of the next case management hearing should be fixed at the conclusion of the **N–14** hearing so that there is no delay in having to fix the date through listing offices, clerks and others.

(b) If one is looking at a trial which threatens to run for months, pre-trial case management on an intensive scale is essential.

(vi) Consideration of the length of the trial

N–15

(a) Case management on the above lines, the procedure set out in paragraph 1(iv), may still be insufficient to reduce the trial to a manageable length; generally a trial of 3 months should be the target, but there will be cases where a duration of 6 months or, in exceptional circumstances, even longer may be inevitable.

(b) If the trial is not estimated to be within a manageable length, it will be necessary for the judge to consider what steps should be taken to reduce the length of the trial, whilst still ensuring that the prosecution has the opportunity of placing the full criminality before the court.

(c) To assist the judge in this task,

(i) the lead advocate for the prosecution should be asked to explain why the prosecution have rejected a shorter way of proceeding; they may also be asked to divide the case into sections of evidence and explain the scope of each section and the need for each section;

(ii) the lead advocates for the prosecution and for the defence should be prepared to put forward in writing, if requested, ways in which a case estimated to last more than three months can be shortened, including possible severance of counts or defendants, exclusions of sections of the case or of evidence or areas of the case where admissions can be made.

(d) One course the judge may consider is pruning the indictment by omitting certain charges and/or by omitting certain defendants. The judge must not usurp the function of the prosecution in this regard, and he must bear in mind that he will, at the outset, know less about the case than the advocates. The aim is achieve [*sic*] fairness to all parties

(e) Nevertheless, the judge does have two methods of pruning available for use in appropriate circumstances:

(i) persuading the prosecution that it is not worthwhile pursuing certain charges and/or certain defendants;

(ii) severing the indictment. Severance for reasons of case management alone is perfectly proper, although judges should have regard to any representations made by the prosecution that severance would weaken their case. Indeed the judge's hand will be strengthened in this regard by rule 1.1(2)(g) of the *Criminal Procedure Rules*. However, before using what may be seen as a blunt instrument, the judge should insist on seeing full defence statements of all affected defendants. Severance may be unfair to the prosecution if, for example, there is a cut-throat defence in prospect. For example, the defence of the principal defendant may be that the defendant relied on the advice of his accountant or solicitor that what was happening was acceptable. The defence of the professional may be that he gave no such advice. Against that background, it might be unfair to the prosecution to order separate trials of the two defendants.

(vii) The exercise of the powers

N–16

(a) The *Criminal Procedure Rules* require the court to take a more active part in case management. These are salutary provisions which should bring to an end interminable criminal trials of the kind which the Court of Appeal criticised in *Jisl* [2004] EWCA 696 at [113]–[121].

(b) Nevertheless these salutary provisions do not have to be used on every occasion. Where the advocates have done their job properly, by narrowing the issues, pruning the evidence and so forth, it may be quite inappropriate for the judge to "weigh in" and start cutting out more evidence or more charges of his own volition. It behoves the judge to make a careful assessment of the degree of judicial intervention which is warranted in each case.

(c) The note of caution in the previous paragraph is supported by certain experience which has been gained of the *Civil Procedure Rules* (on which the *Criminal Procedure Rules* are based). The CPR contain valuable and efficacious provisions for case management by the judge on his own initiative which have led to huge savings of court time and costs. Surveys by the Law Society have shown that the CPR have been generally welcomed by court users and the profession, but there have been reported to have been isolated instances in which the parties to civil litigation have faithfully complied with both the letter and the spirit of the CPR, and have then been aggrieved by what was perceived to be unnecessary intermeddling by the court.

(viii) Expert evidence

(a) Early identification of the subject matter of expert evidence to be adduced by the prosecution and the defence should be made as early as possible, preferably at the directions hearing. **N–17**

(b) Following the exchange of expert evidence, any areas of disagreement should be identified and a direction should generally be made requiring the experts to meet and prepare, after discussion, a joint statement identifying points of agreement and contention and areas where the prosecution is put to proof on matters of which a positive case to the contrary is not advanced by the defence. After the statement has been prepared it should be served on the court, the prosecution and the defence. In some cases, it might be appropriate to provide that to the jury.

(ix) Surveillance evidence

(a) Where a prosecution is based upon many months' observation or surveillance evidence and it appears that it is capable of effective presentation based on a shorter period, the advocate should be required to justify the evidence of such observations before it is permitted to be adduced, either substantially or in its entirety. **N–18**

(b) Schedules should be provided to cover as much of the evidence as possible and admissions sought.

4. Disclosure

In fraud cases the volume of documentation obtained by the prosecution is liable to be immense. The problems of disclosure are intractable and have the potential to disrupt the entire trial process. **N–19**

(i) The prosecution lawyer (and the prosecution advocate if different) brought in at the outset, as set out in paragraph 1(i)(a), each have a continuing responsibility to discharge the prosecution's duty of disclosure, either personally or by delegation, in accordance with the Attorney General's Guidelines on Disclosure.

(ii) The prosecution should only disclose those documents which are relevant (i.e. likely to assist the defence or undermine the prosecution—see s.3(1) of *CPIA* 1996 and the provisions of the *CJA* 2003).

(iii) It is almost always undesirable to give the "warehouse key" to the defence for two reasons:

(a) this amounts to an abrogation of the responsibility of the prosecution;

(b) the defence solicitors may spend a disproportionate amount of time and incur disproportionate costs trawling through a morass of documents.

The judge should therefore try and ensure that disclosure is limited to what is likely to assist the defence or undermine the prosecution.

(iv) At the outset the judge should set a timetable for dealing with disclosure issues. In particular, the judge should fix a date by which all defence applications for specific disclosure must be made. In this regard, it is relevant that the defendants are likely to be intelligent people, who know their own business affairs and who (for the most part) will know what documents or categories of documents they are looking for.

(v) At the outset (and before the cut-off date for specific disclosure applications) the judge should ask the defence to indicate what documents they are interested in and from what source. A general list is not an acceptable response to this request. The judge should insist upon a list which is specific, manageable and realistic. The judge may also require justification of any request.

(vi) In non-fraud cases, the same considerations apply, but some may be different:

(a) It is not possible to approach many non-fraud cases on the basis that the defendant knows what is there or what they are looking for. But on the other hand this should not be turned into an excuse for a "fishing expedition"; the judge should insist on knowing the issue to which a request for disclosure applies.

(b) If the *bona fides* of the investigation is called into question, a judge will be concerned to see that there has been independent and effective appraisal of the documents contained in the disclosure schedule and that its contents are adequate. In appropriate cases where this issue has arisen and there are grounds which show there is a real issue, consideration should be given to receiving evidence on oath from the senior investigating officer at an early case management hearing.

5. Abuse of process

(i) Applications to stay or dismiss for abuse of process have become a normal feature of heavy **N–20** and complex cases. Such applications may be based upon delay and the health of defendants.

(ii) Applications in relation to absent special circumstances [*sic*] tend to be unsuccessful and not to be pursued on appeal. For this reason there is comparatively little Court of Appeal guidance: but see: *Harris and Howells* [2003] EWCA Crim 486. It should be noted that abuse of process is not there to discipline the prosecution or the police.

(iii) The arguments on both sides must be reduced to writing. Oral evidence is seldom relevant.

(iv) The judge should direct full written submissions (rather than "skeleton arguments") on any abuse application in accordance with a timetable set by him; these should identify any element of prejudice the defendant is alleged to have suffered.

(v) The judge should normally aim to conclude the hearing within an absolute maximum limit of one day, if necessary in accordance with a timetable. The parties should therefore prepare their papers on this basis and not expect the judge to allow the oral hearing to be anything more than an occasion to highlight concisely their arguments and answer any questions the court may have of them; applications will not be allowed drag on.

6. The trial

(i) The particular hazard of heavy fraud trials

N–21
    A heavy fraud or other complex trial has the potential to lose direction and focus. This is a disaster for three reasons:

(a) the jury will lose track of the evidence, thereby prejudicing both prosecution and defence;

(b) the burden on the defendants, the judge and indeed all involved will become intolerable;

(c) scarce public resources are wasted. Other prosecutions are delayed or—worse—may never happen. Fraud which is detected but not prosecuted (for resource reasons) undermines confidence.

(ii) Judicial mastery of the case

N–22
(a) It is necessary for the judge to exercise firm control over the conduct of the trial at all stages.

(b) In order to do this the judge must read the witness statements and the documents, so that the judge can discuss case management issues with the advocates on—almost—an equal footing.

(c) To this end, the judge should not set aside weeks or even days for pre-reading (see paragraph 3(i)(b)). Hopefully the judge will have gained a good grasp of the evidence during the case management hearings. Nevertheless, realistic reading time must be provided for the judge in advance of trial.

(d) The role of the judge in a heavy fraud or other complex criminal trial is different from his/her role in a "conventional" criminal trial. So far as possible, the judge should be freed from other duties and burdens, so that he/she can give the high degree of commitment which a heavy fraud trial requires. This will pay dividends in terms of saving weeks or months of court time.

(iii) The order of the evidence

N–23
(a) By the outset of the trial at the latest (and in most cases very much earlier) the judge must be provided with a schedule, showing the sequence of prosecution (and in an appropriate case defence) witnesses and the dates upon which they are expected to be called. This can only be prepared by discussion between prosecution and defence which the judge should expect, and say he/she expects, to take place: See: *Criminal Procedure Rule* 3.10. The schedule should, in so far as it relates to prosecution witnesses, be developed in consultation with the witnesses, via the witness care units, and with consideration given to their personal needs. Copies of the schedule should be provided for the Witness Service.

(b) The schedule should be kept under review by the trial judge and by the parties. If a case is running behind or ahead of schedule, each witness affected must be advised by the party who is calling that witness at the earliest opportunity.

(c) If an excessive amount of time is allowed for any witness, the judge can ask why. The judge may probe with the advocates whether the time envisaged for the evidence-in-chief or cross-examination (as the case may be) of a particular witness is really necessary.

(iv) Case management sessions

N–24
(a) The order of the evidence may have legitimately to be departed from. It will, however, be a

useful for tool for monitoring the progress of the case. There should be periodic case management sessions, during which the judge engages the advocates upon a stock-taking exercise: asking, amongst other questions, "where are we going?" and "what is the relevance of the next three witnesses?". This will be a valuable means of keeping the case on track. Rule 3.10 of the *Criminal Procedure Rules* will again assist the judge.

(b) The judge may wish to consider issuing the occasional use of "case management notes" to the advocates, in order to set out the judge's tentative views on where the trial may be going off track, which areas of future evidence are relevant and which may have become irrelevant (e.g. because of concessions, admissions in cross-examination and so forth). Such notes from the judge plus written responses from the advocates can, cautiously used, provide a valuable focus for debate during the periodic case management reviews held during the course of the trial.

(v) Controlling prolix cross-examination

(a) Setting **rigid** time limits in advance for cross-examination is rarely appropriate—as experience has shown in civil cases; but a timetable is essential so that the judge can exercise control and so that there is a clear target to aim at for the completion of the evidence of each witness. Moreover the judge can and should indicate when cross-examination is irrelevant, unnecessary or time wasting. The judge may limit the time for further cross-examination of a particular witness.   **N–25**

(vi) Electronic presentation of evidence

(a) Electronic presentation of evidence (EPE) has the potential to save huge amounts of time in fraud and other complex criminal trials and should be used more widely.   **N–26**

(b) HMCS is providing facilities for the easier use of EPE with a standard audio visual facility. Effectively managed, the savings in court time achieved by EPE more than justify the cost.

(c) There should still be a core bundle of those documents to which frequent reference will be made during the trial. The jury may wish to mark that bundle or to refer back to particular pages as the evidence progresses. EPE can be used for presenting all documents not contained in the core bundle.

(d) Greater use of other modern forms of graphical presentations should be made wherever possible.

(vii) Use of interviews

The judge should consider extensive editing of self serving interviews, even when the defence want the jury to hear them in their entirety; such interviews are not evidence of the truth of their contents but merely of the defendant's reaction to the allegation.   **N–27**

(viii) Jury management

(a) The jury should be informed as early as possible in the case as to what the issues are in a manner directed by the Judge.   **N–28**

(b) The jury must be regularly updated as to the trial timetable and the progress of the trial, subject to warnings as to the predictability of the trial process.

(c) Legal argument should be heard at times that causes the least inconvenience to jurors.

(d) It is useful to consider with the advocates whether written directions should be given to the jury and, if so, in what form.

(ix) Maxwell hours

(a) Maxwell hours should only be permitted after careful consideration and consultation with the Presiding Judge.   **N–29**

(b) Considerations in favour include:

(i) legal argument can be accommodated without disturbing the jury;

(ii) there is a better chance of a representative jury;

(iii) time is made available to the judge, advocates and experts to do useful work in the afternoons

(c) Considerations against include:

(i) the lengthening of trials and the consequent waste of court time;

(ii) the desirability of making full use of the jury once they have arrived at court;

(iii) shorter trials tend to diminish the need for special provisions *e.g.* there are fewer difficulties in empanelling more representative juries;

      (iv) they are unavailable if any defendant is in custody.

    (d) It may often be the case that a maximum of one day of Maxwell hours a week is sufficient; if so, it should be timetabled in advance to enable all submissions by advocates, supported by skeleton arguments served in advance, to be dealt with in the period after 1:30 pm on that day.

(x) Livenote

N–30   If Livenote is used, it is important that all users continue to take a note of the evidence, otherwise considerable time is wasted in detailed reading of the entire daily transcript.

7. Other issues

(i) Defence representation and defence costs

N–31   (a) Applications for change in representation in complex trials need special consideration; the ruling of HH Judge Wakerley QC (as he then was) in *Asghar Ali* has been circulated by the JSB.

    (b) Problems have arisen when the Legal Services Commission have declined to allow advocates or solicitors to do certain work; on occasions the matter has been raised with the judge managing or trying the case.

    (c) The Legal Services Commission has provided guidance to judges on how they can obtain information from the LSC as to the reasons for their decisions; further information in relation to this can be obtained from *Nigel Field, Head of the Complex Crime Unit, Legal Services Commission, 29–37 Red Lion Street, London, WC1R 4PP.*

(ii) Assistance to the judge

N–32   Experience has shown that in some very heavy cases, the judge's burden can be substantially offset with the provision of a judicial assistant or other support and assistance.

B. Management of Terrorism Cases

N–33   A protocol issued by Sir Igor Judge P.

January 30, 2007

Terrorism cases

N–34   1. This protocol applies to "terrorism cases". For the purposes of this protocol a case is a "terrorism case" where:

    (a) one of the offences charged against any of the defendants is indictable only and it is alleged by the prosecution that there is evidence that it took place during an act of terrorism or for the purposes of terrorism as defined in section 1 of the *Terrorist Act* 2000 [*sic*]; this may include, but is not limited to:

      i. murder;

      ii. manslaughter;

      iii. an offence under section 18 of the *Offences against the Person Act* 1861 (wounding with intent);

      iv. an offence under section 23 or 24 of that Act (administering poison etc);

      v. an offence under section 28 or 29 of that Act (explosives);

      vi. an offence under section 2, 3 or 5 of the *Explosive Substances Act* 1883 (causing explosions);

      vii. an offence under section 1(2) of the *Criminal Damage Act* 1971 (endangering life by damaging property);

      viii. an offence under section 1 of the *Biological Weapons Act* 1974 (biological weapons);

      ix. an offence under section 2 of the *Chemical Weapons Act* 1996 (chemical weapons);

      x. an offence under section 56 of the *Terrorism Act* 2000 (directing a terrorist organisation);

      xi. an offence under section 59 of that Act (inciting terrorism overseas);

      xii. offences under (v), (vii) and (viii) above given jurisdiction by virtue of section 62 of that Act (terrorist bombing overseas);

      xiii. an offence under section 5 of the *Terrorism Act* 2006 (preparation of terrorism acts);

(b) one of the offences so charged includes an allegation by the prosecution of serious fraud that took place during an act of terrorism or for the purposes of terrorism as defined in section 1 of the *Terrorist Act* 2000 [*sic*] and meets the test to be transferred to the Crown Court under section 4 of the *Criminal Justice Act* 1987;

(c) one of the offences charged is indictable only includes [*sic*] an allegation that a defendant conspired, incited or attempted to commit an offence under sub-paragraphs (1)(a) or (b) above;

(d) it is a case (which can be indictable only or triable either way) that a judge of the terrorism cases list (see paragraph 2(a) below) considers should be a terrorism case. In deciding whether a case not covered by sub-paragraphs (1)(a), (b) or (c) above should be a terrorism case, the judge may hear representations from the Crown Prosecution Service.

The terrorism cases list

2. (a) All terrorism cases, wherever they originate in England and Wales, will be managed in a **N–35** list known as the "terrorism cases list" by the Presiding Judges of the South Eastern Circuit and such other judges of the High Court as are nominated by the President of the Queen's Bench Division.

(b) Such cases will be tried, unless otherwise directed by the President of the Queen's Bench Division, by a judge of the High Court as nominated by the President of the Queen's Bench Division.

3. The judges managing the terrorism cases referred to in paragraph 2 will be supported by **N–36** the London and South Eastern Regional Co-ordinator's Office (the "Regional Co-ordinator's Office"). An official of that office or nominated by that office will act as the case progression officer for cases in that list for the purposes of part 3.4 of the *Criminal Procedure Rules*.

Procedure after charge

4. Immediately after a person has been charged in a terrorism case, anywhere in England and **N–37** Wales, a representative of the Crown Prosecution Service will notify the person on the 24 hour rota for special jurisdiction matters at Westminster Magistrates' Court of the following information:

(a) the full name of each defendant and the name of his solicitor of [*sic*] other legal representative, if known;

(b) the charges laid;

(c) the name and contact details of the crown prosecutor with responsibility for the case, if known;

(d) confirmation that the case is a terrorism case.

5. The person on the 24-hour rota will then ensure that all terrorism cases wherever they are **N–38** charged in England and Wales are listed before the Chief Magistrate or other District Judge designated under the *Terrorism Act* 2000. Unless the Chief Magistrate or other District Judge designated under the *Terrorism Act* 2000 directs otherwise the first appearance of all defendants accused of terrorism offences will be listed at Westminster Magistrates' Court.

6. In order to comply with section 46 of the *Police and Criminal Evidence Act* 1984, if a defendant **N–39** in a terrorism case is charged at a police station within the local justice area in which Westminster Magistrates' Court is situated the defendant must be brought before Westminster Magistrates' Court as soon as is practicable and in any event not later than the first sitting after he is charged with the offence. If a defendant in a terrorism case is charged in a police station outside the local justice area in which Westminster Magistrates' Court is situated, unless the Chief Magistrate or other designated judge directs otherwise, the defendant must be removed to that area as soon as is practicable. He must then be brought before Westminster Magistrates' Court as soon as is practicable after his arrival in the area and in any event not later than the first sitting of Westminster Magistrates' Court after his arrival in that area.

7. As soon as is practicable after charge a representative of the Crown Prosecution Service will **N–40** also provide the Regional Listing Co-ordinator's Office with the information listed in paragraph 4 above.

8. The Regional Co-ordinator's Office will then ensure that the Chief Magistrate and the Legal **N–41** Services Commission have the same information.

Cases to be sent to the Crown Court under section 51 of the Crime and Disorder Act 1998

9. A preliminary hearing should normally be ordered by the magistrates' court in a terrorism **N–42** case. The court should ordinarily direct that the preliminary hearing should take place about 14 days after charge.

10. The sending magistrates' court should contact the Regional Listing Co-ordinator's Office who will be responsible for notifying the magistrates' court as to the relevant Crown Court to which to send the case.

11. In all terrorism cases, the magistrates' court case progression form for cases sent to the Crown Court under section 51 of the *Crime and Disorder Act* 1998 should not be used. Instead of the automatic directions set out in that form, the magistrates' court shall make the following directions to facilitate the preliminary hearing at the Crown Court:

> (a) three days prior to the preliminary hearing in the terrorism cases list, the prosecution must serve upon each defendant and the Regional Listing co-ordinator:
>> i. a preliminary summary of the case;
>> ii. the names of those who are to represent the prosecution, if known;
>> iii. an estimate of the length of the trial;
>> iv. a suggested provisional timetable which should generally include:
>>> • the general nature of further enquiries being made by the prosecution;
>>> • the time needed for the completion of such enquiries;
>>> • the time required by the prosecution to review the case;
>>> • a timetable for the phased service of the evidence;
>>> • the time for the provision by the Attorney General for his consent if necessary;
>>> • the time for service of the detailed defence case statement;
>>> • the date for the case management hearing;
>>> • estimated trial date;
>> v. a preliminary statement of the possible disclosure issues setting out the nature and scale of the problem including the amount of unused material, the manner in which the prosecution seeks to deal with these matters and a suggested timetable for discharging their statutory duty;
>> vi. any information relating to bail and custody time limits;
> (b) one day prior to the preliminary hearing in the terrorist cases list, each defendant must serve in writing on the Regional Listing Co-ordinator and the prosecution:
>> i. the proposed representation;
>> ii. observations on the timetable;
>> iii. an indication of plea and the general nature of the defence.

Cases to be transferred to the Crown Court under section 4(1) of the Criminal Justice Act 1987

13. If a terrorism case is to be transferred to the Crown Court the magistrates' court should proceed as if it is being sent to the Crown Court, as in paragraphs 10–12 above.

14. When a terrorism case is so sent or transferred the case will go into the terrorism list and be managed by a judge as described in paragraph 2 above.

The preliminary hearing at the Crown Court

15. At the preliminary hearing, the judge will determine whether the case is one to remain in the terrorism list and if so give directions setting the provisional timetable.

16. The Legal Services Commission must attend the hearing by an authorised officer to assist the court.

Use of video link

17. Unless a judge otherwise directs, all Crown Court hearings prior to the trial will be conducted by video link for all defendants in custody.

Security

18. The police service and the prison service will provide the Regional Listing Co-ordinator's Office with an initial joint assessment of the security risks associated with any court appearance by the defendants within 14 days of charge. Any subsequent changes in circumstances or the assessment of risk which have the potential to impact upon the choice of trial venue will be notified to the Regional Listing Co-ordinator's Office immediately.

[The next paragraph is N–52.]

C. CONTROL AND MANAGEMENT OF UNUSED MATERIAL IN THE CROWN COURT

Introduction

1. Disclosure is one of the most important—as well as one of the most abused—of the procedures relating to criminal trials. There needs to be a sea-change in the approach of both judges and the parties to all aspects of the handling of the material which the prosecution do not intend to use in support of their case. For too long, a wide range of serious misunderstandings has existed, both as to the exact ambit of the unused material to which the defence is entitled, and the role to be played by the judge in ensuring that the law is properly applied. All too frequently applications by the parties and decisions by the judges in this area have been made based either on misconceptions as to the true nature of the law or a general laxity of approach (however well-intentioned). This failure properly to apply the binding provisions as regards disclosure has proved extremely and unnecessarily costly and has obstructed justice. It is, therefore, essential that disclosure obligations are properly discharged—by both the prosecution and the defence—in all criminal proceedings, and the court's careful oversight of this process is an important safeguard against the possibility of miscarriages of justice.

2. The House of Lords stated in *R. v. H. and C.* [2004] 2 A.C. 134 at 147:

> Fairness ordinarily requires that any material held by the prosecution which weakens its case or strengthens that of the defendant, if not relied on as part of its formal case against the defendant, should be disclosed to the defence. Bitter experience has shown that miscarriages of justice may occur where such material is withheld from disclosure. The golden rule is that full disclosure of such material should be made.

3. However, it is also essential that the trial process is not overburdened or diverted by erroneous and inappropriate disclosure of unused prosecution material, or by misconceived applications in relation to such material.

4. The overarching principle is therefore that unused prosecution material will fall to be disclosed if, and only if, it satisfies the test for disclosure applicable to the proceedings in question, subject to any overriding public interest considerations. The relevant test for disclosure will depend on the date the criminal investigation in question commenced (see the section on Sources below), as this will determine whether the common law disclosure regime applies, or either of the two disclosure regimes under the *Criminal Procedure and Investigations Act 1996 (CPIA)*.

5. There is very clear evidence that, without active judicial oversight and management, the handling of disclosure issues in general, and the disclosure of unused prosecution material in particular, can cause delays and adjournments.

6. The failure to comply fully with disclosure obligations, whether by the prosecution or the defence, may disrupt and in some cases even frustrate the course of justice.

7. Consideration of irrelevant unused material may consume wholly unjustifiable and disproportionate amounts of time and public resources, undermining the overall performance and efficiency of the criminal justice system. The aim of this Protocol is therefore to assist and encourage judges when dealing with all disclosure issues, in the light of the overarching principle set out in paragraph 4 above. This guidance is intended to cover all Crown Court cases (including cases where relevant case management directions are made at the magistrates' court). It is not, therefore, confined to a very few high profile and high cost cases.

8. Unused material which has been gathered during the course of a criminal investigation and disclosed by the prosecution pursuant to their duties (as set out elsewhere in this Protocol) is received by the defence subject to a prohibition not to use or disclose the material for any purpose which is not connected with the proceedings for whose purposes they were given it (s.17 *CPIA*). The common law, which applies to all disclosure not made under the *CPIA*, achieves the same result by the creation of an implied undertaking not to use the material for any purposes other than the proper conduct of the particular case (see *Taylor v. Director of the Serious Fraud Office* [1999] 2 A.C. 177, HL). A breach of that undertaking would constitute a contempt of court. These provisions are designed to ensure that the privacy and confidentiality of those who provided the material to the investigation (as well as those who are mentioned in the material) is protected and is not invaded any more than is absolutely necessary. However, neither statute nor the common law prevents any one from using or disclosing such material if it has been displayed or communicated to the public in open court (unless the evidence is subject to continuing reporting restriction), and moreover, an application can be made to the court for permission to use or disclose the object or information.

Sources

9. It is not the purpose of this Protocol to rehearse the law in detail; however, some of the principal sources are set out here.

N-53

10. The correct test for disclosure will depend upon the date the relevant criminal investigation commenced:

> a. In relation to offences in respect of which the criminal investigation began prior to 1 April

1997, the common law will apply, and the test for disclosure is that set out in *R. v. Keane*, 99 Cr.App.R. 1.

b. If the criminal investigation commenced on or after 1 April 1997, but before 4 April 2005, then the *CPIA* in its original form will apply, with separate tests for disclosure of unused prosecution material at the primary and secondary disclosure stages (the latter following service of a defence statement by the accused). The disclosure provisions of the Act are supported by the 1997 edition of the Code of Practice issued under section 23(1) of the *CPIA* (S.I. 1997 No. 1033)

c. Where the criminal investigation has commenced on or after 4 April 2005, the law is set out in the *CPIA* as amended by Part V of the *Criminal Justice Act* 2003. There is then a single test for disclosure of unused prosecution material and the April 2005 edition of the Code of Practice under section 23(1) of the *CPIA* will apply (see S.I. 2005 No. 985).

The *CPIA* also identifies the stage(s) at which the prosecution is required to disclose material, and the formalities relating to defence statements. The default time limit for prosecution disclosure is set out in section 13 of the Act (see further at paragraph 13 below). The time limits applicable to defence disclosure are set out in the *Criminal Procedure and Investigations Act 1996 (Defence Disclosure) Regulations* 1997 (S.I. 1997 No. 684).

10. [*sic*] Regard must be had to the Attorney General's Guidelines on Disclosure (April 2005). Although these do not have the force of law (*R. v. Winston Brown* [1995] 1 Cr.App.R. 191) they should be given due weight.

11. Part 25 of the *Criminal Procedure Rules* 2005 (see S.I. 2005 No. 384) sets out the procedures to be followed for applications to the court concerning both sensitive and non-sensitive unused material. Part 3 of the Rules is also relevant in respect of the court's general case management powers, and parties should also have regard to the Consolidated Criminal Practice Direction.

12. Parts 22 and 23 of the *Criminal Procedure Rules* are set aside to make provision for other rules concerning disclosure by the prosecution and the defence, although at the date of this Protocol there are no rules under those Parts.

The duty to gather and record unused material

N–54

13. For the statutory scheme to work properly, investigators and disclosure officers responsible for the gathering, inspection, retention and recording of relevant unused prosecution material must perform their tasks thoroughly, scrupulously and fairly. In this, they must adhere to the appropriate provisions of the *CPIA* Code of Practice.

14. It is crucial that the police (and indeed all investigative bodies) implement appropriate training regimes and appoint competent disclosure officers, who have sufficient knowledge of the issues in the case. This will enable them to make a proper assessment of the unused prosecution material in the light of the test for relevance under paragraph 2.1 of the *CPIA* Code of Practice, with a view to preparing full and accurate schedules of the retained material. In any criminal investigation, the disclosure officer must retain material that may be relevant to an investigation. This material must be listed on a schedule. Each item listed on the schedule should contain sufficient detail to enable the prosecutor to decide whether or not the material falls to be disclosed. The schedules must be sent to the prosecutor. Wherever possible this should be at the same time as the file containing the material for the prosecution case but the duty to disclose does not end at this point and must continue while relevant material is received even after conviction.

15. Furthermore, the scheduling of the relevant material must be completed expeditiously, so as to enable the prosecution to comply promptly with the duty to provide primary (or, when the amended *CPIA* regime applies) initial disclosure as soon as practicable after:

- the case has been committed for trial under section 6(1) or 6(2) of the *Magistrates' Courts Act* 1980; or
- the case has been transferred to the Crown Court under section 4 of the *Criminal Justice Act* 1987, or section 53 of the *Criminal Justice Act* 1991; or
- copies of documents containing the evidence are served on the accused in according [*sic*] with the *Crime and Disorder Act 1998 (Service of Prosecution Evidence) Regulations* 2005 (S.I. 2005 No. 902), where the matter has been sent to the Crown Court pursuant to section 51 or 51A of the *Crime and Disorder Act* 1998; or
- a matter has been added to an indictment in accordance with section 40 of the *Criminal Justice Act* 1988; or
- a bill of indictment has been preferred under section 2(2)(b) of the *Administration of Justice (Miscellaneous Provisions) Act* 1933 or section 22B(3)(a) of the *Prosecution of Offences Act* 1985.

16. Investigators, disclosure officers and prosecutors must promptly and properly discharge their responsibilities under the Act and statutory Code, in order to ensure that justice is not delayed, denied or frustrated. In this context, under paragraph 3.5 of the Code of Practice, it is provided "an investigator should pursue all reasonable lines of inquiry, whether these point towards or away from the suspect".

17. CPS lawyers advising the police pre-charge at police stations should consider conducting a preliminary review of the unused material generated by the investigation, where this is practicable, so as to give early advice on disclosure issues. Otherwise, prosecutors should conduct a preliminary review of disclosure at the same time as the initial review of the evidence. It is critical that the important distinction between the evidence in the case, on the one hand, and any unused material, on the other, is not blurred. Items such as exhibits should be treated as such and the obligation to serve them is not affected by the disclosure regime.

18. Where the single test for disclosure applies under the amended *CPIA* disclosure regime, the prosecutor is under a duty to consider, at an early stage of proceedings, whether there is any unused prosecution material which is reasonably capable of assisting the case for the accused. What a defendant has said by way of defence or explanation either in interview or by way of a prepared statement can be a useful guide to making an objective assessment of the material which would satisfy this test.

19. There may be some occasions when the prosecution, pursuant to surviving common law rules of disclosure, ought to disclose an item or items of unused prosecution material, even in advance of primary or initial disclosure under section 3 of the *CPIA*. This may apply, for instance, where there is information which might affect a decision as to bail; where an abuse of process is alleged; where there is material which might assist the defence to make submissions as to the particular charge or charges, if any, the defendant should face at the Crown Court; and when it is necessary to enable particular preparation to be undertaken at an early stage by the defence. Guidance as to occasions where such disclosure may be appropriate is provided in *R. v. DPP, ex p. Lee* [1999] 2 Cr.App.R. 304. However, once the *CPIA* is triggered (for instance, by committal, or service of case papers following a section 51 sending) it is the *CPIA* which determines what material should be disclosed.

The judge's duty to enforce the statutory scheme

20. When cases are sent to the Crown Court under section 51 of the *Crime and Disorder Act* **N-55** 1998, the *Crime and Disorder Act 1998 (Service of Prosecution Evidence) Regulations* 2005 allow the prosecution 70 days from the date the matter was sent (50 days, where the accused is in custody) within which to serve on the defence and the court copies of the documents containing the evidence upon which the charge or charges are based (in effect, sufficient evidence to amount to a prima facie case). These time limits may be extended and varied at the court's direction. Directions for service of these case papers may be given at the magistrates' court.

21. While it is important to note that this time limit applies to the service of evidence, rather than unused prosecution material, the court will need to consider at the magistrates' court or preliminary hearing whether it is practicable for the prosecution to comply with primary or initial disclosure at the same time as service of such papers, or whether disclosure ought to take place after a certain interval, but before the matter is listed for a PCMH.

22. If the nature of the case does not allow service of the evidence and initial or primary disclosure within the 70, or if applicable 50, days (or such other period as directed by the magistrates' court), the investigator should ensure that the prosecution advocate at the magistrates' court, preliminary Crown Court hearing, or further hearing prior to the PCMH, is aware of the problems, knows why and how the position has arisen and can assist the court as to what revised time limits are realistic.

23. It would be helpful if the prosecution advocate could make any foreseeable difficulties clear as soon as possible, whether this is at the magistrates' court or in the Crown Court at the preliminary hearing (where there is one).

24. Failing this, where such difficulties arise or have come to light after directions for service of case papers and disclosure have been made, the prosecution should notify the court and the defence promptly. This should be done in advance of the PCMH date, and prior to the date set by the court for the service of this material.

25. It is important that this is done in order that the listing for the PCMH is an effective one, as the defence must have a proper opportunity to read the case papers and to consider the initial or primary disclosure, with a view to timely drafting of a defence case statement (where the matter is to be contested), prior to the PCMH.

26. In order to ensure that the listing of the PCMH is appropriate, Judges should not impose time limits for service of case papers or initial/primary disclosure unless and until they are confident that the prosecution advocate has taken the requisite instructions from those who are actually going to do the work specified. It is better to impose a realistic timetable from the outset than to set unachievable limits. Reference should be made to Part 3 of the *Criminal Procedure Rules* and the Consolidated Practice Direction in this respect.

27. This is likewise appropriate where directions, or further directions, are made in relation to prosecution or defence disclosure at the PCMH. Failure to consider whether the timetable is practicable may dislocate the court timetable and can even imperil trial dates. At the PCMH, therefore, all the advocates—prosecution and defence—must be fully instructed about any difficulties the parties may have in complying with their respective disclosure obligations, and must be in a position to put forward a reasonable timetable for resolution of them.

28. Where directions are given by the court in the light of such inquiry, extensions of time should not be given lightly or as a matter of course. If extensions are sought, then an appropriately detailed explanation must be given. For the avoidance of doubt, it is not sufficient merely for the CPS (or other prosecutor) to say that the papers have been delivered late by the police (or other investigator): the court will need to know why they have been delivered late. Likewise, where the accused has been dilatory in serving a defence statement (where the prosecution has complied with the duty to make primary or initial disclosure of unused material, or has purported to do so), it is not sufficient for the defence to say that insufficient instructions have been taken for service of this within the 14-day time limit: the court will need to know why sufficient instructions have not been taken, and what arrangements have been made for the taking of such instructions.

29. Delays and failures by the defence are as damaging to the timely, fair and efficient hearing of the case as delays and failures by the prosecution, and judges should identify and deal with all such failures firmly and fairly.

30. Judges should not allow the prosecution to abdicate their statutory responsibility for reviewing the unused material by the expedient of allowing the defence to inspect (or providing the defence with copies of) everything on the schedules of non-sensitive unused prosecution material, irrespective of whether that material, or all of that material, satisfies the relevant test for disclosure. Where that test is satisfied it is for the prosecutor to decide the form in which disclosure is made. Disclosure need not be in the same form as that in which the information was recorded. Guidance on case management issues relating to this point was given by Rose L.J. in *R. v. CPS (Interlocutory application under sections 35/36 CPIA)* [2005] EWCA Crim. 2342.

31. Indeed, the larger and more complex the case, the more important it is for the prosecution to adhere to the overarching principle in paragraph 4 and ensure that sufficient prosecution resources are allocated to the task. Handing the defence the "keys to the warehouse" has been the cause of many gross abuses in the past, resulting in huge sums being run up by the defence without any proportionate benefit to the course of justice. These abuses must end.

The defence case statement

32. Reference has been made above to defence disclosure obligations. After the provision of primary or initial disclosure by the prosecution, the next really critical step in the preparation for trial is the service of the defence statement. It is a mandatory requirement for a defence statement to be served, where section 5(5) of the *CPIA* applies to the proceedings. This is due within 14 days of the date upon which the prosecution has complied with, or purported to comply with, the duty of primary or initial disclosure. Service of the defence statement is a critical stage in the disclosure process, and timely service of the statement will allow for the proper consideration of disclosure issues well in advance of the trial date.

33. There may be some cases where it is simply not possible to serve a proper defence case statement within the 14-day time limit; well founded defence applications for an extension of time under paragraph (2) of regulation 3 of the *Criminal Procedure and Investigations Act 1996 (Defence Disclosure Time Limits) Regulations* 1997 may therefore be granted. In a proper case, it may be appropriate to put the PCMH back by a week or so, to enable a sufficient defence case statement to be filed and considered by the prosecution.

34. In the past, the prosecution and the court have too often been faced with a defence case statement that is little more than an assertion that the defendant is not guilty. As was stated by the Court of Appeal in *R. v. Patrick Bryant* [2005] EWCA Crim. 2079 (*per* Judge L.J., paragraph 12), such a reiteration of the defendant's plea is not the purpose of a defence statement. Defence statements must comply with the requisite formalities set out in section 5(6) and (7), or section 6A, of the *CPIA*, as applicable.

35. Where the enhanced requirements for defence disclosure apply under section 6A of the *CPIA* (namely, where the case involves a criminal investigation commencing on or after 4 April 2005) the defence statement must spell out, in detail, the nature of the defence, and particular defences relied upon; it must identify the matters of fact upon which the accused takes issue with the prosecution, and the reason why, in relation to each disputed matter of fact. It must further identify any point of law (including points as to the admissibility of evidence, or abuse of process) which the accused proposes to take, and identify authorities relied on in relation to each point of law. Where an alibi defence is relied upon, the particulars given must comply with section 6(2)(a) and (b) of the *CPIA*. Judges will expect to see defence case statements that contain a clear and detailed exposition of the issues of fact and law in the case.

36. Where the pre-4 April 2005 *CPIA* disclosure regime applies, the accused must, in the defence statement, set out the nature of the defence in general terms, indicate the matters upon which the defendant takes issue with the prosecution and set out (in relation to each such matter) why issue is taken. Any alibi defence relied upon should comply with the formalities in section 5(7)(a) and (b) of the Act.

37. There must be a complete change in the culture. The defence must serve the defence case statement by the due date. Judges should then examine the defence case statement with care to ensure that it complies with the formalities required by the *CPIA*. As was stated in paragraph 35 of *R. v. H. and C.*—

> If material does not weaken the prosecution case or strengthen that of the defendant, there is no requirement to disclose it. For this purpose the parties' respective cases should not be restrictively analysed. But they must be carefully analysed, to ascertain the specific facts the prosecution seek to establish and the specific grounds on which the charges are resisted. The trial process is not well served if the defence are permitted to make general and unspecified allegations and then seek far-reaching disclosure in the hope that material may turn up to make them good. Neutral material or material damaging to the defendant need not be disclosed and should not be brought to the attention of the court.

38. If no defence case statement—or no sufficient case statement—has been served by the PCMH, the judge should make a full investigation of the reasons for this failure to comply with the mandatory obligation of the accused, under section 5(5) of the *CPIA*.

39. If there is no—or no sufficient—defence statement by the date of PCMH, or any pre-trial hearing where the matter falls to be considered, the judge must consider whether the defence should be warned, pursuant to section 6E(2) of the *CPIA*, that an adverse inference may be drawn at the trial. In the usual case, where section 6E(2) applies and there is no justification for the deficiency, such a warning should be given.

40. Judges must, of course, be alert to ensure that defendants do not suffer because of the faults and failings of their lawyers, but there must be a clear indication to the professions that if justice is to be done, and if disclosure to be dealt with fairly in accordance with the law, a full and careful defence case statement is essential.

41. Where there are failings by either the defence or the prosecution, judges should, in exercising appropriate oversight of disclosure, pose searching questions to the parties and, having done this and explored the reasons for default, give clear directions to ensure that such failings are addressed and remedied well in advance of the trial date.

42. The ultimate sanction for a failure in disclosure by the accused is the drawing of an inference under section 11 of the *CPIA*. Where the amended *CPIA* regime applies, the strict legal position allows the prosecution to comment upon any failure of defence disclosure, with a view to seeking such an inference (except where the failure relates to identifying a point of law), without leave of the court, but often it will be helpful to canvass the matter with the judge beforehand. In suitable cases, the prosecution should consider commenting upon failures in defence disclosure, with a view to such an inference, more readily than has been the practice under the old *CPIA* regime, subject to any views expressed by the judge.

43. It is vital to a fair trial that the prosecution are mindful of their continuing duty of disclosure, and they must particularly review disclosure in the light of the issues identified in the defence case statement. As part of the timetabling exercise, the judge should set a date by which any application under section 8 (if there is to be one) should be made. While the defence may indicate, in advance of the cut-off date, what items of unused material they are interested in and why, such requests must relate to matters raised in the accused's defence statement. The prosecution should only disclose material in response to such requests if the material meets the appropriate test for disclosure, and the matter must proceed to a formal section 8 hearing in the event that the prosecution declines to make disclosure of the items in question. Paragraphs 4(iv)–(vi)(a) of the Lord Chief Justice's March 2005 Protocol for the Control and Management of Heavy Fraud and Other Complex Criminal Cases should be construed accordingly.

44. If, after the prosecution have complied with, or purported to comply with, primary or initial disclosure, and after the service of the defence case statement and any further prosecution disclosure flowing there from, the defence have a reasonable basis to claim disclosure has been inadequate, they must make an application to the court under section 8 of the *CPIA*. The procedure for the making of such an application is set out in the *Criminal Procedure Rules*, Pt 25, r.25.6. This requires written notice to the prosecution in the form prescribed by r.25.6(2). The prosecution is then entitled (r.25.6(5)) to 14 days within which to agree to provide the specific disclosure requested or to request a hearing in order to make representations in relation to the defence application. As part of the timetabling exercise, the judge should set a date by which any applications under section 8 are to be made and should require the defence to indicate in advance of the cut-off date for specific disclosure applications what documents they are interested in and from what source; in appropriate cases, the judge should require justification of such requests.

45. The consideration of detailed defence requests for specific disclosure (so-called "shopping lists") otherwise than in accordance with r.25.6, is wholly improper. Likewise, defence requests for specific disclosure of unused prosecution material in purported pursuance of section 8 of the *CPIA* and r.25.6, which are not referable to any issue in the case identified by the defence case statement, should be rejected. Judges should require an application to be made under section 8 and in compliance with r.25.6 before considering any order for further disclosure.

46. It follows that the practice of making blanket orders for disclosure in all cases should cease, since such orders are inconsistent with the statutory framework of disclosure laid down by the *CPIA*, and which was endorsed by the House of Lords in *R. v. H. and C. (supra)*.

Listing

47. It will be clear that the conscientious discharge of a judge' s duty at the PCMH requires a good deal more time than under the old PDH regime; furthermore a good deal more work is required of the advocate. The listing of PCMHs must take this into account. Unless the court can sit at 10am and finish the PCMH by 10.30am, it will not therefore usually be desirable for a judge who is part-heard on a trial to do a PCMH.

48. It follows that any case which raises difficult issues of disclosure should be referred to the Resident Judge for directions. Cases of real complexity should, if possible, be allocated to a specific trial judge at a very early stage, and usually before the PCMH.

49. Although this Protocol is addressed to the issues of disclosure, it cannot be seen in isolation; it must be seen in the context of general case management.

Public interest immunity

50. Recent authoritative guidance as to the proper approach to PII is provided by the House of Lords in *R. v. H. and C. (supra)*. It is clearly appropriate for PII applications to be considered by the trial judge. No judge should embark upon a PII application without considering that case and addressing the questions set out in paragraph 36, which for ease of reference we reproduce here:

"36. When any issue of derogation from the golden rule of full disclosure comes before it, the court must address a series of questions:

(1) What is the material which the prosecution seek to withhold? This must be considered by the court in detail.

(2) Is the material such as may weaken the prosecution case or strengthen that of the defence? If No, disclosure should not be ordered. If Yes, full disclosure should (subject to (3), (4) and (5) below be ordered.

(3) Is there a real risk of serious prejudice to an important public interest (and, if so, what) if full disclosure of the material is ordered? If No, full disclosure should be ordered.

(4) If the answer to (2) and (3) is Yes, can the defendant's interest be protected without disclosure or disclosure be ordered to an extent or in a way which will give adequate protection to the public interest in question and also afford adequate protection to the interests of the defence? This question requires the court to consider, with specific reference to the material which the prosecution seek to withhold and the facts of the case and the defence as disclosed, whether the prosecution should formally admit what the defence seek to establish or whether disclosure short of full disclosure may be ordered. This may be done in appropriate cases by the preparation of summaries or extracts of evidence, or the provision of documents in an edited or anonymised form, provided the documents supplied are in each instance approved by the judge. In appropriate cases the appointment of special counsel may be a necessary step to ensure that the contentions of the prosecution are tested and the interests of the defendant protected (see paragraph 22 above). In cases of exceptional difficulty the court may require the appointment of special counsel to ensure a correct answer to questions (2) and (3) as well as (4).

(5) Do the measures proposed in answer to (4) represent the minimum derogation necessary to protect the public interest in question? If No, the court should order such greater

disclosure as will represent the minimum derogation from the golden rule of full disclosure.

(6) If limited disclosure is ordered pursuant to (4) or (5), may the effect be to render the trial process, viewed as a whole, unfair to the defendant? If Yes, then fuller disclosure should be ordered even if this leads or may lead the prosecution to discontinue the proceedings so as to avoid having to make disclosure.

(7) If the answer to (6) when first given is No, does that remain the correct answer as the trial unfolds, evidence is adduced and the defence advanced?

It is important that the answer to (6) should not be treated as a final, once-and-for-all, answer but as a provisional answer which the court must keep under review.".

51. In this context, the following matter [*sic*] are emphasised:

a. The procedure for making applications to the court is as set out in the *Criminal Procedure Rules* 2005, Pt 25 (r.25.1–r.25.5).

b. Where the PII application is a Type 1 or Type 2 application, proper notice to the defence is necessary to allow them to make focused submissions to the court before hearing an application to withhold material; the notice should be as specific as the nature of the material allows. It is appreciated that in some cases only the generic nature of the material can properly be identified. In some wholly exceptional cases (Type 3 cases) it may even be justified to give no notice at all. The judge should always ask the prosecution to justify the form of notice given (or the decision to give no notice at all).

c. The prosecution should be alert to the possibility of disclosing a statement in redacted form by, for example simply removing personal details. This may obviate the need for a PII application, unless the redacted material in itself would also satisfy the test for disclosure.

d. Except where the material is very short (say a few sheets only), or where the material is of such sensitivity that do so would be inappropriate, the prosecution should have supplied securely sealed copies to the judge beforehand, together with a short statement of the reasons why each document is said to be relevant and fulfils the disclosure test and why it is said that its disclosure would cause a real risk of serious prejudice to an important public interest; in undertaking this task, the use of merely formulaic expressions is to be discouraged. In any case of complexity a schedule of the material should be provided showing the specific objection to disclosure in relation to each item, leaving a space for the decision.

e. The application, even if held in private or in secret, should be recorded. The judge should give some short statement of reasons; this is often best done document by document as the hearing proceeds.

f. The tape, copies of the judge's orders (and any copies of the material retained by the court) should be clearly identified, securely sealed and kept in the court building in a safe or stout lockable cabinet consistent with its security classification, and there should be a proper register of all such material kept. Some arrangement should be made between the court and the prosecution authority for the periodic removal of such material once the case is concluded and the time for an appeal has passed.

Third party disclosure

52. The disclosure of unused material that has been gathered or generated by a third party is **N–59** an area of the law that has caused some difficulties: indeed, a Home Office Working Party has been asked to report on it. This is because there is no specific procedure for the disclosure of material held by third parties in criminal proceedings, although the procedure under section 2 of the *Criminal Procedure (Attendance of Witnesses) Act* 1965 or section 97 of the *Magistrates' Courts Act* 1980 is often used in order to effect such disclosure. It should, however, be noted that the test applied under both Acts is not the test to be applied under the *CPIA*, whether in the amended or unamended form. These two provisions require that the material in question is material evidence, *i.e.*, immediately admissible in evidence in the proceedings (see in this respect *R. v. Reading JJ., ex p. Berkshire County Council* [1996] 1 Cr.App.R. 239, *R. v. Derby Magistrates' Court, ex p. B* [1996] A.C. 487 and *R. v. Alibhai* [2004] EWCA Crim. 681).

53. Material held by other government departments or other Crown agencies will not be prosecution material for the purposes of section 3(2) or section 8(4) of the *CPIA*, if it has not been inspected, recorded and retained during the course of the relevant criminal investigation. The Attorney General's Guidelines on Disclosure, however, impose a duty upon the investigators and the prosecution to consider whether such departments or bodies have material which may satisfy the test for disclosure under the Act. Where this is the case, they must seek appropriate disclosure from such bodies, who should themselves have an identified point for such enquiries (see paragraphs 47 to 51, Attorney General's Guidelines on Disclosure).

54. Where material is held by a third party such as a local authority, a social services department, hospital or business, the investigators and the prosecution may seek to make arrangements to inspect the material with a view to applying the relevant test for disclosure to it and determining whether any or all of the material should be retained, recorded and, in due course, disclosed to the accused. In considering the latter, the investigators and the prosecution will establish whether the holder of the material wishes to raise PII issues, as a result of which the material may have to be placed before the court. Section 16 of the *CPIA* gives such a party a right to make representations to the court.

55. Where the third party in question declines to allow inspection of the material, or requires the prosecution to obtain an order before handing over copies of the material, the prosecutor will need to consider whether it is appropriate to obtain a witness summons under either section 2 of the *Criminal Procedure (Attendance of Witnesses) Act* 1965 or section 97 of the *Magistrates' Court Act* 1980. However, as stated above, this is only appropriate where the statutory requirements are satisfied, and where the prosecutor considers that the material may satisfy the test for disclosure. *R. v. Alibhai (supra)* makes it clear that the prosecutor has a "margin of consideration" in this regard.

56. It should be understood that the third party may have a duty to assert confidentiality, or the right to privacy under article 8 of the ECHR, where requests for disclosure are made by the prosecution, or anyone else. Where issues are raised in relation to allegedly relevant third party material, the judge must ascertain whether inquiries with the third party are likely to be appropriate, and, if so, identify who is going to make the request, what material is to be sought, from whom is the material to be sought and within what time scale must the matter be resolved.

57. The judge should consider what action would be appropriate in the light of the third party failing or refusing to comply with a request, including inviting the defence to make the request on its own behalf and, if necessary, to make an application for a witness summons. Any directions made (for instance, the date by which an application for a witness summons with supporting affidavit under section 2 of the 1965 should be served) should be put into writing at the time. Any failure to comply with the timetable must immediately be referred back to the court for further directions, although a hearing will not always be necessary.

58. Where the prosecution do not consider it appropriate to seek such a summons, the defence should consider doing so, where they are of the view (notwithstanding the prosecution assessment) that the third party may hold material which might undermine the prosecution case or assist that for the defendant, and the material would be likely to be 'material evidence' for the purposes of the 1965 Act. The defence must not sit back and expect the prosecution to make the running. The judge at the PCMH should specifically enquire whether any such application is to be made by the defence and set out a clear timetable. The objectionable practice of defence applications being made in the few days before trial must end.

59. It should be made clear, though, that 'fishing' expeditions in relation to third party material—whether by the prosecution or the defence—must be discouraged, and that, in appropriate cases, the court will consider making an order for wasted costs where the application is clearly unmeritorious and ill-conceived.

60. Judges should recognise that a summons can only be issued where the document(s) sought would be admissible in evidence. While it may be that the material in question may be admissible in evidence as a result of the hearsay provisions of the *CJA* (sections 114 to 120), it is this that determines whether an order for production of the material is appropriate, rather than the wider considerations applicable to disclosure in criminal proceedings: see *R. v. Reading Justices (supra)*, upheld by the House of Lords in *R. v. Derby Magistrates' Court (supra)*.

61. A number of Crown Court centres have developed local protocols, usually in respect of sexual offences and material held by social services and health and education authorities. Where these protocols exist they often provide an excellent and sensible way to identify relevant material that might assist the defence or undermine the prosecution.

62. Any application for third party disclosure must identify what documents are sought and why they are said to be material evidence. This is particularly relevant where attempts are made to access the medical reports of those who allege that they are victims of crime. Victims do not waive the confidentiality of their medical records, or their right to privacy under article 8 of the ECHR, by the mere fact of making a complaint against the accused. Judges should be alert to balance the rights of victims against the real and proven needs of the defence. The court, as a public authority, must ensure that any interference with the article 8 rights of those entitled to privacy is in accordance with the law and necessary in pursuit of a legitimate public interest. General and unspecified requests to trawl through such records should be refused. If material is held by any person in relation to family proceedings (*e.g.*, where there have been care proceedings in relation to a child, who has also complained to the police of sexual or other abuse) then an application has to be made by that person to the family court for leave to disclose that material to a third party, unless the third party, and the purpose for which disclosure is made, is approved by rule 10.20A(3) of the *Family Proceedings Rules* 1991 (S.I. 1991 No. 1247). This would permit, for instance, a local authority, in receipt of such material, to disclose it to the police for the purpose of a criminal investigation, or to the CPS, in order for the latter to discharge any obligations under the *CPIA*.

Conclusion

63. The public rightly expects that the delays and failures which have been present in some   **N–60**
cases in the past where there has been scant adherence to sound disclosure principles will be eradicated by observation of this Protocol. The new regime under the *Criminal Justice Act* and the *Criminal Procedure Rules* gives judges the power to change the culture in which such cases are tried. It is now the duty of every judge actively to manage disclosure issues in every case. The judge must seize the initiative and drive the case along towards an efficient, effective and timely resolution, having regard to the overriding objective of the *Criminal Procedure Rules* (Pt 1). In this way the interests of justice will be better served and public confidence in the criminal justice system will be increased.

TABLE OF CONTENTS

2008

JANUARY

M	T	W	Th	F	Sa	Su
	1	2	3	4	5	6
7	8	9	10	11	12	13
14	15	16	17	18	19	20
21	22	23	24	25	26	27
28	29	30	31			

FEBRUARY

M	T	W	Th	F	Sa	Su
				1	2	3
4	5	6	7	8	9	10
11	12	13	14	15	16	17
18	19	20	21	22	23	24
25	26	27	28	29		

MARCH

M	T	W	Th	F	Sa	Su
					1	2
3	4	5	6	7	8	9
10	11	12	13	14	15	16
17	18	19	20	21	22	23
24	25	26	27	28	29	30
31						

APRIL

M	T	W	Th	F	Sa	Su
	1	2	3	4	5	6
7	8	9	10	11	12	13
14	15	16	17	18	19	20
21	22	23	24	25	26	27
28	29	30				

MAY

M	T	W	Th	F	Sa	Su
			1	2	3	4
5	6	7	8	9	10	11
12	13	14	15	16	17	18
19	20	21	22	23	24	25
26	27	28	29	30	31	

JUNE

M	T	W	Th	F	Sa	Su
						1
2	3	4	5	6	7	8
9	10	11	12	13	14	15
16	17	18	19	20	21	22
23	24	25	26	27	28	29
30						

JULY

M	T	W	Th	F	Sa	Su
	1	2	3	4	5	6
7	8	9	10	11	12	13
14	15	16	17	18	19	20
21	22	23	24	25	26	27
28	29	30	31			

AUGUST

M	T	W	Th	F	Sa	Su
				1	2	3
4	5	6	7	8	9	10
11	12	13	14	15	16	17
18	19	20	21	22	23	24
25	26	27	28	29	30	31

SEPTEMBER

M	T	W	Th	F	Sa	Su
1	2	3	4	5	6	7
8	9	10	11	12	13	14
15	16	17	18	19	20	21
22	23	24	25	26	27	28
29	30					

OCTOBER

M	T	W	Th	F	Sa	Su
		1	2	3	4	5
6	7	8	9	10	11	12
13	14	15	16	17	18	19
20	21	22	23	24	25	26
27	28	29	30	31		

NOVEMBER

M	T	W	Th	F	Sa	Su
					1	2
3	4	5	6	7	8	9
10	11	12	13	14	15	16
17	18	19	20	21	22	23
24	25	26	27	28	29	30

DECEMBER

M	T	W	Th	F	Sa	Su
1	2	3	4	5	6	7
8	9	10	11	12	13	14
15	16	17	18	19	20	21
22	23	24	25	26	27	28
29	30	31				

2009

JANUARY

M	T	W	Th	F	Sa	Su
			1	2	3	4
5	6	7	8	9	10	11
12	13	14	15	16	17	18
19	20	21	22	23	24	25
26	27	28	29	30	31	

FEBRUARY

M	T	W	Th	F	Sa	Su
						1
2	3	4	5	6	7	8
9	10	11	12	13	14	15
16	17	18	19	20	21	22
23	24	25	26	27	28	

MARCH

M	T	W	Th	F	Sa	Su
						1
2	3	4	5	6	7	8
9	10	11	12	13	14	15
16	17	18	19	20	21	22
23	24	25	26	27	28	29
30	31					

APRIL

M	T	W	Th	F	Sa	Su
		1	2	3	4	5
6	7	8	9	10	11	12
13	14	15	16	17	18	19
20	21	22	23	24	25	26
27	28	29	30			

MAY

M	T	W	Th	F	Sa	Su
				1	2	3
4	5	6	7	8	9	10
11	12	13	14	15	16	17
18	19	20	21	22	23	24
25	26	27	28	29	30	31

JUNE

M	T	W	Th	F	Sa	Su
1	2	3	4	5	6	7
8	9	10	11	12	13	14
15	16	17	18	19	20	21
22	23	24	25	26	27	28
29	30					

JULY

M	T	W	Th	F	Sa	Su
		1	2	3	4	5
6	7	8	9	10	11	12
13	14	15	16	17	18	19
20	21	22	23	24	25	26
27	28	29	30	31		

AUGUST

M	T	W	Th	F	Sa	Su
					1	2
3	4	5	6	7	8	9
10	11	12	13	14	15	16
17	18	19	20	21	22	23
24	25	26	27	28	29	30
31						

SEPTEMBER

M	T	W	Th	F	Sa	Su
	1	2	3	4	5	6
7	8	9	10	11	12	13
14	15	16	17	18	19	20
21	22	23	24	25	26	27
28	29	30				

OCTOBER

M	T	W	Th	F	Sa	Su
			1	2	3	4
5	6	7	8	9	10	11
12	13	14	15	16	17	18
19	20	21	22	23	24	25
26	27	28	29	30	31	

NOVEMBER

M	T	W	Th	F	Sa	Su
						1
2	3	4	5	6	7	8
9	10	11	12	13	14	15
16	17	18	19	20	21	22
23	24	25	26	27	28	29
30						

DECEMBER

M	T	W	Th	F	Sa	Su
	1	2	3	4	5	6
7	8	9	10	11	12	13
14	15	16	17	18	19	20
21	22	23	24	25	26	27
28	29	30	31			

2010

JANUARY

M	T	W	Th	F	Sa	Su
				1	2	3
4	5	6	7	8	9	10
11	12	13	14	15	16	17
18	19	20	21	22	23	24
25	26	27	28	29	30	31

FEBRUARY

M	T	W	Th	F	Sa	Su
1	2	3	4	5	6	7
8	9	10	11	12	13	14
15	16	17	18	19	20	21
22	23	24	25	26	27	28

MARCH

M	T	W	Th	F	Sa	Su
1	2	3	4	5	6	7
8	9	10	11	12	13	14
15	16	17	18	19	20	21
22	23	24	25	26	27	28
29	30	31				

APRIL

M	T	W	Th	F	Sa	Su
			1	2	3	4
5	6	7	8	9	10	11
12	13	14	15	16	17	18
19	20	21	22	23	24	25
26	27	28	29	30		

MAY

M	T	W	Th	F	Sa	Su
					1	2
3	4	5	6	7	8	9
10	11	12	13	14	15	16
17	18	19	20	21	22	23
24	25	26	27	28	29	30
31						

JUNE

M	T	W	Th	F	Sa	Su
	1	2	3	4	5	6
7	8	9	10	11	12	13
14	15	16	17	18	19	20
21	22	23	24	25	26	27
28	29	30				

JULY

M	T	W	Th	F	Sa	Su
			1	2	3	4
5	6	7	8	9	10	11
12	13	14	15	16	17	18
19	20	21	22	23	24	25
26	27	28	29	30	31	

AUGUST

M	T	W	Th	F	Sa	Su
						1
2	3	4	5	6	7	8
9	10	11	12	13	14	15
16	17	18	19	20	21	22
23	24	25	26	27	28	29
30	31					

SEPTEMBER

M	T	W	Th	F	Sa	Su
		1	2	3	4	5
6	7	8	9	10	11	12
13	14	15	16	17	18	19
20	21	22	23	24	25	26
27	28	29	30			

OCTOBER

M	T	W	Th	F	Sa	Su
				1	2	3
4	5	6	7	8	9	10
11	12	13	14	15	16	17
18	19	20	21	22	23	24
25	26	27	28	29	30	31

NOVEMBER

M	T	W	Th	F	Sa	Su
1	2	3	4	5	6	7
8	9	10	11	12	13	14
15	16	17	18	19	20	21
22	23	24	25	26	27	28
29	30					

DECEMBER

M	T	W	Th	F	Sa	Su
		1	2	3	4	5
6	7	8	9	10	11	12
13	14	15	16	17	18	19
20	21	22	23	24	25	26
27	28	29	30	31		

2011

JANUARY

M	T	W	Th	F	Sa	Su
					1	2
3	4	5	6	7	8	9
10	11	12	13	14	15	16
17	18	19	20	21	22	23
24	25	26	27	28	29	30
31						

FEBRUARY

M	T	W	Th	F	Sa	Su
	1	2	3	4	5	6
7	8	9	10	11	12	13
14	15	16	17	18	19	20
21	22	23	24	25	26	27
28						

MARCH

M	T	W	Th	F	Sa	Su
	1	2	3	4	5	6
7	8	9	10	11	12	13
14	15	16	17	18	19	20
21	22	23	24	25	26	27
28	29	30	31			

APRIL

M	T	W	Th	F	Sa	Su
				1	2	3
4	5	6	7	8	9	10
11	12	13	14	15	16	17
18	19	20	21	22	23	24
25	26	27	28	29	30	

MAY

M	T	W	Th	F	Sa	Su
						1
2	3	4	5	6	7	8
9	10	11	12	13	14	15
16	17	18	19	20	21	22
23	24	25	26	27	28	29
30	31					

JUNE

M	T	W	Th	F	Sa	Su
		1	2	3	4	5
6	7	8	9	10	11	12
13	14	15	16	17	18	19
20	21	22	23	24	25	26
27	28	29	30			

JULY

M	T	W	Th	F	Sa	Su
				1	2	3
4	5	6	7	8	9	10
11	12	13	14	15	16	17
18	19	20	21	22	23	24
25	26	27	28	29	30	31

AUGUST

M	T	W	Th	F	Sa	Su
1	2	3	4	5	6	7
8	9	10	11	12	13	14
15	16	17	18	19	20	21
22	23	24	25	26	27	28
29	30	31				

SEPTEMBER

M	T	W	Th	F	Sa	Su
			1	2	3	4
5	6	7	8	9	10	11
12	13	14	15	16	17	18
19	20	21	22	23	24	25
26	27	28	29	30		

OCTOBER

M	T	W	Th	F	Sa	Su
					1	2
3	4	5	6	7	8	9
10	11	12	13	14	15	16
17	18	19	20	21	22	23
24	25	26	27	28	29	30
31						

NOVEMBER

M	T	W	Th	F	Sa	Su
	1	2	3	4	5	6
7	8	9	10	11	12	13
14	15	16	17	18	19	20
21	22	23	24	25	26	27
28	29	30				

DECEMBER

M	T	W	Th	F	Sa	Su
			1	2	3	4
5	6	7	8	9	10	11
12	13	14	15	16	17	18
19	20	21	22	23	24	25
26	27	28	29	30	31	

Archbold
paragraph
numbers

AL–5

AL–5

Archbold's Criminal Pleading—2012 ed.

2012

JANUARY							FEBRUARY							MARCH						
M	T	W	Th	F	Sa	Su	M	T	W	Th	F	Sa	Su	M	T	W	Th	F	Sa	Su
	3	4	5	6	7	1			1	2	3	4	5				1	2	3	4
2	10	11	12	13	14	8	6	7	8	9	10	11	12	5	6	7	8	9	10	11
9	17	18	19	20	21	15	13	14	15	16	17	18	19	12	13	14	15	16	17	18
16	24	25	26	27	28	22	20	21	22	23	24	25	26	19	20	21	22	23	24	25
23	31					29	27	28	29					26	27	28	29	30	31	
30																				

APRIL							MAY							JUNE						
M	T	W	Th	F	Sa	Su	M	T	W	Th	F	Sa	Su	M	T	W	Th	F	Sa	Su
	3	4	5	6	7	1		1	2	3	4	5	6					1	2	3
2	10	11	12	13	14	8	7	8	9	10	11	12	13	4	5	6	7	8	9	10
9	17	18	19	20	21	15	14	15	16	17	18	19	20	11	12	13	14	15	16	17
16	24	25	26	27	28	22	21	22	23	24	25	26	27	18	19	20	21	22	23	24
23						29	28	29	30	31				25	26	27	28	29	30	
30																				

JULY							AUGUST							SEPTEMBER						
M	T	W	Th	F	Sa	Su	M	T	W	Th	F	Sa	Su	M	T	W	Th	F	Sa	Su
	3	4	5	6	7	1			1	2	3	4	5						1	2
2	10	11	12	13	14	8	6	7	8	9	10	11	12	3	4	5	6	7	8	9
9	17	18	19	20	21	15	13	14	15	16	17	18	19	10	11	12	13	14	15	16
16	24	25	26	27	28	22	20	21	22	23	24	25	26	17	18	19	20	21	22	23
23	31					29	27	28	29	30	31			24	25	26	27	28	29	30
30																				

OCTOBER							NOVEMBER							DECEMBER						
M	T	W	Th	F	Sa	Su	M	T	W	Th	F	Sa	Su	M	T	W	Th	F	Sa	Su
1	2	3	4	5	6	7				1	2	3	4						1	2
8	9	10	11	12	13	14	5	6	7	8	9	10	11	3	4	5	6	7	8	9
15	16	17	18	19	20	21	12	13	14	15	16	17	18	10	11	12	13	14	15	16
22	23	24	25	26	27	28	19	20	21	22	23	24	25	17	18	19	20	21	22	23
29	30	31					26	27	28	29	30			24	25	26	27	28	29	30
														31						

Supplement No. 3—July, 2012

AL–6
Archbold
paragraph
numbers

AL–6

2013

JANUARY

M	T	W	Th	F	Sa	Su
	1	2	3	4	5	6
7	8	9	10	11	12	13
14	15	16	17	18	19	20
21	22	23	24	25	26	27
28	29	30	31			

FEBRUARY

M	T	W	Th	F	Sa	Su
				1	2	3
4	5	6	7	8	9	10
11	12	13	14	15	16	17
18	19	20	21	22	23	24
25	26	27	28			

MARCH

M	T	W	Th	F	Sa	Su
				1	2	3
4	5	6	7	8	9	10
11	12	13	14	15	16	17
18	19	20	21	22	23	24
25	26	27	28	29	30	31

APRIL

M	T	W	Th	F	Sa	Su
1	2	3	4	5	6	7
8	9	10	11	12	13	14
15	16	17	18	19	20	21
22	23	24	25	26	27	28
29	30					

MAY

M	T	W	Th	F	Sa	Su
		1	2	3	4	5
6	7	8	9	10	11	12
13	14	15	16	17	18	19
20	21	22	23	24	25	26
27	28	29	30	31		

JUNE

M	T	W	Th	F	Sa	Su
					1	2
3	4	5	6	7	8	9
10	11	12	13	14	15	16
17	18	19	20	21	22	23
24	25	26	27	28	29	30

JULY

M	T	W	Th	F	Sa	Su
1	2	3	4	5	6	7
8	9	10	11	12	13	14
15	16	17	18	19	20	21
22	23	24	25	26	27	28
29	30	31				

AUGUST

M	T	W	Th	F	Sa	Su
			1	2	3	4
5	6	7	8	9	10	11
12	13	14	15	16	17	18
19	20	21	22	23	24	25
26	27	28	29	30	31	

SEPTEMBER

M	T	W	Th	F	Sa	Su
						1
2	3	4	5	6	7	8
9	10	11	12	13	14	15
16	17	18	19	20	21	22
23	24	25	26	27	28	29
30						

OCTOBER

M	T	W	Th	F	Sa	Su
	1	2	3	4	5	6
7	8	9	10	11	12	13
14	15	16	17	18	19	20
21	22	23	24	25	26	27
28	29	30	31			

NOVEMBER

M	T	W	Th	F	Sa	Su
				1	2	3
4	5	6	7	8	9	10
11	12	13	14	15	16	17
18	19	20	21	22	23	24
25	26	27	28	29	30	

DECEMBER

M	T	W	Th	F	Sa	Su
						1
2	3	4	5	6	7	8
9	10	11	12	13	14	15
16	17	18	19	20	21	22
23	24	25	26	27	28	29
30	31					

2014

JANUARY

M	T	W	Th	F	Sa	Su
		1	2	3	4	5
6	7	8	9	10	11	12
13	14	15	16	17	18	19
20	21	22	23	24	25	26
27	28	29	30	31		

FEBRUARY

M	T	W	Th	F	Sa	Su
					1	2
3	4	5	6	7	8	9
10	11	12	13	14	15	16
17	18	19	20	21	22	23
24	25	26	27	28		

MARCH

M	T	W	Th	F	Sa	Su
					1	2
3	4	5	6	7	8	9
10	11	12	13	14	15	16
17	18	19	20	21	22	23
24	25	26	27	28	29	30
31						

APRIL

M	T	W	Th	F	Sa	Su
	1	2	3	4	5	6
7	8	9	10	11	12	13
14	15	16	17	18	19	20
21	22	23	24	25	26	27
28	29	30				

MAY

M	T	W	Th	F	Sa	Su
			1	2	3	4
5	6	7	8	9	10	11
12	13	14	15	16	17	18
19	20	21	22	23	24	25
26	27	28	29	30	31	

JUNE

M	T	W	Th	F	Sa	Su
						1
2	3	4	5	6	7	8
9	10	11	12	13	14	15
16	17	18	19	20	21	22
23	24	25	26	27	28	29
30						

JULY

M	T	W	Th	F	Sa	Su
	1	2	3	4	5	6
7	8	9	10	11	12	13
14	15	16	17	18	19	20
21	22	23	24	25	26	27
28	29	30	31			

AUGUST

M	T	W	Th	F	Sa	Su
				1	2	3
4	5	6	7	8	9	10
11	12	13	14	15	16	17
18	19	20	21	22	23	24
25	26	27	28	29	30	31

SEPTEMBER

M	T	W	Th	F	Sa	Su
1	2	3	4	5	6	7
8	9	10	11	12	13	14
15	16	17	18	19	20	21
22	23	24	25	26	27	28
29	30					

OCTOBER

M	T	W	Th	F	Sa	Su
		1	2	3	4	5
6	7	8	9	10	11	12
13	14	15	16	17	18	19
20	21	22	23	24	25	26
27	28	29	30	31		

NOVEMBER

M	T	W	Th	F	Sa	Su
					1	2
3	4	5	6	7	8	9
10	11	12	13	14	15	16
17	18	19	20	21	22	23
24	25	26	27	28	29	30

DECEMBER

M	T	W	Th	F	Sa	Su
1	2	3	4	5	6	7
8	9	10	11	12	13	14
15	16	17	18	19	20	21
22	23	24	25	26	27	28
29	30	31				

Supplement No. 3—July, 2012

AL–8

Archbold
paragraph
numbers

AL–8

2015

JANUARY

M	T	W	Th	F	Sa	Su
			1	2	3	4
5	6	7	8	9	10	11
12	13	14	15	16	17	18
19	20	21	22	23	24	25
26	27	28	29	30	31	

FEBRUARY

M	T	W	Th	F	Sa	Su
						1
2	3	4	5	6	7	8
9	10	11	12	13	14	15
16	17	18	19	20	21	22
23	24	25	26	27	28	

MARCH

M	T	W	Th	F	Sa	Su
						1
2	3	4	5	6	7	8
9	10	11	12	13	14	15
16	17	18	19	20	21	22
23	24	25	26	27	28	29
30	31					

APRIL

M	T	W	Th	F	Sa	Su
		1	2	3	4	5
6	7	8	9	10	11	12
13	14	15	16	17	18	19
20	21	22	23	24	25	26
27	28	29	30			

MAY

M	T	W	Th	F	Sa	Su
				1	2	3
4	5	6	7	8	9	10
11	12	13	14	15	16	17
18	19	20	21	22	23	24
25	26	27	28	29	30	31

JUNE

M	T	W	Th	F	Sa	Su
1	2	3	4	5	6	7
8	9	10	11	12	13	14
15	16	17	18	19	20	21
22	23	24	25	26	27	28
29	30					

JULY

M	T	W	Th	F	Sa	Su
		1	2	3	4	5
6	7	8	9	10	11	12
13	14	15	16	17	18	19
20	21	22	23	24	25	26
27	28	29	30	31		

AUGUST

M	T	W	Th	F	Sa	Su
					1	2
3	4	5	6	7	8	9
10	11	12	13	14	15	16
17	18	19	20	21	22	23
24	25	26	27	28	29	30
31						

SEPTEMBER

M	T	W	Th	F	Sa	Su
	1	2	3	4	5	6
7	8	9	10	11	12	13
14	15	16	17	18	19	20
21	22	23	24	25	26	27
28	29	30				

OCTOBER

M	T	W	Th	F	Sa	Su
			1	2	3	4
5	6	7	8	9	10	11
12	13	14	15	16	17	18
19	20	21	22	23	24	25
26	27	28	29	30	31	

NOVEMBER

M	T	W	Th	F	Sa	Su
						1
2	3	4	5	6	7	8
9	10	11	12	13	14	15
16	17	18	19	20	21	22
23	24	25	26	27	28	29
30						

DECEMBER

M	T	W	Th	F	Sa	Su
	1	2	3	4	5	6
7	8	9	10	11	12	13
14	15	16	17	18	19	20
21	22	23	24	25	26	27
28	29	30	31			

Archbold
paragraph
numbers

AL–9

AL–9

Archbold's Criminal Pleading—2012 ed.

Holidays and Notable Dates

Holiday, etc.	2008	2009	2010	2011	2012	2013	2014	2015
New Year's Day	Jan. 1	Jan. 1	Jan. 1	Jan. 1	Jan. 1	Jan. 1	Jan. 1	Jan. 1
New Year Holiday (England)	—	—	—	Jan. 3	Jan. 2	—	—	—
New Year Holiday (Scotland)	Jan. 2	Jan. 2	Jan. 4	Jan. 4	Jan. 3	Jan. 2	Jan. 2	Jan. 2
St David's Day (Wales)	Mar. 1	Mar. 1	Mar. 1	Mar. 1	Mar. 1	Mar. 1	Mar. 1	Mar. 1
St Patrick's Day (Ireland)	Mar. 17	Mar. 17	Mar. 17	Mar. 17	Mar. 17	Mar. 17	Mar. 17	Mar. 17
Good Friday	Mar. 21	Apr. 10	Apr. 2	Apr. 22	Apr.6	Mar. 29	Apr. 18	Apr. 3
Easter Monday	Mar. 24	Apr. 13	Apr. 5	Apr. 25	Apr.9	Apr. 1	Apr. 21	Apr. 6
St George's Day (England)	Apr. 23	Apr. 23	Apr. 23	Apr. 23	Apr. 23	Apr. 23	Apr. 23	Apr. 23
May Day Holiday	May 5	May 4	May 3	May 2	May 7	May 6	May 5	May 4
Queen's Diamond Jubilee					Jun.4			
Spring Bank Holiday	May 26	May 25	May 31	May 30	Jun.5	May 27	May 26	May 25
August Bank Holiday	Aug. 25	Aug. 31	Aug. 30	Aug. 29	Aug.27	Aug. 26	Aug. 25	Aug. 24
St Andrew's Day (Scotland)	Nov. 30	Nov. 30	Nov. 30	Nov. 30	Nov. 30	Nov. 30	Nov. 30	Nov. 30
Christmas Day	Dec. 25	Dec. 25	Dec. 25	Dec. 25	Dec. 25	Dec. 25	Dec. 25	Dec. 25
Boxing Day	Dec. 26	Dec. 26	Dec. 26	Dec. 26	Dec. 26	Dec. 26	Dec. 26	Dec. 26
Christmas Holiday(s)	—	—	—	—	—	—	—	—

Measurement Conversion Tables

The measurements set out below are based upon the following standards set by the *Weights and Measures Act* 1985, Sched. 1, Pts I to V:

YARD = 0.9144 metre; GALLON = 4.54609 cubic decimetres or litres; POUND = 0.45359237 kilograms

Measurements of Length

Imperial Units of Length		Metric Equivalents
Mil	1/1000 inch	0.0254 millimetres
Inch	1000 mils	2.54 centimetres
Link	7.92 inches	20.1168 centimetres
Foot	12 inches	0.3048 metres
Yard	3 feet	0.9144 metres
Fathom	6 feet	1.8288 metres
Cable	60 feet or 10 fathoms	18.288 metres
Chain	22 yards (100 links)	20.1168 metres
Furlong	220 yards	201.168 metres
Mile	1,760 yards (8 furlongs)	1.609344 kilometres
Nautical mile	6080 feet	1.853184 kilometres

Metric Units of Length		Imperial Equivalents
Micron	1/1000 millimetre	0.03937007 mils
Millimetre	1/1000 metre	0.03937007 inches
Centimetre	1/100 metre	0.3937 inches
Decimetre	1/10 metre	3.937 inches
Metre	Metre	1.09361329 yards
Kilometre	1000 metres	0.62137712 miles or 0.53961 nautical miles

Archbold
paragraph
numbers
AL-11

AL-11

Archbold's Criminal Pleading—2012 ed.

Measurements of Area

Imperial Units of Area	Metric Equivalents
Square inch	6.4516 square centimetres
Square foot	929.0304 square centimetres
Square yard	0.83613 square metres
Square chain	404.685642 square metres
Rood	1011.714 square metres
Acre	4046.85642 sq. ms or 40.4685642 acres
Square mile	258.998811 hectares

Imperial Units of Area	Metric Equivalents
1/144 square feet	
1/9 square yard	
Square yard	
484 square yards	
1,210 square yards	
4 roods or 4840 square yards	
640 acres	

Metric Units of Area	Imperial Equivalents
Square millimetre	0.00155 square inches
Square centimetre	0.155 square inches
Square decimetre	15.5 square inches
Square metre	1.1959 sq. yards or 10.7639 sq. ft.
Are	119.599 sq. yds or 0.09884 roods
Dekare	0.2471 acres
Hectare	2.47105 acres
Square kilometre	247.105 acres or 0.3861 square miles

Metric Units of Area	
1/100 square centimetre	
1/100 square decimetre	
1/100 metre	
Square metre	
100 square metres	
10 ares	
100 ares (1,000 square metres)	
100 hectares	

Measurements of Volume

Imperial Units of Volume		Metric Equivalents
Cubic inch		16.387064 cubic centimetres
Cubic foot	1,728 cubic inches	28.3168465 decimetres
Cubic yard	27 cubic feet	0.76455485 cubic metres

Metric Units of Volume		Imperial Equivalents
Cubic centimetre	1,000 cubic millimetres	0.06102374 cubic inches
Cubic decimetre	1,000 cubic centimetres	0.03531466 cubic feet
Cubic metre	1,000 cubic decimetres	1.30795061 cubic yards or 35.3147 cu. ft.

Measurements of Capacity

Imperial, Apothecaries and US Units of Capacity		Metric Equivalents
Minim	Minim	0.0591938 millilitres
Fluid Drachm	60 minims	0.35516328 centilitres
Fluid ounce	8 fluid drachms	2.84130625 centilitres
US fluid ounce	1.0408 UK fluid ounces	29.573522656 millilitres
Gill	5 fluid ounces	1.42065312 decilitres
Pint	4 gills or 20 fluid ounces	0.56826125 litres
US pint	0.8327 UK pints or 16 US fluid ounces	0.47317636 litres
Quart	2 pints or 8 gills	1.1365225 litres
Gallon	4 quarts or 1.20095 US gallons	4.54609 litres
US gallon	0.08327 UK gallons	3.7854109 litres
Peck	2 gallons or 16 pints	9.09218 litres
Bushel	4 pecks or 8 gallons	36.36872 litres
Quarter	8 bushels or 36 pecks	2.9094976 hectolitres
Chaldron	36 bushels or 4½ quarters	13.0927392 hectolitres

Metric Units of Capacity		Imperial Equivalents
Millilitre	Millilitre	0.28156064 fluid drachms
Centilitre	10 millilitres	0.35195080 fluid ounces
Decilitre	10 centilitres	0.70390160 gills
Litre	10 decilitres	1.75975398 pints or 0.21996924 UK gallons
Dekalitre	10 litres	2.196924 UK gallons
Hectolitre	10 dekalitres or 100 litres	21.996824 UK gallons

Measurements of Weight

Imperial and Apothecaries Units of Weight		Metric Equivalents
Grain	Grain	64.79891 milligrams
Scruple	20 grains	1.2959782 grams
Pennyweight	24 grains	1.55517384 grams
Drachm	3 scruples or 60 grains	3.8879346 grams
Troy ounce	8 drachms or 480 grains	31.1034768 grams
Dram	1/16 ounce	1.77184519 grams
Ounce	16 drams or 437.5 grains	28.3495231 grams
Troy pound (US)	12 troy ounces or 5,760 grains	373.241721 grams
Pound	16 ounces or 7,000 grains	453.59237 grams or 0.45359237 kilograms
Stone	14 pounds	6.35029318 kilograms
Quarter	28 pounds or 2 stone	12.7005863 kilograms
Cental	100 pounds	45.359237 kilograms
Hundredweight	4 quarters or 112 pounds	50.8023454 kilograms
Short hundredweight (US)	100 pounds	45.359237 kilograms
Ton (UK or long ton)	20 cwt or 2,240 pounds	1.0160469 metric tonnes (tonne)
Ton (US or short ton)	2,000 pounds	0.9071847 metric tonnes

Metric Units of Weight		Imperial Equivalents
Milligram	.001 grams	0.012432 grains
Centigram	.01 grams	0.15432 grains
Decigram	.1 grams	1.5432 grains
Gram	1 gram	0.03527396 ounces or 0.03215 troy ounces
Dekagram	10 grams	0.35273961 ounces
Hectogram	100 grams	3.52739619 ounces
Kilogram	1,000 grams	2.20462262 pounds
Myriagram	10 kilograms	22.0462 pounds
Quintal	100 kilograms	1.9684 hundredweight
Tonne	1,000 kilograms	0.984207 UK tons or 1.10231 US tons

Measurements of Velocity

Per Hour	Per Minute	Per Second
Mile	88 feet	17.6 inches per second
1.609344 kph	26.8224 metres	44.704 centimetres per second
Kilometres	16.6667 metres	27.7778 centimetres
0.62137 mph	54.6806 feet	10.9361 inches

SYSTÈME INTERNATIONALE D'UNITES OR SI UNITS

1. SI units are increasingly being used to report laboratory results. They have largely replaced   **AL–16**
earlier systems such as c.g.s. units (centimetre, gram, second), m.k.s. or Giorgi units (metre,
kilogram, second), and Imperial units (yard, pound, second).

2. S.I. Units comprise 7 base units and 2 supplementary units. Other units are derived from
these. 18 derived units are currently widely accepted.

Base SI Units

Physical Quantity	Unit	Symbol
Length	metre	m
Mass	kilogram	kg
Time	second	s
Electric current	ampere	A
Temperature	kelvin	K
Luminosity	candela	cd
Amount of substance	mole	mol
Plane angle*	radian*	rad
Solid angle*	steradian*	sr

*Supplementary Units

Archbold
paragraph
numbers
AL–18

AL–18

Archbold's Criminal Pleading—2012 ed.

Derived SI Units

Physical Quantity	Unit	Symbol
Frequency	hertz	Hz
Energy	joule	J
Force	newton	N
Power	watt	W
Pressure	pascal	Pa
Electric charge	coulomb	C
Electric potential difference	volt	V
Electrical resistance	ohm	Ω
Electric conductance	siemens	S
Electric capacitance	farad	F
Magnetic flux	weber	Wb
Inductance	henry	H
Magnetic flux density	tesla	T
Luminous flux	lumen	lm
Illuminance	lux	lx
Absorbed dose	gray	Gy
Activity	becquerel	Bq
Dose Equivalence	sievert	Sv

Multiples and Subdivisions of SI Units

Prefix	Symbol	Power	Value
exa	E	10^{18}	1,000,000,000,000,000,000
peta	P	10^{15}	1,000,000,000,000,000
tera	T	10^{12}	1,000,000,000,000
giga	G	10^{9}	1,000,000,000
mega	M	10^{6}	1,000,000
kilo	k	10^{3}	1,000
hecto	h	10^{2}	100
deca	da	10	10
–			1
deci	d	10^{-1}	1/10
centi	c	10^{-2}	1/100
milli	m	10^{-3}	1/1,000
micro	μ	10^{-6}	1/1,000,000
nano	n	10^{-9}	1/1,000,000,000
pico	p	10^{-12}	1/1,000,000,000,000
femto	f	10^{-15}	1/1,000,000,000,000,000
atto	a	10^{-18}	1/1,000,000,000,000,000,000

Archbold
paragraph
numbers

AL–20

AL–20

Archbold's Criminal Pleading—2012 ed.

International Time Differences

The following time differences are based upon Greenwich Mean Time (GMT).
British Summer Time (BST) is one hour in advance of GMT.

Country	Hours +/-
Algeria	+ 1 hour
Argentina	– 3 hours
Australia	
South Australia	+ 9½ hours
New South Wales	+ 10 hours
Tasmania	+ 10 hours
Victoria	+ 10 hours
Austria	+ 1 hour
Belgium	+ 1 hour
Bolivia	– 4 hours
Brazil	– 3 hours
Bulgaria	+ 2 hours
Canada	
Newfoundland	– 3½ hours
Atlantic	– 4 hours
Eastern	– 5 hours
Central	– 6 hours
Mountain	– 7 hours
Pacific	– 8 hours
Yukon	– 9 hours
Chile	– 4 hours

Country	Hours +/-
China	+ 8 hours
Columbia	– 5 hours
Czech Lands	+ 1 hour
Denmark	+ 1 hour
Egypt	+ 2 hours
Finland	+ 2 hours
France	+ 1 hour
Germany	+ 1 hour
Ghana	–
Greece	+ 2 hours
Holland	+ 1 hour
Hong Kong	+ 8 hours
Hungary	+ 1 hour
India	+ 5½ hours
Iraq	+ 3 hours
Ireland	–
Israel	+ 2 hours
Italy	+ 1 hour
Jamaica	– 5 hours
Japan	+ 9 hours
Kenya	+ 3 hours

Country	Hours +/-
Luxembourg	+ 1 hour
Malaysia	+ 8 hours
Malta	+ 1 hour
Morocco	—
New Zealand	+ 12 hours
Nigeria	+ 1 hour
Norway	+ 1 hour
Peru	– 5 hours
Philippines	+ 8 hours
Poland	+ 1 hour
Portugal	—
Romania	+ 2 hours
Russia	
Moscow	+ 3 hours
Vladivostock	+ 10 hours
Saudi Arabia	+ 3 hours
Serbia	+ 1 hour
Singapore	+ 8 hours

Country	Hours +/-
South Africa	+ 2 hours
Spain	+ 1 hour
Sri Lanka	+ 5½ hours
Sweden	+ 1 hour
Switzerland	+ 1 hour
Taiwan	+ 8 hours
Thailand	+ 7 hours
Tunisia	+ 1 hour
Turkey	+ 2 hours
Ukraine	+ 3 hours
United Arab Emirates	+ 4 hours
United States	
Eastern	– 5 hours
Central	– 6 hours
Mountain	– 7 hours
Pacific	– 8 hours
Zambia	+ 2 hours
Zimbabwe	+ 2 hours

Stopping Distances

Speed (m.p.h.)	Stopping distance (feet)
20	40
30	75
40	120
50	175
60	240
70	315

Useful Contact Details

	Telephone	*Email*
Courts, etc.		
House of Lords, Judicial Office	(020) 7219 3111	
Royal Courts of Justice	(020) 7947 6000	
Registrar, Criminal Appeals	(020) 7947 6103	
Criminal Appeal Office	(020) 7947 6011	Criminalappealoffice.generaloffice@hmcourts-service.x.gsi.gov.uk
Administrative Court Office	(020) 7947 6205	
Official Bodies		
Home Office	(020) 7035 4848	public.enquiries@homeoffice.gsi.gov.uk
Serious Fraud Office	(020) 7239 7272	public.enquiries@sfo.gsi.gov.uk
H.M. Revenue and Customs	0845 010 9000	Enquiries.estn@hmrc.gsi.gov.uk This address handles all enquiries related to VAT, Excise and other duties formerly administered by HM Customs and Excise (with the exception of International Trade)
New Scotland Yard	(020) 7230 1212	new.scotland.yard@met.police.uk
City of London Police	(020) 7601 2222	postmaster@cityoflondon.police.uk
British Transport Police	0800 40 50 40	
Others		
Justice	(020) 7329 5100	admin@justice.org.uk
Liberty	(020) 7403 3888	
Bar Council	(020) 7242 0082	
Bar Council Ethical Enquiries Line	(020) 7611 1307	
Bar Standards Board	(020) 7611 1444	
Law Society — Lawyerline	0870 606 2588	
Law Society — Practice Advice Service	0870 606 2522	

INDEX

LEGAL TAXONOMY
FROM SWEET & MAXWELL

This index has been prepared using Sweet and Maxwell's Legal Taxonomy. Index entries conform to keywords provided by the Legal Taxonomy except where references to specific documents or non-standard terms (denoted by quotation marks) have been included. These keywords provide a means of identifying similar concepts in other Sweet & Maxwell publications and online services to which keywords from the Legal Taxonomy have been applied. Readers may find some minor differences between terms used in the text and those which appear in the index.

Suggestions to *sweetandmaxwell.taxonomy@thomson.com*

All references are to paragraph numbers.